PRACTICAL ACCOUNTING

PRACTICAL ACCOUNTING

Augustine Benedict and Barry Elliott

FINANCIAL TIMES
Prentice Hall

An imprint of **Pearson Education**

Harlow, England · London · New York · Reading, Massachusetts · San Francisco · Toronto · Don Mills, Ontario · Sydney
Tokyo · Singapore · Hong Kong · Seoul · Taipei · Cape Town · Madrid · Mexico City · Amsterdam · Munich · Paris · Milan

Pearson Education Limited
Edinburgh Gate
Harlow
Essex CM20 2JE

and Associated Companies throughout the world

Visit us on the World Wide Web at:
www.pearsoneduc.com

─────────────────

First published 2001

© Pearson Education Limited 2001

ISBN 0 273 64660 5

British Library Cataloguing-in-Publication Data
A catalogue record for this book is available from the British Library

10 9 8 7 6 5 4 3 2 1
05 04 03 02 01

Typeset in 9/12pt Stone by 35
Printed and bound in Italy by G. Canale & C. S.p.A.

CONTENTS

Part C ACCOUNTING FOR NON-MONETARY ASSETS

Part I PARTNERSHIP ACCOUNTING

Part J ACCOUNTING FOR LIMITED COMPANIES

PREFACE

Choice of name for the book

Accounting is a practical subject that has evolved over the years as the accounting profession has responded to changing commercial practices. The conceptual framework required to underpin the development of the subject is, however, of comparatively recent origin. In our book we consider both these aspects, giving emphasis to both the essentially practical nature of the subject and the application of the concepts using an interactive approach.

Each chapter unfolds progressively, and you will best develop your skills and understanding by drafting a written answer to each of the Interactive Questions as you meet them in the text and checking against the suggested solution before proceeding further. We have also provided Progressive Questions, which we have carefully tailored in order to reinforce and extend what you should have learnt from each chapter. Detailed answers to Progressive Questions appear at the end of the book.

This approach to the subject matter is intended to provide you with an understanding of accounting concepts, a knowledge of accounting techniques, and skills in using the tools available to an accountant. This would put you in a sound position to answer typical examination questions successfully. We are grateful to the various examining bodies that have kindly given us permission to use selected questions from their past examinations, and these appear at the end of the book. Our suggested answers to these exercises are provided in the Lecturer's Resource Pack, which is available from the publishers.

We believe that accounting is a practical discipline that requires understanding and practice. In our book we provide you with an opportunity for both.

Content and target readership

This book contains:

- a comprehensive coverage of financial accounting at foundation and intermediate level;
- an overview of accounting systems and controls;
- an introduction to the use of spreadsheets and computers for the accounting function;
- a comprehensive coverage of the core elements of management accounting.

The book is intended for those:

- preparing for the foundation and intermediate professional qualifications in accounting;
- studying in the first year of a degree course majoring in finance and accounting at universities and colleges;
- taking business-related modules on non-accounting courses (e.g. Law, Engineering, Tourism, Hotel Management, Stock Market Dealing, Charity Finance);
- who are on A-Level, GCSE and NVQ courses;
- seeking a knowledge of the subject for its practical value when managing a business or practising a profession.

We have chosen the topics with the aim of covering the major syllabus requirements of the professional foundation, A-Level and first-year accounting undergraduate courses. The progressive development of each chapter also makes it suitable for use on a selective basis for business-related modules.

The approach adopted

Our material has been developed and successfully used in teaching for many years, both in the United Kingdom and overseas.

You will see that we have taken accounting for cash as our starting point. We have done this because we have found the cash approach more easily understandable and less intimidating to complete beginners. Besides, cash accounting is the starting point in practice for the millions of small and medium-sized businesses. Lecturers who favour the traditional approach through the accounting equation will find that we get on to that approach quite quickly from Chapter 3 onwards.

We have assumed no prior knowledge of the subject and our approach has been calculated to achieve two aims: first, to explain the techniques, so that you can record business transactions, prepare financial statements and interpret them for non-accountants to assist decision making; and, second, to encourage you to challenge the time-hallowed conventions of the subject and be able to justify what you are doing.

Other resources

At www.booksites.net/benedictelliott students and teachers will have access to a website that contains multiple choice questions, corresponding to each chapter, together with their answers. You are encouraged to look up this website and use its resources.

In addition, a Lecturer's Resource Pack is available, free of charge from the publishers, to lecturers adopting this textbook. The resource pack contains:

- a set of questions for use as a teaching aid on matters dealt with in Part A of the book;
- detailed answers to progressive questions for which clues only were included in the book;
- the authors' suggested answers to the selection of questions from past examinations included in the book.

Augustine Benedict and Barry Elliott
December 2000

A Companion Web Site accompanies
PRACTICAL ACCOUNTING
by Benedict and Elliott

Visit the *Practical Accounting* Companion Web Site at *www.booksites.net/benedictelliott* to find valuable teaching and learning material including:

For Students:
- Study material designed to help you improve your results
- Annotated weblinks to further your study
- Multiple choice questions to test your learning
- An international section explaining how the general principles of the book relate to specific countries

For Lecturers:
- A secure, password protected site with teaching material
- A downloadable version of the full Lecturer's Resource Pack
- Extra question material
- Answers to the progressive questions and exam questions
- A syllabus manager that will build and host your very own course web page

Also: This regularly maintained site also has search functions.

ACKNOWLEDGEMENTS

We are grateful for inputs from experienced lecturers/examiners and particularly thank Walter Hamilton for inputs on inflation accounting, Mike Rimmington for inputs on management accounting topics, and David Towers for inputs on spreadsheet, computers in accounting, and accounting systems and controls.

We thank Viv Murphy, David Murphy, Steve Dungworth, Neil Marriot, Anon Batch, Philip McDonald, Harold Alakeson, Eric Cohen, Deva Rodrigo and Vimal Perera for their constructive review comments on the draft manuscript.

We should like to thank also Catherine Newman, Stuart Hay, Lorna Sharrock, Richard Lamprecht, Colin Reed, Laura Prime and Bridget Allen at Pearson Education, for their professional assistance in bringing our manuscript to its present attractive appearance.

Finally we should like to thank our wives, Doris and Di, for their tolerance and continuous support.

Publisher's acknowledgements

We are grateful to the following examining bodies for permission to reproduce accounting examination questions:

Assessment and Qualifications Alliance (AQA) for questions from *A Level Accounting* Summer 1997, 1998, 1999 and *Specimen Paper* 1998; Association of Accounting Technicians (AAT) for a question from a past *Association of Accounting Technicians* examination; Association of Chartered Certified Accountants (ACCA) for twelve questions from past *Chartered Certified Accountants* examinations; The Chartered Institute of Management Accountants (CIMA) for eight questions from past *Chartered Institutes Accountants* examinations; Edexcel – London Examinations for two questions from *A Level Accounting* June 1999; Northern Examinations & Assessment Board (NEAB) for questions from *GCE Accounts Advanced Paper 2* June 1998 and *GCE Principles of Accounts Advanced Paper 1* June 1996; Northern Ireland Council for the Curriculum Examinations and Assessment (CCEA) for a question from *GCSE Accounting Paper 1 Higher Tier* May 1998 and OCR for questions from *Final Accounts* June 1999, *Costing* June 1999, *Accounting Business Studies* June 1998 and *Financial Accounting* November 1998.

The examining bodies accept no responsibility for any answers to questions provided in the Lecturer's Resource Pack.

Whilst every effort has been made to trace the owners of copyright material, in a few cases this has proved impossible and we take this opportunity to offer our apologies to any copyright holders whose rights we may have unwittingly infringed.

Part A

THE FINANCIAL ACCOUNTING SYSTEM

Chapter 1

THE NEED FOR ACCOUNTING

In this chapter
_____

● We will learn of the meaning and significance of accounting

1.1 WHAT IS ACCOUNTING?

The word 'accounting' usually conjures up images of work that is mathematical, tedious and distinctly unexciting. This book sets out to establish that if the subject is approached from a practical point of view, then:

● the mathematical ability required is modest;
● with the assistance of computer technology the tedium can be reduced to a minimum;
● accounting can prove exciting when the information that an accountant provides is properly interpreted and applied for decision making by both managers and investors.

Accounting in its basic form means keeping count in quantities or money. A farmer keeps count of his sheep, and every one of us keeps count of the amount of cash we have. A trader, too, keeps count of the cash in his business but, as we shall soon find out, has to do more than that if the business is to survive. Over the years the technique of keeping count has been developed and improved and is today practised as an art. The art of recording, classifying and summarizing the transactions of a business is known as **_bookkeeping_**. It is called bookkeeping because, until the advent of the computer age, accounting records were maintained in books of account.

Accounting, on the other hand, is what an accountant does, which includes the following:

● setting up and overseeing a system for recording, classifying and summarizing transactions, i.e. the bookkeeping system;
● establishing and enforcing adequate controls to ensure the accuracy and completeness of the bookkeeping process;
● communicating information to those having a legitimate claim to it;
● assisting with interpreting the information and in the making of economic decisions.

The most accepted definition of accounting is the one stated in the box here.

> Accounting is the 'process of identifying, measuring and communicating information to permit informed judgements and decisions by the users of the information'. _The American Accounting Association_

1.2 WHY KEEP ACCOUNTS?

Let us first consider the reasons why a one-person trading entity – referred to as a *sole proprietor* – would keep accounting records. These include:

1. to safeguard the cash and every other asset of the business, such as premises, machinery, furniture, vehicles and goods held for sale, from being stolen or improperly used;
2. to monitor the amount of cash available to the business, to make certain that there is sufficient to pay the bills as they fall due and to maintain and replace assets;
3. to keep track of the amounts payable for goods bought on a promise to pay later;
4. to keep track of the amounts receivable for goods sold on customers' promises to pay later;
5. to check at regular intervals that the business is making a profit – otherwise there would be no justification for it continuing;
6. to use records of past performance to give confidence that the business could meet its commitments in the future, e.g. when seeking a bank loan or trade credit;
7. to satisfy the requirements of the VAT inspectors, where a business must register for VAT when its turnover exceeds a stated threshold (fixed at £52,000 per annum from 1 April 2000);
8. to be able to prepare accounts when submitting returns to the Income Tax authorities in order to show the profit or loss on which tax is assessed.

When two or more individuals pool their resources to carry on a business, it is known as a *partnership*. Accounting records then become necessary to avoid disputes and safeguard their respective interests.

When, as is now common, the business is carried on as a *limited company*, maintenance of proper accounts is insisted on by company law and is monitored by the Registrar of Companies. Since, in a company set-up, the resources are provided by many (shareholders, banks and other creditors) and the management delegated to a few (directors), the management team is legally obliged to keep proper books of account and to report financial information to those providing the resources. A company whose shares are quoted on a stock exchange also has to comply with additional accounting requirements. Since investors seek to assess the future prospects of a business in the light of its past performance, it is essential that accounting information is provided in a manner that assists such assessment.

Today, with the need to survive in a highly competitive market, accounting has become an indispensable management tool for all sizes of business, from the sole proprietor to the multinational corporation trading across national boundaries. Accounting information assists in:

● protecting assets;
● establishing strategies;
● maintaining competitive advantage;
● controlling costs;
● making other day-to-day management decisions.

Such accounting, aimed at satisfying the needs of the business's internal managers, has become known as *management accounting*. Accounting to satisfy the needs of those external to the business (such as profit trends, tax liabilities, or the ability to pay creditors) has become known as *financial accounting*. It is important to recognize, however, that for millions of small and medium-sized businesses this distinction is blurred because the same person or persons might be providing all of the information.

Chapter 2

RECORDING CASH RECEIPTS AND PAYMENTS

In this chapter

We will learn:

- the importance of controlling cash
- some basic methods of exercising control
- some accounting terminology

and you should be able to:

- write up the Cash account of a business

2.1 THE NEED TO CONTROL CASH

The majority of businesses operate on a cash basis. Such businesses cover a wide range of types, including restaurants, retail stores, bakers, newsagents and farmers – the list is virtually endless. The owners and managers of these businesses concentrate on their cash position. Their concerns are whether there will be enough to pay their trade creditors and meet all expenses, allowing them sufficient to live on and to pay their tax at the end of the year. They will be aware that cash also needs to be properly controlled to avoid it being stolen or misused. Therefore, they should have a system whereby all receipts are accounted for and nothing can be paid without proper authority.

In addition, if they are registered for VAT, they will be required to maintain a detailed record of the cash received and paid. VAT inspectors will periodically check these records and will want to be able to see that all receipts are accounted for and what the money coming in has been spent on. Business owners and managers will also need to keep detailed records so that they can prepare accounts at the end of the year for the tax authorities.

2.2 CONTROLLING CASH RECEIPTS AND PAYMENTS

For controlling cash, the primary requirement is that there should be written evidence of each amount received or paid. Such written evidence is known as a *voucher*. For example, on receipt of an amount, a written acknowledgement of the amount received is given and a copy of it retained as the voucher. Similarly, on payment of an amount, the written acknowledgement obtained from the payee is retained as the voucher. The second requirement is that these vouchers should be systematically recorded in a cash book with a cross-reference to the voucher. This means that when the owner or VAT inspector wants to check why cash was paid out, such persons can refer back to the voucher.

It is important, therefore, that there are controls in place to satisfy anyone checking that all the vouchers are available and that the cash book actually records all the vouchers.

Interaction 2.1	**Controlling the vouchers**
	Explain how you could ensure that all vouchers for receipts and payments are available.

Interaction 2.2	**Controlling the receipts and payments**
	Explain what you would do as manager to ensure that all receipts have been recorded in the cash book and that no bill has been paid twice, either by error or through dishonesty.

Control is exercised by counting the cash in hand at regular interval (say daily) and comparing it with the balance appearing in the Cash account. If the two agree, it is presumed that the amount in hand is correct and that receipts and payments have been correctly accounted for. This presumption is not, however, necessarily correct. In many small organizations it is often necessary to rely on one person to receive and pay out the cash. Therefore, there can be no certainty that all receipts and payments are accurately recorded in the Cash account. In these cases, it may be possible to carry out other control tests. For example, sales in a tobacconist's may be expected to be at least 125 per cent of the cost of the items sold, and an amount less than that would lead to an investigation. Such tests are routinely carried out by tax inspectors and other regulatory authorities.

2.3 RECORDING CASH RECEIPTS AND PAYMENTS

We will first consider how an individual, say Beatrice in our example, keeps a record of her personal cash receipts and payments. Beatrice had cash of £125 in hand on 1 January 20X0. Her *transactions*, i.e. her receipts and payments, during the month of January were as follows:

Date	Item	Date	Item
1.1	Received £400 as a maintenance grant.	14.1	Paid £55 to settle the telephone bill.
1.1	Paid £175 as rent for her room.	17.1	Paid £45 for clothes.
2.1	Received a loan of £600 from Simon.	24.1	Paid £30 as share of electricity bill.
4.1	Paid £40 for books and stationery.	26.1	Paid £25 as share of the gas bill.
7.1	Paid £400 for a mountain bike.	30.1	Received £240 for evening work.
11.1	Paid £285 as her contribution for food.	31.1	Paid £250 back to Simon.

Beatrice has prepared a calculation of her cash in hand using two methods, the Running Total Method and the Cash Account Method, as follows:

RUNNING TOTAL METHOD	
20X0	**£**
1.1 Balance in hand	125
1.1 Maintenance grant	400
	525
1.1 Room rent paid	(175)
	350
2.1 Loan received	600
	950
4.4 Books bought	(40)
	910
7.1 Bike bought	(400)
	510
11.1 Food	(285)
	225
14.1 Telephone	(55)
Balance on 14th January	170

CASH ACCOUNT METHOD							
Date	V	Particulars	Amount	Date	V	Particulars	Amount
2000			£	2000			£
1.1		Balance b/f	125	1.1	PV1	Room rent	175
1.1	R1	Maintenance	400	4.1	PV2	Books	40
2.1	R1	Loan	600	7.1	PV3	Bicycle	400
30.1	R3	Earnings	240	11.1	PV4	Food	285
				14.1	PV5	Telephone	55
				17.1	PV6	Clothing	45
				24.1	PV7	Electricity	30
				26.1	PV8	Gas	25
				31.1	PV9	Loan re-paid	250
						Total payment	1,305
						Balance c/d	60
			1,365				1,365
1.2		Balance b/d	60				

In both methods the receipts and payments are listed chronologically, i.e. in the sequence in which they occurred. There are, however, significant differences:

• Receipts and payments are mixed together, the payments being stated in parentheses (brackets). • The balance is calculated after every transaction. • There is a risk of arithmetic error unless calculation is computerized.	• Receipts are listed separately from payments. Receipts are supported by vouchers (with a prefix of R) Payments are supported by vouchers (with a prefix of PV) • The balance is calculated only at the end of the month. • There is less risk of arithmetic errors, although this is not relevant if computerized.

2.4 BALANCING THE ACCOUNT

The Cash account shown above has been balanced at the end of the month. Balancing involves the following steps:

1. Add all amounts received (as £1,365).
2. Add all amounts paid (as £1,305).
3. Find the difference between the two totals (£1,365 – £1,305 = £60), which should be the balance of cash remaining in hand at the end of the period.
4. State that balance also on the payment side of the Cash account, so that the total of all amounts stated on the payment side equals that of those stated on the receipt side. To draw attention to this equality state the totals in level with each other (i.e. on the same line), with a double line drawn beneath each to show that the Cash account for the period ends there.
5. Thereafter enter the same balance as the starting amount, this time on the receipt side, in order to commence writing up the Cash account for the next period.
6. Note the use of the abbreviation c/d standing for 'carried down' and b/d standing for 'brought down'.

Interaction 2.3	**Correctness of a Cash account**
	How would you verify whether Beatrice's Cash account has been prepared correctly?

Interaction 2.4	**Does the cash balance measure performance?**
	Do you think that Beatrice's financial position is worse at the end of the month, in comparison with that at the beginning, bearing in mind that she had less cash in hand?

2.5 A BUSINESS CASH ACCOUNT

A Cash account for a *business* is prepared following the same principles as for an *individual*. There will, however, be differences in:

- **the type of transactions**, for example:
  - the *acquisition* of fixed assets that are to be retained and used in carrying on the business;
  - the *disposal* of fixed assets that had been retained and used in carrying on the business but are no longer required;
  - *purchases* of goods for resale to make a profit, and the *sale* of these goods;
  - the purchase of *consumable items* (such as stationery) for use in the business, which will be treated as an expense rather than a fixed asset;
  - *expenditure* on the payment of business expenses to run the premises, pay staff and promote sales;
- **the terminology used**, where, for example:
  - the pages used to record transactions are referred to as *folios*;
  - entries in the Cash account are *prime entries* because the Cash account is the first place the transactions are recorded;
  - adding up is known as *casting*;

- a regular period by reference to which accounts are prepared is known as the *accounting period*;
- cash as well as any item that is expected to be of value beyond the current period is referred to as an *asset*; whereas if the benefit of the item does not extend beyond the current period, it is referred to as an expenditure.

The greater complexity of the transactions, the fact that they are more numerous, the need to satisfy VAT inspectors and the need to control the cash more tightly have led to the development of a more systematic procedure for recording cash transactions in a business. Let us ascertain the procedure that is followed by the majority of businesses using manual recording. The principles also apply to computerized systems although the arithmetic is then automated.

Accounting terminology

Complete the blanks with an accounting terminology word or phrase chosen from the following list:

| acquisition | asset | casting | disposal | balancing the account | sale |
| expenditure | folio | purchase | prime entry | accounting period | voucher |

Accountants have their own language in which they refer to:

(a) an item that gives future economic benefit as an ....;

(b) an item, the benefit from which is immediately used up, as an ....;

(c) the buying of any item intended for sale as a ....;

(d) the buying of any item intended for use in the business as an ....;

(e) the encashment (converting into cash) of an item intended for sale as a ....;

(f) the encashment of an item intended for use (rather than for sale) as ....;

(g) a regular period chosen for the purposes of accounting as an ....;

(h) the first accounting record made of any transaction as a ....;

(i) a page in any book of account as a ....;

(j) adding together all amounts written on a folio as ....;

(k) proving the accuracy of the Cash account as ....;

(l) the document retained to prove the accuracy of any prime entry as a ....

A separate folio is used for each accounting period to record the receipts and payments in voucher number order. At the end of the month, or other agreed period, the receipts are cast, the payments are cast, the difference between the total receipts and total payments is calculated (the process known as balancing the account) and the balance is compared with the actual cash in hand.

Writing up a trader's Cash account

Andy Small requests you to take charge of a new shop that he is equipping to sell portable telephones. The product to be sold is a standard model costing Andy £100 and selling at £150. The trading commenced on 1 January 20X0. The cash transactions during the first week of business are as follows:

Date	Item	£	Date	Item	£
1.1	Received as capital from Small	5,000	3.1	Paid for staff tea	18
	Acquired as fixed assets for			Purchased 25 portable telephones	?
	office use:			Paid for a rubber stamp	15
	A wooden desk	125		Paid for advertising	40
	a steel filing cabinet	85		Sold 24 portable telephones	?
	four wooden chairs	120		Paid the office telephone bill	60
	Purchased ten portable		4.1	Paid for advertising	125
	telephones for sale	?		Paid for postage stamps	15
	Paid for advertising	60		Sold 11 portable telephones	?
	Sold two portable telephones	?		Received from staff (for a	
	Paid for stationery as follows:			personal call)	11
	Pads of A4 papers	10		Purchased 15 portable telephones	?
	Ball point pens	5	5.1	Paid as staff salary	780
	Rulers and correcting fluid	6		Purchased ten portable	
	A Cash book	15		telephones	?
2.1	Received as a loan from			Paid for staff tea	10
	Jim Jones	1,500		Repaid to Jim in part	
	Purchased 24 portable			settlement of loan	300
	telephones	?		Paid for advertising	130
	Paid for staff tea	12		Sold all portable telephones	
	Paid for an electric typewriter	300		in hand	?
	Paid for typewriter ribbons	4			
	Sold 12 portable telephones	?			

Required:

(a) Prepare a Cash account for the first week's trading.

(b) Comment on whether the business is doing well or not.

(c) Explain how you will ascertain whether the Cash account had been written up correctly.

2.6 ACCOUNTING FOR CASH TAKEN BY THE OWNER FOR PERSONAL USE

If the owner (Andy in our example) takes cash out of the business for his own use, the cashier of the business will record the amount as a payment and describe it as *drawings*. The cashier would not be concerned with the use to which Andy Small puts the cash; whether Andy keeps the cash with him, invests it or spends it on living expenses or a holiday would not be of concern to the business. The only information required is the amount and the fact that Andy Small has taken it. Assuming that, in IQ 2.6 above, Andy Small took £200 from the business on 5 January, the Cash account in Andy Small's business would appear as follows:

CASH ACCOUNT

Date	V	Particulars	F	Amount	Date	V	Particulars	F	Amount
20X0					20X0				
5.1	CS05	Sales		5,250	5.1	PV21	Advertising		130
					5.1	PV22	Drawings		200
									10,835
							Balance c/d		8,276
				19,111					19,111
6.1		Balance b/d		8,276					

SOLUTIONS TO INTERACTIVE QUESTIONS

IQ 2.1 Controlling the vouchers

- Vouchers issued by a business in support of amounts it receives should be pre-numbered and a duplicate retained as evidence of every amount received.
- Vouchers supporting payment for goods or services would be those issued by others, and these should be numbered in sequence when received.
- The vouchers should be kept in safe custody.
- The numbering sequence of the vouchers accounted for should be checked at regular intervals to ensure that none is missing.

IQ 2.2 Controlling cash receipts and payments

- The number sequence of the vouchers accounted for should be checked at regular intervals to ensure that every amount received and paid has been accounted for in the cash book.
- If the number sequence is broken, evidencing that a voucher has been missed out, an adequate explanation is required.
- Vouchers supporting every payment should bear the initials of the person who authorized the payment.

IQ 2.3 Correctness of a Cash account

- Balancing the Cash account indicates that there should be a balance of £60 in hand on 31 January.
- If the actual money in hand is exactly that amount, it may be presumed (provided that all receipts and payments have been recorded) that the Cash account has been correctly written up.

IQ 2.4 Does the cash balance measure performance?

- A person's financial position is more than just the cash balance.
- It cannot be assessed whether Beatrice's financial position is better or worse merely because the cash in hand has fallen from £125 to £60.
- Consideration needs to be given to the fact that Beatrice now has a bicycle (an asset) worth £400, which she did not have at the beginning, but on the other hand there is a debt (a liability) of £350 owed to Simon, which obligation did not exist at the beginning.

IQ 2.5 Accounting terminology

Accountants have their own language in which they refer to:

(a) an item that gives future economic benefit as an asset;
(b) an item, the benefit from which is immediately used up, as an expenditure;
(c) the buying of any item intended for resale as a purchase;
(d) the buying of any item intended for use in the business as an acquisition;
(e) the encashment of an item intended for sale as a sale;
(f) the encashment of an item intended for use as a disposal;
(g) a regular period chosen for purposes of accounting as an accounting period;
(h) the first accounting record made of any transaction as a prime entry;
(i) a page in any book of account as a folio;
(j) adding together all amounts written on a folio as casting;
(k) proving the accuracy of the Cash account as balancing the account;
(l) the document retained to prove the accuracy of any prime entry as a voucher.

IQ 2.6 Writing up a trader's Cash account

(a) Preparing the account

CASH ACCOUNT

Date	V	Particulars	F	Amount	Date	V	Particulars	F	Amount
20X0				£	20X0				£
1.1	R01	Capital		5,000	1.1	PV1	Furniture		330
1.1	CS01	Sales		300	1.1	PV2	Purchases		1,000
2.1	R02	Jim's Loan		1,500	1.1	PV3	Advertising		60
2.1	CS02	Sales		1,800	1.1	PV4	Stationery		36
3.1	CS03	Sales		3,600	2.1	PV5	Purchases		2,400
4.1	CS04	Sales		1,650	2.1	PV6	Staff Welfare		12
4.1	R03	Telephone		11	2.1	PV7	Office Equipment		300
5.1	CS05	Sales		5,250	2.1	PV8	Stationery		4
					3.1	PV9	Staff Welfare		18
					3.1	PV10	Purchases		2,500
					3.1	PV11	Stationery		15
					3.1	PV12	Advertising		40
					3.1	PV13	Telephone		60
					4.1	PV14	Advertising		125
					4.1	PV15	Postage		15
					4.1	PV16	Purchases		1,500
					5.1	PV17	Salaries		780
					5.1	PV18	Purchases		1,000
					5.1	PV19	Staff Welfare		10
					5.1	PV20	Jim's Loan		300
					5.1	PV21	Advertising		130
									10,635
					5.1	–	Balance c/d		8,476
				19,111					19,111
6.1		Balance b/d		8,476					

(b) Whether the shop has done well
- The shop started with a cash balance of £5,000 and finished the week with £8,476, representing an increase of £3,476.
- However, it is not possible to say whether the shop has done well, because the performance of a business cannot be measured solely by the amount of cash in its hand at any one point in time.

(c) Checking the accuracy of cash accounting
- If, on physically counting the money in the till at close of business on 5 January, the cash in hand is found to be exactly £8,476, the Cash account may be presumed (assuming all receipts and payments have been accurately and fully recorded) to have been correctly written up.
- This is why it is said that balancing the Cash account should prove the accuracy of a Cash account.

PROGRESSIVE QUESTIONS

PQ 2.1 Sorting out the side

As the cashier in a retail shop, you maintain a Cash account that has two sides divided by a double line drawn vertically down the centre. The first side (on the left of the double line), in which you record all amounts received, is identified by you as 'IN', while the second side (on the right of the centre line), in which you record all payments, is identified by you as 'OUT'.

Required: State on which of these sides of the Cash account you will record each of the following transactions:

	In (x)	Out (y)	None (z)
(a) £56 paid for postage;			
(b) £15 received on sale of goods held for sale;			
(c) £65 paid for staff refreshments;			
(d) £500 received as a loan from Dave, a friend of the shop owner;			
(e) £1,000 paid as rent for shop premises;			
(f) Two £10 notes given to a customer as change for a £20 note.			

PQ 2.2 Multiple-choice question

You, as the cashier, are required to check the accuracy of your Cash account by ascertaining whether the cash physically in your custody matches the amount stated as the balance in the Cash account.

Required: Tick the appropriate grid to identify the amount by which the cash physically in your hand will differ from the Cash account balance if the only mistake is each of the following:

(a) £4,620 paid for purchasing goods for sale is recorded on the payment side of the Cash account as £462.

£462 more (x)	
£4,158 less (y)	
£4,158 more (z)	

(b) £460 received from sales is not recorded at all in the Cash account.

£460 less (x)	
Same (y)	
£460 more (z)	

(c) £620 paid for stationery was recorded on the payment side of the Cash account as £260.

£620 more (x)	
£360 more (y)	
£360 less (z)	

(d) £106 paid for staff tea was not recorded at all in the Cash account.

£106 more (x)	
£106 less (y)	
Same (z)	

(e) £1,200 paid for office furniture was recorded on the payment side of the Cash account and stated as purchases.

£1,200 less (x)	
£1,200 more (y)	
Same (z)	

(f) £165 paid for advertising was recorded on the receipts side of the Cash account.

£165 less (x)	
£330 less (y)	
£330 more (z)	

PQ 2.3 Writing up the Cash account – Arnold

Arnold commenced business on 1.1.20X0 and has made the following transactions:

(a) 1.1 Started business with £15,000 cash.
(b) 2.1 Made purchases of £300 for cash.
(c) 2.1 Paid rent of £1,500 cash.
(d) 2.1 Bought stationery for £90 cash.
(e) 2.1 Cash sales £1,500
(f) 3.1 Made purchases of £150 for cash.

(g) 4.1 Bought stationery for £60 cash.
(h) 5.1 Paid motor expenses £225 in cash.
(i) 6.1 Paid Peter £1,500 for vehicle
(j) 6.1 Used £450 cash for living expenses.
(k) 7.1 Cash sales £150

Required: Show how these transactions would be recorded in the Cash account and use the Voucher column to cross-reference to the transaction.

PQ 2.4 Writing up the Cash account – Bennett

Bennett started in business on 1 April 20X0 with a capital of £12,000 in cash selling toys. The following transactions took place during his first six months' trading:

Date	Item	£	Date	Item	£
1.4	Paid rent demand for 6 months' rent	1,000	9.5	Paid electricity bill	500
1.4	Paid invoice for acquisition of shop fittings	1,200	1.6	Paid telephone bill	220
5.4	Paid invoice for purchase of toys	2,400	3.6	Cash sales recorded in till roll	7,400
7.5	Paid wages of assistant	1,200	3.6	Cash drawn by Bennett for own use	3,200

Required: Show how these transactions would be recorded in the Cash account.

Chapter 3

DOUBLE ENTRY BOOKKEEPING

In this chapter

We will learn:

- of the need to analyse entries in the Cash account
- that ledger accounts analyse the transactions
- the double entry system and the accounting equation

and you should be able to:

- post cash transactions to appropriate ledger accounts
- classify accounts into the four recognized categories
- prepare a list of balances in all accounts

3.1 THE NEED TO ANALYSE CASH TRANSACTIONS

In a fiercely competitive world there is strong pressure on a business to keep its costs down. This means the managers and owners being aware of what cash is being spent on. We know from Chapter 2 that a Cash account allows us to record all receipts and payments and to check the cash balance. What it does not do, however, is to allow us to see quickly how much was spent on stationery, salaries or any of the other expenses incurred in running a business. The reason for this is that in a Cash account all receipts and payments are recorded in the order in which they occur, i.e. their chronological sequence, with receipts from different sources being intermingled as are payments for different purposes.

What we need is an analysis so that we can see:

- the amount received from sales and paid out for each category of expenditure;
- the amount of growth that the business has achieved – growth being measured as the difference between the cumulative amount of cash received from the sale of goods and the cumulative amounts of cash paid out, both for the purchase of goods and for expenses;
- amounts that the business owes, e.g. loans that have been obtained;
- amounts that the business owns, e.g. furniture, equipment and cash.

3.2 PERFORMING THE ANALYSIS

One way to obtain such an analysis would be simply to analyse the cash transactions in order to obtain cumulative totals. This, in the case of Andy Small's telephone business (IQ 2.6), may be done as follows:

Particulars	Individual amounts involved £	Cumulative £
Cash received as Capital	5,000	5,000
Cash received as a Loan	1,500	1,500
Cash repaid to settle loan	300	300
Cash received from Sales	300 + 1,800 + 3,600 + 1,650 + 5,250	12,600
Cash paid for Purchases	1,000 + 2,400 + 2,500 + 1,500 + 1,000	8,400
Cash paid for Telephone	60	60
Cash received back for a personal call	11	11
Cash paid for Advertising	60 + 40 + 125 + 130	355
Cash paid for Stationery	36 + 4 + 15	55
Cash paid for Salaries	780	780
Cash paid for Staff expenses	12 + 18 + 10	40
Cash paid for Postage	15	15
Cash paid to buy Furniture	330	330
Cash paid to buy Office Equipment	300	300

But how do we organise the cumulative totals to provide information the owners need? Conceptually, we can classify the transactions into four categories:

● liabilities: sources of cash that are repayable (e.g. loans)
● income: sources of cash that are not repayable (e.g. sales)
● assets: uses of cash that have future value (e.g. furniture, equipment)
● expenditure: uses of cash that have no ongoing value (e.g. the telephone bill, rent)

We can then prepare what is known as a Category Quadrant, which summarizes the effect of all transactions by reporting their effect on the four categories stated in the Quadrant. The Category Quadrant for Andy Small, created by separating transactions into the four categories of assets, liabilities, expenditure and income, appears as follows:

ASSETS	LIABILITIES
EXPENDITURE	INCOME

ANDY SMALL

Uses that have value at end of period, i.e. ASSETS £		Sources that are repayable, i.e. LIABILITIES £	
Furniture	330	Capital	5,000
Office equipment	300	Loan	1,200
Cash	8,476		
Sub-total	9,106	Sub-total	6,200

Uses that do not have a value at the end of the accounting period, i.e. EXPENDITURE £		Sources that are not repayable, i.e. INCOME £	
Purchases	8,400	Sales	12,600
Telephone	49		
Salaries	780		
Staff expenses	40		
Stationery	55		
Postage	15		
Advertising	355		
Sub-total	9,694	Sub-total	12,600
TOTAL of assets and expenses	18,800	TOTAL of liabilities and income	18,800

We can see from the Category Quadrant that Andy's business:

(a) has achieved sales of £12,600;
(b) owns assets totalling £9,106;
(c) owes £5,000 to Andy as capital and £1,200 to the loan creditor;
(d) has grown by £2,906 – the amount by which income (£12,600) exceeded expenditure (£9,694) in the period or, put another way, the amount that the assets (£9,106) exceed the liabilities (£6,200).

The important point to remember is that:

$$\text{Total assets} + \text{expenses} = \text{Total liabilities} + \text{income}$$

which is often referred to as the *accounting equation*.

3.3 THE EFFECT OF CASH TRANSACTIONS ON ASSETS, LIABILITIES, INCOME AND EXPENDITURE

We will illustrate the effect of cash transactions on the four categories by using the cash transactions of Richard Brown, who commenced a grocery business on 1 January 20X0 with cash of £10,000 as capital. His transactions during the first day were as follows:

Item	£		£		£
Paid for furniture	6,000	Paid for groceries	145	Paid for groceries	110
Paid for groceries	225	Paid for stationery	35	Paid for staff lunches	35
Paid for advertising	65	Sold groceries	210	Paid for groceries	115
Paid for staff teas	15	Paid for advertising	45	Sold groceries	265
Sold groceries	245	Sold groceries	225		

The table below traces the effect of each transaction on the four categories. Notice that every transaction is entered (recorded) twice, once in the Cash account to record the receipt or payment of cash, and for a second time for analysis under an appropriate

RICHARD BROWN

Cash		Assets	Liabilities	Expenditure				Income
Receipts (payments)	Cash	Furniture	Capital	Purchases	Staff Welf.	Stationery	Advert.	Sales
Capital introduced	10,000	–	(10,000)	–	–	–	–	–
Paid for furniture	(6,000)	6,000	–	–	–	–	–	–
Paid for groceries	(225)	–	–	225	–	–	–	–
Paid for advertising	(65)	–	–	–	–	–	65	–
Paid for staff teas	(15)	–	–	–	15	–	–	–
Sold groceries	245	–	–	–	–	–	–	(245)
Paid for groceries	(145)	–	–	145	–	–	–	–
Paid for stationery	(35)	–	–	–	–	35	–	–
Sold groceries	210	–	–	–	–	–	–	(210)
Paid for advertising	(45)	–	–	–	–	–	45	–
Sold groceries	225	–	–	–	–	–	–	(225)
Paid for groceries	(110)	–	–	110	–	–	–	–
Paid for staff lunches	(35)	–	–	–	35	–	–	–
Paid for groceries	(115)	–	–	115	–	–	–	–
Sold groceries	265	–	–	–	–	–	–	(265)
Cumulative total	4,155	6,000	(10,000)	595	50	35	110	(945)

category, e.g. Cash and Capital for the £10,000 of initial capital received from Richard. This system of accounting, based on the recognition of the need for two accounting entries to account for each transaction, is known as the **double entry system**.

For maintaining symmetry, if the first entry in the Cash account (being an amount received) is a positive figure, the second entry is shown (within parentheses) as a negative figure. Accordingly, the amounts in Capital and Sales are stated as negative figures; conversely, every payment recorded in the Cash account as a negative figure (to record amounts going out) is therefore shown in the second entry as a positive figure.

The accuracy of the analysis, and hence of the cumulative totals, can be established by fitting the results into a Category Quadrant as shown here. Since every transaction is recorded by two entries – one of which is positive and the other negative – the total of all positive amounts should naturally equal the total of all negative amounts. The total of all sources equals the total of all uses.

Uses:

ASSETS	
Furniture	6,000
Cash	4,155

EXPENDITURE	
Purchases	595
Staff welfare	50
Stationery	35
Advertising	110
Total uses	10,945

Sources:

LIABILITIES	
Capital	10,000

INCOME	
Sales	945
Total sources	10,945

3.4 ANALYSIS OF TRANSACTIONS BY POSTING TO LEDGER ACCOUNTS

In real life, the large volume of transactions occurring when running a business make it impractical to analyse the figures as above so as to ascertain cumulative totals. Instead, businesses use books of account referred to as **ledgers** to collect the analysed information. Accounting for transactions is then performed as follows:

1. A pair of accounting entries – one positive and one negative – records every transaction. In accounting, the positive entry is known as a **debit entry** and the negative entry as a **credit entry**. This is the double entry system of accounting.
2. In the Cash account, the convention is for positive entries (i.e. debits, amounts received) to be recorded on the left-hand side of the Cash account and for negative entries (i.e. credits, amounts paid) to be recorded on the right-hand side of the cash book. It might seem strange to describe a payment as a credit but the word is not being used in its literal sense but merely as the accounting term for negative. In a computer system, receipts (debits) would be added and payments (credits) deducted from the cash balance.
3. Accordingly, the accounting convention is for the receipts (left-hand) side of the Cash account to be referred to as the debit side and the payments (right-hand) side as the credit side. Debit is abbreviated to Dr and credit to Cr. Since the transaction is usually first recorded by the business's cashier, his entry is referred to as the prime entry (prime meaning first).
4. The second entry, for the purpose of analysis, is made in a separate book, known as a ledger. The ledger has an account for each type of asset, liability, income and expenditure, formatted like the Cash account with a debit side and a credit side. An amount debited by the cashier (such as the £10,000 received from Richard Brown as Capital) is credited by the bookkeeper in the corresponding (in this case, capital) account. Similarly, an amount credited by the cashier (e.g. payment for furniture) is debited by the bookkeeper (in a Furniture account). This process of making a second entry is referred to as **posting**.

In the case of Richard's groceries, the Cash account would appear as follows:

Debit side   **RICHARD BROWN CASH ACCOUNT**   *Credit side*

Date	V	Particulars	F	Amount	Date	V	Particulars	F	Amount
20X0				£	**20X0**				£
1.1		Capital		10,000	1.1		Furniture		6,000
1.1		Sales		245	1.1		Purchases		225
1.1		Sales		210	1.1		Advertising		65
1.1		Sales		225	1.1		Staff Welfare		15
1.1		Sales		265	1.1		Purchases		145
					1.1		Stationery		35
					1.1		Advertising		45
					1.1		Purchases		110
					1.1		Staff Welfare		35
					1.1		Purchases		115
									6,790
					1.1		Balance c/d		4,155
				10,945					10,945
2.1		Balance b/d		4,155					

Every amount debited in the Cash account is posted to the credit of the appropriate account in the ledger.

CAPITAL ACCOUNT

Date	Particulars	Amount	Date	Particulars	Amount
			20X0		£
			1.1	Cash account	10,000

SALES ACCOUNT

Date	Particulars	Amount	Date	Particulars	Amount
			20X0		£
			1.1	Cash account	245
			1.1	Cash account	210
			1.1	Cash account	225
			1.1	Cash account	265
					945

Similarly, every amount from the credit side of the Cash account is posted to the debit side of the appropriate ledger account.

FURNITURE ACCOUNT

Date	Particulars	Amount	Date	Particulars	Amount
20X0		£			
1.1	Cash account	6,000			

PURCHASES ACCOUNT

Date	Particulars	Amount	Date	Particulars	Amount
20X0		£			
1.1	Cash account	225			
1.1	Cash account	145			
1.1	Cash account	110			
1.1	Cash account	115			
		595			

STATIONERY ACCOUNT

Date	Particulars	Amount	Date	Particulars	Amount
20X0		£			
1.1	Cash account	35			

ADVERTISING ACCOUNT

Date	Particulars	Amount	Date	Particulars	Amount
20X0		£			
1.1	Cash account	65			
1.1	Cash account	45			
		110			

STAFF WELFARE ACCOUNT

Date	Particulars	Amount	Date	Particulars	Amount
20X0		£			
1.1	Cash account	15			
1.1	Cash account	35			
		50			

ASSETS			**LIABILITIES**	
Furniture	6,000		Capital	10,000
Cash	4,155			

EXPENDITURE			**INCOME**	
Purchases	595		Sales	945
Staff Welfare	50			
Stationery	35			
Advertising	110			
TOTAL	10,945			10,945

On completion of posting, the information stated on the left may be read off the ledger accounts.

The accounting equation (which states that the total of assets and expenditure would be equal to the total of liabilities and income) confirms that every transaction has been accounted for by a debit as well as a credit entry.

3.5 OPERATION OF THE DOUBLE ENTRY SYSTEM

The following are important features of the double entry system of accounting:

1. The Cash account is written up by the cashier in a cash book. All other accounts, written up by the bookkeeper, are in the ledger. The name 'ledger' is used because, in days gone by, the bookkeeper usually placed his book on a window ledge while he undertook the task of posting.
2. A double line drawn down the centre of every account (the Cash account as well as every account in the ledger) separates the debit side from the credit side.
3. The debit and credit sides of the Cash account have five columns each, whereas the accounts in the ledger have only four. The column not in the ledger accounts is the one for recording the voucher reference. This is because a transaction requires to be substantiated with a supporting voucher only when it is recorded for the *first* time and that is in the Cash account.
4. In the Cash account the name of the account to which the amount should be posted is recorded in the 'Particulars' column. In the 'Particulars' column of a ledger account the bookkeeper records the account from which he posted the amount to that account. This allows for cross-referencing.
5. Receipts recorded by the Cashier on the debit side of the Cash account are of three categories:
   - receipts arising from earnings, which are known as income;
   - receipts that give rise to an owing, which is referred to as a liability;
   - receipts arising from encashing an asset (e.g. selling some furniture) or encashing an expenditure (e.g. recovering a part of the telephone bill from a member of staff for personal calls).

   Accordingly, the receipts debited in the Cash account are credited by the bookkeeper to:
   - an income account according to the nature of the earning (e.g. sales, rental income);
   - a liability account opened in the name of the party to whom the amount is owed;
   - an asset or expense that is converted into cash (e.g. disposal of a vehicle).
6. Payments recorded by the cashier on the credit side of the Cash account are of three categories:
   - payments to acquire or increase the holding of assets;
   - payments to meet expenditure;
   - payments to (partially or fully) discharge a liability.

   Accordingly, payments credited in the Cash account are debited by the bookkeeper to:
   - an asset account in accordance with the class of asset involved (e.g. the Furniture account);
   - an expenditure account according to its nature (e.g. rent, stationery, salaries);
   - the account recording the liability that is reduced or discharged.
7. As a result of posting to the side opposite the one in which the prime entry is made, a regular pattern emerges as follows:
   - asset accounts and expenditure accounts always have their balance on the debit side;
   - liability accounts and income accounts always have their balance on the credit side.

   Reciprocally the obverse applies. If an account has a balance on the credit side, it should be reporting the balance of an income or liability. Similarly, if an account has a debit balance, it should be reporting an expenditure or an asset.

3.6 SUBDIVISION OF THE LEDGER

As the number of accounts to be written up in the ledger grew for businesses in the past, so it became necessary to have separate ledgers. We will, for the time being, focus on two of these ledgers, namely the *Nominal Ledger*, in which income accounts and expenditure accounts are recorded, and the *Real Ledger*, in which asset accounts (other than cash) and liability accounts are set out. There is not nowadays, of course, the same constraint on space as there has been, now that sets of accounts can be computerized, but it is still of value to examine these two ledgers to help in an understanding of accounting principles.

| Interaction 3.1 | **Accounting terminology** |

Complete the blanks with a word or phrase chosen from the following list:

cashier   bookkeeper   real   posting   ledger   nominal   cash book

In the language of accounting:

(a) the Cash account is written up in a ....;

(b) the person writing up the cash book is known as the ....;

(c) copying what has been already entered in any book of prime entries is known as ....;

(d) the person doing the posting is known as the ....;

(e) the book (or several of them, which may be in loose-leaf or computerized form) containing all the accounts to which items entered in books of prime entry are posted is called the ....;

(f) The income accounts and expenditure accounts are found in the .... Ledger.

(g) The asset accounts and liability accounts are found in the .... Ledger.

| Interaction 3.2 | **Posting to the ledger** |

Remember that every cash transaction is first recorded in the cash book (the receipts being entered on the debit side and the payments on the credit side) and then posted to a ledger account, ensuring that the second entry is on the side opposite to the one in the cash book.

State the side (debit or credit) of the named ledger account in which the bookkeeper would post the following transactions:

Transaction	Account	Side
1. Amount received from owner as capital	Capital	
2. Amount paid to acquire a car for business use	Motor Vehicle	
3. Amount paid to purchase goods for sale	Purchases	
4. Amounts received by selling goods	Sales	
5. Amount paid to the landlord as rent	Rent	
6. Amount paid to buy staff refreshments	Staff Welfare	
7. Amount received as a loan from John	John's Loan	
8. Amount paid as staff salaries	Salaries	
9. Amount paid to buy a cash book and a ledger	Stationery	

The class of an account and its balance – emergence of a pattern

State in Column A in the table below the side on which each of the accounts listed should have its balance; and state in Column B whether you would classify each of the named accounts as an asset account, liability account, expenditure account or income account.

Name of account	Column A Debit side or credit side?	Column B Class of account?
1. Capital account		
2. Motor Vehicles account		
3. Purchases account		
4. Sales account		
5. Rent account		
6. Staff Welfare account		
7. John's Loan account		
8. Salaries account		
9. Stationery account		

SOLUTIONS TO INTERACTIVE QUESTIONS

IQ 3.1 Accounting terminology

In the language of accounting:

(a) the Cash account is written up in a cash book;
(b) the person writing up the cash book is known as the cashier;
(c) copying what has been already entered in any book of prime entry is known as posting;
(d) the person doing the posting is known as the bookkeeper;
(e) the book containing all the accounts to which items entered in books of prime entry are posted is called the ledger;
(f) the income accounts and expenditure accounts are found in the *Nominal* Ledger;
(g) the asset accounts and liability accounts are found in the *Real* Ledger.

IQ 3.2 Posting to the ledger

Transactions	Account	Side
1. Amount received from owner as capital	Capital	Credit
2. Amount paid to acquire a car for business use	Motor Vehicle	Debit
3. Amount paid to purchase goods for sale	Purchases	Debit
4. Amounts received by selling goods	Sales	Credit
5. Amount paid to the landlord as rent	Rent	Debit
6. Amount paid to buy staff refreshments	Staff Welfare	Debit
7. Amount received as a loan from John	John's Loan	Credit
8. Amount paid as staff salaries	Salaries	Debit
9. Amount paid to buy a cash book and a ledger	Stationery	Debit

IQ 3.3 The class of an account and its balance – emergence of a pattern

Name of account	Column A Debit side or credit side?	Column B Class of account?
1. Capital account	Credit side	Liability account
2. Motor Vehicles account	Debit side	Asset account
3. Purchases account	Debit side	Expenditure account
4. Sales account	Credit side	Income account
5. Rent account	Debit side	Expenditure account
6. Staff Welfare account	Debit side	Expenditure account
7. John's Loan account	Credit side	Liability account
8. Salaries account	Debit side	Expenditure account
9. Stationery account	Debit side	Expenditure account

PROGRESSIVE QUESTIONS

PQ 3.1 Multiple-choice question

Tick one of the grids as appropriate:

1. As the bookkeeper of your particular business, identify the account to which you will post the following transactions recorded by the cashier in the Cash account:

(a) £300 paid to buy a cash book and a ledger

Audit Books account	(x)	
Postage account	(y)	
Stationery account	(z)	

(b) £15,000 paid to acquire a lorry for business use

Lorry account	(x)	
Motor Vehicle account	(y)	
Transport account	(z)	

(c) £6,000 paid to buy alarm clocks for sale

Purchases account	(x)	
Alarm Clocks account	(y)	
Stock in Trade account	(z)	

(d) £400 paid for servicing the business lorry

Motor Vehicle account	(x)	
General Expenses a/c	(y)	
Vehicle Maintenance a/c	(z)	

(e) £10,000 received as capital from Joe Gardiner, the proprietor of the shop.

Joe Gardiner's account	(x)	
Capital account	(y)	
Cash Introduced account	(z)	

2. Receipts arise from income, create a liability or represent encashment of an asset or an expense. Classify each of the following receipts by using the table provided.

	Income (x)	Liability (y)	Encash (z)
(a) Amount received as capital from the proprietor			
(b) Receipts arising from sale of goods			
(c) Proceeds from disposal of an asset			
(d) Amount borrowed from a friend			
(e) Amount recovered from a member of staff in respect of personal telephone calls			

3. Payments are to acquire an asset, to meet an expenditure or discharge a liability. Classify each of the following payments among the three categories in the table.

	Asset (x)	Expenditure (y)	Liability (z)
(a) Payment for stationery			
(b) Payment of rent for office premises			
(c) Repayment of part of a loan borrowed from a friend			
(d) Payment of salaries for office staff			
(e) Payment for goods bought for sale			
(f) Payment for furniture acquired for office use			

4. As bookkeeper, to which side of the appropriate account will you post the following transactions recorded by the cashier in the Cash account?

	Dr (x)	Cr (y)
(a) Payment of rent for business premises		
(b) Receipt of capital from the proprietor		
(c) Amounts received on sale of goods		
(d) Payment for a vehicle		
(e) Payments for purchasing goods for sale		
(f) Payment of telephone bills		
(g) Receipt of an amount as loan		
(h) Repayment of part of the loan		
(i) Repayment of the sale price to a customer who returned goods		

5. Classify the accounts named below into the appropriate categories in the table.

	Asset (w)	Liabilities (x)	Expenditure (y)	Income (z)
(a) Sales account				
(b) Salaries account				
(c) Motor Vehicles account				
(d) Purchases account				
(e) Stationery account				
(f) Bank Loan account				
(g) Capital account				
(h) Cash account				

PQ 3.2 Preparation of a Category Quadrant

Stated below are the balances in the Cash account as well as all ledger accounts.

Premises	£100,000	Salaries	£3,500
Fixtures	£50,000	Insurance	£200
Vehicles	£30,000	Motor expenses	£1,500
Capital	£105,000	Cash	£8,800
Purchases	£53,000	Sales	£145,000
Rent	£1,000	Office expenses	£1,500
Lighting	£500		

Required:

(a) Fit the balances into a Category Quadrant.

(b) Check that the difference between the assets and liabilities is the same as the difference between income and expenditure.

PQ 3.3 Accounting for business transactions

Bert, who has set up in business as a pharmacist, reports business transactions as stated below. Each transaction is split into two parts: a receipt or payment of cash (a), accounted for by the cashier; and the source or use of the cash movement (b), accounted for by the bookkeeper.

Required: Complete the following table. Transaction 1 has been completed as an illustration.

Transactions		Book of accounts	Name of the account	Class of account	Debit/Credit	Balance* + or −
1	(a) Received £4,000 in cash	Cash book	Cash account	Asset	Debit	Plus
	(b) as capital from Bert	Real Ledger	Capital a/c	Liability	Credit	Plus
2	(a) Paid £100					
	(b) as business rent					
3	(a) Paid £500					
	(b) for business stationery					
4	(a) Paid £150					
	(b) as postage					
5	(a) Paid £10,000					
	(b) for a van					
6	(a) Paid £700					
	(b) for business insurance					
7	(a) Received £6,000					
	(b) from selling medicine					
8	(a) Paid £600					
	(b) for steel cabinets					
9	(a) Received £4,500					
	(b) as a loan from Liza					
10	(a) Repaid £2,500					
	(b) of Liza's loan					
11	(a) Paid £5,250					
	(b) to buy medicine for sale					
12	(a) Paid back £1,000					
	(b) to Bert the owner					

* whether the balance in the named account will increase (plus) or decrease (minus)

Chapter 4

OBTAINING INFORMATION FROM THE ACCOUNTING SYSTEM

In this chapter

We will learn to:

- establish the accuracy of information in the ledger
- be able to cross-reference from the ledger to the voucher

and you should be able to:

- prepare a list of balances in all accounts, separating those with credit balances from those with debit balances

4.1 CROSS-REFERENCING THE DOUBLE ENTRY

The double entry system requires a pair of entries to account for every transaction – a debit in one account matched by a credit in another. To be able to trace quickly the pair of entries recording a single transaction, each account states against its entry the name of the account in which the corresponding second entry is located, and, in a folio column placed immediately prior to the amount column, the book and folio (page) number in which the second entry is located. This means that you can drill down to a voucher from any ledger entry. For example, if you wanted to find out exactly what was bought for the Furniture account entry of £6,000 in the ledger, you would be able to trace back to the entry in the Cash account to identify the voucher – this would probably be the furniture supplier's invoice in this case.

Interaction 4.1

Obtaining information from an account

The Manager of a shop wishes to review the shop's expenses on staff welfare but complains that he has no time to check through every payment for staff welfare recorded in the Cash account because these are intermingled with payments for many other purposes. What advice would you give him?

Confirming that a transaction is authorized

An entry in the Stationery account for a business appears as follows:

STATIONERY ACCOUNT

20X0	Particulars	F	£	20X0	Particulars	F	£
16.5	Cash book	CB7	740				

The manager of the business suspects that the payment of £740 may include the cost of text-books bought for the use of the cashier's undergraduate daughter.

Required:

(a) Explain how the manager's suspicion could be confirmed or allayed.
(b) If the manager's suspicion is confirmed and £280 is received from the cashier as the cost of his daughter's textbooks, how would you account for it?

4.2 ACCURACY OF ACCOUNTING INFORMATION

To establish accounting accuracy, safeguards have to be instituted to ensure that, first, every receipt and payment is entered in the Cash account and, second, the double entry in the ledgers has been made accurately. These safeguards are extremely important.

At the stage of prime entry, in order to ensure that the Cashier has accurately recorded the receipts and payments, safeguards can be implemented by:

● pre-numbering vouchers in support of receipts as well as payments;
● checking whether the number sequence of all vouchers has been accounted for;
● checking whether the amount physically held in hand at the end of each day's business equals the balance shown in the Cash account.

At the posting stage, in order to ensure that every debit cash entry has a corresponding credit ledger entry and every credit cash entry has a corresponding debit ledger entry, safeguards comprise:

● balancing the Cash account and each of the ledger accounts;
● listing each of these balances to check whether the total of all debit balances equals the total of all credit balances.

The foregoing points can be illustrated by looking once more at Richard's grocery business, referred to in Chapter 3. The accuracy of information conveyed by the various ledger accounts depends on whether the transactions have been posted correctly, for if an amount entered in the Cash account is either not posted or posted to a wrong account, or posted to the wrong side of the correct account, the information conveyed by the ledger account would be inaccurate. For instance, if £110 paid for buying groceries had not been posted to the Purchases account, the amount of purchases would have been stated in that account, inaccurately, as £485 (instead of £595). To safeguard against such inaccuracy, a list is prepared of the balances in the Cash account and all the ledger accounts, separating the debit balances from the credit balances. If, in fact, every transaction had been accounted for by a debit entry as well as a matching credit entry, the total of all debits and credits should be equal. If, as was suggested, there had been a failure to post £110 to the Purchases account, with the Purchases account balance stated in the list on the right as £485, the total of the debits would not equal the total of the credits. This would flag up an error.

LIST OF BALANCES AS AT 1.1.20X0		
	Debit £	Credit £
Cash account	4,155	–
Sales account	–	945
Capital account	–	10,000
Furniture account	6,000	–
Purchases account	595	–
Stationery account	35	–
Advertising account	110	–
Staff Welfare account	50	–
	10,945	10,945

Interaction 4.3

Sorting out the side of the balance in an account

In a retail shop owned by Daisy Hall, all the transactions were recorded in a Cash account and posted to appropriate ledger accounts, carefully observing the rule that amounts should be posted to the side opposite the one in which they are recorded in the Cash account. At the year end, the balances in all the accounts have been listed as shown on the right.

Required: Prepare a list in the format shown (below right), stating the balance of each account, either in the debit column or in the credit column as appropriate.

Capital account	£50,000
Salaries account	£12,160
Furniture account	£24,500
Loan from Penny Hall	£10,000
Motor Vehicles account	£36,000
Telephone account	£3,440
Sales account	£269,600
Advertising account	£11,220
Staff Welfare account	£3,230
Cash account	£18,450
Purchases account	£208,600
Rent account	£12,000

	Debit	Credit
Capital account	?	?

4.3 AN ILLUSTRATION OF POSTING FROM A CASH ACCOUNT TO LEDGER ACCOUNTS

In the Cash account prepared for Andy Small's telephone shop (see Chapter 2, and in particular the answer to IQ 2.6) there are two sides (which we now know as the debit side and credit side) and five columns on each side. But only four of these columns were filled in. This is because the cashier is responsible for filling in only those four columns, as he enters in the Cash account every receipt and every payment. The fifth column, marked 'F', is the Folio column. This column is filled in by the bookkeeper, with the folio number of the corresponding account in the Real Ledger (R) or Nominal Ledger (N), after the amount is posted to that account. The Cash account, after the bookkeeper completes the postings, will therefore appear as follows:

CASH ACCOUNT

Date	V	Particulars	F	Amount	Date	V	Particulars	F	Amount
20X0				£	20X0				£
1.1	R01	Capital a/c	R1	5,000	1.1	PV1	Furniture a/c	R4	330
1.1	CS01	Sales a/c	N1	300	1.1	PV2	Purchases a/c	N2	1,000
2.1	R02	Jim's Loan a/c	R2	1,500	1.1	PV3	Advertising a/c	N3	60
2.1	CS02	Sales a/c	N1	1,800	1.1	PV4	Stationery a/c	N4	36
3.1	CS03	Sales a/c	N1	3,600	2.1	PV5	Purchases a/c	N2	2,400
4.1	CS04	Sales a/c	N1	1,650	2.1	PV6	Staff Welfare a/c	N5	12
4.1	R03	Telephone a/c	N6	11	2.1	PV7	Office Equipment a/c	R3	300
5.1	CS05	Sales a/c	N1	5,250	2.1	PV8	Stationery a/c	N4	4
					3.1	PV9	Staff Welfare a/c	N5	18
					3.1	PV10	Purchases a/c	N2	2,500
					3.1	PV11	Stationery a/c	N4	15
					3.1	PV12	Advertising a/c	N3	40
					3.1	PV13	Telephone a/c	N6	60
					4.1	PV14	Advertising a/c	N3	125
					4.1	PV15	Postage a/c	N8	15
					4.1	PV16	Purchases a/c	N2	1,500
					5.1	PV17	Salaries a/c	N7	780
					5.1	PV18	Purchases a/c	N2	1,000
					5.1	PV19	Staff Welfare a/c	N5	10
					5.1	PV20	Jim's Loan a/c	R2	300
					5.1	PV21	Advertising a/c	N3	130
									10,635
					5.1	–	Balance a/c	–	8,476
				19,111					19,111
6.1		Balance b/d		8,476					

Information filled in when transactions were posted has been shown in bold italic print in the Folio column.

We should note that an account built up for analysing receipts will always have its balance on the credit side. For example, see the Capital account (liability), Jim's Loan account (liability) and the Sales account (income):

(R1)   **CAPITAL ACCOUNT**

Date	Particulars	F	Amount	Date	Particulars	F	Amount
20X0			£	20X0			£
				1.1	Cash a/c	CB1	5,000

(R2)   **JIM JONES' LOAN ACCOUNT**

Date	Particulars	F	Amount	Date	Particulars	F	Amount
20X0			£	20X0			£
5.1	Cash a/c	CB1	300	2.1	Cash a/c	CB1	1,500
5.1	Balance c/d		1,200				
			1,500				1,500
				6.1	Balance b/d		1,200

(N1)   **SALES ACCOUNT**

Date	Particulars	F	Amount	Date	Particulars	F	Amount
20X0			£	**20X0**			£
				1.1	Cash a/c	CB1	300
				2.1	Cash a/c	CB1	1,800
				3.1	Cash a/c	CB1	3,600
				4.1	Cash a/c	CB1	1,650
				5.1	Cash a/c	CB1	5,250
							12,600

We should note also that each account to which the bookkeeper posted the payments always has its balance on the debit side:

(R3)   **OFFICE EQUIPMENT ACCOUNT**

Date	Particulars	F	Amount	Date	Particulars	F	Amount
20X0			£	**20X0**			£
2.1	Cash a/c	CB1	300				

(R4)   **FURNITURE AND FITTINGS ACCOUNT**

Date	Particulars	F	Amount	Date	Particulars	F	Amount
20X0			£	**20X0**			£
1.1	Cash a/c	CB1	330				

(N2)   **PURCHASES ACCOUNT**

Date	Particulars	F	Amount	Date	Particulars	F	Amount
20X0			£	**20X0**			£
1.1	Cash a/c	CB1	1,000				
2.1	Cash a/c	CB1	2,400				
3.1	Cash a/c	CB1	2,500				
4.1	Cash a/c	CB1	1,500				
5.1	Cash a/c	CB1	1,000				
			8,400				

(N3)   **ADVERTISING ACCOUNT**

Date	Particulars	F	Amount	Date	Particulars	F	Amount
20X0			£	**20X0**			£
1.1	Cash a/c	CB1	60				
3.1	Cash a/c	CB1	40				
4.1	Cash a/c	CB1	125				
5.1	Cash a/c	CB1	130				
			355				

(N4)   **STATIONERY ACCOUNT**

Date	Particulars	F	Amount	Date	Particulars	F	Amount
20X0			£	**20X0**			£
1.1	Cash a/c	CB1	36				
2.1	Cash a/c	CB1	4				
3.1	Cash a/c	CB1	15				
			55				

(N5)   **STAFF WELFARE ACCOUNT**

Date	Particulars	F	Amount	Date	Particulars	F	Amount
20X0			£	**20X0**			£
2.1	Cash a/c	CB1	12				
3.1	Cash a/c	CB1	18				
5.1	Cash a/c	CB1	10				
			40				

(N6)   **TELEPHONE ACCOUNT**

Date	Particulars	F	Amount	Date	Particulars	F	Amount
20X0			£	**20X0**			£
3.1	Cash a/c	CB1	60	4.1	Cash a/c	CB1	11
				5.1	Balance b/d		49
			60				60
6.1	Balance b/d		49				

(N7)   **SALARIES ACCOUNT**

Date	Particulars	F	Amount	Date	Particulars	F	Amount
20X0			£	**20X0**			£
5.1	Cash a/c	CB1	780				

(N8)   **POSTAGE ACCOUNT**

Date	Particulars	F	Amount	Date	Particulars	F	Amount
20X0			£	**20X0**			£
4.1	Cash a/c	CB1	15				

In all the foregoing, the numbers stated (within parentheses) on the left of the names of each account denote the folio of the ledger in which the account is located. Prefix 'R' refers to the Real Ledger and 'N' to Nominal Ledger. CB1, stated against each amount in the 'Folio' column of all the ledger accounts, indicates that these amounts have been posted from Folio 1 of the cash book.

Two accounts in the ledger have amounts posted to both the debit side and the credit side. The amount received as a loan from Jim Jones was posted to the credit of the Loan account. Thus a credit balance reports the liability. Conversely, £300 repaid to Jim on 5 January is posted to the debit of the Loan account to record the part-settlement of the loan. As a result, the net balance of £1,200 is carried down to the credit side of the Loan account to report the amount of liability still owed to Jim. Another example is the Telephone account. This expenditure account records a debit balance of £60 until £11 (received from a member of staff in respect of personal calls) is posted on 4 January from the Cash account to the credit of the expenditure account. This is referred to as an encashment of an expense.

The information conveyed by ledger accounts cannot be relied on until the accuracy of posting is established by preparing a list of balances in all accounts – the Cash account and Ledger accounts – to check whether the totals of debits and credits are equal.

LIST OF BALANCES AS AT 5.1.20X0			
Name of account	F	Debit	Credit
Cash account	CB1	8,476	
Capital account	R1		5,000
Jim's Loan account	R2		1,200
Sales account	N1		12,600
Office Equipment a/c	R3	300	
Furniture account	R4	330	
Purchases account	N2	8,400	
Advertising account	N3	355	
Stationery account	N4	55	
Staff Welfare account	N5	40	
Telephone account	N6	49	
Salaries account	N7	780	
Postage account	N8	15	
		18,800	18,800

SOLUTIONS TO INTERACTIVE QUESTIONS

IQ 4.1 Obtaining information from an account

The payments for staff welfare, though intermingled with payments for other purposes in the Cash account, would all be listed together in the Staff Welfare ledger account. The Manager has only to check the balance in that account to know the individual and total payments in that regard.

IQ 4.2 Confirming that a transaction is authorized

(a) An amount of £740 has been posted to the Stationery account from folio 7 of the cash book (see Folio (F) column). The manager has, therefore, to investigate the credit entry in folio 7 of the cash book and, on the basis of the cross-reference made against that entry in the voucher column, locate the voucher supporting the payment. The voucher will reveal whether the payment has been for textbooks for the cashier's daughter.

(b) The £280, when received, is accounted for on the debit side of the Cash account and posted to the credit of the Stationery account.

STATIONERY ACCOUNT

20X0	Particulars	F	£	20X0	Particulars	F	£
16.5	Cash book	CB7	740	?	Cash book	?	280

IQ 4.3 Sorting out the side of the balance in an account

LIST OF BALANCES AS AT 31.12.20X0		
	Debit £	Credit £
Capital account	–	50,000
Salaries account	12,160	–
Furniture account	24,500	–
Loan from Penny Hall a/c	–	10,000
Motor Vehicles account	36,000	–
Telephone account	3,440	–
Sales account	–	269,600
Advertising account	11,220	–
Staff Welfare account	3,230	–
Cash account	18,450	–
Purchases account	208,600	–
Rent account	12,000	–
	329,600	329,600

PROGRESSIVE QUESTIONS

PQ 4.1 Multiple-choice question

Place a tick in the appropriate grid to identify the balance that would be brought down in each of the following named accounts, in the books of Rizwy Mohamed:

1. In the Cash account, if Rizwy commenced business with capital in cash of £10,000 and paid £6,000 for a vehicle, £400 as rent and £1,200 for purchases:

(a) Credit: £2,400	
(b) Debit: £2,400	
(c) No balance	

2. In the Nizar Loan account, if Rizwy gave Nizar a loan of £3,000 and has already received back from Nizar two instalments of £300 each:

(a) Credit: £2,400	
(b) Debit: £2,700	
(c) Debit: £2,400	

3. In the Bank Loan account, if Rizwy obtained a bank loan of £20,000 and has repaid to the bank six instalments of £200 each:

(a) Credit: £18,800	
(b) Debit: £21,200	
(c) Debit: £18,800	

4. In the Office Equipment account, if Rizwy paid £3,000 each for three computers and then returned one because it was not suitable for the intended purpose:

(a) Credit: £6,000	
(b) Debit: £6,000	
(c) Debit: £9,000	

5. In the Telephone account, if Rizwy paid £460 to settle the month's telephone bill and then received £80 from his salesmen for personal calls taken by them:

(a) Debit: £540	
(b) Debit: £380	
(c) Credit: £380	

PQ 4.2 Posting from the Cash account to the ledger

Alice Sagar commenced a business on 1 June 20X0 with capital in cash of £30,000. The Cash account recording the transactions during the first week appears below:

CASH ACCOUNT

Date	V	Particulars	F	Amount	Date	V	Particulars	F	Amount
20X0				**£**	**20X0**				**£**
1.6	R01	Capital a/c		30,000	1.6	PV1	Motor Vehicle		18,000
1.6	CS01	Sales a/c		450	1.6	PV2	Purchases		1,540
1.6	CS02	Sales a/c		376	1.6	PV3	Stationery		24
2.6	CS03	Sales a/c		428	1.6	PV4	Staff Welfare		46
2.6	CS04	Sales a/c		540	1.6	PV5	Advertising		124
2.6	R02	Loan – S. Lawrie		2,500	1.6	PV6	Rent		1,000
2.6	CS05	Sales a/c		622	2.6	PV7	Postage		12
3.6	CS06	Sales a/c		568	2.6	PV8	Purchases		624
3.6	CS07	Sales a/c		245	2.6	PV9	Staff Welfare		14
3.6	CS08	Sales a/c		164	2.6	PV10	Advertising		33
3.6	CS09	Sales a/c		322	2.6	PV11	Staff Salary		200
3.6	CS10	Sales a/c		569	2.6	PV12	Purchases		165
4.6	CS11	Sales a/c		345	3.6	PV13	Staff Salary		240
4.6	CS12	Sales a/c		140	3.6	PV14	Purchases		1,262
4.6	R03	Loan – S. Lawrie		1,500	3.6	PV15	Sagar's Drawing		465
4.6	CS13	Sales a/c		250	3.6	PV16	Staff Welfare		16
4.6	CS14	Sales a/c		372	3.6	PV17	Advertising		35
5.6	CS15	Sales a/c		459	4.6	PV18	Stationery		16
5.6	CS16	Sales a/c		165	4.6	PV19	Purchases		755
5.6	CS17	Sales a/c		544	4.6	PV20	Sagar's Drawing		245
5.6	CS18	Sales a/c		386	4.6	PV21	Staff Welfare		22
5.6	CS19	Sales a/c		240	4.6	PV22	Staff Salary		240
					4.6	PV23	Purchases		248
					4.6	PV24	Telephone		45
					5.6	PV25	Postage		15
					5.6	PV26	Staff Welfare		24
					5.6	PV27	Stationery		32
					5.6	PV28	Advertising		65
					5.6	–	Balance c/d	–	15,678
				41,185					41,185
6.6		Balance b/d		15,678					

Required:

(a) Explain why the vouchers supporting amounts received are identified with two different prefixes – some commencing with R and others CS.

(b) The vouchers supporting payments are received from varied third parties to whom the payments were made. How is it that the vouchers carry numbers in the sequence of payment?

(c) Post each transaction to the appropriate ledger account, filling in the folio column of the Cash account, as the bookkeeper would, after each posting. The folios on which each ledger account is located are as on the right.

(d) Check the accuracy of your posting by preparing a list of balances in the Cash account and in all the ledger accounts, as at 5 June 20X0.

A/C name	Folio	A/C name	Folio
Purchases	NL1	Stationery	NL21
Staff Welfare	NL26	Postage	NL30
Salaries	NL34	S Lawrie loan	RL21
Sales	NL11	Advertising	NL24
Rent	NL28	Telephone	NL32
Capital	RL1	Motor vehicle	RL31

NL stands for Nominal Ledger and RL for Real Ledger.

Chapter 5

THE TRIAL BALANCE

In this chapter

We will learn about:

- the Trial Balance and how it helps
- some common accounting errors

and you should be able to:

- extract a Trial Balance from a set of accounts

5.1 WHAT IS A TRIAL BALANCE?

The double entry system requires every transaction to be recorded twice – once as a debit and once as a credit. It follows from this that the total of the debits and credits should always be equal. By preparing what is known as a *Trial Balance*, businesses carry out such a check at regular intervals to confirm that the double entry principle has been applied in full when accounting for transactions.

Interaction 5.1

The class of an account and the side of its balance

Fill in the following grid by:

(a) using Column 2 to classify each account named in Column 1 as an asset, liability, income or expenditure; and

(b) stating in Column 3 the side on which you would expect to find the balance in that account, whether credit or debit.

Column 1 Name of the account	Column 2 Class of account	Column 3 Side of balance
1. Cash account		
2. Rent account		
3. Purchases account		
4. Sales account		
5. Motor Vehicles account		
6. Salaries account		
7. Stationery account		
8. Furniture & Fittings a/c		
9. Telephone and Postage a/c		
10. Land and Buildings account		
11. Advertising account		
12. Staff Welfare account		
13. Capital account		
14. Loan to Sales Rep. account		
15. Bank Loan account		

A Trial Balance is a list of each of the ledger account balances (the Cash account as well as all the income, expenditure, asset and liability accounts in the ledger), extracted at any point in time. In it, the debit balances are listed separately from the credit balances for the purpose of finding out whether the total of all the debit balances equals the total of all the credit balances. If the totals agree, it is presumed that every transaction has been recorded in the books of account by a debit entry as well as a corresponding credit entry. Putting it another way, if every transaction recorded by the cashier in the cash book is accurately posted by the bookkeeper to the appropriate ledger account and the second entry in the ledger is on the side opposite to the one in which it is recorded in the cash book, the Trial Balance must balance.

Preparation of a Trial Balance

Interaction 5.2

The following is a list of balances as at 5 January 20X0 extracted from the books of Andy Small's shop:

LIST OF BALANCES AS AT 5 JANUARY 20X0		TRIAL BALANCE AS AT 5.1.20X0			
			Debit	Credit	Class of account
Cash a/c	8,476	Cash a/c			
Capital a/c	5,000	Capital a/c			
Furniture a/c	330	Furniture a/c			
Purchases a/c	8,400	Purchases a/c			
Sales a/c	12,600	Sales a/c			
Jim's Loan a/c	1,200	Jim's Loan a/c			
Advertising a/c	355	Advertising a/c			
Stationery a/c	55	Stationery a/c			
Staff Welfare a/c	40	Staff Welfare a/c			
Office Equipment	300	Office Equipment a/c			
Telephone a/c	49	Telephone a/c			
Salaries a/c	780	Salaries a/c			
Postage a/c	15	Postage a/c			

Required:

(a) Prepare a Trial Balance as at 5 January 20X0 showing the debit balances separately from the credit balances.
(b) Classify each account as an asset, liability, expenditure or income.

5.2 HOW FREQUENTLY SHOULD A TRIAL BALANCE BE PREPARED?

There is no rule about how often a Trial Balance should be prepared. The exercise should be undertaken when its need is felt (like taking a bath). A business could just extract a Trial Balance on the last day of its accounting period, to check on the accuracy of its postings, before it reports its position to the owners. If, however, the Trial Balance totals fail to agree, it would be necessary to check through the whole period's postings to locate the error(s). It is customary, therefore, to extract Trial Balances at more frequent intervals so as to restrict the period that would need to be investigated. For a trading company, a Trial Balance might be prepared monthly; for an organization such as a bank that is dealing with clients' money it might even be prepared daily.

Interaction 5.3	**Preparation of a Trial Balance when one balance is not stated**

The following is a list of balances extracted from the books of a newsagents called First with the News, as at 31 March 20X0:

Accounts	£	Accounts	£
Cash account	2,500	Furniture account	24,000
Purchases account	170,500	Bank Loan account	3,000
Sales account	295,900	Stationery account	400
Rent account	18,000	Salaries account	21,600
Audit Fees account	1,200	Advertising account	4,200
Motor Vehicles a/c	60,000	Sales Commission a/c	9,200
Loan to Cashier a/c	5,000	Telephone a/c	300
Machinery account	7,000		

The list includes all balances other than the one in the Capital account.

Required:
Prepare a Trial Balance as at 31 March 20X0 assuming that the missing amount is the balance in the Capital account.

5.3 TYPES OF ACCOUNTING ERROR

Errors may arise from:

- clerical error due to the tedium of the job, e.g. omitting transactions or posting to the incorrect account;
- ignorance, e.g. not being aware of the distinction between an asset and an expenditure; or
- fraud, e.g. omitting to account for receipts or paying fictitious vouchers.

Accounting errors may arise at any of the following stages:

(a) **at the stage of making the prime entry:**
 - failure to enter in accounts (both debit and credit) is an *error of omission*;
 - entering and posting an incorrect amount is an *entry error*;
 - entering the same transaction twice is an *error of duplication*;

(b) **at the stage of posting:**
- failure to post an amount entered in a book of prime entry is a *double entry error*;
- posting to an incorrect account of the correct class (for example posting to the Stationery account instead of the Advertising account, both of which are expenditure accounts) is an *error of commission*;
- posting to an account of an incorrect class (to an expenditure account instead of an asset account) is an *error of principle*;

(c) **at the stage of extracting a Trial Balance:**
- failure to include an account balance in the Trial Balance;
- stating the amount wrongly in the Trial Balance;
- stating the balance on the wrong side (debit instead of credit) in the Trial Balance.

In addition, an entry error, which could arise at one or more of stages (a), (b) or (c), could, for instance, arise through omission of a zero (£2,000 entered, posted or extracted as £200) or through transposition of figures (£652 entered or posted as £625 or £562).

The effect of an accounting error on the Trial Balance	**Interaction 5.4**

Assume that the only error in accounting is each of those stated below and identify the side of the Trial Balance that will fall short and the amount by which it will do so, or state if there is no difference:

The accounting error by either the cashier or the bookkeeper	Side	£
1. £100,000 received as capital was posted to the Liability account as £10,000.		
2. A sale of £5,400 has not been posted.		
3. £6,400 paid for purchases was posted as £4,600 in the ledger.		
4. £600 paid for servicing vehicles was posted to the Asset account.		
5. £140 paid for stationery was posted to the Expenditure account as £14.		
6. £12,000 paid for an office computer system was posted to the Office Expenses account.		
7. The debit side of the cash book was stated as £4,600 instead of £5,800 (an undercast).		
8. £1,000 received as a loan from Peter was debited to Peter's Loan account.		

5.3.1 Transposition errors

Unless accounting is computerized, transposition errors are commonplace at each of the accounting stages identified in 5.3 above. If a Trial Balance fails to balance (say by £12,690) and the numerals in the difference added together until the sum is a single numeral $((1 + 2 + 6 + 9 = 18)$ and $(1 + 8 = 9))$ results in an answer of 9, it may suggest that there is a transposition error.

The following table, showing differences arising through transposition errors, can be an aid to identifying such transposition errors:

If the difference is:

9	18	27	36	45	54	63	72	81

The error could be:

01	10	02	20	03	30	04	40	05	50	06	60	07	70	08	80	09	90
12	21	13	31	14	41	15	51	16	61	17	71	18	81	19	91		
23	32	24	42	25	52	26	62	27	72	28	82	29	92				
34	43	35	53	36	63	37	73	38	83	39	93						
45	54	46	64	47	74	48	84	49	94								
56	65	57	75	58	85	59	95										
67	76	68	86	69	96												
78	87	79	97														
89	98																

To illustrate the use of the above set of figures, let us use it to identify the transposition error in the Trial Balance shown on the right. The difference to be located is 27 (105,058 – 105,085). The table of figures listed under 27 indicates that the transposition could be of 03, 14, 25, 36, 47, 58 or 69. One of the lines of enquiry will have to be whether the cash balance stated as £36,436 should correctly have been £36,463, for when the cash balance is stated as £36,463, the total of all the debits matches the total of credits. This confirms that the error was probably in stating the Cash balance wrongly.

TRIAL BALANCE AS AT XXXX

	Dr	Cr
Capital account	–	39,642
Purchases a/c	20,685	–
Sales a/c	–	65,443
Expenses a/c	12,645	–
Fixed Assets a/c	35,292	–
Cash account	36,436	–
	105,058	105,085

5.4 COMPENSATING ERRORS

It is usual to accept a Trial Balance in which the totals agree as providing a *prima facie* proof (though not a conclusive proof) that every debit entry has been matched by a credit entry. There is no guarantee of the accuracy of accounting because, despite errors, a Trial Balance may perfectly balance in circumstances such as the following:

- when the error is at the stage of making the prime entry;
- when the posting error is one of commission;
- when the posting error is one of principle.

Accounting errors that do not disturb the Trial Balance, but which are errors nevertheless, are referred to as *compensating errors*.

The responsibility for, and description of, accounting errors

The Tasty Cake is a confectionery shop owned by Jill Mitchie. Jill employs a cashier and a bookkeeper. When writing up the books of account for the year ended 31.12.20X0 the following errors have been made by the two accounting staff:

1. Sale of cakes for £64 was not recorded in the cash book or ledger.
2. Payment of £800 as rent was recorded as £8,000 in the cash book and ledger.
3. When recording a payment of £8,000 for a vehicle, the cashier classified it as 'purchases'.
4. £35 paid for stationery was posted to the Telephone account in the ledger.
5. £425 paid for advertising has not been posted in the ledger.
6. £4,250 paid for purchases was posted in the ledger as £2,450.
7. £6,400 paid for furniture was posted to the Assets account in the ledger as £640.

Required:
In respect of each of the errors you are to identify:

(a) which member of the staff is responsible for the error;
(b) whether the balancing of the Trial Balance would have been affected;
(c) the classification of the error.

5.5 ACCOUNTING CONTROL PROCEDURES TO PREVENT ERRORS AND FRAUD

There are various control procedures available when recording and posting cash transactions. The control instituted will depend on the nature of the potential error. For example:

- **Control to prevent errors of omission and duplication:** One method is to give each voucher that is passed to the cashier for payment a sequential number and then the manager follows this up by checking that the cashier has entered this sequence of numbers in the Cash account.
- **Control to prevent an entry error by the cashier:** One method is to pre-list (i.e. add up all the amounts of) the vouchers before passing them to the cashier for payment and *then* the manager follows up by checking that the total of cash payments equals the total of the pre-listed vouchers.
- **Control to prevent an unscrupulous cashier from substituting a voucher (payable to the cashier or an associate) for a valid business voucher:** One method is for the manager to authorize each voucher for payment by initialling it and *then* checking on a sample basis that all vouchers that have been paid have been initialled.
- **Control to prevent the bookkeeper making an error of commission or an error of principle:** One method is for the manager to mark on each voucher the correct account to which it should be posted and *then* to test (by sample) the accuracy of the posting. An additional method is to compare the balance on an account with the corresponding balance in the previous period, investigating any material differences.

SOLUTIONS TO INTERACTIVE QUESTIONS

IQ 5.1 The class of an account and the side of its balance

Name of the account	Class of account	Side of balance
1. Cash account	Asset	Debit
2. Rent account	Expenditure	Debit
3. Purchases account	Expenditure	Debit
4. Sales account	Income	Credit
5. Motor Vehicles account	Asset	Debit
6. Salaries account	Expenditure	Debit
7. Stationery account	Expenditure	Debit
8. Furniture & Fittings a/c	Asset	Debit
9. Telephone and Postage a/c	Expenditure	Debit
10. Land and Buildings account	Asset	Debit
11. Advertising account	Expenditure	Debit
12. Staff Welfare account	Expenditure	Debit
13. Capital account	Liability	Credit
14. Loan to Sales Rep. account	Asset	Debit
15. Bank Loan account	Liability	Credit

IQ 5.2 Preparation of a Trial Balance

TRIAL BALANCE AT 5.1.20X0			
	Debit	**Credit**	**Class of account**
Cash a/c	8,476	–	Asset
Capital a/c[a]	–	5,000	Liability
Furniture	330	–	Asset
Purchases a/c	8,400	–	Expenditure[b]
Sales a/c	–	12,600	Income
Jim's Loan a/c	–	1,200	Liability
Advertising a/c	355	–	Expenditure
Stationery a/c	55	–	Expenditure[c]
Staff Welfare a/c	40	–	Expenditure
Office Equipment	300	–	Asset
Telephone a/c	49	–	Expenditure
Salaries a/c	780	–	Expenditure
Postage a/c	15	–	Expenditure
	18,800	18,800	

Notes:

a. The Capital account is classified as a liability. In the eyes of Andy Small, his capital in the business is certainly an asset – but the business is an entity separate from Andy. In the eyes of the business, the £5,000 it received from Andy is owed to him, though not really to be paid back until the business is wound up one day. The accounts must be viewed from the point of view of the business.

b. The Purchases account is regarded as an expenditure account on the assumption that all goods bought for sale are fully sold out by the end of the accounting period.

c. Similarly, the Stationery account is regarded as an expenditure account on the assumption that all items of stationery are fully used up by the year end.

Both assumptions (b) and (c) are likely to be proved wrong and should be adjusted for, as will be seen in Chapter 6.

IQ 5.3 Preparation of a Trial Balance when one balance is not stated

TRIAL BALANCE AS AT 31 MARCH 20X0	Debits	Credits
	£	£
Cash a/c	2,500	–
Stationery a/c	400	–
Sales a/c	–	295,900
Rent a/c	18,000	–
Audit Fees a/c	1,200	–
Furniture a/c	24,000	–
Bank Loan a/c	–	3,000
Purchases a/c	170,500	–
Salaries a/c	21,600	–
Advertising a/c	4,200	–
Motor Vehicles a/c	60,000	–
Sales Commission a/c	9,200	–
Loan to Cashier a/c	5,000	–
Machinery a/c	7,000	–
Telephone a/c	300	–
Capital a/c	–	25,000
	323,900	323,900

Notes:

1. Cash a/c, Motor Vehicles a/c, Furniture a/c, Machinery a/c and Loan to Cashier a/c are all *assets*; they will each have the balance on the *debit* side.
2. Stationery a/c, Rent a/c, Audit Fees a/c, Purchases a/c, Salaries a/c, Advertising a/c, Sales Commission a/c, as well as Telephone and Postage a/c are *expenditure*, having the balance on the *debit* side.
3. Sales a/c, the only *income* account, will have its balance on the *credit* side.
4. The bank loan is a *liability* and will, therefore, have the balance on the *credit* side.
5. Once all these balances are listed, the missing amount of £25,000 is taken as the *credit* balance owed to the owner as *capital*.

IQ 5.4 The effect of an accounting error on the Trial Balance

The error in accounting either by the cashier or the bookkeeper	Side	£
1. £100,000 received as capital was posted to the Liability account as £10,000.	Cr	90,000
2. A sale of £5,400 has not been posted in the ledger.	Cr	5,400
3. £6,400 paid for purchases was posted as £4,600 in the ledger.	Dr	1,800
4. £600 paid for servicing vehicles was posted to the Asset account.	No difference	
5. £140 paid for stationery was posted to the Expenditure account as £14	Dr	126
6. £12,000 paid for an office computer system was posted to Office Expenses account.	No difference	
7. The debit side of the cash book was stated as £4,600 instead of £5,800	Dr	1,200
8. £1,000 received as a loan from Peter was debited to Peter's Loan account.	Cr	2,000

IQ 5.5 The responsibility for, and description of, accounting errors

The error	Who is responsible?	Classification of the error	Whether error will cause the totals to fail to agree
1. Cash sale is not recorded at all	Cashier	Omission (or a fraud)	TB will balance because neither a debit nor a credit entry has been made.
2. Payment of £800 recorded as £8,000	Cashier	Entry error	TB will balance because £8,000 is credited in the Cash account and posted to the Rent account.
3. Payment for an asset stated as for purchases	Cashier	Entry error and an Error of principle	TB will balance because, despite the error the, credit in the Cash account is matched by an equivalent debit, though in a wrong account.

The error	Who is responsible?	Classification of the error	Whether error will cause the totals to fail to agree
4. Posted to a wrong expense account	Bookkeeper	Commission	TB will balance because the credit in the Cash account is matched by a debit, though in a wrong expense account.
5. Expense not posted at all	Bookkeeper	Double entry error	TB will not balance because the credit in the Cash account has no debit anywhere to match.
6. Transposition error in posting	Bookkeeper	Transposition of figures.	TB will not balance because the debit entry in the Purchases account is £1,800 less than the credit in the Cash account.
7. A zero omitted when posting	Bookkeeper	Omission of a zero	TB will not balance because the credit in Cash account is not matched by the debit.

Note: TB = Trial Balance.

PROGRESSIVE QUESTIONS

PQ 5.1 Multiple-choice question

Assuming that each of the errors stated below is the only error in accounting, identify the amount by which the Trial Balance would fail to balance because of that error, by placing a tick in the appropriate box:

(a) £360 received on sales is not posted:

Excess credit of £360	(x)	
Excess debit of £360	(y)	
Excess debit of £720	(z)	

(b) £1,800 paid for purchases is posted as £180:

Trial Balance will balance	(x)	
Excess credit of £1,620	(y)	
Excess credit of £1,800	(z)	

(c) £145 paid for servicing the vehicle was posted to the Motor Vehicles account:

Excess debit of £145	(x)	
Excess credit of £145	(y)	
Trial Balance will balance	(z)	

(d) £500 paid as a loan to John, a sales representative, has been posted to the credit of John's account:

Excess credit of £1,000	(x)	
Excess credit of £500	(y)	
Excess debit of £1,000	(z)	

(e) An amount of £160 received on sales is not recorded at all by the cashier:

Excess debit of £160	(x)	
Excess credit of £160	(y)	
Trial Balance will balance	(z)	

(f) £260 paid for stationery was posted to the Stationery account as £620:

Excess credit of £360 (x)	
Excess debit of £260 (y)	
Excess debit of £360 (z)	

(g) The debit side of the Cash account is overcast by £200:

Trial Balance will balance (x)	
Excess debit of £200 (y)	
Excess credit of £200 (z)	

PQ 5.2 Preparation of a Trial Balance and identification of account balances

On 31 March 20X0, the last day of the accounting period, Jane Barrymore, a retailer, extracted the following balances from all the accounts in her books:

Particulars	£	Particulars	£
Sales account	86,000	Postage account	105
Purchases a/c	62,500	Staff Welfare account	325
Cash account	8,495	Advertising account	1,200
Salaries account	14,250	Office Expenses a/c	165
Rent account	3,000	Furniture account	8,000
Stationery account	240	Capital account	25,000
Motor Vehicles a/c	12,000	Audit Fees account	500
Vehicle Maintenance a/c	220		

Required:

(a) Set out the above balances in the form of a Trial Balance; and
(b) Identify each account as an asset, liability, income or expenditure.

PQ 5.3 Withholding the balance in the Capital account

Jonah Ikhine extracted the following balances from his books of account on 31.12.20X0:

Particulars	£	Particulars	£
Stationery a/c	320	Loan from Peter a/c	3,000
Salaries a/c	12,800	Purchases a/c	68,400
Electricity a/c	660	Office Expenses a/c	1,465
Sales account	94,500	Motor Vehicles a/c	18,000
Heating account	2,650	Delivery Expenses a/c	1,250
Postage account	125	Office Equipment a/c	6,600
Cash account	7,675	Sales commission a/c	2,555
Furniture a/c	12,000		

Assuming that the only balance that Jonah did not extract is the one from the Capital account, you are *required* to set out these balances in the form of a Trial Balance as at 31.12.20X0.

PQ 5.4 Accounting control procedures to prevent errors

Explain an accounting control procedure that could have prevented the following errors:

(a) Some suppliers have been complaining that they have been underpaid. Investigation has shown that, although the vouchers relating to payments to those suppliers were correct, the cashier has been paying and entering incorrect amounts.
(b) Some suppliers have complained that they have not been paid at all. Investigations show that the cashier had mislaid the relevant vouchers.
(c) The manager suspects that the cashier lives beyond her means. Investigations reveal that the cashier has been substituting vouchers payable to her partner in place of authentic business vouchers for identical amounts.

Chapter 6

REPORTING PERFORMANCE AND PERIOD-END POSITION

In this chapter

We will learn about:

- how a trading entity reports its performance and position
- purchases remaining unsold at the period end
- depreciation of fixed assets

and you should be able to:

- prepare a Trading and Profit and Loss account for an accounting period and a Balance Sheet as at its end date

6.1 REPORTING PERFORMANCE USING THE CATEGORY QUADRANT

At regular intervals (known as *accounting periods*) every business entity seeks to compare the total income it has earned in the period with the total expenses it has incurred. The accounting period normally required for reporting to owners and agreeing a tax liability is 12 months; the accounting period required for management control is normally one month. The difference between total income and total expenditure in an accounting period is the *profit* (or *loss*) for the period.

In Chapter 3 we prepared a Category Quadrant for Richard Brown, separating the outcome of his shop's transactions into four categories, namely assets, liabilities, expenditure and income. To calculate the firm's profit, we compare the subtotals of the balances in income and expenditure accounts (as we have on the left). The profit of £115 reported for the period is based on two assumptions, that his furniture will remain in use for ever, and that at the end of the period there are no unsold groceries or unused stationery. Both assumptions are unrealistic and will have to be reconsidered later in this chapter (see Sections 6.6 and 6.7).

It is possible also to calculate the *gross profit* for the period. This is the difference between the sales (£945) and the cost of sales (£595). The gross profit of £350 was available to meet the expenses on staff, stationery and advertising, leaving a *net profit* of £155.

Expenditure	£	Income	£
Cost of sales:		Sales	245
Purchases	225	Sales	210
Purchases	145	Sales	225
Purchases	110	Sales	265
Purchases	115		
Expenses:			
Staff teas	15		
Staff lunch	35		
Stationery	35		
Advertising	65		
Advertising	45		
Total expenditure	790		
PROFIT	155		
	945	**Total income**	945

In real life, a business would not prepare a Category Quadrant. Instead, it prepares a Trading and Profit and Loss account for the period by transferring to it the balances in all its income accounts and expenditure accounts.

6.2 REPORTING PERFORMANCE USING A TRADING AND PROFIT AND LOSS ACCOUNT

SALES ACCOUNT

Trading a/c	945	Cash a/c	245
		Cash a/c	210
		Cash a/c	225
		Cash a/c	265

PURCHASES ACCOUNT

Cash a/c	225	Trading a/c	595
Cash a/c	145		
Cash a/c	110		
Cash a/c	115		
	595		595

To determine how well Richard's grocery store fared on the first day of business, the balance in his income account (Sales being his only income) is transferred to a Trading account, for the purpose of matching it with the balances in the various expenditure accounts. The transfer from each account is done by a pair of debit and credit entries. For example, by debiting the Sales account and crediting the Trading account with £945, the credit balance of that amount in the former is transferred to the latter. The debit balance of £595 in the Purchases account is similarly transferred to the Trading account by another pair of entries. At this stage the Sales and Purchases, now stated in the Trading account, are compared in order to determine the gross profit, which is carried down to a lower compartment of the same account and which in turn is identified as the Profit and Loss account. Thereafter, the debit balance in each of the three remaining expenditure accounts is transferred to the Profit and Loss account – each transfer being effected by a pair of debit and credit entries. Each of these transfers, by removing the whole of the balance in each income and expenditure account, has the effect of closing them. The amount by which the gross profit exceeds all of the expenditure is the profit made by the grocery business in the accounting period – in this case, a single day.

TRADING AND PROFIT AND LOSS ACCOUNT

Purchases a/c	595	Sales a/c	945
Gross profit c/d	350		
	945		945
Stationery a/c	35	Gross profit b/d	350
Advertising a/c	110		
Staff Welfare a/c	50		
	195		
Net profit c/d	155		
	350		350
		Net profit b/d	155

6.3 USING THE CATEGORY QUADRANT TO REPORT THE FINANCIAL POSITION OF A BUSINESS

Let us refer back again to the Category Quadrant that we prepared for Richard Brown in Chapter 3. To report his performance on the first day we compared his income with expenditure. To report his position at the end of the day, we have to compare the other two areas of the quadrant, namely the assets and liabilities, as shown here. The quadrant shows that his assets have grown by £155 during the day and that growth arises from the profit he made that day.

Assets:	£	Liabilities:	£
Furniture	6,000	Capital	10,000
Cash	4,155	Profit – difference	155
	10,155		10,155

6.4 USING A BALANCE SHEET TO REPORT THE FINANCIAL POSITION OF A BUSINESS

A Balance Sheet is a list, usually prepared on the last day of each accounting period, of all accounts remaining open (which have to be asset accounts and liability accounts) after all the income accounts and expenditure accounts have been closed by transferring their balances to a Trading and Profit and Loss account.

The aim is that a Balance Sheet should be a statement of all that a business *owns* and *owes* on that particular date. As we shall learn in due course this aim is difficult to achieve because a business can only report as its assets those that it can measure in money terms. Subject to that limitation, a Balance Sheet states the financial position of a business as at the end of its accounting period. Another name for a Balance Sheet could, therefore, be a position statement.

In a Balance Sheet the assets are usually listed in reverse order of *liquidity*. By 'liquidity' we mean the time it takes to convert an asset into cash. The cash balance is regarded as the most liquid of assets and is therefore stated last among the assets, while those assets that are not intended for sale in the ordinary course of business, and are, for that reason, known as *fixed assets*, are listed first. The liabilities are stated in the reverse order in which the business intends discharging them. Amounts owed to the proprietor, reported in a Capital account, are discharged only when the business is wound down and therefore the Capital account is stated first among the liabilities.

The Balance Sheet of Richard Brown, as at close of business on 1 January 20X0, would appear as shown above (right).

RICHARD BROWN'S GROCERY STORE

BALANCE SHEET AS AT 1.1.20X0	
Assets:	£
Fixed assets:	
Furniture	6,000
Current assets	
Cash	4,155
	10,155
Liabilities:	£
Capital	10,000
Profit	155
	10,155

6.5 PREPARING A TRADING AND PROFIT AND LOSS ACCOUNT AND BALANCE SHEET

In Chapter 2 we met Andy Small, whose shop deals in portable telephones. We prepared in that chapter a Cash account to record his transactions, posted them to appropriate ledger accounts in Chapter 3, and extracted in Chapter 5 a Trial Balance, which appears as stated here. We will now proceed to prepare for his shop: first, the Trading and Profit and Loss account for the five days ending on 5 January 20X0; and, second, the Balance Sheet as at 5 January 20X0.

The procedure is as follows:

1. The balances in the Sales account and Purchases account are transferred to the Trading account.
2. The balances in the Trading account are compared with each other to reveal a gross

TRIAL BALANCE AT 5.1.20X0		
Particulars	**Debit** £	**Credit** £
Cash a/c	8,476	–
Capital a/c	–	5,000
Furniture a/c	330	–
Purchases a/c	8,400	–
Sales a/c	–	12,600
Jim's Loan a/c	–	1,200
Advertising a/c	355	–
Stationery a/c	55	–
Staff Welfare a/c	40	–
Office Equipment a/c	300	–
Telephone a/c	49	–
Salaries a/c	780	–
Postage a/c	15	–
	18,800	18,800

profit of £4,200, which is carried down to the Profit and Loss account.

3. Debit balances from all other expenditure accounts are transferred to the Profit and Loss account.
4. These debit balances are compared with the gross profit and reveal that there is a net profit of £2,906 for five days of business.
5. The net profit is carried down to another layer referred to as a Profit and Loss Appropriation account.
6. The net profit is transferred (appropriated) from the Profit and Loss Appropriation account to the Capital account, again by a pair of entries, so that the position on 5 January is that the business owes Andy £7,906.
7. The accounts still remaining open (asset accounts and liability accounts) are listed in a Balance Sheet, ensuring that the assets are stated in the reverse order of liquidity and the liabilities in reverse order of the date that payment is due.

ANDY SMALL (TELEPHONE SALES)

	TRADING AND PROFIT AND LOSS ACCOUNT FOR THE FIVE DAYS TO 5 JANUARY 20X0					BALANCE SHEET AS AT 5 JANUARY 20X0	
		£			£	ASSETS:	£
TRADING	Purchases a/c	8,400	Sales a/c		12,600	Fixed assets:	
ACCOUNT	Gross profit c/d	4,200				Furniture a/c	330
		12,600			12,600	Office Equipment a/c	300
							630
PROFIT	Advertising a/c	355	Gross profit		4,200		
AND	Stationery a/c	55				**Current assets:**	
LOSS	Staff Welfare a/c	40				Cash account	8,476
ACCOUNT	Telephone a/c	49					9,106
	Salaries a/c	780					
	Postage a/c	15				**LIABILITIES:**	£
	Total Expenditure	1,294				Capital	5,000
	Net profit c/d	2,906				Profit	2,906
		4,200			4,200		7,906
Appropriation	Capital account	2,906	Net profit		2,906	Loan from Jim	1,200
							9,106

Notes:

1. The shaded areas have been used, as an aid to beginners, to state the identity of the three compartments, which together constitute the Trading and Profit and Loss account.
2. An accounting entry made in any account states, in the Particulars column, where the corresponding second entry is made. For example, £2,906 entered in the Profit and Loss Appropriation account states that the double entry is made in the Capital account and vice versa.
3. Once the net profit is transferred to the Capital account, the Profit and Loss account is left with no balance. By this time all income accounts and expenditure accounts in the ledger are closed, leaving only asset accounts and liability accounts remaining open.
4. The Balance Sheet is merely a list of the balances in the accounts that still remain open. It is, however, an organized list, with assets listed in descending order of liquidity and liabilities in descending order of date payment is due.

Finalizing accounts for a year without any adjustments

The Trial Balance of First with the News, which we prepared in answer to IQ 5.3, is stated here. Assume (though not quite realistically) that machinery and furniture do not reduce in value through use and that there are no stocks of unsold goods or unused stationery remaining as at 31 March 20X0.

Required:
You are to prepare:

(a) the Trading and Profit and Loss account for the year ended 31.3.20X0; and
(b) the Balance Sheet as at that date.

TRIAL BALANCE AS AT 31.3.20X0		
Particulars	**Debits** **£**	**Credits** **£**
Cash a/c	2,500	–
Stationery a/c	400	–
Sales a/c	–	295,900
Rent a/c	18,000	–
Audit Fees a/c	1,200	–
Furniture a/c	24,000	–
Bank Loan a/c	–	3,000
Purchases a/c	170,500	–
Salaries a/c	21,600	–
Advertising a/c	4,200	–
Motor Vehicles a/c	60,000	–
Sales Commission a/c	9,200	–
Loan to Cashier a/c	5,000	–
Machinery a/c	7,000	–
Telephone a/c	300	–
Capital a/c	–	25,000
	323,900	323,900

6.6 ACCOUNTING FOR AN UNSOLD PART OF PURCHASES

If a part of purchases made during an accounting period remains unsold by the end of that period, that would have an impact on the reported performance for the period as well as the position at the end of it. For example, in our answer to IQ 6.1 (First with the News; see page 53 and workings below) we report the gross profit for the year as £125,400 and the assets at the end of the year as £98,500. If goods that cost £10,000 remained unsold by the year end, there are two consequences: first, profits improve by that amount because the cost of goods sold would be lower by that amount (see working on left); and, second, the total assets reported as at the year end will be £98,500 plus stock costing £10,000. The stock remaining unsold at year end, referred to as *closing stock*, is accounted for in the ledger by crediting the Purchases account and debiting the Stock in Trade account.

	£
Sales	295,900
Purchases	(170,500)
Gross profit	125,400

		£
Sales		295,900
Purchases	170,500	
Less: Stock	(10,000)	
Cost of goods sold		(160,500)
Gross profit		135,400

Accounting for closing stock

Hari Haran commenced trading from his retail shop on 1 July 20X0. On 30 June 20X1 he extracted the Trial Balance as stated here. A count of the stock in the shop on 30 June 20X1 showed that there was unsold stock that cost £185,000. Hari has assumed that the motor vehicles and furniture will remain in use for ever and his assumption is to be accepted for the time being.

Required:
You are to prepare:

(a) the Trading and Profit and Loss account for the year ending on 30 June 20X1; and
(b) the Balance Sheet as at that date.

TRIAL BALANCE AS AT 30.6.20X1		
Particulars	**£000**	**£000**
Motor Vehicles a/c	240	–
Purchases a/c	680	–
Sales account	–	960
Cash account	120	–
Salaries account	124	–
Advertising account	36	–
Rent account	24	–
Bank Loan account	–	200
Loan to Sales Rep. a/c	60	–
Furniture account	110	–
Stationery account	12	–
Interest Paid account	20	–
Telephone account	14	–
Capital account	–	280
	1440	1440

Note: £000 means that the amounts listed under it are all thousands of pounds sterling.

6.7 ACCOUNTING FOR THE DEPRECIATION OF FIXED ASSETS

The assumption that fixed assets will remain in use for ever is not reasonable. Assets, however well looked after, have a finite economic lifespan – some short and others much longer. When calculating profit, the cost of the asset must be matched against the income generated by it during that lifespan. The portion of the cost of an asset treated as an expenditure in an accounting period is known as *depreciation*.

Consider a motor vehicle, for example. A vehicle, like any fixed asset other than land, has a finite economic life. Beyond that, it will not be economical to continue using the vehicle. Hence the cost of the vehicle has to be viewed as a payment for a bundle of services that the vehicle is capable of providing for generating income. As the income generated in each year is taken account of, an appropriate portion of the cost paid for the corresponding services provided by the vehicle has to be matched against it, for determining the profit in the period.

Accordingly, for instance in the case of First with the News (IQ 6.1), if we reject the unrealistic assumption that fixed assets will remain in use for ever and assume instead that machinery has a life of ten years, furniture 12 years and motor vehicles five years, the profit for the year as well as the assets reported at the year end will reduce by the amount of the depreciation (£14,700, as shown in the box on the right).

	£	£
Net profit as already determined	£	70,500
Less: Depreciation:		
Machinery (£7,000/10 years)	(700)	
Furniture (£24,000/12 years)	(2,000)	
Motor vehicles (£60,000/5 years)	(12,000)	(14,700)
Revised profit after depreciation		55,800

MACHINERY ACCOUNT

20X0		£	20X0		£
31.3	Balance b/f	7,000	31.3	Depreciation a/c	700
			31.3	Balance c/d	6,300
1.4	Balance b/d	6,300			

DEPRECIATION OF MACHINERY ACCOUNT

20X0		£	20X0		£
31.3	Machinery a/c	700	31.3	Profit and Loss	700

As always, a pair of entries are needed to account, in the ledger, for depreciation in respect of each class of fixed asset – crediting the appropriate Asset account (for example, the Machinery account) and debiting the Depreciation account (expenditure).

Interaction 6.3	The rationale and accounting for depreciation

When Lal de Silva was laid off, he used the redundancy pay of £20,000 to start a minicab business on 1 January 20X0. A summary of his Cash account for the first year is shown below. Lal claims to have made a profit of £10,380 in the first year because he ended the year with that amount in hand.

Required:

You are to:

(a) state whether you agree with Lal's claim regarding profit;

(b) explain to Lal why an appropriate portion of the cost of his vehicle should be included within the expenditure in the year;

(c) prepare the Profit and Loss account for the year ended 31.12.20X0 and the Balance Sheet as at that date, on the basis that Lal expects to use the vehicle for five years.

LAL DE SILVA CASH ACCOUNT	
	£
Capital introduced	20,000
Hire receipts	45,500
Cost of a car	(15,000)
Fuel and oil	(19,650)
Insurance	(2,800)
Licence and road tax	(3,200)
Repairs and servicing	(4,220)
Lal's drawings	(10,250)
Cash in hand on 31.12.20X0	10,380

SOLUTIONS TO INTERACTIVE QUESTIONS

IQ 6.1 Finalizing accounts for an year without any adjustments

● The Trading and Profit and Loss Account covers *a period*, usually lasting a year, and the title to the account should clearly state the length of the period.

● The Balance Sheet, on the other hand, lists the balances in the accounts *as at a particular point in time* (e.g. at close of business on 31 March 20X0).

● Assets other than the fixed assets have been grouped as *current assets* to show that they are constantly being converted into cash by the business in the course of its normal activity.

FIRST WITH THE NEWS

TRADING AND PROFIT AND LOSS ACCOUNT FOR THE YEAR ENDED 31 MARCH 20X0				
	£			**£**
Purchases a/c	170,500	Sales a/c		295,900
Gross profit c/d	125,400			
	295,900			295,900
Salaries a/c	21,600	Gross profit b/d		125,400
Stationery a/c	400			
Rent a/c	18,000			
Audit Fees a/c	1,200			
Advertising a/c	4,200			
Sales Commission a/c	9,200			
Telephone a/c	300			
	54,900			
Net profit c/d	70,500			
	125,400			125,400
Capital a/c	70,500	Net profit b/d		70,500

BALANCE SHEET AS AT 31 MARCH 20X0	
	£
Fixed Assets:	
Machinery a/c	7,000
Furniture a/c	24,000
Motor Vehicles a/c	60,000
Current Assets:	
Loan to Cashier a/c	5,000
Cash a/c	2,500
	98,500
	£
Capital a/c	25,000
Profit	70,500
	95,500
Bank loan	3,000
	98,500

IQ 6.2 Accounting for closing stock

When classifying the Purchases account as an expenditure, it was stated that the classification is valid only on the assumption that all goods purchased for sale are fully sold out by the end of the accounting period. If, as is more likely, a portion of the goods remains unsold, the cost of that portion must be *capitalized* – i.e. transferred from expenditure (Purchases account) to an asset account (Stock in Trade account). Only the amount remaining thereafter in the Purchases account represents the cost of goods sold, which, when transferred to the Trading account and matched with sales, reveals the gross profit for the period. The balance in the Stock in Trade account is then reported on the Balance Sheet as a current asset.

PURCHASES ACCOUNT

Balance b/f	680	Stock a/c	185
		Trading a/c	495

STOCK IN TRADE ACCOUNT

Purchases a/c	185		

In relation to the order of assets in the Balance Sheet, Motor Vehicles is listed after Furniture because it is more readily disposable. Furthermore, because stock is normally regarded as the least liquid of the current assets, it is listed first.

With regard to transferring an amount from an expenditure to an asset account, such a transfer is called *capitalization* and the cost of unsold goods has to be capitalized. We will see in later chapters that several such transfers have to be made from one ledger account to another, immediately prior to the finalization of accounts. These transfers, always done on the double entry basis, are called 'year-end adjustments'.

HARI HARAN (RETAIL)

TRADING AND PROFIT AND LOSS ACCOUNT FOR THE YEAR ENDED 30 JUNE 20X1					BALANCE SHEET AS AT 30 JUNE 20X1		
Particulars	£000	**Particulars**	£000			£000	£000
Purchases a/c	495	Sales a/c	960		**Fixed Assets:**		
Gross profit c/d	465				Furniture		110
					Motor vehicles		240
	960		960		**Current Assets:**		
					Stock in trade	185	
Salaries a/c	124	Gross profit b/d	465		Loan to sales rep.	60	
Advertising a/c	36				Cash in hand	120	365
Rent a/c	24						715
Stationery a/c	12						
Interest a/c	20						£000
Telephone a/c	14				Capital – Jill Baker		280
	230				Profit for the year		235
Net profit c/d	235						515
	465		465		Bank loan		200
Capital a/c	235	Net profit b/d	235				715

IQ 6.3 The rationale and accounting for depreciation

(a) **Lal's claim that improvement in the cash balance is profit**

Lal's claim that the cash in hand represents profit is wrong for many reasons, including:

- A cash balance may increase not only because of earnings but also because of either borrowings or the disposal of assets. Neither of these latter amounts improve the profit portion directly.
- A cash balance may decrease not only because of payments for expenditure but also because of an acquisition of assets or discharge of liability.
- A decrease in the cash balance could also be because of drawings by the proprietor (Lal's living expenses) which is not a business expenditure but a repayment to Lal of what the business owes him.
- Profit earned in a period should be determined by matching the income earned in the period with the expenditure incurred, and not by comparing cash balances on two dates.
- The income that should be taken into account for determining the profit earned in a period is what is earned in that period, even if it is not immediately received in cash.
- The expenditure that should be taken into account for determining the profit of a period should include items that are not paid for in cash during the accounting period – such as depreciation.

(b) **A need to depreciate fixed assets**

Continuing to report a vehicle in the balance sheet, year after year, at the amount at which it was acquired will not fairly reflect the resources available to the entity at each point. The situation is analogous to acquiring a property on lease. If a property is leased for five years, at a cost of £100,000, each year a fifth of what was paid for is used up, and therefore the value of the resources available for the use of the entity – say at the end of the first year – should be one-fifth lower than the original cost.

By depreciating a fixed asset, an amount equal to the cost so depreciated is automatically retained within the business, so that it becomes possible to replace the asset (except where inflation spoils the situation) without having to find fresh capital for the purpose. In Lal's case, if he expects to use the vehicle for five years and accordingly decides to write off as depreciation 20 per cent of the cost of the vehicle each year, the profit reported for the year in question, and therefore available for his withdrawal for personal use, will be £3,000 lower than otherwise. Repeated over the five years of the asset's life, an amount equal to the original cost of the asset (£15,000) would have been retained within the business.

(c) Lal's Profit and Loss account and Balance Sheet

PROFIT AND LOSS ACCOUNT FOR THE YEAR ENDED 31.12.20X0			
	£	Hire income	£ 45,500
Fuel and oil	19,650		
Insurance	2,800		
Licence/road tax	3,200		
Repairs/servicing	4,220		
Depreciation	3,000		
	32,870		
Profit c/d	12,630		
	45,500		45,500
Capital a/c	12,630	Profit b/d	12,630

BALANCE SHEET AS AT 31.12.20X0	
	£
Motor vehicle	12,000
Cash in hand	10,380
	22,380
	£
Capital a/c	20,000
Profit – year 20X0	12,630
	32,630
Drawings	(10,250)
	22,380

- For a correct determination of the profit he was able to earn in the first year, Lal has to match against his earnings in the year a reasonable portion of the cost of the vehicle.
- Depreciation will be £3,000, being 20 per cent of £15,000. This amount will be transferred out of the Motor Vehicles account (reducing it to £12,000) and added to a Depreciation account
- Such a transfer is known as **writing off**. The Americans call it **expensing**.
- Where a business is providing a service rather than trading in the buying and selling of goods, the Profit and Loss account may be referred to as an Income and Expenditure account. This is only a difference in the name and does not affect the items that appear in the account or their measurement.

PROGRESSIVE QUESTIONS

PQ 6.1 Balance Sheet equation

Shown on the right is the balance sheet of John Amber, in transport business. Remember that Capital + Liability = Assets. John finds that the cash in hand is grossly inadequate for day-to-day operations such as buying fuel, paying salaries, and meeting the bills for rent, insurance and repairs.

Required:

(a) Identify three alternative ways in which John could improve his cash balance.
(b) Show within the grid below the impact of each of the transactions in January 20X0 on his capital, his liabilities and each class of asset.
(c) Draft a balance sheet immediately after accounting for these transactions.

JOHN AMBER TRANSPORT

BALANCE SHEET AS AT 31.12.20X0	
	£000
Motor vehicles	180
Cash in hand	20
	200
Capital – John Amber	150
Loan from Mark Batty	50
	200

	Capital £150,000	Liabilities £50,000	Vehicle £180,000	Cash £20,000
(a) Introduced £10,000 more as capital				
(b) Received £5,000 as transport charges				
(c) Paid £1,000 as rent				
(d) Paid £800 as salary to staff				
(e) Borrowed £5,000 more from Mark				
(f) Took £3,000 for John's household expenses				
(g) Paid back £10,000 to Mark				
(h) Paid £500 to Mark as interest on the loan				
(i) Acquired another vehicle for £15,000				
Balances on completion				

PQ 6.2 Impact of each transaction on Balance Sheet items

Phillipa Gray buys and sells second-hand clothes for cash. Her Balance Sheet as at 1 July 20X0 appears as shown on the right. During the week commencing 1.7.20X0 her transactions were as follows:

1. Received £3,000 from the sale of clothes that cost £2,400.
2. Paid £5,000 for another van.
3. Paid £3,750 to buy clothes for sale.
4. Received £2,250 from selling clothes that cost her £1,500.
5. Received £4,200 from selling clothes that cost her £3,000.
6. Paid £4,500 to buy more clothes for sale.
7. Paid £600 as staff salary.
8. Paid £375 as week's rent.
9. Phillipa brought into the business £7,500 more of her own cash.
10. Phillipa removed for her own use clothing that cost £300.
11. Repaid £1,500 to Jill.

Required:

(a) Show how each transaction affects the items on the balance sheet.
(b) Prepare a balance sheet as at 7 July 20X0 on completion of the above transactions.

PHILLIPA GRAY

BALANCE SHEET AS AT 1 JULY 20X0	
Fixed assets:	**£**
Shop premises	82,500
Furniture	12,750
Delivery van	6,000
Current assets:	
Stock – clothing	18,000
Cash	6,000
	125,250
	£
Capital	75,000
Loan from Jill	50,250
	125,250

PQ 6.3 Adjusting for closing stock and depreciation

The Trial Balance prepared in answer to PQ 5.2 appears on the right. You are further informed that goods costing £6,500 remain unsold as at 31 March 20X0; and Jane, the owner, wishes to write off one-fifth of the cost of motor vehicles and one-tenth of the cost of furniture as depreciation for the period.

Required:

(a) Set out the accounting adjustments necessary with regard to each of the extra pieces of information provided above.
(b) Prepare the Trading and Profit and Loss account for the year ended 31.3.20X0 and the Balance Sheet as at that date.

JANE BARRYMORE

TRIAL BALANCE AS AT 31 MARCH 20X0

	Debit	Credit
Sales account	–	86,000
Purchases a/c	62,500	–
Cash account	8,495	–
Salaries account	14,250	–
Rent account	3,000	–
Stationery account	240	–
Motor Vehicles account	12,000	–
Vehicle Maintenance a/c	220	–
Postage account	105	–
Staff Welfare account	325	–
Advertising account	1,200	–
Office Expenses account	165	–
Furniture account	8,000	–
Capital account	–	25,000
Audit Fees account	500	–
	111,000	111,000

PQ 6.4 Adjusting for closing stock, an expense stock and depreciation

The Trial Balance prepared from the books of Jonah Ikhine (in the answer to PQ 5.3) appears as stated on the right. In addition, as at 31 December 20X0 goods purchased for sale at £15,300 remain unsold, and stationery acquired for £45 remains unused. Furthermore, it has been decided that the business's motor vehicles, furniture and office equipment are to be depreciated by 20 per cent, 10 per cent and 5 per cent of cost respectively.

Required:

(a) Account for each of the extra pieces of information stated above.
(b) Prepare the Trading and Profit and Loss account for the year ended 31 December 20X0 and the Balance Sheet as at that date.

JONAH IKHINE

TRIAL BALANCE AS AT 31 DECEMBER 20X0

	Debit	Credit
Stationery account	320	–
Salaries account	12,800	–
Electricity account	660	–
Sales account	–	94,500
Heating account	2,650	–
Postage account	125	–
Cash account	7,675	–
Furniture account	12,000	–
Loan from Peter account	–	3,000
Purchases account	68,400	–
Office Expenses account	1,465	–
Motor Vehicles account	18,000	–
Delivery Expenses account	1,250	–
Office Equipment account	6,600	–
Sales Commission account	2,555	–
Capital account	–	37,000
	134,500	134,500

PERIOD-END ADJUSTMENTS

In this chapter

We will learn of:

- Common period-end adjustments, such as for prepayments and accruals
- the depreciation of fixed assets

and you should be able to:

- Prepare a Trading and Profit and Loss account for an accounting period and a Balance Sheet at its end, in good style and 'vertical' format.

7.1 GENERAL PROCEDURES AT THE END OF AN ACCOUNTING PERIOD

At the end of each accounting period, the accountant finalizes the accounts. This means in practice the following:

1. **balancing the ledgers**: each ledger account is balanced, and then a Trial Balance is extracted, including in it each ledger balance for the purpose of confirming that the debits equal the credits;
2. **making period-end adjustments to the balances in the ledger accounts**: the theme for this chapter;
3. **calculating the profit or loss for the period**: all income and expenditure account balances are transferred to a Trading and Profit and Loss Account;
4. **preparing a Balance Sheet as at the end of the period**: all ledger balances remaining at this stage, plus the closing balance on the Profit and Loss account, are listed in a Balance Sheet.

After balancing the ledgers and extracting a Trial Balance, it is necessary to ensure that the amounts being transferred to the Trading and Profit and Loss account actually represent the income and expenditure applicable to that particular financial period – neither more nor less. It may be necessary to reduce or increase the amount of expenditure or income being transferred. Period-end adjustments take the form of transfers from one account to another.

There are two main reasons for adjusting downwards the balance in an expenditure account. First, the expenditure may include an amount for goods that needs to be capitalized. (By capitalized we mean, remember, that the balance should be classified as an asset rather than an expense.) For example, we transfer the cost of unsold goods from the Purchases account to a Stock in Trade account, which is then reported as an asset in the balance sheet. Second, the expenditure may include an amount for a future benefit that needs to be capitalized, e.g. payment that applies to the following account period such as the prepayment of insurance, where it needs to be removed from the expenditure account to a prepayment account so as to be reported as an asset in the Balance Sheet.

There are two main reasons for increasing the balance in an expenditure account. First, the expenditure account may not include an amount for an expense that has been incurred but not paid for. For example, salaries remaining unpaid in respect of the last week of a financial year (because they are due to be paid next payday) would need to be added to the year's expenditure and also reported as a liability to appear in the Balance Sheet. Such unpaid portions of expenses are referred to as *accruals*. Second, the consumed portion of fixed assets may not have been accounted for as expenditure. For example, we may need to transfer the appropriate portion of the cost of vehicles, representing the value consumed within the period, from the asset account to an expenditure account named the Depreciation account.

There may also be reason to reduce the balance in an income account. Such an account may include an amount that has been received but that relates to the next accounting period. For example, the Rent Received account may include an amount that has been received in advance for the next period. Such amounts should be transferred away from the income account to a Deferred Income account, which is treated as if it were a liability.

And there may be good reason for increasing the balance in an income account. Such an account may not include an amount that is earned in the period but that has not been received. For example, rent due to the business may not have been received by the date of the Balance Sheet, and the amount owing will have to be credited to the Rent Received account and debited to a Rent Receivable account, which is reported as an asset in the Balance Sheet.

| **Typical period-end adjustments** | | | **Interaction 7.1** |

Bill Renton, a retailer, has made payments for the following five items in the year ended 31.12.20X0

Item	£	Further information relating to each item
1. Purchases	214,500	Goods costing £14,500 remain unsold by year end
2. Stationery	3,600	Stationery costing £600 remains unused by year end
3. Rent	15,000	Annual rent for 20X0 is agreed at £1,000 per month
4. Salaries	22,800	Staff salaries of £2,200 remain unpaid at the year end
5. Vehicle	18,000	Wear and tear of vehicle is estimated at 20% of cost

Required: Show in the ledger accounts involved the appropriate period-end adjustments to be made as at 31 December 20X0.

7.2 PREPAYMENTS AND ACCRUALS ILLUSTRATED DIAGRAMMATICALLY

Care is needed to see that expenditure deducted from gross profit is correctly calculated and represents a fair match of income and expenditure.

7.2.1 A scenario when more is paid than is required for the accounting period

The Food Store, an imaginary grocery business, prepares its accounts on 31 December each year. Assume that The Food Store entered into an agreement on 30 November 20X0 for an annual rent on its premises of £12,000, payable three monthly (quarterly)

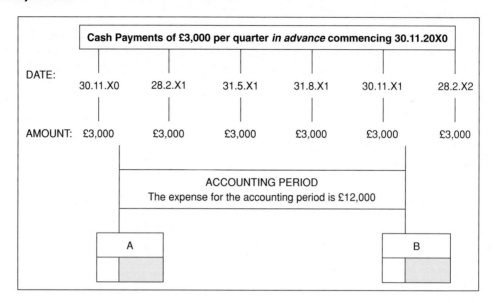

in advance, the first payment being made on 30.11.20X0 itself. The situation is depicted diagrammatically as shown in the box above.

The block marked 'A' in the diagram represents £3,000 paid as rent on 1.11.20X0 and the portion shaded within it is the portion of this amount (£2,000) prepaid as at 1.1.20X1 when the 20X1 accounting period commenced. The prepaid rent, reported as an asset on the balance sheet as at 31.12.X0, is stated as the opening balance in the Rent account. Four rental payments in the accounting year are posted from the Cash account to the Rent account, making up a balance in that account of £14,000. The block marked 'B' in the diagram represents the rental payment on 30.11.X1 and the shaded portion within the block is the prepayment (of £2,000) as at the end of the 20X1 financial year. The prepaid portion of rent, though an asset and reported as such on the Balance Sheet, is carried down as a debit balance in the Rent account. (This is found more convenient in practice, rather than transferring that amount to an asset account on 31 December 20X0 and transferring it back to the expenditure account the next day.)

RENT ACCOUNT

20X0			20X0		
1.1	Balance b/f	2,000	31.12	Profit and Loss a/c	12,000
28.2	Cash a/c	3,000	31.12	Balance c/d	2,000
31.5	Cash a/c	3,000			
31.8	Cash a/c	3,000			
30.11	Cash a/c	3,000			
		14,000			14,000
20X1					
1.1	Balance b/d	2,000			

7.2.2 A scenario when less is paid than is required for the accounting period

Let us amend the situation of The Food Store, assuming instead that, in accordance with an agreement signed on 30.11.20X0, it pays a rent of £3,000 per quarter but makes the payment this time quarterly in arrears – i.e. it makes the first payment on 28.2.20X1. Diagrammatically, the situation may be depicted as shown in the box following.

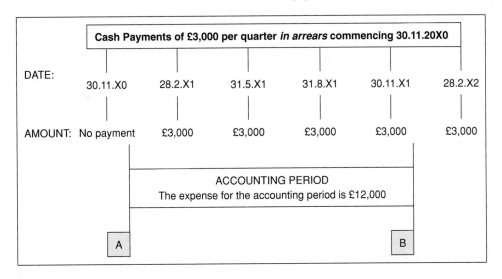

This time, a month's rent is in arrears as at 31.12.X0 (depicted by block 'A') and an identical amount is in arrears by the year end on 31.12.X1 (block 'B'). The rent in arrears on 31.12.X0, included on the Balance Sheet of that date as a liability, is recorded as an opening credit balance in the Rent account (rather than the writing-up of a separate liability account for the purpose). This would make sense because the rental payment on 28.2.X1 would

RENT ACCOUNT

20X1			20X1		
28.2	Cash a/c	3,000	1.1	Balance b/f	1,000
31.5	Cash a/c	3,000	31.12	Profit and Loss a/c	12,000
31.8	Cash a/c	3,000			
30.11	Cash a/c	3,000			
31.12	Balance c/d	1,000			
		13,000			13,000
			20X2		
			1.1	Balance b/d	1,000

discharge this liability. In the same way, the rent remaining unpaid as at 31.12.X1 is debited to the Rent account and, instead of crediting a separate liability account, is carried down as a credit balance in the same account and reported in the Balance Sheet on 31 December 20X1 as a liability.

It must be observed that, irrespective of the payment pattern, the Profit and Loss account for an accounting period records as expenditure the amount contracted to be paid in respect of that period. If the amount of cash outflow (payment) does not exactly coincide with the amount contracted to be paid for the period, an accrual or prepayment will necessarily arise.

| **Accounting for expenditure at the amount contracted for** | Interaction 7.2 |

With regard to The Food Store referred to above, *you are required to*:

(a) explain why the rent expenditure stated in the Profit and Loss account remains as £12,000 irrespective of whether the payments are made in advance or in arrears;

(b) identify the amount of rental expenditure to be stated in the Profit and Loss account if, in the scenario given in Section 7.2.2, the cash payment due on 30 November 20X1 was not made until 1 January 20X2.

7.3 ACCOUNTING FOR OPENING AND CLOSING STOCK

Stock remaining unsold at the end of an accounting period is capitalized. 'Capitalized', in accounting jargon, you will remember simply means that it is reported as an asset on the Balance Sheet rather than as an expense in the Trading account. These goods will be sold in the following year along with those purchased in that year.

Let us illustrate the situation by referring back to Andy Small who, as you may recall, buys portable phones at £100 each and sells them at £150 each. Let us assume that, commencing business on 1.1.20X0, Andy purchased 300 phones and sold 240 in the year 20X0, and that in 20X1 he purchased 400 more phones and sold 360 of them.

By the end of year 20X0, the cost of 60 unsold phones (£6,000) will be capitalized, and the cost of the 240 phones sold in that year will be transferred to the Trading account, to reveal a gross profit of £12,000 earned on 240 phones at £50 per phone. In

PURCHASES ACCOUNT

20X0		£	20X0		£
?	Cash a/c	30,000	31.12	Stock a/c	6,000
			31.12	Trading a/c	24,000

TRADING ACCOUNT

		£
Sales		36,000
Purchases	30,000	
Less: Stock a/c	(6,000)	(24,000)
Gross profit		12,000

20X1 Andy thus has an opening stock of 60 phones (reported in the Stock in Trade account) and 400 more phones bought in the year (reported in the Purchase account). If all 460 phones are sold by the year end, the balances in both the Stock account and the Purchase account would be transferred to the Trading account and the cost of goods sold in the year would then have been £46,000. In that he has 100 unsold phones in hand at 31.12.20X1, his problem will be one of determining whether those remaining unsold are out of those brought forward from the previous year or those purchased in 20X1. If Andy feels certain that those remaining in hand were all purchased in the current year, he would capitalize £10,000 of the balance in the Purchases account and write

OPENING STOCK ACCOUNT

20X1		£	20X1		£
1.1	Balance b/f	6,000	31.12	Trading a/c	6,000

PURCHASES ACCOUNT

20X1		£	20X1		£
?	Cash a/c	40,000	31.12	Trading a/c	40,000

CLOSING STOCK ACCOUNT

20X1		£			
31.12	Trading a/c	10,000			

TRADING ACCOUNT
FOR THE YEAR ENDED 31.12.X1

	£	£
Sales		54,000
Opening Stock	6,000	
Purchases	40,000	
Less: Closing stock	(10,000)	
Cost of sales		(36,000)
Gross profit		18,000

off to the Trading account the remainder in the Purchases account as well as the whole balance in the opening Stock account. What is more likely is that the phones remaining unsold are a mixture of those purchased in the year and others left over from the previous year. In the circumstances, all that Andy can do is to transfer to the Trading account the whole of the balances in both the (Opening) Stock account and the Purchases account and then to transfer back from the Trading account to a Closing Stock account the cost of 100 phones remaining unsold. This would leave in the Trading account a net amount of £36,000, which is the cost of phones sold in 20X1. At £50 on each phone sold, Andy makes a gross profit of £18,000 by selling 360 phones in the year.

It should be observed that the cost of goods remaining unsold on 31.12.X1, (£10,000), debited to the Closing Stock account, is also credited to the Trading account, presented this time in the horizontal format with a debit side and a credit side – see Section 7.5.

TRADING ACCOUNT FOR THE YEAR ENDED 31.12.X1			
Opening stock a/c	6,000	Sales a/c	54,000
Purchases a/c	40,000	Closing Stock a/c	10,000
Gross profit c/d	18,000		
		Gross profit b/d	18,000

7.4 ACCOUNTING FOR GOODS REMOVED FOR OWN USE BY THE PROPRIETOR

Any goods removed from the business by its owner for personal use cannot be accounted for as a sale because the owner would feel entitled to pay no more than the cost for these goods. Therefore, the removal of goods by the owner is accounted for at cost as personal drawings, by debiting the Capital account and crediting the Trading account. The reason for crediting the Trading account is, once again, to avoid having to determine whether the goods removed were out of those stated in the Opening Stock account or the Purchases account. For example, if in 20X1 Andy Small removes one phone for his personal use, the stock remaining unsold will be one less and the Trading account will appear as shown on the right.

TRADING ACCOUNT FOR THE YEAR ENDED 31.12.X1		
	£	£
Sales		54,000
Opening Stock	6,000	
Purchases	40,000	
Less: Drawings	(100)	
Less: Closing Stock	(9,900)	
Cost of sales		(36,000)
Gross profit		18,000

7.5 IMPROVEMENTS TO THE APPEARANCE OF FINANCIAL STATEMENTS

7.5.1 The 'vertical' format of presenting financial statements

We have so far presented the balance sheet in what is known as the *vertical format*, or 'statement' format, of presentation. We have deliberately avoided the alternative format – referred to as the *horizontal format* – where the Balance Sheet, like ledger accounts, has two sides, stating the assets on one side and liabilities on the other. Instead, we have stated the assets first and the capital plus liabilities later.

On the other hand, we have always presented the Profit and Loss account in the horizontal format; this was necessary to impress that the Profit and Loss account is another ledger account and therefore has a debit side, recording expenditure, and a credit side, recording income. When reporting the performance of an entity to those not versed in the language of the double entry system, the information in the Profit and Loss account is better stated in a vertical format. The vertical format commences with sales, deducts therefrom the cost of goods sold to arrive at the gross profit, and then proceeds to deduct all other expenditure to arrive at the net profit for the period.

7.5.2 Grouping expenditure sensibly

Since, in real life, a business entity would incur expenditure under many and varied headings, instead of reporting them all in a long and motley list, it would be more meaningful if expenses were to be grouped under appropriate headings. The headings in use are as follows:

- **Administrative expenses**: These are expenses incurred on office maintenance and administration. They include salaries, audit fees, staff welfare, rent, rates, stationery, telephone, postage, bank charges and similar expenses. Usually depreciation of buildings, furniture and office equipment are included in this group.
- **Distribution costs**: This heading comprises expenses incurred in selling goods and then distributing the goods to customers after sale. This grouping includes advertising, sales commission, and costs relating to the packing and carriage of goods to the extent they relate to goods moving out. Usually depreciation and maintenance expenses on vehicles are included here on the basis that vehicles are mostly used for delivery. There is divided opinion on bad debts; there are those who prefer to include bad debts within administrative expenses on the grounds that they arise because of bad credit administration; however, it would appear more plausible to recognize bad debt as part of the cost of selling arising from indiscriminate sales efforts.
- **Interest**: This is the cost of finding cash, if necessary by borrowing it.

7.5.3 Improving the layout of the Balance Sheet

Items in the Balance Sheet are also grouped to make it easier for the user to understand the significance of the figures. The groupings are as follows:

- **fixed assets**: assets intended for continuous use in the business;
- **current assets**: assets continuously changing in the course of business, comprising stock, debtors, prepayments, and cash both in hand and at the bank.
- **current liabilities**: liabilities intended to be repaid within the next accounting period;
- **non-current liabilities**: liabilities other than current liabilities;
- **capital employed**: the capital provided by the owner plus long-term liabilities;
- **working capital**: that part of the capital employed that is not tied down in fixed assets. It is the amount by which current assets exceed current liability. Working capital is referred to also as 'net current assets'.

Period-end adjustments

Bill Hardy Retail extracted the following Trial Balance at 30.6.20X1. You are informed as follows:

(a) As at 30.6.20X1 stock costing £120,000 remained unsold and stationery costing £3,000 remained unused.

(b) Salary £6,000 and electricity £1,000 remain unpaid at 30.6.20X1.

(c) Rent for business premises is agreed at £1,500 per month.

(d) Interest is payable on the City Bank loan at 10% per annum.

(e) Depreciation is to be written off on the Motor Vehicles and Furniture accounts at 20% and 10% of the value to which they have been written down by the end of the previous accounting period.

BILL HARDY RETAIL

TRIAL BALANCE AS AT 30.6.20X1

	£000	£000
Motor vehicles	320	–
Stationery	12	–
Sales	–	950
Advertising	46	–
Staff loans	85	–
Salaries	65	–
Purchases	725	–
Rent	24	–
Furniture	120	–
Heat and light	19	–
Cash in hand	14	–
City Bank loan	–	150
Staff welfare	20	–
Capital a/c	–	350
	1,450	1,450

Required:

You are to prepare, in vertical format, the Trading and Profit and Loss account for the year ended 30 June 20X1 and the Balance Sheet as at that date, paying attention to their appearance.

Note: The amounts in the Trial Balance are listed under £000, which means that each amount has been rounded off to the nearest one thousand pounds sterling.

7.6 AN INTRODUCTION TO ACCOUNTING RATIOS

A ratio traces the relationship between two related figures. If, for example, the figures concerned are the heights of two brothers and the younger is 3 ft and the elder is 6 ft, then this could be expressed as a ratio in the following forms:

- Pure ratio form   3:6 or simplified as 1:2
- Fraction form   3/6 or simplified as 1/2
- Percentage form $3/6 \times 100\% = 50\%$
- Times cover form   6/3 = twice

Accounting ratios trace, in any of the four forms above, the relationship between two figures reported in a set of accounts. The choice of form depends on which is regarded as the best-suited to convey the significance of the relationship being considered.

7.6.1 Gross profit percentage

This is a common ratio, expressed usually in the form of a percentage (and thus a special case of the percentage form of ratio), to explain the relationship between gross profit and sales. The gross profit ratio of Andy Small, for example, is 33.33%.

FORMULA

$$\frac{\text{Gross profit}}{\text{Sales}} \times 100\%$$

COMPUTATION

$$\frac{£18,000}{£54,000} \times 100\% = 33.33\%$$

Though a ratio traces the relationship between two figures, it is expressed only in terms of one of them. For example, Andy buys his phones for £100 and sells them for £150. Andy could express his profit margin in terms of his cost by saying that his profit margin is half (or 50%). On the other hand, he would be expressing his profit in terms of his sale price when he claims that his gross profit ratio is one-third (or 33.33%). One should appreciate that:

(a) the expression 'gross profit ratio' is used only when the profit loading is expressed in terms of the *sale price*; and

profit margin	gross profit
1/2 of cost price	= 1/3 of sale price
1/3 of cost price	= 1/4 of sale price
1/4 of cost price	= 1/5 of sale price
1/5 of cost price	= 1/6 of sale price
1/6 of cost price	= 1/7 of sale price
1/10 of cost price	= 1/11 of sale price
2/10 of cost price	= 2/12 of sale price
3/10 of cost price	= 3/13 of sale price
6/10 of cost price	= 6/16 of sale price
Do you see the pattern?	

(b) whichever way one chooses to express the profit margin, the other way could be arrived at because there exists a clear relationship between the two, as shown above.

Interaction 7.4

Accounting for unsold stock and stock taken by owner for personal use

Tony Rodriguez deals in alarm clocks of a standard model. He buys each clock for £40 and sells each at a price calculated to give him a profit of 50 per cent on cost. The Trial Balance extracted from his books appear as stated on the right. You are informed as follows:

(a) Tony has taken one alarm clock home for personal use. This has yet to be accounted for.

(b) Tony acquired the business's motor vehicles for £200,000 on 1.7.20X2 and the furniture for £100,000 on 1.7.20X0. He depreciates his vehicles and furniture using the straight-line method at 20% and 10% p.a. respectively.

(c) The loan from Tina Small is repayable when able, but interest has been agreed at 10% per annum.

(d) Rent for office premises has been agreed at £24,000 per annum.

(e) Salaries of £4,000 remain accrued as at 30th June 20X5.

TONY RODRIGUEZ CLOCKS

TRIAL BALANCE AS AT 30 JUNE 20X5

	£000	£000
Motor vehicles	120	–
Furniture	60	–
Stock on 30.6.20X4	116	–
Purchases	640	–
Sales	–	960
Salaries	72	–
Stationery	12	–
Advertising	39	–
Postage	8	–
Sales commission	5	–
Loan to manager	10	–
Loan from Small	–	150
Light & heat	12	–
Rent	30	–
Carriage outward	9	–
Cash in hand	12	–
Capital – T. Rodriguez	–	35
	1,145	1,145

Required:

(a) Calculate the stock of unsold alarm clocks as at 30 June 20X5.

(b) Prepare, in vertical format, the Trading and Profit and Loss account for the year ended 30 June 20X5 and the Balance Sheet as at that date.

Note: The straight-line method for depreciation means that the same amount is written off each year. (So a £15,000 computer system depreciated over three years by the straight-line method would have £5,000 put to a Depreciation account for each of the three years.)

SOLUTIONS TO INTERACTIVE QUESTIONS

IQ 7.1 Typical period-end adjustments

1. Unsold goods

The cost of unsold goods is capitalized, by transfer from the Purchases account to a Stock in Trade account. The remainder in the Purchases account represents the cost of goods sold and is transferred to the Trading account. The Stock in Trade appears on the Balance Sheet.

PURCHASES ACCOUNT				STOCK IN TRADE ACCOUNT			
	£		£		£		£
Cash a/c	214,500	Stock a/c	14,500	Purchases	14,500		

2. Unused stationery

Stationery remaining unused, akin to goods unsold, is capitalized by transferring the cost to a Stock of Stationery account.

STATIONERY ACCOUNT				STOCK OF STATIONERY ACCOUNT			
	£		£		£		£
Cash a/c	3,600	Stock	600	Stationery	600		

3. Prepayment

The expenditure by way of rent, at £1,000 per month, would be £12,000 for the year. Therefore the remainder out of the £15,000 paid in the year (i.e. £3,000) is capitalized by transfer to a Prepaid Rent account because benefit of that payment is expected next year.

RENT ACCOUNT				PREPAID RENT ACCOUNT			
	£		£		£		£
Cash a/c	15,000	Pre-paid	3,000	Rent a/c	3,000		

4. Accrual

The Salaries account, reporting the payment of £22,800, does not record the full expense for the year until the amount of £2,200, accrued as at 31.12.20X0, is also accounted for by a debiting of the Salaries account and a crediting of a liability account (which might be named Salaries Accrued or Salary Payable).

SALARIES ACCOUNT				SALARIES ACCRUED ACCOUNT			
	£		£		£		£
Cash a/c	22,800						2,200
Accrued	2,200						

5. Write-off (or expensing)

Motor vehicles, though an asset, have a finite life. Therefore the cost of the vehicles has to be allocated, in a systematic manner, among the different accounting periods benefiting from their use. The portion of cost so allocated to an accounting period is called the depreciation.

MOTOR VEHICLES ACCOUNT				DEPRECIATION ACCOUNT			
	£		£		£		£
Cash a/c	18,000	Depreciation a/c	3,600	Motor Vehicle a/c	3,600		

IQ 7.2 Accounting for expenditure at the amount contracted for

For The Food Store:

(a) The amount of £12,000 was written off to the Profit and Loss account in order to match the income and expenditure. This is achieved by charging the amount due for the year under the rental agreement – whether or not this amount was paid in the year.

(b) If the payment due under the agreement on 30 November 20X1 was not made until 1 January 20X2, then there would be four months' rent due (September–December) and an accrual for £4,000 would appear in the Balance Sheet as at 31.12.20X1.

IQ 7.3 Period-end adjustments

For Bill Hardy Retail, we have the following:

PURCHASES ACCOUNT

	£		£
Cash a/c	725	Stock a/c	120
		Trading a/c	605

STOCK IN TRADE ACCOUNT

	£		£
Purchases a/c	120		

STATIONERY ACCOUNT

	£		£
Cash a/c	12	Stock a/c	3
		Profit and Loss a/c	9

STOCK OF STATIONERY ACCOUNT

	£		£
Stationery a/c	3		

SALARIES ACCOUNT

	£		£
Cash a/c	65	Profit and Loss a/c	71
Balance c/d	6		
		Balance b/d	6

INTEREST ACCOUNT

	£		£
Balance c/d	15	Profit and Loss a/c	15
		Balance b/d	15

HEAT AND LIGHT ACCOUNT

	£		£
Cash a/c	19	Profit and Loss a/c	20
Balance c/d	1		
		Balance b/d	1

MOTOR VEHICLES ACCOUNT

	£		£
Balance b/f	320	Depreciation a/c	64
		Balance c/d	256
Balance b/d	256		

RENT ACCOUNT

	£		£
Cash a/c	24	Profit and Loss a/c	18
		Balance c/d	6
Balance b/d	6		

DEPRECIATION OF MOTOR VEHICLES ACCOUNT

	£		£
Motor Vehicles a/c	64	Profit and Loss a/c	64

DEPRECIATION OF FURNITURE ACCOUNT

	£		£
Furniture a/c	12	Profit and Loss a/c	12

FURNITURE ACCOUNT

	£		£
Balance b/f	120	Depreciation a/c	12
		Balance c/d	108
Balance b/d	108		

BILL HARDY RETAIL

TRADING AND PROFIT AND LOSS ACCOUNT FOR THE YEAR ENDED 30 JUNE 20X1		
		£000
Sales:		950
Purchases	725	
Less: Stock on 30.6X1	(120)	
Cost of goods sold		(605)
Gross profit		345
Administrative expenses:		
Salaries	71	
Rent	18	
Depreciation – furniture	12	
Stationery	9	
Heat and light	20	
Staff welfare	20	(150)
Distribution cost:		
Advertising	46	
Depreciation – vehicles	64	(110)
Interest		(15)
Profit for the year		70

BALANCE SHEET AS AT 30 JUNE 20X1				
				£000
Fixed assets:				
Furniture				108
Motor vehicles				256
				364
Current assets:				
Stock in trade			120	
Staff loans			85	
Prepaid rent			6	
Stationery stock			3	
Cash in hand			14	
			228	
Current liabilities:				
Salary accrued		6		
Lighting accrued		1		
Interest accrued		15	(22)	
Working Capital				206
Capital employed				570

	£000
Capital – Bill Hardy	350
Profit for the year	70
	420
Long-term liabilities:	
City Bank loan	150
Capital employed	570

Note: The amounts payable as at 30.6.20X1 for salary and electricity, though appearing (for convenience) as credit balances in the respective nominal accounts, are reported as liabilities in the Balance Sheet. Conversely, prepaid rent is reported as an asset, although in the ledger it appears as a debit balance in the nominal account.

IQ 7.4 Accounting for unsold stock and stock taken by owner for personal use

(a) **Calculating the closing stock figure for alarm clocks**

Since each clock costs £40 and a profit margin at 50% thereof is £20, the sale price is £60. Calculations on the right show that, after selling 16,000 clocks and after the proprietor has taken one for personal use, 2,899 clocks remain in hand. Their cost = 2,899 @ £40 each = £115,960.

CLOSING STOCK CALCULATION

	£000	Units
Stock on 30.6.20X4	116	
Purchases	640	
Total (@ £40)	756	18,900
Sales (@ £60)	960	(16,000)
Removed by Tony R.		(1)
Stock on 30.6.20X0		2,899

(b) Trading and Profit and Loss account, plus Balance Sheet

TONY RODRIGUEZ CLOCKS

TRADING AND PROFIT AND LOSS ACCOUNT FOR THE YEAR ENDED 30 JUNE 20X5	£	£
Sales:		960,000
Stock at 30.6.20X4	116,000	
Purchases	640,000	
Capital (goods drawn)	(40)	
Stock at 30.6.20X5	(115,960)	
Cost of sales		(640,000)
Gross profit		320,000
Administrative expenses:		
Salaries	(76,000)	
Rent	(24,000)	
Depreciation – furniture	(10,000)	
Stationery	(12,000)	
Postage	(8,000)	
Light and heat	(12,000)	(142,000)
Distribution costs		
Advertising	(39,000)	
Sales commission	(5,000)	
Depreciation – motor vehicle	(40,000)	
Carriage outwards	(9,000)	(93,000)
Interest		(15,000)
Profit		70,000

BALANCE SHEET AS AT 30.6.20X5		£	£
Fixed assets:			
Furniture and fittings			50,000
Motor vehicles			80,000
			130,000
Current assets:			
Stock in trade		115,960	
Loan to manager		10,000	
Prepaid rent		6,000	
Cash in hand		12,000	
Current liabilities:			
Interest accrued		(15,000)	
Salaries accrued		(4,000)	
Net current assets			124,960
			254,960
			£
Capital a/c			35,000
Profit for the year			70,000
Trading a/c – goods drawn			(40)
			104,960
Non-current liability			
Loan from Tina Small			150,000
			254,960

PROGRESSIVE QUESTIONS

PQ 7.1 Relations between payments and expenditure

The following information relates to a business that commenced trading this year. Fill in the empty cells in the grid with appropriate figures.

ACCOUNT	DURING THE CURRENT YEAR		AS AT THE END OF THE YEAR	
	Payments	Expense	Prepayment	Accrual
(a) Vehicle maintenance	£135	£160	–	
(b) Insurance	£500		–	£125
(c) Salaries		£2,600	–	£55
(d) Rates		£260	95	–
(e) Telephone	£290		–	£80

PQ 7.2 Relations among payments, expense, assets and liability

The information stated below is in respect of a business that started up several years ago. Fill in the empty cells of the grid with appropriate figures.

	BALANCE SHEET AS AT 31.12.20X0		DURING THE YEAR ENDED 31.12.20X1		BALANCE SHEET AS AT 31.12.20X1	
	Asset	Liability	Payment	Expense	Asset	Liability
(a) Rent	£400	–	£1,600	£1,600		–
(b) Fuel	–	–	£855		£155	–
(c) Office equipment	£8,000	–	–			–
(d) Motor vehicles	£5,500	–	£2,500			–
(e) Salaries	£300	–	£6,200		–	£400
(f) Insurance	–	£300		£1,200	–	£300
(g) Telephone	£160	–		£420	£100	–

Office equipment and motor vehicles are depreciated at 20% and 25% respectively of the balance at the year end.

PQ 7.3 Accounting for income on an accruals basis

An accruals basis, in relation to income, means that income is recognized, in each accounting period, not in accordance with the amount received in the period but in accordance with the amount earned in the period. Fill in the empty cells of the grid with appropriate figures.

	BALANCE SHEET AS AT 31.12.20X0		DURING THE YEAR ENDED 31.12.20X1		BALANCE SHEET AS AT 31.12.20X1	
	Asset	Liability	Receipts	Income	Asset	Liability
(a) Commission earnings	£50	–	£565		£35	–
(b) Interest receivable	£100	–	£900	£1,000		
(c) Rent receivable	–	£150	£1,300		£100	–
(d) Commission earnings	£120	–	£1,600		–	£250
(e) Interest receivable	£100	–	£1,300	£1,500		–
(f) Rent receivable	£500	–		£6,000	–	£500

PQ 7.4 Accounting for rent receivable

In the premises used by Free-Range Stores there is an apartment that is rented out to three university students at £2,000 per quarter. Particulars of the rent received are as follows:

CASH RECEIVED DURING YEAR 20X0	
Amount	In respect of the period
£2,000	1.1.20X0 to 31.3.20X0
£2,000	1.4.20X0 to 30.6.20X0
£2,000	1.7.20X0 to 30.9.20X0

CASH RECEIVED DURING THE YEAR 20X1	
Amount	In respect of the period
£2,000	1.10.20X0 to 31.12.20X0
£2,000	1.1.20X1 to 31.3.20X1
£2,000	1.4.20X1 to 30.6.20X1
£2,000	1.7.20X1 to 30.9.20X1
£2,000	1.10.20X1 to 31.12.20X1
£2,000	1.1.20X2 to 31.3.20X2

The store makes up its accounts to 31st December each year.

Required:

(a) Calculate the amounts to be included as rental income in the Profit and Loss accounts in 20X0 and 20X1.
(b) Calculate the amount that should be reported as either current asset or current liability in the Balance Sheets at the end of each of these years.

PQ 7.5 Accounting for expenses on an accruals basis

In her business's balance sheet as at 1 June 20X1, Rosemary Briggs, a retailer, reported rent accrued at £400, while insurance prepaid and rates prepaid were reported at £360 and £350 respectively. During the year ended 31 May 20X2 the following payments were made:

Date	Item	Amount	Period covered
11.7.20X1	Rent	£600	Three months to 30 June 20X1
24.9.20X1	Insurance	£1,200	One year to 30 September 20X2
3.10.20X1	Rates	£700	Six months to 29 February 20X2
14.11.20X1	Rent	£800	Four months to 31 October 20X1
16.3.20X2	Rent	£800	Four months to 29 February 20X2
8.4.20X2	Rates	£800	Six months to 31 August 20X2

Required: Post these payments to appropriate accounts in the ledger, make the year-end adjustments, and identify how each item will be reported in the Profit and Loss account for the year ended 31 May 20X2 and the Balance Sheet as at that date.

PQ 7.6 Trial Balances extracted at different stages of accounting

Mike Sigham commenced business on 1.1.20X0 with a capital in cash of £100,000. He acquired some furniture on the same date for £12,000 and a vehicle on 1.4.20X0 for £20,000. Purchases and sales are strictly on a cash basis and Mike effects his sales at cost plus 25 per cent. Sales during the year amounted to £492,500. Payments during the year to 31 December 20X0 are summarized in the box on the right.

Mike expects to use his furniture for 10 years and his vehicle for five. He reports that as at 31 December 20X0 he owes £1,800 as salaries and £800 for heating, while the rent for the shop premises has been agreed at £500 per month.

	£
Purchases	436,800
Postage and telephone	1,260
Sales commission	4,650
Staff welfare	3,750
Salaries and wages	28,200
Lighting and heating	2,280
Rent	9,000
Advertising	9,400

Required:

(a) Account for the above transactions.
(b) Extract a Trial Balance as at 31.12.20X0 but prior to making any year-end adjustments.
(c) Extract another Trial Balance as at 31.12.20X0 after making all year-end adjustments.
(e) Prepare a Trading and Profit and Loss account for the year ended 31.12.20X0 and a balance sheet as at that date.

Chapter 8

SUBSIDIARY BOOKS OF ACCOUNT

In this chapter	
We will learn of:	and you should be able to:
• credit transactions and credit terms	• account for an entity that transacts business on credit terms as well as on a cash basis
• more books of prime entry	

8.1 INTRODUCTION TO CREDIT TRANSACTIONS

Up to now we have learnt to account for a trader who conducts his business on a cash basis. For a cash-based business the prime entries are made by the cashier and posting of those entries to the ledger is made by the bookkeeper. The bookkeeper must ensure that every transaction is accounted for on a double entry basis. Let us now consider the accounting process when sales and purchases are made on credit terms.

We have already used the word 'credit' to identify a side in each account. When we talk about *credit transactions*, however, the word credit has another meaning. The word is derived from the Latin word *credere* which means to believe or trust. Credit sales, therefore, means selling goods to a customer trusting in that customer's *willingness and ability* to pay on the terms agreed at the time of making the sale. Of course, if the customer is unknown to the trader, he will obtain trade references to assess how much credit to allow before supplying any goods. He will then agree credit terms with the customer. The credit terms normally include: a credit limit – the maximum amount (say £3,000) up to which goods will be sold on credit; and a credit period – the length of time (say 30 days) permitted to the customer to pay for the goods, usually referred to as 'settling the account'.

8.1.1 Accounting for credit sales

To understand how to account for credit sales, whether goods or services, let us assume that a trader makes a cash sale of £500 and also sells goods on credit to Jill West for £400. The cash sale is of course recorded by the trader's cashier on the debit side of the Cash account and then posted by the trader's bookkeeper to the credit side of the Sales account. The credit sale of £400 also needs to be credited to the Sales account, so that the Sales account (stated on the right) would report the total income of £900. Note that if the credit sale had been debited to the Sales account (instead of being credited) the balance in that account would become £100 (rather less than the £900 it should be).

SALES ACCOUNT

			Cash account	500
			Jill West a/c	400
				900

Posting to the Debtors Ledger

To account for the credit sale on the double entry basis, the bookkeeper makes the second entry by debiting an account opened in the name of Jill West. Because Jill's account in the books has a debit balance, the trader refers to Jill as a debtor. The trader regards Jill West as an asset because Jill's account in the books represents a benefit to be received in future when Jill settles her account. The asset is not the physical person of Jill, of course, but the amount she has undertaken to pay. To notify Jill that a debit account has been opened in her name, the trader sends Jill a note that is appropriately called (in technical parlance) a *debit note*. However, a more common name for that note is an *invoice*. Some call it a *credit sales memo*.

JILL WEST ACCOUNT

Sales a/c	400		

To accommodate the personal accounts of those who owe amounts for sales (debtors) and others to whom amounts are owed for purchases (creditors), a separate ledger may be maintained, called a *Personal Ledger*. If there are a large number of debtors, a separate ledger may be required for them and this ledger is known as the *Debtors Ledger*, *Sales Ledger* or *Sold Ledger*.

Accounting for goods returned by a customer

What if Jill changes her mind and returns a part of the goods sold to her, say those for £50? The trader will then have to reverse the entries that have already been made. The trader debits the Sales account (reducing the income to £850) and credits Jill's account (reducing to £350 the amount reported as due from her). A note, known as a *credit note*, is sent to Jill West, to notify her that her account has been credited. (In Chapter 9 we will learn to record the sales returns in another account rather than in the Sales account.)

SALES ACCOUNT

Jill West a/c	50	Cash account	500
Balance c/d	850	Jill West a/c	400
		Balance b/d	850

JILL WEST ACCOUNT

Sales a/c	400	Sales a/c	50
		Balance c/d	350
Balance b/d	350		

8.1.2 Accounting for credit purchases

We account for credit purchases along similar lines. For example, a credit purchase of goods amounting to £400 from City Stores is accounted for by debiting the Purchases account in the Nominal Ledger and crediting the City Stores account in the *Creditors Ledger* (see below). Because the account opened for City Stores has a credit balance, the trader refers to City Stores as a creditor. A creditor is one to whom an amount is owed. The creditor's account represents a liability to be settled in due course in accordance with the agreed credit terms. If the trader returns any part of the goods purchased to the creditor, the return outwards is accounted for by debiting the City Stores account (reducing the amount owed to it) and crediting the Purchases account (reducing the expenditure).

Creditors Ledger

The personal accounts of those who are owed amounts for purchases (creditors) are recorded in a Creditors Ledger, which is known also as *Purchase Ledger* or *Bought Ledger*.

8.2 THE SALES DAY BOOK

A *Sales Day Book* is a book of prime entry. It is a list prepared from the copy invoices of all the credit sales made, showing the name of the customer and the amount due in respect of goods that have been supplied on credit. Whereas the prime entry for all cash transactions is in the cash book, the prime entry for credit sales is made in the Sales Day Book. Moreover, the bookkeeper accounts for the credit sales on a double entry basis by debiting each credit sale to the personal account of the customer concerned and crediting the (daily, weekly or monthly) total of credit sales to the Sales account. Thus the two entries, accounting for each credit sale, are both made by the bookkeeper. The Sales Day Book, unlike the cash book, is not therefore part of the double entry system. Hence the Sales Day Book is a book of prime entry but only a *subsidiary book of account*.

Why is a Sales Day Book necessary? There are many reasons. For example:

1. **It helps the bookkeeper**:
   - It reduces the workload of the bookkeeper. If there were, say, credit sales to 400 different customers in a day, with someone listing them in a Sales Day Book and ascertaining the total credit sales for the day, the bookkeeper would have to make 401 entries rather than having to make 400 entries in the Sales account along with 400 more corresponding entries in the customers' accounts.
   - A small trader who may not have more than a few credit sales in each day may permit the bookkeeper to post monthly totals to the Sales account. If, however, the total is not posted to the Sales account in the nominal ledger until the end of the month, a Trial Balance cannot be extracted until the last day of each month. The trader should insist, however, that postings to the personal accounts of customers are done on a daily basis. If this were not done, it would be impossible to know when the customer had reached the agreed credit limit or to respond to a customer's enquiry as to any amount outstanding.
   - It relieves the bookkeeper of the responsibility for retaining and filing the vouchers (i.e the copy invoices); these are retained by the person making the prime entry in the Sales Day Book. It allows the bookkeeper to concentrate on maintaining accurate ledgers.
2. **It provides a means for easy access to any voucher**: Recording every single credit sale in a prime entry book in the chronological sequence in which it took place means that it is possible, in the event of a query, to trace the voucher (usually a copy of the sales invoice) showing the amount and the identity of the customer for every credit sale.
3. **It provides a bridge between a single credit and corresponding many debits**: Where the arrangement is that daily or monthly totals of credit sales are posted to the Sales account, the Sales Day Book plays the important role of relating a single credit with its corresponding many debits.

8.2.1 Illustrating the Sales Day Book format

The Sales Day Book is drawn with columns to record the date, the voucher (which is the sequential number of the invoice sent to each customer), the name of the customer whose account should be debited, the ledger folio, and the value of the sale. The Folio column is filled by the bookkeeper, after she posts each transaction, with the folio number of each customer's account debited by her and the folio number of the Sales account credited by her. What this does is to provide a daily or monthly total that is used within the double entry system. Such a subsidiary book of account is not included in a Trial Balance because only accounts within the double entry system are listed on it to ensure that each transaction has been accounted for by a debit as well as a credit.

SALES DAY BOOK				
Date	Voucher	Customer's name	F	Amount £
20X0				
1.1	SV712	Jill West	?	400
1.1	SV713	Peter May	?	250
1.1	SV714	S. Kumar	?	325
1.1	SV715	M. Nizar	?	185
		Sales account	?	1,160

Writing up the Sales Day Book

Reginald Mendis started trading with capital in cash of £20,000 on 1 January 20X0. On the first day of business he paid £8,000 for furniture, £800 for expenses and £4,600 to purchase goods for sale. He made a cash sale of £2,800 and sold goods on credit as stated on the right. Ignore depreciation and he had no unsold stock.

John Lyon	£450
Duncan Brown	£725
Liza Lester	£975
Ron Dyer	£845

Required:

(a) Record the transactions in the appropriate book of prime entry.
(b) Post the transactions to the Nominal Ledger and Debtors Ledger.
(c) Extract a Trial Balance at close of business on 1.1.20X0.
(d) Prepare a Trading and Profit and Loss account for the day and a Balance Sheet.

8.3 THE PURCHASES DAY BOOK

The prime entry for all credit purchases (of goods intended for sale) is made in a Purchases Day Book, with columns corresponding to those in the Sales Day Book. The identification numbers printed on each invoice, received from different suppliers, would not of course be in any sequence. Before listing them in the Purchases Day Book, new sequential numbers are written on them. The bookkeeper credits the value of each invoice, individually to the account of each of the suppliers, and debits the (daily or monthly) total of credit purchases to the Purchases account.

The Purchases Day Book, just like the Sales Day Book, stands outside the double entry system and is, therefore, another subsidiary book of account.

PURCHASES DAY BOOK				
Date	V	Supplier's name	F	Amount £
20X0				
1.1	PV 1	Dave Butler	?	2,450
1.1	PV 2	Susan Moore	?	1,676
1.1	PV 3	M. Ramanathan	?	745
1.1	PV 4	City Stores	?	3,256
1.1	PV 5	G.M. Fawzy	?	948
		Purchases a/c	?	9,075

Interaction 8.2

Writing up the Purchases Day Book

Betty Floyd commenced trading as a greengrocer on 1 July 20X0 with a capital in cash of £5,000. She sold strictly on a cash basis. Her sales on the first day were £3,150. Her purchases, on one month's credit, were as stated on the right. On her first day of trading she paid £150 for purchases, £210 for expenses and £400 as school fees for her son.

Suppliers	£
Dave Super Market	600
Stella Grocers	550
Maniam & Co.	420

Required:

(a) Record the first day's transactions in the appropriate books of prime entry.
(b) Post the transactions to appropriate accounts in the ledgers.
(c) Extract a Trial Balance at close of business on first day.
(d) Prepare a Trading and Profit and Loss account for the day and a Balance Sheet at the end of the day, assuming that she has no unsold stock.

8.4 RETURNS DAY BOOKS

The prime entry for goods returned (outwards) to suppliers is made in a *Purchases Returns Day Book* and that for goods returned (inwards) by the business's own customers is made in a *Sales Returns Day Book*. The vouchers supporting returns outwards will be the credit notes issued by suppliers; those for returns inwards will be copies of credit notes issued to customers.

Interaction 8.3

Writing up all four day books

Jane Butt, who commenced trading via a wholesale store on 1.8.20X0, has summarized her transactions during the first week of business as set out here.

CASH RECEIPTS

Date	Particulars	£
1.8	Capital	10,000
1.8	Sales	526
2.8	Sales	412
3.8	Paul Russel	1,236
3.8	Sales	168
4.8	Allen Stern	1,214
4.8	Sales	320
5.8	Allen Stern	1,425
5.8	Sales	460

PURCHASES (ON CREDIT)

Date	Supplier	Purchases	Returns
1.8	Stella Naylor	£1,460	–
1.8	Chris Meall	£580	–
2.8	Luke Perera	£345	–
3.8	Chris Meall	–	£65
3.8	Stella Naylor	£795	–
4.8	Chris Meall	–	£70
4.8	Luke Perera	£1,225	–
4.8	Stella Naylor	–	£45
4.8	Chris Meall	£1,565	–

CASH PAYMENTS			SALES (ON CREDIT)			
Date	Particulars	£	Date	Customer	Sales	Return
1.8	Furniture	8,000	1.8	Paul Russel	£765	–
1.8	Salaries	140	1.8	Allen Stern	£650	–
2.8	Drawings	165	1.8	Simon de Silva	£425	–
2.8	Rent	1,000	2.8	Tony Martin	£468	–
2.8	Salaries	140	2.8	Allen Stern	£684	–
3.8	Chris Meall	515	2.8	Paul Russel	£526	–
3.8	Drawings	120	3.8	S. Tarrimo	£722	–
3.8	Advertising	140	3.8	Allen Stern	–	£120
3.8	Salaries	140	3.8	Allen Stern	£900	–
3.8	Stationery	36	3.8	Simon de Silva	£544	–
4.8	Salaries	140	3.8	Paul Russel	–	£55
4.8	Drawings	90	4.8	Allen Stern	£525	–
5.8	Stella Naylor	1,415	4.8	S. Tarrimo	–	£30
5.8	Salaries	140	4.8	Tony Martin	£488	–
			4.8	Simon de Silva	–	£75
			5.8	Paul Russel	£265	–
			5.8	S. Tarrimo	£186	–
			5.8	Allen Stern	£342	–

Stock in hand on 5 August cost Jane £845.

Required:

(a) Record Jane's transactions in the appropriate books of prime entry.

(b) Post the transactions to the Real Ledger, Nominal Ledger, Debtors Ledger and Creditors Ledger.

(c) Extract a Trial Balance as at 5 August 20X0.

(d) Prepare the Trading and Profit and Loss account for the five days to 5.8.20X0 and the Balance Sheet as at that date. Ignore depreciation of furniture.

8.5 TRADE DISCOUNTS

How does a trader who buys and sells any product make a profit? Generally the trader obtains the product (say calculators) from a fellow trader at a discounted price, which then allows for a profit on resale. The discount is known as a *trade discount*. It is usual for such discounts to be calculated at an agreed percentage of the sale price and to be stated on the invoice requesting payment. For example, on receipt of the invoice shown below, Unimax Ltd records only £5,625 (i.e. the amount due, net of a trade discount) in the Purchases Day Book. Accordingly Unimax's bookkeeper credits the General Equipment Supplies plc account with £5,625 and (as part of the total credit purchases for the day or month, as the case may be) debits the same amount to the Unimax Purchases account. Thus in the system of accounting as practised in the United Kingdom, trade discounts are not recorded at all in the books of accounts.

GENERAL EQUIPMENT SUPPLIES PLC

70A Midmore Road, London N2 4JD
Tel: 0208 965 6852
VAT REGISTRATION: R567842

INVOICE NO: BT765248
YOUR ORDER NO: N4369

TO: Unimax Ltd.
30 Eden Road, Croydon CR0 5BA

DATE: 17 May 20X0

	Per unit £	TOTAL £	p
10 units of Egmore personal computers Model G286	625	6,250	00
Less: 10% Trade discount		625	00
		5,625	00
E&OE			

Note: The 'E&OE' usually printed at the bottom of an invoice is a commercially accepted abbreviation which stands for 'errors and omissions excepted' to safeguard the trading entity that has issued the invoice from the effects of any error or omission made when issuing it (e.g. a mistype by a PC operator).

Trade discount should not be confused with a cash discount or settlement discount, to be met in Chapter 13.

8.6 THE JOURNAL

The four day books we have illustrated in this chapter are the modern version of what was once known as '*the Journal*'. The word 'journal' is derived from the French word meaning a daily record or diary. Originally the prime entry for all transactions was made in a single journal before the bookkeeper posted them to the ledger. With the passage of time, specialized journals such as the ones we have met were developed to make the first entry for repetitive routine transactions. Hence a Sales Day Book is known alternatively as the Sales Journal, the Purchases Day Book as the Purchase Journal, and so on. The Journal itself, sometimes referred to as the *General Journal*, is now used for the prime entry of those transactions for which no specialized journal is available. We will enquire into the transactions recorded in the General Journal in Chapter 10.

Distinguishing prime entry books from subsidiary books

(a) Explain what you understand by the term 'subsidiary books of account'.
(b) Name the books of prime entry that you have come across so far.
(c) Which of the books of prime entry are also referred to as subsidiary books of account?

8.7 THE PETTY CASH BOOK

As a method of giving relief to the cashier, it has become usual to delegate to another person – known as the petty cashier – the responsibility for making specified routine payments of less than a predetermined amount. The cashier, who still remains respons-ible for accounting for all cash receipts and payments, is required to maintain control of the petty cash payments, achieved in general by making an arrangement with the petty cashier as follows:

1. The cashier pays the petty cashier an agreed amount (say £50), the amount depend-ing on the nature and value of payments delegated to the petty cashier and the duration of the regular period. At the end of the period, the cashier reimburses the amount paid out by the petty cashier. The amount left with the petty cashier for making payments is known as the *imprest*.
2. The petty cashier is authorized only to pay specified types of routine expenses (such as for travelling, buying postage stamps, buying stationery, and so on) and up to an agreed limit for each individual payment (say £10). Petty cashiers are usually warned against giving loans to staff.
3. Every petty cash payment must be supported by a petty cash docket, explaining its nature, bearing the signature of the payee and to which should be attached, wher-ever possible, external evidence of the payment.
4. At an agreed interval (say every week) the petty cashier should produce to the cashier the vouchers (dockets) to support the payments and the petty cash balance in hand and the two together should make up the amount of the imprest. At this point the cashier reimburses the petty cashier with the amount of petty cash payments so that the petty cashier commences each period with the same amount of imprest. For example, if the imprest is £50 and in a given week the payments (supported by vouchers) are £38, after checking on £12 still being in hand and vouchers for £38, the cashier should pay £38 to the petty cashier so as to top up the amount held to £50 again.
5. The petty cashier should write up a Petty Cash Book recording the amounts received from the cashier and the petty cash payments made.

The petty cashier usually writes up the Petty Cash Book so as to analyse his payments by main categories. The bookkeeper posts weekly or monthly totals of those categories rather than the individual payments to the appropriate nominal accounts.

For illustration, let us assume that the petty cash balance of £14 was topped up with £86 on 17.1.20X0, the first day of a new week, to bring the balance to the imprest of £100. The Petty Cash Book, with analysis columns, then appears as follows in our example:

PETTY CASH BOOK

RECEIPTS			PAYMENTS				ANALYSIS				
20X0	Folio	£	20X0	V	Particulars	£	Travel	Cleaning	Car maint.	Postage	Stationery
Balance b/f		14.00	17.1	PC51	Bus fare	2.40	2.40	–	–	–	–
17.1	CB1	86.00	18.1	PC52	Rubber stamp	11.00	–	–	–	–	11.00
			18.1	PC53	Postage stamp	4.50	–	–	–	4.50	–
			19.1	PC54	Petrol for car	18.00	18.00	–	–	–	–
			19.1	PC55	Mopping floor	7.50	–	7.50	–	–	–
			19.1	PC56	Taxi to bank	4.50	4.50	–	–	–	–
			20.1	PC57	Servicing car	22.00	–	–	22.00	–	–
			20.1	PC58	Desk stapler	7.60	–	–	–	–	7.60
			21.1	PC59	Janitor's tip	3.00	–	3.00	–	–	–
			21.1	PC60	Car wipers	7.50	–	–	7.50	–	–
						88.00	24.90	10.50	29.50	4.50	18.60
			21.1		Balance c/d	12.00	NL21	NL16	NL32	NL19	NL8
		100.00				100.00					
Balance b/f		12.00									

When, as shown, the Petty Cash Book is written up with analysis columns, instead of posting each (often trivial) petty cash payment individually to the appropriate nominal account, the bookkeeper is able to post the weekly (or monthly) totals, debiting the Travelling account with £24.90, the Cleaning account with £10.50, and so on.

Interaction 8.5	**Is the Petty Cash Book a main or a subsidiary book of account?**

We have seen that the Petty Cash Book is a book of prime entry in which the first entry is made of routine payments undertaken by the petty cashier, who retains and files the voucher supporting each payment.

Required: State whether the Petty Cash Book is a subsidiary book of account or whether, like the cash book and the ledgers, it is one of the main books account that have to be included in any Trial Balance.

8.8 DAY BOOKS WITH ANALYSIS COLUMNS

The technique of using analysis columns could be applied to any of the day books if the trading entity wishes to monitor any aspect of transactions. For example, an entity retailing ready-made clothing may wish to identify how well it is doing in each separate line of business by writing up its Sales Day Book with analysis columns as follows:

SALES DAY BOOK

Date	V	Customer	F	£	ANALYSIS BY LINE OF BUSINESS		
					Menswear	Ladies' wear	Children's wear
20X0					£	£	£
1.8	A426	Paul Russel & co.	DL1	76,500	21,400	38,500	16,600
1.8	A427	Allen Stern Bros	DL8	28,856	4,815	19,566	4,475
1.8	A428	Simon de Silva	DL6	54,258	11,965	36,245	6,048
1.8	A429	Tony Martin Ltd.	DL9	34,658	5,450	21,256	7,952
1.8	A430	S. Tarrimo plc	DL2	16,250	5,600	7,250	3,400
		Sales account	NL2	210,522	49,230	122,817	38,475

8.9 VALUE ADDED TAX – AN INTRODUCTION

Value Added Tax, abbreviated as VAT, is an indirect tax at rates (generally 17.5 per cent currently in the United Kingdom) reckoned on the value of goods and services. We will focus on VAT in Chapter 20 and will confine ourselves here to a mere introduction to the topic. VAT is a tax not on the trader but on the final consumer. But the trader is required to act as an unpaid agent for the UK government to collect the tax. This means (for something rated at the standard rate) that an item that a trader would usually sell for £100 is required to be sold for £117.50 and the VAT portion remitted periodically to HM Customs and Excise (who collect and account for VAT). On receiving £117.50 from a cash sale, the trader has to account for £100 as income in the Sales account and £17.50 as a liability in a VAT account. If the sale had been on credit terms, the customer's account is debited with £117.50 (i.e. the sale price inclusive of VAT) while the Sales account is credited with £100 and the difference is credited to the VAT account. Posting of credit sales would be made easier by drawing up the Sales Day Book with appropriate columns (see specimen above). While each customer's account is debited with the sale price inclusive of VAT (Claire Stevens with £6,110, for instance) each sale is analysed to separate the amount to be credited to the Sales account and VAT account so that the periodical totals may be credited to these accounts (i.e. £17,120 to the Sales account and £2,996 to the VAT account).

On the matter of purchases, the trader is invoiced for the price inclusive of VAT but is able to reclaim the VAT from the government. If the trader buys on credit an item with a price tag of £80, the supplier's invoice will be for £80 plus £14 as VAT. The trader will account for this purchase by crediting the supplier with £94 (the amount owed) and debiting the Purchases account with only £80, while the difference is debited to the VAT account as an offset from what is owed to the VAT department. Accounting for credit purchases would be made easier if the Purchases Day Book is also drawn up with similar analysis columns.

SALES DAY BOOK					
Date: 17 June 20X1				**ANALYSIS**	
Voucher	**Customer**	**F**	**£**	**Sales**	**VAT**
P7456	Claire Stevens	?	6,110	5,200	910
P7457	Peter Silva	?	1,645	1,400	245
P7458	Guy Nathan	?	8,225	7,000	1,225
P7459	S. Ruperalia	?	3,290	2,800	490
P7460	Nick Robert	?	846	720	126
				17,120	2,996
				NL?	RL?

SOLUTIONS TO INTERACTIVE QUESTIONS

IQ 8.1 Writing up the Sales Day Book

BOOKS OF PRIME ENTRY

CASH ACCOUNT

Capital a/c	20,000	Furniture a/c	8,000
Sales a/c	2,800	Expenses a/c	800
		Purchases a/c	4,600
		Balance c/d	9,400
Balance b/d	9,400		

SALES DAY BOOK

Date	V	Customers	F	£
1.1.X0	?	John Lyon's a/c	?	450
1.1.X0	?	Duncan Brown's a/c	?	725
1.1.X0	?	Liza Lester's a/c	?	975
1.1.X0	?	Ron Dyer's a/c	?	845
		Sales account	?	2,995

THE LEDGER ACCOUNTS

FURNITURE ACCOUNT

1.1	Cash a/c	CB1	8,000			

CAPITAL ACCOUNT

				1.1	Cash a/c	CB1	20,000

PURCHASES ACCOUNT

1.1	Cash a/c	CB1	4,600			

SALES ACCOUNT

				1.1	Cash a/c	CB1	2,800
					Sales Day Bk	SDB1	2,995
							5,795

EXPENSES ACCOUNT

1.1	Cash a/c	CB1	800			

LIZA LESTER'S ACCOUNT

1.1	Sales D.Bk	SDB1	975			

JOHN LYON'S ACCOUNT

1.1	Sales D.Bk	SDB1	450			

RON DYER'S ACCOUNT

1.1	Sales D.Bk	SDB1	845			

DUNCAN BROWN'S ACCOUNT

1.1	Sales D.Bk	SDB1	725		

SUMMARY ACCOUNTS

TRAIAL BALANCE AS AT 1.1.20X0

	Dr	Cr
Cash account	9,400	–
Capital account	–	20,000
Furniture a/c	8,000	–
Purchases a/c	4,600	–
Sales account	–	5,795
Expenses a/c	800	–
John Lyon a/c	450	–
Duncan Brown	725	–
Liza Lester a/c	975	–
Ron Dyer a/c	845	–
	25,795	25,795

TRADING AND PROFIT AND LOSS ACCOUNT

	£
Sales	5,795
Purchases	(4,600)
Gross profit	1,195
Expenses	(800)
Profit for the day	395

BALANCE SHEET AS AT 1.1.20X0

		£
Furniture		8,000
Debtors:		
John Lyon	450	
Duncan Brown	725	
Liza Lester	975	
Ron Dyer	845	2,995
Cash		9,400
		20,395

	£
Capital	20,000
Profit	395
	20,395

IQ 8.2 Writing up the Purchases Day Book

BOOKS OF PRIME ENTRY

CASH ACCOUNT

			£				£
1.7	Capital a/c	?	5,000	1.7	Purchases	?	150
1.7	Sales a/c	?	3,150	1.7	Expenses	?	210
				1.7	Capital a/c	?	400
					Balance c/d		7,390
	Balance b/d		7,390				

PURCHASES DAY BOOK

Date 20X0	V	Supplier	F	£
1.7	X	Dave Super Market	?	600
1.7	X	Stella Grocers	?	550
1.7	X	Maniam & Co.	?	420
		Purchases a/c	?	1,570

THE LEDGER ACCOUNTS

CAPITAL ACCOUNT

Cash a/c	CB1	400	Cash a/c	CB1	5,000
Balance c/d		4,600			
			Balance		4,600

PURCHASES ACCOUNT

Cash a/c	CB1	150	
Purchase D.Bk	PDB	1,570	
		1,720	

EXPENSES ACCOUNT

Cash a/c	CB1	210

SALES ACCOUNT

			Cash a/c	CB1	3,150

DAVE SUPER MARKET ACCOUNT

			Purch. D.Bk	PDB	600

STELLA GROCERS ACCOUNT

			Purch. D.Bk	PDB	550

MANIAM & CO. ACCOUNT

			Purch. D.Bk	PDB	420

SUMMARY ACCOUNTS

TRIAL BALANCE AS AT 1.7.X0

	Dr	Cr
Cash account	7,390	–
Capital account	–	4,600
Purchases a/c	1,720	–
Sales account	–	3,150
Expenses	210	–
Dave Super Mkt	–	600
Stella Grocers	–	550
Maniam & Co.	–	420
	9,320	9,320

PROFIT AND LOSS ACCOUNT FOR 1 JULY 20X0

	£
Sales	3,150
Purchases	(1,720)
Gross profit	1,430
Expenses	(210)
Profit for the day	1,220

BALANCE SHEET AS AT 1.7.20X0

		£
Cash		7,390
Creditors:		
Dave Super Mkt	600	
Stella Grocers	550	
Maniam & Co.	420	(1,570)
		5,820

	£
Capital	5,000
Profit	1,220
Drawings	(400)
	5,820

IQ 8.3 Writing up all four day books

BOOKS OF PRIME ENTRY

CASH ACCOUNT

Date	V	Particulars	F	£	Date	V	Particulars	F	£
20X0					20X0				
1.8	?	Capital account	RL1	10,000	1.8	?	Furniture account	RL2	8,000
1.8	?	Sales account	NL2	526	1.8	?	Salaries a/c	NL5	140
2.8	?	Sales account	NL2	412	2.8	?	Capital – drawing	RL1	165
3.8	?	Paul Russel a/c	DL1	1,236	2.8	?	Rent a/c	NL6	1,000
3.8	?	Sales account	NL2	168	2.8	?	Salaries a/c	NL5	140
4.8	?	Allen Stern a/c	DL2	1,214	3.8	?	Chris Meall a/c	CL2	515
4.8	?	Sales account	NL2	320	3.8	?	Capital – drawings	RL1	120
5.8	?	Allen Stern a/c	DL2	1,425	3.8	?	Advertising a/c	NL4	140
5.8	?	Sales account	NL2	460	3.8	?	Salaries a/c	NL5	140
					3.8	?	Stationery a/c	NL3	36
					4.8	?	Salaries a/c	NL5	140
					4.8	?	Capital – drawings	RL1	90
					5.8	?	Stella Naylor a/c	CL1	1,415
					5.8	?	Salaries a/c	NL5	140
									12,181
					5.8		Balance c/d		3,580
				15,761					15,761
6.8		Balance b/d		3,580					

SALES DAY BOOK

Date	V	Customers	F	Amount
20X0				£
1.8	?	Paul Russel	DL1	765
1.8	?	Allen Stern	DL2	650
1.8	?	Simon de Silva	DL3	425
2.8	?	Tony Martin	DL4	468
2.8	?	Allen Stern	DL2	684
2.8	?	Paul Russel	DL1	526
3.8	?	S. Tarrimo	DL5	722
3.8	?	Allen Stern	DL2	900
3.8	?	Simon de Silva	DL3	544
4.8	?	Allen Stern	DL2	525
4.8	?	Tony Martin	DL4	488
5.8	?	Paul Russel	DL1	265
5.8	?	S. Tarrimo	DL5	186
5.8	?	Allen Stern	DL2	342
		Sales account	NL2	7,490

SALES RETURNS DAY BOOK

Date	V	Customers	F	Amount
20X0				£
3.8	?	Allen Stern	DL2	120
3.8	?	Paul Russel	DL1	55
4.8	?	S. Tarrimo	DL5	30
4.8	?	Simon de Silva	DL3	75
		Sales account*	NL2	280

PURCHASES DAY BOOK

Date	V	Suppliers	F	Amount
20X0				£
1.8	?	Stella Naylor	CL1	1,460
1.8	?	Chris Meall	CL2	580
2.8	?	Luke Perera	CL3	345
3.8	?	Stella Naylor	CL1	795
4.8	?	Luke Perera	CL3	1,225
4.8	?	Chris Meall	CL2	1,565
		Purchases a/c	NL1	5,970

PURCHASES RETURNS DAY BOOK				
Date	V	Suppliers	F	Amount
20X0				£
3.8	?	Chris Meall	CL2	65
4.8	?	Chris Meall	CL2	70
4.8	?	Stella Naylor	CL1	45
		Purchases a/c*	NL1	180

* Sales returns are accounted for as a reversal of Sales, and purchases returns as reversal of Purchases. It is more common to maintain a separate Sales Returns account for the former and a Purchases Returns account for the latter. This method of accounting and the rationale for it are explained in Chapter 9.

REAL LEDGER

RL1 — CAPITAL ACCOUNT

2.8	Cash a/c	CB1	165	1.8	Cash a/c	CB1	10,000
3.8	Cash a/c	CB1	120				
4.8	Cash a/c	CB1	90				
5.8	Balance		9,625				
				6.8	Balance		9,625

RL2 — FURNITURE ACCOUNT

1.8	Cash a/c	CB1	8,000				

NOMINAL LEDGER

NL1 — PURCHASES ACCOUNT

5.8	Purchases Day Book	PDB1	5,970	5.8	Purchases Returns Day Bk	PRDB1	180
				5.8	Balance c/d		5,790
6.8	Balance b/d		5,790				

NL2 — SALES ACCOUNT

5.8	Sales Returns Day Bk	SRDB1	280	1.8	Cash account	CB1	526
				2.8	Cash account	CB1	412
				3.8	Cash account	CB1	168
				4.8	Cash account	CB1	320
				5.8	Cash account	CB1	460
5.8	Balance c/d		9,096	5.8	Sales Day Book	SDB1	7,490
				6.8	Balance b/d		9,096

NL3 STATIONERY ACCOUNT

3.8	Cash account	CB1	36				

NL4 ADVERTISING ACCOUNT

3.8	Cash account	CB1	140				

NL5 SALARIES ACCOUNT

1.8	Cash account	CB1	140				
2.8	Cash account	CB1	140				
3.8	Cash account	CB1	140				
4.8	Cash account	CB1	140				
5.8	Cash account	CB1	140				
			700				

NL6 RENT ACCOUNT

2.8	Cash account	CB1	1,000				

DEBTORS LEDGER

DL1 PAUL RUSSEL'S ACCOUNT

1.8	Sales Day Book	SDB1	765	3.8	Sales Returns Day Book	SRDB1	55
2.8	Sales Day Book	SDB1	526	3.8	Cash account	CB1	1,236
5.8	Sales Day Book	SDB1	265	5.8	Balance c/d		265
6.8	Balance b/d		265				

DL2 ALLEN STERN'S ACCOUNT

1.8	Sales Day Book	SDB1	650	3.8	Sales Returns Day Book	SRDB1	120
2.8	Sales Day Book	SDB1	684	4.8	Cash account	CB1	1,214
3.8	Sales Day Book	SDB1	900	5.8	Cash account	CB1	1,425
4.8	Sales Day Book	SDB1	525				
5.8	Sales Day Book	SDB1	342	5.8	Balance c/d		342
6.8	Balance c/d		342				

DL3   SIMON DE SILVA'S ACCOUNT

1.8	Sales Day Book	SDB1	425	4.8	Sales Returns Day Book	SRDB1	75
3.8	Sales Day Book	SDB1	544	5.8	Balance c/d		894
6.8	Balance b/d		894				

DL4   TONY MARTIN'S ACCOUNT

2.8	Sales Day Book	SDB1	468				
4.8	Sales Day Book	SDB1	488	5.8	Balance c/d		956
6.8	Balance b/d		956				

DL5   S. TARRIMO'S ACCOUNT

3.8	Sales Day Book	SDB1	722	4.8	Sales Returns Day Book	SRDB1	30
5.8	Sales Day Book	SDB1	186	5.8	Balance c/d		878
6.8	Balance b/d		878				

CREDITORS LEDGER

CL1   STELLA NAYLOR'S ACCOUNT

4.8	Purchase Returns Day Bk	PRDB1	45		Purchases Day Book	PDB1	1,460
5.8	Cash account	CB1	1,415		Purchases Day Book	PDB1	795
	Balance c/d		795				
				6.8	Balance b/d		795

CL2   CHRIS MEALL'S ACCOUNT

3.8	Purchase Returns Day Bk	PRDB1	65	1.8	Purchases Day Book	PDB1	580
3.8	Purchase Returns Day Bk	PRDB1	70	4.8	Purchases Day Book	PDB1	1,565
4.8	Cash account	CB1	515				
5.8	Balance c/d		1,495				
				6.8	Balance b/d		1,495

CL3   LUKE PERERA'S ACCOUNT

				2.8	Purchases Day Book	PDB1	345
5.8	Balance c/d		1,570	4.8	Purchases Day Book	PDB1	1,225
				6.8	Balance b/d		1,570

SUMMARY ACCOUNTS

TRIAL BALANCE AS AT 5.8.20X0

	F	Dr	Cr
Cash account	CB1	3,580	–
Capital account	RL1	–	9,625
Furniture a/c	RL2	8,000	–
Purchases a/c	NL1	5,790	–
Sales account	NL2	–	9,096
Stationery a/c	NL3	36	–
Advertising a/c	NL4	140	–
Salaries a/c	NL5	700	–
Rent account	NL6	1,000	–
Paul Russel's a/c	DL1	265	–
Allen Stern's a/c	DL2	342	–
Simon de Silva's	DL3	894	–
Tony Martin's a/c	DL4	956	–
S. Tarrimo's a/c	DL5	878	–
Stella Naylor's a/c	CL1	–	795
Chris Meall's a/c	CL2	–	1,495
Luke Perera's a/c	CL3	–	1,570
		22,581	22,581

TRADING AND PROFIT AND LOSS ACCOUNT FOR FIVE DAYS TO 5 AUGUST 20X0

		£
Sales		9,096
Purchases	5,790	
Less: Stock in hand	(845)	(4,945)
Gross profit		4,151
Salaries	700	
Rent	1,000	
Advertising	140	
Stationery	36	(1,876)
Profit		2,275

BALANCE SHEET AS AT 5.8.20X0

			£
Furniture			8,000
Stock		845	
Debtors:			
Paul Russel	265		
Allen Stern	342		
Simon de Silva	894		
Tony Martin	956		
S. Tarrimo	878	3,335	
Cash		3,580	
Creditors:			
Stella Naylor	795		
Chris Meall	1,495		
Luke Perera	1,570	(3,860)	3,900
			11,900

	£
Capital	9,625
Profit	2,275
	11,900

Note: The accounting arrangement is that the bookkeeper should not make any entry except on the basis of a prime entry. We have still to learn what the prime entry would be to account for 'closing' stock and for any year-end adjustments, which (though conveniently avoided in this question) are bound to be necessary. The prime entry for these are made in the Journal, to be met with in Chapter 10.

IQ 8.4 Distinguishing prime entry books from subsidiary books

(a) **Subsidiary books of account** are books of prime entry that are outside the double entry system and serve to support the main books of account. The main books of account are those containing the accounts in which one of the two entries constituting the double entry is made.

(b) **Prime entry books are:**
- cash book (in which the Cash account is written up);
- Purchases Day Book (also known as Purchases Journal);
- Sales Day Book (also known as Sales Journal);
- Purchases Returns Day Book (also known as Return Outwards Journal);
- Sales Returns Day Book (also known as Return Inwards Journal);
- Journal (also known as General Journal).

(c) **Subsidiary books of account:** All prime entry books other than the cash book are subsidiary books of accounts. This is because they are merely prelistings of transactions on the basis of which the book-keeper accounts for the transactions, making both a debit entry and a credit entry.

IQ 8.5 Is the Petty Cash Book a main or a subsidiary book of account?

Whether the Petty Cash Book is a main or a subsidiary book of account depends on the accounting arrangements within each particular business.

As a main book of account

In the example used for illustration, the Petty Cash Book is regarded as one of the main books of account. The weekly reimbursement is posted from the cash book to the Petty Cash Book, and the weekly totals of each classification of expense are posted from the Petty Cash Book to the respective nominal accounts. Thus the Petty Cash Book is part of the double entry system. Therefore, when a Trial Balance is prepared, the balance in the Petty Cash Book should also be included in it.

As a subsidiary book of account

An alternative arrangement could be to use the Petty Cash Book as only a prime entry book falling, like the day books, outside the double entry system. In that case a Petty Cash account is maintained in the ledger. The amounts of the reimbursements are posted from the cash book to the Petty Cash account. The Petty Cash Book is then only used as a book of prime entry on the basis of which the bookkeeper credits the weekly total payment to the Petty Cash Account and debits the individual nominal accounts with the weekly sub-totals of the corresponding petty cash payments. In our example, this results in the following position:

NL21   **TRAVELLING ACCOUNT**

17.1	Balance b/f		?				
24.1	Petty Cash Book	PCB1	24.90				

NL16   **CLEANING ACCOUNT**

17.1	Balance b/f		?				
24.1	Petty Cash Book	PCB1	10.5				

NL32   **CAR MAINTENANCE ACCOUNT**

17.1	Balance b/f		?				
24.1	Petty Cash Book	PCB1	29.50				

NL19   **POSTAGE ACCOUNT**

17.1	Balance b/f		?				
24.1	Petty Cash Book	PCB1	4.50				

NL8   STATIONERY ACCOUNT

17.1	Balance b/f		?				
24.1	Petty Cash Book	PCB1	18.60				

PETTY CASH ACCOUNT

Balance b/f		14	Petty Cash Bk	PCB?	88
Cash a/c	CB?	86	Balance c/d		12
Balance b/d		12			

Within this alternative arrangement the Petty Cash Book, being outside the double entry system, would be a subsidiary book of account. Instead of the balance in the Petty Cash Book being included in the Trial Balance, the one in the Petty Cash account will be included in the Trial Balance.

PROGRESSIVE QUESTIONS

PQ 8.1 Accounting terminology

Complete the blanks in the following sentences with words or phrases in the list below:

friendship	allowance	delivery note	cash discount
trust	invoice	credit limit	settlement discount
waiver	credit note	credit period	trade discount
bad debt	debit note	credit terms	credit sales memo

(a) The word 'credit', in relation to permitting a customer to delay paying for goods sold, means ....

(b) The conditions subject to which credit is allowed to anyone are called ....

(c) The maximum period a trader agrees to wait for cash in respect of a completed sale is the ....

(d) The maximum amount up to which a trader agrees to sell on credit to a customer is the ....

(e) The document that a customer is required to sign acknowledging the amount owed with regard to a credit sale is known alternatively as an ...., a ...., or a ....

(f) A reduction in price permitted usually to a fellow trader is known as a ....

PQ 8.2 Appropriate book of prime entry for every transaction

A retail trader makes the prime entry for all his cash transactions in the cash book (CB) and other routine transactions in one of the four special books of prime entry as follows: Purchases Day Book (PDB); Purchases Returns Day Book (PRDB); Sales Day Book (SDB); and Sales Returns Day Book (SRDB).

Identify (placing a tick in the appropriate cell in the grid) the book of prime entry in which each of the following transactions will be entered:

	CB	PDB	PRDB	SDB	SRDB	NONE

(a) Paid £650 to purchase goods for sale.

(b) Purchased goods for £7,200 from Selma Ltd.

(c) Paid £15,000 for a motor vehicle for business use.

(d) Received £20,000 as a loan from Jim Mitchie.

(e) Cash sales £450.

(f) Repaid £30 on return of cash sales.

(g) Returned to Selma Ltd goods purchased for £600.

(h) Repaid £500 to Jim Mitchie.

(i) Sold to Dave Prichard goods for £9,000.

(j) Dave Prichard returned goods sold to him for £450.

(k) Acquired office furniture for £1,500 from City Traders.

PQ 8.3 The ledgers

The main books of account maintained by Lovelace and Co. consist of a cash book (CB) and four ledgers, as follows: Nominal Ledger (NL); Real Ledger (RL); Debtors Ledger (DL); and Creditors Ledger (CL).

Identify (by ticking the appropriate cell in the grid) the book in which you would find each of the following accounts:

	CB	NL	RL	DL	CL

(a) Electricity account

(b) Plant and Machinery account

(c) Timothy Ltd account (a customer)

(d) Sales account

(e) Salaries and Wages account

(f) Wren plc account (a supplier)

(g) Cash account

(h) Capital account

(i) Bad Debts account

(j) Depreciation of Machinery account

PQ 8.4 Prime entry for sales and returns inwards

Stated on the right are the credit sales of Joe Prentice, a wholesaler, in January 20X0. He requests you to:

(a) record them in appropriate books of prime entry; and

(b) post them to the ledger accounts.

He is agreeable to your posting a monthly total to the nominal account.

Date	Voucher	Customer	Sale	Return
2.1	INV 484	S. Ally	£14,500	–
4.1	INV 485	Peter Gill	£6,800	–
7.1	INV 486	Jane Butt	£11,200	–
9.1	CN 14	Peter Gill	–	£1,400
11.1	INV 487	S. Ally	£6,200	–
12.1	INV 488	Bob Smith	£3,600	–
14.1	CN 15	S. Ally	–	£2,200
16.1	INV 489	Sally John	£5,400	–
19.1	CN 16	Bob Smith	–	£400
22.1	INV 490	Jane Butt	£3,200	–
25.1	INV 491	S. Ally	£2,600	–
29.1	INV 492	Peter Gill	£2,900	–

PQ 8.5 Impact of errors on the Trial Balance

Assuming that each of those listed below is the only accounting error in a set of books, identify (placing a tick in the appropriate grid) the amount by which the Trial Balance will disagree:

(a) A sale of £2,100 to Jim David was not entered in the Sales Day Book.

x	£2,100	
y	0	
z	£4,200	

(b) A sale of £3,400 to Sally John was recorded in the Sales Day Book as £4,300.

x	£3,400	
y	0	
z	£4,300	

(c) A sale of £6,200 to Tim Davies was posted to the Customer's account as £2,600.

x	£3,600	
y	£6,200	
z	£2,600	

(d) A purchase invoice for £3,600 from City Stores was posted to the debit of the Supplier's account.

x	£7,200	
y	£3,600	
z	£1,800	

(e) Goods purchased from Darren's plc, invoiced for £9,600 less 10% trade discount, have been recorded at £9,600 in the Purchases Day Book.

x	£8,640	
y	0	
z	£9,600	

(f) A credit note for £300 issued by City Stores has been recorded in the Purchases Day Book.

x	0	
y	£300	
z	£600	

(g) An invoice for £4,500 from Electro Ltd for a desktop computer for use of the accounts staff was entered in the Purchases Day Book.

x	£4,500	
y	£9,000	
z	0	

(h) The Sales Day Book was added as £149,200 instead of £148,200.

x	£2,000	
y	0	
z	£1,000	

PQ 8.6 Source documents

Grace Bert commenced business on 1 January 20X0 with capital in cash of £10,000. Her transactions in the first month were as follows:

Ref	Date	Transaction
(a)	1.1	Purchased goods from City Stores for £8,200
(b)	1.1	Purchased more goods for sale for £3,800
(c)	2.1	Sold goods for £1,200
(d)	2.1	Sold goods to Sally Jones for £4,200
(e)	2.1	Acquired a motor vehicle for £6,000
(f)	4.1	Paid £300 for office stationery
(g)	4.1	Returned to City Stores goods purchased from them for £1,200
(h)	5.1	Sold goods to Jim Mitchie for £7,200
(i)	6.1	Received £5,000 as a long-term, interest-free loan from Zoë Budd
(j)	7.1	Paid £250 for advertising
(k)	7.1	Jim Mitchie returned goods sold to him for £1,500

Required: For each of the items in the table, state the document that would be retained to support the prime entry.

PQ 8.7 From commencement to first finalization – Grace Bert

Grace Bert commenced business on 1 January 20X0 with a capital in cash of £10,000. Her transactions in the first month were as follows:

Date	Transaction
1.1	Purchased goods from City Stores for £8,200
1.1	Purchased more goods for sale for £3,800
2.1	Sold goods for £1,200
2.1	Sold goods to Sally Jones for £4,200
2.1	Acquired a motor vehicle for £6,000
4.1	Paid £300 for office stationery
4.1	Returned to City Stores goods purchased from them for £1,200
5.1	Sold goods to Jim Mitchie for £7,200
6.1	Received £5,000 as a long-term, interest-free loan from Zoë Budd
7.1	Paid £250 for advertising
7.1	Jim Mitchie returned goods sold to him for £1,500
9.1	Sold goods for £1,500
9.1	Sold goods to S.M. Patel for £3,600
10.1	Purchased goods for sale for £2,400
11.1	Received £3,000 from Jim Mitchie
11.1	Purchased goods for £4,600 from VC Ltd.
14.1	Sold goods for £1,400
14.1	Sold goods to Bob Cameron for £1,600
14.1	Paid £150 for stationery
17.1	Grace Bert took £500 for household expenses
19.1	Sold goods to S.M. Patel for £2,200
19.1	Purchased goods from City Stores for £3,800
19.1	Paid £150 for advertising
22.1	Paid £90 for vehicle fuel and oil
22.1	Sold goods to Jim Mitchie for £4,200
24.1	Paid £1,800 as staff salaries
24.1	Purchased goods for £5,400 from Latiff Bros
27.1	Sold goods for £1,800
27.1	Sold goods to R. Rajan for £3,400
27.1	Purchased goods from City Stores for £2,600
27.1	Paid £1,000 as rent
29.1	Rajan returned goods sold to him for £900

You are informed as follows:

1. If a transaction identifies the other party, assume it to be on credit terms.
2. Stock as at 31 January 20X0 is determined to be £6,800.
3. The motor vehicle is to be depreciated at 20 per cent per annum on cost.

Required:

(a) Record the transactions in appropriate books of prime entry.
(b) Post them to the Real Ledger, Nominal Ledger, Debtors Ledger and Creditors Ledger, as appropriate.
(c) State any transaction for which you could not identify a book of prime entry.
(d) Extract a Trial Balance from the books of Grace Bert as at 31.1.20X0.
(e) Prepare a Trading and Profit and Loss account for the month ended 31.1.20X0 and a Balance Sheet as at that date.

PQ 8.8 From commencement to finalization – Jacob

Jacob commenced business as a wholesaler on 1 January 20X0. His transactions during the first week were as follows:

Date	Transaction
January 1	Commenced business with capital in cash of £15,000
	Paid £4,000 to acquire shop furniture and fittings
	Purchased goods for sale from Larry Bros for £7,500
	Paid £300 for advertising
January 2	Returned to Larry Bros goods purchased for £250
	Sold goods to Essex plc for £4,500
	Paid £150 for stationery
	Purchased goods for £4,500 from Wembly Traders
	Sold goods to Nord plc for £6,000
January 3	Essex Ltd returned goods sold to it for £400
	Sold goods to Westmore Ltd for £5,600
	Purchased goods for £3,000 from Larry Bros
	Received £4,100 from Essex Ltd
	Westmore Ltd returned goods sold to it for £400
	Paid the whole amount due to Larry Bros on this date
January 4	Purchased goods for £5,250 from Larry Bros
	Sold goods for £3,000 to Southey Ltd
	Returned to Larry Bros goods purchased for £250.
	Paid £200 for advertising
	Purchased goods for £4,000 from Wembly Traders
	Paid £1,000 as rent
January 5	Southey Ltd returned goods sold to it for £150
	Sold goods for £8,600 to Essex plc
	Westmore Ltd returned goods sold to it for £300
	Sold goods to Nord plc for £5,800
	Received £6,000 from Nord plc
	Paid £4,500 to Wembly Traders
	Paid £1,800 as salaries

Required:

(a) Record the transactions in the appropriate books of prime entry.
(b) Post the transactions, assuming that day books' totals are posted to the nominal accounts only at the end of each week.
(c) Extract a Trial Balance as at 5 January 20X0.
(d) Assuming that Jacob effects his sales at cost plus 50 per cent and does not depreciate furniture, prepare a Trading and Profit and Loss account for the week ending on 5 January 20X0 and a Balance Sheet as at that date.

Note: If a transaction names the other party to it, assume that it is on credit terms.

Chapter 9

SUPPORTING ACCOUNTS

In this chapter

We will learn of:

- a fifth class of account, which we shall refer to as supporting accounts
- the reasons for setting up such accounts

and you should be able to:

- account for returns inwards and outwards
- account for bad and doubtful debts
- account for the disposal of fixed assets

9.1 INTRODUCTION TO SUPPORTING ACCOUNTS

In Chapter 3 we learnt that there are four categories of account, namely, asset and expenditure accounts, which always have a debit balance, and liability and income accounts, which always have a credit balance. We will now discuss a fifth class of account, which we shall refer to as a *supporting account*.

A supporting account is one created for a specific reason in order to accommodate an accounting entry that would otherwise have been made in a main account. In this chapter we will consider the following main and supporting accounts:

Main account	Supporting account
Sales account	Sales Returns account
Purchases account	Purchase Returns account
Capital account	Drawings account
Fixed Asset accounts (for each class of them)	Provision for Depreciation account
Debtor accounts	Provision for Doubtful Debts account
Fixed Asset accounts (if necessary)	Provision for Impairment account
Debtor accounts (if necessary)	Sales in Suspense account

As we meet these supporting accounts one by one, we should first of all make an attempt to understand the reason for setting up the account. Furthermore, notice that each supporting account usually – though not always – has a balance opposite the one in the main account, e.g. there will be a debit balance on the Sales Returns account whereas there is a credit balance on the Sales account. This is because the supporting account is usually set up temporarily to accommodate an entry that, if made in the main account, would have had the effect of reducing its balance.

9.2 THE SALES RETURNS ACCOUNT

We learnt in Chapter 8 to account for credit sales by crediting Sales account (income) in the Nominal Ledger and debiting a debtor's account (asset) in the Debtors Ledger, and to account for goods returned by the customer by reversing the original entry – i.e. debiting the Sales account and crediting the debtor's account. Accounting for returns in this way is technically correct; but there is, from the senior management point of view, a disadvantage in that only the figure of sales *net of returns* will appear in the Trial Balance presented to senior management.

Imagine a scenario in which a manager chooses deliberately to boost profits in one year by crediting the Sales account with fictitious sales (and debiting a fictitious debtor) and then reversing the entry as returns in the following year – and repeating the process, year after year at an increasing rate. If sales had been recorded in one account and sales returns in another, the progressively higher proportion of sales getting returned would have been drawn to senior management's attention and the fraudulent practice exposed. Businesses therefore use a Sales Returns account as a supporting account.

To illustrate, let us assume that goods were sold to Richard for £4,000 and he returns goods to the value of £1,000. The accounting entries will be as set out:

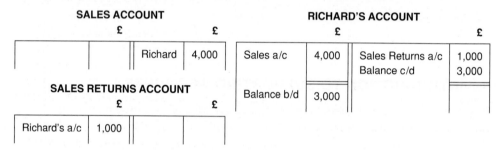

Thus the Sales Returns account is a supporting account that accommodates the debit balance that would otherwise have been made in the Sales account. The balance in the supporting account is on the (debit) side opposite the one on which the main account (Sales) has its balance. The Trial Balance will have two balances relating to sales, namely the Sales account and the Sales Returns account. These balances are reported in the Trading account as shown on the right. Sales returns are known also as 'returns inwards'.

TRADING ACCOUNT FOR THE YEAR ENDED	
	£
Sales	4,000
Less: Returns	(1,000)
	3,000

9.3 THE PURCHASES RETURNS ACCOUNT

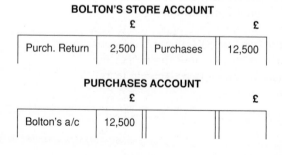

Similarly, management would be interested in keeping a watch on the proportion of purchases that are being returned. Indiscriminate returns could alienate suppliers, prejudice favourable supply terms and possibly result in refusal of supplies. It makes sense, therefore, that the Trial Balance presented to management should report purchases separately from purchase returns. This is achieved by accounting for returns of purchases by debiting the supplier's account in the Creditors Ledger and crediting, not the Purchases account, but a Purchases Returns account.

For example, on returning a fifth of goods purchased for £12,500 from Bolton's Store, Bolton Store's account is debited with £2,500 (reducing the amount owed) and the same amount credited, not to the Purchases account but temporarily to a supporting account that is named the Purchases Returns account. Again, the supporting account has a balance on the (credit) side opposite the one in which the main account has its balance. Purchase returns are referred to also as returns outwards.

PURCHASES RETURNS ACCOUNT

£			£
		Bolton's a/c	2,500

9.4 THE DRAWINGS ACCOUNT

The amount received from a proprietor as capital is posted from the Cash account to a Capital account in the Real Ledger to record the liability owed by the business entity. Therefore, it would appear logical that, when cash is paid back to the owner for personal use, the payment should be posted from the Cash account to the debit of the Capital account, thus reducing the amount reported as liability.

This would have been acceptable but for the fact that the credit balance recorded in the Capital account, although a liability, is not normally regarded as available for the proprietor's withdrawal at will. The common practice is to restrict amounts withdrawn for personal needs during an accounting period to the profits earned during the period. However, there is a difficulty in that the profit for the period is not calculated until the end of the period, and many proprietors need cash to meet their living expenses during the year and cannot wait until accounts are prepared at the end of the year.

However, posting such amounts taken out by the proprietor from the Cash account to the Capital account may well send the wrong message, i.e. that he is free to keep on drawing until the limit of the balance in the Capital account is reached. This would reduce the assets available to run the business – indeed, the cash received from the proprietor might have already been spent on fixed assets and stock. To guard against conveying such an impression, amounts withdrawn for personal use, known as drawings, are posted from the Cash account to the debit of a supporting account, named the Drawings account.

Let us assume that the capital received from a proprietor is £100,000 and his drawings in the year are £5,000. The cash drawn by the proprietor is posted from the Cash account to the debit not of the Capital account but of a Drawings account. The supporting account thus has a (debit) balance, opposite the one in its main account. When accounts for the year are finalized, the debit balance in the supporting account is set against profit for the year. At that point the Capital account is increased if drawings are less than the profit for the year and decreased if more. The final effect is the same, i.e. capital is increased or decreased; but the psychological message is different.

Assuming that capital at the commencement of the year was £100,000, that the

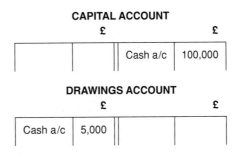

CAPITAL ACCOUNT

£			£
		Cash a/c	100,000

DRAWINGS ACCOUNT

£			£
Cash a/c	5,000		

BALANCE SHEET AS AT XXXXX		£
Capital 1.1.XX		100,000
Profit for the year	30,000	
Less: Drawings	(24,000)	6,000
		106,000

profit for the year is £30,000 and that the proprietor drew £2,000 per month, these particulars will be reported on the Balance Sheet at year end as stated above.

9.5 THE PROVISION FOR DEPRECIATION ACCOUNT

We learnt in Chapter 6 that because assets cannot always continue to provide economic benefits for ever, they have to be depreciated over an estimated period of the assets' useful life. We accounted for depreciation by debiting a Depreciation account in the Nominal Ledger and crediting an asset account in the Real Ledger. For example, assuming that machinery, acquired for £100,000, is estimated to have a useful life of 20 years, £5,000 is written off as depreciation in the first year, by crediting the asset account and debiting an expenditure account named Depreciation as follows:

MACHINERY ACCOUNT

	£		£
Cash a/c	100,000	Depreciation a/c	5,000
		Balance c/d	95,000
Balance b/d	95,000		

DEPRECIATION ACCOUNT

	£		£
Machinery	5,000	Profit and Loss a/c	5,000

This accounting treatment, though correct, may (as happened, for example, in the Royal Mail case[1]) provide opportunities for manipulating accounts. For example, having acquired the machinery for £100,000, the entity may choose deliberately to mask excessive profits in that year by depreciating the machinery aggressively, say by 20 per cent. Next year it could mask a poor performance by clawing back the excess depreciation. When it reports its machinery at £90,000 at the end of the second year, having reported it at £80,000 at the end of the first, it may convey a false impression of having acquired more machinery. In order to prevent such manipulation, there is a company law requirement[2] that fixed assets should be reported at cost and that *accumulated* depreciation written off up to the date of the balance sheet should be reported separately. In order to collect the accumulated depreciation, a supporting account, named Provision for Depreciation, is maintained in the Real Ledger.

MACHINERY ACCOUNT

	£		£
Y1 Cash a/c	100,000	Y1 Depreciation a/c	20,000
		Y1 Balance c/d	80,000
Y1 Balance	80,000		
Y2 Profit and Loss a/c	10,000		

For example, assuming that there is a depreciation charge of £5,000 to be written off in a particular year, the accounting entries will be to debit a Depreciation account (expense). The credit is not to the Machinery account but to a supporting account, which is named Provision for Depreciation. The accounts will appear as follows:

MACHINERY ACCOUNT

	£		£
Cash a/c	100,000		

DEPRECIATION ACCOUNT

	£		£
Provision for Depreciation a/c	5,000		

PROVISION FOR DEPRECIATION ACCOUNT

	£		£
		Depreciation	5,000

Once again, the supporting account has a balance on the (credit) side opposite the one in which its main account (asset) has its balance. But unlike in the case of the three supporting accounts met with so far, at the point of finalizing accounts the balance in the supporting account is not transferred to the main account; instead, the credit balance in the Provision for Depreciation account continues to remain in that account from year to year, accumulating the amounts written off annually as depreciation.

BALANCE SHEET AS AT XXX	£
Machinery at cost	100,000
Provision for depreciation	(5,000)
	95,000

On the balance sheet, the balance in the supporting account is shown as a deduction from the balance in the corresponding main account, to reveal the amount to which the capital outlay on the asset has been written down by that date. The debit balance in the Depreciation account (expense) is transferred, as usual, to the Profit and Loss account when the accounts are finalized.

DEPRECIATION ACCOUNT

	£		£
Provision for Depreciation a/c	5,000	Profit and Loss a/c	5,000

9.5.1 Disposal of partially depreciated assets

What are the accounting entries when there is a disposal of a partially depreciated asset? On the disposal of an asset, the balances in the asset account and the Provision for Depreciation account are both transferred to a Disposal account. The purpose of the Disposal account is to allow comparison of the net book value (the written-down value) of an asset at the date of disposal with the proceeds of sale, so as to determine any gain or loss on disposal.

For illustration, let us assume that machinery, acquired at a cost of £100,000 and depreciated annually by £5,000, is disposed of for £36,000 at the end of the fourth year of use. At the point of disposal, the debit balance of £100,000 appearing in the asset account and the credit balance of £20,000 in the supporting account are both transferred to a Disposal account to reveal that the machinery had been written down to £80,000 by that date. When the proceeds of disposal (£36,000) are posted from the Cash account to the credit of the Disposal account, a loss on disposal of £44,000 is identified and written off to the Profit and Loss account.

MACHINERY ACCOUNT

	£		£
Balance b/f	100,000	Disposal a/c	100,000

PROVISION FOR DEPRECIATION ACCOUNT

	£		£
Disposal a/c	20,000	Balance b/f	20,000

DISPOSAL ACCOUNT

	£		£
Machinery a/c	100,000	Provision for depreciation a/c	20,000
		Cash account	36,000
		Profit and Loss a/c	44,000

Posting depreciation to a separate supporting account (the Provision for Depreciation account) would have drawn attention to the manipulation referred to earlier. If the information on the asset had been presented on Balance Sheets of Year 1 and Year 2 as shown below, it would have been clear that the improved value of machinery in Year 2 arose not because of any new acquisition but because of clawing back from the amount written off in prior periods as depreciation.

BALANCE SHEET AS AT END OF YEAR 1		BALANCE SHEET AS AT END OF YEAR 2	
	£		£
Machinery at cost	100,000	Machinery at cost	100,000
Provision for depreciation	(20,000)	Provision for depreciation	(10,000)
	80,000		90,000

Interaction 9.1

Accounting for disposal, focusing on a single fixed asset

A motor vehicle, acquired for £20,000 on 1.4.20X0 and depreciated by the straight-line method at 20 per cent per year, was disposed of for £12,000 on 30 June 20X2.

Required: Show how these transactions will be recorded in the relevant ledger accounts for the year ended 31 December 20X2.

Interaction 9.2

Disposal of one of a class of assets and an acquisition

Machinery acquired for £600,000 was reported on the balance sheet as at 30 June 20X4 at a written-down value of £484,000. Depreciation is written off on machinery at 5 per cent of cost per annum (i.e. using the straight-line method). During the year ended 30 June 20X5, two things happened: machinery, acquired for £120,000 on 1.10.20X0, was sold for £35,500 on 31.12.20X4; and new machinery was acquired for £160,000 on 1 April 20X5.

Required: Show how these transactions will be:

(a) recorded in relevant ledger accounts;
(b) reported in the Profit and Loss account for the year ended 30 June 20X5 and in the Balance Sheet as at that date.

Interaction 9.3

Disposal of asset depreciated using the reducing balance method

Required: Answer IQ 9.2 above on the amended basis that the accounting policy has been to depreciate machinery every year by 10 per cent of the amount to which the asset has been written down by the end of the previous year (i.e. using the reducing balance method).

9.6 THE PROVISION FOR DOUBTFUL DEBTS ACCOUNT

When goods are sold on credit terms, the Sales account (income) in the Nominal Ledger is credited and an account opened in the Debtors Ledger in the name of the customer is debited. The customer is regarded as an asset as long as there is a reasonable assurance that the amount is recoverable, even if it is necessary to resort to legal process.

9.6.1 Accounting for bad debts

Should a debt for some reason prove irrecoverable (e.g. the debtor becomes bankrupt with no funds to make any payment towards the debt), the amount owing would be transferred from the customer's account (asset) to a Bad Debts account (expense).

For example, let us assume that a business, J & B Watersports, sold goods on credit to Jim Gee for £10,000 on 1.1.20X0; that Jim is made bankrupt and the Trustee in

Bankruptcy advises on 31.12.20X0 that there will be no distribution to creditors. The accounting entries within J & B Watersports' books would be as follows:

JIM GEE'S ACCOUNT				BAD DEBTS ACCOUNT			
£		£		£		£	
1.1.20X0		31.12.20X0		31.12.20X0		31.12.20X0	
Sales a/c	10,000	Bad Debts a/c	10,000	Jim Gee's a/c	10,000	Profit and Loss a/c	10,000

On the other hand, if the advice from the Trustee in Bankruptcy had been that there would be a distribution to the bankrupt's creditors of £0.25 in the £, on 1.3.20X1, the accounting entries would be as follows:

JIM GEE'S ACCOUNT				BAD DEBTS ACCOUNT			
£		£		£		£	
1.1.20X0		31.12.20X0		31.12.20X0		31.12.20X0	
Sales a/c	10,000	Bad Debts a/c	7,500	Jim Gee's a/c	7,500	Profit and Loss a/c	7,500
		Balance c/d	2,500				

The debit balance of £2,500 would remain as a balance on Jim Gee's account until the cash was received on 1.3.20X1. It would also, of course, be included in the total of the debtors that appears in the Balance Sheet as at 31.12.20X0.

9.6.2 Accounting for recovery of a bad debt that has been written off in earlier years

If a debt written off (i.e. wiped from the books of account) in an earlier year is recovered, the amount is posted from the Cash account to a Bad Debt Recoveries account, and the credit balance in that account is reported as an income in the Profit and Loss account.

9.6.3 Accounting for debts of doubtful recovery

We have made it sound as though it is always possible to demarcate debts as either recoverable or irrecoverable. In real life the situation it is not always so clear-cut. There could well be debts that are probably irrecoverable and yet it would be premature to write off the asset (i.e. to transfer the balance from the individual debtor account in the Debtors Ledger, to the debit of the Profit and Loss account) until all avenues of recovery are fully explored.

Accounting treatment of specific doubtful debts

By 'specific' in the subheading we mean that we are considering a debt relating to a specific debtor – in our example it is Jim Gee. Let us now assume the same sales transaction but that it is not definite that Jim Gee is unable to pay. In such a situation, where it appears doubtful that the debt is recoverable, we could debit the Bad Debts account and credit Jim Gee's account to record the likely loss. However, if Jim's account is credited, that asset account would be closed and hence the debt could be completely lost sight of. This would mean that, when reminders are sent out for the overdue accounts in the Debtors Ledger, there would be no account for Jim and no further reminders would therefore be sent to him requesting settlement. In practice this could mean that whatever slim chance there was of recovering the debt might be forfeited. The credit entry is, therefore, made not in Jim's account but in a supporting account named the Provision for Doubtful Debts account. This account carries, until the position is clarified, the credit that would otherwise have been made in Jim's account. The Provision for Doubtful Debts account supports the Debtors account; its balance is on the side opposite that in the main (Debtors) account.

JIM GEE'S ACCOUNT

	£		£
Sales a/c	10,000		

BAD DEBTS ACCOUNT

	£		£
Provision for Doubtful Debts a/c	10,000	Profit and Loss a/c	10,000

PROVISION FOR DOUBTFUL DEBTS ACCOUNT

	£		£
		Bad debts a/c	10,000

In the Balance Sheet, the balance in the Provision for Doubtful Debts account is shown as a deduction from the balance in the Debtor's account – and the effect is to report the asset at nil value. When all efforts at recovering the debt have been exhausted and the time is ripe to wipe off the asset from the ledger, the credit balance in the supporting account is transferred to the main account, closing both accounts. Thus:

JIM GEE'S ACCOUNT

Sales a/c	10,000	Provision for Doubtful Debts a/c	10,000

PROVISION FOR DOUBTFUL DEBTS ACCOUNT

Jim Gee	10,000	Bad Debts a/c	10,000

Accounting treatment of general doubtful debts

It is not always possible specifically to identify debts that may not be recoverable. What is more likely to happen is that an estimate will be made of the percentage of debtors outstanding at a year end that may prove irrecoverable. For making this estimate, individual debts and the extent of their compliance with credit terms granted to them will of course be considered. It is also a common practice to base the estimate of doubtful debts on an age analysis of debtors outstanding. For example, let us assume that J & B Watersports usually allows 30 days' credit to its customers and that their experience is that the incidence of bad debts is as stated in the box. Accordingly they would estimate a general provision for doubtful debts as at 31 December 20X1 as stated below:

Debts outstanding: 30–45 days	5%
Debts outstanding: 46–60 days	10%
Debts outstanding: 61–90 days	20%
Debts outstanding: 91+ days	30%

Debtors as at 31.12.20X1	£	Incidence of bad debt	Provision required £
Within 30-day credit limit	642,500	0%	0
Outstanding 31–45 days	112,400	5%	5,620
Outstanding 46–60 days	76,500	10%	7,650
Outstanding 61–90 days	24,800	20%	4,960
Outstanding 91+ days	15,200	30%	4,560
A general provision for doubtful debts is required of			22,790

Let us assume that the business has 250 individual debtors (including Jim Gee), who owe a total of £881,400. The accounting entries would be as follows:

TRADE DEBTORS ACCOUNTS

	£		£
Balances b/f	881,400		

PROVISION FOR DOUBTFUL DEBTS ACCOUNT

	£		£
		Bad Debts a/c	10,000
		Bad Debts a/c	22,790
			32,790

BAD DEBTS ACCOUNT

	£		£
Provision for Doubtful Debts a/c	10,000	Profit and Loss a/c	32,790
Provision for Doubtful Debts a/c	22,790		

J & B WATERSPORTS

BALANCE SHEET AS AT 31.12.20X1

	£
Debtors*	881,400
Provision for doubtful debts	(32,790)
	848,610

* This includes Jim Gee's debt of £10,000.

Writing off a specific bad debt and creating a general provision

Tim's transactions in the year ended 31.12.20X0 include those stated in the box. Tim wishes to set up a provision for doubtful debts calculated at 5 per cent of debtors outstanding on 31.12.20X0.

Required: Record the transactions in appropriate ledger accounts and show how they will appear in the Profit and Loss account for the year ended 31.12.20X0 and the Balance Sheet on that date.

	£
Debtors as at 1 January 20X0	120
Credit sales in the year	3,640
Sales returns during the year	25
Cash received from debtors during the year	3,420
Debt written off in the year as not recoverable	35

9.6.4 Adjusting a provision for doubtful debts in subsequent years

Year after year, when finalizing its accounts, a business entity has to confront the problem of providing for doubtful debts. By repeating its own version of the exercise we have already seen here, the entity has to determine the amount of provision required at the end of the accounting year and, if that amount is different from the one already brought forward from the previous year, to make adjustments.

For example, let us continue with J & B Watersports. Remember that its trade debtors as at 31.12.20X1, including £10,000 due from Jim Gee, owed £881,400 and it had a provision for doubtful debts on that date of £32,790. Assume that the position one year later, on 31 December 20X2, is as follows:

(a) Jim Gee has paid only 40 per cent of his debt – the remainder is definitely irrecoverable;

(b) there is a specific doubtful debt of £3,300 due from K. Benar;

(c) the debtors, excluding Jim Gee and K. Benar who have been dealt with specifically, are as follows:

Debtors as at 31.12.20X1	£	Incidence of bad debt	Provision required £
Within 30-day credit limit	700,500	0%	0
Outstanding 31–45 days	100,400	5%	5,020
Outstanding 46–60 days	70,500	10%	7,050
Outstanding 61–90 days	44,000	20%	8,800
Outstanding 91+ days	12,000	30%	3,600
A general provision for doubtful debts is required of			24,470

These figures tell us the following four things:

1. We have recovered £4,000 from Jim Gee and the balance of £6,000 is to be written off.
2. We need at the end of the year to have a specific provision for doubtful debts of £3,300 (for K. Benar) and a general provision for doubtful debts of £24,470, i.e. a total of provision of £27,770 is required.
3. We already have a provision brought forward from the previous year of £32,790.
4. The provision has an excess of £5,020 (£32,790 – £27,770), which is no longer required. This figure is therefore transferred from the Provision account to the credit of Bad Debts account so that Jim's bad debt is offset against it. As a result, only £980 remains in the Bad Debts account to be written off to the Profit and Loss account.

The accounting entries to record the movement on the Provision for Doubtful Debts account are as follows:

BAD DEBTS ACCOUNT

1	Jim Gee a/c	6,000	Provision for Doubtful Debts a/c	5,020	3

PROVISION FOR DOUBTFUL DEBTS ACCOUNT

3	Bad Debts a/c	5,020	Balance b/f	32,790	
2	Balance c/d	27,770			
			Balance b/d	27,770	

The steps we follow are thus (see marginal numbering in the accounts):

1. The amount remaining unpaid in Jim's account is transferred to the Bad Debts account by crediting Jim Gee's account and debiting the Bad Debts account.
2. The amount of provision (£27,770) required to appear in the Balance Sheet as at 31.12.20X2 is entered in the Provision account as a carry down figure.

3. The excess amount of £5,020 is transferred from the Provision account to the Bad Debts account.
4. The balance on the Bad Debts account (£980) is transferred to the Profit and Loss account.

Adjusting the provision for doubtful debts each year

Tina Gray carries on a business as a food wholesaler. She has judged it necessary, based on her past experience, to maintain a 5 per cent provision for doubtful debts. Amounts receivable from credit customers, i.e. debtors, before any provision are £126,200 on 31.12.20X1 and were £196,800 on 31.12.20X0. During the year ended 31.12.20X1, Tina Gray's credit sales were £468,400, sales returns £11,200 and bad debts written off £16,400.

Required:

(a) Prepare ledger accounts to record these transactions.
(b) Show how they will be reported in the Profit and Loss account for the year ended 31.12.20X1 and the Balance Sheet as at that date.

9.6.5 Where the Provision account and Bad Debts account are combined

For the sake of economy, an entity may opt not to have a Bad Debts account (expense) separately from a Provision for Doubtful Debts account. Instead, both these accounts may be combined. In that case, any bad debt written off is transferred from the Debtors account to the Provision account. All that is necessary, at the point of finalizing accounts, is to adjust the balance in the Provision account to the amount necessary, by either debiting or crediting the difference to the Profit and Loss account.

Combined Bad Debts and Provision for Doubtful Debts account

Information relating to debtors of Tina Gray is stated in IQ 9.5 above. Set out the ledger accounts of this entity on the basis that they need to maintain a single account to record bad debts as well as the provision for doubtful debts.

9.7 A PROVISION FOR IMPAIRMENT ACCOUNT

Every debit balance that is included as an asset in the Balance Sheet is tested to check that, in the judgement of the business managers, it is not overstated. It is for this purpose that an *impairment review* is conducted (see Chapter 16). If, when such a review takes place, the recoverable amount on an asset is lower than its net book value, the asset is written down to the lower (recoverable) amount. Estimation of recoverable amounts involves uncertainty because it is based on estimates of income that an asset is expected to generate in future years. In the circumstances, if an entity finds that an asset (costing £200,000, say, and already written down to £80,000) has a recoverable amount of only £60,000, it has to recognize the loss on impairment of £20,000 by debiting an Impairment Loss account. But, in view of the uncertainty, instead of crediting the asset account, the entity may prefer to credit a supporting account, which may be named a Provision for Impairment account.

The ledger accounts will in these circumstances appear as follows:

FIXED ASSET ACCOUNT

	£000		£000
Balance b/f	200		

IMPAIRMENT LOSS ACCOUNT

	£000		£000
Provision for Impairment a/c	20	Profit and Loss a/c	20

PROVISION FOR DEPRECIATION ACCOUNT

	£000		£000
		Balance b/f	120

PROVISION FOR IMPAIRMENT ACCOUNT

	£000		£000
		Impairment loss	20

BALANCE SHEET AS AT XXXXXXX

	£000	£000
Fixed asset at cost	200	
Provision for depreciation	(120)	
Provision for impairment	(20)	60

9.8 AN ACCOUNT, ITS CLASS AND ITS BALANCE

Thus a pattern emerges with regard to the class of an account and its balance. While an asset account or expense account always has its balance on the debit side and a liability account or income account always has its balance on the credit side, a supporting account usually has its balance on the side opposite the one in which its main account has the balance.

Interaction 9.7	**An account, its class and its balance**

(a) In Column 2 in the grid below classify, as appropriate, each of the accounts named in Column 1 as an asset account, a liability account, an expenditure account, an income account or a supporting account.

(b) State in Column 3 whether you would expect to find a debit balance or a credit balance in the account named.

	Column 1	Column 2	Column 3
1	Plant and Machinery account		
2	Carriage Inwards account		
3	Carriage Outwards account		
4	Stationery account		
5	Entertainment account		
6	Motor Vehicles account		
7	Cash account		
8	Audit Fees account		
9	Loan Received from Mr Rich a/c		

	Column 1	Column 2	Column 3
10	Loan to Sales Rep. account		
11	Postage account		
12	Depreciation of Motor Vehicles a/c		
13	Provision for Depreciation on Vehicles a/c		
14	Land and Buildings account		
15	Bad Debts account		
16	Office Equipment account		
17	Sales account		
18	Vehicle Maintenance account		
19	Purchases account		
20	Rent Payable a/c (expenditure)		
21	Rent Payable a/c (owing)		
22	Prepaid Rent account		
23	Salaries Accrued account		
24	Returns Inwards account		
25	Returns Outwards account		
26	Drawings account		
27	Provision for Doubtful Debts account		
28	Commission Earnings account		
29	Rent Received in Advance account		
30	Stock in Trade account		

9.9 SALES MADE ON 'SALE OR RETURN' BASIS

Each of the supporting accounts met with so far was opened to temporarily accommodate an entry that, if made in the main account, would have reduced its balance. This
is the reason why the supporting account always has a balance on the opposite side to
the one in the corresponding main account. Exceptionally, a supporting account may
be opened to accommodate an entry that would have increased the balance in the
main account, but it is premature to recognize that transaction as having taken place
and to make a record in a main account. In such a situation the supporting account will
have a balance on the *same* side as its main account. Let us now consider one example
of this.

9.9.1 Goods sent on approval

Where traders deliver goods to customers on approval, the customer may be permitted a 'cooling-off period' of, say, a week or two within which the customer is free to decide whether to return the goods or retain them. The sale is not made until the cooling-off period is over, unless prior to that the customer notifies an intention to retain.

Let us illustrate by assuming that a trader, Digital Relay Ltd, delivers six digital television sets to as many customers on a sale or return basis, pro-forma invoicing each customer for £1,200. (A pro-forma invoice indicates the amount that will be debited to the customer if the item referred to is sold.) At the point of delivering the sets, the Debtors account in Digital Relay's books is debited, but the Sales account cannot be credited because a sale has yet to be made. It is important to remember that the balance on the Sales account is transferred to the Profit and Loss account and results in profit being recognized in the Profit and Loss account. This is not correct where the sale might not actually materialize.

The credit entry is not, therefore, made in the Sales account. Instead, a supporting account is opened named a Sales in Suspense account. If and when a sale qualifies to be recognized, the credit entry in the supporting account is transferred to the main Sales account. If, on the other hand, a customer decides to return the set, that customer's account is credited and the Sales in Suspense account is debited.

Let us assume that by the year-end the customers had retained three sets, returned one and in respect of the remaining two the cooling-off period has still to be completed. The position will be recorded in the relevant ledger accounts as shown here. The invoice price of three sets retained by the customers would qualify for recognition as a sale and is therefore transferred from the supporting account to the Sales account. Having reversed out the value of the set returned by the customer, £2,400 is left behind in the supporting account because that amount (representing the two sets still being considered by customers) is not yet a sale but may still become one.

DEBTORS ACCOUNT

Sales in Suspense a/c	7,200	Sales in Suspense a/c	1,200
		Balance c/d	6,000
Balance b/d	6,000		

SALES IN SUSPENSE ACCOUNT

Debtors account	1,200	Debtors account	7,200
Sales account	3,600		
Balance c/d	2,400		
		Balance b/d	2,400

SALES ACCOUNT

		Sales in Suspense a/c	3,600

9.9.2 Accounting treatment at period end if there are outstanding goods on approval

Debtors

If there is a balance on the Sales in Suspense account at the year end, the treatment in the Balance Sheet is to offset the balance against the Debtors account so that the asset reported as receivable from debtors is only what they actually owe in respect of the sets they have agreed to retain.

Sales

Sales are recognized only in respect of the three sets retained by customers, and not in respect of the two with regard to which the customers still have a right of return.

Stock

How are the two television sets that are still out on approval dealt with in the Balance Sheet at the year end? The two sets within the cooling-off period, though remaining with the customers on this date, are part of the unsold stock of the trader. Digital Relay Ltd should remember to include the cost of these two sets as closing stock at the Balance Sheet date – this will affect the assets in the Balance Sheet and also the calculation of the cost of sales.

Accounting for sales on a sale or return basis   Interaction 9.8

Kitchenaids, dealers in consumer durables, have extracted their Trial Balance as stated on the right. You are informed as follows:

(a) The stock of unsold goods in hand on 30 June 20X1 cost £188,000.

(b) Stated as Sales in Suspense is the sale price of goods delivered to customers on a sale or return basis. Goods with a sale value of £64,000 (cost £48,000) with customers on 30.6.20X1 are within the returnable period.

(c) Fixed assets are to be depreciated at 10 per cent of cost annually.

Required: Prepare the Trading and Profit and Loss account for the year ended 30.6.20X1 and the Balance Sheet as at that date.

KITCHENAIDS

TRIAL BALANCE AS AT 30.6.20X1	£000	£000
Fixed assets	240	
Provision for depreciation	–	66
Stock at 30.6.20X0	228	
Salaries	114	
Debtors and creditors	486	365
Rent	48	
Administration expenses	54	
Sales		844
Advertising	29	
Sales Suspense a/c		154
Bad debts	14	
Capital account		500
Purchases	684	
Cash and bank	32	
	1,929	1,929

References

1. *R. v. Lord Kylsant* (1932) 1 KB 442.
2. Companies Act 1985, Schedule 4 paragraph 42(3).

SOLUTIONS TO INTERACTIVE QUESTIONS

IQ 9.1 Accounting for disposal, focusing on a single fixed asset

N   MOTOR VEHICLES ACCOUNT   **N**

N	20X2		£	20X2		£	N
1	1.1	Balance b/f	20,000	30.6	Disposal a/c	20,000	4

PROVISION FOR DEPRECIATION OF VEHICLES ACCOUNT

N	20X2		£	20X2		£	N
4	30.6	Disposal a/c	9,000	1.1	Balance b/f	7,000	2
				30.6	Depreciation a/c	2,000	3

DEPRECIATION OF MOTOR VEHICLES ACCOUNT

N	20X2		£	20X2		£	N
3	30.6	Provision for Depreciation a/c	2,000	31.12	Profit and Loss a/c	2,000	6

DISPOSAL OF MOTOR VEHICLES ACCOUNT

N	20X2		£	20X2		£	N
4	30.6	Motor Vehicle a/c	20,000	30.6	Provision for Depreciation a/c	9,000	4
6	31.12	P and L – Gain	1,000	30.6	Cash a/c	12,000	5

Notes (see the marginal numbering in the accounts):

1. The vehicle acquired on 1.4.20X0 for £20,000 will continue to appear at its cost in the asset account, until disposal (or revaluation).
2. In the year of acquisition, the vehicle would have been depreciated for only nine months, and in the year 20X1 for the full year. Hence depreciation at 20 per cent of £20,000 for one year and nine months would have accumulated to £7,000 by 1.1.20X2.
3. In 20X2, until disposal on 30 June, the motor vehicle has been used for six months and should therefore be depreciated at 20 per cent of £20,000 for six months.
4. On the date of disposal, the cost of the vehicle from the asset account, and the provision for depreciation up to that date from the supporting account, are transferred to a Disposal account.
5. £12,000 received on disposal is posted from the Cash account to the Disposal account.
6. The Disposal account reveals a gain on disposal of £1,000, which is transferred to the Profit and Loss account for the year as an income along with depreciation written off in the year as an expense.

IQ 9.2 Disposal of one of a class of assets and an acquisition

N		PLANT AND MACHINERY ACCOUNT					N
			£			£	
1	1.7.20X4	Balance b/f	600,000	31.12.20X4	Disposal account	120,000	4
6	1.4.20X5	Cash account	160,000	30.6.20X5	Balance c/d	640,000	
	1.7.20X5	Balance b/d	640,000				

PROVISION FOR DEPRECIATION OF PLANT AND MACHINERY ACCOUNT

			£			£	
4	31.12.20X4	Disposal a/c	25,500	1.7.20X4	Balance b/f	116,000	2
				31.12.20X4	Depreciation a/c	3,000	3
	30.6.20X5	Balance c/d	119,500	30.6.20X5	Depreciation a/c	26,000	7
				1.7.20X5	Balance b/d	119,500	

DEPRECIATION OF MACHINERY ACCOUNT

			£			£	
3	31.12.20X4	Provision for Depreciation a/c	3,000	30.6.20X5	Trading account	29,000	
7	30.6.20X5	Provision for Depreciation a/c	26,000				

DISPOSAL OF MACHINERY ACCOUNT

			£			£	
4	31.12.20X4	Plant and Machinery a/c	120,000	31.12.20X4	Provision for Depreciation a/c	25,500	4
				31.12.20X4	Cash account	35,500	5
				30.6.20X5	P and L a/c – Loss	59,000	

Notes:

1. The total cost of £600,000 of machinery in use appears as a debit balance in the asset account, irrespective of when each was bought and the individual cost.
2. Since, by 1.7.20X4, the machinery had been written down to £484,000, the accumulated depreciation until that date amounts to (£600,000 – £484,000) = £116,000.
3. The machinery sold on 31.12.20X4 should be depreciated for the six months of use in the year, calculated as 5 per cent of £120,000 for six months.
4. Having been acquired on 1.10.20X0, the machinery sold on 31.12.20X4 had been in use for a total period of four years and three months. Hence the accumulated depreciation over this period would be 5% of £120,000 for four years and three months = £25,500. On the date of disposal, transfers should be made to the Disposal account of the cost of the asset (£120,000) from the Plant and Machinery account and accumulated depreciation up to that date (£25,500) from the supporting account.
5. The proceeds on disposal of £35,500 are posted from the Cash account to the Disposal account.
6. The amount of £160,000 paid for the new machinery on 1.4.20X5 is posted from the Cash account to the Plant and Machinery account.
7. Older machinery continuing in use must have been acquired for

5% of £480,000 paid for other machinery	£24,000
5% of £160,000 for new machinery for three months only	£2,000
	£26,000

(£600,000 – £120,000) = £480,000. Hence depreciation for the current year on these items and on the newly acquired machinery amounts to £26,000.

PROFIT AND LOSS ACCOUNT FOR THE YEAR ENDED 30.6.20X5	
	£
In the trading account as a manufacturing expense:	
Depreciation of machinery	(29,000)
In the Profit and Loss account:	
Loss on disposal of machinery	(59,000)

BALANCE SHEET AS AT 30.6.20X5	
	£
Fixed assets:	
Plant and machinery at cost	640,000
Accumulated depreciation	(119,500)
	520,500

IQ 9.3 Disposal of asset depreciated using the reducing balance method

PLANT AND MACHINERY ACCOUNT

N			£			£	N
1	1.7.20X4	Balance b/f	600,000	31.12.20X4	Disposal account	120,000	3
	1.4.20X5	Cash account	160,000	30.6.20X5	Balance c/d	640,000	
	1.7.20X5	Balance b/d	640,000				

PROVISION FOR DEPRECIATION OF PLANT AND MACHINERY ACCOUNT

			£			£	
3	31.12.20X4	Disposal a/c	43,127	1.7.20X4	Balance b/f	116,000	1
				31.12.20X4	Depreciation a/c	4,046	2
	30.6.20X5	Balance c/d	121,227	30.6.20X5	Depreciation a/c	44,308	4
				1.7.20X5	Balance b/d	121,227	

DEPRECIATION OF MACHINERY ACCOUNT

			£			£	
2	31.12.20X4	Provision for Depreciation a/c	4,046	30.6.20X5	Trading account	48,354	
4	30.6.20X5	Provision for Depreciation a/c	44,308				

DISPOSAL OF MACHINERY ACCOUNT

			£			£	
3	31.12.20X4	Plant and Machinery a/c	120,000	31.12.20X4	Provision for Depreciation a/c	43,127	3
				31.12.20X4	Cash account	35,500	3
				30.6.20X5	P and L a/c – Loss	41,373	

Notes:

1. The opening balances in the asset account and the Provision for Depreciation account, being provided by the question, would be the same as in the previous answer.
2. The first intricacy involved in the reducing balance method of depreciation is the calculation of the depreciation on the machine for the period up to the date of disposal. Thus:

	£	Accumulated Depreciation £
1.10.X0 Acquisition at a cost of	120,000	
Depreciation @ 10% of £120,000 for nine months to 30.6.X1	(9,000) >	9,000
1.7.X1 Written down value	111,000	
Depreciation @ 10% of £111,000 for year to 30.6.X2	(11,100) >	11,100
1.7.X2 Written down value	99,900	
Depreciation @ 10% of £99,900 for the year to 30.6.X3	(9,990) >	9,990
1.7.X3 Written down value	89,910	
Depreciation @ 10% of £89,990 for year to 30.6.20X4	(8,991) >	8,991
1.7.X4 Written down value	80,919	39,081
Depreciation @ 10% of £80,919 for six months to 31.12.20X4	(4,046) >	4,046
31.12.X4 Written down value of 31.12.20X0 and accumulated depn.	76,873	43,127

Thus the depreciation for six months up to the date of disposal is £4,046 and the accumulated depreciation is £43,127. Hence the cost of the machine from the asset account as well as the accumulated depreciation from the supporting account are transferred to the Disposal account.

3. The cost of the asset as well as the accumulated provision for depreciation of that asset until the date of disposal (see note 2 for the calculation thereof) are transferred to the Disposal account from the asset account and the supporting account respectively. The disposal proceeds of £35,500 are posted from the Cash account to the Disposal account.

4. The second intricacy is the calculation of depreciation for the year on the old machinery other than the one sold, as follows:

Cost of other machinery continuing in use (£600,000–£120,000)			£480,000
Accumulated depreciation up to 30.6.20X4 on other machinery:			
Accumulated depreciation on all machinery as at 30.6.20X4		£116,000	
Accumulated depreciation on machine sold – see above		(£39,081)	(£76,919)
Written down value of other machinery on 30.6.20X4			£403,081
Depreciation on other machinery: 10% of £403,081			£40,308
Depreciation on new machinery: 10% of £160,000 for three months			£4,000
			£44,308

PROFIT AND LOSS ACCOUNT FOR THE YEAR ENDED 30.6.20X5	£
In the trading account as a manufacturing expense:	
Depreciation of machinery	(48,354)
In the Profit and Loss account:	
Loss on disposal of machinery	(41,373)

BALANCE SHEET AS AT 30.6.20X5	£
Fixed assets:	
Plant and machinery at cost	640,000
Accumulated depreciation	(121,227)
	518,773

IQ 9.4 Writing off a specific bad debt and creating a general provision

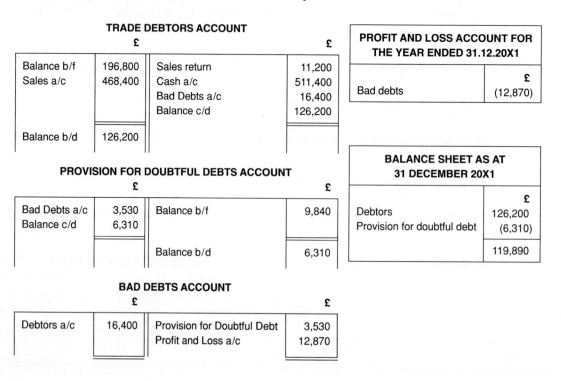

TRADE DEBTORS ACCOUNT

	£		£
Balance b/f	120	Sales return	25
Sales a/c	3,640	Cash a/c	3,420
		Bad Debts a/c	35
		Balance c/d	280
Balance b/d	280		

PROVISION FOR DOUBTFUL DEBTS ACCOUNT

	£		£
		Bad Debts a/c	14

BAD DEBTS ACCOUNT

	£		£
Debtors a/c	35	Profit and Loss a/c	49
Provision for Doubtful Debt	14		

PROFIT AND LOSS ACCOUNT FOR THE YEAR ENDED 31.12.20X0

	£
Bad debts	(49)

BALANCE SHEET AS AT 31 DECEMBER 20X0

		£
Debtors	280	
Provision for Doubtful Debts a/c	(14)	266

IQ 9.5 Adjusting the provision for doubtful debts each year

TRADE DEBTORS ACCOUNT

	£		£
Balance b/f	196,800	Sales return	11,200
Sales a/c	468,400	Cash a/c	511,400
		Bad Debts a/c	16,400
		Balance c/d	126,200
Balance b/d	126,200		

PROVISION FOR DOUBTFUL DEBTS ACCOUNT

	£		£
Bad Debts a/c	3,530	Balance b/f	9,840
Balance c/d	6,310		
		Balance b/d	6,310

BAD DEBTS ACCOUNT

	£		£
Debtors a/c	16,400	Provision for Doubtful Debt	3,530
		Profit and Loss a/c	12,870

PROFIT AND LOSS ACCOUNT FOR THE YEAR ENDED 31.12.20X1

	£
Bad debts	(12,870)

BALANCE SHEET AS AT 31 DECEMBER 20X1

	£
Debtors	126,200
Provision for doubtful debt	(6,310)
	119,890

IQ 9.6 Combined Bad Debts and Provision for Doubtful Debts account

BAD AND DOUBTFUL DEBTS ACCOUNT

	£		£
Debtors a/c	16,400	Balance b/f	9,840
Balance c/d	6,310	Profit and Loss a/c	12,870
		Balance b/d	6,310

IQ 9.7 An account, its class and its balance

	Column 1	Column 2	Column 3	N
1	Plant and Machinery account	ASSET	DEBIT	
2	Carriage Inwards account	EXPENDITURE	DEBIT	1
3	Carriage Outwards account	EXPENDITURE	DEBIT	1
4	Stationery account	EXPENDITURE	DEBIT	
5	Entertainment account	EXPENDITURE	DEBIT	
6	Motor Vehicles account	ASSET	DEBIT	
7	Cash account	ASSET	DEBIT	
8	Audit Fees account	EXPENDITURE	DEBIT	
9	Loan received from Mr Rich account	LIABILITY	CREDIT	
10	Loan to Sales Rep. account	ASSET	DEBIT	
11	Postage account	EXPENDITURE	DEBIT	
12	Depreciation of Motor Vehicles account	EXPENDITURE	DEBIT	
13	Provision for Depreciation on Vehicles a/c	SUPPORTING	CREDIT	
14	Land and Buildings account	ASSET	DEBIT	
15	Bad Debts account	EXPENDITURE	DEBIT	
16	Office Equipment account	ASSET	DEBIT	
17	Sales account	INCOME	CREDIT	
18	Vehicle Maintenance account	EXPENDITURE	DEBIT	
19	Purchases account	EXPENDITURE	DEBIT	
20	Rent Payable a/c (expenditure)	EXPENDITURE	DEBIT	2
21	Rent Payable a/c (owing)	LIABILITY	CREDIT	2
22	Prepaid Rent account	ASSET	DEBIT	2

	Column 1	Column 2	Column 3	N
23	Salaries Accrued account	LIABILITY	CREDIT	
24	Returns Inwards account	SUPPORTING	DEBIT	3
25	Returns Outwards account	SUPPORTING	CREDIT	3
26	Drawings account	SUPPORTING	DEBIT	
27	Provision for Doubtful Debts account	SUPPORTING	CREDIT	
28	Commission Earnings account	INCOME	CREDIT	4
29	Rent Received in Advance account	LIABILITY	CREDIT	5
30	Stock in Trade account	EXPENDITURE/ASSET	DEBIT	6

Notes:

1. Carriage inwards as well as carriage outwards are both expenses that the business has to pay for, the first for transporting goods to the business and the second for taking the goods to customers. The two have to be segregated in separate accounts because the carriage inwards is an expense incurred on placing the goods in the location from which it is sold, and is, therefore, included in the Trading account, whereas carriage outwards is a distribution cost to be reported in the Profit and Loss account.
2. The name Rent Payable account is confusingly used for both the expenditure account and the liability account. The use for the expenditure account is explained away by asserting that it includes the total expenditure for the year – both paid and yet to be paid – and is therefore aptly called the amount payable for the year. The use for the liability account is justified on the premise that the account reports the amount still to be paid. The portion of rent prepaid for use in a future period is of course an asset.
3. Return inwards is another name for sales returns, as is return outwards for purchase returns.
4. Commission earnings is an income earned by the business on services it provides.
5. Rent received is an income, but the portion relating to a future period is yet to be earned and is a liability.
6. The Stock in Trade account reports an expenditure if it is the opening stock that it records and an asset if what it records is the year-end stock.

IQ 9.8 Accounting for sales on a sale or return basis

SALES IN SUSPENSE ACCOUNT			
	£000		£000
Sales a/c	90	Balance b/f	154
Balance c/d	64		
		Balance b/d	64

SALES ACCOUNT			
	£000		£000
		Balance b/f	844
Trading a/c	934	Sales in Suspense a/c	90

Only goods with a sale price of £64,000 remain returnable. Hence the remainder is recognized as sales in the period. Care should be taken to add the cost (£48,000) of the goods in the hands of customers into the stock in hand (£188,000) to report unsold stock on 30 June 20X1 as £236,000.

TRADING AND PROFIT AND LOSS ACCOUNT FOR THE YEAR ENDED 30 JUNE 20X1		
	£000	£000
Sales		934
Stock on 30.6.1999	228	
Purchases	684	
Stock on 30.6.20X4	(236)	(676)
Gross profit		258
Administration expenses:		
Salaries	114	
Rent	48	
Administrative expenditure	54	
Depreciation – fixed asset	24	
Distribution cost:		(240)
Advertising	29	
Bad debts	14	(43)
Loss for the year		(25)

BALANCE SHEET AS AT 30 JUNE 20X1			
	Cost	Acc depn	£000
Fixed assets	240	(90)	150
Current assets:			
Stock in trade		236	
Debtors	486		
Less: Sales in suspense	(64)	422	
Cash and bank balance		32	
Creditors		(365)	325
			475
			£000
Capital			500
Loss for the year			(25)
			475

Note: Here and hereafter, 'Acc depn' stands for 'Accumulated depreciation'.

PROGRESSIVE QUESTIONS

PQ 9.1 Accounting for a fixed asset depreciated using the straight-line method

Hardy Stores acquired a lathe for £24,000 on 1 January 20X1 and a drilling machine on 1 April 20X2 for £30,000. On 1 July 20X3 it disposed of the lathe for £12,500 and replaced it on the same day with another for £36,000. Assuming that Hardy Stores depreciates its machinery at 10 per cent per annum on cost and maintains a separate account in its ledger to record the accumulated depreciation, *you are required to set out*:

(a) the ledger accounts recording the above stated transactions in each of the three years;
(b) how the machinery will be stated on the Balance Sheet as at 31.12.20X3;
(c) a statement of movement of machinery during the year ending on 31 December 20X3.

PQ 9.2 Accounting for a fixed asset depreciated using the reducing balance method

Answer PQ 9.1 on the revised basis that the machinery is depreciated at 20 per cent per annum using the reducing balance method.

PQ 9.3 Assets involving conversion costs and enhancement costs

The fixed assets of Silverstones were stated in its Balance Sheet on 31.3.20X4, as shown on the right. The machinery had been acquired as stated below (right). The following transactions took place during the year ended 31 March 20X5:

BALANCE SHEET AS AT 31 MARCH 20X4			
	Cost	Dep.	Written down value
	£000	£000	£000
Machinery	640	(126)	514
Motor vehicles	280	(80)	200

1 April: A new motor costing £21,500 was fitted to machine M39, improving its fuel efficiency by 300 per cent. The fitting charges amounted to £5,500.

1 July: £72,000 was paid for a luxury coach to transport staff. The cost is made up as shown on the right.

1 October: A vehicle was sold for £9,000 that had originally been acquired for £16,000 on 1 July 20X0.

1 January: Acquired machine M42 for £222,000. Particulars of this transaction are stated on the invoice as shown below:

Machine	Acquired	Cost
M34	1.4.20X1	£180,000
M38	1.4.20X2	£260,000
M39	1.4.20X3	£200,000

Luxury coach	£
Price of the coach	36,000
Freight	8,000
Insurance	2,000
Duty	24,000
Road tax	300
Extended warranty	1,700

Cost of machine M42	£
List price of machine M42	320,000
20% trade discount	(64,000)
Delivery of machine M42	4,000
Allowance for trading in M34	(40,000)
Removal of machine M34	2,000
	222,000

Silverstone depreciates machinery by the straight-line method at 10 per cent per year, and motor vehicles on the reducing balance method at 20 per cent per year.

Required: Record the transactions in the appropriate ledger accounts and show how the assets will appear in the Balance Sheet as at 31 March 20X5.

PQ 9.4 Bad and doubtful debts

Copperband maintains a provision for doubtful debts at 5 per cent of debtors outstanding at the close of business in each accounting period. All customers are allowed one month's credit, but customers who settle within a week are permitted a 10 per cent settlement discount. Debtors, net of provision for doubtful debts, were reported as £405,080 on 30 June 20X0. Transactions during the year to 30 June 20X1 include the following:

Transaction	£
Sales during the year	1,240,000
Amounts received from debtors within a week of a sale	585,540
Amounts received from debtors after more than a week	420,800
Sales returns during the year	36,200
Bad debts written off in the year	28,600

Required:

(a) Make entries in a Debtors account to show total amounts receivable from all customers.
(b) Make entries in a Provision for Doubtful Debts account, which also includes bad debts written off (i.e. a combined bad debt and doubtful debt approach).
(c) Show how these transactions will be reported in the Profit and Loss account for the year ended 30 June 20X1 and the Balance Sheet as at that date.

Note: **Settlement discount** is a waiver of part of the amount due from the customer if the customer pays within a stipulated period. The settlement discount, if allowed, is an expense.

PQ 9.5 A Trial Balance featuring supporting accounts

TRIAL BALANCE AS AT 30 JUNE 20X1		
	£000	**£000**
Motor vehicles at cost	180	–
Provision for deprn – 30.6. 20x0	–	64
Stock in trade – 30.6. 20X0	142	–
Trade debtors	248	–
Stationery	14	–
Purchases	748	–
Purchases returns	–	21
Advertising	35	–
Provision for doubtful debts	–	10
Rent	21	–
Sales	–	965
Sales returns	15	–
Sales commission	16	–
12% Loan from Joe Rover	–	100
Telephone/postage	11	–
Cash and bank balance	31	–
Capital	–	400
Drawings	25	–
Salaries and wages	74	–

Parkside Store extracted its Trial Balance on the last day of business for the year, as shown on the left. You have ascertained the following:

1. The stock of unsold goods at hand is £172,000.
2. Vehicles are depreciated at 20% of cost.
3. Rent is payable at £1,500 per month.
4. Interest on Joe Rover's loan is still to be paid.
5. £18,000 due from Bill Lad, a customer, is to be written off as bad and the provision for doubtful debts adjusted to 10 per cent of the debtors outstanding.
6. Expenses relating to the year and remaining unpaid as at 30.6.20X1 are as stated in the box below.

	£000
Salaries	11
Telephone	3
Audit fees	4
Sales commission	1

Required:

(a) Prepare a Trading and Profit and Loss account for the year ended 30 June 20X1.
(b) Prepare the Balance Sheet as at that date.

PQ 9.6 Recognizing the point at which a Trial Balance was extracted

Brimstones depreciates its motor vehicles and furniture by the straight-line method at 20 per cent and 10 per cent per annum respectively. The firm's Trial Balance as at the end of its financial year appears as shown on the right.

You are also informed as follows:

1. Certain goods with customers on a 'sale or return basis', pro forma invoiced to them for £240,000 have been accounted in error as sales. These goods cost £210,000.
2. A debt of £20,000 should be written off and the provision adjusted to cover 6 per cent of debtors outstanding.

Required:

(a) Identify whether the stock included in the Trial Balance is 'opening' stock or 'closing' stock.
(b) Ascertain whether the Trial Balance was extracted prior to or after writing off the current year's depreciation on furniture and motor vehicles.
(c) Prepare the Trading and Profit and Loss account for the year ended 31.3.20X1 and the Balance Sheet as at that date.

TRIAL BALANCE AS AT 31 MARCH 20X1		
	£000	**£000**
Motor vehicles	960	–
Accumulated deprn – vehicles	–	528
Furniture at cost	540	–
Accumulated deprn – Furniture	–	189
Salaries	628	–
Bad debts	32	–
Cost of sales	11,840	–
Provision for doubtful debts	–	195
Stock in trade on ?	1,428	–
Cash and bank balance	169	–
Sales	–	14,480
Depreciation – Motor vehicles	176	–
Depreciation – Furniture	45	–
Debtors and creditors	2,460	1,580
Capital account	–	2,200
Drawings account	112	–
Advertising	218	–
Other administrative expense	564	–
	19,172	19,172

Chapter 10

THE JOURNAL

In this chapter

We will learn of:

- The Journal as a book of prime entry
- The use of suspense accounts

and you should be able to:

- journalize a transaction that cannot be accommodated in any other book of prime entry
- correct errors, including ones involving a suspense account

---

10.1 THE NEED FOR A JOURNAL

Accounting procedures as operated today restrict any bookkeeper to the task of posting the transactions that have already been recorded in one of the books of prime entry. For all cash transactions, the prime entry is made by the cashier in the cash book. For all non-cash transactions, the prime entry was once made in a single book known as the Journal. The word *journal*, in French, merely means a daily record or diary. In the course of time, the number of transactions necessitated specialized journals to be developed for recording the prime entry of routine transactions such as purchases, sales, and their returns. We have met some of these specialized journals, often referred to as day books, in Chapter 8. It is not uncommon to refer to them as the Sales Journal, Purchases Journal, and so on.

Nowadays, it is customary to regard the Journal (or General Journal, to distinguish it from the specialized ones) as a book of prime entry for first recording any transaction that cannot be recorded in the cash book or in any of the specialized journals.

10.2 TRANSACTIONS USUALLY JOURNALIZED

The act of recording a transaction in a journal is referred to as *journalizing*. The transactions that are journalized are those for which a specialized book of prime entry has not been set aside. Depending on the nature of business, further specialised journals could be used for recording any repetitive transactions.

The transactions typically recorded in a journal include the following:

- opening entries when starting a business;
- acquisition or disposal of fixed assets on credit terms;
- correction of errors and transfers between accounts;
- year-end adjustments;
- reversal of settlement discount (see Chapter 13);
- closing entries – i.e. either closing the nominal accounts when financial statements are prepared at the year end or closing all the accounts when the business is wound up.

10.3 THE STYLE OF PRESENTING A JOURNAL ENTRY

The task of journalizing is usually restricted to a responsible person on the accounting staff who has the necessary level of authority. This would explain the following features in a journal entry:

- A journal entry sounds like a command, naming the account to be debited and the one credited.
- The account to be debited is usually named first, followed, on another line and set slightly inset, by the one to be credited.
- The name of the account to be debited ends with the suffix 'Dr' and the name of the account to be credited begins with a prefix 'To', so that, when read, the journal entry sounds as though the first named account feels indebted to the second named account.
- The journal entry is completed with an explanation clarifying the need for the entry. This explanation is known as a *narration* and the narration traditionally begins with the word 'Being' (just as nursery tales always commence with the words 'Once upon a time').
- Built into each journal entry are columns to record the date of the entry, a cross-reference to the relevant voucher, and the folio numbers of the accounts to which the book-keeper will be posting the journal entry. The folio number is filled in by the book-keeper after he completes the posting.

For illustration, let us journalize the acquisition of a motor vehicle for £18,000 from Belgravia Garages. The journal entry appears as follows:

Date	Voucher	Particulars	F	Debit £	Credit £

20X1
11.2
	D721	Motor Vehicles account Dr
		    To Belgravia Garages account
		Being the acquisition of a saloon car on three months credit
		    as per vending agreement dated 4 February 20X1.
			
			–
			
				18,000	–
					18,000

Thus, when one reads the journal entry as 'Motor vehicles debtor to Belgravia Garages', the impression is conveyed that the asset could not have been obtained but for the credit terms permitted by the named supplier. The bookkeeper debits the Motor Vehicles account with £18,000 and credits the Belgravia Garages account with the same amount. The two accounting entries constituting the double entry are both made by the bookkeeper and the journal is, therefore, a book of prime entry, just as the various day books are.

10.4 COMPOSITE JOURNAL ENTRIES

It may well happen that the accounts to be debited and credited to record a single transaction may be several. Let us assume, for example, that a vehicle costing £15,000, furniture costing £10,000 and a computer costing £5,000 are all acquired from General Stores Ltd. The acquisition of each of these assets may well be journalized by an independent entry. This will be time-consuming and it would be more convenient to make a single composite journal entry as follows:

Date	Voucher	Particulars		F	Debit £	Credit £
20X1 14.9	D942	Sundries	Dr		–	–
		To General Stores account			–	30,000
		Furniture account			10,000	
		Motor Vehicles account			15,000	
		Computer account			5,000	
		Being acquisition of assets as per vending agreement dated 12.9.20X1.				

With more than one account to be debited, the name of the account to be debited is stated as 'Sundries' and the individual accounts debited are named after stating the account to be credited. If the debits as well as the credits are to be made in more than one account, the first two lines of the journal entry will read 'Sundries Dr To Sundries'.

10.5 JOURNAL ENTRIES COMMONLY USED

10.5.1 Journal entries for recording asset acquisitions and disposals

When a fixed asset is acquired on credit terms, the prime entry for it cannot be made in the Purchases Day Book. This is because the periodical totals of the transactions recorded in the Purchases Day Book are posted to the debit of the Purchases account, whereas the asset should be debited to an appropriate asset account. That is why the acquisition of assets on credit terms has to be journalized, as shown in both illustrations given above.

Interaction 10.1

Journalizing the acquisition and disposal of assets

For the purpose of improving the production capacity, Electroplastics acquired machinery for £180,000 on credit from Dando plc and scrapped some obsolete machinery, which had originally cost £60,000 and had been written down by this date to £15,200.

Required: Journalize the acquisition and disposal of this machinery.

Interaction 10.2

Journalizing the acquisition of an expense stock

A new business bought its supply of office stationery for £18,000 on credit from City Traders.

Required: Set out the prime entry for the transaction.

10.5.2 Journal entries for the correction of errors and transfers

A common error requiring correction is when a sale is posted to an incorrect customer with the same or similar name. For example, if a sale of £6,500 to Joe Nathan is posted in error to Jim Nathan, the journal entry for correcting the error will appear as follows:

Date	Voucher	Particulars	F	Debit £	Credit £
20X1 15.11	P621	Joe Nathan account Dr To Jim Nathan account Being the correction of an error in posting.		6,500 –	– 6,500

Probably a letter of protest from Jim would have been referenced as P621 and filed as the voucher. The debit in Joe's account would make him a debtor for the value of goods sold to him, while the credit to Jim's account would relieve that account of the wrong debit.

Journalizing the correction of compensating errors

Interaction 10.3

The following accounting errors were detected in the course of an annual audit:

(a) £16,000, the cost of furniture acquired for office use from Smiths Ltd has been recorded in the Purchases Day Book;

(b) £1,050 paid for servicing vehicles has been posted to the Motor Vehicles account;

(c) £6,400 received from Bob Martin, a credit customer, has been posted in error to the Sales account;

(d) a sale of £9,400 to Joe Budd has been recorded in the Sales Day Book as £4,900 and posted to Jill Budd.

Required: Set out journal entries necessary for correcting the foregoing errors.

Impact of error correction on reported performance and position

Interaction 10.4

Required: Disclose the impact of the corrections you made, in respect of the errors stated in IQ 10.3, on the income, expenditure, liabilities and assets reported for the business.

10.5.3 Journal entries for period-end adjustments

As we saw in Chapter 7, a variety of period-end adjustments are necessary for the proper preparation of financial statements. To effect each adjustment, the bookkeeper has to credit one account and debit another. She is prohibited from making any such entry except on the basis of an appropriate prime entry. For example, to write off as a bad debt £6,250 due from Richard Grey, a customer, the bookkeeper cannot credit Richard's account and debit the Bad Debts account unless the following journal entry authorizes her to make those entries:

Date	Voucher	Particulars	F	Debit £	Credit £
20X1 31.12	B214	Bad debts account Dr To Richard Grey's account Being a trade debt written off as irrecoverable.		6,250 –	– 6,250

Journalizing period-end adjustments

The Trial Balance extracted from the books of a retailer on the last day of the accounting period includes those listed below on the right. You are further informed as follows:

(a) Rent is payable at £3,000 per month.
(b) Salary unpaid at the year end is £21,000.
(c) A trade debt of £16,000 is to be written off and provision for doubtful debts adjusted to cover 10 per cent of debts.
(d) Motor vehicles are to be depreciated annually at 10 per cent of cost.

Required: Set out the journal entries necessary for making the period-end adjustments described in (a)–(d) above.

	£000	£000
Motor vehicles	240	
Provision for depreciation		96
Salaries	216	
Rent	40	
Trade debtors	456	
Provision for doubtful debt	–	21

10.5.4 Journal entries for opening new books of account

If a person commences business introducing his capital in cash, the amount introduced should be recorded in the Cash account (prime entry) and posted from there to the Capital account. No other book of prime entry is needed. If, on the other hand, the capital introduced consists of furniture valued at £10,000, a car valued at £20,000, and £50,000 in cash, although the prime entry for the cash will be in the cash book, a journal entry is still needed to account for the other two assets:

Date	Voucher	Particulars		F	Debit £	Credit £
20X1						
1.1	A001	Sundries	Dr		–	–
		To Capital account			–	30,000
		Furniture account			10,000	–
		Motor Vehicles account			20,000	–
		Being assets introduced at commencement of business as part of capital.				

The bookkeeper posts the amount of cash from the cash book to the Capital account; and by posting the above-stated journal entry, the bookkeeper ensures that the Capital account reports the whole of the capital introduced at the commencement of the business.

CAPITAL ACCOUNT

	£		£
		Cash account	50,000
		Journal	30,000
			80,000

Journalizing net assets introduced at commencement

When he commenced business as a car tyre dealer, Carl introduced as capital a vehicle valued at £36,000, a stock of tyres valued at £80,000, and £24,000 in cash. He also wanted the business to take over the £35,000 he owed to the tyre supplier Horatio Ltd.

Required: Set out the journal entry necessary to account for the capital introduced.

10.6 SUSPENSE ACCOUNTS

Suspense is associated with uncertainty. Confronted with a position (such as when a Trial Balance fails to balance) where the total of the debits fails to match the total of the credits, the difference is placed for the time being in a Suspense account because of the uncertainty as to how it should be dealt with. When, upon detecting the cause (or, probably, causes) of the difference, the uncertainty is resolved and the amount in the Suspense account can be transferred to where it belongs. To be able to place the difference in a Suspense account, and to eliminate the amount so placed, as errors are detected and rectified, journal entries are necessary and, as will be seen, not all of them consist of a pair of matching debit and credit entries.

To illustrate, let us consider a situation where the amounts recorded in a Sales Day Book are overcast by £300 – i.e. they sum to £7,838 instead of £7,538. The total is credited to the Sales account and is inflated by £300, whereas the individual amounts debited to respective customers will add up to only £7,538. As a result, the credit side of the Trial Balance will in this regard exceed the debit side by £300. To correct the imbalance, the difference is placed in a Suspense account, until the reason for the imbalance is ascertained and remedied. For the bookkeeper to debit £300 in the Suspense account, a journal entry is needed, as shown on the right. This journal entry, unlike those met with so far, requires an entry to be made in the named account without requiring a corresponding second entry. This is because, if a second entry is made in another account, the Trial Balance will again become imbalanced. When the overcasting of the Sales Day Book is detected, another journal entry becomes necessary (right) for the bookkeeper to transfer the debit balance from the Suspense account to the Sales account, closing the former and reducing the balance in the latter to the correct amount.

SALES DAY BOOK DATE: 7 MAY 20X0			
Invoice	Customer	F	Amount £
G712	Sally Davies	L85	1,468
G713	Joe Brooks	L46	945
G714	Peter Folly	L68	3,250
G715	Mike Brown	L77	1,875
	Sales a/c	L12	7,838

Particulars	F	Debit £	Credit £
Suspense account Dr Being difference in Trial Balance placed in Suspense a/c		300	–

Particulars	F	Debit £	Credit £
Sales account Dr To Suspense a/c Being correction of an overcast on folio xx of the Sales Day Book		300 –	– 300

Interaction 10.7	Correction of errors that affect the Trial Balance

When the Trial Balance extracted from the books of Darwin Stores on 31 March 20X1 failed to balance, the difference was placed in a Suspense account. Subsequent inquiries confirmed the imbalance to have arisen because of the following four errors:

1. A sale of £9,600 to Sally Brown was not posted to the customer.
2. A monthly total of the Return Inwards Journal had been posted to the Nominal account as £12,400 instead of £21,400.
3. A credit note issued for £1,200 to Peter Collins, a customer, recorded in the Return Inwards Journal, has been posted to the debit of the customer's account.
4. The balance of £4,250 in the Return Outwards account was stated in the Trial Balance as a debit balance.

Required:

(a) Set out the journal entries necessary for correcting the four errors.
(b) Set out the Suspense account, showing how it is closed.

Interaction 10.8	Impact of error corrections on reported performance and position

Refer back to the four errors stated in IQ 10.7 and identify the impact of each correction on the store's income, expenditure, liabilities and assets.

SOLUTIONS TO INTERACTIVE QUESTIONS

IQ 10.1 Journalizing the acquisition and disposal of assets

Date	Voucher	Particulars		F	Debit £	Credit £
?	?	Plant and Machinery account	Dr		180,000	–
		To Dando plc account			–	180,000
		Being acquisition of machinery on credit.				–
?	?	Sundries	Dr		–	–
		To Plant and Machinery account			–	60,000
		Provision for depreciation on Machinery account			44,800	–
		Loss by asset obsolescence			15,200	–
		Being scrapping of machinery which has become obsolete.				

IQ 10.2 Journalizing the acquisition of an expense stock

Date	Voucher	Particulars		F	Debit £	Credit £
?	?	Stationery account	Dr		18,000	–
		To City Traders account			–	18,000
		Being acquisition of stationery on credit terms.				–

IQ 10.3 Journalizing the correction of compensating errors

(a) The acquisition of furniture, recorded in the Purchases Day Book, would have been debited to Purchases a/c. It should be transferred to Furniture a/c.

Date	V	Particulars		F	Debit £	Credit £
?	?	Furniture account	Dr		16,000	
		To Purchases account				16,000
		Being correction of error.				

(b) The payment for servicing vehicles, capitalized in error, has to be expensed by transferring from the asset account to the expenditure account.

Date	V	Particulars		F	Debit £	Credit £
?	?	Vehicle maintenance a/c	Dr		1,050	–
		To Motor Vehicles a/c			–	1,050
		Being correction of error.				

(c) The receipt from a customer, posted from the cash book to the Sales a/c, should be transferred to Bob Martin, the customer.

Date	V	Particulars		F	Debit £	Credit £
?	?	Sales account	Dr		6,400	–
		To Bob Martin's account			–	6,400
		Being correction of error.				

(d) If the error is more complicated than one that requires merely a transfer from one account to another, one of two approaches may be taken for correcting it. The first and more simplistic way is to wipe off the erroneous entries by one journal entry (as shown in the first box here on the right) and then to account for the transaction anew and, this time, correctly by another journal entry (second box). The alternative approach is to make corrections to account balances, without wiping off the entries made already (third box). It should be observed that the second way makes a single journal entry, which, in fact, combines the two made in the first way.

Date	V	Particulars		F	Debit £	Credit £
?	?	Sales account	Dr		4,900	
		To Jill Budd				4,900
		Being correction of error.				

Date		Particulars		F	Debit £	Credit £
?	?	Joe Budd account	Dr		9,400	–
		To Sales account			–	9,400
		Being correction of error.				

Date		Particulars		F	Debit £	Credit £
?	?	Joe Budd account	Dr		9,400	–
		To Jill Budd account			–	4,900
		Sales account			–	4,500
		Being correction of error.				

IQ 10.4 Impact of error correction on reported performance and position

Impact of IQ 10.3 error correction	Income £	Expenditure £	Liabilities £	Assets £
(a) Recording an asset acquisition in the Purchases Day Book	–	(16,000)	–	16,000
(b) Capitalization of the cost of servicing vehicles	–	1,050	–	(1,050)
(c) A debt recovery accounted for as an income	(6,400)	–	–	(6,400)
(d) Income understated and posted to the wrong customer	4,500	–	–	4,500

IQ 10.5 Journalizing period-end adjustments

(a) £4,000 is transferred from the Rent account in order to report the prepaid portion of rent as an asset at the period end.

Date	V	Particulars		F	Debit £	Credit £
?	?	Prepaid Rent account	Dr		4,000	–
		To Rent account			–	4,000
		Being transfer.				

(b) Salary remaining unpaid at year end is accrued to record full expenditure of the period whether paid for or otherwise.

Date	V	Particulars		F	Debit £	Credit £
?	?	Salaries account	Dr		21,000	–
		To Salary Payable a/c			–	21,000
		Being accrual of unpaid salary.				

(c) If preferred, the writing-off of the debt may be done by one journal entry and the adjustment of the provision by another.

Date	V	Particulars		F	Debit £	Credit £
?	?	Bad Debts a/c	Dr		39,000	–
		To Trade Debtors a/c			–	16,000
		Provison for doubtful debt			–	23,000
		Being writing off a bad debt and adjusting the provision to cover 10% of debtors.				

(c) The depreciation of motor vehicles for the year is provided for by debiting the expenditure account and crediting the Provision account.

Date	V	Particulars		F	Debit £	Credit £
?	?	Depreciation of vehicle	Dr		24,000	–
		To Provision for depreciation			–	24,000
		Being provision for depreciation.				

IQ 10.6 Journalizing net assets introduced at commencement

Date	V	Particulars		F	Debit £	Credit £
?	?	Sundries	Dr			
		To Sundries				
		Motor Vehicles account			36,000	–
		Stock in Trade account			80,000	–
		Creditors – Horatio Ltd			–	35,000
		Capital account			–	81,000
		Being net assets introduced as capital at commencement of business.				

The Journal is used as the book of prime entry only in the absence of any other book of prime entry. The capital introduced in cash is entered in the cash book and does not have to be journalized. When the bookkeeper completes the posting, the Capital account will report the net assets introduced at commencement as capital of £105,000.

CAPITAL ACCOUNT

	£		£
		Cash account	24,000
		Journal	81,000
			105,000

IQ 10.7 Correction of errors that affect the Trial Balance

(a) Journal entries

1. The Trial Balance would have shown a debit shortfall of £9,600 because of the failure to post the sale to the customer's account. The debit balance, placed in a Suspense account to make good the shortfall, is transferred to Sally.

Particulars		Debit £	Credit £
Sally Brown's a/c	Dr	9,600	–
To Suspense a/c		–	9,600
Being correction of error.			

2. The Trial Balance would have shown again a debit shortfall of £9,000 because the debit in the Return Inwards account was £12,400 instead of £21,400. The debit balance of £9,000, placed in suspense, is transferred to Return Inwards.

Particulars		Debit £	Credit £
Return Inwards a/c	Dr	9,000	–
To Suspense a/c		–	9,000
Being correction of error.			

3. The Trial Balance would have shown a credit shortfall of £1,200 × 2 because the failure to credit the customer with £1,200 leaves a shortfall of that amount; and wrongly debiting the customer leaves another credit shortfall of the same amount. The amount of £2,400, credited to a Suspense account, is transferred to Peter Collins.

Particulars		Debit £	Credit £
Suspense account	Dr	2,400	–
To Peter Collins a/c		–	2,400
Being correction of error.			

4. The error this time is not in the books of account but in the Trial Balance. By wrongly listing, on the Trial Balance, a credit balance as a debit, a credit shortfall of double that amount has been created and placed as a credit balance in a Suspense account. It is necessary to remove the credit in the Suspense account (by debiting it) without making another entry.

Particulars		Debit £	Credit £
Suspense account	Dr	8,500	–
Being correction of an error.			

(b) Suspense account

The opening balance in the Suspense account, which is the amount by which the Trial Balance would have failed to balance, is arrived at as the balancing amount.

SUSPENSE ACCOUNT

		£		£	
	Balance	7,700	Journal	9,600	1
3	Journal	2,400	Journal	9,000	2
4	Journal	8,500			
		18,600		18,600	

IQ 10.8 Impact of error corrections on reported performance and position

Impact of IQ 10.7 error correction	Income £	Expenditure £	Liabilities £	Assets £
(a) Sale not posted – double entry error	–	–	–	9,600
(b) Transposition error when posting to Nominal Ledger	(9,000)	–	–	–
(c) Posting to wrong side of customer – double entry error	–	–	–	(2,400)
(d) Error in extracting the Trial Balance	–	–	–	–

PROGRESSIVE QUESTIONS

PQ 10.1 Opening the books of a new retail outlet

Sheila West commenced trading via a retail outlet, introducing as part of her initial capital the following:

Assets:		Liabilities:	
Furniture	£36,000	Trade creditors	£39,000
Motor vehicle	£24,000	Loan from Martin West	£30,000
Stock in trade	£42,000		
Cash	£50,000		

Required: Account for this transaction, showing both the prime entry and the entries in the ledger accounts.

PQ 10.2 Journal entries to account for transactions

Jeremy Jefferies, a motor spares manufacturer, entered into the following transactions during the year ended 30 June 20X1:

(a) Bob Salmon, a trade debtor experiencing cash flow problems, hands in his vehicle valued at £15,000 in part-settlement of the amount of £18,000 due from him. Jeremy agrees to waive the remainder of the debt.
(b) £12,000 was paid to repair a machine. It was agreed that 50 per cent of the cost of repair should be deducted from the salary of the foreman whose negligence necessitated the repair. Accordingly, from September 20X0 for ten months the foreman was paid a salary of £2,400 per month instead of £3,000 per month.
(c) Motor spares costing £26,000 are gifted to charity.
(d) A machine acquired for £40,000 and written down to £12,000 was given in part-exchange, along with a cash payment of £38,000 to acquire an improved model.

Required: Identify the prime entry to account for each of the above transactions.

PQ 10.3 Journal entries for the correction of errors

The audit of the books of Collin Drake, dealer in word processors, during the year to 30 April 20X1 revealed the following errors and omissions:

(a) A sale invoiced to Sue Robert at £14,200 was recorded in the Sales Journal as £12,400.
(b) A purchase invoice of £16,450 from Calico plc, a regular supplier, was omitted from the Purchases Journal.
(c) An invoice of £400, again from Calico plc but this time for stationery, was listed in the Purchases Journal.
(d) £11,500 received in respect of a debt written off in the previous year was credited to the Sales account.
(e) £16,000 paid on 1 August 20X0 for office equipment was posted to the Stationery account. Such equipment is usually depreciated at 10 per cent per annum by the straight-line method.
(f) Included in Rent and Rates account is £2,000 paid as Council Tax on Collin's private residence.
(g) Included in stock as at 30 April 20X1, at its cost of £6,000, is a word processor that had been used for demonstration purposes and is expected to be sold for £2,500.

Required: Set out the journal entries necessary for rectifying each of the above errors.

PQ 10.4 Impact of error corrections on reported profit

The draft financial statements of Collin Drake, prior to detection and correction of the errors stated in PQ 10.3, reported for the year ended 30 April 20X1 a gross profit of £976,800 and an operating profit of £172,400.

Required: Identify the impact that the correction of the errors would have on these figures.

PQ 10.5 Establishment of a Suspense account

When the Trial Balance extracted from the books of Kevin Enterprises at the year end failed to balance, the difference was placed in a Suspense account. Assuming that the error that caused the difference was each of the following, identify (by ticking the appropriate grid) the amount that would have been placed in the Suspense account.

(a) A folio in the Purchases Journal has been added as £34,680 instead of £36,480.

a	Dr 3,640	
b	Cr 1,800	
c	Dr 1,800	

(b) £4,200 paid to solicitors for conveyancing a property has been written off as legal expenses instead of being capitalized.

a	Dr 4,800	
b	None	
c	Cr 2,400	

(c) £2,400, being the prepaid portion of insurance, was brought forward from the previous year as a credit balance in the nominal account.

a	Dr 4,800	
b	None	
c	Cr 2,400	

(d) £218,400 paid to a supplier has been posted to the supplier's account as £214,800.

a	Cr 3,600	
b	Dr 3,600	
c	Dr 218,400	

(e) A sale of £13,600 was recorded in the Sales Journal as £3,600 and posted to Guy Bernard, the customer, as £6,300.

a	Dr 2,700	
b	Dr 12,700	
c	Cr 2,700	

(f) The recovery of a staff loan, on the pay sheet at £300 per month for nine months in the year, has not been accounted for.

a	Cr 2,700	
b	Dr 2,700	
c	None	

(g) The year-end Trial Balance records the balance of £116,200 in the Sales Returns account as a credit balance.

a	Dr 116,200	
b	Dr 232,400	
c	Cr 232,400	

PQ 10.6 Correction of errors that may affect the Trial Balance

The Trial Balance extracted from the books of City Grocers on 31.3.20X1 failed to balance. The difference was placed in a Suspense account. Since then, the following errors have been detected:

(a) A folio in the Purchases Day Book has been cast as £214,600 instead of £213,400.
(b) £800 paid to Lal Jason, a supplier, had not been posted to his personal account.
(c) A daily total in the Sales Returns Day Book of £1,200 was not posted to the Nominal account.
(d) £120 paid for stationery was posted to the Office Equipment account.
(e) £4,000 paid as rent was posted as £400.
(f) £360 paid for advertising was posted as £630.
(g) £3,000 received from Mike Shane, a customer, was posted to the debit side of his personal account.
(h) £4,200, the total of Return Outwards Day Book, was debited to the Sales Returns account in the Nominal Ledger.
(i) A sale of £6,250 to Joe Rogers was recorded as £2,650 and posted to Jill Rogers as £265.
(j) Prepaid rent amounting to £6,000 was brought forward from the previous year as a credit balance in the Nominal account.
(k) Accrued rent amounting to £3,000 at the year end is reported in the Trial Balance as a debit balance.
(l) A balance of £3,000 in the Commission Received account is not listed in the Trial Balance.

Required: Set out the journal entries necessary for correcting each error; and, on the basis that the correction of the above errors eliminates the whole balance placed in suspense, show the Suspense account.

PQ 10.7 Elimination of the Suspense account to finalize the accounts

The Trial Balance stated here was extracted from the books of Joe's Retail on the last day of its accounting period, having placed in a Suspense account the amount by which it failed to balance. Subsequent enquiries revealed the following:

(a) Cash sales of £24,000 were not accounted for.
(b) A folio of the Sales Journal was cast as £264,500 instead of £294,500.
(c) Goods included in purchases at £24,000 were left out of stock as at 30 June 20X1 because they remained in transit on the day of stocktaking.
(d) £12,000 paid as sales commission was posted to the Nominal account as £21,000.
(e) One month's rent of £3,000, prepaid as at 1 July 20X0, has been brought forward in the Rent account as a credit balance.
(f) Salary and rent, amounting to £36,000 and £6,000 respectively, remain unpaid as at 30 June 20X1.
(g) Goods costing £16,000, removed by Joe for his own use, have not been accounted for.

TRIAL BALANCE AS AT 30.6.20X1		
	£000	£000
Fixed assets	2,460	–
Accum. depreciation	–	1,640
Depreciation	369	–
Rent	24	–
Salaries	476	–
Sales	–	2,872
Cash and bank	133	–
Stock – 30.6.20X1	416	–
Sales commission	78	–
Debtors & creditors	396	509
Cost of sales	1,708	–
Advertising	84	–
Drawings	115	–
Telephone/postage	28	–
Stationery	17	–
Capital	–	1,250
Suspense account	–	33
	6,304	6,304

Required: Set out the journal entries required for rectifying the errors and making year-end adjustments, and the Trading and Profit and Loss account for the year ended 30 June 20X1 and the Balance Sheet as at that date.

PQ 10.8 Post-Balance Sheet elimination of the Suspense account balance

Mackie Stores proceeded to finalize its accounts for the year ended 31.12.20X0 by placing the difference from the Trial Balance in a Suspense account and reporting the Suspense account balance on the Balance Sheet, which appears as shown on the right. Since then, the auditors were able to detect the following errors:

1. Included within Sales was £24,000 realized on disposal of a vehicle that had been acquired for £60,000 and written down by the date of disposal to £15,000.
2. £17,000, being the cost of goods returned to suppliers, was posted from the Returns Outwards Journal to the credit of the supplier's account.
3. £24,000 paid for advertising was posted to the Nominal account as £42,000.
4. £58,000 paid to suppliers was not posted.
5. £48,000 paid for carriage inwards was posted to the Carriage Outwards account.

Mackie Stores' draft accounts reported a gross profit of £758,000 for the year ended 31 December 20X0.

MACKIE STORES

BALANCE SHEET AS AT 31.12.20X0	Cost	Depn.	£000
Fixed assets	640	(280)	360
Current assets:			
Stock in trade		546	
Debtors		396	
Suspense account		74	
Cash and bank		54	
Current liabilities			
Creditors	(498)		
Accrued expenses	(34)	(532)	538
			898

	£000
Capital	750
Profit for the year	198
Drawings	(50)
	898

Required:

(a) Set out the journal entries necessary to rectify the errors detected by the auditors, bearing in mind that all nominal accounts for the year ended 31 December 20X0 have been closed by transfer to the Profit and Loss account.

(b) Identify the impact of the corrections on the gross profit and net profit reported for the year ended 31 December 20X0.

(c) Set out the amended Balance Sheet as at 31 December 20X0.

Chapter 11

FINALIZATION OF ACCOUNTS

In this chapter

We will learn of:

- the accounting processes undertaken prior to reporting the performance in respect of an accounting period and the position on the last day

and you should be able to:

- undertake more period-end adjustments
- present financial statements in good style

11.1 WHAT FINALIZATION OF ACCOUNTS INVOLVES

Finalization of accounts involves the following

- checking the accuracy of the accounting balances
- making period-end adjustments
- preparing the financial statements for the year which, for the time being, consist of
  - a Trading and Profit and Loss account for the year ending on a particular date
  - a Balance Sheet as at that date.

11.2 CHECKING THE ACCURACY OF THE ACCOUNTING BALANCES

We have seen that there are a number of tests to check the accuracy of the balances in the ledger accounts. These include:

- balancing the cash book and checking the balance with the amount of cash in hand;
- extracting a Trial Balance to establish the arithmetical accuracy of the double entry postings by the bookkeeper;
- undertaking a physical inventory of stock to ensure that year-end stock is accurately determined.

Other means used to check the accuracy of accounting will be considered in later chapters and include the following:

- preparation of bank reconciliation to ensure that money at the bank is correctly stated (Chapter 13);
- verification of the accuracy of individual ledger balances by checking whether the sum of the balances in that ledger equals the balance in the corresponding control account (Chapter 14);
- accounting controls over the sales, purchases and wages systems (Chapter 30).

11.3 PERIOD-END ADJUSTMENTS: QUESTIONS TO CONSIDER

Period-end adjustments are the steps essential for ensuring that, first, the Trading and Profit and Loss account reports the performance for an accounting period by comparing all income earned in the period with related expenses and, second, that the Balance Sheet reports the resources of that entity and its obligations as at the last day of the period. To achieve this, assurance is sought on a number of questions, relating to income (I), expenditure (E), assets (A) and liabilities (L):

1. (I) **Has the income earned in the period been fully accounted for (i.e. credited to the Trading and Profit and Loss account) whether or not it has been received in the form of cash?** If not received, any amount yet to be received should be accounted for as income and also as an asset. For example, interest earnings yet to be received would be credited to the Interest Receivable account (income) and debited to the Interest Receivable account (an asset – though both accounts are identically named).

2. (I) **Does an income account include an amount that has yet to be earned as at the end of the period?** If it does, that portion should be removed from the income account, to be reported instead as a deferred income. For example, if rental earnings received are in respect of more than the 12 months in the period, the amount received in advance for the period after the Balance Sheet date should be transferred from the Rent Receivable account (income) to a Rent Received in Advance account (a deferred income, treated as a liability).

3. (E) **Have the expenses incurred in the period been fully accounted for whether or not they have been paid for in the period?** If not, the amount remaining unpaid should be accrued. For example, the amount of salary remaining unpaid is debited to the Salaries account (expenditure) and credited to the Salaries Accrued account (liability).

4. (E) **Does an expenditure account include an amount that deserves to be recognized as an asset?** If it does, that amount should be capitalized. For example, the cost of any unused stationery needs to be transferred from the Stationery account (expenditure) to the Stock of Stationery account (asset).

5. (A) **Have all resources that are expected to yield economic benefits in the future been recognized as assets (i.e. included in the Balance Sheet)?** If not, the asset should be included. For example, if an error is discovered in casting the stocktaking sheets whereby a stock figure has been undercast, then the correct figure should be entered in the Balance Sheet, with any consequential changes also being made (e.g. cost of sales reduced).

6. (A) **Does an asset account include amounts paid for benefits already used up within the accounting period?** If it does, such amounts should be expensed. For example, amounts paid for any fixed asset should be expensed to the extent that they represent benefits, which have been consumed by the last date of each accounting period.

7. (L) **Have all obligations to transfer economic benefits in the future been recognized and accounted for as liabilities?** If not, the liability should be included. For example, an amount due to, say, the telephone company might only have been billed after the Balance Sheet date, although it covers in part charges arising before the Balance Sheet date.

11.4 PRESENTATION OF THE FINANCIAL STATEMENTS

The aim of accounting is to communicate reliable information, relevant for decision making, to those entitled to such information. To be *reliable*, the information must be accurate and complete. Steps spelt out in Sections 11.2 and 11.3 are designed to take care of this. An important aid to making information *relevant* is to present it so that it is understandable and brings into focus aspects that deserve attention. To achieve this, the presentation of financial statements is being continuously improved.

Such improvements include the following:

● Financial statements (when prepared other than for internal use by management) are usually presented in vertical format rather than in a two-sided account format (where debits are separated from credits by vertical lines).
● In the Profit and Loss account:
  – the gross profit is reported so as to show the results of trading activity and the operating profit so as to show the net result of the entity's usual operations, before proceeding to list any non-operating income and expenditure;
  – expenditure is classified and collected under appropriate headings. For example, all expenses incurred for administration and running the establishment are labelled 'administrative expenses', while expenses incurred for selling and delivery to customers are labelled 'distribution costs'. The cost of obtaining finance for the entity is entitled 'interest'.
● On the Balance Sheet:
  – the long-term finance available to the entity, in the form of capital contributed by the proprietor(s) plus any long-term loans, is identified as the 'capital employed'.
  – that portion of capital employed that is not tied down in fixed assets and is, therefore, available for day-to-day running of the business operations is identified as **working capital**, or 'net current assets'.

The formats of these financial statements, currently in use, are as follows:

TRADING AND PROFIT AND LOSS ACCOUNT FOR THE YEAR ENDED XX.XX.XXXX		
		£000
Sales		xxxxx
Opening stock	xxx	
Purchases	xxxxx	
Carriage inwards	xxx	
Less: Closing stock	(xx)	
Cost of goods sold		xxxxx
Gross profit		xxxx
Administrative expenses:		
Salaries and wages	xxxx	
Rent and rates	xxxx	(xxx)
Distribution cost:		
Advertising	xxxx	
Delivery expenses	xxxx	(xxx)
Operating profit		xxx
Exceptional items*	xx	
	xx	xx
Interest receivable		xx
Interest payable		(xx)
Profit for the year		xxxx

* 'Exceptional items' will be explained in Chapter 43.

BALANCE SHEET AS AT X.X.XXXX	Cost	Acc dep	£000
Fixed assets:			
Furniture and fittings	xxxx	(xxx)	xxxx
Motor vehicles	xxxx	(xxx)	xxxx
			xxxx
Current assets:			
Stock in trade		xxxx	
Trade debtors	xxx		
Provision for doubtful debt	(xx)	xxxx	
Cash and bank		xx	
Current liabilities:			
Trade creditors	xxxx		
Accrued expenses	xxx		
Bank overdraft	xxx	(xxx)	
Working Capital			xxxx
CAPITAL EMPLOYED			xxxxx
			£000
Capital		xxxxx	
Profit for the year		xxx	
Drawings		(xxx)	xxxxx
Loan			xxx
Capital employed			xxxxx

Focus on presentation of financial statements

Jill Grey operates the Town Shop on premises leased for ten years from 1.1.20X0, paying £200,000 for the period. The upper floors of the premises contain two flats. Jill occupies one and has let out the other for £250 per week.

She has also invested cash that is surplus to the immediate requirements of the shop in National Savings Certificates. The shop's Trial Balance is stated on the right. You are also informed as follows:

(a) Stock on 31 December 20X4 is £312,000. In addition, stationery costing £2,000 remains unused.

(b) Jill estimates that one-tenth of the cost of the lease may be allocated to each flat and she depreciates furniture at 5 per cent per year using the straight-line method.

(c) A debt of £8,000 is to be written off and the provision for doubtful debts adjusted to cover 10 per cent of the outstanding debts.

(d) Salary and electricity of £18,000 and £3,000 respectively remain unpaid as at 31.12.20X4.

(e) One-third of the cost of electricity and gas is to be recovered from Jill.

(f) Interest of £3,000 earned on the savings certificates is to be accounted for.

JILL GREY'S TOWN SHOP

TRIAL BALANCE AS AT 31.12.20X4

	£000	£000
Lease of shop premises	120	–
Furniture at cost	200	–
Depreciation to 31.12.20X3	–	28
Stock – 31.12.20X3	248	–
Sales	–	1,426
Investments	45	–
Electricity and gas	21	–
Rent received account	–	15
Postage and telephone	14	–
Purchases	987	–
Debtors and creditors	148	267
Salaries	302	–
Advertising	44	–
Stationery	16	–
Provision for doubtful debts	–	11
6% Loan from Jack Grey	–	300
Carriage inwards	24	–
Capital account	–	200
Cash and bank balance	78	–
	2,247	2,247

Required: Prepare the Trading and Profit and Loss account for the year ended 31.12.20X4 and the Balance Sheet as at that date.

11.5 FURTHER PERIOD-END ADJUSTMENTS

We will now consider two further period-end adjustments, namely those for accrued wages and deductions, and insurance claims on loss of stock. These are discussed in more detail in the following Subsections.

11.5.1 Accounting for accrued wages, salaries and pay-sheet recoveries

The amount paid at periodic intervals (weekly or monthly) to employees is referred to as wages (where the payment is to manual workers) or salaries (where the payment is to other staff). These, like payments for any other expense, are posted from the Cash account to appropriate expenditure accounts and written off, at the point of finalization, to the Trading and Profit and Loss account. Complications arise, however, because of the following:

● periodic payments to be made may include, in addition to the contracted amount, other amounts such as special allowances, overtime, bonus, holiday pay and amounts due under incentive schemes;

- staff loans may be recovered by deduction from pay;
- third parties may require the trading entity to act as their agent to deduct from the pay amounts due to them. Such third parties include:
  - the Department of Inland Revenue (which requires the recovery of income tax under the Pay as You Earn – PAYE – Scheme);
  - the Department of Social Security (which requires the recovery of National Insurance contributions);
- employees themselves may request amounts to be deducted from pay as their contribution to trade union or saving schemes.
- the employer is obliged also to make his own contribution to National Insurance.

To properly account for this expenditure, a Wages (or Salaries) Book should be prepared with appropriate columns to show the make-up of each pay packet, and detailing each addition and deduction. To illustrate, let us assume that the Wages Book of a business entity appears as follows:

WAGES BOOK FOR WEEK ENDING 6 MAY 20X1

	Basic pay	Overtime	Bonus	Gross wages	DEDUCATIONS				NET PAY
					PAYE	Nat. Ins.	Loan	Total	
	£	£	£	£	£	£	£	£	£
Louise Tolworth	420	60	–	480	(96)	(38)	(15)	(149)	331
A. Sothilingham	360	20	–	380	(72)	(30)	(25)	(127)	253
Senaka de Silva	540	40	20	600	(120)	(48)	(40)	(208)	392
G. Mamuya	380	30	–	410	(82)	(33)	(10)	(125)	285
	1,700	150	20	1,870	(370)	(149)	(90)	(609)	1,261

Let us assume also that the staff loan outstanding at the beginning of this week was £14,500 and that the entity is obliged to pay 10 per cent of gross wages as the employer's contribution to National Insurance. The accounting entries will be as follows:

(a) Net pay of £1,261 is posted from the Cash account to the Wages account. This is the amount that will be paid to the four members of staff.

(b) The total of £609 for deductions is debited to the Wages account (so that the expenditure is fully recorded in the Wages account at £1,870) and credited to the PAYE account, National Insurance account and Staff Loan account as £370, £149 and £90 respectively. The amounts so reported as owed in respect of PAYE (to the Inland Revenue) and National Insurance contribution (to the Department of Social Securities) will be reported as liabilities until, on appropriate dates, cheques are sent to settle these dues.

(c) The employer's contribution to National Insurance, calculated at 10 per cent of £1,870, is debited to the Wages account and credited to the National Insurance account.

(d) At the end of the year, the total of the Wages account will be transferred to the Trading and Profit and Loss account.

The relevant ledger accounts will appear as shown below:

WAGES ACCOUNT

	£		£
Cash a/c	1,261		
PAYE a/c	370		
Nat. Insurance a/c	149		
Staff Loan a/c	90		
Nat. Insurance a/c	187		

PAYE ACCOUNT

	£		£
		Wages a/c	370

NATIONAL INSURANCE ACCOUNT

	£		£
		Wages a/c	149
		Wages a/c	187

STAFF LOAN ACCOUNT

	£		£
Balance b/d	14,500	Wages a/c	90
		Balance c/d	14,410

Interaction 11.2

Accounting for deductions from pay

Wetherbury Carpet Store extracted its Trial Balance on the last day of its accounting period as stated here. You are also informed as follows:

(a) The manager was given a housing loan of £20,000 on 1.11.20X0. The loan is being recovered by deducting £400 per month from pay from November 20X0 onwards. The recoveries have not been accounted for.

(b) Staff salaries have been accounted for by posting to the expenditure account the net salary paid to staff.

(c) National Insurance contribution at 8 per cent of gross pay have been deducted on the pay sheet, and the employers' contribution is 10 per cent of gross pay.

Required: Prepare the Trading and Profit and Loss account for the year ended 31.3.20X1 and the Balance Sheet as at that date.

TRIAL BALANCE AS AT 31.3.20X1

	£000	£000
Fixed assets	660	238
Stock at 31.3.20X1	614	–
Staff salaries	320	–
Debtors/creditors	512	468
Other admin. expenses	486	–
Cost of sales	3,642	–
National insurance	56	–
Sales	–	4,990
Loan to Manager	20	
Distribution costs	263	–
Capital account	–	900
Cash and bank	23	–
	6,596	6,596

11.5.2 Accounting for insurance claims on loss of stock

We saw in Section 7.3 that the stock level at the end of an accounting period is accounted for by debiting the Stock in Trade account and crediting the Trading account – rather than either the Opening Stock account or the Purchases account. This is because of the uncertainty on whether the units remaining in hand are those left over from the preceding period or those purchased in the current period.

LOSS OF STOCK BY FIRE ACCOUNT

	£		£
Trading a/c	xxx		

LOSS OF STOCK BY FIRE ACCOUNT

	£		£
Trading a/c	xxx	Insurance Claim a/c	xx
		Profit and Loss a/c	xx

LOSS BY FIRE ACCOUNT

	£		£
Asset account	xxx	Provision for Depreciation a/c	xxx
		Profit and Loss a/c	xxx

LOSS BY FIRE ACCOUNT

	£		£
Asset account	xxx	Provision for Depreciation a/c	xx
Trading account	xxx	Insurance Claim a/c	xx
		Profit and Loss a/c	xx

The same situation applies when goods are lost by fire, theft or other ways. The cost of these goods is removed from the cost of goods sold, by crediting the Trading account and debiting a Loss of Goods account, as shown here.

In the event that the loss is covered by insurance, the amount of the loss recoverable under insurance is credited to the Loss of Goods account, while the remainder is written off to the Profit and Loss account.

If loss by fire is that of a fixed asset, accounting will be similar to disposal in other ways, as shown on the left.

If there were both a loss of fixed assets and of stock, and a part of that loss is recoverable under insurance, the Loss by Fire account would appear as shown on the left (bottom).

Interaction 11.3

Accounting for an insurance claim

A week prior to the extraction of the Trial Balance, on the last day of its accounting period, Knick Knacks had a fire that destroyed part of its stock and a vehicle that had been acquired for £60,000 on 1.1.X0. The insurance claim has been admitted at £95,000, but neither the loss nor the claim has been accounted for.

You are further informed as follows:

(a) Knick Knacks effects its sales consistently at cost plus 25 per cent.
(b) Motor vehicles and furniture are depreciated at 20 per cent and 10 per cent per annum by the straight-line method.
(c) Stock as at 30.6.20X2 was £7,000

TRIAL BALANCE AS AT 31.6.20X2		
	£000	£000
Motor vehicles	240	
Accumulated depreciation at 30.6.20X1		78
Furniture	280	
Accumulated depreciation at 30.6.20X1		99
Stock at 1.7.20X1	346	
Purchases	2,064	
Sales		2,870
Salaries	212	
Capital account		724
Advertising	28	
Rent and rates	32	
Other administrative expenses	264	
Debtors/creditors	420	243
Cash and bank	128	
	4,014	4,014

Required: Prepare the Trading and Profit and Loss account for the year ended 30 June 20X2 and the Balance Sheet as at that date.

11.6 COMMON DIFFICULTIES IN EXAMINATIONS

Students of accountancy often find it difficult to establish at what point the Trial Balance has been extracted. When, therefore, a Trial Balance is presented with a requirement to prepare financial statements, particular attention should be paid to determining *when* the Trial Balance figures were extracted and *what* the figures represent.

11.6.1 Determining when

A Trial Balance always states the date on which it was extracted from the books of account. However, it is unlikely to expressly identify the precise point in the accounting process that had been reached when the Trial Balance was extracted. That point will have to be inferred from the information contained in the Trial Balance.

For example, the Trial Balance might have been extracted from the books at the close of business on the last day of the accounting period, but it could be at any one of the following points in the accounting process:

- **Prior to making any year-end adjustments**: In this case the stock figure in the Trial Balance would be that for opening stock.
- **After making some or all of the period-end adjustments**: For example, if the Trial Balance includes a Depreciation account with a debit balance, this would establish that it is an expenditure for the current period and the corresponding asset has already been depreciated for the period. It does *not* follow, however, that all other accruals and prepayment adjustments have been made.
- **After determining the cost of sales** (by adding together the opening stock and the purchases and deducting closing stock): In this case there would be a debit for cost of sales in the Trial Balance and the stock figure would be that at the year end.
- **After determining the gross profit** (by offsetting the cost of sales from sales): In this case there would be an entry for gross profit in the Trial Balance and the stock figure would be that at the year end.

The precise point reached in the accounting process at which the Trial Balance has been extracted can only be inferred from the information contained within the Trial Balance.

11.6.2 Determining what

If the question lists accounting errors that have been made, the errors will clearly have affected the balances in one or more accounts. For example, if the Trial Balance reports the balance in the Motor Vehicles account as £264,000 and yet you are aware that £18,000 paid for servicing vehicles had been capitalized in error, it should be clear that the correct balance in the Motor Vehicles account prior to the commission of the error would have been £246,000. By transferring the cost of servicing (£18,000) from the asset account to the Motor Veh-

MOTOR VEHICLES ACCOUNT

	£		£
Balance b/f	246,000		
Cash account	18,000	Balance c/d	264,000
Balance b/d	264,000	M.V. Maintenance a/c	18,000
		Balance c/d	246,000

icle Maintenance account, the correct balance is restored to the asset account. (The shaded area in the account here in our example shows what happened prior to the extraction of the account balance as reported in the Trial Balance.)

MOTOR VEHICLES ACCOUNT

	£		£
Balance b/f	226,000		
Cash account	20,000		
Cash account	18,000	Balance c/d	264,000
Balance b/d	264,000	M.V. Maintenance a/c	18,000
		Balance c/d	246,000

If, in addition, you are presented with information that (for example) a vehicle was acquired halfway through a year for a sum of £20,000, the shaded area of the above account would have appeared as shown on the left. This clarifies that the trading entity had vehicles costing £226,000 at the commencement of the year. Hence depreciation has to be written off on vehicles costing £226,000 for the whole year and on one costing £20,000 for half of the year.

Interaction 11.4

The Trial Balance in perspective

Lombard Store's Trial Balance for 31.12.20X3 has been extracted as shown on the right. You are also informed as follows:

(a) On 1 July 20X3 the store acquired furniture for £60,000 and on 1 September 20X3 it acquired a vehicle for £90,000. A vehicle acquired for £30,000 on 1.5.20X0 was sold for £10,000 on 1.5.20X3. Apart from crediting the proceeds to the Motor Vehicles account, the disposal has not been accounted for.

(b) The store depreciates furniture and vehicles at 10 and 20 per cent per annum, respectively, using the straight-line method.

(c) Rent, agreed at £1,000 per month, has been paid in advance until 31 March 20X4, while rates are in arrears at the year end to the tune of £1,000.

TRIAL BALANCE AS AT 31.12.20X3		
	£000	£000
Motor vehicles	280	78
Furniture	360	144
Stock in trade	566	–
Salaries	184	–
Sales account	–	2,168
Rent and rates	18	–
Depreciation – furniture	33	–
Postage and telephone	24	–
Advertising	45	–
Carriage outwards	26	–
Debtors and creditors	404	296
Cost of sales	1,658	–
Capital account	–	950
Cash and bank	38	–
	3,636	3,636

Required: Determine, giving your reasons, the exact point in the accounting process at which the Trial Balance has been extracted. In addition, you must prepare the Trading and Profit and Loss account for the year to 31.12.20X3 and the Balance Sheet as at that date.

11.7 THE EXTENDED TRIAL BALANCE

The use of an extended Trial Balance is a convenient method of recording adjustments when preparing the financial statements without losing sight of the double entry principle. This method is particularly appropriate when computer spreadsheets are used for preparing financial statements. Let us illustrate the method.

Julian Morely extracted a Trial Balance from the books of his retail shop, as stated on the right, on the last day of his accounting period. He informs you further as follows:

(a) Stock at 31.12.20X1 is £324,000.
(b) Shop premises have been rented at £2,000 per month.
(c) Salaries and audit fees, amounting to £12,000 and £4,000 respectively, remain unpaid by the year end.
(d) A trade debt of £14,000 is to be written off and the provision for doubtful debts adjusted to cover 10 per cent of debts outstanding by the year end.
(e) Fixed assets are to be depreciated at 10 per cent per annum using the straight-line method.

TRIAL BALANCE AS AT 31.12.20X1		
	£000	£000
Fixed assets	720	–
Acc.depreciation	–	288
Stock 31.12.20X0	264	–
Salaries	186	–
Rent	27	–
Debtors/Creditors	354	268
Purchases	1,256	–
Sales	–	1,952
Stationery	16	–
Advertising	48	–
Telephone/postage	26	–
Provision for doubtful debt	–	22
Cash and bank	33	–
Capital account	–	400
	2,930	2,930

An extended Trial Balance with the year-end adjustments, together with the Profit and Loss account for the year ended 31 December 20X1 and the Balance Sheet as at that date, would appear as follows:

JULIAN MORELY

TRIAL BALANCE AS AT 31.12.20X1			Year-end Adjustments			Adjusted Trial Balance		Trading and Profit and Loss account		Balance Sheet	
	£000	£000	£000	£000		£000	£000	£000	£000	£000	£000
Fixed assets	720	–	–	–		720	–	–	–	720	–
Accumulated depreciation	–	288	–	72	E	–	360	–	–	–	360
Stock at 31.12.20X0	264	–	–	264	A	–	–	–	–	–	–
Salaries	186	–	12	–	C	198	–	198	–	–	–
Rent	27	–	–	3	B	24	–	24	–	–	–
Debtors	354	–	–	14	D	340	–	–	–	340	–
Creditors	–	268	–	–		–	268	–	–	–	268
Purchases	1,256	–	–	1,256	A	–	–	–	–	–	–
Sales	–	1,952	–	–		–	1,952	–	1,952	–	–
Stationery	16	–	–	–		16	–	16	–	–	–
Advertising	48	–	–	–		48	–	48	–	–	–
Telephone/postage	26	–	–	–		26	–	26	–	–	–
Provision for doubtful debt	–	22	–	12	D	–	34	–	–	–	34
Cash and bank	33	–	–	–		33	–	–	–	33	–
Capital account	–	400	–	–		–	400	–	–	–	400
Cost of sales			1,196	–	A	1,196	–	1,196	–	–	–
Stock at 31.12.20X1			324	–	A	324	–	–	–	324	–
Prepaid rent			3	–	B	3	–	–	–	3	–
Audit fees			4	–	C	4	–	4	–	–	–
Accrued expenses			–	16	C	–	16	–	–	–	16
Bad debts			26	–	D	26	–	26	–	–	–
Depreciation			72	–	E	72	–	72	–	–	–
Profit for the year			–	–		–	–	342	–	–	342
	2,930	2,930	1,637	1,637		3,030	3,030	1,942	1,942	1,420	1,420

Notes:

A: The balances in the Opening Stock account and the Purchases account, net of the amount capitalized as the closing stock, are the cost of goods sold in the year, namely £1,196,000 made up of £264,000 + £1,256,000 − £324,000.

B: Since rent is agreed at £24,000 for the year, the prepaid portion is capitalized.

C: Unpaid salaries and audit fees are accounted for as accrued expenses (liabilities).

D: A debt of £14,000 is written off and the provision for doubtful debts is increased by £12,000 to cover 10 per cent of the debtors outstanding at the year end.

E: Depreciation is written off at 10 per cent of the cost of fixed assets.

F: Every item in the adjusted Trial Balance is slotted into either the Profit and Loss account or the Balance Sheet.

G: The difference between sales income and all the expenses is the year's net profit, which is transferred to the Balance Sheet to be shown as an addition to the Capital account.

The Debit and Credit columns are checked at each stage to ensure that the double entry principle is being observed, i.e. Trial Balance totals, Adjustment totals, Adjusted Trial Balance totals, the Profit and Loss account and the Balance Sheet.

SOLUTIONS TO INTERACTIVE QUESTIONS

IQ 11.1 Focus on presentation of financial statements

A lease is an example of an **intangible asset**. An intangible asset is one that does not have a corporeal existence and cannot therefore be seen or touched. Depreciation of an intangible asset is usually called **amortization**. The cost of the lease is amortized equally over its ten-year lifespan at £20,000 per year. A tenth of this amount is regarded as the expenditure directly relating to the rental income and is therefore reported as an offset from that income. Another tenth relates to the flat occupied by Jill and is therefore transferred to the Drawings account.

At £250 per week, rental earnings from the flat are £13,000 for the year. The extra £2,000 received as rent (for £15,000 is shown in the Trial Balance) must relate to the next accounting year and should therefore be identified as deferred income. The £2,000 could be transferred from the Rental Income account to a Deferred Income account at the end of the period and the entries reversed on the first day of the next period. However, instead of opening a separate Deferred Income account, £2,000 may simply be carried down as a credit balance in the Rental Income account because by next year this amount would be regarded as income.

Similarly, the unpaid portion of electricity, debited to the expenditure account, is carried down in the same account (instead of opening a separate liability account), as a credit balance that is reported as a liability on the Balance Sheet. One-third of the cost of electricity and gas is also transferred to the Drawings account. The total of expenses remaining unpaid (in respect of both salaries and electricity) is referred together on the Balance Sheet as 'accrued expenses', which merely means expenses owed on that date.

An amount of £8,000 from the Debtors account is written off against the Provision for Doubtful Debts account; and to adjust the balance in the Provision account to £14,000 it becomes necessary to charge £11,000 as a bad debt to the Profit and Loss account.

Carriage inwards, being part of the cost of placing the goods sold in the location from which they were sold, is counted within the cost of goods sold.

Taking all the given information, plus the foregoing inferences, into account, the various accounts for Jill Grey's Town Shop are as set out below.

LEASE OF SHOP PREMISES ACCOUNT

	£		£
Balance b/f	120,000	Amortization	20,000
		Balance c/d	100,000
Balance b/d	100,000		

AMORTIZATION OF LEASE ACCOUNT

	£		£
Lease a/c	20,000	Expenditure on letting	2,000
		Drawings a/c	2,000
		Profit and Loss a/c	16,000

RENT RECEIVED ACCOUNT

	£		£
Profit and Loss a/c	13,000	Balance b/f	15,000
Balance c/d	2,000		
		Balance b/d	2,000

ELECTRICITY AND GAS ACCOUNT

	£		£
Balance b/f	21,000	Drawings a/c	8,000
Balance c/d	3,000	Profit and Loss account	16,000
		Balance b/d	3,000

DEBTORS ACCOUNT

	£		£
Balance b/f	148,000	Prov. for doubt	8,000
		Balance c/d	140,000
Balance b/d	140,000		

PROVISION FOR DOUBTFUL DEBTS ACCOUNT

	£		£
Debtors a/c	8,000	Balance b/f	11,000
Balance c/d	14,000	Profit and Loss a/c	11,000
		Balance b/d	14,000

JILL GREY'S TOWN SHOP

TRADING AND PROFIT AND LOSS ACCOUNT FOR THE YEAR ENDED 31.12.20X4

		£000
Sales		1,426
Stock – 1.1.20X4	248	
Purchases	987	
Carriage inwards	24	
Stock – 31.12.20X4	(312)	
Cost of goods sold		(947)
Gross profit		479
Administrative expenses:		
Salaries	320	
Electricity and gas	16	
Amortization – lease	16	
Stationery	14	
Depreciation – Furniture	10	
Postage and telephone	14	(390)
Distribution cost:		
Advertising	44	
Bad debts	11	(55)
Operating profit		34
Rent receivable	13	
Letting expenses	(2)	11
Interest receivable		3
Interest payable		(18)
Profit for the year		30

BALANCE SHEET AS AT 31.12.20X4

	Cost	Acc depn	£000
Fixed assets:			
Lease of premises			100
Furniture	200	(38)	162
Current assets:			262
Stock in trade		312	
Debtors	140		
Provn for doubtful debt	(14)	126	
Stock of stationery		2	
Interest receivable		3	
Investments		45	
Cash and bank		78	
		566	
Current liabilities:			
Creditors	267		
Deferred income	2		
Accrued expenses	21		
Interest payable	18	(308)	
Working Capital			258
CAPITAL EMPLOYED			520

		£000
Capital	200	
Profit for the year	30	
Drawings – Amortisation	(2)	
Electricity/gas	(8)	220
6% Loan		300
CAPITAL EMPLOYED		520

IQ 11.2 Accounting for deductions from pay

Loan recoveries on the pay sheet, of £400 per month over five months, are credited to the Staff Loan account and debited to the Salaries account.

Salaries paid, net of National Insurance recovery from staff members at 8 per cent, amounted to £322,000. Hence the amount recovered was [£322,000 × 8/(100 − 8)] = £28,000. This amount is accounted for by crediting the National Insurance account (liability) and debiting the Salaries account (expenditure). The employer's contribution, at 10 per cent of gross salaries (10% × £350,000 = £35,000), is accounted for by crediting the National Insurance account (liability) and debiting the Salaries account.

SALARIES ACCOUNT

	£000		£000
Balance b/f	320	Profit and Loss a/c	385
Staff Loan a/c	2		
National Insurance a/c	28		
National Insurance a/c	35		

STAFF LOAN ACCOUNT

	£000		£000
Balance b/f	20	Salaries a/c	2
		Balance c/d	18
Balance b/d	18		

NATIONAL INSURANCE ACCOUNT

	£000		£000
Balance b/f	56	Salaries a/c	28
Balance c/d	7	Salaries a/c	35
		Balance b/d	7

WETHERBURY CARPET STORE

TRADING AND PROFIT AND LOSS ACCOUNT FOR THE YEAR ENDED 31.3.20X1

		£000
Sales		4,990
Cost of goods sold		(3,642)
Gross profit		1,548
Administrative expenses:		
Salaries	385	
Other administrative expenses	486	(871)
Distribution costs		(263)
Profit for the year		214

BALANCE SHEET AS AT 31.3.20X1

	Cost	Acc depn	£000
Fixed assets:			
Furniture	660	(238)	422
Current assets:			
Stock in trade		614	
Debtors		512	
Staff loan		18	
Cash and bank		23	
Current liabilities:			
Creditors	468		
National Insurance	7	(475)	692
			1,114

	£000
Capital	900
Profit for the year	214
	1,114

IQ 11.3 Accounting for insurance claims on loss of stock

MOTOR VEHICLES ACCOUNT

	£000		£000
Balance b/f	240	Loss by fire	60
		Balance c/d	180
Balance b/d	180		

PROVISION FOR DEPRECIATION ACCOUNT

	£000		£000
Loss by fire	30	Balance b/f	78
Balance c/d	96	Depreciation	48
		Balance b/d	96

LOSS BY FIRE ACCOUNT

	£000		£000
Motor vehicle	60	Prov. for deprec[a]	30
Trading a/c	107	Insurance claim	95
		Profit and Loss – loss	42

a. The vehicle destroyed by fire would have been depreciated at 20% of £60,000 for two-and-a-half years.

b. Cost of stock lost by fire is the balancing figure in the Trading account.

KNICK KNACKS

TRADING AND PROFIT AND LOSS ACCOUNT FOR THE YEAR ENDED 30.6.20X2

		£000
Sales		2,870
Stock at 1.7.20X1	346	
Purchases	2,064	
Loss by fire[b]	(107)	
Stock at 30.6.20X2	(7)	(2,296)
Gross profit		574
Administrative expenses:		
Salaries	212	
Rent	32	
Depreciation – furniture	28	
Loss by fire	42	
Other administrative expenses	264	(578)
Distribution cost:		
Advertising	28	
Depreciation – vehicles	48	(76)
Loss for the year		(80)

BALANCE SHEET AS AT 30.6.20X2

	Cost	Acc. depn	£000
Fixed assets:			
Furniture	280	(127)	153
Motor vehicles	180	(96)	84
Current assets:			
Stock in trade		7	
Debtors		420	
Insurance claim		95	
Cash and bank		128	
Creditors		(243)	407
			644

	£000
Capital	724
Loss for the year	(80)
	644

IQ 11.4 The Trial Balance in perspective

The Trial Balance has been extracted on the last day of the accounting period after making some – but not all – of the year-end adjustments. In particular:

- The 'cost of sales' included in the Trial Balance would have been arrived at by adding the opening stock and the purchases and deducting the closing stock. This means that the stock included in the Trial Balance is the closing stock.
- Depreciation on the Furniture account appears on the Trial Balance with a debit balance. This means that furniture has been already depreciated for the year, but not motor vehicles.

- The Trial Balance can be seen to have been extracted before capitalizing prepaid rent (because the prepaid rent is not reported on it as an asset) and before accruing for unpaid rates (because the amount of rates in arrears is not reported on it as a liability).

MOTOR VEHICLES ACCOUNT

		£000		£000	
1	Balance b/f	200	Cash – disposal	10	1
1	Cash – acquisition	90	Balance c/d	280	
	Balance b/d	280	Disposal a/c	30	2
2	Disposal a/c	10	Balance c/d	260	
	Balance b/d	260			

PROVISION FOR DEPRECIATION ACCOUNT

			£000		£000	
2	Disposal a/c		18	Balance b/f	78	
				Depreciation	2	2
	Balance c/d		108	Depreciation	46	3
				Balance b/d	108	

RENT AND RATES ACCOUNT

		£000		£000	
	Balance b/f	18	Profit and Loss	16	
4	Balance c/d	1	Balance c/d	3	4
4	Balance b/d	3	Balance b/d	1	4

DISPOSAL OF MOTOR VEHICLE ACCOUNT

		£000		£000	
2	Motor Vehicle a/c	30	Provision for Depreciation a/c	18	2
			Motor vehicle a/c	10	2
			Profit and Loss a/c – Loss a/c	2	

Notes:

1. The Motor Vehicle account balance (£280,000) stated in the Trial Balance is after crediting that account incorrectly with the proceeds on disposal of a vehicle. Taking into account the vehicle acquired on 1 September for £90,000, the balance in that account at the commencement of the accounting year is calculated (as the balancing figure) at £200,000.
2. To account for the disposal of the vehicle, three steps are necessary, as follows:
   - STEP ONE: Depreciate the vehicle for the period that it was used in the year of disposal. The depreciation is at 20% of £30,000 for four months, amounting to £2,000.
   - STEP TWO: Transfer to a Disposal of Vehicle account the cost of the vehicle sold (£30,000) from the asset account, and transfer the accumulated provision on it (20% of £30,000 for three years = £18,000) from the supporting account.
   - STEP THREE: Transfer the proceeds of disposal (£10,000) from the Motor Vehicle account to the Disposal account to ascertain the gain or loss arising from the disposal.
3. Depreciation on other vehicles is 20% of £200,000 plus 20% of £90,000 for four months only.
4. The prepaid portion of rent (£3,000) could have been transferred to an asset account named Prepaid Rent. But in the next year the amount has to be expensed and therefore transferred back to the Rent account. It would be simpler to carry down the prepaid portion as a debit balance in the Rent account, while taking care to report the amount as an asset on the year-end Balance Sheet. For identical reasons, the unpaid portion of rates (£1,000) is carried down as a credit balance in the expenditure account and reported on the Balance Sheet as a liability.

LOMBARD STORES

TRADING AND PROFIT AND LOSS ACCOUNT FOR THE YEAR ENDED 31.12.20X3		
		£000
Sales		2,168
Cost of sales		(1,658)
Gross profit		510
Administrative expenses:		
Salaries	(184)	
Rent and rates	(16)	
Depreciation – furniture	(33)	
Postage and telephone	(24)	
Loss on disposal	(2)	(259)
Distribution cost:		
Advertising	(45)	
Carriage outwards	(26)	
Depreciation – vehicles	(48)	(119)
Profit for the year		132

BALANCE SHEET AS AT 31.12.20X3			
	Cost	Acc. depn	£000
Fixed assets:			
Furniture	360	(144)	216
Motor vehicles	260	(108)	152
Current assets:			368
Stock in trade		566	
Debtors		404	
Prepaid rent		3	
Cash and bank		38	
Current liabilities:			
Creditors	(296)		
Rates accrued	(1)	(297)	714
			1,082
			£000
Capital account			950
Profit for the year			132
			1,082

PROGRESSIVE QUESTIONS

PQ 11.1 An account and the side of its balance

The qualified accountant employed by Jim Hill to write up the books of account in his retail shop resigned the post after writing up the books until the year end on 31 December 20X1. Jim, who is not conversant with the double entry system, extracted the Trial Balance from the books as shown here. You are assured that all information from the books is included, although every balance may not appear on the side it should. You are further informed as follows:

(a) Stock at 31.12. 20X1 was £38,400.
(b) Expenses unpaid as at 31.12.20X1 are as stated in the box.

Salaries	£3,200
Advertising	£800
Telephone	£900

(c) Rent for the premises is £1,000 per month.
(d) Vehicles are depreciated at 20 per cent per year on cost.
(e) A trade debt of £400 is to be written off and the provision set up at 5 per cent of debts.
(f) Employees have been promised one-third of the net profit as bonus.

Required: Redraft the Trial Balance as at 31.12.20X1, and prepare in vertical format and in good style the Trading and Profit and Loss account for the year ended 31.12.20X1 and the Balance Sheet as at that date.

TRIAL BALANCE AS AT 31.12.20X1

	£	£
Purchases	210,400	–
Stock on 31.12.20X0	29,600	–
Trade debtors	46,400	–
Sales	–	306,800
Rent	15,500	
Discount allowed	–	2,400
Sales returns	–	5,200
Salaries	16,400	–
Advertising	–	6,850
Stationery	–	2,650
Capital	30,000	–
Discount received	–	2,100
Postage and telephone	–	950
Motor vehicles	24,000	–
Accum. deprn on vehicles	–	8,000
Drawings	–	2,500
Cash and bank balance	800	–
Staff welfare expense	–	6,100
Trade creditors	–	26,200
Light and heat	–	3,350
	373,100	373,100

PQ 11.2 Personal accounts and their balances

City Electronics has a personal account in its ledger for every one of the following parties:

Jeremy Holden	who owes £14,600 for goods sold to him.
Sony Rickman	to whom £16,200 is owed in respect of goods purchased.
Mike Johnson	to whom £4,000 is owed as rent on the business premises.
London Electricity	to whom £240 is owed in respect of the electricity used in the previous quarter.
Nancy Shaw	who still owes £2,400 of the sum of £4,000 loaned to her.
Tim Morely	who owes £400 as rent for part of the office premises occupied by him.
City Bank	which is owed £60,000 as a loan and £18,000 as interest accrued on it.
London Truckers	with whom a deposit of £5,000 is left for providing trucking services.

Required:

(a) State on which side of each party's personal account the balance will be reported.
(b) Identify which of the following categories each of these parties falls into:

Expense creditors	*Trade creditors*	*Loan creditors*
Prepayments	*Trade debtors*	*Loan debtors*

PQ 11.3 A Trial Balance after all period-end adjustments

On 31 March 20X2, the last day of his accounting period, Cecil Morgan extracted from the books of his retail shop the balances shown here, other than that in the Capital account. You are also informed as follows:

LIST OF BALANCES ON 31.3.20X2	
	£000
Cash in hand	37
Trade debtors	212
Trade creditors	186
Land and building at cost	900
Provision for depreciation on building	96
Furniture and fittings	80
Provision for depreciation on furniture	32
Motor vehicles	160
Provision for depre on vehicles	48
Rent paid	30
Rent received from tenant	18
Sundry expenses	31
Salaries	96
Sales	2,146
Stock on 31.3.20X1	232
Advertising	43
Electricity	21
Return inwards	32
Return outwards	18
Provision for doubtful debt	26
Purchases	1,468
Loan from Investment bank	150
Heating	7
Drawings	19

(a) Stock in hand on 31.3.20X2 was £280,000.
(b) Cecil owns the premises used as sales outlets, but the one used as headquarters is rented at £3,000 per month. A flat on the upper floor of the rented premises has been sublet at £1,000 per month. £24,000 was received as rent in advance from the subtenant on 1.10.20X0.
(c) A cheque for £14,000, received in respect of a debt written off two years earlier, was posted from the cash book to the Sales account.
(d) Expenses remaining unpaid on 31.3.20X2 are as stated in the box on the right.

	£000
Salaries	24
Electricity	3
Sundry expenses	4

(e) A trade debt of £12,000 is to be written off and the provision adjusted to cover 10 per cent of debtors outstanding as at 31 March 20X2.
(f) Assuming that one-third of the cost relates to land, Cecil depreciates his assets by the straight-line method at the rates stated in the box on the right.

Buildings	2%
Motor vehicles	20%
Furniture	10%

(g) Interest is payable on the bank loan at 8 per cent p.a.
(h) Goods costing £2,000 removed by Cecil for personal use are still to be accounted for.

Required: Prepare a Trial Balance for the shop as at 31 March 20X2, after making all year-end adjustments, including the determination of the cost of goods sold in the year. In addition, set out the Trading and Profit and Loss account of the shop for the year ended 31 March 20X2 and the Balance Sheet as at that date.

PQ 11.4 Accounting for deductions from pay and an insurance claim

Raybens retails all items at cost plus a third. It employs 26 employees and maintains proper pay sheets, which have been summarized for the year ended 30.4.20X1 as follows:

Basic salary	London weighting	Overtime payments	National Insurance	Income tax PAYE	Staff loan recovery	Net pay
£246,400	£32,900	£20,700	(£24,000)	(£72,000)	(£38,000)	£166,000

The employer's contribution to National Insurance is fixed at 10 per cent of gross staff pay. Part of the stock was destroyed in a fire in March 20X1, and a payment of £27,000 was received under an insurance claim. You are further informed as follows:

(a) An inventory taken on 6.5.20X1 revealed stock in hand as £126,000. Within the six days after 30 April 20X1 the following transactions took place:
  – Sales £42,000
  – Purchases £17,000
  – Return inwards £2,000
  – Return outwards £3,000
(b) Premises have been rented at £3,000 per month. Bill Seymour, who owns Raybens, occupies a part of these premises. One-third of the rent and one-fifth of electricity costs are to be recovered from Bill.
(c) £56,000 realized on 1.10.20X0 on disposal of a vehicle acquired on 1.1.20X0 for £60,000 was credited to the Sales account.
(d) £5,000 due from a customer is to be written off and the provision adjusted to cover 5 per cent of amounts receivable from customers.
(e) Vehicles and furniture are to be depreciated at 20 per cent and 10 per cent respectively per annum by the straight-line method.

TRIAL BALANCE AS AT 30.4.20X1		
	£000	£000
Debtors	665	312
Stock on 30.4.20X0	234	–
Rent account	30	–
Electricity	15	–
Salary	166	–
Carriage inwards	64	–
Duty on goods imported	32	–
Purchases	1,648	–
Sales	–	2,468
Return inwards	12	–
Staff loan	126	–
Carriage outwards	26	–
Insurance claim	–	27
Discounts allowed	10	–
Motor vehicles	460	–
Depreciation – vehicles	–	117
Furniture	220	–
Depreciation – furniture	–	42
Provision for doubtful debt	–	16
PAYE remittances	60	–
National Insurance paid	49	–
Capital account	–	883
Cash and bank balance	48	–
	3,865	3,865

Required: Prepare the Profit and Loss account for the year ended 30 April 20X1 and the Balance Sheet as at that date.

PQ 11.5 Asset disposal, trade-in and remaining in use after write-off

The Trial Balance extracted from the books of Rushme appears as shown on the following page. You are further informed as follows:

(a) Stock in trade on 31.12.20X3 was £264,000.
(b) Machinery, acquired for £88,000 ten years earlier, was scrapped in the year but continues to be reported as an asset.
(c) For the purpose of significantly enhancing the fuel efficiency of a machine acquired for £180,000 on 1.7.20X0, a new motor was fitted on 1.7.20X3 at a cost of £40,000. The cost has been posted to the Machinery Maintenance account. The amount should be capitalized as an enhancement cost.

(d) New furniture was acquired on 1.5.20X3 for £30,000.

(e) £18,000 paid as an annual charge for servicing vehicles has been posted to the Motor Vehicles account.

(f) An articulated lorry was acquired on 1 July 20X3, trading in another acquired for £60,000 on 1.1.20X0, and paying £32,000 as the difference in the value of the two vehicles. The only accounting entry made of this transaction is the posting of £32,000 from the Cash account to the Motor Vehicles account.

(g) Rushme depreciates its fixed assets on the straight-line method at the following annual rates:
- Machinery: 12.5%
- Furniture: 10%
- Motor vehicles: 20%

(h) Assets continuing in use include machinery acquired for £80,000 nine years earlier and furniture acquired for £60,000 twelve years earlier.

TRIAL BALANCE AS AT 31.12.20X3		
	£000	£000
Furniture at cost	280	–
Provision for depreciation of furniture	–	63
Motor vehicles at cost	420	–
Provision for depreciation of vehicles	–	64
Machinery at cost	560	–
Provision for depreciation of machinery	–	312
Stock – 31.12.20X2	144	–
Advertising	16	–
Sales	–	968
Cash and bank balance	49	–
Salaries	126	–
Purchases	524	–
Trade investments	115	–
Dividend received	–	12
Rent	36	–
Postage and telephone	12	–
Staff welfare	17	–
Debtors and Creditors	116	162
Sales commissions	14	–
Discount received	–	29
Machine maintenance	54	–
Bad debts	6	–
Vehicle maintenance	11	–
Capital	–	900
Other expenses	10	–
	2,510	2,510

Required: Prepare the Trading and Profit and Loss account for the year ended 31 December 20X3 and the Balance Sheet as at that date.

Chapter 12

ACCOUNTING USING SPREADSHEETS

In this chapter

- We will learn how spreadsheets could assist in the bookkeeping function
- and you should be able to account by using a spreadsheet

12.1 INTRODUCTION

Writing up books of account manually – as it has been done for centuries – is undoubtedly tedious and error-prone. This prompts many to invest in a personal computer to automate the bookkeeping function. This can be done in one of two ways. One is to use what has become known as a spreadsheet to take the place of the cash book and other summaries that would otherwise have been written up in books. The other and more sophisticated way is to delegate the accounting function to a specially designed software application. This chapter explores how spreadsheets can assist in the bookkeeping function.

Spreadsheets were invented in the late 1970s in the early days of the development of the microcomputer. The first spreadsheet was called VISICALC, which was used on Apple and Commodore computers prior to IBM introducing the PC in 1981. Very soon after the introduction of the IBM PC, a new spreadsheet called LOTUS 1-2-3 was introduced. It was very similar to VISICALC in its mode of operation and the commands it used, but it allowed larger spreadsheets to be developed and it had a greater range of commands. LOTUS 1-2-3 continues to be used (Lotus now being owned by IBM) and other spreadsheets have been developed by competitors, the best known being EXCEL. We will use the EXCEL format.

12.2 FORMAT OF A SPREADSHEET

A spreadsheet is the computer equivalent of a very large sheet of analysis paper with rows and columns marked out to form a grid (see on right). Each opening in the grid (in which a narrative or an amount can be inserted) is known as a 'cell' and each cell is given an 'address', which is determined by the row and the column in which that cell is situated. For example, the address of the cell in row 8 of column D would be D8 (shaded). The width of the cell and the number of rows and columns can be adjusted.

A large variety of tasks can be performed using a spreadsheet and the range of commands available is too great to be included in this text. The common tasks performed by a spreadsheet include the following:

	A	B	C	D	E
1					
2					
3					
4					
5					
6					
7					
8					

- summing amounts stated in cells identified by a command (or formula);
- proving the accuracy of a set of figures by checking whether their total matches that of another set;
- transferring individual amounts, totals or texts to another area of the spreadsheet;
- recalculating totals (and differences) instantaneously when an amount stated in a row or a column is added to, deleted or altered.

The main inputs that an accountant would make in a spreadsheet include narrative (e.g. sales, salary, rent, vehicles) and numeric data (e.g. 8,000). This data can be manipulated using commands. The main commands an accountant would use in a spreadsheet include the arithmetical commands such as to add, deduct, multiply or divide and to transfer a text, an amount or a command from one cell to another. The command formula would differ, depending on the version of spreadsheet being used, but by and large the formula operates as follows:

- **=Sum(B34+B35)**: the amounts stated in the identified cells (B34 and B35) are added together.
- **=Sum(B34−B35)**: the amount in the latter (B35) is deducted from that in the former (B34).
- **=Sum(B5:B34)**: the amounts in all cells from B5 to B34 are added together.
- **=C5**: the amount, narrative or a command stated in cell C5 is transferred.

Usually the summation symbol appears on the top panel of the EXCEL program. Having moved the cursor down to the appropriate cell, a click on that symbol would produce the formula in the cell. All that is then necessary is to make any adjustment to the formula and press enter.

The accountant can design the output from a spreadsheet exactly as on a manual report. This process requires planning the outline report, entering the formula referencing through to the input, and calculating the report output.

12.2.1 Illustration of inputs and commands

An accountant transferring balances manually from the ledgers into a spreadsheet would wish to check whether the total of debit entries equals the total of credit entries. This is shown in the following example:

Step (1): Enter the narratives in rows as:

Row/Column	A	B	C
1	Sales		
2	Cost of sales		
3	Expenses		
4	Capital		
5	Drawings		
6	Cash at bank		
7	Total		
8	Difference		

Step (2): Enter the amounts in columns B and C, using B cells for debits and C for credits:

Row/Column	A	B	C
1	Sales	−	8,000
2	Cost of sales	3,500	−
3	Expenses	1,400	−
4	Capital	−	5,000
5	Drawings	2,600	−
6	Cash at bank	5,500	−
7	Total		
8	Difference		

Step (3): Get the spreadsheet to total the amounts in each column by stating a formula in appropriate cells (i.e. in cell B7 for debits and C7 for credits). The formula is: =**Sum(B2:B6)** for debit balances. If you try this example on a PC, move down to cell B7 and click on the summation symbol on the top panel of the computer screen. The formula =**Sum(BX:BX)** would appear in the cell. Amend the formula as necessary and press enter to produce the position shown on the right.

Row/Column	A	B	C
1	Sales	–	8,000
2	Cost of sales	3,500	–
3	Expenses	1,400	–
4	Capital	–	5,000
5	Drawings	2,600	–
6	Cash at bank	5,500	–
7	Total	13,000	13,000
8	Difference		

Step (4): Get the spreadsheet to check whether the debits equal the credits. This is done by stating in cell C8 the formula =**Sum(B7–C7)**. If the answer is zero (as it is on the right) the totals agree. If not, as every amount in each cell is checked for error and correction made, the spreadsheet keeps automatically adjusting the totals as well as the difference. The correction process will have to continue until the difference becomes zero and you are satisfied that no more errors exist.

	A	B	C
1	Sales		8,000
2	Cost of sales	3,500	
3	Expenses	1,400	
4	Capital		5,000
5	Drawings	2,600	
6	Cash at bank	5,500	
7	Total	13,000	13,000
8	Difference		0

12.3 DESIGNING A FINANCIAL REPORT

To produce a Profit and Loss account and a Balance Sheet using the amounts entered in a spreadsheet, we proceed as follows (assuming there is no stock, accruals or prepayments):

Step (1): Enter the narratives

PROFIT AND LOSS ACCOUNT

	A	B	C
21	Sales		
22	Cost of sales		
23	Gross profit		
24	Expenses		
25	Profit		

We need not really type in 'sales' in cell A21; since the word 'sales' would already have been entered in cell A1, if we instead type in =**A1** in cell A21 and press enter, the spreadsheet does the entering.

Step (2): Enter the appropriate formula in column B

	A	B	C
21	Sales	=C1	
22	Cost of sales	=B2	
23	Gross profit	=Sum(B21–B22)	
24	Expenses	=B3	
25	Profit	=Sum(B23–B24)	

The formula for stating the amount in cell B21 is to type in =**C1**, and =**B2** in cell B22. But in cell B23 the formula should instruct that the amount in B22 should be deducted from that in B21 and in cell B25 that the amount in cell B24 should be deducted from that in cell B23.

Step (3): Prepare the required report, as shown on the right
An important feature in EXCEL is that the formula (stated in
B21 to B25) can be protected from being tampered with by
others. This facilitates production of routine reports (such as
Profit and Loss accounts at, say, monthly intervals) with
minimum effort.

	A	B	C
26	Sales	8,000	
27	Cost of sales	3,500	
28	Gross profit	4,500	
29	Expenses	1,400	
30	Profit	3,100	

Interaction 12.1

Preparing a Balance Sheet using a spreadsheet

Required: Prepare a Balance Sheet (starting in cell A31) from the figures in the Trial Balance
stated in step (4) of Section 12.2.1 following the three following steps: (a) Enter the narrative
(b) Enter the formulae (c) Calculate the output.

12.3.1 Spreadsheet used for writing up a Cash account

A spreadsheet can be produced for the majority of exercises that appear in this book. For
example, we could produce a spreadsheet for a Cash account exercise such as the one
that we undertook manually for Andy Small in Chapter 2. See (a)–(c) following.

(a) The cash transactions for the first week.

Andy Small requests you to take charge of a new shop that he is equipping to sell
portable telephones. The product to be sold is a standard model costing £100 and
selling at £150. Trading commences on 1 January 20X0. The cash transactions during
the first week of business are as follows:

Date	£	Date	£
1.1 Received as capital from Small	5,000	3.1 Paid for staff tea	18
Acquired as fixed assets for		Purchased 25 portable telephones	?
office use:		Paid for a rubber stamp	15
A wooden desk	125	Paid for advertising	40
A steel filing cabinet	85	Sold 24 portable telephones	?
Four wooden chairs	120	Paid the office telephone bill	60
Purchased ten portable telephones		4.1 Paid for advertising	125
for sale	?	Paid for postage stamps	15
Paid for advertising	60	Sold 11 portable telephones	?
Sold two portable telephones	?	Received from staff (for a personal call)	11
Paid for stationery as follows:		Purchased 15 portable telephones	?
Pads of A4 papers	10	5.1 Paid as staff salary	780
Ball point pens	5	Purchased ten portable telephones	?
Rulers and correcting fluid	6	Paid for staff tea	10
A cash book	15	Repaid to Jim in part settlement	
2.1 Received as a loan from Jim Jones	1,500	of loan	300
Purchased 24 portable telephones	?	Paid for advertising	130
Paid for staff teas	12	Sold all portable telephones in hand	?
Paid for an electric typewriter	300		
Paid for typewriter ribbons	4		
Sold 12 portable telephones	?		

Required: Enter the receipts and payments into the cash book spreadsheet

(b) A skeleton EXCEL spreadsheet (known as a 'template') is prepared, with formulae to calculate the total receipts, total payments and the closing balance.

1	A	B	C	D	E	F	G	H	I	J
2					CASH ACCOUNT					
3	Date	Voucher	Particulars	Folio	Amount	Date	Voucher	Particulars	Folio	Amount
4	20X0				£	20X0				£
5										
6										
7										
8										
9										
10										
11										
12										
13										
14										
15										
16										
17										
18										
19										
20										
21										
22										
23										
24										
25									Note 2	0
26						05 Jan		Balance c/d	Note 4	0
27			TOTAL	Note 1	0			TOTAL	Note 3	0
28	06 Jan		Balance b/d	Note 5	0					

The formulae for the notes are:

Note 1 =SUM(E5:E26)   Note 2 =SUM(J5:J24)   Note 3 =E27
Note 4 =SUM(J27–J25)   Note 5 =J26

(c) Each receipt and payment is entered and the spreadsheet makes the calculations.

CASH ACCOUNT									
Date 20X0	Voucher	Particulars	Folio	Amount £	Date 20X0	Voucher	Particulars	Folio	Amount £
01 Jan	R01	Capital		5,000	01 Jan	PV1	Furniture		330
01 Jan	CS01	Sales		300	01 Jan	PV2	Purchases		1,000
02 Jan	R02	Jim's Loan		1,500	01 Jan	PV3	Advertising		60
02 Jan	CS02	Sales		1,800	01 Jan	PV4	Stationery		36
03 Jan	CS03	Sales		3,600	02 Jan	PV5	Purchases		2,400
04 Jan	CS04	Sales		1,650	02 Jan	PV6	Staff Welfare		12
04 Jan	R03	Telephone		11	02 Jan	PV7	Equipment		300
05 Jan	CS05	Sales		5,250	02 Jan	PV8	Stationery		4
					03 Jan	PV9	Staff Welfare		18
					03 Jan	PV10	Purchases		2,500
					03 Jan	PV11	Stationery		15
					03 Jan	PV12	Advertising		40
					03 Jan	PV13	Telephone		60
					04 Jan	PV14	Advertising		125
					04 Jan	PV15	Postage		15
					04 Jan	PV16	Purchases		1,500
					05 Jan	PV17	Salaries		780
					05 Jan	PV18	Purchases		1,000
					05 Jan	PV19	Staff Welfare		10
					05 Jan	PV20	Jim's Loan		300
					05 Jan	PV21	Advertising		130
									10,635
					05 Jan	–	Balance c/d		8,476
				19,111					19,111
06 Jan		Balance b/d		8,476					

Interaction 12.2

Write up a Petty Cash Book using a spreadsheet

Refer back to the Petty Cash Book used as an illustration in Section 8.7.

Required: Write up the Petty Cash Book using the following three steps: (a) Enter the narrative and amounts (b) Enter the formulae (c) Calculate the results.

12.4 THE 'WHAT IF?' ANALYSIS

Spreadsheets can be developed to perform different and more complex tasks than the simple ones we have referred to so far. They are very helpful in developing a budget for a single period or budgets for a number of periods, where each column represents an accounting period and each row a revenue or cost. It is then possible quickly to get the answer to the question 'What if . . . ?'. For example, a monthly budgeted Profit and Loss account can be prepared, from which a cash flow forecast and Balance Sheet can be developed; from there, the effect that a change in sales and gross profit would have on the profit and cash flow can be calculated by the spreadsheet.

The range of possibilities is great. For instance, the spreadsheet can calculate the effect on profit, cash flow and the Balance Sheet of:

- achieving 90 per cent or 110 per cent of budgeted sales;
- reducing the gross profit margin from 30 per cent to 25 per cent and 20 per cent;
- allowing a longer credit period to debtors;
- taking a longer credit period from creditors.

Changes in the first two entries in the above list could have a significant impact on the profit, whereas the effect of changing creditor and debtor credit policy may be significant as regards the cash flow but less so on the profit, which will probably anyway include interest charged on the increased borrowing.

A spreadsheet is able to perform calculations such as these almost instantaneously. This not only saves time but it gives an accountant a much better understanding of the effect of changes in various factors on profit and cash flow. The cash flow projection is important, since it will enable the accountant to see whether the borrowing limit is going to be exceeded. If the budget shows the borrowing limit *is* likely to be exceeded, other changes can be made to compensate (e.g. reducing debtors' age or increasing creditors' age), or a request can be made to the bank for additional borrowing.

Designing a spreadsheet for sales of golf clubs and squash racquets   Interaction 12.3

Woody Ltd supplies three qualities of golf clubs and squash racquets. Sales (in £) for the period 20X1–20X4 are as follows:

	20X1	20X2	20X3	20X4
Premium clubs	100,000	80,000	60,000	40,000
Premium racquets	110,000	120,000	130,000	140,000
Standard clubs	200,000	180,000	160,000	140,000
Standard racquets	320,000	360,000	420,000	500,000
Economy clubs	700,000	780,000	760,000	740,000
Economy racquets	450,000	350,000	250,000	150,000

Required: Design a spreadsheet to record the total annual sales from the above information.

12.5 CHARTING DATA

There is a useful yet easy facility within EXCEL for producing a chart of the data. You should consider using it for output reports.

As an example, the following chart has been produced for the sales forecast in IQ 12.3:

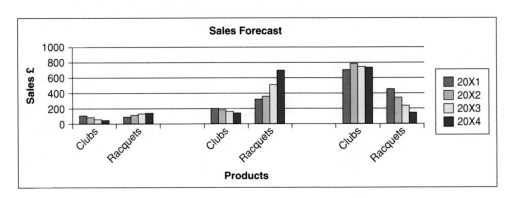

From the chart we can see that the growth product over the four years is the Standard Racquet and that Premium Clubs and Economy Racquets are facing falling sales.

Interaction 12.4	**Designing a spreadsheet to calculate the total value of stock**
	Required: Explain to a colleague how to set up a spreadsheet to calculate the stock value for the Balance Sheet at the year end.

12.6 OVERALL CONSIDERATIONS

Spreadsheets can thus be prepared for simple accounting tasks such as preparation of a Cash account, as well as for more complex tasks such as preparing final accounts from a Trial Balance. The strength of the spreadsheet is that it can be designed with formulae that are instantly recalculated to provide a report. They speed up calculations and perform analysis that would be time-consuming and possibly not cost-effective to carry out manually. They are particularly valuable in calculating the effect of changing one or more variables on key items such as profit and cash. However, in order to design the inputs and formulae in a spreadsheet and interpret the outcome, it is necessary to have an appropriate level of accounting knowledge and skill.

It is generally helpful to design the spreadsheet on paper first, in order to avoid being overcome by either the detail or the sheer mechanics of using the spreadsheet. This allows time to consider general questions such as:

- Why is the spreadsheet being produced, i.e. what is its purpose?
- Who will produce it, and what is that person's level of expertise?
- Who will input the data, i.e. will it be necessary to build a front end for data entry?
- Who will be using the results, i.e. how much explanation will need to be included in the report?
- How frequently will it be used, i.e. how much effort might be needed on the protection of formulae, preparing a foolproof data-input facility, and design of the output?

Specific considerations may also need to be made, depending on the nature of accounting task, such as:

- What will be in final report, i.e. budget projections? Depreciation calculations? Stock valuations?
- What period(s) will be covered by the spreadsheet, i.e. a series of years? An annual calculation? An ad hoc single figure such as a Net Present Value?
- How reliable is the output?

This last consideration, relating to reliability of the output, is a major aspect that influences management reliance on the spreadsheet report. For, from a management point of view, spreadsheets have considerable risks, mainly because there is little or no record of changes, and they are frequently produced by the person who uses them, and so there is little or no independent check that they are accurate. A user will make changes to a spreadsheet and save these changes. Saving the current spreadsheet deletes the previous version of the spreadsheet. With most spreadsheets, there is no record of changes made each time the spreadsheet is used, and so changes made to a spreadsheet may result in inherent errors (or even fraud or manipulation of the results). These are matters that managers should not overlook.

Taking a simple example, the spreadsheet user may overlook having to ensure that the Trial Balance does balance. If the Trial Balance does not balance, the Balance Sheet will not balance, but the user may not notice these differences and so there will be an error in the Profit and Loss account and/or the Balance Sheet. In more complex situations, a Trial Balance may have many accounts, which will be used to produce the financial statements. In this situation it is quite easy either to miss an account or to include it twice when producing the financial statements, which will result in the balance sheet not balancing. If this has not been detected by the user, there will be an error in the financial statements (due to the error in the spreadsheet). Clearly this should be picked up on the annual audit of accounts, but it may not be so readily identified if the exercise is a non-routine one.

One way of preventing uncontrolled changes to a spreadsheet is to lock (or protect) certain cells. This could include the headings and formulae. However, there is unlikely to be any evidence that an apparently 'locked' cell has been 'unlocked', changed and then 'locked' again.

When the same person designs the spreadsheet, puts in the figures and prints the results, that person is likely to be poor at detecting errors in the design of the spreadsheet and the input of data. So there is a relatively high risk that there will be undetected errors in the spreadsheet. These will only be detected if an independent person checks the figures carefully and determines how they have been derived on the spreadsheet. A well-established spreadsheet, where there have been no changes for some time, is likely to contain few (or no) errors.

In writing computer programs, it is said that programmers make an error on 2–3 per cent of instructions, but in correcting errors their error rate is 30 per cent. As the person who designs the spreadsheet is likely to be less experienced and less skilled than a programmer at acting in a logical, methodical matter, the risk of errors in each cell of a spreadsheet is likely to be even higher!

12.7 CONCLUSIONS

So, in summary we can say:

(a) Spreadsheets are a very valuable and flexible tool for accountants.
(b) The risk of in-built and undetected errors in a spreadsheet is high, particularly when the same person both designs the spreadsheet and inputs the accounting figures; and because no one in general checks the work of a designer of a spreadsheet and the input of the accounting figures, there is a weakness in the system of internal control, which means there is a high risk of undetected errors (and, less commonly, fraud).
(c) Frequently, it is impossible to detect changes to spreadsheets, particularly changes in the formulae used to produce the results. This lack of an 'audit trail' means that it will not be possible to detect when errors – and even fraud or manipulation of the figures – have taken place.

The objective of this chapter has been to explain the uses that an accountant might make of a spreadsheet and give some examples. It is not the intention to teach EXCEL programming and there are many texts on the market that do this very well.

SOLUTIONS TO INTERACTIVE QUESTIONS

IQ 12.1 Preparing a Balance Sheet using a spreadsheet

(a) Enter the narrative

	A	B	C
31	**Balance Sheet**		
32	Capital		
33	At start of period		
34	Profit		
35	Drawings		
36			
37	At end of period		
38	**Represented by**		
39	Cash at bank		
40	Difference		

(b) Enter the formulae

	A	B	C
31	**Balance Sheet**		
32	Capital		
33	At start of period	=C4	
34	Profit	=B30	
35	Drawings	=B5	
36		=Sum (B34–B35)	
37	At end of period	=Sum(B33+B36)	
38	**Represented by**		
39	Cash at bank	=B6	
40	Difference	=Sum(B37–B39)	

(c) The spreadsheet calculates

	A	B	C
31	**Balance Sheet**		
32	Capital		
33	At start of period	5,000	
34	Profit	3,100	
35	Drawings	2,600	
36		500	
37	At end of period	5,500	
38	**Represented by**		
39	Cash at bank	5,500	
40	Difference	0	

Note: The difference has been calculated in cell B40 and it is zero, showing that the Balance Sheet balances.

IQ 12.2 Write up a Petty Cash Book using a spreadsheet

(a) Enter the narratives and the amounts:

	A	B	C		D	E	F	G		H	I	J	K	L
1														
2	**PETTY CASH BOOK**													
3		**RECEIPTS**				**PAYMENTS**						**ANALYSIS**		
4	**20X0**	**Folio**	**£**		**20X0**	**V**	**Particulars**	**£**		**Travel**	**Cleaning**	**Car maint.**	**Postage**	**Stationery**
5	**Balance b/f**		14.00		17.1	PC51	Bus fare	2.40						
6	17.1	CB1	86.00		18.1	PC52	Rubber stamp	11.00						
7					18.1	PC53	Postage stamp	4.50						
8					19.1	PC54	Petrol for car	18.00						
9					19.1	PC55	Mopping floor	7.50						
10					19.1	PC56	Taxi to bank	4.50						
11					20.1	PC57	Servicing car	22.00						
12					20.1	PC58	Desk stapler	7.60						
13					21.1	PC59	Janitor's tip	3.00						
14					21.1	PC60	Car wipers	7.50						
15														
16					21.1		Balance c/d							
17	Balance b/d													

(b) Enter the formula:

	A	B	C		D	E	F	G		H	I	J	K	L
1														
2	**PETTY CASH BOOK**													
3		**RECEIPTS**				**PAYMENTS**						**ANALYSIS**		
4	**20X0**	**Folio**	**£**		**20X0**	**V**	**Particulars**	**£**		**Travel**	**Cleaning**	**Car maint.**	**Postage**	**Stationery**
5	**Balance b/f**		14.00		17.1	PC51	Bus fare	2.40		=G5				
6	17.1	CB1	86.00		18.1	PC52	Rubber stamp	11.00						=G6
7					18.1	PC53	Postage stamp	4.50					=G7	
8					19.1	PC54	Petrol for car	18.00		=G8				
9					19.1	PC55	Mopping floor	7.50			=G9			
10					19.1	PC56	Taxi to bank	4.50		=G10				
11					20.1	PC57	Servicing car	22.00				=G11		
12					20.1	PC58	Desk stapler	7.60						=G12
13					21.1	PC59	Janitor's tip	3.00			=G13			
14					21.1	PC60	Car wipers	7.50				=G14		
15								(b)		(c)	(d)	(e)	(f)	(g)
16					21.1		Balance c/d	(h)						
17			(a)					(a)						
18	Balance b/d		(h)											

The formulae referred to by the letters stated above are as follows:

(a) =Sum(C5:C16)   (b) =Sum(G5:G14)   (c) =Sum(H5:H14)   (d) =Sum(I5:I14)
(e) =Sum(J5:J14)   (f) =Sum(K5:K14)   (g) =Sum(L5:L14)   (h) =Sum(C17–G15)

To verify whether the analysis is correct: =Sum(H15:L15)–(G15) and the answer must be zero.

(c) Calculate:

	A	B	C	D	E	F	G	H	I	J	K	L
1												
2	PETTY CASH BOOK											
3	RECEIPTS			PAYMENTS				ANALYSIS				
4	20X0	Folio	£	20X0	V	Particulars	£	Travel	Cleaning	Car maint.	Postage	Stationery
5	Balance b/f		14.00	17.1	PC51	Bus fare	2.40	2.40				
6	17.1	CB1	86.00	18.1	PC52	Rubber stamp	11.00					11.00
7				18.1	PC53	Postage stamp	4.50				4.50	
8				19.1	PC54	Petrol for car	18.00	18.00				
9				19.1	PC55	Mopping floor	7.50		7.50			
10				19.1	PC56	Taxi to bank	4.50	4.50				
11				20.1	PC57	Servicing car	22.00			22.00		
12				20.1	PC58	Desk stapler	7.60					7.60
13				21.1	PC59	Janitor's tip	3.00		3.00			
14				21.1	PC60	Car wipers	7.50			7.50		
15							88.00	24.90	10.50	29.50	4.50	18.60
16				21.1		Balance c/d	12.00					
17			100.00				100.00					
18	Balance b/d		12.00									

IQ 12.3 Designing a spreadsheet for sales of golf clubs and squash racquets

	Premium		Standard		Economy		Total
Years	Clubs	Racquets	Clubs	Racquets	Clubs	Racquets	
	£000	£000	£000	£000	£000	£000	£000
20X1	100	80	200	320	700	450	1,850
20X2	80	120	180	360	780	350	1,870
20X3	60	130	160	520	760	250	1,880
20X4	40	140	140	500	740	150	1,710

IQ 12.4 Designing a spreadsheet to calculate the total value of stock

The procedure could be as follows:

1. Each stock line will be listed and the quantity entered from the stock sheets.
2. The price per unit will be entered.
3. The cost of each line of stock will be the product of the number of units and the price per unit.
4. The sum of the values of each line of stock will be the total value of the stock (at cost). If the stock value is determined from a stocktake each month, then the stock quantity can be entered in the standard spreadsheet.
5. Any changes in the purchase price of stock can be entered.
6. Then the spreadsheet will automatically calculate the value of the stock (at cost).

Part B

ACCOUNTING FOR BANK BALANCES, RECEIVABLES AND PAYABLES

## Chapter 13

THE BANK ACCOUNT AND BANK RECONCILIATION

In this chapter

We will learn:

- of banking terminology
- to account for transactions through a bank

and you should be able to:

- write up a three-column cash book
- prepare bank reconciliation statements

13.1 THE BANK ACCOUNT

When a business has surplus cash, the owner needs to decide where to keep it. This depends on how quickly the cash will be required to meet commitments. If it is required the next day (e.g. as a cash float in the till or to pay suppliers who do not allow credit), then it remains as cash on the premises. If it is required to pay suppliers of goods and services at the end of the month (e.g. when the suppliers submit their accounts), then it is normal to open a bank account in the name of the business and make payments by cheque at the month end. Any cash surplus to the amount required to pay creditors or other claims is usually put into an interest-earning deposit account or possibly invested in the stock market.

We have already seen that the cashier of a business is responsible for recording the cash receipts in the cash book. Where there is a business bank account he is responsible also for recording the amount of money held in the bank account. Bank and cash transactions are both recorded in the cash book.

The Bank account in the cash book has all the columns that a Cash account has plus, on the payment side, an additional column for recording the sequential numbers of the cheques that have been issued. By checking that the sequence of cheque numbers is unbroken, it is possible to ensure that all cheques drawn have been accounted for (i.e. to check that there are no missing cheque numbers). There is, of course, no purpose in having a cheque number column on the debit side of the Bank account because the cheques received from customers will be from different banks and therefore with different series of numbers.

13.1.1 Accounting for amounts received

A business may receive payment for goods and services either directly at its own office or directly into its bank account.

Amounts received by the cashier directly at the business's own office, in cash, cheques and other ways (such as bank drafts and money orders), are accounted for in the Cash account. At convenient times in the day, cash that is surplus to immediate needs, together with receipts other than in cash, are deposited in the bank. A bank paying-in slip is normally signed by the bank staff to acknowledge receipt of the amounts deposited, and this slip is the voucher retained by the cashier to substantiate the deposits made in the bank. The accounting entry to record the bank deposit is to credit the Cash account and debit the Bank account. If an amount is received in the form of a credit card transaction, the business will periodically (say monthly) collect the amount from the credit card company. A cheque received from the credit card company is dealt with by the cashier just like any other cheque.

Amounts received directly into the business's bank account may include giro credits, standing orders and direct debits. The cashier, when informed of such amounts received directly at the bank, accounts for them by debiting the Bank account and crediting either the customer's account or an income account as appropriate. It is not unusual for a cashier to get information on such amounts received directly by the bank only when he receives a bank statement. If a loan is obtained from the bank, on receiving confirmation of this from the bank, the cashier accounts for it by debiting the Bank account and crediting a Bank Loan account.

13.1.2 Accounting for cash and bank payments

The cashier accounts for payments made by the business by crediting either the Cash account or the Bank account, depending on whether the payment is made in cash or out of the bank balance, in the latter case usually by drawing a cheque. Payments could be out of the bank balance also when:

- the business itself has, by means such as a direct debit or standing order, instructed its bank to effect specified payments, e.g. a monthly, quarterly or annual payment of insurance premiums;
- the bank deducts from the business current account bank charges or interest;
- a customer's cheque that was deposited by the business into its bank account is subsequently dishonoured.

If the business should require cash from the bank account, a cheque will be drawn to withdraw the required amount – such a cash withdrawal is accounted for by crediting the Bank account and debiting the Cash account.

Interaction 13.1	**Writing up a Cash and a Bank account**

Andy Small has a cash balance of £26,450 on 1 May 20X0. He opens a current account on that date, with City Bank, depositing £25,000. His transactions during the next three days include the following:

1 May
- Cash sales £2,250.
- Received a cheque for £12,600 from Mike Ridley, a customer.
- Paid £1,200 as rent by cheque number 0001.
- Paid £24 as wages in cash.
- Paid the petty cashier £84 as the week's imprest. The petty cashier has a cash float of £250 at the beginning of each week and has produced vouchers to the cashier to evidence the payment out of petty cash of £84 in the last week of April.
- Deposited all amounts into bank, leaving a cash float with the cashier of £2,000.

2 May
- Paid £38 for stationery by cheque number 0002.
- Cash sales £1,840.
- £2,400 is paid as business rates by a Standing Order.
- Paid £145 for electricity by cheque number 0003.
- Paid £36 as wages in cash.
- Received a cheque for £18,400 from John Bolton, a customer.
- Deposited all amounts into bank retaining a float of £2,000.

3 May
- Mike Ridley's cheque for £12,600 is returned to Andy Small marked 'refer to drawer'. Andy telephoned Mike, who apologized that he was temporarily short of funds and requested Andy to re-present the cheque to the bank on 4 May.
- Bank approves a loan to the business of £10,000.
- Paid £28,000 for a car by cheque number 0004.
- Wrote cheque number 0005 to draw £600 in cash for office use.
- Andy drew £1,000 cash for his personal use.

Required: In the format shown below, write up the Cash account and the Bank account.

CASH ACCOUNT

Date	V	Particulars	F	Amount	Date	V	Particulars	F	Amount
20X0				£	20X0				£

BANK ACCOUNT

Date	V	Particulars	F	Amount	Date	Chq. no	V	Particulars	F	Amount
20X0				£	20X0					£

13.2 BANKING TERMINOLOGY

It may be useful to clarify the meaning of some banking terminology used in this chapter.

A *current account* with a bank is an account maintained with a bank or building society with a view to operating it regularly by making deposits into it and making payments out of it by writing out cheques. To facilitate making deposits, the bank provides its customer with a pad of paying-in slips (see below) and for making payments out of it a cheque book. At agreed intervals the bank reports to the customer in a bank statement (see format below) the full particulars of the position of the bank account from the bank's perspective, detailing deposits and withdrawals individually.

Olive May Stores	in account with			
CITY BANK plc 501 Pall Mall, London SW1 4AN				
Date	Details	Withdrawals	Deposits	Balance
20X0 1.1	Balance b/f	£ –	£ –	£ 12,645

Paying-in slips are pre-printed forms provided by the bank to facilitate documentation of the amounts paid into the bank. As shown in the pro forma below the account holder's name (Olive May Stores) and the bank account number are preprinted, and a grid is provided in which can be stated the value of cheques deposited and, in the case of cash deposits, individually the value of notes and coins of different denominations.

..........20.....	Paid in by		Notes £50		
CITY BANK plc, Pall Mall branch			£20		
			£10		
			£5		
	Olive May Stores		Coins £1		
Fees			Other coins		
			Total cash		
Cheque	56-28-08	27480259	14276	Cheques	
	Sort Code	Account No.	Transaction	£	
	DO NOT WRITE BELOW THIS LINE				

A *cheque* is a written order from an entity addressed to a bank in which it has a current account, requiring the bank to pay a specified sum of money, usually to a named third party. For recognizing whether the customer's order is authentic, the bank retains the customer's specimen signature. For writing out such orders, the bank provides each customer with a pad of forms, which is known as a *cheque book*. Each cheque in the book (see the pro forma below) is numbered in sequence. Cheques issued by banks in the United Kingdom are printed at the bottom with a number that may appear as (say): 126745 56-28-08 27480259. The first six of these digits are usually the sequential number of the cheque. The six (hyphenated) digits in the centre are known as the *sorting code* and are specific to each branch of every bank. The remaining numbers identify the account number of the customer (Olive May Stores) who writes out the cheque.

CITY BANK PLC		**56-28-08**
501 Pall Mall London SW1 4AN		Date: ....20.....
Pay		£
Sum of		
	Olive May Stores	
	....	
126745 Cheque No.	56-28-08 Sort Code	27480259 Account No.

Cheque clearing (also known as realization of a cheque) occurs when a cheque received by the entity from its customer and deposited into the entity's bank account, will in due course move through the banking system and be presented for payment (*clearance*) to the bank in which the customer maintains his account. Cheques may take around three working days to clear unless special clearing arrangements are made, and a charge is levied for those. Deposits made in the bank but not included in the bank statement (because they are still moving through the clearance process) are referred to as 'deposits awaiting clearance'. When there is a refusal by the customer's bank to make the payment in accordance with the customer's order, this is the *dishonouring* of a cheque. The refusal may be because the customer has insufficient funds in his current account for the purpose or because of a variety of other reasons such as the signature differing from the specimen, some irregularity in drawing the cheque (such as the amount stated in words being different from the one in figures), or the cheque becoming 'stale' six months from the date it was drawn.

An *overdraft* is a situation where the entity draws out from its bank more than the amount it had in its current account with the bank. Unless prior agreement is reached with the bank for this purpose and a limit negotiated, the cheque drawn by the entity may be dishonoured. Whereas a Bank account is an asset and would, therefore, normally have a debit balance, if the bank is overdrawn the Bank account will have a credit balance because it will then be reporting a liability.

A *direct debit* is an authority given to the bank by its customer to make payments to a specified third party, the amount depending on what the third party claims from time to time. This arrangement is useful where the amounts to be paid are likely to vary (such as a quarterly telephone bill or an annual membership fee). A *standing order* is an order given to the bank by its customer to pay a *specified* amount to a named third party at a *specified* interval.

Credit cards are cards (for example Visa and Access) issued by banks and building societies to their customers. These cards entitle the customer to make payments to anyone simply by signing on special forms or phoning instructions through. A credit card may be used even when a customer has insufficient funds with the card issuer, but of course up to an agreed limit. If, for example, an amount owed to a business is settled by credit card, the arrangement might be for the credit card company to send a cheque direct to the business (having deducted its commission of, say, 2%) or to make a payment directly into the business's bank account. A card is known as a *debit card* if the customer is permitted to use the card for making payment *only* on the basis of having adequate funds for the purpose with the issuer of the card.

A business might draw a single cheque to settle amounts owed to several creditors and take this cheque, together with the individual payment forms, to the business's bank. The bank will then make the appropriate individual payments and deduct the total from the business account. This kind of transaction is known as a *bank giro credit (BGC)*.

13.3 A TWO-COLUMN CASH BOOK

Instead of writing up the Cash account and the Bank account on two different folios of the cash book, it is more convenient to accommodate them both side by side, in parallel columns on the same folio. A folio in the cash book will then appear as follows:

CASH BOOK

Date	V	Particulars	F	Cash	Bank	Date	V	Chq.no	Particulars	F	Cash	Bank
20X0				£	£	20X0					£	£
1.5		Balance b/f		26,450	–	1.5		–	Cash a/c	C	25,000	–
1.5	X	Cash a/c	C	–	25,000	1.5	X	A001	Rent a/c		–	1,200
1.5	X	Sales a/c		2,250	–	1.5	X	–	Wages a/c		24	–

The Folio column remains to be filled in by the bookkeeper with the folio number of the account to which she posts each entry in the cash book. You will observe that in our example the cashier has made in the cash book both the debit and the credit entries to account for amounts deposited with the bank. Against each of these entries, in the Folio column, the cashier has written the letter 'C' (which is an abbreviation for the word *contra*, meaning 'opposite' in Latin) in order to state in respect of each of the entries that the corresponding second entry is on the opposite side of the same folio.

Interaction 13.2	Writing up a two-column cash book
	You are required to record Andy Small's transactions stated in IQ 13.1 above in a two-column cash book.

13.4 ACCOUNTING IN THE BOOKS OF THE BANK

The bank will naturally write up its accounts from its own point of view. On receiving a deposit of £25,000 from Andy Small (see IQ 13.1), it records the amount as a receipt in its cash book and posts it to the credit of an account opened in the name of its customer – Andy Small. From its own records the bank would report that Andy's shop has a credit balance of £25,000 on that date, whereas in Andy's books the corresponding amount would be a debit balance in the Bank account.

If we assume that all deposits made by Andy cleared on the same date and also assume – less realistically – that everyone to whom Andy issued a cheque rushed to the bank to obtain the money on the same date, Andy Small's account in the bank's books would appear as stated on the left. The bank supplies its customer with a bank statement. In the ideal world contemplated by our assumptions, the credit balance of £24,413 stated in the bank statement will tally with the bank balance reported in Andy's cash book. There will then be no need for a 'bank reconciliation'.

ANDY SMALL ACCOUNT

2000		£	2000		£
1.5	CHQ 0001	1,200	1.5	Cash a/c	25,000
2.5	CHQ 0002	38	1.5	Cash a/c	14,192
2.5	Standing order	2,400	2.5	Cash a/c	20,204
2.5	CHQ 0003	145	3.5	Loan a/c	10,000
3.5	Dishonour	12,600			
3.5	CHQ 0004	28,000			
3.5	CHQ 0005	600			
3.5	Balance c/d	24,413			
			4.5	Balance	24,413

13.5 BANK RECONCILIATION

Bank reconciliation is the process of agreeing information from two different sources. If the two sources are independent of each other then this provides some confidence that the data is accurate.

In the real world the amount stated in a bank statement, as a customer's bank balance on a particular date, is unlikely to be the same as the balance in that customer's cash book. This is because of reasons such as the following:

● deposits into that customer's bank account are awaiting clearance on that date;
● cheques issued by that customer are yet to be presented to the bank for payment;
● amounts have been paid in directly to that customer's bank account (such as by bank giro credit) without being accounted for in its cash book;
● amounts (such as bank charges and interest) have been recovered by the bank directly from that customer's account without being accounted for by the customer;
● errors in the customer's cash book and, very rarely, in the bank's accounting have crept in.

If, for any or all of the reasons, the balance confirmed in a bank statement disagrees with the bank balance stated in the cash book, a bank reconciliation statement is prepared. When preparing a bank reconciliation statement, the following points should be remembered:

1. The reconciliation is always as at a specific date. The date does not necessarily have to be the last day of the accounting period or even the last date of a calendar month. Reconciliation could well be the balance as at a particular date as reported in the cash book and as at the same date as stated in the bank statement.
2. The reconciliation involves two aspects.
   - Each item in the bank statements needs to be traced to the Bank account in the cash book in order to identify all items which appear in the bank statements but are not in the Bank account of the cash book. All such items should then be included in the Bank account of the cash book.
   - Each item in the Bank account (of the cash book) should be traced to the bank statement so as to identify bank deposits and cheques drawn that are not appearing on the bank's statement because the former are awaiting clearance and the latter are yet to be presented to the bank for payment. The bank reconciliation statement (see specimen on the right) should include all such items.

BANK RECONCILIATION STATEMENT	
AS AT 31 DECEMBER 20X0	£
Balance as stated in bank statement	
Add: Deposits yet to clear	
Less: Cheques not yet presented	
Bank balance as stated in cash book	

3. The aim of the bank reconciliation statement is as follows:
   - to ensure that the cash book reports the bank balance accurately; and
   - to obtain evidence of the accuracy from a third party.

The bank balance included in the Balance Sheet is the one stated in the cash book and not the one in the bank statement.

Bank reconciliation statement

Interaction 13.3

Andy Small's shop has written up its Bank account (see answer to IQ 13.2), reporting a balance at the bank on 3 May of £24,413. The bank statement is shown below.

Andy Small   in account with
CITY BANK plc, 501 Pall Mall, London SW1 4AN

Date	Particulars	Debits	Credits	Balance
20X0		£	£	£
2.5	Deposit	–	25,000	25,000
2.5	Deposit	–	14,192	39,192
3.5	Standing order	2,400	–	36,792
3.5	Cheque 0001	1,200	–	35,592
3.5	Loan	–	10,000	45,592
3.5	Cheque 0003	145	–	45,447
3.5	Cheque dishonour	12,600	–	32,847
3.5	Cheque 0005	600	–	32,247
3.5	Bank charges	10	–	32,237

Required: Prepare a bank reconciliation statement as at 3 May 20X0.

13.6 A THREE-COLUMN CASH BOOK

A three-column cash book is required to record cash discounts (also known as settlement discounts). Although traders allow customers to delay payment for an agreed period as a method of promoting sales, the customers are usually encouraged to settle their dues earlier if possible. Such encouragement is given by way of an offer of a discount for settlements received within a specified number of days.

For example, refer to the invoice from Longman plc in the illustration in Section 20.2. You will find a cryptic message printed on the left-hand bottom corner of the invoice stating 'Terms 5/7 n/30'. The message conveyed to the customer (Nancy Doe) is as follows: '5/7' informs Nancy that if she settles the amount of the invoice within seven days she will receive a 5 per cent discount, which is the cash discount intended to induce early settlement; and 'n/30' confirms to Nancy that she has anyway been allowed a 30-day credit period. The trader offers a cash discount on the premise that it may be more economical than paying interest on a bank overdraft. Conversely, the trader may earn a cash discount by early settlement of a supplier's accounts.

13.6.1 Accounting for discount allowed

A customer becomes entitled to a cash discount at the time the cash is received by the trader in settlement. Hence a trading entity's cashier, who would be the first to become aware of such an entitlement, is best placed to make the prime entry for discounts allowed. The prime entry is made in a special column on the debit side of the cash book, immediately before the Cash account column. Assuming that on 4 May 20X0 a cashier receives from customer Ted Smith a cheque for £9,500, net of a 5 per cent cash discount on £10,000 due from Ted, and on 5 May receives a cheque from Azim Habib for £19,000 (net of a 5 per cent discount), the receipts are recorded in the cash book as shown on the left. The debit entries

CASH BOOK

Date	V	Particulars	F	Discount	Cash	Bank
20X0				£	£	£
4.5		Ted Smith's a/c		500	9,500	–
5.5		Azim Habib's a/c		1,000	19,000	–

in the Cash account constitute one of the pair of double entries; the bookkeeper has only to make the corresponding credits in the personal accounts of Ted Smith and Azim Habib to complete the double entry. The Discount column in the cash book, by contrast, is regarded as a prime entry. The bookkeeper has, therefore, to account for the information in that column by making a credit in the personal accounts of Ted Smith (£500) and Azim Habib (£1,000), and a debit in a Discount Allowed account to record the total expenditure of £1,500. The Discount column in the cash book is treated just as the day books are. As with the information recorded in (say) the Purchases Day Book, the individual personal accounts of each customer are credited with the relevant discount entitlement, while the *periodical* total is posted to the debit of the Discount Allowed account. The relevant ledger accounts, after the bookkeeper completes the postings, would appear as shown on the left.

TED SMITH ACCOUNT

Sales Day Bk	SDBX	10,000	Cash a/c	CBX	9,500
			Discount allowed	CBX	500

AZIM HABIB ACCOUNT

Sales Day Bk	SDBX	20,000	Cash a/c	CBX	19,000
			Discount allowed	CBX	1,000

DISCOUNT ALLOWED ACCOUNT

Cash book	CBX	1,500			

Accounting for discount allowed

Ridley's Novelties is a wholesaler selling to retailers on one month's credit. It allows the retailers 4 per cent as a cash discount if remittance is received within a week of sale. The receipts from customers during March 20X0 were as follows:

Date	Customer	Cheque	Received within seven days
4.3	Robinson Ltd	£25,800	£17,280 of the amount
9.3	Tomlinson Bros	£13,440	Whole amount
14.3	Samuel & son	£43,200	Whole amount
17.3	Patricia and Co	£19,500	£14,400 of the amount
25.3	Gamage plc	£16,800	Whole amount

Required: Account for the above transactions, showing the prime entry as well as the ledger accounts. Assume that discounts allowed are posted in total at the end of the month.

13.6.2 Accounting for discount received

Discounts earned by an entity by settling its suppliers within agreed periods are accounted for similarly. The cashier makes the prime entry in a special Discount column built, this time, on the credit side of the cash book. Both of the pair of entries necessary to account for discount received are made by the bookkeeper when each supplier's account is individually debited and the Discount Received (income) account is credited in total, usually periodically.

Accounting for discount received

Date	Customer	Cheque amt
2.5	Bragabout plc	£68,150
6.5	Tellaround plc	£22,500
16.5	Whocares plc	£32,524
24.5	Sowhat plc	£27,072

Ridley Novelties purchases its supplies on one month's credit, on terms that allow a 6 per cent discount if payment is made within a week of purchase. Payments to suppliers in May 20X0 were as stated on the left. All payments, other than the one on 6 May, were made within the discount period.

Required: Account for these payments showing prime entry and ledger accounts.

A cash book with Discount columns built into either side is called a *three-column cash book* and would appear as shown below:

CASH BOOK

Date	V	Particulars	F	Discount	Cash	Bank	Date	V	Chq	Particulars	F	Discount	Cash	Bank
2000					£	£	2000						£	£

13.6.3 Reversal of discount allowed

A customer who was allowed a cash discount when a cheque was received in settlement will forfeit the discount if his cheque is dishonoured. In such circumstances a journal entry is required to reverse the discount. For example, in IQ 13.4 Gamage plc was allowed a discount of £700 upon receiving a cheque for £16,800. If the cheque is dishonoured, the discount allowed needs to be reversed, journalizing as shown below.

	£	£
Gamage plc Dr	700	–
To Discount Allowed a/c	–	700
Being reversal of discount allowed, upon dishonour of the cheque received.		

SOLUTIONS TO INTERACTIVE QUESTIONS

IQ 13.1 Writing up a Cash and Bank account

CASH ACCOUNT

Date	V	Particulars	F	Amount	Date	V	Particulars	F	Amount
20X0				£	**20X0**				£
1.5		Balance b/f		26,450	1.5	X	Bank account		25,000
1.5	X	Sales account		2,250	1.5	X	Wages account		24
1.5	X	Mike Ridley's		12,600	1.5	X	Petty Cash a/c		84
2.5	X	Sales account		1,840	1.5	X	Bank account		14,192
2.5	X	John Bolton's		18,400	2.5	X	Wages account		36
3.5	–	Bank account		600	2.5	X	Bank account		20,204
					3.5	X	Drawings a/c		1,000
					3.5	–	Balance c/d		1,600
				62,140					62,140
4.5	–	Balance b/d		1,600					

BANK ACCOUNT

Date	V	Particulars	F	Amount	Date	Chq.no	V	Particulars	F	Amount
20X0				£	**20X0**					£
1.5	X	Cash account		25,000	1.5	0001	X	Rent account		1,200
1.5	X	Cash account		14,192	2.5	0002	X	Stationery a/c		38
2.5	X	Cash account		20,204	2.5	–	X	Business Rates		2,400
3.5	X	Bank Loan a/c		10,000	2.5	0003	X	Electricity a/c		145
					3.5	–	X	Mike Ridley's		12,600
					3.5	0004	X	Motor Vehicles		28,000
					3.5	0005	–	Cash account		600
					3.5	–	–	Balance c/d		24,413
				69,396						69,396
4.5		Balance b/d		24,413						

IQ 13.2 Writing up a two-column cash book

CASH BOOK

Date	V	Particulars	F	Cash	Bank	Date	V	Chq.no	Particulars	F	Cash	Bank
20X0				£	£	20X0					£	£
1.5		Balance b/f		26,450	–	1.5		–	Cash a/c	C	25,000	–
1.5	X	Cash a/c	C	–	25,000	1.5	X	0001	Rent a/c		–	1,200
1.5	X	Sales a/c		2,250	–	1.5	X	–	Wages a/c		24	–
1.5	X	M. Ridley's		12,600	–	1.5	X	–	Petty Cash		84	–
1.5	X	Cash a/c	C	–	14,192	1.5	X	–	Bank a/c	C	14,192	–
2.5	X	Sales a/c		1,840	–	2.5	X	0002	Stationery		–	38
2.5	X	John Bolton's		18,400	–	2.5	X	–	Bus. Rates		–	2,400
2.5	X	Cash a/c	C	–	20,204	2.5	X	0003	Electricity		–	145
3.5	X	Bank Loan		–	10,000	2.5	X	–	Wages a/c		36	–
3.5	–	Bank a/c	C	600	–	2.5	X	–	Bank a/c	C	20,204	–
						3.5	X	–	M. Ridley's		–	12,600
						3.5	X	0004	Motor Vehicle		–	28,000
						3.5	–	0005	Cash a/c	C	–	600
						3.5	X	–	Drawings a/c		1,000	–
									Balance c/d		1,600	24,413
				62,140	69,396						62,140	69,396
4.5		Balance b/d		1,600	24,413							

Notes:

1. Whenever the double entry is between the Cash account and Bank account, the cashier writes 'C' for 'contra' in the folio column.
2. Whenever a cheque number is not stated, the payment is assumed to be on a cash basis.

IQ 13.3 Bank reconciliation statement

By tracing each debit and credit in the Bank account of the cash book to its counterpart in the bank statement, the following have been identified as the reasons for a disagreement between the two:

- deposit of £20,204 on 2 May is awaiting clearance;
- cheque numbers 0002 and 0004 for £38 and £28,000 respectively have not yet been presented for payment;
- a bank charge of £10 is yet to be accounted for in the cash book.

Note: The reconciliation identifies the correct balance at bank on 3 May as £24,403.

BANK RECONCILIATION STATEMENT AS AT 3 MAY 20X0		
		£
Balance at bank as per cash book		24,413
Bank charges not accounted for		(10)
Correct balance at bank on 3.5.00		24,403
Cheques not presented:		
Cheque no 0002 for	38	
Cheque no 0004 for	28,000	28,038
Less: Deposits awaiting clearance		(20,204)
Balance as per bank statement		32,237

IQ 13.4 Accounting for discount allowed

CASH BOOK

Date	V	Particulars	F	Discount	Cash	Bank	Date	V	Chq.no.	Particulars
20X0				£	£	£	20X0			
4.3	X	Robinson Ltd	DL?	720	25,800	–				
9.3	X	Tomlinson Bros	DL?	560	13,440	–				
14.3	X	Samuel & son	DL?	1,800	43,200	–				
17.3	X	Patricia and Co	DL?	600	19,500					
25.3	X	Gamage plc	DL?	700	16,800	–				
				4,380						
				NL?						

NL?

DISCOUNT ALLOWED ACCOUNT
£

	Balance b/f		?				
31.3	Cash book	CB?	4,380				

ROBINSONS LTD ACCOUNT
DL?
£

Balance b/f	?	4.3	Cash a/c	CB?	25,800
		4.3	Cash bk	CB?	720

TOMLINSON BROS ACCOUNT
DL?
£

Balance	?	9.3	Cash a/c	CB?	13,440
			Cash bk	CB?	560

SAMUEL & SONS ACCOUNT
DL?
£

Balance	?	14.3	Cash a/c	CB?	43,200
		14.3	Cash bk	CB?	1,800

PATRICIA AND CO ACCOUNT
DL?
£

Balance	?	17.3	Cash a/c	CB?	19,500
		17.3	Cash bk	CB?	600

GAMAGE PLC ACCOUNT
DL?
£

Balance	?	25.3	Cash a/c	CB?	16,800
		25.3	Cash bk	CB?	700

IQ 13.5 Accounting for discount received

CASH BOOK

	Cash	Bank	Date	V	Chq.no.	Particulars	F	Discount	Cash	Bank
			20X0					£	£	£
			2.5	X	XXX	Bragabout plc	CL?	4,350	–	68,150
			6.5	X	XXX	Tellaround plc	CL?	–	–	22,500
			16.5	X	XXX	Whocares plc	CL?	2,076	–	32,524
			24.5	X	XXX	Sowhat plc	CL?	1,728	–	27,072
								NL?		

CL?	BRAGABOUT PLC ACCOUNT					CL?	WHOCARES PLC ACCOUNT				
			£						£		
2.5	Cash a/c	CB?	68,150	Balance	?	16.5	Cash a/c	CB?	32,524	Balance	?
2.5	Cash bk	CB?	4,350			16.5	Cash bk	CB?	2,076		

CL?	TELLAROUND PLC ACCOUNT					CL?	SOWHAT PLC ACCOUNT				
			£						£		
6.5	Cash a/c	CB?	22,500	Balance	?	24.5	Cash a/c	CB?	27,072	Balance	?
						24.5	Cash bk	CB?	1,728		

NL?	DISCOUNT RECEIVED ACCOUNT					
						£
			31.5	Cash book	CB?	8,154

PROGRESSIVE QUESTIONS

PQ 13.1 Multiple-choice question

Place a tick in the appropriate box to confirm whether each of the following statements is true or false:

	True	False

(a) A debit balance in a business's bank account in the cash book appears as a credit balance in the bank statement

(b) A bank reconciliation statement is not part of the double entry system

(c) An overdraft in the bank statement is included in the Balance Sheet as a current asset

(d) If the bank reconciliation statement started with a debit balance from the Bank account in the cash book, bank charges appearing in the bank statement would be added

(e) A cash payment as petty cash imprest would appear in the bank statement

(f) If the bank reconciliation statement started with a favourable balance as stated in the bank statement, unpresented cheques would be added

(g) A reconciliation statement is prepared because the Bank account in the cash book is always correct and the bank statement is not

(h) An instruction to a bank to make payments at regular interval is a standing order

PQ 13.2 Two-column cash book

Olive May commenced business on 1.1.20X0 introducing capital in cash of £10,000. Among others, the following transactions on her store took place in January:

Date	Item
1.1	Deposited £9,000 in an account opened with City Bank.
	Paid £24 for stationery in cash.
	Paid £2,400 by cheque number 0001 for purchases.
	Paid £65 for advertising in cash.
	Sold goods for £300 cash.
2.1	Received a cheque for £1,250 from Peter Dudd, a customer.
	Paid £1,500 for rent by cheque 0002.
	Paid £3,000 by cheque 0003 to Rocco Ltd, a supplier.
	Sold goods for £800 for cash.
	Received a cheque for £1,600 from Phil. Richard, a customer.
	Deposited into the bank all amounts, leaving a float in hand of £1,000.
	Instructed the bank to pay £275 for business rates on 5th of every month.
3.1	Received notification that bank has approved a loan of £15,000 and made the funds available.
	Paid £16,500 for a motor vehicle by cheque 0004.
	Sold goods for £600 for cash.
	Paid £240 for advertising by cheque 0005.
	Received a cheque for £1,500 from Sam Brown, a customer.
	Paid £40 for staff tea in cash.
	Paid £3,850 to City Stores, a supplier, by cheque 0006.
	Deposited into the bank Sam's cheque, as well as £1,200 in cash.
4.1	Sold goods for £850.
	Received a cheque for £2,800 from Tom Dexter, a customer.
	Paid £450 for advertising, by cheque 0007.
	Paid £1,650 to Dawn Black, a supplier, by cheque 0008.
	Paid £420 for repairs to the motor vehicle in cash.
5.1	Cashed cheque 0009 for £500 to pay weekly wages.
	Bank returned Sam's cheque marked 'Refer to drawer'.
	Received a cheque for £1,450 from Sonny Mohamed, a customer.
	Bank advises a Bank Giro Credit receipt of £3,200 from Richard Day, a customer.
	Paid £650 as weekly wages to casual workers in cash.
	Deposited into bank the cheques received from Tom and Sonny.
	Bank notifies a charge of £30 for 'unauthorised overdraft'.
	Received a cheque for £3,260 from Laso plc, a credit card company, in respect of sales made on their credit card.

Required: Record these transactions in a two-column cash book.

PQ 13.3 Tracing items for a bank reconciliation statement

In respect of the transactions reported in PQ 13.2 above, Olive May received the following bank statement from City Bank.

Olive May Stores in account with				
CITY BANK plc 501 Pall Mall, London SW1 4AN				
Date	Details	Withdrawal	Deposits	Balance
20X0		£	£	£
1.1	Deposits	–	9,000	9,000
1.1	Chq. 0001	2,400	–	6,600
2.1	Loan	–	15,000	21,600
4.1	Chq. 0004	16,500	–	5,100
4.1	Deposit	–	3,861	8,961
4.1	Chq. 0002	1,500	–	7,461
4.1	Deposit	–	1,200	8,661
5.1	Standing order	275	–	8,386
5.1	Chq. 0006	3,850	–	4,536
5.1	Chq. 0009	500	–	4,036
5.1	Chq. 0003	3,000	–	1,036
5.1	Chq. 0008	1,650	–	614 O/D
5.1	Bank charges	30	–	644 O/D
5.1	Giro credit	–	3,200	2,556

Required: Prepare a bank reconciliation statement as at 5th January 20X0.

PQ 13.4 Ascertaining the actual balance at bank

The following information relates to three separate business entities:

● Business A:
  – The balance on 30.6.20X0, according to the bank statement, was £26,800.
  – Deposits yet to be credited by the bank amount on this date to £6,500.
  – Cheques yet not presented to the bank for payment amount to £18,600.
● Business B:
  – The balance on 30.6.20X0, according to bank statement, was £42,750.
  – Effects awaiting clearance by the bank on this date amount to £14,650.
  – Cheques drawn by this date but presented after it amount to £74,200.
  – The bank has erroneously credited to this account a cheque for £4,500, which was drawn in favour of another entity with a similar name.
● Business C:
  – The overdraft at the bank on 30.6.20X0, according to the bank statement, was £72,400.
  – Deposits awaiting clearance on this date amount to £116,200.
  – Cheques issued by the business yet to be presented for payment amount to £28,200.

Required: With regard to each of the above, determine the amount that will appear in the Bank account in the cash book for each business as at 30 June 20X0.

PQ 13.5 Bank reconciliation statements prepared as at two dates

An extract from the cash book maintained by Bill Sach's retail shop appears as follows:

BANK ACCOUNT

Date	Details	Bank	Date	Chq.	Details	Bank
20X0		£	20X0			£
21.1	Balance	1,260	21.1	26	P. Godwin	1,200
22.1	Cash a/c	4,440	21.1	27	Purchases	1,360
22.1	Loan a/c	8,000	23.1	28	Cash a/c	600
23.1	Cash a/c	2,150	23.1	29	Equipment	2,000
26.1	Cash a/c	1,840	23.1	30	Electricity	760
26.1	Balance	2,210	24.1	31	Lucy Gill	1,180
			24.1	32	Rent	1,500
			25.1	33	S. Nathan	750
			25.1	34	Stationery	650
			25.1	35	Mike Shaw	2,600
			26.1	36	Salaries	5,460
			26.1	37	R. Spring	1,280
			26.1	38	Heating	560
		19,900				19,900
			1.2		Balance	2,210

The bank statement in respect of the period ending on 26 January 20X0 is as follows:

Bill Sachs   in account with

MIDWEST BANK

20X0	Details	Debit	Credit	Balance
21.1	Balance	–	–	150 O/D
21.1	Deposits	–	3,250	3,100
22.1	Loan	–	8,000	11,100
23.1	Chq. 28	600	–	10,500
23.1	Chq. 26	1,200	–	9,300
23.1	Standing order – Rates	400	–	8,900
24.1	Chq. 25	1,620	–	7,280
24.1	Dividend – mandate	–	1,500	8,780
24.1	Chq. 29	2,000	–	6,780
25.1	Chq. 24	220	–	6,560
25.1	Deposit	–	4,440	11,000
25.1	Charges	55	–	10,945
25.1	Chq. 31	1,180	–	9,765
26.1	Deposit	–	2,150	11,915
26.1	Chq. 35	2,600	–	9,315

Required: Prepare a bank reconciliation statement as at 21 January 20X0 and another at 26 January 20X0.

PQ 13.6 Adjusting the cash book prior to bank reconciliation

The following items were identified in the course of bank reconciliation as at 31 May 20X0:

(a) The bank balance on that day as per cash book was £46,400.
(b) Bank charges of £36 have been entered twice in the cash book.

(c) A favourable balance at bank of £23,400 has been carried forward from one folio of the cash book to the next as £32,400.

(d) The debit side of the Bank account in the cash book has been added as £64,250 instead of £64,130.

(e) £11,400 received from John Curry, a customer, through the bank giro credit system is not accounted for in the cash book.

(f) £3,400 paid as insurance by direct debit is not accounted in the cash book.

(g) Deposits not cleared by this date were £22,700.

(h) Cheques drawn but yet to be presented for payment amount to £36,840.

Required:

(a) Set out an amended Bank account to report the actual balance held with the bank on 31 May 20X0.

(b) On the basis that any difference arising in the Trial Balance because of these errors has already been placed in a Suspense account, state any journal entry necessary to eliminate the Suspense account balance.

(c) Prepare a bank reconciliation statement as at 31.5.20X0 to reconcile the balance in the amended Bank account with the balance on the bank statement.

PQ 13.7 Bank balance – actual, and as stated in the bank statement

As at 14 September 20X1, the balance in the Bank account in the cash book of Beta Fruit Suppliers was £14,680. The cashier ascertained the following information:

(a) Three cheques drawn in payment of creditors, for a total value of £18,260, do not appear in the bank statement.

(b) A debit balance at the bank of £11,560 had been carried from one folio of the cash book to the next as £15,160.

(c) The cashier was not aware of bank charges stated on the bank statement as £136.

(d) £32,200 deposited in the bank is not reported on the bank statement.

(e) A cheque for £900 drawn by the proprietor for his own use is not recorded in the cash book but it appears in the bank statement.

(f) The bank has credited to the current account a deposit of £10,000 made into a deposit account.

Required: Ascertain the bank balance to be reported in the Balance Sheet as at 14 September 20X1, and the current account bank balance as it would be stated on the bank statement on 14 September 20X1.

PQ 13.8 Role of bank reconciliation when finalizing accounts

Joy's Minimarket finalized its accounts for the year 20X0, reporting a net profit of £348,600 and a balance at the bank of £79,800 on 31.12.20X0. The Trial Balance extracted as at 31.12.20X0, however, failed to balance. The difference in the Trial Balance was placed in a Suspense account and, when finalizing the accounts for the year, the amount was written off against profit. A bank reconciliation was not prepared as at 31.12.20X0.

As the newly appointed accountant for Joy's Minimarket, your enquiries in January 20X1 reveal as follows:

(a) Bank charges of £16, business rates paid by direct debit amounting to £2,800, as well as dividend income of £3,600 collected on a mandate, were not taken account of when finalizing the accounts for the year ended 31.12.20X0.

(b) A cheque for £11,600 received from Mercy Alles, a credit customer, has been posted in error to the Sales account as £1,160.

(c) Cheques yet to be presented for payment to the bank on 31.12.20X0 amounted to £72,400; and deposits awaiting realization on this date came to £22,600.

(d) A cheque for £2,600, drawn in payment of sales commission, had been replaced by another. The only entries made in this connection were posting of both cheques from the cash book to the appropriate nominal account.

Required:

(a) Show Journal entries to correct these errors in January 20X1.

(b) Identify the impact of the corrections on the profit for the year ended 31.12.20X0 and the bank balance on 31.12.20X0.

(c) Prepare the bank reconciliation statement as at 31.12.20X0.

PQ 13.9 A three-column cash book

On 1.1.20X0 Hilda Stores had £650 in hand and £12,740 at the bank. The transactions on that day were as follows:

● Paid £450 for advertising by cheque 476.

● Paid £13,800 to Peter Tell, a supplier, by cheque 477, taking advantage of an 8 per cent cash discount on offer.

- Received a cheque for £7,600 from Guy Thomas, a customer, who is entitled to a 5 per cent cash discount.
- Cash sales were made for £2,350.
- Paid £120 for staff tea.
- Received a cheque for £6,175 from Jerry Wren, a customer, who is entitled to a 5 per cent cash discount.
- Paid £5,850 by cheque 478 to Peter Paul, to settle an amount due, net of a 10 per cent cash discount.
- Mike Saunter, to whom goods had been sold two days earlier for £7,500, returns goods sold for £300 and settles his dues in full, taking advantage of a 5 per cent cash discount on offer for prompt payment.
- All amounts are deposited at the bank, leaving a cash float of £1,000.

Required: As cashier, record the transactions in a three-column cash book and explain how each transaction will be posted by the bookkeeper.

PQ 13.10 Focus on discounts allowed and received

Ted Smile, a wholesaler, buys his requirements on a month's credit from three reputed suppliers – Alpha, Beta and Gamma. All of them allow a 10 per cent settlement discount if purchases are paid for within three days. Ted in turn has approved a month's credit to his customers – Peter, Paul, James, John and Mark – who have all been assured of cash discount on the scale stated on the right but warned that goods sold may only be returned within three days.

> 5% if payment is received at least by the third day; or
> 3% if payment is received after 3 days but within the calendar month.

On 1 May 20X0, Ted owed Alpha, Beta and Gamma £214,600, £346,500 and £126,400 respectively. £38,500 of the amount owed to Beta was in respect of purchases made on 30

	Peter	Paul	James	John	Mark
Sales on 29/30 April 20X0	£25,600	–	£12,500	–	£4,200
Sales prior to 28.4.20X0	£114,200	£69,300	£36,700	£136,800	£12,400
Total receivable	£139,800	£69,300	£49,200	£136,800	£16,600

April 20X0, while rest of the purchases were made several days earlier. A breakdown of amounts due from customers on 1.5.20X0 is stated above.

Transactions within the week commencing on 1 May 20X0 include the following:

Date	Item
1 May	Sales to Paul of £22,200, to John of £18,000 and to Mark of £6,000.
	Purchases from Alpha of £16,400 and from Gamma of £15,600.
	Return to Beta of goods bought on 30.4.20X0 for £6,500.
	Paid Beta in full by cheque 287.
	Received a cheque in full settlement from James.
2 May	Sales to Peter of £17,500.
	Mark returns goods sold for £1,200.
	Returned to Alpha goods purchased for £1,800.
	Received cheques in full settlement from John and Mark.
3 May	Cheques from James, John and Mark are banked.
	Sales to James of £13,600 and to Paul of £8,200.
	Purchases made from Alpha at a cost of £16,400 and from Gamma at £11,200.
	Returned to Beta goods bought for £1,500.
4 May	Sales to Peter of £7,400, Paul of £8,600 and John of £4,500.
	Purchased from Alpha for £6,500 and from Gamma for £12,500.
	Paid £214,600 to Alpha by cheque 296.
5 May	Mark's cheque is returned by the bank endorsed 'Refer to Drawer'.
	Sales to Peter of £11,200 and to James of £26,400.
	Received a cheque from Peter for £174,445.
	Settled Gamma in full by cheque 299.

Required: Record these transactions in the Sales Day Book, Sales Returns Book, Purchases Day Book and Purchases Returns Book, as appropriate; and post transactions to the Debtors, Creditors and Nominal Ledgers, as appropriate.

PQ 13.11 Correction of errors and use of a Suspense account

Sid Taylor, a retailer, balanced his Trial Balance on the last day of the year, placing the difference in a Suspense account. Making a determined effort, he has identified the following errors:

(a) Rent accrued at year end of £2,400 is listed in the Trial Balance as a debit balance.
(b) The Returns Inwards Day Book has been added as £13,600 instead of £15,700.
(c) An amount of £4,250, the total of the discount column on the debit side of the cash book, was posted to the credit of the Discount Received account.
(d) On receiving a cheque for £7,980 from Tim Hall, Hall was allowed a 5 per cent discount. When the cheque was dishonoured, the only entry made was posting the cheque to the debit of his personal account.

Required: Prepare Journal entries to correct the errors; and prepare a Suspense account on the basis that the correction of the errors fully eliminated its balance.

Chapter 14

CONTROL ACCOUNTS

In this chapter

We will learn:

- of the usefulness of Control accounts
- that it is not only in respect of personal ledgers that Control accounts are maintained

and you should be able to:

- prepare Control accounts and
- reconcile a Control account balance with the sum of corresponding individual balances

14.1 INTRODUCTION TO CONTROL ACCOUNTS

A Control account records in total a large number of entries that are individually entered in many accounts in a ledger. For example, numerous accounts of individual debtors will be found in the Debtors Ledger, each reporting the amount receivable from a particular debtor. A Debtors Control account is prepared so that its balance equals the sum of all the individual debtors' balances in the Debtors Ledger.

The need for writing up Control accounts was appreciated when business entities, dealing with a large number of individual debtors and creditors, found that extraction of a Trial Balance became too laborious and time-consuming, because they had to extract balances from a large number of personal accounts. As a solution to this, they decided to maintain just one account to record in total the transactions with all debtors and, similarly, another to record in total those with all creditors. These became known as Total accounts or Control accounts. Maintenance of a Total Debtors account does not mean that the maintenance of individual accounts for each debtor can be dispensed with, however; without the individual accounts the amount receivable from each debtor cannot be ascertained.

14.2 WRITING UP A CONTROL ACCOUNT

The sources of information for writing up a Control account are the books of prime entry. If one decides, for example, to write up a Total Debtors account, say from 1 May 20X0, one would start by calling for a list of debtors on that day to be extracted from the Debtors Ledger. Let us assume that the list was as stated on the right. By the end of the month he will call for the total of credit sales made in May, information that is available in the Sales Day Book (see following page) and, from the cashier, the receipts from credit customers in that month (see following page). Preparing a Total Debtors account is just a matter of piecing together all three of these bits of information. Thus the Total Debtors account identifies the total

DEBTORS AS AT 1.5.20X0	
	£
Robert	1,000
Samuel	1,250
Timothy	5,200
	7,450

Extract from cash book	
	£
Robert	900
Samuel	1,250
Timothy	3,000
	5,150

TOTAL DEBTORS ACCOUNT

	£		£
Balance b/f	7,450	Cash	5,150
Sales	19,200	Balance c/d	21,500
	26,650		26,650
Balance b/d	21,500		

SALES DAY BOOK

May 20X0	£
Robert	6,000
Samuel	4,150
Timothy	9,050
	19,200

amount to be received from customers (debtors) as at 31 May 20X0 as £21,500. In the meantime, individual accounts of each customer would have been written up in the Debtors Ledger (as shown below) and a list extracted of the amounts due from each of them as at 31 May 20X0. The sum of the balances due from individual debtors (see list below) should be the same as the balance in the Total Debtors account. If so, the accuracy of both the Total Debtors account balance and the balances in the individual debtors' accounts are established, by one corroborating the other.

ROBERT'S ACCOUNT

	£		£
Balance b/f	1,000	Cash a/c	900
Sales Day Bk	6,000	Balance c/d	6,100
Balance b/d	6,100		

SAMUEL'S ACCOUNT

	£		£
Balance b/f	1,250	Cash a/c	1,250
Sales Day Bk	4,150	Balance c/d	4,150
Balance b/d	4,150		

TIMOTHY'S ACCOUNT

	£		£
Balance b/f	5,200	Cash a/c	3,000
Sales Day Bk	9,050	Balance c/d	11,250
Balance b/d	11,250		

LIST AS AT 31 MAY 20X0 OF SALES LEDGER BALANCES

	£
Robert's account	6,100
Samuel's account	4,150
Timothy's account	11,250
	21,500

14.2.1 Distinction between Control accounts and Total accounts

A Total account, if and only if written up under a strict control environment, may be referred to as a Control account. If, for example, the three items of information we required for writing up a Total Debtors account are provided by the same person, that person would be in a position to mask any irregularities. A misappropriation of £1,250 received from Samuel, for example, may be masked by omitting that amount both from the amounts of cash received and the sales for the month. On the other hand, if the three items of information we used for writing up the Total account were obtained from three independent persons, the Total account would have been written up within a controlled environment, which makes it difficult to mask irregularities. In that case the Total account qualifies to be called a Control account.

Note that a Control account maintained in respect of the personal accounts of credit customers is known as a Debtors Control account, **Sales Ledger Control account** or Sold Ledger Control account; the corresponding one maintained in respect of the accounts of suppliers is known as a Creditors Control account, **Purchases Ledger Control account** or Bought Ledger Control account.

14.2.2 Benefits of writing up Control accounts

Control accounts are maintained in respect of personal ledgers because of several benefits derived from them. These include the following:

- It improves the control system because the work of those writing up numerous personal accounts of individual customers and suppliers is proved by matching the results against the balance in the Control account – provided that there is a separation of duties such as issue of invoices, collecting cheques and listing debtor balances.
- It expedites the preparation of a Trial Balance because a single figure of total debtors or creditors is available instead of having to balance off and add together the balances in the accounts of a large number of individual debtors and creditors.
- It enables the tracing of errors by localizing the error, if possible to one of the subsidiary ledgers. There will be no need to check all the accounts in full when looking for an error. For example, if a Trial Balance balances when it includes the balance in the Debtors Control account, but does not do so when the total of individual debtors' balances is substituted, the presumption (which might be wrong) is that the error is in the Sales Ledger.

14.3 ALTERNATIVE WAYS OF MAINTAINING CONTROL ACCOUNTS

Control accounts may be maintained using three alternative procedures. These are as set out next.

14.3.1 Procedure One

In the first procedure, the Control accounts are maintained on a memorandum basis only so that the personal accounts of debtors and creditors remain within the double entry system. This means that every credit sale is posted individually to the debit of, and every amount received individually to the credit of, the account of the customer concerned. In the meantime, a Debtors Ledger Control account is maintained, usually by a senior official, on a *memorandum basis*, i.e. outside the double entry system. The expression 'memorandum basis' means that the information is retained in the form of a note to aid memory. On a vertical format, the Control account would appear as shown here on the right.

MEMORANDUM DEBTORS LEDGER CONTROL ACCOUNT		
20X0		**£**
1.5	Balance b/f	7,450
	Sales in May	19,200
		26,650
	Cash received in May	(5,150)
31.5	Balance c/d	21,500

The aim of this exercise is to use the Control account balance to monitor the accuracy of the balances reported in the many accounts of individual customers, maintained in the Debtors Ledger.

14.3.2 Procedure Two

In the second procedure, the Control accounts (in the Real Ledger) are the actual accounts and it is the individual personal accounts that are maintained on a memorandum basis: Individual accounts of customers and suppliers are no longer posted as part of the double entry system. Instead, they are replaced by a Sales Ledger Control account and a Purchases Ledger Control account in the Real Ledger. The double entry system now requires the periodic totals of the Sales Day Book to be credited to the Sales account and debited to the Sales Ledger Control account.

There is still, of course, an absolute commercial need to keep track of the amounts receivable from each customer and the amounts payable to each supplier. This is taken care of by keeping the individual accounts written up for each customer and supplier – the only difference is that the entries are outside the double entry system. Some businesses recognize this by renaming the Debtors Ledger as a 'Debtors Register'.

14.3.3 Procedure Three

Here, the Control accounts are included in self-balancing ledgers, which is an improvement on the second procedure. Having relegated the accounts of individual customers (and suppliers) away from the double entry system, instead of simply maintaining them on a memorandum basis in a register, arrangements are made to maintain them in a special self-contained subsidiary ledger. The subsidiary ledger in which customers' accounts are written up may be still be named the Sales Ledger, and the one for suppliers' accounts the Purchases Ledger. In the Sales Ledger, when individual customers' accounts are debited with the appropriate amount of sales, crediting the total sale to an 'Impersonal Ledger Adjustment account' completes the double entry. When the amounts received from customers are credited to their individual ledger accounts, debiting the Adjustment account completes double entry. Thus each ledger becomes self-balancing in that a Trial Balance can be extracted in respect of each of them. Just as a Trial Balance can be extracted with balances from both the Real Ledger and the Nominal Ledger, it is possible to extract another Trial Balance in respect of the Debtors Ledger and a third in respect of the Creditors Ledger.

14.4 A SALES LEDGER CONTROL ACCOUNT

Items of information required for writing up a Debtors Ledger Control account (i.e. a Sales Ledger Control account) would in real life be more than the three we identified in Section 14.2 above. The source of information for each of these is as follows:

Opening debtors	List of debtors outstanding on this day extracted from Debtors Ledger
Credit sales	Periodic totals of the Sales Day Book
Receipts from customers	From the cash book. To obtain this information more conveniently, it is usual to build into the cash book appropriate analysis columns into which receipts from credit customers are extended.
Returns inwards	Periodic totals of the Sales Returns Day Book
Discounts allowed	Periodic totals of the Discount column in debit side of the cash book
Bad debts written off	Journal
Reversal of discount	Journal
Setting off	Journal

A Sales Ledger Control account would appear as follows:

PRO FORMA SALES LEDGER CONTROL ACCOUNT

	£		£
Balance b/f	XX	Balance b/f *	X
Sales (on credit)	XXX	Cash/cheques	XXX
Dishonoured cheques	XX	Discounts allowed	X
Discount (reversed)	XX	Sales returns	X
		Bad debts w/off	X
		Set off by contra **	X
Balance c/d *	X	Balance c/d	XX
Balance b/d	XX	Balance c/d *	X

Two items in the pro forma account deserve explanation. The first (marked *) is how a credit balance could exist in customers' accounts. A customer may temporarily be in credit if that customer returns goods after paying for them. The second (marked **) is a 'set-off by contra'. An entity may possibly purchase goods from the same party to whom it also sells. If we name that party 'John', and assume that John is reported as a debtor (in the Sales Ledger) for £10,000 and a creditor (in the Purchases Ledger) for £4,000, it is likely that we would receive only the net amount of £6,000 from John in full settlement. To account for the settlement, we have to offset £4,000 remaining in the Debtors Ledger against the corresponding credit balance in the Creditors Ledger.

Interaction 14.1

Sales Ledger Control account balance

Jasmine Smith's trade debtors as at 1.1.20X0 amount to £12,500 and her transactions include the following:

	January 20X0	February 20X0
Cash sales	£1,500	£2,400
Credit sales	£15,500	£18,600
Returns by credit customers	£200	£540
Settlement discount allowed	£160	£210
Collection from credit customers	£13,650	£16,250
Reversal of discount allowed	£40	–
Bad debts written off	£240	£180
Recovery of debt earlier written off	–	£80

Required: Ascertain the balance that Jasmine would carry down in her Sales Ledger Control account as at 31.1.20X0 and 29.2.20X0.

Interaction 14.2

Multiple-choice review

Tick one of the following grids as appropriate.

1. A source of information for preparing Control accounts is
   (a) bank statements
   (b) Trial Balance
   (c) the books of prime entry
   (d) the ledgers.

2. A credit balance could arise in the Debtors Ledger because of
   (a) a customer returning goods after paying for them
   (b) a customer overpaying the account
   (c) a customer not taking a cash discount available
   (d) all of these.

Sales Ledger Control account

Interaction
14.3

The following information has been obtained from the books of a wholesale trader:

Balances in customers' accounts as at 1.3.20X0:	£
Debit balances	148,650
Credit balances	14,200
Totals for March 20X0:	
Sales Day Book	984,050
Sales Returns Day Book	62,450
Discount column on debit side of the cash book	11,600
Receipts from credit customers	846,240
Information from the Journal:	
Bad debts written off	12,460
Discount reversed	1,200
Offset against balance in Creditors Ledger	22,660
Credit balances in Debtors Ledger as at 31.3.20X0	24,280

Required: Prepare a Debtors Ledger Control account for March 20X0.

14.5 A PURCHASES LEDGER CONTROL ACCOUNT

Similarly to the previous section, to write up a Creditors Ledger Control account (i.e. a Purchases Ledger Control account) the information is obtained as follows:

- Opening balances: obtained from a list of creditors' balances at commencement of the period.
- Credit purchases: obtained from periodic totals of the Purchases Day Book.
- Purchases returns: obtained from periodic totals of the Returns Outward Day Book.
- Payments to suppliers: obtained by analysing the payment side of the cash book.
- Discount received: obtained from periodic totals of the Discount column on the payment side of the cash book.

PRO FORMA **CREDITOR'S CONTROL ACCOUNT**

	£		£
Balance b/f	X	Balance b/f	XX
Cash/cheque	XXX	Purchases (cr)	XXX
Purchase returns	X		
Discount received	X		
Set off by contra	X		
Balance c/d	XX	Balance c/d	X
Balance c/d	X	Balance b/d	XX

The Purchases Ledger Control account will appear as set out above right.

Purchases Ledger Control balance

Interaction
14.4

Raymond Stores owes its suppliers £224,200 on 1 March 20X0. Its transactions in the next two months include the following:

In 20X0	March	April
Purchases for cash	£11,500	£8,600
Purchases on credit	£286,400	£296,800
Payments to credit suppliers	£256,200	£288,500
Returns to credit suppliers	£12,500	£9,600
Cash discount earned	£11,200	£5,400

Required: Ascertain the Purchases Ledger Control account balance on 31 March 20X0 and on 30 April 20X0.

Interaction 14.5

Purchases Ledger Control account

The following information has been obtained from the books of a wholesale trader:

	£
Balances in suppliers' accounts as at 1.3.20X0:	
Debit balances	11,450
Credit balances	214,840
Totals for March 20X0:	
Purchases Day Book	627,550
Purchases Returns Day Book	22,340
Discount column on credit side of cash book	42,800
Payments to suppliers	586,750
Information from the Journal:	
Offset against balance in Debtors Ledger	22,660
Debit balances in Creditors Ledger as at 31.3.20X0	5,160

Required: Prepare a Purchases Ledger Control account for March 20X0.

Interaction 14.6

Set-off by contra

Mervin's Enterprises maintains its personal ledgers on a self-balancing basis. As at 30 June 20X0, an amount of £24,500 owed to City Stores is reported in the Creditors Ledger and £7,200 due from the same party is reported in the Debtors Ledger, though a set-off has been agreed with City Stores.

Required: Lay out in the form of Journal entries how the set-off should be accounted for in the Real Ledger, Debtors Ledger and Creditors Ledger.

14.6 A FAILURE TO MATCH

When a Control account balance fails to match the sum of the corresponding individual account balances, the error could be in:

- making entries to the Control account;
- calculating the balance on the Control account;
- making entries to the individual customers'/suppliers' accounts;
- calculating the balances of the individual customers'/suppliers' accounts;
- extracting the list of balances;
- casting the list of balances.

This means that, if the Control account balance does not reconcile to the total of the list of balances, either might be incorrect. For example, if the Trial Balance balances when the Control account balance is included but not when the sum of the individual accounts is included, it would not necessarily imply that the error is in determining the individual account balances. It could perhaps be that there has been an error in casting the Sales Day Book – this would mean that the Control account balance would be wrong and yet the Trial Balance would balance with the Control account balance included.

Reconciliation with the Control account

Simple Simon maintains in his Real Ledger the Control accounts for customers and suppliers – and the individual personal accounts are written up outside the double entry system. He is pleased that his year-end Trial Balance (summarized on the right) balanced perfectly. His worry, though, is that his Control Account balances fail to match with the sum of the individual debtors and creditors, which amount to £203,000 and £147,000 respectively. His investigations reveal the following errors: a folio in

SUMMARISED TRIAL BALANCE AS AT 30.6.20X0		
	£000	£000
Purchases/Sales	632	984
Debtors Ledger Control	216	–
Creditors Ledger Control	–	156
All other item balances	2,944	2,652
	3,792	3,792

the Sales Day Book has been added as £18,600 instead of £14,600; the Control accounts fail to reflect a debt of £9,000 that was offset against a corresponding amount in the Creditors Ledger.

Required:

(a) Prepare a reconciliation of Control account balances with the sum of individual debtors' accounts and creditors' accounts.
(b) Show Journal entries to correct any error(s).
(c) Set out the revised summarized Trial Balance.

14.7 CONTROL ACCOUNTS FOR OTHER ASSETS

We have explained the use of a Sales Ledger Control account to control debtors and a Purchases Ledger Control account to control creditors. We have also shown how they can produce totals quickly for use in a Trial Balance.

We can apply the same principle to other assets and liabilities, e.g. fixed assets and stock. For example, a Motor Vehicles account reports the total cost of all the vehicles owned by an entity. Particulars of each vehicle (such as those in the box) would be recorded in a Motor Vehicle Register. The sum of the costs of each vehicle stated in the register should equal the balance in the Motor Vehicle account.

A *Motor Vehicle Register* may contain the following particulars of each vehicle:

1. The make and model
2. The registration number
3. The chassis number
4. Engine capacity
5. The cost and improvements
6. Who keeps custody
7. Supplier's particulars
8. Any guarantee/warranty
9. Mileage particulars
10. Service history
11. Major repairs
12. Insurance particulars

In the case of a limited liability company, a Share Capital account records in total the called-up value of shares held by all shareholders. Particulars of each shareholder and the value of shares held by each are reported in a Share Register.

SOLUTIONS TO INTERACTIVE QUESTIONS

IQ 14.1 Sales Ledger Control account balance

SALES LEDGER CONTROL ACCOUNT – JANUARY 20X0	£		£
Balance b/f	12,500	Returns	200
Credit sales	15,500	Discount allowed	160
Disc. reversed	40	Cash received	13,650
		Bad debts	240
		Balance c/d	13,790
	28,040		28,040

SALES LEDGER CONTROL ACCOUNT – FEBRUARY 20X0	£		£
Balance b/f	13,790	Returns	540
Credit sales	18,600	Discount allowed	210
		Cash received	16,250
		Bad debts	180
		Balance c/d	15,210
	32,390		32,390

IQ 14.2 Multiple-choice review

(1) c   (2) d

IQ 14.3 Sales Ledger Control account

SALES LEDGER CONTROL ACCOUNT	£		£
Balance b/f	148,650	Balance b/f	14,200
Sales	984,050	Sales returns	62,450
Discount allowed – reversal	1,200	Discount allowed	11,600
		Cash book	846,240
		Bad debts written off	12,460
		Creditors Ledger – contra	22,660
Balance c/d	24,280	Balance c/d	188,570
	1,158,180		1,158,180
Balance b/d	188,570	Balance b/d	24,280

IQ 14.4 Purchases Ledger Control account balance

CREDITORS LEDGER CONTROL ACCOUNT – MARCH 20X0	£		£
Cash – paid	256,200	Balance b/f	224,200
Return outw..	12,500	Purchases	286,400
Discount recd	11,200		
Balance c/d	230,700		
	510,600		510,600

CREDITORS LEDGER CONTROL ACCOUNT – APRIL 20X0	£		£
Cash – paid	288,500	Balance b/f	230,700
Return outw..	9,600	Purchases	296,800
Discount recd	5,400		
Balance c/d	224,000		
	527,500		527,500

IQ 14.5 Purchases Ledger Control account

PURCHASES LEDGER CONTROL ACCOUNT

	£		£
Balance b/f	11,450	Balance b/f	214,840
Purchase returns	22,340	Purchases	627,550
Discount received	42,800		
Cash book	586,750		
Debtors Ledger – contra	22,660		
Balance c/d	161,550	Balance c/d	5,160
	847,550		847,550
Balance b/d	5,160	Balance b/d	161,550

IQ 14.6 Set-off by contra

In the Real Ledger:	Creditors Control a/c	Dr	£7,200	–
	To Debtors Control a/c		–	£7,200
	Being offset by contra			

In the Creditors Ledger:	City Stores a/c	Dr	£7,200	–
	To Impersonal Ledger Adjustment a/c		–	£7,200
	Being offset by contra			

In the Debtors Ledger:	Impersonal Ledger Adjustment a/c	Dr	£7,200	–
	To City Stores a/c		–	£7,200
	Being offset by contra			

IQ 14.7 Reconciliation with the Control account

(a) Reconciliation of the Control account balances with the sum of the individual personal account balances:

	Debtors Ledger £000	Creditors Ledger £000
Balances in the Control accounts	216	156
Casting error in the Sales Day Book	(4)	–
Failure to record the amount offset by contra	(9)	(9)
Sum of the individual personal account balances	203	147

(b) Journal entries

Sales a/c	Dr	£4,000	
To Sales Ledger control a/c			£4,000
Being correction of error			
Purchase Ledger Control a/c	Dr	£9,000	
To Sales Ledger Control a/c			£9,000
Being correction of error			

Both errors are of a compensating nature. Therefore they did not disturb the Trial Balance. The overcasting in the Sales Day Book inflated both the Sales account and the Debtors Control account balances. The failure to account for the contra offset left an inflated balance in both control accounts.

(c) Revised Trial Balance

	£000	£000
SUMMARIZED TRIAL BALANCE AS AT 30.6.20X0		
Purchases/Sales	632	980
Debtors Ledger Control	203	–
Creditors Ledger Control	–	147
All other items	2,944	2,652
	3,779	3,779

PROGRESSIVE QUESTIONS

PQ 14.1 Writing up Personal Ledger Control accounts

The following information relates to the personal accounts of a trader during March 20X0:

	£
Cash purchases	62,400
Credit purchases	264,600
Carriage inwards	102,450
Carriage outwards	412,200
Paid to suppliers	198,500
Return inwards	26,450
Return outwards	11,500
Cash sales	102,450
Credit sales	412,200
Bad debts	3,800
Settlement discount allowed to customers	15,950
Settlement discount received from creditors	9,450
Receipts from customers	368,500
Dishonour of cheques received from customers	6,650
Reversal of discount allowed to customers	350
Debt collection expenses charged to customers	150
Debt recovered by contra set-off	15,500
Interest charged on a customer who persistently overstepped credit period	225

	Sales Ledger balances		**Purchases Ledger balances**	
As at 1 March 20X0	Debit balance	£348,250	Debit balances	£9,400
	Credit balance	£16,200	Credit balances	£225,700
As at 31 March 20X0	Credit balance	£17,200	Debit balance	£11,500

Required: Prepare the Sales Ledger Control account and the Purchases Ledger Control account for the above business.

PQ 14.2 Sales Ledger control from source information

Michael Scott maintains a Receipts Cash Book separately from a Payments Cash Book, each with appropriate analysis columns to facilitate writing up the personal ledger Control accounts. He maintains the individual personal accounts of his customers and suppliers in subsidiary ledgers operated on a self-balancing basis. The list of amounts due from his customers on 1 May 20X0 were as listed here.

AMOUNTS DUE FROM CUSTOMERS

	Debit	Credit
	£	£
W.B. Rajaguru	62,450	–
Lisa Jenkins Ltd	26,780	–
Parker and sons	14,265	–
Rik Hunt and Co	34,550	–
Jerry Haines plc	–	6,400
Rob Murdoch	26,460	–
Adam Young	36,595	–
M. Ramanathan	–	11,250

The Receipt Cash Book in respect of May 20X0 appears as follows, and other records are as set out thereafter.

Date	V	Particulars	Discount	Cash	Bank	Sales	SL Control	Misc	F
			RECEIPTS CASH BOOK			ANALYSIS COLUMNS			
20X0			£	£	£	£	£	£	
1.5	–	Balance b/f	–	2,150	28,450	–	–	–	
1.5	X	Sales account	–	1,460	–	1,460	–	–	
1.5	X	Jerry Haines a/c	1,202	28,848	–	–	28,848	–	
3.5	X	Sales account	–	2,140	–	2,140	–	–	
3.5	X	Cash account	–	–	29,650	–	–	29,650	CB?
3.5	X	Lisa Jenkins Ltd	1,696	40,704	–	–	40,704	–	
4.5	X	Cash account	–	–	40,704	–	–	40,704	CB?
7.5	X	Sales account	–	1,640	–	1,640	–	–	
9.5	X	Bank Loan a/c	–	–	50,000	–	–	50,000	RL?
11.5	X	W.B. Rajaguru	3,396	81,504	–	–	81,504	–	
11.5	X	Sales account	–	2,425	–	2,425	–	–	
12.5	X	Cash account	–	–	83,200	–	–	83,200	CB?
16.5	X	Sales account	–	1,645	–	1,645	–	–	
18.5	X	Adam Young	1,914	45,936	–	–	45,936	–	
19.5	X	Parker & sons	1,716	41,184	–	–	41,184	–	
19.5	X	Sales account	–	2,145	–	2,145	–	–	
19.5	X	Cash account	–	–	90,100	–	–	90,100	CB?
24.5	X	Rik Hunt and Co	2,140	51,360	–	–	51,360	–	
25.5	X	Jerry Haines plc	676	16,224	–	–	16,224	–	
26.5	X	Cash account	–	–	67,584	–	–	67,584	CB?
29.5	X	M. Ramanathan	2,096	50,304	–	–	50,304	–	
30.5	X	Sales account	–	1,645	–	1,645	–	–	
30.5	X	Lisa Jenkins Ltd	2,468	59,232	–	–	59,232	–	
31.5	X	Cash account	–	–	111,181	–	–	111,181	CB?
			17,304	430,546	500,869	13,100	415,296		
			NL?			NL?	RL?		

SALES JOURNAL				
Date	V	Customer	F	Amount
20X0				£
1.5	X	Parker and sons	DL?	28,635
1.5	X	Jerry Haines plc	DL?	36,450
3.5	X	Adam Young	DL?	11,255
3.5	X	W.B. Rajaguru	DL?	26,200
3.5	X	Lisa Jenkins Ltd	DL?	17,460
7.5	X	Rik Hunt and Co	DL?	20,200
9.5	X	W.B. Rajaguru	DL?	36,250
11.5	X	Jerry Haines plc	DL?	18,560
11.5	X	Lisa Jenkins Ltd	DL?	39,200
15.5	X	M. Ramanathan	DL?	36,420
19.5	X	Parker & sons	DL?	34,140
22.5	X	W.B. Rajaguru	DL?	17,650
26.5	X	Jerry Haines plc	DL?	29,260
27.5	X	M. Ramanathan	DL?	27,230
27.5	X	Rik Hunt and Co	DL?	46,540
30.5	X	Adam Young	DL?	17,480
30.5	X	Lisa Jenkins Ltd	DL?	22,500
31.5	X	M. Ramanathan	DL?	18,640
				484,070

RETURNS INWARDS JOURNAL				
Date	V	Customer	F	Amount
1.5	X	Lisa Jenkins Ltd	DL?	£ 1,840
9.5	X	Rik Hunt and Co	DL?	1,250
11.5	X	W.B. Rajaguru	DL?	3,750
11.5	X	Jerry Haines plc	DL?	1,660
21.5	X	Parker and sons	DL?	2,860
31.5	X	Lisa Jenkins Ltd	DL?	3,940
				15,300

JOURNAL					
				£	£
27.5	X	Bad debts a/c Dr		26,460	–
		To Rob Murdoch		–	26,460
		Being debt written off			

Required:

(a) Explain the posting of transactions recorded in the Receipts Cash Book with the analysis columns.
(b) Prepare a Sales Ledger Control account for the month of May 20X0.
(c) Match the balances in the Control account with the sum of individual ledger balances.

PQ 14.3 Reconciliation of Debtors Control account balance with sum of individual balances

Bruce Stationers maintains a Sales Ledger Control account in the Real Ledger and has organized the Debtors Ledger on a self-balancing basis. On 31 March 20X0, the Sales Ledger Control account (in the Real Ledger) showed a debit balance of £346,800 and a credit balance of £16,200. These do not agree with the sum of the balances extracted from the individual accounts in the Sales Ledger. Subsequent enquiries reveal as follows:

(a) A sale of £12,400 has been posted to the customer in the Sales Ledger as £21,400.
(b) The January 20X0 total of the Sales Day Book has been added as £116,400 instead of £114,800.
(c) The dishonour of a cheque for £6,800 has been posted to the credit of the customer's account.
(d) A credit balance of £2,800 in a customer's account has been listed as a debit balance in the list of balances.
(e) The Discount column on the Receipts side of the cash book has been totalled as £21,600 instead of £22,200.
(f) A payment of £160 for delivering goods to a customer's residence has been posted in error to the customer's account (as well as the Control account) instead of to the Delivery Expense account in the Nominal Ledger.
(g) £2,600 written off as a bad debt has not been entered in the Control account.
(h) A customer is reported as a debtor for £26,700, instead of £29,700, because of a casting error when balancing the personal account in the Sales Ledger.
(i) A debt-collecting expense of £650, incurred in obtaining judgement against a debtor, remains unpaid. This item has still to be charged to the customer in the Debtors Ledger and to be included in the Control account.
(j) The recovery of £7,200 in respect of debts written off in the previous financial year has been posted to the credit of the Control account.
(k) The recovery of a debt of £8,200 by offset contra is yet to be recorded in either of the Control accounts.
(l) A 5 per cent settlement discount, claimed by a customer from whom a cheque for £4,275 was received, though approved, is still to be accounted for.

Required: Prepare a reconciliation of the Debtors Ledger balances with the debit and credit balances in the Control account in the format immediately below, and explain your reasons for the adjustments made.

RECONCILIATION OF THE SALES LEDGER CONTROL ACCOUNT (Balance on 31.3.20X0 with the sum of the individual debtors' balances, in the Sales Ledger, on the same date)	Control account balance £	Sum of individual balances £
Balance on 31.3.20X0	330,600	322,800

PQ 14.4 Reconciliation of Creditors control account balance with sum of individual balances

In the books of Morden Textiles, the Purchases Ledger Control account reports as at 31.12.20X0 a credit balance of £326,200 and a debit balance of £4,500. The list of individual creditors' balances, extracted from the Purchases Ledger on the same date, shows credit balances totalling £333,600 and debit balances of £2,800. The following errors have been identified since then:

(a) A debit balance of £1,700 in a supplier's account has been listed in error as a credit balance.
(b) A credit note received from a supplier for £3,600 is still to be accounted for.
(c) A contra entry of £8,200 with the Debtors Ledger is posted to the credit side of the Purchases Ledger Control account.
(d) A Returns Outwards Day Book folio is totalled as £43,000 instead of £40,000.
(e) The remainder of the errors arose from the failure to post a payment to the supplier's account.

Required: Prepare a reconciliation of Purchases Ledger balances with those in the Control account, and explain your reasons for the adjustments made.

Part C

ACCOUNTING FOR NON-MONETARY ASSETS

Chapter 15

ACCOUNTING FOR ASSETS

In this chapter

We will learn:

- that the identification of assets from expenditure is crucial to accounting
- the criteria for such identification
- of the amount at which an asset may be reported in a set of accounts
- that exceptionally intangible assets may also be accounted for
- to account for a capital grant

15.1 IMPORTANCE OF DISTINGUISHING AN ASSET FROM AN EXPENDITURE

We learnt in Chapter 3 that when the transactions of the telephone shop owned by Andy Small are accounted for, the accounts written up are of four classes – asset, liability, income and expenditure. The balances in the income and expenditure accounts are transferred to a Trading and Profit and Loss account so as to report the results of the performance as a profit of £2,906 (see below); balances in the asset and liability accounts are listed in a Balance Sheet (see below) to report the financial position on the last day of the period. The Balance Sheet identifies that the assets exceed the liabilities by £2,906 and the Profit and Loss account explains how that excess arose.

BALANCE SHEET AS AT 5.1.20X0	
	£
Furniture	330
Office equipment	300
Cash	8,476
	9,106
	£
Capital	5,000
Profit	2,906
	7,906
Loan	1,200
	9,106

TRADING AND PROFIT AND LOSS ACCOUNT FOR FIVE DAYS ENDING 5.1.20X0	
	£
Sales	12,600
Purchases	(8,400)
Gross profit	4,200
Telephone	(49)
Salaries	(780)
Staff expenses	(40)
Stationery	(55)
Postage	(15)
Advertising	(355)
Profit	2,906

From this we can see that it is essential clearly to demarcate an asset from an expenditure. If an expenditure is wrongly identified as an asset (e.g. £400 paid for Purchases is identified as an asset – say office equipment), the profit of Andy Small's business will be overstated by £400 (£2,906 + £400) and the assets will be overstated by £400 (£9,106 + £400). Conversely, if an asset is wrongly identified as an expense, the profit as well as the assets in the Balance Sheet will be understated. This means that if the performance, as reported in the Profit and Loss account, and the financial position as reported in the Balance Sheet are to be correct, assets should be identified correctly from expenditure. Besides, if accounts of different entities are to be comparable, it is essential to standardize the basis of making the identification and to set uniform criteria.

15.2 SETTING UNIFORM CRITERIA – THE ACCOUNTING STANDARDS BOARD

In the United Kingdom, the responsibility for standardizing accounting and reporting practices and setting uniform criteria has been entrusted, since 1990, to an *Accounting Standards Board (ASB)*. The Board succeeded the Accounting Standards Committee (ASC), which had been functioning since 1971. The official pronouncements of the ASB are known as *Financial Reporting Standards (FRSs)*, while those of the ASC were known as *Statements of Standard Accounting Practice (SSAPs)*. The SSAPs are gradually being replaced by FRSs. A *Financial Reporting Review Panel (FRRP)* has been appointed to monitor compliance with accounting standards. We will learn more about these standards in Chapter 22.

15.3 THE CRITERIA FOR IDENTIFYING AN ASSET

In layman's language, an asset is usually regarded as an item of property that is owned. In accounting terminology, an *asset* is defined as a 'right or other access to future economic benefits controlled by an entity as a result of past transactions or events'.[1] Note therefore the following:

- The asset is not the item of property from which economic benefits are derived, but the right or access to some or all of the future economic benefits expected from that property.
- 'Economic benefit' may take the form of an ability to generate an inflow of cash or reduce an outflow. The economic benefits could include the ability to:
  – use the property;
  – sell or exchange the property;
  – exploit its value, for example by pledging it as security for borrowing.
- 'Future' means that the benefit should flow after the completion of the current accounting period.
- 'Control' means that the right or access should be within the entity's control (though not necessarily within its possession). The control may take the form of the ability (either custodial or legal) to deny or restrain others from having access to the benefits. However, neither legal title nor ownership is essential for the recognition of an asset – it is whether in commercial reality the entity controls the right or access to future economic benefits.
- 'A past transaction or event' means that an intention to transact is not sufficient. There must have been a past transaction such as a payment or a contract to pay.

15.3.1 Physical existence is not essential for recognition as an asset

In everyday conversation, we tend to assume that an asset requires physical existence. In accounting terms, this is not so. For example, when the cost of a factory is capitalized, the asset is not the physical structure of that factory but the right to occupy that structure and use it to gain economic benefits. This could result in the same physical structure being recognized as an asset by different parties. For example, the lessee, who has the physical possession of the leased premises, may recognize it as an asset by reference to the period of tenancy assured; and so would the legal owner, on the basis of the reversionary right owned. The criterion for asset recognition is that there is evidence that it will produce economic benefit.

15.3.2 How do we know when the asset recognition criteria have been satisfied?

Tests carried out for recognition as an asset include the following:

- **Matching**. The 'matching' concept requires that the relationship between the cost of establishing the control and the economic benefit expected to flow in the future should be established, or at least justifiably assumed.
- **Prudence**. The 'prudence' concept requires that the right or access to future economic benefits should be certain, or at least probable.
- **Materiality**. The 'materiality' concept requires that the cost of establishing the right or access should be sufficiently material to justify recognition as an asset.
- **Measurement**. The 'money measurement' concept requires that the cost and economic benefits are capable of being measured in monetary terms.

15.4 THE CRITERIA FOR IDENTIFYING AN EXPENSE

The event or transaction is classified as an expense (rather than an asset) if any of the tests stated above for an asset is not satisfied. Following are some examples:

- The relationship between the cost and the benefit expected to arise in a future accounting period under the 'matching' concept cannot be established or justifiably assumed, such as payments for advertising and on cultivating customer relations;
- The future economic benefit is uncertain and fails the 'prudence' concept, such as the cost of researching for a new product, which may or may not materialise;
- The cost is not sufficiently material to warrant recognition as an asset, such as the cost of an office stapler or lever-arch file;
- The 'future' aspect of the definition is not satisfied, e.g. the expenditure may not give access to benefit in subsequent accounting periods but only in the current accounting period, such as payments for current salaries, rent or electricity.

Asset recognition criteria   Interaction 15.1

Explain, with reasons, whether you agree with the following being categorized as assets:

1. A leasehold property in the accounts of (a) the lessor and (b) the lessee.
2. An amount paid to a manufacturer for a machine, which has yet to be manufactured, in the accounts of the purchaser.
3. An amount owed by a customer for goods sold.
4. Prepaid rent, where a refund would not be available if the tenancy were to be terminated before the expiration of the rental period.

| Interaction 15.2 | **No property should be reported as an asset by more than one entity** |

The draft *Statement of Principles* issued by the Accounting Standards Board in 1999 states that 'the requirement that the rights or other access should be controlled by the entity treating them as its asset means that no item of property will be the asset of more than one entity'.[2] How is it then possible for a leasehold property to be stated as an asset by both the lessor and the lessee?

Required: Consider this question.

| Interaction 15.3 | **Expense recognition criteria** |

Explain, with reasons, whether you agree with the following being categorized as expenses:

1. A screwdriver acquired for £18.
2. Substantial amounts spent on an elaborate and well-orchestrated advertising campaign to launch a new product, which is expected to generate economic benefits over several years.
3. The charm, industry and selling ability of an exceptionally capable salesperson.

15.5 TANGIBLE FIXED ASSETS

Some of the assets that satisfy the tests for recognition as an asset may also satisfy further tests for recognition as a *tangible fixed asset*. A tangible fixed asset is an asset that has a physical substance and is:

● held for use in the production or supply of goods or services;
● for rental to others; or
● for administrative purposes on a continuing basis in the reporting entities' activities.[3]

| Interaction 15.4 | **Classification as a tangible fixed asset** |

Explain, with reasons, whether you would classify the following assets of a business entity as a tangible fixed asset:

1. a standby machine that has remained idle during the current accounting period and that is intended to maintain production in the event of a fault with a machine currently in use (rather than to enhance production capacity);
2. premises that are used to store goods rather than for producing goods;
3. residential quarters built to provide accommodation for administrative staff;
4. machinery that is owned by the business but has been leased out to others.

15.6 INTANGIBLE FIXED ASSETS

Some assets that satisfy the tests for recognition as an asset may lack physical substance. What this means is that the asset has no three-dimensional physical presence and therefore, in the absence of such corporeal existence, cannot be seen or touched – although its existence can be felt because of the economic benefits that flow from it. Examples of such *intangible fixed assets* are goodwill, patents and brand names. For example, the aggregate of the current worth of all individual net assets of a business may be £500,000 and yet someone may acquire the business for £800,000 because, considering the earning capacity of the business, the business is regarded as worth that amount. The excess of £300,000 is the cost of goodwill. Goodwill, therefore, consists of a variety of attributes (such as its location, customer loyalty, reputation of its product) that enable the business to earn more than what is commensurate with the value of its tangible assets.

The accepted practice[4] on accounting for intangible fixed assets is as follows:

- Goodwill, when purchased as part of a business acquisition, should be capitalized at cost and amortized (written off), on a systematic basis, over its estimated useful life, which is expected usually to be 20 years or less.
- Internally generated (home-grown) goodwill should not be capitalized.
- Other intangible assets, purchased separately from a business (i.e. when a brand name is acquired without acquiring the whole business) should be capitalized at the amount it cost and amortized over its estimated useful life.
- Intangible assets acquired as part of a business acquisition should be capitalized separately at market value but only if such value can be reliably measured. Otherwise, such intangible assets shall be included within the amount paid for goodwill.
- Exceptionally, intangible assets that are home-grown may be capitalized but only if they have a readily ascertainable market value. This, in real life, would be a rarity. For example, if a business develops a new design and patents it, although the business would know the probably negligible amount it incurred in the process, the market value of the design cannot be but a conjecture. The product (the patent) would be unique and there cannot at that stage be an active market for it.

15.7 RESEARCH AND DEVELOPMENT COSTS

When substantial costs are incurred over several years on developing a product that is expected to produce future economic benefits when, in due course, the product is commercially exploited, it would appear reasonable that the costs should not be written off in the periods in which they were incurred. Instead, the costs should be deferred until the benefits are reaped. This, known as deferring development cost, is justified on the following grounds:

1. **It meets the asset criterion**. The costs are incurred in anticipation of reaping future economic benefit and would, therefore, satisfy the criteria for recognition as an asset.
2. **To comply with the matching concept**, SSAP 2 *requires* the deferral of costs if its relationship with income to be generated in future periods can be established or justifiably assumed.
3. **Impairment of performance reporting**. Unless the costs are deferred and are to be matched with the corresponding income when they arise, the performance is understated during the periods when costs were incurred and overstated during the periods when benefits arise.
4. **Discouragement of research**. The insistence that costs must be written off in the periods in which these are incurred may tend to discourage development effort.
5. **Impairment of comparison with products purchased**. Instead of developing its own product, if a business acquires one already patented by someone else, it is permitted to capitalize the total cost of acquisition, including any cost incurred by that person on the development of the product.

Nevertheless, the accountancy profession the world over prefers to write off the cost of research and development in the year in which it is incurred for reasons such as the following:

- **Inadequate satisfaction of asset recognition criteria.** To qualify for recognition as an asset, the future economic benefits that are expected to arise should be capable of being identified and measured with a degree of certainty that is not always available.
- **It is a period expense.** In today's fiercely competitive world, research and development costs should be regarded more as recurring period expenses, not really for improving the business's revenue-earning capacity but for maintaining the current share of the market.
- **For the sake of prudence.** Empirical evidence gathered in the United States in the 1970s revealed that:
  - not all development projects prove technically feasible;
  - not all technically feasible projects prove commercially viable; and
  - not all viable projects are accepted by the management for implementation.

  The findings in that survey were that only 2 per cent of new product ideas and 15 per cent of product development projects proved commercially successful. In view of such a poor correlation between the costs and the inflow of future economic benefits, prudence would demand that all such costs should be written off as incurred.
- **Deferral could aggravate liquidity.** When development costs are deferred, there is a danger that the cash outflow implications may be lost sight of when making decisions such as those on dividends and investments.

The stand taken by the accounting profession in the UK[5] is as follows:

1. To be considered for deferral, the expense should involve research. To qualify to be so regarded, the expense should involve an element of innovation and the activity concerned should be one that departs from the routine and breaks new ground.
2. Research and development expenses are classified as follows:
   (a) pure research, involving experimental or theoretical work undertaken primarily to acquire new scientific or technical knowledge of underlying foundation of phenomena or observable facts;
   (b) applied research, which is original or critical investigation carried out to gain new scientific or technical knowledge directed towards a specific practical aim; and
   (c) development, which is the use of scientific or technical knowledge to produce new or substantially improved materials, devices or products or to install new processes, systems or services, prior to commencing commercial production.

   Hence, experimental work to learn of the potential of microchips would be pure research; a search for computer hardware capable of responding to oral commands would be applied research; and the production of some sorts of prototypes would be development. All expenses on research and development, irrespective of the classification, are required to be written off in the year in which they are incurred.
3. However, exceptionally, if it is the policy of the business, it is permitted to defer development costs alone, provided that all of the following five conditions are met:
   (a) the costs should have been those incurred on a clearly defined project;
   (b) the related expenses on that project should be separately identifiable;
   (c) the outcome of that project should have been assessed, with reasonable certainty, as technically feasible and commercially viable;
   (d) the aggregate costs of the project, including those yet to be incurred, should be reasonably expected to be recovered in full; and

(e) adequate resources should be either available or expected to be available to complete the project.

15.8 FIXED ASSETS IN THE BALANCE SHEET

Initially[6] a fixed asset should be recorded at its cost. Cost should include the purchase price and cost directly attributable to bringing the asset into working condition for its intended use. Directly attributable costs include labour costs of own employees arising directly from construction or acquisition, and the incremental costs that could have been avoided if the asset was not constructed or acquired.

Note that directly attributable costs should cease to be capitalized (i.e. should be expensed) when substantially all the activities that are necessary to get the asset ready for use are complete, even if the asset has not yet been brought into use. Start-up and commissioning costs may be capitalized but only when without such costs the asset would have been incapable of operating at normal levels.

Remember that the term 'capitalize', when used in relation to expenditure, is the accounting jargon for treating the expenditure as an asset and showing it in the Balance Sheet rather than treating it as an expense and transferring it to the Profit and Loss account.

Measurement of a fixed asset

Interaction
15.5

Explain, with reasons, the values at which these assets may be capitalized:

1. A cattle farm bought a used heavy-goods lorry for £12,000, paid £4,000 to fit a larger body for transporting cattle, and paid a further £3,000 to make the vehicle roadworthy. In addition, insurance costs and road tax for the year amounted to £340 and £250 respectively.
2. A steel rolling mill paid £180,000 for a machine, £1,500 for delivery to the factory, and £4,500 for having it installed. Start-up costs, including material wastage during the start-up period, amounted to £3,000.

15.8.1 Capitalization of finance costs incurred before usage

The cost of the amount borrowed to finance the construction (not acquisition) of an asset may (optionally) also be capitalized, provided the following five conditions are *all* complied with:

1. **Uniform policy**. It must be the policy of the entity to capitalize such finance costs, and the same policy should be adopted for all tangible fixed assets constructed.
2. **Actually incurred**. The interest (and similar charges) so capitalized must be those actually incurred during the period of production.
3. **Overall borrowing rate**. Where the funds used to finance the construction were part of the entity's general borrowings, the amount of interest to be capitalized is determined by applying the firm's overall borrowing rate to the expenditure on the asset.
4. **Timing**. Capitalization should:
   - begin when the expenditure on the asset is incurred;
   - be suspended during any extended periods when active work on the asset construction is interrupted; and
   - cease when substantially all work necessary to get the asset ready for use is complete.

5. **Disclosures**. If finance costs are capitalized, there must be disclosure of:
   - the accounting policy adopted;
   - the amount of finance costs capitalized;
   - the amount of finance costs written off in the Profit and Loss account; and
   - the capitalization rate used to determine the amount capitalized in the year.

Interaction 15.6	**Capitalization of finance costs**

Quick Build plc has an accounting period ending on 31 December. It commenced construction of its head offices on 1 March 20X0. Construction was still in progress as at 31.12.20X0, with a cost of £324,000 incurred up to then. Because of local flooding, construction work had been suspended for the four months ending on 1 August 20X0. The construction is financed by a bank loan carrying interest at 14 per cent per annum. It is the company's policy to capitalize interest on self-constructed assets.

Required: Determine the amount at which the building in progress should be reported as an asset in the Balance Sheet of Quick Build plc on 31.12.20X0.

15.8.2 Costs incurred on an asset subsequent to commencing usage

Costs incurred on an asset after its use has commenced should be treated as an expense if the intention is to maintain the asset at its previously assessed standard of performance. There are, however, three circumstances in which such subsequent costs may be capitalized:

- if the cost is an improvement (i.e. it enhances the economic benefit substantially in excess of previously assessed levels);
- if the cost replaces or restores an asset component treated separately for depreciation purposes;
- if the cost arises from a major inspection or overhaul that restores the economic benefits that had been consumed and written off as depreciation.

Interaction 15.7	**Capitalization of costs incurred subsequent to commencing asset usage**

Your advice is sought as to how the following payments should be dealt with when preparing accounts for the year ended 31.12.20X0:

1. £1,200 paid for replacing a vehicle's crankshaft when that became necessary following an accident.
2. £14,500 paid for an additional thermostat fitted to the cold storage room for the purpose of improving the freezing capacity by 150 per cent.
3. £12,000 paid for replacing a lining on a furnace. The furnace had been installed four years earlier at a cost of £96,000 and at that time the business's managers were advised that the furnace would remain in economic use for at least 20 years but that the lining would require replacement every four years.
4. £7,500 paid for overhauling and restoring to a roadworthy condition a pick-up truck acquired at a cost of £24,000 and fully depreciated by 30 September 20X0.

15.9 ACCOUNTING FOR GRANTS

A grant is some form of assistance, in cash or in kind, received usually from the government but it could well be from other sources. Grants are usually intended to induce an entity to pursue a course of action that may be socially or economically desirable. For example, a grant may be made for inducing an entity to locate itself in a particular area for purposes such as generating employment or bringing about a balanced growth of the country. Furthermore, a grant may be made for the purpose of nurturing a small industry or to encourage modernization of industrial machinery for the purpose of restoring the competitive edge to British industry. An industry may even be given a grant to share its cost of cleaning its industrial waste, and this would be for the protection of the general environment.

A grant is known as a *capital grant* if it meets in full or in part the cost of an asset. Other grants, intended to reimburse an expense, share a cost or make good a loss, are known as *revenue grants*.

15.9.1 Deferral method of accounting for capital grants

A grant, when received, is posted from the cash book to a Deferred Income account. In every accounting period, a reasonable portion of the grant is treated as an income (i.e. released to the Profit and Loss account), while the remainder is reported in the Balance Sheet as a deferred income (though included among the liabilities). To ensure that the grant is released to income on a systematic manner, the relevant Accounting Standard[7] requires the release to be over the expected useful life of the corresponding asset on a basis consistent with the business's depreciation policy. To illustrate, let us assume that a business acquires machinery for £100,000, depreciates it using the straight-line method at 10 per cent per year, and has received a grant of £60,000 toward the cost of acquiring the machinery. At the end of the first year the Capital Grant account and the Profit and Loss extract will appear as shown below. The amount of £54,000 carried down in the Capital Grant account will be included in the Balance Sheet, at the year end, as a deferred income.

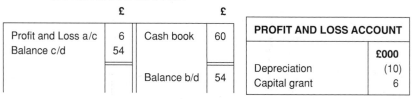

15.9.2 Offset method of accounting for capital grants

The accounting standard SSAP 4 allows an alternative method of accounting for capital grants. This is the offset method. Upon receipt, a capital grant is offset from the cost of the corresponding asset so that the asset is accounted for only at the net amount (i.e., in our example, £100,000 less £60,000 = £40,000). When the net cost of the asset is depreciated on the same basis, the amount written off in each year would be the same (£4,000) as on the deferral method. The offset method, however, is not available to limited companies because company law prohibits such offsetting.

15.9.3 Accounting for revenue grants

Revenue grants are accounted for as follows:

- Where the grant relates to a specific expenditure (say the cost of dealing with waste), the two should be so accounted for as to match one with the other.
- Where the grant finances general activities (say those of a charity) over a specific period, account for the grant as income in the period to which it relates.
- Where the grant reimburses loss of income in a period, account for the grant as income in that period.
- Where the grant is intended to make good expenses or losses incurred in past years, account for the grant as income in the period in which it is receivable.

References

1. FRS 5: *Reporting the Substance of Transactions* (December 1994).
2. *The Statement of Principles* – revised exposure draft (March 1999), paragraph 4.20.
3. FRS 15: *Tangible Fixed Assets* (February 1999).
4. FRS 10: *Goodwill and Intangible Assets* (December 1997).
5. SSAP 13: *Accounting for Research and Development* (December 1977, revised in January 1989).
6. FRS 15 as in n3 above.
7. SSAP 4: *The Accounting Treatment of Government Grants* (April 1974).

SOLUTIONS TO INTERACTIVE QUESTIONS

IQ 15.1 Asset recognition criteria

1. **Leasehold property**: The asset recognized is not the physical property that is in the custody of the lessee, e.g. if custody were to be the sole criterion for asset recognition, then the lessee alone could recognize it in its Balance Sheet.
   (a) The lessor (the legal owner of the property) recognizes the property as an asset because he holds the freehold rights – evidenced in a title deed – and expects future economic benefits from that right in the form of both lease rental during the lease period and reversion of the property on completion of the lease.
   (b) The asset recognised by the lessee is his right of access and the right to occupy the property during the period of the lease. The right, which is legally established and protected, is acquired usually on the basis of a cash outlay on the expectation that future economic benefits will flow from it
2. **Machine yet to be produced**. A machine in this category may be recognized as an asset, irrespective of whether it has been manufactured or paid for, provided an event that has already taken place (such as the signing of a contract of purchase) establishes access to the future economic benefits expected to flow from the machine in the form of its outputs.
3. **A trade debtor**. An asset recognized for accounting purposes is not the physical person of the customer concerned but the legally enforceable right to recover the debt arising from the sale, provided the sale has been legally completed. The future economic benefit is the cash flow expected from the customer in due course.
4. **Prepaid rent**. This is recognized as an asset on the basis that, through the payment(s) made, the right to occupy the premises has been secured along with the economic benefits expected to arise from the occupation. Whether the payment is recoverable in the event of termination of tenancy is irrelevant because financial statements (as we will see in Chapter 23) are prepared on the assumption that the entity will remain operational (the Going Concern concept) and therefore that termination of tenancy is not under consideration.

IQ 15.2 No property should be reported as an asset by more than one entity

What an entity reports as an asset is not the property itself but the right or access to specific future economic benefits expected from the property. For example, a property leased for ten years by A (lessee) from B (lessor) would be reported as an asset both by A and B. Reported as an asset is not the property itself but access to the different benefits (identified in the answer to IQ 15.1) that each entity controls, though the property underlying these benefits is the same.

IQ 15.3 Expense recognition criteria

1. **A screwdriver**. By the payment of £18 the entity apparently acquires an asset because it gains access to economic benefits in the form of reduction of cash outflows (from not having to hire the tool) or improvements to cash inflows (from what the tool could help to produce). The economic benefit may be expected to last several years. Yet, because the cost is immaterial, recognition as an asset is denied.
2. **An advertising campaign**. The campaign would not be undertaken if future economic benefits, in the form of sales promotion and consequent cash inflows, were not expected to result from the campaign. However, because it is difficult to establish or justifiably assume a relationship between the cost of the campaign and a discernible portion of the future income, asset recognition is refused.
3. **Human resources** may be a business's major asset and capable of generating future economic benefit. If there is a service contract, it could be argued that the employer has established the right of access to the resource which it is in a position to deny to all others. However, normal accounting practice is to treat items such as salaries for the use of labour in the same way as rent for the use of property, i.e. as a period cost to be transferred to the Profit and Loss account in the period in which it is paid. In contrast a payment specifically calculated to secure future benefits (such as training costs, or substantial capital outlay to buy a prestigious football player) might be recognized as an asset.

IQ 15.4 Classification as a tangible fixed asset

1. A standby machine is classified as a tangible fixed asset because it is held for use in production and the machine clearly has a physical substance and so is a tangible fixed asset. The definition of a fixed asset does not specify enhancement of productive capacity (as distinct from maintenance thereof) as a criterion for classification as fixed asset.
2. The property used for storage is a warehouse, which is classified as a tangible fixed asset because it is held (though not for production) for the supply of goods and is clearly a physical item.
3. Residential quarters are classified as tangible fixed assets because they are physical units and are held for administrative purposes on a continuing basis.
4. Machinery leased out to others is a tangible fixed asset because the machinery is held for rental to others on a continuing basis and so is a fixed asset (that is also tangible).

IQ 15.5 Measurement of a fixed asset

1. **Lorry**. The purchase price (£12,000) and all directly attributable expenses (£4,000 + £3,000) to place the lorry in a condition for its intended use (transporting cattle) can be capitalized. But the payments for the year's insurance and road tax are expenditure to be written off by transfer to the Profit and Loss account.
2. **Machine**. All costs (£180,000 + £1,500 + £4,500 + £3,000) may be capitalized because these were all necessary to place the machine in the condition for its intended use. Capitalization of the start-up costs, however, is permitted only if it was necessary to run in the machinery to ensure its proper functioning.

IQ 15.6 Capitalization of finance costs

The interest to be capitalized is 14% of £324,000 for the actual period in the year when construction work was in progress:

$$£324,000 \times 14\% \times 6 \text{ months} = £22,680$$

BUILDING UNDER CONSTRUCTION

	£		
Cash a/c	324,000		
Interest	22,680		
	346,680		

IQ 15.7 Capitalization of costs incurred subsequent to commencing asset usage

1. **Crankshaft**. £1,200 paid for the crankshaft should be written off as repairs and maintenance because the expenditure was necessary for restoring (rather than enhancing) the vehicle to its previously assessed levels of performance.
2. **Thermostat**. £14,500 paid for the additional thermostat should be capitalized by adding the cost to the cost of the cold storage room because it enhances the performance of the room to newly required levels.
3. **Furnace lining**. From the time of acquisition of the furnace, the cost of the lining (£12,000) would have been depreciated over four years (see Section 16.5), while the cost of the furnace (£84,000) would have been depreciated over 20 years. Therefore the cost of the new replacement lining (£12,000) is capitalized and reported as an addition to the cost of the furnace because it replaces an asset component treated separately for depreciation.
4. **Pick-up truck**. The amount of £7,500 for overhauling and restoring the roadworthiness of the pick-up truck is capitalized by posting it to the Motor Vehicles account because it restores the economic benefits that have been written off by way of depreciation.

PROGRESSIVE QUESTIONS

PQ 15.1 Distinction of an asset from an expense

(a) Explain why you would regard the following accounting treatments to be incorrect:
  (i)   £14,200 paid during the year for the monthly servicing of machinery was capitalized.
  (ii) When the motor in a machine ceased because an electrical fault burnt the armature, the £7,500 paid for replacing the dynamo was capitalized.
  (iii) In relation to the acquisition of a property, £12,500 paid as stamp duty fees and £10,000 paid to the solicitor for conveyancing were posted to the Property Maintenance account.
  (iv) £120,000 paid for a set of computer terminals was posted to the Stationery account.
(b) Identify the effect of each of the above errors, which occurred during the year ended 31 December 20X0, on the profit that has been reported as £1.246 million and the net assets at the year end that have been reported as £4.985 million. (Ignore the effect of depreciation.)

PQ 15.2 The case of an intercontinental transport company

A business, engaged in intercontinental transportation of heavy goods, makes the following payments during its financial year ended 30.9.20X0:

1. *Payments relating to the property*
  (a) £585,500 to acquire the freehold of a garage site.
  (b) £25,000 as compensation to the previous owner of the garage for personal relocation expenses.
  (c) £2,500 as stamp duty, £300 as land registry fees, and £2,500 as solicitor's conveyancing fees for the transfer of the title to the garage.
  (d) £14,500 for constructing a security fence around the property's perimeter.
  (e) £145,500 for structural changes to the building, £17,800 for fitting shatterproof window glass, £400 for fixing electric bulbs of a higher wattage, and £12,600 for redecoration.
  (f) £37,400 in legal fees defending a decision to restrict the right of way of neighbours across the property.
  (g) £126,200 for constructing a compound for parking containers.
  (h) £35,500 for entertaining business contacts on moving into the property.

2. *Payments relating to machinery*
    (a) £214,500 on ordering machinery, from Japan, for servicing trucks.
    (b) £12,400 for freight and insurance and £46,500 for duty when the machinery arrived from Japan.
    (c) £12,600 for reinforcing the garage floor and £8,800 for constructing a base for the machine.
    (d) £1,200 for lubricating the machine and £1,100 for test runs.
    (e) £21,400 for relocating the machine following a complaint by senior management of noise pollution.

Required: State the criteria you would use to identify the payments to be treated as part of the cost of asset and determine, with explanation, the value at which you would report the assets.

PQ 15.3 Costs incurred subsequent to the commencement of asset usage

A business manufacturing machine tools entered into the following transactions in the year ending 30 June 20X4:

(a) £246,500 was paid for computerizing the designing of machine tools.
(b) Machinery used for producing tools had been purchased for £465,000 in 20X0 and had been expected to have a useful economic life of ten years. However, modifications costing £125,000 were required in 20X4 to meet changing customer needs.
(c) Conveyor belts were installed at a cost of £85,000 when the company commenced business in 20X0 and had an expected useful economic life of five years. They were repaired in January 20X4 at a cost of £6,000 for damage arising from vandalism.
(d) £25,000 was spent in 20X4 on refurbishment of the conveyor belts referred to in (c), extending their useful life by three years.

Required: Explain, with reasons, how you would account for each of the payments reported above.

Chapter 16

DEPRECIATION OF TANGIBLE FIXED ASSETS

In this chapter

We will learn of:

- depreciation and the alternative methods of measuring it
- depreciation of buildings and infrastructure assets

and you should be able to account for variations to:

- the method of depreciation
- the estimate of an asset's useful economic life

16.1 WHAT IS DEPRECIATION?

We saw in Chapter 15 that, on acquisition, tangible fixed assets are accounted for initially at either their purchase price or their production cost. In each accounting period, as the asset is used, a corresponding portion of that amount, representing the consumption of the asset in that period, is written off. We refer to that amount as depreciation. This means that at the end of each period the amount at which the asset is accounted for is reduced by the total of various amounts written off as depreciation to its **written down value** (or **net book value**).

Put another way (see Chapter 6), depreciation is 'the measure of the cost (or revalued amount) of the benefits of tangible fixed assets consumed during the period'.[1] For example, if furniture were acquired for £330 (cost) to be used for ten years (i.e. have a useful economic life of ten years), and it was expected to realize no value at the end of that period (i.e. have no residual value), then it would appear reasonable to assume that the consumption of the asset in each of the ten accounting years is an equal amount of £33 per year, this amount being known as the depreciation for the year and the method being known as the **straight-line method** because the depreciation is the same amount each year. (There are other methods – see Section 16.4.)

16.2 WHY SHOULD FIXED ASSETS BE DEPRECIATED?

For a tangible asset, the normal reason for the consumption of economic benefits is usage, often referred to as 'wear and tear'. However, there could be other factors as well, including:

- physical deterioration of the asset through the effluxion (passing) of time;
- economic obsolescence, e.g. the use of the asset is no longer economical;
- technological obsolescence, e.g. older production processes are replaced by newer methods;
- legal and other limitations on the use of the asset, e.g. a fixed expiry date on leases.

Company law and accounting standards[2] require 'the depreciable amount of a tangible fixed asset to be allocated on a systematic basis over its useful life'. The need for such depreciation arises from several sources.

In relation to the prudence concept, all fixed assets (other than land) have a finite life, on completion of which the economic benefits from the asset would cease to flow. Prudence demands that this fact should be recognized by writing off in each year a proportion of the cost of the asset to represent the amount of the economic benefit consumed during that year.

Second, in relation to the matching concept, in order to determine profit the income earned in a period is matched with all expenditure incurred in the earning process. If an expense is omitted, the profit for the period is overstated. For example, assume that:

- X and Y each earned £30,000 during the year from driving minicabs;
- X used his own car, acquired for £20,000, and Y hired a car for £6,000 per year;
- other expenses amounted to £10,000.

If X does not depreciate his car, he would report a profit of £20,000 (£30,000 – £10,000) whereas Y would report only £14,000 (£30,000 – £10,000 – £6,000). X's profit is overstated because it fails to take into account the expense of using his own car. As X's car will not remain in use for ever, an appropriate proportion of the cost of his car should be recognized as an expense and matched with what he earned during the year.

Third, for sake of a true and fair view, unless fixed assets are depreciated and the depreciation expense matched with income, the report of performance within the accounting period (in the Profit and Loss account) and the position at the end of the period (in the Balance Sheet) will both fail to present a true and fair view – the profit will be exaggerated because it fails to take into account the consumption during the period of fixed assets, and the Balance Sheet will overstate the fixed assets by not reducing its cost by the amount consumed.

For the sake of asset replacement, in the illustration stated above, if X were to depreciate his car by (say) £5,000 per year, then he would report his profit as only £15,000. If living expenses were restricted to the amount of profit, then he could only withdraw £15,000 for living expenses. As a result, an amount equal to the amount written off as depreciation would be retained every year within the business. Repeated over four years, X would have retained within the business £20,000 by the end of the fourth year, when the car needs replacement (see workings). The effect of depreciation is to ensure that an amount equal to the amount of the asset consumed is retained within the business, so as to facilitate asset replacement. This amount may not be sufficient, of course, if there have been price rises during the four years.

	Year 1	Year 2	Year 3	Year 4
	£	£	£	£
Earnings (in cash)	30,000	30,000	30,000	30,000
Expenses (in cash)	(10,000)	(10,000)	(10,000)	(10,000)
Cash available (at bank)	20,000	20,000	20,000	20,000
Drawings by X (limited to profit)	(15,000)	(15,000)	(15,000)	(15,000)
Cash retained at bank each year	5,000	5,000	5,000	5,000
Cumulative amount at bank	5,000	10,000	15,000	20,000

Lastly, for the sake of capital maintenance, if, X did not depreciate his car, and withdrew for living expenses all of the profit (reported at £20,000), at the end of the fourth year (when the car has to be replaced) he would have to introduce fresh capital for the replacement. Alternatively, if he had depreciated over the four years, at the end of the fourth year he would maintain his capital at the amount he introduced originally to buy the car.

Note also that depreciation is an *allocation* of cost, not a valuation process. It is not intended to maintain the asset at its net realizable value in the Balance Sheet.

16.3 ACCOUNTING FOR DEPRECIATION

As we saw in Chapter 9, depreciation for a year is accounted for by debiting the Depreciation account (expenditure) and crediting the Provision for Depreciation account (an account set up to support the asset account of any class). To focus on accounting for depreciation, let us assume that the financial statements of an entity, without writing off depreciation, would have appeared as stated on the left and that it has been decided to write off depreciation of fixed assets at a tenth of their cost. Because one-tenth of the cost of a fixed asset is recognized as an additional expense, the profit for the year is reduced by that amount and the fixed asset's value stated in the Balance Sheet reduced by the same amount.

Revised financial statements at the end of the first year of the asset's life are shown on the left. The process of writing down the asset is repeated year after year until, by the end of the asset's estimated useful life, the asset is fully written off. It should be noted, however, that depreciation written off each year lowers the year's profit of the entity without lowering its cash balance. For this reason, depreciation is referred to as a non-cash expense.

TRADING AND PROFIT AND LOSS ACCOUNT FOR THE YEAR ENDED 31.12.20X0

	£
Sales	100,000
Cost of sale	(60,000)
Gross profit	40,000
Expenses	(28,000)
Profit	12,000

BALANCE SHEET AS AT 31.12.20X0

	£
Fixed asset	40,000
Stock	22,000
Cash	18,000
	80,000

	£
Capital	68,000
Profit	12,000
	80,000

TRADING AND PROFIT AND LOSS ACCOUNT FOR THE YEAR ENDED 31.12.20X0

	£
Sales	100,000
Cost of sale	(60,000)
Gross profit	40,000
Depreciation	(4,000)
Expenses	(28,000)
Profit	8,000

BALANCE SHEET AS AT 31.12.20X0

	£
Fixed asset at cost	40,000
Prov. for depreciation	(4,000)
	36,000
Stock	22,000
Cash	18,000
	76,000

	£
Capital	68,000
Profit	8,000
	76,000

16.3.1 Calculating depreciable amount

Depreciation, effectively, is a portion of the depreciable amount of a fixed asset allocated to each period of its use. The depreciable amount is the aggregate depreciation, which is the difference between the cost of the asset and its residual value after the period of its intended use. The residual value is the net realizable amount expected from its disposal at the end of its economic life, based on prices prevailing at the date of acquiring the asset. What this means is that the effect of inflation on the residual value should be ignored.

Depreciable amount and depreciation

City Stores acquires a Ford Escort van at a cost of £20,000 on 1.1.20X0. It expects to use the van for four years. It learns from *Autotrader* that at current prices a four-year-old Escort van may be sold for £2,000. Taking account of the current rate of annual inflation of 4 per cent, it is anticipated that on completion of its economic life on 31.12.20X3 the van will probably fetch £2,340. Selling expenses at that date are expected to amount to 5 per cent of the sale price.

Required: Determine the depreciable amount of the van as at 1.1.20X0, and, assuming that City Stores wishes to write off depreciation at a constant amount in each of the four years (i.e. the straight-line method), calculate the amount to be written off as depreciation in each year.

The depreciable amount of the fixed asset needs to be allocated over the accounting periods in which economic benefit is expected from the asset – this is known as the expected *useful economic life (UEL)*. An asset's expected UEL is not based simply on the technical specification from the manufacturer. The manufacturer's specification may, for example, be that a vehicle should last for five years, whereas the management of a business that buys the vehicle may decide on a UEL of four years or even less (based on their experience). Expected UEL is therefore determined by the management's own asset management policy.

16.3.2 Depreciating major components

It is possible that the estimated economic life of a major component of an asset may be different from that of the remainder of the asset. For example, machinery acquired for £100,000 and expected to remain in use for 20 years may require regular replacement of linings at a cost of (say) £5,000 every four years. This would necessitate the cost of the lining to be depreciated over four years and £95,000 (being the cost of the remainder) to be depreciated over 20 years. If residual value is assumed to be negligible and the straight-line method of depreciation is in use, depreciation would be written off as follows:

Cost	Depreciation
£95,000/20 years	£4,750
£5,000/4 years	£1,250
Annual depreciation	£6,000

MACHINERY ACCOUNT

Cash a/c	100,000	Depreciation	6,000
		Balance c/d	94,000
	100,000		100,000

16.4 METHODS OF ALLOCATING DEPRECIABLE AMOUNTS TO DIFFERENT ACCOUNTING PERIODS

Over the years, different methods have been developed for allocating the depreciable amount of fixed assets to the different accounting periods. Whatever method is used, the allocation must be on a systematic basis and must reflect as fairly as possible the pattern in which the asset's economic benefits are consumed in each accounting period.

The common methods in use for allocating depreciable amount are as set out next.

16.4.1 **The straight-line method**

This method allocates the depreciable amount equally over the accounting periods in which the asset is consumed. For example, if an entity that finalizes accounts annually on 31 December acquires a machine for £100,000 (cost) and hopes to dispose of it after ten years' use (UEL) for £4,000 (residual value), the depreciable cost of the machine (£100,000 less £4,000) is allocated equally among each of the ten years at £9,600 per year. If the residual value is assumed to be nil, then 10 per cent of the cost (£100,000) would be written off as depreciation in each year. Since the annual depreciation charged to the Profit and Loss account would remain constant from year to year, this method is known also as the fixed instalment system or straight-line method.

Acquisition or disposal of an asset part-way through a year

If an asset is acquired or sold part-way through a year, it might be the accounting policy in a real-life situation to depreciate the fixed asset for a whole year in the year it is acquired and abstain from depreciating it in the year of disposal. Unless this policy is specifically stated to be in use the annual depreciation charge will have to be time-apportioned.

Advantages

The advantages of the straight-line method include the following:

- Operation of this method is simple and easily understood.
- Unless a more justifiable alternative method of allocating depreciable cost is found, the fairest method is probably to allocate the depreciable amount equally among the different accounting periods in which the asset assists the earning process.
- Under this method the asset is completely eliminated from the books by the end of its useful economic life. This ensures that the whole of depreciable amount is charged against the income generated by the asset. This makes the method particularly suitable in respect of assets (like a lease) that have a specifically fixed economic life.

Disadvantages

The disadvantages of this method may include the following:

- The method may wrongly assume that depreciation is a function of time rather than of the use or output.
- By charging a constant amount to the various years of its use, it overlooks factors such as deterioration in performance or increase in costs of maintenance and repairs. However, it could be argued that the increasing total cost of using the asset is offset by the returns generated by the funds retained by depreciation.
- If the asset outlives its anticipated useful economic life, the asset may continue to generate income without a charge being made against it in respect of its cost.
- This method could become inconvenient because, if additions are made or enhancement costs are incurred during the asset's expected useful economic life, fresh calculations become necessary to ensure that these too are written off over the remaining period of useful economic life. This is not, of course, a problem if proper asset registers are maintained to record for each asset the date purchased, the cost, the expected useful economic life and the amount of depreciation that has been charged since the date of acquisition.

The straight-line method of depreciation

A transport company, Rapid Deliveries, has a fleet of four vehicles, the first acquired for £40,000 in 20X0, the second for £36,000 in 20X1, the third for £48,000 in 20X2 and the fourth for £42,000 in 20X3. The acquisitions were at the commencement of each of the years. The accounting policy is to depreciate vehicles at 20 per cent per annum using the straight-line method.

Required:

(a) Prepare the Motor Vehicles account to show the written down values as at 31 December 20X0, 20X1, 20X2 and 20X3 for the vehicle acquired on 1.1.20X0 for £40,000.
(b) Prepare the Motor Vehicles account as well as the Provision for Depreciation account, identifying the written down values as at 31 December 20X0, 20X1, 20X2 and 20X3 for all vehicles.

16.4.2 The reducing balance method

In this method the depreciation written off in each accounting period is a fixed percentage not of the cost but of the *value to which the asset has been written down* by the end of the previous period. If the residual value is assumed to be nil, with regard to an asset acquired for £100,000 at commencement of Year 1 and expected to remain in use for ten years, the depreciation in the first year, on the reducing balance method, is 10 per cent of cost (just as it would be on the straight-line method). But in the second year, the depreciation written off on the reducing balance method is 10% of the remaining value of £90,000. Notice, in the workings shown here,

		Straight-line method	Reducing balance method
		£	£
1.1.Yr 1	Cost	100,000	100,000
	Depreciation @ 10%	(10,000)	(10,000)
1.1.Yr 2	Written down value	90,000	90,000
	Depreciation @ 10%	(10,000)	(9,000)
1.1.Yr 3	Written down value	80,000	81,000
	Depreciation @ 10%	(10,000)	(8,100)
1.1.Yr 4	Written down value	70,000	72,900

that the annual depreciation charge reduces in each successive year – hence the name. Since the amount written off each year becomes smaller (being a fixed percentage of a diminishing balance), it is necessary to use a higher depreciation rate if the asset is to be written off over its expected useful economic life of, say, 10 years. The method is known also as the diminishing balance method.

Calculation of an appropriate depreciation rate for the reducing balance method

$$r = (1 - \sqrt[n]{s/c}) \times 100\%$$
Where:
r = the rate of depreciation
n = the useful economic life
s = the residual value
c = the cost

The depreciation rate for writing off the depreciable cost of an asset over its estimated useful life, on the reducing balance method, is arrived at by using the formula given on the left. If we apply the formula to an asset that cost £100,000 and that is expected to realize £4,000 on completion of an expected economic life of ten years, the annual rate of depreciation, on the reducing balance method, would be calculated, as shown on the right, as 27.52%.

$$r = 1 - \sqrt[10]{4,000/100,000} \times 100\%$$
$$= 27.52\%$$

Advantages

The advantages claimed for this method are the following:

- Simplicity of operation because, on this method, the annual charge for depreciation is arrived at merely by applying the appropriate rate to the net book value, i.e. the value brought forward in the asset account from the previous year, plus any acquisitions and less any disposals in the year.
- The diminishing amount of depreciation charge appears equitable because it more closely reflects the pattern of consumption of economic benefits of the asset. Arguably greater benefits are obtained when the asset is new and technologically novel than when it is older, more prone to breakdown and technologically overtaken by further developments.
- The total expenditure related to an asset over successive years tends to even out when progressively diminishing levels of depreciation are considered along with both increasing costs of maintenance and repairs and the deterioration in performance associated with the asset's age.
- It is suggested that heavier depreciation in earlier years may be justified because the written down value of the asset will then be more in line with the asset's resale value, since resale values are known to decline more in early years.
- This method never fully eliminates an asset from the books unless it is deliberately done. This is because in each successive period only a given percentage of written down value is written off as depreciation, even when the written down value is already a negligible amount. This ensures that assets that remain in use well past their estimated economic life are reflected in the books even by a token amount.

Disadvantages

The disadvantages of this method are as follows:

- In this method the rate of depreciation charge is substantially higher than in others. For example, in the case used above for illustration, the rate of depreciation on this method has to be 27.52% as against 10% of cost written off on the straight-line method. For this reason the method is referred to also as the 'double declining method'.
- Since on this method the amount written off is a given percentage of the diminishing balance, the asset will never be fully eliminated from the ledger account unless care is taken deliberately to do this at the end of its economic life.
- Because of its simplicity of operation, adequate registers may not be kept and in that event it would become difficult to identify individual assets within the written down values brought forward in the ledger. There is a danger, then, that residues of assets may be left behind long past their disposal.

Interaction
16.3

Reducing balance method of depreciation

Rapid Deliveries maintains a separate account for recording accumulated depreciation from year to year.

Required:

(a) Assuming that Rapid Deliveries has only a single vehicle, acquired for £40,000 on 1 January 20X0, and that it depreciates the cost of the vehicle at 40 per cent per annum on the reducing balance method, set out the Motor Vehicle account to show the written down values of the vehicle as at 31 December 20X0, 20X1, 20X2 and 20X3.

(b) Assuming that Rapid Deliveries owns four vehicles acquired as stated in IQ 16.2, and depreciates them at 40 per cent per annum on the reducing balance method, set out the Motor Vehicles account and the Provision for Depreciation account, identifying the written down values as at 31 December 20X0, 20X1, 20X2 and 20X3.

16.4.3 Sum of the year's digits method

With this method, the depreciable amount (assumed in a worked example here to be £20,000) is allocated to each accounting period within its useful economic life in accordance with the proportion of its life remaining as at the commencement of each year. Assuming an estimated UEL of four years, the proportion of life remaining at the start of each year would be as stated in the box shown here. Accordingly, depreciation written off in the first year would be 4/10th of £20,000 = £8,000, in the second 3/10th of £20,000 = £6,000, and so on.

Year	Remaining UEL	Depreciation in the year
1	4 years	4/10 × (cost – scrap value)
2	3 years	3/10 × (cost – scrap value)
3	2 years	2/10 × (cost – scrap value)
4	1 year	1/10 × (cost – scrap value)
	10 years	Sum of the digits

Interaction
16.4

The sum of the year's digits method

Use the information stated in IQ 16.2 above, but assume this time that the accounting policy is to depreciate vehicles over four years using the sum of the year's digits method, and that the first, second, third and fourth years of use will have a weighting as 4:3:2:1 respectively.

Required:

(a) Prepare the Motor Vehicles account and the Provision for Depreciation account, identifying the written down values of vehicles as at 31.12.20X0, 20X1, 20X2 and 20X3 for the vehicle purchased on 1.1.20X0 for £40,000.

(b) Prepare the Motor Vehicles account and the Provision for Depreciation account of *all* the vehicles, identifying their written down values as at the 31 December 20X0, 20X1, 20X2 and 20X3.

16.4.4 Machine-hour rate

This method, mainly appropriate when depreciating machinery, allocates the depreciable amount over the different periods in accordance with how the number of hours of the machine's use in the period compares with the estimated total hours of use expected from the machine. For example, if the depreciable cost of a machine is £80,000 and it is expected to run for 20,000 hours in all, the depreciation expense in Year 1 for 3,000 hours' use would be calculated as 3,000/20,000 of £80,000 = £12,000.

16.4.5 Production unit method

This method, appropriate mainly for depreciating productive assets, allocates the depreciable amount over the different periods in accordance with how the productive output of the asset within the year compares with the total output expected over its useful economic life. For example, if an asset costing £80,000 is capable of producing 120,000 units and its output in the first year is 30,000 units, then 30,000/120,000 × £80,000 = £20,000 is written off as depreciation in the year.

16.4.6 Depletion unit method

This method resembles the machine-hour rate method and is appropriate for wasting assets. (A 'wasting asset' is any asset (especially a natural resource, such as a mine) whose value decreases with its depletion and that cannot be replaced or renewed – *Chambers English Dictionary* 1998.) The cost of a mine, for example, is divided by the estimated output from it to arrive at a rate per tonne of (say) ore extracted from the mine. The actual tonnage extracted in an accounting period is evaluated at that rate to determine the amount to be written off the asset as depletion occurs.

16.4.7 Revaluation method

The depreciation to be written off in an accounting period on this method is determined by valuing the asset on each Balance Sheet date and comparing the closing value with the opening one for the period, the difference being the depreciation amount allocated. This method is commonly applied to loose tools; but is not suitable for machinery.

16.4.8 Sinking fund method

The amount of depreciation to be written off as an expense in each period is determined using one of the other methods. The distinctive feature of this method is that an amount equal to the annual depreciation expense is invested outside the entity in readily realizable securities, so that at the time the asset requires replacement the cash could be more readily found by realizing the securities.

16.4.9 Annuity method

The capital tied up in an asset is assumed to earn interest at a notional rate. The annual depreciation is therefore calculated so as to write off not only the cost of the asset but also the notional interest on the capital tied up in the asset. BOC group is known to be using this method for depreciating certain tonnage plants.

16.5 CHANGES OF METHODOLOGY

16.5.1 Alteration to the depreciation method

We have seen above that the depreciation expense will vary according to the method used and that, as a result, the profit after depreciation has been charged will vary. For example, an entity may be able to report an improved profit simply by shifting from the reducing balance method to the straight-line method and it would be very tempting to use a change of method to influence the profit figure. If this were permitted, it would be impossible to compare performance from year to year. To prevent such manipulation, the accounting treatment is required to be applied *consistently*. To safeguard such consistency, a change from one method of depreciation to another is prohibited unless such a change is regarded as necessary for the fairer reporting of the entity's performance and position. If an alteration becomes necessary for the sake of fairer reporting, the net book value (i.e. the cost less amounts written off as depreciation until then) of the asset is depreciated from that point using the new method.

16.5.2 Alteration to the estimated useful economic life

Although there is a requirement to be consistent with the measurement of depreciation, it is recognized that there may be circumstances where it is necessary to revise the amount that is being charged as depreciation. This is because the parameters used for measuring depreciation – such as (mainly) the estimate of useful economic life and (to a lesser extent) the expected residual value – are only estimates, and estimates by their very nature require revision in the light of experience and developments. Besides, the accounting profession is wary of a situation where an asset might have been fully written off by depreciation but still remains in use. In this situation, while income in the period is benefiting from the use of that asset there would be no matching expense by way of a depreciation charge. The only way in which the profession expects that particular situation to be avoided is by keeping the estimate of the asset's useful life constantly under review.

Accordingly, the accepted accounting practice[3] requires that, first, the entity must review the estimate of economic life of each class of asset at the end of every accounting period, and, second, in the event of any change in the estimate of economic life, the net book value of the asset (i.e. the cost less depreciation written off up to that point) should be written off over the remainder of the revised economic life, using the same depreciation method.

In deference to this requirement, British Airports Authority (BAA) found it necessary, when preparing their 1990 accounts, to extend the UEL of the airport terminal buildings and the airport runways from 40 years to 100 years. Similarly when preparing their 1993 accounts Cable and Wireless found it necessary to reduce the UEL of analogue cables from 15 to 7 years because of the need to replace them with digital technology by the year 2000.

Revision of UEL   **Interaction 16.5**

Wimbledon Mills acquired a machine on 1.1.20X0 for £80,000 and has been depreciating it at 5 per cent of cost per annum. On 1.1.20X6 it was decided that to keep up with market trends the machinery should be replaced by 31 December 20X9. Determine the depreciation to be written off in the year to 31 December 20X6. Assume that a separate account is maintained for accumulated depreciation.

16.6 DEPRECIATION OF BUILDINGS

Buildings differ from machinery and equipment in that the economic life of buildings is significantly longer. However, although the economic life may be long, it is not infinite and the cost of buildings should therefore also be depreciated.

Even so, many hotels, banks and building societies that have large property portfolios are known to resist the requirement to depreciate buildings on the grounds set out below, and we comment in places on their arguments.

- **Difficulty of identifying the cost of a building separately from that of land**. This can occur because the land and buildings were acquired together many years ago. The difficulty, however, is not real, because the Royal Institution of Chartered Surveyors has sufficient records, which help in identifying the cost of buildings.
- **Determination of economic life is a difficult exercise** – in the case of buildings and more particularly in the cases of dams, reservoirs, airport terminals and runways. This difficulty cannot, though, be an excuse for not depreciating. What needs to be done is to estimate the economic life on the basis of past experience and keep the estimate under review at regular intervals or, alternatively, to consider renewal accounting (which is described below in Section 16.7).
- **Immateriality of the amount**. It has been argued that the economic life of buildings, if well maintained, might tend toward infinity or at least be so long that the annual charge for depreciation would be immaterial. For example, the Trusthouse Forte group claimed in its 1992 accounts that 'it is the group's practice to maintain these assets in a continual state of sound repair and extend and make improvements thereto from time to time and accordingly the directors consider that the lives of these assets are so long and residual values, based on prevailing prices at the time of acquisition, . . . are so high that their depreciation is insignificant'.

  Although one can concede that exceptionally good maintenance could correspondingly extend the economic life of a building, and therefore that the amount of depreciation in each year would be correspondingly small, one might be reluctant to accept that as justification for not depreciating at all. Taken by itself, the annual amount might be small, but when accumulated over many years it could result in a significant amount. However, in practice, immateriality of the annual amount is accepted as a valid reason for not depreciating. There is a safeguard, however, in that impairment reviews (see Section 16.8) are required to be carried out at the end of every accounting period if it appears that depreciation has actually occurred and the Balance Sheet figure is excessive.
- **Depreciation amounts to a double charge on profits**. This is said to happen when the high cost of maintenance is also taken into account. This argument misses the point, that the cost of maintenance (like the cost of servicing a vehicle) is part of the recurrent expense, while the depreciation is an allocation to each accounting period of an appropriate portion of the cost of the asset. It is conceded, however, that high maintenance costs, by extending the asset's economic life, will lower the annual depreciation charge.
- **Buildings have no depreciable cost because their residual value tends to appreciate with time**. Admittedly, the ageing process tends to add value to certain assets such as buildings, timber and wine. Trusthouse Forte's 1992 report refers to such an improvement when it identifies improvements in value other than those attributable to inflation. The question, however, is whether such improvement in residual value should be permitted to mask the depreciable cost of an asset.

Interaction
16.6

Focus on absence of a depreciable cost

(a) A vintner buys two casks of wine at £50 each. One he sells for £75, and the other, remaining in stock, has a market value of £80. Is it acceptable for him to capitalize (i.e. to record as an asset in the Balance Sheet) the unsold cask at £80 and to report the cost of the one sold at £20?

(b) The Trusthouse Forte group in 1992 explained its failure to depreciate its buildings as follows:

- it maintains its buildings in a continual state of sound repair, making renovations and building extensions;
- the life of the buildings is so long that annual depreciation becomes immaterial;
- the residual values of buildings at prices that prevailed at the time of acquisition are so high that there is no depreciable cost.

Required: Explain whether you would accept these reasons.

16.7 DEPRECIATION OF INFRASTRUCTURE ASSETS BY RENEWAL ACCOUNTING

Renewal accounting is the term used to describe the practice of charging the cost of replacements against the profits for the year instead of a depreciation figure arrived at by allocating cost. For example, in order to remain effective in their professional practice, solicitors have by necessity to maintain an up-to-date library, which involves having to replace existing volumes with newer editions. In these circumstances it is usual accounting practice for solicitors to report their library at initial cost and to write off the cost of replacements in lieu of depreciation.

Company law[4] permits the adoption of the 'renewal accounting' for fixed assets that are constantly being replaced, provided (a) the overall value is not material for assessing the company's state of affairs and (b) the quantity, value and composition of the assets are not subject to material variation. Cinemas and theatres use renewal accounting when accounting for seats in their auditorium; and so do hotels when they account for crockery and cutlery.

Accounting standards[5] permit renewal accounting as an alternative to depreciation when public utilities account for infrastructure assets. This is because entities such as the water companies have a statutory responsibility to maintain in perpetuity their infrastructure assets (such as the network of mains, raw-water storage reservoirs and sludge pipelines). The annual expenditure they incur to maintain the infrastructure asset is treated as equivalent to depreciation, and the practice is acceptable provided the following criteria are met:

(a) the infrastructure asset is a system or network that, as a whole, is intended to be maintained at a specified level of service potential by the continuing replacement and refurbishment of its components;

(b) the level of annual expenditure required to maintain the operating capacity of the infrastructure asset is calculated from an asset management plan that is certified by a person who is appropriately qualified and independent; and

(c) any identifiable major components within the infrastructure asset with a determinable finite life are depreciated over that economic life.

When renewal accounting is used, the actual cost of renewal or refurbishment is capitalized, while the amount of renewal necessary for maintaining the infrastructure asset at specified levels is written off as depreciation in each period. For example, if an entity reports its infrastructure asset on 1.1.20X0 at £214 million and during the year to 31.12.20X0 incurs £48 million more on renewals, whereas, according to the certified plan for asset maintenance, it should have incurred £72 million, it has to report the asset at £190 million on 31 December 20X0 (see account to the right). The actual cost of renewals is capitalized, while the amount it should have incurred in accordance with the certified plan is written off as depreciation.

INFRASTRUCTURE ASSET ACCOUNT

	£m		£m
Balance b/d	214	Depreciation	72
Cash a/c	48	Balance c/d	190
	262		262
Balance b/d	190		

16.8 IMPAIRMENT REVIEWS

We have seen that different methods of depreciation result in different net book values in the Balance Sheet at the end of each financial year. There is an additional test to check that the depreciation has not been materially understated and the net book value of the asset overstated. This test is known as an impairment review and its objective is to ensure that the asset should not be reported in a Balance Sheet at higher than its recoverable amount.

The recoverable amount of an asset is defined as the higher of *value in use* (the present value of the economic benefits that the asset is expected to generate over its economic life, i.e. the discounted cash flows associated with the asset) and *net realizable amount* (the amount the asset can be sold for on that date, less selling expenses).

For example, let us assume that a machine acquired for £100,000 and depreciated at 10 per cent per annum by the straight-line method is reported on 1.1.20X0 at £40,000. Let us consider two alternative scenarios as follows:

MACHINE ACCOUNT

20X0		£	20X0		£
1.1	Balance	40,000	31.12	Depreciation a/c	10,000
			31.12	Balance c/d	30,000
		40,000			40,000

MACHINE ACCOUNT

20X0		£	20X0		£
1.1	Balance	40,000	31.12	Depreciation a/c	6,500
			31.12	Impairment	14,000
			31.12	Balance c/d	19,500
		40,000			40,000

1. The present value of the income that this machine could generate over the remaining four years of its economic life is £52,000; but if the asset is sold on 1.1.20X0, it would realize only £18,000. The machine would continue to be reported at £40,000 (and depreciated as usual by £10,000 per annum) because the recoverable amount (£52,000) is higher.

2. The present value of the income that this machine could generate over the remaining four years is £24,000; but if the asset is sold on 1.1.20X0, it would realize £26,000. Hence as at 1.1.20X0 the asset should be written down to £26,000 (its recoverable amount) by writing off the difference of £14,000 as impairment loss. The revised book value of £26,000 is then depreciated, by the straight-line method, over the remaining four years.

16.8.1 When is it necessary to carry out an impairment review?

There is a requirement[6] for an impairment review to be carried out at the end of each accounting period, in certain circumstances such as any one of the following:

- the asset is one that has not been depreciated either because (like land) its economic life is not finite or because its economic life is so long that depreciation would be immaterial;
- the remaining economic life is estimated at more than 50 years;
- a significant adverse change has occurred in the market in which the fixed asset is involved;
- there has been a major loss of key employees;
- there is evidence of obsolescence or physical damage to the asset;
- there are current, and possibly future, operating losses.

16.9 ACCOUNTING FOR DISPOSAL OF A FIXED ASSET

Each year that a fixed asset is being used productively, there will be an annual depreciation expense transferred away from the asset account to the Depreciation account and finally to the Profit and Loss account. If the original estimates of the number of years of economic life and the residual value were accurate, then the sales proceeds will be exactly equal to the written down value of the asset on the date of disposal. To illustrate this (highly improbable) scenario, let us assume that a fixed asset, a computer, was acquired for £4,000 on 1 January 20X0 and it was estimated that it would have an economic life of five years and a residual value of £700, i.e. the amount that would be received as sales proceeds on 31 December 20X4.

The Computer account would appear as follows:

COMPUTER ACCOUNT

		£			£
20X0			**20X0**		
1.1	Cash a/c	4,000	31.12	Depreciation a/c	660
			31.12	Balance c/d	3,340
20X1		4,000	**20X1**		4,000
1.1	Balance b/d	3,340	31.12	Depreciation a/c	660
			31.12	Balance c/d	2,680
20X2		3,340	**20X2**		3,340
1.1	Balance b/d	2,680	31.12	Depreciation a/c	660
			31.12	Balance c/d	2,020
20X3		2,680	**20X3**		2,680
1.1	Balance b/d	2,020	31.12	Depreciation a/c	660
			31.12	Balance c/d	1,360
20X4		2,020	**20X4**		2,020
1.1	Balance b/d	1,360	31.12	Depreciation a/c	660
			31.12	Cash	700
		1,360			1,360

Note that the cash of £700 exactly equals the net book value after five years' depreciation at £660 per annum. However, it is very unlikely that the estimates of both the economic life and the residual value (made on 1.1.20X0) will be accurate by the end of 20X4.

What if economic life is less than five years? Assume that at 31 December 20X2 the computer becomes obsolete and is scrapped. There will be a loss of £2,020 and the Computer account will then appear as follows:

COMPUTER ACCOUNT

		£				£
20X0			**20X0**			
1.1	Cash a/c	4,000	31.12	Depreciation a/c		660
			31.12	Balance c/d		3,340
20X1		4,000	**20X1**			4,000
1.1	Balance b/d	3,340	31.12	Depreciation a/c		660
			31.12	Balance c/d		2,680
20X2		3,340	**20X2**			3,340
1.1	Balance b/d	2,680	31.12	Depreciation a/c		660
			31.12	Profit and Loss account		2,020
		2,680				2,680

Now assume that at the end of five years the computer is sold for £800. This is £100 more than expected and there will be a profit transferred to the Profit and Loss account. The implication is that the depreciation of £660 charged in each of the five years of use should have been £20 per year less (£100/5). The accounting approach is to record the profit of £100 at the date of sale and not to go back over the five years reducing the depreciation expense and increasing the profit by £20 per year. The ledger account would appear as follows:

COMPUTER ACCOUNT

		£			£
20X4			**20X4**		
1.1	Balance b/d	1,360	31.12	Depreciation a/c	660
31.12	Profit and Loss account	100	31.12	Cash	800
		1,460			1,460

Interaction 16.7

Accounting for asset disposal

Wimbledon Mills acquired machinery for £120,000 on 1.1.20X0 and depreciated annually at 5 per cent of cost. To keep up with change in technology, the business had to dispose of the machinery for £25,000 on 30 June 20X6, replacing it with other machinery costing £150,000.

Required: Set out, in respect of the year ended 31.12.20X6: (a) the Machinery account; (b) the Provision for Depreciation account; and (c) the Disposal of Machinery account.

References

1. FRS 15: *Accounting for Tangible Fixed Assets* (February 1999).
2. FRS 15, *ibid.*
3. FRS 15, *ibid.*
4. Companies Act 1985, Schedule 4 paragraph 25.
5. FRS 15: *Accounting for Tangible Fixed Assets* (February 1999).
6. FRS 11: *Impairment of Fixed Assets and Goodwill* (July 1998).
7. W.T. Baxter, *Depreciation* (Sweet and Maxwell, London, 1971).

SOLUTIONS TO INTERACTIVE QUESTIONS

IQ 16.1 Depreciable amount and depreciation

Realizable value is to be based on current prices (i.e. without the impact of any future inflation).

   Depreciation = £18,100/4 = £4,525 per annum.

Cost of Escort Van		£20,000
Less: Realizable value	£2,000	
Selling expenses @ 5%	(£100)	
Net realizable value		(£1,900)
Depreciable amount		£18,100

IQ 16.2 The straight-line method of depreciation

(a)

MOTOR VEHICLES ACCOUNT

			£				£
20X0				**20X0**			
1.1	Cash a/c	40,000		31.12	Depreciation a/c	8,000	
				31.12	Balance c/d	32,000	
20X1			40,000	**20X1**			40,000
1.1	Balance b/d	32,000		31.12	Depreciation a/c	8,000	
				31.12	Balance c/d	24,000	
20X2			32,000	**20X2**			32,000
1.1	Balance b/d	24,000		31.12	Depreciation a/c	8,000	
				31.12	Balance c/d	16,000	
20X3			24,000	**20X3**			24,000
1.1	Balance b/d	16,000		31.12	Depreciation a/c	8,000	
				31.12	Balance c/d	8,000	
20X4			16,000	**20X4**			16,000
1.1	Balance b/d	8,000					

(b) Columnar worksheet is as follows:

Vehicles		First	Second	Third	Fourth	Total
		£	£	£	£	£
Cost		40,000	36,000	48,000	42,000	166,000
Depreciation at 20% p.a.	20X0	(8,000)	–	–	–	(8,000)
	20X1	(8,000)	(7,200)	–	–	(15,200)
	20X2	(8,000)	(7,200)	(9,600)	–	(24,800)
	20X3	(8,000)	(7,200)	(9,600)	(8,400)	(33,200)
Written down value – 31.12.20X3		8,000	14,400	28,800	33,600	84,800

MOTOR VEHICLES ACCOUNT

		£			£
1.1.X0	Cash bk	40,000			
1.1.X1	Cash bk	36,000			
1.1.X2	Cash bk	48,000			
1.1.X3	Cash bk	42,000			

PROVISION FOR DEPRECIATION ACCOUNT

	£				£
			31.12.X0	Deprn a/c	8,000
			31.12.X1	Deprn a/c	15,200
			31.12.X2	Deprn a/c	24,800
			31.12.X3	Deprn a/c	33,200

BALANCE SHEET (EXTRACT) AS AT 31 DECEMBER

		At cost	Acc. depre.	Written down value
20X0	Motor vehicles	£40,000	(£8,000)	£32,000
20X1	Motor vehicles	£76,000	(£23,200)	£52,800
20X2	Motor vehicles	£124,000	(£48,000)	£76,000
20X3	Motor vehicles	£166,000	(£81,200)	£84,800

IQ 16.3 The reducing balance method of depreciation

(a)

MOTOR VEHICLES ACCOUNT

		£				£
20X0			**20X0**			
1.1	Cash a/c	40,000	31.12	Depreciation a/c	16,000
			31.12	Balance c/d	24,000
20X1		40,000	**20X1**		40,000
1.1	Balance b/d	24,000	31.12	Depreciation a/c	9,600
			31.12	Balance c/d	14,400
20X2		24,000	**20X2**		24,000
1.1	Balance b/d	14,400	31.12	Depreciation a/c	5,760
			31.12	Balance c/d	8,640
20X3		14,400	**20X3**		14,400
1.1	Balance b/d	8,640	31.12	Depreciation a/c	3,456
			31.12	Balance c/d	5,184
20X4		8,640	**20X4**		8,640
1.1	Balance b/d	5,184			

(b) Columnar worksheet is as follows:

Date	Vehicles	First	Second	Third	Fourth	Total
		£	£	£	£	£
1.1.X0	Cost	40,000				40,000
31.12.X0	Depreciation: 40% of cost	(16,000)				(16,000)
31.12.X0	Written down value	24,000				24,000
1.1.X1	Cost	–	36,000			36,000
31.12.X1	Depreciation: 40% of wdv	(9,600)	(14,400)			(24,000)
31.12.X1	Written down value	14,400	21,600			36,000
1.1.X2	Cost	–	–	48,000		48,000
31.12.X2	Depreciation: 40% of wdv	(5,760)	(8,640)	(19,200)		(33,600)
31.12.X2	Written down value	8,640	12,960	28,800	–	50,400
1.1.X3	Cost	–	–	–	42,000	42,000
31.12.X3	Depreciation: 40% of wdv	(3,456)	(5,184)	(11,520)	(16,800)	(36,960)
31.12.X3	Written down value	5,184	7,776	17,280	25,200	55,440

MOTOR VEHICLES ACCOUNT

		£						£
1.1.X0	Cash bk	40,000						
1.1.X1	Cash bk	36,000						
1.1.X2	Cash bk	48,000						
1.1.X3	Cash bk	42,000						

PROVISION FOR DEPRECIATION ACCOUNT

		£			£
			31.12.X0	Deprn a/c	16,000
			31.12.X1	Deprn a/c	24,000
			31.12.X2	Deprn a/c	33,600
			31.12.X3	Deprn a/c	36,960

BALANCE SHEET (EXTRACT) AS AT 31 DECEMBER

		At cost	Acc. depre.	Written down value
20X0	Motor vehicles	£40,000	(£16,000)	£24,000
20X1	Motor vehicles	£76,000	(£40,000)	£36,000
20X2	Motor vehicles	£124,000	(£73,600)	£50,400
20X3	Motor vehicles	£166,000	(£110,560)	£55,440

IQ 16.4 The sum of the year's digits method

(a) Written down values

MOTOR VEHICLES ACCOUNT

		£				£
1.1.X0	Cash bk	40,000				

PROVISION FOR DEPRECIATION ACCOUNT

		£			£
			31.12.X0	Deprn a/c	16,000
			31.12.X1	Deprn a/c	12,000
			31.12.X2	Deprn a/c	8,000
			31.12.X3	Deprn a/c	4,000

MOTOR VEHICLE ON 31 DECEMBER

	Cost	Acc. depre.	WDV
20X0	£40,000	(£16,000)	£24,000
20X1	£40,000	(£28,000)	£12,000
20X2	£40,000	(£36,000)	£4,000
20X3	£40,000	(£40,000)	00

(b) Columnar worksheet is as follows:

Vehicles		First	Second	Third	Fourth	Total
		£	£	£	£	£
Cost		40,000	36,000	48,000	42,000	166,000
Depreciation	20X0	(16,000)				(16,000)
	20X1	(12,000)	(14,400)			(26,400)
	20X2	(8,000)	(10,800)	(19,200)		(38,000)
	20X3	(4,000)	(7,200)	(14,400)	(16,800)	(42,400)
Written down value – 31.12.20X3		00–	3,600	14,400	25,200	43,200

MOTOR VEHICLES ACCOUNT

		£			£
1.1.X0	Cash bk	40,000			
1.1.X1	Cash bk	36,000			
1.1.X2	Cash bk	48,000			
1.1.X3	Cash bk	42,000			

PROVISION FOR DEPRECIATION ACCOUNT

	£			£
		31.12.X0	Deprn a/c	16,000
		31.12.X1	Deprn a/c	26,400
		31.12.X2	Deprn a/c	38,000
		31.12.X3	Deprn a/c	42,400

BALANCE SHEET (EXTRACT) AS AT 31 DECEMBER

		At cost	Acc. depre.	Written down value
20X0	Motor vehicles	£40,000	(£16,000)	£24,000
20X1	Motor vehicles	£76,000	(£42,400)	£33,600
20X2	Motor vehicles	£124,000	(£80,400)	£43,600
20X3	Motor vehicles	£166,000	(£122,800)	£43,200

IQ 16.5 Revision of UEL

		£			£
1.1.X0	Cash bk	80,000			

PROVISION FOR DEPRECIATION OF MACHINERY ACCOUNT

		£			£
			1.1.X6	Balance b/f	24,000
			31.12.X6	Deprn a/c	14,000

Assuming nil residual value and an economic life of 20 years, the machinery would have been depreciated at £4,000 per year for six years until 31.12.20X5. On 1.1.20X6, upon revising the estimate of useful economic life to four more years, the written down value (£56,000) on that date is written off on the same method over the remaining useful economic life.

IQ 16.6 Focus on absence of a depreciable cost

(a) In the case of the vintner, the application of unrealized gain of £30 on the cask yet remaining in hand, in order to reduce the cost of the cask sold, is unacceptable for two reasons. First, in principle and practice, accounting is transactions-based, so that profit can be recognized only when goods are sold. The gain on the unsold cask will not be objectively established until that also is sold. Second, the profit is the difference between the sale price of the cask and the amount paid to purchase that cask. That cost remains £50 irrespective of other events.

Prof. W.T. Baxter refers[7] to similar circumstances when he asks whether it would be fair for a person owning a pile of stones, from which he used a few every year, to use the unrealized gains expected from the stones remaining unused to reduce the cost of those used.

(b) The reasons advanced by Trusthouse for not depreciating buildings appear dubious for the following reasons:

- The avoidance of depreciation of buildings pointing to the high cost of maintenance is not far removed from endeavours to avoid depreciation of machinery pointing to superlative maintenance.
- Though admittedly, because of very long economic lives, annual depreciation could be immaterial, over the long years of economic life, the amount would accumulate significantly.
- The buildings are not intended for disposal. Therefore, appreciation in value of buildings is not relevant for the determination of depreciable cost; just as in the case of the appreciation in value of the unsold cask of wine and unused stones.

IQ 16.7 Accounting for asset disposal

PLANT AND MACHINERY ACCOUNT

			£				£	
a	1.1.X0	Cash book	120,000	30.6.X6	Disposal a/c	120,000	d
a	30.6.X6	Cash book	150,000	31.12.X6	Balance c/d	150,000	
	1.1.X7	Balance	150,000				

PROVISION FOR DEPRECIATION OF MACHINERY ACCOUNT

			£				£	
d	30.6.X6	Disposal	39,000	1.1.X6	Balance b/f	36,000	b
				30.6.X6	Deprn a/c	3,000	c
	31.12.X6	Balance c/d	3,750	31.12.X6	Deprn a/c	3,750	e
				1.1.X7	Balance b/f	3,750	

DISPOSAL OF MACHINERY ACCOUNT

			£				£	
d	30.6.X6	P&M a/c	120,000	30.6.X6	Prov. for dep	39,000	d
				30.6.X6	Cash book	25,000	
				31.12.X6	P&L – loss	56,000	f

Notes:

(a) The costs of the old machine and its replacement are capitalized.
(b) Annual depreciation is £6,000 per year, written off over six years until 31.12.20X5.
(c) Depreciation is at the rate 5 per cent of cost on the old machinery for six months until disposal.
(d) There is a transfer of cost as well as accumulated depreciation of the machinery disposed of.
(e) Depreciation of new machinery for six months to 31.12.20X6.
(f) Loss on disposal written off.

PROGRESSIVE QUESTIONS

PQ 16.1 The concept of depreciation

Place a tick in the appropriate column of the grid to identify whether each of the following statements is true or false:

	TRUE	FALSE

(a) By depreciation an entity sets aside cash resources which will be readily available to pay for the eventual replacement of existing assets. Therefore depreciation may be regarded as a source of funds.

(b) Depreciation is not a valuation process. All that it does is to allocate the depreciable cost of tangible assets over the years that constitute their economic life in a reasonable and systematic manner.

(c) Factors to be considered when determining the depreciation charge are:

(i) the cost of the asset;

(ii) the residual value (also known as scrap value or salvage value);

(iii) the method of depreciation in use;

(iv) the market value at the end of each accounting period;

(v) expenses to keep the asset in a working condition.

PQ 16.2 An assessment of the straight-line method of depreciation

Fill the blanks in the sentences that follow with an appropriate word selected from the set below:

increasing	low	useful	negative
adjustment	high	stolen	disposal
knowledge	nil	working	accurate
experience	cost	estimation	

(a) The disadvantage of the straight-line method is that every year depreciation remains the same, whereas in early years repairs should be .... In later years there will be an .... charge to the Profit and Loss account in that there will be a .... repair charge with the same depreciation.

(b) Another disadvantage of the straight-line method is that if the asset is reduced to ...., care must be taken to see that the asset is not .... or depreciated to a .... figure.

(c) The assessment of depreciation involves the consideration of three factors: the .... of the asset, which is known; the probable value realizable on ultimate ...., which can generally be estimated only within fairly wide limits; and the length of time during which the asset will be commercially .... to the organization, where in most cases the last factor cannot be calculated precisely. Depreciation is therefore in most cases matters of .... based upon the available .... and .... rather than of .... determination. The values require .... from time to time in the light of changes in experience and expenditure, including prolongation of useful .... life through exceptional maintenance expenditure, curtailment due to excessive use, or obsolescence not allowed for in the original estimation of the commercially useful life of the asset.

PQ 16.3 The common depreciation methods

Place a tick in the appropriate grid to identify whether each of the following statements refers to the straight-line method (SLM) or reducing balance method (RBM) of depreciation:

	SLM	RBM

(a) Once computed, the annual depreciation charge remains the same.

(b) It is difficult to determine a fair rate at which to depreciate the asset. If too low a rate is adopted, a large balance remains to be written off when the asset is discarded; and if too high a percentage is used, there will be an excessive depreciation charge in earlier years of the asset's life.

(c) The charge for depreciation fails to correspond with the real life fall in the market value of the asset.

(d) Its virtue is its simplicity of calculation.

(e) The steadily decreasing charge for depreciation corresponds to the asset's declining earning power and loss of efficiency arising with age.

(f) An asset fully written off may still remain in good condition and be of use.

(g) Since the expenditure on repairs is likely to increase with the age of the asset, a diminishing depreciation charge tends to equalize the total charge to revenue as regards the asset.

(h) The charge to revenue tends to increase with the age of the asset because repair costs tend to rise as the asset gets older.

PQ 16.4 Impact of depreciation on cash flow and asset replacement

(a) John Smith owns and operates a taxicab. On 1 January 20X0 he bought a taxi for £2,400 and depreciated it on the straight-line basis using an expected useful life of three years and a trade-in value after three years of £600. All his cash takings are banked and all business expenditure is paid by cheque. His drawings for each of the last three years have been exactly equal to his profits. He has never borrowed any money, and has no creditors, debtors or stocks.

  Required: Calculate the bank balance at 31 December 20X0, 20X1 and 20X2 assuming that Smith's bank balance was nil after paying for the taxi at the beginning of 20X0.

(b) On 1 January 20X3 the best trade-in allowance he can obtain for his taxi is £600, as originally estimated, but the replacement cost of an identical vehicle is now £3,600, and although he has never drawn out more from his business than the profits shown by his accounts, he now has insufficient funds to replace his taxi. He blames you, his accountant, for this unhappy situation, and suggests that the depreciation written off must have been inadequate.

  Required: Briefly discuss the issues involved in this scenario.

PQ 16.5 Comparison of four depreciation methods

A company acquires a new machine on 1 January 20X0 for £50,000. It is estimated that the machine will have a useful life of four years, after which time it is expected to be sold for £10,000. State, by placing a tick in the appropriate box, the depreciation to be written off in the year ending 31 December 20X0, when the basis of depreciation is:

1. The straight-line method.

(a)	£8,000	
(b)	£12,500	
(c)	£10,000	

2. The reducing balance method, using the formula stated in Section 16.4.2.

(a)	£12,252	
(b)	£13,252	
(c)	£16,565	

3. Machine hour rate, on the basis that machine capacity is 40,000 hours and the intended use of the machine is 10,000 hours in 20X0, 12,000 hours in 20X1, 10,000 hours in 20X2, and 8,000 hours in 20X3.

(a)	£12,500	
(b)	£5,500	
(c)	£10,000	

4. Sum of the year's digits method.

(a)	£4,000	
(b)	£5,000	
(c)	£16,000	

PQ 16.6 Further comparison of depreciation methods

Lambeth Industries, finalizing accounts annually on 31 December, acquired a machine on 1.1.20X0 for £280,000. Assume the residual value to be nil.

Required:
Determine:

(a) the depreciation expense in the year ended 31.12.20X4; and
(b) the amount at which the asset is reported on the Balance Sheet on that date, in each of the following alternative methods of depreciation:
  (i) the straight-line method at 10 per cent per annum;
  (ii) the reducing balance method at 20 per cent;
  (iii) the sum of the year's digits method over ten years;
  (iv) the machine-hour method, where the machine is expected to have a capacity for 864,000 hours of work and during the year ended 31.12.20X4 it clocked up 108,000 hours;
  (v) the production unit method, where the machine is capable of 1.62 million units of output and during the year the output was 260,357 units.

PQ 16.7 Comparison of straight-line method with sum of the year's digits method

Y and Z acquired identical equipment having an estimated useful economic life of five years. Y uses the straight-line method of depreciation; Z uses the sum of the year's digits method. Assuming the businesses of Y and Z are identical in all respects:

(a) Z will charge more in depreciation on this asset over the five-year service life than Y;
(b) if the asset is sold at the end of the second year, Y is more likely to report a loss than Z;
(c) Y's depreciation expense will be higher during the first year than Z's;
(d) Y's net income will be higher during the fifth year than Z's.

Only one of the above statements is correct. Identify that statement.

PQ 16.8 Change of estimate of useful economic life

On 1.1.20X4 the production manager of a business reports that, in view of technological innovations, a machine, acquired for £320,000 on 1 July 20X0 and depreciated at 5 per cent per annum by the straight-line method, requires replacement not later than 31.12.20X6.

Required: Determine the depreciation expense to be written off in the year ending 31.12.20X4.

Chapter 17

STOCK IN TRADE

In this chapter

We will learn of:

- alternative methods used for ascertaining the quantity and cost of unsold stock
- the non-aggregation rule

and you should be able to:

- ascertain the cost of unsold goods:
  (a) when stock-take is not on the last day of the year
  (b) on the basis of alternative cost flow assumptions

17.1 SIGNIFICANCE OF STOCK IN ACCOUNTING

A Franciscan friar Luca Pacioli[1] reported that the system of accounting on a double entry basis, as we know it today, was practised even in the middle ages by Venetian merchants. These merchants would typically enter into a venture (e.g. shipping a consignment of silk from Asia to Europe) and would only prepare an account on the completion of the venture, which would have been on sale of the whole consignment. In such a scenario there would be no unsold stock to value because the accounts would only be finalized when all stock had been sold.

Today it is no longer appropriate to apply the 'venture' concept, as it came to be known. Instead, businesses now apply the 'time interval' concept, under which accounting reports are prepared at regular intervals – which, typically, is annually. But the trade cycle of a business does not always coincide with the accounting period, and a trader is not always able to sell the whole of his purchases within the accounting period. Hence, on completion of each accounting period, a trader has to determine the cost of his unsold purchases for the purpose of:

- reporting it on the Balance Sheet as an asset named 'stock in trade', because it is expected to bring him economic benefit by way of sales, hopefully in the next period;
- removing it from the balance in the Purchases account so that the remainder can be written off as the cost of goods sold in the period.

How does stock affect profit? A trader measures his (gross) profit by comparing his sales income with the cost of what he sold; and he determines the cost of what he sold by removing from the balance in the Purchases account the cost of what remains unsold at the end of his accounting period. In this context the accuracy of determining the quantity of goods remaining unsold, and their cost, is crucial. Let us assume, for example, that Cyber Model's Trading account should have appeared as shown below. If the quantity of items in hand by the year end was mistakenly counted as three items, the cost of sales would have been incorrectly stated as £81,000 (£108,000 – £27,000) and the gross profit as £19,000. Similarly, if the error was in valuation of the items remaining unsold – say the items were each valued at £19,000 instead of £9,000

TRADING ACCOUNT

	£	£
Sales (10 items @ £10,000)		100,000
Purchases (12 items @ £9,000)	108,000	
Less: Stock (2 items @ £9,000)	(18,000)	
Cost of goods sold (10 items @ £9,000)		(90,000)
Gross profit		10,000

– the cost of sales would be incorrectly reported as £70,000 (£108,000 – £38,000) and the gross profit as £30,000.

Notice that the profit will be increased (or decreased) on a £-for-£ basis with the error in the stock figure. Because the profit figure is often significantly smaller than the stock figure, the effect of an error is proportionately greater.

For example, for Cyber Models, the stock count error is only 10 per cent of the stock (£9,000:£90,000) whereas it is 90 per cent of the profit (£9,000:£10,000). This means that the Balance Sheet would fail to present a true and fair view of the assets because the stock is inaccurate and the profit is inaccurate.

Interaction 17.1

Stock is crucial to financial reporting

On completion of his first year's business as a dealer in fashionware, Bernard prepared his financial statements as follows:

TRADING AND PROFIT AND LOSS ACCOUNT FOR YEAR ENDED 31.12.20X0	
	£000
Sales	640
Purchases	(516)
Gross profit	124
Expenses	(94)
Depreciation	(18)
Profit	12

BALANCE SHEET AS AT 31.12.20X0		
		£000
Fixed assets		360
Provision for depreciation		(18)
		342
Debtors	114	
Cash	22	
Creditors	(216)	(80)
		262

	£000
Capital	250
Profit for the year	12
	262

Bemard's attention is drawn to his failure to account for the stock of fashionware, costing £112,000, which remained unsold as at 31 December 20X0.

Required: Prepare amended financial statements for the year.

17.2 KEEPING TRACK OF THE COST OF GOODS SOLD

Ideally, a trader should know the cost of goods at the time he sells them. This certainly would be the case when the item being sold is of a high value and individually identifiable by, say, a serial number or description (e.g. a motor car, computer or valuable item of jewellery). It is possible in these situations to match the cost of sales with the individual sales and to identify the items still unsold at the year end.

Let us illustrate this situation by referring to a trader who sells yachts. Assume that his transactions in the year were as follows:

Date of purchase	Item purchased	Serial number	Cost price (£)	Date of sale	Sale price (£)	Profit (£)
3.1.20X0	Yacht	SK100	100,000	30.10.20X0	189,000	89,000
14.3.20X0	Yacht	PV300	58,000	28.9.20X0	69,000	11,000
26.7.20X0	Yacht	XR251	102,000	–	–	–

The performance for the year and the position at the end thereof are as shown on the right.

Often, however, a trader finds it impossible, or not cost-effective, to keep track of the quantity and cost of the items he sells. The more important reasons for this are twofold. First, stocks often consist of numerous items, very diverse in kind and each of such insignificant cost that it is difficult and not

TRADING ACCOUNT FOR YEAR ENDED 31.12.20X0		
		£
Sales		258,000
Cost of sale:		
SK100	100,000	
PV300	58,000	(158,000)
Gross profit		100,000

BALANCE SHEET AS AT 31.12.20X0	
	£
Stock in trade (XR251)	102,000

always cost-effective to keep count of them even if there was no variation in the unit prices paid for them. The stock held by a grocer, for example, could range from perishable foodstuffs such as milk and bread, to non-perishables such as canned foods, to household products such as toiletries and cleaning items, with each of the items stocked in a variety of brand names, sizes and packaging. Similarly, the stock held by a dealer in electronic goods may range from very expensive, technologically sophisticated, computer hardware to basic pocket calculators. Given such a situation, it may even appear absurd that they are all reported together as a single item in the same ledger account. The second reason is that purchases may be made at different prices and it is difficult to keep track of the cost of each item. Where, as is usually the case, the units of stock are purchased at different prices, the task of identifying the actual individual cost of the units sold may be impossible, as in the case of a builders merchant selling sand.

17.3 ASCERTAINING QUANTITIES OF GOODS REMAINING UNSOLD

Business entities use one of the following methods for ascertaining quantity of goods remaining unsold.

17.4.1 The perpetual inventory system

An ideal, though laborious, system of keeping a constant track of goods held for sale is known as the perpetual inventory system. In this system, a continuous record is maintained of the quantities of that item coming in (on purchase) and going out (on sale, or for use in production). Periodically, the accuracy of the balance reported on the bin card is established by taking a physical inventory of the item concerned. The greatest advantage of this method is that it offers management repeated opportunities for checking the accuracy of the perpetual records and for monitoring the quantities held so as to guard against loss, overstocking, deterioration and slow-moving items.

17.4.2 Physical inventory

Many businesses, however, do not keep an updated record of the cost of goods held by them for sale. Instead, they wait until the end of the accounting period and then physically count and value the stock of unsold goods. The physical inventory (another name for a stock count) is done at close of business on the last day of the accounting period or, more commonly, on a convenient day shortly thereafter. The quantities in hand are physically counted, under proper controls, and are listed on pre-numbered stock sheets. The opportunity is taken also to assess the condition of the goods – keeping watch for those that are damaged, out of date or shop-soiled or that have in any way deteriorated. The results of the physical count will require adjustment for the following:

1. Items for which an invoice might have been received and that have been accounted for as purchases but the goods are not yet in the entity's custody. There could be various reasons why this happens; for example, the items might be in transit, there might be an unexpected production holdup at the manufacturer's, or the items might be held in a bonded warehouse pending payment of import duty etc. These items should be added to the stock if title to the goods has passed to the business (or, exceptionally, be deducted from the amount stated as Purchases if the title to the goods remains with the supplier).
2. Items might belong to the business but not have been included in the stock count, e.g. items in the custody of customers (on approval or a sale-or-return basis) or with third parties such as agents or consignees. Such items, too, should be added to the results of the stock count.
3. Items accounted for as sold but remaining in the entity's hands because of reasons such as a delay in delivery to customers. These items should be deducted from the stock count (because it is necessary to include the cost of these items in the cost of sales).
4. Items of expense stock (such as stationery or packing material) may have been incorrectly included within the count and treated as stock for resale. The cost of these items will need to be adjusted against the appropriate head of expenditure, rather than with purchases.

17.4.3 Consistent profit margin system

The easiest way of ascertaining stock at an end date, commonly used by retail corner shops, is the consistent profit margin system. This system is available only to those who so fix their sale price as to give a constant profit margin. By expressing the merchandise in hand, at any time, at the fixed sale price (see illustration on right), they are able to keep constant track of the potential sale (£150,000 in the case illustrated). Actual sales as and when made are deducted from that figure to reveal the unsold stock at the constant sale prices. By removing the profit margin, the cost of goods in hand is ascertained (at £8,000 in our case). At convenient points, the stock in hand would be physically counted in order to verify whether or not the actual stock matches the expectation.

	£000
Opening stock	20
Purchases	100
Total at cost price	120
Profit margin:	
@ 25% of cost	30
Stock at sale price	150
Sales (to year end)	(140)
Stock at sale price	10
Less: Profit margin	(2)
Cost of stock held	8

Counting stock on a day subsequent to the year end

Hanson Stores finalized its accounts on 31 March 20X1 but was unable to perform a physical inventory until 6 April 20X1. The stock was then physically counted and entered on stock sheets. Every item on the stock sheets was priced at cost. The total value of stock on hand, at cost price, was determined as £216,400. You have ascertained as follows:

(a) Adjustments are required for movements between the year end and the date of the stock count. Between 1.4.20X1 and the time of the stocktake, purchases amounted to £48,400, sales to £74,100 and sales returns to £2,100. The figure of sales referred to includes goods invoiced at £6,000 but not delivered to customers until 8.4.20X1, which was after the time the inventory was taken. Hanson Stores fixes sale price to yield a profit margin of 50 per cent on cost.

(b) Adjustments are required for errors in the stocktake. A subtotal of £156,500 has been carried forward from one stock sheet to the next as £165,500; and the stock sheets include, at £1,600, the cost of packing material and, at £2,800, the cost of unused stationery.

(c) Adjustments are required for stock held by third parties at the time of the stocktake. Certain goods costing £164,400 included within purchases in the year to 31.3.20X1 were not cleared from a bonded warehouse until the second week of April 20X1.

(d) Adjustments are required for stock held by customers. Stock with customers on sale-or-return basis on 31 March 20X1 had been pro-forma invoiced to them (as usual at cost plus 50 per cent) for £5,400. One-third of these goods had been returned by 6 April and the rest had been retained by customers. (A *pro-forma invoice* is a sample invoice – no sale is recognised until the customer confirms that the goods are not to be returned.)

(e) Adjustments are required for items not realizable at least at cost. Included in the stock sheets at a cost of £14,400 are certain shop-soiled items that are expected to be sold at £12,000 and subject further to payment of a sales commission of 5 per cent.

Required: Determine the value of stock to be included in the Trading account for the year ended 31 March 20X1 and the Balance Sheet as at 31 March 20X1.

17.4 THE COST OF STOCK IN TRADE

For a trader who buys, rather than manufactures, the goods he sells, the cost of stock is set at the purchase price plus all expenses incurred for placing the goods in the condition in which they are sold and at the location from which they are sold. This means that the cost of stock includes, in addition to the price paid to purchase the items, the costs associated with carriage inwards, freight, insurance, import duty and clearance expenses, as well as the cost of any further processing performed before the merchandise is offered to the customer. It follows, therefore, that all these expenses, to the extent that they relate to goods sold in the period, have to be stated in the Trading account, as part of the cost of goods sold.

Where goods sold are those manufactured by the entity, the cost of stock includes:

- the cost of raw materials purchased from outside;
- wages paid to workers engaged in the production process;
- depreciation of machinery;
- payments for production work subcontracted out.

Whether the cost should also include overheads (such as factory power, rent, and the supervisors' salaries) and interest paid to finance the production will be discussed in Chapter 29 when manufacturing activity is focused upon.

Turning either one of these formulae for stock cost into a means of costing the stock at the end of an accounting period is nevertheless not straightforward. For where, as is usually the case, a business entity purchases its merchandise at different prices, unless the individual units purchased are of high value (as would apply in the case of yachts, which we used as an example earlier, or vehicles or pianos) it is not always cost-effective to identify the actual cost of each unit remaining unsold by the year end. The alternative often resorted to is to assume a cost flow, often arbitrarily, to associate the costs paid during the year with the units remaining unsold at the end of it. There are many such *cost-flow assumptions* (as they are known) in use, though the common ones are the 'first in first out' (FIFO) and the 'simple average cost'.

Let us use the case of Samuel, a builders' merchant, to illustrate the alternative cost-flow assumptions that could be made to associate cost with the units remaining unsold. Samuel's purchases and sales of sand in 20X0 are as follows:

PURCHASES				SALES			
Date 20X0	Quantity (tonnes)	Unit cost per tonne	Total Cost (£)	Date 20X0	Quantity (tonnes)	Unit price per tonne	Total sales (£)
1.1	100	£10	£1,000	4.2	90	£30	£2,700
17.4	400	£20	£8,000	26.5	310	£35	£10,850
28.6	1,200	£25	£30,000	14.9	450	£40	£18,000
11.10	100	£35	£3,500	5.11	200	£40	£8,000
	1,800		£42,500		1,050		£39,550

It is clear that the amount of profit that Samuel would report for the year depends on the cost he could associate with 750 tonnes of sand remaining unsold by the year end. There is no correct answer because there is no way he could identify the actual cost of the pile in hand. All that can be done in the circumstances is to make one of the following assumptions:

17.4.1 First in first out (FIFO)

By far the commonest cost-flow assumption adopted in the United Kingdom and almost everywhere else (other than Germany, Italy, South Africa and some countries of South America) assumes that the merchandise leaves the shop in the sequence in which it arrived. On this premise the items remaining unsold are presumed to be those purchased at the most recently paid prices. Such an assumption would probably correspond to reality in businesses to which stock rotation is important – such as those dealing in perishables (like fruits, vegetables and eggs) and date-marked processed food. In such cases a deliberate effort will be made to ensure that early arrivals are cleaved from stock well prior to deterioration or expiry dates. On the other hand, a dealer in consumer durables may not succeed in unloading a particular unit to a reluctant customer purely on the premise that it was the next in line according to the sequence of arrival.

For example, assuming that the first lot to come in was the first to be sold, those in stock would be the ones bought at the latest prices paid on 28 June and on 11 October.

COST OF CLOSING STOCK

Tonnes	Bought on	Unit cost	Cost
650	28.6.X0	£25	£16,250
100	11.10.X0	£35	£3,500
750			£19,750

TRADING ACCOUNT FOR YEAR ENDED 31.12.20X0

		£000
Sales		39,550
Purchases	42,500	
Less: Stock	(19,750)	(22,750)
Gross profit		16,800

The advantages of using FIFO include the following:

- The assumed sequence of stock movement usually reflects reality.
- The Balance Sheet will report stock at values that approximate to those currently prevailing.
- The method is acceptable to the UK tax authorities.

The disadvantages of using FIFO include the following:

- Expenditure charged to the Profit and Loss account is based on outdated prices. This may distort profit.
- In the context of rising prices, the cost charged against sales revenue will not reflect the cost of replacing the items sold.
- If the whole of the profit calculated on this assumption were to be distributed, capital maintenance would be affected, i.e. there would be insufficient funds retained to replace the same number of items sold.

17.4.2 Last in first out (LIFO)

In this approach it is assumed that goods move out in the reverse order of their arrival. Hence, the items remaining unsold are presumed to be ones that arrived the earliest and the items on the stock sheets would, therefore, be evaluated (priced) at the earliest-paid prices. Though permitted by company law, the use of this method in the United Kingdom is discouraged[2] because, by valuing stock for Balance Sheet reporting at outdated costs, 'it does not provide the fairest approximation to actual cost'. The sequence of stock movement assumed here would probably accord with the one obtaining in Samuel's business. One could imagine Samuel piling up sand as it arrives so that the latest lot to arrive would probably be on top and likely to be next to be sold. This method is in common use in a few countries, including Italy.

If Samuel opts to make this assumption, he would account as shown below. Assuming that the last goods to come are the first to leave, those remaining unsold would be those bought at the earliest prices paid.

COST OF CLOSING STOCK

Tonnes	Bought on	Unit cost	Cost
100	1.1.X0	£10	£1,000
400	17.4.X0	£20	£8,000
250	28.6.X0	£25	£6,250
750			£15,250

TRADING ACCOUNT
YEAR ENDED 31.12.20X0

		£000
Sales		39,550
Purchases	42,500	
Less: Stock	(15,250)	(27,250)
Gross profit		12,300

The main advantage of LIFO is that profit reported on this assumption is more accurate because the prices at which goods are matched with sales revenue will be closer to the latest prices. The disadvantages of this method are as follows:

- As inflation builds up, the value at which stock is reported on the Balance Sheet will progressively become farther removed from contemporary market prices. This is the most serious disadvantage.
- The assumption is not in keeping with the sequence of most stock movements in real life.
- Copious records are needed to keep track of historical prices.
- This method is not acceptable to the tax authorities in the United Kingdom (but it is in the United States).

17.4.3 Average cost

This approach is a compromise between FIFO and LIFO. Hence it shares to a lesser extent the merits and demerits of both. This method makes no assumption regarding the sequence in which the goods move. Instead, it values the unsold units at the average of the various prices paid. The method takes various forms.

Simple average cost

If Samuel opts for simple average cost, he will value 750 tonnes remaining unsold at the average of the four different prices he paid in the year, without taking into account the quantities purchased at each of these prices. The average would be £22.50 per tonne (i.e. [£10 + £20 + £25 + £35]/4). Stock of 750 tonnes @ £22.50 would amount to £16,875.

TRADING ACCOUNT IN THE
YEAR ENDED 31.12.20X0

		£000
Sales		39,550
Purchases	42,500	
Less: Stock	(16,875)	(25,625)
Gross profit		13,925

Weighted average cost

If Samuel opts, instead, for the weighted average cost, he would calculate the average of various prices paid for purchases by weighting the price by the quantity purchased at that price. The cost per tonne will then be £23.61 (i.e. £42,500/1,800 tonnes) × 750 tonnes, and the cost of the closing stock would be accounted for at £17,708.

TRADING ACCOUNT IN THE
YEAR ENDED 31.12.20X0

		£000
Sales		39,550
Purchases	42,500	
Less: Stock	(17,708)	(24,792)
Gross profit		14,758

Weighted average cost is larger than simple average cost in our example because a greater quantity was purchased at the higher prices involved.

Moving average cost

On this method, instead of calculating the average cost (whether a simple or a weighted average) at the year end, the average cost is calculated immediately after each purchase, so that the items being sold and the items remaining in hand are valued at that average cost.

The advantages of the average cost method (whichever form it takes) are twofold. First, the cost charged against profit is a closer approximation to the actual cost than in FIFO; and, second, the value of stock reported on the Balance Sheet reflects the current prices better than in LIFO. However, there are also two disadvantages: the price used may not be one ever paid for any of the purchases; and (when the moving average cost is used) a new average has to be calculated at the point of each purchase.

The simple or weighted average is described as 'periodic' when it is calculated at the end of each period (rather than immediately after each purchase).

17.4.4 Other IFO methods

Certain variations on FIFO and LIFO are in use, although not commonly. Following are two examples:

- Next in first out (NIFO) is one such variant, which adopts the premise that if the cost of an item should reflect what it would cost to replace it, the price used to charge the items sold to the Trading account should not be the price last paid but the one negotiated for the goods next to be purchased.
- Highest in first out (HIFO) invokes the prudence concept to require that the goods that cost the maximum should be the first to be rid of, so that stock is reported at prices paid for the cheaper ones.

17.4.5 Base stock method

This method is rarely used and is actively discouraged by the accounting standards authorities,[3] for it assumes that a minimum level of stock is always maintained. That level is referred to as the base stock and items within it are consistently valued at the original price at which they were purchased.

17.4.6 Standard cost method

On this method, the management estimates in advance what the cost levels will be, taking into account the prevailing price levels, operational efficiency and other relevant factors, to establish a standard price at which stock is valued. The standard needs to be kept under review to ensure that the values bear a reasonable relationship to actual costs prevailing.

Interaction 17.3	**Alternative cost-flow assumptions**

Unicombs deals in personal computers of a standard make and model. During the year ended 31.12.20X1 it made its purchases at different prices but retailed them consistently at £1,200 per unit, until 1.10.20X1 when the business increased the sale price by 10 per cent. A stock of 320 units was reported in Unicombs' Balance Sheet on 31.12.20X0, at £128,000. Particulars of the purchases and sales in the year ended 31.12.20X1 are as follows:

PURCHASES			SALES	
Date	Units	Unit cost	Month of sale	Units
16.2.20X1	600	£725	Jan. to March	620
7.4.20X1	800	£850	April to June	860
11.7.20X1	1,200	£975	July to Sept.	920
5.10.20X1	1,000	£1,050	October to Dec.	810

Required:

(a) Determine the cost of stock held by Unicombs on 31.12.20X1 on each of the following alternative cost-flow assumptions: (i) FIFO (ii) LIFO (iii) periodic simple average (iv) periodic weighted average and (v) moving average.

(b) Trace the effect of each of the above-stated cost-flow assumptions on the performance as well as the position reported by the company.

17.5 REPORTING STOCK AT COST OR LOWER REALIZABLE VALUE

Accounting standards require that 'the amount at which stocks and work in progress . . . is stated in periodic financial statements should be the total of the lower of cost and net realisable value of the separate items of stock and work in progress or of groups of similar items'.[4] Four aspects of this requirement should be focused on, as follows:

● Stock should be reported at cost. Thus reporting stock at an amount *above* cost is prohibited because the excess would be profit, which cannot be recognized for accounting until it is realized by a sale.

● Stock should be written down to its realizable value if the realizable value is lower than cost because accounting prudence demands that all foreseeable losses should be accounted for immediately. This means that the loss is recognized in the current accounting period even though the stock may not be sold until a later period, and the asset in the Balance Sheet is at an amount that is reasonably certain to be realized when the stock is sold.

● Realizable value is defined as the actual or estimated selling price (net of trade but before settlement discount) less . . . all costs expected to be incurred in marketing, selling and distributing.

● The comparison of cost with realizable value cannot be done for the whole of stock taken together. The comparison should be done either for each item of stock or for groups of fungible (interchangeable) items of stock. The aim of this requirement, known as the **non-aggregation rule**, is to avoid an anticipated loss on some items in stock being offset against a gain expected on other items.

| | | | | Interaction 17.4 |

Comparison of cost with net realizable value (NRV) of fungible groups

The year-end stock of Reyney's Electronics consists of following items:

Model of television	Units in stock	Unit cost	Unit sale price
PYE 28" Colour	320 sets	£380	£450
SATCHI 28" Colour	106 sets	£320	£375
GODWIN 25" Colour	85 sets	£175	£160
SELKIRK 15" Colour	64 sets	£190	£150

Required: Ascertain the value at which the stock should be reported at year end.

What if the item of stock is to be incorporated into another product? There is no need to write down an item of stock from its cost to its lower sale price if the item is not intended for sale at that lower price. As an example, assume that, because of falling prices, a component purchased for £1,000 can only be sold for £800. Normally that component would have to be written down to its lower realizable value of £800. If, however, that component is to be incorporated into another product that the entity usually deals with, and that product is realizable at an amount higher than its cost, then the component does not have to be written down to its lower realizable value.

17.6 DISCLOSURES REQUIRED IN RELATION TO STOCK

When reporting the performance and position of a business to those who have a legitimate claim for such information, disclosure is required of the accounting policies that are being applied in respect of stock in trade, i.e. that stock is valued at the lower of cost and net realizable value. If the business is a manufacturer, there is also a requirement for the stock to be subclassified into its elements as raw material, work in progress, and finished goods. This information is helpful in that a build-up of finished stock might indicate a collapsing market for the product, whereas a build-up of raw materials might indicate preparation for increasing sales.

References

1. *Summa de Arithmetica, Geometria, Proportioni et Proportionalita* [All about Arithmetic], a treatise in Italian by Luca Pacioli (1445–1517).
2. SSAP 9: *Stocks and Long-term Contracts* (1975).
3. SSAP 9, *ibid.*
4. SSAP 9, *ibid.*

SOLUTIONS TO INTERACTIVE QUESTIONS

IQ 17.1 Stock is crucial to financial reporting

TRADING AND PROFIT AND LOSS ACCOUNT FOR THE YEAR ENDED 31.12.20X0		
		£000
Sales		640
Purchases	516	
Less: Stock	(112)	(404)
Gross profit		236
Expenses		(94)
Depreciation		(18)
Net profit		124

BALANCE SHEET AS AT 31.12.20X4		
		£000
Fixed assets		360
Provision for depreciation		(18)
		342
Stock	112	
Debtors	114	
Cash	22	
Creditors	(216)	32
		374
		£000
Capital		250
Profit for the year		124
		374

Thus, within the first year the business achieved a return of 49.6% (124/250 × 100%), whereas if end-of-year stock had been left out of the accounting, the return would have been a mere 4.8%.

IQ 17.2 Counting stock on a day subsequent to the year end

HANSON STORES

	£	£	N
Stock as per inventory taken on 6 April 20X1		216,400	
(a) Purchases subsequent to Balance Sheet date		(48,400)	1
Sales subsequent to Balance Sheet date	74,100		
Sales returns subsequent to Balance Sheet date	(2,100)		
Sales not delivered until date of stocktaking	(6,000)		
Sales in post-Balance Sheet period that involved exit of goods	66,000		
Profit margin in sale price = one-third of £66,000	(22,000)	44,000	1
(b) Error in carry forward that would have inflated inventory results		(9,000)	2
Expense stock: packing material £1,600 + stationery £2,800		(4,400)	3
(c) Stock remaining in bonded warehouse (left out of the inventory)		164,400	4
(d) Goods with customers on approval	5,400		
One-third returned by date of stocktaking and hence counted	(1,800)		
Stock with customers not counted during the stocktaking	3,600		
Profit margin at one-third of £3,600	(1,200)	2,400	4
Cost of stock not sold in the year (to be credited to Trading a/c)		**365,400**	5
(e) Shop-soiled goods at sale price	12,000		
Less: Sales commission	(600)		
Realizable value of shop-soiled goods	11,400		
Cost of the shop-soiled good	(14,400)	(3,000)	5
Stock to be reported on the Balance Sheet at lower of cost and net realizable value.		**362,400**	

Notes:

1. To determine the unsold stock, on the basis of an inventory taken six days later (on 6 April), goods that arrived during the intervening six days should be removed and the goods that exited during the same period should be added.
2. The error in carry forward would have inflated the results of the stock count by £9,000.
3. Expense stocks, erroneously included in stock during stocktaking, should be excluded to determine the stock in trade.
4. The entity's stock that was not counted during stocktaking (because it was in a bonded warehouse or with customers on approval) should be added to the stocktake results.
5. For determining the cost of goods sold, the cost of unsold goods should be removed from the Trading account. But prudence demands that unsold stock should be reported on the Balance Sheet at cost or lower realizable value. Hence the amount reported on the Balance Sheet should be reduced by the expected loss of £3,000 in respect of shop-soiled goods.

IQ 17.3 Alternative cost-flow assumptions

(a) A stock sheet recording the physical movement of the personal computers during the year to 31.12.20X1 would appear as shown on the right, reporting a stock of 710 units in hand on 31 December 20X1. These units would have been purchased during the accounting year (or even earlier) at different prices. To determine the cost of these units, ideally, each unit should have been cost-tagged so that the actual price paid for each unit would have been known. An alternative is to allocate a presumed cost to each unit, adopting one of the many cost-flow assumptions as set out below.

STOCK SHEET			
Date	Receipts	Issues	Balance
Yr. 20X1			
1.1	–	–	320
16.2	600	–	920
31.3	–	620	300
7.4	800	–	1,100
30.6	–	860	240
11.7	1,200	–	1,440
30.9	–	920	520
5.10	1,000	–	1,520
31.12	–	810	710

1. **On the FIFO basis**

   If the first to arrive are assumed to be the first to be sold, 710 units remaining would be out of 1,000 purchased at £1,050 per unit on 5.10.20X1. Cost of 710 units at £1,050 = £745,500.

2. **On the LIFO basis**

   710 units will be reported at a cost of £410,750 (see box on right).

3. **On a periodic simple average basis**

   The simple average of the five separate prices paid for purchases in the year, calculated after the year end, is: (£400 + £725 + £850 + £975 + £1,050) divided by 5 = £800. Though no units were purchased at that price, stock of 710 units valued at £800 per unit amounts to £568,000.

320 units purchased in prior year @ £400	£128,000
390 units purchased on 16.2.X1 @ £725	£282,750
710 units are reported at a cost of	£410,750

4. **On a periodic weighted average basis**

   The average price paid per unit is determined, again at the year end but this time taking into account the quantities purchased at each price. The total cost of £3,463,000, divided by 3,920 units purchased, gives an average price of £883, at which the cost of 710 units remaining amounts to £627,227. The weighted average happens to be higher than the simple one in item 3 above because larger quantities were purchased at the higher prices.

Units	Unit price	Cost
320 @	£400	£128,000
600 @	£725	£435,000
800 @	£850	£680,000
1,200 @	£975	£1,170,000
1,000 @	£1,050	£1,050,000
3,920 @	£883	£3,463,000

5. On a moving average basis

Instead of calculating the average cost (whether a simple one or a weighted one) at the year end, the average cost is calculated immediately after each purchase, so that the items exiting by sale or otherwise, as well as the units remaining in hand, are valued at that average cost. Weighted average cost is used in this illustration. The average cost of stock held at the beginning of the year is £400. On acquiring 600 more units at £725 each, Unicombs will find that the moving average cost is then determined at £612, by dividing the total cost up to that point (£563,000) by the number of units held at that point (920). This process of determining the weighted moving average cost is repeated after each successive purchase. The stock held at year end (710 units) is valued at the moving average cost of £1,014, amounting to £719,762.

Date	Transaction	Units	Unit cost	Cumulative	Moving avr
20X1		Sets	£	£	£
1.1	In hand	320	400	128,000	400
16.2	Purchases	600	725	435,000	
		920		563,000	612
31.3	Sales	(620)	612	(379,440)	
		300		183,560	612
7.4	Purchases	800	850	680,000	
		1,100		863,560	785
30.6	Sales	(860)	785	(675,100)	
		240		188,460	785
11.7	Purchases	1,200	975	1,170,000	
		1,440		1,358,460	943
30.9	Sales	(920)	943	(867,560)	
		520		490,900	944
5.1	Purchases	1,000	1,050	1,050,000	
		1,520		1,540,900	1,014
31.1	Sales	(810)	1,014	(821,138)	
31.1	Stock in trade	710		719,762	1,014

(b) Impact of cost-flow assumption on profit and stock value on gross profit.

	FIFO	LIFO	SIMPLE AV.	WEIGHTED AV.	MOVING AV.
Sales	3,949,200	3,949,200	3,949,200	3,949,200	3,949,200
Stock 1.1.20X1	128,000	128,000	128,000	128,000	128,000
Purchases	3,335,000	3,335,000	3,335,000	3,335,000	3,335,000
Stock 31.12.20X1	(745,500)	(410,750)	(568,000)	(626,930)	(719,762)
	(2,717,500)	(3,052,250)	(2,895,000)	(2,836,070)	(2,743,238)
Gross profit	1,231,700	896,950	1,054,200	1,113,130	1,205,962
Gross profit Rating (FIFO = 100)	100	72.8	85.6	90.4	97.9
Stock in trade	£745,500	£410,750	£568,000	£626,930	£719,762
Rating (FIFO = 100)	100	55.1	76.2	84.1	96.5

IQ 17.4 Comparison of cost with net realizable value (NRV) of fungible groups

REYNEY'S ELECTRONICS: VALUATION OF STOCK AT COST OR LOWER NET REALIZABLE VALUE						
Model of stock	Units	Unit cost	Unit sale price	Value at cost	Value at sale price	Lower of cost or NRV
PYE 28"	320	£380	£450	£121,600	£144,000	£121,600
SATCHI 28"	106	£320	£375	£33,920	£39,750	£33,920
GODWIN 25"	85	£175	£160	£14,875	£13,600	£13,600
SELKIRK 15"	64	£190	£150	£12,160	£9,600	£9,600
TOTAL				£182,555	£206,950	£178,720

Although, on comparison, it would appear that in aggregate the stock at the end of the accounting period should be reported at £182,555 (because the aggregate market value is higher at £206,950), the entity is obliged to reports its stock at £178,720, making the comparison in groups of fungible items.

PROGRESSIVE QUESTIONS

PQ 17.1 Where physical stock is lower than expected

Jerry Noel retails computer software, fixing his sale price consistently at cost plus one-third. The results of his trading transactions during the year ending 31.12.20X0 have been reported as shown on the right. On the basis of a physical stocktake, he has ascertained that his stock as at 31.12.20X0 is £546,000.

	£000
Stock: 1.1.20X0	324
Purchases	4,620
Sales	5,840
Return inwards	124
Return outwards	76

Required:

(a) Explain whether Jerry has any reason to be unhappy with the results of his stocktaking.
(b) Identify the reasons that may have caused the results of stocktaking to be different from what the stock figure should have been on 31.12.20X0.

PQ 17.2 Impact on profit of errors in accounting for stock

Sally Smith, dealer in domestic appliances, determines her year-end stock by undertaking a physical inventory of stock on or shortly after the last date in the year. A four-year review of the business's accounts, undertaken immediately after 31 December 20X3, reveals the following errors in accounting for stock:

(a) Because of a casting error in the stock sheets recording stock as at 31.12.20X0, stock on that date had been reported at £236,400 instead of £254,800.
(b) Goods costing £16,000, removed by Sally for personal use on 11 May 20X1, have never been accounted for.
(c) Goods costing £34,200, accounted for as part of purchases in the year to 31.12.20X1 but not received until a week later, were omitted from the figure of stock as at that date.
(d) Only on 7 February 20X3 was it realized that floods that occurred in August 20X2 had damaged certain domestic appliances so badly that they had had to be scrapped. These appliances were accounted for as part of the stock on 31.12.20X2 at cost, amounting to £48,000, and written off as scrap in the year 20X3.
(e) Stock as at 31.12.20X3 includes certain items at their cost of £36,800. These items have been damaged by negligent handling and may be sold for £10,000 if they are reconditioned at a cost of £2,000.

Sally Smith's business has reported its performance in each of the four years ending on 31.12.20X3 as stated on the right.

Year ended 31.12.20X0	Profit	£76,500
Year ended 31.12.20X1	Loss	£58,000
Year ended 31.12.20X2	Profit	£124,600
Year ended 31.12.20X3	Profit	£96,800

Required:

(a) Revise the performance reported in respect of each of the four years on the basis of the errors revealed.
(b) Clarify whether the failure to recognize the loss by flood (information d above) at the time the accounts for year 20X2 were prepared would have affected the gross profit reported for that year.

PQ 17.3 A trader takes stock after the year end

The financial year of Ladybird Ltd ends on 31 December. In order to avoid interference with production, the stocktaking for the year ended 31 December 20X0 was carried out on Saturday and Sunday, 3 and 4 January 20X1, when the stock on the company's premises, at cost, amounted to £117,567. You are additionally informed as follows:

(a) Selling prices in 20X0 yielded a gross profit of 25 per cent on sales. On and after 1 January 20X1, they were determined by adding 20 per cent to the cost of goods sold.
(b) Sales (goods invoiced) for the month of December 20X0, not dispatched until 20X1, amounted to £2,800. These goods were all dispatched during the period 1–2 January, with the exception of goods sold for £80, which were not dispatched until 8 January.
(c) Sales for the period 1–2 January 20X1 amounted to £19,590, of which goods sold for £2,700 were not dispatched until the week commencing 5 January.
(d) During the period 1–2 January 20X1, credit notes for returns inwards, amounting to £496 (selling price), were issued and the relevant goods were received in the same period. £400 of these returns related to goods sold and dispatched in 20X0, and the remainder was in respect of goods sold and dispatched on 1 January 20X1.
(e) Purchases for the period 1–2 January 20X1 amounted to £14,685 and all the goods were received in the same period.
(f) Goods purchased on 31 December 20X0 for £150 and entered in the books on that date were not received until 6 January 20X1.

Required: Ascertain the amount at which the stock should be included in the annual accounts made up to 31 December 20X0.

PQ 17.4 A manufacturer ascertains stock on the basis of a delayed inventory

Furniture Mart manufactures and retails household and office furniture and accounts for sales at the point the furniture is ready for delivery. It prepares accounts annually up to 30 June. On the basis of an inventory conducted on 5 July 20X1, Furniture Mart ascertained that its stock in hand on that date was £865,200. You are provided with the following additional information:

(a) On the stock sheets, 1,200 sets of furniture rollers have been valued at £20 per set where as they actually cost £20 per dozen.
(b) Sales during the first five days of July amounted to £144,000, though one-third of these were not delivered to the customer until 6 July. Sales are effected at cost plus one-third.
(c) Purchases during the five days to 5 July amounted to £200,000, but only 25 per cent of this amount was delivered by the time of the inventory.
(d) A shipment of wood, for which £75,000 was paid on 18 June 20X1 and accounted for as purchases in the year, was not received at Furniture Mart until 6 July.
(e) Included in the stock sheet at its cost of £15,000 are brass cabinet hinges, the market value of which have since gone down by 20 per cent. These hinges are intended for making cabinets.
(f) Four hundred pieces of office shelving, included in the stock sheets at a cost of £300 each, are no longer in fashion and cannot be retailed at more than £225 a piece.
(g) A dining-room suite, made to a customer's order at an agreed price of £6,000, has been included in the stock sheets at its cost of £4,800. To abide by a recent change in legislation, the suite cannot be delivered to the customer until it is re-upholstered in non-flammable material, and that work is expected to cost £1,500.

Required: Determine the stock in trade to be reported on the Balance Sheet as at 30 June 20X1.

Part D

FURTHER ASPECTS OF FINANCIAL REPORTING

Chapter 18

LIABILITIES, PROVISIONS AND CONTINGENCIES

In this chapter

We will learn:

- to identify and account for liabilities
- when and how a liability of uncertain timing and amount is accounted for as a provision
- whether and when contingencies should be accounted for or disclosed

18.1 WHAT IS A LIABILITY?

Correct identification of liabilities from income is just as important for accurate reporting of an entity's performance and position as the correct identification of assets from expenditure (as we saw in Chapter 15). If a liability is wrongly identified as income (e.g. £2,000 due to a creditor identified as income), the profit of the entity will be overstated (by £2,000) and the liabilities understated by the same amount. Conversely, if income has been wrongly identified as a liability, the profit will be understated and the liabilities overstated.

A liability is defined in the Statement of Principles issued by the Accounting Standards Board as 'an obligation to transfer economic benefits as a result of past transactions or events'.[1] To be accounted for, a liability should possess all four of the following qualities:

- it should be a present obligation;
- it should result from a past transaction;
- the obligation to pay or transfer resources must be certain, or at least probable;
- the amount of the payment or transfer must be capable of being estimated reliably.

An *obligation* would arise only if there has been an obligating event. *Obligating event* is new accountancy jargon meaning that there has to be an event committing the entity to an obligation (i.e. a commitment) to pay *and* allowing it no realistic alternative except to pay. The obligation has to be a present obligation (as distinct from possible obligation), and if the entity can avoid the obligation by some future action then it has no present obligation. The obligation does not necessarily have to be a legal one (arising, for example, from a contract); it may also be a constructive one (arising from a statement made or the past behaviour of an entity that creates a valid expectation in other parties).

The *transfer of economic benefits* may take the form of a payment of cash or a transfer of an asset other than cash. Such a commitment to transfer economic benefit is assumed to have arisen if:

- there is no possibility of avoiding the obligation by taking some future action;
- the need to pay (i.e. to transfer economic benefit) is certain;
- the amount of the obligation is measurable with a fair degree of reliability, on the basis of a contract, invoice, agreement, past experience or expert advice.

A liability resulting from a *past transaction* means that a mere intention to transact is not sufficient. There must have been a transaction already, e.g. a contract to pay or transfer some other asset.

Interaction 18.1	Recognition as a liability

Sylvia carries on business as a baker, trading as The French Confection. When finalizing the accounts of The French Confection for the year ending on 31 March 20X1, she seeks your advice on whether she should account for the following claims on her resources (i.e. record them in the ledgers and report them in the Profit and Loss account and/or Balance Sheet):

(a) She is planning to acquire a new convector oven for £7,500 on 1 April 20X1.

(b) She hired the services of a pastry cook in September 20X0 on the understanding that the chef would be trained in oriental culinary, and this training is expected to cost £9,000.

(c) She acquired a kitchen grinder for £12,000 on 1.7.20X0, intending to use it for five years. The manufacturers advised her that its motor would require replacement annually at a cost of £500.

(d) The Public Health Inspector notified her on 1 March 20X1 that The French Confection was required to pay a penalty of £1,000 for a minor breach of health and safety laws.

(e) One of her regular customers, a reputable restaurant, complained on 10 March 20X1 that a consignment of pastries, invoiced to the restaurant at £14,000, was not fresh. To defend her reputation as a supplier of fresh pastries Sylvia's policy usually is to make a refund of 125 per cent of the value of any defective products.

Required: Explain how each of the items (a) to (e) should be accounted for, and complete the following table for each of them:

Account to be debited	Account to be credited	Effect on Profit and Loss account	Effect on Balance Sheet
a.			
b.			
c.			
d.			
e.			

18.2 ACCOUNTING FOR LIABILITIES

A liability may be accounted for as an accrual or as a provision. A key consideration is whether or not it is possible to make a *reliable estimate* of the amount. If it is possible, then we make an accrual; if it is not possible then we make a provision.

18.2.1 Liabilities of known amount: accruals

We have already discussed the accounting treatment of accruals in Chapter 7, where we saw that it is quite usual for a business to estimate at the end of the accounting year any amounts outstanding for services (such as rent, light, heat, telephone or wages) for the period from the date of the last payment to the year end. This happens at the end of every accounting year and it is normally possible to make a reliable estimate based on evidence such as past experience, recorded usage or hours worked. The accounting treatment is to include the estimated amount as an expense in the Profit and Loss account and as an accrued liability in the Balance Sheet.

18.2.2 Liabilities of uncertain amount or timing: provisions

Where it is not possible to make a reliable estimate of the amount, a provision is created. A *provision* is defined as 'a liability of uncertain timing and amount'.[2] To be accounted for as a provision, an obligation should:

- qualify for recognition as a liability, i.e. it should be a present obligation, arising from a past transaction, the commitment to pay should be certain (or at least probable), and it should be possible to estimate the amount with *some* degree of reliability; and
- there should be uncertainty as to the *timing* of the payment or the *amount*.

It is important to note that the uncertainty cannot relate to *whether or not* there will be a payment. If there were any uncertainty as to whether there would be a payment, then the item would have failed to satisfy one of the liability criteria given in Section 18.1. Similarly, unless the amount is measurable with *some degree of reliability*, the item fails a liability recognition criterion.

When there is uncertainty as to amount, how is a reliable estimate made?

The problem of uncertainty as to amount is resolved by providing for the *best estimate* of the amount that the entity would *rationally pay* to settle the obligation on the Balance Sheet date. In assessing that amount, the entity uses management's judgement, past experience and, if necessary, expert opinion.

However, it is necessary to take into account all the uncertainty surrounding the amount. Future events that may affect the amount required to settle the obligation should also be taken into account where there is sufficient objective evidence that such events will occur. For example, if the obligation under consideration is one to remedy manufacturing defects in a product sold, due consideration should be given to the possibility that the defect may not be remedied at the very first attempt. However, gains from expected disposal of assets should not be taken into account when measuring the amount of the provision.

How is a provision accounted for?

The accounting is the same as for an accrual. The only difference is that the liability, when stated on the Balance Sheet, is given a modified label – including the prefix Provision – for the purpose of drawing attention to the element of uncertainty.

To illustrate the accounting, let us assume that Michael is a farmer carrying out field trials of genetically modified corn and that one of his neighbours, an organic farmer, has obtained a Court Order (a) restraining Michael from sowing more GM seeds and (b) awarding damages to be assessed when the neighbour harvests his crop. The damages would be the difference in selling price between organically certified corn and non-certified corn. The amount will not be known for certain until the harvest in the summer but the best estimate, based on acreage and expected market prices, is £3,000. This scenario satisfies all of the liability criteria except that there is uncertainty as to the amount. Michael has to account for the damages of £3,000 as an additional expense in the Profit and Loss account and as a liability on the Balance Sheet, making sure that he labels the liability as a provision for the purpose of drawing attention to the uncertainty of the amount.

Interaction 18.2	**Accrued liability or a provision?**

Warren Industries manufactures and retails domestic appliances. The business had prepared draft accounts by 30.4.20X1 and seeks your advice on how they should account for the following claims in the accounts for the year ended 31.12.20X0:

(a) The audit fees for the year ended 31.12.20X0 (£15,000 in the preceding year) remain to be negotiated.

(b) Holiday pay (usually ranging between £60,000 and £72,000) is yet to be calculated and accounted for.

(c) A claim for damages, at £40,000, is received from a customer on 7.3.20X1 in respect of injuries sustained within the company premises on 29.11.20X0. The legal advisers are of opinion that the company will be held liable for an amount probably of around £20,000 because of its failure to display a 'wet floor' sign.

(d) The domestic appliances are sold under warranty, by which the company undertakes to either remedy at no cost to the customer or to replace an appliance, should any manufacturing defects become apparent within six months of the date of sale. As at 31.12.20X0, £6,240,000 of sales are within the warranty period. The company's experience in previous years has been that 80 per cent of the appliances sold had no defect, 15 per cent had minor defects and about 5 per cent required replacement. Based on this experience, it estimated that if minor defects are detected in all appliances sold, it would cost £400,000 to rectify. If major defects are detected in all appliances sold, it would cost £5.2 million to replace the appliances.

(e) A customer has filed an action against the company claiming £1 million on the premise that an electrical fault in the appliance sold by the company was responsible for the electrocution of his wife. The company solicitors are of opinion that the claim is unlikely to succeed because the company's appliances are produced strictly in accordance with British Standards and are rigorously tested prior to delivery.

Required: Advise the company on the accounting treatment of the items listed above, identifying whether each claim should be accounted for as an accrued liability or a provision. State clearly how each satisfies the criteria for recognition as an accrual or provision.

18.3 REQUIREMENTS RELATING TO PROVISIONS

The following requirements[3] relate to accounting for a provision

● The amount of the provision should be reviewed at every Balance Sheet date, adjusted by increasing or decreasing it to reflect the current best estimates, and reversed when no longer needed.

● A provision should be applied only for the purpose for which it was originally established.

- When some or all of the payments required to settle a provision are expected to be reimbursed by another party, and such reimbursement is virtually certain:
  - the reimbursement should be accounted for as a separate asset in the Balance Sheet;
  - the amount so recognized as an asset cannot exceed the provision;
  - the expense relating to the provision may be reported, in the Profit and Loss account, net of the amount recognized as a reimbursement.
- If the assumption of the obligation, recognized as a provision, in turn gives access to future economic benefits that are expected to accrue over more than one accounting period, the part of the provision that corresponds to the future economic benefits is capitalized.

Accounting for provisions

Interaction 18.3

A building contractor seeks your advice on how the following claims should be treated when finalizing accounts for the year ended 31.12.20X1:

(a) When the scaffolding at a building site collapsed, a worker sustained head injuries and was paralysed. In the opinion of the company solicitors, damages of around £400,000 may be awarded. The insurance company refuses to meet the claim on the premise that the worker concerned was not wearing a protective helmet at the time of the accident.

(b) The contractor's practice is to take responsibility for all remedial work relating to any construction work for three years from the date of completion. In respect of a building handed over in December 20X0, a provision of £40,000 for remedial action was made when the accounts were prepared for the year ending 31.12.20X0. Remedial actions on that building during 20X1 have already cost £28,000; investigations into major cracks on the building reveal the need for underpinning and the additional work may cost £30,000 and perhaps a further £5,000 in the event of any price escalation.

(c) A worker has filed legal action claiming £100,000 on the basis that his ailments arose from the vibration of working with angle grinders. He has produced medical opinion to support this claim. It may be possible to come to an out-of-court settlement at an amount of around £50,000. The insurance company is prepared to admit this claim at £40,000.

(d) A customer has claimed £25,000 as the cost of luxury bath suites damaged because of negligence of the contractor's workers. Negligence of the workers has been established. The contractor will be able to realize £10,000 by disposing of the damaged bath suites.

Required: Advise the contractor on items (a) to (d) above.

18.4 CONTINGENT LIABILITIES

A *contingent liability* is defined[4] as either a *possible* obligation that arises from a past event and whose existence will be confirmed only by the occurrence of one or more uncertain future events not wholly within the entity's control, or a *present* obligation that arises from past events but that is not recognized (i.e. included in the ledgers or financial statements) because it is *not probable* that a transfer of economic benefits will be required to settle the obligation or the amount of the obligation *cannot be measured with sufficient reliability*. We can see from the definition that a contingent liability consists of two entirely different categories, as follows:

- **Category 1** comprises *possible liabilities*, not actual liabilities. The fact that there is uncertainty as to whether they would crystallize into a liability and that crystallization depends on future events, over which the entity has no control, differentiates this category from a liability.

- **Category 2** comprises *liabilities* that are omitted from the ledgers and financial statements because they fail to satisfy one of the criteria necessary for such recognition in the financial statements in that:
  - the transfer of economic benefit is less than probable; or
  - the amount of the transfer cannot be measured with reasonable reliability.

Items in Category 2 may therefore be referred to as 'quasi liabilities'.

18.4.1 Accounting for contingent liabilities

The accounting requirement[5] is that contingent liabilities should *not* be accounted for (by inclusion in the ledgers or financial statements) so long as the conditions described above remain. Users of the financial statements need to be aware of the existence of such contingent claims, and there is a twofold accounting requirement that contingent liabilities should be disclosed to those who have a legitimate claim for such information (i.e. owners, in the case of a sole proprietorship, and shareholders in the case of a limited liability company) unless the prospect of a transfer of economic benefit is remote, and that the disclosure should be made irrespective of whether or not the amount involved can be estimated reliably.

Some areas in which contingent liabilities usually arise are as follows:

- unsettled legal claims by customers, employees or others on matters including those stated in the box;
- arbitration and other pending labour awards;
- obligations under product warranties/guarantees;
- bills of exchange with recourse, if discounted;
- pensions liability not provided for in accounts;
- performance guarantees given to or on behalf of subsidiaries or others;
- liabilities arising from regulations – say one prohibiting release of toxic chemicals;
- commitments in futures markets.

> – faulty goods
> – breach of contract
> – violation of copyrights or patents
> – injury to health or welfare
> – environmental pollution
> – breach of regulations

When is a contingent liability included in the ledgers and financial statements?

A contingent liability needs to be accounted for only when any development converts it into an actual liability. This will be the case in the following circumstances:

- for Category 1 items, the uncertain future event takes place (or is virtually certain to take place) and at that point confirms the existence of the liability;
- for Category 2 items, a change in circumstances may have made the transfer of economic benefits probable or may have made it possible to measure the amount with reasonable reliability.

18.5 CLASSIFYING ACCRUED LIABILITIES, PROVISIONS AND CONTINGENT LIABILITIES

The lines of demarcation between accrued liability, provision and contingent liability may be summarized as follows:

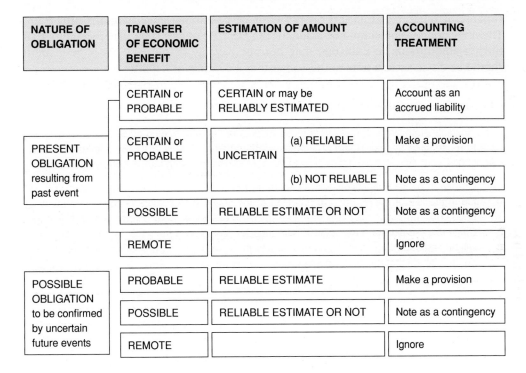

NATURE OF OBLIGATION	TRANSFER OF ECONOMIC BENEFIT	ESTIMATION OF AMOUNT		ACCOUNTING TREATMENT
PRESENT OBLIGATION resulting from past event	CERTAIN or PROBABLE	CERTAIN or may be RELIABLY ESTIMATED		Account as an accrued liability
	CERTAIN or PROBABLE	UNCERTAIN	(a) RELIABLE	Make a provision
			(b) NOT RELIABLE	Note as a contingency
	POSSIBLE	RELIABLE ESTIMATE OR NOT		Note as a contingency
	REMOTE			Ignore
POSSIBLE OBLIGATION to be confirmed by uncertain future events	PROBABLE	RELIABLE ESTIMATE		Make a provision
	POSSIBLE	RELIABLE ESTIMATE OR NOT		Note as a contingency
	REMOTE			Ignore

18.6 THE THRESHOLDS FOR DETERMINING WHETHER PROBABLE, POSSIBLE OR REMOTE

We can see from the above that a contingent liability is accounted for in the financial statements, disclosed as a note to the financial statements or ignored, depending on the entity's opinion as to whether or not the transfer of future economic resources to settle the obligation is virtually certain, probable, possible or remote. However, there is no official guidance given on such demarcation. The authors suggest the ranges stated on the right; these, however, are no more than suggestions. What is important is not the accuracy of the suggested range so much as a uniform approach by all entities so that users of the information

	Range
Virtually certain	>95%
Probable	50 to 95%
Possible	5 to 50%
Remote	<5%

are not misled when comparing the financial performance of different companies.

As an example, let us apply the range to the following scenario. Assume that in IQ 18.3 the situation with regard to the paralysed worker was as follows in more detail. When the scaffolding at a building site collapsed, a worker sustained head injuries and was paralysed. In the opinion of the company solicitors, damages of between £400,000 and £600,000 may be awarded depending on whether the paralysis is temporary or permanent. As at 31.12.20X1 the medical opinion is that there is a 25 per cent chance that the paralysis will be permanent. The insurance company refuses to meet the claim on the premise that the worker concerned was not wearing a protective helmet at the time of the accident. The reasoning will be as follows. The obligating event is the accident met with by the worker within company premises and while on legitimate company work. The worker has sustained serious injuries and therefore a transfer of economic benefits (i.e. a cash payment) appears probable, if not certain. The amount, though capable of reliable estimation on the basis of past experience, remains uncertain. Therefore, a provision should be made for the estimate of £400,000. The possibility that further amounts up to £200,000 may become payable if the paralysis is permanent should be disclosed in a note to the accounts as a contingent liability.

Interaction 18.4

Accrued liability, provision and contingent liability

The financial statements of Casserole plc in respect of the year ending on 31 December 20X0 are to be adopted by their Board at a meeting scheduled for 7 May 20X1. By a letter dated 15 April 20X1 your advice is sought on how to account for the following transactions and events:

(a) Casserole plc has cancelled, with effect from 30.9.20X0, a franchise it had granted to Pan Ltd in the Isle of Wight. Pan Ltd has filed action claiming liquidated damages in a sum of £300,000 and further punitive damages of £400,000. The legal opinion is that because Casserole plc did not have sufficient grounds for premature termination of the franchise, it will be liable for the liquidated damages, and the award of any punitive damages depends on the attitude that the court adopts.

(b) On 4 March 20X1 Casserole plc received a claim for £250,000, in addition to £50,000 paid as compensation on terminating the services of a branch manager with effect from 30.11.20X0. Because there were several instances of provable managerial inadequacies, the chance of the claim being enforced against the company is estimated at less than 5 per cent.

(c) A batch of goods sold in November/December 20X0 has proved defective. Customers have, as a result, made claims for repayment as follows:
 – Claims received by 31.12.20X0: £180,000
 – Claims received by 14.4.20X1: £90,000
 – Further claims expected to be received: £30,000
 These goods had been sold at cost plus 25 per cent, but have no value upon return. Casserole plc considers that it is possible to make a counterclaim against the supplier from whom it had acquired the goods.

(d) The company is currently subject to an investigation by the Director General of Fair Trading in respect of possible contravention of orders made by the Restrictive Practices Court. Though the charges are strenuously contested and Casserole plc is doing its utmost to vindicate its trading practices, the legal advisors are unable to foresee the outcome. In the event that the findings are adverse, damages awarded against the company may range from £100,000 to ten times that amount. The company is averse to admitting to such an investigation because of the damage it may cause to its reputation, and it is unwilling to account for any claim that may arise because that could amount to an admission of guilt.

Required: In respect of each of the above claims, clarify whether the obligation to transfer future economic benefit should be accounted for either as an accrued liability or as a provision, or disclosed in a note to the accounts as a contingent liability.

18.7 CONTINGENT ASSETS

For the sake of completeness we will also consider the treatment of contingent assets in this chapter. A contingent asset is defined[6] as 'a possible asset that arises from past events and whose existence will be confirmed only by the occurrence of one or more uncertain future events not wholly within the entity's control'.

An example of a contingent asset can be seen in the case of the scaffolding collapse referred to in IQ 18.3 above, where the insurance company is being pursued for reimbursement of any damages paid to the injured worker. The contractor is seeking to recover an amount and whether that amount is an asset or not depends on whether the worker would succeed in making a recovery. At the point where efforts are successful and the inflow of economic benefits become certain (or virtually certain), the benefit is recognized and the contingent asset is reclassified as an asset.

The accounting requirements[7] are that contingent assets are:

- never accounted for in the financial statements;
- disclosed only when the inflow of economic benefit is *probable*;
- ignored when the inflow of benefits is *either possible or remote*.

References

1. *Statement of Principles*, revised exposure draft, March 1999.
2. FRS 12: *Provisions, Contingent Liabilities and Contingent Assets*, September 1998.
3. FRS 12, *ibid.*
4. FRS 12, *ibid.*
5. FRS 12, *ibid.*
6. FRS 12, *ibid.*
7. FRS 12, *ibid.*

SOLUTIONS TO INTERACTIVE QUESTIONS

IQ 18.1 Recognition as a liability

(a) The obligation to transfer £7,500 of her resources for a convector oven is not a present obligation arising from a past transaction. It is expected to arise next year from a proposed transaction. Therefore, it has not satisfied the criteria to be recognized and accounted for as a liability as at 31.3.20X1.

(b) The future obligation to provide training to the chef at a cost of £9,000 arose from a past obligating event – which was hiring the chef's services on the stated terms. The obligation could be a legal one arising from a contract of employment or a constructive one arising from an understanding between the parties. In view of the commitment to provide the training, Sylvia has no realistic alternative or possibility of avoiding the obligation by means of a future action. She has, therefore, to account for the obligation at the best estimate at which it is expected to be discharged, as an accrued liability.

(c) The need to replace the motor for the kitchen grinder at a cost of £500 is not a present obligation because Sylvia can avoid the obligation by her future action. For example, by replacing the grinder she may avoid the need to replace its motor. Hence it does not satisfy criteria for classification as a liability. The appropriate accounting treatment is to treat £500 as a period cost to be written off each year as the motor is replaced, and to depreciate the remainder of the grinder's cost (£11,500) over its five years of expected economic life.

(d) The penalty of £1,000 is a present obligation. The obligating event giving rise to it is the breach of the health and safety laws. There is a legal obligation to pay this penalty and its amount is reliably established. Therefore the penalty of £1,000 should be accounted for as an accrued liability.

(e) With regard to the defective pastries Sylvia has to account for an accrued liability of £17,500 (being 125% of the £14,000 sale price of the product). The obligating event is the sale of defective pastries. She faces a constructive obligation to pay because, by her past practice, she has created a valid expectation that she would.

Account to be debited	Account to be credited	Effect on P and L account	Effect on Balance Sheet
a. None	None	None	None
b. Chef's training	Provision for training	Profit reduced	Additional liability
c. None	None	None	None*
d. Penalty account	Penalty payable	Profit reduced	Additional liability
e. Compensation	Compensation payable	Profit reduced	Additional liability

* The need to replace the motor is not accounted for, but is taken into account when determining the depreciation charge for the year.

IQ 18.2 Accrued liability or a provision?

(a) The audit fees should be accounted for as an accrued liability at £15,000 (adjusted for any fee escalation as expected). The obligating event is the conduct of the audit. The company has no realistic alternative but to pay the audit fees.

(b) Despite uncertainty on the amount payable, the degree of uncertainty is insufficient to make holiday pay a provision. From past experience and using management judgement, it should be possible to make a reliable estimate of the amount of pay likely to be due. Since there is a commitment (either legal or constructive) to transfer economic benefits to discharge this present obligation resulting from a past event (service provided by the employees), the company has to account for the best estimate of the liability as an accrued liability.

(c) The failure to take reasonable precautions for customer safety (namely not displaying a 'wet floor' sign) is the obligating event. The transfer of economic benefit to discharge the present obligation to pay appears probable. The judgement of the court serves only to crystallize the amount and not to determine whether there is a payment necessary. The expert advice is that £20,000 may become payable. Since, until the judgement, there is no certainty on the amount and considering the degree of uncertainty involved, a provision should be made for £20,000.

(d) The obligation to remedy manufacturing defects is assumed under the terms of the warranty. The obligating events are the sale of the appliances under the stated terms. The transfer of economic benefit to discharge the obligation is at least probable. The amount, though, is uncertain, depending as it would on various factors. Because of the degree of uncertainty involved in this case, a provision should be made for £320,000. Calculation of the amount is shown here in the box.

Estimate of expense involved:	£000
Minor defects: 15% of £400,000	60
Major defects: 5% of £5,200,000	260
	320

(e) In relation to the £1 million claim on electrocution, although it is founded on a past event the possible obligation will only involve a payment if and when a court confirms the obligation. Such a legal confirmation is regarded as remote. The obligation to transfer future economic benefit is not probable. Therefore, the claim may be ignored.

IQ 18.3 Accounting for provisions

(a) The obligating event is the accident met by the worker within company premises and while on legitimate company work. The worker has sustained serious injuries and therefore a transfer of economic benefits (i.e. a cash payment) appears probable if not certain. The amount, though capable of reliable estimation on the basis of past experience, remains uncertain. Therefore, a provision should be made for the best amount estimate of £400,000.

(b) The contractor has committed himself to an obligation to remedy the construction defects within three years of delivery. The obligating event is the construction within such terms. Transfer of economic benefits to carry out the remedial work is probable but the amount remains uncertain, though measurable with some degree of reliability. Accordingly, a provision of £40,000 was made in the accounts to 31.12.20X0. When there is uncertainty regarding the amount, the liability is identified as a provision and the amount is kept annually under review. The expenses on remedial work done in the year 20X1 are offset against the provision, which is as a result reduced to £12,000. As further remedial work yet to be carried out is estimated at £30,000, the balance in the Provision account should be increased to £30,000 by charging the difference of £18,000 to the Profit and Loss Account. The additional cost of £5,000, which

PROVISION FOR REMEDIAL WORK ACCOUNT

Cash account	28,000	Balance b/f	40,000
Balance c/d	30,000	Profit & Loss a/c	18,000
	58,000		58,000
		Balance b/d	30,000

could arise from cost escalation, is ignored because it is not a liability on 31.12.20X1, since the need to pay that amount may be avoided by management action – for instance by buying the material prior to price escalation.

(c) On the basis of the medical evidence, it appears probable that the contractor has an obligation to transfer to the worker an amount estimated at £50,000. In view of the uncertainty as to the amount, a provision is made for £50,000, which is the best estimate. At the same time, the counterclaim on the insurance company, admitted by them (and therefore virtually certain) at £40,000, is accounted for as an asset in the Balance Sheet. The amount of the provision to be charged in the Profit and Loss account is reduced by the amount expected from the insurance company to £10,000 (£50,000 – £40,000).

(d) Since negligence on the part of the contractor's workers has been established, the contractor has a present obligation on 31.12.20X1 to pay £25,000 for the damaged bathroom suites. The amount payable is the cost of the suite. Hence there is no uncertainty on the amount. Therefore £25,000 should be accounted for as an accrued liability rather than as a provision. The assumption of the liability entitles the contractor to a corresponding future economic benefit of the amount he expects to realize by disposing of the damaged bathroom suite for £10,000. But FRS 12 prohibits the recognition of such a gain until it is realized. Hence the contractor's profit in the year goes down by £25,000.

IQ 18.4 Accrued liability, provision and contingent liability

(a) The obligating event is the premature cancellation of the franchise, which took place on 30.9.20X0. Hence, as at 31.12.20X0 there is an obligation to transfer economic benefit in the future, arising from a past event and, in accordance with legal opinion, the transfer of economic benefit is probable. A reliable estimate of the amount is made for liquidated damages at £300,000. Taking into account the element of uncertainty in the amount, a provision is made for £300,000 rather than accounting for it as an accrued liability. Because the obligation to pay any punitive damages is yet to be confirmed by an uncertain event (court's verdict) the claim for punitive damages is reported as a contingent liability.

(b) Because the company apparently is justified in doing what it did, the obligating event is not the apparently wrongful dismissal on 30 November 20X0 but the court's confirmation of the obligation to pay further damages. It seems remote that the court will uphold the claim. Therefore the claim is ignored.

(c) The claims in respect of a batch of defective goods convert the sales income into a liability. Accordingly, the Sales account is debited with £300,000 and the Claims for Refund account credited with the same amount. The obligating event is the sale of defective goods; the obligation to make refunds appears certain, and the amount is measured with reliability. Since a counterclaim against the supplier is only a possibility, the claim, though actively pursued, cannot be either accounted for or disclosed in a Note to the accounts. The cost of these goods (£300,000 × 100/125 = £240,000) is transferred from a Cost of Goods Sold account (Trading account) to a Loss on Defective Goods account (Profit and Loss account).

(d) Sentiments (such as the protection of image or reputation) and potential consequences cannot sway the need to account accurately to convey a true and fair view of the entity's performance and position. Notwithstanding the entity's confidence in its defences, it is unlikely that investigations would have commenced without a basis. But this is only a *possible* obligation, the outcome of which is to be confirmed by uncertain events; and it is not possible to make a reliable estimate of the amount of future economic benefits, which may have to be transferred. In the circumstances, the entity should disclose the position in a Note. However, FRS 12 allows exemption from disclosure, in extreme cases, where disclosure of the information may seriously prejudice the position of the entity in a dispute with other parties.

PROGRESSIVE QUESTIONS

PQ 18.1 Accounting for claims on a publisher

Nick Boy is the chief executive of Teenstar Ltd, publishers of a newspaper targeting the teenage market. The financial statements for the year have been prepared as follows:

INCOME STATEMENT FOR THE YEAR ENDED 30.6.20X1	
	£000
Sale of newspaper	640
Cost of production	(210)
Gross profit	430
Distribution cost	(185)
Administrative expenses	(145)
Profit for the year	100

BALANCE SHEET AS AT 30.6.20X1	Cost	Dep.	£000
Fixed assets	480	(160)	320
Current assets			
Stock		210	
Prepayments		35	
Cash/bank balance		45	
Creditors		(180)	110
			430

	£000
Capital – 1.7.20X0	330
Profit for the year	100
	430

When preparing these financial statements the following claims were not taken account of:

1. An article that appeared on 15.5.20X1 in Teenstar's newspaper commented disparagingly on the personal life of Jane Russell, a journalist working with a rival paper. Jane filed a legal action on 9 June 20X1, claiming damages in a sum of £500,000.
2. On 26.8.20X0, Tim Henry, a publisher, served notice on Teenstar claiming damages at an amount of £35,000 because a piece published by Nick on 14.6.20X0 infringed copyright.
3. Jason David, an employee dismissed by Nick on 31.3.20X1, served notice claiming £200,000 as compensation for wrongful dismissal.

You have gathered further information from Teenstar's solicitors as follows:

(a) It would be difficult to substantiate the information reported on Jane's personal life or to establish that it was in the public interest to give it publicity. The damages awarded could be £150,000, extending up to the amount claimed if the court adopts the view that intrusion of privacy must be resolutely prevented in order to protect human dignity.
(b) There is evidence that Teenstar infringed Henry's copyright, although every effort will be made to deny it. If infringement is upheld by the court, the liquidated damages could range from £25,000 to £35,000 – but more likely to be the former than the latter.
(c) Because Jason's dismissal was for provable misconduct while on duty, the claim is without merit and can be successfully resisted.

Required: Advise Nick on the accounting treatment of each of the three claims above, and redraft the financial statements accordingly.

PQ 18.2 Accounting for claims on an oil explorer

Transoil plc is in the business of worldwide explorations for, and extraction of, oil. When finalizing its financial statements for the year ended 31.12.20X0, it is confronted with the following claims:

(a) In 20X0 Transoil plc had found oil on the island of Bolonia and had commenced extraction. On 30.11.20X0 it received a letter from Bolonia's Ministry of the Environment claiming £12 million as compensation for environmental contamination. The company's lawyers advise that although the claim cannot be enforced within the island's current legislation, it could be if a Bill before the Island's National Assembly is enacted, and that the amount claimed is reasonable because it represents a very insignificant fraction of the income expected from drilling in Bolonia.

(b) Having successfully completed explorations in Desmania the company finds that, because of recent changes in environmental laws of that country, the extraction of oil cannot commence without carrying out capital constructions to protect Desmania's road infrastructure, involving an outlay of £26 million more than what was envisaged.

(c) Transoil has been extracting oil offshore in Barona over several years. New legislation passed in October 20X0 requires the company to remove the rig and restore the seabed when extraction is completed. These activities are estimated to cost £38 million.

(d) Many legal suites have been filed in the Republic of Godavi, claiming in excess of £54 million as damages on the premise that the environmental pollution arising from the exploration efforts of the company was responsible for the spread of lung cancer in villages nearby.

(e) On a visit to the Republic of Godavi in December 20X0, the Chief Executive of Transoil plc announced that, as reparation for the inconvenience caused to residents of neighbouring villages, the company would donate a hospital complex, which is expected to cost not less than £40 million.

Required: Advise Transoil plc on how these obligations should be treated when preparing financial statements for the year ended 31.12.20X0.

Chapter 19

POST-BALANCE SHEET EVENTS

In this chapter

We will learn of events occurring within the immediate post-Balance Sheet period, where:

- some events necessitate adjustments to the financial statement
- others require disclosure as notes to the financial statements

19.1 WHAT ARE POST-BALANCE SHEET EVENTS?

When a business reaches the end of its financial period (say 31 December 20X0), there are a number of steps it has to take before presenting its accounts to the tax authorities or other external parties entitled to receive a copy of the accounts. The steps include the following:

- To begin with, the accountant lists in a Trial Balance all the ledger balances to confirm the arithmetical accuracy of the postings.
- A physical stocktake is conducted on the last day of the year (or other convenient date).
- The accountant obtains information required to make adjustments to the ledger balances in the Trial Balance (e.g. the information to make adjustments for accruals, prepayments and provisions) and to evaluate the stock (i.e. pricing the items on the stock sheets and calculating a total for closing stock).
- The information obtained by the accountant is entered into the adjustment columns of an extended Trial Balance.
- A draft Trading and Profit and Loss account and Balance Sheet are prepared.

    It might well take a couple of months (say to end of February 20X1) to reach this stage.

- The draft accounts are then passed to the auditors, who carry out their audit procedures to verify whether the accounts show a true and fair view – i.e. that the Trading and Profit and Loss account does not materially misreport the income and expenditure, and that the Balance Sheet does not materially misreport the assets and liabilities. The audit may take several weeks.
- When the financial statements are ready in their final form, the owner (in the case of a company, a director and the company secretary) signs the financial statements, approving them, and immediately thereupon the auditor signs its report. (Let us assume that the auditor and the owner both signed on 31 March 20X1.)
- Upon such approval (on 31 March 20X1) the financial statements can be communicated to anyone external to the entity that is entitled to receive them.

Thus there would inevitably be a time gap of many weeks between the last day of the accounting period (31 December 20X0) and the date on which the financial statements are approved (say 31 March 20X1).

Post-Balance Sheet events are events that take place between the Balance Sheet date and the date on which financial statements are approved by the owners (or, in the case of a limited company, by the Board of Directors).

An accounting standard[1] requires that when financial statements are prepared, *material* post-Balance Sheet events must be reviewed, for the following purposes:

- **Amending the information in the Profit and Loss Account and Balance Sheet**. This means identifying those events that necessitate the information in the financial statements being adjusted. This is an outcome of applying the Time Interval rule. Because of the necessity to report its performance and position at regular interval, an entity has to make estimates and judgements about a number of substantial uncertainties that inevitably remain on the date of reporting. Events that happen after the end of the year allow the entity to have the benefit of hindsight and may clarify or resolve some of those uncertainties. Post-Balance Sheet events are therefore an aid to establishing the position as at the Balance Sheet date.
- **Adding a note to the accounts**. This means identifying the events that, although not relevant to the position as at the Balance Sheet date, are of such significance to the decisions made on the basis of the financial statements that they must be disclosed as notes to the financial statements, although the amounts in the statements are not adjusted.
- **Revising the basis on which Balance Sheet values were determined**. This means identifying events that may invalidate the *going concern* assumption (see Sections 19.3 and 23.2.4) on the basis of which financial statements are prepared, and that require the amounts to be adjusted.
- **Draw attention to any 'window dressing'**. This means recognizing any efforts at window dressing the financial statements (see Section 19.5 below) and taking appropriate action.

19.2 CLASSIFICATION OF POST-BALANCE SHEET EVENTS

For the purposes of determining how they should be dealt with, the Post-Balance Sheet events are classified into two groups, namely those requiring adjustment to the accounts and those requiring disclosure, as follows:

19.2.1 Group 1: Adjusting events

These are post-Balance Sheet events on the basis of which the financial statements have to be adjusted. There are three subcategories of such adjusting events as follows:

1. Those events that crystallize (i.e. make clear) the position as at the Balance Sheet date. Such events could affect any category of item appearing in the financial statements – assets, liabilities, income or expenditure. For example, insolvency proceedings initiated against a customer during the post-Balance Sheet period would establish that the debt concerned was not after all an asset as at the Balance Sheet date, and it should be written off as an expense. Similarly, an invoice received in the post-Balance Sheet period (e.g. a telephone invoice) would establish the amount at which a liability should be recognized on the Balance Sheet – before receiving the invoice the accountant would have had to estimate the amount of the telephone liability. The adjustment that arises from the invoice will affect both the liabilities in the Balance Sheet and also the corresponding expense in the Profit and Loss account.

2. Those events that invalidate the assumption that the entity will remain a going concern.
3. Those events that, although definitely relating to the period after the Balance Sheet, are reflected in the Balance Sheet because of statutory or conventional requirements.

19.2.2 Group 2: Non-adjusting events

These are post-Balance Sheet events that, although not relevant to the conditions existing as at the Balance Sheet date, are so significant to the users of the accounts when making decisions that they require disclosure as notes to the financial statements. There are two categories of such events: first, there are events that are crucial for decision making because of their relevance to the assessment of an entity's performance, prospects, liquidity and so on; and, second, there are events that reveal efforts at window dressing.

19.3 ADJUSTING EVENTS

Balance Sheets are prepared on the basis of conditions existing on the Balance Sheet date. The following are examples of events that, although occurring after the Balance Sheet date, would require adjustments to be made to the items and/or to the value of items stated in the Balance Sheet together with consequential changes in the Profit and Loss account:

1. **Events that establish the existence of an asset at the Balance Sheet date:**
   (a) A debt time-barred or apparently irrecoverable at the Balance Sheet date but collected in the post-Balance Sheet period (which would establish that the debt was an asset and not an expense).
   (b) Information received in the post-Balance Sheet period, which confirms that risks and rewards relating to an asset have been transferred to the entity prior to Balance Sheet date, e.g. receiving in the post-Balance Sheet period notification of the shipment of goods ordered prior to the Balance Sheet date.
2. **Events that establish the non-existence of an asset at the Balance Sheet date:**
   (a) A debt that appeared recoverable at the Balance Sheet date but later proves otherwise because of reasons such as insolvency ascertained in the post-Balance Sheet period.
   (b) A physical inventory of stock or any other asset, undertaken after the Balance Sheet date, establishing the non-existence of stock at the Balance Sheet date.
3. **Events that establish the value of an asset at the Balance Sheet date:**
   (a) The receipt of an invoice, subsequent to Balance Sheet date, that establishes the cost of an asset (which would have been estimated previously), and where the disposal of stock in the post-Balance Sheet period establishes that the realizable value of stock is lower than cost.
   (b) The disposal or valuation of a fixed asset in the post-Balance Sheet period, which establishes that there has been a permanent impairment in the value of the asset, unless there is reasonable evidence to show that the impairment arose in the period *after* the Balance Sheet date.
4. **Events that establish the existence or extent of a liability at the Balance Sheet date:**
   (a) A claim may be discharged or notified in the post-Balance Sheet period but relating to the period ending at the Balance Sheet date, which establishes the existence as well as the extent of the liability at the Balance Sheet date. It is usual to review entries in the cash book in the post-Balance Sheet period so as to identify any items of this nature.

(b) Crystallization within the post-Balance Sheet period of a liability that had been accounted for as a contingent liability at the Balance Sheet date.

5. **Events that invalidate the going concern assumption:**

Any event occurring or identified in the post-Balance Sheet period that indicates that the business will not be able to continue operating. In accounting terminology, we say that such an event invalidates the assumption of going concern on the basis of which financial statements are usually prepared. There are various events that could lead to a business being unable to continue, e.g. the loss of a major market or a crucial line of business, denial of a significant line of credit, loss of key personnel, crystallization at a significant amount of a contingent liability, and so on.

6. **Events recognized in the Balance Sheet because it is conventional to so do:**

Dividends for the year ending on the Balance Sheet date, proposed by the directors after the Balance Sheet date.

Adjusting post-Balance Sheet events

Interaction 19.1

Robin Dale, a wholesaler, prepared his draft Balance Sheet as stated here on the right. The following events happened before the financial statements were approved on 4 August 20X0:

(a) Stock, stated in the draft Balance Sheet at cost at £34,000, realized only £26,000 on 17 July.

(b) Collin Dare, a customer, was adjudicated bankrupt on 29 July and, in a letter dated 2 August, the Trustee in Bankruptcy warns not to expect any part of the debt of £46,000 due from Collin, which is stated as part of the debtors' figure.

(c) Included within the investments, at £54,000, are 90,000 ordinary shares in Weltodo plc, quoted on the London Stock Exchange on 30 June 20X0 at 80p per share. These shares were sold on 3 August for £46,800.

BALANCE SHEET AS AT 30.6.20X0			
	Cost	Ac. dep.	£000
Fixed assets	364	(112)	252
Current assets:			
Stock in trade		826	
Debtors		468	
Investments		112	
Cash and bank		34	
Creditors		(582)	858
			1,110

	£000
Capital	1,000
Profit for the year	110
	1,110

Required: Advise Robin on how these post-Balance Sheet events should be treated when accounts are finalized for the year ended 30 June 20X0. On the basis that your advice is accepted, prepare a revised Balance Sheet as at 30 June 20X0.

19.4 NON-ADJUSTING EVENTS

Non-adjusting events are those that are not relevant to the condition existing on the Balance Sheet date but require disclosure because of their significance to decision making. The significance arises because of the impact that these events have on the predictive value of the information stated in the financial statements. The events may require disclosure, for example, because they affect – either favourably or unfavourably – the following:

1. **The entity's future performance:**
   - acquisition or disposal of new business or new lines of activity;
   - changes in physical capacity or performance of the entity;
   - changes in the environment in which the entity operates – exchange rates, interest rates, or the general political or economic climate.
2. **The entity's liquidity position:**
   - changes in the capital base, e.g. introduction of new capital;
   - reconstructions or reorganizations;
   - crystallization of contingent liabilities;
   - obtainment or loss of lines of credit.

19.4.1 Disclosures required of non-adjusting events

The following disclosures are required[2] to be made: the nature of the event; and an estimate (if practicable) of its financial implications, including the tax implications (if that is necessary for a proper understanding of the situation).

| Interaction 19.2 | **Non-adjusting post-Balance Sheet events** |

Sophie Peters produces ladies' designerwear of fine quality. Her order books are full and she counts among her customers several leading retailers in the City of Birmingham. Her problem, however, is that despite working three shifts and stretching her capacity to its limits, she is unable to meet the orders on time. She requires £180,000 to improve production capacity and £200,000 more to meet her liabilities.

Her draft Balance Sheet appears as shown here on the right.

She is happy to report as follows:

(a) On 11.4.20X0 she obtained a loan of £380,000, pledging her machinery as security.
(b) Additional machinery acquired on 15 April for £180,000 improved her production capacity by 25 per cent.

Required: Advise Sophie on the amendments required to her financial statement on 31.3.20X0, in the light of the developments since then.

BALANCE SHEET AS AT 31 MARCH 20X0		
		£000
Fixed assets		640
Machinery at cost		(280)
		360
Current assets:		
Stock in trade	116	
Debtors	248	
Cash and bank	6	
Creditors	(468)	
Salary payable	(42)	
Rent accrued	(24)	
Rates accrues	(18)	(182)
		178
		£000
Capital		120
Profit for the year		58
		178

19.5 WINDOW DRESSING

'Window dressing' is the expression commonly used to refer to a situation where a deliberate effort has been made to so prepare financial statements as to convey not a falsehood but an appearance that may not exactly correspond with reality. The objective of the exercise is usually deception, prompting decisions that would not otherwise have

been made. In his book *Accounting for Growth*[3], Terry Smith refers to this as the 'accounting sleight of hand' that, he claims, was responsible for 'much of the apparent growth of profits which had occurred in 1980s'. Real-life examples of this abound in his book. To keep it simple, let us illustrate using an imaginary example.

A company that usually carries three months' requirements as stock, receives one month's credit from its suppliers and permits an equal period of credit to its customers finds itself with a cash flow problem and is, consequently, significantly in arrears to its creditors. The real position of the entity would have appeared on the Balance Sheet as stated on the right. Because the company wishes to submit its financial statements to its bank in support of an application for a substantial loan, it finds the position as

BALANCE SHEET AS AT 31.12.20X0			
	Cost	Ac. dep.	£000
Fixed assets	600	(120)	480
Stock in trade		540	
Debtors		240	
Cash/bank balance		160	
Creditors		(675)	265
			745

stated in the Balance Sheet undesirable. This is because banks tend to gauge creditworthiness by comparing the total of (debtors + cash) to the creditors, and a healthy business is expected to have (debtors + cash) at least equalling the creditors. The Balance Sheet for this company clearly shows that this is not the position, because the creditors total exceeds the total of debtors and cash by £275,000.

The business, therefore, takes two steps to present a position that will please the bank. As Step 1 it instructs the Purchasing Department to defer purchases from December 20X0 to January 20X1 so as to run down the stock held on 31.12.20X0 from three months' supply to one month's. As Step 2 it instructs the cashier on the last day of the year to draw cheques for the full amount available in payment of suppliers, and while the payments so made are accounted for, the cheques are not mailed to the suppliers for several weeks until the entity's liquidity position improves.

BALANCE SHEET AS AT 31.12.20X0			
	Cost	Ac. dep.	£000
Fixed assets	600	(120)	480
Stock in trade		180	
Debtors		240	
Cash/bank balance		0	
Creditors		(155)	265
			745

By reducing the stock to one month's supply, the entity reduces its creditors by £360,000. By pretending to pay out the whole of its bank balance to creditors, the amount reported as owed to them is reduced to £155,000. The position resulting from these arrangements would be as stated on the Balance Sheet above. The Balance Sheet no doubt shows a true and fair view of the position on 31 December 20X0. What it fails to reveal, however, is that the position then applying is one that has been carefully stage-managed to achieve a *temporary* situation in which the debtors are 1.55 times greater than the creditors – a situation that would no doubt be far more pleasing to the company's bank.

This accounting sleight of hand is described in accounting terminology as 'a reversal or maturity after the year end of a transaction entered into before the year end, the substance of which was primarily to alter the appearance of the company's balance sheet'.[4]

The accounting treatment required by the standard setters[5] is one of disclosure by way of a note to the accounts:

- reporting the stage-managed position on the Balance Sheet;
- making an admission, in the note only, that the running-down of stock and the pretended payment of creditors were both no more than a charade to satisfy the banker's requirements.

The accountancy profession draws a distinction between a fraudulent window dressing and a benign one, and it suggests that disclosure alone will be sufficient in respect of the latter.[6] It is the authors' view that deliberate deception is unacceptable, whether it is fraudulent or benign.

References

1. SSAP 17: *Accounting for Post-Balance Sheet Events* (August 1980).
2. SSAP 17, *ibid*.
3. Century Business, London, 1992.
4. SSAP 17, *op. cit.*, paragraph 23(b).
5. SSAP 17, *op. cit.*
6. Technical release TR398, *Statement by the Accounting Standards Committee on the publication of SSAP 17*.

SOLUTIONS TO INTERACTIVE QUESTIONS

IQ 19.1 Adjusting post-Balance Sheet events

The Balance Sheet reports the position on 30 June 20X0. Events occurring after that date are irrelevant unless they serve to crystallize the position as at that date.

(a) Realization of part of the stock at £8,000 less than cost establishes that the goods in question had a realizable value of £8,000 lower than cost on the Balance Sheet date. Therefore, in accordance with accepted accounting practice, these goods have to be accounted for at the lower realizable value unless it can be established that the goods fell in value *after* the Balance Sheet date.

(b) The customer's adjudication as an Insolvent, in the post-Balance Sheet period, establishes that the amount of £46,000 was not an asset on the Balance Sheet date because – with benefit of hindsight – it is known that no future economic benefit can be expected to flow therefrom.

(c) The investments, acquired at 60p per share, had a market value of 80p per share on the Balance Sheet date and could well have been realized at that value on the London Stock Exchange. It was only in the next year that these share prices fell to 52p per share. Hence the lower amount at which the shares were realized is irrelevant for the position as at 30 June 20X0.

BALANCE SHEET AS AT 30.6.20X0			
	Cost	Ac. dep.	£000
Fixed assets	364	(112)	252
Current assets:			
Stock in trade		818	
Debtors		422	
Investments		112	
Cash and bank		34	
Creditors		(582)	804
			1,056
			£000
Capital			1,000
Profit (110 − 8 − 46)			56
			1,056

IQ 19.2 Non-adjusting post-Balance Sheet events

The second post-Balance Sheet event reported by Sophie conveys significant improvement to the production capacity (and hence the profit-making ability) of the entity; and the first conveys a significant improvement to the liquidity position. Both these pieces of information are crucial to anyone who, on the basis of the financial statements, has to make decisions such as whether to invest in the entity or to grant it credit facilities. Thus, the information should be reported as notes to the financial statements. However, the contents of the financial statements do not have to be adjusted because the information does not in any way affect the position as at the Balance Sheet date.

PROGRESSIVE QUESTIONS

PQ 19.1 A case study

Angela Noall, a recent graduate in business studies, produces as well as retails fashionable women's wear. Her auditors have raised several significant reservations, to which her response is that the auditors are 'as usual nit-picking'. The draft financial statements are as shown here.

BALANCE SHEET AS AT 31.12.20X0			
	Cost	Ac. dep.	£000
Fixed assets:			
Machinery	380	(212)	168
Furniture	160	(46)	114
Current assets:			
Stock of ladies' wear		242	
Debtors		240	
Investments		145	
Cash and bank balance		23	
Creditors/accruals		(185)	465
			747
			£000
Capital – Angela Noall			525
Profit for the year 20X0			122
			647
Loan at 12% interest p.a.			100
			747

PROFIT AND LOSS ACCOUNT FOR THE YEAR ENDED 31.12.20X0	
	£000
Sales	1,050
Cost of goods sold	(430)
Gross profit	620
Distribution cost	(214)
Administrative expenses	(162)
Loss on investment	(110)
Interest	(12)
Profit for the year	122

The items in dispute are summarized as follows:

1. **Facts**: An order for an industrial sewing machine was placed with a Korean supplier on 9.12.20X0. An invoice received on 8.1.20X1 confirms the date of shipping as 27.12.20X0 and the price of the machine as £200,000 Free on Board.
   Auditors: At the point of shipment the title to the goods passes to Angela. Therefore her Balance Sheet as at 31.12.20X0 should state the machinery as an asset at £200,000 and the supplier as a creditor for the same amount.
   Angela: The Balance Sheet as at 31.12.20X0 cannot report as an asset an item the existence of which we were not aware of on that date.
2. **Facts**: Ladies' wear produced at a cost of £18,000 and stated on the draft Balance Sheet at cost, has been damaged by rain seepage from a roof leak, not detected until 5.1.20X1. Damaged garments have since been destroyed – they had no salvage value.
   Auditors: The loss, though detected after the Balance Sheet date, obviously occurred prior to it. Therefore these garments cannot be stated as an asset on the Balance Sheet.
   Angela: The Balance Sheet should be prepared on the basis of information available as at the Balance Sheet date because that is the cut-off date for accounting.
3. **Facts**: To have the cash ready to pay the Korean supplier, Angela invested in shares quoted on the London Stock Exchange. These investments include 80,000 shares bought for £110,000 in Joel plc which went into compulsory liquidation in January 20X1. No dividends are expected. Therefore these shares have been deleted from the investments stated on the Balance Sheet. On 31.12.20X0 the shares were quoted at 142 pence per share.
   Auditors: At 142p per share, the investment in Joel plc could have been realized on 31.12.20X0 at £113,600, which is more than the cost. The loss should be recognized only in the accounts for 20X1.
   Angela: The prudence concept requires that all foreseeable losses should be fully provided for.
4. **Facts**: The Balance Sheet as at 31.12.20X0 includes within debtors an amount of £45,000 due from Joel plc.
   Auditors: The post-Balance Sheet events establish that the debt is not recoverable and should therefore be written off.
   Angela: This is a shift in attitude from the one taken in respect of shares in Joel plc.

5. **Facts**: £24,000 was received in January 20X1 in respect of a debt written off in 20X0.

   Auditors: The debt is an asset to be recognized in the Balance Sheet on 31.12.20X0 because its recoverability has been established by the post-Balance Sheet event.

   Angela: This is unreasonable. After all, if the cheque had been delayed in the post for a few days more, the writing-off would have been accepted as correct.

6. **Facts**: In an accident on 7.11.20X0, a seamstress lost her thumb. Her claim for £75,000 as compensation, ignored when the accounts for 20X0 were drafted, was settled at the amount claimed following a Court Order in her favour.

   Auditors: The Court Order merely crystallized the extent of the liability existing on the Balance Sheet date. The liability should be recognized on the Balance Sheet as a provision.

   Angela: Inclusion of the liability prior to the Court Order would amount to an admission of liability. In fact no liability existed until the Court Order was made.

7. **Facts**: About a third of the turnover in the year consisted of exquisitely embroidered ladies' garments made by Sue, a highly skilled dressmaker, who left Angela's services with effect from 15.1.20X1.

   Auditors: This information should be stated as a note to the financial statement.

   Angela: In that case, notes should also communicate Angela's intention to marry in 20X1 and the enrolment by Angela's sister Clara in an embroidery class.

Required: Advise Angela as to how each of the post-Balance Sheet events should be dealt with when finalizing accounts for the year ended 31.12.20X0.

PQ 19.2 A second case study

The management of Leeway Stores seeks your advice on how the following post-Balance Sheet events should be dealt with when finalizing the accounts for the year ended 30.6.20X0:

(a) Owing to an acute cash flow problem, the company relied heavily on a revolving credit arrangement approved by the bank. By a letter dated 27.7.20X0 the bank withdraws this facility, pointing to the company's failure to abide by the terms on which the credit line was approved.

(b) Goods that lay dormant for more than six months were disposed of in July 20X0 at a trade discount of 25 per cent. These goods, included in the Balance Sheet on 30.6.20X0 at their cost of £214,500, are usually sold at cost plus 20 per cent.

(c) Machinery, included in the Balance Sheet on 30.6.20X0 at its written down value of £240,000, was destroyed by fire on 19.8.20X0. The insurance company refuses to meet the claim, blaming the fire on the company's negligence.

(d) Leeway Stores lost access to the market in a country in the Far East because of a political upheaval that occurred in that country in August 20X0. In recent years, that country had accounted for 12–20 per cent of the company's turnover.

(e) At the Board meeting on 27 August 20X0, Hardput Ltd proposed a 10 per cent dividend in respect of the year ending on 30 June 20X0. Leeway Stores holds 9,000 of the 120,000 ordinary shares of £1 each that Hardput Ltd has in issue.

You may assume that the senior management of Leeway Stores is expected to meet in the second week of September 20X0 to approve the financial statements.

Required: Advise the management on the accounting implications of the above events.

## Chapter 20

ACCOUNTING FOR VALUE ADDED TAX

In this chapter

We will learn to account for both input and output Value Added Tax

20.1 WHAT IS VALUE ADDED TAX?

Value Added Tax, abbreviated to VAT, is an indirect tax on the sale of goods and services. The government expects only the final consumer (not traders) to pay VAT; but it expects the traders to act as its agent in collecting the tax. VAT was known in France since 1954 and has operated in European countries in one form or another since then. It was introduced in the United Kingdom by the EEC First Directive and has applied in the UK to the sale of goods and services since April 1973.

Some services connected with education, health, banking and insurance are exempt from VAT. Otherwise, most goods and services supplied in the UK are liable to VAT. The rate at which VAT is charged is fixed from time to time in the government's annual Budget. Currently, the standard rate applicable to the sale of most goods and services is 17.5 per cent. There is a reduced rate of 5 per cent on domestic fuel and power and on energy-saving material installation. Some items (see box) are liable to VAT at zero rate. Section 20.4 explains how charging VAT at zero rate (rather than being exempted from VAT) places those selling such items in a privileged position.

> **Examples of items zero-rated for VAT**
> Goods sold abroad
> Food and drinks (except in the catering trade)
> Water and sewerage services
> Books, newspapers and periodicals
> Drugs and medicine on prescription
> Children's clothing and footwear

For the purposes of understanding the operation of VAT and accounting for it, we have assumed in some of the examples following that the VAT rate is 10% because that is arithmetically more convenient.

20.2 TRADING IN GOODS OR SERVICES LIABLE TO VAT

20.2.1 Registration for VAT

Under the Value Added Tax Act 1983 a person in business:

- is *required* to obtain VAT registration if his taxable supplies have exceeded a specified threshold in the previous 12 consecutive months; and
- is *allowed* to obtain VAT registration if his taxable supplies within the subsequent 12 months are expected to exceed the specified threshold.

The threshold set by the government varies from year to year and has been fixed at £52,000 from April 2000. The 12-month period mentioned in the regulations is any consecutive 12 months on a rolling basis. Registration for VAT gives a trading entity authority to charge customers, in addition to the normal selling price, VAT at the relevant rate. When that is done, the entity's invoices (see following page) should carry certain prescribed particulars, such as the VAT registration number, the VAT rate and the amount charged as VAT. Where a customer is offered a cash discount to induce prompt payment, VAT is charged on the price net of the maximum cash discount the customer is entitled to, irrespective of whether or not the customer takes advantage of the offer. So, in our example, Longman's invoice offers a cash discount of 5 per cent if payment is received within seven days; hence VAT is calculated at 17.5% × (£40,000 less 5% cash discount).

The VAT charged from customers is referred to as *output VAT*. In the UK, a trader has to account to the Customs and Excise Department for the amount received as output VAT.

LONGMAN PLC			
Bill and tax point			
CUSTOMER: Nancy Doe		**DATE:**	
REFERENCE: 784562		31.7.1999	
	Price £	**Qty**	**Total £**
Longs p.c. Model G 524	1,000	40	40,000
CURRENT NET TOTAL			40,000
VAT @ 17.5%			6,650
BROUGHT FORWARD TOTAL			0
TOTAL BALANCE NOW DUE			46,650

TERMS: 5/7 n/30
REGISTERED IN ENGLAND: NO. 6245895
VAT REG. NO: 326 4791 27

20.2.2 Accounting for output VAT on sales

To understand the mechanics of accounting for VAT in the books of a VAT-registered trader, let us focus on a business entity that retails portable hi-fis, one model of which sells at £100. On obtaining VAT registration, assume that the entity sells one unit for £110 (i.e. £100 plus 10 per cent VAT). Although £110 is received and accounted for in the cash book, only £100 of the amount is treated as income and posted to the Sales account. The remaining £10 is payable to HM Customs and Excise Department, on whose behalf the trader acts as an unpaid collecting agent. Accordingly, this amount is accounted for as a liability, posted therefore to a VAT account – or, if preferred, a Customs and Excise Department account.

The accounting process is repeated for all portable hi-fis sold on credit. For each unit sold, the customer is debited with £110, while £100 is credited to the entity's Sales account and £10 is credited to the VAT account. It should be noted, therefore, that sales will be reported (in the Profit and Loss account) without VAT, but debtors will be reported (on the Balance Sheet) with VAT because the amount to be recovered from them is inclusive of VAT. To facilitate this accounting process, the entity writes up its Sales Day Book in columnar format with columns to report the sales value separately from the VAT amount so that the total of the Sales column can be credited to the Sales account and the total of the VAT column can be credited to the Liability account.

Interaction 20.1

Sales Day Book with VAT analysis column

Richard, a wholesale dealer, reports his sales (inclusive of VAT at 10 per cent) as stated on the right.

Required: Record the sales in a Sales Day Book, and post them to the appropriate ledger. Assume that the Sales account is in Nominal Ledger folio 21, the VAT account is in Real Ledger folio 78 and customers' accounts are in the Debtors Ledger. The Debtors Ledger folios are Pointer DL52, Curry DL36, West DL22, Holmes DL61 and Upton DL16.

Date	Invoice	Customer	£
20X0			
5.1	SN458	B.K. Pointer	2,640
9.1	SN459	J.N. Curry	6,325
11.1	SN460	Sheila West	6,424
17.1	SN461	P.S. Holmes	9,086
24.1	SN462	D. Upton	3,916

20.2.3 Accounting for input VAT on purchases

Let us next assume that the trader in our example purchases its hi-fis from a supplier, paying for each a normal price of £60 plus VAT at 10 per cent. When the trader pays £66 for one unit, £6 of that amount is the VAT element. That latter amount is referred to as *input VAT*. Although having to pay input VAT, traders with VAT registration can reclaim the input VAT in the UK from the HM Customs and Excise Department. Hence the units held for sale actually cost the trader only £60. Accordingly, only £60 of the payment of £66 credited in the Cash account is debited to the Purchases account, while the remainder is debited to the VAT account. The input VAT paid by the trader is offset from the output VAT owed to the Customs and Excise Department, so that it is the net amount that is to be remitted to that department.

Similarly, when the entity purchases two more units from its supplier at a VAT-inclusive price of £66 each, although £132 is credited to the supplier's account (because that amount is owed to the supplier), only £120 is debited to the Purchases account while the VAT element of £12 is debited to the VAT account.

To facilitate this accounting, the Purchases Day Book will be maintained with a suitable columnar format for VAT.

20.2.4 Accounting for unsold stock of items purchased subject to VAT

If we were to assume that the trader purchased three portable hi-fis and sold two, then the one remaining unsold would have cost the trader only £60 because the trader would have reclaimed the VAT element relating to it. Stock should therefore be reported on the Balance Sheet at £60, i.e. its cost without VAT.

20.2.5 Accounting for fixed assets acquired subject to VAT

In the same way, although VAT-inclusive payments are made for fixed assets and other expenses, the input VAT is always reclaimed. Fixed assets and expenses are therefore generally stated in the Balance Sheet and Profit and Loss account respectively *without* VAT.

However, not all fixed assets and expenses are treated in this way. A VAT-registered trader is refused the right of reclaiming input VAT when paying for motor vehicles (except where the vehicle is intended for resale or is to be used for hire, as a taxi or for driving instruction) and for entertainment (unless it is staff entertainment). Accordingly, motor vehicles are stated on the Balance Sheet and entertainment is stated in the Profit and Loss account *with* VAT added. The input VAT can be reclaimed, however, where it relates to fuel, repairs and maintenance of vehicles used in business, and on car leases started after 1 August 1995.

Shown on the right is a summary of how the VAT element affects amounts at which items are accounted for and reported in the Profit and Loss account or Balance Sheet (as appropriate) in the case of a VAT-registered trader.

Accounting standards confirm that turnover (sales) should be reported in the Profit and Loss account after deducting VAT,[1] although,

HOW VAT IS STATED ON THE FINANCIAL STATEMENTS		
Profit and Loss account	Sales	without VAT
	Cost of sales	without VAT
	Expenses	without VAT
	Entertainment expenses	with VAT
Balance Sheet	Motor vehicles	with VAT
	Other fixed assets	without VAT
	Stock in trade	without VAT
	Trade debtors	with VAT
	Trade creditors	with VAT
	Accruals (if liable to VAT)	with VAT
	Accruals (if not liable to VAT)	without VAT

if it is thought to be more appropriate, sales may be reported with VAT and then VAT shown as a deduction.

Interaction 20.2

A trader with VAT registration

Jane Richards, registered for VAT purposes, extracted her Trial Balance as shown on the right.

You are informed as follows:

(a) VAT-inclusive prices of £8,800 and £11,000, paid on 1.1.20X1 for furniture and motor vehicles respectively, are included in the corresponding asset accounts.

(b) Furniture and motor vehicles are depreciated by the straight-line method at 10 per cent and 20 per cent per annum respectively.

(c) Unsold stock on 30.6.20X1 cost £2,420 inclusive of VAT.

(d) The VAT rate is 10 per cent.

Required: Prepare a Trading and Profit and Loss account for the year ended 30.6.20X1 and a Balance Sheet as at that date.

TRIAL BALANCE AS AT 30 JUNE 20X1	Dr	Cr
Sales with VAT	–	94,864
Purchases with VAT	63,360	–
Stock without VAT	2,840	–
Furniture account	12,600	–
Ac. depre. on furniture	–	4,744
Motor vehicles	21,000	–
Ac. depre. on vehicle	–	4,000
Expenses with VAT	20,075	–
Entertainment with VAT	440	–
Debtors and creditors	1,946	1,452
Payments of VAT	212	–
Cash and bank	587	–
Richards Capital account	–	18,000
	123,060	123,060

20.2.6 The payment of VAT

The Local VAT Office (LVO) requires every VAT-registered trader to submit a VAT Return (Form VAT 100) every quarter. A quarter is a period of three months beginning on a day that the LVO decides. If the Return shows that during the quarter the output tax exceeded the input tax, a cheque for the difference should accompany the return. If the reverse is the case, the trader is entitled to receive the difference from HM Customs and Excise Department. The failure to pay the proper amount when it is due can result in the imposition of a surcharge, which may range from 2 per cent of the amount owed to 15 per cent.

20.2.7 When a debt inclusive of VAT is written off

A trader is required to account for output VAT at the point that customers are invoiced, without waiting until the amount is received. For example, if the credit sales in a period, inclusive of VAT at (say) 10 per cent, is £11,000, the trader owes the Customs and Excise Department £11,000 × 10/110 = £1,000 as output VAT, although the amount has yet to be received from customers. This would not be unfair because the trader is permitted to reclaim from the Department unpaid input VAT included within creditors' amounts.

The trader has a problem, however, if the debt (along with VAT) has to be written off as irrecoverable. The trader is given relief in this situation by being allowed to claim the VAT portion of the bad debt from the Department, provided that, first, the debt has been written off from the trader's books and, second, at least six months have elapsed from the date the payment was due.

Bad debt relief

Trade debtors as at 30.6.20X1, the last day of the year, amount to £609,870 and the balance in the Provision for Doubtful Debts account is £10,500. Two debts are to be written off as follows:

(a) £81,620 due from Alpha Ltd which is in compulsory liquidation;
(b) £8,250 due from Nancy Dewar, whose whereabouts cannot be traced.

The Provision for Doubtful Debts account is to be adjusted to 5 per cent of debtors receivable at the year end. VAT is charged on sales at 10 per cent.

Required: Calculate the amount of bad debts written off as expenditure in the year, and determine the amount that may be claimed from the Customs and Excise Department in respect of bad debts.

20.2.8 Goods taken by a trader for own use

The intention is that Value Added Tax should be borne by the ultimate user. Goods with an intermediary, such as a trader, will be VAT-free only so long as they are held for sale or (other than in the case of motor vehicles) held for business use. If a trader removes some goods for personal use, then the VAT relief should be reversed and the trader charged for the cost of the goods inclusive of VAT.

Goods removed for own use by a trader

In addition to the information stated in IQ 20.2 above, you are informed that removal for the personal use of the proprietor of goods purchased for £1,650 (inclusive of VAT) has yet to be accounted for.

Required: Set out the amended Trading and Profit and Loss account for Jane Richards for the year ended 30.6.20X1 and the Balance Sheet as at that date.

20.3 TRADING WHEN NOT REGISTERED FOR VAT PURPOSES

A business may not be registered for VAT either because it deals in goods and services that do not attract VAT, or because taxable supplies fall below the threshold at which registration is required and the business has opted not to be registered for VAT. Businesses in these categories cannot charge their customers with Value Added Tax on sales. At the same time, such businesses will not be able to claim from the Customs and Excise Department the input VAT paid on its purchases and expenses. In such circumstances, VAT should be accounted for as part of the item of expenditure to which it corresponds.[2]

A trader without VAT registration

Hassan Javiz, who is not registered for VAT, provides you with his Trial Balance as shown on the right, with the following additional information:

(a) VAT-inclusive prices of £8,800 and £11,000, paid on 1.1.20X1 for furniture and motor vehicles respectively, are included in the asset accounts.

(b) Furniture and motor vehicles are depreciated by the straight-line method at 10 per cent and 20 per cent per annum respectively.

(c) Unsold stock on 30.6.20X1 cost £1,056 inclusive of VAT.

(d) The VAT rate is 10 per cent.

Required: Prepare the Trading and Profit and Loss account for the year ended 30.6.20X1 and the Balance Sheet as at that date.

TRIAL BALANCE AS AT 30.6.20X1		
	Dr	Cr
Sales without VAT	–	47,200
Purchases with VAT	28,600	–
Stock with VAT	880	–
Furniture account	12,600	–
Ac. depre. on furniture	–	4,744
Motor vehicles	21,000	–
Ac. depre. on vehicle	–	4,000
Expenses with VAT	3,630	–
Entertainment with VAT	440	–
Debtors and creditors	646	962
Cash and bank	110	–
Hassan Javiz's capital	–	11,000
	67,906	67,906

20.4 TRADING IN ITEMS ZERO-RATED FOR VAT

A trader registered for VAT but dealing in zero-rated products is in a doubly privileged position. First, such a trader does not add a VAT charge on sales to customers. Second, because the trader is VAT-registered, there is eligibility to claim all input VAT payments from the Customs and Excise Department.

A trader dealing in zero-rated product lines

Jo Minard, registered for VAT, but dealing with zero-rated items, provides you with her trial balance as shown. She informs you further as follows:

(a) VAT-inclusive prices of £8,800 and £11,000, paid on 1.1.20X1 for furniture and motor vehicles respectively, have been included in the appropriate asset accounts.

(b) Furniture and motor vehicles are depreciated by the straight-line method at 10 per cent and 20 per cent per annum respectively.

(c) Unsold stock on 30.6.20X1 cost £1,056 inclusive of VAT.

(d) The VAT rate is 10 per cent.

Required: Prepare the Trading and Profit and Loss account for the year ended 30.6.20X1 and the Balance Sheet as at that date.

TRIAL BALANCE AS AT 30.6.20X1		
	Dr	Cr
Sales without VAT	–	47,200
Purchases with VAT	28,600	–
Stock without VAT	800	–
Furniture account	12,600	–
Acc. deprec. on furniture	–	4,744
Motor vehicles	21,000	–
Acc. deprec. on vehicle	–	4,000
Expenses with VAT	3,630	–
Entertainment with VAT	440	–
Debtors and creditors	646	962
Cash and bank	190	–
Jo Minard's capital	–	11,000
	67,906	67,906

In real life it is unlikely that such an ideal position would exist. A pharmacist, for example, who deals in zero-rated prescription medicine and drugs, is likely also to have other lines of activity (toiletries, food items, sweets) that are liable for VAT at the standard rate.

References

1. SSAP 5: *Accounting for Value Added Tax* (1974).
2. SSAP 5, *ibid.*

SOLUTIONS TO INTERACTIVE QUESTIONS

IQ 20.1 Sales Day Book with VAT analysis column

		THE SALES DAY BOOK				
2000	Voucher	Customer	Folio	£	Sales	VAT
5.1	SN458	B.K. Pointer	DL52	2,640	2,400	240
9.1	SN459	J.N. Curry	DL36	6,325	5,750	575
11.1	SN460	Sheila West	DL22	6,424	5,840	584
17.1	SN461	P.S. Holmes	DL61	9,086	8,260	826
24.1	SN462	D. Upton	DL16	3,916	3,560	356
				28,391	25,810	2,581
					NL21	RL78

DL16   D. UPTON'S ACCOUNT £   £

Sales Day Book   3,916

DL22   SHEILA WESTS'S ACCOUNT £   £

Sales Day Book   6,424

DL36   J.N. CURRY'S ACCOUNT £   £

Sales Day Book   6,325

DL52   B.K. POINTER'S ACCOUNT £   £

Sales Day Book   2,640

Note: Since the VAT-inclusive price is 110%, the VAT is price × 10/110, e.g. £2,640 × 10/110 = £240.

DL61   P.S. HOLMES' ACCOUNT £   £

Sales Day Book   9,086

RL78   VAT ACCOUNT £   £

Sales Day Book   2,581

NL21   SALES ACCOUNT £   £

Sales Day Book   25,810

IQ 20.2 A trader with VAT registration

FURNITURE ACCOUNT

	£		£
Balance b/f	3,800		
Cash a/c	8,800	Balance c/d	12,600
Balance b/d	12,600	VAT a/c	800
		Balance c/d	11,800
Balance b/d	11,800		

Notes:

1. Depreciation on furniture: 10% of 3,800:
   10% of £8,000 for six months only
2. The entity being VAT-registered, VAT can be reclaimed on all expenses and payments for fixed assets, other than those on entertainment and vehicles.
3. Depreciation on motor vehicles:
   20% of £10,000
   20% of £11,000 for six months only
4. Since, at the point of purchase, VAT *is* reclaimed, stock is reported at cost (i.e. without VAT).

	£
	380
	400
	780

	£
	2,000
	1,100
	3,100

PROVISION FOR DEPRECIATION – FURNITURE

	£		£
		Balance b/f	4,744
Balance c/d	5,524	Depreciation	780
		Balance b/d	5,524

PROVISION FOR DEPRECIATION – VEHICLES

	£		£
		Balance b/f	4,000
Balance c/d	7,100	Depreciation	3,100
		Balance b/d	7,100

MOTOR VEHICLES ACCOUNT

	£		£
Balance b/f	10,000		
Cash a/c	11,000	Balance c/d	21,000
Balance b/d	21,000		

VALUE ADDED TAX ACCOUNT

	£		£
Cash a/c	212	Sales a/c	8,624
Purchases	5,760		
Furniture a/c	800		
Expenses a/c	1,825		
Balance c/d	27		
		Balance c/d	27

TRADING AND PROFIT AND LOSS ACCOUNT FOR THE YEAR ENDED 30 JUNE 20X1

		£
Sales		86,240
Stock on 1.7.20X0	2,840	
Purchases	57,600	
Stock on 30.6.20X1	(2,200)	(58,240)
Gross profit		28,000
Expenses		(18,250)
Depreciation – furniture		(780)
Entertainment		(440)
Depreciation – vehicles		(3,100)
Profit for the year		5,430

BALANCE SHEET AS AT 30 JUNE 20X1

	Cost	Ac. dep.	£
Fixed assets:			
Furniture	11,800	(5,524)	6,276
Motor vehicles	21,000	(7,100)	13,900
			20,176
Current assets:			
Stock in trade		2,200	
Trade debtors		1,946	
Cash and bank		587	
Creditors	1,452		
VAT	27	(1,479)	3,254
			23,430

	£
Capital account	18,000
Profit for the year	5,430
	23,430

IQ 20.3 Bad debt relief

TRADE DEBTORS ACCOUNT

Balance b/f	609,870	Bad Debts a/c	81,620
		Bad Debts a/c	8,250
		Balance c/d	520,000
Balance b/d	520,000		

PROVISION FOR DOUBTFUL DEBTS ACCOUNT

		Balance b/f	10,500
Balance c/d	26,000	Bad debts	15,500
		Balance b/d	26,000

Bad debt relief claimable from Customs and Excise is the VAT element of both specific bad debts – assuming that six months have elapsed since amounts were due from the respective debtors.

BAD DEBTS ACCOUNT

Debtors a/c	81,620	VAT a/c	8,170
Debtors a/c	8,250	P&L a/c	97,200
Provision for Doubtful Debtors a/c	15,500		

IQ 20.4 Goods removed for own use by a trader

TRADING AND PROFIT AND LOSS ACCOUNT FOR THE YEAR ENDED 30 JUNE 20X1

	£	£
Sales		86,240
Stock on 1.7.20X0	2,840	
Purchases	57,600	
Stock on 30.6.20X1	(2,200)	
Drawings	(1,500)	(56,740)
Gross profit		29,500
Expenses		(18,250)
Depreciation – vehicles		(3,100)
Entertainment		(440)
Depreciation – furniture		(780)
Profit for the year		6,930

BALANCE SHEET AS AT 30 JUNE 20X1

	Cost	Ac. dep.	£
Fixed assets:			
Furniture	11,800	(5,524)	6,276
Motor vehicles	21,000	(7,100)	13,900
			20,176
Current assets:			
Stock in trade		2,200	
Trade debtors		1,946	
Cash and bank		587	
Creditors	(1,452)		
VAT	(177)	(1,629)	3,104
			23,280

	£
Capital	18,000
Profit for the year	6,930
Drawings	(1,500)
VAT	(150)
	23,280

Note: When goods, on which VAT relief was obtained, are removed for personal use of the proprietor, the relief is clawed back. Accordingly, the Drawings account is debited, in addition to the cost of the goods, with the corresponding VAT amount, which is owed to the Customs and Excise Department.

IQ 20.5 A trader without VAT registration

A trader not registered for VAT has to bear all his input VAT. He accounts for the input VAT as part of the expenditure to which it relates.

Depreciation on furniture:	£
10% of £3,800 for whole year	380
10% of £8,800 for six months	440
	820

Depreciation on motor vehicles:	£
20% of £10,000 for whole year	2,000
20% of £11,000 for six months	1,100
	3,100

TRADING AND PROFIT AND LOSS ACCOUNT FOR THE YEAR ENDED 30.6.20X1

		£
Sales		47,200
Stock on 1.7.20X0	880	
Purchases	28,600	
Stock on 3.6.20X1	(1,056)	(28,424)
Gross profit		18,776
Expenses		(3,630)
Depreciation – furniture		(820)
Entertainment		(440)
Depreciation – vehicles		(3,100)
Profit for the year		10,786

BALANCE SHEET AS AT 30.6.20X1

Fixed assets:	Cost	Ac. dep.	£
Furniture	12,600	(5,564)	7,036
Motor vehicles	21,000	(7,100)	13,900
			20,936
Current assets:			
Stock in trade		1,056	
Debtors		646	
Cash and bank		110	
Creditors		(962)	850
			21,786

	£
Capital account	11,000
Profit for the year	10,786
	21,786

IQ 20.6 A trader dealing in zero-rated product lines

A trader, registered for VAT but dealing in zero-rated products, can claim his input VAT (other than on entertainment and motor vehicles) from the Customs and Excise Department.

Depreciation on furniture:	£
10% of £3,800 for whole year	380
10% of £8,000 for six months	400
	780

Depreciation on motor vehicles:	£
20% of £10,000 for whole year	2,000
20% of £11,000 for six months	1,100
	3,100

CUSTOMS AND EXCISE DEPARTMENT

Furniture a/c	800		
Purchases a/c	2,600		
Expenses a/c	330		
	3,730		

TRADING AND PROFIT AND LOSS ACCOUNT FOR THE YEAR ENDED 30.6.20X1

		£
Sales		47,200
Stock on 1.7.20X0	800	
Purchases	26,000	
Stock on 30.6.20X1	(960)	(25,840)
Gross profit		21,360
Expenses		(3,300)
Depreciation – furniture		(780)
Entertainment		(440)
Depreciation – motor vehicles		(3,100)
Profit for the year		13,740

BALANCE SHEET AS AT 30.6.20X1

Fixed assets:	Cost	Ac. dep.	£
Furniture	11,800	(5,524)	6,276
Motor vehicles	21,000	(7,100)	13,900
			20,176
Current assets:			
Stock in trade		960	
Debtors		646	
Customs and Excise Dept		3,730	
Cash and bank		190	
Creditors		(962)	4,564
			24,740

	£
Capital – Jo Minard	11,000
Profit for the year	13,740
	24,740

PROGRESSIVE QUESTIONS

PQ 20.1 Accounting for transactions of a VAT-registered trader

On 1.1.20X0 Bob Cameron commenced business as a wholesale dealer in air-conditioning (AC) systems, with capital in cash of £100,000. He is registered for VAT purposes with the UK's Customs and Excise Department. He arranged to obtain his supplies on a month's credit from Coolit Ltd. The value of his transactions, listed below, is inclusive of VAT at 17.5 per cent unless stated otherwise:

January 1	Paid £28,200 for office furniture and £38,775 for a motor vehicle.
	Paid £517 for advertising.
	Purchased 12 AC system units from Coolit Ltd for £34,545.
January 3	Paid £1,000 as rent for the month (no VAT is payable).
January 5	Sold to Comfy plc three AC system units for £14,100.
January 6	Sold to Deckchair Ltd four AC system units for £18,800.
	Purchased six AC system units from Coolit for £17,625.
January 9	Sold two AC system units for £9,400.
January 14	Sold three AC systems to Easy plc for £14,100.
January 17	Paid £235 for stationery.
January 20	Sold one AC systems for £4,700.
January 21	Paid £705 for advertising.
January 22	Received £18,800 from Deckchair Ltd.
January 23	Bob removed an AC system for personal use in his home.
January 24	Sold three AC systems to Deckchair Ltd for £14,100.
January 27	Paid £3,600 as salary (no VAT is payable).
January 30	Paid £282 for electricity, £423 for gas and £188 for telephone.

Required:

(a) Record these transactions in appropriate books of prime entry, drawing the day books with analysis columns for reporting related VAT.
(b) Extract a Trial Balance as at 31 January 20X0 after posting all transactions other than the removal by Bob of an AC system for personal use.
(c) Set out a journal entry to account for Bob's removal of the AC system for personal use.
(d) Prepare the Trading and Profit and Loss account for the month ended 31 January 20X0 and the Balance Sheet as at that date, assuming that (i) Bob depreciates his motor vehicles and furniture on the straight-line method at 20 per cent and 10 per cent per annum and (ii) Bob uses the FIFO method for determining the cost of unsold goods.

PQ 20.2 Prime entry books with analysis columns to account for VAT

Riyaz Supplies commenced business as a wholesale supplier of sporting equipment on 3 April 20X0. The business is registered for VAT. Transactions during the first week have been recorded in the books of prime entry as shown here.

SALES DAY BOOK					
20X0	Customer	Sales	VAT	Total	F
		£	£	£	
3.4	Camilus Ltd	3,600	630	4,230	
3.4	Albert & sons	5,800	1,015	6,815	
4.4	Dale and Co	6,200	1,085	7,285	
4.4	Berty Bros	3,000	525	3,525	
5.4	Camilus Ltd	1,800	315	2,115	
6.4	Edwin and son	4,200	735	4,935	
7.4	Berty Bros	6,000	1,050	7,050	
7.4	Albert & sons	12,400	2,170	14,570	
		43,000	7,525		

PURCHASES DAY BOOK					
20X0	Supplier	Purchases	VAT	Total	F
		£	£	£	
3.4	Verona plc	9,000	1,575	10,575	
3.4	Sarena Ltd	12,000	2,100	14,100	
4.4	Wimala Ltd	8,000	1,400	9,400	
5.4	Verona plc	5,000	875	5,875	
6.4	Wimala Ltd	8,000	1,400	9,400	
		42,000	7,350		

		RECEIPTS CASH BOOK				ANALYSIS COLUMNS			
20X0	V	Particulars	Cash	Bank	Sales	VAT	Others	F
3.4	X	Capital – Riyaz	50,000	–	–	–	50,000	
3.4	X	Cash a/c – deposit	–	48,000	–	–	48,000	C
4.4	X	Sales a/c	1,175	–	1,000	175	–	
5.4	X	Sales a/c	4,700	–	4,000	700	–	
5.4	X	Bank Loan a/c	–	25,000	–	–	25,000	
6.4	X	Camilus Ltd	4,230		–	–	4,230	
6.4	X	Sales a/c	2,350	–	2,000	350	–	
6.4	X	Cash a/c – deposit	–	12,000	–	–	12,000	C
7.4	X	Albert and Sons	6,815	–	–	–	6,815	
			69,270	85,000	7,000	1,225		
				Folio				

		PAYMENTS CASH BOOK						ANALYSIS COLUMNS				
20X0	V	Particulars	Cash	Bank	Purchase	Wages	Stationery	Sundry	VAT	Advt.	Others	F
3.4	X	Bank a/c	48,000	–	–	–	–	–		–	48,000	C
3.4	X	Advertising	–	1,410	–	–	–	–	210	1,200	–	
3.4	X	Purchases	–	3,525	3,000	–	–	–	525	–	–	
3.4	X	Rent	–	4,000	–	–	–	–	–	–	4,000	
4.4	X	Wages	225	–	–	225	–	–	–	–	–	
4.4	X	Stationery	–	141	–	–	120	–	21	–	–	
4.4	X	Furniture	–	15,275	–	–	–	–	2,275	–	13,000	
4.4	X	Sundry exp.	47	–	–	–	–	40	7	–	–	
5.4	X	Wages	225	–	–	225	–	–	–	–	–	
5.4	X	Purchases	4,700	–	4,000	–	–	–	700	–	–	
5.4	X	Stationery	94	–	–	–	80	–	14	–	–	
5.4	X	Vehicle	–	28,200	–	–	–	–	–	–	28,200	
5.4	X	Advertising	–	2,115	–	–	–	–	315	1,800	–	
6.4	X	Bank a/c	12,000	–	–	–	–	–	–	–	12,000	C
6.4	X	Wages	225	–	–	225	–	–	–	–	–	
6.4	X	Serena Ltd	–	14,100	–	–	–	–	–	–	14,100	
6.4	X	Sundry exp.	141	–	–	–	–	120	21	–	–	
6.4	X	Purchases	–	4,935	4,200	–	–	–	735	–	–	
7.4	X	Wages	225	–	–	225	–	–	–	–	–	
7.4	X	Verona plc	–	10,575	–	–	–	–	–	–	10,575	
7.4	X	Sundry exp.	54	–	–	–	–	–	54	–	–	
			65,936	84,276	11,200	900	200	214	4,823	3,000		
7.4	X	Balance c/d	3,334	724								

You are further informed as follows:

(a) Unsold stock at close of business on 7 April cost £14,570, inclusive of VAT.
(b) Rent is payable at £1,000 per week.
(c) Unpaid telephone and electricity as at 7.4.20X0 were £705 and £846, inclusive of VAT.
(d) Value Added Tax applies at 17.5 per cent.
(e) Each of the ledger accounts is in the folios stated below:

REAL LEDGER		NOMINAL LEDGER		DEBTORS LEDGER		CREDITORS LEDGER	
Capital account	RL01	Sales a/c	NL01	Camilus Ltd	DL01	Serena Ltd	CL01
VAT account	RL02	Purchases a/c	NL02	Albert & sons	DL02	Verona plc	CL02
Bank Loan a/c	RL03	Wages a/c	NL03	Dale & Co	DL03	Wimala Ltd	CL03
Furniture a/c	RL04	Stationery a/c	NL04	Berty Bros	DL04		
Vehicles a/c	RL05	Rent a/c	NL05	Edwin and son	DL05		
		Advertising a/c	NL06				
		Sundries a/c	NL07				

Required:

(a) Post the transactions to appropriate ledger accounts and then insert into the white area of each book of prime entry the folio number of the respective ledger account.
(b) Prepare a Trial Balance as at 7 April 20X0, prior to making period-end adjustments.
(c) Set out the Trading and Profit and Loss account for the week ending 7 April 20X0 and the Balance Sheet as at that date. You may ignore the depreciation of fixed assets.

PQ 20.3 Finalization of accounts of a VAT-registered trader

Allen Grumpy is a VAT-registered dealer in domestic appliances. The balances extracted from his books appear as stated here. You are further informed as follows:

(a) Stock in trade as at 30 June 20X1, at cost inclusive of VAT, is £423,000.
(b) The Furniture account stated in the Trial Balance includes a VAT-inclusive price of £94,000 paid for furniture on 1.10.20X0, while the Motor Vehicles account includes a VAT-inclusive price of £47,000 paid for a vehicle on 1.1.20X1.
(c) A trade debt of £47,000 is to be written off because the customer has been pronounced bankrupt; and the provision for bad or doubtful debts has to be adjusted to cover 5 per cent of the debtors outstanding.
(d) Allen Grumpy depreciates motor vehicles and furniture by the straight-line method at 20 per cent and 10 per cent per annum respectively.
(e) Assume that the standard rate of VAT is 17.5 per cent.

Required: Prepare Allen's Trading and Profit and Loss account for the year ended 30 June 20X1 and the Balance Sheet as at that date.

TRIAL BALANCE AS AT 30 JUNE 20X1		
	£000	£000
Motor vehicles	442	196
Furniture	196	72
Salaries	216	–
Rent	24	–
Telephone (including VAT)	47	–
Sales (including VAT)	–	3,525
Purchases (including VAT)	2,115	–
Entertainment (including VAT)	94	–
Debtors and creditors	687	324
Stationery (including VAT)	141	–
VAT paid to Customs & Excise	54	–
Stock (excluding VAT)	480	–
Provision for doubtful debts	–	28
Capital account	–	520
Cash and bank balance	169	–
	4,665	4,665

Chapter 21

INTERPRETATION OF FINANCIAL STATEMENTS

> **In this chapter**
>
> We will learn to interpret the information in financial statements for the purposes of assessing profitability, liquidity and management's performance with a trading entity

21.1 IMPORTANCE OF CORRECT INTERPRETATION

Accounting is not an end in itself, but a means to an end. The objective of accounting is to maintain reliable and adequate records of an entity's transactions and events and to present financial statements as a basis for making informed decisions. Those making such decisions have to interpret (i.e. fully comprehend the meaning of) the information contained in these statements. Having so far studied the maintenance of accounts in the ledgers and the preparation of financial statements, let us now assist with their interpretation.

The initial requirement is to identify the priorities and interest of the party for whom the interpretation is undertaken. For example, you need to know whether the interpretation is for the benefit of the entity's manager, or its owner, or the bank manager or a creditor. This is really important because each of them may have a different priority in gleaning information about the business. For example:

- the priority of the owner may be to maximize profitability and hence the return on investment;
- the priority of a manager may be to maximize personal remuneration, achieving satisfactory profitability and keeping the business going to secure employment;
- the priority of the bank manager may be the liquidity of the business, i.e. its ability to service any overdraft or bank loan by paying interest or repaying capital on time;
- the priority of a creditor may again be liquidity, but over a much shorter time-scale – one that demonstrates an ability to settle the account within the agreed credit terms.

Although their priorities differ, all of them have a *common interest* in the business, and specifically in three areas:

- profitability, because the performance of a business is usually assessed in terms of profit and, in the absence of profit, liquidity is likely to get eroded;
- liquidity, because the entity's ability to meet bills and exploit opportunities depends on whether it can find ready cash when needed; and
- management performance and the discharge of prudent stewardship, because the owners of the entity may have delegated its management to others.

21.2 ACCOUNTING RATIOS AS THE TOOL FOR INTERPRETATION

The size of the amounts stated on financial statements reveals how well the business is doing and how good its financial position is. What is more important for making informed decisions is the extent of progress that the entity has made and the prospects for growth in the future. For assessing these, more important than the size of the amounts in the financial statements are the relationships between amounts in the Profit and Loss account and the Balance Sheet, and how these relationships compare with those of the same entity in previous years, the budgeted amounts for the period, and those of other entities comparable with it.

The tool commonly used for tracing these relationships is **accounting ratios**. An accounting ratio is a mathematical expression of the relationship between two amounts. For example, assuming the two amounts to be sales during the year of £100,000, and gross profit of £10,000, the relationship between them may be expressed in any one of four different forms as follows:

1. in pure ratio form (e.g. the gross profit to sales ratio is 1:10);
2. in fraction form (e.g. the gross profit is (£10,000/£100,000) = one-tenth of sales);
3. in percentage form (e.g. the gross profit is (£10,000/£100,000 × 100) = 10% of sales);
4. as times cover (e.g. the sale is (£100,000/£10,000) = ten times the gross profit);

The usefulness of accounting ratios is mainly as comparators. They assist us to understand changes that have occurred by enabling comparisons to be drawn between current relationships, what they were in the past, and what they are in other similar entities. The form chosen to express the relationship should be the one best suited for conveying the relationship. For example, the relationship between gross profit and sales is called the **gross profit ratio** and is always expressed in percentage form.

An attempt to trace a relationship between two amounts would be futile unless it is reasonable to expect that there would be a meaningful relationship between the two. For example, in the Profit and Loss account we would expect the distribution cost for the year to have a meaningful relationship with the amount of sales for the year. However, it is important to recognize that there may be a number of reasons for a change in a relationship. A change in a relationship puts us on notice and prompts us to enquire further. For example, a rise in distribution costs despite a significant fall in sales could indicate something negative, like a failing on the part of management to control costs effectively. On the other hand, there could equally well be a positive explanation – such as that the business had entered into a contract with a carrier and to ensure priority attention the business had agreed to a fixed charge that increases with time.

Significance of a change in relationship

Interaction 21.1

On reviewing the accounts of a client, you notice that the debtors at the end of the year had risen by 10 per cent, although the sales had fallen by 20 per cent.

Required: Suggest reasons why this change in the relationship might have occurred.

Accounting ratios may be classified into three groups, according to the source of the information:

- ratios tracing relationships between two items within a Balance Sheet are called 'Balance Sheet ratios' or 'point of time ratios' or 'static ratios';
- ratios tracing relationships between two items in the Profit and Loss account are referred to as 'Profit and Loss account ratios' or 'flow ratios' or 'dynamic ratios';
- ratios tracing relationships between an item in the Balance Sheet and one in the Profit and Loss account are referred to as either 'inter-statement ratios' or 'point/period ratios'.

These are discussed in the three sections following.

21.3 BALANCE SHEET RATIOS

By tracing the relationship between two amounts in a Balance Sheet, we can assess whether:

- the business is adequately financed;
- the business is likely to face liquidity problems;
- the business relies too heavily on borrowed capital.

As an illustration, let us consider Simpleton's Balance Sheet as at 31 December 20X0, as given here. Let us seek answers to the following questions by focusing on the relationships stated against each:

BALANCE SHEET AS AT 31.12.20X0	
	£000
A **Fixed assets**	185
B **Current assets**	
Stock	62
Debtors	36
Cash/bank	22
	120
C **Current liabilities**	
Trade creditors	(60)
Working capital	60
Net assets employed	245

Finance by		**£000**
D **Capital**	100	
Retained profit	65	165
E **Non-current liabilities**		80
		245

Questions	Relationship
How are fixed assets financed?	Is D + E > A?
Do current assets exceed current liabilities?	Is B > C?
Do liquid assets exceed current liabilities?	Is B − stock > C?
Is the business borrowing too much?	Is D > E × 2?

These questions are discussed in turn as set out next.

21.3.1 How are fixed assets financed?

This aspect of the business may be regarded as satisfactory provided the capital (D) plus loans (non-current liability, E) exceeds the amount tied up in fixed assets (A). Such a relationship means that a part of the capital employed in the business is available as working capital. On the other hand, if fixed assets had been acquired through current liabilities, there is a risk that, when the short-term credit period expires and creditors seek payment, there could be insufficient cash available because it is tied up in fixed assets. This could place the business at risk because its creditors are entitled to seek recovery through the courts and may possibly pursue the business into bankruptcy.

21.3.2 Do current assets exceed current liabilities? (The current ratio)

The relationship of current assets (B) to current liabilities (C) is referred to as the *current ratio* or *working capital ratio*. In the Simpleton illustration, the current assets exceed the current liabilities. It is generally suggested that current assets should be twice the current liabilities, so that if, at worst, the current assets realize only 50 per cent of their book value, the entity would still be able to meet its current liabilities in full. However, this rule of thumb depends on the nature of the business: businesses such as supermarkets operate on a 'just in time' stock policy and aim at very high stock turnaround, and this means that they can survive with a much lower current ratio than 2:1.

21.3.3 Do liquid assets exceed current liabilities? (The acid test ratio)

The relationship of current assets (B) less stock (i.e. debtors + cash) to current liabilities is referred to as the *acid test ratio* or *liquidity ratio* or *quick assets ratio*. In the Simpleton illustration, the liquid current assets are equal to the current liabilities. This gives a ratio of approximately 1:1, which is normally regarded as the minimum acceptable. The reason for this is that, in a going concern, the shelves have to remain filled up with goods, which means that the resources tied up in stock cannot be released to meet liabilities. Therefore, to be regarded as satisfactory, current assets without stock should at least be equal to the current liabilities, so that the former would be adequate to settle the latter.

21.3.4 Is the business borrowing too much? (The gearing ratio)

The relationship between the ownership interest (i.e. capital contributed by the owner, plus retained earnings) and loan capital is referred to as the *gearing ratio*. It is believed that, normally, the ownership interest should be at least twice the loan capital. If the loan capital is more than 50 per cent of the equity capital plus retained profit, the entity is described as 'highly geared'. The question to be asked, if an entity is highly geared, is whether it will continue to have the ability to service its loans (i.e. pay interest regularly and repay capital at the agreed time).

21.3.5 Summary analysis

We are now in a position to analyse the relationships in Simpleton's Balance Sheet as follows:

	Form of expression	Formula	Workings for Simpleton	Ratio
Financing of fixed assets	Percentage	$\dfrac{\text{Capital} + \text{retained earnings} + \text{loan}}{\text{Fixed assets}} \times 100\%$	$\dfrac{100 + 65 + 80}{185} \times 100\%$	132%
Current ratio	Times cover	$\dfrac{\text{Current assets}}{\text{Current liabilities}}$	$\dfrac{120}{60}$	2
Acid test ratio	Times cover	$\dfrac{\text{Current assets} - \text{stock}}{\text{Current liabilities}}$	$\dfrac{(120 - 62)}{60}$	0.97
Gearing ratio	Percentage	$\dfrac{\text{Loan capital}}{\text{Capital} + \text{retained earnings}} \times 100\%$	$\dfrac{80}{(100 + 65)} \times 100\%$	48%

From the above analysis we are able to make some initial observations about Simpleton, as follows:

- The first of the above ratios shows that the business is adequately financed because the capital plus retained profit has financed the whole of fixed assets, leaving 32 per cent of the capital as working capital.
- The second and third ratios suggest that it is unlikely that the business faces liquidity problems because its current or working capital ratio is 2 and the acid test ratio is almost one. As a rule of thumb, these levels are regarded as the ideal ones.
- The fourth ratio reveals that the business is geared but that the gearing, being less than 50 per cent, is regarded as low.

| Interaction 21.2 | **Comparison of liquidity** |

The Balance Sheets as at 31.12.20X0 of three entities are as follows:

BALANCE SHEETS AS AT 31 DECEMBER 20X0	Peter £000	John £000	Russell £000
Fixed assets	420	380	980
Current assets:			
Stock in trade	462	164	112
Debtors	594	492	12
Cash/bank	28	32	16
	1,084	688	140
Current liabilities:			
Trade creditors	(462)	(418)	(394)
Net current asset/liability	622	270	(254)
	1,042	650	726
Capital	750	550	500
Profit for the year	192	50	176
	942	600	676
Loan	100	50	50
	1,042	650	726

Required:

(a) State your assessment of the liquidity of these three entities.
(b) How assured are the trade creditors in the most liquid of these businesses of receiving payment within the agreed credit period?
(c) Will your answer to question (a) above be different if you are informed that:
 – Peter is a wholesale dealer in consumer durables;
 – John is a wholesale dealer in children's toys; and
 – Russell's business is a supermarket?

21.4 PROFIT AND LOSS ACCOUNT RATIOS

By tracing the relationship between two amounts stated in the Profit and Loss account we can assess whether:

- the entity's trading policy is one appropriate to its product and the market in which it operates;
- any class of expenditure requires greater control;
- profit levels are adequate to justify continuing with the business and servicing the interest payable on any loan capital;
- there is any threat to the safety margin available to loan creditors, with regard to interest (and, as we shall see in Chapter 42, the safety margin available to shareholders as regards dividend).

Some of the ratios, which trace the relationship between amounts stated in a Profit and Loss account, are as follows:

21.4.1 Gross profit ratio

The gross profit ratio is always expressed as a percentage. It traces the relationship between the gross profit and the sales. If an entity reports a gross profit of £30 and its sales as £300, its gross profit ratio is reported as (30/300 × 100%) = 10%. All that a gross profit ratio of 10% means is that every £100 of sale generates £10 of gross profit. In considering the ratio, we ask ourselves whether it is appropriate to its product and the market in which it operates.

The gross profit ratio, on its own, is not an indicator of the amount of profit achieved. For example, an entity dealing in designer clothing would report a much higher gross profit ratio than a supermarket. The profitability of the supermarket may nevertheless be much better because it may have a much larger volume of sales. Clearly, even a 4% gross profit ratio on a sales volume of £120 million is substantially higher than a 30% gross profit ratio on a sales volume of only £10 million.

The significance of the gross profit ratio is in two areas. First, it reveals the trading policy of the business – conveying whether the entity aims at higher gross profit ratio catering (say) to fastidious tastes or opts for larger sales volume at lower profit margins. Second, it is important for control purposes – to establish the accuracy of accounting. Any significant variations in gross profit ratio would cause questions to be asked as to the reason(s) for the changes.

There can be a number of reasons for a variation in the gross profit ratio over time. These include:

- **Commercial reasons:**
  - changes in the sale price;
  - changes in cost of goods sold;
  - changes in the *sales mix* (the variation in the mix of more profitable lines and less profitable ones);
- **Management failings:**
  - inadequacy of controls, which results in pilferage by staff and shoplifting by customers;
  - failing to ensure that goods accounted for as opening stock or purchases are also accounted for, either within sales or stated as closing stock;
  - inaccuracies in stocktaking;
  - inaccuracies in pricing the items remaining unsold;

- Manipulations:
  - overstating or understating the quantity of closing stock;
  - overstating or understating the price used to calculate closing stock;
  - inflating sales by the owner introducing cash and describing it as sales revenue;
  - understating the purchases by concealing invoices from suppliers.

21.4.2 Expense to sales ratios

Any individual expense classification may be expressed as a percentage of sales. The classification of costs may be by function (e.g. distribution cost, administrative expenses) or by type of expense (e.g. advertising, carriage outwards).

An expense ratio is useful, first, for establishing whether the particular cost has remained in line with changes in sales. Second, an entity bent on improving profitability may wish to review each class of expenditure with a view to pruning them if possible. A first step in this effort is to establish the relative size of each expense classification by expressing it as a percentage of the sales.

Some of the steps an entity may consider as part of pruning its expenses include reducing:

- establishment expenses – by moving the head office from a city centre to a less expensive location;
- administration expenses – by downsizing and making middle managers redundant;
- selling expenses – by cutting the advertising expenditure or rates of sales commission;
- distribution costs – by using carriers instead of operating the entity's own delivery fleet;
- financial costs – by renegotiating the terms of a loan and replacing it with a loan at a lower rate of interest.

21.4.3 Net profit to sales ratio

Whereas the expense to sales ratio concentrates on the individual expense classification, the net profit to sales ratio focuses on the profit-generating ability of the sales by identifying, as a percentage, what portion of the sales remains as profit after meeting all expenses incurred in the year.

21.4.4 Return on capital to sales ratio

This ratio focuses on the return generated to the ownership interest (i.e. the providers of capital) and the loan capital, as measured against the level of sales. The net profit plus the interest on loan capital is expressed as a percentage of sales. Assuming that net profit is £28,000 after paying interest of £8,000, and that sales are valued at £300,000, the return on capital to sales ratio is calculated as $(28,000 + 8,000)/300,000 \times 100\% = 12\%$.

21.4.5 Interest cover ratio

This ratio focuses on the safety margin available to meet interest payments. It states the relationship between earnings available to meet interest payments (i.e. gross profit less all expenses except interest) and the interest payable. The ratio is expressed in the form of times cover and it is calculated as (profit + interest)/interest.

If the interest cover is, say, six times, then the loan creditors may feel secure in the knowledge that business earnings are more than six times what is needed to pay interest. Their concern is not that the payment of interest will be refused if profits disappear (because interest is payable even when making losses) but that continuous losses would erode liquidity and this could, in time, jeopardize the entity's ability to pay interest.

21.4.6 Simpleton's Profit and Loss account ratios

To assist with an assessment of the identified areas, let us assume that Simpleton's Profit and Loss account for the year ended 31 December 20X0 is as shown here.

Simpleton's Profit and Loss account ratios computed from this information are stated below. No conclusions can be drawn from them in the absence of comparator ratios from previous years, from budgets or from competitors. For example, the gross profit ratio of 30% would be of little significance except in comparison with what it was in the previous year. A reduction in the ratio would prompt an inquiry into whether it arose from a deliberate commercial decision or it reflects an error in accounting.

PROFIT AND LOSS ACCOUNT FOR THE YEAR ENDED 31.12.20X0		
		£000
Sales		950
Stock on 1.1.20X0	48	
Purchases	679	
Stock on 31.12.20X0	(62)	(665)
		285
Administrative expenses		(152)
Distribution cost		(56)
Interest		(12)
Profit for the year		65

	Express as	Formula	Workings for Simpleton	Ratio
Gross profit ratio	Percentage	$\dfrac{\text{Gross profit}}{\text{Sales}} \times 100\%$	$\dfrac{£285,000}{£950,000} \times 100\%$	30%
Distribution cost to sales ratio	Percentage	$\dfrac{\text{Distribution cost}}{\text{Sales}} \times 100\%$	$\dfrac{£56,000}{£950,000} \times 100\%$	5.9%
Net profit to sales ratio	Percentage	$\dfrac{\text{Net profit}}{\text{Sales}} \times 100\%$	$\dfrac{£65,000}{£950,000} \times 100\%$	6.8%
Return on capital to sales ratio	Percentage	$\dfrac{\text{Net profit} + \text{interest}}{\text{Sales}} \times 100\%$	$\dfrac{£65,000 + £12,000}{£950,000} \times 100\%$	8.1%
Interest cover	Times cover	$\dfrac{\text{Net profit} + \text{interest}}{\text{Interest}}$	$\dfrac{£65,000 + £12,000}{£12,000}$	6.4 Times

A fall in gross profit ratio

Tarrant Electronics' Trading account appears as follows:

Year to 31.12	20X1		20X0	
	£000	£000	£000	£000
Sales		884		876
Stock on 1.1	128		116	
Purchases	726		652	
Stock on 31.12	(164)	(690)	(128)	(640)
Gross Profit		194		236

Required: Identify any variation in the entity's gross profit ratio, and (if any exists) explain the possible reasons for this variation.

21.5 INTER-STATEMENT RATIOS

Inter-statement ratios focus on the relationship of an item in the Balance Sheet to an item in the Profit and Loss account. These ratios are very useful for the assessment of:

● the operational efficiency of the business;
● the profitability of the business;
● the liquidity of the business.

It should be observed that the way in which a ratio (tracing relationships between two identical items) is expressed might vary depending on the particular reason for looking at the relationship. Each of the three reasons given above is examined in turn hereafter.

21.5.1 Assessing operational efficiency

In relation to assessing operational efficiency, there are a number of relevant ratios. We often hear reference by managers to 'making the assets work harder'; this means making the assets generate more sales. Such effort can be measured by dividing the sales in a year by the amount of capital tied up in any class of asset. Ideally, the sales should be divided by the average value of the assets of a class rather than the value reported on a Balance Sheet at the end of the year. However, in the absence of opening and closing figures, the year-end value is accepted as a proxy for the average. This ratio, and others, are discussed next.

Total asset turnover ratio

This ratio expresses the relationship between sales in the year and the average capital tied up in the business assets, and it is presented as times cover. For example, if a total investment of £500,000 in the net assets of a business generates £800,000 in sales income, the total asset turnover ratio is (800,000/500,000) = 1.6 times. The ratio may be broken down further to ascertain the turnover ratios separately for fixed assets and net current assets. Indeed, many business entities go even further when they calculate physical ratios, evaluating the sales per square metre of selling space and the sales per sales staff member.

An increase in the ratio means that the entity is working the assets harder. It is possible for the ratio to become *too* high when a business is said to suffer from **undercapitalization**. What this means is that the entity does not have sufficient assets (i.e. resources) to support the present level of sales. On the other hand, a low asset turnover ratio could be a symptom of **overcapitalization**, meaning that the entity has an excess of assets that are failing to generate adequate sales.

Stock turnover ratio

This ratio is calculated by dividing the cost of sales by the *average* stock carried in the year. The ratio is an indication of the number of times that stock is turned over (i.e. sold and replaced) during the accounting period. If the cost of sales in a year was £120,000 and the average stock carried (i.e. opening stock plus closing stock, divided by 2) was £20,000, the stock turnover in the year is (120,000/20,000) or six times. Sometimes, because of lack of data, it is necessary to use the closing stock in place of the average stock.

The stock turnover ratio reveals the buying efficiency of an entity. The buying function is regarded as efficient when what is bought is sold as quickly as possible. Assume that Andy Small (we have referred to him in earlier chapters) buys each mobile phone for £100, sells it for £150 and buys a second only after selling the first. By the time he has made the first replacement of stock he will have earned £50. The amount of profit he makes in a year would depend on how many times he turns around his stock of a single phone.

An entity with a high stock turnover is of course more efficient, not only because it earns more profit but also because it ties up less capital in stock, incurs less storage cost, and suffers less by way of obsolete goods. However, care should be exercised when comparing two entities in this regard, and for the following reasons:

- The stock turnover ratio has, by necessity, to be high in businesses such as bakeries, dairies and any others that deal with perishables or products with a sell-by date (such as newspaper publishers). The industry context needs to taken into account, therefore.
- The stock turnover ratio will differ in accordance with whether the entity is a wholesaler, retailer, exporter, importer, trader or manufacturer and (having particular regard to the last in the list) how long the manufacturing process takes.
- The stock turnover ratio is usually exaggerated because entities tend to fix their accounting period to end when their stock holdings are at the lowest.
- The stock turnover ratio is susceptible to manipulations by such means as deliberately running down stock, postponing reordering, conducting heavily discounted sales, and undertaking the aggressive write-down of stock.

Debtors turnover ratio

This ratio shows the relationship between debtors and *credit* sales. For example, if the credit sales in a year are £800,000 and the average debtors are £140,000, the debtors turnover ratio is (800,000/140,000) = 5.7 times.

Although a business may sell goods on credit in an effort to promote sales, it remains conscious that amounts tied up in debtors are unproductive. That is why it sets a credit period and endeavours to enforce it. The measure of its success in this endeavour is the debtors turnover ratio. Whether the ratio is satisfactory can only be judged in accordance with the nature of the business, the type of product it sells, the kind of customers it has, the credit terms on offer by competitors, the length of credit offered by the business, whether the business offers discounts for prompt payment, and so on. A high ratio is generally better because it means that less of the amounts generated by credit sales remain tied up in debtors. However, care is needed that the pressure to increase the rate of turnover does not adversely affect the level of sales.

Creditors turnover ratio

This ratio is determined by dividing the *credit* purchases during the year by the average creditors outstanding. If we assume that credit purchases in a year were £600,000 and average creditors £150,000, the creditors turnover ratio is (600,000/150,000) = 4 times. A business would aim at the lowest possible ratio, without alienating its creditors, because liquid resources would then be available for alternative uses.

Operational efficiency of Simpleton's business

Let us now assess the operational efficiency of Simpleton's business using inter-statement ratios. We have to assume that all sales and purchases were made on credit terms, and accept the debtors and creditors at close of business to be representative of the average. The relevant ratios are as follows:

	Express as	Formula	Workings for Simpleton	Ratio
Total asset turnover ratio	Times cover	$\dfrac{\text{Sales}}{\text{Total assets}}$	$\dfrac{£950,000}{£245,000}$	3.88
Fixed asset turnover ratio	Times cover	$\dfrac{\text{Sales}}{\text{Fixed assets}}$	$\dfrac{£950,000}{£185,000}$	5.14
Net current asset turnover ratio	Times cover	$\dfrac{\text{Sales}}{\text{Net current assets}}$	$\dfrac{£950,000}{£60,000}$	15.8
Stock turnover ratio	Times cover	$\dfrac{\text{Cost of sale}}{\text{Average stock}}$	$\dfrac{£665,000}{(£48,000 + £62,000)/2}$	12
Debtors turnover ratio	Times cover	$\dfrac{\text{Credit sales}}{\text{Average debtors}}$	$\dfrac{£950,000}{£36,000}$	26.4
Creditors turnover ratio	Times cover	$\dfrac{\text{Credit purchases}}{\text{Average creditors}}$	$\dfrac{£679,000}{£60,000}$	11.3

We can see from the table that the stock turnover of 12 times shows that the business carries only one month's supply of stock; the debtors turnover of 26 times during the year shows that the debtors do not remain outstanding for more than two weeks; and the creditors turnover of 12 times during the year shows that creditors are settled strictly within a month's credit period. However, it is not possible to assess whether Simpleton's business is efficient in the utilization of its assets without comparative information of its past performance and the average ratios for the industry.

21.5.2 **Assessing profitability**

Return on capital employed (ROCE)

This ratio shows the relationship between the profit for the year (before the deduction of interest on loan capital and taxation) and the capital employed in the business (i.e. the ownership interest and the loan capital). This ratio, abbreviated as **ROCE**, is regarded as the *primary ratio* because it is the most important measure of an entity's profitability.

By way of illustration let us assume that the net profit, after paying £10,000 as interest, is £70,000 (ignoring taxation for the time being), so that the figure to be used for the ROCE is the sum of the two, namely £80,000. Let us further assume that the owner's capital is £400,000 and the loan capital is £100,000. The ROCE, expressed as a percentage, is then $(80,000/500,000) \times 100\% = 16\%$.

Let us now assume that the sales for the year amounted to £800,000. We can then identify how the ROCE of 16% was achieved, by the following three steps:

- Step 1: Total asset turnover ratio = £800,000/£500,000 = 1.6 times
- Step 2: Return on capital to sales ratio = $[(£70,000 + £10,000)/£800,000] \times 100\% = 10\%$
- Step 3: ROCE : $10\% \times 1.6 = 0.16$, i.e. 16%.

This can be shown diagrammatically as follows:

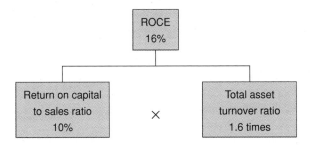

We can see from this diagram that a business is able to increase its ROCE by either improving its return on capital to sales ratio or by increasing the total asset turnover ratio.

Return on capital employed

Interaction 21.4

The following particulars relate to Simpson Enterprises. For the year ended 30.6.20X1, sales were £462,000 and net profit was £15,720 after paying interest at 12 per cent per year on a long-term loan of £100,000. Furthermore, at 1.7.20X0, Simpson's capital was £216,280 and during the year Simpson drew £2,000 per month for living expenses.

Required:

(a) Calculate the following ratios:
   - return on capital to sales ratio;
   - total asset turnover ratio;
   - return on capital employed.
(b) Comment on whether Simpson can afford to continue with the loan capital, paying 12% per annum.

Return on equity capital ratio (ROE)

This ratio shows the relationship between the net profit (after tax in the case of a company) as a percentage of the ownership interest, i.e. capital plus retained profit. The ratio focuses on whether the owner is obtaining adequate return from the business. For example, if the net profit for the year is £24,500 and the owner's capital by the end of the year is £312,500, ROE is (24,500/312,500 × 100%) = 7.84%. Here again, if information is available, the comparison of the net profit should be with the owner's average capital rather than the year-end capital.

Let us now assess the profitability of Simpleton's business as follows:

	Express as	Formula	Workings for Simpleton	Ratio
Return on capital employed (ROCE)	Percentage	$\dfrac{\text{Profit before interest (\& tax)}}{\text{Average capital employed}} \times 100\%$	$\dfrac{£65,000 + £12,000}{£165,000 + £100,000} \times 100\%$	29.0%
Return on equity	Percentage	$\dfrac{\text{Net profit after tax}}{\text{Average owner's capital}} \times 100\%$	$\dfrac{£65,000}{£165,000} \times 100\%$	39.4%

The capital employed in the business is earning 29%. Therefore the business can well afford to pay 12% interest on loan capital. The return on equity is very high, but whether it is the best that can be achieved can only be assessed in the context of returns that may be expected from alternative investments.

21.5.3 Assessing liquidity

We have already learnt to use Balance Sheet ratios for assessing liquidity. Further to that, we can now work out how many days' sales are tied up in stock and debtors.

Stock days

We can look at the amount of stock carried to determine how many days' sales this represents. Since stock is not valued at selling price, the comparison should be of stock with the cost of goods sold. For example, if the sales in the year amount to £400,000 and goods are sold at cost plus one-third, then the cost of goods sold is £300,000 and this is the figure used in the stock days calculation. If we assume that the stock at the end of the year is £72,000, we would arrive at the stock days as (72,000/300,000 × 365 days) = 87.6 days.

You will remember that we have already traced the relationship between stock and the cost of sales for assessing management efficiency, and we have expressed the ratio in that context as a number of times that stock turns over. We are now looking at the same relationship again, but this time to assess liquidity, and we express the relationship in terms of stock days.

What we should remember is that the business has to finance the stock, and the more days' stock is held, the more finance the business must commit to it. We can compare the number of stock days with those of previous years and of other comparable businesses, to assess whether it was acceptable.

Interaction
21.5

Changing stock turnover

Riverdale Holdings effects its sales at cost plus one-quarter. In respect of the year to 31.12.20X0, it reports sales of £426,000 and stock days as 108. Please place a tick in one or more of the following grids to indicate your agreement with each of the following statements, bearing in mind that more than one answer may be correct.

(1) If the stock days are reduced to 90 next year:
  (a) profitability of the business would improve
  (b) liquidity of the business would improve
  (c) operational efficiency would improve.

(2) It is *not* sensible to reduce the stock days if:
  (a) the business suffers a cash shortage
  (b) sales are affected by stock shortage
  (c) creditors are pressing for payment.

(3) If sales next year improve by 20 per cent while other circumstances remain unchanged, the stock days next year will:
  (a) rise proportionately by 20 per cent
  (b) rise, but not by as much as 20 per cent
  (c) remain at 108 days.

(4) Improvement in sales by 20 per cent next year may cause a cash shortage because of having to:
  (a) hold proportionately higher stock levels
  (b) finance more trade debtors
  (c) acquire more fixed assets.

Interaction
21.6

Ascertaining stock days

Prichard's sales in the year to 30 June 2000 were £390,000. The sales produced a gross profit ratio of 30%. Answer the following questions by placing a tick in an appropriate grid:

(1) If Prichard's stock at cost on 30 June 2000 was £78,000, the stock days were:

(a)	73 days	
(b)	95 days	
(c)	104 days	

(2) If Prichard's stock days were 72, what would be the cost of stock he carries?

(a)	£53,852	
(b)	£59,178	
(c)	£49,710	

(3) If sales next year were to rise to £520,000, though stock turnover remained unchanged at 104 days, what will be his stock at the year end?

(a)	£113,973	
(b)	£103,715	
(c)	£148,164	

Debtors days

We can ascertain the number of days' sales tied up in debtors by tracing again the relationship between sales and debtors at the year end. For example, if the sales in the year amount to £400,000 and debtors by the year end amount to £102,000, then the debtors days figure is worked out as $(102,000/400,000 \times 365 \text{ days}) = 93$ days.

Whether this is good or bad depends on the nature of business, the types of product being sold, and in particular the credit terms offered to customers. If the business allows its customers one month's credit, 93 debtors days could signal a breakdown in credit control. In contrast, if the debtors days were, say, 10 days, then this could signal possible liquidity problems, with the business feeling compelled to collect debts more quickly.

Interaction 21.7	**Extending debtors days**

Offord Mills is in business as a wholesale dealer in textiles. Sales in the year ended 31.3.20X0 were £365,000 and Offord allows its customers 45 days' credit, with sales taking place consistently throughout the year. You are required to tick the grid or grids below to state your answer, bearing in mind that there may may be more than one correct answer:

(1) If sales next year increase by one-third, while credit terms remain unchanged, Offord's working capital required will:
(a) increase
(b) remain unaffected
(c) decrease.

(2) If, in the wake of an expansion in sales, there is an increase in debtors, that increase will have to be funded by:
(a) obtaining more credit from suppliers
(b) retaining more profit in the business
(c) introducing additional capital.

(3) It is not sensible for Offord to reduce the credit period allowed to customers to less than 45 days when:
(a) competitors allow 45 days
(b) the business is short of cash
(c) Offord has too much stock in hand.

(4) It is *not* sensible for Offord to extend the credit period allowed to customers to more than 45 days when:
(a) the business has cash-flow problems
(b) stocks are low
(c) customers have difficulty in paying.

Interaction 21.8	**Ascertaining debtors days**

Marlin's Wholesale reported its sales for the year ended 31 March 20X0 as £511,000. Its sales are always made on one month's credit.

1. If trade debtors on 31 March 20X0 came to £63,000, calculate the debtors days.

(a)	60 days	
(b)	45 days	
(c)	30 days	

2. Ascertain the trade debtors as at 31.3.20X0 if they state their debtors days as 63.

(a)	£126,400	
(b)	£321,930	
(c)	£88,200	

3. Ascertain the trade debtors as at 31.3.20X0 if they state their debtors days as 33.

(a)	£54,600
(b)	£46,200
(c)	£168,630

4. Ascertain their debtors as at 31.3.20X1 if they expect sales to increase by 20 per cent while debtors days remain at 45.

(a)	£75,600
(b)	£49,737
(c)	£54,200

5. If sales in the year to 31.3.20X1 are 10 per cent lower and one-sixth of the sales remain outstanding by the year end, ascertain the debtors days.

(a)	54 days
(b)	61 days
(c)	45 days

Creditors days

By similarly comparing creditors at the year end (assumed to be £72,000) with the purchases during the year (say £368,000), we can ascertain the creditors days that the business has taken advantage of as (72,000/368,000 × 365 days) = 71 days. If the credit period allowed by the suppliers is one month – or even two months – the business is defaulting on the credit terms and this may signal that it is experiencing liquidity problems.

Changing creditors days

Respond to the following questions by ticking the appropriate grid or grids, bearing in mind that there could be more than one correct answer:

1. An increase in creditors days may result in:
   (a) additional stock
   (b) additional stock and debtors
   (c) additional stock, debtors and cash.

2. A business should aim at lowering creditors days if:
   (a) it has too much stock
   (b) it has too much cash
   (c) it breaches supplier's credit terms.

3. A fall in creditors days may signal:
   (a) a reduction in profitability
   (b) better liquidity in the business
   (c) worsening operational efficiency.

Ascertaining creditors days

In respect of the year ended 31.12.20X0, Hussain reports his purchases as £624,000. Then:

1. If his creditors at the year end amount to £114,000, calculate the creditors days.

(a)	94 days
(b)	67 days
(c)	48 days

2. If creditors days are stated as 62, determine the creditors outstanding.

(a)	£105,995
(b)	£134,546
(c)	£78,654

Summary analysis

Let us continue with our assessment of the liquidity of Simpleton's business, this time taking into consideration the inter-statement ratios as follows:

	Express as	Formula	Workings for Simpleton	Ratio
Stock days	Days	$\dfrac{\text{Stock at end}}{\text{Cost of sales}} \times 365\ \text{days}$	$\dfrac{\pounds62,000}{\pounds665,000} \times 365\ \text{days}$	34 days
Debtors days	Days	$\dfrac{\text{Debtors at end}}{\text{Sales}} \times 365\ \text{days}$	$\dfrac{\pounds36,000}{\pounds950,000} \times 365\ \text{days}$	13.8 days
Creditors days	Days	$\dfrac{\text{Creditors at end}}{\text{Purchases}} \times 365\ \text{days}$	$\dfrac{\pounds60,000}{\pounds679,000} \times 365\ \text{days}$	32.3 days

Simpleton is carrying just about a month's supply of goods; he appears to be allowing 14 days' credit to his customers and strictly enforcing it; and he appears to be receiving a month's credit from his suppliers and is more or less complying with their terms.

21.6 ACCOUNTING RATIOS GROUPED BY AREA OF FOCUS

So far we have looked at a large number of ratios according to the source of information necessary for calculating each. Let us now attempt at grouping the ratios we have come across in accordance with their area of focus, as set out in the box below.

Operational performance[a]

1. Gross profit ratio
2. Expense to sales ratio
3. Net profit to sales ratio
4. Return on capital to sales
5. Total asset turnover
   Fixed asset turnover
   Working capital turnover
6. Stock turnover[b]
7. Debtors turnover[b]
8. Creditors turnover[b]

Profitability

1. Return on capital employed
2. Return on equity

Liquidity

1. Working capital ratio
2. Liquidity ratio
3. Stock days[b]
4. Debtors days[b]
5. Creditors days[b]

Capital structure

1. Financing of fixed assets
2. Gearing

Notes:

a. These focus on management action such as those with regard to trading policy and how hard the assets are worked.
b. Though tracing the relationship between two identical items, they each have a different focus and, accordingly, they are expressed in different forms.

21.7 SOME WORDS OF CAUTION ON ACCOUNTING RATIOS

There are a number of issues relating to accounting ratios where caution needs to be exercised. These are set out below.

21.7.1 Background information is important as it raises an expectation of what changes are likely to have occurred

Someone endeavouring to interpret accounting ratios should first do the necessary background reading to obtain as much information as is possible in the time and with the resources available. This should, as a minimum, include identifying the industry in which the business operates, and obtaining some financial history (e.g. copies of the last three years' accounts).

Additional information that could be useful includes:

- press comment relating to the industry, the business and its competitors;
- management comment, possibly from the directors' report, relating to past performance;
- management comment, possibly from the chairman's report, relating to future prospects;
- local knowledge of the business, if within your own area:
  - customers: contracts not likely to be renewed; failure of an important customer; customer taken over by a competitor; legal action being taken that might threaten the customer's business;
  - suppliers: main supplier refusing or unable to continue to supply; possible price increases;
  - employees: key personnel likely to leave; the business having problems recruiting staff; or problems with labour disputes.

21.7.2 Ratios indicate symptoms

Accounting ratios are to the accountant what physical symptoms are to the doctor. A reading from a thermometer or a blood pressure gauge would in itself have no significance unless the medical practitioner is able judiciously to interpret the reading. The relationship traced by an accounting ratio is only a symptom; the symptom is useful provided it helps with a correct diagnosis and the diagnosis is corroborated by other symptoms. To seek corroboration the person interpreting the financial statements must seek further information. Those who prepared the financial statements may be prepared to supply the information if either to do so would be to their benefit (say to obtain a bank loan) or the information requirement can be legally enforced, e.g. by the auditors or the Inland Revenue.

When cooperation is forthcoming, every effort must be made to identify possible bias. For example, an owner of a business proposing to sell it may be tempted to inflate the gross profit. Similarly, a manager interested in a management buy-out may be tempted to deflate the gross profit in order to be able to buy the business at a lower price. Failing cooperation, alternative sources of information have to be sought such as from credit agencies, bank references, comments in the trade press, and so on.

21.7.3 Ratios need comparators

A ratio in isolation would be of little use, unless the ratio has a norm with which it can be compared or a standard against which it can be judged. The relationship traced by a ratio would be meaningful only in comparison with:

- what the relationships were in the past;
- what relationships were aimed at when the business established its budget;
- what relationship competitors and others achieve in the same industry.

Comparative information may be obtained from membership of a trade association, where members submit their financial data, have it analysed according to a set pattern, and receive an inter-firm comparison report that compares each member's performance with the other members whilst maintaining each firm's anonymity. An inter-firm comparison report allocates the ratios tracing each relationship, achieved by firms within kindred groups, into four quartiles, so that a business can identify the quartile into which it falls to learn how its position compares with the average in the industry.

21.7.4 Ratios are red flags

The ratios are simply red flags that should raise questions; they do not supply the answers. The accounting ratios are incapable of providing answers to the numerous questions raised by the users of accounting reports. All that they can do is to provide a basis for comparison and to indicate trends. For example, we learnt that the ROCE in Simpleton's business for the year is 29%. This does not tell us what the yield could have been in the circumstances of the business or how best such a yield could have been achieved.

21.7.5 Knowledge of a business's commercial thinking is essential

A relationship traced by a ratio is meaningless unless it is interpreted in the light of the circumstances of the business involved. For example, a business may deliberately build up high stock levels, resulting in a poorer stock turnover ratio as well as a deterioration in the liquidity ratio. But this may be a deliberate move, either to launch a significant sales push or in anticipation of a price rise. An interpretation of accounting ratios, without full awareness of the attendant circumstances, may well lead to incorrect conclusions and, hence, inappropriate decisions.

Besides, the symptoms revealed by the same set of ratios are capable of several – sometimes conflicting – interpretations. For example, significantly high stock turnover ratios and debtors turnover ratios may well be interpreted as signs, respectively, of super efficiency and effective credit control. What these ratios may mask is that the entity is losing business because of inadequate stock levels to meet customer needs and that customers are being alienated by an overly severe credit policy.

21.7.6 Trends are vital

Much more important than a relationship currently existing is the trend in relationships over the years. The trend throws into relief the significance of any change taking place. Taking note of such changes is crucial where the ratios are used as the basis for predicting the future.

21.8 INTERPRETING FINANCIAL INFORMATION BY OTHER MEANS

There are, of course, alternative ways of placing the information in a financial statement in proper perspective. These include the following two forms.

First, graphical representations, such as the drawing of pie charts and bar charts (see examples below), can be used to portray the comparative sizes of each item (say in a Profit and Loss account) as slices of a pie or bars, each proportional in size to the amount or percentage it represents.

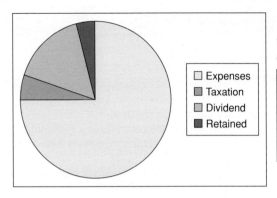

What happened to the earnings in the year 20X0:

Expenses	£84,100
Taxation	£6,000
Dividend	£18,000
Retained	£4,400
Sales	£112,500

Projected performance

	20X0	20X1	20X2	20X3
Sales	£112,500	£132,800	£158,200	£196,500
Profits	£28,400	£38,200	£40,600	£52,400
Dividend	£18,000	£24,000	£30,000	£40,000

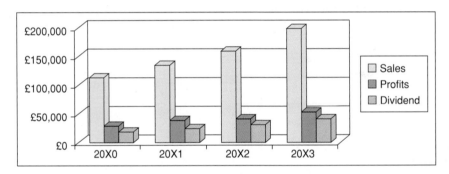

Second, component percentages can be used to equate the focal point of attention in a financial statement to 100 and then to express all other significant figures in that statement as percentages of that figure. For example, Simpleton's Profit and Loss account for the year ended 31.12.20X0 (below left) if presented as component percentages, equating sales to 100%, will appear as shown on the right.

PROFIT AND LOSS ACCOUNT FOR THE YEAR ENDED 31.12.20X0	
	£000
Sales	950
Cost of sales	(665)
Gross profit	285
Administrative expenses	(152)
Distribution cost	(56)
Interest	(12)
Profit for the year	65

PROFIT AND LOSS ACCOUNT FOR THE YEAR ENDED 31.12.20X0	
	£000
Sales	100%
Cost of sales	(70)%
Gross profit	30%
Administrative expenses	(16)%
Distribution cost	(6)%
Interest	(1)%
Profit for the year	7%

SOLUTIONS TO INTERACTIVE QUESTIONS

IQ 21.1 Significance of a change in relationship

There are a number of possible reasons, as set out below.

- **Commercial reasons:**
  - The credit terms offered by competitors in the industry might have changed.
  - There is greater competition in the industry, with a need to offer longer credit as a marketing tool.
  - There might have been a change in the customer base, so that certain customers have been able to negotiate better credit terms.
  - There might have been a change in the risk attaching to debts, e.g. the business might have taken out debt indemnity insurance.
  - It is part of the business marketing strategy to maintain sales in a declining market.
- **Financial reasons:**
  - The business liquidity has improved so that it is able to offer better credit terms.
  - There might be a possible increase in the bad debt risk, with customers unable to settle within agreed credit terms.
- **Management reasons:**
  - There might have been a possible breakdown of credit control.

IQ 21.2 Comparison of liquidity

(a) Accounting ratios for assessing liquidity:

	Peter	John	Russell
Current ratio:	$\dfrac{£1,084}{£462} = 2.35$	$\dfrac{£688}{£418} = 1.65$	$\dfrac{£140}{£394} = 0.36$
Liquidity ratio	$\dfrac{£622}{£462} = 1.35$	$\dfrac{£524}{£418} = 1.25$	$\dfrac{£28}{£394} = 0.07$

The rule of thumb is that for the current ratio to be regarded as satisfactory it must be at least 2. Only Peter meets that requirement, while John is a close second. The liquidity ratio should be at least unity. Both Peter and John meet this requirement. According to the rules of thumb, Russell appears to be in desperate straits on both fronts. Peter is obviously the best in this regard.

(b) **How assured are creditors in Peter of receiving payment in time?**
- The ratios merely reflect the *ability* to pay, not the willingness.
- Though Peter has current assets that cover current liabilities more than twice, £462,000 (43%) of it is tied up in stock and £594,000 (55%) of it is in debtors. How quickly and at what value these could be converted into cash, to meet an emergency, depends on so many factors, including the type of business, the nature of the product, the type of customers, and so on.
- The ratios we have worked out do not reflect further cash commitments, which are not yet recorded in the accounts; nor whether the timing and amounts of cash expected to flow from these assets would match the payment needs. The latter aspect can only be focused on by preparing a cash projection.

(c) **How the nature of business impacts liquidity assessment**
Based only on the ratios, Peter appears to be the most liquid and Russell the least. Information on the nature of their businesses gives a completely different complexion to the situation, as follows:
- John's current ratio appears less satisfactory than Peter's because his stock of children's toys would be at the lowest level immediately after the Christmas season.
- Russell's situation is typical of most supermarkets in real life. Supermarkets effect their sale strictly for cash, and so maintain stock levels as to rotate them within a matter of days. This explains the low

levels of stock and debtors; whereas the amount of creditors may represent (say) one month's credit, which they have obtained from their suppliers. Despite negative working capital (where current liabilities exceed current assets), supermarkets do not appear to experience cash flow problems. This is because the cash resources with which they settle their liabilities are not those reflected on the Balance Sheet but those that are yet to be generated during the weeks following the Balance Sheet.

IQ 21.3 A fall in gross profit ratio

	Year to 31.12.20X0	Year to 31.12.20X1
Gross profit ratio	$\dfrac{£236,000}{£876,000} \times 100\% = 26.9\%$	$\dfrac{£194,000}{£884,000} \times 100\% = 21.9\%$

The fall in Tarrant Electronics' gross profit ratio may have occurred on account of one, or a combination, of the following reasons:

- **Commercial reasons:**
  - a fall in the market price of the items sold;
  - an increase in the purchase price, processing costs, carriage inwards, freight and duty paid on imported items, and so on, which could not be passed on by way of a corresponding increase in the sale price;
  - an adverse variation in sales mix – in the sense that, even though overall sales have improved, more is being sold of the less profitable lines.
- **Accounting errors:**
  - not establishing a correct cut-off to ensure that all goods accounted for as part of opening stock or purchases are included within closing stock if they are not accounted for as sales;
  - an error in the stock count, such as failing to count some items, or overlooking items with customers on approval or in transit, or in bonded warehouses;
  - an error in ascribing cost to the items on stock sheets.
- **Inadequacy of controls:**
  - pilferage of goods by staff;
  - shoplifting by customers;
  - a failure to account for goods removed for personal use by Mr Tarrant's family.
- **Manipulations** intended to understate the entity's performance.

IQ 21.4 Return on capital employed

(a1) Return on capital to sales ratio:

Return on capital:

	£	£	
Net profit	15,720		
Interest	12,000	$\dfrac{27,720}{462,000} \times 100\% = 6\%$	
Sales			

(a3) Return on capital employed (ROCE):

	£	
Return on capital employed	$\dfrac{27,720}{308,000} = 9\%$	

(a2) Total asset turnover:

	£	
Sales	462,000	= 1.5 times
Capital	308,000	
Capital (working)		
Capital on 1.7.20X0	216,280	
Profit for the year	15,720	
Less: Drawings	(24,000)	
Owner's capital	208,000	
Loan capital	100,000	
Capital employed	308,000	

(b) Comment on the affordability of 12% loan capital

Simpson's Enterprises is earning an annual return of only 9% on its capital. Therefore it cannot afford an interest rate of 12% per annum on its loan capital.

IQ 21.5 Changing stock turnover

1. (a), (b) and (c)   2. (b)   3. (c)   4. (a), (b) and (c)

IQ 21.6 Ascertaining stock days

1. (c)   2. (a)   3. (b)

IQ 21.7 Extending debtors days

1. (a)   2. (a), (b) and (c)   3. (a) and (c)   4. (a) and (b)

IQ 21.8 Ascertaining debtors days

1. (b)   2. (c)   3. (b)   4. (a)   5. (b)

IQ 21.9 Changing creditors days

1. (c)   2. (a), (b) and (c)   3. (b)

IQ 21.10 Ascertaining creditors days

1. (b)   2. (a)

PROGRESSIVE QUESTIONS

PQ 21.1 A basic interpretation of financial statements

Small Fry's business submits to you the following financial statements:

PROFIT AND LOSS ACCOUNT FOR THE YEAR ENDED 31.12.20X0		
		£000
Sales		625
Stock on 1.1.20X0	54,500	
Purchases	415,000	
Depreciation – machinery	18,000	
Stock on 31.12.20X0	(62,500)	
Cost of sales		(425)
Gross profit		200
Administrative expenses		(118)
Distribution cost		(48)
Interest on loan		(9)
Profit for the year		25

BALANCE SHEET AS AT 31.12.20X0			
	Cost	Ac. dep.	£000
Fixed assets:			
Machinery	180	(45)	135
Motor vehicles	27	(12)	15
			150
Current assets:			
Stock		62,500	
Debtors		31,250	
Cash and bank		6,250	
		100,000	
Current liabilities:			
Trade creditors		(50,000)	
Working capital			50
			200

Financed by	£000
Capital	100
Profit for the year	25
	125
Loans	75
	200

Required: Assess the profitability, the liquidity and the operational efficiency of the business, *calculating two accounting ratios* that, in your opinion, best report each of the above aspects.

PQ 21.2 Progress of an entity from one year to the next

The summarized financial statements of a business are stated below:

20X0	BALANCE SHEET AS AT 30 SEPTEMBER	20X1
£		£
	Fixed assets:	
40,000	Premises	98,000
65,000	Plant and equipment	162,000
105,000		260,000
	Current assets:	
31,200	Stock	65,300
19,700	Trade debtors	25,700
15,600	Cash and bank	11,500
66,500		102,500
	Current liabilities:	
(52,300)	Trade creditors	(96,700)
14,200	**Working capital**	5,800
119,200	**Net assets employed**	265,800
£		£
	Financed by:	
100,000	Capital	119,200
19,200	Retained earnings	46,600
119,200		165,800
–	7% Loan	100,000
119,200		265,800

20X0	PROFIT AND LOSS ACCOUNT FOR YEAR TO 30 SEPTEMBER	20X1
£		£
386,400	**Sales**	764,200
29,600	Stock on 1.10.20X0	31,200
310,720	Purchases	682,400
(31,200)	Stock on 31.9.20X0	(65,300)
(309,120)	**Cost of sale**	(648,300)
77,280	Gross profit	115,900
(43,400)	Administrative expenses	(37,650)
(14,680)	Distribution cost	(24,650)
–	Interest	(7,000)
19,200	**Profit**	46,600

Required: Report on:

(a) the operational performance;
(b) the profitability;
(c) the liquidity; and
(d) the capital structure of the business, substantiating your findings with as many accounting ratios as you can calculate.

Remember: there is no justification for using year-end amounts as proxy for the average for the year if information is available for working out the average.

PQ 21.3 Return on capital employed

Stated below are particulars with regard to six different companies 'a' to 'f'. Each of these companies has borrowed £2,500 at 8 per cent interest per annum. Fill the white grids with appropriate figures.

	Sales for the year	Net profit for the year	Interest on loan capital	Capital employed	Return on capital to sales ratio	Total asset turnover	Return on capital employed (ROCE)
(a)	£10,000	£800	£200	£5,000			
(b)	£15,000		£200	£8,000	12%		
(c)	£10,000		£200		5%		20%
(d)		£800	£200			4	20%
(e)			£200	£10,000	10%	4	
(f)	£20,000		£200			4	10%

PQ 21.4 Interpretation from an investor's focus

William commenced business on 1 April 20X0, using as initial capital an amount provided by his mother. The accounts for the first two years of business have been prepared as follows:

TRADING AND PROFIT AND LOSS ACCOUNTS YEAR TO 31 MARCH		
	20X1	20X2
	£	£
Sales	70,000	98,000
Cost of sales	(42,000)	(63,000)
Gross profit	28,000	35,000
Overheads – variable	(14,000)	(24,500)
– fixed	(8,400)	(11,200)
Net profit (loss)	5,600	(700)

BALANCE SHEETS AS AT			
	1.4.20X0	31.3.20X1	31.3.20X2
Fixed assets	49,000	49,000	56,000
Net current assets:			
Stock in trade	3,500	7,500	4,000
Trade debtors	–	9,700	16,800
Bank balance	9,100	2,400	(2,800)
Creditors	(2,100)	(3,500)	(9,600)
	10,500	16,100	8,400
Capital employed	59,500	65,100	64,400

In an effort to persuade his mother to lend him a further amount, William points out that:

(a) The sales in the second year were 40 per cent more than that in the first, and the sales next year will probably be around £150,000.
(b) The net loss in the second year results from the increase in fixed costs because of renting more spacious premises, big enough to allow for the anticipated expansion in sales.
(c) A cash injection is urgently needed to maintain the business at the intended scale. Currently the business is unable to comply with the suppliers' terms of one month's credit and the stock levels are inadequate to meet customer demand.
(d) A bank overdraft has not been negotiated.

The mother's concern, however, is that William is capable of earning around £7,000 per year if he finds employment elsewhere, and she herself could earn 8 per cent per year on her savings.

Required: Your advice is sought by William's mother on the implications of the financial information set out above.

PQ 21.5 Creating accounts from ratios

The following information is available for the year ended 31 May 20X0:

1. Working capital at 31 May 20X0 was £11,500.
2. Drawings during the year were £3,000.
3. Depreciation of fixed assets during the year @ 10 per cent on cost was £1,500. No new fixed assets were acquired during the period.
4. Assume that stock and debtors remained constant through out the year.
5. General expenses (without depreciation) were 25 per cent of sales.
6. The following ratios applied:

   Acid test ratio: 1.25 times;
   Current ratio: 1.5 times;
   Total asset turnover: 2 times;
   Stock turnover: 5 times;
   Debtors turnover: 8 times

Required: Prepare a list of calculations in respect of items 1–6 above, and prepare a Trading and Profit and Loss account and a Balance Sheet as at 31.5.20X0.

Part E

STANDARDIZATION OF ACCOUNTING AND CONCEPTUAL FRAMEWORK

Chapter 22

ACCOUNTING STANDARDS

In this chapter

We will learn of the accounting standards and

- examine the case for setting standards,
- identify the extant accounting standards in the UK, enquiring how they are set and enforced.

22.1 WHAT ARE ACCOUNTING STANDARDS?

Accounting standards are a set of professional pronouncements that establish the norm to be maintained and the level of excellence to be achieved for accounting and communicating accounting information. The Accounting Standards Board defines 'accounting standards' as follows:[1]

Accounting standards are authoritative statements of how particular types of transactions and other events should be reflected in financial statements and accordingly compliance with accounting standards will normally be necessary for financial statements to give a true and fair view.

In some countries, such as Japan, the responsibility for setting accounting standards is assumed by the legislature; and in most countries of Europe, too, the standards – though influenced by the profession – are laid down in statutes. In a few countries, such as the United States and the United Kingdom, the responsibility for standard setting and enforcing has for a long time been the responsibility of the accounting profession, although in the *recent* past there has been a deliberate effort to involve others in the task rather than just members of the accounting profession, and to provide some form of legal backing to ensure that standards are complied with.

With the 1989 amendment to company law in the United Kingdom,[2] the function of setting and enforcing standards received legal recognition. Company law in the UK thereby requires that on financial statements published by companies

it shall be stated whether the accounts have been prepared in accordance with applicable accounting standards and particulars of any material departures from those standards and reasons for it shall be given.[3]

22.2 THE CASE FOR SETTING ACCOUNTING STANDARDS

There are a number of very positive reasons for having accounting standards. These reasons are set out in the remainder of this section.

22.2.1 Setting of accounting standards promotes greater comparability of financial reports

If financial reports are to serve their purpose as the basis for making informed decisions, they should be prepared on a consistent basis. This consistency takes two forms:

(a) from year to year, so that one year's performance and position may be compared with those of another (known as inter-temporal comparison);
(b) among different entities engaged in similar activities, which makes it possible to make sensible comparisons.

Setting accounting standards promotes consistency in accounting in two ways: by standardizing the techniques of accounting for transactions and events; and also, where a standard approves alternative accounting techniques, by requiring disclosure of the technique used and the reason for the choice.

If standardization is to be achieved in the context of the globalization of economic activity, there needs to be a harmonization of accounting standards in all countries of the world. Hence there is a case for *international* accounting standards.

22.2.2 Accounting standards encourage the making of meaningful disclosures when reporting

To constitute a sound basis for making informed decisions, financial reports must not only be reliable but also complete in all material particulars. For example, a company reporting a profit of £1.5 million without providing for the £4 million depreciation of its buildings would not have done better than another that reports a loss of £2 million after writing off £4 million as depreciation. Without a disclosure of the accounting policy on depreciation, wrong conclusions will be drawn when the performances of both entities are compared.

Until efforts at standardization commenced in 1970, companies in the United Kingdom generally confined themselves to only disclosing the minimum required by company law extant at that stage. Even though successive amendments to company law increased the volume of disclosures required, the disclosure requirements tended to be identified on an ad hoc basis, mainly with reference to particular company failures. Efforts to identify the purpose of accounting and the disclosures required to achieve the identified purposes followed efforts at standard setting.

22.2.3 Standard setting assists the users of accounting reports

First, standard setting assists users by defining the concepts and spelling out the accounting techniques. In this way the standards assist the users to understand both the information presented to them and the limitations of such information.

Second, standards help by prescribing particular accounting techniques and demanding minimum disclosures. The accounting standards then provide an (albeit limited) assurance on the relevance and completeness of the information presented, as well as on the consistency of the underlying accounting treatment.

Finally, the standard-setting effort itself has been found to instil confidence in users.

22.2.4 **Standard setting assists the preparers of accounting reports**

Standards serve as a handbook that, when an accountant is confronted with a new or unfamiliar situation, draws to the accountant's attention the alternative accounting techniques that may be used and, having inquired into the merits and demerits of each, prescribes a particular technique of accounting.

Furthermore, standards usually spell out the concepts on which a technique is founded, the various hypotheses on which the adoption of a given technique is advocated and the circumstances in which that technique is most suited. This gives the accountant the maximum information and assistance without depriving him of his professional discretion on whether to adopt the technique. When an accountant decides against adopting a prescribed technique he is required to disclose the fact, explain the circumstances and quantify the impact of non-compliance.

Accounting standards thus provide accountants with an invaluable defensive mechanism to resist management pressures brought on them to present biased information. The backing of a well-prepared handbook – particularly if founded on a sound conceptual framework – enhances the quality of an accountant's work and adds prestige to professionalism.

22.2.5 **Setting accounting standards inevitably promotes the search for a theoretical base for accounting**

Until the commencement of standard setting, the accounting techniques in use were no more than 'distilled practices' handed down from generation to generation, as was pointed out by Prof. Edward Stamp.[4] Particular accounting techniques were in use either because that was how it was done in the past or because it best suited those who prepared the accounts to convey the view they wished. The situation changed only with commencement of standard setting.

If a standard is to uphold a particular accounting technique as more appropriate to a given circumstance than its alternatives, the choice has to be justified. This provokes a search for a theoretical base. The quest for a theoretical base became all the more compelling when, in the second half of this century, accountants – like economists – were expected to possess predictive ability. In order to be able to predict the impact of interest rate changes, for example, on price levels and exchange rates, economists were compelled by circumstance to make a set of assumptions, to identify an hypothesis, and to then pronounce their theories. Correspondingly, when those active in the share markets wished to make predictions on the basis of accounting information, the accountants themselves were compelled to make their assumptions, identify an hypothesis and pronounce appropriate theories.

22.2.6 **The majority view**

Most would agree on the need for accounting standards. Professor Baxter[5] draws an analogy with a nation having to avoid chaos on the roads by issuing a rule prescribing the side of the road on which cars should be driven. He submits that a theoretical basis for the rule would be good but is not essential for achieving the objective.

22.3 THE CASE AGAINST SETTING ACCOUNTING STANDARDS

In the debate about standard setting, there are some who argue *against* having accounting standards. Their reasoning is set out below, with comment.

22.3.1 It is impossible to establish a theoretical base for accounting

It is pointed out that a valid theoretical base may be built for chemistry, where reactions of molecules are predictable, and in physics, where theory can be proven by controlled experiments undertaken within a laboratory. In social sciences such as economics and accounting, the claim for a scientific approach to developing a theory is that the assumptions made, the hypothesis put forward and the theory pronounced are validated by empirical studies. But invariably all such theories can only be advanced on the basis of the assumption *ceteris paribus* (which is the Latin for 'assuming all other things remain unchanged'). Such an assumption is never true to life because in the real world other things never remain the same.

22.3.2 In the real world, the existence of a variety of accounting techniques is a position that has to be accepted

This acceptance is unavoidable, it is argued, because business transactions are so numerous and the factors that have to be taken into account when choosing an accounting technique are so varied and affected by so many nuances that it is impossible to standardize.

22.3.3 Financial statements are multipurpose

For want of a better alternative, the same set of financial statements has to serve the many and disparate requirements of a variety of information users, and therefore they cannot be based on the same accounting techniques because a technique suitable for one user group may well not suit another. For example, one user group may prefer financial statements based on the assumption that the entity will remain a going concern, whereas another may prefer the break-up value basis for the purpose of assessing the security available for a loan advanced. Similarly, one group may be interested in the profit available for immediate distribution, whereas another's interest is in the amount of profit that is likely to be repeated in future years.

22.3.4 Standardization, even if possible, is not desirable

The reasons supporting this view are fourfold:

1. Prescription of working rules make accounting bureaucratic and rigid.
2. Compliance with standards can be costly and not commensurate with benefits.
3. Standards can compromise the accountant's professionalism.
4. Standards offer the information user a placebo, giving the impression that it is an effective medicine.

The following comments are made in relation to reasons (3) and (4).

22.3.5 Setting standards places the accountant's professionalism in jeopardy

Some take the view that, by prescribing rules on how accounting is to be performed in stated circumstances, the standards tend to circumscribe the accountant's work, saddle him with rigid rules and deny him the opportunity to exercise professional judgement. Professor W.T. Baxter[6] points out that this could have repercussions on an accountant's training as well – requiring concentration on familiarization with relevant rules, instead of a focus on the development of critical thought and the ability to react to unforeseen circumstances.

There is, however, an opposite point of view – that standards enhance professionalism. Instead of a slavish application of time-honoured accounting techniques, the standards brief accountants on all available alternative techniques and promote use of professional judgement when selecting one, which may or may not be the one prescribed.

22.3.6 The assurances provided by the standards are akin to those of a placebo

It is submitted that the confidence instilled and assurances provided by accounting standards are similar to those felt by patients who have been administered a placebo (rather than a medicine). The standards tend to provide the users of accounting information with levels of assurance that may not really always be available. On the strength of the belief that the technique prescribed by the standards is indeed the one best suited for the purpose, and the hope that the standards are always complied with, the user of accounting information may attribute qualities to the information that are not justified.

Professor David Myddelton of Cranfield School of Management takes the view that a better way of instilling confidence in information users is to educate them to accept accounting information on the basis of *caveat lector* (Latin for 'let the reader take care'). The user must be made aware, for example, that despite best efforts the accounting information cannot be bestowed with more than a limited degree of accuracy, reliability and comparability. For instance, under the time interval concept, accountants cannot but make assumptions and estimates, and these are invariably influenced not only by the skill levels and the experience of the one making them but also by her or his age and temperament.

22.4 EFFORTS AT STANDARDIZATION OF ACCOUNTING IN THE UK PRIOR TO 1970

Prior to 1970, the only significant – though marginal – efforts at standardising the information disclosed in financial statements took the form of disclosure requirements contained in successive enactments of company law. The normal thrust of the law, in keeping with the desire to maintain confidentiality of company management policies and practice, is to call for the *minimum* of disclosure. But based on experience gained, particularly from management lapses that resulted in court cases, efforts were made to forestall such lapses by means of purposeful increases in the volume of disclosures required. Not until the passing of the Companies Act 1981, in response to the EEC Fourth Directive, was a limited attempt made to standardize accounting concepts, accounting techniques and the format of presenting information in published financial statements.

Since the end of the Second World War, the need to provide guidance and to evaluate alternative accounting techniques used in respect of similar transactions was recognized by some of the major professional bodies. Between 1942 and 1969 the Institute of Chartered Accountants in England and Wales issued 29 sets of 'recommendations', providing guidance to its members on all manner of accounting matters. But their impact on standardizing the accounting practices in the United Kingdom was limited, and for several reasons. First, the recommendations were more persuasive than mandatory. Second, because of a pervasive desire to achieve a semblance of unanimity and to accommodate different points of view, the recommendations tended to be vague and often left room for discretion.

22.5 RECOGNITION IN THE UK OF THE NEED FOR ACCOUNTING STANDARDS

The need for setting and enforcing accounting standards was recognized in the United Kingdom in the late 1960s, and in the United States more than three decades prior to that (during the Wall Street Crash of 1929), when a spate of company collapses drew the attention of the public and the government to startling instances of bias and 'creativity' in reporting accounting information. Accounting techniques used for identical transactions were often handled in a variety of ways, some of them inappropriate and others (depending on circumstances) inconsistent. When preparing accounts, some businesses deliberately chose from a range of accepted practices those that would make their business appear in the most favourable light.

One such instance in UK was the set of accounts prepared by the directors of Associated Electrical Industries (AEI) to fend off a hostile take-over bid mounted by the General Electric Company Ltd (GEC). GEC made the bid in September 1967 and on 20 October, within two months of the financial year end, AEI published a profit forecast of £10 million for the year 1967, duly certified as true and fair by Deloittes, the company's auditors. When, after the take-over succeeded, the results for the year 1967 were reported as a loss of £4.5 million, an investigation into the turnaround, undertaken jointly by Price Waterhouse and Deloittes, found that £5 million of the discrepancy related to matters of fact and £9.5 million substantially to those of judgement.

Another of these instances was the set of audited accounts prepared for 1968 by Pergamon Press Ltd, reporting a profit of £2.1 million. American Lease Data Processing Equipment Corp., interested in a take-over, commissioned an investigation of the accounts by Price Waterhouse, who reported that the performance in the year 1968 resulted really in a loss of £495,000. An investigation by the Department of Trade and Industry revealed that none of Pergamon's accounts for the period 1964 to 1969 showed a true and fair view. This provoked the late Robert Maxwell to exclaim that 'accountancy is not the exact science which some of us thought it was'.

Public consternation at these and several other such cases was reflected in the banner headlines in the financial press on the 'watchdog that failed to bark'. Sir Frank Kearton, chairman of the Industrial Reorganisation Corporation, wrote to the President of the Institute of Chartered Accountants in England and Wales expressing concern at the 'plethora of generally accepted accounting principles'. The accounting profession had to react to these and, in particular, to Edward Stamp, then Professor of Accounting at Edinburgh University, who probably did more than anyone else to provoke the profession by writing an article in *The Times* in September 1969 entitled 'The need to audit the auditors'.[7] Professor Stamp pointed out that 'serious doubt has been cast on the usefulness, let alone the theoretical validity, of the figures prepared and "authenticated" by accountants'.

22.5.1 A Statement of Intent

The reaction of the accounting profession in the United Kingdom took the form of a Statement of Intent[8] to publish accounting standards, issued by the Institute of Chartered Accountants in England and Wales (ICAEW) towards the end of 1969, followed in early 1970 by the formation of the Accounting Standards Steering Committee (ASSC). The Institutes of Chartered Accountants of Scotland and of Ireland joined the committee almost immediately, while the Association of Certified Accountants and the Institute of Cost and Management Accountants joined a year later. In 1976 the Chartered Institute of Public Finance and Accountancy joined the committee.

The ASSC changed its name to the Accounting Standards Committee (ASC) and was reconstituted, from 1 February 1976, as a joint committee of the six member bodies. From then on, the six member bodies acted collectively through a Consultative Committee of Accountancy Bodies (CCAB). From 1 January 1986, the ASC functioned like a committee of CCAB Ltd.

Between 1971 and July 1990, when its functions were taken over by the newly formed Accounting Standards Board (ASB), the ASC published 25 Statements of Standard Accounting Practice (SSAPs), 55 Exposure Drafts (EDs), and many discussion papers. The principal method used for establishing a standard was that, before an approved method of accounting was stated in a SSAP, the proposed method was announced in an ED for discussion and comment and, in the light of these, the final version was formulated.

22.6 ACCOUNTING STANDARD SETTING IN THE UK BETWEEN 1970 AND 1990

During the period between 1970 and 1990, the SSAPs were prepared by the Accounting Standards Committee, approved by the governing council of each of the six members of CCAB, issued by the CCAB, and enforced on their members by the individual professional bodies. The standard-setting effort was inadequately financed. Members of the Accounting Standards Committee worked part time and were not remunerated for their services.

The following committees undertook early reviews of the standard-setting process:

1. A committee, chaired by T.R. Watts, in 1978 drew attention to the following:[9]
   - the need for a conceptual framework to constitute the basis for setting accounting standards;
   - the need for a supervisory body to monitor compliance with accounting standards;
   - the need for restricting the application of some standards to larger entities alone;
   - the need to resource the standard-setting efforts better.
2. Another committee, chaired by Sir James Mckinnon, in 1983 focused on procedural aspects with a view to expediting the issue of standards.[10] Their suggestions included the following:
   - that approval of accounting standards should require a 75 per cent vote instead of a unanimous vote;
   - introduction of the Statements of Recommended Practice (SORPs) and Franked SORPs;
   - that at the initial stage of standard making, a Statement of Intent should be issued.
3. A Statement of Recommended Practice differed from an SSAP in the following ways:
   - An SSAP dealt only with 'matters of major or fundamental importance [that] affect the generality of companies', while a SORP dealt with matters that, though of widespread application, were not of fundamental importance, and with matters that are of limited application, say to a specific industry;
   - SORPs were issued by the ASSC whereas SSAPs were issued by the CCAB; and
   - Whereas compliance with a SSAP was mandatory, SORP was only a recommendation with the expectation that those who expressly confirm compliance with it would enhance the credibility of their financial statements. The two SORPs applying at that time were:
     - SORP(1): Pension Schemes accounts   May 1986
     - SORP(2): Accounting by charities   May 1988

Franked SORPs are those applicable to a particular activity, developed by and at the expense of those engaged in that activity but approved by the ASC, stating thereby that they represent the current best accounting practice. Since 1990 the ASB has confined itself to giving 'negative assurances' to SORPs.

22.7 THE DEARING REPORT[11]

Another committee, chaired by Sir Ron Dearing, was appointed in 1986 to inquire into the accounting standard setting and enforcing process. Some of the factors that prompted this inquiry were as follows:

- **The ASC's inability to respond promptly to the changing needs of the profession and increasingly complex accounting issues.** In the context of changes in the economic and political climate at that time, the business entities were (and still are) called upon to operate in a fast-moving, highly competitive, and increasingly complex environment. The standard-setting machinery, as it then existed, was underfinanced and depended on unpaid part-time staff, and so it could not provide the support expected in the circumstances. Failure promptly to address issues such as the accounting for price-level changes, off-Balance Sheet financing, the issue of a variety of capital instruments by companies (explained later), and accounting for intangibles including brand names were some of the specific instances cited of the inadequacy of the standard-setting system.
- **The call to permit wider interests than the accounting profession to partake in the standard-setting process.** On the recommendations of the Wheat Committee (1972), action had been taken already in the United States to involve representatives of all accounting information user groups in the process of setting standards. The need to do the same thing in the United Kingdom had been recognized as early as in 1982.
- **The need to insulate the standard-setting process from pressure groups and from conflicts of interest.** A widespread criticism was that the standards were not neutral and free from bias, being influenced by pressure groups. To overcome this, it became important that standard setting should be better resourced and undertaken by paid and full-time staff, who would be free from any conflict of interest.
- **Frequent amendments, revisions and withdrawals of standards, and shuffling of concepts.** It was felt that the way of effectively overcoming this problem was the development of a generally accepted conceptual framework.
- **Inadequate monitoring of compliance with accounting standards.** There were several problems in this area. First, in the scenario then obtaining, only the members of the professional accounting bodies could – if at all – be penalized for non-compliance, whereas the decision to comply or not was usually made at a higher level. There was no legal requirement on the directors of companies to comply. Second, when instances of non-compliance were identified and inquired into by the Department of Trade and Industry (as in the case of Midland Bank), the outcome, at worst, was an assurance by the guilty party that it would not recur.

The main recommendations of the Dearing Committee included the following:

- Development of a conceptual framework to underlie accounting standards. The report identified that the absence of an adequate conceptual framework constrained the work of both the standard setters and those required to comply with them. Therefore it was recommended that:

- further work should be undertaken, on a modest scale, building on the work done by the Financial Accounting Standards Board in the United States and the International Accounting Standards Committee;
- every standard should be accompanied by a 'statement of principles', underlying it and explaining why alternative techniques were rejected.

● Standard setters should focus on quality and timeliness of standards, reduction of permitted options and enforcement of the standards rather than increasing the number of standards.

● Whether accounting standards should apply to small entities should be decided individually for each standard, taking into account the cost of compliance and the comparable benefit expected.

● The application of each standard to those within the public sector should be agreed between the government and the standard setters. This is because the government departments are increasingly working on a commercial basis and therefore there should be an underlying unity of approach to accounting in both the public and the private sectors.

● The enforcement of standards by a legal process – as done in countries such as Japan and Canada – was not recommended because 'this inescapably requires a legalistic approach and a reduction in the ability of the financial community to respond quickly to new developments'. Instead, the enforcement of standards should be approached as follows:
  - The directors of large companies should be required to state, in notes to financial statements, whether or not they have been prepared in accordance with applicable accounting standards, drawing attention to material departures and explaining the reasons for the departures.
  - Where any accounts fail to show a true and fair view, a Secretary of State or a body authorized for the purpose should have power to apply to the courts for an order requiring the revision thereof.
  - Where there has been a material departure from any accounting standard, the onus of proving that the financial statements do indeed show a true and fair view should be on the party who compiled the financial statements and the auditor who reported an unqualified opinion on them.
  - In legal proceedings there should be a general presumption that all accounting standards would have the support of the courts unless it could be demonstrated that, despite material departures, the financial statements gave a true and fair view.

● A new process for setting accounting standards was recommended.

22.8 THE ACCOUNTING STANDARD-SETTING PROCESS IN THE UK SINCE 1990

Several bodies share the accounting standard-setting and enforcing process in the United Kingdom. A description of these bodies and relevant aspects of their work is set out next.

22.8.1 Financial Reporting Council (FRC)

The Financial Reporting Council is registered with the Registrar of Companies as a company registered by guarantee. It has a wider interest than those in the accounting profession alone. The aim of the FRC is to mobilize the participation of information users in the standard-making process and to secure their acceptance of the accounting standards. The wider group of 'information users' is to include the government, the Stock Exchange, banks, academics, industry etc.

The chairman of the FRC is appointed jointly by the Secretary of State for Trade and Industry and the Governor of the Bank of England, in consultation with the chairman of the CCAB. Membership of the FRC consists of:

- three deputy chairmen representing the profession, industry and commerce, and the city;
- the chairman of the Accounting Standards Board;
- the chairman of the Financial Reporting Review Panel;
- members selected (by a subcommittee of the FRC) from the highest levels in the profession, in industry and commerce, in the city, and from amongst others with an interest in good financial reporting.

The functions of the FRC have been spelt out as threefold:

1. to promote good financial reporting and, in that context, from time to time to make public its views on reporting standards. In this role, it will, when appropriate, make representation to the government on the current working of legislation and on any desirable development;
2. to provide guidance to the ASB on work programmes and on broad policy issues;
3. to verify that the arrangements are conducted with efficiency and economy and that they are adequately funded.

The FRC has four operational bodies as follows:

- the Accounting Standards Board (ASB);
- the Financial Reporting Review Panel (FRRP);
- the Urgent Issues Task Force (UITF);
- the Public Sector Liaison Committee (PSLC).

22.8.2 Accounting Standards Board (ASB)

The Accounting Standards Board is responsible for setting, amending, issuing and withdrawing accounting standards. Entrusted with this power by the Secretary of State for Trade and Industry, it issues standards on its own right and needs no external approval for its actions.

The ASB consists of:

- a full-time chairman;
- a full-time technical director;
- seven members drawn from the profession, industry and commerce, and the city, serving part-time but (unlike before) remunerated for their work.

The standards issued by the ASB are called *Financial Reporting Standards (FRSs)* and their Exposure Drafts are identified as *Financial Reporting Exposure Drafts (FREDs)*.

22.8.3 The Financial Reporting Review Panel (FRRP)

The Companies Act 1985, as amended in 1989 (s 245), empowers courts to order companies to rectify defective accounts. The application to courts to secure such an order has to be made by the Secretary of State for Trade and Industry, who has delegated the power, with regard to large and public companies, to the Financial Reporting Review

Panel. The FRRP consists of a chairman and 22 members, who are accountants, bankers or lawyers. Because the FRRP lacks the capacity to examine every set of accounts, it operates on a referrals basis – i.e. focusing only on those companies referred to it by the London Stock Exchange, or commented on in the media, or complained of by anyone.

When a case is brought to its attention FRRP proceeds as follows:

1. Its staff examines the set of accounts for the purpose of establishing whether there is a *prima facie* case to answer of material non-compliance with either the law or a standard.
2. If there is a case to answer, FRRP staff draw it to the attention of the company concerned, inviting the directors of the company (and, if they wish, its auditors) to meet a panel of about five members of the FRRP.
3. Only where no mutual agreement can be reached does the FRRP refer the matter to the courts.

The FRRP makes an endeavour (with 100 per cent success to date) to secure by voluntary means the revision of the defects in the accounts. But it proclaims its seriousness about seeking a court order, should necessity arise, by maintaining for the purpose a bank balance of £2 million.

22.8.4 The Urgent Issues Task Force (UITF)

The Urgent Issues Task Force is chaired by the ASB chairman and consists of 15 members. It has two main functions, as follows:

1. to assist the ASB in areas where an accounting standard or a company law provision exists, but where unsatisfactory or conflicting interpretations have developed or seem likely to develop, by endeavouring to reach a consensus on the desirable accounting treatment for the matter in question;
2. when new issues emerge that have to be dealt with urgently, without awaiting the usual process of consultation that occurs for setting standards, to endeavour to reach a consensus and expect companies to accept it as the technique that would convey a true and fair view. Any such consensus reached by the UITF is conveyed from time to time in UITF 'Abstracts'.

22.8.5 The Public Sector Liaison Committee (PSLC)

This committee aims to minimize the differences in accounting techniques and reporting practices adopted by the public sector and the private sector. For this purpose, it is entrusted with the following four functions:

1. to endeavour to minimize the differences by apprising the ASB of helpful points;
2. to advise the ASB on any proposed public-sector SORPs;
3. to comment on the ASB's materials from the point of view of the public sector;
4. to foster a common developmental philosophy for public- and private-sector reporting.

22.9 THE EXTANT ACCOUNTING STANDARDS IN THE UK

Set out in the table following are all the accounting standards extant at July 2000.

	Issued by the Accounting Standards Committee	Issue date
SSAP 2	Disclosure of Accounting Policies	Nov. 1971
SSAP 4	The Accounting Treatment of Government Grants	April 1974
SSAP 5	Accounting for Value Added Tax	April 1974
SSAP 8	The Treatment of Taxation under the Imputation System	Aug. 1974
SSAP 9	Stocks and Long-term Contracts	May 1975
SSAP 13	Accounting for Research and Development	Dec. 1977
SSAP 15	Accounting for Deferred Tax	Oct. 1978
SSAP 17	Accounting for Post-Balance Sheet Events	Aug. 1980
SSAP 19	Accounting for Investment Properties	Nov. 1981
SSAP 20	Foreign Currency Translation	April 1983
SSAP 21	Accounting for Leases and Hire Purchase Contracts	Aug. 1984
SSAP 24	Accounting for Pension Costs	May 1988
SSAP 25	Segmental Reporting	June 1990
	Issued by the Accounting Standards Board	:
FRS 1	Cash Flow Statements (originally published in 1991)	Oct. 1996
FRS 2	Accounting for Subsidiary Undertakings	July 1992
FRS 3	Reporting Financial Performance	Nov. 1992
FRS 4	Capital Instruments	Dec. 1993
FRS 5	Reporting the Substance of Transactions	Dec. 1994
FRS 6	Acquisitions and Mergers	Sept. 1994
FRS 7	Fair Values in Acquisition Accounting	Sept. 1994
FRS 8	Related Party Disclosures	Oct. 1995
FRS 9	Associates and Joint Ventures	Nov. 1997
FRS 10	Goodwill and Intangible Assets	Dec. 1997
FRS 11	Impairment of Fixed Assets and Goodwill	July 1998
FRS 12	Provisions, Contingent Liabilities and Contingent Assets	Sept. 1998
FRS 13	Derivatives and other Financial Instruments: Disclosures	Sept. 1998
FRS 14	Earnings per Share	Oct. 1998
FRS 15	Tangible Fixed Assets	Feb. 1999
–	Financial Reporting Standard for Smaller Entities	March 1999
FRS 16	Current Tax	Dec. 1999

22.10 RELEVANCE OF ACCOUNTING STANDARDS TO SMALL BUSINESS ENTITIES

The general expectation is that accounting standards should be complied with by all entities, whether incorporated in law or otherwise, and irrespective of size. This is because the focus of all financial reports is to show a true and fair view of the performance of an entity during a year and its position at each year end. This is indeed what the accounting standards aim at. However, taking into account the particular situation of smaller entities and trading off the cost of compliance with resulting benefits, the Financial Reporting Standard for Smaller Entities (see table above), issued by the ASB originally in 1997 and amended in March 1999, exempts small entities from mandatory compliance with many of the accounting standards so far laid down.

References

1. Exposure Draft, *Forward to Accounting Standards*.
2. Companies Act 1989.
3. Companies Act 1985, Schedule 4 paragraph 36A.
4. Prof. Edward Stamp, 'The need to audit the auditors', *The Times*, September 1969.
5. Prof. W.T. Baxter, 'Recommendations on accounting theory', *The Accountant*, October 1953.
6. Prof. W.T. Baxter, *ibid*.
7. Prof. Edward Stamp, *op. cit.*
8. *Statement of Intent on Accounting Standards in 1970s*, ICAEW 1969.
9. *Setting Accounting Standards* – a consultative document by a committee chaired by T.R. Watts, 1978.
10. *Review of the Standard Setting Process* – by a committee chaired by Sir James Mckinnon, 1983.
11. *The Making of Accounting Standards* – by a committee chaired by Sir Ron Dearing, September 1988.

## Chapter 23

ACCOUNTING CONCEPTS

In this chapter

We will learn that accounting for transactions is done on the basis of a number of agreed assumptions, complying with agreed working rules and conforming to accepted conventions

23.1 DISTINGUISHING ACCOUNTING ASSUMPTIONS, WORKING RULES AND CONVENTIONS

Although, over several centuries, accountants are known to have practised their techniques and continually sought to perfect them, their endeavours to identify and evaluate the concepts (meaning the ideas and thinking) that underlie the techniques are of comparatively recent origin. In recent times the efforts in this direction gathered momentum because of the interest in promulgating accounting standards. The Accounting Standards Board continues to be enthusiastic about these efforts and committed to establishing a conceptual framework.

We find it helpful to break accounting concepts down into three categories, namely assumptions, working rules and conventions:

- Assumptions are the premises that are taken for granted.
- Working rules are the minimum codes that those in accounting are expected to abide by for achieving results.
- Conventions are the norms that determine the choice of a particular course of action, when there is discretion concerning alternative courses.

To illustrate the differences, consider the situation in relation to enrolling in a class of study. The *assumption* on which one would enrol is that the teachers are qualified and competent. A *working rule* is that the teacher and students are punctual. The *conventions* are that a teacher should behave with decorum and cater to the needs of students without any discrimination based on race, gender, religion, and so on. Conventions are not assumptions; nor are they working rules to abide by – they are the agreed view of what is thought to be proper behaviour. This view will constitute the norm in accordance with which any available discretion is exercised.

In relation to accounting, we will consider four main assumptions, six working rules and five conventions, as set out in the box opposite and described more fully hereafter.

ACCOUNTING CONCEPTS		
Assumptions	**Working rules**	**Conventions**
• Separate entity • Money measurement • Stable value of money • Going concern*	• Time interval (periodicity) • Accruals/matching* • Realization • Historical cost • Valuation • Non-aggregation †	• Materiality • Objectivity • Prudence* • Consistency* • Substance over form

Four of these concepts (marked*) are identified in SSAP 2[1] as 'Fundamental accounting concepts', while the same four plus a fifth (marked †) have been named in company law[2] as 'accounting principles', in accordance with which companies are required to prepare financial statements.

23.2 ACCOUNTING ASSUMPTIONS

23.2.1 Separate entity

When accounting for transactions, it is assumed that the entity in respect of which the accounting records are maintained is separate from (a) its owner or owners and (b) other entities owned by the same person(s). For example, looked at from the point of view of the business entity, the capital contributed by the owner is a liability and is accounted for as such; whereas, from the point of view of the one who contributed it, the capital would be an asset. In a strictly legal sense this assumption is true only with regard to limited companies, which on incorporation are recognized as separate entities not only distinct from but also having rights against those who own it. Without the clear demarcation that incorporation provides, it is difficult to identify the position of the thin line dividing the resources and activities of the entity from those of its owner, although it is necessary to do so for tax purposes. For example, a sole trader carrying on business from home will need to establish the proportion of the household running costs that relate to the business and the proportion that constitute personal use.

23.2.2 Money measurement

The responsibility to account for an entity's transactions may well be discharged in physical terms, without necessarily involving money values. The assets of an entity could be expressed, for example, as consisting of X hectares of land, Y tonnes of coal or Z litres of wine. The expression in such physical terms would of course be more meaningful particularly when comparing the entity's performance or position now with those several years earlier, because physical values remain stable over time. A hectare of land remains the same in extent today as it was centuries ago.

The problem with measuring in physical terms, however, is that the physical values cannot be aggregated so as to identify the total wealth of an entity in a single figure. For example, debtors, creditors and cash cannot be aggregated with physical measures such as tonnes or litres. Without aggregation using a common unit of measurement, it is not possible to compare different entities or the same entity over time.

For these reasons, accountants prefer to measure what they have to account for in terms of money. Money values, established by market transactions, are traditionally accepted as more objective, freer from bias and, therefore, more reliable for reporting an entity's performance and progress. Having therefore decided to use money values for accounting, the inevitable problem arises that any transaction or event that cannot be measured in terms of money cannot then be accounted for. To overcome this problem, accountants assume that what cannot be measured in terms of money need not be accounted for.

| Interaction 23.1 | **Business information that money cannot measure** |

Accountants assume that what is not measurable in terms of money does not have to be accounted for. They are aware, however, of significant areas that cannot be measured in terms of money and yet that are of interest to those to whom accounting reports are intended.

Required: Identify some business information that may be important to the successful running of a business but that money cannot measure. In addition, explain how such information is communicated to those interested in it.

23.2.3 Stable value of money

Accountants in each country use their national currency as the yardstick for measuring transactions and events for purpose of accounting. In the United Kingdom, therefore, the pound sterling is generally used. This gives rise to three problems:

- Whereas physical measures (e.g. hectares) remain as a stable measure over time, monetary measures do not. A pound sterling today is worth less than two-thirds of its value ten years ago and around one-fifth of its value 30 years ago.
- Each asset does not always have a constant money value over time. For example, because of a limitation in supply, land is bound to increase in money value over time.
- Measurements made in terms of money can be distorted by variations in exchange rates. For example, a machine bought from Japan 20 years ago would be worth much more today purely because of the appreciation in the exchange value of the Japanese yen.

Yet money remains the yardstick of accounting measurement because it provides the only means of aggregating fixed assets, current assets and current liabilities and making comparisons possible over time and between entities.

Reasons why the assumption is unrealistic

Accountants have to choose whether to assume that money is stable in value or to adjust all of the figures in the financial statements to take account of the changes in value. Rather than do this, they have made the assumption that the value of money remains constant over time. On the basis of this assumption, the financial statements seem to imply that an entity earning £20 million this year has performed better than when it earned £19 million a year earlier and that an entity X with resources of £100 million is better resourced than an entity Y with £90 million. Neither of these assertions may be valid if, because of inflation, the value of money has diminished.

Consider the following two examples:

1. If there is an inflation rate of 10 per cent, the earning this year of £20 million is worth only (£20m × 100/110) = £18.18 million in terms of last year's money values. In that case the performance is worse than the £19 million of the last year.

2. If an entity Y acquired most of its assets in 1960, when the Retail Price Index was 12.5, and has the same sterling amount of fixed assets in 1999 as an entity X that acquired its fixed assets in 1998 when the Retail Price Index was 163, then clearly entity Y is far better resourced than entity X.

Variations in the value of money, therefore, not only distort comparison over time and with other entities, but they also inhibit performance reporting as well as position reporting. For example, performance reporting is bound to be distorted to the extent that earnings measured in terms of current (lower) monetary units are compared with expenditure at least some of which (like depreciation of assets and opening stock) are measured in monetary units of a prior period. Position reporting is inhibited because the assets reported on a historical cost basis will be stated at the different money values that prevailed at the time each of them was acquired.

The assumption is only questioned in times of high inflation

Accountants are fully aware that measurements are distorted by changing values of their unit of measurement. The distortion is of course greater in times of more pronounced inflation. That is why the accounting profession tends to intensify its efforts at finding a solution to the problem during periods of accelerated inflation, as was the case in the 1970s when standard setters actively searched for ways of accounting for price-level changes. Currently inflation is low and there is little pressure to take it into account.

Alternative to historical cost accounting	Interaction 23.2

Accounting on the basis of historical cost is valid only if it is assumed that the value of money remains constant over time. This constraint would be overcome if accounting used current values rather than historical costs.

Required: Explain the reluctance to record accounting information using current values.

23.2.4 Going concern

The financial statements of an entity are prepared on the assumption that the entity 'will continue in operational existence for the foreseeable future' and that there is no intention or necessity to close down the business or to significantly curtail the scale of its operations. It is on the basis of the assumption that the entity will remain a 'going concern' that a fixed asset continues to be reported at depreciated historical cost, even if its realizable value is lower. It is again on the basis of the assumption that the entity will survive to complete its current commitments that income is anticipated on long-term contracts even prior to completing them.

Those responsible for preparing financial statements are required to satisfy themselves on the validity of the going concern assumption by making inquiries into areas such as:

● adequacy of capital – both working capital as well as long-term finances;
● operational prospects – considering the size of the order book, the market share, the market trends, intensity of competition and so on;
● availability of resources, including raw material, manpower, know-how and so on.

It must be conceded, however, that financial statements prepared on an assumption of going concern may not be adequate for evaluating, say, the security available to a lending bank, which may have also to contemplate prospects of a forced realization in the event of an emergency.

Interaction
23.3

The going concern assumption

Unless expressly stated otherwise, financial statements are assumed to have been prepared on the assumption that the entity will remain in the business as a going concern for the foreseeable future.

Required: Explain how assets and liabilities are valued on the basis of the assumption that the entity will remain in operation at the current scale for the foreseeable future.

23.3 WORKING RULES

23.3.1 Time interval (or periodicity)

In the distant past, the accounts for voyages and trade across the seas were based on the 'venture' concept and prepared only on completion of a venture when there had been a full disposal of the merchandise. Such accounting was more reliable in that it did not have to assign a value for any merchandise remaining unsold nor to predict how the remainder of the venture would fare. The current scenario, however, is one in which those with a legitimate claim for information on any entity prefer to have accounting information at regular intervals and with greater frequency than on final completion of the venture. As a result, the venture concept has been rejected in favour of 'time interval' rule.

The time interval rule requires accounting information to be communicated to those external to the entity (i.e. outside those who manage the entity) at regular intervals, typically of 12 months' duration. To comply with the time interval working rule, accountants find it necessary:

● to associate income and expenditure with specific time periods; and, because transactions often span accounting periods, develop accounting bases (see Section 23.5) to allocate costs and income to different accounting periods;

● to make estimates with regard to transactions, such as taking and valuing year-end stock, determining the consumption of fixed assets arising from depreciation, and providing for expenses remaining unpaid. If these cannot be precisely measured at the time of reporting, they have to be estimated. Estimation inevitably involves subjectivity.

23.3.2 Accruals and matching

For reporting the performance of an entity within a given period, its accomplishments in that period are matched with the corresponding efforts, both being measured in terms of accruals (i.e. amounts earned and expenses incurred) rather than on the basis of the cash flows.

SSAP 2[3] spells out the accruals rule as follows:

● Income and expenditure shall be recognized as they are earned and incurred – not as money is received and paid.

● Income and expenditure shall be matched with one another so far as their relationship can be established or justifiably assumed.

● Income shall be matched with associated expenditure so far as they are material and identifiable.

● Where the accruals concept is inconsistent with the prudence concept, the latter prevails.

Although these rules are clear, abiding by them is fraught with problems, as is illustrated next:

1. If income is to be accounted for as it is earned, at what precise point is it earned and when exactly would it be prudent to account for income yet to be received in cash?
2. If expenditure is to be matched with corresponding income in so far as their relationship can be justifiably assumed, how prudent would it be to regard as an asset the cost of developing a product in the hope that it will generate income in future periods?

The accruals and matching rule

Interaction 23.4

Susan Pizzy, a young graduate operating as a dealer in computer software, requests your help to finalize the accounts of her shop for the year ended 31 December 20X0. After you have completed the task, she writes to you, making, among others, the following points:

(a) The total price paid for software in the year should be regarded as expenditure. There is no point showing the cost of the unsold portion as an asset in the Balance Sheet.
(b) She had deliberately avoided paying the last half year's rent and the last quarter's bills for gas and electricity, hoping that there would be a corresponding improvement in profit in the first year.
(c) The amount of £36,000 she had received up front on subletting a portion of her shop for three years, at £1,000 per month, should all have been treated as her income for the current year because she has no intention of repaying any portion of it even if the tenant were to leave early.

Required: Draft your response to the points made by Susan.

23.3.3 Realization

The realization working rule requires that income should not be recognized for the purpose of accounting until it is realized. As we shall see in Chapter 25, income is not realized until all uncertainties relating to the earning process are substantially resolved. This means, in the case of a business that produces what it sells, that:

- the production should be completed, so that no uncertainty remains as to whether raw material can be found and whether production will be completed;
- the sale must be agreed, so that there is no uncertainty about whether a buyer can be found and on the price that can be obtained;
- the sale proceeds should have been received, or there should at least be a reasonable assurance of receiving it.

In relation to the prudence concept, SSAP 2 states that to be regarded as realized the income should be received '*in the form of cash or of other assets the ultimate cash realisation of which can be assessed with reasonable certainty*'. This means, for example, that sales income should not be recognized until the goods have been produced and are sold, and in exchange the entity has received either cash or another asset (debtor, in the case of credit sale) the cash realization of which is reasonably certain. To draw attention to the importance that company law attaches to the realization rule, some of its provisions are stated in the box on the right.

Realization under the law

1. Only profits realized by the Balance Sheet date shall be included in the Profit and Loss account (Sched. 4, para. 12).
2. Only realized profits are distributable (s 263).
3. Any distribution other than what is distributable can be reclaimed whether shareholders knew of the position or ought to have known of it (s 277).

<table>
<tr><td>Interaction
23.5</td><td>Realization rule inhibits performance reporting</td></tr>
</table>

Two sisters, Tessa and Venessa, commenced a business on 1.1.20X0 with capital in cash of £50,000 each. On that day each of them invested that amount in 50,000 ordinary shares of £1 each, paying no more than £1 per share. By 31 December 20X0 these shares were quoted in the London Stock Exchange at 120p per share. Tessa encashed her holding on that date, but Venessa held on to them, expecting the shares to go up even further.

Required: Set out the Balance Sheet of the business activity of each sister as at 31 December 20X0. State also whether you regard Venessa's performance in the year as poorer or better when compared with that of Tessa.

At what point is income realized?

A major problem with the realization rule is the determination of the precise point at which an income may be regarded as having been realized. Professionals, such as solicitors, who are usually not permitted by rules of professional etiquette to sue their clients for professional fees, have regarded their fees income as deserving accounting recognition only when received in cash. A club or association may also adopt the same attitude. If realization in the form of cash is to be the criterion for accounting for income, then credit sales cannot be accounted for as income. But they *are*, because the sale gives rise to an asset (referred to as a debtor) the cash realization of which can be assessed with reasonable certainty because the due process of law would assist in collecting it. It is important to note that the point at which the income may be regarded as realized, though critical to accounting, may not always be clear. The practice in this area has still not been standardized in the United Kingdom.

<table>
<tr><td>Interaction
23.6</td><td>Determination of the point when income is realized</td></tr>
</table>

Tom Lovedale is a carpenter specializing in producing drawing-room suites of an exquisite design, which he sells for £3,600 per suite. On completing his first year's operations, he stated his accomplishments as given in the box here.

Received orders for	11,200 suites
Bought materials for making	9,000 suites
Completed production of	7,500 suites
Delivered to customers	7,400 suites
Invoiced customers for	7,250 suites
Customers paid in full for	5,850 suites

Required: Advise Tom on the amount he should recognize as income in the year.

23.3.4 Historical cost

The time-hallowed method that accountants have always used is to measure the resources of an entity as well as the expenditure incurred at *historical cost* (i.e. the actual amount paid). The value is based on the amount actually paid and, being established by an arm's-length market transaction, it is objective, verifiable and reliable. It is seen as the basis for sound stewardship, i.e. making it clear what a business has done with the resources entrusted to it.

The shortcomings of accounting on the historical cost rule should, however, be admitted, as follows:

- **Resources are not shown at current value**. The Balance Sheet, reporting resources at their historical cost, fails to reflect the current value of the resources available at the disposal of the entity. This distorts the reported value of the business as well as the calculation of accounting ratios such as the return on capital employed. Besides, the amounts stated on a Balance Sheet become meaningless because assets are stated at costs paid at different times, when money values were different.
- **Performance is not accurately reported**. The Profit and Loss account would not accurately report the performance in a period because it matches the current period's earnings against expenses, at least a part of which were incurred in an earlier period when money had a different value. The extent of distortion arising as a result would depend on the level of inflation and the time gap between the acquisition of assets and utilizing them for income-generating activity.

For these reasons, accountants tend to stray away from the historical cost rule and have obtained legal approval for doing so through the Companies Act 1981, which introduced the **Alternative Accounting Rule**, permitting assets (freehold property in particular) to be accounted for at the market value rather than at historical cost.

23.3.5 Valuation

Three of the valuation rules adopted by accountants are as follows:

1. Fixed assets are valued at cost less depreciation up to the date of reporting.
2. Stock is valued at the lower of cost and net realizable value.
3. A liability is stated as the amount of cash or cash equivalent that, on the reporting date, is deemed to be necessary to fully discharge the obligation existing on that date.

23.3.6 Non-aggregation

The non-aggregation rule applies when, with regard to assets such as stock in trade, cost is compared with realizable value for determining which is the lesser. The rule, introduced for the first time in the Companies Act 1981, demands that the comparison should be made separately for each individual asset or for groups of 'fungible' (meaning interchangeable – one being as good as another) assets. The objective is identified and the operation of the rule is illustrated in IQ 17.4.

23.4 CONVENTIONS

23.4.1 Materiality

When, faced with alternative courses of action, an accountant is required to use discretion, one of the norms to fall back on is provided by the materiality convention. For example, materiality is the criterion that determines the answer to questions such as those in the box here.

> Capitalize or write off?
> Report separately or include with other items?
> Accord special accounting treatment?

Subjectivity is inevitable here, for the materiality convention inevitably introduces an element of subjectivity into accounts. Materiality means 'significance' and significance cannot be objectively quantified. What the accountant is required to consider is whether the information, its accounting treatment or its disclosure, non-disclosure or the manner of its disclosure would be significant for the decisions to be made on the basis of the accounts. The judgement of what is material could be influenced by subjective factors. The Trusthouse Forte group of companies does not depreciate its buildings on the premise that the amount of depreciation in each year would be immaterial, taking into consideration the long life of its buildings because of the high quality of maintenance. Others, in an identical position, *do* depreciate their buildings because, although the amount for a single year may be relatively small and thus immaterial, accumulated over the long life of the property the amount is bound to become material. A sole trader would probably regard the cost of a personal computer as being sufficiently material to warrant capitalization; but for international conglomerates the cost may be so immaterial that it deserves to be expensed. Most companies, when publishing their annual financial statements, round off the amounts to the nearest thousand pounds; whereas companies like ICI round them to the nearest million pounds.

Interaction 23.7	**Materiality as the norm for a decision**

Accountants apply the materiality convention when exercising their discretion at various stages in the accounting process, e.g. for deciding whether to capitalize an item or write it off as expenditure.

Required: Explain why such a convention is necessary and give examples where accountants apply this convention.

23.4.2 Objectivity

If accounting information is to be the basis for informed decision making, then it is essential that it should be credible. By 'credible' we mean that it must be accurate and, more importantly, free from the personal opinions and bias of those responsible for its preparation.

Objectivity safeguards credibility. The adherence to the historical cost rule is one of the means that accountants use to safeguard objectivity. For example, by reporting fixed assets at the cost actually paid, the accountant avoids the subjective judgement involved when assets are valued. Yet there are occasions when the accounting process requires subjective judgements to be made. Some such occasions are as follows:

- determining depreciation, when the useful economic life of assets is estimated;
- making provision for doubtful debts, when the recoverability of the debt is assessed;
- accruing for unpaid bills, when estimates have to be made because actual amounts are yet unknown;
- valuing stock, when the cost of unsold stock is compared with its net realizable value, which is an estimated figure.

23.4.3 Prudence

Prudence was once regarded as synonymous with pessimism. This was regarded as the way accountants took care of the risks and uncertainties immanent in business. This position was perhaps acceptable at a time when the main focus of accounting was to discharge stewardship, where the owners of the entity preferred to be told the worst scenario possible, with the knowledge that reality would probably be better. The contemporary position is that accounts constitute the basis for predicting future possibilities for making informed investment/divestment decisions. While conceding that the future would not exactly be a repetition of the past, the performances of the current period and the present financial position are expected to constitute a reasonable premise for predicting the future.

The aim today, therefore, is not to report the worst possible scenario but to report the most likely scenario. Accordingly, when faced with discretion in relation to alternative courses of action, the prudence convention demands that:

- income is not anticipated, being recognized only when realized;
- all known expenditure and liability are fully provided for, irrespective of whether the amount is known with certainty or is the best estimate in the light of the information available;
- where an asset may be valued in several ways, the one chosen should be the most realistic and the one that accords with consistency.

23.4.4 Consistency

To constitute a reliable basis for making informed decisions, the accounting information must be reported consistently. This is because decisions are made by determining how the information available for this year compares with those of prior years (intertemporal comparison) and how they compare with those of other similar entities (inter-firm comparison). For facilitating this comparison, company law insists that 'accounting policies shall be applied consistently from one year to another';[4] while SSAP 2 demands that 'there shall be consistency of accounting treatment of like items within each accounting period and from one period to the next'.

An accounting policy, once adopted, is not permitted to be changed except where the change can be justified as necessary for showing a true and fair view. The position in this regard is probably stricter in the UK than in the United States. There, the 'convention of preferability' permits a policy change if the new one is preferable to the existing one.[5] In the United Kingdom the need for a change has to be more compelling. In the event of a change in accounting policy, SSAP 2 demands the disclosure of the nature of the change, the reason for the change, and the quantified impact of the change.

The Financial Reporting Review Panel (the body supervising compliance with accounting standards – see Section 22.8.3) had to draw to the attention of Ptarmigan Holdings plc (now Graystones plc) the need to justify and explain accounting inconsistency when, in its accounts for the year ending on 30 June 1992, it changed the policy with regard to goodwill from writing off to capitalization.

Inconsistency to manipulate accounts

Interaction 23.8

Mary Jones sells exquisitely hand-painted Chinese ornamental vases at £100 each. On 1 July 20X0 she had in stock 800 vases, which she valued at £30 each. During the year ended 30 June 20X1 she bought vases in three batches of 1,000 vases each, paying £40 per vase for those in the first batch, £50 for those in the second and £60 for those in the third. During the year she sold 2,200 vases. She has no way of determining the batch to which the unsold vases belong. For accounting for the vases remaining unsold, she usually applied the simple average cost. Since she wishes to apply for a bank loan, she feels that her performance would appear better if she shifts to first in first out (FIFO).

Required: Determine Mary's business performance during the year ended 30 June 20X1, using both FIFO and simple average cost, and advise Mary on whether she may change her policy.

Consistency refers to the policy adopted

The consistency that is demanded relates to the *policy adopted* with regard to accounting for transactions and not the detailed *application* of a policy in use. On the detailed application of a policy, corrections and amendments may become necessary and that is encouraged because it may be essential for conveying a true and fair view. For example, having adopted a policy of depreciating machinery equally over its useful life, estimated (say) at 20 years, an entity may find that the machinery has to be replaced by the end of the seventh year if its market position is to be maintained.

In the area of facilitating inter-firm comparison by maintaining consistency of accounting treatment in similar entities, very little has been achieved, although the efforts at standardization and the disclosure requirements assist in inter-firm comparisons.

23.4.5 Substance over form

When a business entity enters into a transaction that appears to be one sort of transaction in its legal form but quite another in commercial reality, the convention of **substance over form** requires the accounting to be in accordance with the commercial substance.

An example of this convention is an asset acquired on lease terms. In legal form the asset belongs to the lessor. The commercial reality, however, is that the lessee has all the risks and rewards related to that asset. If the item leased is machinery, the lessee assumes all the risks, such as having to insure it, repair it and maintain it. Since the lessee is denied the option of cancelling the lease within a stated period (which is known as the primary period) the lessee bears also the losses arising from excess capacity or obsolescence. In the meantime, the lessee is entitled to all the rewards from the machinery, such as the benefit from what it produces, custody of the item, and the right of uninterrupted usage. If, in these circumstances, the lessee does not account for the leased item as an asset, on the premise that it legally belongs to another, the position reported in the Balance Sheet of the lessee will not be true and fair for the following reasons: the lessee fails to report as an asset a resource in respect of which all risks and rewards are his; and the lessee fails to report, as a liability, the corresponding uncancellable obligation to pay, assumed in terms of the lease agreement.

For these reasons, SSAP 21[6] requires the lessee to capitalize leased items if, in terms of the agreement with the lessor, the risks and rewards belong to the lessee. In parallel circumstances, FRS 5[7] requires also the capitalization of other assets such as stock, debtors and investments, if the risks and rewards relating to them are those of the entity.

23.5 ACCOUNTING BASES AND ACCOUNTING POLICIES

23.5.1 Accounting bases

Having chosen to abide by the working rule of time interval and confronted with a situation where accounting periods do not always coincide with business cycles, accountants have to find acceptable ways by which income and expenses, which cut across accounting periods, could be allocated to one of them. **Accounting bases** are the alternative techniques developed by the accounting profession for the purpose of allocating costs and income to different accounting periods. SSAP 2 defines accounting bases as:

methods developed for applying fundamental accounting concepts to financial transactions or items for . . .

(a) determining the accounting period in which a revenue and cost should be recognised in the Profit and Loss account; and

(b) determining the amounts at which material items should be stated in the Balance Sheet.

23.5.2 Accounting policies

Particular accounting bases selected by an entity as ones most appropriate to its own circumstances and consistently adopted by it are known as the accounting policies of the entity.

SSAP 2 requires every entity to disclose its accounting policies in a note to the accounts, and to limit the disclosure to those policies that are material to the determination of profit in the Profit and Loss account and to the critical appreciation of the financial position in the Balance Sheet. SSAP 2 further requires every entity to disclose the policies as clearly, as fairly and as briefly as possible.

References

1. SSAP 2: *Disclosure of Accounting Policies* (November 1971).
2 Companies Act 1985, Schedule 4 Part 2, paragraphs 10 to 15.
3. SSAP 2, *op. cit.*
4. Companies Act 1985, Schedule 4 Part 2 paragraph 11.
5. APB Opinion No.20: *Accounting Changes* (July 1971).
6. SSAP 21: *Accounting for Leases and Hire Purchase Contracts* (August 1984).
7. FRS 5: *Reporting the Substance of Transactions* (December 1994).

SOLUTIONS TO INTERACTIVE QUESTIONS

IQ 23.1 Business information that money cannot measure

Significant business information of interest to those who have a claim for information cannot be accounted for because they are not measurable in terms of money. Such information may include the following:

- the quality and competence of the entity's employees;
- the morale among the staff, their motivation, and threat of industrial action;
- the quality of the entity's assets and how well they are maintained;
- the competitive edge that the entity has over its rivals, in such form as reputation, location, brand names and past history.

Such information, which cannot be measured in terms of money, is communicated by being narrated in financial statements as footnotes or in management or directors' reports.

IQ 23.2 Alternative to historical cost accounting

The reluctance to substitute current values for historical cost arises from several factors, including the following:

- The 'value' of an asset or a transaction is subjective and therefore could vary according to the thinking and mood of the person doing the valuation.
- 'Value' could mean different things to different people. For example, value in use is different from market value. Value in use would vary according to the intended use to which the item is to be put; market value could itself refer to the value at which the item could be disposed of (realizable value) or the value at which the item could be replaced (the replacement value).
- The value cannot be verified (for example during an audit) and that may affect the credibility of the information provided in the accounts.

IQ 23.3 The going concern assumption

- Assets are recognized for inclusion in a Balance Sheet on the basis that the entity will remain ongoing. For example, a prepaid portion of rent is recognized as an asset on the assumption that the entity will remain ongoing and continue to occupy the premises.
- Liabilities are recognized on the basis that the entity will remain in operation. For example, if the entity ceases business and lays off employees, the compensation it may have to pay its employees is not accounted for unless such cessation of business is under contemplation.
- Assets are valued on the premise that the entity will continue to operate and at the present scale. For example, assume that machinery of a specialized nature, acquired for £500,000 and written down to £250,000, has a realizable value of only £50,000. The lower realizable value is ignored so long as disposal of the machinery is unlikely and the written down value of the machinery is recoverable from its use. Similarly, the amounts realizable on stock and recoverable from debtors are likely to be lower in the forced realization that cessation of business entails, and they are not yet taken into account when preparing annual financial statements.
- Liabilities are accounted for at the amount needed for their discharge if the business remains ongoing. Any penalties that may arise, for example from settling a loan earlier than the agreed date, are again ignored.
- In a Balance Sheet, assets are classified as 'fixed' and 'current' in accordance with whether they are intended to be realized or used within the next accounting period. Such a classification is valid only on the going concern assumption. In the event of closure of the business, all assets are for realization and would fall within a single category. Similarly the Balance Sheet classification of liabilities as 'current' and 'long-term' depends on the intended period of repayment, if the business remains ongoing. In the event of winding-up, the whole classification has to be altered to identify preferential creditors, secured creditors and unsecured ones.

IQ 23.4 The accruals and matching rule

(a) **Reporting unsold purchases as an asset:**
- Unless the cost of goods not sold is removed from the Trading account, the sales income will not be 'matched' properly with the cost of what was sold.
- The goods remaining in hand are expected to be sold in the next period. Their *cost* has therefore to be deferred to the next period because the relationship between this cost and the income to be earned in the next period is 'established or justifiably assumed'.

(b) **Accounting for expenses remaining unpaid:**
The rule of accruals requires that the results of performance within an accounting period should be determined by comparing accomplishments in the period (whether matched by cash inflows or not) with the efforts made for the purpose, as measured by expenditure (whether paid for or not). Hence unpaid expenditure (on rent, electricity and gas) has to be accounted for.

(c) **Deferral of income yet to be earned:**
Under the accruals rule, income is recognized only to the extent earned within the period. Though £36,000 is received in the period, only a third of it, relating to the current period, is earned by the reporting date. The remainder is, therefore, accounted for as a deferred income and stated on the Balance Sheet along with liabilities even though there is no intention to repay.

IQ 23.5 Realization rule inhibits performance reporting

TESSA'S BALANCE SHEET	
	£000
Cash and bank	60
	60

	£000
Capital	50
Profit for the year	10
	60

VENESSA'S BALANCE SHEET	
	£000
Investments	50
	50

	£000
Capital	50
Profit for the year	0
	50

Applying the realization rule, Tessa is able to report a profit because she has realized it by selling the shares. Although by holding the shares for a year Venessa too has earned some profit, she cannot account for the so-called 'holding gain' until it is realized.

Venessa's decision to hold the shares until the prices improve further may be wiser and yet, under the realization rule, she appears to have performed worse than Tessa.

IQ 23.6 Determination of the point when income is realized

The process of earning income by sales consists of a series of related activities. At one point in that series the uncertainties involved in the earning process are substantially resolved and at that point the sale is effected and therefore the income is recognized for accounting purposes. The precise identification of that point is a legal matter. It varies from business to business and depends essentially on the precise wording of the contract of sale. The evidence of, and therefore the trigger for, recognizing the sale is usually the act of invoicing because it is at that point that uncertainties such as the consent of the customer and the value of the sale are resolved.

Delivery usually precedes invoicing but the sequence thereof may not be crucial because it is normally assumed that *the property (the risks) in the goods* passes to the customer at the point of invoicing, even if the customer is yet to take delivery, provided the item involved is segregated from the rest. There are exceptions to this. For example, where goods are made to order, the contract with the customer is made (and, therefore, most uncertainties are resolved) when the customer places the order, so that the income may be recognized at the point the production is completed (even prior to invoicing and delivery).

In the case of Tom Lovedale, it would appear that he produces drawing-room suites to meet orders placed by customers. He may recognise his sales as 'realized' at the point he completes production. On that basis his income for the year is (7,500 suites × £3,600) = £27 million. If he opts to adopt the more common approach by recognizing income at the point of invoicing, his income for the year will be (7,250 × £3,600) = £26.1 million. This may well be an understatement of his performance in the year because he has in fact delivered 7,400 suites and clearly the risks and rewards related to them have passed to the customers. Therefore he should rather recognize an income of (7,400 × £3,600) = £26.64 million in the year.

What is important, however, is that first he should disclose the basis on which he recognizes his income and, second, he should adopt that basis consistently from year to year.

IQ 23.7 Materiality as the norm for decision

Accounting reports are intended to communicate information on the basis of which economic decisions may be made by those to whom the reports are intended. This aim will be defeated unless the information is communicated in such a manner that it could be understood and acted upon. To safeguard these qualities, the focus has to be on whether the information included is material for decision making.

Instances of applying materiality convention are as follows:

- Materiality is the threshold criterion for determining whether or not a transaction should be separately reported in the financial statements.
- On a decision whether to capitalize a cost or to write it off, the materiality convention is crucial.
- Unless a transaction or event is material (either in its nature or in amount), it will not be considered for any special accounting treatment, such as reporting the transaction as an exceptional item or accounting for it as a prior-period adjustment (see Chapter 43).
- When preparing financial statements for publication, companies round off the figures to the nearest thousand pounds (the nearest million in the case of very large companies) on the premise that amounts less than that are not material for those to whom the statements are intended.

IQ 23.8 Inconsistency to manipulate accounts

On each of the alternative cost-flow assumptions, performance will be reported as follows:

PERFORMANCE FOR THE YEAR ENDED 30 June 20X1					
	Average cost		FIFO		
	£000	£000	£000	£000	
Sales		220		220	a
Stock – 1.7.20X0	24		24		
Purchases	150		150		
Stock – 30.6.20X1	(72)	(102)	(90)	(84)	b
Gross profit		118		136	

(a) Sales of 2,200 vases @ £100 are given.
(b) Stock in hand on 30.6.20X1 is calculated thus:
  ● **On average cost:**
  Average price: £(30 + 40 + 50 + 60)/4 = £45
  1600 vases @ £45 = £72,000
  ● **FIFO:** 600 vases @ £50 = £30,000
  1,000 vases × £60 = £60,000
  £90,000

The convention of consistency prevents Mary from shifting away from her usual cost-flow assumption. By sacrificing consistency, she will manipulate profit by £18,000.

PROGRESSIVE QUESTIONS

PQ 23.1 The governing accounting concept

When preparing its financial statements for the year ended 31 December 20X0, the following accounting adjustments were made by Hornbill plc:

(a) £16,500 due from a customer was written off as irrecoverable.
(b) 20 per cent of the cost of vehicles was written off as depreciation.
(c) An item of stock costing £6,000 was written down to its realizable value of £4,500.
(d) School fees paid to the proprietor's son was debited to the Drawings account.
(e) £2,500 paid for a photocopying machine was written off (instead of being capitalized).
(f) Insurance paid for the period after the Balance Sheet date was transferred to a Prepayments account.
(g) The cost of stock in hand at the year end was determined, as usual, on a FIFO basis.
(h) The dividend proposed for the year in respect of shares held in a limited company was not accounted for as income because it was not received.

Required: Identify the main accounting concept or concepts on the basis of which the above adjustments were made.

PQ 23.2 Conflict among accounting concepts

In the recent past, accountants have shown an interest in identifying the concepts that underlie the techniques they use when accounting for transactions. They acknowledge that some among the accounting concepts are fundamental ones, but they also observe that occasionally there is a conflict between concepts.

Required:

(a) Illustrate with a transaction a conflict between the following concepts:
  ● The Matching working rule and the Materiality convention;
  ● The Materiality convention and the Objectivity convention;
  ● The Matching working rule and the Prudence convention;
  ● The Separate entity assumption and the Substance over form convention.
(b) Explain how you would resolve the conflict, pointing out whether your judgement will be swayed because one of the concepts at conflict is identified as a 'fundamental' one.

PQ 23.3 The assumption of going concern in jeopardy

Norwich Tanners and Curriers (NTC) finds that due to a cash-flow crisis it has to cease operation soon. The Trial Balance extracted on the last day of the accounting period appears as stated here. You are further informed as follows:

(a) Stock on 30.6.20X1, costing £840,000, would normally realize 25 per cent more, but in a forced realization it is usual to allow a 50 per cent discount.

(b) In the event of closing down the business, 20 per cent of the debtors are expected to default.

(c) Motor vehicles should fetch not less than their written down value, but the machinery is not likely to realize more than £100,000.

(d) The following expenses remain unpaid as at 30 June 20X1: salaries £32,000; rent £12,000; and advertising £18,000.

(e) When the services of employees are dispensed with, compensation will become payable at an amount of £116,000.

Required: Prepare the Trading and Profit and Loss account of the business for the year ended 30 June 20X1, on a basis where the business is not a going concern.

TRIAL BALANCE AS AT 30 JUNE 20X1		
	£000	£000
Machinery at cost	340	–
Depreciation on machinery	–	180
Motor vehicles at cost	420	–
Depre. on motor vehicles	–	240
Stock in trade 1.7.20X0	826	–
Salaries	268	–
Depreciation on machinery	34	–
Depreciation on vehicles	42	–
Sales	–	2,690
Purchases	2,086	–
Advertising	164	–
Motor vehicle maintenance	28	–
Machinery maintenance	46	–
Debtors and creditors	485	698
16% bank loan	–	150
Rent	36	–
Provision for doubtful debt	–	25
Lighting and heating	29	–
Bank overdraft	–	60
Cash in hand	16	–
Other admin. expenses	198	–
Capital	–	975
	5,018	5,018

## Chapter 24

CONVEYING ACCOUNTING INFORMATION

In this chapter

We will learn of:

- stakeholders who have a legitimate claim for information and the nature of their interest
- qualitative characteristics of information to be included in financial statements
- the elements of financial statements, their recognition and measurement

---

24.1 FINANCIAL REPORTS AND FINANCIAL STATEMENTS

Financial reports are the means used by an entity to communicate information on the financial effect of its activities to those external to it. There are two types of financial reports, namely special-purpose reports and general-purpose reports.

24.1.1 Special-purpose reports

Financial reports addressed to those in a position to demand special-purpose reports (such as returns to the Registrar of Companies, and tax returns to the Inland Revenue) are tailor-made to meet the individual requirements with regard to contents and format of presentation.

24.1.2 General-purpose reports

Financial reports other than those specially prepared are known as general-purpose financial reports. They provide a wide range of users with financial statements such as the Profit and Loss account, the Balance Sheet and the Cash Flow Statement, including explanatory notes. And they supply narrative reports such as the Chairman's Statement, Directors' Report, and Operational and Financial Review.

Limited companies, which are the commonest form of business organization, are legally required to publish specified general-purpose financial reports. These reports are required to be made available to certain parties who are identified in law (e.g. the shareholders) and they are also available to members of the public as documents of public record, filed with the Registrar of Companies.

The format of these reports, as well as their contents, is specified in company law; and there has been a progressive extension of the disclosure that a company is required to make. The disclosures to be made, however, have been reactively identified on an ad hoc basis. Each additional disclosure has been designed usually to deal with failings identified by investigations into company failures.

There is, however, a need for a proactive approach to disclosure requirements. It is now appreciated that the general-purpose financial reports could be made more meaningful, if their contents and format of presentation were to be determined after considering the following:

(a) Who are the different parties, known as 'stakeholders', who have a legitimate claim for information and to whom financial information should be communicated?
(b) What are the main areas of interest each of those parties has?
(c) Which items of information will be of relevance to those areas of interest?
(d) What are the qualitative characteristics that these parties will expect of the information provided?
(e) Which means will prove most effective for communicating the identified information?

Interest in seeking answers to these questions arose when the accounting profession launched its quest for a 'conceptual framework'.[1] An attempt was made in the United States in 1971 to identify the different groups that have a legitimate claim for information from a business entity and how best such needs may be satisfied effectively. This study was undertaken by a Study Group on the Objectives of Financial Statements, appointed by the American Institute of Certified Public Accountants (AICPA) and chaired by Robert Trueblood. A similar study was commissioned in the United Kingdom around the same time by the Accounting Standards Committee. This study resulted in the publication in 1975 of a discussion paper, which was called *The Corporate Report*.

The latest position in this UK study is contained in the *Statement of Principles* for financial reporting published by the Accounting Standards Board in 1999. This statement is referred to hereafter as the SoP.

Limitations of financial statements

Interaction
24.1

There is a view that traditional financial statements prepared by business entities are inadequate for communicating fully the performance and financial position of business entities.

Required: Explain the reasons for such a view.

24.2 STAKEHOLDERS AND THEIR INTERESTS

24.2.1 Identification of the stakeholders

The parties with a legitimate claim for information from profit-orientated entities have been identified in the SoP as follows:

1. *investors*, being those who have provided or intend to provide risk capital;
2. *lenders* (present and prospective), being the providers of loan capital;
3. *suppliers* and other trade creditors, being providers of credit facilities;
4. *employees*, whose financial security and prospects are entwined with those of the entity;
5. *customers*, who expect to be served as well as serviced by the entity;
6. *government* and its agencies, whose interest is usually met by special-purpose reports;
7. *the public*, whose welfare is affected by the activities of the entity.

The variety of different parties who have a legitimate claim for information from an entity were referred to in *The Corporate Report* as **stakeholders**.

24.2.2 **Main areas of stakeholder interest**

The main areas of interest to a range of stakeholders may be identified as follows:

- **Discharge of stewardship**. In a limited company, even though the resources of the entity are owned usually by numerous shareholders, the management of these resources (the stewardship) is entrusted to a small number of directors. The divorce of ownership from management places the management in a fiduciary relationship with the owners and hence with a responsibility to account to the owners for protection, proper application and efficient use of the resources, and achieving returns on the resources that are acceptable to the owners. Note that by 'fiduciary' we mean that the directors are required to act in good faith in the best interests of the business, avoiding conflict with personal interests.

- **Profitability of the entity's activities** within the constraints of the entity's own norms on risk levels, steady growth and customer satisfaction. Profitability is paramount because losses erode the capital base of the entity and may, in time, jeopardize its very existence. Profitability is one of the measures used for assessing stewardship.

- **Liquidity** provides the means to satisfy debts and to achieve financial adaptability. It is gauged on the basis of the ability of the entity to meet its bills as and when they fall due, and to find the resources to avail itself of profit-making opportunities. SoP defines 'financial adaptability' as the entity's 'ability to take effective action to alter the amount and timing of its cash flows so that it can respond to unexpected needs or opportunities'. If liquidity is weak, then this will ring alarm bells with suppliers and loan creditors with regard to the creditworthiness of the entity, and inhibit profitability by both having to miss out on profit-making opportunities and having to incur high costs to find a means of meeting its bills.

- **Solvency**, which is the ability of the entity, in the event that it is wound up, to meet in full all claims on its resources. If the entity is a limited liability company, then solvency requires close attention because the owners' obligation to meet claims against the entity is restricted to the amount they agreed to contribute to the entity.

- **National goals and public welfare**, which an entity is obliged to seek in order to maintain its customer loyalty, social image and a conducive operating environment. National goals that entities may aim at include geographically balanced growth of the country, welfare of the disabled, and preservation of the national identity and its moral values. Public welfare is advanced by protecting the environment, providing employment, conserving foreign exchange holdings, improving the local or national standard of living, and so on.

- **Employee welfare** has to be secured to reap the benefits of staff contentment and avoid difficulties such as those arising from industrial action. The extent to which an entity secures the welfare of its staff may be gauged not only on the basis of remuneration levels but also taking into account other aspects of interest to employees, such as:
  - the rate of staff turnover;
  - training and staff development facilities and promotional prospects;
  - work ethics, office atmosphere and staff motivation;
  - debt relief;
  - facilities for airing grievances;
  - participation in the management process.

24.2.3 The information needs of stakeholders are not congruent

SoP declares that 'the objective of financial statements is to provide information that is useful to those for whom they are prepared'. The same set of financial statements is expected to satisfy the information needs of a variety of stakeholders (as identified in Section 24.2.1). The problem is that their interests are not always congruent. For example:

- A supplier considering an entity's application for credit would find the annually prepared financial statements inadequate for the purpose and would have to fall back on reports of credit protection agencies.
- A bank, placed in similar circumstances, would find it necessary to insist additionally on special-purpose reports containing management reports, budgets and monthly cash-flow forecasts.
- The information needs of different stakeholders may even be in conflict. A bank, for example, may prefer the borrower's balance sheet to be prepared on a break-up value basis in order to assess the security for the loan; an investor, on the other hand, is more interested in one prepared on the going concern basis.

The authors suggest that the primary, secondary and tertiary focus of each group of stakeholders in different areas of interest could probably be as stated below:

Stakeholders	Stewardship	Profitability	Liquidity	Solvency	National goals	Employee welfare
1. Investors	Primary	Primary	Secondary	Tertiary	Tertiary	Tertiary
2. Lenders	Tertiary	Secondary	Primary	Tertiary	Tertiary	Tertiary
3. Suppliers	Tertiary	Secondary	Primary	Tertiary	Tertiary	Tertiary
4. Employees	Secondary	Secondary	Secondary	Tertiary	Tertiary	Primary
5. Customers[a]	Secondary	Tertiary	Tertiary		Secondary	Tertiary
6. Government[b]	Secondary	Primary	Secondary	Tertiary	Primary	Secondary
7. Public					Primary	

a. Customers' primary interest will be on whether supply is steady and price is competitive.
b. Government's primary interest varies. The primary interest of the revenue-collecting agency is on profit, while that of a regulatory agency is on employee welfare, attainment of national goals and so on.

24.2.4 Satisfying the investors' information needs predominates

General-purpose reports are expected to provide the information on the basis of which the wide range of stakeholders has to make informed economic decisions. We can see from the above that the economic decisions for which different stakeholders require information are not always the same, and different economic decisions require different information. There is, however, a degree of overlap in the information requirements of the different groups, to the extent that all of them are interested, to varying degrees, in the financial performance and financial position of the entity, and the entity's ability to generate cash and respond to unexpected needs and opportunities.

The SoP considers that there is sufficient overlap to assume that if an entity satisfies the information needs of the predominant group, then the information needs of other stakeholders will also be satisfied. It has, accordingly, identified the investors (present and potential) as the defining group and made a rebuttable assumption that meeting the information needs of this group would satisfy those of all others. Other groups of stakeholders should be conscious of this assumption so that, when making their decisions, they would regard the information in financial statements only as a broad frame of reference against which to evaluate more specific information they should obtain.

24.3 INFORMATION TO BE INCLUDED IN FINANCIAL STATEMENTS

24.3.1 Information of relevance

Information that should be included in financial statements because they are of relevance for assessing the main areas of interest to a cross-section of stakeholders is that which is relevant to an assessment of the following:

Topic	Performance in each period	Financial position	Generation and use of cash
1. Stewardship	X	X	X
2. Profitability	X	X	
3. Liquidity/financial adaptability		X	X
4. Solvency	X	X	X

Supplementary information useful for the assessment of the above areas and others necessary for assessing the entity's efforts at securing national goals and employees' welfare would be stated in other financial reports.

Interaction 24.2

Information needs of a loan creditor

In support of its application for a £60 million loan, Presage plc has submitted its Balance Sheets and Cash Flow Statements for the preceding five years to the organization considering the loan. The financier has called also for:

(a) the Profit and Loss accounts for the same period;
(b) the break-up value of the company's freehold premises and machinery;
(c) the corporate plan, the management budgets and the cash-flow forecasts for the next year.

The managing director of Presage plc is reluctant to provide this information, being of the opinion that:

1. the Profit and Loss accounts should be of no concern to a financier because the loan, together with interest, is payable irrespective of the company's performance;
2. break-up values are irrelevant because the company is expected to remain in operational existence for a long time; and
3. corporate plans, management budgets and cash-flow forecasts are sensitive and prepared only for internal use and should not be disclosed.

Required: Advise the managing director.

24.3.2 Qualitative characteristics

The accountant's aim is to produce a general-purpose report that presents a true and fair view of the performance during an accounting period and the financial position on the last day of that period. The ultimate test on whether to include accounting information in a financial statement is, therefore, whether the inclusion of the information is necessary in order to achieve a true and fair view.

To convey a true and fair view, the financial statements should contain information 'sufficient in quantity and quality to satisfy the reasonable expectations of the readers to whom [it is] addressed'.[2] We suggest that this overall quality could be achieved if the information included in the financial statement possesses certain qualities as follows:

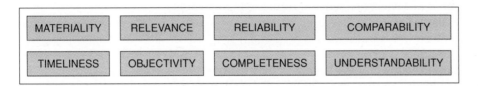

To place these qualities in proper perspective, the SoP structures them as follows:

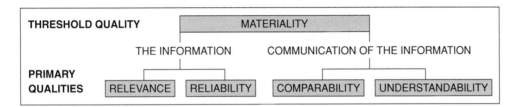

Relevance requires information to be timely; reliability requires information to be objective and complete. When determining the relevance and reliability of information to be included in financial statements, there has to be a trade-off, taking into account both the timeliness of preparing the information and the cost/benefit balance in doing so.

Materiality

Materiality is the threshold criterion for determining whether or not information should be included in a financial statement. Inclusion of immaterial information would result in clutter, which would impair understandability. An item of information is material if its mis-statement or omission might reasonably be expected to influence economic decisions or assessment of stewardship. Whether information is material depends on its nature and size:

- The *nature* of the information relates to its relevance to decisions likely to be made, taking into account factors such as legality, sensitivity, normality, potential consequences, and the identity of the parties involved.
- The *size* is comparative and is determined by use of professional judgement, taking into consideration factors such as those stated in the box on the right.

> Materiality of size may have to be gauged in comparison with:
>
> 1. the items in the whole report;
> 2. the size of related items;
> 3. its significance within the transaction it relates to;
> 4. comparative figure of earlier years;
> 5. the size it was expected to be.

Relevance

Relevance is the usefulness of that information for making economic decisions. The usefulness could arise because of the significance of the information for:

- confirming or correcting past evaluations and assessments;
- evaluating or assessing the present;
- predicting the future.

Reliability

For the information to be reliable it should:

- faithfully represent reality (taking into account the substance of transactions and the commercial effect of a series of connected transactions);
- be neutral – i.e. be free from deliberate or systematic bias intended to influence decisions;
- be free from material error;
- be complete (within the bounds of materiality);
- be prudent – so that, in conditions of uncertainty, a degree of caution should be used when making estimates and exercising judgement.

Comparability

To facilitate decision making, the information should be prepared and presented in such a way that it is comparable both over time within the entity and with that of other similar entities. The comparability is achieved through:

- consistency throughout the entity, within each accounting period and from one period to the next and also between different entities; and
- disclosure of accounting policies for the purpose of ascertaining consistency and making comparisons despite inconsistencies.

Understandability

Understandability is whether the users of financial statements will be able to perceive the significance of the information. That depends on:

- the way the information is presented (e.g. reported as assets, liabilities, income and expenditure; included within clusters of kindred nature; classified into subgroups such as fixed and current assets; and reported in a structured format);
- the capability of the users (assuming that users have a reasonable knowledge of the business, economic activities and accounting and that the users are willing to study the information with reasonable diligence).

Interaction 24.3	**Conflict between qualities of information**
	'Relevance' and 'reliability' are accorded equal primary status as qualitative characteristics of information to be included in financial statements.
	Required: Discuss the possibility of conflict between the two qualities and how such conflict should be resolved.

24.4 THE ELEMENTS OF FINANCIAL STATEMENTS

We have seen that transactions can be aggregated and classified. This process is based on separating items into elements.

24.4.1 Definition of elements

The following are the elements that are recognized within the financial statements, with a brief definition of each:

- **Assets:** rights or other access to future economic benefits controlled by an entity as a result of past transactions or events (see Chapter 15);
- **Liabilities:** obligations of an entity to transfer economic benefits as a result of past transactions or events (see Chapter 18);
- **Ownership interest:** the residual amount found by deducting all of the entity's liabilities from all of the entity's assets, normally consisting of the net amount of capital that the owners have contributed, plus gains less distributions and losses;
- **Contributions from owners:** increases in ownership interest resulting from transfers from owners in their capacity as owners;
- **Distributions to owners:** decreases in ownership interest resulting from transfers to owners in their capacity as owners.
- **Gains and losses:** increases in ownership interest not resulting from contributions from owners (gains) and decreases in ownership interest not resulting from a distribution to the owners (losses). Assuming that there are no contributions from or distribution to owners, any increase in assets not matched by an increase in liabilities is reported as a gain.

Assets, liabilities and ownership interest are included in the Balance Sheet; gains and losses are included in the performance statement (which we know as the Profit and Loss account).

Elements of financial statement

Interaction
24.4

Resources of Sally Smith's shop were as follows in the years stated:

	31.12.20X0	31.12.20X1
Fixed assets at cost less depreciation	£256,400	£314,800
Stock in trade at cost	£124,500	£168,200
Trade debtors	£64,600	£89,500
Trade creditors	£82,400	£78,600
Bank balance	–	£26,200
Bank overdraft	£16,600	–
10% loan	£80,000	£60,000

You are also informed that Sally took £200 per week regularly from the business for her own expenses and on 7 September 20X1 introduced into the business £100,000 received as a legacy from her deceased father.

Required:

(a) Set out the elements in appropriate financial statements so as to report the performance in the year ended 31 December 20X1 and the position of the shop as at that date and one year earlier.
(b) Compare the contents of the performance report prepared as the answer to (a) with the Profit and Loss account that a trader usually prepares.

24.4.2 Recognition of an element and its changes

Recognition of an element in a financial statement is both the depiction of the 'elements' in a financial statement by words and by monetary amounts and the inclusion of the amount in the statement totals. The SoP advocates as follows.

Initial recognition of asset/liability

Initial recognition may be made if there is both an element certainty (i.e. sufficient evidence of the existence of the asset or liability) and a measurement certainty (i.e. a sufficiently reliable measure of its monetary value). Transactions involving the provision of services and goods for net gain are recognized on the occurrence of the critical event in the operating cycle. See Chapter 25 for a fuller coverage of the whole topic of revenue recognition.

The SoP adopts a Balance Sheet approach to revenue recognition when it insists that 'the starting point to the recognition process is the effect the transaction or other event involved has had on the reporting entity's assets and liabilities, because it is the assets and liabilities that demonstrate the lasting effect of changes in other elements'.[3] It concedes, however, that 'the notions of matching and the critical event in the operating cycle will often help in identifying these effects'.[4]

What triggers the recognition of an asset or a liability is usually a transaction. However, the trigger could as well be *any* event, such as the passage of time, a fire, a discovery, a court's verdict, and so on. The trigger may:

- create a new or additional asset or liability;
- provide evidence for recognition of an asset or liability already in existence;
- signal the need to amend the record (measurement or description or classification).

Subsequent re-measurement

This involves changing the amount at which an already recognized asset/liability is stated in the financial statements.

Derecognition

This is the cessation of recognition when either the asset/liability no longer exists or the recognition criteria (stated above) are no longer met.

24.4.3 Measurement of an element

Measurement of an element to be included in a financial statement involves the selection of an appropriate base for measurement and the measurement of the asset/liability on the chosen base. We will consider each of these.

Selection of the appropriate base for measurement

Assets and liabilities may be measured in one of the following bases:

- the historical cost system, which measures assets and liabilities at their historical cost;
- the current value system, which measures assets and liabilities at current values;
- the mixed measurement system (referred to also as the modified historical cost system), which measures some categories of assets/liabilities on historical cost and others at current value, as appropriate in the circumstances surrounding each category.

The SoP favours the mixed measurement system on the premise that information provided under this system is more relevant for decision making.

Measurement of the asset/liability on the chosen base

Initial measurement is the measurement for the first recognition of an asset or liability. Where, as is usually the case, an asset is acquired or a liability is assumed as a result of transactions carried out at fair value (usually referred to as 'arm's-length transactions'), the measurement will be at transaction cost (which is assumed to be the fair value of the transaction). Where the asset/liability is acquired on the basis of other transactions or as a result of other events, the initial measurement will be at current value (which is explained below).

A limited amount of subsequent re-measurement of assets/liabilities also usually takes place. Although an entity opting to report its elements at historical cost could continue with the amount at which they were initially measured (subject to adjustments such as depreciation), for the purpose of making the information more relevant to the needs of users a limited amount of re-measurement usually takes place. Such a re-measurement is needed, for example, to ensure that an asset is not reported at more than its recoverable amount.

If an entity opts to measure its assets/liabilities (or selected categories of assets/liabilities) at current values, re-measurements are necessary to ensure that the reporting is at up-to-date current values. The current value, in the case of an asset, is the 'value to the business', which is the loss the entity would suffer if it were deprived of the asset. So long as the asset could be used profitably within the business, the amount recoverable from the use of the asset will exceed the cost of replacing the asset. In such circumstances the current value of the asset is its replacement cost. On the other hand, if the cost of replacing the asset exceeds the amount recoverable from its most profitable use, the current value of the asset is (see box above) the higher of:

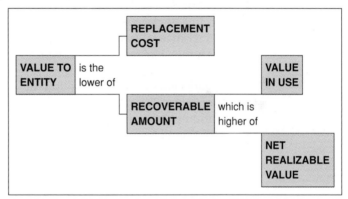

(a) the amount, net of disposal expenses, realizable on the asset's disposal;
(b) the present value of the amounts that are expected to arise from the continued use of the asset and its ultimate disposal.

The current value of a liability is the lowest amount at which the entity could divest itself of the obligation involved (i.e. the minimum payable for settling the liability).

24.5 PRESENTATION OF FINANCIAL INFORMATION

Financial statements, together with supporting notes, are the primary vehicles for communicating financial information to those who have a legitimate claim for such information. To enhance the usefulness of the information for decision making, the SoP advocates that the presentation of information should pay attention to the following eight points:

1. The objective of presentation should be to communicate clearly and effectively and in as simple and straightforward a manner as is possible without loss of relevance and reliability and without significantly increasing the length.

2. The financial statements should be highly structured and aggregated. Instead of communicating a mass of detail that obscures the message, the presentation of the statements should involve interpretation, simplification, abstraction and aggregation, with a view to:
   - conveying information which would otherwise have been obscured;
   - highlighting the most significant items and their relationships;
   - enhancing comparability and understandability.

3. Items that are similar should be classified together and distinguished from dissimilar ones, so as to highlight similarities and relationships.

4. In the statement of financial performance (the Profit and Loss account), with a view to enhancing the assessment of performance and the predictive value of the information, the components should be clearly demarcated in accordance with:
   - the nature, cause and function;
   - relative continuity (possibility of recurrence);
   - stability, risk, predictability;
   - reliability.

   Furthermore, there should be an identification of:
   - amounts affected by changes in economic conditions and business activity;
   - items unusual in amount or incidence;
   - expenses related primarily to the profits of future periods.

5. In the statement of financial position (the Balance Sheet), the entity's resource structure should be delineated – showing major classes of assets, their function, those held on a continuing basis and liquidity of available resources; and the entity's financial structure should be made clear – showing ownership interest as well as major classes of liability, with information on their nature, amounts and timing.

6. In the Cash Flow Statement, the extent of cash generation and use by the entity's activities (differentiating those related to operations from others) should be shown.

7. Supporting notes to financial statements are an integrated part of the financial statements and should amplify and explain the information on the financial statements. However, a disclosure in the notes is not a substitute for recognition as an element in the financial statements, nor can it justify misrepresentation in, or omission from, the financial statement.

8. Other accompanying information, such as five-year trend information, operating and financial reviews, the directors' report, and the chairman's statement, may complement information in the financial statements.

References

1. *The Scope and Implications of the Conceptual Framework Project* (1967), FASB, Stanford, Conn.
2. *Statement of Principles for Financial Reporting* (December 1999), paragraph 12 of the Introduction.
3. *Statement of Principles, ibid.*, para 5.4.
4. *Statement of Principles, ibid.*, para 5.27.

SOLUTIONS TO INTERACTIVE QUESTIONS

IQ 24.1 Limitations of financial statements

Traditional financial statements are intended to serve two main objectives. The first is as a vehicle for discharging stewardship. The second is as a basis for making informed economic decisions. On both counts the financial statements are inadequate for the following four reasons:

1. The financial statements are only capable of reporting the financial effects of transactions and events. These statements do not communicate non-financial effects, which are nonetheless valuable for assessment of performance and position.
2. The information contained in financial statements is largely historical and fails to reflect future possibilities that could enhance or impair the entity's performance and financial position and are, therefore, of inadequate significance for decision making.
3. Since the natural operating cycle of an entity does not always coincide with its accounting periods, the financial statements relating to the accounting periods have necessarily to be prepared on the basis of allocating continuous operations to discrete accounting periods, and of sorting uncertainties remaining at the end of each period by making assumptions and estimates. These requirements introduce an element of conjecture, subjectivity and tentativeness to the performance and financial position stated in financial statements.
4. Financial statements, by their very nature, convey their message in numerical terms. This message may not be meaningful unless it is interpreted and placed into context by a description of the business environment, the features of the market and the strategies adopted by the entity. Such descriptions can only be provided in additional narrative reports.

IQ 24.2 Information needs of a loan creditor

1. Admittedly, the primary interest of a loan creditor will be in the area of the entity's liquidity because the entity's ability to pay interest at agreed intervals and repay capital on the due dates would depend on the liquidity of its resources. Nevertheless the loan creditor would be concerned also with profitability because inadequacy in that area will, over time, erode liquidity and may imperil the existence of the entity and its continuing capacity to service the loan.
2. Financial statements are prepared on the assumption that the entity will remain in operational existence for the foreseeable future. This is because those to whom financial statements are intended require financial information from that perspective for making their decisions. A loan creditor, however, is concerned with the security available in the unlikely event of a winding-up and requires for that purpose information on the break-up value of the entity's resources.
3. Although, in theory, the financial statements are prepared to communicate information of interest to a cross-section of (seven) groups of stakeholders, in practice it caters mainly to the interest of investors. The draft Statement of Principles identifies the investors as the defining group and makes the presumption that 'focus on the interest that investors have . . . will, in effect also be focusing on the common interest that all users have . . .'. Although a loan creditor shares with the investor interests in such areas as profitability and liquidity, the degree of assurance that a loan creditor requires with regard to future prospects is usually greater than that sought by the investor. An investor is usually content with an ability to forecast the future prospects on the basis of the current performance. A loan creditor, on the other hand, requires more positive evidence of (a) how the entity plans to perform in future, seeking evidence of this from copies of corporate plans and management budgets, and (b) the entity's ability to meet its commitments within prescribed time-frames, seeking assurance of this from cash forecasts.

IQ 24.3 Conflict between qualities of information

The following provide some instances of conflict between the relevance of information and the reliability of information:

1. To report the financial position of an entity and, reciprocally, its performance, information on all its assets and liabilities would be relevant. Yet one (or more) of these elements may have to be left out of financial statements because of uncertainty about its existence or measurement.

2. Awaiting a resolution of uncertainties would imperil timeliness of information because out-of-date information would be irrelevant for decision making.
3. Reliability of information demands neutrality as well as prudence, and these two may be mutually conflicting. Neutrality is freedom from deliberate and systematic bias; prudence requires a deliberate effort at conservatism when reporting performance.

The SoP identifies these conflicts and suggests that in the event of conflict between relevance and reliability, financial statements should use 'the most relevant of whichever information is reliable'. It also suggests that the tension between neutrality and prudence should be 'resolved by finding a balance that ensures that deliberate and systematic understatement of assets or gains and overstatement of liabilities or losses do not occur'.

IQ 24.4 Elements of financial statement

(a) Financial statements

BALANCE SHEET AS AT 31 DECEMBER		
	20X0	**20X1**
Assets:	£	£
Fixed assets at w.d.v	256,400	314,800
Stock in trade	124,500	168,200
Trade debtors	64,600	89,500
Bank balance	–	26,200
Liabilities:		
Trade creditors	(82,400)	(78,600)
Bank overdraft	(16,600)	–
10% Loan	(80,000)	(60,000)
Ownership Interest	266,500	460,100

PERFORMANCE STATEMENT FOR THE YEAR ENDED 3 DECEMBER 20X1	
	£
Gains in the year	104,000

WORKING:	£
Ownership interest on 31.12.20X1	460,100
Ownership interest on 31.12.20X0	(266,500)
Increase in ownership interest	193,600
Add: Drawings 52 weeks @ £200	10,400
Less: Capital contribution	(100,000)
Gains in the year to 31.12.20X1	104,000

(b) The Performance Statement identifies the results of the entity's performance in the year from the Balance Sheet perspective. The gain (or loss) in a period is arrived at as the increase (or decrease) in the ownership interest, which in turn is arrived at by deducting the liabilities from the assets. This approach fails to:

● identify the nature of the activities that gave rise to revenue;
● classify the components of expenses incurred during the operating activity;
● draw attention to non-operating expenses (such as the 10 per cent interest paid on the loan);
● convey information (such as items of unusual size or incidence) necessary for using the performance in the year as the basis for predicting future prospects.

## Chapter 25

REVENUE RECOGNITION

In this chapter

We will learn of the point and the amount at which earnings may be recognized for accounting

25.1 DEFINITION AND DISCUSSION

'Revenue' is defined in the Concise Oxford Dictionary as 'income'. Income may be earned or gained. It is earned if it arises from a business activity and gained if it arises in other ways, for example from a legacy received by a charity. Income, whether earned or gained, is associated with an inflow of an asset, often in the form of cash. 'Revenue recognition' is the determination of both the point and the amount at which income is to be recognized for accounting purposes.

The problems relating to revenue recognition arise mainly because of the substitution of the venture concept by the time interval rule. Every business has its own revenue-earning cycle. For example, for a farmer the cycle would be the time between getting the field ready and reaping the harvest, which might be three to five months depending on the crop. A bridge construction business may, on the other hand, take several years to complete a task. If each of these businesses adopted the venture concept, the farmer would prepare his accounts after the crop was harvested and the bridge builder after the bridge was constructed. In each case, at the point of accounting, all transactions relating to the venture would have been completed, and all uncertainties relating to the venture would have been resolved.

When the time interval rule replaces the venture concept, the problem confronted is that the accounting period rarely coincides with the revenue-earning cycle. As a result, there could be incomplete transactions at the point of reporting. This gives rise to many problems, as discussed below.

25.1.1 The problem of recognizing income when the *production* process is incomplete

When the income-generating activity (say the production of goods) cuts across more than one accounting period, how much of the income is to be regarded as being earned in each period?

One solution to the problem is to recognize a proportion of the total expected profit on the basis of the efforts made during each period, even though substantial uncertainties remain as regards measurement of the total profit and the timing of the cash inflow as income. For example, if an entity builds a house estimating that it would cost £150,000 to build and could be sold for at least £50,000 profit, then, if it spends £75,000 during the period, it may recognize half that profit in the accounting period and report income for the accounting period as £100,000, so that in comparison with the expenditure (£75,000) profit is recognized as £25,000.

An alternative solution might be to delay recognition of the income until the income-generating activity is fully completed so that (when the house is sold) there would be a resolution of significant uncertainties such as those relating to measurement of the accomplishment and receipt of the proceeds.

25.1.2 The problem of measuring income when the *sale* process is incomplete

Where the income-generating activity is the sale of goods, how much of the total income arising from a single venture, which cuts across several accounting periods, may be recognized as earned within an accounting period? To illustrate, let us assume that an entity purchased 300 logs of fine ebony at £200 per log. Within the accounting period, it sold 200 logs at £300 each. Demand is buoyant and it is reasonably certain that the remainder can be sold at the same price. The whole venture is expected to yield a profit of £100 per log on 300 logs, namely £30,000. The problem is how much of that profit should be recognized within the current accounting period.

The normal solution would be to recognize the profit only in respect of the logs sold within the period, ignoring those relating to the logs in hand until they too are realized. Another solution is to recognize within a period also at least a part of the profit relating to unsold logs, perhaps on the premise that these logs improved in value during the period because of the impact of time on the logs.

If the entity opts for the normal solution, it has still to confront the problem of determining the precise point at which the sale takes place. This is because the movement of goods does not always correspond in time-scale with the movement of title (ownership) and the proceeds; and, further, terms and covenants may be built into the transaction, making it completely different in commercial reality from what it appears to be on the face of it or in legal form.

25.1.3 The problem of recognizing income when there are outstanding commitments

The accounting recognition of income received in the period may have to be deferred, at least partially, to a future period because a portion of income may relate to efforts yet to be made and expenses yet to be incurred. This applies, for example, to products sold with a promise of after-care or with a maintenance guarantee, and to subscriptions received in advance for periodicals yet to be produced.

25.2 RELEVANCE OF ACCOUNTING CONCEPTS

The approach to be adopted for revenue recognition should be founded on the accepted accounting concepts, including the following:

- **Money measurement**. To be accountable, the income must be measurable in terms of money. For example, a charity would be unable to account for the participation of a popular film star in a fund-raising event because of its inability to measure in terms of money the value of the film star's efforts.
- **Accruals**. If we were to abandon the accruals rule, opting instead to account for income on the basis of receipts (and expenses on the basis of payments), most problems involved in revenue recognition would be overcome. It is the commitment to recognizing income on the basis of accomplishments (rather than cash inflow) that

requires the determination of the precise point at which, and the manner in which, the accomplishments are measured for the purpose of accounting.

- **Prudence**. The prudence convention is paramount for determining the point of revenue recognition. Prudence demands that revenue should not be recognized in respect of incomplete transactions until all major uncertainties involved are substantially resolved or are capable of reliable measurement.
- **Objectivity**. For the purpose of maintaining objectivity, accounting is usually transaction-based, so that the amount to be recognized is established by an arm's-length market transaction. Objectivity is paramount for safeguarding the credibility of the accounting information.
- **Consistency**. Consistency in the approach taken to revenue recognition is paramount if the performance in a period is to be compared over time. For example, where the income-earning process progresses through distinct stages and it is possible to recognize revenue, with equal justification, at more than one of these stages, what is crucial is whether the practice adopted for revenue recognition remains consistent from period to period.
- **Substance over form**. If an entity habitually recognizes income on the basis of completed sales, there needs to be a critical review of the terms of what appears to be a sale to ensure that the revenue-earning process has in fact been completed. The terms, contained in what appears legally to be a sale, may well retain to the seller substantial rewards and risks related to the item sold.

25.3 THE MAIN APPROACHES

In compliance with accepted accounting concepts, the accountancy profession has recognized three alternative approaches to revenue recognition, as follows:

- the critical event approach;
- the accretion approach;
- the revenue allocation approach.

Each is discussed further below.

25.3.1 The critical event approach

The income earning process may involve a cycle of any or all of nine related stages, as shown in the box (though not necessarily in that sequence).

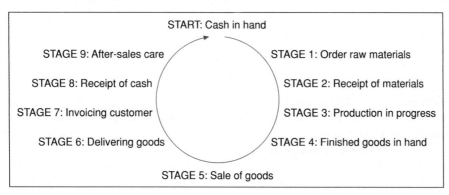

The critical event approach assumes that, at a particular stage in the cycle, a crucial decision is made or a critical action taken that is acceptable as an appropriate basis to recognize revenue. The criteria applied under this approach to identify such an event are that the income should have been substantially earned at the stage selected, and that any uncertainty remaining at that stage should be capable of estimation with sufficient accuracy that it could be taken into account when measuring the revenue. For identifying that stage, several factors are taken into account, including the following:

- the terms of the agreement between the parties;
- the custom of trade and practices followed in the type of business;
- the provisions in the applicable law as well as case law.

Let us now consider each of the above stages to assess whether it might be appropriate as the critical event that triggers revenue recognition:

Stage 1: Placing an order with a supplier to acquire materials

At this stage in the cycle there will be no accounting entries because there would have been no transactions involving money or money's worth. The stage is unlikely to trigger revenue recognition because there would remain substantial uncertainty on matters such as the cost of production, selling the product, the sale price achievable and collectability of any credit sale. Would the situation change if the acquisition of material was specifically for meeting a firm order from a customer? The existence of a firm order would resolve major uncertainties in respect of finding a customer and the measurement of the income. Yet substantial uncertainties would remain such as those relating to whether and when production will be completed, and at what cost.

Stage 2: Receipt of materials from the supplier

The business will now hold stock in its warehouse and the transactions involved would have been accounted for. But, as regards revenue recognition, the same considerations apply to this stage as at Stage 1.

Stage 3: Production in progress

While the production process is still ongoing, the uncertainties as to whether the production could be completed and at what cost will still remain. In addition, there are uncertainties as to whether a customer could be found, the sale price achievable and the collectability of the proceeds. However, where the production is to meet a firm order and where the production process cuts across more than one accounting period, as in the case of long-term contracts, revenue recognition takes place as each stage of production is completed.

Stage 4: Production process completed

If the business is producing finished goods to hold in its warehouse as stock to meet customer orders as they arise, then uncertainty still remains as to the possibility of achieving a sale, as to the selling price, and as to whether the proceeds can be collected. Therefore there cannot be any revenue recognition. On the other hand, in a transaction in which the greatest uncertainty concerns production, the completion of production could be the critical event triggering the revenue recognition. By that stage the uncertainties as to whether the goods could be produced and at what cost will have been resolved. If the further uncertainties regarding whether a buyer could be found and the selling price achievable can also be resolved, then revenue can be recognized. Such a situation would apply, for example, when:

- production is against a firm order;
- the product might be a mined precious metal, the sale of which is virtually certain at a price fixed in the international market; or
- the products are periodicals produced in respect of subscriptions that have been received in advance.

Stage 5: The sale of goods

This stage is commonly regarded as the crucial stage for revenue recognition for most trading transactions. This is because selling resolves the most crucial of a trader's uncertainties, which are whether a buyer can be found and the price at which the item can be sold. The uncertainties that remain at this stage (such as whether the sales may be rescinded and goods returned, and whether the proceeds will be received) are usually capable of reasonable estimation. This would not be the case, however, where the sale contract permits the buyer to rescind the contract within a stipulated period or where the contract includes commitment to onerous after-sales care. A problem with revenue recognition at this stage, however, is the identification of the precise point at which the sale is completed. The UK's Sale of Goods Act 1979 provides that the ownership of goods passes from the seller to the buyer when all of certain conditions (stated in the box here) are met. The invoicing and delivery of goods are not crucial to the revenue-recognizing process.

> 1. A contract of sale is made;
> 2. Goods are physically capable of immediate delivery;
> 3. This position is notified to the buyer.

Stage 6: The delivery of the goods

The common practice in the United Kingdom is to recognize revenue at the point of delivering the goods to customers. This is the position approved in the United States as well.[1] In real life, delivering the goods into the custody of the customer is accepted as the cut-off point at which the sale may be *prudently* regarded as having taken place. It also satisfies the accounting concepts in that the transaction may be *measured in monetary terms* and the income measurement is *objective*, having been agreed with a third party at arm's length. Some uncertainties remain with regard to the collection of the sales proceeds and the cost of after-sales service, but these are usually capable of reasonable estimation on the basis of past experience.

Stage 7: Raising an invoice for a credit sale

In the UK this is regarded as a mere routine procedure to confirm to the customer the terms of the sale and is usually not considered a critical event for revenue recognition. Outside the United Kingdom, however, this stage is commonly regarded as the revenue recognition stage in most trading transactions.

Stage 8: Receiving sale proceeds

Unless the debt is time-barred and cannot be legally enforced, due process of the law normally assures the collection of sale proceeds. The collection of proceeds could, however, replace Stage 6 as the critical event triggering revenue recognition in cases such as where sales are made to overseas customers (particularly in countries with exchange restrictions) or where considerations of professional etiquette prevent pursuit through legal process of bills for services performed.

Stage 9: After-sales care

The costs involved in after-sales care could well be substantial (in cases such as the sale of vehicles and in respect of rectification work arising from civil engineering contracts). Yet revenue recognition is usually not delayed until this stage because the costs that could arise are capable of measurement on the basis of past experience and can therefore be taken account of when recognizing revenue.

| Interaction 25.1 | Illustration of the critical event approach |

Ajit Singh commenced business on 1.1.20X0 producing a single product, a high-quality drawing-room suite. He sells each suite for £1,250 to retailers on one month's credit. The demand for his product exceeded supply. His activities during the first year are summarized as follows:

ACTIVITIES OF AJIT SINGH IN THE YEAR ENDED 31.12.20X0				
Stage	Activity completed	Units	Unit cost	Unit MV
1.	Acquisition of raw materials	320	£225	£225
2.	Construction/assembly of carcass	290	£540	£675
3.	Completion of upholstery	260	£680	£920
4.	Lacquer coating, polishing, finishing	240	£750	£1,250
5.	Sale of the finished product	200	£750	£1,250
6.	Delivery of the finished product	190	£750	£1,250
7.	Invoicing of units delivered	185	£750	£1,250
8.	Receipt of the sale proceeds	145	£750	£1,250

Unit cost: this does not include carriage outwards and the expenses of issuing invoices and receipts.
MV: market value is the net amount realizable at that stage of completion, based on a comparison with competitors.

Ajit provides also the following information:

1. Customers have yet to pay for 40 units because these were delivered to them within a month of the year end.
2. Five units, delivered on 31.12.20X0, were not invoiced until the next day.
3. Delivery and invoicing were delayed on ten units sold on 31.12.20X0 because of a transport breakdown.
4. Forty units, completed by 31.12.20X0, were sold within the next three days.

Ajit claims that his profit for the year is £128,850, calculated as follows:

	Profit per suite (£)		Total (£)
190 suites delivered by 31.12.20X0	500	:	95,000
10 more suites delivered next day	500	:	5,000
40 more suites completed in current year	500	:	20,000
20 more suites completed to stage 3	240	:	4,800
30 more suites completed to stage 2	135	:	4,050
			128,850

Required:

(a) Would you agree with Ajit's claim?
(b) Identify the circumstances in which Ajit could recognize revenue on any part of his unsold stock of completed or partially completed suites.

25.3.2 The accretion approach

Instead of awaiting a critical event to trigger revenue recognition, the accretion approach allows revenue to be recognized as the value of the product improves, either on the basis of the continuing production process or the passage of time. This approach is not consistent with the transactions approach adopted in historical cost accounting because there is no objective and verifiable arm's-length transaction with a third party. This approach to revenue recognition is, however, accepted accounting practice in three specific areas as follows:

1. **Where income is earned by permitting others the use of one's asset.** Depending on the terms of the contract and the established custom of trade, income is recognized on a time basis to the extent that time enhances the claim against the other party. This would be the case with regard to interest earned on loans, rent earned on premises let out, and royalties earned on a patent or copyright assigned to others. The recognition of income would be permitted provided any remaining uncertainties (such as the collectibility of the dues) are capable of reliable estimation.
2. **Where income recognized is on long-term contracts.** SSAP 9, *Stocks and Long-term Contracts*, requires the adoption of the accretion approach in respect of long-term contracts, recognizing revenue as progress is made with the efforts.
3. **Where income arises from natural growth or ageing.** Some products improve in value because of the passage of time. This would be the case with timber, spirits and wine, all of which mature with age. It would also be the case with growing crops and livestock. The accretion approach to recognizing income is adopted in these cases provided the following conditions are met:
   - the product should have a verifiable market value at different stages of its growth;
   - there should not remain any significant uncertainty other than those that can be reliably measured;
   - the revenue recognition is for the purpose of reporting the earnings and not for the purpose of distributing the amount earned, because the distribution has to await the realization of the earning.

Illustration of the accretion approach   Interaction 25.2

Tim Dole raised capital of £50,000 in cash from four friends, to invest in 3,250 casks of vintage wine. He is convinced that these casks, if held in storage for ten years, should realize at least £150,000. Pressed by the friends for a report of his performance by the end of the first year, he feels entitled to report as profit in the year one-tenth of the amount anticipated, by reporting the casks in storage at £60,000.

Required: Advise him on whether this is permitted under currently accepted accounting practice.

25.3.3 The revenue allocation approach

This is a combination of the other two approaches. For example, an entity adopting the critical event approach to revenue recognition, if confronted with substantial uncertainty (say with regard to onerous after-sales service or the possibility that the sale may be rescinded) at the stage when it usually recognizes revenue, would adopt one of two solutions as follows:

- adhere to the critical event approach, making the best possible estimation of the uncertainty; or

- adopt the revenue allocation approach, allocating appropriate portions of revenue between, for instance, the sales activity and the after-sales activity.

Reference

1. FAS 48 *Revenue Recognition When Right of Return Exists*.

SOLUTIONS TO INTERACTIVE QUESTIONS

IQ 25.1 Illustration of the critical event approach

(a) **Ajit's claim of earning a profit of £128,850 for the year is unacceptable** because Ajit should account for his income using the critical event approach. Normally, the critical event in a trading business like his is the sale of furniture. Section 18 of the Sale of Goods Act 1979 does not require delivery of goods as essential for recognizing a sale. Yet, if Ajit wishes to abide by the practice common among traders in the UK, he should recognize sale only at the point of delivery. Accordingly, his profit for the year would be £500 per suite on 190 suites delivered = £95,000. At the point the sale is made, all major uncertainties (such as those in respect of saleability and the amount realizable) are resolved and further uncertainties as remaining are capable of being reliably estimated.

(b) **Revenue recognition on unsold goods is not permitted** because the accretion approach to revenue recognition is not available for application to trading transactions, and the prudence concept would deter any income being recognized until the major uncertainty on finding a buyer is resolved (notwithstanding the fact that, for his products, Ajit's prospects are excellent).

Exceptionally, however, Ajit could recognize profit on the units yet to be sold, in the following circumstances:

- **If his product qualifies for recognition as a long-term contract**. If the units under production are of a substantial size, the production process cuts across more than one accounting period and lasts more than the duration of one accounting period, then the units produced by Ajit will qualify for recognition as long-term work in progress, and under SSAP 9 these units can be valued on the accretion approach.
- **If Ajit's production is based on a firm order**. If goods are produced to order, the critical event triggering the revenue recognition is the completion of production. Hence, if Ajit produces his units only on the basis of firm contracts to produce these units, the uncertainties in respect of saleability and the sale price would be resolved at the point of receiving the order – so that income may be recognized at the point the production is completed but prior to sale, delivery or invoicing. Income on the 50 units yet to be completed cannot be recognized, however, because until the production is completed, the uncertainties relating to the ability to complete and the costs related thereto would remain unresolved.

IQ 25.2 Illustration of the accretion approach

What Tim Dole is proposing to do is to adopt the accretion approach to revenue recognition. Whilst this method, not being transaction-based, is generally discouraged, it is acceptable in activities such as the one Tim is engaged in – because there is accretion of value arising from the ageing process.

Attention should be paid, however, to the following conditions, which must all be satisfied:

- **Active market**. There should be an active market providing prices, by reference to which Tim is able to set the value of wine in stock at £60,000, as he proposes to. In the absence of such a market, there would be no objective measure as to value – Tim's valuation would then have to be subjective, with the possibility of falling anywhere within a wide range, and this would make the valuation unreliable and inappropriate for comparing performance with other similar businesses.
- **Future costs**. It should be possible to estimate the future costs on such matters as the storage and selling of wine.
- **Distribution**. Though income may be recognized for purposes of reporting performance in the year, that income cannot be distributed until the profit is realized upon a sale.

PROGRESSIVE QUESTION

PQ 25.1 A case study

As a financial consultant, your advice is sought on whether and to what extent revenue may be recognized in each of the following independent circumstances:

(a) Your client 'A' publishes medical journals. At the beginning of the first year's trading the business received £15,000 in advance, being a three-year subscription for the journal. It is now preparing its accounts at the end of the first year.

(b) Your client 'B' accepted an order for 5,000 tonnes of sugar and received payment in full of £90,000. The client has placed an order for sugar to satisfy its customers but the sugar was not in stock at the year end.

(c) Your client 'C' received £150,000 for granting a franchise to another company, allowing that company to deal exclusively in the products of C within a defined area for five years.

(d) Your client 'D', a mail-order company, dispatches goods to its customers 'on approval', on terms that the goods may be returned, without obligations, within two weeks of delivery. On the last day of the year, goods with a sales value of £214,600 remained with customers within the approval period.

(e) Your client 'E' sold a machine to a customer on three months' credit, stating on the invoice, in small print, that the title to the goods would remain with E until the goods are paid for. The goods are still to be paid for by the year end.

(f) Your client 'F', a company owning tea estates in Sri Lanka, reports that as at the year end it holds a stock of 3,250 tonnes of *pinkpechoe* highland tea, which realized £297,400 in the following week's London tea auctions. The expenses of realization amounted to £6,000.

Required: Advise your clients as to how to handle these transactions with regard to revenue recognition, giving reasons to support your advice.

Part F

ACCOUNTING IN
DIFFERING CONTEXTS

Chapter 26

SINGLE ENTRY AND INCOMPLETE RECORDS (1)

In this chapter

We will learn:
- the rules of preparing financial statements from incomplete records

and you should be able to:
- report the performance and position of an entity with incomplete records

26.1 THE DIFFERENCE BETWEEN A SINGLE ENTRY SYSTEM AND INCOMPLETE RECORDS

A single entry system of accounting is one in which a transaction is accounted for by just one entry in an appropriate book of accounts, for instance when recording particulars of the family's cash inflows and outflows. Instead of a double entry system, it is more convenient to record every amount received and paid by just a single entry. In contrast, 'incomplete records' is an expression used to refer to a situation where books that were normally maintained on the double entry system have become incomplete for one reason or another – such as negligence or a natural calamity such as a fire. In either case – in one by choice and in the other by accident – the books of account do not provide the double entry aspect that allows us to extract a Trial Balance and finalize the accounts by transferring the income and expenditure ledger balances to a Profit and Loss account and listing the remaining balances in a Balance Sheet.

Confronted with either situation, an entity has to adopt the same approach, namely to do whatever is necessary to analyse the information available to obtain the information normally provided by the double entry system, so that the entity is in a position where it can prepare the Profit and Loss account and the Balance Sheet. We need to remember, however, that there are varying degrees of incompleteness. Hence the procedure to obtain the information normally available from a complete double entry system must depend on the nature of records and the extent of the information actually available.

26.2 INSUFFICIENT INFORMATION FOR A PROFIT AND LOSS ACCOUNT

In an extreme case, the information available may be so scanty as to render futile any efforts at recording the transactions on a double entry basis. For example, there might be no record of amounts received from sales and paid for purchases, which would make it impossible to prepare a Trading account to calculate the gross profit.

All that may be possible, in such a scenario, is to attempt to *estimate* (rather than determine on a double entry basis) the profit (or loss) made within an accounting period. This has to be done by endeavouring to ascertain the owner's capital in the business at the end of a year and comparing it with the capital at the beginning. For example, if the owner's capital in the business at the end of a year was £150,000 and that at the beginning was £100,000, the profit for the year is assumed to be the difference of £50,000.

This assumption of £50,000 profit would be correct unless there had been any drawings or capital introductions during the year. If there had been drawings of £1,000 per month during the year, obviously the capital at the year end, but for the drawings, would have been £162,000 and that would indicate a profit of £62,000 (i.e. £162,000 – £100,000). If, in addition, £5,000 had been introduced during the year as new capital, the year's profit would be £57,000, as calculated here.

	£000
Capital at year end	150
Less: Capital at commencement	(100)
	50
Add: Drawings (£1,000 × 12)	12
Less: Capital introduced	(5)
Profit for the year	57

Interaction 26.1

Inadequate information to recreate a double entry system

Chris Jones, a retailer, is a new client in your accountancy business. At the first interview with Chris on 1.3.20X2, you ascertain that he started trading on 1.1.20X0 but he has failed to maintain proper books of account. You have prepared

	31.12.20X0 £	31.12.20X1 £
Fixed assets at written down value	180,000	215,000
Stock in trade at cost	284,200	326,600
Trade debtors	16,500	21,400
Cash and bank balance	11,400	26,800
Trade creditors	(165,800)	(158,500)

an estimate of the profit for 20X0 and are now required to prepare an estimate for the tax authorities for the year ended 31.12.20X1.

You have been able to gather the following information:

(a) Chris has no source of income other than from his shop.
(b) Considering the style and standard of his living, Chris' monthly living expenses should be at least £1,500.
(c) The assets and liabilities of the shop are ascertained as stated in the box above.

Required: Estimate the shop's profit for the year ended 31 December 20X1; and make a revised estimate of the profit for the year, taking into account the following additional information:

● private education for Chris's three children have cost £24,000 per year;
● Chris bought a luxury car for personal use in September 20X1 for £27,500, disposing of his Toyota for £8,000;
● Chris won £14,500 from the National Lottery in March 20X1 and ploughed it into his business.

26.3 ADEQUATE INFORMATION TO SET UP A DOUBLE ENTRY SYSTEM

The first step for establishing the incomplete accounting records of an entity on a double entry basis is the preparation of a list of assets and liabilities for that entity at the beginning of the period. This list is known as a *Statement of Affairs* because it sets out the state of affairs of the business as at that date and enables the owner's capital to be determined as the difference between the sum of assets and the sum of liabilities.

In appearance and content a Statement of Affairs is identical to a Balance Sheet (see the example here). The difference in principle is that the name 'Balance Sheet' is used only where the books of account are already on a double entry basis, for then the preparation of the Balance Sheet consists merely of listing out the account balances after writing up the Trading and Profit and Loss account. On the other hand, where the records are incomplete, the preparation of a Statement of Affairs could involve exhaustive inquiry and sifting of evidence to ascertain the assets and liabilities existing on that date, and determine the values at which they should be reported.

STATEMENT OF AFFAIRS AS AT 1 JANUARY 20X1		
	£	£
Motor vehicles		60,000
Furniture		24,000
Stock	10,000	
Debtors	18,000	
Cash/bank	6,000	
Creditors	(15,000)	19,000
Capital		103,000

The next step is to open appropriate ledger accounts for each item on the list, placing the values on the correct side – i.e. on the debit side if it is an asset account and on the credit side if it is a liability account. By this stage the books of the entity are already set on a double entry basis.

The transactions of the entity are, thereafter, accounted for on a double entry basis, a Trial Balance is extracted at the year end to ascertain double entry accuracy, and the Trading and Profit and Loss account for the year and a Balance Sheet as at the end of the year are prepared in the usual way.

26.4 FOUR POINTS TO REMEMBER ON INCOMPLETE RECORDS

The four points to remember are set out in this section and discussed.

26.4.1 Remember the basic bookkeeping rule

Every asset account and expenditure account has its balance on the debit side, while every liability account and every income account has its balance on the credit side. A supporting account usually has its balance on the side opposite to the one in which the corresponding main account has its balance.

26.4.2 In incomplete record exercises, certain assumptions are always made

The following assumptions apply unless the data suggest otherwise:

- All purchases and sales, in the normal course of business, are made on credit terms.
- All acquisitions and disposals of fixed assets are made on cash terms.

26.4.3 Ascertain missing information by assembling the information available

This is rather like doing a crossword puzzle where we know some of the letters and are searching for the remaining letters to complete a word. Similarly, when answering an incomplete-record question we have to be aware of the number of different amounts that an account comprises, and by slotting in the amounts stated in the question we can ascertain any missing amount. Let us focus on specific examples to develop this technique.

Calculating sales

A Total Debtors account will comprise, as a minimum, four different amounts, as identified by the numerals one to four on the right. If three of them are stated in the question (or can be ascertained when completing another account) the fourth can be derived as the difference that makes both sides of the account balance. If we assume that the question states the opening balance, sales for the year, and the closing balance of trade debtors as £40,000, £280,000 and £65,000 respectively (see the account on the left), the amount of cash received from all debtors can be derived as £255,000 to make the columns balance.

TOTAL DEBTORS ACCOUNT

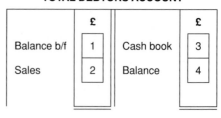

TOTAL DEBTORS ACCOUNT

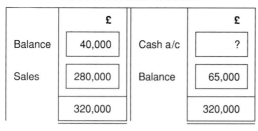

Alternatively, the question may state the opening balance, closing balance and cash takings from debtors as £40,000, £65,000 and £255,000 respectively; and in that case it will be the amount of sales that has to be ascertained as the balancing figure (of £280,000).

TOTAL DEBTORS ACCOUNT

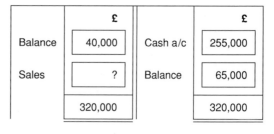

Calculating purchases

The same approach is taken to ascertain the purchases figure. A Total Creditors account will comprise, as a minimum, four different amounts, as stated on the right. If three of them are stated (or can be ascertained when completing another account), the fourth can be derived as the difference to make both sides of the account balance. If, for example, a question states the amounts of the opening creditors balance, the closing balance and the purchases for the year as £20,000, £32,500 and £140,000 respectively (see account on the left), the amount of cash paid to creditors can be derived as £127,500.

TOTAL CREDITORS ACCOUNT

	£		£
Cash a/c	1	Balance	3
Balance	2	Purchases	4

TOTAL CREDITORS ACCOUNT

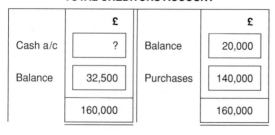

Alternatively the question may state the opening and closing creditors along with the cash paid to them during the year as £20,000, £32,500 and £127,500 respectively, leaving the amount of purchases to be ascertained as £140,000.

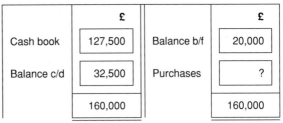

TOTAL CREDITORS ACCOUNT

	£		£
Cash book	127,500	Balance b/f	20,000
Balance c/d	32,500	Purchases	?
	160,000		160,000

The Trading account

Similarly, to complete a Trading account, a minimum of four items are needed. These have been identified by numerals one to four in the *pro forma* account shown below (left). The question marks identify the amounts that can be calculated, if the amounts identified by the numerals are available. For example, if opening stock, purchases, sales and closing stock are stated as £80,000, £360,000, £480,000 and £56,000 respectively (see the Trading account shown below, right), the cost of sales can be calculated as £384,000 and the gross profit as £96,000.

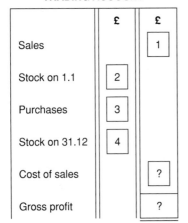

TRADING ACCOUNT

	£	£
Sales		1
Stock on 1.1	2	
Purchases	3	
Stock on 31.12	4	
Cost of sales		?
Gross profit		?

TRADING ACCOUNT

	£000	£000
Sales		480
Stock on 1.1	80	
Purchases	360	
Stock on 31.12	(56)	
Cost of sales		(384)
Gross profit		?

If, out of the four items comprising a Trading account, one is missing (see, for example, the Trading account set out on the right), then we cannot make progress unless we are provided with a clue for the purpose. One such clue could be that the business effects all its sales at standard prices calculated to produce a profit margin of 25 per cent of cost. We already know that one-quarter of cost is the same as one-fifth of sales. With the help of that clue we can proceed to complete the Trading account as follows:

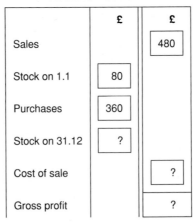

TRADING ACCOUNT

	£	£
Sales		480
Stock on 1.1	80	
Purchases	360	
Stock on 31.12	?	
Cost of sale		?
Gross profit		?

- Step (1): Calculate the gross profit as £96,000 (i.e. 1/5 of sales amounting to £480,000).
- Step (2): Calculate the cost of sales as £384,000 (i.e. sales minus the gross profit).
- Step (3): Ascertain the closing stock as £56,000 by removing the cost of goods sold from the total of opening stock and purchases.

Use all the information provided

When attempting to find missing information by calculating a balancing figure, we have to be very careful to ensure that the information stated in the problem has been fully taken into account. Failure to do this will give us the wrong answer. For example, if we are informed that the opening debtors, credit sales and cash takings are £40,000, £280,000 and £220,000 respectively, we may be tempted to arrive at the amount of closing debtors as £100,000. This answer, although appearing to be correct at that point, would be found wrong if, later on, the amount of closing debtors is stated to be £65,000. Accordingly, the Total Debtors account would appear as shown above. To balance that account, one or more amounts are needed and these could either be bad debts written off or settlement discounts allowed, or both, depending on what the problem suggests.

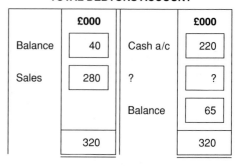

TOTAL DEBTORS ACCOUNT

	£000		£000
Balance	40	Cash a/c	220
Sales	280	?	?
		Balance	65
	320		320

26.4.4 Take care to distinguish income from receipts and expenditure from payments

This pointer means looking carefully at the way an item is described. For example, the *sales* would be an income figure to be credited to the Sales account and debited to the Total Debtors account; whereas *cash takings* refer to the amounts collected from debtors, to be debited to the Cash account and credited to the Total Debtors account.

Interaction 26.2

Distinguishing receipts from income and payments from expenditure

Green Wholesalers commenced business on 1.1.20X0. All sales and purchases were on credit. The following are some of its transactions during the year:

(a) Sales during the year	£448,200
(b) Cash takings during the year	£386,400
(c) Purchases during the year	£368,600
(d) Payments for purchases during the year	£296,500
(e) Paid as salary	£63,240
(f) Rent is agreed as	£3,000 per month
(g) Payment for rent	£45,000

Required: Complete the following table, identifying whether the transaction is a receipt, an income, a payment or an expenditure, and the accounts in which you would record the transaction.

Transaction	£	Classification	Account to debit	Account to credit
(a) Sales	448,200			
(b) Cash takings	386,400			
(c) Purchases	368,600			
(d) Settlement	296,500			
(e) Salary paid	63,240			
(f) Rent	36,000			
(g) Rent paid	45,000			

Show also how these transactions will be stated on the Profit and Loss account for the year ended 31.12.20X0 and the Balance Sheet as at that date, assuming that goods are sold at cost plus 50 per cent and that one week's salary amounting to £1,240 remains unpaid.

A basic question on incomplete records

Interaction
26.3

Betty Harrow assumed duties as accountant of a retail shop, Tongdean Hardware, on 7 January 20X2. The only records available were:

- a schedule of fixed assets;
- cash sales memos for fixed assets acquired during 20X1;
- stocktaking sheets for stock at 31.12. 20X0 and 20X1;
- purchase invoices;
- a list of purchase invoices that were unpaid at 31.12.20X0 and 20X1;
- a list of copy sales invoices outstanding at 31.12.20X0 and 20X1;
- a record in a diary of amounts paid for rent, salaries and other expenses.

The owner also provided Betty with an estimate of amounts he drew out to meet his personal household expenses. From these records she was able to gather information as follows:

(a) Assets and liabilities of the shop were as stated on the right.

(b) Purchases in the year to 31 December 20X1 amounted to £486,200.

(c) Fixed assets have been acquired during the year for £60,000.

(d) Information stated in the diary reveals payments made during the year as stated on the right (below).

(e) The proprietor draws £200 per week to meet his household expenses.

	31.12.20X0 £	31.12.20X1 £
Fixed assets at w.d.v	240,000	284,000
Stock in trade at cost	112,400	138,200
Trade debtors	136,800	164,600
Cash and bank bal.	12,600	15,400
Trade creditors	62,500	77,800

	£
Rent	24,000
Salaries/wages	48,800
Other expenses	16,400

Required: Carry out the following steps:

- Step 1: Prepare a Statement of Affairs as at 1 January 20X1 to calculate Tongdean Hardware's opening capital.
- Step 2: Open appropriate ledger accounts to record opening assets and liabilities.
- Step 3: Account for each transaction by entries in the ledger accounts.
- Step 4: Enter the closing balances into the ledger accounts.
- Step 5: Enter balancing figures in the ledger accounts and decide what each balancing figure represents.
- Step 6: Prepare a Trading and Profit and Loss account for the year ended 31.12.20X1.
- Step 7: Prepare a Balance Sheet as at 31.12.20X1.

26.5 THE CHALLENGE OF ASCERTAINING MISSING INFORMATION

When accounting records are incomplete, the challenge faced by the accountant is to ascertain the information needed to build up the accounts on a double entry basis. The task may well appear daunting. Let us assume, for illustration, that all that we have managed to ascertain on debtors is that they owed us £40,000 at the beginning of the year and £65,000 at the end.

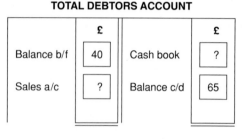

TOTAL DEBTORS ACCOUNT

	£		£
Balance b/f	40	Cash book	?
Sales a/c	?	Balance c/d	65

The information missing is the sales and the cash takings. Given one of these, the other can be ascertained as the balancing figure. The accountant has to think through a way of ascertaining one of the two missing pieces of information.

One approach could be to arrive at the figure of sales in the year using the following steps:

● Step (1): By preparing a Statements of Affairs at the beginning of the year, ascertain the net asset on that date; and by preparing a Balance Sheet as at the end of the year, ascertain the net assets on that date.
● Step (2): Ascertain the profit for the year by comparing the net assets on both dates, adjusting the difference for any capital introductions and drawings within the year.
● Step (3): Ascertain the gross profit in the year by adding on to the profit all administrative expenses and distribution cost.
● Step (4): If the gross profit ratio usually applicable to the business can be ascertained, the sales in the year can be arrived at from the amount of gross profit.

Interaction 26.4

The challenge of ascertaining missing information

Rick Alderman owns a shop. Because of a recent bereavement, he has neglected to maintain full accounting records. To prepare the financial statements for the year ended 31.12.20X2, he has gathered the following information:

(a) Sales are always effected at cost plus 50 per cent.
(b) The total of administrative expenses and distribution cost, other than depreciation, was reported as £214,500 during the year ended 31 December 20X1. The corresponding amount for the current year is expected to be 20 per cent more.
(c) The assets and liabilities of the shop were as stated here.
(d) Apart from new furniture acquired on 1.10.20X2, others had been acquired on 1 January 20X0 when business commenced. Furniture is depreciated at 10 per cent per annum using the reducing balance method.
(e) Rick's living expenses, including mortgage payments on his private residence, are estimated at £1,500 per month. Rick has no other source of income.

	31.12.20X1 £	31.12.20X2 £
Furniture at cost	240,000	300,000
Stock at cost	426,400	316,500
Trade debtors	48,200	64,400
Prepaid rent	6,000	–
Cash and bank	38,600	55,200
Trade creditors	185,200	212,600
Accrued expenses	12,600	17,800

Required: Prepare the Trading and Profit and Loss account for the year ended 31 December 20X2 and the Balance Sheet as at that date.

SOLUTIONS TO INTERACTIVE QUESTIONS

IQ 26.1 Inadequate information to recreate a double entry system

During the year to 31.12.20X1 the net assets have improved by £105,000 (£431,300 – £326,300), even after Chris drew £18,000 in the year (see table to right). He has no other source of income. Therefore the profit of the business for the year must be (£105,000 + £18,000) = £123,000.

	1.1.20X1 £	31.12.20X1 £
Fixed assets	180,000	215,000
Stock in trade	284,200	326,600
Trade debtors	16,500	21,400
Cash and bank	11,400	26,800
Creditors	(165,800)	(158,500)
Net assets	326,300	431,300

REVISED ESTIMATE BASED ON MORE INFORMATION	£	£
Net assets (as before)		105,000
Living expenses	18,000	
Education of children	24,000	
Replacing car	19,500	
Lottery winnings	(14,500)	47,000
Estimate of profit		152,000

IQ 26.2 Distinguishing receipts from income and payments from expenditure

Transaction	£	Classification	Account to debit	Account to credit
(a) Sales	448,200	Income	Debtors account	Sales account
(b) Cash takings	386,400	Receipt	Cash account	Debtors account
(c) Purchases	368,600	Expenditure	Purchases account	Creditors account
(d) Settlement	296,500	Payment	Creditors account	Cash account
(e) Salary paid	63,240	Payment	Salaries account	Cash account
(f) Rent	36,000	Expenditure	Rent (expense) a/c	Rent (liability) a/c
(g) Rent paid	45,000	Payment	Rent (liability) a/c	Cash account

Notes:

(a) Purchases (£386,400) less goods remaining unsold.
(b) 50% (gross profit ratio) of sales.
(c) Agreed rental for the year, though more was paid.
(d) Salary relating to the year, though it remains partly unpaid.
(e) Sales (£448,200) less cash takings (£386,400).
(f) Excess of payment (£45,000) over amount agreed (£36,000).
(g) Unpaid portion of salary.

PROFIT AND LOSS ACCOUNT

	£	N
Sales	448,200	
Cost of sales	(298,800)	a
Gross profit	149,400	b
Rent	(36,000)	c
Salary	(64,480)	d

BALANCE SHEET AS AT 31.12.20X0

	£	
Stock	69,800	
Debtors	61,800	e
Prepaid rent	9,000	f
Salary owed	(1,240)	g

IQ 26.3 A basic question on incomplete records

- **Step 1**: Prepare a Statement of Affairs as at 1.1.20X1, listing the assets and liabilities on that day and establishing the owner's Capital as the difference. See on right.

- **Step 2**: Open appropriate ledger accounts for each of the items on the Statement of Affairs, remembering to state assets as debit balances and liabilities (including Capital) as credit. The cash and bank balance is stated in a combined Cash account. The stock, though an asset, will soon be expended when sold and is therefore stated as opening stock in the Trading account. By this stage, Betty's books would be on a double entry basis.

- **Step 3**: Account for each transaction stated in the question by entries in the ledger accounts.

- **Step 4**: Enter the closing balances in the ledger accounts, carrying down in the appropriate ledger accounts the assets as debit balances and liabilities as credit balances.

- **Step 5**: Enter the balancing figure in each ledger account, deciding what it represents and accounting for it accordingly.

  In the ledger accounts set out on the right, the tilde symbol (~) indicates a balancing figure in an account and the hash symbol (#) indicates how that amount is accounted for by completing double entry with another account.

STATEMENT OF AFFAIRS AS AT 1.1.20X1

	£
Fixed assets	240,000
Stock at cost	112,400
Debtors	136,800
Cash/bank balance	12,600
Creditors	(62,500)
Capital	439,300

CASH ACCOUNT

		£		£	
	Balance b/f	12,600	Rent	24,000	
#	Total debtors	633,300	Salaries/wages	48,800	
			Other expenses	16,400	
			Fixed assets	60,000	
			Drawings	10,400	
			Total creditors	470,900	~
			Balance c/d	15,400	
		645,900		645,900	

FIXED ASSETS ACCOUNT

	£		£	
Balance b/f	240,000	Depreciation	16,000	#
Cash a/c	60,000	Balance c/d	284,000	

TOTAL DEBTORS ACCOUNT

	£		£	
Balance b/f	136,800	Cash a/c	633,300	~
Sales a/c	661,100	Balance c/d	164,600	

TOTAL CREDITORS ACCOUNT

		£		£
#	Cash a/c	470,900	Balance	62,500
	Balance c/d	77,800	Purchases	486,200

● **Step 6:**

TRADING AND PROFIT AND LOSS ACCOUNT FOR THE YEAR ENDED 31 DECEMBER 20X1		
	£	£
Sales		661,100
Stock on 1.1.20X1	112,400	
Purchases	486,200	
Stock on 31.12.20X1	(138,200)	(460,400)
Gross profit		200,700
Rent		(24,000)
Salaries and wages		(48,800)
Other expenses		(16,400)
Depreciation		(16,000)
Profit for the year		95,500

● **Step 7:**

BALANCE SHEET AS AT 31.12.20X1		
	£	£
Fixed assets		284,000
Stock at cost	138,200	
Debtors	164,600	
Cash and bank balance	15,400	
Creditors	(77,800)	240,400
		524,400
		£
Capital – 1.1.20X1		439,300
Profit for the year		95,500
Drawings		(10,400)
		524,400

IQ 26.4 The challenge of ascertaining missing information

Opening Statement of Affairs

STATEMENT OF AFFAIRS AS AT 1.1.20X2			
	£	£	£
Furniture	240,000	(45,600)	194,400
Stock in trade		426,400	
Debtors		48,200	
Prepaid rent		6,000	
Cash/bank		38,600	
Trade creditors		(185,200)	
Accrued expenses		(12,600)	321,400
Capital – Rick Alderman			515,800

The preparation of the Statement of Affairs as at 1.1.20X2 is a matter merely of listing the information tabulated in paragraph (c) of the question. The only difficulty is the calculation of the accumulated depreciation on furniture by the reducing balance method. The arithmetic involved in the method is as shown below.

Furniture	Book value	Accm deprn.
	£	£
At cost	240,000	
Depreciation @ 10%	(24,000)	24,000
At written down value	216,000	
Depreciation @ 10%	(21,600)	21,600
At written down value	194,400	45,600

Depreciation for the current year is calculated as shown on the right. Expenses (other than depreciation) in the year are estimated at 120 per cent of the previous year's amount of £214,500, namely £257,400. When one proceeds to account for all the information stated in the question, one finds that, because of insufficiency of information, many accounts have more than one blank space to fill. Observe the question marks in the following accounts:

	£
10% of 194,400	19,440
10% of 60,000 for 3 mths	1,500
	20,940

TOTAL DEBTORS ACCOUNT				
	£			£
Balance b/f	48,200	Cash a/c		?
Sales a/c	?	Balance		64,400

TOTAL CREDITORS ACCOUNT				
	£			£
Cash a/c	?	Balance b/f		185,200
Balance c/d	212,600	Purchases		?

CASH ACCOUNT

	£		£
Balance b/f	38,600	Furniture	60,000
Debtors	?	Drawings	18,000
		Expend.	246,200
		Creditors	?
		Balance	55,200

If an account is short of just one item, that is ascertained as the balancing figure. This is not possible when more than one item is missing. The only way out of this impasse is to work backwards (as one would in the case of a crossword puzzle) by preparing a Balance Sheet at the year end.

BALANCE SHEET AS AT 31.12.20X2

	£	£	£	
Furniture	300,000	(66,540)	233,460	
Stock in trade		316,500		
Trade debtors		64,400		
Cash/bank balance		55,200		
Trade creditors		(212,600)		
Accrued expense		(17,800)	205,700	
			439,160	
			£	
Capital on 1.1.20X1			515,800	
Loss in the year			(58,640)	#
Drawings			(18,000)	
			439,160	

FURNITURE AND FITTINGS ACCOUNT

	£		
Balance b/f	240,000		
Cash a/c	60,000		

PROVISION FOR DEPRECIATION ACCOUNT

			£
		Balance b/f	45,600
		Depreciation	20,940

TOTAL DEBTORS ACCOUNT

	£		£	
Balance b/f	48,200	Cash a/c	642,900	#
Sales a/c	659,100	Balance c/d	64,400	

TOTAL CREDITORS ACCOUNT

		£		£	
#	Cash a/c	302,100	Balance b/f	185,200	
	Balance c/d	212,600	Purchases	329,500	~

TRADING AND PROFIT AND LOSS ACCOUNT FOR THE YEAR ENDED 31.12.20X2

		£	
Sales		659,100	
Stock – 1.1.20X1	426,400		
Purchases	329,500		#
Stock – 31.12.20X1	(316,500)	(439,400)	
Gross profit		219,700	
Expenditure		(257,400)	
Depreciation		(20,940)	
Loss for the year 20X1		(58,640)	

TOTAL EXPENDITURE ACCOUNT

		£		£
	Balance b/f	6,000	Balance b/f	12,600
#	Cash a/c	246,200	Profit and Loss a/c	257,400
	Balance c/d	17,800		

CASH ACCOUNT

		£		£	
	Balance b/f	38,600	Furniture	60,000	
~	Debtors	642,900	Drawings	18,000	
			Expenditure	246,200	~
			Creditors	302,100	~
			Balance c/d	55,200	

 # Balancing figure in the account.
~ A figure derived from another account.

PROGRESSIVE QUESTIONS

PQ 26.1 Multiple-choice question

Place a tick in a space in the grids as appropriate:

1. Able's capital was £274,400 on 31.12.20X0 and £224,000 a year earlier. There were no drawings or capital introductions during the year. Estimate Able's profit for the year.

a	£50,400 profit	
b	£50,400 loss	
c	Cannot calculate	

2. During the year to 31.12.20X0, Basil's gross profit was £40,000. Basil sells his goods adding 20 per cent to cost. What were the sales in the year?

a	£260,000	
b	£240,000	
c	£200,000	

3. Camilus sells his goods adding one-third to his cost. His sales in the year were £240,000. Determine the gross profit for the year.

a	£36,000	
b	£48,000	
c	£60,000	

4. Dorothy drew £8,437 during the year as living expenses and reports her shop's assets and liabilities as follows:

	Property	Stock	Debtors	Bank	Creditors
As at 1.4.20X1	£56,250	£7,650	£5,287	£2,025	£9,664
As at 31.3.20X2	£56,250	£10,912	£6,300	£4,050	£10,462

a	£5,502 profit	
b	£2,935 loss	
c	£13,939 profit	
d	Cannot calculate	

Ascertain her profit for the year to 31 March 20X2.

5. In December 20X0 Epsilon introduced into its business £25,000 which was raised by selling a privately owned sail cruiser. In March 20X1 the business obtained a bank loan of £20,000 repayable in three years. The business assets and liabilities on 1.10.20X0 were £364,500 and £300,000 respectively. As at 30.9.20X1, business assets were £368,200 and liabilities (excluding the bank loan) £310,000. During the year Epsilon's owner had drawn £34,500 for living expenses. Ascertain Epsilon's profit.

a	£85,800 loss	
b	£16,800 loss	
c	£6,300 profit	

6. Determine the amount Felician paid its creditors during the year, when it reports that its creditors on 31.3.20X1 were £4,500 and £3,000 a year earlier, its purchases during the year to 31.3.20X1 were £150,000 and it had received £7,500 as a cash discount.

a	£141,000	
b	£144,000	
c	£148,500	
d	£156,000	

7. Debtors as at 1.1.20X0 were reported by George as £66,250 and at 31.12.20X0 as £84,375. George received £816,000 from debtors during the year, after allowing £6,000 for cash discount and writing off £8,000 as a bad debt. Ascertain George's sales during the year.

a	£822,000	
b	£832,125	
c	£836,125	
d	£848,125	

8. Gregory, a wholesaler, permits 6 per cent cash discount, which is always availed of by all his customers. During the year the sales were £296,500 and the amount received from customers was £269,498. Debtors at the beginning of the year were £35,000 and at the end £31,500. Ascertain his bad debts.

a	£7,000	
b	£3,500	
c	£13,300	

9. Helen was owed £51,030 by her customers on 1.2.20X2. During the year to 31.1.20X3 she received £157,430 from customers. By 31.1.20X3, after making a contra entry of £6,370 for a customer who was also a supplier, and after increasing the provision for doubtful debts by £4,200, customers owed her £55,090. Ascertain what Helen's sales for the year were.

a	£155,120	
b	£159,320	
c	£167,860	
d	£172,060	

PQ 26.2 A mini question on incomplete records

Ilford states its assets and liabilities as below (right).
Transactions during the year to 31.12.20X1 were as follows:

(a) Drawings by the proprietor	£40,000
(b) Payments to suppliers	£1,731,600
(c) Receipts from customers	£2,160,000
(d) Paid salaries	£180,000
(e) Paid for other expenses	£154,800

	1.1.20X1 £	31.12.20X1 £
Fixed assets at cost	96,400	112,800
Accumulated depreciation	(24,600)	(32,400)
	71,800	80,400
Stock in trade	234,500	252,800
Debtors	43,200	46,800
Bank balance	2,160	?
Creditors	97,200	109,800

Required: Set out Ilford's summarized cash book, its Trading and Profit and Loss account for the Year to 31.12.20X1, and its Balance Sheet as at that date.

PQ 26.3 Involving acquisition and disposal of fixed assets

Jeane's Shop provides you with the information on the right. Transactions during the year ended 31.3.20X1 were as follows:

(a) Furniture, acquired for £16,200 and written down to £5,400, was scrapped in the year.
(b) A vehicle acquired for £54,000 was sold in the year for £30,000, making a gain of £8,000.
(c) Sales, amounting to £846,200 in the year, yielded a gross profit ratio of 25%.
(d) Expenses incurred in the year include:
 ● Bad debts £2,100;
 ● Depreciation on furniture £4,200;
 ● Administration/selling expenses other than depreciation £68,200.
(e) No record has been maintained of amounts drawn from time to time by Jeane.

Net assets as at	31.3.20X0 £	31.3.20X1 £
Furniture at cost	36,400	54,200
Depreciation	(18,200)	?
Motor vehicles	124,000	132,400
Depreciation	(86,800)	(68,400)
Stock in trade	154,500	216,800
Debtors	216,400	254,200
Cash/bank	16,200	9,600
Creditors	(208,300)	(245,900)
Accrued expense	(16,400)	(32,500)

Required: Set out the shop's summarized cash book, the Trading and Profit and Loss account for the year ended 31.3.20X1, and the Balance Sheet as at that date.

PQ 26.4 Information on assets and liabilities may be scattered

On 1 July 20X0 Lorna Hill started retailing computer software. Overwhelmed by her efforts to break into the market, she neglected the accounting function. Her bank has recently rejected her application for a bank accommodation, insisting on the latest financial statements. At Lorna's request you were able to gather the following information:

(a) The shop's assets and liabilities include those stated in the table on the right.
(b) All fixed assets, including a Ford Escort van, were acquired when the business commenced. The van, acquired for £20,000, was sold for £4,000 on 1.4.20X3 when it was replaced by a Volkswagen van. Lorna agrees to depreciate all fixed assets at 10 per cent per annum using the straight-line method.

	31.12.20X2 £	31.12.20X3 £
Fixed assets at cost	480,000	520,000
Stock of computer software	246,800	362,500
Unpaid supplier's invoices	112,400	198,600
Salaries and wages accrued	24,500	36,800
Cash	12,600	1,400

(c) Lorna allows one month's credit to all her customers and maintains a 'pending' file for retaining the carbon copies of invoices issued in respect of each sale. Upon receiving payment from a customer, she stamps 'received' on the related copies of the invoice and transfers it to a Receipted Invoices file. However, one invoice for £6,000 was destroyed by her when she failed with her best efforts to trace the customer. The total value of invoices issued in the year, including that of the one destroyed, was £982,600. The value of invoices remaining in the pending file on 31.12.20X3 was £184,000 and on 31.12.20X2 was £162,000. Lorna believes that a provision of 5 per cent would cover possible bad debts.

(d) Rent for the business premises, agreed at £24,000 p.a., had been paid three years in advance at the commencement of business.

(e) A summary of the payments in the year, as recorded in a diary, is as on the right. No record has been maintained, however, of amounts drawn by Lorna from time to time for her personal use.

(f) Business rates, at £6,000 per annum, have never been paid since commencement of business.

	£
Salaries and wages	136,400
Advertising	26,600
Rent for business premises	8,000
Other expenses	75,200
Payment to Suppliers	628,200

Required: Prepare:

(a) the Statement of Affairs as at 1.1.20X3;
(b) the Trading and Profit and Loss account for the year ended 31 December 20X3; and
(c) the Balance Sheet as at that date.

## Chapter 27

SINGLE ENTRY AND INCOMPLETE RECORDS (2)

In this chapter

We will learn to finalize accounts of entities which, though with incomplete records, have transacted mainly through bank accounts and may even be VAT registered.

27.1 BANK TRANSACTIONS

Where bank transactions are involved, as well as cash, it helps to write up a two-column cash book bearing in mind that initially all takings (meaning collections), including those in the form of cheques, will be accounted for in the Cash account (i.e. the Cash column of the cash book). Normally, two steps are required as follows:

- **Step 1**: Ascertain the amount deposited into the bank during the year, as shown on the right, and account for it by debiting the Bank account and crediting the Cash account.

	£
Closing balance at bank	XX
Sum of all cheque payments	XXX
Less: Opening balance at bank	(XX)
Amount deposited into bank[a]	XXX

- **Step 2**: Ascertain the amount received from customers during the year (shown on the right) and account for the amount by debiting the Cash account and crediting the Debtors Control account.

	£
Amount deposited into the bank	XXX
Amounts paid out in cash	XXX
Closing balance of cash in hand	XX
Less: Opening balance of cash in hand	XX
Amount received from customers[b]	XXX

a. If there is information on direct deposits into the bank (such as bank giro credit, mandates or when a bank loan, on approval, is placed directly into the bank account), the amount ascertained as the sum deposited into the bank will have to be reduced accordingly.

b. If there is information that there have also been other sources of receipts during the year (such as capital introductions or disposal of assets), the amount ascertained as receipts from customers will have to be reduced accordingly.

| Transactions including cheque receipts and payments | | Interaction 27.1 |

School Supplies has £12,400 at the bank and £400 in hand on 1.1.20X0. By 31.12.20X0 the balance at the bank has risen to £16,200 and the cash in hand is £150. Payments made during the year are as stated here.

Required: Write up the two-column cash book for the year ending on 31 December 20X0.

	Cash £	Cheque £
For a vehicle	–	30,000
To creditors	620	96,400
As salary	140	8,450
As rent	–	6,000
For advertising	–	650

| Transactions including other sources of money input | | Interaction 27.2 |

In addition to what was stated in IQ 27.1, you are informed that:

(a) in May 20X0, a bank loan of £20,000 was approved for School Supplies;
(b) a vehicle was sold for £7,500 in August 20X0.

Required: Write up the two-column cash book for the year ending 31 December 20X0.

27.2 FINDING MISSING INFORMATION IN INCOMPLETE RECORDS

Sales	£32,000
Stock on 1.1	£5,400
Purchases	£24,800
Stock on 31.12	£2,800

The challenge of an incomplete records situation (see Section 26.5) is that information essential for writing up a set of accounts may not be readily available. For example, let us assume that during the year a part of stock was destroyed by fire. The information available is just that stated above. If we decide to ignore the fire and prepare a Trading account on the basis of the available information, the gross profit reported would be £4,600 (as shown on the right). This would be wrong because the cost of goods lost in the fire is stated as part of the cost of goods sold. If, on further inquiry, we ascertain that the business consistently fixes its sale price by adding a profit margin of one-third to its cost price, it would be clear that on £32,000 sales the gross profit should have been one-quarter (i.e. £8,000 rather than £4,600). This would mean that the cost of goods sold should have been £32,000 less £8,000, namely £24,000. Accordingly, we should be able to identify the cost of goods lost by fire as £3,400 (being the difference between £27,400 and £24,000. The cost of goods lost by fire is admittedly an expense, but not one to be taken into the account when ascertaining the gross profit. Therefore, the loss by fire should be removed from the Trading account to be stated (net of any amount recoverable from insurance) in the Profit and Loss account (see presentation above).

TRADING ACCOUNT FOR THE YEAR ENDED 31.12.XX

		£
Sales		32,000
Stock 1.1	5,400	
Purchases	24,800	
Stock 31.12	(2,800)	
Cost of sales		(27,400)
Gross profit		4,600

TRADING ACCOUNT FOR THE YEAR ENDED 31.12.XX

		£
Sales		32,000
Stock 1.1	5,400	
Purchases	24,800	
Stock 31.12	(2,800)	
Loss by fire	(3,400)	
Cost of sales		(24,000)
Gross profit		8,000
Loss by fire		(3,400)

Interaction 27.3	Involving a loss by fire

Bruce Drake requests your assistance to prepare the financial statements of his shop for the year ended 30 June 20X1, and he has provided you with the following information:

(a) The shop's assets and liabilities are as stated here.

(b) Shops of this type and size usually achieve a gross profit ratio of 25%.

(c) Motor vehicles, acquired for £28,000 and written down to £12,000 by 1 July 20X0, were sold on that date for £9,000.

(d) Bruce habitually banks all his takings intact at close of business each day, leaving a float of £500 for making minor payments in cash.

(e) Payments made in the year were recorded in a diary and are summarized as stated on the right.

(f) Rent is payable at £2,000 per month. One-third of the premises is occupied by Bruce and his family.

(g) A fire in May 20X1 destroyed a substantial amount of stock. The insurance claim was admitted at £32,500 but the cheque was not received until 6.8.20X1.

	30.6.20X0 £	30.6.20X1 £
Motor vehicles at w.d.v	82,000	106,000
Office equipment at w.d.v	24,500	28,400
Stock in trade at cost	142,400	96,500
Trade debtors	98,500	106,400
Prepaid insurance	1,200	?
Balance at bank	21,300	19,700
Trade creditors	68,600	114,200
Salaries accrued	18,200	15,600

	In cash £	By cheque £
For purchases	12,400	662,800
Rent	–	30,000
Salaries and wages	3,600	108,500
Motor vehicles	–	60,000
Office equipment	–	16,000
Living expenses – family	3,400	14,200
Other admin/distribution expenses	7,800	44,600
Insurance – year to 30.9.20X1	–	6,000

Required: Set out:

(a) the two-column cash book recording the above stated transactions;
(b) the Trading and Profit and Loss account for the year ended 30.6.20X1;
(c) the Balance Sheet as at that date.

27.3 THE NEED FOR BANK RECONCILIATION

One reason for incompleteness of records may well be loss or destruction of a part or all of the records. In an extreme situation, one may even confront an accounting jigsaw in which the information needed to reconstruct the accounts may have to be pieced together, as best as one can, by steps such as the following:

● Obtain a copy of the opening Balance Sheet from the auditor's file.
● Obtain copies of bank statements and, by summarizing them, build up a profile of transactions that have gone through the bank.
● Confirm the debtors and creditors by circularizing them.
● Determine the cost of stock and, if necessary, the value of each class of fixed asset, by conducting physical inventories.

When dealing with the information gathered from bank statements, it should be remembered that they report the transactions from the bank's point of view. You will need to prepare a bank reconciliation to identify the transactions that would have appeared in the cash book.

Preparing a bank reconciliation to identify figures for the cash book

Interaction 27.4

An analysis of bank statements for the year reveals that payments made in the year to 31.12.20X1 include the following:

- Payments to suppliers for purchases   £246,840
- Payment for rent   £18,000

The bank reconciliation as at 31 December 20X1 reveals that three cheques amounting to £42,500 sent to suppliers and one cheque for £3,000 sent to the landlord for rent, all drawn within the two weeks before the year end, had not been presented to the bank for payment until the first week in January 20X2.

Required: Determine the payments for purchases and rent that should be accounted for in the cash book for the year ending on 31.12.20X1:

(a) on the basis of the information stated above and assuming that, as at 1.1.20X1, the balance at the bank stated in the cash book was the same as that stated in the bank statement;

(b) on the basis that there had been a bank reconciliation prepared on 1 January 20X1 in respect of cheques not presented for payment to the bank as at 31.12.20X0 by suppliers for £56,200 and by the landlord for £6,000.

Bank reconciliations both at commencement and at end

Interaction 27.5

A shop's bank statements reveal that its bank balance on 1.1.20X1 was an overdraft of £16,200, total payments into the bank during the year were £368,240, and its bank balance on 31.12.20X1 was £28,560. Your inquiries further reveal as follows:

	31.12.20X0	31.12.20X1
In-payments not credited by the bank	£42,640	£28,450
Cheques not presented to the bank	£18,660	£36,760

Required: State the amounts to be included in the cash book as:

(a) the bank balance as at 1 January 20X1;
(b) bank in-payments during the year ended 31.12.20X1;
(c) payments through bank during the year ended 31.12.20X1;
(d) the bank balance as at 31 December 20X1.

27.4 WHERE TRANSACTIONS INVOLVE VALUE ADDED TAX

If the incomplete records are those of a business registered for VAT (see Chapter 20), we should bear in mind that the entity would have collected output VAT, which the business has to account for as a liability, and would have paid input VAT, which it should claim back in the UK from HM Customs and Excise. We should recall, however, that

- input VAT cannot be claimed back if it relates to motor vehicles and entertainment;
- bad-debt relief is available when a debt is written off; and
- the reclaimed input VAT becomes payable to Customs and Excise if the item is taken for personal use.

Interaction 27.6

Incomplete records of a VAT-registered trader

Following a raid from the local VAT Office, John Bond seeks your assistance in preparing the financial statements of his VAT-registered shop for the year ended 31.12.20X2. You have ascertained as follows:

(a) Assets and liabilities of the shop include those listed on the right.

	31.12.20X1 £		31.12.20X2 £	
Motor vehicles at cost	172,500	#	207,750	#
Computers at cost	–		9,400	#
Stock in trade at cost	169,200	#	144,760	#
Trade debtors	332,580	#	419,175	#
Rent prepaid	–		12,000	
Cash and bank	26,865		42,710	
Trade creditors	272,320	#	336,375	#
Salaries accrued	16,400		21,600	
Other accruals	2,415	#	8,625	#
VAT account (owed)	3,250		11,650	

Amounts marked with a hash (#) include VAT at 17.5%.

(b) A vehicle was acquired on 1.5.20X2 for £35,250 (inclusive of VAT at 17.5 per cent). All other vehicles were acquired when the business commenced in January 20X0.

(c) Two computers were acquired on 1.7.20X2 for £4,000 each plus VAT at 17.5 per cent. One is for use by the Accounts Department and the other for use by John's undergraduate son.

(d) The vehicles and the computers are to be depreciated at 20 per cent and 10 per cent p.a. respectively using the straight-line method.

(e) Income and expenses during the year ended 31.12.20X2 have been recorded in a diary as stated on the right.

	£	VAT @ 17.5% £	TOTAL £
Sales	1,524,800	266,840	1,791,640
Purchases	993,600	173,880	1,167,480
Salaries	184,600	–	184,600
Rent	48,000	–	48,000
Entertainment	9,000	1,575	10,575
Other expenses	115,600	20,230	135,830

(f) To tide over a cash-flow crisis in May 20X2, £114,000 was collected from customers permitting them a 5 per cent settlement discount.

(g) £84,600 due from a customer was written off as bad during the year.

(h) John regularly draws £350 per week to meet his household expenses; but he cannot recall the amount he drew recently to prepare to celebrate his son's graduation.

Required: Prepare the Trading and Profit and Loss account for the year ended 31 December 20X2 and the Balance Sheet as at that date.

SOLUTIONS TO INTERACTIVE QUESTIONS

IQ 27.1 Transactions including cheque receipts and payments

CASH BOOK

		Cash £	Bank £			Cash £	Bank £
Balance b/f		400	12,400	Motor Vehicles account		–	30,000
Cash account	c	–	145,300	Creditors Control account		620	96,400
Debtors Control a/c		145,810	–	Salaries account		140	8,450
				Rent account		–	6,000
				Advertising account		–	650
				Bank account	c	145,300	–
				Balance c/d		150	16,200
Balance b/d		150	16,200				

IQ 27.2 Transactions including other sources of money input

CASH BOOK

		Cash £	Bank £			Cash £	Bank £
Balance b/f		400	12,400	Motor Vehicles account		–	30,000
Bank loan account		–	20,000	Creditors Control account		620	96,400
Disposal of vehicle		7,500	–	Salaries account		140	8,450
Cash account	c	–	125,300	Rent account		–	6,000
Debtors Control a/c		118,310	–	Advertising account		–	650
				Bank account	c	125,300	–
				Balance c/d		150	16,200
Balance b/d		150	16,200				

IQ 27.3 Involving a loss by fire

Because there are both cash and bank transactions, a two-column cash book is prepared. *Cash paid into the bank* is calculated as £940,500 by adding together all amounts paid by cheque during the year (£942,100) and the closing balance at the bank (£19,700) and deducting from the total the opening bank balance (£21,300). *Collection from the customers*: Since the cash in hand remains constant (at £500), the sum of all cash payments, plus bank deposits, less the proceeds of asset disposal, is the amount collected from customers.

CASH BOOK

		Cash £	Bank £			Cash £	Bank £
Balance b/f		500	21,300	Creditors a/c		12,400	662,800
Disposal a/c		9,000	–	Rent		–	30,000
Cash a/c	c	–	940,500	Salaries and wag.		3,600	108,500
Debtors a/c		958,700	–	Motor vehicle		–	60,000
				Office equipment		–	16,000
				Drawings		3,400	14,200
				Other expense		7,800	44,600
				Insurance		–	6,000
				Bank a/c	c	940,500	–
				Balance c/d		500	19,700
Balance b/d		500	19,700				

Preparing a Statement of Affairs as at commencement: In addition to all assets and liabilities stated in paragraph (a) of the question, the statement should include the cash float of £500.

The cost of goods lost by fire is ascertained as follows:

(a) Purchases, adjusted for opening and closing stock, reveals the cost of goods disposed of in the year – either by sale or otherwise – as £766,700.
(b) The cost of goods sold, at 75% of £966,600, is £724,950.
(c) The cost of goods lost by fire (i.e (a) minus (b)) is £41,750.

The amount by which the cost of goods lost by fire exceeds the insurance claim is the loss stated in the Profit and Loss account.

STATEMENT OF AFFAIRS AS AT 30.6.20X0

		£
Motor vehicles		82,000
Office equipment		24,500
Stock	142,400	
Debtors	98,500	
Prepayment	1,200	
Bank balance	21,300	
Cash float	500	
Creditors	(68,600)	
Accrued expenses	(18,200)	177,100
Capital at 1.7.20X0		283,600

MOTOR VEHICLES ACCOUNT

	£		£	
Balance b/f	82,000	Disposal	12,000	
Bank a/c	60,000	Depre. a/c	24,000	#
		Balance c/d	106,000	

OFFICE EQUIPMENT ACCOUNT

	£		£	
Balance b/f	24,500	Depre. a/c	12,100	#
Bank a/c	16,000	Balance c/d	28,400	

DISPOSAL OF VEHICLE ACCOUNT

	£		£
M. Vehicle	12,000	Cash a/c	9,000
		P&L – Loss	3,000

INSURANCE ACCOUNT

	£		£	
Balance b/f	1,200	P&L a/c	5,700	#
Bank a/c	6,000	Balance c/d	1,500	

GOODS LOST BY FIRE ACCOUNT

	£		£
Trading a/c	41,750	Insurance	32,500
		P&L a/c	9,250

TOTAL CREDITORS ACCOUNT

	£		£	
Cash a/c	12,400	Balance b/f	68,600	
Bank a/c	662,800	Purchases	720,800	#
Balance c/d	114,200			

TOTAL DEBTORS ACCOUNT

		£		£	
	Balance b/f	98,500	Cash a/c	958,700	~
#	Sales a/c	966,600	Balance c/d	106,400	

SALARIES AND WAGES ACCOUNT

	£		£	
Cash a/c	3,600	Balance b/f	18,200	
Bank a/c	108,500	P&L a/c	109,500	#
Balance c/d	15,600			

RENT ACCOUNT

	£		£
Bank a/c	30,000	Drawings	8,000
		P&L a/c	16,000
		Balance c/d	6,000

\# Balancing figures
~ Use of figures derived elsewhere.

TRADING AND PROFIT AND LOSS ACCOUNT FOR THE YEAR ENDED 30.6.20X1		
		£
Sales		966,600
Stock – 1.7.20X0	142,400	
Purchases	720,800	
Goods lost by fire	(41,750)	
Stock – 30.6.20X1	(96,500)	(724,950)
Gross profit		241,650
Salaries and wages		(109,500)
Rent		(16,000)
Other expenses		(52,400)
Depreciation – vehicles		(24,000)
Depreciation – equipment		(12,100)
Insurance		(5,700)
Loss on disposal of vehicle		(3,000)
Loss of goods by fire		(9,250)
Profit for the year		9,700

BALANCE SHEET AS AT 30 JUNE 20X1		
		£
Motor vehicles		106,000
Office equipment		28,400
Stock in trade	96,500	
Debtors	106,400	
Insurance claim	32,500	
Prepaid insurance	1,500	
Prepaid rent	6,000	
Bank balance	19,700	
Cash in hand	500	
Creditors	(114,200)	
Salaries accrued	(15,600)	133,300
		267,700

	£
Capital – 1.7.20X0	283,600
Profit for the year	9,700
Drawings	(17,600)
Rent	(8,000)
	267,700

IQ 27.4 Preparing a bank reconciliation to identify figures for the cash book

		To suppliers £	As rent £
(a)	Payments as per bank statement	246,840	18,000
	Cheques drawn in the year yet to be presented to the bank	42,500	3,000
	Payment to be accounted for in the cash book	289,340	21,000

		£	£
(b)	Payments as per bank statement	246,840	18,000
	Cheques drawn in the year yet to be presented to the bank	42,500	3,000
		289,340	21,000
	Less: Corresponding unpresented cheques a year earlier	(56,200)	(6,000)
	Payment to be accounted for in the cash book	233,140	15,000

IQ 27.5 Bank reconciliations both at commencement and at end

Workings: Payments through bank as per bank statement is arrived at as shown here.

	£
Lodgement as reported	368,240
Overdraft as at 1.1.20X1	(16,200)
Balance as at 31.12.20X1	(28,560)
Payments through bank	323,480

Ascertainment of amounts to be stated in the bank column of the cash book	Opening balance	Bank lodgements	Payments by cheque	Closing balance
	£	£	£	£
As stated in the bank statements	(16,200)	368,240	(323,480)	28,560
On 1.1.20X1: deposits yet to be credited	42,640	(42,640)	–	–
cheques yet to be presented	(18,660)	–	18,660	–
On 31.12.20X1: deposits yet to be credited	–	28,450	–	28,450
cheques yet to be presented	–	–	(36,760)	(36,760)
To be stated in the cash book	7,780	354,050	341,580	20,250

IQ 27.6 Incomplete records of a VAT-registered trader

Notes:

1. The balancing figure in each ledger account is identified as #, and the use of that figure as input in another account as ~.
2. The input VAT on motor vehicles is regarded as part of the cost of the vehicle because it cannot be recovered from HM Customs and Excise.
3. The accumulated depreciation, on 1.1.20X2, of vehicles acquired at the commencement of business is 20 per cent of £172,500 over two years. The current year's depreciation is 20 per cent of £172,500 plus 20 per cent of £34,500 for eight months only.
4. Because VAT in respect of purchases is fully recoverable, stock remaining unsold is reported excluding VAT.
5. Amounts recoverable from debtors or payable to creditors are inclusive of VAT.
6. The VAT related to the computer acquired for business use can be claimed back. Therefore the cost (excluding VAT) is capitalized and depreciated at 10 per cent p.a. for six months of use.
7. The settlement discount allowed is 5/95 of £114,000.
8. The VAT element of bad debt is claimed as bad debt relief.
9. Transactions stated in paragraph (e) of the question are income or expenditure – not receipts or payments.
10. Payment for the computer for the use of the proprietor's son should be accounted for as a drawing. The VAT involved cannot be claimed from Customs and Excise. The £350 drawn weekly for household needs and the amount drawn for celebrating the son's graduation are also further drawings by the proprietor.
11. VAT in respect of entertainment expenses also cannot be reclaimed from Customs and Excise.

STATEMENT OF AFFAIRS AS AT 31.12.20X1

	£	£	N
Motor vehicles		172,500	2
Accum. depreciaton		(69,000)	3
		103,500	
Stock in trade	144,000		4
Debtors	332,580		5
Cash/bank	26,865		
Creditors	(272,320)		5
Salary accrued	(16,400)		
Accrued exp.	(2,415)		5
VAT owed	(3,250)	209,060	
CAPITAL – 31.12.20X1		312,560	#

TOTAL DEBTORS ACCOUNT

N		£		£	N
5	Balance b/f	332,580	Discount all	6,000	7
5	Sales a/c	1,524,800	Bad debts	84,600	8
5	VAT a/c	266,840	Cash/bank	1,614,445	#
			Balance c/d	419,175	

TOTAL CREDITORS ACCOUNT

N		£		£	N
#	Cash/bank	1,103,425	Balance b/f	272,320	5
	Balance c/d	336,375	Purchases a/c	993,600	5
			VAT a/c	173,880	5

BAD DEBTS ACCOUNT

N		£		£	N
	Trade Debtors	84,600	Profit and Loss a/c	72,000	
			VAT a/c	12,600	8

MOTOR VEHICLES ACCOUNT

N		£		£	N
2	Bal. b/f	172,500			
2	Cash book	35,250			

PROVISION FOR DEPRECIATION OF VEHICLES ACCOUNT

N		£		£	N
			Bal. b/f	69,000	3
			Depre. a/c	39,200	3

COMPUTER ACCOUNT

N		£		£	N
6	Cash book	4,000			

PROVISION FOR DEPRECIATION OF COMPUTER ACCOUNT

		£		£	
			Depre. a/c	200	6

VAT ACCOUNT

N		£		£	N
6	Computer	700	Bal. b/f	3,250	
5	Creditors	173,880	Debtors	266,840	5
5	Expenses	20,230			
8	Bad debts	12,600			
#	Cash book	51,030			
	Balance	11,650			

SALARIES ACCOUNT

N		£		£	N
#	Cash book	179,400	Bal. b/f	16,400	
	Bal. c/d	21,600	Profit and Loss a/c	184,600	9

OTHER EXPENSES ACCOUNT

N		£		£	N
#	Cash book	129,620	Bal. b/f	2,415	
	Bal. c/d	8,625	Profit and Loss a/c	115,600	9
			VAT a/c	20,230	5

RENT ACCOUNT

N		£		£	N
#	Cash book	60,000	Profit and Loss a/c	48,000	9
			Bal. c/d	12,000	

DRAWINGS ACCOUNT

N		£		£	N
10	Equipment	4,700			
10	Cash book	18,200			
10	Cash book	1,700			

CASH BOOK

		£		£		N
	Balance b/f	26,865	Entertainment		10,575	11
~	Debtors	1,614,445	Motor vehicle		35,250	2
			Computer	4,000		
			VAT a/c	700	4,700	6
			Drawings		4,700	10
			Drawings		18,200	10
			Creditors		1,103,425	~
			Salaries		179,400	~
			Other expense		129,620	~
			Rent		60,000	~
			VAT a/c		51,030	~
			Drawings		1,700	#
			Balance c/d		42,710	

TRADING AND PROFIT AND LOSS ACCOUNT FOR THE YEAR ENDED 31.12.20X2		
		£
Sales		1,524,800
Stock – 31.12.20X1	144,000	
Purchases	993,600	
Stock – 31.12.20X2	(123,200)	(1,014,400)
Gross profit		510,400
Salaries		(184,600)
Rent		(48,000)
Entertainment		(10,575)
Other expenses		(115,600)
Depreciation – vehicles		(39,200)
Depreciation – computer		(200)
Discount allowed		(6,000)
Bad debts		(72,000)
Profit for the year		34,225

BALANCE SHEET AS AT 31.12.20X2			
	Cost	Ac. depn	£
Motor vehicles	207,750	(108,200)	99,550
Computer	4,000	(200)	3,800
Stock in trade		123,200	
Trade debtors		419,175	
Prepaid rent		12,000	
Cash and bank balance		42,710	
Trade creditors		(336,375)	
Salary accrued		(21,600)	
Accrued expenses		(8,625)	
VAT accrued		(11,650)	218,835
			322,185

	£
Capital – 31.12.20X2	312,560
Profit for the year	34,225
Drawings	(24,600)
	322,185

PROGRESSIVE QUESTIONS

PQ 27.1 Incomplete record involving bank reconciliations

John Dyson is in business trading wholesale in consumer durables. He purchases from reputable manufacturers and sells at a price calculated to yield a profit margin of 25 per cent on cost. His accounts are in a state of disarray and you have been assigned the task of preparing the financial statements in respect of the year ended 30.9.20X1. The Balance Sheet as at 30.9.20X0, obtained from the auditors, appears as shown here. Your investigations reveal as follows:

(a) Unpaid invoices on 30.9.20X1 amount to £196,700.
(b) By the sending of a standard letter, the debtors as at 30.9.20X1 were confirmed as £168,500. Although John knows that the amount is substantially lower than the actual amount, he agrees that the difference has to be written off as bad.
(c) John depreciates fixed assets at 10 per cent per annum by the straight-line method.
(d) On the basis of a physical inventory, the cost of stock in hand on 30.9.20X1 is ascertained to be £284,600.
(e) The bank statements for the year have been summarized as shown on the following page (top right).

BALANCE SHEET AS AT 30.9.20X0			
	Cost	Ac. depn	WDV
Furniture	60,000	(24,000)	36,000
Equipment	45,000	(10,400)	34,600
Stock in trade		242,600	
Trade debtors		312,400	
Bank balance		51,600	
Cash in hand		300	
Trade creditors	(245,400)		
Accrued expense	(32,800)	(278,200)	328,700
			399,300
Capital			312,500
Profit for the year			98,600
Drawings			(11,800)
			399,300

(f) An amount of £17,500, deposited on 29.9.20X1, was not reflected on the bank statement until three days later. The corresponding uncleared amount a year earlier was £24,400. A cheque for £46,800, drawn in favour of a supplier on 27.9.20X1, was not presented to the bank until a week later.

(g) John habitually banks all his takings intact on the same day, leaving a float of £300 for meeting incidental expenses. Payments made out of this float during the year were as stated on the right (below).

	£		£
Balance – 1.10.20X0	27,200	Purchases	724,500
Bank lodgement	962,300	Rent	36,000
		Salaries and wages	88,400
		Furniture – 1.1.20X1	80,000
		John's life insurance	15,000
		Other expenses	27,400
		Balance 30.9.20X1	18,200
	989,500		989,500

(h) An analysis of payments made after 30 September 20X1 reveal that £22,400 of these payments were in respect of administrative expenses incurred prior to 30.9.20X1. Provision should be made in the accounts also for £8,500 accrued as staff salary and £5,000 you intend to claim for accounting work. The staff salary accrued as at 30.9.20X0 of £12,600 has been reported as part of accrued expenses.

	£
Paid to suppliers	12,400
Other expenses	9,600
John's drawings	11,800

Required: Complete the following Bank Reconciliation table, and then prepare the Trading and Profit and Loss account for the year ended 30 September 20X1 and the Balance Sheet as at that date.

BANK RECONCILIATION

	As stated in the question	Deposits not cleared as at 30.9.20X0	Deposits not cleared as at 30.9.20X1	Cheques not presented by 30.9.20X1	Correct position to state in the cash book
Balance – 1.10.20X0	27,200				
Bank lodgements	962,300				
Purchases	(724,500)				
Rent	(36,000)				
Salaries and wages	(88,400)				
Furniture	(80,000)				
Drawings	(15,000)				
Other expenses	(27,400)				
Balance – 30.9.20X1	18,200				

PQ 27.2 Another incomplete record involving bank reconciliations

On 1 April 20X0, when his services with an estate agent were terminated, Dave Twist commenced a vehicle valeting and cleaning business, with capital of £40,000 that he had received as redundancy pay. In addition, he obtained a loan of £100,000 from Highland Bank on the following terms:

(a) He would settle the loan in 20 equal half-yearly instalments commencing 30 September 20X0;

(b) Interest, calculated at 15 per cent per annum at annual rests (i.e. where interest is calculated at annual intervals), is payable half-yearly in arrears along with the capital payments.

The high-tech valeting and cleaning equipment, installed on 1.4.20X0 at a cost of £120,000, is depreciated at 10 per cent per annum on cost. The premises were rented at £30,000 per annum, but a portion thereof is sublet to a sweet shop at £500 per month.

Though quite disciplined in conducting his business and regular in meeting all commitments to the bank, Dave has failed to maintain proper books of account. All takings, however, have been banked intact, and payments were usually made by cheque.

The Inland Revenue has called for a set of financial statements and Dave seeks your assistance to prepare them in respect of the year ended 31 March 20X3. The following are the facts to have emerged so far:

(a) Your assistant has summarized the bank statements for the year ended 31 March 20X3 as shown on the right. A cheque for £2,400, drawn in favour of a supplier on 27 March 20X2, was presented to the bank for payment on 4 April 20X2. Several cheques drawn prior to 31 March 20X3 but presented for payment after that date are summarized as stated below:

To supplier of cleaning materials	3,400
London Electricity plc	2,200
School fees for Dave's son	8,500

	£
Overdraft as at 1 April 20X2	24,600
Suppliers of cleaning materials	84,600
Wages to valets and cleaners	128,200
Other administrative staff salary	46,800
Capital and interest: Highland Bank	22,000
Advertising	2,400
Motor vehicle (bought on 1.7.20X2)	30,000
Insurance – year ended 30.4.20X3	7,200
Rent for business premises	25,000
Electricity and heating	4,400
Other administrative expenses	17,100
Maintenance of equipment	4,600
Cheques dishonoured	7,200
Dave's living expenses	29,500
Balance on 31 March 20X3	32,200
Bank lodgements in the year	465,800

Bank lodgements awaiting clearance on 31.3.20X3 totalled £11,400 and on on 31.3.20X2 totalled £27,500.

(b) One of the cheques, for £2,500, which had been dishonoured in the year, was replaced with cash, while the others were honoured on subsequent re-presentation.

(c) A motor vehicle, acquired for £24,000 on 1.7.20X0, was sold for £11,500 on 30.6.20X2. Dave depreciates motor vehicles at 20 per cent per annum by the reducing balance method.

(d) Assets and liabilities of the business, other than those already referred to, are as stated in the table on the right.

	31.3.20X2	31.3.20X3
	£	£
Stock – cleaning material	7,780	11,200
Due from customers	17,600	29,400
Rent due from shop	1,500	3,500
Insurance prepaid	500	?
Owed to suppliers	16,400	28,500
Admin. staff salary owed	8,800	9,200
Rent accrued	5,000	?

Required: Complete the following table to ascertain the correct amounts to be included in the cash book, and then prepare a Profit and Loss account for the year ended 31.3.20X3 and a Balance Sheet as at that date.

BANK RECONCILIATION

	As stated in the question	Cheques not presented by 31.3.20X2	Deposits not credited by 31.3.20X2	Cheques not presented by 31.3.20X3	Deposits not credited by 31.3.20X3	The correct position
Overdraft – 1.4.20X2	(24,600)					
Bank lodgements	465,800					
Payments:						
Creditors	(84,600)					
Wages	(128,200)					
Staff salaries	(46,800)					
Capital and interest	(22,000)					
Advertising	(2,400)					
Motor vehicle	(30,000)					
Insurance	(7,200)					
Rent	(25,000)					
Electricity	(4,400)					
Other admin.	17,100					
Equip. maintenance	4,600					
Dishonoured cheque	(7,200)					
Drawings	(29,500)					
Balance – 31.3.20X3	32,200					

PQ 27.3 Incomplete records of a VAT-registered trader

BALANCE SHEET AS AT 30.6.20X4

	Cost	Ac. depn	£
Vehicles	120,000	(48,000)	72,000
Equipment	86,000	(25,800)	60,200
Stock at cost		194,600	
Debtors less provision		152,950	
Cash and bank		34,250	
Trade creditors		(188,945)	
Salaries accrued		(18,400)	
Other accruals		(10,810)	
VAT account		(10,845)	152,800
			285,000
			£
Capital – Carl Moss			265,500
Profit for the year			77,800
Drawings			(58,300)
			285,000

Carl Moss, a wholesale dealer in ready-made menswear, achieves a gross profit ratio of 50 per cent. The Balance Sheet of the business as at 30.6.20X4 is shown on the left. Since then, the accounting function has been neglected, though on the basis of records in his personal diary Carl confirms as follows:

(a) As at 30.6.20X5, £276,000 is due from customers and £216,200 is owed to suppliers.
(b) During the year ended 30.6.20X4, the payments set out in the table below have been made.

	£
Paid for purchases (including VAT @ 17.5%)	501,495
Staff salaries	200,260
Rent for shop premises	24,000
Entertainment (including VAT @ 17.5%)	4,025
Office equipment (including VAT @ 17.5%)	29,375
Motor vehicles (including VAT @ 17.5%)	35,250
Other expenses (including VAT @ 17.5%)	66,035
Personal expenses	26,500
HM Customs and excise department	32,500

You are further informed as follows:

(a) A vehicle acquired for £30,000 on 1.4.20X0 was sold for £7,660 in the year.
(b) Motor vehicles and equipment are depreciated at 20 per cent and 10 per cent p.a. on cost, respectively. The depreciation policy is to charge a full year's depreciation in the year of acquisition and none in the year of disposal.
(c) A provision for doubtful debts is maintained at 5 per cent of debtors outstanding at the year end.
(d) Debts amounting to £43,475 were written off in the year.
(e) Accruals as at 30.6.20X5 consisted of salaries £21,200, rent £6,000 and other expenses inclusive of VAT at 17.5 per cent, amounting to £27,025.
(f) Cash in hand and at bank on 30.6.20X5 is £815.
(g) Stock in trade on 30.6.20X5, valued at cost including VAT at 17.5 per cent, is £198,810.
(h) Carl's teenage sons have been regularly helping themselves to ready-made garments from the shop.

Required: Prepare the Trading and Profit and Loss account for the year ended 30 June 20X5 and the Balance Sheet as at that date.

Chapter 28

ACCOUNTING FOR NON-TRADING CONCERNS

In this chapter

We will learn to account for entities other than those engaged in trading activity and observe that accounting is still on double entry basis, although the accounting terminology is different

---

28.1 DIFFERENT ACCOUNTING TERMINOLOGY

Our focus so far has been on *trading* concerns. We have now to consider the accounting systems of other concerns, which are referred to as *non-trading* concerns. They include entities engaged in a variety of activities ranging from not-for-profit entities to those very much in the profit sector.

The not-for-profit sector includes:

- members' fellowships, which might be known as associations, clubs, societies, unions or groups, the primary focus of which is the welfare of the members rather than pursuit of profit;
- *organizations* such as charities, universities, churches, local government authorities, and trade unions, all of which operate with identified aims and work for the benefit of those who are targeted by them.

The profit-motivated service sector consists of concerns that, though not engaged in trading of goods, sell services in pursuit of profit. They include:

- professionals in public practice, such as accountants, solicitors, architects and doctors;
- providers of services, such as transport, telecommunications, entertainment, banking, insurance, finance and the like.

Non-trading concerns, whether not-for-profit or profit-motivated, have to maintain proper books of account in order to provide the information to report properly their performance and financial position. This means recording their activities and events, when measurable in money value, on the double entry system. The main difference, though, is that non-traders have their own accounting terminology, as stated below:

Trading concerns	Non-trading concerns	
	If profit-motivated	If not profit-motivated
Cashier	Cashier	Treasurer
Cash account	Receipts and Payments account	Receipts and Payments account
Capital account	Capital account	Accumulated Fund
Trading and Profit and Loss	Income and Expenditure account	Income and Expenditure account
Profit (or Loss)	Profit (or loss)	Surplus (or deficiency)
Balance Sheet	Balance Sheet	Balance Sheet

28.2 ACCOUNTING FOR MEMBERS' FELLOWSHIPS: CLUBS, ASSOCIATIONS AND SOCIETIES

28.2.1 The accounting system

There are special aspects of the accounting system that need to be highlighted. Some are in accordance with the table above; those and others are discussed below.

The counterpart of a cashier in a not-for-profit concern is a treasurer, sometimes with a prefix honorary if he or she is not remunerated for the services provided.

The summarized Cash account is called a Receipts and Payments account. The receipts and payments of cash are recorded in this account and are then posted to appropriate ledger accounts, the accuracy of posting being checked from time to time by extracting a Trial Balance.

The usual period-end adjustments are made to the ledger balances. Income, including membership subscriptions (which typically are the main source), is accounted for on an accruals basis, as are the expenses. At the end of each accounting period the income and expenditure balances are transferred to an **Income and Expenditure account** (see format on the right) to determine whether the result of the period's activity is a 'surplus' (if income exceeds expenditure) or a 'deficiency' (if expenditure exceeds income).

The assets and liabilities reported in the ledger, on the last day of each accounting period, are listed in a Balance Sheet (see format on the right) in exactly the same way as for traders. The most noticeable difference is that *capital* is replaced by an **Accumulated Fund**. As always, the Accumulated Fund plus the surplus denotes the capital employed and equals the net assets on that date.

INCOME AND EXPENDITURE ACCOUNT FOR THE YEAR ENDED XXXXX	
	£
Income	400
Less: Expenses	(280)
Surplus (deficiency)	120

BALANCE SHEET AS AT XXXXXXXX		
	£	£
Fixed assets		300
Current assets	120	
Less: Current liabilities	(80)	40
		340
Accumulated Fund		220
Add: Surplus for the year		120
		340

Interaction 28.1	**The accounts of a society**

Peter Hews, honorary treasurer of the newly formed Dowell University Alumni Society, submits to the Annual General Meeting of the Society the following account, with a claim that the Society made a profit of £39,000 in the first year to 31 December 20X0.

	£
Membership subscriptions received	116,500
Sale of dance tickets	22,650
Loan from Dowell University	50,000
Less: Rent for three years to 31.12.20X2	(36,000)
Vehicles (bought on 1.4.20X0)	(40,000)
Furniture (bought on 1.1.20X0)	(24,000)
Caretaker's salary	(8,800)
Printing and stationery	(3,650)
Lighting and heating	(2,250)
Membership welfare	(15,600)
Dance night expenses – May Ball	(18,750)
Telephone/postage	(1,100)
Balance at bank on 31 December 20X0	39,000

Required:

(a) What would you call the account shown above?
(b) Do you agree with Peter's claim?
(c) Prepare the society's Income and Expenditure account and Balance Sheet for the year ended 31.12.20X0, taking into account the information stated below:

	£
Caretaker's salary remaining unpaid	800
Owed to the caterer for May Ball	7,650
Telephone bill outstanding	350

Assume that subscriptions due have all been received and that vehicles and furniture are to be depreciated at 20 per cent and 10 per cent respectively on cost.

28.2.2 Accounting for membership subscriptions

When individuals organize themselves into a club, society or association, the main income usually is membership subscription, which is accounted for in one of two methods, as set out next.

Method 1

Subscriptions received are posted from the Receipts and Payments account to an income account named Subscriptions Receivable. Let us assume that in addition to £18,000 received as subscriptions in the year, £2,000 more is receivable as at the year end. The entries will be:

SUBSCRIPTIONS RECEIVABLE (INCOME) ACCOUNT

	£		£
		Receipts and payments	18,000
		Subs receivable – asset	2,000

SUBSCRIPTIONS RECEIVABLE (ASSET) ACCOUNT

	£		£
Subs receivable – Inc	2,000		

Confusion may be created because both the income account and the asset account are often named identically. The income account records the amount of subscriptions received in the year as well as the amount yet to be received by the year end, so that the total earning of £20,000 could be transferred to the Income and Expenditure account. The asset account records the unreceived portion of the income, which is stated as an asset on the Balance Sheet.

Method 2

An alternative method that is met in practice is, at the very commencement of each year, to credit the Subscriptions Receivable (income) account and debit a Subscriptions Receivable (asset) account with the total subscriptions expected in the year. Amounts, as received, are posted from the Receipts and Payments account to the Subscriptions Receivable (asset) account. The balance in the latter account would then represent the amount of subscriptions yet to be collected. The accounts would then appear as follows:

SUBSCRIPTIONS RECEIVABLE (INCOME) ACCOUNT

	£		£
		Subs receivable	20,000

SUBSCRIPTIONS RECEIVABLE (ASSET) ACCOUNT

	£		£
Subs receivable	20,000	Receipts and payments	18,000
		Balance c/d	2,000

Interaction 28.2

Accounting for subscription income

The following particulars relate to two different associations. Each accounts for subscription income on an accruals basis.

- The first association uses Method 1. It received £246,000 as membership subscriptions during the year ended 31.12.20X0 and £48,000 is still receivable as at that date.
- The second association uses Method 2. It has 2,400 members, each paying £5 per month, and has received £105,600 as subscriptions for the year to 31.12.20X0.

Required: Set out the relevant ledger accounts and state how these transactions will be reported in the Income and Expenditure account and the Balance Sheet of each association.

Subscriptions Receivable account as a Debtors' Control account

As an association continues in existence and accounts for subscription income on an accruals basis, it is likely that at any point of time some members will be in arrears for subscription while others will have paid in advance. Just as the former is reported as an asset, the latter should be reported as a liability. In order to keep a track of the amounts that individual members owe or are owed, it is usual to keep a register (or, if necessary, a subsidiary ledger) and it is convenient to write up the Subscription Receivable account (the one we identified as an asset) as a Control account. In that case, it is like a Debtors Control account in that, on the same date, it could have a debit balance (of amounts in arrears) as well as a credit balance of subscriptions received in advance. The Control account format will appear as follows:

SUBSCRIPTIONS RECEIVABLE (ASSET) ACCOUNT

Balance b/f (*arrears*)		Balance b/f (*advance*)	
Subs receivable (*income*)		Receipts and payments	
Balance c/d (*advance*)		Balance c/d (*arrears*)	
Balance b/d (*arrears*)		Balance b/d (*advance*)	

Interaction 28.3

Subscriptions Receivable account

Tooting Jazz Club has 640 members, each paying a monthly subscription of £10. The Subscriptions Register of Members reveals as follows:

	31.3.20X0	31.3.20X1
Subscriptions in arrears	£42,800	£54,400
Subscription received in advance	£6,200	£9,600

Required: Set out the Subscriptions Receivable (Control) account of the club and state how the information provided will feature in the Income and Expenditure account for the year ended 31.3.20X1 and the Balance Sheet as at that date.

28.2.3 Accounting for membership enrolment (or joining) fees

There are two points of view on how an association should account for enrolment (joining) fees. Either method of accounting is acceptable, provided the method is disclosed and is adopted *consistently* from year to year.

Spreading the fee

The first viewpoint is that the benefit of such fees should accrue in a systematic manner to the many years over which that person is expected to remain a member. The reasoning is that a club may levy substantial enrolment fees for the purpose of keeping the recurrent annual subscriptions low. Unless the fees are spread over the years, the performance in later years will tend to be understated and, as clubs tend to focus on recruitment mainly in the early years, they may give a misleading appearance of doing well in those years.

Crediting the fee to income in the year of receipt

The opposite view is that enrolment fees are earnings in the year in which they are received. The reasoning is that, to remain ongoing, a club has to continuously focus on the enrolment of new membership.

28.2.4 Accounting for life membership fees

Some clubs or associations may, for a single large fee, grant life membership. Clearly, it is not possible to estimate precisely each member's life expectancy and it is normal practice to spread the amount received on a reasonable and systematic basis using an estimated average number of years. The accounting procedure in this case is to credit the fees received to a Life Membership account, from which a reasonable portion is released annually to the Income and Expenditure account, with the remainder reported in the Balance Sheet as deferred income. The proportion released each year depends on the policy adopted by the club.

28.2.5 Collections for a specified purpose

Any amounts collected for a particular charitable or other purpose are posted from the Receipts and Payments account to a Liability account maintained in the name of that charity or activity. Payments made for the purpose are accounted for as an offset from the amount owed to the charity or set apart for the activity.

28.2.6 Special funds

Though the totality of resources available to a non-profit-motivated organization is usually stated in an Accumulated Fund, it may exceptionally set apart portions of its resources to special funds devoted, for example, to a particular kind of charitable work or any other special intention. Resources collected for an identified purpose have to be reported as a separate fund and, if so instructed by the provider of the funds, the assets representing the fund may also have to be segregated from other assets.

28.2.7 Trading activity of a non-trading concern

If a non-trading concern engages in a trading activity – such as running a bar for its members – it has to prepare a Trading account to report the results of the related transactions. Normally it should be possible to include the Trading account as an inset within the Income and Expenditure account (see illustration below).

INCOME AND EXPENDITURE ACCOUNT FOR THE YEAR ENDED XXXXX			
	£	£	£
Subscriptions receivable			7,500
Sales of refreshments		185	
Opening stock	20		
Purchases	150		
Less: Closing stock	(30)		
Cost of refreshments sold		(140)	
Surplus/(Deficit) on refreshments			45
Less: Expenses			(6,800)
Surplus of income over expenses			745

Income and Expenditure account

Accounting Juniors, an association of accountancy students, submits to you its Balance Sheet (as stated on the right) and a summary of its bank statements (as stated below).

		£
Bank balance – 1.1.20X1		526
Subscriptions for	20X0	162
Subscriptions for	20X1	4,464
Subscriptions for	20X2	94
Sale of text books		9,064
Purchase of text books		(7,725)
Meeting expenses		(418)
Membership welfare		(874)
Rent of premises		(1,750)
Admin. expenses		(965)
Balance on 31.12.20X1		2,578

BALANCE SHEET AS AT 31.12.20X0	
	£
Fixed assets at wdv	12,400
Stock of text books	5,850
Subscription in arrears	342
Bank balance	276
Creditors for text books	(1,625)
Subscriptions for 20X1	(78)
Rent in arrears	(500)
Accumulated Fund	16,665

You are informed as follows:

(a) Premises have been rented at £250 per month.

(b) A cheque drawn in payment of one month's rent had not been presented to the bank for payment as at 31.12.20X0.

(c) The membership register reveals that subscriptions due for the year to 31.12.20X1 were £5,968.

(d) As at 31.1.20X1, creditors for text books are owed £1,925.

(e) Accounting text books, purchased in bulk, are sold to members at cost plus 10 per cent.

(f) Fixed assets are depreciated by 10 per cent of book value.

(g) Subscription income is accounted for on an accruals basis.

Required: Prepare the Income and Expenditure account of the association for the year to 31.12.20X1 and the Balance Sheet as at that date.

28.3 ACCOUNTING FOR MEMBERSHIP SUBSCRIPTIONS ON A RECEIPTS BASIS

A club, and others in a similar position, may not always be able to recover arrears of membership subscriptions. The members might have moved or it is too expensive to seek to recover the arrears through courts of law. Thus it may be prudent for the club or association to account for the subscriptions income only to the extent received (i.e. on a receipts basis). An Income and Expenditure account in which subscription income is accounted on a receipts basis is sometimes called (though not quite correctly, because it would be wrong to use the words 'receipts' and 'income' as synonyms), a *Receipts and Expenditure account*.

Interaction
28.5

Receipts and Expenditure account

Answer question IQ 28.4 again, on the basis this time that the association accounts for sub-scriptions income on a receipts basis. Remember that, on a receipts basis, subscriptions in arrears would not have appeared as an asset in the Balance Sheet on 31.12.20X0 and, accord-ingly, the Accumulated Fund as at that date would have amounted to £16,323.

Although an association might choose to account for subscriptions income in the Income and Expenditure account on a receipts basis, it might still decide to maintain a record in the ledger of any subscriptions in arrears, for the purpose of keeping track of these amounts and attempting to recover them. This can be done by accounting for the subscriptions in arrears as if applying the accruals basis and then setting up a 'Provision for subscriptions not received' to cover the whole of the amount in arrears. Assuming that the year's subscriptions due amount to £10,000 and that £9,400 has been received, the position will be reported on a receipts basis as shown below. As we can see, the effect of these entries is to maintain a record on the face of the Balance Sheet of the amount unpaid but not to state it as an asset (by including it in the Balance Sheet total).

INCOME AND EXPENDITURE ACCOUNT FOR YEAR ENDED XXXXX		BALANCE SHEET AS AT XXXXXXX	
	£		£
Subscription receivable	10,000	Subscriptions receivable	600
Provision for subs not received	(600)	Provision for subs not received	(600)
Subs on a receipts basis	9,400		–

Interaction
28.6

Income on a receipts basis with a provision to cover arrears

Answer IQ 28.4 again, assuming that the association opts to account for subscriptions in arrears on a receipts basis and yet wishes to record in the ledger the amount of the arrears.

SOLUTIONS TO INTERACTIVE QUESTIONS

IQ 28.1 The accounts of a society

(a) **Receipts and Payments account** is the non-trading concern's equivalent of a Cash account, listing all receipts and payments.

(b) **The performance within a period cannot be gauged from the cash balance alone.** This is because of the following:

   1. The performance in an accounting period is measured not by comparing receipts with payments but by comparing accomplishment (measured in terms of income) with effort (measured in terms of costs incurred in the process). This is done, in a trading concern, by preparing a Trading and Profit and Loss account and, in a non-trading concern, by preparing an Income and Expenditure account.

   2. Changes in cash balance do not always correspond with the performance in a period. The cash bal-ance may improve because of borrowings (the loan from the university, for instance) or a delay in meeting expenses; or the cash balance may be reduced by the acquisition of assets (the vehicle and furniture as well as rent prepaid) or because of discharging liability.

   3. Earnings may not be reflected in the cash balance because they are yet to be received in cash.

   4. Expenses such as depreciation and bad debts do not involve immediate cash outflow.

(c) The society's financial statements

INCOME AND EXPENDITURE ACCOUNT FOR THE YEAR ENDED 31.12.20X0			N 1
		£	
Membership subscription		116,500	2
Dance night sale	22,650		3
Related expense	(26,400)	(3,750)	4
Caretaker's salary		(9,600)	4
Rent		(12,000)	5
Printing and stationery		(3,650)	
Lighting and heating		(2,250)	
Telephone and postage		(1,450)	4
Membership welfare		(15,600)	
Depreciation – vehicles		(6,000)	6
Depreciation – furniture		(2,400)	6
Surplus of income over expenditure		59,800	7

BALANCE SHEET AS AT 31.12.20X0					
	Cost	Ac. dep	£		
Vehicles	40,000	(6,000)	34,000		
Furniture	24,000	(2,400)	21,600		
Prepaid rent		24,000			5
Bank balance		39,000			
Salary accrued		(800)			4
Owed to caterer		(7,650)			4
Telephone accrued		(350)	54,200		4
			109,800		
			£		
Accumulated Fund			59,800		7
Loan – Dowell University			50,000		
			109,800		

Notes:

1. The counterpart of a Trading and Profit and Loss account, in a non-trading concern, is the Income and Expenditure account.
2. For associations, clubs and societies, the main income is the membership subscription.
3. By matching income with related expenses, an effort is being made to focus on the results of a particular activity.
4. Expenses remaining unpaid have been accrued.
5. The pre-paid portion of rent is capitalized.
6. Though not profit-motivated, clubs and societies too have to depreciate their assets so that they may be able to replace the assets in time.
7. The excess of income over expenses is called a 'surplus' rather than profit. Such surpluses, accumulated over the years, are appropriately referred to as the Accumulated Fund.

IQ 28.2 Accounting for subscription income

First Association:

SUBSCRIPTION RECEIVABLE (INCOME) ACCOUNT[a]			
	£		£
		Cash a/c	246,000
		Subs receivable	48,000
			294,000

SUBSCRIPTION RECEIVABLE (ASSET) ACCOUNT[b]			
	£		£
Subs receivable	48,000		

Second Association:

SUBSCRIPTION RECEIVABLE (INCOME) ACCOUNT[a]				SUBSCRIPTION RECEIVABLE (ASSET) ACCOUNT[b]			
	£		£		£		£
		Subs receivable	144,000	Subs receivable	144,000	Rec. & Paym. a/c	105,600
						Balance c/d	38,400
				Balance b/d	38,400		

a. The balance in the income account is transferred to the Income and Expenditure account.
b. The balance in the asset account, being subscriptions in arrears at year end, is reported as an asset on the Balance Sheet.

IQ 28.3 Subscriptions Receivable account

SUBSCRIPTIONS RECEIVABLE (CONTROL) ACCOUNT

		£			£
31.3.20X0	Balance b/f	42,800	31.3.20X0	Balance b/f	6,200
	Subs receivable (income)	76,800		Cash account	68,600
31.3.20X1	Balance c/d	9,600	31.3.20X1	Balance c/d	54,400
1.4.20X1	Balance b/d	54,400	1.4.20X1	Balance b/d	9,600

The Income and Expenditure Account will report the subscription income as £76,800. The Balance Sheet as at 31.3.20X1 will report the subscriptions in arrears of £54,400 as an asset, and the subscription received in advance of £9,600 as a liability.

IQ 28.4 Income and Expenditure account

INCOME AND EXPENDITURE ACCOUNT FOR THE YEAR ENDED 31 DECEMBER 20X1			
	£	£	£
Subscriptions receivable			5,968
Sales of text books		9,064	
Stock – 1.1.20X1	5,850		
Purchases	8,025		
Stock – 31.12.20X1	(5,635)	(8,240)	824
Less: Expenses:			
Rent		(3,000)	
Meeting expenses		(418)	
Membership welfare		(874)	
Admin. expenses		(965)	
Depreciation		(1,240)	(6,497)
Surplus of income over expense			295

BALANCE SHEET AS AT 31.12.20X1	
	£
Fixed assets at written down value	11,160
Stock of text books for sale	5,635
Members' subscription receivable	1,606
Balance at bank	2,578
Rent in arrears	(2,000)
Subscriptions received in advance	(94)
Creditors for text book supply	(1,925)
	16,960

	£
Accumulated Fund – 1.1.20X1	16,665
Surplus for the year to 31.12.20X1	295
	16,960

SUBSCRIPTIONS RECEIVABLE (CONTROL) ACCOUNT

	£		£
Balance b/f	342	Balance b/f	78
Subs receivable	5,968	Receipts and payments	4,720
Balance c/d	94	Balance c/d	1,606
Balance b/d	1,606	Balance b/d	94

RENT ACCOUNT

	£		£
Receipts and payments	1,500	Balance	500
Balance c/d	2,000	Inc. & Exp.	3,000

CREDITORS FOR TEXT BOOK SUPPLY ACCOUNT

	£		£
Receipts and payments	7,725	Balance b/f	1,625
Balance c/d	1,925	Purchases	8,025
		Balance b/d	1,925

IQ 28.5 Receipts and Expenditure account

RECEIPTS AND EXPENDITURE ACCOUNT FOR THE YEAR ENDED 31.12.20X1

			£
Subscriptions on receipts basis			4,704
Sales of text books		9,064	
Stock – 1.1.20X1	5,850		
Purchases	8,025		
Stock – 31.12.20X1	(5,635)	(8,240)	824
Less: Expenses:			
Rent		(3,000)	
Meeting expenses		(418)	
Membership welfare		(874)	
Admin. expenses		(965)	
Depreciation		(1,240)	(6,497)
Deficiency for the year			(969)

BALANCE SHEET AS AT 31.12.20X1

	£
Fixed assets at written down value	11,160
Stock of text books for sale	5,635
Balance at bank	2,578
Rent in arrears	(2,000)
Subscription received in advance	(94)
Creditors for text book supply	(1,925)
	15,354

	£
Accumulated Fund – 1.1.20X1	16,323
Deficiency for the year	(969)
	15,354

SUBSCRIPTIONS RECEIVABLE (CONTROL) ACCOUNT

	£		£
Subs receivable	4,704	Balance b/f	78
Balance b/d	94	Receipts and payments	4,720
		Balance b/d	94

When accounting for subscription income, arrears at the end of each year are ignored but subscriptions received in advance are taken into account.

IQ 28.6 Income on a receipts basis with a provision to cover arrears

INCOME AND EXPENDITURE ACCOUNT FOR THE YEAR ENDED 31 DECEMBER 20X1	£	£	£
Subscriptions receivable			5,968
Sales of text books		9,064	
Stock – 1.1.20X1	5,850		
Purchases	8,025		
Stock – 31.12.20X1	(5,635)	(8,240)	824
Less: Expenses:			
Rent		(3,000)	
Meeting expenses		(418)	
Membership welfare		(874)	
Administ expenses		(965)	
Provision for subs in arrears*		(1,264)	
Depreciation		(1,240)	(7,761)
Deficiency for the year			(969)

BALANCE SHEET AS AT 31.12.20X1	£	£
Fixed assets at written down value		11,160
Stock of text books for sale		5,635
Subscription receivable	1,606	
Provision for subs. in arrears	(1,606)	–
Balance at bank		2,578
Rent in arrears		(2,000)
Subscriptions received in advance		(94)
Creditors for text book supply		(1,925)
		15,354
		£
Accumulated Fund – 1.1.20X1		16,323
Deficiency for the year		(969)
		15,354

* The provision for subscriptions in arrears may be stated in the Income and Expenditure account as a deduction from subscriptions income.

SUBSCRIPTION RECEIVABLE (CONTROL) ACCOUNT

	£		£
Balance b/f	342	Balance b/f	78
Subs receivable	5,968	Receipts and payment	4,270
Balance c/d	94	Balance c/d	1,606
Balance b/d	1,606	Balance b/d	94

PROVISION FOR ARREARS OF SUBSCRIPTION

	£		£
		Balance b/f	342
Balance c/d	1,606	Income and exp.	1,264
		Balance b/d	1,606

PROGRESSIVE QUESTIONS

PQ 28.1 Accounts of a social club

The Treasurer of the Seaford Social Club has prepared his accounts for 20X1 as stated on the right. The following additional information is available:

	1.1.20X1	31.12.20X1
	£	£
Club house at cost	140,000	140,000
Fixtures and fittings	16,800	21,120
Stock of bar supplies	6,440	5,880
Creditors for bar supplies	4,760	4,564
Subscriptions receivable	1,850	1,820
Accrued clubhouse expenses	–	1,120

RECEIPTS AND PAYMENTS ACCOUNT FOR THE YEAR ENDED 31.12.20X1	
	£
1.1　Balance	1,456
Subscriptions for 20X1	58,828
Subscriptions for 20X0	1,400
Bar takings	98,560
Salaries	(85,400)
Ground maintenance	(2,128)
Office supplies	(812)
Clubhouse expenses	(4,480)
Bar supplies	(59,920)
Fixtures and fittings	(7,000)
31.12　Balance	504

Required: Prepare the Income and Expenditure account for the year ended 31 December 20X1 and the Balance Sheet as at that date.

PQ 28.2 Accounting for subscriptions receivable

The following particulars relate to three different associations, 'A' 'B' and 'C'.

Association 'A'

At 1.1.20X1, subscriptions in arrears were £21,600 and those received in advance were £9,460. In the year to 31.12.20X1, subscriptions were received totalling £124,580. At 31.12.20X1, subscriptions in arrears amounted to £34,580 and those received in advance amounted to £11,400.

Association 'B'

This association has 460 members, each paying a monthly subscription of £10. At 1.1.20X1 the members had paid 30 months' subscriptions in advance; and were in arrears for 54 months' subscription overall. At 31.12.20X1, 24 month's subscription had been received in advance, but members were in arrears for 66 months' subscription.

Association 'C'

Subscriptions in arrears were £82,600 on 1.1.20X1 and £106,400 on 31.12.20X1. The amount of £368,500 received as subscription in the year to 31.12.20X1 includes £44,600 for the previous year and £15,800 for 20X2. As at 31.12.20X0, £21,400 of year 20X1's subscriptions and £6,200 of year 20X2's subscriptions had been received in advance.

Required: Calculate the membership subscription income to be accounted for by each association in respect of the year to 31 December 20X1 on (a) an accruals basis, and (b) a receipts basis.

PQ 28.3 The accounts of an association

When a Welfare Association was formed on 1.1.20X0, the tenants of all 420 flats on Greenwood Lane Complex joined as members. The membership fee was agreed at £10 per month. Two hundred and eighty of these tenants agreed also to pay an additional fee of £25 per month for crèche facilities. The borough council reciprocated by allocating a three-roomed flat, rent-free, for use as offices of the Association and approving an annual grant of £25,000. On completing the first year of activities, the Association prepared its Receipts and Payments account as follows:

GREENWOOD LANE FLAT TENANTS' WELFARE ASSOCIATION
RECEIPTS AND PAYMENTS ACCOUNT FOR THE YEAR TO 31.12.20X0

	£		£
Membership fees for year 20X0	46,800	Watchman's salary	19,600
Membership fees for year 20X1	6,400	Crèche attendants	38,800
Crèche fees for year 20X0	75,500	Furniture	16,400
Crèche fees for year 20X1	1,250	Garden maintenance	12,800
Grant from borough council	25,000	Snooker tables	16,000
Sale: Xmas raffle tickets	7,450	Crèche consumables	21,450
		Xmas party raffle	4,500
		Xmas party expenses	5,150
		Sports consumables	11,200
		Admin. expenses	13,650
		Balance at bank	2,850
Balance b/d	2,850		

You are further informed as follows:

(a) Sports consumables costing £1,500 remain unused as at 31.12.20X0.
(b) Membership fees and crèche fees due for a seven-month period were written off because a tenant had left the country.
(c) Expenses stated in the box on the right remain unpaid as at 31.12.20X0.
(d) One-tenth of the cost of furniture and a snooker table should be written off as depreciation.

Crèche attendants' salary	£12,800
Watchman's salary	£1,350
Supplier of crèche consumables	£6,750

Required: Prepare the Income and Expenditure account for the year ended 31 December 20X0 and a Balance Sheet as at that date.

PQ 28.4 Enrolment fees and special-purpose collections

Surbiton West Cricket Club, though formed in 20X0, never maintained proper books of account. Their transactions, however, were always through a bank account. They have two types of membership: sporting members pay £20 per month and social members pay £15 per month. A non-refundable fee of £250, charged on joining, is regarded as part of the income for the year. The bank statements for the year ended 31.12.20X3 have been summarized as stated on the following page.

	£
Balance at bank on 1.1.20X3	4,250

	In respect of the years			
	20X0/20X2	20X3	20X4	
Sporting membership fees	11,200	118,800	1,920	131,920
Social membership fees	13,440	58,050	3,960	75,450

	£
Joining fees	21,500
Collections for mentally handicapped charity	7,650
Bar takings	65,480
Sale of refreshments	21,345
Staff salary	(74,480)
Purchase of refreshments	(16,850)
Furniture and fittings	(30,000)
Donations to the mentally handicapped	(6,200)
Repayment of mortgage loan	(25,000)
Interest on the mortgage loan	(6,875)
Purchase of sporting consumables	(22,600)
Bar purchases	(66,600)
Membership welfare	(14,260)
Administrative expenses	(26,680)
Clubhouse maintenance	(22,450)
Travel expenses on away matches reimbursed	(14,260)
Balance at bank on 31 December 20X3	1,340

You have gathered the following additional information:

(a) £12,440 of sporting membership subscriptions and £4,250 of social membership subscriptions are to be written off in the year.
(b) Regular till collections are made on match days for the benefit of those mentally handicapped.
(c) The assets and liabilities of the club include the following:

	31.12.20X2	31.12.20X3
	£	£
Clubhouse at cost	240,000	240,000
Furniture at book value	72,500	?
Debtors for sporting membership fees	28,400	40,510
Debtors for social membership fees	19,450	28,460
Stock of sporting consumables	11,250	14,550
Stock of bar supplies	24,650	21,500
Debtors for bar sales	6,450	16,550
Subscription in advance – sporting membership	1,450	?
Subscription in advance – social membership	2,550	?
Creditors for bar supplies	5,650	4,400
Creditors for refreshment supplies	1,560	3,450
Owed to mentally handicapped charity	4,250	?
Loan on mortgage of club house premises	125,000	?

(d) The clubhouse is not depreciated; one-fifth of the year-end book value of furniture is written off as depreciation.

Required: Prepare the Income and Expenditure account of the club for the year ended 31 December 20X3 and the Balance Sheet as at that date.

PQ 28.5 Receipts and Expenditure account

The chairman of the Governing Committee of the Surbiton West Cricket Club (see PQ 28.4) rejects the financial statements prepared by you on two premises, as follows:

1. Reporting the arrears of membership subscriptions as an asset is meaningless because members in default are not going to be pursued through the courts. It is more prudent to account for subscriptions on a receipts basis.
2. Since the sales at the bar are always effected at cost plus 20 per cent, it would appear that there has been a misappropriation of bar takings, the extent of which should be determined and recovered from the pay of the bar attendants.

Required: Prepare the club's financial statements for the year to 31.12.20X3 again, complying with the chairman's wishes.

PQ 28.6 Life membership fees and special funds

A Single Parents Association of Great Britain (SPAGB) was formed on 1 April 20X0. The joining fee was fixed at £50 and quarterly subscriptions at £20 per member. The quarters commence on 1 April, 1 July, 1 October and 1 January. A member joining at any point within a quarter has to pay subscription for the whole quarter. Life membership is offered at £1,000 per member. The membership register shows that, as at 31.3.20X1, there were 78 life members and 12,350 other members, whose position as regards membership fees is stated in the table here.

Quarters ending on:	Numbers joining in each quarter	NUMBERS IN ARREARS AS AT 31.3.20X1 FOR MEMBERSHIP FEES IN RESPECT OF		
		2nd, 3rd, and 4th quarters	3rd and 4th quarters	4th quarter only
30.6.20X0	1,650	150	275	500
30.9.20X0	3,150	–	300	450
31.12.20X0	4,700	–	–	250
31.3.20X1	2,850	–	–	–
TOTAL	12,350	150	575	1,200

During the year to 31.3.20X1, a legacy of £100,000 was received, on the death of Philomin Rutlish, a single parent. The terms of the legacy are that the amount should be held separately in gilt-edged securities to be used, as necessity arises, to offer relief to single parents in financial distress.

The Treasurer of SPAGB has prepared a Receipts and Payments account of the Association for the year ended 31 March 20X1, as shown on the right. The Management Committee of the Association requests you to prepare the Association's financial statements for submission to its first Annual General Meeting. It has instructed you as follows:

(a) The amount of cash lost by misappropriation, which probably happened during the early days, should be written off.
(b) Life membership fees should be spread equally over ten years.
(c) Motor vehicles and furniture are to be depreciated at 20 per cent and 10 per cent per annum respectively, using the straight-line method.
(d) One-tenth of any surplus of income over expenditure in a year should be transferred to the Rutlish Fund. For purposes of this transfer, income from membership subscription should be accounted for on a receipts basis.

Required: Prepare the Income and Expenditure account of the Association for the year ended 31 March 20X1 and the Balance Sheet as at that date.

RECEIPTS AND PAYMENTS ACCOUNT	
	£
Twenty-year lease of office premises	250,000
Furniture (acquired 1.4.20X0)	80,000
Motor vehicles (acquired 1.7.20X0)	68,000
Staff salaries	178,500
Publication of SPA VOICE (a monthly) (newsletter)	118,560
Legal consultation and fees	72,500
Commission – canvassing membership	12,550
Insurance	14,500
Administrative expenses	185,580
Advertising/publicity	29,420
Campaign expenses on:	
Protect single mother's privileges	16,650
Stop tracking absentee fathers	8,450
Queen's Speech Day demonstrations	6,600
Cultivation of political lobby	45,690
Rutlish Fund investments	62,500
Distress relief (paid from Rutlish Fund)	42,635
Balance at bank on 31.3.20X1	89,570
Receipts during the year	1,281,705

Chapter 29

ACCOUNTS IN MANUFACTURING

In this chapter

We will learn of:

- the accounting processes in a manufacturing entity
- the need to allocate or apportion factory overheads to determine the factory cost of the item produced
- royalties and how they are accounted for

and you should be able to:

- prepare a manufacturing account
- allocate and apportion overheads
- value and account for work in progress
- adjust for unrealized profit if it occurs

29.1 THE NEED FOR A MANUFACTURING ACCOUNT

Our focus, until now, has been on traders who sell what they buy and ascertain their gross profit by comparing the sales income with the costs they incur to place the items sold in the *condition* in which they sold them and in the *location* from which they sold them. We have now to consider the case of those who sell goods *of their own manufacture*.

Clearly, for ascertaining gross profit, the manufacturer would compare sales income with the manufacturing cost of goods sold and the comparison would again be done in a Trading account. The process of ascertaining the manufacturing cost, however, would be done in a Manufacturing account, before it is transferred to the Trading account. The manufacturing cost of a product comprises both the prime (or direct) costs and the factory overheads, and these terms are explained further in the next two sections.

29.2 PRIME COSTS OF MANUFACTURE

A business producing what it sells has to select a unit (known as the *unit of cost*) with which its costs may be directly and conveniently associated. Such a unit of cost, for someone who manufactures high-quality wardrobes to order, would obviously be a wardrobe. On the basis of how readily costs can be associated with the unit of cost, the costs are classified as direct costs, which comprise those for directly used materials, labour and related expenses, and indirect costs, or overheads. For the first category (direct costs):

- **Direct materials** are the raw materials that are easily identified with a particular unit of cost. In the case of our wardrobe manufacturer, these would include the wood for the manufacture of the wardrobe and other items such as hinges, locks and sliding gear. Some materials of low value (such as nails, glue and screws), although capable of being identified with the unit of cost and therefore of being reckoned as 'direct', are nevertheless regarded as 'indirect' because it is not cost-effective to do otherwise.

- **Direct wages:** These are wages paid to employees who are directly engaged in the production process, e.g. cabinet-makers and joiners in the case of wardrobe manufacturers.
- **Direct expenses:** These are costs other than materials or wages that can nevertheless be directly associated with the unit of cost. An example, in the case of manufacturing wardrobes, would be the cost of designing the wardrobe or the royalties paid to the holders of a patent for the design.

The total of the above direct costs is called the ***prime cost*** of manufacture.

Ascertaining the prime cost

Light Engineering Works extracted the following balances as at the last day of the year:

Balances as at 30 June 20X1	£000	£000
Purchase of raw material	12,650	–
Productive wages	6,250	–
Royalty paid for design of the product	1,250	–
Stock of raw materials on 1.7.20X0	1,560	–

The stock of raw materials, at cost, as at 30.6.20X1 was £1,500,000.

Required: Calculate the prime cost of manufacture for the year ended 30.6.20X1 and the Balance Sheet entry as at that date.

29.3 TOTAL COST OF PRODUCTION

Expenses other than those reckoned as 'direct' are regarded as 'indirect' expenses, or **overheads** as they are otherwise known. They are functionally classified into three groups, as:

1. factory overheads;
2. administrative overheads;
3. selling and distribution overheads.

As stated in Section 29.1, prime cost together with factory overheads is referred to as the manufacturing (or factory) cost. Factory cost together with administrative overheads and selling and distribution overheads is referred to as the total cost of manufacture.

The make-up of costs may be shown diagrammatically as follows:

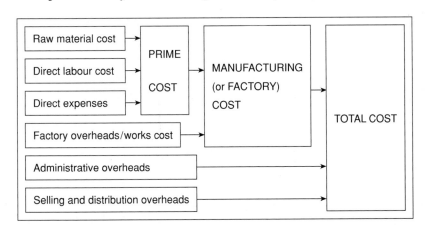

Factory overheads (also known as works costs) are indirect expenses incurred on the production function rather than on the administrative or distribution functions. They include:

- **Indirect materials** (also known as consumable stores), which themselves include materials of such insignificant value that it is not worthwhile identifying them individually with the unit of cost. For example, for a wardrobe manufacturer, the cost of glue, sandpaper and nails falls into this category.
- **Indirect wages**, which form the remuneration of those (such as supervisors, cleaners, caretakers and machine maintainers) who, though in the production department, are not directly engaged in the production process.
- **Machinery depreciation, repairs and maintenance**.
- **Power** for operating machinery.
- **Other expenses of the factory**, such as rent, insurance, heating, water and electricity.

MANUFACTURING ACCOUNT FOR THE YEAR ENDED XX.XX.XX	£000	£000
Raw materials consumed:		
Opening stock	124	
Purchases	3,260	
Less: Closing stock	(185)	3,199
Productive wages		1,462
Direct expenses		312
Prime cost		4,973
Factory overheads		
Depreciation of machinery	250	
Power	24	
Factory rent	180	
Consumable stores	48	502
Factory cost of goods manufactured		
transferred to Trading account		5,475

The prime cost as well as the factory overheads are stated in the Manufacturing account (as shown here), while the administrative as well as the selling and distribution overheads are stated in the Profit and Loss account.

Preparing a Manufacturing account

The Trial Balance extracted from the books of Light Engineering Works, by the year end, includes the following:

TRIAL BALANCE AS AT 30 JUNE 20X1	£000	£000
Sales		54,925
Machinery at cost	1,200	–
Stock on 1.7.20X0 – raw materials	214	–
Finished goods	628	–
Factory power	172	–
Purchase of raw materials	12,845	–
Salaries and wages	32,620	–
Rent and rates	6,000	–
Advertising	226	–
Other administrative expenses	852	–
Consumable stores	54	–

You are further informed as follows:

(a) Stock in hand as at 30 June 20X1 consisted of raw materials costing £315,000 and finished goods costing £476,000.
(b) Forty per cent of salaries and wages had been paid to workers directly engaged in the production process and ten per cent to others servicing the factory. One-third of rent relates to the factory.
(c) Machinery is to be depreciated using the straight-line method at 10 per cent per annum.

Required: Show how this information will appear in the Manufacturing account and the Trading and Profit and Loss account for the year ended 30.6.20X1, and in the Balance Sheet as at that date.

29.4 FINISHED GOODS REMAINING UNSOLD

The manufactured goods remaining unsold at the year end should be reported as an asset at their factory cost. Unless this is done, the whole of the factory cost incurred for producing units that have been sold in the year, as well as those remaining unsold, would be charged against the profit generated by those that were sold. This would understate the profit for the current year and overstate the profit in the following year when they are sold. Besides, it is the requirement of accepted accounting practice[1] that the cost of unsold manufactured goods should include 'production overheads'. The problem with ascertaining the factory cost of unsold goods is that, while the direct cost of each unit can easily be identified, some acceptable basis needs to be found to add on to each such unit an appropriate portion of factory overheads. In search of such an acceptable basis, let us enquire into the manner in which overheads are controlled.

29.4.1 Cost centres to collect and control overheads

For the purpose of controlling costs, activities can be organized into sections, which are referred to as cost centres, with a manager taking responsibility for collecting information on costs relating to that centre and for controlling them. In some cases it may be possible to identify an overhead with a particular cost centre. For example, if the Maintenance Department is a cost centre, then the wages of the maintenance staff could be specifically associated with that centre. Such expenses are, therefore, *allocated* to that centre. In other cases, however, the overhead may be of such general nature applicable to the business as a whole (e.g. rent) that an acceptable way has to be found to associate a portion thereof to each cost centre benefiting from it. This is known as *apportionment*. A reasonable way of apportioning rent among the different cost centres would be on the basis of the floorspace used by each centre.

29.4.2 The problem with service cost centres

Cost centres can be divided into two types:

- production cost centres, which (as the name implies) provide the organization's products; and
- service cost centres, which provide ancillary services to the production departments (e.g. maintenance, canteen, internal transport, boiler-house).

Having identified the costs with cost centres – whether production or service – if we are to achieve our objective of adding on a portion of all overheads to the product (the unit of cost), the service cost centres' expenses must be apportioned to the production cost centres before being absorbed into the product cost. There might be a complication if two service cost centres provide reciprocal services to each other – for example, the boiler-house may provide hot water to heat the canteen, which in turn provides meals for the boiler-house staff.

29.4.3 Apportioning overheads

Unlike when overheads are allocated to cost centres, apportioning overheads is a rather arbitrary division of overheads among cost centres. When seeking the most appropriate basis for apportionment, the focus should be on identifying the reason for the cost being incurred and on spreading the cost on a base related to that reason. For example, the annual rent and rates payable are normally based on the area of land or buildings (£ per square metre) and this would suggest that the most appropriate method of apportioning such costs would be on the area occupied by each cost centre.

Some bases for apportioning overhead and the types of cost which may be apportioned on such bases are as follows:

Base	Costs apportioned using the stated base
Floor area	Rent, rates, fire prevention
Cubic capacity	Heating, cleaning
Number of employees	General supervision (as distinct from the supervision of a specific cost centre), personnel and welfare costs, canteen
Capital value of assets	Depreciation, insurance
Metered consumption	Electricity, gas, water
Weight or volume of material	Material handling costs, storage costs

Allocation and apportionment of overheads

Dave Bell's wardrobe manufacturing business has three production departments (A, B and C) and two service departments (L and M). Forecast overheads for the year, other than £7,100 specifically allocated, are as follows:

	£
Rent and rates	12,800
Machine insurance	6,000
Telephone charges	3,200
Depreciation of machinery	18,000
Production supervisors' salaries	24,000
Heating and lighting	6,400
	70,400

The three production departments and the two service departments are housed in new premises, the details of which, together with other statistics and information, are listed below:

BASES FOR APPORTIONING

	Production Depts			Service Depts	
	A	**B**	**C**	**L**	**M**
Floor area occupied (sq. metres)	3,000	1,800	600	600	400
Machine value (£000)	24	10	8	4	2
Forecast direct labour hours	3,200	1,800	1,000	–	–
Labour rate per hour	£3.80	£3.50	£3.40	£3.00	£3.00
Number of telephones	3	2	1	1	1
Overheads allocated to each (£000)	2.80	1.70	1.20	0.80	0.60

Required: Prepare a statement showing the overhead cost for each department and the bases of apportionment used. You are not required to apportion the service departments over the three production departments.

29.4.4 Apportioning service department costs

As stated already, service departments often serve each other. If the costs involved are insignificant, or if the service departments are of a similar nature and could therefore be spread over the production departments on the same basis, there would be no need to concern ourselves with the apportionment of interdepartmental costs. However, in real life the service departments can be very dissimilar (e.g. maintenance and canteen); therefore, the apportionment to production departments would be distorted if appropriate steps were not taken to distribute the interdepartmental costs.

There are two methods of apportioning interdepartmental costs, namely the repeated distribution method and the simultaneous equations method. Each is described next.

Repeated distribution method

The procedure is as follows:

● **Step 1**. Share out among the other service departments the costs of the service department that provides the most services to the others, using any basis regarded as appropriate in the circumstances (e.g. floor area, number of personnel).
● **Step 2**. Share out, similarly, the costs of the second most serving department. Note that in doing this we will have charged a cost to the first department.
● **Step 3**. Steps 1 and 2 are repeated until the final amount charged is insignificant and all the costs have been redistributed to production departments alone.

Interaction 29.4	Repeated distribution method for service department overheads

Refer back to the information stated in IQ 29.3. Assume that the service department costs are to be distributed among other departments in the following proportions:

	A	B	C	L	M
Service department L	30%	25%	20%	–	25%
Service department M	20%	20%	40%	20%	–

Required: Complete the following statement showing the total overhead cost of each production department (including the service department costs) using the repeated distribution method.

ALLOCATION AND APPORTIONMENT OF OVERHEADS

	Production departments			Service depts	
	A	B	C	L	M
	£	£	£	£	£
	37,800	20,100	11,400	5,000	3,200
Service Dept L apportioned	1,500	1,250	1,000	–	1,250
					4,450
Service Dept M apportioned					
Service Dept L apportioned					
Service Dept M apportioned					
Service Dept L apportioned					
Service Dept M apportioned					
Total					

Simultaneous equations method

We will illustrate this method by applying it to Dave Bell's wardrobe business IQ 29.3 as follows:

● Step 1: Let £x be the total overhead of the service department L after the apportionment of the overheads of the service department M.
● Step 2: Let £y be the total overheads of service department M after the apportionment of the overheads of the service department L.

- Step 3: Write the simultaneous equations applicable for his business, according to the information given in IQ 29.3:

$$x = 5{,}000 + 0.20y$$
$$y = 3{,}200 + 0.25x$$

- Step 4: To solve these simultaneous equations, we can substitute y's expression (in terms of x) into the first equation of the two, to obtain

$$x = 5{,}000 + 0.20(3{,}200 + 0.25x)$$
$$= 5{,}000 + 640 + 0.05x$$

Getting the x's on one side and the numbers on the other, we obtain

$$0.95x = 5{,}640$$
$$x = 5{,}936.84$$

- Step 5: Substituting this value of x into the second simultaneous equation, we get

$$y = 3{,}200 + 0.25(5{,}936.84)$$
$$= 3{,}200 + 1{,}484.21$$
$$= 4{,}684.21$$

Thus the total overhead cost (x) of service department L to the nearest whole number is £5,937 and the total overhead cost (y) of service department M is £4,684. These costs can now be apportioned among the three production departments. Remember that the apportionment will be in proportion to the services provided to the production departments – which in the case of service department L is in the ratio 30:25:20 to production departments A, B and C respectively, and in the case of service department M is in the ratio 20:20:40 respectively.

If the service department overheads, arrived at as above on the simultaneous equation method, are allocated to the production departments on the basis of how each service department served the various production departments, the overheads ultimately apportioned to the production departments would more or less be as arrived at in the answer to IQ 29.4 (see working below).

Service	Overhead	Proportion of service to			Apportionment on basis of service provided		
		A	B	C	A	B	C
Dept L	£5,937	30%	25%	20%	£1,781	£1,484	£1,188
Dept M	£4,684	20%	20%	40%	£937	£937	£1,873
Overheads already apportioned (see IQ 29.3)					£37,800	£20,100	£11,400
Total apportioned to production departments					£40,518	£22,521	£14,461

29.4.5 Absorption of factory overheads into a product

After identification of the total overhead for each production department, what is yet to be determined is the amount of such overheads to be added onto the cost of each individual unit produced. The approach is to calculate **overhead absorption rates** (referred to also as **recovery rates**). The overhead absorption rate tells us how much of the overheads to add to the direct costs of a unit of product. It is possible to calculate one overhead absorption rate for the whole product of the factory. This, however, may give unfair proportions of overheads to different products. For example, if there are production departments with widely differing manufacturing methods (with, say, one very machine-intensive and another very labour-intensive), then a single rate would be unfair. The normal approach is therefore to calculate a separate absorption rate for each production department and add on to the cost of a product in accordance with its use of each department.

29.4.6 Bases for absorption of overheads into the cost of the product

There are several common bases for absorbing overheads. These include cost bases and activity bases as follows:

- Cost bases:
  - percentage of direct material cost;
  - percentage of direct labour cost;
  - percentage of prime cost.
- Activity bases:
  - rate per unit (only applicable if all units produced are identical);
  - rate per direct labour hour;
  - rate per machine hour.

The underlying principle in selecting a base is that the method of absorbing overheads into a product should be linked to the factors that have contributed to the overhead cost being incurred. In other words, whatever caused the overhead should form the basis for its recovery. For example, if a production department is highly mechanized with significant machine-associated costs (such as depreciation, maintenance, and power consumption), then the base for the absorption rate should be machine hours. Conversely, in a labour-intensive department an appropriate base would be percentage of direct labour cost or rate per direct labour hour.

29.4.7 Use of overhead absorption rates

The total cost of a product comprises:

- the cost of materials consumed (obtained from purchase invoices and stores requisitions);
- the direct labour costs (obtained from time sheets filled in by the work force);
- the appropriate departmental overhead obtained by applying absorption rates.

It is possible to calculate the overhead absorption rate based on actual costs incurred in an accounting period. However, this can only be done at the end of the period and would be appropriate for the purpose of determining the cost of finished goods remaining unsold by the year end. Yet the management requires overhead absorption rates during the year as well, for purposes of control and for decision making (e.g. setting the sale price of a unit). It is usual, therefore, to calculate the overhead recovery rate at the beginning of the financial year, based on estimates. The procedure is as follows:

- Step 1: Estimate the overhead cost likely to be incurred for this financial period.
- Step 2: Estimate the appropriate level of production (e.g. the number of machine hours).
- Step 3: Divide the estimated overhead cost by the estimated level of activity – for instance:

Rate per machine hour = overhead costs (£)/machine hours, or
Percentage of direct labour cost = overhead cost (£)/direct labour cost (£) × 100%

Calculation of absorption rates

The estimated cost of manufacture for a manufacturing company is as stated on the right. It is also estimated that 100,000 direct labour hours and and 200,000 machine hours will be worked during the period.

Required: Calculate the overhead absorption rates based on:

(a) direct material cost
(b) direct labour cost
(c) prime cost
(d) machine hours and
(e) direct labour hours.

	£000
Direct material	80
Direct labour	120
Prime cost	200
Factory overhead	60
Factory cost	260

29.4.8 **Overabsorption and underabsorption of overheads**

Because overhead absorption rates are based on estimates, it is inevitable that at the end of the financial period the amount of overhead absorbed will differ from the actual overheads incurred. This could arise because the actual overhead cost incurred was different from estimated overhead costs, and/or the estimated base used for absorption (i.e. labour hours or machine hours) differed from the actual. At the end of the financial period, therefore, an adjustment will have to be made in the Manufacturing account in respect of any over/under-recovery.

29.5 **WORK IN PROGRESS**

The manufacturing process that takes place in an accounting period produces:

- units of finished goods that have been sold during the accounting period;
- units of finished goods that remain unsold and that are therefore reported as an asset;
- units of goods that by the year end are at various stages of completion.

The last of these is referred to as *work in progress*. The direct and indirect costs incurred on those units up to that point are removed from the costs incurred in the current year so that only the cost of units completed in the year are transferred to the Trading account as the cost of goods which are available for sale. The costs are also transferred to a Work in Progress account and included in the Balance Sheet as an asset. In the following year, the direct and indirect costs of work in progress brought over are added on to the costs incurred that year to produce finished goods.

The valuation of work in progress is at cost, including, in addition to the direct costs of manufacture, any indirect costs that may appropriately be added on, taking into account the stage of completion. To illustrate, let us refer back to wardrobes manufactured by Dave Bell and assume that the manufacturing cost per wardrobe is as follows:

Cost element	£
Material	100
Wages per unit	50
Direct expenses per unit	20
Prime cost per unit	170
Factory overheads @ appropriate overhead recovery rate (10% of prime cost)	17
Factory cost of completed wardrobes as at end of year	187

If, as at the year end, work is in progress on 20 wardrobes and these are 100 per cent complete as to material and 30 per cent complete as to labour and direct expenses, then work in progress is valued as follows:

Cost element of each incomplete wardrobe	£
Material	100
Wages per unit	15
Direct expenses per unit	6
Prime cost per unit	121
Factory overheads @ appropriate overhead recovery rate (10% of prime cost)	12
Factory cost of an incomplete unit as at end of year	133

Work in progress in the Manufacturing account and Balance Sheet will then be £2,660 (20 × £133).

Interaction 29.6 — Accounting for work in progress

Light Engineering Works extracted its Trial Balance as at the last day of its first year of business as follows:

TRIAL BALANCE AS AT 30 JUNE 20X1		
	£000	£000
Machinery at cost	720	–
Motor vehicles at cost	240	–
Purchase of raw material	2,845	–
Productive wages	765	–
Factory overheads	620	–
Sales for the year	–	4,925
Administrative expenses	612	–
Distribution cost	78	–
Debtors and creditors	168	694
Capital account	–	500
Cash and bank balance	71	–
	6,119	6,119

You are further informed as follows:

(a) As at 30 June 20X1:
 – the stock of raw materials, at cost, was £154,000;
 – work in progress, at cost up to the present state, was £16,000;
 – the stock of unsold completed goods, at cost, was £268,000.
(b) Machinery and motor vehicles are to be depreciated by the straight-line method at 10 per cent and 20 per cent per annum.

Required: Prepare the Manufacturing, Trading and Profit and Loss account for the year to 30.6.20X1 and the Balance Sheet as at that date.

Valuation of work in progress

Dave Bell commenced business on 1.1.20X0 making wardrobes of a standard size and model. The wardrobes, made of hardwood, have a reputation for being well designed. On commencement, he installed lathes at a cost of £75,000 and acquired office furniture for £26,000. His production staff consist of lathe operators and cabinet makers, who work on a piecework basis (i.e. they are paid per item of work). Lathe operators cut and shape the wood and are paid £60 per wardrobe, while the cabinet makers attend to the remainder of the production process and are paid £100 per wardrobe. The wardrobe fittings, comprising sliding gears, hanger bars and locks, cost £45 per wardrobe. Each wardrobe is sold for £600. During the year ended 31.12.20X0, the sales amounted to £592,800 and expenses were as listed below:

	£
Purchase of wood	242,750
Wages to lathe operators	66,000
Wages to cabinet makers	103,600
Wages to factory staff (foremen, cleaners)	33,100
Salary to administrative staff	64,500
Cost of sliding gear, hanger bars, hinges and locks	47,340
Cost of glue, sand paper, nails etc	4,719
Administrative expenses	38,496
Maintenance of lathes	4,250
Rent for premises (one-third for administration)	30,000
Advertising expenses	16,450
Delivery of wardrobes to customers' residence	8,250
Power for operating lathes	4,675

You are further informed that:

(a) As at 31.12.20X0 Dave holds unused wood costing £50,250 and 48 completed wardrobes available for sale; while on 64 more wardrobes the lathe operations only have been completed.

(b) Lathes and office furniture are to be depreciated by the straight-line method at 20 per cent and 10 per cent per annum respectively.

(c) For the purpose of valuing unsold units and work in progress at factory cost, Dave adds on to the prime cost of these units a percentage as factory overheads (i.e. the overheads are recovered as a percentage of prime cost).

Required: Prepare the Manufacturing account and a Trading and Profit and Loss account of Dave Bell for the year ended 31 December 20X0.

29.6 UNREALIZED PROFIT

Some entities may prefer to transfer the completed units from the Manufacturing account to the Trading account not at the factory cost of these units but instead:

● at the price at which they would have been bought from outside, so that the benefit of producing a unit rather than buying it would become apparent;

● in any case, at a price higher than the cost, so as to report a manufacturing profit in addition to a trading profit.

When this is done, the Profit and Loss account begins by reporting two different types of profit, namely one arising from the manufacturing activity and the other from trading activity. The problem, however, is that whereas the trading profit is recognized only in respect of items sold, the manufacturing profit is recognized at the point the goods are ready for sale, although some of them might not really be sold by the year end. This means that, to the extent that the manufacturing profit relates to items remaining unsold at the year end, the profit is yet to be earned. Such profit, yet to be earned, is referred to as *unrealized profit* and must be deducted from the earnings reported for the year.

29.6.1 Accounting for unrealized profit

It is necessary, therefore, to remove the unrealized profit from the Profit and Loss account by transferring it to a Provision for Unrealized Profit account. To illustrate, let us assume that a manufacturer produced completed units at a cost of manufacture of £800, transferred these completed units to his sales depot at cost plus 10 per cent profit (namely £880), and that 75 per cent of the units were sold by the year end for £1,200 each. This means that units remaining unsold at the year end, reported at 25 per cent of £880 (namely £220), include an unrealized profit of £20. The unrealized profit is transferred from the Profit and Loss account to a Provision for Unrealized Profit account, and the balance in the Provision account is reported on the Balance Sheet as a deduction from the value of stock, so that stock in hand is stated at cost.

The transactions would feature in the financial statements of the year as follows:

MANUFACTURING, TRADING AND PROFIT AND LOSS ACCOUNT FOR THE YEAR ENDED XXXXXXX		
	£	£
Factory cost of goods manufactured		800
Manufacturing profit c/d		80
Transfer to Trading account		880
Sales account		1,200
Transfer from Manufacturing a/c	880	
Less: Stock in trade	(220)	(660)
Gross profit b/d		540
Manufacturing profit b/d	80	
Less: Unrealized profit	(20)	60
		600

BALANCE SHEET AS AT XXXXXXXXX		
	£	£
Current assets:		
Stock in trade	220	
Less: Provision for unrealized profit	(20)	200

The Provision for Unrealized Profit account is another supporting account that temporarily records a profit embedded in the year-end stock. The balance in the supporting account is deducted from that of the main account to state the unsold stock at cost on the Balance Sheet.

Provision for unrealized profit

The Trial Balance extracted at the year end from the books of Loyds, manufacturers of sporting helmets, includes the items stated here. Further information is as follows:

(a) Upon manufacture, the completed helmets are transferred to the sales depots at cost plus 20 per cent.

(b) Stock as at 31.3.20X1 has been ascertained as:
   - Raw materials: £186,000
   - Work in progress: £48,000
   - Finished goods: £978,000

Required: Prepare the Manufacturing, Trading and Profit and Loss account for the year ended 31.3.20X1. Furthermore, state how the stock will be shown on the Balance Sheet as at 31 March 20X1.

TRIAL BALANCE AS AT 31 MARCH 20X1		
	£000	**£000**
As at 1 April 20X0:		
Stock of raw material	116	–
Work in progress	72	–
Finished goods	810	–
Purchases – raw material	5,474	–
Sales	–	11,685
Productive wages	1,846	–
Depreciation – machinery	340	–
Depreciation – vehicles	72	–
Provision for unrealized profit	–	135
Factory power	32	–
Manufacturing overheads	434	–
Administrative expenses	1,436	–
Distribution costs	684	–

29.7 ROYALTIES

The owner of premises is called a *landlord* and rent is charged as payment for the privilege of being able to use the premises. One who patents an idea, a design, or a method of production is also referred to as the landlord and the amount paid for the permission to commercially exploit what has been patented is called a *royalty*.

The terms agreed with the landlord may require the amount of royalty payable to be calculated based on either the number of units produced or the number sold. The terms agreed may also provide for the landlord to receive in each period an amount not less than a minimum. The minimum so stipulated is known as the *minimum rent*. In such cases the agreement is likely to stipulate that any excess paid to make up the difference between the agreed minimum and what would have been payable otherwise could be recovered from the landlord, subject to terms agreed upon. The amount so recoverable is referred to as *shortworking* and is, of course, an asset for the one paying the royalty, so long as it is recoverable.

29.7.1 Accounting for royalties

For illustration, let us assume that Masons publishes Lisa's fictional work on the understanding that Masons will pay Lisa £1 per copy of the book published. If the number of copies published in year 20X0 is 1,500, Masons will account for the expenditure, debiting its Royalty account (expenditure) and crediting Lisa's personal account (liability) with £1,500.

The royalty is part of the expenditure of publishing the book and, therefore, the balance in the Royalty account would be transferred to the Manufacturing (in this case Publishing) account. The amount owed to Lisa will appear as a liability, until it is settled by payments made as agreed. For example, if the royalty were to be paid in two instalments of £900 in the current year and £600 in the following year, the ledger accounts would appear as follows and £600 would be reported in the Balance Sheet as a liability:

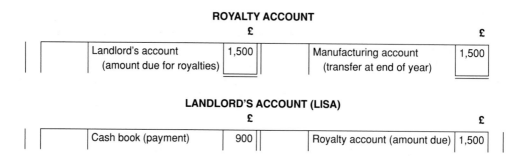

ROYALTY ACCOUNT

	£		£
Landlord's account (amount due for royalties)	1,500	Manufacturing account (transfer at end of year)	1,500

LANDLORD'S ACCOUNT (LISA)

	£		£
Cash book (payment)	900	Royalty account (amount due)	1,500

If, as happens sometimes, the publisher agrees to a minimum rent per year of (say) £2,500, Lisa has to be reported as a liability not for £1,500 but for £2,500. The extra £1,000 payable because of the minimum stipulation is regarded as a loan to Lisa, to be recovered on terms that the parties have mutually to agree upon.

The extra £1,000 is shortworking and is accounted for by debiting a Shortworkings account (asset) and crediting Lisa's personal account (reporting her as a liability for the minimum agreed upon). The agreement with Lisa would have stipulated the period over which Masons is entitled to recover the shortworking. The accounts will then appear as follows:

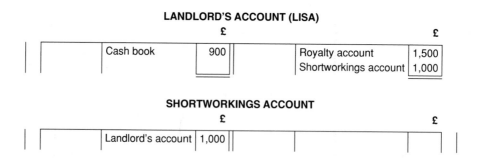

LANDLORD'S ACCOUNT (LISA)

	£		£
Cash book	900	Royalty account	1,500
		Shortworkings account	1,000

SHORTWORKINGS ACCOUNT

	£		£
Landlord's account	1,000		

Recovery will be possible only in a year when the number of copies published exceeds 2,500. For example, if royalties in the following year were £3,250, then crediting the Shortworkings account and debiting the Landlord's account would make a recovery of £750. If at any point the shortworking becomes irrecoverable, it has to be written off as an expense in the Profit and Loss account. Shortworkings that are recoverable are reported as an asset on the Balance Sheet.

Accounting for royalties

Richard patented an Electronic Personal Organizer and on 1.1.20X0 assigned the exploitation rights to Dynamics plc on an agreement as follows:

- Dynamics to pay Richard a royalty of £8 per unit sold, merging into a minimum rent of £40,000 per year.
- The royalty is payable annually on 31 December.
- Shortworkings are recoverable within the first five years of the contract.

The number of units of the personal organizer sold in each year were as follows:

Year 20X0	3,200	Year 20X2	6,600	Year 20X4	5,400
Year 20X1	5,800	Year 20X3	4,100	Year 20X5	4,700

As the accountant of Dynamics, you are *required* to record these transactions in appropriate ledger accounts, and to state how they will be reflected in the Profit and Loss accounts and Balance Sheets of each of the six years to 31 December 20X5.

Reference

1. SSAP 9: *Stocks and Work in Progress* (May 1975), paragraph 19.

SOLUTIONS TO INTERACTIVE QUESTIONS

IQ 29.1 Ascertaining the prime cost

MANUFACTURING ACCOUNT FOR THE YEAR ENDED 30.6.20X1		
	£000	£000
Raw materials consumed:		
Stock on 1.7.20X0	1,560	
Purchases	12,650	
Less: Stock on 30.6.20X1	(1,500)	12,710
Productive wages		6,250
Royalty paid		1,250
Prime cost		20,210

Unused raw material would be reported at £1,500,000 under current assets in the Balance Sheet.

IQ 29.2 Preparing a Manufacturing account

MANUFACTURING ACCOUNT FOR THE YEAR ENDED 30.6.20X1	£000	£000
Raw material consumed:		
Stock 1.7.20X0	214	
Purchases	12,845	
Stock 30.6.20X1	(315)	12,744
Productive wages		13,048
Prime cost		25,792
Factory overheads:		
Rent	2,000	
Consumable stores	54	
Wages	3,262	
Depreciation	120	
Factory power	172	5,608
Factory cost of goods manufactured carried to Trading account		31,400

TRADING AND PROFIT AND LOSS ACCOUNT FOR THE YEAR ENDED 30 JUNE 20X1	£000	£000
Sales		54,925
Stock on 1.7.20X1	628	
Manufactured goods	31,400	
Stock on 30.6.20X1	(476)	(31,552)
Gross profit		23,373
Administrative expenses:		
Salaries	16,310	
Rent	4,000	
Other admin. expenses	852	(21,162)
Distribution expenses:		
Advertising		(226)
Profit for the year		1,985

BALANCE SHEET AS AT 30 JUNE 20X1	£000	£000
Stock of raw materials	315	
Stock of finished goods	476	791

IQ 29.3 Allocation and apportionment of overheads

Overheads	£000	Basis of apportioning	Production Dept. A	B	C	Service Dept. L	M
Specific costs	7.10	Allocation	2.80	1.70	1.20	0.80	0.60
Rent and rates	12.80	Floor area	6.00	3.60	1.20	1.20	0.80
Machine insurance	6.00	Machine value	3.00	1.25	1.00	0.50	0.25
Telephone	3.20	No. of telephones	1.20	0.80	0.40	0.40	0.40
Depreciation	18.00	Machine value	9.00	3.75	3.00	1.50	0.75
Supervision	24.00	Labour hours	12.80	7.20	4.00	–	–
Heat and light	6.40	Floor area	3.00	1.80	0.60	0.60	0.40
Total	77.50		37.80	20.10	11.40	5.00	3.20

IQ 29.4 Repeated distribution method for service department overheads

ALLOCATION OF SERVICE DEPARTMENT OVERHEADS ON REPEATED DISTRIBUTION METHOD

	Production departments			Service departments	
	A	B	C	L	M
Overhead already allocated/apportioned	37,800	20,100	11,400	5,000	3,200
Overheads of Service Dept L	1,500	1,250	1,000	(5,000)	1,250
Overheads of Service Dept M	890	890	1,780	890	(4,450)
Overheads of Service Dept L	267	223	178	(890)	222
Overheads of Service Dept M	44	44	89	45	(222)
Overheads of Service Dept L	14	11	9	(45)	11
Overheads of Service Dept M	2	2	5	2	(11)
Overheads of Service Dept L	1	1	–	(2)	
Total apportioned to Production Depts	40,518	22,521	14,461		

IQ 29.5 Calculation of absorption rates

	Based on	Formula	Calculation	Answer
(a)	Direct material cost	Factory overheads / Direct material cost	£60,000 × 100 / £80,000	75% of direct material cost
(b)	Direct labour cost	Factory overheads / Direct labour cost	£60,000 × 100 / £120,000	50% of direct labour cost
(c)	Prime cost	Factory overheads / Prime cost	£60,000 × 100 / £200,000	30% of prime cost
(d)	Machine hours	Factory overheads / Machine hours	£60,000 / 200,000	£0.30 per machine hour
(e)	Direct labour hours	Factory overheads / Direct labour hours	£60,000 / 100,000	£0.60 per direct labour hour

IQ 29.6 Accounting for work in progress

MANUFACTURING, TRADING AND PROFIT AND LOSS ACCOUNT FOR THE YEAR ENDED 30.6.20X1		
		£000
Raw material consumed:		
Purchases	2,845	
Less: Stock 30.6.20X1	(154)	2,691
Productive wages		765
Prime cost		3,456
Factory overheads	620	
Depreciation of machinery	72	692
		4,148
Less: work in progress		(16)
Cost of goods manufactured		4,132

Sales		4,925
Cost of goods manufactured	4,132	
Less: Stock on 30.6.20X1	(268)	(3,864)
Gross profit		1,061
Administrative expenses		(612)
Distribution cost	78	
Depreciation of vehicles	48	(126)
Profit for the year		323

BALANCE SHEET AS AT 30 JUNE 20X1			
			£000
Fixed assets:			
Machinery	720	(72)	648
Motor vehicles	240	(48)	192
			840
Current assets:			
Stock:			
Raw materials	154		
Work in progress	16		
Finished goods	268	438	
Debtors		168	
Cash and bank		71	
Creditors		(694)	(17)
			823

	£000
Capital on 1.7.20X0	500
Profit for the year	323
	823

IQ 29.7 Valuation of work in progress

MANUFACTURING ACCOUNT FOR THE YEAR ENDED 31.12.20X0		£
Raw materials consumed:		
Purchases	242,750	
Stock – 31.12.20X0	(50,250)	192,500
Productive wages		169,600
Direct expenses		46,620
Prime cost		408,720
Factory overheads		
Indirect wages	33,100	
Indirect materials	4,719	
Deprn – lathes	15,000	
Lathe maintenance	4,250	
Factory power	4,675	
Factory rent	20,000	81,744
		490,464
Work in progress – 1.1.20X0		–
Work in progress – 31.12.20X0		(18,048)
Factory cost of goods produced		
carried to Trading account		472,416

TRADING AND PROFIT AND LOSS ACCOUNT FOR THE YEAR ENDED 31 DECEMBER 20X0		£
Sales		592,800
Stock on 1.1.20X0	–	
Fact. cost of goods produced	(472,416)	
Stock on 31.12.20X0	21,888	(450,528)
Gross profit		142,272
Administrative expenses:		
Salaries	64,500	
Office rent	10,000	
Administrative expenses	38,496	
Depreciation of furniture	2,600	(115,596)
Distribution costs:		
Advertising	16,450	
Carriage outwards	8,250	(24,700)
Profit for the year		1,976

Workings:

	Units
1. Number of wardrobes sold = £592,800/£600	988
Number of wardrobes completed but remaining unsold by the year end	48
Number of completed wardrobes produced within the year	1,036
Number of incomplete wardrobes reckoned as work in progress	64
Number of wardrobes on which wood was used and lathe operators were paid.	1,100

2. Factory overheads as a percentage of prime cost: £81,744/£408,720 × 100%.	20%

3. Cost per unit of incomplete wardrobes:	£
Wood = £192,500/1,100 units	175
Lathe operator's wages @ £60	60
Prime cost as at 31.12.20X0	235
Factory overheads @ 20% of prime cost	47
Factory cost of an incomplete wardrobe as at 31.12.20X0	282

   Factory cost of work in progress: 64 wardrobes @ £282 = £18,048.

4. Factory cost of unsold wardrobes: (£472,416/1,036) × 48 = £21,888.

5. Cost of sliding gear, hinges etc. is treated as direct expenses. Alternatively, such items may be regarded as direct materials. On the premise that these would be fitted only when the wardrobes are ready for sale, the cost written off is calculated at £45 per set needed for 1,036 units = £46,620.

IQ 29.8 Provision for unrealized profit

MANUFACTURING, TRADING AND PROFIT AND LOSS ACCOUNTS FOR THE YEAR ENDED 31 MARCH 20X1		
	£000	£000
Raw materials consumed:		
Stock as at 1.4.20X0	116	
Purchases	5,474	
Stock on 31.3.20X1	(186)	5,404
Productive wages		1,846
Prime cost		7,250
Factory overheads:		
Manufacturing exp.	434	
Factory power	32	
Depreciation – machinery	340	806
Work in progress 1.4.20X0		72
Work in progress 31.3.20X1		(48)
Factory cost of helmets		8,080
Manufacturing profit: 20%		1,616
Transferred to Trading account		9,696

Sales			11,685
Stock on 1.4.20X0		810	
Transfer from Trading a/c		9,696	
Stock on 31.3.20X1		(978)	(9,528)
Gross profit			2,157
Manufacturing profit		1,616	
Provision for unrealized profit		(28)	1,588
			3,745
Administrative expenses		1,436	
Distribution cost	684		
Depreciation of vehicles	72	756	(2,192)
Profit for the year			1,553

BALANCE SHEET AS AT 31.3.20X1		
		£000
Stock:		
Raw materials		186
Work in progress		48
Finished goods	978	
Provision for unrealized profit	(163)	815
		1,049

Workings:

Unrealized profit embedded in the closing stock of finished goods:

$$£978,000 \times 20/120 = £163,000$$

PROVISION FOR UNREALIZED PROFIT ACCOUNT

	£		£
		Balance b/f	135
Balance c/d	163	Profit and Loss a/c	28
		Balance b/d	163

IQ 29.9 Accounting for royalties

ROYALTY ACCOUNT

a	31.12.20X0	Landlord's account	25,600	31.12.20X0	Manufacturing account	25,600	
a	31.12.20X1	Landlord's account	46,400	31.12.20X1	Manufacturing account	46,400	
a	31.12.20X2	Landlord's account	52,800	31.12.20X2	Manufacturing account	52,800	
a	31.12.20X3	Landlord's account	32,800	31.12.20X3	Manufacturing account	32,800	
a	31.12.20X4	Landlord's account	43,200	31.12.20X4	Manufacturing account	43,200	
a	31.12.20X5	Landlord's account	37,600	31.12.20X5	Manufacturing account	37,600	

LANDLORD'S ACCOUNT   £

	31.12.20X0	Cash book	40,000	31.12.20X0	Royalty account	25,600	a
				31.12.20X0	Shortworkings account	14,400	b
c	31.12.20X1	Shortworkings account	6,400	31.12.20X1	Royalty account	46,400	a
	31.12.20X1	Cash book	40,000				
c	31.12.20X2	Shortworkings account	8,000	31.12.20X2	Royalty account	52,800	a
	31.12.20X2	Cash book	44,800				
	31.12.20X3	Cash book	40,000	31.12.20X3	Royalty account	32,800	a
				31.12.20X3	Shortworkings account	7,200	b
c	31.12.20X4	Shortworkings account	3,200	31.12.20X4	Royalty account	43,200	a
	31.12.20X4	Cash book	40,000				
	31.12.20X5	Cash book	40,000	31.12.20X5	Royalty account	37,600	a
				31.12.20X5	Profit and Loss account	2,400	e

SHORTWORKINGS ACCOUNT

b	31.12.20X0	Landlord's account	14,400	31.12.20X1	Landlord's account	6,400	c
				31.12.20X1	Balance c/d	8,000	
	1.1.20X1	Balance b/d	8,000	31.12.20X2	Landlord's account	8,000	c
b	31.12.20X3	Landlord's account	7,200	31.12.20X4	Landlord's account	3,200	c
				31.12.20X4	Profit and Loss account	4,000	d

Notes:

(a) The royalty on the number of units produced in each year @ £8 per unit is part of the cost of production of the units in the year, to be reported in the Manufacturing account.

(b) The amount by which the royalty payable in respect of units produced in the year falls short of the minimum rent (£14,400 in year 20X0 and £7,200 in 20X3) is recorded as an asset in the Shortworkings account because these amounts are recoverable.

(c) Shortworkings are recovered from amounts payable as royalty to the extent that the recovery does not reduce the payment to less than the minimum rent.

(d) Since the recovery of shortworkings is limited to the first five years of the contract, the shortworkings remaining unrecovered in the fifth year are written off to the Profit and Loss account.

(e) Any shortfalls arising after the fifth year cannot be recovered and should therefore be written off at once.

The transactions are reflected on financial statements thus:

Year	In Manufacturing a/c as royalty	In Profit and Loss account as shortworking w/off	In the Balance Sheet (shortworking as a current asset)
20X0	£25,600	–	£14,400
20X1	£46,400	–	£8,000
20X2	£52,800	–	–
20X3	£32,800	–	£7,200
20X4	£43,200	£4,000	–
20X5	£37,600	£2,400	–

PROGRESSIVE QUESTIONS

PQ 29.1 Accounting for a manufacturer

Liz McDermot, manufacturer and dealer in vanity cases made of imported hide, extracted the Trial Balance from the books as at the year end as stated below. Liz informs as follows:

TRIAL BALANCE AS AT 30.6.20X1

	£000	£000
Freehold land and building	620	48
Plant and machinery	640	280
Furniture and fittings	260	117
Motor vehicles	320	152
Stock on 30.6.20X0:		
~ Raw materials at cost	264	–
~ Work in progress at factory cost	93	–
~ Finished goods at factory cost	187	–
Purchase of raw materials	926	–
Sale of vanity cases	–	2,702
Rent	60	–
Electricity	20	–
Power	37	–
Advertising	106	–
Debtors and creditors	428	217
Capital – Liz McDermot		1,200
Bad debts	21	–
Audit fees	15	–
Consumable stores	27	–
Wages and salaries	364	–
Drawings by Liz McDermot	115	–
Freight and carriage inwards	75	–
Insurance	30	–
Provision for unrealized profit	–	17
Stationery	12	–
Telephone and postage	13	–
Sales commission	67	–
Duty on raw materials	22	–
Cash and bank balance	11	–

(a) Buildings, machinery, furniture and motor vehicles are to be depreciated using the straight-line method at 2, 5, 10 and 20 per cent p.a., assuming that the buildings cost £400,000.

(b) Stock as at 30.6.20X1:

	£000
Raw materials at cost	164
Work in progress at factory cost	109
Finished goods at factory cost	154
Stationery	2
Consumable stores	4

(c) Analysis of wages and salaries:

	£000
Directly in production function	122
In supervisory/ancillary roles	65
Administrative and accounting staff	135
Sales staff	24
Drivers and cleaners of vehicles	18

(d) Expenses may be apportioned as follows:

	Factory	Admin.	Sales
Electricity	20%	60%	20%
Rent	50%	30%	20%
Insurance	60%	30%	10%
Deprn-buildings	25%	50%	25%

(e) The vanity cases are transferred from the factory to sales depots at cost plus 10 per cent.

Required: Prepare the Manufacturing, Trading and Profit and Loss account for the year ended 30 June 20X1 and the Balance Sheet as at that date.

PQ 29.2 Accounting for royalties

Sanguine plc agrees to publish a fictional work of Tony Gardner based on the following agreement:

(a) Tony will receive a royalty, on the number of copies published in each year, at 10 per cent of the sale price per copy published, merging into a minimum rent of £15,000 p.a.
(b) Shortworkings are recoverable only within two years following the date they arise.
(c) £6,000 will be paid as an advance on 1 July each year and the balance of the royalty will be settled annually in arrears on each 1 January.
(d) The sale price per copy is fixed at £12.

The book was published on 4.1.20X0. The particulars of sales in each year and the number of copies remaining unsold at the end of each year have been tabulated here.

Year ending on	Sales	Copies in hand
31.12.20X0	£75,000	3,750
31.12.20X1	£113,520	1,790
31.12.20X2	£154,320	2,930
31.12.20X3	£170,640	6,710
31.12.20X4	£187,800	1,560

Required: Prepare:

(a) The Royalty account
(b) Minimum Rent account
(c) Landlord account
(d) Shortworkings account,

for the five years, showing how the accounts will be dealt with when finalizing the accounts of Sanguine plc at the end of each year.

PQ 29.3 To buy or to produce?

Automobile Electronics deals in car alarms which it retails at £400 per unit. Until recently, the alarms were imported from Japan at £300 per unit. Since April 20X0, Automobile Electronics has manufactured the units locally by an agreement with the Japanese suppliers, dated 1.4.20X0, as follows:

● The royalty payable to the Japanese firm, annually in arrears on 1 April, is to be calculated at £25 per unit manufactured, merging into a minimum rent of £60,000 per year.
● Shortworkings are recoverable within two years following the year in which they arose.

The retail price of alarms has been maintained at £400 per unit. The locally manufactured units were transferred to the sales division at £300 per unit. Though the import of alarms from Japan ceased in July 20X0, some Japanese-made units remain unsold. A newly appointed accountant has finalized the accounts for the year ending on 31 March 20X3 as on the following page.

Rejecting these accounts, the owner of the business calls for a revision, pointing out that:

(a) The format of presentation could be substantially improved.
(b) Because of the failure to reflect the transfer of locally manufactured units from the factory to the sales division at £300 per unit, the wisdom of producing the units locally, rather than importing them from Japan, is not reflected in the financial statements.
(c) The shortworkings as well as the provision for unrealized profit are stated at the same amounts at which they appeared in the previous year's financial statements. The shortworkings consist of £12,400 that arose in the year to 31.3.20X1 and £6,600 that arose next year. It should be possible to recover at least a part of these in the current year.

BALANCE SHEET AS AT 31.3.20X3			
			£
Plant and machinery	300,000	(90,000)	210,000
Furniture	180,000	(135,000)	45,000
Motor vehicles	240,000	(168,000)	72,000
Stock of raw materials		82,450	
Work in progress		50,400	
Finished goods		144,000	
Shortworking recoverable		19,000	
Trade debtors		202,450	
Cash and bank balance		14,200	
Creditors and accruals		(83,100)	
Royalty payable		(63,500)	365,900
			692,900
			£
Capital – 1.4.20X2			607,630
Profit for the year			139,925
Drawings			(54,655)
			692,900

TRADING AND PROFIT AND LOSS ACCOUNT FOR THE YEAR ENDED 31 MARCH 20X3			
			£
Sales			982,000
Stock on 1.4.20X2:			
~ Raw materials	74,200		
~ Work in progress	24,600		
~ Finished goods	118,500	217,300	
Purchases – raw materials		111,850	
Duty on raw materials		21,650	
Freight on raw material		11,250	
Salaries and wages		363,750	
Sales commission		14,140	
Royalty payable		63,500	
Advertising		68,450	
Consumable stores		22,500	
Administrative expenses		142,000	
Bad debts		11,260	
Depreciation – machinery		30,000	
– vehicles		48,000	
– furniture		18,000	
Stock on 31.3.20X3:			
~ Raw materials	82,450		
~ Work in progress	50,400		
~ Finished goods	144,000	(276,850)	(866,800)
			115,200
Provision for unrealized profit			24,725
Profit for the year			139,925

You have ascertained as follows:

(a) The balance in the Salaries and Wages account is analysed as stated in the box on the right.
(b) The work in progress is valued at prime cost.
(c) The alarm units in stock at year end are as follows:

	£
Paid to a Japanese factory manager	45,000
Paid to workers engaged in production function	168,500
Paid to support staff at the factory	33,800
Paid to administrative and accounting staff	116,450

	31.3.20X2	31.3.20X3
Locally made units	215	420
Japanese-made units	180	60

(d) Fifteen per cent of administration expenses may be apportioned to the factory.

Required: Revise the financial statements for the year to 31.3.20X3.

Part G

THE CONTROL FUNCTION

Chapter 30

ACCOUNTING SYSTEMS AND CONTROLS

In this chapter

We will learn of the systems and controls without which the effectiveness of the accounting process and hence the validity of the financial statements would both be in jeopardy

30.1 INTRODUCTION TO ACCOUNTING SYSTEMS

An accounting system is the co-ordinated arrangement that ensures that:

- complete and authentic records are maintained of all transactions entered into by an entity within an accounting period;
- these records are analysed and summarized in accordance with accepted accounting principles;
- the financial statements, prepared on the basis of these records, show a true and fair view of the entity's performance in an accounting period and the position on the last day of that period.

If an entity transacts business strictly on a cash basis, its accounting system could be structured as illustrated on the following page.

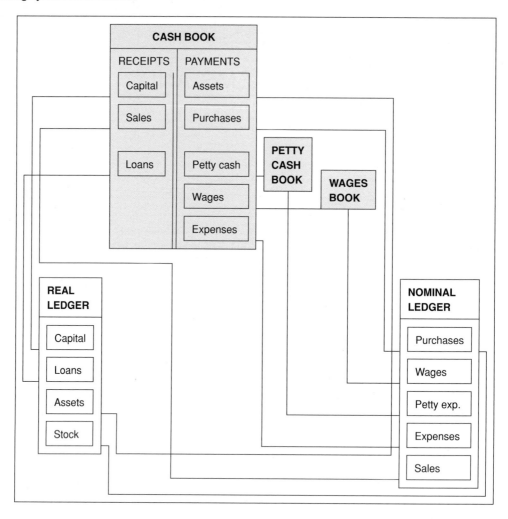

If, on the other hand, the business entity transacts business on credit terms as well, as we have already learnt, the prime entry for its transactions will be made not only in the cash book but also in various day books. In such a scenario the accounting system in operation might be structured as illustrated opposite.

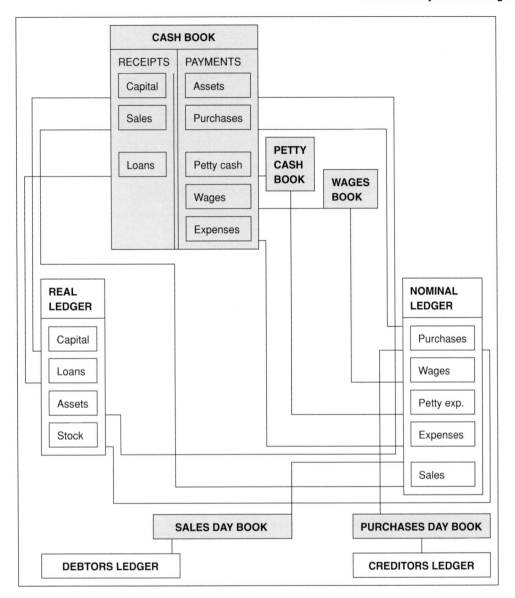

30.2 ACCURACY IN ACCOUNTING RECORDS

When seeking the accuracy of accounting records, every business should consider:

- the risk of error and fraud;
- how to deal with errors or fraud that have occurred;
- how to counter the risk, and how to prevent errors and fraud.

Each of these aspects is discussed further below.

30.2.1 The risk of error and fraud

Errors occur far more frequently than fraud.

An *error* is an accidental mistake in recording transactions in accounting systems. Errors can take many forms, including not recording a transaction, recording a figure incorrectly, making a mistake in adding up a set of figures, or posting an item to a wrong account. Computer systems tend to reduce the frequency of errors, although they do not eliminate them. An error can result in an increase in profit, a reduction in profit or have no effect on profit at all. Some of the errors may be revealed when a Trial Balance fails to balance (see Chapter 5).

Fraud is the deliberate manipulation of accounting records in order to obtain a personal benefit. The following are some examples of common fraud:

- understating income by such means as misappropriation of sales proceeds or pilfering stock;
- overstating expenditure by such means as fictitious expense claims by an employee or paying fictitious suppliers, or paying more than once for the same supply, or exaggerating wage payments by inclusion in wage sheets of fictitious names, hours, rates of pay (known as 'padding');
- covering up misappropriation of an amount recovered from a debtor, writing off the debt as bad, transfering it to an expense account or issuing false credit notes;
- misappropriating an amount received from a customer and then, to prevent the account from falling markedly into arrears, crediting that customer's account with part of an amount received from another (known as 'teeming and lading').

Fraud usually involves stealing and, in accounting terminology, it is referred to as *misappropriation*. It typically consists of stealing cash or pilfering stock but it can also be more elaborate, involving other parties in it. For example, an employee may arrange for a supplier to be paid more than is due and subsequently split the excess payment with the supplier.

A more serious fraud, perpetrated usually by those at the highest levels of management and not necessarily involving misappropriation of money, is the manipulation of accounts to show a position different from the actual. The aim of the manipulation is usually to influence the decision to be made on the basis of the accounts, either by an investor or by a party from whom a loan is sought. 'Window dressing' (see Section 19.5) is an example of manipulation. Performance-related payments to staff or tax evasion could also motivate manipulation.

30.2.2 Dealing with errors (or fraud) that have occurred

When errors are detected, the extent to which the entity would go to seek out its ramifications and remedy its effects would depend on the *materiality* of the errors. An error is regarded as material if it could influence the economic decisions of users. For example, overstating the stock at the year end to change a loss to a profit when applying to the bank for an extension of an overdraft facility would be material. However, many errors do not have such a dramatic impact.

30.2.3 How to counter the risk

To minimize the risk of error and fraud, and to detect them when they occur, a business must have *internal controls* in place to ensure that accounting transactions are recorded accurately. We have already discussed two examples of controls – over cash, with the preparation of a bank reconciliation (Chapter 13), and over debtors and creditors, with the preparation and reconciliation of control accounts (Chapter 14).

30.3 INTERNAL CONTROLS

Internal controls instituted in an entity to protect its accounting function are in fact a whole system of controls, which the management of an entity establishes to ensure that:

1. the business is carried on in an efficient and orderly manner in accordance with the entity's policies;
2. the assets of the entity are safeguarded;
3. the completeness and accuracy of accounting records are secured;
4. fraud and errors are prevented and those that occur are detected.

The more important forms of internal control include the following:

- establishment of proper procedures for the selection and training of staff, in order to ensure that personnel are competent to carry out their responsibilities at every level;
- establishment of proper organizational plans in which the duties, responsibilities and limits of authority of individuals are clearly defined and demarcated;
- carefully thought-out subdivision of work among staff – the important element of internal check (see below);
- physical control over the custody of assets;
- insistence on authorization of every transaction at appropriate levels;
- other forms of management controls such as reconciliations, use of control accounts, budgetary control, and internal audit.

30.3.1 Internal check

The establishment of a well-conceived system of internal check is the most effective way of minimizing the risk of error and fraud. *Internal check* is an expression used to refer to working arrangements in which responsibilities (such as authorizing a transaction, executing it, recording it, and keeping custody of resultant assets) are carefully spread among as many persons as possible so that:

- each person's work falls within the automatic and subsequent scrutiny of at least one other;
- no one person can carry through a transaction and record it without the intervention of at least one other.

Internal controls to forestall problems   Interaction 30.1

Cavendish Secondary School, with 12,000 students, is buying a new cooker for the canteen.

Required: Identify the controls and internal check that ought to be in operation to ensure that:

(a) this does not create cash-flow problems for the school;
(b) the make, model and size of the cooker acquired are not unsuitable for the purpose;
(c) the price paid for the cooker is not one privately negotiated with the supplier by either the canteen manager or purchasing officer at a level that permits a portion thereof to be illegitimately siphoned off;
(d) the payment is not made without the cooker being received.

It should be appreciated, however, that:

- the best-conceived system of internal check would not prevent a fraud in which two or more employees co-operate for perpetrating it (this is known as **collusion**);
- the internal check is bound to be ineffective in smaller entities because the division of work cannot be other than limited and the chances of collusion within a closely-knit group is greater.

30.4 THE CASH SYSTEM

The cash book interacts with every one of the ledgers, as well as with the wages system and the petty cash system. Hence, aspects of the cash book will be considered in our discussion of other systems such as the sales, purchases and wages systems. Sound internal control requires that the cashier does not have access to any of the ledgers.

Interaction 30.2	**Inadequate internal check**
	In the Small Forge Company, the cashier enters the copy sales invoices in the Sales Ledger, receives cheques, and records the receipt in the cash book and Sales Ledger. Explain what the risks are of error or fraud to the business.

30.4.1 Cheques received from debtors

Monthly statements are normally sent to debtors (as a request for payment), and they in turn send back cheques in the post. It is important that the post should be opened by two people, who should list the cheques received and only then give them to the cashier. The cashier will record details of the cheques in the receipts side of the cash book and subsequently pay them into the bank. The cheques will thereafter be posted by the bookkeeper to the Sales Ledger account of the appropriate customer.

Interaction 30.3	**Pre-recording of cheques received from customers**
	Required: Explain why it is important that two independent people open the mail and record cheques received, and why is it unacceptable for the cashier to open the mail and record the cheques received.

30.4.2 Cheque payments

Ideally, almost all payments by a business should be made by cheque, as cheques are very secure and it is extremely difficult for a cheque to be paid into a bank account other than that of the payee as stated on the cheque.

Cheques for Purchase Ledger payments, prepared by either the Purchase Ledger staff, the Purchase Ledger computer system or the cashier, should be signed by two signatories authorized for the purpose. Evidence to support the payment – such as remittance advices, invoices, and goods received notes – to establish the reason for and legitimacy of the payment should be produced to, and effectively cancelled in, the presence of a signatory to the cheque.

Wage payments are discussed further in Section 30.8 below.

30.4.3 **Bank reconciliation**

By performing the bank reconciliation, the cashier derives considerable assurance on the accuracy of the information in the cash book. The bank reconciliation explains the difference between the bank balance recorded in the bank statement and that recorded in the cash book. The cashier will probably prepare the bank reconciliation, and not only make amendments to the cash book when errors are found but also make entries for fresh items that appear on the bank statement, such as direct debits, credit transfers, and charges made by the bank.

The main differences occurring from a bank reconciliation, which account for the difference between the cash book balance and that on the bank statement, are:

● cheques and cash paid into the bank that have not been recorded on the bank statement;
● cheques issued by the entity that have not been presented to the bank for payment.

If cheques or cash stated as deposits in the bank column of the cash book do not appear in the bank statement, it could be either because these were not actually deposited until a later date, or because the cheques have yet to complete the clearance process.

Whether the position is the former could be established by checking the bank paying-in slips. Usually no more than the previous day's collections should be undeposited. If there appears to be a significant delay in paying cheques into the bank, there is a risk of 'teeming and lading'. If it appears, for example, that three days' cheques have not been paid into the bank, the cashier should be holding the cheques (and cash) for these three days. If some or all of these cheques (and cash) are 'missing', then the cashier will have committed a fraud by misappropriating the difference. Although frauds are uncommon, a teeming and lading fraud is one of the most common frauds. A person – someone other than the cashier – should verify whether the cheques that remain in the clearance process at the time of reconciliation are, upon clearance, reported in the next bank statement. The dates the cheques are cleared should be recorded on the bank reconciliation.

Similarly, cheques that had not been presented for payment on the date of the reconciliation should be traced into future bank statements. Understandably, there will be some delay in presenting some cheques, but if there are a large number of cheques where there is a significant delay in their appearing on the bank statement, it is possible that the business has delayed sending the cheques to the suppliers (in order to minimize the bank overdraft and the bank overdraft interest).

On a regular basis, an independent person should check the bank reconciliation to confirm that:

(a) the bank balance agrees with the bank statement;
(b) the Cash account balance agrees with the cash held;
(c) the uncleared bankings (receipts) (commonly called 'uncleared lodgements') agree with the cash book and are cleared by the bank promptly after the month end;
(d) cheques issued but not reported as withdrawals on the bank statement are subsequently cleared in the bank statement after the end of the month;
(e) any other reconciling items (such as any items in dispute with the bank) are reasonable;
(f) the additions on the bank reconciliation are correct.

30.5 THE PETTY CASH SYSTEM

Petty cash payments should be controlled on an 'imprest' system (see page 81). As part of the internal control the cashier should:

- verify the vouchers in support of petty cash payments;
- count the balance held by the petty cashier on that date;
- ensure that the amount reimbursed and the amount held by the petty cashier equal the imprest.

As the total of each week's petty cash payments is likely to be different, the amount of each cheque reimbursing the petty cash system will be different. An independent person should periodically check that each petty cash imprest payment in the cash book is matched by a receipt recorded in the Petty Cash Book. This check may prove difficult if the amount of reimbursement of the petty cash is the same value each time.

30.6 CASH SALES SYSTEMS

The most common example of a cash sales system is that found in retail shops. Much of their income is received in the form of coins and notes, but cheques, credit card and debit card settlements are also received. Most credit and debit card transactions are made using a machine connected from the seller's business to the credit card or debit card company. The value of the transaction is credited immediately to the business's bank account and the card company makes a transaction charge to the business. Occasionally, the retail store may have its own credit card, but the transaction is similar to that for any other credit card, and the collection of money from the customer is undertaken by the business's finance company (which issues the credit card).

Thus, the characteristic of a cash sales system is that the business receives cash from the customer when the transaction takes place, either in the form of coins or notes or by use of a cheque, credit card or debit card. The proceeds from the transaction will be received by the company immediately or within a day. No credit is given and the business has no risk of the amount due being unpaid (though there are infrequent risks of forged banknotes and stolen credit/debit cards). The cheques received do not constitute a risk because the business will insist that the customer provides a cheque guarantee card to support the cheque.

30.6.1 When cash is received

Ideally, a cash till should be used by only one employee. When there is a change of employee using the till, a subtotal should be obtained of the cash received and the till drawer should be removed to a safe place. A new till drawer should be put in the till with a 'float', which is sufficient to give change to the first few customers (after which the cash received in the till should provide sufficient change for new customers). The cash in the previous till drawer should be counted and checked to the subtotal on the till roll, after taking into account the 'float' when the employee took over the till. Any significant differences should be investigated.

The till may provide separate subtotals of the amounts received as coins and notes, cheques, and credit and debit card transactions, in which case the individual amounts in the till for these transactions can be checked to the subtotals. Discrepancies of a few pence are acceptable, but larger differences should be investigated. A history of discrepancies should be allocated to each employee, and further action should be taken if there are consistent problems with an employee.

Admittedly, collection of sales revenue through till operators weakens the internal check. However, recent developments have reduced the risks. Coins and notes continue to be a problem, but they are nowadays used less and less frequently by customers. The Cheques Act 1995 has, since its inception, made it almost impossible to negotiate a cheque (i.e. make it payable to a person other than the one named as the payee on the cheque), and so employees will not be able to pay customer cheques into their own bank accounts. Credit and debit card transactions undertaken using the telephone system can only be directed to the business's account. Even with manually input credit and debit card transactions the machine that records the transaction on the slip has the business's name and address as the payee; hence the proceeds can only be paid into the business's bank account.

Bar-coding of products is a major development that reduces the risk of fraud. The bar code is used to price the product on the till, and so the till operator cannot use a lower price for a 'friend'. Also, each sale deducts one unit from the stock quantity held on the computer. By carrying out periodic stocktakes and comparing the actual stock quantities with those on the computer, discrepancies will be highlighted and the business will be able to take action where there is an apparent loss of stock. Prior to the use of bar codes, the business could have been aware of stock losses (as the gross profit margin would have been lower than predicted), but they would have been unable to determine which lines of stock had been responsible for the loss.

When shopping at our local supermarket, we are aware that some products are sold at a lower-than-normal price when they are close to their 'sell-by date'. The till operator inputs the lower price manually and then scans the product (which deducts one unit from the computer stock quantities). The label giving the lower price is put in the till. The computer can be asked to print out products sold at a lower price, and these lower prices can be checked to the labels in the till. So, an independent person can check that where there is a lower selling price, there is a label in the till, and he/she will be able to detect when the till operator has used an unauthorised lower price.

There is a risk that the till operator may not scan certain products, thus giving a friend these products 'free'. This can be detected using a video camera and recorder to see the actions of till operators.

30.7 SALES AND PURCHASES SYSTEMS

In this section we propose to look simultaneously at the sales and purchases systems in so far as these are on credit terms. When sales are made on credit, customers are sent the goods for which payment is received at a later date – typically at the end of the month after. Similarly, purchases from suppliers are also made on credit terms. Thus, the seller's sales system interacts with the purchaser's purchasing system. The operations of purchases and sales systems are as follows:

	Purchases system	Sales system
1	The user department raises a purchase requisition in duplicate and sends one copy to the Purchasing Department.	
2	The Purchasing Department check that the requisition is from an authorized person and is for goods required by the business. They raise a purchase order, sending copies to: ● the supplier of the goods (the original) ● the requisitioning department ● the Goods Received Department ● the Accounts Department and a copy is retained for follow-up.	The Sales Department receives the customer's order. It checks that goods are available, and the credit controller checks that the customer's credit is satisfactory. The Sales Department then sends details of the goods to be dispatched to the Dispatch Department.
3	The goods are received by the Goods Received Department. It checks the goods to the copy order and to the advice note accompanying the goods. If this check is satisfactory, the department raises a goods received note (GRN), a copy of which they send to: ● the Accounts Department; ● the Purchasing Department.	The Dispatch Department sends the goods to the customer with an advice note (or delivery note), which gives details of the quantity, description and part numbers of the goods sent. If the goods are being sent through a carrier, the carrier will be asked to sign for receipt of the goods.
4	The Accounts Department receives the purchase invoice, which it checks to the GRN and purchase order. When everything is satisfactory, the accounting manager authorizes the purchase invoice for posting to the Purchase Ledger.	The Accounts Department raises a sales invoice, a copy of which is sent to the customer.
5	The purchase invoice is posted to the Purchase Ledger and filed (frequently in alphabetical order by supplier).	The sales invoice is posted to the Sales Ledger and filed.
6	Based on the balances and age of the items on the Purchase Ledger, a cheque and remittance advice are raised by the Accounts Department. The cheque is signed by an authorized signatory and sent with the remittance advice to the supplier.	A cheque and remittance advice are received from the customer. The remittance advice states which invoices are being paid.
7	The cheque (paying the supplier) is recorded in the cash book by the cashier.	The cheque (received from the customer) is recorded in the cash book by the cashier.
8	The cheque is posted to the Purchase Ledger by the Accounts Department.	The cheque is posted to the Sales Ledger by the Accounts Department.
9	Statements are received from the supplier.	Statements are sent to customers, showing outstanding invoices, cash received in the month, and the outstanding balance.
10	The statements are checked by an independent person to the balances on the Purchase Ledger.	

As described above, one company's purchasing system interacts with another company's sales system. Individual systems of businesses may vary in detail but the basic systems are very similar to that described above. Some businesses, particularly small ones, have less formal systems for ordering goods (for example the requisitioning department may order goods verbally from the purchasing department, who may place orders by phone with no written documentation). The important thing is to recognize that when this happens there is a greater risk of error and fraud.

A specimen invoice, issued by Reeve Ltd to Mapperley plc, would appear as shown below. To Reeve Ltd it is a sales invoice and to Mapperley plc it is a purchase invoice.

INVOICE NO: C10462　　　　　　　　　　　　　　　　　　**Reeve Limited**

Account no: D004　　　　　　　　　　　　　　　　　　11, Colwick Lane

　　　　　　　　　　　　　　　　　　　　　　　　　　　Anytown 2RU 5TA

INVOICE TO:　　　　　　　　　**DELIVER TO:**

　　　　　　　　　　　　　　　　　　　　　　　　　　TEL: 0123 654 987

Mapperley plc　　　　　　　　　　Invoice address
　　　　　　　　　　　　　　　　　　　　　　　　　　FAX: 0123 654 988
31 Church Lane

Anytown AN3 5WU

Customer order: C10156	Delivery Note: D7467	Date: 5/5/20X0		
Code	**Item**	**Quantity**	**Price**	**Total Value**
N423	Widgets (brown)	25	1.23	30.75
Carr:	Carriage, packing & insurance	1	5.00	5.00
	Goods			35.75
	VAT			6.26
				42.01

VAT Reg. No: GB 240 3468 52

TERMS: Payment is due, without discount, within one month of invoice date

A delivery note would be similar in appearance except that it would not have any prices stated on it. The supplier's Statement of Account, which Reeve Ltd would send to Mapperly plc, would appear as follows:

STATEMENT FOR THE MONTH OF: May 20X0						**Reeve Limited**

Account no: D004

11, Colwick Lane

Anytown 2RU 5TA

TO:

TEL: 0123 654 987

Mapperley plc

FAX: 0123 654 988

31 Church Lane

Anytown AN3 5WU

DATE 31.5.20X0		**T/Over** 500		**Cr. Limit** £100		
Date	**Type**	**Reference**	**Status**	**Debit**	**Credit**	**Balance**
13.2.X0	Invoice	C10111	Paid	53.24		53.24
15.3.X0	Invoice	C10124		31.62		84.86
12.4.X0	Invoice	C10148		36.82		121.68
1.5.X0	Receipt	G123	Allocated to C10111	–	53.24	68.44
5.5.X0	Invoice	G10156		42.01		110.45

3 months	**2 months**	**1 month**	**Current**			**Total due**
0.00	31.62	36.82	42.01			£110.45

Reeve Ltd itself would prepare an Aged Debtors' List as shown below, and the particulars relating to customer D004, Mapperly plc, are stated at the foot of the statement sent to them.

REEVE LIMITED AGED DEBTORS' LIST	AS AT 31 MAY 20X0					
Customer No.	3 months + £	2 months £	1 month £	Current £	Total £	Cr. Limit £
A003	0.00	25.34	6.23	36.41	67.98	100.00
B005	56.17	0.00	63.46	25.21	144.84	150.00
D004	0.00	31.62	36.82	42.01	110.45	100.00
TOTAL	56.17	56.96	106.51	103.63	323.27	

Notes:

(a) Account D004 is over the credit limit by £10.45.
(b) Account B005 has £56.17 in debts that are three months old – this needs investigation.
(c) Though the company policy is to permit a credit period of one month from invoice date, accounts A003, B005 and D004 have overstepped the credit period.
(d) It would be useful for Reeve Ltd to prepare an Aged Creditors List on similar lines, particularly when cash flow is strained, to identify suppliers who should be settled on a priority basis.

30.8 WAGES SYSTEMS

The term 'wage' is used to include all payments to employees, including salaries. The wages system involves three separate tasks as follows:

- calculation of gross pay;
- determination of net pay and deductions, usually using a standard computerized payroll system;
- paying the net wage.

30.8.1 Calculation of gross pay

The gross wage of an employee is likely to fall into one of the following categories:

(a) a fixed weekly or monthly sum, usually based on an annual salary. The payment will be for a specified number of hours worked per week;
(b) item (a), plus additional payments for working overtime (which requires authorization);
(c) a variation on (a), such as payments for part-time employees at a fixed rate per hour, or payments based on the number of units produced (traditionally in manufacturing trades).

The gross wages may be calculated manually, or more expeditiously using a computer. Large businesses may have specially written software to calculate the gross wages.

30.8.2 Determination of net pay

Use of a software package to calculate the deductions and net pay for each employee has many advantages, including saving employee time, ensuring the calculations are accurate and ensuring that current legislation is used for calculating the deductions.

30.8.3 Paying the net wage

Wages payment may be organized in any one or a combination of the following ways:

(a) The payments are made by cheque, after the authorized signatory verifies that the amounts stated on each cheque tally with the particulars on the payroll.

(b) The payments are made by direct credit from the company's bank account to the employee's bank account. This method of payment is common because it is more economical and reduces fraud. The particulars of payments to be made to each employee will be listed by the payroll system. Before paying the wages, a responsible official should inspect the payroll to check there are no unexpected amounts of gross or net pay (which could be due to an error, or possibly a fraud). This official should also sign the list that asks the business's bank to pay the wages directly into each employee's bank account.

(c) The payments are made in cash (i.e. banknotes and coins). This is becoming less and less common.

Controls required when wages are paid in cash include the following:

● The computerized payroll system lists the number of each type of banknote and coin required to pay the employees. A cheque, written out for the total net pay, is signed by a responsible official in order to obtain from the bank the notes and coins necessary. The notes and coins will be divided by wages staff to make up each employee's wage packet.

● Each wage packet will contain a statement detailing the employee's gross pay, deductions and net pay. When all the wage packets have been filled, all the cash should have been used. There should be no surplus or shortage.

● At an appointed time, the wage packets are handed to each employee, who should sign for the wage. Where an employee is not present at the wages pay-out, the wage packets should be returned to the cashier (or other independent person, but not the wages staff), who should record them by writing the details in an Unclaimed Wages Book. An independent person should check that an unclaimed wage packet exists for each entry in the Unclaimed Wages Book. When such unclaimed wages are claimed on a subsequent date, the employee should sign the Unclaimed Wages Book. After a specified period, any unclaimed wage packets should be paid back into the bank as this avoids the risk of them being stolen. Details of the wage packets paid back into the bank should be recorded in the Unclaimed Wages Book, and the amount banked should be equal to the total net wage of the wage packets unclaimed by the specified date.

● Ideally, a person other than the cashier and wages staff should be responsible for dealing with disputes about wages.

30.9 FIXED ASSET SYSTEMS

The acquisition of fixed assets will probably be processed through the purchases system, but there will be additional controls because of their high value. The business should have an agreed procedure over the acquisition of, and accounting for, fixed assets. Controls in this area should be strong, particularly for the acquisition of high-value items. The directors of the business should have approved for the year a budget, which will include the agreed value of fixed assets to be acquired in the year.

For acquisition of small-value fixed assets (e.g. under £500) the procedure may be similar to other purchases and the items may be expensed rather than included in fixed assets. However, there are likely to be annual limits to the amount of such expenditure by each department. As some fixed assets can be used privately (e.g. computers) the Purchases Department should ensure that the items are being acquired for use in the business and are not going to be taken home by employees.

At the next level of cost (say £500 to £5,000), a senior manager or director should be allowed to authorize the acquisition of the fixed asset. Above a specified amount (say £5,000), the acquisition of the fixed asset is authorized by the Board of Directors. Such authorization requires a form to be signed by either the directors or the company secretary (who attends and records minutes of board meetings). Upon authorization, the fixed asset is purchased through the normal purchasing system.

For complex acquisitions of fixed assets, such as the construction of a new retail store, a senior person would manage the project and be responsible for ensuring that the fixed asset is completed at the agreed time and within the agreed cost. For the purchase of land and buildings, the procedure becomes more complex and it is likely to be undertaken by the company secretary and the company's solicitor. For land and buildings, a senior person should keep the documents of title, such as the conveyance, land registry certificate or lease. These documents should be kept in a secure place (e.g. in a safe or at the company's bank).

Details of fixed assets are recorded in a Fixed Asset Register, maintained manually or on a computer. The Fixed Asset Register records details of the fixed asset, including its:

- description;
- serial number;
- original cost;
- purchase date;
- location in the company's premises;
- depreciation rate;
- depreciation charge for each year and the accumulated depreciation.

Usually, the control of fixed assets that do not have a serial number is much weaker because it is much more difficult to identify an individual item – for instance, there may well be hundreds of similar office desks and chairs. There may be no record of these items in a Fixed Asset Register, and the only evidence of them in the accounts will be the cost and accumulated depreciation in the Real Ledger. As controls over such fixed assets are weak, there is correspondingly a higher probability of fraud and error. Nevertheless, their value is relatively small, and an employee is likely to complain if his/her desk has been stolen! Periodically, an independent person should check the existence and condition of fixed assets.

The Fixed Asset Register provides the information on the cost, depreciation charge for the year, accumulated depreciation and net book value for the individual fixed assets and for each type of fixed asset. The total for each type of fixed asset should agree with the figure in the Real ledger and in the annual financial statements. Any difference should be investigated. Frequently, the depreciation charge for the year is arrived at from the Fixed Asset Register, as this will allow for fixed assets that have been written down to nil value in previous periods (and no depreciation will be charged on these).

30.10 NOMINAL LEDGER SYSTEMS

Most entries in the Nominal Ledger result from transactions in other systems described in earlier sections. Additional entries that a company's accountant might make in the Nominal Ledger are those to:

- correct errors (e.g. an expense posted to a wrong account);
- include the closing stock and depreciation on fixed assets for the period;
- make adjustments for changes in the bad and doubtful debt provision.

An independent person should check the adjustments made by an accountant. At the end of each period, before the financial statements are prepared, the accuracy of the values in the Nominal Ledger should be established by cross-checking them with other records. For example, the income, and particularly the expenses, should be compared with the budget and the corresponding amounts of the previous year, and any significant difference should be investigated. Allowance should be made for sales being different from the budget, but most expenses should be either mainly fixed or mainly variable (i.e. change at the same rate as the change in sales).

30.11 STOCK CONTROL SYSTEMS

With the introduction of the bar-coding of products, many companies use a computerized system to record stock quantities. In such a system:

- receipts of goods will either be input from the bar code on the product or entered manually (using a keyboard to enter the bar code number and quantity into the computer);
- sales will be recorded at the till or the dispatch point, so that when the bar code is scanned, the computer records the selling price and sales value on the customer's invoice (bill) and deducts one unit from the stock quantity;
- for each product, the number of units in stock should be the opening stock plus the quantity received less the quantity sold in the period.

Periodically, a stocktake should be carried out, where the quantity in stock is counted and compared with the quantity shown by the computer. The stock quantity on the computer is adjusted for small differences; larger differences are investigated. It might be necessary to decide, for instance, whether a difference has arisen from some 'missing' stock in the store or from an error in inputting goods received into the computer.

There should be few, if any, errors in recording details of goods sold, although this may occur when the product's number has been input manually from the till because the scanner is not able to read it. Most of the differences found at the stocktake will be stock shortages, where the stock in the store is less than that shown on the computer. Where there appears to be a significant loss of stock, more controls need to be implemented, such as the store detective keeping an eye on the stock or video surveillance equipment being used for the same purpose. In a supermarket there is likely to be a greater loss in fresh produce than in other stock items, mainly because of wastage where the product passes its sell-by date or in some other way deteriorates and becomes unsuitable for sale.

Stock control systems are an effective way of identifying loss of stock and are a deterrent to employees stealing products. Furthermore, because the stock control system records stock levels and sales, it can be used to order stock for the store. Also, it identifies stock that is selling slowly, so that the management can reduce the price to sell the remaining stock and they may well decide not to trade in the line in the future. In a super-market or shop, the hourly sales can be used to determine the number of employees required on the tills – more individuals being employed when sales are high and fewer when sales are low.

Stock control systems in manufacturing companies are more complex, because a single product comprises a number of individual items. When a product is completed, the individual components making up the product have to be deducted from their various stock quantities. Further problems arise where there is wastage during manufacture of the product.

SOLUTIONS TO INTERACTIVE QUESTIONS

IQ 30.1 Internal controls to forestall problems

Focus is on the controls and the number of persons involved in the buying process.

(a) To guard against cash flow problems:
  ● The school budget, approved in advance by its Board of Governors, should have an allocation established for capital expenditure.
  ● The capital expenditure requisition for the cooker, completed by the canteen manager, cannot be forwarded for action by the school's principal until the school's treasurer has checked the requisition against the budget provision.
(b) To assure suitability of make, model and size:
  ● The canteen manager specifies exact requirements on the capital expenditure requisition.
  ● The purchasing officer invites quotations from several approved suppliers for the supply of cookers of alternative makes and models.
  ● The canteen manager comments on the suitability of the alternatives.
  ● The decision on the cooker to be bought is made either by the principal, or, if necessary by the Board of Governors.
(c) To guard against possible siphoning of the price paid for the cooker, the chances of privately negotiating an excessive price are minimized because:
  ● the purchasing officer does the negotiation;
  ● the canteen manager makes the recommendation;
  ● the principal or the Board of Governors makes the choice of the supplier.
  Unless there is collusion among all three and the supplier, siphoning off part of the price would prove difficult.
(d) To ensure that no payment is made except on receipt of the cooker:
  ● The cooker, when received, is inspected by the stores officer, who completes a material received note and records particulars of the cooker in an Asset Register.
  ● A copy of the material received note is appended to the supplier's invoice, when received, by the purchasing officer, before it is passed on to the treasurer for payment.
  ● The treasurer makes the payment by cheque, properly crossed, directly to the supplier.
  ● Prior to signing the cheque, the principal checks on whether all controls have operated satisfactorily and effectively, and cancels the invoice as well as the material received note to prevent these from being produced again fraudulently to support another payment.

IQ 30.2 Inadequate internal check

Having misappropriated an amount collected from a customer, the cashier could prevent that customer's account from falling markedly into arrears by writing off the debt, transferring the debt to an expense account, or accounting for a fictitious credit note.

IQ 30.3 Pre-recording of cheques received from customers

An employee opening the mail has custody of the asset (cheques and cash in the mail) and is charged with recording the transaction (recording cheques and cash received). So, if one person performs this task, there is a weakness in the internal check; there is a need for two people to undertake these tasks, so that one person can check the other person's work. The cheques and a copy of the record of the cheques should be given to the cashier to record in the cash book and to bank the cheques. The system of internal check will then be an effective control, provided there is no collusion between the two people opening the mail and recording the cheques received.

It is unacceptable for the cashier to open the mail and record the cheques because the cashier would then be having custody of the asset *and* be responsible for recording the transaction.

PROGRESSIVE QUESTIONS

PQ 30.1 Inadequacy of internal check at the tills

In a retail shop a person at the till collects the proceeds of sales.
  Required:

(a) Explain why the internal check is inadequate.
(b) Give some examples of the ways in which the till operator could carry out a fraud.
(c) Describe the controls that the shop can exercise to minimize the risk of fraud by the till operator.

PQ 30.2 Internal controls in the sales system

Required:

(a) Describe what should be checked before the goods are dispatched to a customer after receipt of an order.
(b) Describe how delivery of goods to customers is normally documented.

PQ 30.3 Weaknesses in a purchases system

The procedures in the purchasing system of Sherwood Wholesalers Ltd are as follows:

(a) The user department telephones the Purchasing Department with details of the products required.
(b) The Purchasing Department finds a suitable supplier and issues a Purchase Order, which they send to the supplier. Copies of the purchase order are sent to the user department and the Purchase Accounts Department.
(c) The Goods Received Department checks details of the goods received to the supplier's delivery note. If the details of the goods received agree to the supplier's delivery note, the Goods Received Department staff sign the delivery note and send it to the Purchase Accounts Department. They file a copy of the supplier's delivery note.
(d) When the Purchase Accounts Department receives the purchase invoice, they check it to the supplier's delivery note. If the details agree, the Purchases Accounts Department posts the purchase invoice to the Purchase Ledger.
(e) When the supplier's invoices are due for payment, the cashier writes out a cheque for the unpaid invoices, and the chief accountant signs the cheque.
(f) The Purchase Accounts Department checks the balances on the Purchase Ledger to suppliers' statements, investigates differences, and corrects any errors on the Purchase Ledger.

Required: Identify the weaknesses in the purchasing system described above.

PQ 30.4 Internal controls in the purchases system

A file maintained by the Accounts Department for one of Sherwood's suppliers includes:

● copy of purchase requisition
● goods received note
● advice note (delivery note)

● purchase invoice
● copy of remittance advice
● supplier's statement.

Required: Explain the following:

(a) Why is it important that a department other than the Purchasing Department should raise a purchase requisition?
(b) Even with a separate Purchasing Department (i.e. separate from the department that raises the purchase requisition), there is still a risk of fraud by staff in the Purchasing Department. In what way could a fraud take place, and how could controls be instituted to minimize the risk of such a fraud?
(c) Why is each purchase invoice not sent with the goods to the Goods Received Department?
(d) Why should the Goods Received Department not accept goods where there is no purchase order?
(e) What items on a purchase invoice should the Accounts Department check, or get authorized by another department?
(f) Why should the person checking suppliers' statements with the balances on the Purchase Ledger be independent of other staff involved in purchasing transactions?
(g) What matters should the person checking suppliers' statements pay attention to, and what errors may he/she find?

PQ 30.5 Control weaknesses in wages systems

(a) Explain why there is a weakness in control when the Wages Department staff deal with disputes about wages.
(b) Identify the control weaknesses where the Wages Department: (i) makes up the wage packets and (ii) pays the wages to employees.
(c) Employees in the Wages Department will usually be responsible for calculating and paying their own wage. Explain why this is a weakness and describe controls to overcome this weakness.

PQ 30.6 Checks in the petty cash system

Required: List the checks that an independent person should perform when checking a petty cash system.

PQ 30.7 Verification of fixed assets

Required:

(a) Describe the matters that should be checked when inspecting a fixed asset for verifying its existence and value.
(b) State the additional checks needed if the fixed asset is a motor vehicle.

PQ 30.8 Disposing of fixed assets

Required: Describe the risks of fraud in relation to the disposal of fixed assets.

PQ 30.9 Nominal Ledger – checking the accountant's entries

Required: Describe why is there a need for an independent person to check the entries made by the accountant in the Nominal Ledger.

PQ 30.10 Controls to minimize abuse of company facilities

The managing director of Moberley Enterprises is concerned about the use of the company's equipment and facilities by employees for their personal use. She has asked you to describe the controls that could minimize personal use of the company's equipment and facilities. Her main concerns relate to:

● the use of the company's telephone for personal calls;
● the use of the company's photocopier;
● the use of the company's computer for playing computer games and accessing the Internet;
● using the company to pay for postage of personal letters.

Required: In respect of the concerns listed above, describe what you would recommend to the managing director. Explain why the company might not be able to establish controls that would prevent all of the potential frauds listed.

Chapter 31

FIXED ASSETS: APPRAISAL AND FINANCING

In this chapter

We will learn of:

- methods of appraising capital investment
- alternative methods of financing the acquisition of fixed assets

and you should be able to:

- appraise and choose between capital investments
- account for assets acquired on hire purchase and finance lease terms

31.1 INTRODUCTION

In today's competitive markets, if a business is to remain viable it must make capital investments to replace obsolete and worn-out fixed assets and acquire additional ones. As capital investment often involves large sums of money and long-term commitments, management decisions in regard to them cannot be taken lightly. Several issues have to be considered, such as:

- Appraising the viability of the investment:
  - Will the business recover the outlay (cost) on the investment?
  - Will the investment give an adequate return?
  - What will that return be?
  - If there are alternative investments, which one should be chosen?
- Deciding how the investment is to be financed:
  - Is the asset to be acquired on a cash basis, on credit terms or on a hire purchase or lease?
- Financial reporting:
  - How will the transaction be accounted for?

31.2 APPRAISING THE INVESTMENT

There are three main methods of appraising the viability of a capital investment proposal. Each of these can be used to identify whether a single project is worthwhile, or to compare two or more alternatives in order to select the one most suitable. These methods are as follows:

1. payback;
2. annual accounting rate of return;
3. discounted cash flow, through either the 'net present value' approach or the 'internal rate of return' approach.

31.2.1 Payback

Under the payback method the choice of an investment project is based on the length of time it takes to recover the outlay on the project from the stream of cash generated by it. Thus the focus is on the cash inflow rather than profit. For example, if an asset acquired at a cost of £30,000 is expected to generate a constant cash flow of £10,000 per year, the payback period for that asset can be considered as three years. If the expected cash flow from year to year is not constant, the cash flows in successive years are added together to determine how long it takes for the cash inflow to equal the outlay on the project. If the cash flows from the asset costing £30,000 are £5,000, £14,000 and £22,000 in the first, second and third years respectively, the payback period is two-and-a-half years (when the cash inflow of £5,000 + £14,000 + £11,000 equals the £30,000 initial outlay).

Although simple to apply and to understand, this method suffers from two major setbacks:

- Cash flows beyond the point when the recovery of the original outlay has been achieved are ignored. One project may have a shorter payback period than another but the aggregate cash inflow therefrom may be markedly lower than that from the other project.
- When reckoning the cost of the investment, the payback method focuses on the cash outlay, ignoring the time value of money – i.e. the interest that could have been earned on that outlay had it not been tied down in the asset.

The payback method tends to consider safety as the major criterion in capital-investment decision making and is most appropriate where the market for the output of the project is highly volatile and uncertain. A reason for this could be rapid and unexpected changes in fashion or technological development.

Investment appraisal by the payback method

Interaction 31.1

Walbar plc carries on business as a children's playgroup. It is considering three capital investment suggestions involving three separate projects. Project (1) is to acquire minibuses to transport children from outlying areas of a town it operates in, with the expectation that it would be a couple of years before competitors counteracted this initiative. Project (2) is to acquire new canteen equipment to provide meals in-house and replace the outside caterers. Project (3) is to acquire new premises to accommodate additional playgroup classes. Each project requires an initial capital outlay of £50,000 and the anticipated cash inflow from each is as stated here.

Required: Using the payback method of project appraisal, select the project that you regard as the most viable. You are to assume that cash flows occur evenly throughout each year. Using all of the information available, can you see any argument for choosing another project?

	Minibuses	Canteen	Premises
	Cash inflows (£)		
Year 1	28,000	10,000	30,000
Year 2	22,000	20,000	18,000
Year 3	8,000	30,000	12,000
Year 4	4,000	20,000	6,000
Year 5	–	10,000	2,000

31.2.2 Annual accounting rate of return (AARR)

The accounting rate of return method, unlike the payback method, focuses on the project's profitability rather than its cash inflow, and takes account of profitability over the asset's whole lifespan. The calculation of the AARR is done in two steps, as follows:

1. **Calculate the average annual profit (AAP) from the project.** Isolate the incremental (extra) profit arising from the investment (i.e. cash flow generated by the project over its whole life, less the depreciation of the asset) and, by dividing it by the expected life of the asset, determine the AAP. To illustrate let us assume that a new machine costing £100,000 will generate a cash flow of £30,000 per year over five years and that the machine is to be depreciated over five years using the straight-line method. The average annual profit in each of the five years is found as follows:

Average annual profit	Formula	Calculation	AAP
	$\dfrac{\text{Incremental cash flow less depreciation}}{\text{Expected life of the project}}$	$\dfrac{(£30,000 \times 5) - £100,000}{5 \text{ years}}$	£10,000

2. Work out the AARR by dividing the AAP by:
   - either the whole outlay on the project;
   - or (if preferred) the average outlay. If one assumes that the investment declines in a linear fashion as the asset ages, the average outlay may be taken to be one-half of the original outlay (plus, if there is any scrap value, one-half of that scrap value).

Average accounting rate of return	If calculated on whole outlay $\dfrac{£10,000}{£100,000} \times 100\% = 10\%$	If calculated on average outlay $\dfrac{£10,000}{£100,000/2} \times 100\% = 20\%$

A major defect of AARR, however, is that it ignores the time value of money. For example, it may identify one project as superior to another even though the profit generated by the former is more toward the end of its life whereas that of the latter occurs early in its life.

Interaction 31.2

AARR based on the original investment

Walbar plc acquires an asset for an outlay of £200,000, which it estimates will last for five years. During its life the average annual cash flow will be £70,000 per annum. Depreciation is calculated using the straight-line method and there will be no residual value.

Required: Calculate the annual accounting rate of return based on the original investment.

AARR based on the average investment

Required:

(a) Using the information stated in IQ 31.2, calculate the annual accounting rate of return based on the average investment.

(b) Compare, using the annual accounting rate of return based on average investment, the acquisition of the above-stated asset with an alternative project that involves a capital outlay of £300,000 and is expected to yield a cash flow in years one, two, three, four and five of £180,000, £150,000, £70,000, £15,000 and £5,000 respectively. Assume that, in the alternative project also, the asset is depreciated by the straight-line method and has no residual value.

(c) Comment on any defect in the comparison of the two projects.

31.2.3 Discounted cash flow (DCF)

Unlike both previous methods, discounted cash flow (DCF) takes into account the time value of money. It recognizes that £1 in a year's time is not worth as much as £1 today since it ignores the fact that £1 could be invested today and in a year's time would have increased in value by the amount of the interest it had earned. DCF is based on cash flows not profits, and it converts the future cash flows generated by a project into their present value by the application of a discount factor. The resultant figure can then be compared with the original outlay, thereby comparing like with like. Once this is done, it can be ascertained whether a project is giving a return in real terms and, if necessary, what it represents when expressed as a percentage return on the original investment.

The discounted cash flow method uses either the net present value in its calculations or an internal rate of return. Each of these is discussed next.

Net present value (NPV)

The net present value approach uses the principle of DCF and is employed where the required rate of return is known. The rate used is usually the minimum acceptable to the business. The rate is used to discount the net cash inflows of a project to their present values, and this present value is then subtracted from the original outlay so as to determine the net present value. If the resultant answer is positive, it indicates that the project under scrutiny gives a better return than the rate used for the discounting, and therefore the project is seen as viable. For example, let us assume that an investment of £600 on a project is expected to generate £200, £300, £400 and £200 in years one to four respectively and that the minimum rate of return acceptable to the business is 10 per cent per annum. £1 received one year later, discounted at 10 per cent p.a. would be worth (£1 × 100/110) = £909 today. If the expected returns from the project are discounted in this manner, the present value of the project (calculated below) is £866.60 and the amount by which this exceeds the investment (of £600) is the net present value of £266.60.

As this value is positive, the project is deemed viable.

The net present value approach is useful also when making a choice between alternative projects. The project with the higher NPV would be the one chosen.

Year	Return	Discounted value of £1 @ 10% p.a.	Net present value (£)
1	£200	0.909	181.80
2	£300	0.826	247.80
3	£400	0.751	300.40
4	£200	0.683	136.60
Present value of returns			866.60

The net present value approach

Walbar plc plans to invest £200,000 in a new machine. Over the next six years the cash inflows from the project are expected to be as follows:

Year	1	2	3	4	5	6
Cash inflows (£)	40,000	50,000	70,000	60,000	40,000	10,000

At the end of year 6 the machine will be sold for scrap and will realize £5,000 (this amount not being included in the above cash inflows). Assume that the initial outflow is immediate and that all inflows occur at each year end. The company policy is that all capital expenditure projects must return at least 10 per cent per annum on the original investment.

Required: Using the net present value approach, identify whether the company should go ahead with the project.

Internal rate of return (IRR)

The internal rate of return is the actual interest rate earned on an investment over the course of its economic life. In this approach, unlike in the net present value approach, the expected rate of return is not known. Instead, we look for a rate of return that, when used to discount all cash flows from the investment, will equate the present value of all cash flows to the cash outlay on the project. If we can calculate the point when the discounted future cash flow is exactly equal to the outlay (i.e. when the net present value of a project is zero), whatever discount rate was used to obtain this situation is the actual return for the project. A judgement can then be made by management as to whether this rate of return is adequate.

It would be possible to keep discounting the cash flow by every possible rate of return until such a zero point is reached. It is simpler, however, if, on a trial-and-error basis, the cash flow is discounted at a rate that gives a positive net present value and then recalculated using a higher discounting rate until a negative net present value is arrived at. This means that the true rate for the project is somewhere between the two. The actual rate is arrived at by using a technique called interpolation, which presumes (as an adequate approximation) a straight-line relationship between the positive and negative points. The following illustration shows how interpolation works.

Year	Cash flow	Discount factor @ 16%	Net present value @ 16%	Discount factor @ 18%	Net present value @18%
	£		£		£
0	(100,000)	1.000	(100,000)	1.000	(100,000)
1	30,000	0.862	25,860	0.847	25,410
2	40,000	0.743	29,720	0.718	28,720
3	50,000	0.641	32,050	0.609	30,450
4	25,000	0.552	13,800	0.516	12,900
			1,430		(2,520)

The actual rate in our example lies between 16 and 18 per cent because NPV ranges between £1,430 positive and £2,520 negative. Starting with the lower rate, we can calculate the proportional point at which NPV is zero:

$$\text{Actual rate of return} = 16\% + [1,430/(1,430 + 2,520)] \times (18\% - 16\%)$$
$$= 16\% + 0.724\% = 16.724\%$$

The actual rate of return for the project, when ascertained, is compared with the company's required rate of return to determine whether investment in the project is acceptable to management.

Internal rate of return	**Interaction 31.5**

Required: If the investment needed and the expected cash flows are as stated in IQ 31.4, and on the basis of calculating discount factors for 10 and 16 per cent, calculate the internal rate of return for the project.

31.2.4 Summary of investment appraisal

We have seen that investment appraisal techniques vary from the very simple to the complex, each having its place in the decision-making mechanism. Each, too, can be used singly or in conjunction with any one of the other techniques. No one method is correct. The situation will determine the most appropriate method or methods to be employed.

31.3 FINANCING THE ACQUISITION

Having selected a project on the basis of its viability and how it compares with alternatives, the next decision to be made is how it is to be financed.

31.3.1 Acquisition for cash or credit

An outright purchase of the asset, on cash or credit terms, is accounted for by debiting the asset account and crediting the Cash account or a supplier's account, as the case may be. The effect on the Profit and Loss account is felt when the asset is depreciated. However, the acquisition of expensive fixed assets can cause serious cash-flow problems. To ease these problems, rather than acquiring for cash or on normal trade credit terms, assets may be acquired by way of a hire purchase contract or by leasing.

31.3.2 Hire purchase

A *hire purchase* (HP) contract is a contract for the hire of an asset, which contains a provision giving the hirer an option to acquire legal title to the asset upon the fulfilment of certain conditions stated in the contract. These conditions are usually the payment of an agreed number of instalments plus the payment of a notional sum at the end of the contracted hire period. During the period of the contract, legally the asset remains the property of the supplier; the payments made are technically hire charges. However, the commercial substance is that the business enjoys the benefit of the asset as if it had been acquired and the asset acquired under hire purchase contracts should be accounted for as one that is owned. Only the cash price equivalent (i.e. the hire purchase price less interest) is capitalized and depreciated using the method and rate of depreciation appropriate to the class of asset and in accordance with the organization's depreciation policy. The interest element is written off to the Profit and Loss account.

In most hire purchase contracts there is provision for interest to be paid to the supplier. The interest element in a hire purchase contract is the excess of the hire purchase price over the cash price that would have been paid if the goods had been bought outright.

Interest is treated by the customer as an expense. There are two methods of recording these transactions.

To illustrate both methods let us assume that on 1.1.20X0 Soya Ltd acquired a machine on hire purchase terms from Beans plc, paying £4,000 immediately and agreeing to pay three further annual instalments of the same amount, annually in arrears, commencing on 31 December 20X0. The cash price of the machine is £13,947 and the company's policy is to write off one-third of the cost of this class of asset annually as depreciation. When spelling out the terms, interest has been included at 10 per cent per annum.

Hire purchase interest: the common method

In the common method of recording HP transactions, the identification of the interest is deferred until it becomes due.

MACHINERY ACCOUNT

			£			£	
a	1.1.X0	Beans plc	13,947				

PROVISION FOR DEPRECIATION – MACHINERY ACCOUNT

			£			£	
				31.12.X0	Depreciation	4,649	b
				31.12.X1	Depreciation	4,649	b
				31.12.X2	Depreciation	4,649	b

BEANS PLC – (HIRE PURCHASE VENDOR) ACCOUNT

			£			£	
c	1.1.X0	Cash account	4,000	1.1.X0	Machinery	13,947	a
	1.1.X0	Balance c/d	9,947				
e	31.12.X0	Cash account	4,000	1.1.X0	Balance b/d	9,947	
	31.12.X0	Balance c/d	6,942	31.12.X0	Interest a/c	995	d
e	31.12.X1	Cash account	4,000	1.1.X1	Balance b/d	6,942	
	31.12.X1	Balance c/d	3,636	31.12.X1	Interest a/c	694	d
e	31.12.X2	Cash account	4,000	1.1.X2	Balance b/d	3,636	
				31.12.X2	Interest a/c	364	

Notes:

(a) The cash price of the machine capitalized on the date of acquisition.
(b) Depreciation of the cost, in accordance with company policy.
(c) Downpayment made on the date of acquisition.
(d) Interest calculated at 10% of the amount outstanding
(e) Three more instalments, paid annually in arrears.
(f) Cost of the machine less depreciation written off until that point is stated as a fixed asset on each Balance Sheet.
(g) The Profit and Loss account for each year would report as expense the depreciation as well as the interest relating to that year.

Hire purchase interest: a second method of recording

In the second accounting method, the total amount owing on the contract is acknowledged at the point of acquisition. Hence it becomes necessary to debit to an Interest Suspense account the difference between the total amount payable on the HP contract and the cash price of the asset. The interest expense so recorded in the Interest Suspense account is allocated to each year of the contract, either in accordance with how it actually arose or apportioned on an approximate basis.

The acquisition of the machinery on HP terms stated in our illustration would be accounted for on this method as shown by the journal entry on the right. The amount owed to the HP vendor would be discharged by the downpayment and the three annual instalments. The machinery would be depreciated in accordance with the company's policy. If the actual rate of interest accrued under the HP contract is known (as it is in the case used for illustration) the balance in the Interest Suspense account would be allocated to each of the three years as shown on the right. This is known as the as the *actuarial method*. The balance in the Interest Suspense account at every year end would be offset from the balance in the HP vendor's account so that the actual amount owed to the vendor on that date is stated as the liability (see on the right how the liability as at 31 December 20X0 is stated on the Balance Sheet).

Sundries	Dr	£	£
To Beans plc (HP vendor)		–	16,000
Machinery account		13,947	–
Interest Suspense account		2,053	–
Being acquisition of machinery on hire purchase terms			

INTEREST SUSPENSE ACCOUNT

		£			£
1.1.X0	HP vendor's a/c	2,053	31.12.X0	Profit and Loss a/c	995
			31.12.X0	Balance c/d	1,058
1.1.X1	Balance b/f	1,058	31.12.X1	Profit and Loss a/c	694
			31.12.X1	Balance c/d	364
1.1.X2	Balance b/d	364	31.12.X2	Profit and Loss a/c	364

BALANCE SHEET AS AT 31.12.20X0	
Creditors:	£
Owed to HP vendor	8,000
Less: Interest Suspense a/c	(1,058)
	6,942

Hire purchase interest rate not known

If the actual rate of interest built into a hire purchase contract is not known,[1] it becomes necessary to apportion the interest to each of the three years. The easiest method of doing this is to apportion the interest cost equally to the number of years involved. This method is not acceptable unless there are a large number of hire purchase contracts of relatively small value.[2] An alternative and acceptable method of apportioning the interest is known as the **sum of the year's digits method**. On this method, interest is allocated to each year in proportion to the number of instalments outstanding in each of these years. For example, in the case used for illustration, throughout the first year (until the instalment paid on 31.12.20X0) three instalments were outstanding; in the second year two were outstanding and, in the third, just one. Accordingly, the interest (£2,053) is allocated to years one, two and three in the ratio 3:2:1 respectively. If an agreement provides for 12 annual instalments, the sum of the digits assigned in this way to each of the 12 years would be (12 + 11 + 10 + 9 + 8 + 7 + 6 + 5 + 4 + 3 + 2 + 1) = 78. For this reason this method of apportioning interest is often known also as the 'rule of 78'.

Summary

The effect of using each of the three methods (as shown below) clarifies that the sum-of-the-year's-digits method achieves results fairly close to the actuarial method.

Interest written off	20X0	20X1	20X2
Actuarial method	£995	£694	£364
Sum of the year's digits method	£1,026	£684	£343
Equally to each year (common method)	£685	£684	£684

Interaction 31.6

Acquisition of asset on hire purchase terms

A machine price marked at £35,500 could be acquired subject to a trade discount of 7 per cent. BMC Ltd acquired the machine on 1 January 20X1 on hire purchase terms, paying £15,000 as a downpayment on that date and undertaking to pay three more annual instalments of £7,500 commencing from 1 January 20X2. An interest rate of 12 per cent p.a. has been built into the terms. BMC Ltd depreciates assets of this class at 20 per cent per year using the straight-line method.

Required:

(a) Show the ledger accounts to reflect the above transactions up to 31 December 20X5. Interest is to be charged to the Profit and Loss account on an actuarial basis.
(b) Work out the amount of interest charged to the Profit and Loss account using the sum-of-the-year's-digits method.

31.3.3 Acquiring an asset on finance lease terms

To get the concept in perspective, let us use a story. Polly and Nelly, two sisters, both equally clever at making ladies' garments, received £100,000 each from their father to set themselves up in business from 1 January 20X0. Polly acquired machinery for £60,000 and with working capital left over of £40,000 proceeded to make a net profit of £20,000 in the first year after writing off one-tenth of the cost of machinery as depreciation. Nelly began by frittering away £60,000 and found herself left with only the working capital but not the resources to buy the machinery. Her attempt to acquire machinery on hire purchase terms from a supplier was unsuccessful because the supplier found that the interest rates were too high to undertake trading on such terms. In the circumstances, Nelly applied for a bank loan of £60,000. Though aware that Nelly was a credit risk, the bank did not wish to miss out on a business opportunity. Therefore, the bank acquired the machinery for £60,000 and leased it to Nelly on the following terms:

● Nelly to pay a lease rental of £21,016 annually in arrears for four years commencing from 31 December 20X0.
● During the four years (i.e. until the bank recovered the capital tied up, along with interest at 15 per cent per annum), the lease agreement cannot be cancelled. This is because if Nelly cancels the agreement and returns the machinery, the bank will have no use for it. The period within which the agreement cannot be cancelled is referred to as the 'primary period'.

- Thereafter Nelly may continue to use the machinery for however long she wishes, paying no more than £1 per year. Such a nominal rent, payable after the primary period is completed, is known as **peppercorn rent**. Nelly intends to use the machinery for five years.
- Although legally the machinery belongs to the bank, Nelly will have its custody and uninterrupted usage of it; but she should also take responsibility for servicing, repairing, maintaining and insuring the machinery.

With the leased machinery, Nelly launched herself into the same business as her sister and by the year end reported a profit of £20,000. On the premise that the machinery does not belong to her, Nelly did not capitalize the cost of the leased machinery and wrote off as expenditure the annual lease rental of £21,016. As at the last day of the first year, Polly's Balance Sheet appears as shown on the left and Nelly's as shown on the right.

POLLY'S BALANCE SHEET AS AT 31.12.20X0

	£000
Machinery	60
Accum. depreciation	(6)
	54
Working capital	66
	120

	£000
Capital	100
Profit	20
	120

NELLY'S BALANCE SHEET AS AT 31.12.20X0

	£000
Working capital	60
	60

	£000
Capital	40
Profit	20
	60

The accounts of both businesses are audited by the same person, who feels unhappy with the comparative position of the two. It appears that Nelly's performance is far better than Polly's because Polly's return on capital employed (£20,000/£100,000 × 100%) is 20%, whereas Nelly's (£20,000/£40,000 × 100%) is 50%. He suggests that to establish the comparability of the position of both businesses, Nelly should capitalize the cost (excluding the interest element) of the machinery, notwithstanding the fact that legally the machinery belongs to the bank. He makes his case by pointing out that although legally the machinery belongs to the bank, in commercial substance it is as good as belonging to Nelly. This is because Nelly, just like her sister, has all the rewards and risks relating to the machinery.

The rewards are as follows:

- Nelly, like Polly, has the custody and uninterrupted usage of the machinery.
- Nelly, like Polly, is entitled to benefit from all that the machinery can produce.

The risks are as follows:

- Like Polly, Nelly is responsible for repairs, maintenance and insurance of the machinery.
- Because the lease agreement is uncancellable within the primary period, Nelly, like her sister, will have to bear any loss from excess capacity or obsolescence of the machinery.

Besides, if Nelly does not capitalize the machinery, her Balance Sheet would fail to show a true and fair view because it would fail to report as an asset the resource it controls for generating income, and it would not report as a liability an uncancellable obligation that Nelly has to the bank. For these reasons it is a requirement of an accounting standard[3] that assets acquired on finance lease terms should be capitalized. A *finance lease* is defined as a lease that transfers to the lessee the risks and rewards of the asset leased. The accounting standard provides a rule of thumb that there is a rebuttable presumption that all risks and rewards are transferred to the lessee if, at the inception of the lease, the present value of the minimum lease obligation to which the lessee is committed amounts to the whole of, or substantially the whole of (i.e. not less than 90 per cent of), the fair value of the asset acquired. In the case of Nelly, if the four instalments of £21,016 she has committed herself to are discounted at the interest rate of 15 per cent p.a., the present value of her obligation is £60,000, which is the whole of the fair value (market price) of the machinery.

Nelly has, therefore, to capitalize the finance-leased machinery and depreciate it over the five years she intends to use it. The transaction will have to be accounted for as follows:

MACHINERY (ON FINANCE LEASE) ACCOUNT

			£				£	
a	1.1.X0	Oblig. on F.L.	60,000					

OBLIGATIONS ON FINANCE LEASE ACCOUNT

			£			£	
c	31.12.X0	Cash book	21,016	1.1.X0	Machinery a/c	60,000	a
	31.12.X0	Balance c/d	47,984	31.12.X0	Interest a/c	9,000	b
c	31.12.X1	Cash book	21,016	1.1.X1	Balance b/d	47,984	
	31.12.X1	Balance c/d	34,166	31.12.X1	Interest a/c	7,198	b
c	31.12.X2	Cash book	21,016	1.1.X2	Balance b/d	34,166	
	31.12.X2	Balance c/d	18,275	31.12.X2	Interest a/c	5,125	b
c	31.12.X3	Cash book	21,016	31.12.X3	Balance b/d	18,275	
				31.12.X3	Interest a/c	2,741	

PROVISION FOR DEPRECIATION ON MACHINERY ACCOUNT

		£	
31.12.X0	Depreciation a/c	12,000	d
31.12.X1	Depreciation a/c	12,000	d
31.12.X2	Depreciation a/c	12,000	d
31.12.X3	Depreciation a/c	12,000	d
31.12.X4	Depreciation a/c	12,000	d

Notes:

(a) Present value of the minimum lease payments (i.e. the four lease rentals discounted by the interest rate of 15 per cent per annum).

(b) Interest at 15 per cent p.a. of the amount owed at beginning of the year.

(c) Annual payment of lease instalments.

(d) Depreciation of the finance leased asset over the number of years of intended use.

Instead of the lease instalment of £21,016, Nelly would write off to the Profit and Loss account the interest (£9,000) and depreciation (£12,000). Her revised profit in the first year would then be (£20,000 + 21,016 less interest and depreciation) = £20,016. Nelly's Balance Sheet as at 31.12.20X0 will appear as shown on the right. Nelly's return on capital employed will be (£20,016/£108,000 × 100%) = 18.53%, which is broadly comparable with that of Polly.

The main differences between an acquisition on hire purchase and finance lease terms are, therefore, that:

- a hire purchase agreement is with the supplier (it is a trading transaction) whereas a finance lease agreement is with a financing institution (it is a financing transaction);
- assets acquired on an HP agreement would be owned in due course by the party who hired the item, whereas an item acquired on finance lease terms would never be owned, at least under the arrangements currently prevailing in the United Kingdom.

NELLY'S BALANCE SHEET AS AT 31.12.20X0	
	£
Machinery on finance lease	60,000
Accumulated depreciation	(12,000)
	48,000
Working capital	60,000
	108,000
	£
Capital	40,000
Profit for the year	20,016
	60,016
Obligation under finance lease	47,984
	108,000

If the lease terms on which an asset was acquired do not qualify the lease to be regarded as a finance lease (so that the asset does not have to be capitalized), it is referred to as an *operating lease*.

Identification of a finance lease

Interaction 31.7

In 20X2 Growth plc acquired the following machinery on lease terms:

Date 20X2	Cash price	Deposit	Instalments	Terms
1.1	£60,000	None	5 of £15,000	Annually in arrears
1.4	£135,000	£30,000	4 of £30,000	Annually in advance
1.10	£180,000	£20,000	2 of £20,000	Annually in advance

The lease terms are known to include interest at 8 per cent per annum. The cumulative present value factors for 8 per cent are stated on the right. Bear in mind the rule of thumb that if the present value of minimum lease payments amounts to the whole of the fair value of the asset, the lease is presumed to have transferred the risks and rewards of the asset to the lessee and is, therefore, to be treated as a finance lease.

Year	Present value
1	0.926
2	1.783
3	2.577
4	3.312
5	3.993

Required: Identify each lease as a finance lease or an operating lease.

31.4 SUMMARY

An asset obtained under a hire purchase agreement or finance lease terms is considered similar to an acquisition financed by a loan upon which interest is charged. It follows therefore that the hirer/lessee will account for the asset as if it had been acquired and debit the asset account while reporting as a liability the present (discounted) amount of the outstanding hire purchase or finance lease commitment. Any interest under the agreement is treated as any other interest payable and written off to the Profit and Loss account. The asset is depreciated over the period of hire/lease or intended use.

References

1. The actual rate of interest can be ascertained using the Present Value Tables. These will be introduced in the next volume of this series.
2. SSAP 21: *Accounting for Leases and Hire Purchase Contracts* (August 1984).
3. SSAP 21, *ibid.*

SOLUTIONS TO INTERACTIVE QUESTIONS

IQ 31.1 Investment appraisal by the payback method

Projects	Outlay	Stream of cash inflows						Payback period
		Year 1	Year 2	Year 3	Year 4	Year 5	Total	
Minibus	£50,000	£28,000	£22,000	£8,000	£4,000	–	£62,000	2 years
Canteen	£50,000	£10,000	£20,000	£30,000	£20,000	£10,000	£90,000	2 yrs 8 mths
Premises	£50,000	£30,000	£18,000	£12,000	£6,000	£2,000	£68,000	2 yrs 2 mths

Although the Minibus project would be the choice using the payback method, it can be seen that both of the other alternatives generate more cash in the later years, with the Canteen project being particularly impressive.

IQ 31.2 Annual accounting rate of return based on the original investment

AAP: [(£70,000 × 5 years) less depreciation of £200,000]/5 years = £30,000.
AARR: AAP/original investment × 100% = (£30,000/£200,000) × 100% = 15%.

IQ 31.3 Annual accounting rate of return based on the average investment

(a) AARR: £30,000/one-half of original investment × 100% = £30,000/£100,000 × 100% = 30%.
(b) AAP = [(£180,000 + £150,000 + £70,000 + £15,000 + £5,000) less depreciation of £300,000]/5 years = £24,000. AARR = [£24,000/£150,000 (one-half of the investment)] × 100% = 16%.
(c) AARR points to the acquisition of the first asset (AARR of 30%) as better than the alternative project (AARR of 16%). But what the comparison overlooks is the fact that most of the returns from the alternative project are in the early stages of its life, and therefore when the time value of money is taken into account (depending on the discount factor) the alternative project may prove better value for money.

IQ 31.4 The net present value approach

Year	Cash flow £	10% discount factor	Net present value £
0	(200,000)	1.000	(200,000)
1	40,000	0.909	36,360
2	50,000	0.826	41,300
3	70,000	0.751	52,570
4	60,000	0.683	40,980
5	40,000	0.620	24,800
6	15,000	0.564	8,460
			+ 4,470

The net present value after year 6 remains positive at the 10 per cent rate of return, and so the project should be considered viable.

IQ 31.5 Internal rate of return

Year	Cash flow £	10% discount factor	NPV £	16% discount factor	NPV £
0	(200,000)	1.000	(200,000)	1.000	(200,000)
1	40,000	0.909	36,360	0.862	34,480
2	50,000	0.826	41,300	0.743	37,150
3	70,000	0.751	52,570	0.641	44,870
4	60,000	0.683	40,980	0.552	33,120
5	40,000	0.620	24,800	0.476	19,040
6	15,000	0.564	8,460	0.410	6,150
			+ 4,470		(25,190)

Interpolating between 10 per cent and 16 per cent on the basis of the above figures, we devise the break-even point to be 10.904%.

IQ 31.6 Acquisition of asset on hire purchase terms

MACHINERY (ON HP TERMS) ACCOUNT

			£				£
a	1.1.X1	HP vendor	33,015				

PROVISION FOR DEPRECIATION – MACHINERY ACCOUNT

			£			£	
				31.12.X1	Depreciation a/c	6,603	e
				31.12.X2	Depreciation a/c	6,603	e
				31.12.X3	Depreciation a/c	6,603	e
				31.12.X4	Depreciation a/c	6,603	e
				31.12.X5	Depreciation a/c	6,603	e

HIRE PURCHASE VENDOR'S ACCOUNT

			£			£	
b	1.1.X1	Cash book	15,000	1.1.X1	Machinery a/c	33,015	
	31.12.X1	Balance c/d	20,177	31.12.X1	Interest a/c	2,162	c
d	1.1.X2	Cash book	7,500	1.1.X2	Balance b/d	20,177	
	31.12.X2	Balance c/d	14,198	31.12.X2	Interest a/c	1,521	c
d	1.1.X3	Cash book	7,500	1.1.X3	Balance b/d	14,198	
	31.12.X3	Balance c/d	7,500	31.12.X3	Interest a/c	802	c
d	1.1.X4	Cash book	7,500	1.1.X4	Balance b/d	7,500	

Notes:

(a) Fair value of machine calculated as follows: list price (£35,500) less 7% discount (£2,485) = cash price (£33,015)

(b) Downpayment of £15,000 on the date of acquisition.

(c) Interest at 12 per cent p.a. on the opening balance, less the instalment paid at the commencement of each year.

(d) Payment of instalments.

(e) Machinery depreciated using the straight-line method over five years.

If the sum-of-the-year's-digits method had been used for apportioning the interest:

TOTAL PAYMENT ON HP		AMOUNT OUTSTANDING			INTEREST APPORTIONED	
	£			**Digits**	Year 20X1: 3/6	£2,242.50
					Year 20X2: 2/6	£1,495.00
Downpayment	15,000	In year 20X1	£22,500	3	Year 20X3: 1/6	£747.50
Instalment (£7,500 × 3)	22,500	In year 20X2	£15,000	2		
		In year 20X3	£7,500	1		–
	37,500	In year 20X4	–			
Cash price of machine	(33,015)					£4,485.00
		Sum of the year's digits		6		
Interest paid	4,485					

IQ 31.7 Identification of a finance lease

Lease	Present value of minimum lease payment	Percentage of fair value	Type of lease
1	£15,000 @ 3.993 = £59,895	59,895/60,000 × 100% = 99.8%	Finance lease
2	(£30,000 @ 3.312) + £30,000 = £129,360	129,360/135,000 × 100% = 95.8%	Finance lease
3	(£20,000 @ 1.783) + £20,000 = £55,660	55,660/180,000 × 100% = 30.9%	Operating lease

PROGRESSIVE QUESTIONS

PQ 31.1 Comparative appraisal of two investments

Your company is considering the acquisition of a new machine for its factory and has a choice from two machines, the 'President' and the 'Royal'. Both the machines meet the production requirements of the engineering department. In such circumstances it is company policy to select the machine that gives maximum cost reduction using a criterion of a minimum 25 per cent DCF return coupled with a three-year payback period.

The relevant details given by the Costings Department are as follows:

	President	Royal
	£	**£**
Capital outlay	40,000	60,000
Estimated total annual savings (i.e. cost reductions including labour and overheads):		
Year 1	12,000	20,000
Year 2	16,000	20,000
Year 3	16,000	30,000
Year 4	16,000	40,000
Year 5	16,000	20,000

An extract from the relevant page of a set of discount tables for 25%, to determine the present value of a single payment received a number of years from the present, is as follows:

Years	1	2	3	4	5	6	7	8	9	10
Factor	0.800	0.640	0.512	0.410	0.328	0.262	0.210	0.168	0.134	0.107

Required: Calculate for each machine the payback period (assuming savings accrue evenly over each year) and the net present value. Give your recommendation, with reasons, as to which machine should be purchased.

PQ 31.2 Appraising the viability of a project

The Directors of Capleigh Ltd are considering making an investment in a project that could lead to the development of a new product that the company could market. The project requires the purchase of new equipment costing £165,000. This equipment is expected to have a life of four years but no scrap value at the end of that time. It is company policy to depreciate all equipment on the straight-line basis.

When the product is ready for marketing the sales in units are expected to be as stated on the left. The details of unit cost of production and the anticipated sale price are as stated on the right. The fixed factory overheads will be incurred in any case, whether or not the project is adopted. The company requires a minimum rate of return of 15 per cent on capital employed. The directors have been informed that the present value of £1 at 15 per cent per year is as stated in the table on the left. Receipts and payments are deemed to take place at relevant year end.

Year	Sales (units)
1	1,000
2	1,250
3	1,400
4	1,600

Year 1	£0.870
Year 2	£0.756
Year 3	£0.658
Year 4	£0.572

Cost per unit:	£	£
Direct material		5
Direct Labour		5
Factory overheads:		
Fixed	10	
Variable	3	13
		23
Selling price per unit		60

Required:

(a) Calculate the payback period.
(b) Calculate the net present value of the project and state whether the project is acceptable using this method.
(c) Write a report to the directors explaining:
  ● two advantages of using the payback method as a basis of decision making;
  ● why the emphasis is on cash flow and not profits when using discounted cash flow techniques to evaluate projects.

PQ 31.3 Acquisition on hire purchase terms payable quarterly in advance

On 1 October 20X0 WBM Ltd acquired a machine from REH Ltd under a hire purchase contract. The contract called for a deposit of £2,000 and seven further instalments of £2,000 paid quarterly in advance commencing on 1 January 20X0. The cash price of the machine is £14,500.

Required: Show how the above transactions would appear in the Balance Sheet and Profit and Loss account of WBM Ltd for the period of the contract. WBM Ltd depreciates machines of this class over four years using the straight-line method. The rate of interest implicit in the contract is 11.65 per cent per annum calculated quarterly. WBM uses the actuarial method of allocating interest and finalizes accounts annually on 31 December.

PQ 31.4 Acquisition on HP terms including a trade-in

On 1 April 20X0, MCL Ltd acquired a light crane, priced at £41,844, on hire purchase terms, making a downpayment of £12,000 followed by three further annual instalments of the same amount commencing on 1 April 20X1. On 1 July 20X2, this crane was traded in for a heavier one, price-marked £62,550. The hire purchase terms for the heavier crane comprised a downpayment of £15,000 followed by four more annual instalments of the same amount commencing on 1 July 20X3. As the trade-in value of the light crane, the amount due on that crane as well as the deposit due on the heavier one were waived. The interest rate implicit in the hire purchase terms is 10 per cent per annum. MCL Ltd depreciates assets of this class at 20 per cent per annum on the reducing balance method.

Required: Set out the accounts recording these transactions and explain how the transactions will be reported in the Profit and Loss accounts of each of the four years ending on 31 December and in the Balance Sheets as at each year end.

PQ 31.5 Finance lease

On 1 April 20X1, Sinclair plc leased a machine on an agreement to pay four annual instalments of £20,000 commencing on 1 April 20X2. The cash price of the machine is £64,000. The company intends to use the machine for five years and usually depreciates machinery of this class using the straight-line method.

The terms of each lease include an interest rate of 10 per cent per annum. Stated on the right is a table of the cumulative present value of an annual year-end payment of £1 at 10% interest per year.

Required: Show how the lease is accounted for in the year to 31.12.20X1, and show how the transaction will be reported in the Profit and Loss accounts in each year until 31 December 20X5 and the Balance Sheets as at each year end.

End of year	PV Factor @ 10%
1	0.909
2	1.736
3	2.487
4	3.170
5	3.791
6	4.355

PLANNING AND CONTROL: BUDGETING

In this chapter

We will learn of:

- the need, for business survival, to plan the future by setting up targets in the form of budgets and to endeavour to achieve them

and you should be able to:

- prepare the cash budget and various functional budgets
- prepare flexible budgets for different levels of activity

32.1 WHAT ARE BUDGETS?

Every business needs to plan for the future. The plan might simply be to carry on as in the current year – i.e. to supply the same goods or services to the same customers. In times of change and intense competition, as we witness in many sectors at present, this outlook may not suffice to ensure survival.

A business needs to set clear targets on such matters as its pricing structure, levels of costs, profits and safe cash levels; it also needs to set up the mechanism to achieve these targets and inquire into any failure to meet them. Such targets are set in the form of *budgets*.

If the financial statements for a period are to be as budgeted, there is a need to:

> 'A budget is a plan quantified in monetary terms; prepared and approved prior to a defined period of time; usually showing planned income to be generated and/or expenditure to be incurred during that period; and the capital employed to attain a given objective.'
> ~ *Chartered Institute of Management Accountants*

- set up operating budgets for each area of operation, such as sales, stock levels, production, purchases, and cash;
- delegate to appropriate executives the responsibility to achieve the budgets;
- undertake a continuous comparison of the actuals with budgeted results;
- take appropriate action either to achieve the budgeted results or to provide a basis for its revision.

All these procedures together are referred to as *budgetary control*.

32.2 PURPOSES OF BUDGETARY CONTROL

The main objective of budgetary control is:

- **planning** as a means of achieving the stated objectives, such as (say) maximizing trading profits or the return on capital employed;

- **co-ordination** of the activities of the various operations, functions or departments of the business;
- **control** of these activities, measured in either quantitative or monetary terms by comparison of the actual achievement with the budget, leading to corrective action.

There are, of course, other benefits to be obtained, such as the motivation of staff by the measurement and evaluation of performance, with suitable rewards where appropriate, and the achievement of more efficient communication.

32.3 RESPONSIBILITY FOR BUDGET PREPARATION AND IMPLEMENTATION

A company's strategic policy is usually formulated by the Board of Directors. However, it is not their responsibility to carry out the day-to-day activities associated with budgetary control. They delegate this role, generally to a Budget Committee.

The **Budget Committee** is made up of senior executives and managers who act in a collaborative manner. The duties of the Budget Committee include the following:

- **Before budgets are agreed**
  - the Committee acts in an advisory capacity, both upwards to senior management and downwards to functional managers, reviewing the various budgets and either accepting them or calling for their amendment;
  - it liaises with functional managers regarding their budgets in order to ensure that they conform to the company's policy and fit in with other budgets;
  - it appoints a Budget Officer.
- **After budgets have become operational** the Budget Committee considers requests for revisions and identifies procedures for correcting deficiencies.

The **Budget Officer** is responsible for carrying out the day-to-day administrative work relating to the budgets. This includes the following:

- checking the various budgets submitted by the functional managers to ensure that they are free from errors and inconsistencies;
- collating actual figures to compare with budgets;
- presenting budget/actual reports to the functional managers;
- highlighting any variances and calling for their explanations;
- following up the explanations to ensure that corrective action is taken or the budget revised, if necessary.

32.4 BUDGET PREPARATION

Before we illustrate the preparation of operating budgets in detail, we will explain the information flow for one of the costs (that for raw materials purchases) going into the Manufacturing account and into the cash budget.

To start with, the amount of raw materials to be purchased is determined and this is done in accordance with the number of units of the finished product that the business plans to sell, the amount of finished goods to be held in stock, and the stocks of raw materials to be held. The Manufacturing account is prepared on an accruals basis with no adjustment for the terms of credit obtained from suppliers and the timing of the payments.

The focus at this stage is when the purchases of raw material should be paid for. This will depend on whether the purchases are for cash or credit and, if for credit, the credit terms (e.g. 30 days) and whether discount is available for early payment.

The information flow can be shown diagrammatically as set out below.

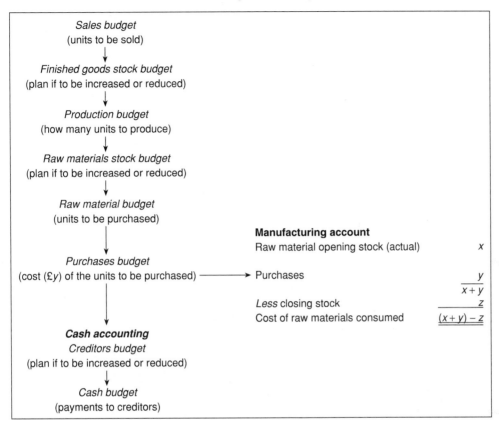

32.4.1 **The limiting factor**

A major point to recognize is that in any business there is bound to be a factor that will restrict activity. It would, for example, be pointless to accept orders for more items than the business is able to produce. This factor is known as the key factor or *limiting factor*.

Weak demand for the product is often a major limiting factor, where for instance foreign markets become difficult if the home currency is strong and foreign products are therefore relatively cheaper. There are, of course, other factors, such as:

- the lack of a production facility, e.g. raw material, skilled labour, plant capacity;
- a lack of storage space;
- a lack of finance to acquire fixed assets and provide adequate working capital.

Although it is sometimes possible to take action to eliminate a limiting factor (e.g. boosting sales demand by an advertising campaign or subcontracting work to overcome labour or machine shortages), it is likely that such solutions may only be short-term and/or expensive. Realistically, therefore, budgets have to be formulated bearing the limiting factor in mind. The major limiting factor will usually determine the first budget to be produced, and this will form the base for all the other budgets.

32.5 THE SALES BUDGET

If we assume that the sales demand is the limiting factor, the first budget to be produced would be the sales budget. This budget would estimate the volume of sales in terms of units and evaluate that volume in monetary terms by the application of selling prices. Because other functional managers (e.g. the production manager and the advertising manager) will then be preparing their budgets to support the level of sales activity, it is important that the sales budget should be realistic. This means taking into consideration the following:

- past experience;
- changes in the state of the market;
- changes in the company's and competitors' policies on pricing, marketing and credit terms;
- any new products on the market;
- salesmen's estimates;
- the state of the order book compared with previous periods.

Interaction 32.1

Preparation of a sales budget

Growell Ltd produces three grades of fertilizer. On 20X0 its sales were as follows:

Grade 1		Grade 2		Grade 3	
Quantity (sacks)	Price (£) per sack	Quantity (sacks)	Price (£) per sack	Quantity (sacks)	Price (£) per sack
45,000	£6.20	35,000	£6.70	55,000	£7.20

As a result of market research and the observations of the company's own salesforce, it has been estimated that for 20X1 the sales for each grade of fertilizer could be increased by 5,000 sacks if the selling price for each grade were to be reduced by £0.20 per sack.

Required: Prepare a sales budget in quantity and value for the year 20X1 for each grade of fertilizer, on the following format:

	Grade 1	Grade 2	Grade 3
Quantity in previous year			
Increase anticipated			
Sales budget (in sacks)			
New selling price (£)			
Sales budget (£)			

32.6 FUNCTIONAL BUDGETS

A 'functional' budget is defined as a budget of income and/or expenditure applicable to a particular function. A function may refer to a department or a process. Examples of functional budgets are as follows:

- sales budget
- production budget
- direct materials budget
- purchasing budget
- creditors budget
- direct labour budget
- production overhead budget
- production cost budget
- administration budget
- selling costs budget
- plant utilization budget
- cash budget.

We will consider each of these budgets in turn (apart from the sales budget, which has already been discussed in Section 32.5).

32.6.1 The production budget

When preparing the production budget, we must consider not only the quantity required to satisfy the sales budget but also any adjustment we decide to make to the amount of stock that is held.

The timing of production is vital if the smooth running of the business is to be achieved. It is, for example, necessary to plan the production to take account of any seasonal variations in sales demand (i.e. to produce for stock when demand is low in order that there is less pressure on production facilities when demand is heavy) but to ensure at the same time that excessive stockholding costs and possible obsolescence are avoided.

The production budget is in a quantitative form and provides the basis for the preparation of other budgets, such as the direct materials budget and the direct labour budget, which are required to meet the budgeted production levels and timing.

Interaction 32.2

Preparation of a production budget

The sales budget prepared in answer to IQ 32.1 reported the forecast sales for 20X1 as Grade (1) 50,000 sacks, Grade (2) 40,000 sacks and Grade (3) 60,000 sacks. The stock of finished goods on 1.1.20X1 was Grade (1) 5,000 sacks, Grade (2) 5,500 sacks and Grade (3) 7,500 sacks. The management of Growell Ltd has identified a need to increase the stock levels by 60 per cent by the end of 20X1.

Required: Prepare the production budget, by grade, for 20X1 in the following format:

	Grade 1	Grade 2	Grade 3
Produced for sale (sacks)			
Produced for stock increase (sacks)			
Production budget (sacks)			

32.6.2 The direct materials budget

The direct materials budget sets out the quantity of raw materials required to ensure that the budgeted production levels established in the production budget are met.

Interaction 32.3

Preparation of direct materials budget

Growell Ltd produces three grades of fertilizers, in 50 kg sacks, by mixing three ingredients G, R and Q in amounts stated on the right.

Required: Using the quantity of grades obtained from the production budget in the answer to IQ 32.2 to satisfy the sales budget and the stock increase of 60 per cent, produce the direct materials budget by ingredient in the following format:

Ingredient	Grade 1	Grade 2	Grade 3
G	25 kg	15 kg	5 kg
R	20 kg	25 kg	30 kg
Q	5 kg	10 kg	15 kg

Ingredient	G			R			Q		
	Qty	kg	kg (000s)	Qty	kg	kg (000s)	Qty	kg	kg (000s)
Grade 1									
Grade 2									
Grade 3									
Total									

32.6.3 The purchasing budget

On completion of the direct materials budget, the business is in a position to place orders for the amount of raw materials required to produce the three grades of fertilizer required to satisfy the sales budget and to meet the increase of 60 per cent in the stock of finished goods, i.e. sacks of the three grades. In addition to the production requirements, consideration must be given to the possible need to adjust the level of the raw materials stockholding of ingredients G, R and Q. This can arise for a number of reasons such as:

- a change in the physical facilities (e.g. a decrease or increase in storage space);
- a commercial change (e.g. if the purchasing department has information that a particular ingredient may be in restricted supply sometime in the coming year, it may be prudent to purchase additional quantities whilst it is available).

Preparation of purchasing budget

Growell Ltd, producer of fertilizers in sacks of 50 kg, held stocks of ingredients on 1 January 20X1 as stated on the right. In view of supply shortage anticipated by the purchasing manager, it is decided that stock levels should be increased by 31 December 20X1 to those stated on the left.

Ingredients	kg
G	200,000
R	400,000
Q	100,000

Ingredients	kg
G	220,000
R	440,000
Q	110,000

Required: Prepare a purchases budget on the following format:

	G (kg, 000s)	R (kg, 000s)	Q (kg, 000s)
Production quantity			
Add: increase in stock			
Less: decrease in stock			
Totals			

32.6.4 The direct labour budget

The direct labour budget is similar to the direct materials budget in that the basic data for its preparation is obtained from the production budget. The hours required to satisfy the needs of the production budget can be estimated using work-study techniques and past experience.

Preparation of direct labour budget

Growell Ltd produces three grades of fertilizer, in 50 kg sacks. The labour hours required to produce each sack are stated on the right. Using the quantity of grades obtained from the production budget (see IQ 32.2) to satisfy the sales budget as well as a 60 per cent increase in the stock of finished goods, produce the direct labour budget in the format shown on the right.

Grade 1	Grade 2	Grade 3
0.2 hours	0.3 hours	0.4 hours

	Production quantity (sacks)	Hours per sack	Production hours
Grade 1			
Grade 2			
Grade 3			

32.6.5 The production overhead budget

The production overhead budget is prepared on a departmental or cost-centre basis, with the advice and co-operation of departmental managers. The budget is based on detailed information from previous periods, as adjusted for expected changes in activity levels and economic circumstances.

Budgeted overhead recovery rates can be calculated and applied to the production on an appropriate basis, e.g. the percentage use on direct labour cost or machine-hour rate. It should be noted that overhead costs can be fixed or variable, and it may be advantageous to prepare a flexible budget. This concept is discussed later in this chapter (see Section 32.10).

32.6.6 The production cost budget

The production cost budget is a summary of the other budgets expressed, this time, in monetary terms. Once the direct materials and direct labour budgets have been prepared in quantitative terms, they are evaluated in monetary terms by applying material prices and labour rates. The expertise of the purchasing and personnel managers will be utilized to arrive at these prices and rates. As stated in Section 32.6.5, production overheads are included by the application of overhead recovery rates.

Interaction 32.6	**Preparation of a production cost budget**

In addition to Growell's direct materials budget of IQ 32.3 and the direct labour budget of IQ 32.5, you have been informed as follows:

- direct material prices for the three input materials are thus: G £0.20 per kg; R £0.25 per kg; Q £0.40 per kg;
- the direct labour rate is £5 per hour;
- overheads are recovered at the rate of 50 per cent of direct labour.

Required: Prepare a production cost budget in the following format:

		Quantity (kg, 000s)	Cost (£) per kg	£
Direct materials:	Ingredient G			
	Ingredient R			
	Ingredient Q			
Direct labour cost Production overheads				

32.6.7 The administrative and selling overhead budget

This is similar to the production overhead budget in its method of preparation, i.e. by department or cost centre. It is also made up of fixed and variable costs, although the administrative costs tend to be mainly fixed. As with the production overheads, appropriate recovery rates are calculated and applied if a total cost budget is required.

32.6.8 The plant utilization budget

This budget identifies the extent to which plant and machinery capacity is available to meet production requirements and, by comparing availability with requirement, over- or under-utilization is identified. Steps are then taken to correct the situation. If, for example, there is spare capacity, it may be necessary to attempt to increase sales or alternatively take in subcontract work. In extreme circumstances, disposal of spare capacity may be considered. If, however, there is a shortfall of plant availability, the following actions may be appropriate:

- overtime working
- additional shift working
- subcontracting work to outside firms
- acquiring additional plant.

If the need to acquire additional plant is identified and agreed, then this will give rise to a capital expenditure budget (see Section 32.7).

32.6.9 The cash budget

This is a key budget and is a summary of the cash movements for the budget period. Note that, unlike the other budgets, the cash budget is prepared on a receipts-and-payments basis rather than on an accrual income-and-expenditure basis, which means that non-cash items such as depreciation are excluded. Care must also be taken to allow for the timing of cash movements because of factors such as credit periods allowed to debtors and allowed by creditors. If a month's credit is allowed and received, then the cash budget for 20X1 will include the cash flows relating to transactions in the last month of 20X0 and 11 months of 20X1.

The cash budget for Growell Ltd for the year ended 31.12.20X1 would appear in the following format:

	20X1											
Receipts:	Jan	Feb	Mar	Apr	May	Jun	July	Aug	Sep	Oct	Nov	Dec
Amounts collected from debtors												
Payments:												
Materials: amounts paid to creditors												
Labour: wage and salary payments												
Production overheads (less depreciation)												
Administrative & selling overheads												
Balance as at 1.1.20X1												
Balance as at 31.12.20X1												

The items under the Receipts and Payments headings will depend on the circumstances of the business and may include additional items such as those stated on the right.

Receipts:	
Sales:	Cash sales
	Takings from debtors
Other income:	Rent received
Finance:	Interest received
	Additional capital
	Additional loans
Disposals:	Of fixed assets
Payments:	
Purchases:	Cash purchases
	Payments to creditors
Labour:	Wages
	Salaries
Overheads:	Administrative expenses
	Selling expenses
	Distribution costs
Finance:	Repayment of capital
	Repayment of loan
Acquisitions:	Payment for new assets

32.7 THE CAPITAL EXPENDITURE BUDGET

In addition to the purchase of additional plant to meet a shortfall identified by the plant utilization budget, the capital expenditure budget will include amounts for planned replacements and expansion programmes where fixed assets have to be obtained and financed, as already discussed in Chapter 31. This budget will, of necessity, be long-term and is usually set for three to five years on a rolling-programme basis. Because of the large amounts of finance required, there might be the need for cash injections if sufficient is not available from within the business.

32.8 THE MASTER BUDGET

After preparation of budgets for each subsection of the organization, it is necessary to collate these in order to ensure that they are compatible with each other and, in total, they are 'congruent' with the overall policies and goals of the business (e.g. they achieve a target return on capital employed).

This result of bringing together of all the detailed budgets into one is known as the master budget. It usually takes the form of a projected Profit and Loss account and Balance Sheet.

32.9 MANAGING THE CASH BUDGET

The cash budget, especially when prepared on a month-to-month basis, highlights when there may be a need to take management action – for example to invest surplus cash or to deal with a cash shortage that may appear in any month.

Preparation of a monthly cash budget

As accountant of Sunstand Ltd, your duties include the preparation of budgets, one of which is the cash budget. This is prepared on a monthly basis and monthly forecasts have been prepared for eight months ending December 20X3 as stated on the right.

Other information on the timing of receipts and payments and credit terms is available as follows:

	Purchases	Sales	Overheads	Wages
	£000	£000	£000	£000
May	100	200	20	40
June	120	180	22	38
July	80	120	21	40
August	160	110	24	34
September	40	100	20	35
October	80	160	23	38
November	100	180	24	40
December	120	240	25	41

(a) All purchases are on a monthly credit term, suppliers being paid, less 2.5 per cent cash discount, in the month following purchase.

(b) Twenty per cent of all sales are for cash, and the remainder are sales to customers of whom half pay in the month following sale and the rest pay two months after the sale.

(c) Overhead expenses include depreciation amounting to £3,000 each month. Payments are made in the month in which the expenses are incurred.

(d) Salaries and wages are paid in the month that they are incurred.

(e) A computer is to be acquired for office use for £25,000 in August 20X3.

(f) Furniture is expected to be sold in October 20X3 for £1,000.

(g) The bank balance at 1 July 20X3 is expected to be £20,000.

Required: Prepare a month-by-month cash budget for the six months to 31 December 20X3 showing the balance at the bank at the end of each month. Recommend the overdraft facility that should be negotiated with the bank.

32.10 FLEXIBLE BUDGETS

As mentioned earlier in this chapter, some costs vary with activity whilst others remain constant, these being known as variable and fixed costs respectively. In the context of planning business operations, it is necessary to start with a budget at a single anticipated level of activity that it is hoped will be achieved and at which profits should be maximized. However, if the actual activity differs from the level planned, then for control purposes a comparison of actual with this fixed budget will not provide meaningful variances since like is not being compared with like. Sales and/or production targets may not be met and, as a result, certain costs would be expected to increase/decrease in line with any upwards/downwards movement. For example, it would be expected that material costs would rise in proportion to units produced since this is a variable cost. Even where a cost is expected to vary with activity, if the variance was greater than expected then the difference would need to be investigated.

It may be beneficial, therefore, to provide managers with a series of budgets based on a range of activity levels, taking into consideration the behaviour of different types of cost. When the actual level of activity is known, then the costs incurred can be compared with the appropriate budget, thereby eliminating variances caused simply by a change in quantity and concentrating on the remaining variances that warrant further investigation.

Preparing a flexible budget

Barmic Ltd has set its budget for 20X0 at 9,000 sales units (a fixed budget). Listed below are changes that may affect the assumptions made when preparing the fixed budget:

- Sales volume: Market research reveals that sales are price-sensitive and would change as stated on the right.
- Raw materials: The supplier of raw materials has offered a quantity discount. The unit cost would be £1.50 per unit up to 9,000 units and £1.25 per unit on *all* units if the quantity exceeded 9,000 units.
- Direct labour: Direct labour costs would remain constant at £1.25 per unit for all levels.
- Overheads: Fixed costs would remain constant at £15,000 up to 10,000 units and would increase to £17,500 if more than 10,000 units were to be produced.

Unit price	Expected sales
£5.00	8,000 units
£4.75	9,000 units
£4.50	10,000 units
£4.25	11,000 units

Required: Prepare a flexible budget covering the range of sales, showing the budgeted profit at each level.

32.11 BUDGETING IN THE SERVICE SECTOR

So far we have concentrated on the preparation of budgets within the manufacturing industry. However, the principles we have identified apply equally to the service sector. The purpose of budgetary control and setting up a Budget Committee with the appointment of a Budget Officer to ensure that the organization's strategic policy is achieved are common factors, and although limiting factors may differ, they will still exist and form a vital consideration in the budget process. No longer will shortage of production facilities, such as raw materials and machine availability, be relevant; but we must still consider the potential demand for this service, the availability of finance, and the ability to supply the service. For example, are there enough staff with the appropriate skills? Are there sufficient funds to pay staff? Is there sufficient office space? Can we obtain more space if required? If the answer is 'no' to any of these questions, then we would be restricted in the level of future activities.

Within the service sector the nature of costs may change. For example, what was classed as indirect labour in a manufacturing business may well be classed as direct in a service business. This means that the format of the various functional budgets in the service sector may take a form more in line with the administration or selling and distribution cost budgets of the manufacturing sector. Nevertheless their purpose remains the same, i.e. the planning of the activities, the co-ordination of the various parts, and the control of its functions and costs by the identification of variances from budget and the subsequent taking of corrective action.

32.12 THE BUSINESS PLAN

So far in this chapter we have concentrated on the preparation and use of budgets from the perspective of the managers of the business in order that they may achieve the targets set. This is particularly relevant to the well-established, ongoing business.

However, new businesses and those going through initial expansion stages have to satisfy outside parties, such as banks and venture capitalists, if they are to secure the financial backing they need to become successful. As there will be no historical figures to support requests for finance, a greater emphasis has to be placed on the estimates of future expectations. These are known as **business plans** and are comprehensive documents that will include all of the following:

- marketing strategy, i.e. the market to be targeted and details of competitors;
- the means of supply, i.e. to manufacture or to buy in;
- any existing financial commitments;
- pricing policy;
- product costings.

In addition, projected Manufacturing, Trading and Profit and Loss accounts and a projected Balance Sheet for the first year of trading will be prepared, along with a projected Cash Flow Statement. These will be similar in form to the master budget described above. Finally, it is likely that the prospective investor will require a summary of the longer-term plans of the business and what rate of return they may expect and when it might be increased.

SOLUTIONS TO INTERACTIVE QUESTIONS

IQ 32.1 Preparation of a sales budget

	Grade 1	Grade 2	Grade 3
Previous year's quantity	45,000	35,000	55,000
Increase anticipated	5,000	5,000	5,000
Sales budget (units)	50,000	40,000	60,000
New selling price (£)	£6.00	£6.50	£7.00
Sales budget (£)	£300,000	£260,000	£420,000

IQ 32.2 Preparation of a production budget

	Grade 1	Grade 2	Grade 3
For sales	50,000	40,000	60,000
Stock increase	3,000	3,300	4,500
Production budget (units)	53,000	43,300	64,500

IQ 32.3 Preparation of direct materials budget

Ingredient	G			R			Q		
	Quantity	kg	kg (000s)	Quantity	kg	kg (000s)	Quantity	kg	kg (000s)
Grade 1	53,000	25	1,325.0	53,000	20	1,060.0	53,000	5	265.0
Grade 2	43,300	15	649.5	43,300	25	1,082.5	43,300	10	433.0
Grade 3	64,500	5	322.5	64,500	30	1,935.0	64,500	15	967.5
TOTAL			2,297.0			4,077.5			1,665.5

IQ 32.4 Preparation of purchasing budget

	G (kg, 000s)	R (kg, 000s)	Q (kg, 000s)
Production quantity	2,297.0	4,077.5	1,665.5
Add: increase to stock	20.0	40.0	10.0
	2,317.0	4,117.5	1,675.0

IQ 32.5 Preparation of direct labour budget

	Production quantity	Hours per sack	Production hours
Grade 1	53,000	0.20	10,600
Grade 2	43,300	0.30	12,990
Grade 3	64,500	0.40	25,800
			49,390

IQ 32.6 Preparation of a production cost budget

		Quantity (kg, 000s)	Cost (£) per kg	£
Direct materials cost	Ingredient G	2,297.0	0.20	459,400
	Ingredient R	4,077.5	0.25	1,019,375
	Ingredient Q	1,665.5	0.40	666,200
				2,144,975
Direct labour cost	(49,390 × £5)			246,950
Production overheads	(£246,950 × 0.5)			123,475
				2,515,400

IQ 32.7 Preparation of a monthly cash budget

CASH BUDGET FOR SUNSTAND LTD FOR SIX MONTHS ENDING 31 DECEMBER 20X3						
	July	August	September	October	November	December
Opening balance	20,000	21,000	5,000	(91,000)	(71,000)	(70,000)
Receipts:						
Cash sales	24,000	22,000	20,000	32,000	36,000	48,000
Credit sales	152,000	120,000	92,000	84,000	104,000	136,000
Sale of fixed asset	–	–	–	1,000	–	–
	196,000	163,000	117,000	26,000	69,000	114,000
Payments:						
Wages	40,000	34,000	35,000	38,000	40,000	41,000
Overheads	18,000	21,000	17,000	20,000	21,000	22,000
Creditors	117,000	78,000	156,000	39,000	78,000	97,500
Computer	–	25,000	–	–	–	–
	175,000	158,000	208,000	97,000	139,000	160,500
Closing balance	21,000	5,000	(91,000)	(71,000)	(70,000)	(46,500)

(b) The maximum overdraft requirement of £91,000 (required in September 20X3) should be negotiated.

IQ 32.8 Preparing a flexible budget

Sales in units	8,000	9,000	10,000	11,000
Selling price	£5.00	£4.75	£4.50	£4.25
Sales income	£40,000	£42,750	£45,000	£46,750
Less:				
Direct materials @ £1.50	(12,000)	(13,500)	–	–
Direct materials @ £1.25	–	–	(12,500)	(13,750)
Direct labour @ £1.25	(10,000)	(11,250)	(12,500)	(13,750)
Fixed costs	(15,000)	(15,000)	(15,000)	(17,500)
Forecast profit	3,000	3,000	5,000	1,750

PROGRESSIVE QUESTIONS

PQ 32.1 Monthly cash budget

Jill Askey and Partners commenced trading on 1 October 20X1 selling garden gnomes with a capital of £680,000. The entity prepared a cash budget from the following information:

(a) **Fixed asset acquisition:**
  ● Freehold property to be purchased on 1 October 20X1 for £238,000.
  ● Equipment to be purchased on 1 October 20X1 for £102,000.
  ● Fixtures to be purchased on 1 November 20X1 for £60,000. The purchase price was to be paid for in three equal monthly instalments, commencing on 1 November 20X1.
  ● Vehicles to be purchased on 1 December 20X1 for £30,600.
(b) **Purchases:** The following quantities of gnomes are to be purchased at £17 each:

October	November	December
1,900	1,900	2,200

  The credit terms are that half will be paid for in the month of purchase and half in the month following.
(c) **Employees:** Wages of £13,600 to be paid each month. Income tax deductions of £11,050 to be paid on 1 December 20X1.
(d) **Sales:** Sales are estimated (in quantity) to be:

October	November	December
1,080	1,760	2,040

  The selling price per unit will be £20 each. The credit terms are that one-quarter of each month's sales will be paid for in cash and payment for the remaining three-quarters will be received in the month following the sale.
(e) **Expenses:** Expenses of £14,790 will be incurred each month – one-third to be paid for in cash and the remaining two-thirds in the month following. Partners' salaries are to be £2,720 per month in total.
(f) **Depreciation:** Depreciation is to be calculated on a monthly basis using the straight-line method and the following annual rates:
  ● equipment   10%
  ● fixtures   5%
  ● vehicles   25%

Required: Prepare a monthly cash budget for the period October–December 20X1, and comment on the results.

PQ 32.2 Purchases budget and cash budget

Zeus Devereaux is planning to open a retail shop on 1 July 20X0 with a cash capital of £125,000 and a bank overdraft facility of £20,000. The shop will sell two models of diving suits – an Inshore model and a Deepsea model. Market research indicates that the monthly level of sales can be expected as follows:

	£
July	100,000
August	150,000
September	200,000
October	250,000
November	300,000
December	350,000
January	350,000

In addition:

- It is anticipated that 75 per cent of the sales will be for the Inshore model with a gross profit of 10 per cent, and 25 per cent of the sales for the Deepsea model with a gross profit of 20 per cent.
- It is expected that half of the sales will be made for cash and half on credit. The credit terms will be one month's credit on Inshore sales and two months' credit on Deepsea sales.
- Stock for July 20X0 will be delivered on 1 July 20X0, and it is planned that the monthly opening stock thereafter will equal monthly sales. Suppliers have offered one month's credit on all purchases.
- Wages of £12,500 will be paid in the month in which they are incurred. Other expenses are estimated at £7,500 per month, which includes depreciation of £1,250 on shop fittings. These other expenses are paid one month in arrears.

Required:

(a) Calculate the monthly purchases budget, in value, for each of the months July to December 20X0.
(b) Prepare a monthly cash budget for the period July to December 20X0 inclusive, highlighting the maximum overdraft requirement.
(c) Consider how to deal with any adverse implication.

PQ 32.3 Reconciliation of budgeted profit with actual

Flexible Friend Ltd manufactures credit cards to order. It has introduced a system of flexible budgeting and the following information is available for January 20X1:

Budgeted sales and production	200,000 cards
Actual sales and production	160,000 cards

The budgeted selling price, cost and profit on 100 cards are:

	£	£
Selling price		40.00
Direct materials	12.00	
Direct labour	8.00	
Variable overheads	3.00	
Fixed overheads	11.35	
Total cost per 100 cards		34.35
Profit		5.65

Actual costs varied from budget during the month of January 20X1, with direct materials, direct labour and variable overheads increasing over budget by 10 per cent, 5 per cent and 6 per cent respectively.

Required: Prepare a Profit and Loss account for the month on each of the actual, budget and flexible-budget bases, and reconcile the budgeted profit and actual result.

## Chapter 33

STANDARD COSTING AND VARIANCE ANALYSIS: AN INTRODUCTION

In this chapter

We will learn of:

- the usefulness of standard costing
- the need to set appropriate standards
- the importance of identifying the precise cause for the actual differing from the standard

and you should be able to calculate:

- material price and usage variances
- labour rate and efficiency variances
- overhead expenditure and recovery variances
- fixed overhead volume variance
- sales price and volume variances

33.1 INTRODUCTION: BUDGETARY CONTROL V. STANDARD COSTING

In Chapter 32 we looked at budgetary control as a means of exercising control over the financial aspects of a business by the comparison of actual results with predetermined budgets. However, budgetary control, although focusing on each function of the business (i.e. production, sales, administration, etc.), looks at these from the point of view of total income and expenditure. Therefore, when employing a system of budgetary control it is only possible to identify *total variances* from the original targets.

Standard costing, on the other hand, looks at the individual production activities and provides a base for the identification of variances for each element of cost (i.e. materials, labour and overheads) in detail. In other words, budgetary control sets targets in order to control expenditure of departments or cost centres, whereas standard costing draws to managers' attention the cause of the difference between the actual expenditure and budgeted expenditure.

33.2 DEFINITION OF STANDARD COSTING

Standard costing is a method of accounting that uses predetermined (standard) levels for each element of cost – materials, labour and overheads – for each unit of production. When actual costs are known, they are compared with the standard and the difference (or variance) is analysed into causes. The causes as well as the extent of variance arising from each cause are reported to the persons responsible for the particular area in order that appropriate remedial action may be taken. For example, the purchasing manager will be responsible for action when the price of material deviates from the original standard. Likewise the production manager will be responsible for investigating variances identified as being caused by labour inefficiency.

The purpose of standard costing depends on when it is being used, and it can be expressed thus:

- at the beginning of an accounting period:
  - to assist in the preparation of budgets;
  - to provide a means for assessing efficiency and to maximize profits;
- during an accounting period:
  - to speed up reporting;
  - to measure ongoing efficiency;
  - to provide the means for taking remedial action on variances;
  - to give a basis for estimating quotations for jobs and fixing selling prices;
- at end of an accounting period:
  - to give a basis for the valuation of stocks;
  - to measure efficiency over the accounting period.

33.3 THE SETTING OF STANDARDS

For the system to be effective and the managers to feel committed, the procedure for setting the standards must be reliable and accurate. Consideration must be given to all aspects of the product and the production facilities. Whilst past experience may be an important factor in setting standards, a more detailed forward-looking view is needed. For example, the amount and quality of materials required should be obtained from material specifications and drawings, and the price of materials obtained from current quotations. Similarly, the length of time to be allowed for the labour element should be based on work-study techniques and the labour rates ascertained by negotiations between the workers' representatives and the personnel department. The standard-setting is essentially a forward-looking exercise.

33.3.1 Types of standard

There are basically two types of standard: an ideal standard and an attainable standard.

An *ideal standard* is a target set based on the assumption that the most favourable circumstances will prevail – that is, that workers and machinery will work at maximum levels and the buyer will achieve the best terms when purchasing of materials. No deviation is permitted from these very high levels and, as a result, it is inevitable that all variances will be unfavourable and require maximum attention and investigation. The standards are not adjusted even if it is subsequently found that the variance was not caused by inefficiency within the business. The effect of setting ideal standards is that they are virtually impossible to attain and, as a result, this can have a demotivating effect on the workforce.

An *attainable standard* is one that can be attained provided that (conditional) extra effort is made. The approach taken is to examine closely all aspects of the business to identify what can reasonably be expected with extra effort and to set a target that a motivated workforce will endeavour to achieve. One drawback to this is that, if the standard is set too low, it will be achievable without the need for extra effort and the benefit of standard setting will be lost.

33.3.2 Procedure for fixing the standard cost of a product

As stated earlier, the procedure for setting direct standard costs is forward-looking and direct standard costs will be based on material specifications, price quotations and personnel assessment on labour required and wages rates applying. Indirect standard costs are set by applying overheads using overhead recovery rates based on budgeted levels of activity and expenditure as described in Chapter 29. It is useful, at this stage, to refresh our memory on how these rates are calculated and applied.

Fixing the standard cost of a product

Interaction
33.1

The following specifications have been supplied by the technical departments for product XYZ:

Direct material content: 10 kilos @ £2 per kilo
Direct labour content: 3 hours @ £5 per hour

Overheads are recovered on direct labour hours at the rate of £3 per direct labour hour.

Required: Calculate the standard cost of product XYZ.

33.4 CALCULATION OF VARIANCES

Once we have calculated standard costs for each of our products (showing the detailed breakdown of costs into the various elements), we have the basis for comparison with actual costs when these become available. The normal procedures for the recording of the accounting data will give us the information we require regarding actual costs, i.e. material invoices, wage time sheets, etc. If actual expenditure exceeds the standard, then this is known as an adverse variance. If actual expenditure is lower than standard then the variance is favourable.

The purpose of standard costing is to provide information that can be used to maximize profits and to remedy overspending arising from inefficiencies. For this purpose the systems should highlight only those variances in respect of which remedial action can be taken.

Direct material and direct labour costs are by nature variable with the level of activity; for instance, if we produce less we will use less material. It would therefore be meaningless to report a material variance that arose simply because we used less material on account of our output being less than planned. The starting point for the calculation of variances for direct costs is, therefore, always the *actual* levels of production. The questions to be asked are:

1. How many articles did we produce?
2. What should they have cost?
3. What *did* they cost?

The answers to these three questions form the basis for calculating all variances for variable cost.

The procedure for fixed costs is slightly different because these costs do not vary with activity. This means that, although we may not incur any additional expenditure on fixed overheads as a result of an increase in production, we will recover more overheads. This cause of variance is meaningful and requires calculation.

33.4.1 Materials cost variances

The total materials cost variance can be subdivided into two in accordance with whether it arises from a change in the price of the material (known as *material price variance*) or from a change in the amount of material used (known as *material usage variance*). The total material variance is the sum of the two lesser variances.

Starting with the actual level of activity in terms of production, we want to know how much material we should have used and at what price, in order to compare with the amount of material we *did* use and the price we *did* pay. This can be expressed in the form of a formula:

**Material cost variance = (Actual quantity × Actual price) –
(Standard quantity × Standard price)**

Interaction 33.2

Total material cost variance

In addition to the information provided in IQ 33.1, with regard to product XYZ, you are provided with those stated here.

Actual production	100 units
Actual material used	950 kilos
Actual material price	£2.50 per kilo

Required: Calculate the total material cost variance for the product.

Although we now know how to calculate a total material cost variance, we still do not know the cause of the variance. It could be due to a price change or a change in usage, or a combination of both. To isolate the precise cause of the variance so that we can take it up with the responsible manager, we need to break it down into its price and usage elements. In this effort we may find the following diagram helpful:

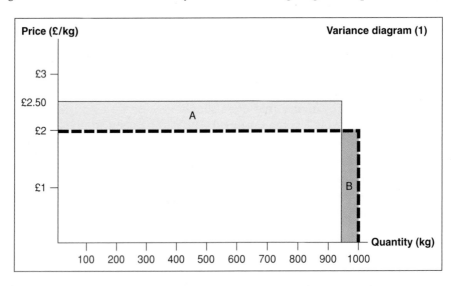

The standard (1,000 kg at £2 per kg) is depicted by the thicker line and the actual (950 kg at £2.50) is depicted by the thinner one. The area marked by 'A' represents material price variance, and the area marked by 'B' represents material usage variance.

Material price variance = (Actual price – Standard price) × Actual quantity

Material usage variance = (Actual quantity – Standard quantity) × Standard price

Material price and usage variances

On the basis of the information provided in IQ 33.1 and IQ 33.2, *you are required* to calculate the material price variance and the material usage variance for product XYZ.

The isolation of the material price variance from the material usage variance could be calculated conveniently and depicted clearly on the variance diagram (1) because one of these variances (usage) was favourable and

	Standard	Actual
Material used in kilos	50 kg	60 kg
Material price per kilo	£5	£6

the other (price) adverse. The isolation of the two becomes blurred, however, in a situation where both variances are in the same direction (see variance diagram (2) below). In this example, the actual cost of material used was 60 @ £6 = £360, whereas the standard was 50 @ £5 = £250. Price as well as usage was adverse and the combined effect was an adverse variance of £360 − £250 = £110. Depicted on a variance diagram (2) the position appears as follows:

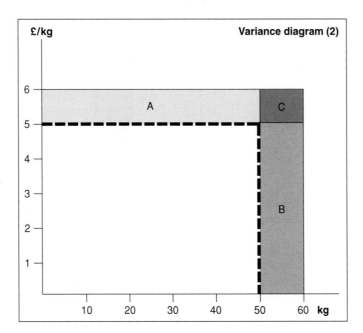

The standard cost is depicted by the rectangle enclosed by the thicker dashed line while the higher actual cost is depicted by the area enclosed within the continuous lines. There is agreement that the material price variance is the rectangle identified as 'A' and the material usage variance is rectangle marked 'B'. Whether the rectangle marked 'C' (which is common to both) should be included within the former or the latter (or should be identified on its own as a separate variance) is a matter for further inquiry. For the present it is submitted that the rectangles A plus C should be regarded as material price variance. Accordingly, the total material cost variance (A + B + C) has arisen as shown on the left.

Material price variance	(£6 − £5) × 60 kg	£60 adverse
Material usage variance	(60 kg − 50 kg) × £5	£50 adverse
Total material cost variance		£110 adverse

33.4.2 Labour cost variances

Labour cost variances are calculated similarly to material cost variances because both direct labour and direct materials are variable costs. Therefore the formulae for calculating variances with regard to direct labour are the same as for materials, except that wage rate is substituted for material price and labour hours for material quantity. As with material, to be useful the total labour variance has to be broken down to those elements arising from a change in the wage rates and those arising because of change in hours worked – a process in which variance diagram (3) would be useful. The rectangle marked by 'A' identifies the labour rate variance, while the one marked by 'B' identifies the labour efficiency variance.

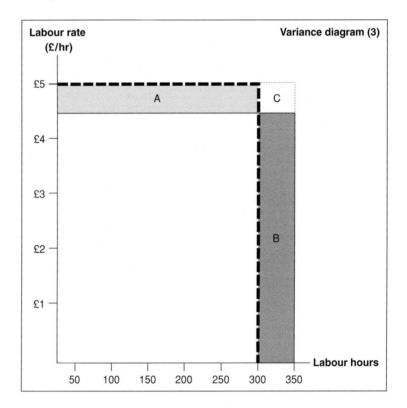

To draw into focus the cost saving that arises from paying 50p less for 350 hours actually worked, area 'C' is included with both area 'A' (rate variance) and area 'B' (efficiency variance).

$$\text{Total labour cost variance} = (\text{Actual hours} \times \text{Actual rate}) - (\text{Standard hours} \times \text{Standard rate})$$

To isolate the effect of a wage rate change, and again using actual hours worked:

$$\text{Labour rate variance} = \text{Difference in wage rate } (\pounds0.50) \times \text{Actual labour hours } (350)$$

To isolate the effect of change in labour efficiency:

$$\text{Labour efficiency variance} = \text{Difference in labour hours } (50) \times \text{Standard wage rate } (\pounds5.00)$$

Labour cost, rate and efficiency variances

In addition to the information provided in IQ 33.1 you are informed that 100 units were produced and that particulars of direct labour were as stated here.

Actual hourly rate of pay: £4.50
Actual hours worked: 350 hours

Required: Calculate the total labour cost variance, the labour rate variance, and the labour efficiency variance.

33.4.3 Overhead variances

The calculation of overhead variances is somewhat different from that for material and labour variances in that, in addition to the anticipated expenditure and the actual expenditure, a third element enters the equation. This is the overhead recovered figure. As a result, the use of formulae becomes a little more complicated and so a different approach is suggested.

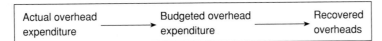

If we take the two extremes (i.e. actual expenditure and recovery) we have the difference between what we spent and what we got back. This represents the total overhead variance. If we then compare the two extremes each with the central item (budgeted overheads), the total overhead variance can be split into two elements:

● *Overhead expenditure variance*, caused by spending more than we budgeted for, where

$$\text{Overhead expenditure variance} = \text{Actual overhead expenditure} - \text{Budgeted overhead expenditure}$$

● *Overhead recovery (or efficiency or volume) variance*, caused by producing a different level of output from that budgeted for, where

$$\text{Overhead recovery variance} = \text{Budgeted overhead expenditure} - \text{Recovered overheads}$$

Overhead variances

A company budgeted to spend £500,000 on overheads in an accounting period, but actual overheads were £550,000. Budgeted production was 100,000 units and each unit has a standard production time of 2 hours. Overheads are recovered on the basis of production hours, giving an hourly recovery rate of £2.50 per production hour. Actual production was 95,000 units.

Required: Calculate the total overhead variance and the subvariances for expenditure and volume.

On the variable costs side, we should not forget that, as with other variable costs, the budgeted figure is flexed – in the case of variable overhead expenditure it is flexed according to hours worked. This means that the budgeted variable overhead figure is the *actual* hours worked multiplied by the standard variable overhead recovery rate per hour. The variable overhead efficiency variance is the difference between overheads absorbed at actual hours worked (i.e. budgeted overheads) and the overheads absorbed on the output achieved, measured in standard hours, during the actual hours worked (i.e. recovered overheads). It is similar in principle to the labour efficiency variance.

For fixed overheads, the recovery (or volume) variance is

**Budgeted fixed overheads – (Standard labour hours of actual output ×
Standard fixed overhead recovery rate)**

It can be divided into two separate variances:

- The *capacity usage variance*, namely the difference between the budgeted hours of activity and the actual hours worked, at the standard fixed overhead recovery rate;
- The *efficiency variance*, namely the difference between the actual hours worked and the standard hours of output achieved, at the standard fixed overhead recovery rate.

These two subvariances indicate that the overall fixed overhead volume variance is affected by the level of activity in terms of hours worked and the level of efficiency during those hours, as measured in terms of the output achieved.

Interaction 33.6

Fixed overhead volume variance

A company had a budget of 200,000 direct labour hours for a period. This was used as the basis for establishing standard factory overhead absorption rates. Fixed factory overhead was budgeted to be £400,000 and variable factory overhead £200,000. Output was budgeted at 400,000 units. In the period, 420,000 units were completed in 220,000 direct labour hours, at a labour cost of £787,000. No labour rate variance occurred. The factory overhead incurred during the period was £620,000.

Required: Calculate the fixed overhead volume variance, and explain both the meaning and significance of the fixed overhead volume variance, and how the fixed overhead volume variance may be further analysed.

33.5 REASONS FOR VARIANCES

33.5.1 Material cost variances

Price and usage variances may arise from a variety of reasons.

Price variance can occur through:

- an unexpected change in the price;
- a failure to take advantage of bulk-buying discounts;
- the purchase of alternatives at a different price, if original materials are unavailable;
- the use of an alternative supplier because the original supplier fails to provide the materials;
- changes in costs (such as carriage inwards) that are part of the cost of materials.

Usage variance can occur through:

- defective material;
- inefficiencies of employees in use of materials;
- abnormal wastage due to cheaper grades of material being used;
- abnormal wastage due to an unskilled workforce being used;

- pilfering;
- deterioration due to poor storage facilities.

33.5.2 Labour cost variances

This type of variance can similarly arise from a variety of reasons:

Labour rate variance can occur through:

- an unexpected change in wage rates;
- additional overtime worked at premium rate;
- use of employees with different skills, and therefore different wage rates, than those planned.

Labour efficiency variance can occur through:

- variations in the quality of the workforce;
- inadequate training;
- unsatisfactory working conditions;
- defective or obsolete machinery;
- poor organization and supervision, leading to delays;
- use of low-quality material, leading to extra production time required to avoid spoilage; or, conversely, high-quality material being easier to work and requiring less time to work.

33.5.3 Overhead variance

Expenditure variance can occur because of over- or under-spending by the various cost centres. This may be due to lack of control over expenditure by cost-centre managers, or it may be due to factors outside their control – for instance, increased costs imposed from outside such as unanticipated rises in items such as rent, rates or power costs.

Volume variance can arise from inefficiencies. For example, there may be delays in production caused by factors such as a machine breakdown, use of defective materials, and labour disputes. Other circumstances causing volume variance include a shortage of materials, poor planning of production schedules, a failure to achieve expected orders, power cuts and the like.

There may be efficiencies giving rise to extra production and consequently over-recovery of overheads, although additional production without additional sales may not necessarily be advantageous. Such efficiency may be due to:

- extra effort on the part of the workforce;
- extra sales orders being obtained;
- fewer machine breakdowns than allowed for in the standard adopted;
- fewer labour disputes than allowed for in the standard;
- less defective material than allowed for in the standards.

33.5.4 Summary

Although the above lists of reasons are fairly comprehensive, they may not be the only ones; neither will they all occur together. The very purpose of variance analysis is to investigate variances and to identify their causes, which in some circumstances may be peculiar to specific types of business.

33.6 STOCK VALUATION

We need to check from time to time that the standard cost for each product is acceptable. This requires us to consider any variances that may have arisen and to decide whether they affect the current year's profit or can be carried forward in the stock valuation, when they will affect the profits of the following year. The general principle is that if the variance has arisen from an inefficiency in the current year, then it should be taken account of in the current year's profit calculation and not included in the stock valuation. For example, if the material usage variance is adverse because the buyer purchased substandard material, then this variance should be written off in the current year.

33.7 SALES VARIANCES

The results of the performance in an accounting period would differ from that budgeted for, not only because of the cost variances that we have focused on so far but also because of sales variances. Let us assume, for illustration,

	Budgeted	Actual
Sales in units	10,000	9,000
Sale price per unit	£5	£4

that the sales were as stated in the box here. Accordingly, the actual sales in the period were 9,000 at £4 = £36,000, whereas the budgeted sales were 10,000 units at £5 = £50,000. The cause of the adverse variance of £14,000 may be identified as:

$$\text{Sales price variance} = (£5 - £4) \times 10,000 \text{ units} = £10,000$$

$$\text{Sales volume variance} = (10,000 - 9,000 \text{ units}) \times £4 = £4,000$$

In addition, the profit achieved in a period could differ from that budgeted for because of a change in sales mix. For example, where a business deals with several lines of activity, although the number of units sold is more than that budgeted for, profit could be affected if more units of a less profitable line had accounted for the increased sales volume.

Interaction 33.7

Sales variances

A company budgeted to sell during the year 25,000 mobile phones at £60 per unit. Faced with intense competition, which it did not anticipate, it permitted a 10 per cent trade discount and yet was able to sell only 21,000 units during the year.

Required: Calculate the sales variance.

33.8 SUMMARY

It is worthwhile repeating that standard costing and the calculation of variances only provide the information to managers that activities have not gone as planned. In itself, standard costing solves no problems. The problem solving is only achieved by the managers responsible for the various aspects of the business identifying the cause of the variances and taking appropriate remedial action.

SOLUTIONS TO INTERACTIVE QUESTIONS

IQ 33.1 Fixing the standard cost of a product

Direct material cost	10 kilos @ £2 per kilo	£20
Direct labour cost	3 hours @ £5 per hour	£15
Overhead cost	£3 per direct labour hour for 3 hours	£9
Standard cost of product XYZ		£44

IQ 33.2 Total material cost variance

Standard total cost of material	1,000 kilos @ £2	£2,000
Actual total cost of material	950 kilos @ £2.50	(£2,375)
Total material cost variance	(adverse)	(£375)

IQ 33.3 Material price and usage variances

Material price variance:	Actual quantity × Standard price = 950 @ £2	£1,900
	Actual quantity × Actual price = 950 @ £2.50	(£2,375)
	Material price variance (adverse)	(£475)

Material usage variance:	Standard quantity × Standard price = 1,000 @ £2	£2,000
	Actual quantity × Standard price = 950 @ £2	(£1,900)
	Material usage variance (favourable)	£100

Material price variance (£475 negative) + material usage variance (£100 positive) = total material cost variance of £375 (adverse).

IQ 33.4 Labour cost, rate and efficiency variances

Total labour cost variance:	Actual hours @ actual wage rate: 350 hrs @ £4.50	(£1,575)
	Standard hours @ standard wage rate: 300 hrs @ £5.00	£1,500
	Total labour cost variance (adverse)	(£75)

Labour rate variance:	Difference in wage rate: £5 − £4.50	£0.50
	× Actual hours worked	× 350hrs
	Labour rate variance (favourable)	£175

Labour efficiency variance:	Difference in hours: 350 − 300 hours	50 hours
	× standard wage rate	× £5
	Labour efficiency variance (adverse)	£250

Labour rate variance (£175 favourable) + labour efficiency variance (£250 adverse) = total labour cost variance of £75 adverse, which matches the figure obtained.

IQ 33.5 Overhead variances

Total overhead variance:	Actual fixed overhead expenditure	(£550,000)
	Overhead recovery: 95,000 units @ 2 hrs @ £2.50	£475,000
	Total fixed overhead variance (adverse)	(£75,000)

Overhead expenditure variance:	Actual fixed overhead expenditure	(£550,000)
	Budgeted fixed overhead expenditure	£500,000
	Fixed overhead expenditure variance (adverse)	(£50,000)

Overhead recovery variance:	Budgeted recovery: 100 units × 2 hrs @ £2.50	(£500,000)
	Actual recovery: 95 units × 2 hrs @ £2.50	£475,000
	Fixed overhead recovery variance (adverse)	(£25,000)

Total overhead variance can be seen to equal overhead expenditure variance + overhead recovery variance.

IQ 33.6 Fixed overhead volume variance

Fixed overhead volume variance = Budgeted fixed overhead − (standard labour hours of actual output × standard fixed overhead recovery rate per hour).

Fixed overhead rate per hour = £400,000 budgeted overhead/200,000 hours = £2 per hour

Variance = £400,000 − (210,000 × £2) = £400,000 − £420,000 = £20,000 (favourable)

The fixed overhead volume variance represents the difference between the amount of fixed overhead budgeted and that absorbed at standard rate by actual output. The volume variance therefore arises from the actual volume of output differing from that budgeted – in this case 20,000 units over budget. The existence of a fixed overhead volume variance will provide an indication of whether fixed overheads are being recovered in product costs.

The volume variance can be subdivided into a capacity usage variance and an efficiency variance. The capacity usage variance is the difference between budgeted hours of activity and the actual hours of activity, at the standard fixed overhead rate. The efficiency variance is the difference between actual hours of activity and the standard hours of output achieved, at the standard fixed overhead rate. The overall volume variance is therefore influenced by both the level of activity in terms of hours worked and also the level of efficiency achieved during actual hours worked, in relation to budget.

IQ 33.7 Sales variances

Total sales variance:		£			£
Budgeted	25,000 units @ £60	1,500,000	**Sale price variance**	(£60 − £54) × 25,000	150,000
Actual	21,000 units @ £54	1,134,000	**Sale volume variance**	(25,000 − 21,000) × £54	216,000
Adverse variance		366,000			366,000

PROGRESSIVE QUESTIONS

PQ 33.1 The purpose of and case for standard costing

Your company's managing director is shortly going to attend a conference on standard costing and you have been asked to prepare a report explaining the purpose of standard costing. You have decided to include some figures to illustrate the points you wish to make and you have made up the following data:

Standard prime cost per unit of output:		£
Direct material	10 kg @ £2.00 per kg	20
Direct labour	3 hours @ £5 per hour	15
	Prime cost per unit	35

Actual cost of 200 units of output:		£
Direct material	1,950 kg	4,290
Direct labour	590 hours	3,245

Required: Prepare a report to the managing director, as requested, including two benefits of standard costing. Using the above data you should include the following variances with one possible explanation for each:

- direct material price variance;
- direct material usage variance;
- direct labour rate variance;
- direct labour efficiency variance.

PQ 33.2 Variance analysis with flexed budget

Carrogs Ltd is a small private company that manufactures a range of healthfood breakfast cereals, which it sells to local healthfood shops. Rizabix is its top of the range product, selling at £1.25 per packet. Accountant of Carrogs has produced, as stated on the right, the standard cost statement for Rizabix, based on production of 360,000 packets. During the year ended 31 May 20X0 the

Raw materials	240,000 kg at 40p/kg
Direct labour	42,000 hours at £5.40/hr
Total fixed overheads	£75,000 per year

actual output of the product was 300,000 packets which were all sold at £1.25 each. The directors of Carrogs expect this pattern of sales to continue for the foreseeable future. The actual costs for the year ended 31 May 20X0 were as stated on the left.

Raw materials	210,000 kg at 38p/kg
Direct labour costs	34,000 hours at £5.50/hour

Required:

(a) Calculate the total raw material cost variance and its analysis into material usage variance and material price variance.
(b) Calculate the total direct labour variance and its analysis into direct labour efficiency variance and direct labour rate variance.
(c) Prepare a profit statement for May 20X0 showing the budgeted and actual profits.

PQ 33.3 Variance analysis and its use

Trusch plc manufactures a single product. The company has recently introduced a system of budgeting and variance analysis. The following information is available for March 20X0:

March 20X0	Budget	£000
Sales	31,250 units at £48	1,500
Direct material	40,000 kg at £6 per kg	240
Direct labour	120,000 hours at £3.25	390
Variable manufacturing overheads		75
Variable sales overheads		80
Administrative costs (fixed)		180
Selling and distribution costs (fixed)		60

Actual		£
30,000 at £50; 2,000 at £56		1,612,000
40,500 kg at £5.90 per kg		238,950
118,000 hours at £3.40		401,200
5% more than the budget		
2% more than the budget		
3% less than the budget		
10% more than the budget		

There were no finished goods or work in progress as at 31 March 20X0. Assume that all variable costs are expected to vary in direct proportion to sales quantity.

Required:

(a) Calculate the total direct material cost variance and the total direct labour cost variance, with an analysis of these variances.
(b) Prepare revenue statements for March 20X0 showing budgeted and actual profits or losses.
(c) Show what uses the management can make of the variances calculated in (a) and (b) above.
(d) Write a report to the management of Trusch plc suggesting possible action that could be taken to eradicate any adverse variances.

## Chapter 34

SHORT-TERM DECISION MAKING: PROFIT, VOLUME AND COST ANALYSIS

In this chapter

We will learn of:

and you should be able to:

- how short-term decisions to utilize spare capacity are made on the basis of marginal costing

- calculate contributions and break-even points
- draw break-even charts

34.1 INTRODUCTION

In Chapter 29 (Manufacturing accounts) we learnt about the following:

1. Identifying three types of cost:
   - *variable costs*: costs that increase or decrease in direct proportion to levels of activity;
   - *fixed costs*: costs that remain unchanged irrespective of any change in the level of activity;
   - *semi-variable costs*: costs that remain stable up to a particular level of activity but change when that level is exceeded, containing a fixed element and a variable element. Examples are items where there is a fixed standing charge plus a cost per unit, such as in some gas and electricity bills.
2. SSAP 9 requires that the cost of unsold stocks must include a share of the manufacturing overheads, both fixed and variable. This is done by either allocation or apportionment of overheads.

Determination of the cost of goods, as required by SSAP 9,[1] is known as the *full cost basis* or the *absorption costing* basis, and this is, of course, relevant for reporting performance in each accounting period. However, when it comes to decision making, the inclusion of fixed costs may create problems and result in erroneous decisions.

For illustration, let us examine a decision that Rita had to make. Rita manufactures vanity cases, which she retails at £60 per unit. She expects to sell 30,000 units during the year and maintains stock levels constant. The costs in the year are expected to be as stated here. Her calculation, therefore, is that each vanity case costs her (£1,620,000/30,000) = £54.

Her sales manager had been exploring prospects of selling in continental Europe, but had failed until now because the strength

Costs of producing 30,000 units of vanity cases	£000
Materials: 30,000 units at £20	600
Labour: 30,000 units at £10	300
Manufacturing costs – variable: 30,000 at £8	240
Manufacturing costs – fixed	80
Administrative, selling and distribution – fixed	400
Total costs	1,620

of the pound sterling made the product too expensive for European customers. He has, however, just obtained an order for 5,000 vanity cases from a French supermarket at £45 per case. Rita was quick to refuse the order on the ground that the sale price (£45) is lower than the cost per unit (£54). She agreed to reconsider her decision when her accountant explained as follows how the business would benefit from accepting the order:

- Raw material and labour for producing 5,000 more cases are readily available at the same rates and the business has sufficient spare capacity to produce this additional quantity without increasing the fixed overheads.
- In the circumstances, if the French order were to be accepted, the business would perform as set out below (left). On the other hand, if the French order is refused, Rita's profit would have been as shown on the right.

Performance in the year		£000	£000
Sales 30,000 units locally at £60		1,800	
5,000 units to France at £45		225	2,025
Less Variable costs:			
Materials	35,000 at £20	700	
Labour	35,000 at £10	350	
Manufacturing overheads	35,000 at £8	280	
Marginal cost		1,330	
Fixed overheads:			
Manufacturing overheads		80	
Administrative, selling and distribution		400	(1,810)
Profit for the year			215

	£000
Sales: 30,000 units at £60	1,800
Total cost as stated above	(1,620)
Profit	180

Thus the acceptance of the French order improves Rita's profit by £35,000, although she is selling each unit at a price that is £9 less than the full cost of the unit. This situation, though seemingly strange, arises because the fixed overheads remain constant, despite the production of 5,000 more units. This means that the additional expenses incurred on producing each unit sold in France is (£20 + £10 + £8) = £38. This figure, calculated without taking fixed costs into account, is known as the *marginal cost* per unit. Hence, when each of these units is sold for £45, it makes a *contribution* of £7 (i.e. sale price less marginal cost) towards meeting the fixed overheads and then leaving a profit. The contribution of £7 per unit from the 5,000 additional units accounts for the improved profit of £35,000.

34.2 MARGINAL COSTING

Marginal costing is a system in which costs are ascertained by differentiating between fixed and variable costs in order to identify the effect on profits brought about by a change in the level of activity. The marginal cost is the variable cost of one unit of output (i.e. ignoring fixed costs).

34.2.1 Contribution: a definition

'Contribution' is the difference between the sales income and the marginal (or variable) cost. This can be calculated per unit or in total. The contribution accumulates and pays, first, the fixed costs and, after these have been met, any further contribution is profit.

For example, let us assume that we are planning a training course for which we are charging £90 per trainee. Let us assume that the fixed costs are the room rent of £250 and the lecturer's fees of £350. These expenses remain fixed irrespective of the number enrolling on the course. On the other hand, the Training Manual we propose to issue to each trainee costs £30. This then is a variable cost. The fee received from each trainee (£90) would cover the variable cost (£30 – which is known as the marginal cost) and makes a contribution of £60 towards the fixed costs.

34.2.2 How the contribution is used to make decisions

The identification of the amount of the contribution enables us to make two calculations. These deal with points such as the following:

1. How many trainees should enrol on the course so that we will be at a point where we make no profit or loss – a situation referred to as the 'break-even' point? With a contribution of £60 per trainee, the number of trainees required to break even is arrived at by dividing the total fixed costs (£600) by the contribution per trainee (£60), yielding ten trainees as the break-even point.
2. What will be the profit if 15 trainees enrol? The profit we make would be the contribution we receive from each trainee after we reached the break-even point – i.e. 5 extra @ £60 = £300.

In other business situations a knowledge of the contribution allows management to identify matters such as the most profitable product mix and the most profitable departments. From this kind of information, informed decisions can be made (e.g. whether to cease a product line or close a department).

34.2.3 Semi-variable costs

Identifying and measuring variable and fixed costs is relatively simple. Semi-variable costs, however, create a problem, because it is necessary to identify that proportion of costs that will vary with activity and that will remain constant. The simplest method of splitting semi-variable costs into their two elements is known as the 'high–low' method whereby expenses

Activity level	Units	£
High	6,750	2,750
Low	2,750	1,750
Difference	4,000	1,000

The variable rate = $\dfrac{£1,000}{4,000 \text{ units}}$ = 25p per unit

and the levels of activity are identified at two different points (high and low points). The difference in expense can be measured and compared with the difference in activity level, to identify the portion of the expense that is the variable element, as seen from the example stated above. By applying the variable rate to the original figures (as done on the right) the fixed element of cost is identified. When the fixed and variable elements are identified, it will be possible to calculate the expenses at various levels of activity.

CALCULATION OF FIXED COST

	High	Low
Total semi-variable expense	£2,750.00	£1,750.00
Less: Variable expense @ 25p per unit	£1,687.50	£687.50
Fixed element of semi-variable	£1,062.50	£1,062.50

| Interaction 34.1 | **The contribution and the profit determination** |

Walbar plc manufactures miniature London Eyes at a variable cost of £1.50 each. Fixed costs for the period, in which 10,000 miniatures were produced, amounted to £6,000, whilst semi-variable costs were £2,000. In the previous period, when 5,000 miniatures were produced, the semi-variable costs were £1,500. The miniatures sell for £2.50 each.

Required: Calculate the variable element of the semi-variable cost, and the contribution per miniature to the fixed costs. Calculate also the profit when 10,000 miniatures are sold.

34.3 BREAK-EVEN ANALYSIS

As we have seen already in the previous section, the contribution is the difference between selling price and variable costs. This can be expressed as the following formula:

$$C = S - VC$$

where C = contribution, S = selling price, and VC = variable cost per unit. The point at which contribution is exactly the same as fixed costs is known as the 'break-even' point and it implies that at this level of activity all costs will be covered and neither a profit nor a loss will be made. The formula for the break-even point is:

$$\text{Break-even point in units} = \frac{\text{Fixed costs}}{\text{Unit contribution}}$$

We can use this formula to identify the level of activity (in units) required to cover our fixed costs or, by the addition of a profit figure, the level of activity required to give a specific return:

$$\text{Level of activity} = \frac{\text{Fixed costs} + \text{required profit}}{\text{Unit contribution}}$$

| Interaction 34.2 | **The break-even point** |

Required: Using the information given in IQ 34.1, calculate the level of activity required to break even and to make a profit of £3,000.

34.3.1 Break-even charts

The calculations made above can be represented in graphical form with the values in £s being represented on the vertical axis and the level of activity represented on the horizontal axis as follows:

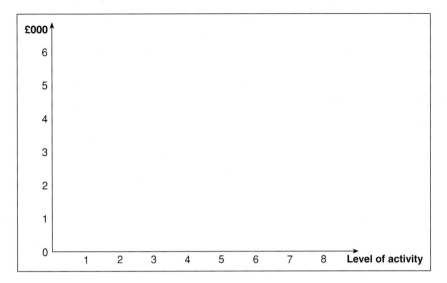

Fixed costs are represented by a straight line drawn parallel to the horizontal axis, while variable costs start at the point where the fixed cost line intersects the vertical axis and rises uniformly as activity increases to give the total cost line.

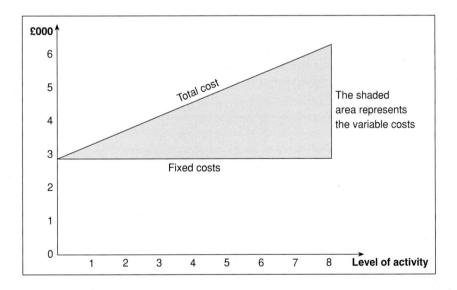

If we draw the sales line starting at zero and rising uniformly, we will be able to identify the point at which it intersects with the total cost line. This enables us to read down on the horizontal axis the level of activity where sales equal total cost, i.e. the break-even point. The area to the right of the break-even point between the total cost line and the sales line is the area of profit and that to the left of the break-even point is the area of loss.

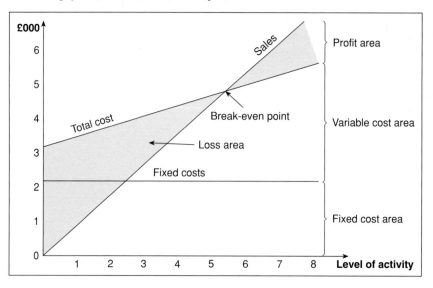

The distance between the level of activity at which break-even occurs and the actual level of activity is known as the margin of safety and illustrates how far activity should fall before we reach break-even point.

34.3.2 **Alternative form of break-even chart**

In the previous break-even chart, fixed costs were shown as a line parallel to the horizontal axis and variable costs commencing at the point at which the fixed-cost line intersected the vertical axis. An alternative presentation shows the variable costs line commencing at zero with the fixed costs line rising parallel to this. The sales line remains as in the previous graph.

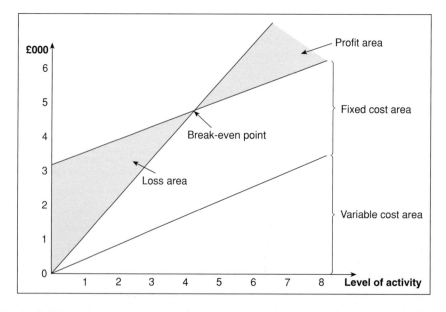

The benefit of using this type of chart is that it shows clearly how, as sales progress, the contribution to fixed cost increases until break-even point is reached, and after this profits are generated.

Using a break-even chart

Required: Estimate from the following diagram:

(a) the total fixed costs;
(b) the break-even point (in 000s units);
(c) the total cost, fixed cost, variable cost, margin of safety and profit when 50,000 units are produced.

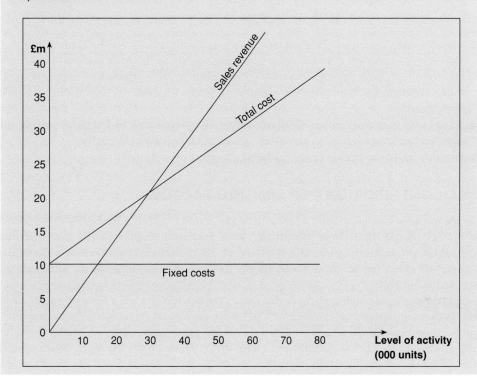

34.3.3 The use of break-even charts and analysis in decision making

Break-even analysis can be employed to aid management decisions by building models based on changes in any of the constituent elements, such as a change in selling price or in the cost of materials. On the other hand, what would happen if fixed costs were to increase, as a result (say) of moving premises or purchasing new plant and equipment? Before answering this questions, have a go at IQ 34.4.

Impact of changes in scenario

In addition to the information stated in IQ 34.1 you are informed that the management of Walbar is contemplating the following alternatives:

(a) to use cheaper materials, which would reduce the variable cost by 25p per miniature but would also lead to a reduction of 20 per cent in the number of miniatures sold; or
(b) to reduce the selling price to £2, which would lead to an expected increase of 30 per cent in the number of miniatures sold.

Required: In respect of each of the alternative scenarios in (a) and (b) above, calculate the break-even point and the revised profit.

It can be seen from IQ 34.4 that alternative strategies, such as increasing sales by reducing prices, increasing fixed costs by marketing expenditure (which in turn should increase sales) or variations in the marginal cost structure, can be tested through break-even analysis to examine their viability before putting them into practice in the real environment.

34.3.4 Limitations of break-even analysis

There are limitations in the use of break-even analysis. These include the following:

- Variable costs and sales revenues are shown as straight lines on the assumption that they remain constant per unit. This is not necessarily so, because material prices may change due to bulk buying discounts, labour costs may be affected by overtime working to meet production demands and selling prices may fall as a result of goods sold at a discount.
- Fixed costs may not remain constant during the period due to increases outside the company's control – such as rent rises or rises in the price of electricity.
- Production methods may change, having an effect on both fixed and variable costs.

34.4 CONTRIBUTION PER LIMITING FACTOR

So far we have considered the contribution per unit of output where only one product is manufactured. If there is a limiting factor (i.e. some aspect of the business that constrains production), such as a shortage of a key material or a lack of a particular labour skill, then the business would simply produce as many units as it could with the resources available.

If a company manufactures more than one product and there is a limiting factor, then it is important to determine which product takes priority. If the objective is to maximize profit, then the approach is to concentrate on the production of those articles that give the greatest contribution per limiting factor rather than simply choosing those articles that give the best contribution per unit.

To illustrate the scenario, let us assume that Birdsong plc sells two types of bird seeds – a Premium Mix and a Standard Mix – and that both mixes contain sunflower seeds, which are in short supply (only 10,000 kg being available). The Premium Mix uses 6,000 kg and the Standard Mix uses 4,000 kg. The contributions from Premium Mix and Standard Mix are £10,000 and £8,000 respectively. Which mix should Birdsong produce in order to maximize profits if it had to concentrate on one product only? We focus on the contributions from each product as follows:

	Contribution	Limiting factor	Contribution per limiting factor
Premium Mix	£10,000	6,000 kg	£1.67
Standard Mix	£8,000	4,000 kg	£2.00

These figures indicate that Birdsong should choose to produce the Standard Mix because:

- by producing Premium Mix the contribution will be 10,000 kg × £1.67 = £16,700
- by producing Standard Mix it will be 10,000 kg × £2.00 = £20,000.

The second option is therefore preferable.

Choice of product in terms of a limiting factor

A company manufactures two products, X and Y. Particulars of cost structure and selling prices are as stated here.

Required: Calculate the contribution per unit of each product and also a contribution in terms of each of the following:

Product	Material	Wages	Variable overhead	Sales
	£	£	£	£
X	90	30	35	250
Y	150	100	100	530

(a) per £ worth of material;
(b) per £ worth of labour;
(c) per £ of sales.

34.4.1 Making the choice between multiple products

It may well be that there are commercial reasons why Birdsong needs to supply both the Premium Mix and the Standard Mix to regular customers and it would be commercially imprudent to decide to supply only Standard Mix.

Where a company produces more than one article and where there is both a limiting factor and a commitment to supply a *minimum* quantity of all products, the company should maximize production of the product that gives the best contribution per limiting factor and should produce the minimum quantity of the product with the worst contribution per limiting factor.

34.5 CONTRIBUTION ACCOUNTING IN OTHER DECISION-MAKING SITUATIONS

We have seen that there are several circumstances in which contribution accounting aids management to make its decisions regarding its product policies. There are other areas too where this concept can be useful. Such areas include when a decision is required on the following:

● acceptance of an order below the normal selling price;
● whether to discontinue a particular product line;
● whether to close a department or branch;
● whether to manufacture a part or buy in from an outside supplier.

34.5.1 Acceptance of an order at a price below total cost

Marginal costing is where the focus is only on the variable cost of a product. The alternative is absorption costing, where the focus is on the whole cost including fixed costs. Products are normally priced to recover direct costs and their share of absorbed overheads. However, there may be commercial reasons for a product to be sold at a price lower than full cost. For example, where the company has spare facilities, there may be justification for acceptance of an order at less than the full cost, provided that the selling price obtained exceeds the marginal cost (i.e. it makes a contribution to fixed costs). Care must be taken to ensure that the acceptance does not lead to the company incurring additional fixed costs or to normal production being disrupted.

34.5.2 Discontinuance of a product line

Again, on a full cost basis, it may appear that a particular product no longer makes a profit. If, however, it makes a contribution to the fixed costs, which will be incurred even if production is discontinued, it would be better to continue the manufacture of the product. Otherwise overall profits will be reduced. This, however, would be conditional on there not being another product with a better contribution.

34.5.3 Closure of a department or branch

The same approach may be used when determining whether to close a branch or department. It might be loss-making when the calculation is based on total costs, but it may be making a contribution to general overheads, without which overall profitability of the company as a whole may suffer. Even if closure seems logical on a financial basis, there may be other factors to be taken into consideration such as the social effects – for example, worsening unemployment in an area of high unemployment, an adverse effect on staff morale, or a reduction in the reputation of the business as a whole.

34.5.4 Make-or-buy decisions

There are times when a decision has to be made on whether to manufacture a part or to buy from an outside supplier. If a business is considering a new item, it may be that because of the need to invest in new capital equipment and train staff in new skills, the best solution is to buy from a specialized manufacturer. When the business already has the facilities for production to be carried out economically, it may be better for the business to produce the item itself since this would give control of quality and supply. If, however, the decision is being made purely on the grounds of cost, we must not forget that cessation of production may only save the variable or marginal cost and that fixed cost will still have to be met. Therefore, a comparison must be made between the outside purchase price and the *marginal* cost of production, and only if this comparison shows a saving by purchase should that choice be made, however attractive the outside price may at first appear.

Interaction 34.6	**Make-or-buy decision**

Walbar manufactures a component used in its regular product. The cost of the component is as stated on the right. Walbar has received an offer to supply the component at £34 per unit. You are to assume that if production ceases, no material, wage or variable overhead costs will be incurred and a saving on fixed costs of £2 per unit will be made as a result of not having to store materials or provide services for the workers.

Material	£15
Labour	£12
Overhead – variable	£4
Overhead – fixed	£6
Total cost	£37

Required: Advise Walbar plc on whether it should accept the offer from the outside supplier. Support your answer with workings.

Reference

1. SSAP 9: *Stocks and Long-term Contracts* (May 1975).

SOLUTIONS TO INTERACTIVE QUESTIONS

IQ 34.1 The contribution and the profit determination

Variable element of semi-variable expense	Units	Expense
High	10,000	£2,000
Low	(5,000)	(£1,500)
Difference	5,000	£500

Semi-variable £500/5,000 = 10p per miniature

The fixed element of semi-variable expense	High	Low
Semi-variable expense	£2,000	£1,500
Variable element at 10p	(£1,000)	(£500)
Fixed element	£1,000	£1,000

Contribution per unit to fixed cost		£
Sale price		2.50
Variable cost	1.5	
Semi-variable	0.1	(1.60)
Contribution per unit		0.90

Profit when 10,000 units are sold	
Contribution: 10,000 @ 90p	£9,000
Less: Fixed costs	(£6,000)
Semi-variable (fixed element)	(£1,000)
Profit	£2,000

IQ 34.2 The break-even point

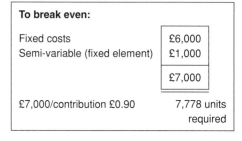

To break even:	
Fixed costs	£6,000
Semi-variable (fixed element)	£1,000
	£7,000
£7,000/contribution £0.90	7,778 units required

To make a profit of £3,000:	
Fixed and semi-variable	£7,000
Profit anticipated	£3,000
	£10,000
£10,000/contribution £0.90	11,111 units required

IQ 34.3 Using a break-even chart

(a) The total fixed costs are £10 million.

(b) The break-even point (in units) is 30,000 units.

(c) At 50,000 units level of activity the total cost is £27.5 million; the fixed costs are £10 million; the variable costs are £17.5 million and the profit is £6.5 million. The margin of safety is 30,000 units.

IQ 34.4 Impact of changes in scenario

	(a)	(b)
Sale price	£2.50	£2.00
Variable costs	(£1.25)	(£1.50)
Semi-variable (v)	(£0.10)	(£0.10)
Contribution	£1.15	£0.40

Break-even point:		
£7,000/£1.15	6,087	
£7,000/£0.40		17,500

Profit statement:		
Proposal	(a)	(b)
Fixed costs	(£6,000)	(£6,000)
Semi-variable (fixed)	(£1,000)	(£1,000)
Contribution:		
8,000 units @ £1.15	£9,200	
13,000 units @ £0.40		£5,200
Profit (Loss)	£2,200	(£1,800)

IQ 34.5 Choice of product in terms of a limiting factor

	X	Y
Sales	£250	£530
Material	(£90)	(£150)
Labour	(£30)	(£100)
Overhead	(£35)	(£100)
Contribution	£95	£180

Limiting factor:	X	Y
Contribution per £ worth of material	£1.056	£1.200
Contribution per £ worth of labour	£3.167	£1.800
Contribution per £ worth of sales	£0.380	£0.340

Dependent on which was in limited supply, the company would decide on which product to focus on.

IQ 34.6 Make-or-buy decision

Cost savings (buying out):	£
Variable cost: £15+12+4	31
Fixed cost (saved)	2
Savings effected	33
Outside purchase price	34

The decision may be checked as follows:	£
Outside purchase price	34
Remaining fixed cost (£6 less £2)	4
Total cost of component when bought	38
Cost of component if manufactured	37

Therefore do not accept the offer from the outside supplier.

PROGRESSIVE QUESTIONS

PQ 34.1 Absorption costing v. marginal costing

Proctor plc manufactures yo-yos. During its first year of business, to 31.12.20X1, Proctor sold 15,000 yo-yos at £5 each and produced 22,500 yo-yos at costs as stated on the right.

Direct material	£22,500
Direct labour	£45,000
Overheads – variable	£9,000
Overheads – fixed	£18,000

Required:

(a) Calculate the profit for the year using first absorption costing and then marginal costing.
(b) Explain and illustrate why the two methods give different results.

PQ 34.2 Profit using marginal costing

Delcoop plc, producing and selling a single product, provides you with costs as stated here. During the period just ended, 390,000 units of the product were produced and 345,000 units were sold at £3.50 per unit. At the beginning of the period, 60,000 units were in stock and these had been valued at the budgeted costs. The actual costs incurred in the year were as per budget.

Budgeted costs for 360,000 units	£000
Direct material and labour	396
Variable production overheads	72
Fixed production overheads	216
Variable selling and distribution costs	36
Fixed selling and distribution costs	144

Required: Calculate the profit for the period using marginal costing.

PQ 34.3 Contribution and break-even point

Information on three perfume products now manufactured by Aroma plc is tabulated here. Annual fixed costs are currently £3 million.

	Selling price per unit	Variable cost per unit	Current annual sales in units
Lavender	£6.00	£2.40	500,000
Passion	£4.90	£3.34	1,200,000
Musk	£8.00	£5.20	480,000

Required: Calculate:

(a) the weighted average contribution per £ of sales;
(b) the current break-even sales revenue of the business;
(c) the margin of safety.

PQ 34.4 Contemplated changes to product price and quality

Further to the information stated in PQ 34.3, assume that, in respect of the Lavender perfume, Aroma plc plans for additional fixed costs of £365,000 to employ quality-control inspectors and for a decrease in the selling price to either £5.50 or £5.10. The sales manager advises that the expected sales volumes at these prices would be 700,000 and 800,000 units respectively.

Required:

(a) Determine whether to proceed with price reduction and the employment of the quality-control inspectors.
(b) Calculate the sales volume needed to be achieved in order to maintain the same level of profit if it were decided to decrease the price to £5.50.

Part H

COMPUTERIZED ACCOUNTING

Chapter 35

COMPUTERS IN ACCOUNTING

In this chapter

We will learn of the benefits and the use of computers in the accounting and control functions

---

35.1 INTRODUCTION

Computerized accounting systems may appear frightening and difficult to understand because it is not immediately apparent where the entries of transactions go. The entries go into computer files, which are held invisibly on magnetic discs. They can only be 'seen' when the transactions input into the system are printed out.

Although it is a common fear that computerized systems are prone to more errors than manual accounting systems, the reverse is true. Many of the errors made in manual systems (such as arithmetical errors and failure to account by a pair of entries) cannot occur in computerized systems. Also, it is easier to locate a problem in a computer system, by printing out accounts or transactions in the problem area; with manual systems it may be much more difficult to locate problems, particularly when there are computation errors, items posted to the wrong account, or items posted only once in a double entry system. The Trial Balance in a computerized system, unlike that in a manual system, will always balance. Computerization does not, however, prevent errors of omission, commission or principle. For example, it is still possible to make entries that satisfy the double entry rule but that may be to the wrong account.

Computerization of accounting systems nevertheless bestows several advantages:

- computerized systems have fewer errors than manual systems;
- computers allow data to be processed much more quickly;
- analysis of this data provides more information more speedily to enable management to run a business more effectively.

There are two types of files in computer systems. Although alternative names are in use, this chapter refers to them as:

1. *standing data files*, which are files that change infrequently – for example, in a sales ledger system they will comprise the files containing customer's account number, name, address, credit rating, bank details etc.;
2. *transaction files*, which contain details of all transactions occurring. The transaction file in a sales ledger system, for example, will comprise, for each customer account, unpaid sales invoices and cash received in the current month. There will be a separate transaction file containing details of sales invoices, cash received and other items posted in the month.

Processing by the computer generally comprises five steps:

- Step 1: Open data files for Standing and Transaction data.
- Step 2: Input data. In a sales ledger system this comprises sales invoices, cash received and other items.
- Step 3: Perform edit checks, which will be made on the data input into the system. In a sales ledger system this will include checking whether the account number for the transaction (e.g. sales invoice, cash etc.) is valid.
- Step 4: Process the input data. The transactions will be posted to the individual sales ledger accounts.
- Step 5: Print the input data and the contents of data files. For input of sales invoices into a sales ledger system, the computer can print the sales invoices input today and for the month to date. The main printout of the contents of data files will be, for each customer, the outstanding items on their sales ledger account.

In Chapter 12 we considered the use of spreadsheets. In this chapter we consider:

(a) computerized electronic point of sale (EPOS) systems in shops;
(b) computerized Sales and Purchase Ledgers;
(c) a computerized Nominal Ledger.

The most popular accounting packages for microcomputers (for Sales and Purchase Ledgers, Nominal Ledger, sales invoicing, stock control and payroll) are from Sage and Pegasus. The system described in (b) and (c) above is similar to these popular accounting packages. This chapter provides only an introduction to the use of computers in accounting; the manuals for commercially available accounting packages should be studied for more specific information on computerized systems.

35.2 COMPUTERIZED ELECTRONIC POINT OF SALE SYSTEMS

Computerized electronic point of sale (EPOS) systems are being considered here, first, because we may well encounter them at least once a week. We will consider an EPOS system in a food supermarket.

35.2.1 Purpose of the system

The purpose of an EPOS system is to:

(a) price the products sold to customers;
(b) calculate and print customers' bills and record cash received;
(c) record stock movement arising from sales and purchases;
(d) determine the quantity of stock of each product;
(e) record the transactions in the accounting records.

35.2.2 The computer system

A schematic diagram of an EPOS system is shown opposite. It comprises:

(a) a central processor and the data files;
(b) a terminal in the Goods Received Department to record receipt of goods;
(c) a number of checkouts, where the bar codes on the products are scanned, the bill for the customer is printed, and cash or credit for the sale is received;
(d) a terminal to control the computer, input changes in product details and adjustments to stock quantities.

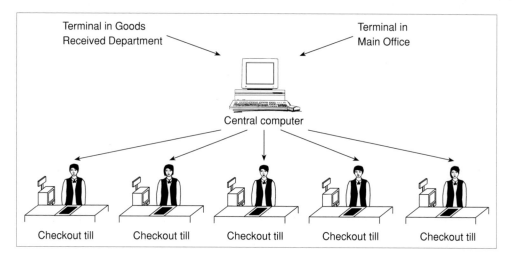

In real life, the computer system may be more complex. In most systems, some processing occurs at the checkouts. A checkout will have details of a limited number of products, so that the description and price can be printed on the customer's bill without having to obtain this information from the main computer. This reduces the electronic traffic from the checkouts to the main computer, and minimizes delays created by the main computer becoming too busy.

Failure of the stock control system will have very serious consequences. It will be impossible to process sales, and so the store would have to be closed. The following features are normally included to minimize the risk of such system failure:

- Having two computers that run in parallel, so that the second computer takes over if the first computer fails. Two separate disk drives will be used to store the data, and the individual transactions will be recorded on each. Data files should be copied to a backup file each day. This will minimize the consequences of failure of a disk drive, the main computer and/or corruption of the data.
- The system should continue to operate if part of the system crashes. The system should be fault-tolerant and the software that processes the data should be tried and tested so there are relatively few 'bugs' in the computer programs. 'Bugs' in computer programs commonly result in the system crashing and/or corruption of the data files.
- There should be a backup electrical supply to allow the system to continue when there is a power failure. There should be filters in the main power supply to prevent voltage 'spikes' from reaching the computer. Data lines between the main computer and the terminals should be screened to prevent electrical interference from entering the data cables.

35.2.3 Data files

The data files in an EPOS system will comprise at least one standing data file – containing the bar-code numbers of products, their description and their selling price – as well as a transaction file recording products purchased and sold and the current stock balance. In addition, the system will be integrated into the 'back office' accounting system, i.e. the Nominal Ledger, where it will record sales, VAT, and cash received (in the cash book).

More sophisticated systems will contain additional files that record the sales of each line of stock and the stock age. This will highlight slow-moving stock, and it can be used to reorder items. There can be records of sales during each day, or even during each hour of the day.

35.2.4 Input sales data

An example of the data input into the system is shown on the right. This unprocessed data is not very meaningful. The procedure for entering the data is thus:

Item No.	Bar Code No.	Number/Quantity
1	G20362225M	
2	G21148941M	
3	5000166029537	
4	G20375232M	5
5	141	0.315 kg

(a) The bar code on the product is scanned and the computer translates it into a bar-code number.
(b) If no quantity is input, it is assumed to be one item.
(c) With item 4, the till operator has input the quantity (5) and scanned the bar code on one product.
(d) Item 5 represents an input for fresh fruit and vegetables. The till operator has input a three digit code for a certain fruit (bananas), and the scale beside the till has weighed the product.
(e) The products starting 'G' and ending 'M' are the supermarket's own brand products.

Where it is not possible to read the bar code, the till operator will input it manually from the keyboard. Where the product is sold at a lower-than-normal price, the till operator will input the price on the keyboard and then scan the bar code.

35.2.5 Perform edit checks

The main edit check is on the bar-code number. The computer will check that the bar-code number is on the computer's standing data file. If the bar-code number is not on the computer's standing data file, a warning buzzer will sound at the till and an indicator light will be set to red. The till operator will reinput the bar code. The computer will check that the number of items is reasonable (e.g. it would not accept 1,000 cartons of milk) and that the weight is reasonable (e.g. negative or nil weights would be rejected).

35.2.6 Process the data

The computer will look up the descriptions of the products and their selling prices from the standing data file, using the bar-code numbers. This will produce the following information:

Bar Code No.	Number	Description	Price per unit	Total cost
G 2036 2225 M	1	Margarine	0.35	0.35
G 2114 8941 M	1	Vegetable soup	0.46	0.46
5 000166 029537	1	Cat food	0.48	0.48
G 2037 5232 M	5	Skimmed milk	0.27	1.35
141	0.315 kg	Bananas	@ £0.92/kg	0.29
			Balance	2.93

Processing of the input data would produce information that the customer understands. The customer's bill would appear as shown on the right. The customer will pay in cash, by cheque, credit or debit card:

Number	Description	Total cost
1	Margarine	0.35
1	Vegetable soup	0.46
1	Cat food	0.48
5@ £0.27	Skimmed milk	1.35
0.315 kg @ 0.92/kg	Bananas	0.29
	BALANCE	2.93

(a) With payment by cash, the cashier will input the cash received and the computer will calculate the change.
(b) With the other methods of payment (cheque, credit or debit card), the charge will be exactly equal to the total on the bill.
(c) With cheques and debit cards, the customer can request 'cashback'. If a customer asks for £10 cashback, the cheque or debit card will be made out for £10 more than the grocery bill and the customer will be given £10 as cash.

When the transactions are complete, they will be processed to the computer's transaction files:

● Stock: the stock will be reduced by one (or more) item for each product sold.
● Cash: the cash received will be posted to the cash book. A cash book will be allocated to each till, so that the amount in the till for each operator can be checked to the computer record.
● Sales: the system will record the sales value and VAT of each item sold, and calculate the total sales and VAT for each sale. This will be posted to the Nominal Ledger, probably via a Sales Day Book.

35.2.7 Input of purchases data (supplier not customer)

Goods purchased will be entered into the stock control system when they are received. The staff will enter the bar-code number of the product, either using a scanner or by inputting the figures manually. The quantity will be entered when the bar code is scanned. The normal control procedures over input of purchase transactions will be carried out (see Chapter 30). These will comprise the following:

(a) The goods received will be checked to the supplier's advice note and a goods received note may be written out.
(b) The purchase invoice from the supplier will be received shortly after the receipt of goods. The purchase invoice will be checked to the goods received, and the price per unit of the items on the purchase invoice will be checked to the purchase order.
(c) The purchase invoice will be posted to the Purchase Ledger and the Nominal Ledger.
(d) The company may have a system of matching the purchase invoice to the goods received, as recorded on the computer file. In this way, the computer can print out details of goods received for which no purchase invoice has been posted to the Purchase Ledger.

If the system records purchase prices, these will be amended when changes are made by the supplier.

35.2.8 Updating the standing data file(s)

A standing data file for purchases normally contains details of the products the company sells, e.g. the bar-code number; the description; the selling price; the purchase price; and the VAT category of the product. The file will be amended if there are any changes, e.g. changing prices of products; deleting details of products that are discontinued; inputting details of new products; and correcting errors made in the past on existing products.

There should be strong controls over changing entries in a standing data file. These will include the use of passwords, and only allowing changes to be made from certain terminals in the system (e.g. the computer terminal in the office).

Where a company has a large number of supermarkets, changes in prices of products may be instigated by Head Office and transferred to individual supermarkets. This can be performed using the telephone system or by sending an updating disk to each supermarket.

When there are changes to the prices of products, the price label on or beside the product should be changed at the same time. Periodically, the company should check the price beside the product to the price on the computer's standing data file, and any discrepancies should be investigated. Most price changes will be made overnight, when the supermarket is closed or has relatively few customers.

35.2.9 Periodic stocktakes

A supermarket should count its stock periodically and compare it with the computer records. Any discrepancies should be investigated. Most discrepancies arise through stock being stolen, damaged or deteriorating so that it can no longer be sold. Where stock loss is due to deterioration, either the stockholding period can be reduced or measures can be taken to minimize deterioration (e.g. by putting tomatoes in a cool cabinet). The store detective or a video camera can be used to investigate where stock appears to be being stolen.

Many food supermarkets sell televisions and video recorders. These high-value items are attractive for customers or employees to steal. So, those not on display should be kept in a locked area within the storeroom. The key should be kept by the manager, and a record kept of all receipts into and movements out of the locked area. The stock in this area should be counted more frequently than other stock items.

The use of EPOS systems permits excellent controls over stock, so it is able to minimize the loss of stock through stealing or deterioration. If the computer stock records accurately reflect the quantities of stock in the store, it indicates that losses of stock are low and it allows further analyses to be made, including using the computer stock records to value the stock at the year end.

Interaction 35.1	**Costs and benefits of an EPOS system**

Required:

(a) List the nature of costs of setting up an EPOS system.
(b) List the day-to-day costs of running an EPOS system.
(c) Describe the benefits of using an EPOS system.

Your answer to part (c) should include examples of how the EPOS system can assist management in running the supermarket (e.g. ordering of goods from suppliers).

35.3 SALES LEDGER SYSTEM

A basic Sales Ledger system is used to record amounts owed by customers. Most of these systems record sales (and VAT) and cash received, which can be posted manually or automatically to the Nominal Ledger. There is a need to record sales so as to produce a Profit and Loss account, and the recording of VAT must satisfy the requirements of HM Customs and Excise (who collect the tax and are able to inspect the company's records).

35.3.1 Data files

The standing data file will contain for each customer account the name and address of the customer and his or her credit limit. The main transaction file will contain details of transactions on each customer account and the current balance. Transactions will comprise such things as sales invoices, credit notes, cash received, discounts for early settlement of debts, cash paid back (i.e. refunds), and any adjustments.

Other transaction files will contain:

- the transaction file entries above, made in the current month (and there may be a separate file for the batch of the transactions which are posted today, although this file may be kept in the computer's memory (RAM));
- the age of the debts on each Sales Ledger account;
- the total of the aged debtors and the total balance on the Sales Ledger;
- records of the current month's entries that are to be posted to the Nominal Ledger.

35.3.2 Input of data

The transactions mentioned for the main transactions file stated above will be posted to the appropriate accounts. When posting a sales invoice, for instance, such as that below, to the Sales Ledger, the operator will first input the account number, and the customer's name will be displayed on the terminal's screen. If the name is correct, the transaction can be posted to the Sales Ledger.

Account No.	Date	Transaction type	Invoice No.	Value	VAT		
B001	22.04.00	I	364296	235.00	35.00		
					Analysis		
				Code			**Value**
				S001			200.00

Transaction types

The following are typical transaction types that would appear in column 3 above:

- Sales invoices (transaction type 'I') will be produced manually (e.g. typed or handwritten) and certain details of the sales invoice will be posted to the Sales Ledger.
- Credit notes (transaction type 'C') will be produced manually and the total value of the credit note will be posted to the Sales Ledger. Authorization of the credit note may be required before it can be posted to the Sales Ledger.
- Cash received (transaction type 'R') and discounts will come from either customers' remittances or the list of cash received when the post is opened. Where the operator inputs individually the cash received and discount allowed, the total value of these

two items should be input. The computer will only accept the data if the value of cash and discount input equals the total value of the transaction.

- Refunds to customers (transaction type 'F') – here, the system may require authorization by a senior member of staff before such a transaction can be posted to the Sales Ledger.
- Adjustments (transaction type 'A') will be to correct small differences and write off bad debts. There should be an explanation for each adjustment, and it should be authorized if it is above a specified figure (e.g. over £100). Staff should be discouraged from using adjustments. Instead, they should correct errors using one of the items above.

Control over the data

The following are typical control procedures:

- Data should be entered into the Sales Ledger system in batches, each of up to 50 similar items.
- Taking the example of input of sales invoices, the operator should find the total value of the invoices to be posted using a calculator – this is known as pre-listing.
- The sales invoices should then be posted to the Sales Ledger and printed out.
- The total value of the sales invoices accepted by the computer should be checked as being equal to the total determined using the calculator. If there are any differences, they should be investigated. Any errors in inputting sales invoices to the computer should be corrected.
- A further check of the value of sales invoices accepted can be made by recording the total Sales Ledger balances both before and after the items are posted. The increase in the total Sales Ledger balances is equal to the value of invoices accepted by the computer and it should be equal to the total determined manually using the calculator.
- For 'cash and discount', it should be allocated to the sales invoices being paid. The Sales Ledger system should check that the total value of sales invoices allocated is equal to the cash and discount posted to the Sales Ledger. The system will put a 'paid' against the invoices that have been paid and 'allocated' against the cash that has been received for these items. These annotations to the file will be included in the printout of the account at the end of the month.

35.3.3 Perform edit checks

Let us refer back to the sales invoice shown in Section 35.3.2 above and consider additional computer checks necessary when inputting. Four typical edit checks performed by computers when inputting the sales invoice would be a format check, a standing data file check, a reasonableness check and a computation check. We will briefly describe each of these checks.

A format check

This means:

- there are only alphabetic characters where they are required (e.g. the first letter of an account number must be alphabetic);
- there are only numeric characters where required (e.g. the final three characters of the account number);
- where numbers are input, a '.' will be acceptable as a decimal point and a '-' for negative (if this is permitted).

A standing data file check

This is a consistency and compatibility check, e.g. the software checks there is a sales account with the number 'B001'.

A reasonableness check

Such a check includes the following:

- **Value**. There may be a limit to the value of a sales invoice. For a small accounting package, it may be limited to £999,999.99.
- **Quantity**. When a quantity is input, the system will check that it is not excessive (e.g. a customer purchasing 1,000 litres of milk). Negative quantities would generally not be allowed.
- **Credit limit**. A warning would be given if the sales invoice results in the balance on a customer's account exceeding the permitted credit limit.

A computation check

Such a check can comprise the following:

- **Ex VAT value**. The 'analysis' on the sales invoice should be the total value less the VAT (in our example from 35.3.2, £235 – £35 VAT = £200). The software will only allow processing of the sales invoice if the total of the 'analysis' items equals £200.
- **VAT rate**. The system may give a warning, when, for standard-rated sales, the value of the VAT element of the sales invoice is not close to the goods value ex VAT.

Edit checks on the input of a sales invoice   Interaction 35.2

Required: List the edit checks that the Sales Ledger software should perform when the data in the sales invoice (shown in Section 35.3.2) is entered into the computer.

35.3.4 Process the data

Processing will involve entering the credit transaction and the cash settlement in the Sales Ledger transaction file and obtaining reports out.

Credit sales

These involve:

(a) **Entering**. The sales invoice number, the account number, the date and value of each credit transaction.

(b) **Posting**. In the Nominal Ledger, the entries will be as shown on the right. Note that the system may either post the Nominal Ledger entries at the same time that the sales invoice is posted or it may accumulate these items and post

		£	£
D001	Dr Sales Ledger control	235	
S001	Cr Sales		200
V001	Cr Output VAT		35

them to the Nominal Ledger at the end of the month. Posting items at the end of the month has the advantage that the number of transactions recorded in the Nominal Ledger is reduced, thus reducing the length of the printouts of the Nominal Ledger (see the comment in Section 35.3.6 below).

(c) **Reporting**. Most systems will keep a record of the age of debts on each account and the total value of debtors on the Sales Ledger. Thus, the system will record the value as a current-month balance on the aged debtors file, and the total value of debtors on the Sales Ledger will be increased by the value of the sales invoice.

Cash receipts

These involve:

(a) **Entering**. Cash and discount, the account number, the date and value will be recorded in the Sales Ledger transaction file. A marker will be included against those sales invoices on the transaction file that are being paid by cash with a discount.

(b) **Posting**. The total value of debtors on the Sales Ledger will be reduced by the cash and discount posted to the Sales Ledger. For £235 received in cash, the transaction processed to the Nominal Ledger will be as shown here.

		£	£
B001	Dr Cash book	235	
D001	Cr Sales Ledger control		235

(c) **Reporting**. On the aged debtors list, if an invoice three months old is settled, the system will reduce the aged balance on the customer's account at three months old by the value of the invoice settled.

35.3.5 Reports

In addition to the aged analysis reports, at the end of inputting credit and cash received transactions, the Sales Ledger system should print out a list of the transactions posted to the Sales Ledger on that day. Normally, each batch of transactions should be only a single type, such as sales invoices. Also, the system may print out entries posted to the Nominal Ledger (or it may leave such a printout until the end of the month). In addition to the printouts described here, the system should have the facility to display on the screen for any customer account the ageing of the debt and the outstanding transactions on the Sales Ledger. Such information will be helpful to the credit controller.

35.3.6 Month-end procedures

Printouts

At the end of each month, the system should print out:

- all the individual transactions posted to the Sales Ledger by type: sales invoices; credit notes; cash and discounts; cash paid; adjustments;
- the outstanding transactions on each account, a copy of this printout being sent to each customer, when it is called a 'supplier's statement' (see example opposite);
- all the accounts in the business's Sales Ledger at the end of the month;
- an aged list of debtors – a copy of which will be sent to the credit controller, for 'chasing' slow-paying customers. An example of the list is given on page 540 (top).

STATEMENT FOR THE MONTH OF: May 20X0

Reeve Limited

Account no: M004

11, Colwick Lane

Anytown 2RU 5TA

TO:

TEL: 0123 654 987

Mapperley plc

FAX: 0123 654 988

31 Church Lane

Anytown AN3 5WU

DATE 31.5.20X0		**T/Over** 500		**Cr. Limit** £100		
Date	**Type**	**Reference**	**Status**	**Debit**	**Credit**	**Balance**
13.2.X0	Invoice	C10111	Paid	53.24		53.24
15.3.X0	Invoice	C10124		31.62		84.86
12.4.X0	Invoice	C10144		36.82		121.68
1.5.X0	Receipt	G123	Allocated to C10111	–	53.24	68.44
4.5.X0	Invoice	G10156		42.01		110.45

3 months	**2 months**	**1 month**	**Current**			**Total due**
0.00	31.62	36.82	42.01			£110.45

Note that the £53.24 received from Mapperley Limited on 1 May '00 was allocated to invoice C10111.

Reeve Limited						
Aged Debtors List as at 31 May 20X0						
Customer No:	**3 months +**	**2 months**	**1 month**	**Current**	**Total**	**Cr. Limit**
A003	0.00	25.34	6.23	36.41	67.98	100.00
B005	56.17	0.00	63.46	25.21	144.84	150.00
M004	0.00	31.62	36.82	42.01	110.45	100.00
TOTAL	56.17	56.96	106.51	103.63	323.27	

1. Account M004 has exceeded its credit limit by £10.45.
2. Account B005 has £56.17 of its total debt three months old or over – this should be investigated.
3. Accounts A003 and M004 have amounts which are two months owing, which is over the company's credit limit of one month after the date of the invoice.

Backup

After these procedures have been carried out, a copy of the standing data and transaction files should be stored on a separate backup disk. This backup disk can be used to recreate the files if there is a subsequent failure of the system.

Clearing

Finally, a month-end procedure will be carried out that eliminates matched cash and sales invoices on the sales ledger (e.g. the £53.24 entries in the supplier's statement example on page 539), and makes all the balances on the aged list of debtors one month older (i.e. the current month's debtors become one month old etc.). The files of the current month's transactions will be set to zero.

If the system posts transactions to the Nominal Ledger at the end of the month, then this procedure will be carried out at the same time as the month-end procedure for the Sales Ledger. The system will print out details of the individual entries to each account in the Nominal Ledger, and it will post the *totals* to the Nominal Ledger. So, in the Nominal Ledger there will be only one entry per month for items posted from the Sales Ledger. Details of the individual transactions will be obtained from the month-end printout. With this system, there will be very few entries made in the Nominal Ledger, thus making the printout of the Nominal Ledger of a manageable length.

Nominal Ledger posting

With systems that post individual transactions to the Nominal Ledger, the number of entries in the sales and output VAT accounts will be the same as the number of sales invoices posted to the Sales Ledger, and so there may be hundreds of individual entries in a single account in the Nominal Ledger. After the month-end transfer of items from the sales system to the Nominal Ledger has been made, the Sales Ledger system will clear the transaction file that records Nominal Ledger transactions.

35.4 SALES LEDGER SYSTEM INTEGRATION WITH SALES INVOICING AND STOCK RECORDS

The next two stages in developing a computerized accounting system are normally to integrate the Sales Ledger with both sales invoicing and stock control. Businesses develop their computerized systems by adding these two aspects to their Sales Ledger system. Integration may occur progressively, rather than all at once, and the order in which a business integrates them may vary.

35.4.1 Integration with sales invoicing

Sales invoicing and stock control have been covered earlier in Section 35.2 when describing the electronic point of sale (EPOS) system. Thus, the only new concept at this stage is the integration of these systems with the Sales Ledger rather than with the cash book (the point of sales system was for a cash sales system).

In Chapter 30, on credit sales systems, we saw that a multipart advice note was prepared to describe the goods dispatched and was sent with the goods to the customer. The sales invoice was produced from the advice note and posted to the Sales Ledger. With a computerized system, the sales department will input into the computer details of goods to be dispatched, and the date of dispatch (usually the current date).

The computer will check to the stock records that the goods are in stock. If they are not in stock, normally the computer will not allow processing of the transaction. Because of time delays in inputting goods received into the stock control system, the computer may allow goods to be dispatched if they are not recorded in stock, provided authorization is given by a responsible official. This responsible official may be the sales manager, who should check the goods are available before he gives authorization.

The computer will also check that the customer is not over the credit limit, or put on 'stop' by the credit controller. If the customer is over the credit limit or has been put on 'stop', authorization by the credit controller will be required before the dispatch is allowed. The computer system should calculate the customer's Sales Ledger balance after including the invoice for the goods to be dispatched, to see whether this balance is over the customer's credit limit. The term 'put on stop' means that the credit controller prevents any dispatches of goods to the customer without his/her authority. This may occur even when the customer's Sales Ledger balance is not over the limit, if the credit controller becomes aware that the customer is in financial difficulties.

Provided everything is satisfactory, the computer prints copies of the advice notes (preferably on a printer in the Dispatch Department), and the Dispatch Department sends the goods, with the copy advice note, to the customer.

At the same time as producing the advice note, the computer will produce a sales invoice. In generating the advice note, the sales department will have input:

(a) the customer account number – the computer will display the matching name and address of the customer on the screen for staff visual confirmation;
(b) the part number(s) of the product(s) being sold – the computer will display the description(s) of the part(s) being sold;
(c) the number of items being sold.

Production of the sales invoice will not normally require any additional information being input by the operator, as the computer will find the price per unit of the products from the computer's price file (standing data), and then calculate the value of the goods dispatched, the VAT and the total value of the invoice. This will allow printing of the sales invoice. Then, the invoice will be posted to the Sales Ledger.

Some systems are designed to produce the sales invoice when the dispatch department has confirmed the goods have been sent to the customer.

35.4.2 Integration with the stock control system

If the sales invoicing system is integrated to the stock control system, when the sales invoice is produced the items sold will be deducted from the quantities in stock. With this system, however, a problem arises if there is a delay between the time when the goods to be dispatched are input into the computer, and the time when the goods are dispatched to the customer and the computer stock records are updated. In such circumstances there is the risk that, when later details are input of goods to be dispatched, there may be insufficient items in stock when the goods are actually dispatched. For instance, consider the situation when

(a) 15 items are in stock at 9am;
(b) a dispatch of 10 items is entered into the computer at 10am, but the goods are not dispatched until 12 noon;
(c) a dispatch of 12 items is entered into the computer at 11am, but the dispatch does not take place until 2pm;
(d) 10 items are dispatched at 12 noon (per order (b)).

At 11am (item (c)) it would appear that there are 15 items in stock, so it would appear that the order for 12 items can be satisfied. However, at 12 noon ten items will be dispatched, leaving a stock of five items. When the dispatch department come to assemble the goods for item (c), there will be only five items in stock, which will be insufficient to fulfil the order of 12 items.

A way of overcoming this problem is to allocate order (b) to the stock at the time the order is input into the computer, and say that ten items are 'committed', leaving five items available for future orders. Then, when item (c) is entered into the computer, it will be apparent there is insufficient stock to complete this delivery.

35.4.3 Integration with the Nominal Ledger

		£	£
D001	Dr Sales Ledger Control a/c	235	
S001	Cr Sales account		200
V001	Cr VAT (assuming rate of 17.5%)		35

When a sales invoice is produced, its value (say £235) is posted to the Sales Ledger. The entries in the Nominal Ledger will be as shown on the left. The business may have a number of sales accounts in the Nominal Ledger (to enable the value of each sale line to be reported), and either an individual sales account will be allocated to each product or the person inputting dispatch details into the computer will enter the sales accounts to which the different types of sale on the invoice will be posted.

Thereafter, either the individual sales invoices will be printed out at the end of the month and the *total* of the entries will be posted to the Nominal Ledger at the end of the month (as in some Pegasus systems), or the sales invoices will be posted to the Nominal Ledger individually, at the same time as they are posted to the Sales Ledger (as in some Sage systems).

35.5 PURCHASE LEDGER SYSTEMS

Purchase Ledger systems are similar to Sales Ledger systems, except that they show amounts owing to suppliers rather than amounts owed by customers. In this way, they are very similar to the basic Sales Ledger system described in Section 35.3 above. However, as the purchase invoice is prepared by the seller of the goods, there is no equivalent in a purchasing system of the sales invoicing and stock control system. A further, minor, difference in a Purchase Ledger system (compared with a Sales Ledger system) is that there will be no equivalent of the credit limit in sales systems (or it will be of much less importance).

A basic Purchase Ledger system is used to record amounts owed to suppliers. Most of these systems record purchases (and VAT) and cash paid, which can be posted manually or automatically to the Nominal Ledger. There is a need to record purchases and other expenses so as to produce a Profit and Loss account, and the recording of VAT must be good so as to satisfy the requirements of HM Customs and Excise (who collect the tax and are able to inspect the company's records).

35.5.1 Data files

The standing data file will contain, for each supplier account, the name and address of the supplier and the credit limit (it is not essential to have a credit limit for purchases systems, although many systems provide this facility).

The main transaction file will contain details of transactions on each supplier account and the current balance. Transactions will comprise:

- purchase invoices (I);
- credit notes (C);
- cash paid (P) and discounts for early settlement of debts;
- cash received (i.e. refunds) (F);
- adjustments (A).

Other transaction files will contain:

(a) the entries above made in the current month (and there may be a separate file for the batch of transactions posted today, although this file may be kept in the computer's memory);
(b) the age of the debts on each Purchase Ledger account;
(c) the total of the aged creditors and the total balance on the Purchase Ledger;
(d) records of the current month's entries that are to be posted to the Nominal Ledger.

35.5.2 Input data

The entries when posting a purchase invoice will comprise (for example):

Account No.	Date	Transaction type	Invoice No.	Value	VAT		
R001	19.04.00	I	263462	117.50	17.50		
					Analysis		
					Code		**Value**
					P001		100.00

The procedures for inputting this data and the edit checks are almost identical to those for inputting sales ledger data.

Edit checks on the input of a purchase invoice

Interaction
35.3

Required: List the edit checks that the Purchase Ledger software should perform when the data in a purchase invoice (see above example) is entered into the computer.

35.5.3 **Reports**

At the end of inputting transactions, the Purchase Ledger system should print out:

● a list of the transactions posted to the Purchase Ledger on that day – normally, each batch of transactions should comprise only those of a single type, such as purchase invoices;
● entries posted to the Nominal Ledger (or it may leave such a printout until the end of the month).

In addition to the printouts described above, the system should have the facility to display on screen, for any supplier account, the ageing of debts and the outstanding transactions on the Purchase Ledger. Such information will be helpful to the person who deals with disputes and payment of suppliers.

35.5.4 **Month-end procedures**

Printouts

At the end of each month, the system should print out:

● all the individual transactions posted to the Purchase Ledger by type:
  – purchase invoices;
  – credit notes;
  – cash paid and discount received;
  – cash received (i.e. refunds);
  – adjustments;
● the outstanding transactions on each account, which would be the company's Purchase Ledger; this is not sent to suppliers but an independent person will check suppliers' statements with the balances on the Purchase Ledger accounts and investigate differences;
● an aged list of creditors, a copy of which will be sent to the chief accountant and the employee who pays suppliers. This will help them decide which suppliers' accounts should be paid.

Backup

After these procedures have been carried out, a copy of the standing data and transaction files should be stored on a separate back-up disk. This back-up disk can be used to recreate the files if there is a failure of the system.

Clearing

Finally, a month-end procedure will be carried out. This procedure eliminates matched cash and purchase invoices on the Purchase Ledger, and it makes all the balances on the aged list of creditors one month older (i.e. the current month's creditors become one month old). The files of the current month's transactions will be set to zero.

Posting to the Nominal Ledger

After a month-end transfer of items from the purchases system to the Nominal Ledger has been made, the Purchase Ledger system will clear the transaction file that records Nominal Ledger transactions.

35.6 NOMINAL LEDGER SYSTEM

The Nominal Ledger is a record of financial transactions of the company. Most computerized accounting systems call this the 'Nominal Ledger system', but in this book the Nominal Ledger system comprises both the Nominal Ledger and the Real Ledger.

The Nominal Ledger includes accounts for all income, expenses and Balance Sheet items in the periodic accounts. The most common way of recording items in the Nominal Ledger is to treat the Sales Ledger, Purchase Ledger and cash books as 'memo' accounts. The equivalent accounts in the Nominal Ledger will be the Sales Ledger Control account, Purchase Ledger Control account and the cash book (sometimes called the 'Cash Control account'). The Sales Ledger Control account will comprise individual transactions posted to the Sales Ledger, but it will be a single balance. The Sales Ledger has a separate account for each customer, and the sum of the balances on each of these accounts should equal the balance on the Sales Ledger Control account in the Nominal Ledger. Just as we learnt in Chapter 14, the Sales Ledger will have many balances (one for each customer), whereas the Sales Ledger Control account in the Nominal Ledger will be a single balance (which should be equal to the total of the balances on the individual Sales Ledger accounts).

Thus (for example), a sales invoice of £235 to Mr A. Smith will appear as an entry on A. Smith's account on the Sales Ledger as 'Dr S001 Invoice 235.00', where the £235 invoice comprises £200 of sales and £35 of VAT. The entry in the Nominal Ledger will be as shown here. The entry in the individual Sales Ledger

		£	£
D001	Dr Sales Ledger Control a/c	235	
S001	Cr Sales account		200
V001	Cr Output VAT		35

account is called a 'memo' (or memorandum) transaction, as it duplicates the £235 entry in the Sales Ledger Control account in the Nominal Ledger.

The Nominal Ledger system will only allow entries to be made if the total of the debit entries is equal to the total of the credit entries. In this way, the Nominal Ledger system ensures that the Trial Balance always balances (i.e. the total of the debit balances from the Nominal Ledger accounts equals the total of the credit balances). In manual systems, differences between the total of the debit and credit balances on the Nominal Ledger are common and, because of the large number of entries in a period, it can be impractical for the difference to be eliminated. This is an advantage of computerized accounting systems – the Trial Balance always balances.

35.6.1 Payroll entries

We have already considered the integration of Sales Ledgers and Purchase Ledgers into the Nominal Ledger system. What other transactions are required to complete the accounting entries in a Nominal Ledger? The first such missing transactions relate to wages costs. Payroll systems can be integrated into Nominal Ledger systems in a similar way to Purchase and Sales Ledger systems. The employees can be allocated to a particular expense, such as production labour or accounting wages, and the gross costs can be posted to the Nominal Ledger. Thus for an accounts department employee the week's wages expense could be as stated on the right. As the wages will be paid within a few days of preparing the payroll, the cash book entry can be made in the Nominal Ledger, as the date of payment of the net wages is effectively the

		£	£
W003	Dr Accounting wages	550	
B001	Cr Cash book		360
T001	PAYE (income tax)		95
N001	Employer's Nat. insurance		50
N002	Employee's Nat. insurance		45

		£	£
T001	Dr PAYE	1,500	
N001	Employer's Nat. insurance	700	
N002	Employee's Nat. insurance	600	
B001	Cr Cash book		2,800

same as the date the transactions were entered in the Nominal Ledger. The accounts for PAYE (pay as you earn – income tax), employer's and employee's National Insurance contributions record the amounts owing for these in the Balance Sheet. When the tax and National Insurance are paid (usually monthly), the cash book and other entries in the Nominal Ledger will be as stated on the left.

For a number of reasons, it is less common to integrate payroll systems into the Nominal Ledger than Sales and Purchase Ledger systems. The reasons include the fact that an employee may work on a number of projects in a week, where each project is recorded in a separate Nominal Ledger account. Thus allocating an employee to a single expense account is not practicable. However, there are computer systems that allow an employee's wage to be allocated to a number of accounts in a single week.

35.6.2 Other entries in the Nominal Ledger system

With the Sales Ledger, Purchase Ledger and payroll integrated into the Nominal Ledger system, some additional transactions will have to be entered into the Nominal Ledger system so that all the company's financial transactions are fully accounted for.

Interaction 35.4

Other entries in the Nominal Ledger

Assuming all transactions from the sales and Sales Ledger system, the purchases and Purchase Ledger system and the payroll system have been entered into the Nominal Ledger, *you are required* to describe the other entries that will need to be made in the Nominal Ledger in order to produce an accurate Trial Balance.

35.6.3 Nominal Ledger and periodic accounts

From the balances on the Nominal Ledger, the periodic accounts can be prepared (e.g. the month's, quarter's or year's accounts). The inclusion of bad debts and depreciation have been covered in IQ 35.4(c), and accruals, prepayments and closing stock have been included in IQ 35.4(d). The Nominal Ledger system can be configured to produce the Profit and Loss account and Balance Sheet for the period.

An alternative to using the Nominal Ledger system to produce the periodic accounts is to use a spreadsheet. Many computerized Nominal Ledger systems can download the names of the Nominal Ledger accounts and their balances to a spreadsheet file. Then the Nominal Ledger balances can be manipulated to produce the Profit and Loss account and Balance Sheet. The advantages of using a spreadsheet over the standard Nominal Ledger package include the following:

1. Adjustments can be entered more easily, the effect of the adjustment can be found and the accounts printed quickly.
2. A spreadsheet is more flexible and allows accounts to be printed in a form more suitable for management and an entity's directors. For instance, the spreadsheet can analyse the company's results into its different activities. It can determine the current month's results and the year to date, and compare them with budget. While standard Nominal Ledger systems can produce similar results, their format tends to be less flexible, and making changes in layouts tends to take longer with a Nominal Ledger package than when using a spreadsheet.

SOLUTIONS TO INTERACTIVE QUESTIONS

IQ 35.1 Costs and benefits of an EPOS system

(a) The costs of setting up an EPOS system include:
  (i)   the costs of the hardware – the main computer(s), disk drives for storing the programs and data, the cash tills at the customer checkouts, the terminal(s) in the Goods Received Department, other terminals (e.g. in the back office for adding new products, changing product prices and quantities, communication links with Head Office, and wiring between the different pieces of equipment), and equipment that allows the system to be run during power failures;
  (ii) the costs of the software – the computer programs that run the EPOS system;
  (iii) the costs of installing the system, and checking that it operates correctly;
  (iv) the costs of setting up the standing data files (of part numbers, descriptions and selling prices of products) and the transaction data file (the quantities of goods in stock at the date the EPOS system starts to be used);
  (v)   the cost of training staff to use the system.

(b) The day-to-day costs of running an EPOS system include the following:
  (i)   electricity for running the system;
  (ii)   the costs of maintenance of the system, including a contract with a maintenance company that will repair the system if it breaks down;
  (iii) the costs of training new staff (commonly, there is a high turnover of staff in retail outlets);
  (iv)   the costs of any upgrades to the system, both hardware and software;
  (v)   the costs of inputting new products, deletion of products and changing product prices, where there will be a saving in the cost of putting prices on individual products, which would be required in a non-EPOS system;
  (vi)   the costs of carrying out periodic stocktakes and changing quantities on the computer when differences between the physical stock quantities and the quantities on the computer are confirmed; and even without an EPOS system, a stocktake will have to be carried out at least annually, so this cost will be deducted from the stocktaking costs of an EPOS system to determine the net cost of having an EPOS system;
  (vii) the costs of entering purchases into the system;
  (viii) depreciation of the items capitalized (e.g. hardware and software).

(c) The benefits of using an EPOS system include the following:
  (i)   There is an accurate record of stock in the store. This will provide information on when new stock should be purchased. Also, it should reduce situations where the company is out of stock or has excessive stock. For fast-moving products (e.g. bread) a 'just in time' system can be used for deliveries to the store, so that bread is delivered to the store just before all the stock has been sold. Overall, there should be just the right amount of stock of each item, which will both minimize the stock in the store and minimize the occasions when the product is out of stock.
  (ii) Records of the level of sales each day (e.g. Friday night and most of Saturday are busy times for supermarkets) will allow the company to match deliveries of stock with sales. Also, the number of staff on the cash checkouts will be matched to sales, so that customers' waiting times are minimized, and the checkout staff are not idle (i.e. have no customers to serve).
  (iii) The system will be able to highlight slow-moving stock. The supermarket will reduce the selling price of this stock, and, in future, order smaller quantities of the stock. If there are 'stock outs', the size of orders can be increased to reduce the chance of this happening again.
  (iv) Differences between physical counts and the quantities on the computer will highlight stock that is either being stolen or wasted. Action can be taken to stop stock being stolen (by the use of store detectives or video cameras) and procedures can be instigated to minimize wastage of stock (e.g. by ensuring that perishable items are slightly unripe, so as to prevent them becoming overripe before they are sold).
  (v)   As the computer puts the prices on the customer's bill, this prevents the till operator from inputting a lower price. Thus, this reduces the risk of fraud and error in pricing of customers' bills. With lower-than-normal prices, there can be a test check by the office staff that there is a label in the till with the same price as the reduced price entered by the till operator.

IQ 35.2 Edit checks on the input of a sales invoice

The edit checks on the input data for a sales invoice should include the following:

(a) Check the customer account number. First the format of the number: it should have four characters, the first character should be a letter and the remainder three numerals. Then check whether there is a customer with the account number B001 on the standing data file. When the account number is entered into the computer, the computer should display the customer's name and address on the screen. The user should check that the invoice being processed is for this customer.

(b) The date entered should be in the correct format. It should be in the form 'DD.MM.YY', where DD is the day of the month, MM is the month, and YY is the last two digits of the year. DD should range from 01 to 31 (a lower figure for some months), MM should range from 01 to 12, and YY should range from 00 to 99. If the system has been used prior to the year 2000, the year should be entered as either four digits (not the abbreviated two numbers) or the system should be able to understand that '99' represents the year 1999 and '00' the year 2000. The system should give a warning when the date entered is significantly different from the current date. It may accept sales invoices entered up to a month in arrears and up to a day in advance; a warning would be given for any other dates. 'Rejection' means the data is not accepted. With a 'warning' the system should ask the user 'Is this correct? Y/N'. If the user replies 'Y', the data should be accepted; otherwise it should be rejected.

(c) A character should be entered for the transaction type. In this example, 'I' is used for sales invoices. If the character entered is not one of the acceptable types, it should be rejected, and the user should be asked to re-enter the character. After entering the transaction type, the system should display on the screen the type of transaction that is being accepted (sales invoices in this example).

(d) The invoice number should be entered. The format of the invoice number may be checked by the computer so see whether it is all numerical digits. However, in a simple Sales Ledger system, there may be no edit checks of this item. In a sales invoicing system, the computer may generate the invoice number automatically, as being one more than the last invoice.

(e) The total value of the invoice. Only numeric characters should be permitted (including a decimal point '.'). The system may require input of pence as well as pounds (£s). A warning should be given if posting the sales invoice to the Sales Ledger results in the customer's credit limit being exceeded. If the credit limit is being exceeded, the computer should ask the operator if he/she still wants the sales invoice to be posted to the Sales Ledger.

(f) The VAT on the invoice should be checked. The item should comprise only numerical characters. The amount of VAT on the total value of the invoice should be checked as being reasonable. If the VAT value appears to be wrong, the computer should give a warning and ask the operator whether the VAT value is satisfactory. The system should process the item only if the operator confirms the VAT value is satisfactory.

(g) The section titled 'Analysis' is the posting of the income element of the invoice to the Nominal Ledger. The amount posted must be equal to the total value of invoice less the VAT element. The first item to check is the account code (abbreviated as 'Code' on the screen) to which the income should be posted in the Nominal Ledger. In this example, the account code is 'S001'. The system should perform a format check by checking the first character is alphabetic and the remaining three characters are numeric. Also, the system should check there is an account with the code 'S001' on the Nominal Ledger.

(h) Under 'value' the system should check the characters input are all numeric (including a decimal point '.'). The operator should input 'E' when the analysed entries are all entered. Then, the system should check that the total of analysed items = total value minus the total VAT. If this analysis does not balance, the system should ask for more details before the operator is allowed to input the next sales invoice.

IQ 35.3 Edit checks on the input of a purchase invoice

The edit checks on the input data for a purchase invoice should include the following:

(a) The supplier account number. First, the system should check the format of the account number is correct. If the account number is 'R001' (in our example), the system should check whether the account number has four characters and the first character is alphabetic and the remaining three characters are numbers. The system should then check that there is a supplier with the account number R001 on the standing data file. When the account number is entered into the computer, the computer should display the supplier's name and address on the screen. The user should check that the invoice being processed is for this supplier.

(b) The date entered should be checked as being in the correct format. It should be in the form 'DD.MM.YY', where DD is the day of the month, MM is the month, and YY is the last two digits of the year. (What has been stated in paragraph (b) of the answer to IQ 35.2 applies here as well.)

(c) A character should be entered for the transaction type. In the purchase invoice system 'I' is used for purchase invoices. If the character entered is not one of the acceptable types, it should be rejected and the user should be asked to re-enter the character. After entering the transaction type, the system should display on the screen the type of transaction that is being accepted (purchase invoices in this example).

(d) The invoice number should be entered. There will be no format of the invoice number because suppliers use many formats. So, for the Purchase Ledger system, there will probably be no edit checks of this item.

(e) The total value of the invoice should be checked. Only numerical characters should be permitted. The system may require input of pence as well as pounds sterling. A warning may be given if posting the purchase invoice to the Purchase Ledger results in the supplier's credit limit for the company being exceeded.

(f) The VAT on the invoice should be checked as comprising only numerical characters. The amount of VAT on the total value of the invoice should be checked as being reasonable. If the VAT value appears to be wrong, the computer should give a warning and ask the operator if the VAT value is satisfactory. The system should process the item if the operator confirms the VAT value is satisfactory.

(g) The section titled 'Analysis' is the posting of the expense element of the invoice to the Nominal Ledger. The amount posted must be equal to total value of invoice less the VAT element. The first item to check is the account code (abbreviated as 'Code' on the screen) to which the expense will be posted in the Nominal Ledger. In this example, the account code is 'P001'. The system should perform a format check by checking the first character is alphabetic and the remaining three characters are numeric. Also, the system should check to the standing data file there is an account with the code 'P001' on the Nominal Ledger. Under 'value' the system should check the characters input are all numeric (including a decimal point '.'). The operator should input 'E' when the analysed entries are all entered. Then, the system should check that the total of analysed items equals the total value less the total VAT. If this analysis does not balance, the system should ask for more details before the operator is allowed to input the next purchase invoice.

IQ 35.4 Other entries in the Nominal Ledger

The additional transactions that should be entered into the Nominal Ledger system will comprise the following:

(a) **Other cash book entries.** These will comprise mainly payments not recorded on either the Purchase Ledger or payroll. It will include payments of tax to the Inland Revenue and National Insurance, payment of loan interest and dividends, repayments of loans, and payments into petty cash. There will be few unrecorded receipts in the cash book, because almost all receipts by businesses are from the Sales Ledger. Other receipts will include cash sales, receipts of cash as loans, and proceeds on disposal of fixed assets.

(b) **Petty cash book entries.** These will comprise receipts from the cash book and payments of petty cash expenses (including VAT). Normally, an analysed petty cash book will be used and the posting of entries to the Nominal Ledger will be from the totals of each of the analysis columns.

(c) **Bad and doubtful debts, depreciation, and disposal of fixed assets.** Journal entries will be made for bad and doubtful debts. The writing-off of bad debts on the Sales Ledger will be performed using the computerized Sales Ledger package. Writing off bad debts will be entered into the system by posting an adjustment to the Sales Ledger. As the other entry to the adjustment will be to the Sales Ledger Suspense account, the entry in this account will have to be transferred to the Bad Debt Charge account using a journal entry. Doubtful debts and depreciation of fixed assets will be entered into the

	£	£
Dr Bad debts	1,000	–
Cr Provision for doubtful debts	–	1,000
Dr Depreciation of machinery	2,000	–
Cr Provision for depn – machinery	–	2,000

Nominal Ledger using a journal entry. An increase of £1,000 in bad debts provision is made in the example above. Machinery is depreciated by £2,000 in the year by another journal entry, as shown.

Proceeds from the disposal of a fixed asset will have been entered into a Fixed Asset Disposal account, when posting the journal for cash receipts (item (a) above). If the proceeds are £1,500, the cost of the fixed asset was £10,000 and its accumulated depreciation was £8,000, the first entry when posting the cash receipt will be as shown to the right. The cost and accumulated depreciation of the asset will then be transferred from the respective accounts to the Disposal account by another journal entry, as shown. The entries in the Disposal account will comprise a debit of £2,000 and a credit of £1,500, giving a net debit of £500, which is the loss on disposal.

	£	£
Dr Cash book	1,500	–
Cr Asset Disposal account	–	1,500
Dr Asset Disposal account	2,000	–
Provision for depn – machinery	8,000	–
Cr Machinery account	–	10,000

(d) **Other adjustments, mainly to correct errors**. It can be seen from the description of the Sales Ledger/Nominal Ledger systems that they allow posting of adjustments where one entry is to the Sales Ledger Control account and the other to the Sales Ledger Suspense account. Adjustments will need to be made to transfer the entries in the Suspense account to the appropriate expense account (e.g. bad debts). Some of these entries may be to include accruals and prepayments at the period end. An accrual for electricity, for example, will be posted as shown on the right. Similarly, a pre-payment for insurance will be posted as shown. To produce periodic accounts, the stock of unsold goods at year end will need to be entered into the system as shown.

	£	£
Dr Electricity account	500	–
Cr Accruals	–	500
Dr Prepayments	1,000	–
Cr Insurance account	–	1,000
Dr Stock account (Balance Sheet)	52,000	–
Cr Stock account (Profit & Loss)	–	52,000

PROGRESSIVE QUESTIONS

PQ 35.1 Benefits of using computer systems

Required: Describe the benefits that accrue from the use of computerized accounting systems (as opposed to using manual or handwritten systems). You should divide your answer into:

(a) accuracy of processing;
(b) speed of processing;
(c) analyses and reports.

PQ 35.2 Edit checks

Required: List the types of edit checks that computer software can perform when data is entered into a computerized accounting system.

Part I

PARTNERSHIP ACCOUNTING

Chapter 36

PARTNERSHIP ACCOUNTS (1): APPROPRIATIONS

In this chapter

We will learn of:

- the concept of 'partnership' and the regulatory environment in which it operates
- appropriation of profit among partners

and you should be able to:

- appropriate profit among partners
- account for interest on their drawings
- give effect to any guarantees

36.1 WHAT IS A PARTNERSHIP?

A business entity, as it grows in size and variety of activities, may require more resources than a single proprietor can provide in terms of time, finance and skills. It is for such reasons that a sole trader seeks one or more persons to form a partnership.

The formation of a partnership requires no formality such as registration or entering into an agreement. The legal definition, provided by the Partnership Act 1890, is that partnership is 'a relationship that subsists between persons carrying on a business in common with a view to profit'. This means that a partnership exists, without any formal documentation, if the relationship between two or more persons has the following features:

- co-ownership of assets;
- conduct of a business;
- intention to share profits and losses.

If these features exist in a relationship one may, even unwittingly, be regarded as a partner. For example, brothers who had co-owned a property inherited from their father and had drawn out equal sums weekly were held by a court to be partners, because they carried on a business and shared profits.[1]

Let us consider a situation where Peter and Paul contributed £100,000 and £50,000 respectively to buy a boat to use for their own leisure purposes. When on the first day as owners of the boat they sailed down the river Thames with friends, Paul suggested that they could earn some money by taking tourists down the river on their boat. Peter thought this was an excellent suggestion. On the following day, before they had been able to insure the boat for business use, Peter phoned to say that the boat had sunk and nothing could be salvaged. Paul's only consolation was his thought that at least his own loss was not as great as Peter's. However, it was not long afterwards that Peter phoned to ask Paul to pay a further £25,000 as his share of the loss. Peter pointed out that they were partners and, as such, in the absence of an agreement to the contrary, they would have to share the loss of £150,000 equally.

Paul was quick to deny the existence of a partnership, pointing out that he never intended to become a partner and that a business was not registered nor was there any formal agreement drawn up between them for that purpose. Paul's legal adviser explained that the existence of a partnership can be legally established if a court is satisfied that they were co-owners, they intended to conduct a business (through Paul's suggestion to take paying passengers) and therefore there was an intention to share profits and losses.

Paul's plea that he would rather share the loss in the ratio in which the capital was contributed was also rejected because, in the absence of an agreement to the contrary, partnership law provides that partners should share profits and losses equally. Paul's protest that he did not have any more money to spare was of no avail because his legal adviser pointed out that, as a partner, he had unlimited liability (i.e. responsibility for making good in full his share of the loss) and Peter could seek judgment in the court and pursue him into bankruptcy if he failed to pay the £25,000. The outcome was that Paul had to pay the extra £25,000. The sharing of the loss equally and the situation that necessitated Paul to pay the extra £25,000 would have been accounted for as follows:

LOSS OF BOAT ACCOUNT

	£000		£000
Boat a/c	150	Peter	75
		Paul	75

PARTNERS' CAPITAL ACCOUNTS

	Peter £000	Paul £000		Peter £000	Paul £000
Loss of boat	75	75	Cash a/c	100	50
Balance c/d	25	–	Balance c/d	–	25
Balance b/d	–	25	Balance b/d	25	–

36.2 A PARTNERSHIP AGREEMENT

Although a partnership may well exist without any written agreement among partners, the need for a formalized agreement should be appreciated. This is because the relationship could well become an onerous one for two main reasons. First, each partner assumes unlimited liability for all debts of the business. This means that if the partnership assets prove insufficient to meet in full the partnership debts, each partner is legally regarded as jointly and severally liable to make good the shortfall. This could place in jeopardy the private possessions of each partner. Second, each partner, as an agent of the others, has authority to bind them all into contractual commitments.

In view of these reasons, and for the purpose of avoiding disputes and possible litigation, potential partners are advised to commence their relationship on the basis of a written agreement, known as a **partnership deed.** Ideally the agreement should cover every possible area of dispute that could be foreseen. Under partnership law, an oral agreement or one that may be inferred from past behaviour (referred to as a 'course of dealing') is also equally acceptable. Some of the items that may be beneficially included in such an agreement are stated in the box on the right.

> **A PARTNERSHIP AGREEMENT**
>
> This may usefully include, among other things, the following:
>
> 1. profit sharing arrangements;
> 2. any additional responsibility and rewards;
> 3. the agreed ratio of holding capital balances;
> 4. limitations on partners' drawings, if any;
> 5. authority to change the nature of the business;
> 6. authority to admit a new partner;
> 7. authority to obtain loans and enter contracts;
> 8. requirements on accounts and audits;
> 9. that audited accounts are binding on all.

In the absence of an agreement, profits and losses are shared equally among partners. If they so agree, however, partners may adjust their share of partnership profit to take account of each partner's:

● capital contribution (by allowing interest on respective capital balances);
● effort contribution (by providing for payment of salaries);
● drawings made ahead of the year end (by charging interest on such drawings).

36.3 LEGAL FRAMEWORK OF PARTNERSHIPS

Partnership is a long-established form of business organization that has been governed throughout the 20th and into the 21st century by the Partnership Act 1890. The main provisions of that Act are as follows.

The number of partners

These can be from two to a maximum of 20. Members of certain professions, however (such as accountants, solicitors and stock exchange brokers), have the permission of the Board of Trade to exceed the maximum limit.

Section 24 provisions

Section 24 of the Act applies either when there is no agreement among partners or when the agreement fails to cover any situation. Requirements of section 24 includes those stated in the box on the right.

> Section 24 of the Partnership Act 1890 provides:
> 1. profits and losses are shared equally among partners;
> 2. no salary to be paid to any partner;
> 3. no interest to be allowed on partners' capital balances;
> 4. no interest to be charged on any partner's drawings;
> 5. interest to be allowed on partner's loans at 5 per cent per year;
> 6. every partner shall introduce capital;
> 7. every partner shall partake in management;
> 8. admission of a new partner requires unanimous consent.

Section 42 provisions

Section 42 of the Partnership Act provides that interest should be paid on any amount owing to an outgoing partner, either at 5 per cent p.a. or at such rate as a court would determine as attributable to the use of the assets of the partner concerned.

Arrangements under the Partnership Act 1890 were generally appropriate when partnerships were small and the partners were of the same profession working closely with one another. However, this is no longer always the case. With the growth in the size of partnerships, not all the partners are known personally to one another. In professional partnerships there has been such an increase in litigation for professional negligence that partners' personal assets have been at risk when a claim exceeds the sum of the assets and insurance cover. In view of these developments, the Limited Liability Partnerships (LPP) Act 2000 received Royal Assent in July 2000. This Bill creates an additional form of business entity with limited liability. In many respects the new entity will be similar to a company but with the organizational flexibility of a partnership. An LLP will be incorporated by registering an incorporation document with the Registrar of Companies showing the entity's name, its registered office and the names of the partners. On incorporation, an LLP would, like a company, have a legal personality and limitation of liability, but, unlike a company, would not have to divorce management from ownership.

36.4 PARTNERS' CAPITAL AND CURRENT ACCOUNTS

Partners normally draw out monies for their personal use during the year in anticipation of profits being agreed at the end of the year. This means that there is a potential risk that individual partners might draw out monies that exceed their share of the potential profit. The effect of this would be twofold: first, a partner may unwittingly draw out monies that had been contributed as capital; second, excessive drawings may deplete the partnership working capital to levels lower than what may be regarded as satisfactory. As a precaution against this, partners usually agree that capital contributions should be recorded in a *Capital account* and that such amount should not normally be regarded as available for their withdrawal until the partnership is dissolved.

To demarcate the amounts that partners may feel free to draw out at will, such amounts are recorded in a *Current account*. For example, the profit when determined annually is transferred from the Profit and Loss (Appropriation) account to each partner's Current account. Amounts drawn by partners from time to time are posted to the debit of the Current account. If partners do not withdraw each year the whole of their share of the profits, a credit balance will accumulate on the Current account.

Interaction 36.1	**Sharing profits among partners**

Jack and Jill are in business as partners, without any formal agreement. They extracted their Trial Balance on the last day of their accounting period as stated on the right.

Required: Record the year's profit as well as drawings in the partners' accounts, and set out the Balance Sheet as at 30 June 20X0.

TRIAL BALANCE AS AT 30.6.20X0	£000	£000
Fixed assets	840	–
Depreciation – 30.6.20X0	–	380
Stock on 30.6.20X0	648	–
Debtors and creditors	584	596
Profit for the year		260
Drawings – Jack	35	–
Drawings – Jill	16	–
Capital account – Jack	–	600
Capital account – Jill	–	300
Cash and bank	13	–
	2,136	2,136

36.5 APPROPRIATION OF PROFIT AND CHARGE AGAINST PROFIT

A partner may carry out a role as a partner for which he receives a proportion of the profit after all expenses have been deducted from the partnership income – this is known as an *appropriation* of profit. A partner may also carry out a role in a capacity other than as a partner. Payment by the partnership for such an extra role is treated as an expense of the partnership and is therefore a 'charge' when ascertaining the partnership profit.

The profit in a partnership organization is the amount available to be shared among partners in their capacity as a partner. Each partner, in the capacity of a partner, is expected to play three roles, namely to:

- **contribute capital** – although the amount each contributes is left to their mutual agreement and it need not be in equal amounts, nor need it necessarily be in the form of cash.

- **participate in management** – although in real life a partner excused from management responsibility is referred to as a 'sleeping partner', such an arrangement is

not recognized by law and a sleeping partner remains fully liable for the debts of the partnership.
● **share the risk** involved in running the business and share the rewards.

The agreement might provide for each of these three activities to be rewarded out of the operating profit in different proportions. For example, partners might receive interest on capital to recognize different levels of capital contribution; they might receive a salary to recognize different levels of management commitment; and they might receive different proportions of profit to recognize the different degrees to which they generate income for the partnership. A reward earned by a partner in relation to any of these three roles (by way of interest on the capital, salary for management services and a share of residual profit) is a share of the partnership profit. Sharing of the partnership profit is known (as stated above) as 'appropriation'.

In contrast, should a partner assume an extra role, the reward for such a role is regarded as an expenditure (a charge) to be deducted before determining the profit of the partnership. Additional roles that a partner might assume include acting as:

● a landlord, providing business premises to the partnership and earning rent;
● a money lender, giving a loan to the partnership and earning interest;
● the owner of a patent or copyright who has assigned the rights to the partnership and earns royalties.

Distinguishing a charge from an appropriation

Interaction 36.2

Tom, Dick and Harriet are partners sharing profits and losses in the ratio 2:1:1 respectively, after allowing Tom a salary of £3,000 per month and interest on fixed capital balances at 6 per cent per annum. The Trial Balance extracted on the last day of the accounting period is stated on the right.

You are also informed as follows:

(a) Stock as at 31.3.20X1 has been ascertained as £412,000.
(b) Dick, as owner of the premises, is to receive a rent of £4,000 per month.
(c) The Salaries account includes an amount of £30,000 paid as salary to Tom.
(d) Depreciation is to be written off at 20 per cent per annum using the reducing balance method.

Required: Prepare a Trading and Profit and Loss for the year ended 31.3.20X1 and a Balance Sheet as at that date, showing the partners' Capital accounts separately from current accounts.

TRIAL BALANCE AS AT 31.3.20X1		
	£000	£000
Fixed assets	640	
Depreciation – 31.3.20X0		300
Stock – 31.3.20X0	365	
Rent paid to Dick	40	
Salaries	214	
Interest paid to Tom	9	
Debtors and creditors	544	428
Purchases	2,172	
Postage and telephone	32	
Sales		3,096
Advertising	165	
Current accounts – Tom		126
Dick		34
Harriet	12	
12% loan from Tom		100
Cash and bank balance	92	
Other admin. expenses	349	
Capital account – Tom		300
Dick		150
Harriet		100
	4,634	4,634

36.6 INTEREST ON PARTNERS' DRAWINGS

If a partner makes drawings during the year, it may be agreed among the partners that interest should be charged at an agreed rate, from the date of the drawing until the year end. This discourages partners from drawing out partnership resources prior to the year end and it is also fair as between the partners.

Partners' drawings at irregular intervals

For illustration of this scenario, let us assume that the accounting period ends on 31 December, that partners agree to charge interest on drawings at 6 per cent per year and that a partner draws £5,000 on 1 March. Interest of £250 (£5,000 × 6/100 × 10/12) is charged on the partner by debiting the respective Current account and crediting the Appropriation account. Individual calculations such as these have to be made in respect of each amount drawn if drawings are at irregular intervals.

Partners drawing a consistent amount and at regular intervals

If a partner draws the same amount at regular intervals, interest may be calculated on the total amount drawn for the *average* period. For example, if partner X draws £3,000 per month consistently on the first day of each month, the total amount drawn in the year would be £36,000. Assuming that the year ends on 31 December, the average period for which these drawings would have been outstanding is calculated as follows.

The first amount, drawn on 1 January, would have been outstanding for 12 months, the second for 11 months and so on until the last, drawn on 1 December, would have been outstanding for one month. Hence 12 + 11 + 10 + 9 + 8 + 7 + 6 + 5 + 4 + 3 + 2 + 1 = 78 divided by 12 separate drawings gives an average period outstanding of 6.5 months. Interest is therefore charged on £36,000 at whatever rate has been agreed for the average period of 6.5 months.

Similarly, if a regular amount is drawn on the last day of each month, the average period works out to 5.5 months; and if the drawing is halfway through each month, the average period works out to six months exactly.

Interaction 36.3	**Calculation of interest on partners' drawings**

Sun, Moon and Star are partners who make up their accounts to 31 December each year. Their agreement provides that interest is chargeable on their drawings at 6 per cent per annum.

Required: Determine the amount of interest to be charged in respect of each partner's drawings in each of the following three scenarios:

SCENARIO (1): Sun draws £5,000 on 31.3.20X0, Moon draws £8,000 on 1.7.20X0 and Star draws £20,000 on 1.8.20X0 and £6,000 more on 1.10.20X0.

SCENARIO (2): Sun, Moon and Star each draw £2,000 per month regularly, Sun drawing on the first day of each month, Moon drawing on the last day of each month and Star in the middle of each month.

SCENARIO (3): Sun drew £4,000 per month on the first day of each month, up to and including 1 September 20X0. Moon drew £5,000 per month, on the last day of each month, commencing on 31.3.20X0. Star drew regularly throughout the year at the middle of each month, but the amount drawn was £2,000 per month until 15.6.20X0 and £3,000 per month thereafter.

36.6.1 Accounting for interest on partners' drawings

The interest charged on partners' drawings is not an additional earning for the partnership. It is merely a device used to ensure that, when profits are shared, the extent of their drawings is taken into account. To illustrate, let us assume that a partnership business earns a profit of £300,000 in the year and the partners A, B and C have agreed to share profits equally. Let us assume also that during the year the drawings of A, B and C were £25,000, £5,000 and £12,500 respectively and the interest on the drawings is calculated as £800 for A, £200 for B and £500 for C. The appropriation of the year's profit would be as shown on the right and the partners' Current accounts as shown below:

PROFIT AND LOSS (APPROPRIATION) ACCOUNT

	£		£
Profit share:		Profit b/d	300,000
A	100,500	Interest on drawing:	
B	100,500	A	800
C	100,500	B	200
		C	500

PARTNERS' CURRENT ACCOUNT

	A	B	C		A	B	C
Cash book	25,000	5,000	12,500	Profit for the year	100,500	100,500	100,500
Interest on drawing	800	200	500				

What we should appreciate is that the net amount shared among the partners is no more than £300,000, which is the net profit of the partnership for the year.

	A	B	C	Total
Profit share	100,500	100,500	100,500	301,500
Interest charged	(800)	(200)	(500)	(1,500)
Net amount	99,700	100,300	100,000	300,000

36.7 A JOINT-LIFE POLICY ON PARTNERS

The amount of the partnership net assets owned by each partner would be the sum of the balances of their Current and Capital accounts. Should the partnership ever have to pay off a partner's interest in the business (for example, when a partner dies or retires) the business could experience a severe strain on its resource base. To provide for such an eventuality it is common for partners to take out a life policy jointly on the lives of all partners. The premium is paid by the business. This action should ensure that the life policy, maturing on the death of any one partner, provides sufficient resources to pay off the deceased partner's interests. The payment of the premium, however, can be a significant financial commitment to the partnership and accounting for the premium deserves special attention.

The partnership has a choice of three methods for accounting for the premium. These are as follows:

- **The life policy is capitalized.** Since the premium paid is realizable on the maturity of the policy or its earlier surrender, the annual premium is regarded as an asset and accordingly capitalized (i.e. cash is credited and the Life Policy account is debited with no charge to the Profit and Loss account). The advantage of this method is that it reports the life policy as an asset on the Balance Sheet. The disadvantage is that (because the cash outflow is not reckoned as an expense when determining the profit for the year) the capital base of the entity tends to get eroded year after year by the amount of the life policy premium paid in that year, if partners draw out the whole amount of the profit available for appropriation.
- **The annual premiums are written off.** Treating the annual premium as an expenditure safeguards the capital from erosion because the profit available for appropriation is reduced by the amount of the premium. However, the disadvantage is that the asset (i.e. the life policy) is not reported on the Balance Sheet.
- **A Life Policy Fund is maintained.** The annual premium is capitalized and at the same time an equal amount is appropriated from the profit to a reserve (which is usually named the Life Policy Fund) for the purpose of protecting the capital base from erosion. A reserve or a provision is known as a 'Fund' when it is represented by an investment of equivalent amount outside the entity. When, in the course of time, the life policy matures or is surrendered, the credit balance in the Life Policy Fund is appropriated among the partners, just as any reserve would be. A variation of this method is to adjust annually the value of the asset (the life policy) to its surrender value on that date, by crediting or debiting the difference to the Life Policy Fund account.

Interaction 36.4 — Accounting for a joint life policy

Rook and Raven, equal partners, draw out all of their share of the profits each year. On 1.1.20X0 they took out a joint life policy at an agreed annual premium of £30,000. The Trial Balance as at 31.12.20X0 is shown on right. The business requires a working capital of not less than £200,000. Depreciation is to be ignored.

Required: Account for the life policy using each of the three alternative methods available for the purpose.

TRIAL BALANCE AS AT 31.12.20X0	£000	£000
Fixed assets at cost	300	
Profit for the year		210
Net current assets	380	
Capital – Rook		250
Capital – Raven		250
Life policy premium	30	
	710	710

36.8 THE ADMISSION OF A NEW PARTNER

When a new partner is admitted there are a number of considerations relating to changes in the existing partners' profit-sharing arrangements and establishing a fair net asset figure for the existing partners at the date of admission. These include questions such as: What percentage share of the profit is the new partner to receive?; How will this affect the percentage shares of the existing partners?; Is the new partner given any guarantee as to the minimum monetary profit entitlement? (This last is of particular interest when a manager, taken into partnership, needs to maintain a base level of income.)

36.8.1 **Revision of existing partners' profit sharing ratios**

When a partner is admitted to a share of profit, the new profit-sharing ratio among all partners should be mutually agreed. It is usual to assume that the remainder is shared among the continuing partners in the ratio in which they shared profits until then. For example, let us assume that A and B, who shared profits in the ratio 2:1 respectively, admit C to a fourth share of the profit. Assuming that the quarter share of profit was given to C by A and B in the ratio 2:1 respectively, the new profit-sharing ratio of A, B and C is determined as follows:

A: 2/3 less (2/3rd of 1/4th)   = 6/12 = 1/2
B: 1/3 less (1/3rd of 1/4th)   = 3/12 = 1/4
C: (2/3rd of 1/4th from A) plus (1/3rd of 1/4th from B) = 3/12 = 1/4

Simplified, A, B and C will, from now on, share profits in the ratio 2:1:1 respectively, i.e. the relationship between A and B is still 2:1.

36.8.2 **Where the admission is during the currency of an accounting period**

If there is a change in the number of partners (or the ratio of their profit sharing) during the course of an accounting period, it becomes necessary to determine the profit or loss up to the date of change separately from that of the period thereafter. It becomes necessary, therefore, to prepare two separate Profit and Loss accounts in respect of that accounting period. The preparation of two Trading accounts is, however, not possible unless the stock in hand on the date of the change is ascertainable. The alternative is to prepare a single Trading account for the whole accounting period (as usual) and apportion the gross profit between the periods prior to and after admission of the new partner, preferably on the basis of sales reported in respect of each.

36.8.3 **Where the new partner is given a minimum income guarantee**

As an inducement to accepting the partnership, either the firm or one of the current partners may guarantee the incoming partner's income from the partnership at a specified amount per year. For illustration let us assume that C had previously been a manager with the partnership and was admitted to a quarter share of profit on 1 September on a guarantee that his share of partnership profit would not be less than £18,000 per year; and further assume that during the year ended 31 December his share of the partnership profit was £1,000 as interest on capital and £3,000 as a share of the profit. Thus C's share of partnership profit is £4,000 as against a guarantee in respect of four months of partnership of £6,000. The shortfall of £2,000 is therefore credited to C's Current account and debited to the Current account of the partner (or partners) who gave the guarantee.

Admission of a new partner within an accounting period

Penny and Sally shared profits in the ratio 3:2 respectively, after allowing Penny a salary of £2,000 per month and interest on partners' fixed capitals at 6 per cent per annum. They admitted Molly to a sixth share of profits from 1.10.20X1 on the following terms:

- Salary to Penny and the interest on the capital balances are to continue.
- Molly's share of income from the partnership is guaranteed by Penny at £120,000 per annum.

You are informed further as follows:

(a) Stock on 31.12.20X1 was £586,000.
(b) Sales in each month after Molly's admission to partnership were 50 per cent better than they had been in each month prior to her admission.
(c) Motor vehicles and furniture are to be depreciated on the reducing balance method at 20 per cent and 10 per cent p.a. respectively.

Required: Prepare the Trading and Profit and Loss account for the year to 31.12.20X1 and the Balance Sheet as at that date.

TRIAL BALANCE AS AT 31.12.20X1		
	£	£
Motor vehicles	320	–
Acc. depreciation	–	170
Furniture	280	–
Acc. depreciation	–	120
Stock – 31.12.20X0	524	–
Salaries	288	–
Rent	48	–
Advertising	72	–
Sales	–	3,159
Drawings – Penny	50	–
Drawings – Sally	28	–
Debtors/Creditors	752	514
Other admin. exp.	96	–
Capital – Penny	–	500
Capital – Sally	–	300
Capital – Molly	–	200
Cash and bank	241	–
Purchases	2,264	–
	4,963	4,963

36.8.4 Where a continuing partner is given a negative guarantee

It may well happen that, at the point of admission of a new partner, one of the continuing partners may give a guarantee to another continuing partner that in the event that the new partner's annual share of partnership profit exceeds a specified amount, the whole of such excess would be borne by the one giving the guarantee.

A negative guarantee

Required: Answer IQ 36.5 again, this time assuming that the guarantee is worded as follows: Penny guaranteed to Sally that if Molly's share of annual income from the partnership exceeded £100,000, then Penny would bear the whole of the excess.

36.8.5 Establishing a fair net asset figure at date of admission

Partnerships frequently maintain fixed assets in their books at depreciated cost, which do not fairly reflect their market value as at the date of admission of a new partner. Where, at the point of admission of a partner, an asset remains fully or partly unrecorded in the books of the partnership, an appropriate adjustment becomes necessary to safeguard the interest of the continuing partners. An unrecorded asset represents unrealized (and hence unaccounted for) earnings that, if not adjusted for, would be prejudicial to the interests of those whose share of partnership profit is adversely affected by any variation in profit-sharing arrangements. One example of such an unrecorded asset is a life policy, where the premium paid for the policy had been treated as an expenditure year after year. This, and further examples of unrecorded assets and the method of adjusting for them, will be explained in Chapter 37.

Reference

1. *Davis v. Davis* (1894) 1 Ch. 393.

SOLUTIONS TO INTERACTIVE QUESTIONS

IQ 36.1 Sharing profits among partners

PARTNERSHIP (APPROPRIATION) ACCOUNT

	£000
Profit for the year	260
Current accounts:	
Jack	(130)
Jill	(130)

BALANCE SHEET AS AT 30.6.20X0

		£000
Fixed assets	840	
Accum. depreciation	(380)	460
Stock in trade	648	
Debtors	584	
Cash and bank	13	
Creditor	(596)	649
		1,109
Capital – Jack	600	
Jill	300	900
Current a/c – Jack	95	
Jill	114	209
		1,109

PARTNERS' CURRENT ACCOUNTS

	Jack £000	Jill £000		Jack £000	Jill £000
Drawings	35	16	P&L a/c	130	130
Balance c/d	95	114			
			Balance b/d	95	114

PARTNERS' CAPITAL ACCOUNTS

	Jack £000	Jill £000		Jack £000	Jill £000
			Cash a/c	600	300

IQ 36.2 Distinguishing a charge from an appropriation

PARTNERS' CURRENT ACCOUNTS

	Tom £000	Dick £000	Harriet £000		Tom £000	Dick £000	Harriet £000
Balance b/f	–	–	12	Balance b/f	126	34	–
Salaries a/c	30	–	–	Rent a/c	–	8	–
				Interest a/c	3	–	–
				P&L (appropriation)			
				Salary	36	–	–
				Interest on capital	18	9	6
Balance c/d	175	62	5	Share of profit	22	11	11

TRADING AND PROFIT AND LOSS ACCOUNT FOR THE YEAR ENDED 31 MARCH 20X1		
		£000
Sales		3,096
Stock 1.4.20X0	(365)	
Purchases	(2,172)	
Stock 30.3.20X1	412	(2,125)
Gross profit		971
Distribution cost		
Advertising		(165)
Administrative expenses		
Salaries	184	
Rent	48	
Depreciation	68	
Postage and telephone	32	
Other admin. expenses	349	(681)
Interest on loan		(12)
Profit for the year		113
Salary to Tom		(36)
Interest on capital:		
Tom	(18)	
Dick	(9)	
Harriet	(6)	(33)
Profit share – Tom	(22)	
Dick	(11)	
Harriet	(11)	(44)

BALANCE SHEET AS AT 31.3.20X1		
		£000
Fixed assets	640	
Acc. Depreciation	(368)	272
Current assets:		
Stock in trade	412	
Debtors	544	
Cash and bank	92	
Creditors	(428)	620
		892
		£000
Capital accounts: Tom	300	
Dick	150	
Harriet	100	550
Current accounts: Tom	175	
Dick	62	
Harriet	5	242
Loan from Tom		100
		892

Note: The salary drawn by Tom (£30,000) is treated as drawings and transferred to the debit of his Current account, which is in turn credited with his salary entitlement when profits are appropriated. Alternatively, £30,000 could have been transferred to a Partner's Salary account, adjusted for the amount accrued of £6,000, before the balance of £36,000 in that account is debited to the Profit and Loss (Appropriation) account.

IQ 36.3 Calculation of interest on partners' drawings

SCENARIO ONE	Sun: £5,000 @ 6% for nine months		= £225
	Moon: £8,000 @ 6% for six months		= £240
	Star: £20,000 @ 6% for five months	£500	
	plus £6,000 @ 6% for three months	£90 =	£590
SCENARIO TWO	Sun: £24,000 @ 6% × 6.5 months		= £780
	Moon: £24,000 @ 6% × 5.5 months		= £660
	Star: £24,000 @ 6% × 6 months		= £720
SCENARIO THREE	Sun: £36,000 @ 6% × (12 + 4/2 =) 8 months		= £1,440
	Moon: £50,000 @ 6% x (9 × 0/2 =) 4.5 months		= £1,125
	Star: £12,000 @ 6% × (11.5 + 6.5/2 =) 9 months	£540	
	£18,000 @ 6% × (5.5 + 0.5/2 =) 3 months	£270 =	£810

IQ 36.4 Accounting for a joint life policy

(a) The life policy is capitalized

P&L APPROPRIATION A/C

	£000
Profit for the year	210
Rook Current a/c	(105)
Raven Current a/c	(105)

NET CURRENT ASSETS

	£000		£000
Balance	380	Rook	105
		Raven	105
		Balance	170
Balance	170		

BALANCE SHEET AS AT 31.12.20X0

	£000
Fixed asset	300
Life policy	30
Net current asset	170
	500

	£000
Capital – Rook	250
Raven	250
	500

PARTNERS' CURRENT ACCOUNT

	Rook £000	Raven £000		Rook £000	Raven £000
Cash a/c	105	105	P&L (approp)	105	105

Note: Year after year, the amount of the premium erodes the net current assets (i.e. working capital).

(b) Annual premiums are written off

P&L (APPROPRIATION) A/C

	£000
Profit for the year	210
Life policy	(30)
	180
Rook Current a/c	(90)
Raven Current a/c	(90)

NET CURRENT ASSETS

	£000		£000
Balance b/d	380	Rook	90
		Raven	90
		Balance c/d	200
Balance b/d	200		

BALANCE SHEET AS AT 31.12.20X0

	£000
Fixed assets	300
Net current asset	200
	500

	£000
Capital – Rook	250
Raven	250
	500

PARTNERS' CURRENT ACCOUNTS

	Rook £000	Raven £000		Rook £000	Raven £000
Cash a/c	90	90	P&L appr.	90	90

Note: Net current assets are no longer eroded by the amount of annual life policy premium; but an asset (the life policy) is not reported on the Balance Sheet.

(c) A Life Policy Fund is established

P&L (APPROPRIATION) A/C			
	£000		
Profit for the year	210		
Life Policy Fund	(30)		
	180		
Rook Current a/c	(90)		
Raven Current a/c	(90)		

NET CURRENT ASSETS			
	£000		**£000**
Balance b/d	380	Rook	90
		Raven	90
		Balance c/d	200
Balance b/d	200		

BALANCE SHEET AS AT 31.12.20X0	
	£000
Fixed assets	300
Life policy	30
Net current asset	200
	530
	£000
Capital – Rook	250
Raven	250
Life Policy Fund	30
	530

PARTNERS' CURRENT ACCOUNTS

	Rook £000	Raven £000		Rook £000	Raven £000
Cash a/c	90	90	P&L appr.	90	90

Note: The life policy is reported as an asset on the Balance Sheet and yet the net current assets are not eroded annually by the amount of the premium.

IQ 36.5 Admission of a new partner within an accounting period

1. Assuming that Penny and Sally gave one-sixth of partnership profit in the ratio in which they shared profits between them, the new profit-sharing ratio would be as follows:

> **Penny: 3/5th of 5/6th = 3/6 = 1/2**
> **Sally: 2/5th of 5/6th = 2/6 = 1/3**
> **Molly:** = 1/6

2. If sales in each month up to September was 2 units, the sales in each month thereafter would have been 3 units. Therefore the ratio of turnover would be as follows:

> **January to September: 9 months @ 2 = 18**
> **October to December: 3 months @ 3 = 9**

Thus the ratio of sales in the period prior to and after admission is 2:1 respectively. The gross profit as well as distribution costs are apportioned between the two periods in the turnover ratio. Administrative expenses are apportioned on the time basis as 3:1.

3. Molly receives £3,000 as interest and £25,000 as a share of profit making, making £28,000 in respect of the three months of partnership; and the corresponding amount Penny guaranteed was £30,000. Hence the shortfall of £2,000 is credited to Molly and debited to Penny.

PARTNERS' CURRENT ACCOUNTS

	Penny £000	Sally £000	Molly £000		Penny £000	Sally £000	Molly £000
Drawings	50	28	–	Up to 30.9.20X1:			
Molly – guarantee	2	–	–	Salary	18	–	–
Balance c/f	186	113	30	Interest on capital	22.5	13.5	–
				Share of profit	108	72	–
				After 30.9.20X1:			
				Salary	6	–	–
				Interest on capital	7.5	4.5	3
				Share of profit	76	51	25
				Penny – guarantee	–	–	2

TRADING AND PROFIT AND LOSS ACCOUNT FOR THE YEAR ENDED 31.12.20X1

	£000	£000	£000	£000
Sales				3,159
Stock – 31.12.20X0		524		
Purchases		2,264		
Stock – 31.12.20X1			(586)	(2,202)
Gross profit for the year				957
Apportioned on turnover basis		638		319
Distribution cost:				
Depreciation – vehicles	(20)		(10)	
Advertising	(48)	(68)	(24)	(34)
Administrative expense:				
Salaries	(216)		(72)	
Rent	(36)		(12)	
Depreciation – furniture	(12)		(4)	
Other admin. expense	(72)	(336)	(24)	(112)
Profit		234		173
Salary to Penny		(18)		(6)
Interest on capital:				
Penny	(22.5)		(7.5)	
Sally	(13.5)		(4.5)	
Molly	–	(36)	(3.0)	(15)
Profit – Penny	(108)		(76)	
Sally	(72)		(51)	
Molly	–	(180)	(25)	(152)

BALANCE SHEET AS AT 31.12.20X1

			£000
FIXED ASSETS			
Furniture	280	(136)	144
Motor vehicles	320	(200)	120
CURRENT ASSETS:			
Stock in trade		586	
Debtors		752	
Cash & bank		241	
Creditors		(514)	1,065
			1,329
			£000
Capital – Penny		500	
Sally		300	
Molly		200	1,000
Current – Penny		186	
Sally		113	
Molly		30	329
			1,329

IQ 36.6 A negative guarantee

In terms of the guarantee given to Sally, Molly's income within the three months of partnership should not exceed £25,000, whereas Molly receives £28,000. The excess of £3,000 should therefore be borne by Penny. If Molly's income had been sealed off at £25,000, Penny and Sally would have shared the excess of £3,000 in the ratio 3:2 respectively. Thus, by failing to seal off Molly's income, Penny has already lost 3/5th of £3,000. In terms of the guarantee, Penny has to take over from Sally the remaining 2/5th of £3,000 = £1,200.

PARTNERS' CURRENT ACCOUNTS

	Penny £000	Sally £000	Molly £000		Penny £000	Sally £000	Molly £000
Drawings	50	28	–	*Up to 30.9.20X1:*			
Sally – guarantee	1.2	–	–	Salary	18	–	–
Balance c/f	186.8	114.2	28	Interest on capital	22.5	13.5	–
				Share of profit	108	72	–
				After 30.9.20X1:			
				Salary	6	–	–
				Interest on capital	7.5	4.5	3
				Share of profit	76	51	25
				Penny – guarantee	–	1.2	–

PROGRESSIVE QUESTIONS

PQ 36.1 Ascertaining each partner's share of profit

Heron, Pelican and Stork, in partnership, fared as stated below in respect of the year ended 30 June 20X1:

Partners	Salary*	Loan interest*	Rent	Drawings	Interest on drawings*	Interest on capital*	Residual profit*
Heron	£12,000	–	–	£30,000	£600	£36,000	£85,815
Pelican	£18,000	–	£36,000	£24,000	£360	£24,000	£57,210
Stork	£6,000	£24,000		£18,600	£186	£18,000	£28,605

* These amounts were determined in accordance with the partnership agreement.

Required:

(a) Set out the appropriation account for the year ended 30 June 20X1.
(b) Set out the journal entry to give effect to each of the following alternative guarantees:
   ● Heron has guaranteed Stork's share of partnership profit at £60,000 per year.
   ● Heron has given a guarantee to Pelican that if Stork's share of profit exceeds £40,000 per year the whole of the excess will be borne by Heron.

PQ 36.2 An introductory question on partnership appropriation

Senkoro, Kibona and Msusa are partners, sharing profits and losses equally after allowing Senkoro a salary at £1,000 per month and interest on fixed capitals at 12 per cent per annum. They extracted their Trial Balance on 31 December 20X1 as shown here.

You are also informed as follows:

(a) Stock on 31.12.20X1 is ascertained at £25,570.
(b) Stock costing £6,250, removed by Senkoro for own use, and others costing £2,400 gifted to Msusa on the occasion of his wedding, are still to be accounted for. The sale prices of these goods were £7,500 and £3,000 respectively.
(c) Rent of the business premises, owned by Msusa, has been agreed at £800 per month.
(d) Motor vehicles and furniture are depreciated using the reducing balance method at 20 per cent and 10 per cent per annum respectively.

Required: Prepare the Trading and Profit and Loss account of the partnership for the year ended 31 December 20X1, and prepare the Balance Sheet as at that date, along with the Current accounts of the partners.

TRIAL BALANCE AS AT 31.12.20X1		
	£	£
Motor vehicles	348,500	88,500
Furniture and fittings	196,600	101,600
Stock on 31.12.20X0	78,450	–
Purchases	416,500	–
Sales	–	744,600
Salary to Senkoro	11,000	–
Rent paid to Msusa	6,000	–
Vehicle maintenance	24,600	–
Staff salaries	96,500	–
Debtors/Creditors	100,250	91,550
Advertising	4,850	–
Drawing – Senkoro	4,000	–
– Kibona	8,000	–
– Msusa	6,000	–
Stationery	640	–
Telephone/postage	1,860	–
Heat and light	1,250	–
Loan from Kibona	–	50,000
Current a/c – Senkoro	–	14,650
Kibona	–	8,200
Msusa	3,650	–
Sundry expenses	11,270	–
Capital a/c – Senkoro	–	100,000
Kibona	–	100,000
Msusa	–	40,000
Cash and bank	19,180	–
	1,339,100	1,339,100

PQ 36.3 Deciding whether a charge on profit or an appropriation

Mark, John and Mathew, partners in a business as publishers and retailers of books, have agreed as follows:

(a) Mark, as the printshop manager, receives a salary of £36,000 p.a., while John and Mathew, as the administrative manager and the sales manager respectively, receive £24,000 each.

(b) Interest at 6 per cent p.a. is to be allowed on the partners' capital balances, which are to remain fixed as stated in the box.

Mark	£200,000
John	£300,000
Mathew	£250,000

(c) John, himself a best-selling author, is paid a royalty of £1 per copy of his book sold.

(d) Mathew, as owner of the shop premises, is paid rent at £2,000 per month.

(e) Interest on a £40,000 loan obtained from John is agreed at 10 per cent per annum.

(f) No interest is to be charged on drawings.

(g) Mark, John and Mathew share profits and losses in the ratio 1:2:2 respectively.

A draft Trading and Profit and Loss account for the year ended 31 March 20X1 has been prepared as shown here.

Required: Explain why the Profit and Loss account is unsatisfactory, and to re-draft the Trading and Profit and Loss account for the year ended 31.3.20X1.

TRADING AND PROFIT AND LOSS ACCOUNT FOR THE YEAR ENDED 31 MARCH 20X1

	£000	£000	£000
Sales			1,640
Stock of publications – 1.4.20X0		280	
Printing costs	734		
Publishing expenses	78		
Royalty to authors	133		
Mark's salary	36	981	
Stock of publications – 31.3.20X1		(315)	(946)
Gross profit			694
ADMINISTRATIVE EXPENSES:			
Staff salaries		(178)	
Postage/telephone		(14)	
Lighting/heating		(11)	
Business rates		(13)	
Other administ. expenses		(72)	
John's salary		(24)	(312)
DISTRIBUTION COST:			
Advertising		(64)	
Carriage outwards		(45)	
Bad debts		(20)	
Mathew's salary		(24)	(153)
PROFIT FOR THE YEAR			229
Royalty to John			(16)
Interest on John's Loan			(4)
Rent paid to Mathew			(24)
Interest on capital – Mark		(12)	
John		(18)	
Mathew		(15)	(45)
Profit share – Mark		(28)	
John		(56)	
Mathew		(56)	(140)

PQ 36.4 Partnership appropriations including a guarantee

Tom and Dick were in partnership, sharing profits and losses in the ratio 3:1 respectively, on the basis of an agreement that provided for interest at 8 per cent p.a. on the fixed capital balances and at 6 per cent p.a. on drawings and for a salary to Tom of £24,000 p.a. Dick is paid rent at £3,000 per month. Harry, their shop manager, was paid a salary of £18,000 p.a. and interest at 12 per cent p.a. on a loan of £50,000 that he had provided to the partnership.

On 1.10.20X1 Harry was admitted to a fifth share of the partnership on the basis of the following agreement:

(a) Tom continues to receive the salary as hitherto.

(b) Interest on capital and drawings is to continue.

(c) Harry's loan is to be treated as his capital.

(d) No adjustment is to be made for goodwill.

(e) Harry's share of income from the partnership is guaranteed by Tom at £24,000 p.a.

The Trial Balance extracted from the partnership books on 31.12.20X1 appears as shown here. You are further informed as follows:

(a) Stock on 31.12.20X1 is ascertained as £134,100.
(b) Goods costing £30,000 donated to charity are still to be accounted for.
(c) The Salaries account includes the salary drawn by Harry until he became a partner and Tom's full year salary.
(d) Motor vehicles and furniture are depreciated using the reducing balance method at 20 per cent and 10 per cent p.a. respectively.
(e) In addition to the salary, Tom and Dick draw £1,000 each per month regularly, Tom drawing on the first day of each month and Dick on the last day.
(f) Unless indicated otherwise, it may be assumed that all income and expenditure have accrued consistently throughout the year.

Required: Prepare the Trading and Profit and Loss account for the year ended 31 December 20X1 and the Balance Sheet as at that date.

TRIAL BALANCE AS AT 31.12.20X1		
	£	£
Motor vehicles	96,000	30,000
Furniture & fixture	44,000	24,000
Stock – 31.12.20X0	116,500	–
Rent	30,000	–
Salaries	157,500	–
Purchases	668,900	–
Sales	–	994,800
Drawings – Tom	12,000	–
Dick	12,000	–
Loan from Harry	–	50,000
Debtors/Creditors	246,800	164,000
Interest on loan	3,000	–
Administr. expense	62,400	–
Advertising	6,000	–
Capital – Tom	–	120,000
Dick	–	80,000
Cash/bank	7,700	–

PQ 36.5 Partnership appropriation with a negative guarantee

Answer PQ 36.4 again but with two amendments as follows:

● Paragraph (e) in the Partnership Agreement after Harry's admission is amended to read as follows: Tom guarantees to Dick that if Harry's income from the partnership exceeds £36,000 p.a., the whole of the excess will be borne by Tom.
● Paragraph (f) of the information is amended to read as follows: Sales in each month after Harry's admission to the partnership were 50 per cent better than those in each of the earlier months.

PQ 36.6 Reappropriation of profits among partners

G. Ebb and T. Flow were in partnership sharing profits and losses in the ratio 2:1 respectively, until 31.12.20X0 when K. Wave was admitted to a fourth share of profit. As from 1.1.20X2 it is agreed that the three partners should share profits and losses equally. During the audit of the accounts for the year ended 31.12.20X2, the following errors have been detected:

(a) Because of an error in the stocktaking procedure, the stock in hand on 31.12.20X0 was understated by £26,000, whereas the stock positions on 31.12.20X1 and on 31.12.20X2 were overstated by £13,000 and £36,800 respectively.
(b) Goods usually sold by the business for £20,000 (at cost plus one-third) were gifted to Flow on the occasion of her marriage, in May 20X2. The gift was accounted for by crediting the Sales account with £20,000 and debiting a Wedding Gift account, which was then treated as an expenditure in 20X2.
(c) Freehold premises, acquired by the partnership for £360,000 on 1.1.20X0, were never depreciated. Warned of the activities of the Financial Reporting Review Panel, the partners wish to depreciate the buildings on the straight-line method, assuming for convenience that one-third of the cost relates to land and that the buildings have a useful economic life of 50 years.
(d) A mainframe computer acquired for £12,000 on 1.7.20X0 was written off in the same year. Since the computer continues in use, the partners agree that it should have been capitalized and depreciated using the straight-line method at 20 per cent per annum.
(e) The nature of the business is such that significant amounts are written off as bad debts from year to year. Yet no Provision for Doubtful Debts account has ever been maintained. It is now felt that, for a more accurate determination of performance in each year, a Provision for Doubtful Debts account should be maintained at 10 per cent of debtors outstanding on the last day of each accounting period. Information needed for this purpose is stated in the box.

Debtors as at	Bad debts in year to
31.12.X0	£260,000	£21,000
31.12.X1	£220,000	£27,000
31.12.X2	£360,000	£33,000

You have been requested by the partners to pass a journal entry as at 31 December 20X2 so as to rectify the above errors, ensuring that the effect of the rectification affects the partners in accordance with their respective profit-sharing ratios in the year to which the error relates.

## Chapter 37

PARTNERSHIP ACCOUNTS (2): UNRECORDED ASSETS

In this chapter

We will learn of:

- the need to make adjustments for any asset remaining unrecorded whenever there is a change in the profit-sharing arrangements among partners

and you should be able to:

- account for any change in profit-sharing arrangements, whether or not it arises from the admission, retirement or death of a partner

37.1 ADJUSTMENT FOR UNRECORDED ASSETS

The fair value of an asset is the amount at which that asset could be sold at arms length in the market. Assets may not be reported in the accounts of a business at their fair value for a number of reasons, such as those stated below:

- The assets are reported (as is common) at depreciated historical cost or at an out-of-date valuation.
- The assets are not reported at all because payments for the asset have been written off as an expense. An example of this is an unrecorded life policy, where the annual premiums have been written off in the year the payments are made.
- The asset has arisen not from a transaction (i.e. paid for) but as a consequence of advantages such as business location, its profitability, or customer loyalty, which together are referred to as '*goodwill*'.

It is important for partners to appreciate that an asset remaining unrecorded implies that the corresponding gain remains unrecognized. Furthermore, they need to recognize that, whenever there is a change in profit-sharing arrangements among partners, unless an unrecognized gain is properly adjusted for, there could be unfairness to one or more partners whose share of profit after the change is lower than that before.

Adjustment is needed for unrecorded assets whenever there is a change in profit-sharing arrangements, such as when:

- there is a change in the profit-sharing arrangements among continuing partners
- a new partner is admitted
- an existing partner leaves the business by retirement or death.

The partner (or partners) whose share of profit after the change is lower than that prior to it would be unfairly affected unless, at the point of this change, the unrecorded asset is accounted for and the corresponding gain appropriated according to the profit sharing arrangement before the change, or the party affected is compensated in some way.

Interaction 37.1	**Unrecorded assets**
	Required: Explain the reasons why assets might not be reported at fair value. Identify the circumstances in which unrecorded assets should be adjusted for.

37.2 IF FAIR VALUE OF ASSETS IS MORE THAN BOOK VALUE

Traditionally, accounting is transaction-based, so that gains are not accounted for until realized by a sale. A single individual who owns a business is not concerned whether or not the market value of an asset is higher than the value at which it is reported in the accounts; this is because he is confident that, whenever the asset is sold and the gain recognized upon realization, the gain would be his. Such an assurance is not always available in a partnership environment. To illustrate, let us assume that:

● Peter and Paul entered into a partnership on 1.1.20X0 with a capital of £300,000 and £200,000 and an agreement to share profits in the ratio 2:1 respectively;
● they acquired a property on 1.1.20X0 for £143,500;
● as at 31 December 20X7 the property is recorded in the books at its depreciated cost of £120,000, although it has a market value of £150,000;
● with effect from 1.1.20X8, Peter and Paul have agreed to share profits equally.

	Peter	Paul
Profit each partner gets in case the property is sold:	**£000**	**£000**
(a) before change in profit-sharing arrangement	20	10
(b) after change in profit-sharing arrangement	15	15
How the change affects each of the parties	−5	+5

If, prior to the change in the profit-sharing arrangements, nothing is done about the unrecognized gain, Peter's interest will be in jeopardy, as shown by the calculations on the left.

One way of safeguarding Peter's interest would be to sell the property prior to 1 January 20X8 and distribute the realized gain to Peter and Paul in their existing profit-sharing ratio. This would clearly be inadvisable if the partnership wishes to continue using the property. The alternative is to take one of the three following courses of action:

1. Paul could pay £5,000 to Peter to compensate him for the amount of unfairness.
2. The asset could be revalued, the gain being credited to the partners' Capital accounts in their profit-sharing ratio prior to the change so that Peter and Paul share the gain as they deserve to. The disadvantage of this is that the higher value of the asset would require correspondingly higher depreciation write-off, which would reduce the profit. The gain on revaluation is credited to the Capital account rather than the Current account of partners because it is not available to be withdrawn by them at will.
3. Having first revalued the asset and shared the gain as earlier, the asset could be restored to its original book value by writing off the difference to the partners' Capital accounts in their new profit-sharing ratio. The partners are debited in the *new* profit-sharing ratio because that would be the ratio they would share the gain whenever it was accounted for in the future. (See account shown here.)

PROPERTY ACCOUNT

	£		£
Balance b/f	120,000	Capital a/c:	
Capital a/c:		Peter	15,000
Peter	20,000	Paul	15,000
Paul	10,000	Balance c/d	120,000
Balance b/d	120,000		

If the third alternative course is taken, partners' Capital accounts would appear as shown below:

CAPITAL ACCOUNTS

	Peter	Paul		Peter	Paul
	£	£		£	£
Property account*	15,000	15,000	Balance b/f	300,000	200,000
Balance c/d	305,000	195,000	Property a/c – gain	20,000	10,000
			Balance b/d	305,000	195,000

* To write down the property back to its depreciated cost.

It should be observed that the effect of this third course of action is identical to the first – in that Paul surrenders to Peter £5,000 of his capital as compensation for the unfairness.

Unrecorded appreciation in asset value

Green and Black, sharing profits in the ratio 2:1 respectively, prepared their Trial Balance on the last day of their accounting period as stated right. Green wishes to admit Red, his son, to a one-quarter share of profit from this date. Black insists that, prior to Red's admission, the freehold land should be sold at its current market value, which has been reported as £750,000.

TRIAL BALANCE AS AT 30.6.20X0

	£000	£000
Freehold land	450	
Other assets	550	
Capital – Green		600
Black		400
	1,000	1,000

Required:

(a) Explain the rationale for Black's insistence.
(b) Is there a way of safeguarding Black's interests without selling the land?
(c) After Red is admitted to partnership with a capital of £300,000, if the partners opt to continue to report the freehold land at its historical cost, state the accounting adjustment necessary for the purpose.
(d) Explain to Red why his capital is reported as £225,000 in your answer to (c) above, whereas he introduced a capital of £300,000.

Interaction 37.2

Journal entry to adjust for unrecorded asset

Hickory and Dickory are in partnership with a capital of £500,000 and £400,000 and sharing profits in the ratio 2:1 respectively. On 1.1.20X1 they admit Dock, with a capital of £300,000, to a one-quarter share of the partnership profits. A property recorded in the books at £280,000 has a market value on 1.1.20X1 of £400,000.

Required: State in the form of a journal entry the adjustment necessary in respect of the unrecorded asset, assuming that the partners wish to continue to report the property at its existing value.

Interaction 37.3

37.3 ASSET NOT ACCOUNTED FOR BECAUSE PAYMENTS HAVE BEEN EXPENSED

An example of such an asset is a joint-life policy, where premiums have been written off and, as we saw in Chapter 36, have correspondingly reduced the profit available for appropriation. It would, therefore, be unfair if the profit-sharing arrangements were to change prior to the maturity or surrender of the life policy unless the fair value of the policy on the date of the change in profit-sharing arrangements is brought into the books of account.

To illustrate, let us assume that:

- Peter and Paul, sharing profits in the ratio 2:1 respectively, admit John to partnership on 1.1.20X0 on the basis that Peter, Paul and John are to share profits in the ratio 2:2:1 respectively;
- Partners maintain a joint-life policy but have written off the premiums annually against profit and on 1.1.20X0 the life policy has a surrender value of £120,000.

If, at the point of John's admission, nothing is done about the unrecorded life policy, Peter's loss would be £32,000 whereas Paul and John would gain £8,000 and £24,000 respectively (see box).

	Peter	Paul	John
The life policy:			
If surrendered prior to John's admission	£80,000	£40,000	–
If surrendered after John's admission	£48,000	£48,000	£24,000
	–32,000	+8,000	+£24,000

The easiest way to adjust for the unrecorded life policy is to bring the policy into the books by debiting a life policy account with £120,000, crediting the amount to the Capital accounts of Peter and Paul in their old profit-sharing ratio (i.e. £80,000 and £40,000 respectively). If, after John's admission, all partners agree to eliminate the life policy from the books, the Life Policy account should be credited with £120,000 and the Capital accounts of Peter, Paul and John debited with £48,000, £48,000 and £24,000 respectively. The net effect of these entries would be that Paul and John hand over £8,000 and £24,000 respectively of their capital balances to Peter as compensation for the unfairness Peter would suffer by leaving the life policy unaccounted for.

Interaction 37.4	**Change of profit-sharing arrangement**

Jack and Jill, with a capital of £400,000 and £200,000, shared profits in the ratio 3:1 respectively. Jack wishes to reduce his management involvement from 1.1.20X1. Consequently, it is agreed that from that date Jack and Jill will share profits in the ratio 1:2 respectively. They maintain a joint-life policy but have written off the annual premium. The surrender value of the policy on 1.1.20X1 is £90,000.

Required: On the basis that the partners wish to continue writing off the life policy premium, show the adjustment for the policy in their Capital accounts, and explain the impact that the adjustment has on Jack's capital.

37.4 WHEN GOODWILL REMAINS UNRECORDED

37.4.1 What is goodwill?

A business, if sold as a going concern, is usually worth more than the aggregate market values of its assets and liabilities appearing in the Balance Sheet. The difference between the going-concern value and the market value of the net assets is known as goodwill. Looked at from the point of view of the one buying the business, goodwill is the extra amount (a premium) paid in excess of the market value of each of the individual assets less liabilities acquired. Looked at from the point of view of those selling the business, goodwill represents an extra gain that the owners could potentially make if they disposed of the whole business as a going concern rather than each asset individually. Since such gain cannot be recognized until the disposal of the business, it is one of the unrecorded assets, which deserves to be taken into account whenever there is a change in the profit-sharing arrangement among partners.

37.4.2 How to value goodwill

The going-concern value of a business as a whole can only be established accurately by a completed market transaction, i.e. sale of the business; if a value is required prior to sale, then it has to be estimated. It is generally agreed that the value of a going concern is correlated to its future earning power and that future earning power is best estimated on the basis of past performance, taking into account any known factors that may affect it in future.

Alternative formulae have been developed to estimate the goodwill as a multiple of the predicted earning power. The formula used has to be one mutually agreed upon by the parties interested in the value. For example, if on the basis of average performance in the past it is expected that the business will continue to earn £50,000 per year, the goodwill could be valued by:

- Multiplying the anticipated annual profit by a multiple, say of three (i.e. £50,000 × 3), valuing goodwill at £150,000, this formula being expressed as 'three-year purchase of the anticipated annual profit'. The multiplying factor would normally be the one generally applicable to the type of business.
- Capitalizing the expected profit at an agreed rate of return of, say, 25 per cent (i.e. the capital, invested at 25% return, that would produce £50,000 annually).
- Capitalizing the expected profit at the current market rate of return and ascertaining the goodwill by deducting from that amount the market value of net assets – for example, if the market rate of return is 8 per cent and the sum of the market values of assets less liabilities is £450,000, goodwill is deemed to be £175,000 (see box).

	£000
Capitalized value at 8% = £50,000 × 100/8	625
Net assets at market value	(450)
Goodwill	175

- Multiplying the super profit by a multiple (say 10). 'Super profit' is defined as the amount by which the partnership profit exceeds the total of (a) a reasonable return on the capital invested at the date of valuation, and (b) a fair remuneration for services of the partners. For example, if we assume that the net assets are £450,000, a reasonable rate of return on net assets is 6 per cent p.a. and the fair remuneration of partners is £12,000 per annum, then super profit (as calculated in the box) is £11,000 and goodwill at 10 times is £110,000.

Average partnership profit per year	£50,000
Reasonable return: 6% of £450,000	(£27,000)
Fair remuneration to partners	(£12,000)
Super profit	£11,000

Interaction 37.5	Valuation of goodwill on alternative formulae

Duck and Drake shared profits in the ratio 2:1 until Swan is admitted to a one-sixth share of profit on 1 April 20X3. Draft accounts for the year ended 31.12.20X3 reveal a profit of £387,000. Performance in prior years were as stated on the right. Assume that profits and losses accrue consistently throughout each of these years.

Year ended		£000
31.12.20X0	Profit	267
31.12.20X1	Loss	75
31.12.20X2	Profit	324

Required: Estimate the value of goodwill on 1 April 20X3 on the basis of each of the following alternative formulae:

FORMULA ONE: Goodwill is to be valued at four-year purchase of the average profits of the three years *preceding* the date of valuation.

FORMULA TWO: Goodwill is to be valued at three-year purchase of the average profits of the three years *ending on* the date of valuation.

FORMULA THREE: Goodwill is to be valued at two-year purchase of the average profits of the three years preceding the date of valuation, giving a weight for the first, second and the most recent of these three years of 1:2:3 respectively.

FORMULA FOUR: Goodwill is valued at the capitalized value at 16 per cent per annum of the average annual profits of the three years *preceding* the date of valuation.

FORMULA FIVE: Goodwill is valued at the capitalized value at 10 per cent of the average super profits of three years *ending on* the date of valuation. Further information required for the goodwill valuation is as stated in the box here.

FORMULA SIX: Goodwill is valued as the amount by which the capitalized value at 8 per cent of the average profits of the three years preceding the date of valuation exceeds the net assets reported by the partnership on the preceding accounting date. The net assets of the partnership on 31.12.20X2 were reported as £1.5 million.

		£000
Capital as at 1.1.20X3	Duck	900
	Drake	600
Drawings per month	Duck	2
	Drake	1
Reasonable return on capital per year		6%
Fair remuneration per partner per month		2

37.4.3 Adjustment for unrecorded goodwill

Unrecorded goodwill (like unrecorded appreciation in the value of any asset) represents a gain already made but unaccounted for as at that date. Whenever profit-sharing arrangements change, failure to make appropriate adjustment for the unrecorded goodwill would adversely affect the party whose profit share reduces from that point.

Goodwill is adjusted for in the same way as suggested in respect of the unrecorded appreciation in the value of assets in Section 37.2 above. The value of goodwill arrived at on the basis of an agreed formula is accounted for by debiting the Goodwill account and crediting the Capital accounts of the existing partners in the profit-sharing ratio from which they propose to change. If, after the change in ratio for admission of a new partner or some other reason, the partners decide that goodwill should not appear in the books, it is eliminated by crediting the Goodwill account and debiting the Capital accounts of the continuing partners in their new profit-sharing ratio.

Interaction
37.6

New partner pays for unrecorded goodwill

Hickory and Dickory are partners holding £500,000 and £400,000 respectively as capital. They share profits in the ratio 2:1 respectively. They admit Dock as a partner with a capital of £300,000. Hickory, Dickory and Dock propose to share profits in the ratio 2:1:1 respectively. The value of the unrecorded goodwill at the date of Dock's admission is £120,000.

Required:

(a) Explain why Dock would make a payment to the two existing partners for unrecorded goodwill.
(b) Prepare partners' Capital accounts on the basis that Dock pays Hickory and Dickory an amount from his Capital account to compensate them for the unrecorded goodwill.
(c) Prepare partners' Capital accounts on the basis that goodwill is entered into the books and then written out.

Interaction
37.7

Journal entry to adjust for goodwill

Knight and Tower, sharing profits in the ratio 3:2 respectively, admit Rook to one-sixth of profit. The goodwill of the business on this date is valued at £180,000.

Required: Journalize the goodwill adjustment in each of the following scenarios:

(a) Goodwill is to be stated in the books at £180,000.
(b) Goodwill is not to appear in the books of account.
(c) Goodwill, already stated in the books at £45,000, is to be retained at that amount.

37.4.5 Gifting of goodwill

One of the parties adversely affected by a variation in profit-sharing arrangement may agree to waive his entitlement for compensation from the party gaining from assets remaining unrecorded. Such a waiver is referred to as the *gifting of goodwill*. What this means is that:

- where only two parties are involved, no adjustment at all is made for unrecorded assets;
- where there are more than two parties involved, adjustment is so made that the party gaining compensates the ones losing but without compensating the one agreeing to waive the compensation.

For example, when answering IQ 37.6 we found that Dock had to compensate Hickory for a loss of £20,000 and Dickory for £10,000. If Hickory agrees to gift his share of unrecorded goodwill, the journal entry necessary to adjust for goodwill will be as stated here.

	£000	£000
Dock Capital a/c Dr	10	
To Dickory Capital	–	10
Being adjustment for goodwill		

Interaction
37.8

Gifting of goodwill

Shabani and Sayore were in partnership with a capital of £500,000 and £300,000, and sharing profits in the ratio 3:1, respectively. Shabani's son Malonga is admitted to a one-sixth share of profit from 1.1.20X1, on the basis of the following agreement:

(a) Unrecorded goodwill on 1.1.20X1 was valued at £120,000.
(b) Shabani is not to be compensated for his share of unrecorded goodwill.
(c) Malonga will introduce £200,000 as his capital.
(d) Goodwill is not to be accounted for in the books.

Required: State the partners' profit-sharing ratio after Malonga's admission, and set out the journal entry to adjust for goodwill on Malonga's admission.

37.5 DEATH OR RETIREMENT OF A PARTNER

When a partner dies or retires from the partnership, he or she (or the estate) is entitled to an appropriate share of not only the profit or loss up to that date but also any unrecorded gain (or loss) as at that date. Unless the partner's entitlement can be fully discharged on that date, the outgoing partner is entitled also to a proportionate share of post-retirement profit or interest at an agreed rate. If there is no agreement on the rate, section 42 of the Partnership Act 1890 provides for interest at 5 per cent per annum.

37.6 REVALUATION ACCOUNT

Whenever there is either a change in profit-sharing ratio or an admission or retirement (or death) of a partner, all assets and liabilities have to be restated at market value. We have considered the accounting treatment when a single asset is revalued. Where there are a number of changes in value involved, it may be convenient to credit the gains and debit the losses to a Revaluation account, so that the net gain (or loss, as the case may be) is credited (or debited) to the partners' Capital accounts as a single figure in the ratio in which they shared profits before the change. If the partners do not intend to incorporate the new values into the books of account, instead of writing up a Revaluation account on the double entry basis, a Memorandum Revaluation account may be written up (outside the books of account) to ascertain the net gain or loss on revaluation, which is then accounted for by a journal entry.

| Interaction 37.9 | **The Revaluation account** |

Jack and Jill were partners sharing profits in the ratio 3:2 respectively. They admitted Hill to a one-sixth share of profit from 1.1.20X1 when their Balance Sheet was as stated here. Hill introduced £250,000 as his capital. The partners agreed that, for purposes of Hill's admission into partnership:

(a) property and machinery are to be valued at £900,000 and £300,000 respectively;
(b) a life policy on partners' lives should be taken into account at its surrender value on that date of £96,000;
(c) the bad debts provision should be adjusted to cover 10 per cent of debtors outstanding on the date of Hill's admission as a partner.

Required: Prepare a Revaluation account and a Balance Sheet as at 1.1.20X1 after Hill's admission, assuming that (a) the partners wish to incorporate the new values into their books, and then that (b) they wish to continue with the existing values in the books.

BALANCE SHEET AS AT 31.12.20X0

	Cost	Dep.	£000
Freehold property			640
Machinery	480	(160)	320
Stock in trade		560	
Debtors	480		
Provision	(12)	468	
Cash and bank		22	
Creditors		(640)	410
			1,370

		£000
Capital – Jack	600	
Jill	400	1,000
Current – Jack	260	
Jill	110	370
		1,370

SOLUTIONS TO INTERACTIVE QUESTIONS

IQ 37.1 Unrecorded assets

Reasons why assets may not be reported at fair value

- The assets are being reported at depreciated cost or at an out-of-date valuation.
- The assets are not reported because payments have been written off as an expense (e.g. unrecorded life policies where the annual premiums have been written off in the year the payments are made).
- The assets have arisen not from a transaction but as a consequence of other factors, such as being in a good location or being profitable. These factors are known as goodwill.

Circumstances in which net book values of asset should be adjusted

Unrecorded assets should be adjusted for whenever there is an alteration in the profit-sharing arrangements among partners. Such alterations arise:

- on a change of the profit-sharing arrangement among continuing partners;
- on admission of a new partner;
- on retirement or death of a partner.

IQ 37.2 Unrecorded appreciation in asset value

(a) **The reason for Black's insistence on selling the land**

The reason for Black's insistence is his unwillingness to forfeit his legitimate share of the unrealized gain from holding the freehold land. The land, acquired for £450,000, currently has a fair value (market value) of £750,000. The gain of £300,000, though yet unrealized and therefore unrecorded in the accounts, has been earned by 30.6.20X0. Black is entitled to receive one-third of that gain, amounting to £100,000; whereas if the land is sold after Red's admission, Black's share of the gain, on the new profit-sharing ratio of one-quarter, will amount to £75,000, which is £25,000 lower.

(b) **Another way of safeguarding Black's interest in the unrecorded asset**

Instead of disposing of the land, it could be revalued, prior to Red's admission, to its current market value and the gain shared between Green and Black in the ratio in which they have shared profits until now. The gain being unrealized, and therefore not available for the partners' withdrawal, is credited to their Capital accounts rather than their Current accounts.

The Capital accounts after Red's admission will appear as shown below. Black cannot complain any longer because he has received what he is entitled to.

FREEHOLD LAND ACCOUNT

		£000		£000
Balance b/f		450		
Capital a/c:				
Green	200			
Black	100	300		
		750		

CAPITAL ACCOUNT

	Green £000	Black £000	Red £000		Green £000	Black £000	Red £000
				Balance b/f	600	400	–
				Land a/c	200	100	–
Balance c/d	800	500	300	Cash book	–	–	300
				Balance	800	500	300

(c) **Restoring the revalued asset to earlier book value**

If after adjusting for unrecorded asset, the partners wish to continue reporting the land at its historical cost, the extra £300,000 is written off by crediting the Land account and debiting the Capital accounts, but this time in the new profit-sharing ratio. The Capital account is as shown on the following page (top).

CAPITAL ACCOUNT

	Green £000	Black £000	Red £000		Green £000	Black £000	Red £000
				Balance b/f	600	400	–
Land a/c	150	75	75	Land a/c	200	100	–
Balance c/d	650	425	225	Cash book	–	–	300
				Balance b/d	650	425	225

(d) New partner's capital reduced by the adjustment for unrecorded assets

As a result of the adjustment for unrecorded asset, Red's capital is stated at £225,000 which is £75,000 lower than what he introduced. This is because £75,000 is his one-quarter share of the assets remaining unrecorded in the books.

IQ 37.3 Journal entry to adjust for unrecorded asset

If the property had been revalued to its market value and the gain shared among the continuing partners, and thereafter the property had been restored to its original book value, debiting the difference to all the partners' Capital accounts in the new profit-sharing ratio, the Capital accounts would have appeared as follows:

PARTNERS' CAPITAL ACCOUNTS

	Hickory £000	Dickory £000	Dock £000		Hickory £000	Dickory £000	Dock £000
				Balance b/f	500	400	–
Property a/c	60	30	30	Property a/c	80	40	–
Balance c/d	520	410	270	Cash account	–	–	300
				Balance b/d	520	410	270

Instead, the net effect of the adjustment for unrecorded assets on the partners' Capital accounts can be identified as shown on the right, and this effect is achieved by journalizing as shown below.

	Hickory £000	Dickory £000	Dock £000
To write up the asset to market value	80 Cr	40 Cr	–
To restore the current book value	60 Dr	30 Dr	30 Dr
Net effect of both entries	20 Cr	10 Cr	30 Dr

JOURNAL ENTRY

		£000	£000
Docks' Capital a/c	Dr	30	–
To Hickory's Capital		–	20
Dickory's Capital		–	10
Being adjustment for market value of property			

When the journal entry is posted to the partners' Capital accounts, the resulting position will be as stated in the Capital accounts shown above.

IQ 37.4 Change of profit-sharing arrangement

As a result of the change in profit-sharing arrangement, Jack's loss is as follows: 3/4 less 1/3 = 5/12. Therefore, if the unrecorded life policy is not adjusted for, Jack would lose 5/12 of £90,000 = £37,500. To compensate for this, Jill surrenders to Jack £37,500 of her capital.

CAPITAL ACCOUNTS

	Jack £000	Jill £000		Jack £000	Jill £000
Life policy a/c	30,000	60,000	Balance b/f	400,000	200,000
Balance c/d	437,500	162,500	Life policy a/c	67,500	22,500
			Balance b/d	437,500	162,500

IQ 37.5 Valuation of goodwill on alternative formulae

Formula one:	£000	£000
20X0 Profit	267	
20X1 Loss	(75)	
20X2 Profit	324	
Total of 3 years	516	
Average: 516/3 years		172
Four year purchase = £172,000 × 4		688

Formula two:	£
20X0 Profit	267,000
20X1 Loss	(75,000)
20X2 Profit	324,000
20X3 Profit	387,000
Total of four years	903,000
Less: First quarter of 20X0 profit	(66,750)
Last three quarters of 20X3 profit	(290,250)
Profit for three years up to 1.4.20X3	546,000
Average profit = £546,000/3 years	£182,000
Three year purchase (£182,000 × 3)	546,000

Formula three:	£000	weight	£000
20X0 Profit	267	× 1	267
20X1 Loss	(75)	× 2	(150)
20X2 Profit	324	× 3	972
Total for six years			1,089
Average: £1,089,000/6			181.5
Two year purchase: 181.5 × 2			363

Formula four:	£000
20X0 Profit	267
20X1 Loss	(75)
20X2 Profit	324
Total for 3 yrs	516
Average	£172
Capitalizing £172,000 @ 16% = £172,000/16 × 100 = £1,075,000	

Formula five:	£		£
Capital on 1.1.20X3	1,500,000	Average profit for three years to 1.4.20X3	182,000
Profit to 31.3.20X3	96,750	6% return on £1,587,750	(95,265)
Drawings to 31.3.20X3	(9,000)	Fair remuneration for management	(48,000)
Capital on 1.4.20X3	1,587,750	Average super profit	38,735
		Capitalized at 10%: £38,735/10 × 100	387,350

Formula six:	£		£
Average for three years	172,000	Capitalized at 8% = £172,000/8 × 100	2,150,000
		Net assets on 1.1.20X0	(1,500,000)
		Goodwill	650,000

IQ 37.6 New partner pays for unrecorded goodwill

(a) At the date of admitting Dock, the business can be disposed of for a value £120,000 higher than the values at which its assets and liabilities are recorded. If the disposal takes place prior to Dock's admission, Hickory and Dickory would share the gain of £120,000 as £80,000 and £40,000 respectively. If, on the other hand, the disposal takes place after Dock's admission, the gain of £120,000 would be shared by Hickory, Dickory and Dock in the ratio £60,000, £30,000 and £30,000 respectively. A comparison of the two positions establishes (see box) that Dock gains £30,000, depriving Hickory of £20,000 and Dickory of £10,000. This would be unfair unless Dock, who gains, compensates the losers.

If upon disposal of business the goodwill is realised at £120,000	Hickory £000	Dickory £000	Dock £000
(a) prior to Dock's admission	80	40	–
(b) after Dock's admission	60	30	30
(Losers) and gainers	(20)	(10)	30

(b) One compensation method is for Dock to hand over £20,000 of his capital to Hickory and £10,000 to Dickory to compensate them for the unfairness. Cash brought in by Dock, recorded in the cash book, is posted to the Capital accounts of Hickory, Dickory and Dock as £20,000, £10,000 and £270,000 respectively. The Capital accounts appear as follows:

PARTNERS' CAPITAL ACCOUNTS

	Hickory £000	Dickory £000	Dock £000		Hickory £000	Dickory £000	Dock £000
				Balance b/f	500	400	–
Balance c/d	520	410	270	Cash account	20	10	270
				Balance b/d	520	410	270

(c) An alternative and more common method of adjusting for unrecorded goodwill is to account for the goodwill by passing the first journal entry (shown on the right) prior to the admission of the new partner and then, if preferred, to eliminate the goodwill from the books by passing a second journal entry.

Goodwill, though admittedly an asset of high value, is usually left out of the accounting records, however, because its value is not established by a market transaction and, in any case, it cannot be realized except when the whole business is disposed of as a going concern. The capital balances of the partners resulting from the use of the alternative method are exactly identical to those from the first method because both achieve the same effect.

Journal entry (1)	£000	£000
Goodwill account Dr	120	–
To Hickory Capital a/c	–	80
Dickory Capital a/c	–	40
Being accounting for goodwill		

Journal entry (2)	£000	£000
Sundries Dr		
To Goodwill account	–	120
Hickory Capital a/c	60	–
Dickory Capital a/c	30	–
Dock Capital a/c	30	–
Being elimination of goodwill		

PARTNERS' CAPITAL ACCOUNTS

	Hickory £000	Dickory £000	Dock £000		Hickory £000	Dickory £000	Dock £000
				Balance b/f	500	400	–
Goodwill a/c	60	30	30	Goodwill a/c	80	40	–
Balance c/d	520	410	270	Cash account	–	–	300
				Balance b/d	520	410	270

IQ 37.7 Journal entry to adjust for goodwill

(a) If goodwill is to be accounted for

		£000	£000
Goodwill account	Dr	180	–
To Knight Capital a/c		–	108
Tower Capital a/c		–	72
Being accounting for goodwill			

(b) If goodwill is not to appear in the books

		£000	£000
Rook Capital a/c	Dr	30	–
To Knight Capital a/c		–	18
Tower Capital a/c		–	12
Being adjustment fo unrecorded goodwill			

	Knight £000	Tower £000	Rook £000
Workings:			
Credit in the old ratio	108	72	–
Debit in the new ratio	(90)	(60)	(30)
Net effect	18 Cr	12 Cr	30 Dr

(c) If goodwill is to be retained in books at existing lower value

		£000	£000
Rook Capital a/c	Dr	22.5	–
To Knight Capital a/c		–	13.5
Tower Capital a/c		–	9
Being adjustment for unrecorded goodwill			

	Knight £000	Tower £000	Rook £000
Workings:			
Credit in the old ratio	81	54	–
Debit in the new ratio	(67.5)	(45)	(22.5)
Net effect	13.5 Cr	9 Cr	22.5 Dr

IQ 37.8 Gifting of goodwill

If Malonga is to receive a one-sixth share of profit, it is understood the remaining five-sixths would be shared between Shabani and Sayore, as they have done up to now. That is:

Shabani gets 3/4 of 5/6th = 15/24
Sayore gets 1/4 of 5/6th = 5/24
Malonga gets 1/6 which is the same as = 4/24

The necessary Journal entry to adjust for goodwill is thus:

	£000	£000
Malonga Capital a/c Dr	5	–
To Sayore Capital a/c	–	5
Being adjustment for goodwill		

	Shabani £000	Sayore £000	Malonga £000
Workings:			
Credit in the old ratio	90 Cr	30 Cr	–
Debit in the new ratio	75 Dr	25 Dr	20 Dr
Net effect	15 Cr	5 Cr	20 Dr
Cancellation (gift)	(15)		(15)
Adjustment is needed	–	5 Cr	5 Dr

IQ 37.9 The Revaluation account

To find the gain on revaluing machinery, the market value should be compared with the net book value. The credit balance of £160,000 in the Provision for Depreciation of Machinery account (the supporting account) should be transferred to the Plant and Machinery account (main account) to arrive at the net book value.

The life policy is not stated as an asset on the Balance Sheet because the premiums paid for it have been written off year after year to the Profit and Loss account.

(a) If the new values are to be incorporated into the books of account

REVALUATION ACCOUNT

	£000		£000
Machinery a/c	20	Freehold property	260
Prov. for bad debts	36	Life Policy a/c	96
Gain on revaluation	300		
Capital accounts:		Gain on revaluation	300
Jack	180		
Jill	120		

FREEHOLD PROPERTY ACCOUNT

	£000		£000
Balance b/f	640		
Revaluation a/c	260		

PLANT AND MACHINERY ACCOUNT

	£000		£000
Balance b/f	480	Prov. for dep	160
		Revaluation a/c	20
		Balance c/d	300
Balance b/d	300		

LIFE POLICY ACCOUNT

	£000		£000
Revaluation a/c	96		

PROVISION FOR DOUBTFUL DEBTS ACCOUNT

	£000		£000
		Balance b/f	12
		Revaluation a/c	36

CASH BOOK

	£000		£000
Balance b/f	22		
Hill's Capital a/c	250		

BALANCE SHEET AS AT 1.1.20X1

		£000
		£000
Freehold property		900
Plant and machinery		300
Life policy		96
Stock in trade	560	
Debtors	480	
Provision for bad debt	(48)	432
Cash and bank	272	
Creditors	(640)	624
		1,920
		£000
Capital – Jack	780	
Jill	520	
Hill	250	1,550
Current – Jack	260	
Jill	110	370
		1,920

Hill's capital is reported at the amount of cash introduced by him because Jack and Jill have been compensated for their share of unrecorded assets.

CAPITAL ACCOUNTS

	Jack £000	Jill £000	Hill £000		Jack £000	Jill £000	Hill £000
				Balance b/f	600	400	–
				Revaluation a/c	180	120	–
				Cash book	–	–	250
					780	520	250

(b) If the new values are not to be incorporated into the books of account

In order to adjust the partners' interests on the basis of the new values, the net gain or loss on a revaluation of assets has to be determined and that could be done, without making any accounting entries, by merely preparing a Memorandum Revaluation account as follows:

MEMORANDUM REVALUATION ACCOUNT

	£000		£000
Machinery a/c	20	Freehold property	260
Prov. for bad debts	36	Life Policy a/c	96
Gain on revaluation	300		
		Gain on revaluation	300

The Memorandum Revaluation account, though called an account, is merely a calculation of the surplus or deficiency arising from a comparison of book values with fair values on the date that profit-sharing arrangements change. The net surplus of £300,000 is adjusted among partners as follows:

	Jack £000	Jill £000	Hill £000
Surplus credited in old ratio	180 Cr	120 Cr	–
Surplus debited in new ratio	150 Dr	100 Dr	50 Dr
Net effect on each partner	30 Cr	20 Cr	50 Dr

BALANCE SHEET AS AT 1.1.20X1

			£000
Freehold property			640
Plant and machinery	480	(160)	320
Stock		560	
Debtors	480		
Provision for bad debts	(12)	468	
Cash and bank		272	
Creditors		(640)	660
			1,620
			£000
Capital – Jack		630	
Jill		420	
Hill		200	1,250
Current – Jack		260	
Jill		110	370
			1,620

CAPITAL ACCOUNTS

	Jack £000	Jill £000	Hill £000		Jack £000	Jill £000	Hill £000
				Balance b/f	600	400	–
Revaluation a/c	150	100	50	Revaluation a/c	180	120	–
Balance c/d	630	420	200	Cash book	–	–	250
				Balance b/d	630	420	200

PROGRESSIVE QUESTIONS

PQ 37.1 Profit-sharing ratio after new partner's admission

Sane and Wise were in partnership sharing profits and losses in the ratio 3:2 respectively. Clever was admitted to partnership on 1 January 20X0. What would be the profit-sharing ratio after the admission in each of the following alternative scenarios:

(a) Clever was admitted to a one-quarter share of profit.
(b) Clever was admitted to a one-quarter share of profit on the basis that he would take over the share equally from Sane and Wise.
(c) Clever was admitted to a one-quarter share of profit taken over from Sane.

PQ 37.2 Adjustment for unrecorded goodwill

Goodwill stated in the books of the partnership in PQ 37.1 at £120,000 is to be retained at that figure, although its market value on the date of Clever's admission to the partnership is agreed to be £480,000. Set out the journal entry necessary for adjusting for the unrecorded asset in each of the alternative scenarios identified in PQ 37.1 above.

PQ 37.3 An elementary question on the admission of a new partner

Polly and Kelly carried on a business in partnership sharing profits in the ratio 2:1 respectively, after allowing 6 per cent interest on their Fixed Capital account balances. Molly was admitted to a one-sixth share of profit on 1 March 20X1. Molly introduced £120,000 as capital and £30,000 as her share of goodwill.

The Trial Balance extracted at year end appears as stated here. You are further informed as follows:

(a) Stock costing £235,000 remained unsold by the year end.
(b) Fixed assets are to be depreciated at 10 per cent per year, using the reducing balance method.
(c) Income and expenditure are to be assumed to have accrued evenly through the year.
(d) Goodwill is to be adjusted for, but is not to be recorded in the books of account.

Required: Prepare the Trading and Profit and Loss account of the partnership for the year ended 30 June 20X1 and the Balance Sheet as at that date. Set out also the partners' Capital accounts and Current accounts in columnar format.

TRIAL BALANCE AS AT 30 JUNE 20X1		
	£000	£000
Fixed assets at cost	480	–
Depreciation to 30.6.20X0	–	220
Drawings: Polly	30	–
Kelly	15	–
Molly	6	–
Stock on 1 July 20X0	214	–
Administrative expenses	1,029	–
Sales	–	3,848
Capital accounts – Polly	–	200
Kelly	–	150
Molly	–	150
Purchases	2,174	–
Debtors and creditors	469	418
Current accounts – Polly	–	18
Kelly	11	–
Distribution costs	484	–
Cash and bank balance	92	–

PQ 37.4 Admission of a partner during an accounting period

Rajan and Kumaran were partners, sharing profits in the ratio 2:1 respectively, after paying Rajan a salary of £24,000 p.a. and allowing interest on capital at 6 per cent p.a. On 1.4.20X2 Akilan was admitted to partnership on the basis of the following agreement:

● Akilan to bring in £100,000 as his capital and £40,000 as his share of goodwill. No account for goodwill is to be raised in the books.
● No salary is to be paid to any partner, but the interest at 6 per cent p.a. on capital is to continue.
● Rajan, Kumaran and Akilan are to share profits and losses in the ratio 3:2:1 respectively.

The Trial Balance extracted from the partnership books on 31.12.20X1 appears as shown here. You are informed further as follows:

(a) Stock on 31.12.20X2 is ascertained at £214,500.
(b) The Salaries a/c includes 11 months' salary drawn by Rajan.
(c) The sales in each month from and after July were 50 per cent better than those in each of the earlier months.
(d) On the day of admission to partnership Akilan received a gift of a car, acquired for the business on 1.1.20X0, for £20,000. Rajan and Kumaran wish to share cost of the gift equally. The gift has still to be accounted for.
(e) The partnership depreciates furniture and vehicles at 10 per cent and 20 per cent p.a. respectively using the reducing balance method.

Required:

(a) Explain to Kumaran why he is not benefiting at all from the adjustment for goodwill on Akilan's admission as partner.
(b) Show the accounting entries necessary to adjust for unrecorded goodwill.
(c) Finalize the accounts of the partnership for the year ended 31 December 20X2.

TRIAL BALANCE AS AT 31.12.20X2		
	£	£
Motor vehicles	200,000	42,600
Furniture	210,000	34,800
Stock – 31.12.20X1	186,400	–
Purchases	692,650	–
Sales	–	984,250
Salaries	112,000	–
Rent	32,000	–
Sales commission	21,800	–
Debtors/Creditors	246,800	161,200
Cash/bank	3,795	–
Advertising	17,805	–
Admin. expenses	32,400	–
Bad debts	7,200	–
Cash from Akilan	–	140,000
Capital – Rajan	–	300,000
Capital – Kumaran	–	100,000

PQ 37.5 Goodwill valued by capitalizing super profits

Anil and Ranil are brothers, in partnership, sharing profits in the ratio 2:1 respectively, after allowing Anil a salary of £30,000 p.a. and allowing interest on the Capital account balances at 6 per cent per annum. Other provisions in the partnership deed include the following:

● Whenever necessity arises, goodwill is to be valued as the capitalized value at 10 per cent of the average super profits for the three years ending on the date of valuation. (Super profit is defined as the amount by which the average earnings exceed the sum of both the 6 per cent return on partners' capital balances at the date of last reporting and a fair remuneration for the services of each of the partners on that date, at £12,000 per year.)
● A joint life policy, with a maturity value of £200,000, shall be maintained; but the premium paid for the policy shall be written off in the year of payment.

Sunil, their youngest brother, is admitted to a one-sixth share of profit from 1 October 20X3. Sunil brought in £100,000 as capital and took over his share of profit *equally* from both Anil and Ranil. There was no other change in the partnership deed.

The Trial Balance of the partnership was extracted as shown on the right. You are also informed as follows:

(a) The premium on the life policy was £3,000 per quarter until Sunil's admission and £5,000 per quarter thereafter. The policy had a surrender value of £24,000 on 1.10.20X3.
(b) The partners have agreed that goodwill should not appear in the books of account.
(c) The operating results in previous years have been reported as stated within the box on the right.
(d) You may assume that, unless indicated otherwise, income and expenses accrued evenly.

TRIAL BALANCE AS AT 31.12.20X3		
	£000	£000
Motor vehicles	310	78
Furniture	180	63
Stock on 31.12.20X3	346	–
Cash from Sunil	–	100
Goodwill	30	–
Admin. expenses	229	–
Debtors/Creditors	362	244
Cost of goods sold	744	–
Distribution cost	142	–
Life policy premium	14	–
Cash and bank	119	–
Sales	–	1,275
Capital – Anil	–	400
– Ranil	–	300
Current – Anil	–	36
Ranil	14	–
Sunil	6	–

Year ended		
31.12.20X0	Profit	£68,800
31.12.20X1	Loss	£21,850
31.12.20X2	Profit	127,650

Required: (a) Prepare the Profit and Loss account for the year ended 31.12.20X3 and the Balance Sheet as at that date, and (b) determine the profit-sharing ratio among Anil, Ranil and Sunil, if Sunil had not taken over his one-sixth share equally from both his brothers.

PQ 37.6 A partnership with incomplete records

Gold, Silver and Copper share profits equally, after allowing Gold a salary of £2,000 per month. Nickel is admitted to a one-tenth share of partnership profits on 1.1.20X4 on the following terms:

● Nickel is to bring in £150,000 as capital.
● Goodwill is to be valued at the capitalized value at 20 per cent of the amount by which the average profits for the three years preceding the date of valuation exceed 8 per cent of the capital employed on that date.
● There is to be no adjustment for goodwill between Gold and Nickel.
● Other terms of the partnership agreement are to remain unchanged.

The partners have failed to maintain proper books of account. You have nevertheless ascertained the following information:

● No current accounts are maintained.
● Partners' capital balances were as stated in box (1).
● Drawings by partners, other than salary drawn regularly by Gold, were as stated in box (2).
● Apart from additional capital introduced by Nickel, the only capital introduction by a partner during this period was £50,000 introduced by Silver on 1 July 20X3.

Required:

(a) Determine the results of the partnership performance in each year until 31 December 20X3.
(b) Value the partnership goodwill as at 1 January 20X4.
(c) If goodwill should remain unrecorded in the books, set out the journal entry to adjust for goodwill on 1.1.20X4.
(d) Write up the partners' Capital accounts from 1.1.20X1 until Nickel's arrival on 1.1.20X4.

BOX (1)
Balances in partners' accounts as on

	31.12.X0 £000	31.12.X1 £000	31.12.X2 £000	31.12.X3 £000
Gold	215	244	201	253
Silver	200	216	163	251
Copper	175	185	131	171
Total	590	645	495	675

BOX (2)
Drawings in each year ending on

	31.12.X1 £000	31.12.X2 £000	31.12.X3 £000
Gold	3	4	–
Silver	16	14	14
Copper	22	15	12
Total	41	33	26

PQ 37.7 Retirement of a partner

Karim, the senior partner of a successful business dealing in reconditioned vehicles, decided to retire with effect from 31 March 20X0 when the position of the business was certified by the auditors as shown here. Karim, Essaj and Gulam worked equally hard to promote the business and shared profits equally. They have agreed, however, that any gains or losses arising other than in dealing with cars should be shared among them in the ratio in which they hold their capital.

The partners agree that as at the date of retirement, the business premises and furniture have a value of £360,000 and £60,000 respectively, while machinery (which had been depreciated on the straight-line method at 10 per cent p.a.) would cost £240,000 to replace. Goodwill of the business is valued at £150,000. The partners wish to report their fixed assets in the books at their current fair values, but prefer to allow goodwill to remain unrecorded.

The partners maintained a joint life policy, the annual premium in respect which was written off. £300,000 is realized on surrendering the policy, although the total premiums paid amounted to £270,000.

Karim is paid £360,000 on the date of retirement and the balance owed to him is treated as a loan to be settled in ten equal half-yearly instalments with interest accruing at 10 per cent p.a.

BALANCE SHEET AS AT 31.3.20X0

	Cost	Ac.dep	£000
Business premises			240
Machinery	180	(72)	108
Furniture	124	(34)	90
Stock in trade		685	
Debtors		145	
Cash and bank		75	
Creditors/accruals		(113)	792
			1,230

		£000
Capital – Karim		600
Essaj		400
Gulam		200
Current – Karim	17	
Essaj	27	
Gulam	(14)	30
		1,230

Required: Prepare:

(a) the Revaluation Account;
(b) the partners' Capital accounts, recording the retirement of Karim;
(c) a revised Balance Sheet on 31.3.20X0 on the basis that all transactions relating to the retirement were completed, without cost, on the same date;
(d) the Appropriation account for the year ended 31 March 20X1, on the basis that the profit for the year, without charging any interest on Karim's loan, is £215,500.

PQ 37.8 Death of a partner

Hard Branson and Soft Paxman, sharing profits in the ratio 2:1 respectively as partners of a retail shop, have extracted their Trial Balance on the last day of the year as shown here.

Their shop operates from the ground floor of premises owned by Hard. Rent for the shop is agreed at £12,000 p.a. Brittle Fleming, their shop manager, employed at a salary of £900 p.m., is also entitled to interest at 12 per cent p.a. on a loan he has given the partnership.

The upper floors of the premises comprise six self-contained flats. One of them is rented to Brittle at £300 per month, the rent being recovered on the pay sheet. The remaining flats are rented out to outsiders at £400 per month, on the basis that Hard bears the cost of all repairs as well as the rates. For a commission fixed at 10 per cent of rent collected, Brittle is responsible for collecting the rent and it is agreed that the transactions relating to the rent, though not of the partnership, are to be accounted for in the partnership books.

Soft died on 30.9.20X1. £120,000 received on maturity of the life policy was handed over to the widow, although the whole transaction is still to be accounted for. From the date of Soft's death, Brittle was admitted to a one-third share of profit on the following agreement:

● As a partner, Brittle continues to receive the salary as earlier, but his loan is converted into his capital.
● Goodwill, valued at £75,000, is not to appear in the books.

Further information provided to you is as follows:

(a) Stock on 31.12.20X1 is ascertained as £284,700.
(b) Salary, net of rent, drawn by Brittle consistently throughout the year is reported in the Salaries account.
(c) The partnership received a cheque for £11,900 from Brittle on 31.12.20X1 with the statement shown here.
(d) Motor vehicles and shop fixtures are to be depreciated at 20 per cent and 10 per cent p.a. respectively, using the fixed instalment method.

Required: Finalize the accounts of the partnership for the year ended 31 December 20X1.

TRIAL BALANCE AS AT 31.12.20X1		
	£	£
Motor vehicles	180,000	72,000
Shop fixtures	96,000	38,400
Stock – 31.12.20X0	216,800	–
Purchases	824,600	–
Sales	–	982,800
Life policy	84,000	–
Shop rent	11,000	–
Salaries	106,400	–
Loan – Brittle	–	100,000
Drawing – Hard	10,500	–
Soft	8,165	–
Debtors/Creditors	115,600	192,600
Life policy fund	–	84,000
Advertising	4,240	–
Light/heat	3,000	–
Brittle's a/c	–	11,900
Other expenses	42,600	–
Capital – Hard	–	150,000
Soft	–	100,000
Cash/bank	28,795	–

STATEMENT OF RENT COLLECTIONS		
for and on behalf of Hard Branson		
		£
Rent collectible: £400 × 12 × 5 flats		24,000
Less: Rent in arrears		(3,000)
Amount collected to date		21,000
Less: Rates		(4,800)
Cost of repairs	(2,400)	
Remaining unpaid	200	(2,200)
Commission @ 10%		(2,100)
Cheque paid in		11,900

## Chapter 38

PARTNERSHIP ACCOUNTS (3): DISSOLUTION AND CONVERSION

In this chapter

We will learn to:

● close the books of a partnership when partners decide to terminate their relationship and

● open the books of a limited company

and you should be able, on dissolution of a partnership, to:

● close its books of accounts

● open the books of a limited company or

● convert partnership books to those of a company

38.1 PIECEMEAL DISPOSAL OF A PARTNERSHIP BUSINESS

When partners wish to terminate the partnership, ideally they would seek to dispose of their business as a going concern because in this way they would realize a value also for goodwill. Should this prove impossible for any reason, it would become necessary to realize each asset as best as possible, discharge the liabilities, and share among the partners whatever is left over.

Let us illustrate such a piecemeal disposal assuming that Rose and Ivy, sharing profits in the ratio 2:1 respectively, decided to terminate their partnership with effect from 31 December 20X0 when their Balance Sheet was as stated on the right. The dissolution progressed as follows:

● Fixed assets realized £295.
● Stock realized 20 per cent more than cost.
● £35 of trade debts proved irrecoverable.
● Creditors were settled subject to a 10 per cent discount.
● The expenses of realization amounted to £5.
● Partners' claims were met and the books were closed.

BALANCE SHEET AS AT 31.12.20X0		
		£
Fixed assets at cost	600	
Prov. for depreciation	(240)	360
Stock in trade	415	
Debtors	385	
Cash and bank	25	
Creditors	(280)	545
		905
		£
Capital – Rose	500	
Ivy	300	800
Current a/c – Rose	15 Cr	
Ivy	(10) Dr	5
Rose Loan account		100
		905

The dissolution of the partnership is accounted for as follows:

- Every asset (other than cash) is transferred to a Realization account and as each asset is realized the proceeds are debited to the Cash account and credited to the Realization account.
- The expenses of realization are posted from the Cash account to the Realization account. (The Realization account may also be called a 'Dissolution account' in these circumstances.)
- The creditors are settled and any gain (the discount) transferred to the Realization account.
- The balance in the Realization account would represent the gain or loss on realization, and this is appropriated among the partners in their profit-sharing ratio.
- The partner's loan is settled prior to paying back what is due to each of them as Capital and Current account balances.

The accounts will appear as follows:

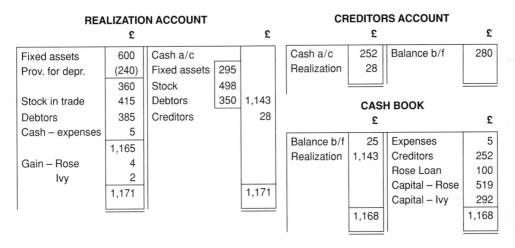

REALIZATION ACCOUNT

	£			£
Fixed assets	600	Cash a/c		
Prov. for depr.	(240)	Fixed assets	295	
	360	Stock	498	
Stock in trade	415	Debtors	350	1,143
Debtors	385	Creditors		28
Cash – expenses	5			
	1,165			
Gain – Rose	4			
Ivy	2			
	1,171			1,171

CREDITORS ACCOUNT

	£		£
Cash a/c	252	Balance b/f	280
Realization	28		

CASH BOOK

	£		£
Balance b/f	25	Expenses	5
Realization	1,143	Creditors	252
		Rose Loan	100
		Capital – Rose	519
		Capital – Ivy	292
	1,168		1,168

PARTNERS' CAPITAL ACCOUNTS

	Rose £	Ivy £		Rose £	Ivy £
Current a/c – transferred	–	10	Balance b/f	500	300
			Current a/c – transferred	15	–
Cash book – balancing figure	519	292	Realization a/c – gain	4	2

Piecemeal dissolution of a partnership

Ebb and Flow, who shared profits in the ratio 3:2 respectively, decided to terminate their partnership with effect from 31.3.20X0 when their Balance Sheet appeared as stated here. The dissolution proceeded as follows:

(a) Flow took over a vehicle that cost £30,000 initially and had been written down to £26,000 by this date.

(b) The remaining vehicles, furniture and stock realized £54,000, £92,000 and £718,000 respectively.

(c) £74,000 of the debts had to be written off.

(d) The expenses of realization were £18,000.

Required: Show the closure of the partnership books. Remember that a partner takes over an asset at its depreciated cost (known also as book value), and that proceeds on disposal of a partnership should be used first to pay any expenses, then to meet claims of outsiders, then to settle partners' loans and finally to meet partners' claims in respect of their Capital and Current account balances.

BALANCE SHEET AS AT 31.3.20X0

	Cost	Depn	£000
Furniture	420	168	252
Motor vehicle	280	140	140
Stock in trade		625	
Debtors	460		
Prov. for bad debt	(24)	436	
Cash and bank		72	
Creditors	(562)		
Bank overdraft	(96)	(658)	475
			867

	Ebb	Flow	£000
Capital a/c	400	400	800
Current a/c	(104)	21	(83)
Loan – Flow			150
			867

38.2 DISPOSAL OF A PARTNERSHIP AS A GOING CONCERN

If a partnership business is disposed of as a going concern, depending on the agreement, every one of its assets, including cash and its bank balance, as well as its liabilities would be sold for the agreed price. Let us assume, this time, that the business owned by Rose and Ivy was sold on 31.12.20X0 as a going concern for a consideration received in cash of £950. The net assets of the partnership were reported on the Balance Sheet of that date at £905, giving the partners a gain on disposal of £45 if we assume that there were no expenses of realization. The Realization account will confirm this position as shown below.

The following points should be noted:

(a) The cash and bank balance on the date of disposal are also among the assets disposed of.

(b) The creditors' balances are transferred to the credit of the Realization account so that the net assets (£1,185 less £280) of £905 may be compared with the amount of £950 for which they were sold.

(c) The gain on disposal of £45 is appropriated among the partners in their profit-sharing ratio.

REALIZATION ACCOUNT

	£		£
Fixed asset	600	Creditors	280
Provision for depn	(240)	Cash	950
	360		
Stock	415		
Debtors	385		
Cash and bank	25		
	1,185		
Gain – Rose	30		
Ivy	15		
	1,230		1,230

(d) The amount received on disposal (£950) is paid to the partners in accordance with their claims stated in their Capital accounts, after settling Rose's Loan account. The cash book and the Capital accounts would appear as follows:

CASH BOOK

	£		£
Balance b/f	25	Realization a/c	25
Realization a/c	950	Rose Loan	100
		Capital – Rose	545
		Capital – Ivy	305

CAPITAL ACCOUNTS

	Rose £	Ivy £		Rose £	Ivy £
Current a/c	–	10	Balance b/f	500	300
Cash book	545	305	Current a/c	15	–
			Realization a/c	30	15

Disposal of a partnership as a going concern   *Interaction 38.2*

Ebb and Flow, who shared profits in the ratio 3:2 respectively, prepared their Balance Sheet on 31.3.20X0 as stated in IQ 38.1. Flow agreed to take over the bank overdraft as well as a vehicle that cost £30,000 initially and had been written down by this date to £26,000. Subject to these points and Flow's loan, the business was taken over by Wave Ltd for a consideration payable in cash of £982,000.

Required: Show how the books of the partnership will be closed upon dissolution.

38.3 PURCHASE CONSIDERATION

In the context of a business disposal, the expression ***purchase consideration*** could, but does not always, refer to the total price for which the assets of a business are disposed of. If the vendee (i.e. the one who acquires the business) does not assume responsibility for discharging the liabilities, then (but then alone) the purchase consideration will equal the price fetched by the assets. When a business is disposed of as a going concern, it is usual for the vendee to take over the assets together with liabilities. In that case the purchase consideration is arrived at by deducting from the agreed price for all of the assets the amount of such liabilities taken over.

Determination of the purchase consideration   *Interaction 38.3*

Asoka Guruge owns a car acquired for £24,000, using a loan of £6,000 from Finco Ltd. When Asoka advertised the car for sale, John Smith agrees to buy it for £25,000.

Required: Account for the disposal of the car in Asoka's books in each of the following scenarios:

- SCENARIO (1): Asoka agrees to settled the Finco loan;
- SCENARIO (2): Asoka expects John Smith to discharge the Finco loan.

Identify also the sale price of the car and the purchase consideration in each scenario.

38.3.1 Purchase consideration received other than in cash

Upon disposal of a business, the purchase consideration may not always be received in cash. Instead, the agreement with the vendee may be that the purchase consideration should be discharged by an allotment of the vendee company's shares and possibly debentures (see Chapters 39 and 40 for more details). When shares are received in discharge of the purchase consideration, there would be a need:

(a) **to account for the shares as an asset in the books of the partnership**. The shares are accounted for as investments (an asset), valued at the amount at which the shares were allotted. For example, if 100,000 ordinary shares of £1 each had been allotted at £1.25 per share (i.e. with a premium of 25p per share), the shares received will be valued at £125,000 and accounted for by crediting the Vendee's account and debiting an Investment account.

(b) **for the partners to agree on the ratio in which each of them is to be allotted these shares**. In the absence of any agreement, the shares may be allotted in one of two ways as follows:

● If it is the wish of the partners that they should continue to receive dividends from the company in the same ratio as the one in which they shared partnership profits, the shares may be allotted in the partnership profit-sharing ratio.

● If the wish of the partners is that they should own the company in the ratio in which they owned the partnership, the shares may be allotted in the ratio of their respective capital balances.

38.3.2 Calculation of the purchase consideration

The calculation of purchase consideration receivable from a vendee who acquires a business as a going concern involves two steps, as follows:

1. Aggregate the price at which each of the assets (including goodwill) is taken over (remembering that where there is no mention of such a sale price it is assumed that the particular asset is taken over at its book value).
2. Deduct the value at which the liabilities are taken over from the total receivable for all the assets.

| Interaction 38.4 | **Purchase consideration calculated based on asset values** |

Having finalized their Balance Sheet as shown here, Gerenia and Petunia decided to sell their business, as a going concern, to Flowers Ltd, on the basis of the following valuation:

● land and buildings at £960,000;
● motor vehicles at £90,000;
● debtors subject to a provision of 10 per cent;
● goodwill valued at £150,000.

Flowers Ltd is to discharge the purchase consideration as follows:

(a) allotment to the partners, in their profit-sharing ratio, of 1,500,000 ordinary shares of £1 each in Flowers Ltd, allotted at a premium of 10p per share;
(b) paying the remainder in cash.

Gerenia and Petunia had shared profits in the ratio 2:1 respectively. Expenses of dissolution amounted to £5,000.

Required: Record the closure in the partnership books.

BALANCE SHEET AS AT 30.6.20X0		
		£000
Land and building	840	
Accum. depn	(196)	644
Motor vehicles	260	
Accum. depn	(156)	104
Stock in trade	574	
Debtors	480	
Provision	(24)	456
Cash and bank		96
Creditors	(492)	
Accruals	(72)	(564)	562
		1,310
		£000
Capital – Gerenia		800
Capital – Petunia		600
Current – Gerenia	(74)	
– Petunia	(16)	(90)
		1,310

Where the values at which the assets are taken over are not fully agreed upon (for example, there might be no agreement on the valuation of goodwill), the amount of the purchase consideration is calculated by valuing the items received from the vendee by way of discharging the purchase consideration.

Purchase consideration based on the value of what is received

Interaction 38.5

Gerenia and Petunia, sharing profits in the ratio 2:1 respectively, have finalized their Balance Sheet on 30 June 20X0 as stated in IQ 38.4. Their business is sold to Flowers Ltd, on this date, valuing land and buildings and motor vehicles at £960,000 and £90,000 respectively. Debtors are to be taken over subject to a 10 per cent provision for doubtful debts. The purchase consideration is to be discharged by an allotment to the partners, in their profit-sharing ratio, of 1.5 million ordinary shares of £1 each in Flowers Ltd, allotted at £1.10 per share, and payment of £88,000 in cash. Expenses of dissolution amounted to £5,000.

Required: Close the books of the partnership. (*Note*: Goodwill has not been valued; hence the purchase consideration should be calculated by valuing the items received from Flowers Ltd for discharging the purchase consideration.)

38.4 DEFICIENT PARTNER: THE *GARNER V MURRAY* RULE

If, upon dissolution of a partnership business, a partner is deficient (i.e. his Capital account, usually after charging him with his share of loss on realization, has a debit balance), such deficiency has to be made good by an appropriate payment in cash. This is because each partner has unlimited liability for any failure to make good such deficiency and may be pursued through courts.

If, however, the deficient partner is insolvent and hence unable to make good the deficiency, unless partners have agreed otherwise, the ruling of a court in England[1] is that the solvent partners should share such deficiency in the ratio of their 'last agreed capital' – i.e. the capital balances in the Balance Sheet prepared immediately prior to dissolution. This rule was made on the premise that when partners agree upon a profit-sharing ratio, such a ratio applies only to losses sustained by the business and not to any deficiency in a partner's capital.

Capital deficiency of an insolvent partner

Interaction 38.6

Sun, Moon and Star shared profits in the ratio 3:2:1 respectively until they decided to dissolve the partnership with effect from 31 March 20X0. The Balance Sheet of the partnership, prepared as at that date, reported the net assets of the partnership at £750,000 (as stated here). The net assets of the partnership realized only £210 and Star was adjudicated bankrupt.

Required: Set out the partners' Capital accounts, showing how:

(a) the loss on realization was appropriated among partners;
(b) the insolvent partner's deficiency is taken over by others;
(c) the final settlement was made of the partners' claims.

Capital:	£000
Sun	500
Moon	100
Star	100
Current:	
Sun	75
Moon	15
Star	(40)
	750

38.5 OPENING THE BOOKS OF THE ACQUIRING COMPANY

We will learn of accounting for limited companies, including shares issued by them, from Chapter 39 onwards. For the limited purpose of this chapter, let us learn:

- how to account for assets and liabilities acquired by a company for an agreed consideration;
- how to account for any shares issued by a company to discharge the purchase consideration.

38.5.1 Accounting for the acquisition of assets and liabilities for an agreed consideration

Every class of asset acquired is debited in the appropriate asset account at the value at which each is acquired, and every liability is credited to the appropriate liability account, the agreed purchase consideration being credited to a Vendor's account (i.e. the opposite number of the vendee). For example, if goodwill, fixed assets, stock, debtors and cash valued respectively at £50, £100, £60, £45 and £15 are acquired together with creditors amounting to £65, for a purchase consideration of £205, the journal entry necessary to account for the acquisition would be as stated in the box.

Sundries Dr	£	£
To Sundries		
Goodwill account	50	
Fixed Assets account	100	
Stock account	60	
Debtors account	45	
Cash book	15	
Creditors account		65
Vendor's account		205
Being an acquisition of a business		

Two points are worthy of note, as follows:

1. If an asset acquired for £100 and written down by the date of disposal to £60 is acquired by a company at a value of £75, the company will account for the asset at £75 because that would be its cost. On the other hand, if debtors amounting to £100 were taken over subject to a provision for doubtful debts of 10 per cent, even though the value at which the debt is taken over is £90 the company would account for £100 as debtors (because that would be the total of the amounts it should endeavour to collect from all the debtors taken over) and credit the difference of £10 in a Provision for Doubtful Debts account.
2. The journal entry stated above is defective in that it includes a cash balance, the prime entry for which should have been in the cash book. As we learnt in Chapter 10, a journal entry is required for making a prime entry for transactions for which no other suitable book of prime entry is available. Ideally, the cash balance should have been posted to the Vendor's account from the cash book, while the journal entry accounted for only the remainder of the purchase consideration (£205 less £15). The Vendor's account would then have appeared as on the right here.

VENDOR'S ACCOUNT

	£		£
		Cash book	15
		Journal	190

38.5.2 Accounting for the issue of shares to discharge a purchase consideration

As we will learn in Chapter 40, it is a requirement of company law that shares issued by a company should be accounted for at their nominal value (i.e. the value stated on the share certificate) in the Share Capital account. If a £1 share is issued at £1.25, the excess (the premium) of 25p over the par value is accounted for in a Share Premium account.

Accordingly, if the purchase consideration of £205 is discharged by issuing 120 ordinary £1 shares allotted at £1.25 each, and a payment of £55 in cash, the accounting for the discharge of the purchase consideration would be as stated in the journal entry here. For the sake of clarity we had again to journalize the cash entry.

		£	£
Vendor's account	Dr	205	–
To Ordinary Share Capital a/c		–	120
Share Premium account	–	–	30
Cash account	–	–	55
Being discharge of the purchase consideration			

Opening the books of a company – journalizing a cash balance Interaction 38.7

A partnership business carried on by Gerenia and Petunia was acquired by Flowers Ltd with effect from 30 June 20X0. All particulars of this acquisition are as stated in IQ 38.4.

Required: Set out the journal entries necessary to account for the acquisition in the books of Flowers Ltd. (You may journalize the cash balance as well.)

Journal entries for opening the books of the company Interaction 38.8

Required: On the basis of the information in question IQ 38.5, set out in the books of Flowers Ltd:

(a) the journal entries to open the books (*note*: you should *not* journalize the cash balance);
(b) the Vendor's account.

38.6 CONVERTING THE BOOKS OF A PARTNERSHIP TO THOSE OF A COMPANY

38.6.1 Where assets of a partnership are taken over at existing book value

If the books of a partnership are to be converted into those of a company and all assets and liabilities are taken over at their existing book values, all that needs to be done is to:

- transfer the balances in the partners' accounts to a Vendor's account (alternatively named a Purchase of Business account);
- account for the discharge of the consideration by issuing shares and/or making payment in other form, as agreed between the parties.

The amount by which the value of the consideration exceeds the amount due to the vendors for tangible net assets taken over is the amount paid for the intangible asset, which is goodwill.

BALANCE SHEET AS AT 31.3.20X0		
		£
Fixed assets		600
Stock	320	
Debtors	440	
Cash/bank	80	
Creditors	(460)	380
		980
		£
Capital – Pansy	600	
Begonia	300	900
Current – Pansy	96	
Begonia	(16)	80
		980

For illustration, assume that Pansy and Begonia, who shared profits in the ratio 3:2 respectively, decided to convert their business into a company as from 31.3.20X0, when their Balance Sheet was prepared as shown here. The company is named Flora Ltd and the purchase consideration was agreed at £1,250 to be settled by issuing to partners 1,000 ordinary shares of £1 each, allotted at £1.20 per share, and a payment in cash of £50.

In the absence of any information to the contrary, it may be assumed that partnership assets and liabilities were all taken over by Flora at existing book values. Instead of closing the books of the partnership and opening new ones for Flora, the partnership books could be converted into those of Flora Ltd by preparing a Purchase of Business account as shown on the left.

The aggregate of balances in the partners' Capital and Current accounts (of £980) is the net asset of the partnership taken over by Flora paying a purchase consideration of £1,250. The excess of £1,250 over the value of tangible net assets taken over (£980) is the value paid for goodwill (£270). The shaded area in the Purchase of Business account arises as the balancing figure between the value of the consideration paid and the value of the tangible net assets taken over from the partners.

PURCHASE OF BUSINESS ACCOUNT

	£		£
Current – Begonia	16	Capital – Pansy	600
Share Capital a/c	1,000	Capital – Begonia	300
Share Premium a/c	200	Current – Pansy	96
Cash book	50	Goodwill a/c	270

38.6.2 Where assets of the partnership are taken over at revised market values

The goodwill, as a balancing figure, will vary if one or more of the tangible fixed assets of the partnership are taken over at a value different from the book value. For example, if Flora took over the partnership fixed asset at a value of £750 (instead of £600), the difference of £150 is debited to the Fixed Asset account and credited to the Purchase of Business account to record the fact that the tangible assets acquired are worth not £980 but £150 more. Accordingly the amount paid for goodwill will be not £270 but £150 less than that.

Interaction 38.9	Conversion of partnership books to those of a company

Refer back to the information stated in IQ 38.4.

Required: Convert the books of the partnership into those of Flowers Ltd and set out the Balance Sheet of Flowers Ltd immediately after the conversion.

38.6.3 Where any partnership asset and/or liabilities are not taken over by the company

The book value of any asset not taken over is debited to the Purchase of Business account to reduce the amount payable to the vendor. Similarly, the amount of any liability not taken over is credited to the Purchase of Business account to increase by that amount the amount owed to the vendor.

Reference

1. The Garner v. Murray rule (1904) 1 Ch. 57 does not apply in Scotland.

SOLUTIONS TO INTERACTIVE QUESTIONS

IQ 38.1 Piecemeal dissolution of a partnership

REALIZATION ACCOUNT

		£000	£000			£000	
	Furniture	420		Flow – motor vehicle		26	a
	Prov. for depn	(168)	252	Cash book:			
a	Motor vehicles	280		Motor vehicle	54		
a	Prov. for depn	(140)	140	Furniture	92		
	Stock in trade		625	Stock	718		
b	Debtors	460		Debtors	386	1,250	
b	Prov. for bad debt	(24)	436	Loss – Ebb Capital		117	c
				Flow Capital		78	c
	Expenses		18				

CASH BOOK

	£000		£000
Balance b/f	72	Expenses	18
Realization a/c	1,250	Bank overdraft	96
		Creditors	562
		Flow Loan a/c	150
		Capital – Ebb	179
		Capital – Flow	317

PARTNERS' CAPITAL ACCOUNTS

	Ebb £000	Flow £000		Ebb £000	Flow £000
Current a/c	104	–	Balance b/f	400	400
Motor vehicle	–	26	Current a/c	–	21
Realization – loss	117	78			
Cash book	179	317			

Notes:

(a) Alternatively, the balances brought to the Realization account from the Motor Vehicles account and the Provision for Depreciation account could have been £250,000 and £136,000 respectively, after transferring to Flow's Capital account the amounts relating to the vehicle taken over by her.

(b) Alternatively £386,000 received from debtors could have been posted to the Debtors account and the bad debt of £74,000, offset against the Provision, bringing only the difference of £50,000 (bad debts not already provided for) as a loss on realization to the Realization account.

(c) The loss on realization is appropriated between the partners in their agreed profit-sharing ratio.

IQ 38.2 Disposal of a partnership as a going concern

REALIZATION ACCOUNT

	£000	£000		£000	
Furniture	420		Flow – motor vehicle	26	b
Provision for depn	(168)	252	Creditors	562	c
			Wave Ltd	982	d
Motor vehicles	280				
Provision for depn	(140)	140			
Stock in trade		625			
Debtors	460				
Provision for bad debt	(24)	436			
a Cash and bank		72			
Gain – Ebb Capital a/c		27			
Flow Capital a/c		18			

WAVE LTD ACCOUNT

	£000		£000
Realization	982	Cash book	982

CASH BOOK

	£000		£000
Balance b/f	72	Realization	72
Wave Ltd	982	Flow Loan	150
		Ebb Capital	323
		Flow Capital	509

Notes:

(a) When a business is disposed of as a going concern, its cash and bank balance are also taken over.

(b) The depreciated cost of the motor vehicle taken over is debited to Flow's Capital account and the bank overdraft is credited to that account.

(c) In addition to paying £982,000 in cash, Wave Ltd is taking over the creditors of the partnership. Hence the total received by the partners in respect of the assets taken over is £982,000 + £562,000 = £1,544,000.

(d) The portion of the total price for the assets (£1,544,000) paid immediately to the partners by the one acquiring the business is referred to as 'purchase consideration' (see Section 38.3).

IQ 38.3 Determination of the purchase consideration

(a) Accounting for the disposal of the vehicle

MOTOR VEHICLE DISPOSAL ACCOUNT (SCENARIO (1))

Motor Vehicle a/c	24,000	John Smith[a]	25,000
Gain on disposal	1,000		

MOTOR VEHICLE DISPOSAL ACCOUNT (SCENARIO (2))

Motor Vehicle a/c	24,000	Finco Loan	6,000
Gain on disposal	1,000	John Smith[b]	19,000

a. In Scenario (1), because John Smith does not take over the liability to Finco, the sale price of the vehicle (£25,000) is equal to what is receivable from John (the purchase consideration).

b. Although the vehicle's sale price remains £25,000 as in Scenario (1), because John Smith undertakes to pay the Finco loan, the amount immediately receivable from John (the purchase consideration) is only £25,000 less the liability taken over of £6,000, i.e. £19,000.

(b) The sale price and purchase consideration

	Scenario (1)	Scenario (2)	Comment
Sale price of the car	£25,000	£25,000	No difference
Purchase consideration	£25,000	£19,000	The difference is because liability is taken over in Scenario (2).

IQ 38.4 Purchase consideration calculated based on asset values

REALIZATION ACCOUNT

	£000	£000		£000
Land and building	840		Creditors	492
Accum. depn	(196)	644	Accrued expenses	72
Motor vehicles	260		Flowers Ltd.#	1,738
Accum. depn	(156)	104		
Stock in trade		574		
Debtors	480			
Prov. for doubt. debts	(24)	456		
Cash and bank		96		
Expenses of realization		5		
Gain – Gerenia	282			
Petunia	141	423		

Purchase consideration calculated as:

		£000
Land and building		960
Motor vehicle		90
Goodwill		150
Stock (at book value)		574
Debtors	480	
Less: Provision doubtful debts	(48)	432
Cash and bank balance		96
Less: Creditors	(492)	
Accrued expenses	(72)	
	#	1,738

CASH BOOK

	£000		£000
Balance b/f	96	Realization	96
Flowers Ltd	88	Expenses	5
Gerenia Capital	92	Petunia Capital	175

FLOWERS LTD ACCOUNT

	£000		£000	
Realization a/c	1,738	Investments a/c	1,650	a
		Cash	88	b

INVESTMENTS ACCOUNT

	£000		£000	
Flowers Ltd	1,650	Gerenia Capital	1,100	c
		Petunia Capital	550	c

PARTNERS' CAPITAL ACCOUNTS

		Gerenia £000	Petunia £000		Gerenia £000	Petunia £000	
	Current a/c	74	16	Balance b/f	800	600	
c	Investments a/c	1,100	550	Gain on realization	282	141	
d	Cash book	–	175	Cash book	92	–	d

Notes:

(a) 1.5 million shares at £1.10 per share.
(b) The difference between the purchase consideration and the value of shares is settled in cash.
(c) Shares allotted to partners in their profit-sharing ratio.
(d) Cash adjustment between partners to close the books.

IQ 38.5 Purchase consideration based on the value of what is received

The answer to this question is the same as for IQ 38.4 because the information provided is identical, except that this question does not place a value on goodwill and, therefore, the purchase consideration has to be calculated (as done in the box on the right) by valuing what was received from Flowers Ltd in discharge of it.

Purchase consideration is calculated as:	
	£000
Value of shares: 1,500,000 @ £1.10	1,650
Cash received	88
	1,738

IQ 38.6 Capital deficiency of an insolvent partner

PARTNERS' CAPITAL ACCOUNTS

		Star £000	Moon £000	Sun £000		Star £000	Moon £000	Sun £000	
	Current a/c	–	–	40	Balance b/f	500	100	100	
a	Realization – loss	270	180	90	Current a/c	75	15	–	
b	Sun – deficiency	25	5	–	Star & Moon	–	–	30	b
	Cash book	280			Cash book		70		c

Notes:

(a) Loss on realization:
- net assets — 750,000
- realized — (210,000)
- loss — 540,000

This amount will be shared in the profit-sharing ratio 3:2:1.

(b) Sun's deficiency £(40,000 + 90,000 – 100,000 = 30,000) is taken over by Star and Moon in the ratio of their last agreed capital (£500,000:£100,000) as £25,000 and £5,000 respectively, in accordance with *Garner v Murray* rule.

(c) Moon, being solvent, has to introduce £70,000 in cash to make good his deficiency.

IQ 38.7 Opening the books of a company – journalizing a cash balance

Date	V	Particulars		F	£000	£000	
1.7.X0		Sundries	Dr				
		To Sundries					
		Goodwill			150	–	
		Land and building			960	–	
		Motor vehicles			90	–	
		Stock in trade			574	–	
		Debtors			480	–	a
		Cash book			96	–	
		Creditors			–	492	
		Accrued expenses			–	72	
		Prov. for doubtful debts			–	48	a
		Vendor's account			–	1,738	
		Being an acquisition of business					
1.7.X0		Vendor's account	Dr		1,738		
		To Ordinary share capital				1,500	
		Share Premium a/c				150	
		Cash book				88	
		Being a discharge of the purchase consideration					

Note:

(a) Debtors, though taken over at a value of £432,000, are recorded in the books at £480,000, the difference being stated as a provision for doubtful debts. All other assets are accounted for at the value at which each is taken over; and so are the liabilities.

IQ 38.8 Journal entries for opening the books of the company

The Vendor's account will appear as on the right.

Date	V	Particulars		F	£000	£000
1.7.X0		Sundries	Dr			
		To Sundries				
		Goodwill			150	–
		Land and building			960	–
		Motor vehicles			90	–
		Stock in trade			574	–
		Debtors			480	–
		Creditors			–	492
		Accrued expenses			–	72
		Prov. for doubtful debts			–	48
		Vendor's account			–	1,642
		Being an acquisition of business				
1.7.X0		Vendor's account	Dr		1,650	
		To Ordinary share capital				1,500
		Share Premium a/c				150
		Being a discharge of the purchase consideration				

VENDOR'S ACCOUNT

	£000		£000
Journal .2	1,650	Cash book	96
Cash book	88	Journal .1	1,642

IQ 38.9 Conversion of partnership books to those of a company

LAND AND BUILDINGS ACCOUNT

	£000		£000	
Balance b/f	840	Provision for depn	196	a
Purchase of business	316	Balance c/d	960	
Balance b/d	960			

MOTOR VEHICLES ACCOUNT

	£000		£000	
Balance b/f	260	Provision for depn	156	
		Purchase of business	14	b
		Balance c/d	90	
Balance b/d	90			

PROVISION FOR DOUBTFUL DEBTS ACCOUNT

	£000		£000	
		Balance b/f	24	
Balance c/d	48	Purchase of business	24	c
		Balance b/d	48	

PURCHASE OF BUSINESS ACCOUNT

		£000		£000	
	Current – Gerenia	74	Capital – Gerenia	800	
	Current – Petunia	16	Capital – Petunia	600	
b	Motor vehicle	14	Land and building	316	a
c	Prov. for d. debts	24	Goodwill	150	d
e	Ordinary share	1,500			
e	Share premium	150			
e	Cash book	88			

FLOWERS LTD			
BALANCE SHEET AS AT 30.6.20X0			
			£000
Fixed assets:			
Goodwill			150
Land and buildings			960
Motor vehicles			90
Current assets:			
Stock in trade		574	
Debtors	480		
Provision for doubtful debts	(48)	432	
Cash and bank		8	
Creditors		(492)	
Accrued expenses		(72)	450
			1,650

Share capital and reserves:	£000
Ordinary shares of £1 each	1,500
Share Premium account	150
	1,650

Notes:

(a) The land and buildings, reported in the partnership books at a written down value of £644,000 are valued on this date at £960,000. Accordingly, the amount owed to the partnership in respect of tangible assets would increase by the difference of £(960,000 – 644,000), namely £316,000.

(b) Similarly, motor vehicles reported in the partnership books at a written down value of £104,000 are taken over valued at only £90,000. Accordingly, Flowers owes £14,000 less for the tangible assets.

(c) It has been agreed that the provision for doubtful debts, stated in the partnership books at £24,000, should be increased by £24,000 more to cover 10 per cent of debtors taken over. Hence the amount owed for tangible assets decreases by £24,000.

(d) Flowers agrees to buy the partnership goodwill for £150,000. Accordingly, the amount owed to the vendor is increased.

(e) The purchase consideration is discharged by issuing 1.5 million shares of £1 each (credited to the Share Capital account) allotted at a premium of 10p each (credited to the Share Premium account) and payment of £88,000 in cash.

(f) The cash and bank balance with Flowers on 30 June 20X0 amount to £96,000 taken over from the vendor less £88,000 paid back to discharge the purchase consideration, a net amount of £8,000.

PROGRESSIVE QUESTIONS

PQ 38.1 Piecemeal disposal of a partnership business

Tarimo, Kito and Mbwilo are in partnership repairing and servicing refrigeration equipment, and they share profits in the ratio 2:2:1 respectively. The Balance Sheet of the partnership appeared as shown on the right when they decided to terminate the partnership, taking steps as follows:

- A machine acquired for £24,000 and written down to £16,000 was taken over by Tarimo who, for a consideration of £18,000, agreed to take care of the maintenance guarantees given to customers. Remaining machinery realized £114,500.
- The stock of spares realized 15 per cent above cost, and the motor vehicles were disposed of for £76,500.
- The prepaid rent couldn't be recovered, and the debtors realized only £24,500; but the suppliers agreed to allow 10 per cent settlement discount.
- Expenses of dissolution were £4,600.
- The bank overdraft had been secured by Tarimo's personal guarantee as well as a pledge of his life policy, which had a surrender value on 31.12.X0 of £60,000.

Required:

(a) Explain why the partners prefer to dispose of their business as a going concern.
(b) Show the closure of the books of the partnership on completion of the dissolution.
(c) Justify your treatment of Tarimo's personal guarantee and the pledge of his life policy.

BALANCE SHEET AS AT 31.12.20X0			
	Cost	Ac. depr.	£
Machinery	348,500	(128,600)	219,900
Vehicles	124,500	(32,600)	91,900
Stock of spares		84,600	
Debtors	46,500		
Provision	(3,500)	43,000	
Prepaid rent		2,500	
Cash in hand		125	
Owed to suppliers		(36,500)	
Maintenance guarantee		(15,000)	
Accrued expenses		(11,250)	
Bank overdraft		(14,225)	53,250
			365,050
			£
Capital – Tarimo			150,000
Kito			100,000
Mbwilo			80,000
Current a/c – Tarimo		3,200	
Kito		(2,150)	
Mbwilo		(6,000)	(4,950)
Loan – Tarimo			40,000
			365,050

PQ 38.2 A basic question on going-concern disposal of a partnership

Happy and Lucky were in partnership sharing profits in the ratio 3:2 respectively, and they prepared their Balance Sheet as shown on the right. They decided to convert their business from this date to a limited company. The company, registered as Cheerful Ltd, took over all asset and liabilities of the partnership at their book values, for a purchase consideration agreed at £600,000 and discharged by an allotment to both partners of 400,000 ordinary shares of £1 each.

Required:

(a) Close the books of the partnership.
(b) Show how different your answer would be if the partners had expressed a wish to continue to share the profits in the company as they did in the partnership.
(c) Open the books of Cheerful Ltd on the basis that all assets were taken over at existing book values, setting out the Balance Sheet immediately after opening the books.

BALANCE SHEET AS AT 31 MARCH 20X1			
	Cost	**Ac. depr.**	**£**
Machinery	285,000	(112,600)	172,400
Vehicles	120,000	(45,000)	75,000
Stock in trade		248,600	
Debtors	164,000		
Provision	(12,500)	151,500	
Cash and bank balance		22,800	
Creditors		(96,600)	326,300
			573,700
			£
Capital – Happy			300,000
Lucky			200,000
Current a/c – Happy		94,600	
Lucky		(20,900)	73,700
			573,700

PQ 38.3 Purchase consideration calculated on the basis of asset valuation

Mandy, Daphne and Olive, sharing profits in the ratio 4:3:3 respectively, decided to convert their business into a limited liability company, named Cosmetics Ltd, with effect 30 June 20X1 when they finalized their Balance Sheet as stated on the right.

All assets, other than the investments and a joint-life policy, and all liabilities other than the bank overdraft are transferred to the company subject to the following revaluation:

- goodwill, premises and machinery are valued at £120,000, £300,000 and £106,500 respectively;
- debtors are transferred with a 10 per cent provision.

The purchase consideration is to be discharged by an allotment to the partners, in their profit-sharing ratio, of 600,000 ordinary shares of £1 each in Cosmetics Ltd, issued at £1.25, with payment of the balance in cash. An amount of £64,000 was realized on surrendering the life policy. The investments held by the partnership were taken over by Mandy at a valuation of £45,000. The expenses of dissolution amounted to £3,250.

Required: Show the closure of the partnership books and set out the journal entries to open the books of Cosmetics Ltd, journalizing the cash entries.

BALANCE SHEET AS AT 30 JUNE 20X1			
	Cost	**Ac.depr.**	**£**
Premises	320,000	(64,000)	256,000
Machinery	164,000	(41,000)	123,000
Furniture	80,000	(24,000)	56,000
Investments			32,500
Stock in trade		168,500	
Debtors	246,400		
Provision	(12,320)	234,080	
Cash		1,420	
Creditors	(196,500)		
Accruals	(26,600)		
Overdraft	(18,800)	(241,900)	162,100
			629,600
			£
Capital – Mandy			250,000
Daphne			200,000
Olive			150,000
Current a/c – Mandy		(15,200)	
Daphne		28,500	
Olive		16,300	29,600
			629,600

PQ 38.4 Calculation of the purchase consideration by reference to how it is discharged

Stated here is the Balance Sheet of Silent and Patient, who share profits in the ratio 3:2 respectively. Recovery Ltd was formed to take over the business from the Balance Sheet date.

The terms of the takeover were agreed as follows:

(a) A trade debt of £12,500 is to be written off because it is time-barred, and the provision adjusted to 5 per cent of the remaining debtors.

(b) Joe Robust, the manager of one of the retail outlets, is to be retired from this date. The compensation to Joe agreed at £24,000 is to be settled by Recovery Ltd in six equal monthly instalments commencing from 31 July 20X0.

(c) Prepayments could not be transferred to Recovery Ltd.

(d) The vehicles and stock were taken over valued at £90,000 and £224,000 respectively.

(e) The purchase consideration was discharged as follows:
  - the allotment to Silent and Patient, in the ratio of the capital account balances, of 1,200,000 ordinary shares of 50p each in Recovery Ltd, issued at a premium of 10 per cent;
  - the allotment of 8 per cent debentures of £90,000 in Recovery Ltd to settle Silent's loan;
  - a cash payment of £16,300.

Required: Close the books of the partnership and set out, in the books of Recovery Ltd, not only the books of prime entry for opening the books but also the Vendor's account.

BALANCE SHEET AS AT 30 JUNE 20X0			
	Cost	Ac. depr.	£
Goodwill at cost			75,000
Furniture	240,000	(48,000)	192,000
Vehicles	180,000	(54,000)	126,000
Stock in trade		284,600	
Debtors	182,500		
Provision	(9,400)	173,100	
Prepayments		3,500	
Cash/bank balance		32,200	
Creditors		(164,800)	
Accruals		(11,200)	317,400
			710,400
			£
Capital – Silent			400,000
Patient			200,000
Current a/c – Silent			35,600
Patient			(15,200)
Loan from Silent			90,000
			710,400

PQ 38.5 Converting the partnership books into those of a company

Refer back to the information stated in PQ 38.3.

Required: Convert the books of the partnership into those of Cosmetics Ltd.

Part J

ACCOUNTING FOR LIMITED COMPANIES

## Chapter 39

COMPANIES (1): AN INTRODUCTION

In this chapter

We will learn:

- how companies are formed, their merits and demerits
- how companies raise their finance

39.1 WHAT IS A LIMITED COMPANY?

We have seen that it is possible for two or more persons to carry on business as a partnership without the need for any formal partnership agreement or official registration. Despite this convenience, business in the form of a partnership is constrained by the following:

- Each partner is liable for the whole debt of the partnership. This means that business creditors can, if the business assets are insufficient, look to the personal assets of the partners to meet the business liabilities.
- Each partner should participate in management. This means that children and others unable to partake in management are denied the opportunity of investing in a business enterprise.
- The number of partners cannot exceed 20 without special dispensation. This means that the resource base of the business is restricted.

To overcome these constraints and promote enterprise, a further type of business organization has been permitted by statute – the limited liability company.

39.1.1 A limited company is a body corporate

A limited company is a *body corporate*. What this means is that it is recognized by law as a person, not only separate and distinct from the humans who constitute it but also having rights even against those human persons. Though not endowed with a physical life, in the eyes of the law it is a separate legal person capable of owning property, entering into contracts, suing and being sued in a court of law and, in fact, undertaking any activity (though acting through its human agents) so long as that activity is within the 'objects clause' in its Memorandum (see Section 39.2).

The legal recognition of the company as a body corporate was well established when the House of Lords upheld Aron Salomon's claim in respect of secured loans (over those of unsecured creditors) against a company in which Aron and his family held all the shares[1]. Aron's claim was upheld on the premise that 'the company is, at law, a different person altogether from its subscribers' (i.e. shareholders).

However, although a company has its own existence as an organization and can raise finance, own assets, incur liabilities and carry on business providing goods or services, being an artificial person it cannot act except through its human agents, i.e. the directors and managers.

39.1.2 Perpetual succession

A limited company comes into existence by a process called *incorporation* during which certain statutory requirements set out in the Companies Act 1985 should be satisfied. It will continue to exist until its existence is terminated by another legal process known as *liquidation*. The ability of a company to outlive humans is described as *perpetual succession*.

Whereas a partnership ceases to exist on the death of a partner, a company continues to remain in legal existence unless a deliberate decision is taken to liquidate it. In the meantime, while the individual shareholders may change, the company continues its legal existence – even over centuries.

39.2 INCORPORATION

The common way of forming a company is by registering it with the Registrar of Companies. There are other ways of incorporation, such as by a Royal Charter or by a Special Act of Parliament, but these are not commonly available. Those not inclined to go through the elaborate process of incorporating their own company may buy one 'off the shelf' from those who sell ready-made companies (currently for approximately £50).

The main steps for incorporating a company include the following:

- choose a name;
- prepare the documentation;
- obtain a Certificate of Incorporation.

Each of these steps is described further below.

39.2.1 Choose a name for the company

The name, when chosen, should be cleared with the Registrar of Companies, who will check that there is no company already registered with the same or similar name. The use of certain words within the name is not permitted, for instance those that suggest Royal patronage, government or local government involvement, or ones calculated to mislead or allow the new company to pass itself off as another already in existence.

39.2.2 Prepare the enabling documents

The documents that must be filed with the Registrar of Companies to enable a company to come into existence are as follows:

(a) Memorandum of Association;
(b) Articles of Association;
(c) A Statement of Registered Office;
(d) A List of Directors with their consent;
(e) A Statutory Declaration in which a solicitor or the secretary of the company confirms compliance with all requirements of incorporation.

We will briefly explain (a), (b) and (c) from this list.

Memorandum of Association

This document establishes the identity of the company. It defines its relationship with those it deals with by stating (in the objects clause) the type of business it is permitted to carry on. Originally, the objects clause was tightly specified (e.g. to mine for gold). Now, however, it has become usual to draft the objects clause to include activities that the company is not even remotely expected to be involved in. This is because if a company engages itself in an activity that is outside its objects clause, the activity is null and void (*ultra vires*). What this means is that if, for example, the activity falling outside the objects clause is a contract, the company cannot legally enforce the contract. The other party to the contract, too, is equally affected, although since 1972 there is a protection to such other party provided that party acted in good faith.[2]

> **The Memorandum of Association**
> contains the following in the sequence stated:
>
> 1. the name of the company;
> 2. domicile (country registered in);
> 3. the objects clause;
> 4. that the liability of members is limited;
> 5. the authorized share capital and its division into shares of fixed par values;
> 6. the association clause – signed by at least seven (two for a private company), each taking at least one share;
> 7. that it is a public company (if so).

The fourth paragraph of the Memorandum is commercially important because it limits the liability of each shareholder to the amount that he or she agreed to pay for the shares. This protects the shareholders from creditors of the company in that, if the company were to be liquidated and the company's assets prove insufficient to meet its liabilities in full, the creditors cannot proceed against the shareholders.

It should be noted that the contents of a company's Memorandum cannot be altered except 'in the cases, in the mode and to the extent' permitted by company law.

Articles of Association

These are a set of internal rules and regulations that govern, among other things, the relationship of the shareholders with those to whom the management of the company is ultimately entrusted – the directors. The Companies (Tables A to F) Regulations 1985, made by the Secretary of State for Trade and Industry, contains a Table 'A' which is a model set of Articles that apply to every company if, and to the extent that, they are not excluded by a company's own set of Articles. Few of the matters usually stated in the Articles of a company are listed within the box on the right.

> **The Articles of Association**
> usually state, amongst other things, the following:
>
> TABLE A: the extent applicable to it.
> SHARES: issues, forfeiture, redemption, and transfer of shares.
> VOTING POWER of each class of share.
> DIRECTORS: the number, qualifications, appointment, remuneration, removal.
> BORROWING POWERS and limits to it.
> DIVIDENDS and transfers to RESERVE
> MEETINGS of members: calling/holding.

The Statement of Registered Office

The Statement of the address of a company's registered office is filed so that the Registrar knows where to contact the company, and so that its creditors know where to send their claims and any related legal documents.

39.2.3 Obtaining a Certificate of Incorporation

On registration of all the enabling documents with the Registrar of Companies and on payment of appropriate fees, the Registrar issues a Certificate of Incorporation, which is the final and conclusive proof that a legal entity has come into existence. A private company (see Section 39.5) may start trading immediately thereafter; a public company cannot do so until it allots a minimum of £50,000 shares and receives the Registrar's consent to do so.

39.3 SHAREHOLDERS, THEIR RIGHTS AND RESPONSIBILITIES

A company is owned by the people who hold the ordinary shares. Ordinary shares are those that are entitled to the residue of profit after the claims of everyone with a prior charge (e.g. loan creditors) have been met in full. Consequently, the shares of this class are likely to be the ones most affected by any downturn or upturn in profits. To convey the proneness to risk and the fact that these shares are entitled to everything remaining after paying those with a priority claim, they are commonly referred to as **equity shares**.

Ordinary shareholders are rewarded by a portion of the company's profit being paid to them as **dividends**. Dividends are usually expressed as so many pence per share, although exceptionally they may be expressed as a percentage of the called-up value of each share. The directors have authority to pay interim dividends (usually on the basis of half-yearly accounts) and to propose the final dividend, which will be paid only if and after the shareholders approve it at the company's Annual General Meeting.

Each ordinary share would normally receive the same amount of dividend, but there are commercial circumstances in which a variety of ordinary shares can be issued, with different rights as to dividend. For example, preferred ordinary shares carry a preferential right to dividend up to a stated maximum before sharing the balance with others. deferred ordinary shares are those that are not entitled to any dividend until others have received dividend at a certain specified amount. Such deferred shares may be issued to those who founded the company and may then be known as 'founders shares'.

Votes at general meetings give control to the shareholders. The voting entitlement of each share is spelt out in the Articles of Association of each company – each share normally carries one vote. Some companies, however, issue non-voting ordinary shares.

39.3.1 Limitation of shareholders' liability

The much sought-after advantage of company formation is the limitation of each shareholder's liability. There are two methods of limiting the liability of shareholders, namely:

- **Method 1**. Each shareholder's liability is limited to the amount he or she agreed to pay for the shares taken up. The failure of the business will not, therefore, place the personal assets of the shareholder in jeopardy. However, the privilege of limited liability will be forfeited if the company carries on in business for more than six months without having at least two shareholders.
- **Method 2**. A *company limited by guarantee* is a company that has chosen to limit the liability of its members, not by reference to the number and value of shares taken up but by reference to an amount they guarantee or promise to pay (often just £1) in

case a deficiency arises when the company is wound up. Such companies are usually formed to promote art, science, commerce, education, religion, charity or profession. A company of this category may be exempted from the requirement to use the word 'limited' as the last word in its name.

There are also unlimited companies but there are few of these. An *unlimited company* is one incorporated in accordance with company law but without limiting the liability of its members. As a result, in the event of winding-up, its members are unlimitedly liable to make good any deficiency, if the assets of the company prove insufficient to meet its liabilities in full. Being in this position bestows on the company several privileges, the most significant among which is that it does not have to file its annual accounts and reports with the Registrar of Companies.

39.3.2 Transacting shares

The capital of a company is usually divided into shares. The names and addresses of individuals who acquire shares in a company, the shareholders, are entered by the Company Secretary in a Share Register. This information is necessary in order to be able to send out notices of meetings and to pay dividends.

A shareholder is issued with a share certificate as evidence of legal title to the share. The share, once issued, is the property of the individual shareholder, who may transfer it – whether by sale or as gift – to anyone. The transfer may be negotiated privately or on a Stock Exchange if the company is a listed one. The information on such transfers is communicated to the company secretary for appropriate amendments to be made in the Share Register.

In a private company there may be restrictions placed on the transferability of shares. For example, the remaining shareholders might have first option on the shares (known as the right of pre-emption) or be able to refuse to accept a transfer to a person that they do not want to join them as a shareholder. In a partnership, by contrast, whenever there is a transfer of ownership, such as that arising on the death of a partner, the partnership ceases to exist.

39.4 THE MANAGEMENT OF A COMPANY

Whereas in a partnership the law expects all partners to participate in its management, a distinctive feature of a company is that, by and large, *ownership is divorced from management*. The ownership of the company lies with the shareholders who, by virtue of their right to appoint the directors, have the ultimate control over the activities of the company. It is the director(s), however, who have strategic and day-to-day control over the affairs of the company. In many small companies there is only one director, who may also be the major shareholder, with a family member holding the remainder of the shares. In larger companies the directors are employees and may perhaps hold no shares, although it is becoming increasingly common for directors to be given share options as part of their remuneration package.

The separation of ownership and management in the larger companies has two benefits in that the company can achieve a larger capitalization and management powers can be delegated to specialists:

● **Larger capitalization.** In a partnership, efforts to raise more capital by finding new partners are usually constrained by the exposure of partners to unlimited liability, by the entitlement of every partner to participate in the management, and by the legal restriction of 20 on the number of partners. The limitation of liability and the separation of ownership from management have made it easier for a company to encourage investors to invest their savings and have made companies attractive as a business organization for undertaking ventures that could be risky. These factors have allowed them to grow and exploit economies of scale. Besides, there is no legal limit on the maximum number of shareholders.

- **Delegation** enables those incapable of (or disinclined to) active participation in management nevertheless to own a business by providing an organization where the management is delegated to specialists with appropriate skills.

However, there is a downside to this separation, in that despite the efforts by successive company legislation to safeguard the ownership rights of the shareholders and to compel the directors adequately to discharge their stewardship responsibilities, the powers of the directors are substantial and real. For example, they are usually in control of their own levels of remuneration, although in principle they are only entitled to such remuneration as the company (i.e. the shareholders) may by ordinary resolution determine. The government is not inclined to provide statutory control over remuneration and has favoured voluntary regulation. For example, companies are encouraged to comply with the Cadbury Code,[3] which recommends that companies should have non-executive directors (i.e. directors who are not full-time employees of the company) and that the non-executive directors should determine the remuneration of the executive directors.

The directors are also in control of the rewards paid as dividends to shareholders because the shareholders cannot approve dividends at a level greater than that recommended by the directors. No court of law will compel directors to pay a larger dividend than they think appropriate. The reason that the court would not interfere is because there is an assumption that the recommendation has taken into account broader strategy issues such as a potential increase in competition or a planned increase in fixed asset expenditure.

39.5 PRIVATE LIMITED COMPANIES AND PUBLIC LIMITED COMPANIES

Limited companies are of two types, as follows:

1. A public company is one that
   - is limited by shares;
   - identifies itself as a public company in its Memorandum;
   - uses the letters 'plc' (abbreviation for public limited company) as the last word in its name;
   - does not commence business nor exercise borrowing powers unless its issued share capital is at least £50,000 and until at least one-quarter of this issued capital and the whole of any premium is paid up.
2. A private company is one that is not a public company and uses the word 'Ltd' (abbreviation for limited) as the last part of its name. It is a criminal offence for a private company to make an offer to the public to subscribe for its shares or debentures. A private company enjoys many privileges (see box below).

The box below also highlights some of the differences and similarities.

	Private company	Public company
Directors	Could have just one	Should have at least two
Company secretary	Each company must have a secretary; a sole director cannot also be the secretary	
	No qualifications prescribed	Shall possess prescribed qualifications
Commencement of business	Could commence business soon after its incorporation	Cannot commence business until obtaining a Trading Certificate
Duty to lay and deliver accounts	Within ten months of the year end	Within seven months of year end
	By elective resolution may dispense with laying accounts at Annual General Meeting	No such privileges are available
Company administration	A private company has privileges (denied to a public company), such as: 1. Dispensing with the annual appointment of the auditor 2. Fewer restrictions on the financial relationship the directors have with the company 3. By resolution, to alter the duration of authority to allot shares and alter the majority required for authorizing shorter notice of meetings 4. A proxy appointed to attend/vote at meetings has same right to speak as a member	
Retention of records	Records must be retained for three years	Retention of records is for six years
Protection of the company's capital base	1. Permitted to buy/redeem own shares out of its capital (CA 1985, s. 171) 2. May provide financial assistance to buy its own shares (CA 1985, s. 155)	1. Strict rules when shares are allotted for considerations other than cash (CA 1985, s. 99) 2. Strict rules on the treatment of its own shares held by it (CA 1985, s. 146) 3. Restrictions on liens/charges on its own shares (CA 1985, s. 150) 4. Greater restriction of profit available for distribution (CA 1985, s. 264) 5. Obliged to call an Extraordinary General Meeting of members if there is a serious loss of capital (CA 1985, s. 142)

Note: CA = Companies Act

39.6 THE LAW GOVERNING COMPANIES IN THE UK

The law governing limited companies in the United Kingdom is largely encapsulated in the Companies Act 1985, as amended in 1989. Various Companies Acts passed until then have been consolidated into the four statutes as stated in the box. The Companies Act 1989 made significant changes to the Companies Act 1985, to give effect in particular to the European Community Seventh Directive, dealing

> 1. Companies Act 1985
> 2. Company Securities (Insider Dealing) Act 1985
> 3. Business Names Act 1985
> 4. Companies Consolidation (Consequential Provisions) Act 1985

with group accounts, and the Eighth Directive dealing with auditors. Other Acts have come into force subsequently but need not be considered at this stage.

39.6.1 Accounting standards regulations

'It shall be stated whether the accounts have been prepared in accordance with applicable accounting standards and particulars of any material departure from these standards and reasons for it shall be given.' (Companies Act 1985, Schedule 4 paragraph 36A) '. . . accounting standards means statements of standard accounting practice issued by such body or bodies as may be prescribed by regulations.' (Companies Act 1985, section 256)

As we learnt in Chapter 22, accounting standards must be complied with by everyone whose financial statements are expected to convey a true and fair view. In addition, specific provisions of company law (see box on left) make it obligatory for the directors to ensure that:

- the financial statements are prepared in compliance with accounting standards in force;
- in the event they do not, to identify instances of and state reasons for any departure from the standards.

39.6.2 Stock Exchange regulations

Any public company of repute may qualify for inclusion in the *Official List* of the London Stock Exchange, but only if it survives a prolonged in-depth investigation. The investigation is calculated to protect the reputation of the Stock Exchange and the interests of those who buy and sell in it. To qualify for 'listing':

- the company's listed securities initially should be likely to exceed £700,000 at market capitalization values (i.e. the number of shares × the share market price); and
- at least 25 per cent of any class of its equity capital should be in the hands of the investing public.

The *Admission of Securities to Listing* (commonly known as the 'Yellow Book') contains the conditions and procedure for listing. Once listed, the securities of the company (its shares and debentures) can be bought and sold in the London Stock Exchange. The companies so listed are obliged to comply with certain rules, which are known as 'continuing obligations' and which are intended to so regulate the volume and timing of price-sensitive information made available by the company that no one is given an advantage. Some of these rules are as follows:

- Annual accounts and reports shall be sent to shareholders within six months of the year end.
- The annual report should include additional information such as follows:
  - accounting standards: instances of non-compliance and the reasons for it;
  - segmental reports: turnover and profit to be segmented on a geographical basis;
  - trading results: any variation from what was forecast to be explained;
  - bank loans/overdrafts: repayments due within one year, 1–2 years, 2–5 years and thereafter to be disclosed;
  - directors' interests in company shares, options and contracts to be disclosed;
  - voting powers: whether there is any substantial holding (i.e. 5 per cent or more);
  - waivers of emoluments by directors and dividends by shareholders;

– subsidiaries: the names and their principal country of operation;
– operating and financial review, to draw out those aspects of the year under review that are relevant to assess the company's prospects, so as to be of assistance to those making investment decisions regarding the company;
– a confirmation of compliance with any voluntary code of best practice adopted by the company with regard to the financial aspects of corporate governance.[4]
- Half-yearly reports and preliminary profit statements are required within four months of the end of each half year, either circulated individually to members or advertised in two daily newspapers.
- Share price-sensitive information must be notified to the Stock Exchange as soon as possible.

39.7 ADVANTAGES AND DISADVANTAGES OF BEING A COMPANY

We have seen that there are many reasons why the company form of business organization is the commonest. These include the following:

- limitation of shareholders' liability so that the failure of the business will not place the personal assets of the shareholder in jeopardy;
- legal entity: by a legal fiction a company is deemed to have an existence;
- divorce of ownership from management so that management can be delegated;
- transferability of shares is possible and is easy if a company is listed on a Stock Exchange;
- a larger capitalization is possible because of the features listed;
- perpetual succession exists whereby a company continues to remain in legal existence unless a deliberate decision is taken to liquidate it.

There are, however, some disadvantages with the company form of business organization, as set out next.

39.7.1 Creditors' interest could be in jeopardy

The company form of business organization, intended to protect the interests of shareholders by granting them limited liability, places in jeopardy the interests of banks, debenture holders, creditors and whoever extends it credit facilities. This is because, should the company's resources prove insufficient to meet its commitments, those who have a claim on it will not have any recourse to the personal resources of those who own or run the company.

Statutory measures to protect creditors

Company law attempts to protect the interests of creditors by seeking to maintain intact the capital base of the company as a buffer for the creditors. The steps taken to protect the creditors' buffer from depletion include the following:

- The capital base of the company cannot be reduced (by such means as repayment of share capital, buying back or redeeming own shares) except by a procedure, and subject to the safeguards provided for, in the law.
- Profits, which may be distributed by the company, are to be determined in accordance with rules specified in the law.

39.7.2 Companies are subject to legal control

For the purpose of protecting the interests of the creditors (for the reasons stated above), the investors (who are not in charge of the management) and all the others who deal with a company in one way or another, company law subjects the management of the company to severe legal controls that include the following:

- **Restriction of activity.** If a company's activity falls outside the scope spelt out in the objects clause of its Memorandum, such activity is null and void (i.e. not enforceable at law).

- **Records.** Accounting records of the company are required to be kept as prescribed by company law (Companies Act 1985, s. 221), and these shall be kept either at the company's registered office or such other place as the directors think fit, but shall be open at all times to inspection by the officers of the company.

- **Audit.** The audit of company accounts is compulsory and the law prescribes the qualifications of the auditor as well as his powers, duties, manner of appointment and removal.

- **Statutory registers and returns.** Every company is legally obliged to maintain specified statutory registers (stated in the box here) at the company's registered office and open to inspection by the public. In addition, every company is required to make returns of specified information (such as those stated in the box) to the Registrar of Companies.

> **The statutory registers:**
>
> 1. Register of members (s. 352)
> 2. Register of debenture holders (s. 190)
> 3. Register of directors and secretaries
> 4. Register of charges (s. 407)
> 5. Register of directors' shareholdings
> 6. Register of interests in shares (s. 211)
> 7. Register of disqualification orders
>
> **Returns to be made to Registrar:**
>
> 1. The Annual Return (s. 363)
> 2. Return of allotment of shares (s. 88)
> 3. Charges on company's property (s. 415)

Note: The section numbers are from the Companies Act 1985.

- **Publicity.** A significant price that a company pays for the many advantages bestowed on it is its inability to protect the confidentiality of information on its performance and position. First, there is the legal requirement that anyone should be permitted access (though on payment of fees by non-members) to the company's statutory registers. Secondly, all information filed with the Registrar of Companies, including the annual financial statements and reports that have to accompany the Annual Returns, is available for anyone's inspection.

Interaction 39.1

Company formation and its consequences

Sen Gupta and his wife Tara are in business making a variety of oriental pickles. Sen proposes to incorporate his business as 'Sentara Ltd'.

Required: Advise Sen and Tara on how they should set about incorporating their business, and the advantages and disadvantages to them of carrying on their business through a private limited company.

39.8 HOW A COMPANY RAISES FINANCE

Investors have different attitudes to the level of risk that they will accept and the level of reward they expect. Company directors are aware of this and raise finance for their company by offering a variety of terms and variety of levels of risk. We can rank them into three broad categories as follows:

- Highest risk/potentially highest return: ordinary shares
- In between: preference shares
- Lowest risk/lowest return: debentures

Companies therefore obtain cash for their business by issuing ordinary shares, preference shares and debentures. These are referred to as **capital instruments**. Let us now consider each of these sources of finance.

39.8.1 Ordinary shares

Ordinary shareholders accept the risk that they might lose the amount they have paid
for their shares and might not receive a dividend, in return for the potential rewards of
capital growth, i.e. an increase in the value of their shares and/or income that exceeds
the rate obtainable from a less risky investment.

39.8.2 Preference shares

Preference shares are part of the issued capital of a company. These are shares that carry
a right to be paid dividends at an agreed percentage prior to the payment of dividends
on other classes of shares. Despite the prior right, there is no guarantee that they will
receive any dividend annually at the agreed rate. All that is agreed is that, until this
prior right is honoured, others will not receive any dividend. The following points may
be noted:

- If a company does not pay a preference dividend, the courts will not compel payment, so long as no dividend is paid to those with an inferior claim.
- Preference shares are assumed to be cumulative irrespective of whether the name
  expressly confirms this position.[5] This means that those with inferior claims for dividends cannot be paid any until all arrears up to and including the current year's preference dividend are fully discharged.
- Unless the terms of issue or the Articles of Association state to the contrary, the word
  'preference' is assumed to confer on the preference shares the preferential claim only
  for dividends. This means that they are not automatically entitled to a preferential
  repayment of capital in the event of liquidation.
- Usually the preference shares do not carry a right to vote at meetings, although exceptionally such a right may be provided, particularly when preferential dividends are
  in arrears.
- A variation, known as participating preference shares, gives such shares a right to a
  further dividend, sharing profits in an agreed proportion with others, after the others
  have received dividends at a stated amount.
- If the Articles of Association or the terms of issue so provide, preference shares may be
  redeemable on terms agreed at the time of the issue, but in accordance with the procedure stated in the law.

39.8.3 Debentures

Another way of raising finance is to borrow by issuing debentures. **Debentures** are written acknowledgement of indebtedness by a company. The acknowledgement is usually
made in a document (known as a debenture deed) that bears the company's seal and states,
among other things, the rate of interest, the nature and type of any security provided,

and the terms of repayment. The ability of a company to borrow long-term is usually controlled by placing restrictions thereon in its Memorandum and setting limits on the amount in the Articles of Association. On the basis of the security provided for the indebtedness, debentures are classified as follows:

- Mortgage debentures
- Debentures supported by a floating charge
- Unsecured debentures (sometimes known as naked debentures).

Each type is described further below.

Mortgage debentures

Where the one to whom the company is indebted is granted a charge on any property of the company, it is known as mortgage debentures. The charge so granted is usually a fixed charge on a particular property – typically a fixed asset such as a freehold property. What this means is that while the company retains the custody and the uninterrupted use of the property, an interest in that property is assigned to the one to whom the company is indebted.

The assignment of interest, known as the 'creation of a charge', should be registered within 21 days with the Registrar of Companies and also recorded in the company's Register of Charges (s. 395 of the Companies Act 1985). By virtue of the interest so assigned, the one to whom it is assigned has the right to demand the disposal of the property and settlement of his claim out of the proceeds, should the company default on any of the terms of the mortgage. The default may be in payment of interest, repayment of capital on due dates, or a failure to insure or otherwise maintain the mortgaged property. So long as the charge remains valid, the company is not allowed to dispose of the mortgaged property without the prior permission of the debenture holder; and if the property is disposed of, the debenture holder has to be repaid (the debenture redeemed) immediately.

Debentures with a floating charge

Whereas it is possible to create a mortgage over fixed assets, it is not possible to do this with current assets such as stock and debtors, which are constantly turned over. To meet this situation, a company can create what is known as a 'floating charge'. Under this arrangement the charge remains floating over the charged assets, allowing the company to dispose of them until such time as it fails to comply with the terms of the charge (e.g. by failing to pay interest or meet the agreed repayment schedule). If it fails to comply with the terms of the charge, it is said to have 'defaulted' and the floating charge 'crystallizes'. **Crystallizing** means that the floating charge becomes a fixed charge at that time and the company is no longer permitted to dispose of the assets.

A floating charge may be created also on certain types of fixed assets (like seats in a theatre) which are systematically replaced over a rotation of years.

Unsecured debentures

Debentures that are not secured by any form of charge over any of the company's assets are merely unsecured loans. They are known as unsecured debentures. In the event of non-payment of interest or capital, these debenture holders have merely the same rights as an unsecured trade creditor (i.e. they can seek a judgement against the company in the court).

Preference shares v. debentures

On the day that Sen Gupta and his wife Tara decided to incorporate their oriental pickle business into a limited company, the Balance Sheet of the partnership business had been finalized as shown here. Sen proposes that he and his wife should each be allotted 400,000 ordinary shares of £1 each at 25p premium per share, in Sentara Ltd. Since Tara requires the amount advanced by her as a loan to be paid back in three years, she is to receive £100,000 8 per cent debentures. Tara wonders whether it would not be better for her to be allotted 8 per cent preference shares rather than debentures.

Required: Your advice is sought on Tara's proposal.

BALANCE SHEET AS AT 31.3.20X1		
	£000	£000
Fixed assets at written down value		648
Stock at cost	365	
Debtors	242	
Cash/bank	94	
Creditors	(249)	452
		1,100
		£000
Capital – Sen Gupta		500
Tara Gupta		500
8% Loan from Tara		100
		1,100

39.9 ACCOUNTING FOR SHARES AND DEBENTURES

39.9.1 Accounting for shares

Company law in the United Kingdom requires that every share should have a par value (also known as its nominal value) assigned to each share, whereas in the United States and other countries shares of 'no par value' are common. Though a Committee appointed by the UK Board of Trade advocated the issue of shares of no par value in the UK,[6] to date no action has been taken in this regard.

Share premium

A successful company may be able to issue its shares at a price that is greater than the par value fixed for each. For example, it may issue a £10 share for, say, £12. Upon receiving £12, the par value is posted to the Ordinary Share Capital account, while £2 (i.e. the difference between the par value and the amount received) is posted to a Share Premium account because that is the requirement of company law (s. 130 of the Companies Act 1985).

Any balance in the Share Premium account is, therefore, a part of the capital received from shareholders. For preserving the capital base in the interest of those who have a claim on the company, company law seeks to protect from erosion any balance in the Share Premium account, as much as it does with the balance in the Share Capital account. Accordingly, company law (Companies Act 1985, s. 130) permits the application of any balance in the Share Premium account only for the purposes stated within the box here.

Share Premium account balance may be applied for:

1. Capital reduction.
2. Issue of bonus shares.
3. Write-off of preliminary expenses.
4. Write-off of expenses of, or commission on, or discount on, the issue of debentures.
5. Write-off of the expenses of, or commission on, the issue of shares.
6. Write-off of the premium on redeeming debentures.
7. Write-off of the premium paid for redeeming shares that had been issued at a premium, provided the redemption is out of a fresh issue (CA 1985, s. 160).

39.9.2 **Accounting for debentures**

Irrespective of whether the debentures are mortgage, floating or unsecured, the accounting treatment is the same, namely, to post the proceeds received from the cash book to the credit of a long-term liability account named the Debentures account. Interest is a period expenditure, to be deducted when determining the company's profit before tax.

References

1. *Salomon v. A. Salomon and Co Ltd/Broderip v. Salomon* (1895) 2 Ch. 323.
2. The European Communities Act 1972, which implemented the EC Council's First Directive.
3. The report of 'The Committee on the Financial Aspects of Corporate Governance', chaired by Sir Adrian Cadbury, was set up in 1991 by the Financial Reporting Council, the London Stock Exchange and the accounting profession to examine the reporting and control functions of boards of directors and the role of auditors.
4. Cadbury report, *ibid*.
5. *Henry v. Great Northern Rly Co* (1857) 1 De G. & J. 606.
6. The Gedge Committee Report 1952.

SOLUTIONS TO INTERACTIVE QUESTIONS

IQ 39.1 Company formation and its consequences

(a) Procedure for incorporating a company

It is unlikely that a company with the name Sentara Ltd can be bought off the shelf. The most convenient way of incorporation is to assign the responsibility to a solicitor specializing in company formation. If Sen and Tara prefer to do it themselves, they must take the following steps:

1. Have the name Sentara Ltd cleared by the Registrar of Companies.
2. Prepare and have printed the enabling documents. When preparing the Memorandum of Association, special attention should be paid to (a) the objects clause, to ensure that all activities that their company intends (even remotely) to undertake are mentioned therein, and (b) the authorized share capital, to ensure that it is adequate for the activities contemplated bearing in mind that company registration fees are calculated on the basis of the amount stated.
3. Upon filing the enabling documents with the Registrar of Companies and payment of requisite fees, they will receive the Certificate of Incorporation.

Sentara Ltd, being a private limited company, can commence business from that date.

(b) Merits and demerits of incorporation

- Merits:
  1. There is a limitation of Sen's and Tara's liability to the amount they agree to contribute to Sentara Ltd by taking up its shares. In the unlikely event that the company is required (by courts, for instance) to compensate food poisoning with a sum more than the total resources of the company, the personal wealth of Sen and Tara will not be in jeopardy.
  2. There is divorce of management from ownership. It becomes possible to delegate the management of Sentara Ltd to specialized hands, while Sen and Tara retain control.
  3. Larger capitalization is possible. Sentara Ltd can raise capital, as required, by issuing debentures or even shares, while Sen and Tara retain control by ensuring that they retain majority votes.
  4. Perpetual succession exists. The business and its supply of oriental pickles may be expected to outlive Sen and Tara.
  5. Legal personality exists. Sentara Ltd is recognized in law as an artificial legal person who can sue and be sued.
  6. The ownership of the business can be transferred conveniently by a mere transfer of shares.

● **Demerits:**
   1. There is a liability to Corporation Tax (see Chapter 41). Unlike the proprietary business of Sen and Tara, Sentara Ltd is liable to Corporation Tax.
   2. The company is subject to legal control. Sentara Ltd has to ensure that its activities are always within the 'objects clause' in its Memorandum of Association, has to maintain proper books of accounts, lay and deliver financial statements (as will be explained in Chapter 42), have those financial statements audited, maintain statutory registers, and make regular statutory returns to the Registrar of Companies.
   3. **Publicity.** Because of the legal requirement to file returns and permit access to its statutory registers, members of the public will have access to information on Sentara Ltd – though, being a private limited company, the amount of such information disclosure will be restricted.

IQ 39.2 Preference shares v. debentures

From Tara's (the investor's) point of view:

● The debenture holder receives interest at the agreed rate irrespective of whether the company has distributable profit. In respect of preference shares, the receipt of the dividend depends first of all on whether the company has distributable profit, and second on whether the directors approve the payment. They may legitimately refuse approval so long as they do not pay dividends to those with an inferior claim.
● The debentures, unlike preference shares, could be secured with a charge (either fixed or floating) on the assets of the company.
● A preference shareholder is a member of the company, whereas a debenture holder is only a creditor. As a member, a preference shareholder may have voting rights if the dividends are in arrears.
● Assuming that debentures are not secured, in a winding-up they will still enjoy a twofold advantage over preference shareholders. First, debentures rank prior to preference shares for repayment of capital. Second, debentures are entitled to claim interest right up to the date of repayment, whereas preference dividends are payable only up to the date of a winding-up order or the resolution to wind up. Whether they are entitled at all would depend on whether the Articles or the terms of their issue provide for it or whether the directors declared the dividend in arrears prior to the date of winding-up.
● On the other hand, the preference shares have an advantage over debentures, within the imputation system of taxation. Under this system any dividend received is imputed to have already suffered taxation at the basic rate of income tax. Assuming the basic rate of taxation to be 20 per cent, what this means is that Tara will receive a return of 10 per cent if she is allotted preference shares (i.e. 8 per cent plus the imputed tax), whereas she will receive only 8 per cent on the debenture.

From the point of view of Sentara Ltd (the company):

● Debenture interest is fully tax-deductible for the company, whereas preference dividend is not. The implication of this is that, assuming a Corporation Tax rate (see Chapter 41) of 20 per cent, the cost that the company incurs on debentures will be only 6.4 per cent (i.e. 8 per cent less a tax saving of 20 per cent thereof) as against 8 per cent on preference shares.
● When the directors decide to redeem the debentures, they could do so without having to comply with all the legal requirements that apply when preference shares are redeemed.
● Viewed from the gearing position of the company (see Section 40.1), there is little to choose between the two methods of raising capital because both debentures and preference shares are prior-charge capital.

## Chapter 40

COMPANIES (2): SHARES AND DEBENTURES

In this chapter

We will learn of:

- shares issue, forfeiture and reissue
- issue, servicing and redemption of debentures

and you should be able to account for:

- issue, forfeiture and reissue of shares
- the servicing and redemption of debentures

40.1 EQUITY AND LONG-TERM FINANCE

A company could finance itself entirely by the issue of ordinary shares and/or by retaining profits as they are earned. However, if the company is able to borrow at a lower rate than the rate of profit it makes on the borrowed funds, then the ordinary shareholders would benefit from borrowing more. This process of operating with borrowed capital rather than equity capital is known as *gearing*. It would seem at first thought that it would benefit the ordinary shareholders for the company to borrow as much as possible. However, the company has to continue paying the interest on the loan even when the earnings become less than the rate of interest. Besides, as the amount borrowed increases, the risk that the lender perceives increases, and therefore the rate of interest required by the lender is very likely to increase.

40.2 PROCEDURE FOR A PUBLIC ISSUE OF SHARES

A public limited company seeking to raise capital by issuing shares would issue a *prospectus* calling upon those interested to apply for shares. The applicants are requested to enclose an amount as *application money*. If applications are received for more shares than the number advertised, the application money is refunded to unsuccessful applicants along with a letter of regret. The successful applicants are allotted shares and requested at that point to pay either the whole of the remainder due or an instalment, which then is called *allotment money*. In the latter case, further instalments will be called for and these are known as *calls*. There may well be more than one call.

40.3 ACCOUNTING FOR SHARE ISSUES

40.3.1 An analogy

To understand accounting for share applications and allotment, let us first consider an analogous situation. Henry owned a vintage car, which he advertised for sale at £15,000. To establish the seriousness of applicants, he requested a refundable deposit of £5,000 with the application, the remainder being payable when the car was delivered. When he received applications from seven different parties, he opened an account for each applicant and posted to its credit the amount received as advance from each. A more convenient alternative would have been to open a single control account for all seven applicants, posting the amount received from the cash book to the credit of this Control account and posting to its debit the refund of £30,000 to unsuccessful applicants. At this point the Control account would have recorded as a credit balance £5,000 owed to the successful applicant. When the car is delivered, the Sales account would be credited and the Control account debited with the *full* sale price of £15,000, so that, net of the amount received already, the successful applicant would, at this point, appear as a debtor for the difference of £10,000.

APPLICATION AND SALE OF A VINTAGE VEHICLE ACCOUNT

		£		£	
2	Cash book – refund	30,000	Cash book – applicants' money	35,000	1
3	Sales a/c	15,000	Balance c/d	10,000	4
4	Balance b/d	10,000			

Notes:

1. When application money is received.
2. When refunds are made to those not successful.
3. When the car is delivered to the successful applicant.
4. The debt carried down in the Control account is cleared when, on receipt, £10,000 is posted from the cash book to the credit of the Control account.

40.3.2 When shares are to be paid for fully at the time of allotment

When accounting for an issue of shares, the application money is posted from the cash book to the credit of a Control account, which is named Application and Allotment account. The refund of application money in respect of unsuccessful applications is posted from the cash book to the debit of the Control account. When shares are allotted to successful applicants, if (as in the case of the vintage car) the full price of the share is payable on allotment, the par value of all shares allotted is credited to the Share Capital account and debited to this Control account.

If we assume, for example, that applications were invited for 10,000 ordinary shares of £1 each, 20p per share payable on application and the remainder on allotment, and that applications were received for 12,000 shares, the accounting entries will be as shown below. When 10,000 shares are allotted, the full price of the shares (£10,000) is debited to the Control account, so that the successful applicants will be reported as debtors for £8,000 (i.e. full share price net of the amount received as application money). The receipt of the allotment money (10,000 shares @ 80p per share), when posted from the cash book to the Control account, will wipe out the debit balance in the Control account.

APPLICATION AND ALLOTMENT ACCOUNT

	£		£
Cash book – refund	400	Cash book – applicants' money	2,400
Share Capital a/c	10,000	Balance c/d	8,000
Balance	8,000		

40.3.3 **When a part of the share price is not payable until called**

Alternatively, a part of the share price may be payable only on call. Let us consider a scenario in which applications are invited for 10,000 ordinary shares of £1 each, 20p per share payable with application, 45p on allotment and the remainder when called. Let us assume this time that applications were received for 15,000 shares, the allotment was made on 15 March, and the call was not made until 5 June. Let us assume also that, by 30 June, the allotment money was received on 9,000 shares but the call money only on 6,000.

To identify separately the amounts of arrears for the allotment money and for the call, it would make sense to write up a Call account separately. When, as in this example, the call is made on 5 June, the Call account is debited and the Share Capital account credited.

An important point to note is that the balance in the Share Capital account, on any date, will always be the *value of the number of shares in issue so far called up*. For example, until the call was made on 5 June, the 10,000 shares in issue appear in the Share Capital account at the value so far called up – at that point, 65p each.

APPLICATION AND ALLOTMENT ACCOUNT

		£				£
?	Cash book – refund	1,000		?	Cash bk – applications	3,000
15.3	Share Capital a/c	6,500		?	Cash bk – allotment	4,050
				30.6	Balance c/d	450
	Balance	450				

CALL ACCOUNT

		£				£
5.6	Share Capital a/c	3,500		?	Cash book	2,100
				30.6	Balance c/d	1,400
1.7	Balance b/d	1,400				

ORDINARY SHARE CAPITAL ACCOUNT

		£				£
				15.3	Applic. & Allotment a/c	6,500
30.6	Balance c/d	10,000		5.6	Call account	3,500
				1.7	Balance b/d	10,000

Accounting for issue of shares at par

Immediately after its incorporation on 1 July 20X0, Tender plc invited applications for 10,000 ordinary shares of £10 each payable as stated below:

- £4 on application;
- £5 on the allotment of the share;
- £1 on call.

Applications are received for 12,500 shares. Allotment was made on 14.9.20X0 and a letter of regret dispatched to unsuccessful applicants on the same date, enclosing a full refund of their application money. The call was made on 1.11.20X0. By 31 December 20X0, the allotment money was in arrears on 1,600 shares and the call on 3,400 shares.

Required: Account for these transactions in the company's cash book and ledger accounts, and state how the balances appear on the Balance Sheet on 31.12.20X0.

40.3.4 **When shares are issued at a premium**

If a company has traded profitably and there is a strong demand for the shares, it becomes possible to issue shares at a premium – i.e. at a price higher than the par value fixed for each. The excess is the premium received on each share. It is usual to assume that the premium is received as part of the allotment money. Accordingly, the premium is accounted for when accounting for the allotment of shares.

Let us account for the allotment of a single share of £10, assuming that the terms of issue required £3 on application, £4 on allotment and £4 more on call. There are three steps involved as follows:

- Step 1: Ascertain the amount of the premium by comparing the total of various amounts receivable in respect of each share with the par value. Under the terms of issue, a total of £11 is receivable for the share of £10, the excess of £1 being, of course, the premium.
- Step 2: Determine the amount to be credited to the Share Capital account, at the point of allotment. The amount to be credited is the value so far called up of the share at that point. This is best calculated by comparing the value of calls yet to be made with the par value of shares. In our example, the par value of each share is £10, the call value is £4 and hence the value so far called up of each share, at the point of allotment, is the difference of £6.
- Step 3: Ascertain the amount to be charged to the applicant (i.e. debited to the Application and Allotment account) at the point of allotment. The amount to be charged is the value of the share so far called up (£6) plus the premium (£1) that is payable upon allotment.

Accordingly the accounting entries for allotting a single share would be as stated by the journal entry shown here.

Application and Allotment a/c	Dr	£7	–
To Ordinary Share Capital a/c		–	£6
Share Premium account		–	£1
Being the allotment of a share of £10,			
£6 called up, issued at a premium of £1.			

Interaction 40.2	**Accounting for issue of shares at premium**

Immediately after incorporation, Sycamore plc invited applications for one million ordinary shares of £1 each, on terms as stated in the box shown here. Applications were received for 1,450,000 shares. The allotment of shares and the refund to unsuccessful applicants were made on 31.3.20X0. The first call was made on 5.7.20X0. By the year end on 30.9.20X0, allotment money was in arrears on 175,000 shares and the first call in arrears on 240,000.

Receivable on each share	
On application	20p
On allotment	35p
On first call	30p
On final call	25p
Total receivable	110p

Required:

(a) Account for the share transactions in the year.
(b) State how the share capital will be stated on the Balance Sheet as at 30 September 20X0.
(c) Explain what is the authorized capital of the company.
(d) Identify the issued capital, called-up capital and paid-up capital of Sycamore plc as at 30.9.20X0.

40.3.5 When shares are allotted *pro rata*

If applications are received for more shares than the number advertised (so that the share issue is 'oversubscribed'), the company has to establish a criterion for deciding which applications to reject and which to accept. Alternatively, a company may decide to meet all applicants' requests but proportionately (*pro rata*). For example, if 12,000 applications are received for 10,000 shares, the decision could be to allot five shares to every request for six. When that happens, the application money received in respect of unsuccessful applications is retained (rather than refunded) as an offset against the amount due on allotment.

Interaction 40.3	*Pro rata* **allotment of shares**

Cavendish plc invited applications for 20,000 ordinary shares of £1 each, payable as 25p on application, 65p on allotment and 20p on a call that is due on 1 May 20X0. Applications were received for 32,000 shares. Applications for 2,000 shares were rejected and the others were allotted shares *pro rata* on 1.3.20X0. By 30.6.20X0, allotment money was in arrears on 1,600 shares and the call was in arrears on 4,600 shares.

Required: Set out the ledger accounts recording the above transactions up to 30 June 20X0.

40.3.6 When shares are offered as a package deal

Traders who find some product lines not moving fast are known to resort to 'package deals', selling them in a parcel along with others in greater demand. The same technique may be resorted to by a company that finds the demand low for (say) its preference shares, perhaps because the dividend rate assigned to them is lower than prevailing in the market. To account for the allotment of shares, one has to know the so far called-up value of the shares allotted. Where allotment is a package of two categories of shares and, at the time of allotment, a call remains to be made, it is necessary that one of the categories of shares should be identified as fully called-up at the point of allotment so that one may know that the call yet to be made relates to the other.

Shares offered in a package deal

Flourishing plc invited applications for 100,000 packages, each consisting of one 8% preference share of £1 each to be allotted at par and two ordinary shares of £1 each to be allotted at £1.25 per share. The preference share is to be regarded as fully called-up at the point of allotment. Applicants for each package were required to pay £1 with the application, £1.25 on allotment, 75p on first call and the balance on final call. Applications were received for 125,000 packages. The applications for 25,000 packages were rejected and allotment made for the others on 5 May 20X0. The first call was made on 1.6.20X0. By 1.10.20X0, all amounts due on shares until this date had been received other than the allotment money and the first call on the ordinary shares in 8,000 packages.

Required: Set out the ledger accounts recording these transactions.

40.4 FORFEITURE AND REISSUE OF SHARES

If those to whom shares are allotted by a company default paying for them on the terms agreed, the directors have the power in Table A to forfeit the shares (by passing a resolution for the purpose, after giving 14 days' notice to those in default), and to resell the shares so forfeited.[1] Three points deserve attention as follows:

1. The person whose shares are forfeited, though ceasing to be a member of the company, remains liable to pay the company the full amount in default, unless the company is able to recover that amount by reissuing the shares involved.[2]
2. The forfeited shares may be held by the company as an asset – but only up to three years,[3] and during this period these shares may be reported on the Balance Sheet as an asset, described as 'investments in own shares'. Otherwise the shares should be either reissued or cancelled. If cancelled, it amounts, in effect, to a reduction of the company's capital and this requires compliance with substantial legal procedures.
3. If forfeited shares are reissued, the proceeds from the reissue plus amounts received prior to the forfeiture should be not less than the par value of the shares. This is insisted upon because otherwise it would amount to issuing shares at a discount, which is legally prohibited.[4]

40.4.1 Accounting for forfeiture of shares

Shares remain in issue until they are cancelled by a resolution of directors. Hence, except upon cancellation, the balance in the Share Capital account is not reduced; all that happens in a forfeiture is that those to whom the shares were originally allotted are deprived of their ownership and the shares held for the time being by the company, reported as 'Investments in own shares' in their Balance Sheet, until they are allotted to someone else by reissue. The amount in default on these shares is the value at which they are capitalized. For example, if an ordinary share of £1 had been forfeited because the call of 20p was in default, the debit balance of 20p that would appear in the Call account is, upon forfeiture, transferred to an asset account named Investments in Own Shares account.

<table>
<tr><td>

**Interaction
40.5**

</td><td>

Forfeiture of shares

Refer back to the case of Tender plc (IQ 40.1). The company's directors resolved on 1.1.20X1 to forfeit all shares in arrears on that date for the allotment money.

Required: Set out the ledger accounts to record the forfeiture, and state how the share transactions will feature in the company's Balance Sheet on 1.1.20X1 immediately after the forfeiture.

</td></tr>
</table>

<table>
<tr><td>

**Interaction
40.6**

</td><td>

Reissue of forfeited shares

On 15.1.20X1, Tender plc (see IQ 40.5) reissued all the forfeited shares at £7 each, payable immediately on reissue.

Required:

(a) Account for the reissue of forfeited shares.
(b) Explain how you would treat the gain on reissue.
(c) State the consequence if the reissue had been at £5.50 per share.

</td></tr>
</table>

40.4.2 Shares forfeited are those that had been issued at a premium

If the shares are in this category and, at the point of forfeiture, allotment money on them had not been received, because the premium is assumed to be received along with the allotment money the unreceived premium should be reversed when accounting for the forfeited shares as an asset.

For example, let us assume that applications were invited for a single share of £10, £4 payable on application and £7 more on allotment. If the share is forfeited for non-payment of the allotment money, the forfeiture will be accounted for by making two entries as follows: the transfer of the debit balance in the Application and Allotment account (£7) to a Forfeited Shares account; and £1 accounted for in the Share Premium account when the share was allotted is transferred to offset that amount from the balance in the Forfeited Shares account. Thus the forfeited shares will be reported, until reissue, as an asset at the amount of the unreceived part of its par value (£6).

<table>
<tr><td>

**Interaction
40.7**

</td><td>

Forfeiture of shares issued at premium

On 1 October 20X0, Sycamore plc (referred to in IQ 40.2) resolved to forfeit all shares in arrears for allotment money on that day. The final call was made on 1 November 20X0, and 100,000 of the forfeited shares are to be reissued on 1.1.20X1 at 85p per share. By 30.9.20X1, all amounts due on shares had been received, other than the first call on 600 shares and the final call on 900.

Required: Account for these share transactions, bearing in mind that:

● each share had been issued at a premium of 10p, which is assumed to be received along with the allotment money;
● shares were forfeited when each was 75p called-up and reissued when fully called.

</td></tr>
</table>

40.5 SHARES ISSUED FOR CONSIDERATIONS OTHER THAN CASH

A company may acquire an asset by paying for it not in cash but by issuing its *own* shares. For example, if a company issued 100,000 ordinary shares of £10 each to acquire a property that has a market value of £1.2 million, the par value of shares issued (to be stated in the Share Capital account) is £1 million, whereas the value of the consideration received is £1.2 million. This means that by

	£000	£000
Freehold property a/c Dr	1,200	–
To Share Capital a/c	–	1,000
Share Premium a/c	–	200

Being allotment of 100,000 ordinary shares of £10, fully called-up, to pay for the acquisition of freehold property.

issuing its own shares the company makes a gain of £200,000 which, in accordance with section 130 of the Companies Act 1985, should be accounted for as share premium. The journal entry for accounting for the transaction would appear as shown above.

Company law is sensitive to possible abuses when shares are issued for consideration other than cash. A director or other related party in a position of influence may be allotted shares the value of which may be excessive in relation to the value of the property transferred or services rendered. For this reason public companies are required to get properties valued by an independent expert when it is paid for by a share allotment,[5] and they are also prohibited from issuing shares for a consideration to be satisfied by rendering of any service or a promise to render service.[6]

40.6 ISSUE OF BONUS SHARES

Shares issued to existing shareholders without making any charge for them are known as bonus shares or a *scrip issue*. Such shares are issued usually for the purpose of bringing the issued capital of the company (£400,000 in the example on the right) more in line with the capital employed by the company (£1,300,000). If the company pays a dividend of £300,000, it would appear to be an excessive

Capital and reserves:	£000
Ordinary shares of £1 each	400
Share Premium account	200
Revaluation Reserve	400
Profit and Loss account	300
	1,300

reward to shareholders because it would represent a 75 per cent return on their capital. If the balances in the Share Premium account and Revaluation account are used to make a bonus issue of three for every two shares currently in issue, the issued capital would become £1,000,000 and then the dividend of £300,000 would appear more reasonable at 30 per cent.

If three bonus shares of £1 each are issued for every two currently in issue, shares of the value of £600,000 (£400,000 × 3/2) would be issued. This is accounted for by credited the Share Capital account and debiting a Bonus Issue account with £600,000. Since these shares are not going to be paid for, the debit balance in the Bonus Issue account would represent a loss that has to be written off. Unless the company deliberately wishes to tie down distributable profits, the loss should be written off against the balance in the Share Premium account (which can never be distributed) and that in the Revaluation Reserve (which is distributable only in certain circumstances, such as when the revalued asset is sold). Hence the cost of the bonus issue should be written off as shown by the journal entry here.

	£	£
Share Premium a/c	200,000	–
Revaluation Reserve	400,000	–
To Bonus issue	–	600,000

Being writing off cost of bonus issue

40.7 RIGHTS ISSUE OF SHARES

A company could raise additional capital and also reward its shareholders by making a rights issue. A £1 share cannot be issued at a price lower than £1 because that amounts to issuing the share at a discount and company law prohibits that. However, if the share is selling in the market at 180p each, the company may give its shareholders the *right* to subscribe less than the market price for the share. For example, if the company makes a rights issue of 10,000 shares at 110p each, the issue, when taken up, would be accounted for as shown here.

Dr Cash book	£11,000
Cr Share Capital account	£10,000
Cr Share Premium account	£1,000

40.8 ACCOUNTING FOR THE ISSUE AND SERVICING OF DEBENTURES

40.8.1 Accounting for debentures issued at par

Debentures represent a liability for the company. Accordingly, the cash received by issuing debentures is posted from the cash book to a liability account, named the Debentures account, which is reported in the Balance Sheet as a non-current liability. The interest incurred for the purpose of obtaining finance is an expenditure written off to the Profit and Loss account.

40.8.2 Accounting for debentures issued at a discount

A company that is unable to pay interest on its borrowings at rates currently prevailing in the market may offer to compensate the other party by issuing its debentures at a discount. For example, if the interest rate prevailing in the market as at 1.1.20X0 is 15 per cent per year, but the company is able to pay only 6 per cent per year and intends to repay the borrowing in five years, it may offer to issue 6% debentures of £100,000 at 30.17 per cent discount. What this means is that it receives only £69,830 in cash upon issuing the debentures, but it has to pay interest at 6 per cent p.a. on £100,000 annually and repay £100,000 to settle the liability on 31.12.20X4. As we see from the calculations in the box, £69,830 plus interest at 15 per cent p.a., less 6 per cent p.a. paid as interest in each of the five years, accumulates to £100,000, which is payable on 31.12.20X4.

Year	Amount owed 1.1	Interest at 15% p.a.	Interest paid in year	Owed by 31 December
20X0	£69,830	£10,475	£6,000	£74,305
20X1	£74,305	£11,146	£6,000	£79,451
20X2	£79,451	£11,918	£6,000	£85,369
20X3	£85,369	£12,805	£6,000	£92,174
20X4	£92,174	£13,826	£6,000	£100,000

FRS 4, *Capital Instruments*, requires accounting as follows:

- At the point of issuing debentures, the liability is accounted for at the amount of net proceeds, i.e. £69,830 is posted from the cash book to a 6% debentures account.
- Expenses incurred directly in relation to the issue of debentures are offset against the proceeds of the issue so as to report the liability at the 'net' proceeds, immediately upon the issue. For the purpose of this illustration we have assumed that there were no such expenses.

- Annually, interest is accounted for at the effective rate of 15 per cent p.a. and not at the 6 per cent actually paid, i.e. an Interest (expenditure) account is debited and a Debentures (liability) account is credited annually with 15 per cent of the amount of liability outstanding at the commencement of each year. For example, interest written off in the year 20X0 is £10,475 (not £6,000).
- Interest actually paid (at 6 per cent) is posted from the cash book to the Debentures account.

Accordingly, the liability (debentures) is reported in the Balance Sheet at the end of the first year at £74,305, being the proceeds of the debenture issue plus interest payable at the effective rate (15 per cent) less interest actually paid (at 6 per cent). See the ledger account shown below:

6% DEBENTURES ACCOUNT

		£			£
31.12.20X0	Cash book – interest @ 6%	6,000	1.1.20X0	Cash book	69,830
31.12.20X0	Balance c/d	74,305	31.12.20X0	P&L – interest @ 15%	10,475
			1.1.20X1	Balance b/d	74,305

Over the next four years the liability increases annually by the difference between the interest effectively incurred in each and the amount actually paid, to appear at the amount (£100,000) at which the liability is to be discharged by the end of the fifth year. See the ledger account below:

6% DEBENTURES ACCOUNT

		£			£
31.12.20X0	Cash bk – interest @ 6%	6,000	1.1.20X0	Cash book	69,830
31.12.20X0	Balance c/d	74,305	31.12.20X0	P&L – interest @ 15%	10,475
31.12.20X1	Cash bk – interest @ 6%	6,000	1.1.20X1	Balance b/d	74,305
31.12.20X1	Balance c/d	79,451	31.12.20X1	P&L – interest @ 15%	11,146
31.12.20X2	Cash bk – interest @ 6%	6,000	1.1.20X2	Balance b/d	79,451
31.12.20X2	Balance c/d	85,369	31.12.20X2	P&L – interest @ 15%	11,918
31.12.20X3	Cash bk – interest @ 6%	6,000	1.1.20X3	Balance b/d	85,369
31.12.20X3	Balance c/d	92,174	31.12.20X3	P&L – interest @ 15%	12,805
31.12.20X4	Cash bk – interest @ 6%	6,000	1.1.20X4	Balance b/d	92,174
31.12.20X4	Cash bk – repayment	100,000	31.12.20X4	P&L – interest @ 15%	13,826

Issue of debentures at a discount

Interaction 40.8

Motorviola plc issued £500,000 worth of 8% debentures on 1.1.20X1 at a 10 per cent discount, incurring £10,747 as expenses directly in respect of the issue. The debentures are to be redeemed at par on 31.12.20X4. The rate of interest applicable to such borrowing is 12 per cent per annum.

Required: State the amount at which the liability will be reported on 31 December 20X1, and identify the debenture interest written off in each year to 31 December 20X4.

40.8.3 **Accounting for the repayment of debentures**

Repayment of debentures is usually referred to as the *redemption* of debentures. The amount paid for redemption is posted from the cash book to the Liability account, as was done in the illustration shown above.

A company unable to borrow at current market rates may borrow at rates lower than the market, agreeing to redeem the debentures at a premium (i.e. paying for them more than the par value of the debentures). This, like issuing debentures at a discount, is another method of disguising the rate of interest effectively paid by a company. For illustration, let us assume that on 1 January 20X1, when interest rates were 12 per cent, a company issued £100,000 8% debentures at par, agreeing to redeem them at a 25 per cent premium by 31.12.20X5. The expenses of issue were £234.

The accounting entries are similar to those stated in respect of the issue of debentures at a discount. On the date of issue, the debentures are reported as the proceeds net of the expenses of issue. The interest written off every year is calculated at the effective rate of 12 per cent per annum on the liability outstanding at the beginning of each year. The liability is settled by the end of the fifth year at £125,000. The Ledger account would appear as follows:

6% DEBENTURES ACCOUNT

		£			£
1.1.X1	Cash bk – expense	234	1.1.X1	Cash book	100,000
1.1.X1	Balance c/d	99,766			
31.12.X1	Cash bk – int. paid	8,000	1.1.X1	Balance b/d	99,766
31.12.X1	Balance c/d	103,738	31.12.X1	P&L – interest	11,972
31.12.X2	Cash bk – int. paid	8,000	1.1.X2	Balance b/d	103,738
31.12.X2	Balance c/d	108,187	31.12.X2	P&L – interest	12,449
31.12.X3	Cash bk – int. paid	8,000	1.1.X2	Balance b/d	108,187
31.12.X3	Balance c/d	113,170	31.12.X3	P&L – interest	12,983
31.12.X4	Cash bk – int. paid	8,000	1.1.X4	Balance b/d	113,170
31.12.X4	Cash bk – redempt.	118,750	31.12.X4	P&L – interest	13,580
31.12.X5	Cash bk – int. paid	8,000	1.1.X5	Balance b/d	118,750
31.12.X5	Cash bk – redempt.	125,000	31.12.X5	P&L – interest	14,250

Interaction 40.9

Redemption of debentures at a premium

Mineret plc issued £600,000 worth of 6% debentures on 1.1.20X1, at a discount of 10 per cent on the basis that they will be redeemed at a 30 per cent premium by 31 December 20X4. Expenses of issue amounted to £8,486. The terms were calculated on the basis of an interest rate of 16 per cent per annum.

Required: Set out the 6% Debentures account, identifying the amounts expensed as interest cost in each of the four years to 31.12.20X4 and showing the redemption on that date.

40.9 APPRAISING THE FINANCING STRUCTURE OF A COMPANY

There are two key ratios that are calculated when a company has a mix of equity and long-term loans. These are the gearing ratio from the Balance Sheet and the interest cover from the Profit and Loss account.

40.9.1 Gearing ratio

We commenced this chapter stating that a company may decide to gear (i.e. borrow) in order to increase the profit available for distribution to the ordinary shareholders. There might, of course, be other reasons, such as the lack of sufficient equity capital and retained profits to carry out a planned investment programme. The *gearing ratio* expresses what percentage of the total resources of a company (i.e. debentures + issued capital + all reserves) is in the form of prior-charge capital. (i.e. those to whom a return has to be paid in priority to equity capital). The formula for the gearing ratio is:

Gearing ratio = Prior charge capital/(long-term loans + issued share capital and reserves) × 100%

To illustrate, let us assume that the capital employed in a company is as stated in the box here. The gearing ratio would be:

Ordinary shares	£100,000
Retained profit	£350,000
6% Debentures	£150,000
Capital employed	£600,000

150,000/(100,000 + 350,000 + 150,000) × 100% = 25%

The company is geared because it relies to some extent on loan capital. A gearing of up to 50 per cent is usually regarded as low and beyond that as high.

A gear in a car is the arrangement by which the car's driving wheel performs more or fewer revolutions relative to the revolutions of the crankshaft. If in a high gear, the car is propelled faster. Similarly, a company is said to be highly geared if its capital structure is such that a given change in its performance is likely to cause more than a proportionate change on the amount available to equity shareholders.

For illustration, let us compare the situation in a low-geared company with that of a highly geared one to trace the impact of a 50 per cent reduction in profit on the amount available to equity shares. Let us assume that each company reported a profit after tax of £200 in year 20X0 and half that amount in 20X1. As we see in the box on the right, in a highly geared company, a 50 per cent fall in profit reduces the amount available to equity shares by almost double that percentage. Hence a highly geared company is regarded as more risky from the point of view of equity shareholders.

GEARING OF THE CAPITAL STRUCTURE

			Low	High
a	Ordinary share capital		£800	£300
b	12% Preference shares		£100	£800
c	Reserves		£300	£100
d	Capital employed	a + b + c	£1,200	£1,200
e	Gearing ratio	b / d × 100	8%	67%
f	Profit available to	Profit after tax		
f_1	equity shares in 20X0	*less* Preference	£188	£104
f_2	in 20X1	dividend	£88	£4
g	Percentage change in f	$(f_1 - f_2)/f_1 × 100$	53%	96%

40.9.2 Interest cover

Interest cover measures how many times the profit before interest and tax covers the interest payable. The formula is as follows:

Interest cover = Profit before interest and tax (PBIT)/interest = ? times

For illustration, let us assume that a company's performance is as stated on the right. The interest cover would be:

(£45,000 + £9,000)/£9,000 = 6 times

Operating profit	£54,000
Interest expense	(£9,000)
Profit before tax	£45,000
Taxation	(£8,500)
Profit after tax	£36,500

This shows that the profits well cover the interest and there would need to be a material fall in turnover or increase in costs before the company would be unable to meet its interest commitment. This in turn indicates that there is little likelihood that the company is at risk of legal action by the lenders for non-payment of the interest.

References

1. Table A, paragraphs 19 and 20.
2. Table A, paragraph 21.
3. Section 146 of the Companies Act 1985.
4. Section 100 of the Companies Act 1985.
5. Section 103(1) of the Companies Act 1985.
6. Section 99(2) of the Companies Act 1985.

SOLUTIONS TO INTERACTIVE QUESTIONS

IQ 40.1 Accounting for issue of shares at par

(a) Accounting for the share transactions:

APPLICATION AND ALLOTMENT ACCOUNT

N	20X0		£		20X0		£	
2	14.9	Cash bk – refund	10,000		?	Cash bk – applicat.	50,000	1
	14.9	Share Capital a/c	90,000		?	Cash bk – allotment	42,000	5
					31.12	Balance c/d	8,000	6
	1.1	Balance b/d	8,000					

Notes:

1. £50,000 received with the application (12,500 @ £4) is credited to the Control account.
2. The refund of £10,000 to unsuccessful applicants (2,500 @ £4) is posted to the debit of the Control account, which at this point reports a liability of £40,000 owed to the successful applicants.
3. Though the par value of each share is £10, £1 of this amount is not due until called. Hence, at the point of allotment, the so far called-up value per share is £9. Accordingly the allotment of shares is accounted for by debiting the Application and Allotment account and

ORDINARY SHARE CAPITAL ACCOUNT

	£			£	
			Applic & allotment	90,000	3
			Call account	10,000	4

crediting the Share Capital account with £90,000, which is the value so far called up (£9) of the number of shares in issue (10,000).

4. The call made on 1 November is accounted for by crediting the Share Capital account (which by now reports the fully called-up value of 10,000 shares in issue) and debiting another Control account opened, this time, for reporting amounts receivable as a call. After the call of £1 each on 6,600 shares has been received by 31.12.20X0, the Call account reports the amount yet to be received as £3,400.

5. Amounts, as received, are posted from the cash book to the appropriate Control accounts.

THE CALL ACCOUNT

		£			£	
4	Share capital	10,000		Cash book	6,600	5
				Balance c/d	3,400	
	Balance b/d	3,400				

CASH BOOK

		£			£	
1	Applic. & allot.	50,000			10,000	2
5	Applic. & allot.	42,000				
5	Call a/c	6,600				

(b) Share transactions are reported on the year-end Balance Sheet as follows:

BALANCE SHEET AS AT 31.12.20X0		
Included among the assets:	£	
Called-up capital not paid	11,400	(Allotment money in arrears plus call in arrears)
As share capital and reserves:	£	
Ordinary shares of £1 each	100,000	(Fully called-up value of number of shares in issue)

IQ 40.2 Accounting for issue of shares at premium

(a) Accounting for the share transactions

APPLICATION AND ALLOTMENT ACCOUNT

		£			£
31.3	Cash book	90,000	?	Cash book	290,000
31.3	Share capital*	450,000	30.9	Cash book	288,750
31.3	Share premium	100,000	30.9	Balance c/d	61,250
1.10	Balance b/d	61,250			

* So far called-up value		£
Par value per share		1.00
Less: Calls not made:		
First call	0.30	
Final call	0.25	(0.55)
		0.45

FIRST CALL ACCOUNT

		£				£
5.7	Share capital	300,000	?	Cash book		228,000
			30.9	Balance c/d		72,000
1.10	Balance b/d	72,000				

ORDINARY SHARE CAPITAL ACCOUNT

		£			£
			31.3	Application & allot.	450,000
			5.7	First Call account	300,000
					750,000

SHARE PREMIUM ACCOUNT

		£			£
			31.3	Application & allot.	100,000

So far called-up value (75p) of the number of shares in issue (one million shares)

(b) How particulars of share capital would be reported on the Balance Sheet

BALANCE SHEET AS AT 30.9.20X0		
Among assets:	£	
Called-up capital not paid up	133,250	(£61,250 + £72,000)
As share capital and reserves:	£	
Ordinary shares of £1, 75p called up	750,000	(So far called-up value (75p) of one million shares)
Share premium account	100,000	(Gain on issuing own shares, not available to be distributed as dividends)

(c) Authorized capital of a company
This is the amount stated in paragraph 6 of the Memorandum of Association.

(d) Issued capital, called-up capital and paid-up capital

In the case of Sycamore plc	£	
Issued capital	1,000,000	(One million shares of £1 each in issue)
Called-up capital	750,000	(One million shares of 75p each called up so far)
Paid-up capital	616,750	(£750,000 less amounts in arrears of £133,250)

IQ 40.3 *Pro rata* allotment of shares

APPLICATION AND ALLOTMENT ACCOUNT

		£				£
1.3	Cash book – refund	500	?	Cash book – applic.		8,000
1.3	Share capital*	16,000	?	Cash book		9,660
1.3	Share premium	2,000	30.6	Balance c/d †		840
1.7	Balance b/d	840				

* So far called-up value of each share at point of allotment		
		£
Par value		1.00
Call yet to be made		(20)
So far called up =		80
20,000 shares @ 80p = £16,000		

† *Pro rata* allocation: Those who applied for 30,000 shares received 20,000. Hence the *pro rata* basis was 2 for every 3. 1,600 shares in arrears for the allotment money would have applied for 2,400 shares – i.e. 800 more – for which they paid 25p each.	
Default: 1,600 shares @ 65p	1,040
Less: excess on application	(200)
Hence the amount in arrears	840

ORDINARY SHARE CAPITAL ACCOUNT

		£			£
			1.3	Applic. & allotment	16,000
			1.5	Call account	4,000
					20,000

SHARE PREMIUM ACCOUNT

		£			£
			1.3	Applic. & allotment	2,000

CALL ACCOUNT

		£			£
1.5	Share capital	4,000	?	Cash book	3,080
			30.6	Balance c/d	920
1.7	Balance b/d	920			

IQ 40.4 Shares offered in a package deal

1. Determination of the final call on each package:

	Par value	Issue price	No.	£
Ordinay shares	£1.00	£1.25	2	2.50
8% Pref. shares	£1.00	£1.00	1	1.00
Price payable for each package				3.50

Payable on application:	£1.00	
On allotment	£1.25	
On first call	£0.75	(3.00)
On final call		0.50

2. The so far called-up value of both ordinary shares in each package, at the point of allotment.

	£
Par value of both ord. shares together	2.00
Calls yet to be made: First call	(0.75)
Final call	(0.50)
So far called-up value of both shares	0.75

100,000 packages @ 75p so far called-up value at point of allotment = £75,000

APPLICATION AND ALLOTMENT ACCOUNT

		£		£	
4	Cash book	25,000	Cash bk – appli.	125,000	3
5	8% Pref. shares	100,000	Cash book	115,000	~
2	Ordinary share capital	75,000			
6	Share premium	50,000	Balance c/d	10,000	8
	Balance b/d	10,000			

8% PREFERENCE SHARE CAPITAL ACCOUNT

		£		£	
			Applc. & allotment	100,000	5

ORDINARY SHARE CAPITAL ACCOUNT

		£		£	
			Applc. & allotment	75,000	2
			First Call a/c	75,000	7

FIRST CALL ACCOUNT

		£		£	
7	Ord. share capital	75,000	Cash book	69,000	~
			Balance c/d	6,000	9
	Balance b/d	4,000			

SHARE PREMIUM ACCOUNT

		£		£	
			Applc. & allotment	50,000	6

3. Application money for 125,000 packages at £1 each.
4. Refund of £1 on 25,000 packages oversubscribed.
5. Allotment of 100,000 preference shares of £1 each, at par, fully called up at the point of allotment.
6. Premium of 25p per share on the 200,000 ordinary shares, recovered with allotment money.
7. First call of 75p per package on 100,000 packages.
8. Allotment money of £1.25 per package in arrears on 8,000 packages.
9. First call of 75p per package in arrears on 8,000 packages.
~ Balancing figure.

IQ 40.5 Forfeiture of shares

Forfeiture does not mean that the shares have been cancelled (i.e. made non-existent). In fact, 100,000 ordinary shares of £1 each remain in issue and are as stated on the Balance Sheet on 31.12.20X0. Confiscating the shares from those to whom they had been allotted, Tender plc holds them as investments in own shares, stating them at the amount in default – i.e. Allotment money 1,600 @ £5; and Call 1,600 shares @ £1. Also, 1,800 other shares not forfeited have still to pay the call of £1 each.

APPLICATION AND ALLOTMENT ACCOUNT

		£				£
20X0			**20X0**			
14.9	Cash book	10,000	?	Cash bk – applic.	50,000
14.9	Share capital	90,000	?	Cash bk – allotm.	42,000
			31.12	Balance c/d	8,000
1.1	Balance b/d	8,000	1.1.X1	Forfeited shares	8,000

THE CALL ACCOUNT

		£				£
1.11	Share capital	10,000	?	Cash book	6,600
			31.12	Balance c/d	3,400
1.1	Balance b/d	3,400	1.1	Forfeited shares	1,600
			1.1	Balance c/d	1,800
1.1	Balance b/d	1,800			

FORFEITED SHARES ACCOUNT

		£			£
1.1	Applic. & allotment	8,000			
1.1	Call account	1,600			
		9,600			

BALANCE SHEET AS AT 31.12.20X0		
Included among the assets:	£	
Called-up capital not paid	1,800	(The call in arrears)
Investments in own shares	9,600	(Own shares forfeited and held for the time being)
	£	
As share capital and reserves:		
Ordinary shares of £1 each	100,000	(The total shares in issue including those forfeited)

IQ 40.6 Reissue of forfeited shares

(a) Accounting for ressue of forfeited shares

FORFEITED SHARES ACCOUNT

		£			£
1.1	Applic. & allotment	8,000	15.1	Cash book	11,200
1.1	Call account	1,600			
		9,600			
15.1	Share premium	1,600			

1,600 shares are reissued at £7 per share, realizing £11,200. This yields a gain of £1,600, which is regarded as a premium received.

(b) Accounting treatment of gain on reissuing forfeited shares

On 1,600 forfeited and then reissued, £4 had been received on application and £7 more on the reissue, making £11 per share, whereas the par value of each share is £10. Section 130 of the Companies Act 1985 requires that the excess of the amount realized on shares over their par value should be regarded as share premium.

(c) Consequence of reissuing forfeited shares at a loss

If the forfeited shares had been reissued at £5.50 each, the total amount received on each share (including £4 received on application) would amount to £9.50, whereas the par value of each share is £10. This would mean that the shares are being issued at a discount, which is prohibited by company law. If the company is unable to reissue the forfeited shares except at a discount, the loss incurred in the process is recoverable from those from whom the shares were forfeited.

IQ 40.7 Forfeiture of shares issued at premium

APPLICATION AND ALLOTMENT ACCOUNT

		£			£	
31.3	Cash book	90,000	?	Cash book	290,000	
31.3	Share capital	450,000	30.9	Cash book	288,750	
31.3	Share premium	100,000	30.9	Balance c/d	61,250	
1.10	Balance b/d	61,250	1.10	Forfeited shares	61,250	1

FIRST CALL ACCOUNT

		£			£	
5.7	Share capital	300,000	?	Cash book	228,000	
			30.9	Balance c/d	72,000	
1.10	Balance b/d	72,000	1.10	Forfeited shares	52,500	1
			1.10	Balance c/d	19,500	
1.10	Balance b/d	19,500	?	Cash book	19,320	~
			30.9	Balance c/d	180	6
1.10	Balance b/d	19,320				

ORDINARY SHARE CAPITAL ACCOUNT

		£			£	
			31.3	Applic. & allotment	450,000	
			5.7	First Call a/c	300,000	
			1.11	Final Call a/c	206,250	3
			1.11	Forfeited shares	43,750	3
					1,000,000	

SHARE PREMIUM ACCOUNT

			£			£	
4	1.10	Forfeited shares	17,500	31.3	Applic. & allotment	100,000	
	30.9	Balance c/d	87,500	1.1	Forfeited shares	5,000	5
				1.10	Balance b/d	87,500	

FORFEITED SHARES ACCOUNT

			£			£	
1	1.10	Applic. & allotment	61,250	1.10	Share premium	17,500	2
1	1.10	First Call a/c	52,500	?	Cash book	85,000	5
3	1.11	Share capital	43,750				
5	1.11	Share premium	5,000	30.9	Balance c/d	60,000	4
	30.9	Balance b/d	60,000				

FINAL CALL ACCOUNT

			£			£	
3	1.11	Share capital	206,250	?	Cash book	206,025	~
				30.9	Balance c/d	225	6
	1.10	Balance b/d	225				

Notes:

1. Upon forfeiture of the 175,000 shares, the allotment money as well as the first call (35p + 30p) in default are transferred to a Forfeited Shares account.
2. Because the amount in default includes a premium of 10p per share, £17,500 of the share premium was never earned. The premium is therefore reversed. Until the final call is made, on 1.11.20X0, the forfeited shares will be accounted for as an asset (investment in own shares) at £96,250 (£61,250 + £52,500 – £17,500).
3. When the final call is made on 1.11.20X0, 175,000 shares are held within the company and only 825,000 held by the shareholders. An accounting entry recording the final call should reflect this position.
4. Forfeited shares are reported, from this point, at £140,000 (i.e. the par value of 175,000 shares, less the amount received in respect of them as application money). Hence the shares not yet reissued (75,000 in number) are accounted for at (£140,000/175,000) × 75,000 = £60,000.
5. Reciprocally, the reissued shares would have been valued at (£140,000/175,000) × 100,000 = £80,000. Reissue of these shares at £85,000 results in a gain of £5,000. This is a gain resulting from the issue of the company's own shares and should, therefore, be regarded as part of share premium.
6. As at 30.9.20X1, 600 shares are in arrears for the first call and 900 shares for the final call.
7. Amounts marked with ~ are balancing figures.

IQ 40.8 Issue of debentures at a discount

As at 31.12.20X1 8% Debentures will be reported as a liability as £451,963. Interest written off to the Profit and Loss account is as follows:

- 20X1: £52,710 (i.e. 12% of £450,000 – £10,747)
- 20X2: £54,236 (i.e. 12% of £451,963)
- 20X3: £55,944 (i.e. 12% of £466,199)
- 20X4: £57,857 (i.e. 12% of £482,143)

8% DEBENTURES ACCOUNT

		£			£
1.1.X1	Cash bk – expense	10,747	1.1.X1	Cash book	450,000
31.12.X1	Cash bk – int. paid	40,000			
31.12.X1	Balance c/d	451,963	31.12.X1	P&L – interest	52,710
31.12.X2	Cash bk – int. paid	40,000	1.1.X2	Balance b/d	451,963
31.12.X2	Balance c/d	466,199	31.12.X2	P&L – interest	54,236
31.12.X3	Cash bk – int. paid	40,000	1.1.X2	Balance b/d	466,199
31.12.X3	Balance c/d	482,143	31.12.X3	P&L – interest	55,944
31.12.X4	Cash bk – int. paid	40,000	1.1.X4	Balance b/d	482,143
31.12.X4	Cash bk – redempt.	500,000	31.12.X4	P&L – interest	57,857

IQ 40.9　Redemption of debentures at a premium

6% DEBENTURES ACCOUNT

		£			£	
1.1.X1	Cash book – expense	8,486	1.1.X1	Cash book	540,000	
1.1.X1	Balance c/d	531,514				
31.12.X1	Cash book – interest @ 6%	36,000	1.1.X1	Balance b/d	531,514	
31.12.X1	Balance c/d	580,556	31.12.X1	P&L – interest @ 16%	85,042	#
31.12.X2	Cash book – interest @ 6%	36,000	1.1.X2	Balance b/d	580,556	
31.12.X2	Balance c/d	637,445	31.12.X2	P&L – interest @ 16%	92,889	#
31.12.X3	Cash book – interest @ 6%	36,000	1.1.X2	Balance b/d	637,445	
31.12.X3	Balance c/d	703,436	31.12.X3	P&L – interest @ 16%	101,991	#
31.12.X4	Cash book – interest @ 6%	36,000	1.1.X4	Balance b/d	703,436	
31.12.X4	Cash book – redemption	780,000	31.12.X4	P&L – interest @ 16%	112,564	#

\# Interest expenses written off in each year.

PROGRESSIVE QUESTIONS

PQ 40.1　Multiple-choice questions

The prospectus inviting applications for ordinary shares of £1 each had stated that 20p per share is payable with application, 45p on allotment, 35p on first call and 30p on final call. Tick the appropriate column in the grid to identify the amount at which each of the following companies would report their share capital and share premium on the Balance Sheet as at 31 December 20X1, if the circumstances were as stated below:

	Share capital			Share premium	
	a	£70,000		a	£30,000
	b	£97,400		b	£20,000
	c	£100,000		c	£10,000

1. 100,000 ordinary shares of £1 each, fully called-up, were in issue as at 31.12.20X1, though 2,800 shares were in arrears for the first call and 5,400 for the final call.

	Share capital			Share premium	
	a	£500,000		a	£151,500
	b	£497,500		b	£149,500
	c	£487,500		c	£150,000

2. 500,000 ordinary shares are in issue, fully called-up, but 12,500 shares, in arrears for both calls, had been forfeited and 80 per cent of them had been reissued at 80p per share in November 20X1.

	Share capital			Share premium	
	a	£280,000		a	£120,000
	b	£390,000		b	£80,000
	c	£400,000		c	£117,000

3. 400,000 ordinary shares are in issue, fully called-up, but, as at 31.12.20X1, 10,000 shares were in arrears for the allotment money as well as both calls. These shares were forfeited on 31.12.20X1.

	Share capital			Share premium	
	a	£200,000		a	£20,000
	b	£140,000		b	£60,000
	c	£141,350		c	£30,000

4. 200,000 ordinary shares are in issue, but the final call was not made until 5.2.20X2. As at 31.12.20X1, 16,200 shares were in arrears for allotment money and 24,000 for first call, while the final call has been received in advance on 4,500 shares.

PQ 40.2 Accounting for share issue and forfeiture

Phoenix plc invited applications for one million ordinary shares of £1, each payable as stated in the box. Share events thereafter in the year were as follows:

Payable on each share:
30p payable on application
65p payable on allotment
35p payable as call on 30.6.20X0
20p payable as call on 31.8.20X0

- By 31 March: applications received for 1.2 million shares;
- On 31 March: excess applications rejected; allotment made;
- By 31 July: 24,000 shares are in arrears for allotment money and 16,000 more for first call;
- On 31 July: shares in arrears for both allotment money and first call are forfeited;
- By 15 August: 18,000 forfeited shares are reissued at 60p per share.

By the year end on 31.12.20X0, 4,000 shares are in arrears for first call, and 6,000 more for the final call.

Required: Set out the cash book and ledger accounts recording the above-stated share events and identify how these events will feature on the Balance Sheet of Phoenix plc on 31 December 20X0.

PQ 40.3 Journal entries to account for share issue and forfeiture

In respect of the share events of Phoenix plc stated in PQ 40.2 above, set out the journal entries necessary to account for these events, bearing in mind that if the prime entry can be made in the cash book, then a journal entry is not necessary.

PQ 40.4 *Pro rata* allotment of shares

Thriving plc, incorporated in 20X0 with a share capital stated in its Memorandum as 600,000 ordinary shares of £10 each, had issued 450,000 ordinary shares at par immediately after its incorporation. The final call of £3 per share is yet to be made on these shares. To fund organic growth, on 1 April 20X2 Thriving plc invited applications for 100,000 more ordinary shares of £10 each, payable as stated in the box here. Applications were received for 148,600 shares. Share allotment was made, *pro rata*, to those who applied for 120,000 shares, having rejected the application of the others. By the year end, on 31 December 20X2, the final call had been received in advance on 1,500 shares, while the allotment money was in arrears on 4,500 shares and the first call in arrears on 2,500 more shares.

Payable on each share:	£
On application	3.00
On allotment	4.50
As first call on 1.10.20X2	1.50
As final call – when made	3.00

Required:

(a) Set out the ledger accounts (not the cash book), accounting for the share issue.
(b) Identify:
- the authorized capital;
- the issued capital;
- the called-up capital;
- the paid-up capital

of the company on 31.12.20X2.

PQ 40.5 Forfeiture and reissue of shares

The directors of Thriving plc (see PQ 40.4) resolved on 1.1.20X3 to forfeit all shares in arrears for either allotment money or first call, and they reissued 5,000 of these shares on 15.1.20X3 at £5 per share, subject to payment of the final call.

Required: Record these share transactions in the books of Thriving plc, and show how they will be stated on the Balance Sheet as at 31.12.20X3.

PQ 40.6 Redemption of debentures

Crest plc extracted its year-end Trial Balance as shown on the right. On 1 January 20X5 they had issued £500,000 5% debentures at a discount of 20 per cent on the basis that they will be redeemed by 31 December 20X9 at a premium of 20 per cent. The cost of issuing the debentures, amounting to £17,889, is stated as part of administrative expenses. The terms on which the debentures were issued are based on an effective interest rate of 15 per cent per annum.

Ignore taxation of the company's profits and assume that directors do not propose to pay any dividends.

Required:

(a) Amend the accounting for debenture issue to fall in line with the requirements of FRS 4, *Capital Instruments*.
(b) Prepare the Trading and Profit and Loss account for the year ended 31 December 20X5 and the Balance Sheet as at that date.
(c) Appraise the financing structure of the company on the basis of appropriate ratios.

TRIAL BALANCE AS AT 31.12.20X5		
	£000	£000
Fixed assets	1,240	–
Depreciation – 31.12.20X5	–	372
Cost of sale	982	–
Administration expenses	296	–
Sales	–	1,618
Distribution cost	112	–
5% Debentures	–	500
Discount on debenture	100	–
Debenture interest	25	–
Stock on 31.12.20X5	365	
Ordinary share capital	–	600
Share Premium account	–	60
Profit and Loss account	–	144
Debtors and creditors	512	392
Cash and bank balance	54	–
	3,686	3,686

Chapter 41

COMPANIES (3): ANNUAL ACCOUNTS FOR INTERNAL USE

In this chapter

We will learn of features in accounting peculiar to companies

and you should be able to prepare financial statements of companies for use of internal management

41.1 ANNUAL ACCOUNTS OF A COMPANY

Like any other form of business organization, companies too have to finalize their accounts, typically at annual intervals, in order to ascertain the results of their performance within that period and their position on the last day of the period. In addition, companies have an obligation to publish their financial statements – an area, that will be dealt with in Chapter 42. This chapter is concerned with the annual accounts prepared by a company for *internal* management use.

A typical format is as follows:

TRADING AND PROFIT AND LOSS ACCOUNT FOR THE YEAR ENDED 31 MARCH 20X1		
	£000	£000
Sales		3,000
Stock on 1.4.20X0	400	
Purchases	2,000	
Stock on 31.3.20X1	(500)	(1,900)
Gross profit		1,100
Distribution cost:		
Sales commission	120	
Advertising	31	
Bad debts	15	
Vehicle depreciation	64	(230)
Administrative expenses:		
Salaries and wages	146	
Directors' emoluments	164	a
Depreciation	38	
Audit fees	35	
Rent and rates	28	
Other admin. expenses	19	(430)

BALANCE SHEET AS AT 31 MARCH 20X1			
Fixed assets:	£000	£000	£000
Land and buildings	840	(72)	768
Plant and machinery	580	(164)	416
Furniture, fittings, tools	218	(98)	120
Investments			74
Sinking Fund Investments			56 e
			1,434
Current assets:			
Stock in trade		500	
Debtors		614	
Cash and bank		92	
Current liabilities:			
Creditors		(425)	
Accrued expenses		(64)	
Taxation		(72)	b
Dividend proposed		(80)	c
Working capital			565
			1,999

TRADING AND PROFIT AND LOSS ACCOUNT FOR THE YEAR ENDED 31 MARCH 20X1			
	£000	£000	
Operating profit		440	
Dividend received		30	
Interest received		10	
Interest paid		(20)	
Profit before taxation		460	
Taxation		(72)	b
Profit after taxation		388	
Interim dividend paid		(30)	c
Final dividend proposed		(80)	c
Retained profit for the year		278	
Profit and Loss balance b/f		525	d
General Reserve		(75)	d
Debenture Redemption S. Fund		(10)	e
Balance carried forward		718	f

BALANCE SHEET AS AT 31 MARCH 20X1		
	£000	
Share capital and reserves:		
Ordinary shares of £1 each	750	
Share Premium account	150	
General Reserve	125	
Debenture Red. Sinking Fund	56	e
Profit and Loss reserve	718	f
	1,799	
Non-current liability:		
10% Debentures	200	
	1,999	

These accounts involve items (shaded and marked by letters) which we have not met with so far and deserve to be introduced.

41.2 DIRECTORS' EMOLUMENTS

Directors are those with particular skills in company management, elected by the shareholders to be entrusted with the management of a company. A private company needs to have only one director, whereas a public company must have at least two.[1] The Articles of Association usually provide that the business of the company shall be managed by the directors, who will collectively act as a board, although the Articles may also provide for the delegation of extensive powers to individual directors or committees of directors.

Within this context, unless 'Table A' is expressly excluded or superseded by a company's own Articles, the remuneration of directors shall from time to time be determined by the company in general meeting.[2] The determination of the remuneration of the managing director and those of executive directors, however, is delegated to the Board of Directors.[3] It has now become commonplace in larger public companies for the determination of directors' remuneration to be delegated to a 'Remuneration Committee', usually composed mainly of non-executive directors. The directors' emoluments may take a variety of forms, including the following:

- remuneration for services (which may consist of salary, commission and bonus);
- fees for attending board meetings;
- pension contribution by the company;
- compensation for loss of office if that should occur.

Directors' emoluments are a charge on profit and not an appropriation. By contrast, the salary paid to partners is an appropriation. This is because the directors, unlike partners, are employees of their company.

41.3 TAXATION OF COMPANIES

Since 1965, companies in the United Kingdom have had to pay Corporation Tax on their profits, at rates fixed from time to time in the annual budget of the government. The rates in 2000–01 were set at:

- 30% for large companies (those earning profit exceeding £1.5 million in the year);
- 20% for small companies (those earning between £50,000 and £300,000 profit in the year);
- 10% for very small companies (those earning less than £10,000 profit in the year);
- various rates for those falling outside the bandings given above.

41.3.1 Computation of Corporation Tax

Corporation Tax at the appropriate rate is not calculated on the profit as reported in the accounts but on the *taxable* profit. To arrive at the taxable profit of a company, the starting point is the accounting profit, adjusted as follows:

1. **Add back expenses that are not allowable for tax purposes** because they were not incurred 'wholly and exclusively' for the purpose of earning the income. Common examples of such disallowed expenses are entertainment (other than of staff) and political contributions.
2. **Deduct income not liable to taxation.** Common examples are:
   - Dividends received from another company resident in the UK. The dividend is exempt from tax because that other company would have paid the dividend out of its profits, which would already have been taxed. Such tax-free dividends are referred to as 'franked investment income'.
   - Interest to the extent it is not received within the year. This is because even though interest is accounted for on accruals basis, it is taxed on a receipts basis. This adjustment, however, should be made only in the year in which the interest, yet to be received, was earned for the first time. In subsequent years, although the interest earned in that year is not taxed, a corresponding amount similarly exempted in the previous year would be.
3. **Substitute depreciation with a taxation capital allowance.** This is because the method and rates of depreciation charges would vary from company to company. Therefore, tax law prefers to substitute the depreciation charge with a corresponding capital allowance calculated in accordance with its own rules.

41.3.2 Accounting for Corporation Tax

When accounting for Corporation Tax, normal double entry principles apply. Two accounts are opened with the same name, debiting one and crediting the other with the estimated amount of the Corporation Tax on the year's profit. The account with the debit balance is the expenditure, which is written off to the Profit and Loss account; the account with the credit balance is the liability, to be stated in the Balance Sheet. The liability should be settled on the day after nine months from the Balance Sheet date.

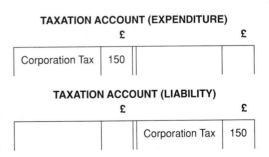

TAXATION ACCOUNT (EXPENDITURE)

	£		£
Corporation Tax	150		

TAXATION ACCOUNT (LIABILITY)

	£		£
		Corporation Tax	150

Adjustment of tax from year to year

An estimate made of Corporation Tax for a year would not always match with the amount finally agreed with the Inland Revenue. Let us assume that the Corporation Tax for the year 20X0, although accounted for at an estimated amount of £150, had to be settled nine months later by a payment of £165. The shortfall of £15, referred to as an *underprovision*, is added to the Corporation Tax bill for 20X1. As shown in the accounts on the left, if Corporation Tax for 2001 is estimated at £180, the amount written off as expenditure in that year's Profit and Loss account would be £195, including as it would the underprovision for the previous year. On the other hand, if the tax payable for 2000 turns out to be less, say only £140, the *overprovision* of £10 will correspondingly reduce the tax expenditure of 2001.

TAXATION ACCOUNT (EXPENDITURE)

		£			£
31.12.20X0	Corporation Tax	150	31.12.20X0	Profit and Loss	150
1.10.20X1	Underprovision	15			
31.12.20X1	Corporation Tax	180	31.12.20X1	Profit and Loss	195

TAXATION ACCOUNT (LIABILITY)

		£			£
1.10.20X1	Cash book	165	31.12.20X0	Corporation Tax	150
			1.10.20X1	Taxation (exp.)	15
			31.12.20X1	Corporation Tax	180

Corporation Tax as an appropriation

Corporation tax is an appropriation in the sense that it is a share of the company's profit appropriated to the government with the intention of helping to create the environment in which the company can thrive. Only the profit remaining after deducting Corporation Tax is available for distribution as dividends to the owners of the company – the shareholders.

41.4 DIVIDENDS OF A COMPANY

A dividend is that portion of a company's distributable profit that the directors choose to distribute among shareholders as reward for the finance provided by them. In other forms of business organizations we have come across so far, the profit for the year has been fully appropriated to the owner or in agreed proportions among the partners. This does not happen in a company. The company, being itself a separate legally recognized entity, retains the profit for itself, distributing as dividend to shareholders only such amounts as approved for the purpose by the directors. The profit in each year, after deducting taxation and any dividends, is referred to as the **retained profit** and this is accumulated from year to year in an account named **Profit and Loss Reserve**.

In a company, provided that it has profits that have been realized and are legally distributable, the directors of the company have authority to pay **interim dividends** during the accounting period and to propose a **final dividend**, to be paid in the next period but only after approval by the shareholders at the Annual General Meeting. At this meeting audited accounts are submitted by the directors, who will report on the past year and outline their strategy for the future.

A dividend is commonly expressed as so many pence per share. Exceptionally (as happens in respect of preference shares), the dividend may be expressed as a percentage. In that case, unless the company's own Articles expressly excludes Table A in this regard, the dividend will be calculated as a percentage of the paid-up capital.[4] If we assume, for example, that a company has in issue 100,000 £10 ordinary shares, £8 called-up, and the calls are in arrears for £15,000, the paid-up capital of the company would then be £785,000. If a dividend is proposed at 6 per cent, the amount payable would be 6 per cent of £785,000 = £47,100. On the other hand, if a dividend is approved as 6p per share, the dividend payable would be 6p on 800,000 shares = £48,000.

41.4.1 Accounting for dividends

Upon payment, the interim dividend is posted from the cash book to an Interim Dividend account, which, being an expenditure, is written off to the Profit and Loss account for the year. It is shown in the Profit and Loss account as a deduction from the amount of profit after taxation. The final dividend, when proposed, is accounted for – as it was in the case of taxation – by opening two accounts with identical names, debiting one and crediting the other. The one with the debit balance is the expenditure, to be written off to the Profit and Loss account and positioned therein immediately after the interim dividend. The one with the credit balance is the liability to be stated on the Balance Sheet, which becomes payable upon approval by the shareholders.

FINAL DIVIDEND PROPOSED (EXPENDITURE) ACCOUNT

	£		£
Final Dividend proposed	150		

FINAL DIVIDEND PROPOSED (LIABILITY) ACCOUNT

	£		£
		Final Dividend proposed	150

Calculation of Corporation Tax and dividends

Interaction 41.1

Alpha Ltd extracted its Trial Balance at year end, as stated here. You are informed as follows:

(a) Stock on 31.12.2001 at cost is £516,000.
(b) Furniture and vehicles are to be depreciated by the straight-line method at 10 per cent and 20 per cent p.a. respectively.
(c) The audit fee for the year is expected to be £6,000.
(d) The Corporation Tax rate is 20 per cent.
(e) The tax capital allowance for the year is estimated at £124,000.
(f) The directors propose a final dividend of 6p per share.

Required: Prepare, for the internal use of the management, the Trading and Profit and Loss account for the year ended 31 December 20X1, and the Balance Sheet as at that date (ignore deferred tax).

TRIAL BALANCE AS AT 31.12.20X1

	£000	£000
Furniture	240	96
Motor vehicles	320	108
Stock – 31.12.20X0	432	–
Salaries and wages	286	–
Sales	–	3,264
Investments	264	–
Rent	72	–
Purchases	2,648	–
Ordinary shares £1	–	900
Share premium	–	90
Telephone/postage	22	–
Advertising	18	–
Debtors/creditors	394	286
Directors fees	42	–
Interim dividend	30	–
Entertainment	26	–
Dividend received	–	30
Profit and Loss a/c	–	58
Cash and bank	38	–
	4,832	4,832

Interaction 41.2

Interest earned and incurred

The year-end Trial Balance of Beta plc appears as shown here.

You are informed further as follows:

(a) Stock held on 30.6.20X1 at cost was £876,000.

(b) Investments include £300,000 12% debentures held in Theta plc. Theta pays interest annually in arrears on 1 July.

(c) Beta plc pays interest on its debentures half-yearly on 1 January and 1 July.

(d) Accruals as at 30 June 20X1 include the following:
- Directors' fees: £28,000
- Audit fees: £30,000

(e) Fixed assets are to be depreciated at 10 per cent of cost per annum.

(f) Other administrative expenses include a political contribution of £20,000.

(g) The Corporation Tax rate is 30 per cent and the tax capital allowance is £311,000.

(h) Directors propose to pay a final dividend of 24p per share.

Required: Create for internal use the Trading and Profit and Loss account for the year ended 30 June 20X1 and the Balance Sheet as at that date (ignore deferred tax).

TRIAL BALANCE AS AT 30.6.20X1		
	£000	£000
Fixed assets	2,140	816
Stock 1.7.20X0	722	–
Salaries and wages	589	–
Debtors and creditors	684	599
Tax paid for 20X0	216	–
Investments	528	–
Sales	–	7,484
Interest paid	24	–
Purchases	5,168	–
Bad debts	16	–
8% debentures	–	600
Provision for 20X0 tax	–	198
Interim dividend	120	–
Advertising	76	–
Rent	48	–
Ordinary shares £1	–	900
Share premium	–	60
Other admin.expenses	528	–
Dividend received	–	45
Duty on imports	152	–
Profit and Loss a/c	–	331
Cash and bank	22	–
	11,033	11,033

41.5 RESERVES

Reserves are accumulations of profits or gains (including retained profits and others such as those arising from revaluation of an asset) that are retained within the company. They can be either revenue reserves or capital reserves.

Revenue reserves are those that would otherwise have been available for distribution as dividends but have been instead retained for enhancing the resource base of the company. Transfers to these reserves are voluntary, so that directors are free to transfer them back to (say) the Profit and Loss reserve if they so choose. It is usual for companies to earmark such reserves for specific purposes such as follows:

- **Asset Replacement Reserve.** Intended to build up amounts that may become necessary when assets have to be replaced at amounts substantially higher than what they originally cost.
- **Dividend Equalization Reserve.** This reserve could be drawn on when the profits in a year are insufficient to pay dividends at levels the company wishes to maintain.
- **Debenture Redemption Reserve.** This is built up from year to year to accumulate the resources necessary to pay off debentures (or other long-term loans) by a particular date.
- **General Reserve.** When a reserve amount is not earmarked for any identified purpose, it goes into here.

Capital reserves, on the other hand, are reserves that, by statute, case law or decision of the directors, are not available for distribution as dividends. Following are some examples:

- **Capital Redemption Reserve**, which is a legal requirement and which we will come across only when we study buyback (redemption) of a company's own shares.
- **Share Premium account**, which is the excess over par value received on the issue of shares and which can be applied only for the purposes permitted by section 130 of Companies Act 1985.
- **Revaluation Reserve**, which arises when a company decides to report its assets not at their historical cost but at a higher (current market) value. Company law restricts the purposes for which this reserve can be applied, though this reserve would become distributable in certain circumstances, such as when a revalued asset is disposed of.

41.5.1 Accounting for reserves

If the directors decide that (say) £25,000 of current year's profit should be transferred to General Reserve, the Profit and Loss (Appropriation) account is debited and the General Reserve credited with that amount.

Transfers to and from reserves

Interaction 41.3

Lullaby plc has in issue one million ordinary shares of £10 each, fully called-up, and wishes to maintain the annual dividend level at 8p per year. On 1.1.20X0 it had £21,400 in Profit and Loss Reserve and £95,000 in a Dividend Equalization Reserve (DER). During the four years from 1.1.20X0 its profit after tax and transfers were as follows:

	31.12.20X0	31.12.20X1	31.12.20X2	31.12.20X3
Profit (loss) after taxation	£96,500	£68,500	£56,000	£112,000
Transfer to (from) DER	£10,000	–	(£15,000)	£20,000

Required: Set out how the following would appear in each of the four years:

(a) the appropriation section of the company's Profit and Loss account;
(b) the Dividend Equalization Reserve.

41.6 SINKING FUNDS

When a company builds up its resource base, by setting aside amounts regularly to a specific reserve (say for repayment of a loan), it is likely that over the years the resources so retained may become tied down in assets such as additional fixed assets, stock, debtors, or a combination of these. As a result, when it is time to repay the loan, the company may find that despite having built up the necessary resources it does not have ready cash for the purpose. Such a predicament could be overcome if, as transfers are made annually to a reserve, an equivalent amount is simultaneously invested outside the company in readily realizable investments. This ensures that, at the time of having to repay the loan, cash can be readily found by realizing the investments.

If a reserve (or a provision) is represented by an equivalent investment outside the business, the reserve (or provision) is referred to as a *Sinking Fund*. If a company maintains a Sinking Fund, say for repaying a loan, it would have sinking fund investments equal in value to the balance in the Sinking Fund. Any earnings from the investments (by way of interest or dividends) will be credited to the Sinking Fund and reinvested in sinking fund investments.

For illustration, let us assume that on 1.1.20X0 a company:

- has an outstanding loan of £400,000;
- proposes to repay one-quarter of the loan every year commencing on 31.12.20X0;
- annually appropriates £65,000 for this purpose;
- has already built up a Sinking Fund of £246,500 with equivalent sinking fund investments.

Let us assume also that during the year ended 31.12.20X0, earnings from the investments amounted to £22,500 and that sinking funds investments that cost £80,000 were realized at £91,200. These transactions and the repayment (redemption) of one-quarter of the loan are accounted for as follows:

SINKING FUND FOR LOAN REDEMPTION

			£				£	
8	31.12	General Reserve	100,000	1.1	Balance b/f	246,500	1
				31.12	SF Cash a/c	22,500	2
				31.12	SF Cash a/c	11,200	4
9	31.12	Balance c/d	245,200	31.12	P&L appropriat.	65,000	5
				1.1	Balance b/d	245,200	9

SINKING FUND INVESTMENTS ACCOUNT

			£				£	
1	1.1	Balance b/f	246,500	31.12	SF Cash a/c	91,200	3
4	31.12	Sinking Fund	11,200	31.12	Balance c/d	166,500	4
	31.12	Balance b/d	166,500				
7	31.12	SF Cash a/c	78,700				
9			245,200				

SINKING FUND CASH ACCOUNT

			£				£	
2	31.12	Sinking Fund	22,500	31.12	Loan a/c	100,000	6
3	31.12	SF Investments	91,200	31.12	SF Investment	78,700	7
5	31.12	Cash book	65,000				

LOAN ACCOUNT

			£				£	
6	31.12	SF Cash account	100,000	1.1	Balance b/f	400,000	
	31.12	Balance c/d	300,000				
				1.1	Balance b/d	300,000	

Notes:

1. The balance in the Sinking Fund will always be equal to the sinking fund investments.
2. To segregate the Sinking Fund cash, a separate Sinking Fund Cash account is maintained. The earnings from the sinking fund investments are posted from the SF Cash account to the Sinking Fund account.
3. The proceeds on disposal of Sinking Fund investments are posted from the Sinking Fund Cash account to the Sinking Fund Investments account.
4. The cost of investment other than that sold (£246,500 − £80,000) is carried down, revealing the gain on disposal, which is transferred to the Sinking Fund.
5. When, as usual, £65,000 is appropriated to the Sinking Fund, an equal amount is transferred from the company's cash book to the Sinking Fund Cash account.
6. The Sinking Fund cash is paid to redeem the loan.
7. The whole of the balance in the Sinking Fund Cash account is invested.
8. When Sinking Fund cash is released for repayment of the loan, an equal amount from the Sinking Fund account should be transferred to General Reserve.
9. The balance in the Sinking Fund account will equal the amount held in the Sinking Fund Investments account.

Redemption of debentures

Interaction
41.4

Hushabye plc has in issue £500,000 8% debentures redeemable at par by 31 December 20X1. To facilitate the redemption, the company has been appropriating £40,000 per year to a Sinking Fund and investing an equal amount annually in gilt-edged securities. By 31 December 20X0, the balance in the Sinking Fund amounted to £412,500. On 31 December 20X1, the company:

- received £38,200 as dividend on the investments;
- realized the whole of the investments at £426,800;
- redeemed the debentures as agreed.

Required: Set out the relevant accounts, showing how they will all be closed.

References

1. Companies Act 1985, s. 282.
2. Table A, art. 82.
3. Table A, art. 84.
4. Table A, art. 104.
5. Companies Act 1985, s. 241.
6. Companies Act 1985, s. 242.

SOLUTIONS TO INTERACTIVE QUESTIONS

IQ 41.1 Calculation of Corporation Tax and dividends

TRADING AND PROFIT AND LOSS ACCOUNT FOR THE YEAR ENDED 31.12.20X1

	£000	£000
Sales		3,264
Stock – 1.1.20X1	432	
Purchases	2,648	
Stock – 31.12.20X1	(516)	(2,564)
Gross profit		700
Distribution cost		
Depreciation	64	
Advertising	18	
Entertainment	26	(108)
Administrative expenses:		
Salaries and wages	286	
Directors' fees	42	
Depreciation	24	
Audit fees	6	
Rent	72	
Telephone/post	22	(452)
Operating profit		140
Dividend received		30
Profit before taxation		170
Taxation		(26)
Profit after taxation		144
Interim dividend		(30)
Final dividend proposed		(54)
Retained profit for 20X1		60
Profit and Loss balance b/f		58
Balance carried forward		118

BALANCE SHEET AS AT 31.12.20X1

	Cost	Ac.dep	£000
Fixed assets:			
Furniture	240	(120)	120
Motor vehicles	320	(172)	148
Investments			264
Current assets:			
Stock		516	
Debtors		394	
Cash and bank		38	
Current liabilities:			
Creditors	286		
Audit fee accrued	6		
Taxation	26		
Dividend proposed	54	(372)	
Working capital			576
			1,108

	£000
Share capital and reserves:	
Ordinary shares of £1	900
Share Premium account	90
Profit and Loss Reserve	118
	1,108

Calculation of Corporation Tax:

		£000
Profit before tax – as per accounts		170
Add: Entertainment		26
Less: Resident company dividend		(30)
Depreciation 64 + 24	88	
Tax capital allowance	(124)	(36)
Taxable profit		130

Tax on £130,000 @ 20% = £26,000

IQ 41.2 Interest earned and incurred

TRADING AND PROFIT AND LOSS ACCOUNT FOR THE YEAR ENDED 30.6.20X1

	£000	£000
Sales		7,484
Stock – 1.7.20X0	722	
Purchases	5,168	
Duty paid	152	
Stock – 30.6.20X1	(876)	(5,166)
Gross profit		2,318
Distribution cost:		
Bad debts	16	
Advertising	76	(92)
Administrative expenses:		
Salaries and wages	589	
Directors' fees	28	
Audit fees	30	
Depreciation	214	
Rent	48	
Other expenses	528	(1,437)
Operating profit		789
Dividend received		45
Interest earned		36
Interest expense		(48)
Profit before taxation		822
Taxation		(228)
Profit after taxation		594
Interim dividend paid		(120)
Final dividend proposed		(216)
Retained profit		258
Balance b/f		331
Balance c/f		589

BALANCE SHEET AS AT 30 JUNE 20X1

	Cost	Ac. dep.	£000
Fixed assets	2,140	(1,030)	1,100
Investments			528
Current assets:			
Stock in trade		876	
Debtors		684	
Interest receivable		36	
Cash and bank		22	
Current liabilities:			
Creditors	599		
Interest payable	24		
Directors' fees accrued	28		
Audit fees accrued	30		
Taxation	210		
Dividend proposed	216	(1,107)	511
			2,149
			£000
Share capital and reserves:			
Ordinary shares of £1 each		900	
Share Premium account		60	
Profit and Loss Reserve		589	1,549
Long-term liability:			
8% debentures			600
			2,149

	£000
Computation of corporation tax:	
Accounting profit for the year	822
Add: Political contributions	20
Less: Dividend from resident co.	(45)
Substitute: Depreciation	214
with tax capital allowance	(311)
	(97)
Taxable profit for the year	700

Corporation Tax: £700,000 @ 30% = £210,000

TAXATION ACCOUNT (LIABILITY)

	£		£
Cash book	216	Balance b/f	198
		Taxation a/c – exp.	18
		Corporation Tax	210

TAXATION ACCOUNT (EXPENDITURE)

	£		£
Underprovision	18	Profit and Loss a/c	228
Corporation Tax	210		

IQ 41.3 Transfers to and from reserves

PROFIT AND LOSS (APPROPRIATION) ACCOUNTS FOR YEARS ENDED 31 DECEMBER				
	20X0	20X1	20X2	20X3
	£	£	£	£
Profit after taxation	96,500	68,500	56,000	112,000
Dividend	(80,000)	(80,000)	(80,000)	(80,000)
Retained profit (Loss)	16,500	(11,500)	(24,000)	32,000
Dividend Equalization Reserve	(10,000)	–	15,000	(20,000)
Profit and Loss balance b/f	21,400	27,900	16,400	7,400
Profit and Loss balance c/f	27,900	16,400	7,400	19,400

DIVIDEND EQUALIZATION RESERVE

		£					£
31.12.20X2	Profit and Loss (appropriation)	15,000		1.1.20X0		Balance b/f	95,000
31.12.20X2	Balance c/d	90,000		31.12.20X0		Profit and Loss (appropriation)	10,000
				1.1.20X3		Balance b/f	90,000
				31.12.20X3		Profit and Loss (appropriation)	20,000

IQ 41.4 Redemption of debentures

SINKING FUND FOR REDEMPTION OF DEBENTURES ACCOUNT

			£				£	
9	31.12	General Reserve	505,000	1.1	Balance b/f	412,500	1
				31.12	SF Cash a/c	38,200	2
				31.12	SF Investment a/c	14,300	4
	31.12			31.12	P&L (appropriation)	40,000	5

SINKING FUND INVESTMENTS ACCOUNT

			£				£	
1	1.1	Balance b/f	412,500	31.12	SF Cash a/c	426,800	3
4	31.12	Sinking Fund	14,300				

SINKING FUND CASH ACCOUNT

			£			£	
2	31.12	Sinking Fund	38,200	31.12	Debenture Redemption a/c	500,000	7
3	31.12	SF Investments a/c	426,800	31.12	Cash book	5,000	8
5	31.12	Cash book	40,000				

DEBENTURE REDEMPTION ACCOUNT

			£			£	
7	31.12	SF Cash a/c	500,000	31.12	8% debentures	500,000	6

Notes:

1. Balance in the fund with equivalent investments.
2. Income from sinking fund investments.
3. Realization of the sinking fund investments.
4. Transfer of the gain on realizing the sinking fund investments.
5. Annual appropriation and cash transfer.
6. An account opened to record redemption.
7. Redemption of the debentures at par.
8. Refunding of cash in excess of requirements.
9. Transfer of the Sinking Fund balance to General Reserve.

PROGRESSIVE QUESTIONS

PQ 41.1 Appropriations of a company profit

As at 31.12.20X0, Bradbury plc had balances of £2,600,000, £1,620,000 and £1,200,000 in its Profit and Loss Reserve, Dividend Equalization Reserve and Asset Replacement Reserve, respectively. Corporation Tax for the year ended 31.12.20X0 had been estimated at £3,624,000. The following particulars relate to the four years to 31 December 20X4:

Year ending 31 December	20X1	20X2	20X3	20X4
	£000	£000	£000	£000
Profit before taxation	12,840	11,650	18,720	21,560
Corporation Tax for the year estimated at	3,965	5,848	5,924	7,255
Payment of Corporation Tax for the previous year	3,862	4,694	5,862	5,448
Interim dividend paid in the year	2,400	2,400	3,600	3,600
Final dividend proposed for the year	6,000	6,000	7,200	7,200
Transfers to (from) Dividend Equalization Reserve	–	(1,500)	1,000	2,000
Transfers to Asset Replacement Reserve	500	500	500	500

Required: Set out the appropriation portion of Bradbury plc's Profit and Loss account in each of the four years to 31 December 20X4.

PQ 41.2 Final accounts of a manufacturing company

Croydon Metalworks plc has extracted its Trial Balance, on the last day of its accounting period, as stated on the right. You are further informed as follows:

(a) The stock of finished goods on 30.6.20X5 has been ascertained as £528,000.

(b) Machinery, acquired for £480,000 on 1 April 20X0, was sold on 31 March 20X5 for £240,000.

(c) The following fixed assets were acquired during the year:
  ● On 1.10.20X4, furniture for £47,000;
  ● On 1.4.20X5, motor vehicle for £80,000.
  Costs stated above are inclusive of VAT at 17.5 per cent, and these costs are included in the amounts at which the respective assets are stated on the Trial Balance.

(d) Plant and machinery, furniture and motor vehicles are to be depreciated for the year by the straight-line method, at 5 per cent, 10 per cent and 20 per cent respectively.

(e) One-quarter of the rent and electricity are to be regarded as relating to various sales outlets.

(f) The provision for doubtful debts is usually maintained to cover 5 per cent of debtors.

(g) The Corporation Tax on the year's profit is estimated at £286,000.

(h) Investments are to be written down by £28,000 because of a permanent fall in their market value.

(i) The directors propose to pay the preference dividend and a final dividend of 9p to ordinary shareholders.

Required: Set out the Trading and Profit and Loss account of the company for the year ended 30 June 20X5, and the Balance Sheet as at that date, both having been prepared for internal use of the company's management.

TRIAL BALANCE AS AT 30 JUNE 20X5		
	£000	£000
Machinery at cost	1,420	–
Machinery depreciation 30.6.20X4	–	639
Furniture and fittings at cost	547	–
Furniture depreciation 30.6.20X4	–	189
Vehicles at cost	720	–
Vehicle depreciation 30.6.20X5	–	234
Stock of finished goods – 30.6.20X5	462	–
Value Added Tax payable	–	112
Provision for 20X4 Corporation Tax	–	214
Stock of raw material – 30.6.20X4	238	–
Work in progress – 30.6.20X4	42	–
Disposal of machinery	–	240
Payment of 20X4 Corporation Tax	236	–
Investments at cost	436	–
9% debentures	–	400
Advertising account	294	–
Dividend received	–	24
Manufacturing cost	6,428	–
Telephone and postage	65	–
Debenture interest paid	18	–
Rent account	116	–
Sales account	–	8,748
Salaries account	618	–
Directors fees	112	–
Sales commission	184	–
Ordinary shares of 50p each	–	800
8% preference shares of £1 each	–	300
Share Premium account	–	120
Interim dividend paid	120	–
Profit and Loss Reserve	–	346
Bad debts	12	–
Cash and bank balance	84	–
Debtors and creditors	760	572
Electricity account	48	–
Provision for doubtful debts	–	22
	12,960	12,960

PQ 41.3 Corrections to financial statements prepared already

When you assumed duties as head of accounting of Eurig plc on 1 January 20X1, you were presented with financial statements prepared by your predecessor as shown opposite. Your enquiries further reveal as follows:

(a) The balance at the bank on 31.12.20X0, as per the bank statement, is £17,000. The difference has arisen from the following:
  ● The cash book does not record bank charges amounting to £1,000, nor £6,000 received by mandate as interest on a loan to Tiny Ltd.
  ● Bank lodgements not credited by the bank and cheques yet to be presented to the bank as at 31.12.20X0 were £8,000 and £46,000 respectively.
  ● Business rates paid by standing order accounts for the remaining difference.

TRADING AND PROFIT AND LOSS ACCOUNT FOR THE YEAR ENDED 31.12.20X0	£000	£000
Sales		9,624
Stock 1.1.20X0	614	
Purchases	7,286	
Stock 31.12.20X0	(752)	(7,148)
Gross profit		2,476
Distribution cost:		
Depreciation	296	
Advertising	104	
Bad debts	11	(411)
Administrative exp.		
Salaries	849	
Directors' fees	72	
Depreciation	84	
Bank charges	6	
Audit fees	25	
Staff welfare	7	
Other expenses	462	(1,505)
Operating profit		560
Dividend received		48
Debenture interest		(32)
Profit before taxation		576
Taxation		(212)
Profit after taxation		364
Interim dividend		(60)
Final dividend		(96)
Retained profit		208

BALANCE SHEET AS AT 31.12.20X0

	Cost	Ac. dep.	£000
Fixed assets			
Furniture	960	(316)	644
Motor vehicles	1,840	(980)	860
Investments			485
Current assets:			
Stock in trade		752	
Debtors	814		
Provision	(41)	773	
Loan to Tiny Ltd		60	
Current liability:			
Creditors	738		
Suspense a/c	8		
Taxation	198		
Bank overdraft	11		
Dividend	96	(1,051)	534
			2,523

	£000
Share capital and reserves:	
Ordinary shares of 50p	1,200
Share Premium account	300
Profit and Loss Reserve	623
Non-current liability:	
8% debentures	400
	2,523

(b) Your predecessor has overlooked the company's policy of maintaining a provision to cover 5 per cent of debtors outstanding. *

(c) Unsold stock as at 31 December 20X0 has been valued at cost plus Value Added Tax at 17.5 per cent.

(d) Personal ledger accounts are maintained in subsidiary ledgers on a self-balancing basis. The sum of the individual debtors' balances on 31.12.20X0 amounts to £808,000 and fails to match the control account balance stated on the Balance Sheet. You have been able to ascertain the reasons for the discrepancy as follows:
  ● a cheque for £4,000 received from a customer has inadvertently been debited to the customer's personal account;
  ● the Sales Day Book has been overcast by £6,000;
  ● the difference arose because the monthly total of the discount column on the debit side of the cash book has been posted to the debit of the Sales Ledger Control account.

(e) The difference arising in the Trial Balance as at 31 December 20X0 has been placed in suspense and carried forward to the Balance Sheet.

(f) Other expenses include £180,000 on forming the company (preliminary expenses).

Required: Redraft the Profit and Loss account for the year ended 31.12.20X0 and the Balance Sheet as at that date.

PQ 41.4 An incomplete list of account balances

Selamander plc has in issue one million ordinary shares of £1 each, which were issued at a premium of 10p per share. So far, 70p per share has been called up. On 30 June 20X1, 120,000 shares were in arrears for the first call of 15p per share, while 10,000 shares have paid the final call of 30p per share in advance. Apart from the balances relating to the above share transactions, remaining balances have been extracted from the company's ledgers as stated on the right.

You are further informed as follows:

(a) Stock on 30 June 20X1 was £712,000.
(b) Fixed assets are to be depreciated by 10 per cent of cost.
(c) £8,000 of trade debt is to be written off, and the provision for doubtful debts is to be adjusted to 5 per cent of debtors outstanding.
(d) £30,000 is to be accounted for as audit fees.
(e) The Corporation Tax on the year's profit is estimated at £214,000.
(f) Directors have resolved to pay a dividend of 8p per share.

Required: Prepare:

(a) for internal use of the management, the Trading and Profit and Loss account for the year ended 30 June 20X1 and the Balance Sheet as at that date;
(b) a revised Balance Sheet as at 30 June 20X1 on the basis that all shares in arrears for the call were forfeited on that date.

TRIAL BALANCE	
	£000
Stock in trade – 30.6.20X0	696
Carriage inwards	142
Trade debtors	568
Trade creditors	662
Cash in hand	16
Bank overdraft	72
Purchases	6,442
Sales	9,478
Salaries	963
Fixed assets at cost	5,900
Depreciation up to 30.6.20X0	3,840
Overprovision – Corporation Tax	22
Investments at cost	286
Advertising	186
Provision for doubtful debts	34
Accrued expenses	168
Rent and rates	246
Stationery, postage, telephone	72
Motor vehicle maintenance	184
Dividend received	42
9% debentures	300
Profit and Loss Reserve b/f	412
Directors' emoluments	114

## Chapter 42

COMPANIES (4): PUBLISHED FINANCIAL STATEMENTS

In this chapter

We will learn of:

- the format in which companies are required to publish financial statements
- ordinary and extraordinary activities
- ratios used by investors

and you should be able to:

- prepare financial statements for publication
- deal with exceptional items and prior-period adjustments
- interpret information in published financial statements

42.1 THE LEGAL REQUIREMENT TO PUBLISH

Company law requires every company to publish (i.e. allow the public access to) its financial statements. The requirement to publish the financial statements is commonly referred to as the duty to 'lay and deliver': within seven months of the end of each financial year (ten months in the case of a private company) every company has a legal duty to lay before the shareholders at a general meeting, and to deliver to the Registrar of Companies, a copy of its financial statements. The copies delivered to the Registrar are available for inspection by any member of the public.

The Profit and Loss account and Balance Sheet prepared for publication differ from those that are prepared for the internal use of management. For example, in answer to IQ 41.2 we prepared the Profit and Loss account for internal use as shown on the following page (top left). The Profit and Loss account when prepared for publication would appear as shown on the following page (top right). The two differ in:

- the format of presentation – see Section 42.3;
- the terminology – marked as 'a' – see also Section 42.2;
- the contents – marked as 'b' – see also Section 42.4.

TRADING AND PROFIT AND LOSS ACCOUNT FOR THE YEAR ENDED 30 JUNE 20X1 (for internal use)			
		£000	
Sales		7,484	a
Stock – 1.7.20X0	722		b
Purchases	5,168		b
Duty paid	152		b
Stock – 30.6.20X1	(876)	(5,166)	b
Gross profit		2,318	
Distribution cost:			
Bad debts	16		b
Advertising	76	(92)	b
Administrative expenses:			
Salaries and wages	589		b
Directors fees	28		b
Audit fees	30		b
Depreciation	214		b
Rent	48		b
Other expenses	528	(1,437)	b
Operating profit		789	b
Dividend received		45	a
Interest earned		36	a
Interest expense		(48)	a
Profit before taxation		822	
Taxation		(228)	
Profit after taxation		594	
Interim dividend paid		(120)	
Final dividend proposed		(216)	
Retained profit		258	
Balance b/f		331	
Balance c/f		589	

PROFIT AND LOSS ACCOUNT FOR THE YEAR ENDED 30 JUNE 20X1 (for publication)		
	£000	
Turnover	7,484	a
Cost of sales	(5,166)	b
Gross profit	2,318	
Distribution cost	(92)	b
Administrative expenses	(1,437)	b
Operating profit	789	a
Income from fixed asset investments	45	a
Interest receivable and similar income	36	a
Interest payable and similar charges	(48)	a
Profit from ordinary activity before taxation	822	
Tax on profit on ordinary activities	(228)	
Profit on ordinary activities after taxation	594	
Interim dividend paid	(120)	
Final dividend proposed	(216)	
Retained profit	258	

Similarly, the Balance Sheet prepared for publication differs from that prepared for internal use in format, terminology and content.

42.2 TERMINOLOGY USED IN PUBLISHED FINANCIAL STATEMENTS

The published accounts use terminology prescribed by company law. If the answer to IQ 41.2 had been prepared for publication, some of the expressions used should be different as shown here.

Terminology we used	Terminology required by company law
Sales	Turnover
Current liability	Creditors: amounts falling due within one year
Long-term liability	Creditors: amounts falling due after more than one year
Working capital	Net current assets

42.3 FORMAT FOR PRESENTING PUBLISHED FINANCIAL STATEMENTS

For the purpose of standardizing the format in which all companies publish their financial statements, company law prescribes four alternative formats for presenting the Profit and Loss account and two for presenting the Balance Sheet. To present its financial statements, every company should adopt one of these formats and use the chosen one consistently, without making alterations to either the sequence of the items or their wording.

Furthermore, the accounting profession is making a continuous endeavour to improve the format. The main thrust of these improvements has been to ensure that:

- the performance and position are reported in the financial statements with clarity to convey a *true and fair view*; and
- the information is so displayed as to enhance the use of the information as the basis for predicting the company's prospects and for assessing its performance, profitability and liquidity.

The combined effect of the legal and the professional requirements is that a Profit and Loss account, prepared in 'Format 1', would appear as shown below. Special points to note are as follows:

- Items marked x in the margin are those required by the legal format and those marked y are the professional requirements.
- Items 1, 2 and 4–6 are required to be broken down to identify the extent to which each of these relate to continuing operations, acquisitions, and discontinued operations (see Section 42.8).
- If necessary for showing a true and fair view, items are required to be identified as 'exceptional' (see Section 42.6.3).
- The legal requirement is that item 8 should identify separately income from subsidiaries, associates and other fixed asset investments.
- The legal requirement is that description of items 13 and 14 should identify them as relating to ordinary activities. Such an identification is now probably superfluous because (as we will see in Section 42.6.2) it is unlikely that a company will have any activity that is other than 'ordinary' (see definition in Section 42.6.1).
- Although, under a legal requirement, it would suffice to disclose in aggregate the dividends paid and proposed, it is usual for the convenience of shareholders to show them separately.

PROFIT AND LOSS ACCOUNT FOR THE YEAR ENDED 31.12.20X0			
		£000	
1	Turnover	800	x
2	Cost of sales	(550)	x
3	Gross profit	250	x
4	Distribution cost	(64)	x
5	Administrative expenses	(112)	x
6	Operating profit	74	y
7	**Exceptional Items:**		y
	Loss on asset disposal	(15)	
8	Income from investments	20	x
9	Interest receivable and similar income	8	x
10	Amounts written off investments	(12)	x
11	Interest payable and similar charges	(9)	x
12	Profit before taxation	66	y
13	Tax on profit on ordinary activities	(14)	x
14	Profit on ordinary activity after taxation	52	x
15	Interim dividend paid	(10)	y
16	Final dividend proposed	(20)	y
17	Retained profit	22	y

BALANCE SHEET AS AT 31.12.20X0		
	£	£
Fixed assets:		
Intangible assets		240
Tangible assets		620
Investments		20
Current assets:		
Stocks	320	
Debtors	415	
Investments	45	
Cash at bank and in hand	25	
Creditors: amounts falling due		
within one year	(325)	
Net current assets		480
Total assets less current liabilities		1,360

		£
Creditors: amounts falling due after		
more than one year:		
Debenture loans		200
Provision for liabilities and charges:		
Pension and similar obligations	35	
Deferred taxation	25	60
Capital and reserves:		
Called-up share capital	800	
Share Premium account	120	
Revaluation reserve	40	
Other reserves	15	
Profit and Loss account	125	1,100
		1,360

The Balance Sheet, presented in the legally prescribed 'Format 1', would appear as set out on the left. Company law requires the breakdown of each item, but permits them to be stated in schedules rather than on the face of the Balance Sheet as set out below.

SCHEDULES	
Intangible assets:	*Tangible assets:*
Development cost	Land and building
Patents, trademarks	Plant and machinery
Goodwill	Fixtures, fittings, tools
	and equipment

Stocks:	
Raw materials	*Creditors:*
Work in progress	Debenture loans
Finished goods	Bank loan/overdrafts
	Payments on account
Debtors:	Trade creditors
Trade debtors	Owed to subsidiary
Due from subsidiary	Owed to associates
Due from associate	Taxation
Other debtors	Accruals
Called-up capital	
not paid	
Prepayments	

The point at which the asset side of the Balance Sheet is separated from the liability side is in accordance with the authors' preference. Company law is silent on this.

42.4 CONTENTS OF PUBLISHED FINANCIAL STATEMENTS

Information requiring separate disclosure
1. Turnover – segmental breakdown
2. Depreciation
3. Fall in value of any fixed asset
4. Directors' emoluments
– remuneration for services
– fees
– pension cost
– compensation for loss of office
5. Audit fees and expenses
6. Hire or lease of plants
7. Employees: average number/breakdown
8. Payments to employees
– salaries and wages
– pension cost
– social security cost
9. Profit – segmental breakdown
10. Taxation – breakdown into components
11. Identity, nature and amount of any exceptional item, extraordinary item or prior-period adjustment
12. Earnings per share (if a listed company)

The information included in published financial statements should conform strictly with the requirements of company law and accounting standards. If extra is provided, the company would resent disclosing more than is required; if there is less, there would be a breach of company law or an accounting standard or both.

The following may be noted:

● Whereas in financial statements prepared for internal use each expense is itemized according to its nature (as salary, rent, stationery etc.), in those for publication the expenses are grouped together (as cost of sales, distribution costs or administrative expenses) and only the subtotal for each group is published.

● Items of specific significance to those entitled to the information, however, are required to be disclosed in Notes, to be published as part of the financial statements. Some of such items have been listed in the box shown above.

- More disclosures on directors' emoluments are required if the total emoluments paid to all of them exceed £60,000 per year.
- The list of disclosures to be made is ever growing.

Let us recall the three groups into which operating expenses are included in the Profit and Loss account:

- **Cost of sales.** This includes production expenses and expenses incurred placing the goods sold in the condition in which, and the location from which, the goods are sold.
- **Distribution costs.** This includes expenses incurred in selling goods and delivering them to customers.
- **Administrative expenses.** This includes expenses incurred in maintaining the establishment and carrying out administration.

Grouping of operating expenses

Interaction 42.1

The Profit and Loss account, when prepared for publication in 'Format 1', states subtotals of groups of operating expenses instead of listing each individually.

Required: Identify the group in which you would include each of the following operating expenses, by stating in the appropriate cell of the following grid the relevant abbreviation as: cost of sales (C), distribution cost (D) and administrative expense (A), assuming that there are no specific instructions to allocate or apportion expenditure.

1	Salaries		16	Depreciation – building	
2	Rent		17	Depreciation – furniture	
3	Postage		18	Depreciation – machinery	
4	Telephone expense		19	Depreciation – vehicles	
5	Advertising		20	Depreciation – equipment	
6	Rates		21	Audit fees	
7	Staff welfare		22	Pension cost	
8	Productive wages		23	Directors' remuneration	
9	Sales commission		24	Directors' fees	
10	Carriage inwards		25	Bad debt	
11	Carriage outwards		26	Development cost – write-off	
12	Stationery		27	Development cost – amortization	
13	Factory power		28	Stock loss – if normal	
14	Raw material consumed		29	Bank charges	
15	Cost of goods sold		30	Vehicle maintenance	

Interaction 42.2

Published accounts – a basic question

Perrins Ltd extracted its year-end Trial Balance as stated here and informs as follows:

(a) Stock of unsold goods as at 30.6.20X1 has been ascertained as £512,000.

(b) The company employs the following:
- Directors 2
- Senior executives 3
- Administrative staff 4
- Salesmen 11
- Junior employees 3

(c) Salaries and wages account includes £46,000 paid to directors.

(d) Expenses yet to be accounted for as at 30 June 20X1 include the following:
- Directors' fees   £15,000
- Rent   £12,000
- Audit fees   £6,000

(e) Other expenses include £4,000 incurred in relation to the audit.

(f) Fixed assets are to be depreciated at 10 per cent per annum using the straight-line method.

(g) Corporation Tax is estimated at £18,000.

(h) Directors propose a final dividend of 6p per share.

Required: Prepare for publication the financial statements of Perrins Ltd.

TRIAL BALANCE AS AT 30.6.20X1	£000	£000
Fixed assets	750	224
Stock on 30.6.20X0	364	–
Purchases	862	–
Sales	–	1,298
Returns inwards	22	–
Salaries and wages	182	–
Advertising	21	–
Debtors and creditors	544	486
Stationery	16	–
Postage and telephone	34	–
Dividend received	–	15
Rent	48	–
Investments	98	–
Provision for doubtful debts	–	26
Other expenses	42	–
Carriage inwards	14	–
Ordinary shares of £1	–	500
Share premium	–	80
Profit and Loss a/c	–	294
Interim dividend	20	–
8% debentures	–	150
Cash and bank	56	–
	3,073	3,073

42.5 STATEMENT OF MOVEMENT OF TANGIBLE FIXED ASSETS

Company law permits the Balance Sheet to report as a single amount the aggregate of the written-down values of the various classes of tangible fixed assets *provided* the details of each class are included as a schedule in a Statement of Movements of Tangible Fixed Assets.

To illustrate, let us assume that:

- as at 1.1.20X0, a company owned equipment costing £800, written down by that date to £540;
- equipment acquired for £120 and written down by 1.1.20X0 to £35 was sold on that day for £45;
- new equipment was acquired on 1.4.20X0 for £160;
- the company's policy is to depreciate equipment at 10 per cent per year using the straight-line method.
- financial statements are prepared annually on 31 December.

These transactions would be accounted for as follows:

EQUIPMENT ACCOUNT

20X0		£	20X0		£
1.1	Balance b/f	800	1.1	Disposal a/c	120
1.4	Cash book	160	31.12	Balance c/d	840
1.1	Balance b/d	840			

PROVISION FOR DEPRECIATION ACCOUNT

20X0		£	20X0		£
1.1	Disposal	85	1.1	Balance b/f	260
31.12	Balance c/d	255	31.12	Depreciation*	80
			1.1	Balance b/d	255

DISPOSAL OF EQUIPMENT ACCOUNT

20X0		£	20X0		£
1.1	Equipment	120	1.1	Provision for depn	85
31.12	P&L – gain	10	1.1	Cash book	45

* Calculation of depreciation at 10% of cost:
10% of (£800,000 less £120,000) = £68,000
10% of £160,000 for nine months = £12,000
£80,000

The movements during the year in the value of equipment are stated within a schedule that forms part of the published accounts. The information in the asset account is stated, in a statement form, in the first box here; and that in the Provision account is stated in the second, while the difference between the balances carried forward in both boxes is stated as the written down value of that class of asset, in the third box. Each box would be equipped with additional columns, if necessary, to report the information relating to each class of tangible fixed asset. The aggregate of the written down values of all classes of tangible assets is stated in the Balance Sheet.

The gain on disposal of equipment is reported in the Profit and Loss account, if material, as an exceptional item (see Section 42.6.3 below).

Cost of equipment	
Balance b/f	£800,000
Acquisition	£160,000
Disposal	(£120,000)
Balance c/f	£840,000

Accumulated depreciation	
Balance b/f	£260,000
Depreciation	£80,000
Disposal	(£85,000)
Balance c/f	£255,000

Written down value	
As at 31.12.20X0	£585,000

Manufacturing company with movements in tangible assets

Interaction 42.3

Tuna Ltd provides you with its year-end Trial Balance as stated below, as well as the following additional Information:

(a) Stock as at 30 June 20X1 consists of:
  ● Raw materials: £244,000;
  ● Work in progress: £26,000;
  ● Finished goods: £328,000.
(b) Acquisition of fixed assets during the year were as follows:
  ● 1.7.20X0: land and building for £150,000;
  ● 1.11.20X0: machinery for £60,000.
(c) Machinery acquired for £80,000 on 1.1.20X0 was sold for £45,000 on 31.12.20X0.
(d) The company's policy is to assume that one-third of the cost relates to land and to depreciate buildings and machinery at 2 per cent and 5 per cent respectively per year, using the straight-line method.
(e) The apportionment on the right has been agreed:

	Factory	Admin.	Dist.
Salaries/wages	40%	50%	10%
Building depreciation	50%	50%	–

(f) A debt of £28,000 is to be written off and the provision adjusted to cover 5 per cent of debtors.

(g) Corporation Tax for the year is estimated at £58,000.

(h) The directors propose a final dividend of 4p per share.

Required: Prepare for publication the Profit and Loss account for the year ended 30 June 20X1 and the Balance Sheet as at that date, along with a Statement of Movement of Tangible Fixed Assets.

Notes:

- Underprovision for tax is the amount by which the amount set aside for the previous year's Corporation Tax falls short of the amount at which it was eventually settled. This amount is added to the current year's tax expenditure.

- Deferred tax is a tax liability, the payment of which is delayed. This arises because, under tax laws, certain income items are not taxed and certain expenditure is not recognized until a later period. The balance in a deferred tax account is recognized as a liability and reported as such in the Balance Sheet under the statutory heading 'Provision for liabilities and charges'.

TRIAL BALANCE AS AT 30 JUNE 20X1		
	£000	£000
Land and buildings	600	–
Provision for depn – Building 30.6.X0	–	96
Plant and machinery	480	–
Provision for depn – Machinery 30.6.X0	–	112
Cash and bank	189	–
Ordinary shares of 50p each	–	600
Share premium account	–	60
Stock as at 30.6.20X0:		
– Raw materials	154	–
– Work in progress	37	–
– Finished goods	286	–
Purchases of raw material	1,466	–
Sales	–	2,276
Salaries and wages	260	–
Factory power	52	–
Debtors and creditors	548	692
Disposal of machinery	–	45
Stationery	11	–
Sales commission	21	–
Postage and telephone	12	–
Directors fees	45	–
Provision for bad debts	–	17
Rent (for sales depots)	12	–
Under-provision for 20X0 tax	16	–
Deferred taxation	–	32
Advertising	64	–
Profit and Loss account	–	392
Staff welfare	33	–
Interim dividend paid	36	–
	4,322	4,322

42.6 THE 'ALL-INCLUSIVE' CONCEPT OF PERFORMANCE REPORTING AND ITS EFFECTS

There are two schools of thought as to what the Profit and Loss account should include for purposes of reporting performance in a period. The first, known as the Current Operating Profit school, advocates that only *current performance* and *operating performance* should be included. This school advocates that income or expenditure other than those of the current period and within the operating activity should be excluded from the Profit and Loss account and included in a Reserve to be stated in the Balance Sheet. Accordingly, this school is known also as the Reserve Accounting school.

The other school of thought is known as the 'All-Inclusive school' and advocates that the Profit and Loss account should include all items of income and expenditure, irrespective of whether or not they are part of the operating activity, they are expected to recur regularly or frequently, or they are within the control of the entity's management.

The accounting profession in the United Kingdom has accepted the All-Inclusive school of thought and accordingly advocates that the Profit and Loss account should include all income and expenditure recognized within the period unless this is prohibited either by law or by an accounting standard. (For example, it is the requirement of company law that no gain should be included in the Profit and Loss account unless it is realised,[1] and any gain arising from revaluation of an asset should be stated in a Revaluation Reserve;[2] accordingly, notwithstanding the adoption of the All-Inclusive school of thought, a gain on revaluation of an asset, though recognized within the period, cannot be stated in the Profit and Loss account.)

Adherence to the All-Inclusive school means that the Profit and Loss account would include the result of all transactions and events irrespective of whether they are part of the normal operations of the entity or, indeed, whether any of them is a rarity or one-off. To trace the progress of operational activity from period to period, it is then necessary to focus on the entity's ordinary activities. Unless the results of any activity that may be regarded as a rarity or one-off are identified, it is difficult to use the performance in an accounting period as the basis for forecasting the future. Hence the accounting standard FRS 3[3] requires identification of:

● ordinary activity;
● extraordinary items;
● exceptional items.

These are each discussed further below.

42.6.1 Ordinary activity

The ordinary activity of a business entity is defined in FRS 3 as stated here. By including within 'ordinary' activity the effect of changes in any environment, it has become impossible to find any transaction or event that is other than ordinary.

> **Ordinary activity is any activity:**
>
> ● undertaken by an entity as part of its business;
> ● related activity in furtherance of, incidental to, or arising from, this activity; and
> ● that includes effects of any change in the various environments within which it operates, including the political, regulatory, economic and geographical environments, irrespective of the frequency or unusual nature . . .

42.6.2 Extraordinary items

If the future performance of an entity is to be predicted on the basis of its current performance, those with an intimate knowledge of the entity (the management) will have to assist by identifying any transaction or event that, in their considered opinion, is unlikely to recur. For example, let us assume that a company reports a reduced profit of £15 million for the year, having suffered a loss of £33 million in a political upheaval in a foreign country from which it has since withdrawn. Unless attention is directed to the fact that the material loss of £33 million is unlikely to recur, the future performance of the company is likely to be underestimated. Therefore, FRS 3 defines 'extraordinary' items as stated here.

> **Extraordinary items are:**
>
> 1. material items
> 2. possessing a high degree of abnormality
> 3. outside the ordinary activities and
> 4. not expected to recur

Furthermore, FRS 3 requires that:

- extraordinary items shall be stated in the Profit and Loss account after 'Profit or Loss on ordinary activities after taxation' and before any appropriations;
- each extraordinary item, shown individually, shall be adequately described so that its nature can be understood and tax implications thereof separately disclosed.

However, it is rare that any company has an extraordinary item to report. This is because, as we saw in Section 42.6.1, FRS 3 has so stretched the definition of ordinary activities that no activity is likely to fall outside it. The loss from the upheaval in a foreign country that we cited above as an example is likely to have arisen from the political environment in that country and would therefore fall within 'ordinary activity'.

42.6.3 Exceptional items

If the performance reported for a year is to constitute a reliable basis for predicting future performance, those preparing the accounts should provide guidance to those making economic decisions on the basis of the accounts, by drawing attention also to any item which may be 'exceptional'. The FRS 3 accounting standard[4] requires such identification and defines exceptional items as those possessing three characteristics, as stated in the box here. The key words are 'size' and 'incidence' and we will consider each in turn:

> **Exceptional items are:**
>
> (a) material items;
> (b) within ordinary activities; and
> (c) need to be disclosed because of their *size* or *incidence* if the financial statement is to show a true and fair view.

- **Size.** If the reported performance in a year is impaired (or boosted) because an item of (say) expenditure (e.g. bad debt) is significantly different from what is normal, unless this is drawn to the attention of interested parties the current year's performance cannot be a reliable basis for predicting the future.
- **Incidence.** The word 'incidence' may be used in two meanings. The first is 'frequency of occurrence' (as in 'the incidence of malaria is greater in a tropical climate'). The word can also mean 'impact' as in 'indirect taxes are those whose incidence is uncertain'. Hence an item may be regarded as abnormal in incidence either because it is a rarity or because it should have impacted the performance in a different period rather than the current one.

The requirements of the FRS 3 accounting standard in this regard are that:

- exceptional items shall be included within the appropriate heading in the legal format and disclosed by way of a Note with adequate description;
- the following three exceptional items, however, shall be disclosed *on the face of the Profit and Loss account*:
  - profit or loss on sale or termination of an operation;
  - cost of fundamental reorganization or restructuring;
  - gain/loss on disposal of fixed assets.

Identification of exceptional items

Herrings plc reported a loss after tax of £228,000 for the current year, whereas the comparative amounts in previous years had been profits ranging between £800,000 and £1 million.

The loss reported in the current year is after taking into account the following items:

(a) a gain of £225,000 on disposing of land that had been used until then as a staff car park;
(b) £375,000 paid to the former Managing Director as compensation for loss of office;
(c) a debt of £418,000 written off as bad upon the compulsory liquidation of a major customer (bad debts usually amounting to around £60,000 per year);
(d) business rates paid in the year, amounting to £32,000, whereas the amount until now had been around £28,000 per year;
(e) £250,000 paid as compensation to a customer for injuries suffered on company premises in the previous year – the claim had been ignored when reporting the previous year's performance;
(f) £420,000 incurred in countering Y2K – i.e. computer problems anticipated from what was known as the millennium bug.

Required: Explain, giving reasons, which of the above items you would identify as 'exceptional', and clarify whether you would draw attention to it on the face of the Profit and Loss account or in the Notes.

42.7 PRIOR-PERIOD ADJUSTMENTS

The retained profit with which a company's annual Profit and Loss account would usually end is accumulated from year to year in a Profit and Loss Reserve. The accumulated total in this reserve is stated as part of the company's reserves in its Balance Sheet. If an expenditure incurred in the year could be written off directly against the balance in the Profit and Loss Reserve, rather than in the Profit and Loss account, the company would report an improved profit performance for the year and therefore better earnings per share (see Section 42.11.1). This, however, is prohibited. An item of income or expenditure cannot be taken directly to the Profit and Loss Reserve unless it qualifies for recognition as a 'Prior-period adjustment'. The FRS 3 accounting standard[5] defines a prior-period adjustment as stated in the box. To be taken directly to the Profit and Loss Reserve, that adjustment should not only be material in amount and one relating to a prior period, but also, more importantly, be one necessitated because of a change in accounting policy or for correcting a fundamental error.

> **Prior-period adjustments are:**
>
> ● material adjustments;
> ● applicable to prior periods;
> ● arising from changes to accounting policy or correction of a fundamental error.

For illustration, let us assume that a company acquired a building for £800,000 on 1.1.20X0 and did not depreciate it. On 1.1.20X6 it changes its policy and decides that the building should be depreciated at 2 per cent of cost per year. To give effect to this new policy, by 31.12.20X6 the building should have been depreciated for seven years – i.e. by £16,000 per year × 7 years = £112,000. Out of this amount, £16,000 would be the current year's depreciation, which is treated as any other expenditure arising in the year. The backlog depreciation of £96,000 (relating to the previous six years) would qualify to be treated as a prior-period adjustment because:

● the amount is material;
● the amount relates to (six) prior years; and
● the adjustment arises from a change of accounting policy.

Therefore, £96,000 can be – and, in fact, *should* be – debited to the Profit and Loss Reserve.

A fundamental error is one so serious that the auditor would have had to give a disclaimer of opinion. For example, it would be a fundamental error if the financial statements had been prepared on the assumption of going concern in a situation where that assumption could not have applied – where, for instance, the company was insolvent.

42.8 DISCONTINUED AND ACQUIRED ACTIVITY

If a company dealing in several lines of activity discontinues (and/or acquires) a line during the year, FRS 3 requires full particulars to be published. Unless full particulars of the extent to which the performance relates to an activity that has been discontinued are identified, the reported performance in the year cannot provide a reliable basis for forecasting future performance.

To illustrate, let us assume that a company dealing in ready-made garments has, in the year, moved out of dealing in menswear and has instead commenced dealing in workwear. Particulars of its performance in the year in each of these lines are stated in the box below. Lines 1 and 2 are being continued with and line 4 is newly acquired in the year, while line 3 has been discontinued. Reporting only the aggregate of the four lines, as stated in the 'total' column, would fail to draw into focus what the performance is likely to be in future years. Therefore, FRS 3 requires that, in respect of each of the five items stated below, the published Profit and Loss account should identify the amounts relating to:

(a) continuing activity – aggregate of lines 1 and 2;
(b) acquisition – line 4;
(c) subtotal of (a) and (b) – because this is likely to mirror the performance in the future; and
(d) discontinued activity – line 3.

	Line 1	Line 2	Line 3	Line 4	Total for the year
	Womenswear	Childrenswear	Menswear	Workwear	
	£000	£000	£000	£000	£000
Sales	654	286	189	189	1,318
Cost of sales	(490)	(172)	(170)	(135)	(967)
Distribution cost	(26)	(18)	(29)	(32)	(105)
Admin. expenses	(24)	(28)	(24)	(20)	(96)
Operating result	114	68	(34)	2	150

Accordingly, the published Profit and Loss account, with the breakdowns required by FRS 3 (when applicable), would appear as shown below. With the loss-making menswear discontinued, the chances are that future performance of the company will resemble the amounts stated in the subtotal column (shaded). If it is felt that all these details will make the Profit and Loss account appear cluttered, FRS 3 permits the breakdown of the items, other than that of turnover and operating profit, to be stated in a schedule rather than on the face of the Profit and Loss account.

PROFIT AND LOSS ACCOUNT FOR THE YEAR ENDED XXXXXXXX					
	Continuing	Acquisition	Subtotal	Discontinued	£000
Turnover	940	189	1,129	189	1,318
Cost of sale	(662)	(135)	(797)	(170)	(967)
Gross profit	278	54	332	19	351
Distribution cost	(44)	(32)	(76)	(29)	(105)
Admin. expenses	(52)	(20)	(72)	(24)	(96)
Operating profit	182	2	184	(34)	150

42.9 REPORTING ASSETS AT VALUATION

A company is permitted to report an asset at its market value rather than at cost. The Alternative Accounting Rule, introduced into company law in the United Kingdom since 1981, permits this. But when an asset is revalued upwards, the gain recognized is not realized – and will not be realized until the asset is sold. Therefore, company law requires that a gain on revaluation should be recorded in a Revaluation Reserve, which is reported in the Balance Sheet along with other reserves.

42.10 ADDITIONAL PRIMARY STATEMENTS

FRS 3[6] also requires companies to publish the following additional primary statements:

- Statement of Total Recognised Gains or Losses;
- Note of Historical Cost Profits and Losses;
- Reconciliation of Movements in Shareholders' Funds;

These are vehicles to draw to shareholders' attention specific matters. Let us consider each in turn.

42.10.1 The Statement of Total Recognised Gains or Losses

This statement reports as one figure the totality of gains and losses recognized in the year, although only the realized portion of such gains is reported in the Profit and Loss account, while unrealized revaluation gains are stated in the Balance Sheet within Revaluation Reserves, and prior-period adjustments are made against the Profit and Loss balance brought forward from prior periods. See a specimen of this statement on the right.

STATEMENT OF TOTAL RECOGNISED GAINS OR LOSSES	
	£000
Profit (after tax)	600
Add: Unrealized gain on revaluation	150
Gain on foreign exchange	15
Less: Prior-period adjustment	(75)
Total recognized gain in the year	690

42.10.2 Note of Historical Cost Profits and Losses

This note has to be used by a company that has departed from the historical cost rule (i.e. that has revalued its assets) to identify what its performance in a period would have been had it adhered to the historical cost rule.

To illustrate, let us assume that during the year a company:

- sold for £425 property that cost £100 but that had been revalued to £400 in a prior year; and
- wrote off £40 as depreciation on revalued machinery, whereas the corresponding amount would have been £10 had it not revalued the machinery.

NOTE OF HISTORICAL COST PROFIT OR LOSS	
	£
Profit (before tax)	500
Additional depreciation because of revaluation	30
Realization of prior recognized revaluation gain	300
Profit on historical cost basis	840

If the company had adhered to the historical cost rule, the gain on disposal of property would have been reported this year as £425 less £100, namely £325 (rather than £25); and the depreciation written off for machinery would have been £30 less. What the company's profit or loss would have been on the historical basis is drawn to the attention of the shareholders in a Note of Historical Cost Profit or Loss, as shown in the example here.

42.10.3 The Reconciliation of Movements in Shareholders' Funds

This information traces the variations that occur during the year in each item constituting the shareholders' funds. The reconciliation is required particularly to trace the movements in share capital (issue or buy-back of shares) and in the share premium account.

42.11 INTERPRETING COMPANY FINANCIAL STATEMENTS

We have already discussed (in Chapter 21) the following ratios:

Profitability ratios	**Asset utilization ratios**
• Return on capital employed	• Fixed asset turnover
• Gross profit to sales	• Current asset turnover
• Net profit to sales	• Stock turnover
	• Debtors' turnover
Liquidity ratios	• Creditors' turnover
• Current ratio	**Long-term solvency ratios**
• Liquidity ratio	
• Stock days	• Ratio of debt to equity
• Debtors' days	• Ratio of debt to total assets
• Creditors' days	• Interest cover

Let us now consider five additional ratios of interest to shareholders:

- earnings per share;
- price/earnings ratio;
- earnings yield ratio;
- dividend yield ratio;
- dividend cover.

And, in discussing each of them further below, let us assume that the information stated on the right are those of a company listed on the London Stock Exchange.

Profit and Loss (extract)	**£000**
Profit before taxation	240
Taxation	(50)
Profit after taxation	190
Preference dividend	(24)
Interim dividend paid	(20)
Final dividend proposed	(80)
Retained profit	66

Balance Sheet (extract)	**£000**
Ordinary shares of £1	4,000
6% Preference shares of £1	400
Price per ordinary share on London Stock Exchange	160p

42.11.1 Earnings per share (abbreviated as EPS)

This is expressed as so many pence per share and is calculated by dividing the profit available to ordinary shares (i.e. profit after tax less any extraordinary items and preference dividend) by the number of ordinary shares in issue. In our example,

$$EPS = (£190,000 \text{ less } £24,000)/4,000,000 \times 100p = 4.15p$$

This shows that each ordinary share of £1 earned 4.15p in the year, although a dividend of only 2.5p is being paid. The EPS should be compared with that in prior years and those of comparable companies to assess whether the company is performing better or worse than others or than itself previously. A company whose shares are publicly traded is obliged to include an EPS figure in its published Profit and Loss account.[6]

42.11.2 Price/earnings ratio (abrreviated as PE ratio)

This ratio is calculated by dividing the market capitalization of the company (i.e. price per share × number of shares) by the profit after tax that is available for distribution to the ordinary shareholders. In our illustration:

- the market capitalization is 4,000,000 shares @ 160p = £6,400,000;
- the profit available to ordinary shareholders (same as above) = (£190,000 less £24,000) = £166,000;
- the PE ratio is therefore £6,400,000/£166,000 = 38.55 times.

An alternative way of calculating the PE ratio is by dividing market price per share by EPS:

$$160/4.15 = 38.55 \text{ times}$$

The PE ratio reflects the level of confidence that investors have in a company – the higher the ratio, the greater the confidence.

42.11.3 Earnings yield ratio

This ratio calculates as a percentage how the earnings available to ordinary shareholders compare with the market capitalization of the share. The ratio may be calculated for the whole company or for a single share to yield the same result, as follows:

Calculated focusing on the whole company:	Calculated focusing on each share:
$\dfrac{\text{Earnings available to all ordinary shares } £166,000}{\text{Market capitalization of all ordinary shares } £6,400,000} \times 100\% = 2.59\%$	EPS/market price × 100 = 4.15/160 × 100% = 2.59%

42.11.4 Dividend yield ratio

This ratio calculates the dividends for the year as a percentage of the market price per share. In our example, we have 2.5 pence per share/160 pence × 100% = 1.56%.

42.11.5 Dividend cover

This calculation measures the ability of the company to maintain equity dividends at current levels by dividing the profit available for ordinary shares (i.e. profit after tax less any preference dividend) by the amount of equity dividends paid and proposed in the current year. For our example we have (£190 less £24)/£100 × 100% = 166%. This shows that the company will be able to maintain equity dividends at current levels even if profits were to fall by as much as (66/166 × 100%), i.e. 40 per cent.

Interaction 42.5

Interpreting company accounts

Shamrock plc's financial statements have been prepared as follows:

PROFIT AND LOSS ACCOUNT FOR YEAR ENDED 30.6.20X1	£000
Turnover	7,484
Cost of sales	(5,166)
Gross profit	2,318
Distribution cost	(92)
Administ. expenses	(1,437)
Operating profit	789
Investment income	45
Interest receivable	36
Interest & similar ch.	(48)
Profit before taxation	822
Taxation	(228)
Profit after taxation	594
Interim dividend	(120)
Dividend proposed	(216)
Retained profit	258

BALANCE SHEET AS AT 30 JUNE 20X1

Fixed assets	Cost	Depn.	£000
Machinery	2,140	(1,030)	1,110
Investments			528
Current assets:			
Stock		876	
Debtors		720	
Cash and bank		22	
Creditors: due within one year		(1,107)	
Net current assets			511
Total assets less current liability			2,149

		£000
Creditors – due after more than I year		
8% debentures		600
Capital and reserves:		
Ordinary shares of £1	900	
Share premium account	60	
Profit and Loss account	589	1,549
		2,149

As at 30 June 20X0 Stock, Debtors and Creditors were £722,000, £648,000 and £484,000 respectively. Trade Creditors on 30 June 20X1 were £714,000. Shamrock plc shares are quoted on London Stock Exchange at 1600p.

Required: Calculate the accounting ratios that would be of interest when evaluating:

(a) profitability;
(b) asset utilization;
(c) liquidity;
(d) long-term solvency; and
(e) for making investment decisions.

References

1. Companies Act 1985, Schedule 4, part II, paragraph 12A.
2. Companies Act 1985, Schedule 4, part II, paragraph 34.
3. FRS 3: *Reporting Financial Performance* (November 1992).
4. FRS 3, *ibid.*
5. FRS 3, *ibid.*
6. FRS 14: *Earnings per Share* (October 1998).

SOLUTIONS TO INTERACTIVE QUESTIONS

IQ 42.1 Grouping of operating expenses

1	Salaries	Admn	16	Depreciation – building	Admn
2	Rent	Admn	17	Depreciation – furniture	Admn
3	Postage	Admn	18	Depreciation – machinery	CoS
4	Telephone expense	Admn	19	Depreciation – vehicles	Dist
5	Advertising	Dist	20	Depreciation – equipment	Admn
6	Rates	Admn	21	Audit fees	Admn
7	Staff welfare	Admn	22	Pension cost	Admn
8	Productive wages	CoS	23	Directors' remuneration	Admn
9	Sales commission	Dist	24	Directors' fees	Admn
10	Carriage inwards	CoS	25	Bad debt*	Dist
11	Carriage outwards	Dist	26	Development cost – write-off	Admn
12	Stationery	Admn	27	Development cost – amortization	CoS
13	Factory power	CoS	28	Stock loss – if normal	Admn
14	Raw material consumed	CoS	29	Bank charges	Admn
15	Cost of goods sold	CoS	30	Vehicle maintenance	Dist

* Bad debt arises because of bad selling and is therefore regarded as a selling expense. An alternative view is that bad debt is an administrative expense because it arises from ineffective credit administration.

IQ 42.2 Published accounts – a basic question

PERRINS LTD – FOR PUBLICATION

PROFIT AND LOSS ACCOUNT FOR YEAR ENDED 30.6.20X1

	£000
Turnover	1,276
Cost of sales	(728)
Gross profit	548
Distribution cost	(21)
Administrative expenses	(430)
Operating profit	97
Income from investment	15
Interest & similar charges	(12)
Profit before taxation	100
Taxation	(18)
Profit after taxation	82
Interim dividend	(20)
Final dividend proposed	(30)
Retained profit	32

BALANCE SHEET AS AT 30.6.20X1

	Cost	Depn	£000
Fixed assets	750	(299)	451
Investments			98
Current assets:			
Stock in trade		512	
Debtors		518	
Cash and bank		56	
Creditors: within one year		(579)	
Net current assets			507
Total asset less current liability			1,056

		£000
Creditors: due after one year		
8% Debentures		150
Capital and reserves:		
Called-up capital:	500	
Share Premium account	80	
Profit and Loss account	326	906
		1,056

NOTES AND SCHEDULES

(a) Expenses written off in the year include:

	£000
Depreciation	75
Directors' emoluments	46
Directors' fees	15
Wages and salary	182
Audit fees and expenses	10

(b) The company employed 23 employees categorized as:

Directors	2
Senior executives	3
Administrative staff	4
Salesmen	11
Minor staff	3

(c) Creditors due within one year

	£000
Creditors	486
Accrued expenses	45
Taxation	18
Dividend proposed	30
	579

Workings:

Cost of sales: $(364 + 862 + 14 - 512) \times £000 = £728,000$

Admin. expenses: $(182 + 60 + 16 + 34 + 42 + 15 + 6 + 75) \times £000 = £430,000$

Accrued expenses: $(15 + 12 + 6 + 12) \times £000 = £45,000$

Dividend proposed: 6p on 500,000 shares = £30,000.

IQ 42.3 Manufacturing company with movements in tangible assets

TUNA LTD – FINANCIAL STATEMENTS FOR PUBLICATION

PROFIT AND LOSS ACCOUNT FOR THE YEAR ENDED 30.6.20X1

	£000
Turnover	2,276
Cost of sales	(1,526)
Gross profit	750
Distribution cost	(160)
Administrative exp.	(235)
Operating profit	355
Exceptional item:	
Disposal of machine	(31)
Profit before tax	324
Taxation	(74)
Profit after tax	250
Interim dividend	(36)
Final dividend	(48)
Retained profit	166

BALANCE SHEET AS AT 30 JUNE 20X1

		£000
Fixed assets:		
Tangible assets		767
Current assets:		
Stocks	598	
Debtors	494	
Cash and bank	189	
Creditors due within one year	(798)	
Net current asset		483
Total asset less current liability		1,250

		£000
Provision for liabilities and charges		
Deferred taxation		32
Capital and reserves:		
Called-up capital – £1	600	
Share Premium account	60	
Profit and Loss a/c	558	1,218
		1,250

NOTES AND SCHEDULES

Stocks:	£000
Raw materials	244
Work in progress	26
Finished goods	328
	598

	£000
Creditors: amount falling due within one year	
Trade creditors	692
Taxation	58
Dividend proposed	48
	798

Tangible assets	Land and buildings	Plant and machinery	Total
Cost	£000	£000	£000
Balance b/f	450	420	870
Acquisition	150	60	210
Disposal	–	(80)	(80)
Balance c/f	600	400	1,000

Accumulated depreciation:	£000	£000	£000
Balance b/f	96	112	208
Depreciation	8	21	29
Disposal	–	(4)	(4)
Balance c/f	104	129	233
Written down value as at 30.6.20X1			
	496	271	767

Expenses written off in the year include the following:

	£000
Directors' fees	45
Depreciation	29

Exceptional item:
Loss on disposal of a machinery, being material and abnormal in size, is disclosed as an exceptional item.

Workings:	Cost of Sales	Distrib. cost	Admin. exp.
Raw material	154		
Work in progress	37		
Finished goods	286		
Purchases	1,466		
Depn – building	4	–	4
Depn – machinery	21		
Power	52		
Salary/wages	104	26	130
Stationery			11
Postage/tel.			12
Directors' fees			45
Staff welfare			33
Rent		12	
Advertising		64	
Sales commission		21	
Bad debts		37	
Raw material	(244)		
Work in progress	(26)		
Finished goods	(328)		
	1,526	160	235

LAND AND BUILDING ACCOUNT

	£000		£000
Balance b/f	450		
Cash book	150	Balance c/d	600
Balance b/d	600		

PROVISION FOR DEPN BUILDINGS A/C

	£000		£000
		Balance b/f	96
Balance c/d	104	Depreciation	8
		Balance b/d	104

PLANT AND MACHINERY ACCOUNT

	£000		£000
Balance b/f	420		
Cash book	60	Balance c/d	480
Balance b/f	480	Disposal	80
		Balance c/d	400
Balance b/d	400		

PROVISION FOR DEPN – MACHINERY A/C

	£000		£000
Disposal a/c	4	Balance b/f	112
Balance c/d	129	Depreciation	21
		Balance b/d	129

Depreciation on buildings:	£000
2% of 300,000	6
2% of 100,000	2
	8

Depreciation on machinery:	£000
5% of 80,000 × 6m	2
5% of 340,000	17
5% of 60,000 × 8m	2
	21

DISPOSAL OF MACHINERY ACCOUNT

	£000		£000
Machinery	80	Prov. for depn	4
		Cash book	45
		P&L – loss	31

DEBTORS ACCOUNT

	£000		£000
Balance b/f	548	Bad debt	28
		Balance	520
Balance b/d	520		

TAXATION (EXPENDITURE) ACCOUNT

	£000		£000
Under prov.	16		
Corp. Tax	58	P&L a/c	74

PROFIT AND LOSS ACCOUNT

	£000		£000
		Balance b/f	392
		Retained	166
			558

PROVISION FOR DOUBTFUL DEBTS ACCOUNT

	£000		£000
Bad debts	28	Balance	17
Balance c/d	26	P&L a/c	37
		Balance b/d	26

IQ 42.4 Identification of exceptional items

Those with a legitimate claim for information from Herrings plc are likely to be misguided by the Profit and Loss account when assessing the current year's performance and forecasting future prospects, unless their attention is drawn to any exceptional items affecting the current year's performance. Thus:

(a) Gain on disposal of property (£225,000), being material, should be identified as exceptional on the face of the Profit and Loss account because that is expressly required by FRS 3.

(b) £375,000 paid as compensation for loss of office to the former managing director will also have to be drawn to attention as an exceptional item because of the abnormal size of the amount involved.

(c) The performance in the current year has been seriously affected by the compulsory liquidation of a major customer. A loss of this magnitude (£418,000) is not normal. Unless this is drawn to attention, by reporting the bad debt as exceptional, the prospects of the company may be wrongly assessed.

(d) A 12.5 per cent increase in business rates, though material, need not be drawn to attention because the rates are likely to be at that level or higher in future as well.

(e) The compensation of £250,000 paid to the customer was for injury sustained in a prior year and ought to have impacted that year's performance. Because the amount is material and is abnormal in incidence (i.e. impacting the wrong year) attention should be drawn to it as an exceptional item.

(f) The problem of countering the millennium bug is a rarity. Therefore the material amount incurred on it should be stated as an exceptional item.

Whether attention should be drawn to any of the exceptional items, other than that referred to in (a), on the face of the Profit and Loss account would depend on whether that is regarded as necessary for showing a true and fair view. Otherwise each of these items may be included within an appropriate statutory heading and attention drawn to them in the Notes published with the financial statements.

IQ 42.5 Interpreting company accounts

(a) Profitability ratios:

	Ratio name	Formula	Calculation for Shamrock	Result
1	Return on capital employed ratio	$\dfrac{\text{Profit before interest \& tax}}{\text{Average capital employed}} \times 100\%$	$\dfrac{\pounds822 + \pounds48}{\pounds2,149} \times 100\%$	40.5%
2	Gross profit ratio	$\dfrac{\text{Gross profit}}{\text{Sales}}$	$\dfrac{\pounds2,318}{\pounds7,484}$	31%
3	Distribution cost to sales ratio	$\dfrac{\text{Distribution cost}}{\text{Sales}} \times 100\%$	$\dfrac{\pounds92}{\pounds7,484} \times 100\%$	1.2%
4	Profit to sales ratio	$\dfrac{\text{Profit before tax}}{\text{Sales}} \times 100\%$	$\dfrac{\pounds822}{\pounds7,484} \times 100\%$	11%
5	Return on capital to sales ratio	$\dfrac{\text{Profit before interest \& tax}}{\text{Sales}} \times 100\%$	$\dfrac{\pounds822 + \pounds48}{\pounds7,484} \times 100\%$	11.6%

(b) Asset utilization ratios

	Ratio name	Formula	Calculation for Shamrock	Result
1	Total asset turnover ratio	$\dfrac{\text{Sales}}{\text{Total assets (i.e. capital empl.)}}$	$\dfrac{\pounds7,484}{\pounds2,149}$	3.5 times
2	Fixed asset turnover	$\dfrac{\text{Sales}}{\text{Fixed assets}}$	$\dfrac{\pounds7,484}{\pounds1,110}$	6.7 times
3	Net current asset turnover	$\dfrac{\text{Sales}}{\text{Net current assets}}$	$\dfrac{\pounds7,484}{\pounds511}$	14.6 times
4	Stock turnover	$\dfrac{\text{Cost of sale}}{\text{Average stock}}$	$\dfrac{\pounds5,166}{(\pounds722 + \pounds876)/2}$	6.5 times
5	Debtors' turnover	$\dfrac{\text{Credit sales}}{\text{Average debtors}}$	$\dfrac{\pounds7,484}{(\pounds648 + \pounds720)/2}$	10.9 times
6	Creditors' turnover	$\dfrac{\text{Credit purchases}}{\text{Average creditors}}$	$\dfrac{(\pounds5,166 + \pounds876 - \pounds722)}{(\pounds484 + \pounds714)/2}$	8.9 times

(c) Liquidity

	Ratio name	Formula	Calculation for Shamrock	Result
1	Working capital ratio	$\dfrac{\text{Current assets}}{\text{Current liabilities}}$	$\dfrac{£1,618}{£1,107}$	1.46 times
2	Liquidity ratio	$\dfrac{\text{Current assets} - \text{stock}}{\text{Current Liabilities}}$	$\dfrac{£742}{£1,107}$	0.67 times
3	Stock days	$\dfrac{\text{Stock at end}}{\text{Cost of sales}} \times 365 \text{ days}$	$\dfrac{£876}{£5,166} \times 365 \text{ days}$	61.9 days
4	Debtors' days	$\dfrac{\text{Debtors at end}}{\text{Sales}} \times 365 \text{ days}$	$\dfrac{£720}{£7,484} \times 365 \text{ days}$	35.1 days
5	Creditors' days	$\dfrac{\text{Creditors at end}}{\text{Purchases}} \times 365 \text{ days}$	$\dfrac{£714}{£5,320} \times 365 \text{ days}$	49 days

(d) Capital structure

	Ratio name	Formula	Calculation for Shamrock	Result
1	Financing fixed assets	$\dfrac{\text{Capital} + \text{reserves} + \text{loan}}{\text{Fixed assets}} \times 100\%$	$\dfrac{£2,149}{£1,110} \times 100\%$	194%

(e) Share market ratios

	Ratio name	Formula	Calculation for Shamrock	Result
1	Return on equity ratio	$\dfrac{\text{Profit before tax}}{\text{Average capital \& reserves}} \times 100\%$	$\dfrac{£822}{£1,549} \times 100\%$	53%
2	Gearing ratio	$\dfrac{\text{Prior charge capital}}{\text{Equity Capital} + \text{Reserves}} \times 100\%$	$\dfrac{£600}{£1,549} \times 100\%$	38.7%
3	Interest cover	$\dfrac{\text{Profit before interest \& tax}}{\text{Interest}}$	$\dfrac{£822 + £48}{£48}$	18 times
4	Earnings per share	$\dfrac{\text{Profit after tax} - \text{pref. div.}}{\text{No. of ordinary shares in issue}} \times 100$	$\dfrac{£594}{900 \text{ shares}} \times 100$	66 pence
5	Price earnings ratio	$\dfrac{\text{Price per share}}{\text{Earnings per share}}$	$\dfrac{1,600\text{p}}{66\text{p}}$	24.2 times
6	Earnings yield	$\dfrac{\text{Earnings per share}}{\text{Price per share}} \times 100\%$	$\dfrac{66\text{p}}{1,600\text{p}} \times 100\%$	4.1%
7	Dividend yield	$\dfrac{\text{Dividend per share}}{\text{Price per share}} \times 100\%$	$\dfrac{£336/900 \text{ shares}}{£16} \times 100\%$	2.3%

PROGRESSIVE QUESTIONS

PQ 42.1 No movements in fixed assets

Dorian Ltd's year-end Trial Balance appears as stated here. You are further informed as follows:

(a) The company employs 54 people, including nine senior executives and three directors.

(b) The directors are entitled to a salary of £24,000 each. By the year end, only £66,000 has been paid as directors' salary and stated within the balance in the Salaries a/c.

(c) The company assumes that one-quarter of the cost relates to land, and it depreciates building and furniture at 2 and 5 per cent respectively per year, using the straight-line method.

(d) A debt of £36,000 is to be written off and the provision adjusted to cover 5 per cent of the debts receivable.

(e) Expenses accrued as at 31.12.20X1 include the following:
- Audit fees   £12,000
- Electricity   £3,000
- Sales commission   £9,000

(f) Included in other administrative expenses is £4,000 incurred on entertaining the auditors and £32,000 on staff welfare.

(g) Unsold stock as at 31.12.20X1 has been ascertained at £427,000.

(h) Corporation Tax on the year's profit is estimated at £28,000.

(i) The Directors propose as follows:
- transfer £25,000 to general reserve
- pay a final dividend of 3p per share.

Required: Prepare for publication the Profit and Loss account for the year ended 31 December 20X1 and a Balance Sheet as at that date, along with any Notes that should be published. (The note on accounting policy is not required.)

TRIAL BALANCE AS AT 31 DECEMBER 20X1		
	£000	£000
Land and building at cost	1,200	–
Prov. for depn – building 31.12.20X0	–	216
Furniture at cost	240	–
Prov. for depn – furniture 31.12.20X0	–	72
Interim dividend	60	–
Fixed asset investments	435	–
Sales	–	4,628
Debenture interest paid	18	–
Debtors and creditors	516	498
Stock in trade on 31.12.20X0	364	–
Return inwards	118	–
Deferred taxation	–	42
Provision for 20X0 Corporation Tax	–	24
Corporation Tax paid on 20X0 profit	16	–
Dividend received	–	36
Cash and bank balance	476	–
Ordinary shares of 50p each	–	1,200
Share Premium account	–	300
Purchases	3,169	–
Profit and Loss account	–	412
Salaries	368	–
Interest received	–	22
Stationery	21	–
Discount allowed	28	–
Discount received	–	12
Rent	180	–
Directors' fees	66	–
Provision for doubtful debts	–	46
Advertising	114	–
Sales commission	212	–
12% debentures	–	300
Electricity and gas	69	–
Telephone and postage	42	–
Bad debts	14	–
Other administrative expenses	82	–
	7,808	7,808

PQ 42.2 Statement of fixed asset movements

Flora plc extracted its year-end Trial Balance as stated here, and provides the following information:

(a) Salaries and wages were paid to staff as follows:

	Number	£000
Production workers	12	216
Factory supervisors	4	124
Administrative staff	3	96
Accounting staff	2	54
Salesmen	8	144
Directors	4	128
		762

(b) Stock as at 31 December 20X4 has been ascertained as follows:

	£000
Raw material	322
Work in progress	54
Finished goods	428

(c) Following assets were acquired in 20X4:

	Date	Cost
Machinery	1 April	£80,000
Furniture	1 July	£40,000

(d) Machinery acquired for £240,000 on 1 October 20X0 was sold on 30.9.20X4 for £72,000.

(e) The company depreciates its buildings, machinery and furniture at 2, 5 and 10 per cent per year respectively, using the straight-line method and assuming that one-third of the cost relates to land, which is not depreciated.

(f) Expenses to be accrued as at 31.12.20X4 include the following:

Audit fees	£15,000
Electricity and gas	£18,000

(g) The following apportionment is agreed:

	Electricity and gas	Depreciation on buildings
Factory	60%	50%
Administration	30%	–
Selling	10%	50%

TRIAL BALANCE AS AT 31 DECEMBER 20X4		
	£000	£000
Land and building at cost	2,100	–
Provision for depn – building 31.12.20X3	–	392
Machinery at cost	840	–
Provision for depn – machinery 31.12.20X3	–	294
Furniture at cost	160	–
Provision for depn – furniture 31.12.20X3	–	64
Stock on 31.12.20X3	–	–
Raw materials	284	–
Work in progress	32	–
Finished goods	396	–
Investments	425	–
Sales	–	6,458
Debenture interest paid	24	–
Debtors and creditors	724	696
Interim dividend paid	120	–
Factory overheads	112	–
Disposal of machinery	–	72
Freight and duty on raw material	284	–
Return inwards	116	–
Deferred taxation	–	56
Provision for 20X0 Corporation Tax	–	218
Corporation Tax paid on 20X0 profit	234	–
Dividend received	–	48
Cash and bank balance	112	–
Ordinary shares of 20p each	–	600
Share Premium account	–	120
Purchase of raw material	2,418	–
Profit and Loss account	–	506
Salaries	762	–
Factory power	54	–
Stationery	21	–
Rent	180	–
Directors' fees	66	–
Provision for doubtful debts	–	68
Advertising	96	–
Sales commission	168	–
12% debentures	–	400
Electricity and gas	42	–
Telephone and postage	34	–
Bad debts	6	–
Sundry expenses	182	–
	9,992	9,992

(h) A debt of £24,000 is to be written off and the provision for doubtful debts adjusted to cover 5 per cent of debtors outstanding.

(i) The Corporation Tax on the year's profit is estimated at £428,000 and £18,000 is to be set aside for deferred tax.

(j) The directors propose a final dividend of 6 pence per share.

Required: Prepare for publication the Profit and Loss account for the year ended 31 December 20X4 and the Balance Sheet as at that date, along with the Statement of Movement of Tangible Assets and as many Notes as you are able to (other than the one on accounting policy).

Notes:

● The amount to be set aside for deferred tax is an additional tax expenditure for the year.
● The make-up of the tax expenditure should be shown as one of the Notes.

PQ 42.3 An investor's decision

Summarized below is information relating to Grill plc and Broil plc, both listed on the London Stock Exchange:

EXTRACT OF PROFIT AND LOSS ACCOUNT FOR YEAR ENDED 31.12.20X0		
	Grill £000	Broil £000
Profit before taxation	1,628	1,096
Taxation	(492)	(332)
Profit after taxation	1,136	764
Preference dividend	(360)	–
Interim dividend	(300)	(240)
Final dividend proposed	(500)	(300)
Retained profit (Loss)	(24)	224

EXTRACT OF BALANCE SHEET AS AT 31 DECEMBER 20X0		
	Grill £000	Broil £000
Ordinary shares of 50p each	8,000	6,000
12% preference shares of £1	3,000	–
Share premium account	1,200	900
Reserves	860	1,840
	13,060	8,740
15% debentures	6,000	–
	19,060	8,740

Grill's shares are quoted at 64p and Broil's at 98p. An investor contemplating investing £50,000 in shares of either company seeks your advice.

Required: Compare the value of shares in both companies on the basis of appropriate accounting ratios.

ADDITIONAL INFORMATION VEHICLES

Chapter 43

CASH FLOW STATEMENTS

In this chapter

We will learn of:

- the usefulness of the Cash Flow Statement for assessing an entity's liquidity, solvency and financial adaptability

and will be able to:

- prepare Cash Flow Statements
- interpret the information in the statement

43.1 CASH GENERATION AND FLOW

We saw in Chapter 32 that as part of its budgeting exercise a business prepares cash flow projections. If its policy is to settle its bills at weekly intervals, the projections will have to be on a weekly basis, tracing the expected inflow and outflow of cash in each week. Managers are then able to take appropriate action. For example, if the projections reveal that in a particular week the cash outflow would not be matched by an appropriate inflow, the managers could arrange for overdraft facilities or delay paying creditors. Projections and the remedial actions are intended for internal management's use and are not made available to people outside the organization.

Although the *performance* of a business entity is usually gauged in terms of its profit-generating ability, experience teaches that its *survival* could depend on its cash-generating ability. To exploit opportunities and to meet its bills as they fall due, the business has to generate the necessary cash – ensuring that the amounts and timing match the needs. An entity making profit but unable to find cash when necessary could face problems such as the following:

- Failure to settle accounts on time could lead to suppliers stopping supplies and other suppliers refusing or limiting credit. Continuing failure could ultimately lead to bankruptcy proceedings.
- Lost opportunities for making profit because of an inability to find the cash outlay, e.g. for buying new fixed assets or investing in a lucrative line of business.
- Enforced borrowing on unfavourable terms to pay its trade creditors or other dues.

Profit-making concerns are known to have failed because of their inability to find the cash to meet their bills when they became due. Although profit increases the capital base of the business, the increase may be tied up (e.g. in more fixed assets, stock or debtors) and may not, therefore, always be represented by an equal amount of cash.

43.2 THE CASH FLOW STATEMENT

Those external to a business but with a legitimate claim for information require a broad assurance that the survival of the business is not threatened by inadequacy of cash to meet its bills. To provide such an assurance, businesses are required[1] to publish as part of their annual report a *Cash Flow Statement*, which is, in effect, a summary of the Cash account for the year. The expectation is that this should provide information to assist in the assessment of the entity's liquidity, solvency and financial adaptability.

43.2.1 A definition of 'cash'

Clearly, the focus of a Cash Flow Statement is on the amount of cash running through a business; after all, 'cash flow' is defined as an increase or decrease in an amount of cash. It is crucial, therefore, that one preparing a Cash Flow Statement should be clear about the definition of cash. Cash is defined as:[2]

> Cash in hand, deposits repayable on demand with any qualifying financial institutions, less overdrafts from any qualifying financial institution repayable on demand. Deposits are repayable on demand if they can be withdrawn at any time without any notice and without penalty or if a maturity or period of notice of not more than 24 hours or one working day has been agreed. Cash includes cash in hand and deposits denominated in foreign currencies.

What this means is that:

- the amount of cash includes amounts held at the bank even in foreign currency;
- overdrafts, payable on demand are netted;
- fixed deposits requiring more than one day's withdrawal notice are *not* to be reckoned as cash (although they would be reported as part of cash in the Balance Sheet).

43.2.2 Readjustment for accruals

When we finalize the accounts at the end of an accounting period, we adjust the information stated in the Cash account for accruals and prepayments. For example, to the amount of salaries paid, as stated in the cash book, we add the amount of any salary accrued to obtain the Profit and Loss account figure. When the Cash Flow Statement is prepared from the information in the Profit and Loss account and Balance Sheet, that process has to be reversed.

Three points have to be noted as follows:

- The adjustments we made in order to state an income or expense on an accruals basis in the Profit and Loss account will have to be reversed to identify the cash flow in the period.
- Expenses recognized in the Profit and Loss account do not always involve a cash outflow. Depreciation, stock and debtor write-offs are examples of such expenses.
- A Balance Sheet may well include assets acquired and capital instruments issued without involving any cash flows either inwards or outwards.

Interaction 43.1

Income and expense items with period-end adjustments reversed

INCOME/EXPENDITURE FOR THE YEAR ENDED 31.12.20X2		AS AT 1.1.20X2		AS AT 31.12.20X2	
	£000		£000		£000
		Debtors	245	Debtors	368
Sales	1,680	Creditors	264	Creditors	296
Purchases	1,246	Prepaid rent	15	Accrued rent	10
Rent	60	Accrued salary	32	Accrued salary	46
Salaries	246				

Required: Calculate the cash inflow/outflow during the year ended 31.12.20X2 on the basis of the information tabulated above.

43.2.3 Preparation of the statement

Given the information in a Profit and Loss account, along with that in the Balance Sheets both at commencement and at end of the period, we should be able to ascertain the cash flows (in either direction) as they would be stated in a Cash account. The cash flows presented as a simple list of receipts and payments (see pro forma on the right) would be a Cash Flow Statement, though it is not organized or classified in any way.

CASH FLOW STATEMENT FOR YEAR ENDED	
	£
Received from debtors	XXX
Paid to creditors	(XX)
Paid for expenditure	(XX)
Paid for fixed assets	(XX)
Paid as interest	(X)
Repayment of loan	(XX)
Repayment of capital	(X)
Inflow/(outflow) of cash	X

Cash flow is a Cash account summary in a statement form

Interaction 43.2

The financial statements of Fulma & Co appear as stated below:

BALANCE SHEET AS AT 31 DECEMBER					
		20X1 £000		20X2 £000	
Fixed assets at w.d.v		540		680	
Stock in trade	240		326		
Debtors	365		425		
Cash and bank	65		64		
Creditors	(326)		(418)		
Accrued expenses	(42)	302	(32)	365	
		842		1045	
		£000		£000	
Capital		525		642	
Profit for the year		162		264	
Drawings		(45)		(11)	
		642		895	
Loan at 12%		200		150	
		842		1,045	

PROFIT AND LOSS ACCOUNT FOR THE YEAR ENDED 31.12.20X2			
			£000
Sales			4,265
Stock 1.1.20X2	240		
Purchases	3,264		
Stock 31.12.20X2	(326)	(3,178)	
Gross profit		1,087	
Expenses		(678)	
Depreciation		(124)	
Interest		(21)	
Profit		264	

Required: Prepare for 20X2 (a) a Cash account and (b) a Cash Flow Statement using the format shown above.

43.3 A UNIFORM FORMAT FOR CASH FLOW STATEMENTS

FRS 1, *Cash Flow Statements*, as amended in 1996, requires that the Cash Flow Statement should be published in a standardized format that consists of eight headings. These headings (shown below) should appear in the sequence as stated.

CASH FLOW STATEMENT FOR THE YEAR ENDED XXXXX		
	£000	£000
1. From operating activity:		
Received from debtors	958	
Paid to creditors	(486)	
Paid as expenses	(214)	258
2. Return on investments and **servicing of finance:**		
Interest received	12	
Dividend received	9	
Interest paid	(36)	(15)
3. Taxation		(47)
4. Capital expenditure and **financial investments:**		
Acquisition of assets	(148)	
Disposal of assets	12	(136)
5. Acquisition and disposal of interest in group companies		–
6. Equity dividend paid		
Interim dividend	(12)	
Final dividend	(18)	(30)
7. Management of liquid resources Temporary investments		(4)
8. Financing		
Loan capital raised (repaid)	(50)	
Equity capital raised (repaid)	60	10
Cash inflow (outflow)		36

The following may be noted:

- The cash flows listed under the first three of the headings and under the sixth relate to revenue items that appear on the Profit and Loss account.
- Four of the remaining headings (the fourth, fifth, seventh and eighth) list cash flows of a capital nature that appear on the balance sheet.
- Heading 5 is for listing acquisitions and disposals of interests in subsidiary and associate companies. Therefore, this heading would not be relevant except for preparing cash flows in a group situation.
- An entity is financed by those who provide loan capital and, more importantly, equity capital. Yet the rewards for servicing the former are stated early within heading 2 because they are obligatory, whereas those to the latter are stated within heading 6 because dividends are discretionary.
- Investments of a temporary nature (meaning those that deploy cash surplus to immediate requirements) and realization of such investments are stated within heading 7.
- Cash flows related to raising or repaying long-term finance (by means such as shares and debentures) is stated within heading 8.

Not all Cash Flow Statements will require entries under each of the eight headings; it will depend on the transactions that have occurred during the year.

Interaction 43.3	**Presenting cash flow in a uniform format**

Refer back to the information stated in IQ 43.2.

Required: Present the Cash Flow Statement for the year ended 31 December 20X2 on the format prescribed in FRS 1.

43.4 CASH FLOW STATEMENTS OF LIMITED COMPANIES

Preparation of a Cash Flow Statement for a limited company is no different from that of other forms of business organizations except that:

- The Profit and Loss account and Balance Sheets provided for the purpose would probably be the ones prepared for publication rather than those for internal use of the directors.
- Additional items would appear in the Profit and Loss account, such as taxation and dividends, and on the Balance Sheet, debentures, share capital and the Profit and Loss account balance.

- When redeeming (i.e. repaying) debentures, the company may have to pay a premium (i.e. pay more than the amount borrowed). Any such premium paid can be written off against the balance in the Share Premium account.[3] Care needs to be taken to identify the amount of cash that was paid for the redemption.

Cash flow of a limited company

Interaction
43.4

BALANCE SHEETS AS AT 31 DECEMBER			PROFIT AND LOSS ACCOUNT FOR THE YEAR ENDED 31.12.20X2	
	20X1 £000	20X2 £000		£000
Fixed assets	720	840	Turnover	1,910
Acc. depreciation	(280)	(320)	Cost of sales	(1,245)
	440	520	Gross profit	665
Investments	75	120	Distribution cost	(76)
Stock in trade	528	612	Administration expense	(218)
Trade debtors	386	484		
Cash and bank	54	72	Operating profit	371
Creditors	(612)	(596)	Dividend received	15
Accrued expense	(24)	(34)	Interest paid	(24)
Taxation	(96)	(112)	Profit before tax	362
Dividend proposed	(45)	(60)	Taxation	(112)
	706	1,006	Profit after tax	250
	£000	£000	Interim dividend	(30)
			Final dividend	(60)
16% debentures	200	150		
Ordinary shares	400	500	Retained profit	160
Share premium	60	150	Balance b/f	46
Profit and Loss	46	206		
	706	1,006	Balance c/f	206

Required: Prepare a Cash Flow Statement for the year ended 31.12.20X2. Note that you will require Total Debtors and Total Creditors accounts to establish the cash movements.

43.5 IMPACT OF ASSET DISPOSALS ON CASH FLOW

If an asset had been disposed of for cash, the proceeds are recognized as an inflow, irrespective of whether the disposal resulted in a gain or a loss. Any gain or loss on disposal, stated in the Profit and Loss account, would not feature as a separate item in the Cash Flow Statement because the impact on the cash flow would have been recognized as part of the proceeds.

For example, assume that an asset acquired for £100,000 and depreciated by £30,000 is sold for £80,000. The proceeds of disposal (£80,000) are posted from the cash book to the Asset Disposal account to be compared with the written down value (£70,000) of the asset on that date. The gain on disposal (£10,000) is transferred from the Disposal account to the Profit and Loss account. When the cash inflow arising from the asset disposal (£80,000) is reported in the Cash Flow Statement, it already includes the gain on disposal (of £10,000).

Interaction 43.5

Cash flow on asset disposal at a profit

Required: Ascertain the cash flows arising in respect of acquisition and disposal of machinery and motor vehicles in the following circumstances:

(a) Machinery acquired for £240,000 and written down to £96,000 was sold, making a gain of £12,000.

(b) Motor vehicles acquired for £180,000 were reported on the Balance Sheet at the commencement of the year at £84,000. During the year £48,000 was written off as depreciation on motor vehicles, and the Profit and Loss account reported £12,000 as a gain on the disposal of motor vehicles that had been acquired for £40,000. The Balance Sheet at the year end reports the cost of motor vehicles as £160,000 and the written down value as £32,000.

Interaction 43.6

Cash flow on asset disposal at a loss

Furniture acquired for £40,000 and written down to £12,000 was sold, incurring a loss of £7,800.
Required: How will this transaction be reported in the year's Cash Flow Statement.

Interaction 43.7

Cash flow involving asset disposal

BALANCE SHEETS AS AT 30 JUNE			PROFIT AND LOSS ACCOUNT YEAR ENDED 30 JUNE 20X2	
	20X1 £000	20X2 £000		£000
Furniture at cost	760	860	Turnover	2,539
Less: Depreciation	(248)	(324)	Cost of sale	(1,828)
Motor vehicles	840	880	Gross profit	711
Less: Depreciation	(360)	(382)	Distribution cost	(112)
			Admin. expense	(284)
	992	1,034	Operating profit	315
Investments	212	326	Gain on disposal	26
Stock in trade	648	592	Dividend received	14
Debtors	542	674	Interest paid	(39)
Cash and bank	74	16	Profit before tax	316
Creditors	(554)	(598)	Taxation	(132)
Accrued expense	(28)	(52)	Profit after tax	184
Taxation	(115)	(132)	Interim dividend	(45)
Dividend proposed	(60)	(75)	Final dividend	(75)
	1,711	1,785	Retained profit	64
	£000	£000		
12% debentures	400	250		
Share capital and reserves:				
Ordinary shares	900	1,000		
Share premium	180	240		
Profit and Loss a/c	231	295		
	1,711	1,785		

You are informed as follows:

(a) Vehicles acquired for £180,000 and written down to £98,000 were sold during the year.

(b) Debentures were redeemed at a premium of 10 per cent.

Required: Prepare a Cash Flow Statement for the year to 30.6.20X2.

Asset acquisition without cash flow

Caterola Ltd's financial statements appear as shown below.

BALANCE SHEETS AS AT 31.12					
	20X2		**20X3**		
	£000	£000	£000	£000	
Fixed assets:					
Machinery	790		965		
Depreciation	(365)	425	(424)		
Furniture	240		320	541	
Depreciation	(88)	152	(144)	176	
Motor vehicle	210		345		
Depreciation	(63)	147	(92)	253	
Investments		245		270	
Current assets:					
Stock in trade	728		688		
Debtors	546		604		
Cash/bank	36		16		
Creditors	(442)		(486)		
Salary accrued	(28)		(54)		
Interest accrued	(18)		(12)		
Taxation	(84)		(102)		
Dividend	(45)	693	(75)	579	
		1,662		1,819	
Creditors due after one year:					
12% debentures		300		200	
Due on machinery		–		150	
Share capital and reserves:					
Ordinary shares: £1		900		1,050	
Share Premium a/c		150		180	
Profit and Loss a/c		312		239	
		1,662		1,819	

PROFIT AND LOSS ACCOUNT FOR THE YEAR ENDED 31.12.20X3	
	£000
Turnover	4,704
Cost of sale	(3,465)
Gross profit	1,239
Distribution cost	(364)
Administrative expenses	(718)
Operating profit	157
Gain on disposal of vehicle	26
Dividend received	36
Fall in value of investments	(12)
Interest and similar charges	(30)
Profit before taxation	177
Taxation	(115)
Profit after taxation	62
Interim dividend paid	(60)
Final dividend proposed	(75)
Retained loss	(73)

You are informed as follows:

(a) Included within cash and bank balance is a three-month fixed deposit of £12,000 on 31.12.20X3 and £25,000 one year earlier.

(b) Machinery acquired for £150,000 on extended credit terms during the year is to be paid for in 20X6.

(c) Debenture interest is paid half-yearly in arrears, on 1 January and 1 July. The debentures were redeemed at 20 per cent premium.

(d) Depreciation written off in the year to 31.12.20X3 was as shown on the right.

	£000
Machinery (included in cost of sale)	59
Furniture (included in admin. expense)	56
Vehicles (included in distribution cost)	47

(e) Sold in 20X3 were vehicles that had been acquired for £120,000 in 20X2.

Required: Prepare the Cash Flow Statement for the year ended 31 December 20X3 and comment on the company's cash and liquidity position. (Note: remember Section 43.2.1 on the definition of 'cash'.)

43.6 THE MANAGEMENT OF LIQUID RESOURCES

Instead of keeping cash idle, putting it on fixed deposit (to earn interest until it is needed) or investing in the stock market makes better business sense. In the case of Caterola Ltd (see IQ 43.8), the cash resources available to it on 31.12.20X3 for meeting its bills amounted to £16,000, although £12,000 of this amount was tied down in fixed deposit and cannot be retrieved except with one month's notice. We can reasonably regard the amounts held on fixed deposit as 'backup' funds. Admittedly, however, resources that are not quite available for immediate use are of a lower degree of liquidity than amounts held in hand or at the bank. Therefore, such 'near' cash amounts are required to be identified and defined as *liquid resources* and the movements thereof reported under heading 6 of the standardized Cash Flow Statement format as 'Management of liquid resources'.

Liquid resources are more closely defined as follows:

> Liquid resources are current asset investments held as readily disposable stores of value. A readily disposable investment is one that:
>
> (a) is disposable by the reporting entity without disrupting or curtailing the business; and
> (b) is either readily convertible into known amounts of cash at or close to carrying amount or is traded in an active market.

When evaluating an entity's liquidity (i.e. its ability to meet its bills as they fall due), we need to take into account not only the cash balance but also the position of the liquid resources that constitute its backup funds. For example, Caterola Ltd, referred to in IQ 43.8, has not only suffered an outflow of cash amounting to £7,000 during the year but it has also run down its liquid resources by another £13,000. Hence, the liquid resource position has worsened in the year to the extent of £20,000.

43.7 RECONCILIATION WITH NET DEBT

For the purpose of assessing the impact of the year's activity on the ability of a business to meet its obligations (i.e. liquidity), FRS 1 requires that the Cash Flow Statement should be accompanied by a reconciliation of the cash flow to net debt.[4] The *net debt* is defined as the amount by which the long-term debts of an entity on any date exceeds its cash *plus* its liquid resources.

Net debt as at 31.12.20X3:	£000
Long-term debt: 12% debentures	(200)
Less: Cash	4
Liquid resources	12
Net debt	(184)

The net debt of Caterola Ltd (IQ 43.8) on 31.12.20X3 would be £184,000. Had cash plus liquid resources on this date exceeded its long-term debt, instead of net debt, Caterola Ltd would have had net fund. As at the beginning of the year Caterola Ltd's net debt was £264,000 (see calculation on the left). During the year the company's liquidity improved because it discharged its long-term debt of £100,000. However, at the same time its liquidity worsened because cash decreased by £7,000 and liquid resources decreased by £13,000. The net effect is that during

Net debt as at 1.1.20X3:	£000
12% debentures	(300)
Cash	11
Liquid resources	25
Net debt	(264)

RECONCILIATION OF NET DEBT WITH CASH FLOW IN YEAR TO 31.12.20X3	
	£000
Debenture redemption	100
Less: Cash balance reduced	(7)
Liquid resources reduced	(13)
Improvement in net debt	80
Net debt as at 1.1.20X3	(264)
Net debt as at 31.12.20X3	(184)

the year there was an improvement of the liquid position by £80,000 and hence the net debt on 31.12.20X3 was £184,000.

Focus on liquidity position

CASH FLOW STATEMENT FOR THE YEAR ENDED 30 JUNE 20X1		
	£000	£000
Operating activity		585
Return on investments and servicing of finance:		
Dividend received	21	
Interest paid	(72)	(51)
Taxation		(174)
Capital expenditure		
Fixed assets	(145)	
Disposal of asset	20	(125)
Dividend on equity		
Interim dividend	(60)	
Final dividend	(90)	(150)
Management of liquid resources		76
Financing		
Debenture redemption	(360)	
Share capital	100	
Share premium	20	(240)
Cash outflow in the year		(79)

Cyberolla Ltd's Cash Flow statement for the year to 30 June 20X1 appears on the left. You are informed further as follows:

AS AT 30 JUNE		
	20X0 £000	20X1 £000
Cash and bank balance	48	7
Bank overdraft	–	38
Current asset investments	172	96
12% debentures	600	300

Required: Determine the extent to which the company's liquidity has improved or become worse during the year ended 30 June 20X1.

43.8 OPERATING PROFIT AND CASH INFLOW

In IQ 43.8 the operating profit was stated as £157,000 whereas the cash flow from operating activity was determined, in the Cash Flow Statement, as £371,000. Such a discrepancy would not arise if all of following conditions obtained:

- all sales in the year were made for cash (i.e. debtors at the end of the year remained the same as at the beginning);
- all purchases were made for cash (i.e. creditors at the end of the year remained the same as at the beginning);
- no stock (other than what remained unsold at the commencement of the year) remains unsold;
- expenses are all fully paid for in cash;
- there is no expenditure (such as depreciation, amortization and asset write-off) that does not involve a cash outflow.

In real life such a set of circumstances does not exist. As a result, the cash generated in the period will be *less* than the operating profit to the extent the cash generated by profit is tied up in additional stock, debtors or for reducing amounts owed to creditors or for accrued expenses. Conversely, the cash generated in a period will be *more* than the operating profit if expenses recognized include items such as depreciation, which do not involve an outflow of cash.

43.8.1 Reconciliation of operating profit to cash flow from operating activity

FRS 1 requires[5] that every Cash Flow Statement should be accompanied by a reconciliation of operating profit with the cash flow from operating activity. The reconciliation would appear as shown on the left. Clearly, cash generation will exceed the operating profit by the amount of non-cash expenses deducted in the Profit and Loss account. The cash generated by operating profit will be depleted to the extent that the cash is tied down in additional stock, debtors or prepayments, or used up for pruning the trade creditors or accrued expenses. Pruning down the stock, debtors or prepayments or obtaining additional credit facilities, on the other hand, will increase the cash flow. The reconciliation should be shown either adjoining the Cash Flow Statement or as a note.

> **RECONCILIATION OF OPERATING PROFIT WITH CASH FLOW FROM OPERATING ACTIVITY**
>
> Operating profit:
> *Add*:   Non-cash expenses such as depreciation and amortization
> *add (deduct)*   Stock decrease (increase)
>   Debtors decrease (increase)
>   Prepayments decrease (increase)
>   Creditors increase (decrease)
>   Accruals increase (decrease)
> Reconcile the result against the cash flow from operating activity

Interaction 43.10

Reconciliation of operating profit and cash flow

Required: On the basis of the information in IQ 43.8, prepare a reconciliation of Caterola's operating profit (£157,000) with the cash flow from operating activity (£371,000).

43.9 A CASH FLOW STATEMENT USING THE 'INDIRECT' METHOD

A Cash Flow Statement (as illustrated up to now) that, when reporting the cash flow from operating activity, identifies the receipts from customers and payments to suppliers and for expenses is said to have been prepared on the 'direct' method. Most business entities are averse to disclosing so much information; they prefer instead to confine themselves merely to deriving the cash flow from operating activity by means of the reconciliation from operating profit (as was carried out in the solution to IQ 43.10). This is known as the 'indirect' method. Both the direct and indirect methods are acceptable in terms of the accounting standards.

Accountants preparing a Cash Flow Statement on the indirect method will benefit from the following hints:

1. If the requirement does not include a Profit and Loss account, in the absence of information on sales, purchases and expenses there is no way of preparing the Cash Flow Statement by the direct method.
2. To prepare the Cash Flow Statement by the indirect method, the operating profit would have to be the starting point, so that by a process of reconciliation the cash

flow from operating activity can be ascertained. To find operating profit, the Profit and Loss account should be built up, starting with the calculation of the retained profit (or loss) by comparing the Profit and Loss account balance carried forward at the end of the year with that at commencement. This is slotted into a Profit and Loss account format (as shown here) along with all information provided (other than of items of operating income or expenditure like depreciation, bad debts, amortization and so on). The balancing figure (£270) would be the amount of operating profit for the year.

To ascertain operating profit:	
Operating profit	?
Gain on asset disposal	45
Dividend received	15
Interest and similar chrg.	(30)
Profit before taxation	300
Taxation	(80)
Profit after taxation	220
Interim dividend paid	(40)
Final dividend proposed	(60)
Retained profit	120

3. To prepare the Cash Flow Statement on the indirect method, there is no need to open the Cost of Sales account, the Expense account, the Debtors Control account and the Creditors Control account. Besides, in the absence of information, cash flows relating to these can never be ascertained.

Cash Flow Statement using the indirect method

Interaction 43.11

Peterola Ltd pays debenture interest quarterly in arrears on 1 January, 1 April, 1 July and 1 October. Any cash surplus to immediate requirements is invested in readily realizable shares quoted on the London Stock Exchange. The Balance Sheets of Peterola Ltd appear as stated here.

BALANCE SHEETS AS AT 31.12				
	20X0		20X1	
	£000	£000	£000	£000
Fixed assets at cost	760		920	
Accumulated depreciation	(288)	472	(318)	602
Investments		186		214
Stock in trade	532		392	
Debtors	396		428	
Cash and bank	32		11	
Creditors	(478)		(396)	
Accrued expenses	(64)		(72)	
Taxation	(84)		(92)	
Dividend proposed	(30)		(42)	
Bank overdraft	0	304	(26)	203
		962		1,019
12% debentures		400		100
Ordinary shares of £1	350		500	
Share Premium account	75		125	
Profit and Loss a/c	137	562	294	919
		962		1,019

You are informed further that during the year ended 31.12.20X1:

(a) a vehicle, which cost £72,000, was sold for £54,000;
(b) £17,000 was received as dividend;
(c) expenses written off include those stated in the box on the right;
(d) debentures were redeemed at 25 per cent premium on 30.9.20X1;
(e) Corporation Tax for the year was estimated at £92,000;
(f) £25,000 was paid as interim dividend in September 20X1;
(g) investments stated on the Balance Sheets include temporary investment of the cash surplus to immediate needs of £48,000 on 31.12.20X1 and £21,000 a year prior to that.

	£000
Salaries and wages	168
Bad debts	17
Depreciation	64
Investments w/off	20

Required: Prepare a Cash Flow Statement for the year ended 31.12.20X1 along with the reconciliation of net debt.

References

1. FRS 1: *Cash Flow Statements* (issued in 1991 and amended in 1996).
2. FRS 1, *ibid.*, paragraph 2.
3. Companies Act 1985, section 130.
4. FRS 1, *op. cit.*, paragraph 33.
5. FRS 1, *op. cit.*, paragraph 12.

SOLUTIONS TO INTERACTION QUESTIONS

IQ 43.1 Income and expense items with period-end adjustments reversed

TOTAL DEBTORS ACCOUNT

	£000		£000
Balance b/f	245	Cash a/c*	1,557
Sales	1,680	Balance c/f	368

TOTAL CREDITORS ACCOUNT

	£000		£000
Cash a/c*	1,214	Balance b/f	264
Balance c/f	296	Purchases	1,246

RENT ACCOUNT

	£000		£000
Balance b/f	15	Profit and Loss	60
Cash a/c*	35		
Balance c/f	10		

SALARIES ACCOUNT

	£000		£000
Cash a/c*	232	Balance b/f	32
Balance c/f	46	Profit and Loss	246

* Cash flows are marked with an asterisk.

IQ 43.2 Cash flow is a Cash account summary in a statement form

FIXED ASSETS ACCOUNT

	£000		£000
Balance b/f	540	Depreciation	124
Cash a/c*	264	Balance c/f	680

LOAN ACCOUNT

	£000		£000
Cash a/c*	50	Balance b/f	200
Balance c/f	150		

TOTAL DEBTORS ACCOUNT						TOTAL CREDITORS ACCOUNT				
	£000		£000				£000			£000
Balance b/f	365	Cash a/c*	4,205			Cash a/c*	3,172	Balance b/f		326
Sales*	4,265	Balance c/f	425			Balance c/f	418	Purchases		3,264

EXPENDITURE ACCOUNT						CAPITAL ACCOUNT				
	£000		£000				£000			£000
Cash*	688	Balance b/f	42			Cash a/c*	11	Balance b/f		642
Balance c/f	32	P&L a/c	678			Balance c/f	895	Profit		264

Figures identified with an asterisk (*) are the balancing figures.

CASH ACCOUNT			
	£000		£000
Balance b/f	65	Creditors a/c	3,172
Debtors a/c	4,205	Expenditure a/c	688
		Fixed Asset a/c	264
		Interest a/c	21
		Loan a/c	50
		Drawings	11
		Balance c/f	64

* Cash-flow items.

CASH FLOW STATEMENT FOR YEAR ENDED 31.12.20X2	
	£000
Received from debtors	4,205
Paid to creditors	(3,172)
Paid for expenditure	(688)
Paid for fixed assets	(264)
Paid as interest	(21)
Repayment of loan	(50)
Drawings by owner	(11)
Outflow of cash in 20X2	(1)

The Cash Flow Statement identifies the net outflow of cash during the year as £1,000.

IQ 43.3 Presenting cash flow in a uniform format

CASH FLOW STATEMENT FOR THE YEAR ENDED 31.12.20X2		
		£000
1. OPERATING ACTIVITY:		
From sales	4,205	
For purchases	(3,172)	
On expenses	(688)	345
2. SERVICING OF FINANCE		
Interest payments		(21)
3. CAPITAL EXPENDITURE		
Acquisition fo assets		(264)
4. RETURN ON EQUITY		
Drawings		(11)
5. FINANCING		
Repayment of loan		(50)
Cash outflow in the year		(1)

IQ 43.4 Cash flow of a limited company

CASH FLOW STATEMENT FOR THE YEAR ENDED 31.12.20X2

	£000	£000	
Operating activity:			
From debtors		1,812	e
To creditors		(1,345)	f
As expenses		(244)	g
		223	
Return on investments and servicing of finance:			
Dividend received	15		x
Interest paid	(24)	(9)	
Taxation		(96)	h
Capital expenditure and financial investments:			
Fixed assets	(120)		a
Investments	(45)	(165)	c
Acquisitions and disposals		–	
Equity dividend paid:			
Interim dividend	(30)		x
Final dividend	(45)	(75)	k
Management of liquid resources:		–	
Financing:			
Debenture redemption	(50)		l
Share capital	100		m
Share premium	90	140	n
Cash inflow in the year		18	y

FINAL DIVIDEND PROPOSED (L) ACCOUNT

	£000		£000	
k	Cash book	45	Balance b/f	45
	Balance c/d	60	Dividend (exp.)	60

SHARE CAPITAL ACCOUNT

	£000		£000	
			Balance b/f	400	
	Balance c/d	500	Cash book	100	m

SHARE PREMIUM ACCOUNT

	£000		£000	
			Balance b/f	60	
	Balance c/d	150	Cash book	90	n

FIXED ASSETS ACCOUNT

		£000		£000
	Balance b/f	720		
a	Cash book	120	Balance c/d	840

PROVISION FOR DEPRECIATION ACCOUNT

	£000		£000	
			Balance b/f	280	
Balance c/d	320	Depreciation	40	b

INVESTMENTS ACCOUNT

		£000		£000
	Balance b/f	75		
c	Cash book	45	Balance c/d	120

COST OF SALE ACCOUNT

		£000		£000
	Stock on 1.1	528	Trading a/c	1,245
d	Purchases	1,329		
	Stock on 31.12	(612)		
		1,245		1,245

DEBTORS CONTROL ACCOUNT

	£000		£000	
Balance b/f	386	Cash book	1,812	e
Sales	1,910	Balance c/d	484	

CREDITORS CONTROL ACCOUNT

		£000		£000	
f	Cash book	1,345	Balance b/f	612	e
	Balance c/d	596	Purchases	1,329	d

EXPENSES ACCOUNT

		£000		£000
b	Depreciation	40	Balance b/f	24
g	Cash book	244	Distrib. cost	76
	Balance c/d	34	Admin. expen.	218

TAXATION (LIABILITY) ACCOUNT

		£000		£000
h	Cash book	96	Balance b/f	96
	Balance c/d	112	Tax (expend.)	112

DEBENTURE REDEMPTION ACCOUNT

		£000		£000
I	Cash book	50	Debentures a/c	50

PROFIT AND LOSS ACCOUNT

		£000		£000
			Balance b/f	46
x	Balance c/d	206	Retained profit	160

Notes:

Letters a to h tie each amount with how it was arrived at.
x: Dividend received and interim dividend paid were given in the Profit and Loss account.
y: Cash inflow is the closing cash balance less opening balance.

IQ 43.5 Cash flow on asset disposal at a profit

(a) Machinery: cash inflow = £108,000
(b) Vehicles: cash outflow = £20,000
                cash inflow = £36,000

MACHINERY DISPOSAL ACCOUNT

	£		£
Balance b/f	240,000	Provision for depn	144,000
P&L – gain	12,000	Cash book	108,000

MOTOR VEHICLES ACCOUNT

	£		£
Balance b/f	180,000	Disposal a/c	40,000
Cash book	20,000	Balance c/d	160,000

PROVISION FOR DEPRECIATION – VEHICLES ACCOUNT

	£		£
Disposal a/c	16,000	Balance b/f	96,000
Balance c/d	128,000	Depreciation	48,000

MOTOR VEHICLE DISPOSAL ACCOUNT

	£		£
Motor vehicle a/c	40,000	Provision for depn	16,000
P&L – gain	12,000	Cash book	36,000

IQ 43.6 Cash flow on asset disposal at a loss

Capital expenditure and financial investments: furniture cash inflow = £4,200.

FURNITURE DISPOSAL ACCOUNT

	£		£
Furniture a/c	40,000	Provision for depn	28,000
		Cash book	4,200
		P&L – Loss	7,800

IQ 43.7 Cash flow involving asset disposal

CASH FLOW STATEMENT FOR THE YEAR ENDED 31.12.20X2

	£000	£000	
Operating activity:			
From debtors		2,407	f
To creditors		(1,728)	h
As expenses		(192)	j
		487	
Return on investments and servicing of finance:			
Dividend received	14		x
Interest paid	(39)	(25)	x
Taxation		(115)	k
Capital expenditure and financial Investments:			
Furniture	(100)		a
Motor vehicles	(220)		c
Investments	(114)		e
Disposal of vehicle	124	(310)	x
Acquisitions and disposals		–	
Equity dividend paid:			
Interim dividend	(45)		x
Final dividend	(60)	(105)	l
Management of liquid resources:			
Financing:			
Debenture redemption	(165)		m
Share capital	100		n
Share premium	75	10	o
Cash outflow in the year		(58)	p

FURNITURE AND FITTINGS ACCOUNT

		£000			£000	
x	Balance b/f	760				
a	Cash book	100	Balance c/d		860	x

PROVISION FOR DEPRECIATION – FURNITURE ACCOUNT

		£000			£000	
			Balance b/f		248	x
x	Balance c/d	324	Depreciation		76	b

MOTOR VEHICLES ACCOUNT

		£000			£000	
x	Balance b/f	840	Disposal a/c		180	x
c	Cash book	220	Balance c/d		880	x

PROVISION FOR DEPRECIATION – VEHICLES ACCOUNT

		£000			£000	
x	Disposal a/c	82	Balance b/f		360	x
x	Balance c/d	382	Depreciation		104	d

DISPOSAL OF MOTOR VEHICLE ACCOUNT

		£000			£000	
x	Motor vehicle	180	Provision for depn		82	x
	P&L – gain	26	Cash book		124	x

INVESTMENT ACCOUNT

		£000			£000	
x	Balance b/f	212				
e	Cash book	114	Balance c/d		326	x

DEBTORS CONTROL ACCOUNT

		£000			£000	
x	Balance b/f	542	Cash book		2,407	f
x	Sales account	2,539	Balance c/d		674	x

CREDITORS CONTROL ACCOUNT

		£000			£000	
h	Cash book	1,728	Balance b/f		554	x
x	Balance c/d	598	Purchases		1,772	g

EXPENSES ACCOUNT

		£000			£000	
b	Depreciation	104	Balance b/f	28	x
d	Depreciation	76	Distrib. cost	112	x
j	Cash book	192	Admin. exp.	284	x
x	Balance c/d	52			

COST OF SALE ACCOUNT

		£000		£000	
x	Stock 1.7.20X1	648	Trading a/c	1,828
g	Purchases	1,772		
x	Stock 30.6.20X2	(592)		
		1,828		1,828

PROFIT AND LOSS ACCOUNT

		£000			£000	
			Balance b/f	231	x
x	Balance c/d	295	Retained	64	x

TAXATION (LIABILITY) ACCOUNT

		£000			£000	
k	Cash book	115	Balance b/f	115	x
x	Balance c/d	132	Tax (exp.) a/c	132	x

ORDINARY SHARE CAPITAL ACCOUNT

		£000			£000	
			Balance b/f	900	x
x	Balance c/d	1,000	Cash book	100	n

FINAL DIVIDEND PROPOSED (LIABILITY) ACCOUNT

		£000			£000	
l	Cash book	60	Balance b/f	60	x
x	Balance c/d	75	Div. prop. (exp.)	75	x

SHARE PREMIUM ACCOUNT

		£000			£000	
m	Deb. red. a/c	15	Balance b/f	180	x
x	Balance c/d	240	Cash book	75	o

DEBENTURE REDEMPTION ACCOUNT

		£000			£000	
x	Cash book	165	Debentures	150	x
			Share premium	15	m

Letters a to o tie up each figure stated with how it was derived.

x: Items stated in the question.

p: Cash outflow during the year is the amount by which the opening cash balance (£74,000) exceeds the closing cash balance (£16,000).

IQ 43.8 Asset acquisition without cash outflow

(a) Cash Flow Statement (and subsidiary workings)

CASH FLOW STATEMENT FOR THE YEAR ENDED 31.12.20X3

	£000	£000	
Operating activity:			l
From sales		4,646	
For purchases		(3,322)	n
Admin. expenses		(636)	o
Distribution cost		(317)	p
		371	
Return on investment and servicing of finance:			
Dividend received	36		x
Interest paid	(36)	–	q
Taxation		(97)	r
Capital expenditure and financial investments:			
Machinery	(25)		a
Furniture	(80)		c
Motor vehicles	(255)		e
Investments	(37)		j
Disposals	128	(269)	h
Equity dividend paid:			
Interim dividend	(60)		x
Final dividend	(45)	(105)	s
Management of liquid resources:		13	k
Financing:			
Debenture redemption	(120)		t
Share capital	150		u
Share premium	50	80	v
Cash outflow during year		(7)	w

PLANT AND MACHINERY ACCOUNT

		£000			£000	
x	Balance b/f	790				
x	Long-term debt	150				
a	Cash book	25	Balance c/d		965	x

PROVISION FOR DEPRECIATION – MACHINERY ACCOUNT

		£000			£000	
			Balance b/f		365	x
x	Balance c/d	424	Depreciation		59	b

FURNITURE AND FITTINGS ACCOUNT

		£000			£000	
x	Balance b/d	240				
c	Cash book	80	Balance c/d		320	

PROVISION FOR DEPRECIATION – FURNITURE ACCOUNT

		£000			£000	
			Balance b/f		88	x
x	Balance c/d	144	Depreciation		56	d

MOTOR VEHICLES ACCOUNT

		£000			£000	
x	Balance b/f	210	Disposal a/c		120	x
e	Cash book	255	Balance c/d		345	x

PROVISION FOR DEPRECIATION – VEHICLES ACCOUNT

		£000			£000	
g	Disposal a/c	18	Balance b/f		63	x
x	Balance c/d	92	Depreciation		47	f

MOTOR VEHICLE DISPOSAL ACCOUNT

		£000			£000	
x	Motor Vehicle a/c	120	Provision for depn		18	g
x	P&L – gain on dis	26	Cash book		128	h

FIXED ASSET – INVESTMENTS ACCOUNT

		£000			£000	
x	Balance b/f	245	P&L – write-off		12	x
j	Cash book	37	Balance c/d		270	x

DEBTORS CONTROL ACCOUNT

		£000		£000	
x	Balance b/f	546	Cash book	4,646	l
x	Sales	4,704	Balance c/d	604	x

CURRENT ASSET – INVESTMENTS ACCOUNT

		£000		£000	
x	Balance b/f	25	Cash book	13	k
			Balance c/d	12	x

CREDITORS CONTROL ACCOUNT

		£000		£000	
n	Cash book	3,322	Balance b/f	442	x
x	Balance c/d	486	Purchases	3,366	m

COST OF SALES ACCOUNT

		£000		£000	
x	Stock 1.1	728	Trading a/c	3,465	x
m	Purchases	3,366			
b	Depreciation	59			
	Stock 31.12	(688)			
		3,465		3,465	

DISTRIBUTION COST ACCOUNT

		£000		£000	
f	Depreciation	47	P&L a/c	364	x
p	Cash book	317			

ADMINISTRATIVE EXPENSES ACCOUNT

		£000		£000	
d	Depreciation	56	Balance b/f	28	x
o	Cash book	636	P&L a/c	718	x
x	Balance c/d	54			

TAXATION (LIABILITY) ACCOUNT

		£000		£000	
r	Cash book	97	Balance b/f	84	x
x	Balance c/d	102	P&L a/c	115	x

DEBENTURE REDEMPTION ACCOUNT

		£000		£000	
t	Cash book	120	Debentures	100	x
			Sh. premium	20	x

FINAL DIVIDEND PROPOSED (L) ACCOUNT

		£000		£000	
s	Cash book	45	Balance b/f	45	x
x	Balance c/d	75	Dividend a/c	75	x

ORDINARY SHARE CAPITAL ACCOUNT

		£000		£000	
			Balance b/f	900	x
x	Balance c/d	1,050	Cash book	150	u

PROFIT AND LOSS ACCOUNT

		£000		£000	
x	Loss in 2003	73	Balance b/f	312	x
x	Balance c/d	239			x

SHARE PREMIUM ACCOUNT

		£000		£000	
x	Debenture red	20	Balance b/f	150	x
x	Balance c/d	180	Cash book	50	v

INTEREST ACCOUNT

		£000		£000	
q	Cash book	36	Balance b/f	18	x
x	Balance c/d	12	P&L a/c	30	x

Items marked x are those stated in the question. Other letters represent the amounts arrived at when balancing each account.

(b) Comment on company's cash and liquidity position

The resources available to the company on 31.12.20X3 for meeting its bills were £16,000, although £12,000 of this amount is tied up in fixed deposit and cannot be retrieved except with one month's notice. We can reasonably regard the amounts held on fixed deposit as backup funds, although the requirement is for these to be shown in the Cash Flow Statement separately from the cash figure and identified as liquid resources. Caterola Ltd has not only suffered an outflow of cash amounting to £7,000 during the year, but also has run down its liquid resources by another £13,000. Hence, the liquid resources of the company have worsened in the year to the extent of £20,000. But, at the same time, the company's long-term debt (debentures) has reduced by £100,000. Taking both together, the liquidity of the company has improved by (£100,000 less £20,000), namely £80,000.

IQ 43.9 Focus on liquidity position

During the year there has been a cash outflow of £79,000, in addition to running down liquid resources by £76,000. Thus it would appear that the liquidity has worsened by £79,000 + £76,000.

Net debt as at 30.6	20X0 £000	20X1 £000
12% Debentures	(600)	(300)
Cash and bank balance	48	(31)
Liquid resources	172	96
Net debt	(380)	(235)

Reconciliation of net debt	£000
Redemption of debenture	300
Cash outflow in the year	(79)
Liquid resources reduced	(76)
Liquidity improves by	145
Net debt as at 30.6.20X0	(380)
Net debt as at 30.6.20X1	(235)

At the same time, the entity's debts (debentures) have been reduced by £300,000. Therefore, as shown by the 'reconciliation of net debt' (see above), the entity's liquidity has improved by £145,000 during the year.

IQ 43.10 Reconciliation of operating profit and cash flow

On this reconciliation, only items that fall within the first heading in the Cash Flow Statement are included. The following, though accrued, are not included because:

- Interest falls under heading 2;
- Taxation falls under heading 3;
- Dividend proposed falls under heading 6.

RECONCILIATION OF OPERATING PROFIT WITH CASH FLOW FROM OPERATING ACTIVITY	
	£000
Operating profit	157
Depreciation (59 + 56 + 47)	162
Stock decrease	40
Debtors increase	(58)
Creditors increase	44
Accrued expenses increase	26
Cash flow from operating activity	371

IQ 43.11 Cash Flow Statement using the indirect method

CASH FLOW STATEMENT
YEAR ENDED 31 DECEMBER 20X1

	£000	£000	
Operating activity:		449	
Return on investment and servicing of finance:			
Dividend received	17		x
Interest paid	(48)	(31)	j
Taxation		(84)	f
Capital expenditure and financial investments:			
Fixed assets	(232)		a
Investments	(21)		d
Disposal of asset	54	(199)	c
Equity dividend paid:			
Interim dividend	(25)		x
Final dividend	(30)	(55)	g
Management of liquid resources:		(27)	e
Financing:			
Debenture redemption	(375)		h
Share capital	150		k
Share premium	125	(100)	l
Cash outflow in the year		(47)	

RECONCILIATION OF OPERATING PROFIT WITH CASH FLOW FROM OPERATION

	£000
Operating profit	342
Depreciation	64
Stock decrease	140
Debtors increase	(32)
Creditors decrease	(82)
Accruals increase	17
Cash flow from operation	449

FIXED ASSETS ACCOUNT

		£000		£000	
x	Balance b/f	760	Disposal a/c	72	x
a	Cash book	232	Balance c/d	920	x

PROVISION FOR DEPRECIATION ACCOUNT

		£000		£000	
b	Disposal a/c	34	Balance b/f	288	x
x	Balance c/d	318	Depreciation	64	x

DISPOSAL OF ASSET ACCOUNT

		£000		£000	
x	Fixed asset a/c	72	Provision for depn	34	b
x	P&L – gain	16	Cash book	54	c

FIXED ASSET INVESTMENTS ACCOUNT

		£000		£000	
x	Balance b/f	165	P&L – write-off	20	x
d	Cash book	21	Balance c/d	166	x

CURRENT ASSET INVESTMENTS ACCOUNT

		£000		£000	
x	Balance b/f	21			
e	Cash book	27	Balance c/d	48	x

TAXATION (LIABILITY) ACCOUNT

		£000		£000	
f	Cash book	84	Balance b/f	84	x
x	Balance c/d	92	Tax (exp) a/c	92	x

DIVIDEND PROPOSED (LIABILITY) ACCOUNT

		£000		£000	
g	Cash book	30	Balance b/f	30	x
x	Balance c/d	42	Dividend (exp.)	42	x

DEBENTURE REDEMPTION ACCOUNT

		£000		£000	
h	Cash book	375	Debentures	300	x
			Share premium	75	m

RECONCILIATION OF CASH FLOW WITH NET DEBT	
	£000
Redemption of debentures	300
Liquid resources improve	27
Cash outflow in the year	(47)
Change in net debt	280
Net debt on 1.1.20X1	(347)
Net debt as at 31.12.20X1	(67)

	£000	
Operating profit	342	x
Gain on disposal	16	
Dividend received	17	
Investments w/off	(20)	
Interest	(39)	
Profit before tax	316	
Taxation	(92)	
Profit after taxation	224	
Interim dividend	(25)	
Dividend proposed	(42)	
Retained profit	157	

INTEREST ACCOUNT

		£000			£000	
j	Cash book	48		Balance b/f	12	x
x	Balance c/d	3		P&L – exp.	39	x

ORDINARY SHARE CAPITAL ACCOUNT

		£000			£000	
				Balance b/f	350	x
x	Balance c/d	500		Cash book	150	k

SHARE PREMIUM ACCOUNT

		£000			£000	
m	Debenture red	75		Balance b/f	75	x
x	Balance c/d	125		Cash book	125	l

PROFIT AND LOSS ACCOUNT

		£000			£000	
				Balance b/f	137	x
x	Balance c/d	294		Retained profit	157	x

Net debt as at:	1.1.20X1	31.12.20X1
Debentures	(£400,000)	(£100,000)
Cash and bank	£32,000	£11,000
Liquid resources	£21,000	£48,000
Bank overdraft	–	(£26,000)
Net debt	(£347,000)	(£67,000)

Notes:

x: Operating profit is the balancing amount. This amount is arrived at by starting at the bottom (with retained profit) and working upwards.

1. Despite cash outflow of £47,000, the company's liquidity has improved by £280,000 – that being the amount of the reduction in its net debt position.

2. One quarter's interest (at 12% per annum) would have remained accrued on each Balance Sheet date.

PROGRESSIVE QUESTIONS

PQ 43.1 Multiple-choice question

In each of the following independent cases, determine the **cash inflow (or outflow)**, on income or expenditure items for the year ended 31.12.20X1, taking into account all of the information provided below:

Cash inflow/outflow
£

(a) Debtors on 1.1.20X1 were £362,400 and on 31.12.20X1 were £416,400. Sales in the year to 31.12.20X1 were £1,846,500. Bad debts written off in the year were £32,200.

x	1,792,500
y	1,760,300
z	1,846,500

(b) Debtors on 1.1.20X1 were £264,800 and on 31.12.20X1 were £292,600. Purchases in the year were £862,600. Stock in hand was £216,400 on 1.1.20X1 and £284,600 on 31.12.20X1. Sales are made at cost plus 50 per cent.

x	1,031,400
y	1,266,100
z	1,163,800

(c) Sales in the year to 31.12.20X1 were £492,600. Goods are sold at cost plus one-third. Stock and creditors were £124,400 and £54,600 on 1.1.20X1 and £118,600 and £62,800 a year later, respectively.

x	(355,450)
y	(314,450)
z	(367,000)

(d) Salary payable in respect of the year ended 31.12.20X1 was £378,400. Salary accrued was £75,500 on 1.1.20X1 and £92,800 on 31.12.20X1.

x	(361,100)
y	(395,700)
z	(342,500)

(e) Rent prepaid on 1.1.20X1 was £8,000 and accrued on 31.12.20X1 was £4,000. Rent was agreed at £4,000 per month.

x	(40,000)
y	(52,000)
z	(36,000)

(f) Interest is paid half-yearly in arrears on 1 January and 1 July. A £400,000 16% loan was outstanding on 1.1.20X1, with £100,000 of this amount having been discharged on 1 July 20X1.

x	(56,000)
y	(72,000)
z	(64,000)

(g) Interest is paid half-yearly in arrears on 1 April and 1 October. A £600,000 12% loan was outstanding on 1.1.20X1 and one-third of this amount was discharged on 1 October 20X1.

x	(72,000)
y	(78,000)
z	(84,000)

PQ 43.2 Cash Flow Statement using the direct method and indirect method

Lincoln Stores' Balance Sheets appear as shown here. You are informed that Lincoln's drawings during the year amounted to £26,000.

Required:

(a) Prepare a Cash Flow Statement for the year on the indirect method.

(b) Prepare the Cash Flow Statement on the direct method, and for this purpose you are given the following additional information:
   - Sales during the year were £966,000.
   - Sales are made at cost plus 50 per cent.

BALANCE SHEETS AS AT 31 DECEMBER		
	20X0	20X1
	£000	£000
Fixed assets at cost	460	540
Accum. depreciation	(180)	(210)
	280	330
Stock in trade	286	354
Debtors	362	396
Cash and bank	24	32
Creditors	(312)	(348)
Accrued expenses	(28)	(39)
Capital	612	725

PQ 43.3 Cash Flow Statement using the indirect method

Electrical Stores, owned by Jerry, submits its Balance Sheets as shown here. Transactions during the year included the following:

(a) A vehicle, acquired for £36,000 and written down to £21,000 by 1.1.20X2, was written off in an accident. £5,000 was recovered from insurance.

(b) Jerry's private motor vehicle was transferred to the business during the year, valued for the purpose at £30,000.

(c) Loan interest is paid annually in arrears on 1 January.

(d) Part of the loan was discharged on 1.1.20X2.

(e) A dividend of £18,000 was received during the year ended 31.12.20X2.

(f) Jerry takes £500 per week for his living expenses.

(g) Reported as part of cash and bank balance is a fixed deposit of £15,000 on 31.12.20X1 and £10,000 on 31.12.20X2.

Required: Prepare a Cash Flow Statement for the year ended 31.12.20X2.

BALANCE SHEETS AS AT 31 DECEMBER				
	20X1		20X2	
	£000	£000	£000	£000
Furniture at cost	280		340	
Accum. depreciation	(98)	182	(128)	212
Motor vehicles at cost	360		480	
Accum. depreciation	(144)	216	(172)	308
Investments		264		296
Stock in trade	568		528	
Debtors	324		385	
Cash and bank balance	24		9	
Creditors	(436)		(454)	
Accrued expenses	(69)	411	(52)	416
16% loan		(400)		(250)
Capital – Jerry Lawson		673		982

PQ 43.4 Cash Flow Statement using the direct method

Will's Electricals submits to you the following financial statements:

BALANCE SHEET AS AT 30 JUNE				
	20X1		20X0	
	£000	£000	£000	£000
Fixed assets:				
Machinery at cost	420		360	
Accum. depreciation	(136)	284	(124)	236
Furniture at cost	190		160	
Accum. depreciation	(72)	118	(54)	106
Motor vehicles at cost	320		280	
Accum. depreciation	(84)	236	(64)	216
Investments		220		195
Current assets:				
Stock in trade	786		654	
Debtors	594		552	
Cash and bank	11		36	
Creditors	(724)		(628)	
Salary payable	(112)		(82)	
Sales commission due	(34)		(21)	
Bank overdraft	(16)		–	
Net current asset		505		511
		1,363		1,264
		£000		£000
Capital – Terry Will		1,013		814
12% loan		350		450
		1,363		1,264

PROFIT AND LOSS ACCOUNT FOR THE YEAR ENDED 30 JUNE 20X1		
	£000	£000
Sales		3,339
Cost of sales		(2,484)
Gross profit		855
Administrative expenses:		
Salaries	(246)	
Rent	(42)	
Depreciation – furniture	(18)	
Stationery	(4)	
Audit fees	(18)	
Other expenses	(38)	(366)
Distribution cost:		
Advertising	(66)	
Sales commission	(72)	
Bad debts	(14)	
Depreciation on vehicles	(54)	(206)
Loss on sale of machinery		(21)
Gain on sale of vehicles		14
Interest		(51)
Profit for the year		225

You are further informed as follows:

(a) Assets disposed of during the year ended 30 June 20X1 consisted of machinery that cost £140,000, which was written down to £62,000, and vehicles that cost £60,000, which were written down to £26,000.

(b) Reported as part of investments are a temporary holding of shares in listed companies costing £26,000 on 30 June 20X0 and £8,000 on 30 June 20X1.

(c) During the year Terry introduced £30,000 as additional capital.

Required: Prepare a Cash Flow Statement using the direct method, a reconciliation of operating profit with cash flow from operating activity, and a reconciliation of cash flow with net debt.

PQ 43.5 Cash Flow Statement for a limited company

Phoenix plc has drafted its financial statements as follows:

PROFIT AND LOSS ACCOUNT FOR THE YEAR ENDED 30 JUNE 20X2	£000
Turnover	15,977
Cost of sales	(12,495)
Gross profit	3,482
Distribution cost	(412)
Administrative expenses	(948)
Operating profit	2,122
Loss on vehicle disposal	(18)
Dividend received	54
Investments written off	(32)
Interest and similar charge	(66)
Profit before taxation	2,060
Taxation	(870)
Profit after taxation	1,190
Interim dividend	(240)
Final dividend proposed	(720)
Retained profit	230

BALANCE SHEETS AS AT 30 JUNE	20X1		20X2	
	£000	£000	£000	£000
Fixed assets:				
Development cost		120		158
Furniture at cost	964		1,122	
Accumulated depreciation	(268)	696	(324)	798
Motor vehicles at cost	1,620		1,845	
Accumulated depreciation	(1,124)	496	(1,346)	499
Investments		364		528
Current assets:				
Stock in trade	1,485		2,128	
Trade debtors	2,168		2,456	
Prepayments	42		68	
Cash and bank	284		396	
Trade creditors	(1,942)		(2,464)	
Interest accrued	(18)		(12)	
Directors' fees accrued	(120)		(180)	
Taxation	(685)		(845)	
Dividend proposed	(540)	674	(720)	827
		2,350		2,810
		£000		£000
Creditors due after one year:				
15% debentures		480		320
Share capital and reserves:				
Ordinary shares of £1	1,200		1,500	
Share Premium a/c	150		240	
Profit and Loss reserve	520	1,870	750	2,490
		2,350		2,810

You are informed as follows:

(a) Expenses written off in the year include those stated on the right.
(b) Debentures were redeemed on 1 April 20X1 at 20 per cent premium.
(c) Vehicles sold in the year had been acquired at a cost of £80,000.
(d) Stated on the Balance Sheet on 30 June 20X2 as investments are shares quoted on the London Stock Exchange held as a readily disposable store of value amounting to £54,000 (£31,000 on 30.6.20X1), and stated within the cash and bank balance is a three-month fixed deposit of £25,000 (£4,000 on 30.6.20X1).

	£000
Depreciation – furniture	56
Depreciation – vehicles	258
Amortization of develop. cost	84
Directors' emoluments	128
Bad debts written off	22

Required: Set out the Cash Flow Statement for the year ended 30 June 20X2 using the direct method, along with a reconciliation of operating profit with cash flow from operating activity and a reconciliation of cash flow with the net debt. In addition, briefly comment on the impact of the year's activities on the liquidity of the company.

PQ 43.6 Profit is not always matched by cash inflow

Richard & Co, wholesalers, sells its product at cost plus 50 per cent and effects its sales on one month's credit. The company obtains supplies also on one month's credit and carries one month's stock. The Balance Sheet of the business on 31 December 20X1 is as stated on the right.

A new sales manager, embarking on a programme of dynamic expansion from this date, acts as follows:

(a) reduces the sale price by 10 per cent;
(b) allows all customers three months' credit;
(c) carries three months' supplies in stock.

Credit facilities from suppliers, however, could not be extended. In addition, you can assume that during the year to 31.12.20X2 sales will improve threefold, expenses (other than on purchases), determined at £1,280,000 in year 20X1, are expected to increase by one-quarter, and no additional fixed assets are acquired.

BALANCE SHEET AS AT 31.12.20X1		
		£000
Fixed assets at written down value		725
Stock in trade	120	
Debtors	240	
Cash and bank	35	
Creditors	(120)	275
Capital		1,000

Required (ignoring depreciation): Prepare a projected Cash Flow Statement and Profit and Loss account for the year ending on 31.12.20X2, and determine the impact of obtaining three months' credit from suppliers on the cash flow of this business.

PQ 43.7 Focus on liquidity position

In each of the following cases, tick an appropriate cell in each grid to indicate the impact of operations during the year on the liquid position of the company:

(a) There was a cash outflow of £68,000, liquid resources were run down by £45,000, but £300,000 of debentures had been redeemed at 20 per cent premium.

	Impact	
a	£113,000 worse	
b	£413,000 better	
c	£187,000 better	

(b) There was a cash inflow of £86,000, despite investing £45,000 in liquid resources and £300,000 debentures being redeemed at 25 per cent premium.

a	£506,000 better	
b	£516,000 better	
c	£431,000 better	

(c) There was a cash inflow of £28,000 after liquid resources were run down by £72,000, and £250,000 of debentures were redeemed paying 20 per cent premium.

a	£350,000 better	
b	£256,000 better	
c	£206,000 better	

(d) There was a cash inflow of £126,000 after investing £35,000 in liquid resources, though £300,000 had been raised in the year by the issue of 14 per cent debentures.

a	£391,000 better	
b	£461,000 better	
c	£139,000 worse	

## Chapter 44

MORE VEHICLES FOR COMMUNICATING INFORMATION

In this chapter

We will learn of:

- continuing efforts to identify more ways for communicating financial information to those with a legitimate claim for it

and you should be able to:

- prepare value added statements
- interpret value added statements

44.1 MORE VEHICLES FOR COMMUNICATION

The information needs of those who have a legitimate claim for information from entities are not adequately met by the Profit and Loss account and Balance Sheet, which have been the traditional vehicles used to provide information. *The Corporate Report*[1]:

- identified the different categories of stakeholders with a legitimate claim for information;
- enquired into their information needs;
- advocated the publication of a Cash Flow Statement (Chapter 43) and a Value Added Statement (Section 44.2), as well as the following reports.

44.1.1 Employment Report

This report is one where an entity reports the extent to which it discharges its social obligations in areas such as:

- employment provision
- wage bill of the entity
- training of school-leavers
- employment of the disabled
- welfare of its employees.

Admittedly, the usefulness of this report is more on the basis of social accounting than stewardship accounting. And it is already a legal requirement that every company should disclose the salaries and wages paid to employees, as well as the average number employed during the year, divided into major categories. Although the publication of an Employment Report is not a legal requirement, most companies include in their Annual Report and Accounts (see box on the following page) some information of interest to, and relating to, their employees.

British Telecommunications plc 1998:

'At BT, we understand the link between being our customers' "supplier of choice" and our people's "employer of choice". That is why we have such a deep commitment to our people and why we are backing it up by seeking accreditation as an investor in people company.'

They proceed to list, amongst other things, the following:

- that 127,000 people are employed at 31.3.1998;
- that over 500 high-calibre graduates and 500 modern apprentices were recruited in the year;
- that real equality of opportunity is promoted by leading-edge programmes and policies;
- that employment, training and career development of people with disabilities are actively encouraged;
- that in March 1998 the top prize in the Opportunity 2000 awards scheme was won;
- that a wide-ranging programme of employee opinion research is conducted;
- that 2 per cent of annual pre-tax profit is allocated to employees under a BT employee share ownership scheme.

44.1.2 Statement of money exchange with government

This is a means whereby an entity could report money flow between the government and the entity, drawing attention to:

- payments to government in the form of taxes, customs, excise, rates, social security;
- receipts from government in the form of grants and subsidy; and
- collections on behalf of government by way of PAYE and VAT.

This proposal from the ASC has not been put into effect.

44.1.3 Statement of transactions in foreign currency

Here, an entity is able to report its earnings in foreign currency as well as its use of foreign currency to pay for goods and services, for paying interest and dividends, and for making investments in other countries.

This, again, has not been put into effect.

44.1.4 Statement of Corporate Objectives

This report is intended to allow an entity to convey its aims and objectives, not only as regards performance and profits expressed in monetary terms but also as regards its aspirations through its social and environmental policies. The report therefore enables an entity to project its image and permits its stakeholders to assess its performance in the context of its targets.

Although such a statement is not legally required, most entities make such a statement at one place or another in their Annual Report and Accounts. Following are extracts from what Anglian Water had to say in its 1998 Report and Accounts.

Anglian Water plc: 1998 Report and Accounts:

- 'The company continues to set industry standards in demand management, customer service and environmental quality measures.
- Despite the worst drought this century . . . Anglian Water maintained supplies to customers without any restrictions.
- In more than quarter of a million tests carried out, 99.6% of water complied with the government standards.
- All 38 bathing waters . . . in the region now meet European Union Standards.
- Since 1990, river quality . . . has improved by 35%.
- We plan to treat sludge to standards over and above the requirements of existing regulations.
- The commissioning of new forms of sewage treatment using Kaldnes media . . . has proved particularly successful in improving wastewater treatment.'

44.1.5 Statement of future prospects

Here, management has the opportunity to project the levels of future profits, employment and investments on the basis of their experience and intimate knowledge of the entity. In the absence of any legal compulsion, companies are loath to venture into making forecasts and projections other than in very general terms, as Somerfield plc has done in the extract shown on the right.

Somerfield plc Report and Accounts 1997/98:

'We are delighted with the progress that our merged business has made in its first few months; we are highly confident of delivering the synergy benefits we envisaged at the time of the merger. Over the next two years we intend to make significant progress towards our goal of becoming the pre-eminent neighbourhood retailer and both consumers and shareholders will feel the benefit.'

44.1.6 Segmental report

This is a report in which turnover, profit and net assets employed are broken down to reveal the extent to which these were contributed to by the different industrial segments (product lines) in which the entity is involved and each geographical segment in which the entity operates. This proposal has been put into effect – the publication of segmental information is now a requirement of company law[2] and accounting standards.[3]

44.1.7 Other reports

The quest continues, however, for additional or alternative vehicles to communicate information of interest to those who have a stake in the entity. For example, FRS 3 requires[4] the publication also of the following primary statements:

- Statement of Total Recognized Gains and Losses;
- Note of Historical Cost Profit and Loss;
- Reconciliation of Shareholders Funds.

44.2 THE VALUE ADDED STATEMENT

The Profit and Loss account is traditionally relied upon to convey the performance of a business entity, reporting the performance in terms of profit. The profit is the residual amount (the bottom-line figure) available to those who provided the risk capital (as distinct from loan capital) of the entity (i.e. the owner or, in the case of companies, the shareholders). It has long been suggested that profit cannot be the only yardstick for measuring performance because other yardsticks of equal (or perhaps greater) significance would include the extent to which the entity was able to:

- achieve the goals it sets itself, in terms of economy, efficiency, output and growth;
- generate employment;
- improve the standard of living and promote social welfare;
- enhance national resources such as foreign-exchange reserves;
- protect the natural environment.

Even if one restricts the measurement of performance to the return for efforts, the owners of an entity are not the only party who contributes to its operations. Measuring the performance in terms of profit alone, therefore, ignores the contribution made by others – such as the employees, providers of loan capital, and the government. To overcome this, *The Corporate Report* by the ASC suggested the publication of an additional performance statement to be called the Value Added Statement (VAS).

The VAS, like the Profit and Loss account, commences with the entity's turnover, and by deducting the expenses incurred for buying inputs from those outside the entity (such as on purchasing goods, paying for rent, electricity, stationery, insurance and so on), identifies the value added by the entity's own efforts. This amount, being what is achieved through the collective efforts of the employees, the providers of capital (both loan capital as well as risk capital) and the government, is shared among these three groups, retaining a portion within the entity for maintaining and enhancing the resource base of the entity.

Pro forma **Value Added Statement** **for the year ended XXXXXXX**	£000
Turnover	XXXX
Less: Bought-in materials & services	(XXXX)
Value added	XXX
Applied as follows:	
Paid to: Employees	(XX)
Providers of capital	(XX)
Government	(XX)
Retained within the entity	(XX)

Although during the years immediately after the proposal for VAS was published many companies were quick to comply with it, the enthusiasm has since waned. One reason for it could be that, burdened as they are with a proliferation of reporting and disclosure requirements, entities no longer feel inclined to publish what is, in any case, optional. Another reason for loss of interest is that, in the absence of any efforts at professional standardization, it has not always been possible to compare the VASs prepared by entities because of the possibility of alternative treatment of the same item.

44.2.1 Preparation of the Value Added Statement

The information contained in the VAS is exactly as in a Profit and Loss account. The difference is the shift of focus from *profit* to *value added*, which requires the rearrangement of items. The VAS comprises two sections: in the first it identifies the amount of value added and in the second it reports how the added value is shared among the parties whose collective effort produced it.

In the following illustration, the items in the Profit and Loss account have been identified as 'a' and 'b' according to whether they fit into the first or the second section of the VAS.

PROFIT AND LOSS ACCOUNT FOR THE YEAR ENDED 31.12.20X0	£000	£000	
Turnover		8,640	a
Cost of sales		(7,816)	a
Gross profit		824	
Administrative expenses:			
Salaries	296		b
Rent	36		a
Rates	16		a
Audit fees	10		a
Depreciation	24		b
Stationery	8		a
Electricity	14	(404)	a
Distribution cost:			
Advertising	82		a
Depreciation	36		b
Carriage out	22	(140)	a
Interest		(30)	b
Profit before tax		250	
Taxation		(80)	b
Profit after tax		170	
Dividends		(60)	b
Retained profit		110	b

VALUE ADDED STATEMENT FOR THE YEAR ENDED 31.12.20X0		£000	**
Turnover		8,640	
Bought-in materials and services*		(8,004)	
Value added		636	100%
Applied as follows:			
To employees:			
Salaries		(296)	46%
To providers of capital:			
Interest paid	30		
Dividend	60	(90)	14%
To government – as tax		(80)	13%
Retained within:			
As depreciation	60		
As retained profit	110	(170)	27%

Notes:

* All items (other than turnover) marked 'a' fall within the first compartment in VAS and are aggregated to be stated as 'Bought-in materials and services'.

** The percentage column is introduced into the VAS to assist with interpretation of what it conveys.

Preparation of Value Added Statement

The Profit and Loss account published by Cherubim Ltd appears as shown on the right. You are further informed as follows:

PROFIT AND LOSS ACCOUNT YEAR ENDED 31.12.20X1	
	£000
Turnover	7,642
Cost of sales	(4,864)
Gross profit	2,778
Distribution cost	(862)
Administrative exp.	(1,264)
Operating profit	652
Investment income	30
Interest paid	(48)
Profit before taxation	634
Taxation	(212)
Profit after taxation	422
Dividend	(240)
Retained profit	182

(a) Cost of sales is made up as:

	£000
Stock on 31.12.20X0	652
Purchases	2,462
Import duty	488
Depreciation – machinery	622
Hire of plant	285
Productive wages	786
Stock on 31.12.20X1	(431)
	4,864

(b) Distribution cost consists of:

	£000
Advertising	344
Bad debts	82
Sales staff salary	212
Depreciation of vehicles	160
Vehicle maintenance	64

(c) Administrative expenses:

	£000
Admin. staff salary	872
Insurance	23
Telephone & postage	36
Audit fees	80
Depreciation of furniture	62
Other admin. expenses	191

Required: Prepare a Value Added Statement for Cherubim Ltd in respect of the year ended 31 December 20X1.

44.2.2 Dispute on treatment of some items in the Value Added Statement

In the absence of an accounting standard on the subject, there have been different treatments for some items in the Value Added Statement. Some examples are considered below.

Depreciation of fixed assets

The dispute is about whether depreciation should appear in the first section as part of 'bought-in materials' (just as comparable amounts such as hire or lease of machinery would) or in the second section of the VAS as a retention of value added for purposes of asset replacement. If depreciation is stated in the second section, as we have, a company owning the asset would report higher value added than another that leased the asset.

Investment income

In the VAS prepared in answer to IQ 44.1 (p. 727), the investment income has been treated as part of the value added by the entity, i.e. it has been included in the first section but identified separately from the value generated within the entity. Those who maintain that such income represents value generated by employees of another entity suggest several alternative treatments:

- leave investment income out of the VAS;
- include income in the first part of the VAS but as a deduction from the cost of bought-in goods and services;
- include income in the second section of the VAS as a deduction from the amount of added value given to the providers of capital.

The authors prefer to include investment income in the first section of the VAS, although separately identified, on the premise that investment income represents value generated by the entity by allocating a part of its resources for use by another entity.

Taxation

Reporting both direct and indirect taxes together in the second section as an application of value added facilitates comparison of the performance of an entity with that of another, operating in a different country, with a different mix of direct and indirect taxes. But there are those who prefer to state in the VAS the same tax figure as reported in the Profit and Loss account, on the premise that an indirect tax represents higher cost of the item consumed by the entity in its effort to generate added value. By the same token it is submitted that rates paid to a local authority should be viewed as part of the cost of services paid for by the entity.

44.2.3 The case for publishing Value Added Statements

The case for publishing VASs may be made as follows:

1. Whereas the Profit and Loss Account reports the performance from the narrow perspective of the providers of risk capital and measures performance with the yardstick of profit, the VAS identifies the performance of an entity as the outcome of the collective effort of other parties as well, and measures performance with the yardstick of the additional value that the entity generates.
2. It is suggested that the size and significance of an entity are better gauged in terms of its value added rather than its turnover, profit, capital employed and so on.
3. By viewing the performance of an entity as the result of the collective effort of several parties, the VAS contributes towards better relations among those parties, encouraging a team spirit among them and greater commitment to each other, while discouraging strife arising from mutual suspicion and industrial action.

4. By putting in perspective the share received by employees against the value generated by the entity, the VAS would probably be more useful in wage negotiations and productivity agreements.

On the other hand, the publication of a VAS is discouraged by those who point out that:

1. The VAS does no more than rearrange the information in the Profit and Loss Account.
2. Proliferation of accounting statements tends to confuse and overwhelm information users.
3. Profit, rather than value added, is still regarded both as the measure of performance and as the criterion for decision making.
4. The concept that a business entity is a collective effort of a team is merely a public relations exercise, which tries to mask the capitalist reality of antagonism between capital and labour. (This suspicion gains ground because a few entities who continue to retain an interest in VASs include them only in their special reports addressed to their employees.)
5. If a business entity is in fact a team effort, perhaps there is a case for recognizing the trade suppliers and landowners also as members of this team, so that payments for purchases and of rent would also have to be regarded as application of the value added (in the second section).
6. When an entity reports a loss, preparation of a VAS could prove an embarrassment because, while employees and loan providers receive a share of value added, the providers of risk capital would fare negatively.

Interaction 44.2	**How beneficial is a Value Added Statement?**

Required: Refer to the Value Added Statement prepared for Cherubim Ltd in answer to IQ 44.1 and comment on salient features of the company's performance in the year, on the basis of accounting ratios extracted from the statement.

References

1. *The Corporate Report* (Accounting Standards Committee, 1975).
2. Companies Act 1985.
3. SSAP 25: *Segmental Reporting* (ASC, June 1990).
4. FRS 3: *Reporting Financial Performance* (ASB, 1992).

SOLUTIONS TO INTERACTIVE QUESTIONS

IQ 44.1 Preparation of Value Added Statement

VALUE ADDED STATEMENT FOR THE YEAR ENDED 31st December 20X1			W
		£000	
Turnover		7,642	
Less: Bought-in materials and services		(3,788)	a
Value added within entity		3,854	
Investment income		30	
Value added in the year		3,884	
Applied as follows:			
To employees		(1,870)	b
To providers of capital:			
As interest	48		
As dividend	240	(288)	
To government:			
As Corporation Tax	212		
As import duty	488	(700)	
Retained for maintenance and expansion			
As depreciation	844		c
As retained profit	182	(1,026)	

Workings (£000):

(a) $652 + 2,462 + 285 - 431 + 344 + 82 + 64 + 23 + 36 + 80 + 191 = 3,788$
(b) $786 + 212 + 872 = 1,870$
(c) $622 + 160 + 62 = 844.$

IQ 44.2 How beneficial is a Value Added Statement?

(a) **Ratio of value added to sales** = $(3,854/7,642) \times 100\% = 50.43\%$
   This shows that, by processing the materials purchased from outside, Cherubim Ltd is able to add substantial value, whereas the ratio is bound to have been much lower had Cherubim been only a retailer of the product, working within narrow trade discounts.
(b) **Ratio of wages to value added** = $(1,870/3,884) \times 100\% = 48.15\%$
   It is of interest to employees to learn that:
   (a) they are receiving almost one-half of the value added;
   (b) their share of the value added is substantially higher than the 7.41% received by those who provided the capital;
   (c) one-quarter of the value added (26.42%) is being ploughed back into the business to safeguard the future prospects.
(c) **Ratio of value added to wages** = $(3,884/1,870) \times 100\% = 208\%$
   This shows that employees deserve the salary they are paid because the value added they helped to generate is more than twice what they are paid.
(d) **Ratio of tax to value added** = $(700/3,884) \times 100\% = 18.02\%$
   This ratio draws to attention whether or not the entity bears an unfair burden of taxation.

PROGRESSIVE QUESTIONS

PQ 44.1 Focus on the vehicles proposed to communicate information

1. It is submitted that the performance of an entity within an accounting period should be assessed not only with a yard-stick of profit but also using other yardsticks, including the ability to:

(a) achieve the goals it sets itself in terms of economy, efficiency, output and growth;
(b) ensure that the amount and timing of cash generation match the needs;
(c) generate employment;
(d) improve the standard of living and promote social welfare;
(e) enhance national resources such as foreign-exchange reserves;
(f) protect the natural environment.

Required: Identify which of the additional vehicles proposed by *The Corporate Report* (1975) provide – or would have provided – the yardsticks for assessing each of the above-stated areas.

2. For informed decision making with regard to making investments in business entities, the investors seek information with a predictive value.

Required: Explain which vehicle would be most useful for this purpose.

PQ 44.2 Preparation of Value Added Statement

The published financial statements of Seraphim Ltd includes the following:

PROFIT AND LOSS ACCOUNT FOR THE YEAR ENDED 30.6.20X1	£000
Turnover	8,684
Cost of sales	(5,268)
Gross profit	3,416
Distribution cost	(962)
Administrative expenses	(1,825)
Operating profit	629
Loss on asset disposal	(124)
Dividend received	48
Interest paid	(60)
Profit before taxation	493
Taxation	(148)
Profit after taxation	345
Interim dividend paid	(60)
Final dividend proposed	(120)
Retained profit	165

STATEMENT OF MOVEMENT OF TANGIBLE FIXED ASSETS AS AT 30.6.20X1

	Building £000	Machinery £000	Furniture £000	Vehicle £000
Balance b/f	1,450	864	620	460
Acquisitions	–	226	120	80
Disposal	–	(465)	–	(120)
Balance c/f	1,450	625	740	420

Accumulated depreciation:

	£000	£000	£000	£000
As at 30.6.20X0	406	324	248	162
Depreciation	29	106	68	88
Disposal	–	(242)	–	(72)
As at 30.6.20X1	435	188	316	178
Net Book Value	1,015	437	424	242

Expenses in the year 20X1:	£000
Duty on import of materials	214
Salaries and wages (including to directors)	1,428

Required: Set out the Value Added Statement of Seraphim Ltd for the year ended 30.6.20X1.

Chapter 45

GROUP ACCOUNTS

In this chapter

We will learn to prepare consolidated balance sheet to report the combined position of a group of companies

45.1 PARENTS AND SUBSIDIARIES

We have learnt to write up the financial statements of a limited company. Let us now consider a situation where a limited company acquires control of *another* company by investing in its shares. We will still prepare financial statements for each company separately; but, if we wish to see the combined performance and the financial position of both together, we need to combine their Profit and Loss accounts and the Balance Sheets into a third set of financial statements. We refer to this third set as **group accounts**.

Let us assume that Tyrone Ltd invests £100,000 to buy all of the shares in Cork Ltd and that the Balance Sheets as at the date of acquisition appears as set out here. Each of these companies maintains its own books of accounts on a double entry basis. The Balance Sheets can be combined to produce a third Balance Sheet by merely aggregating the amounts stated in each line of the individual Balance Sheets. The combined Balance Sheet would then appear as shown on the following page (top left), but would suffer from a serious flaw. Making an investment of £100,000, Tyrone Ltd acquired the assets (net of liabilities) of Cork Ltd. The investment stated as an asset by Tyrone Ltd represents the individual assets and liabilities reported in Cork's Balance Sheet. Hence, by listing the investment as well as the net assets of Cork Ltd, the combined Balance Sheet would be double-counting the net assets in Cork. To avoid such double-counting, the investment reported as an asset by Tyrone should be offset against the Share Capital reported as a liability by Cork. The Consolidated Balance Sheet will then appear as shown on the following page (top right).

BALANCE SHEETS AS AT 31.12.20X0				
	Tyrone Ltd		Cork Ltd	
	£000	£000	£000	£000
Fixed assets		360		80
Investment in Cork		100		–
Stock in trade	420		160	
Debtors	275		115	
Cash and bank	45		15	
Creditors	(360)	380	(270)	20
		840		100
		£000		£000
Share Capital		740		100
Profit and Loss account		100		
		840		100

Where one company owns (or is in a position to control) another, the one controlling is referred to as a **parent company** and the one controlled as a **subsidiary**. Company law requires[1] every parent company to prepare group accounts in the form of a Consolidated Balance Sheet and a Consolidated Profit and Loss account.

CONSOLIDATED BALANCE SHEET AS AT 31.12.20X0			
		£000	£000
Fixed assets	360 + 80		440
Investments in Cork Ltd			100
Stock	420 + 160	580	
Debtors	275 + 115	390	
Cash and bank	45 + 15	60	
Creditors	360 + 270	(630)	400
			940
			£000
Share Capital – Tyrone			740
Share Capital – Cork			100
Profit for the year – Tyrone			100
			940

CONSOLIDATED BALANCE SHEET AS AT 31.12.20X0			
		£000	£000
Fixed assets	360 + 80		440
Stock	420 + 160	580	
Debtors	275 + 115	390	
Cash and bank	45 + 15	60	
Creditors	(360 + 270)	(630)	400
			840
			£000
Share Capital – Tyrone			740
Profit – Tyrone			100
			840

45.2 CONSOLIDATION AS A MEMORANDUM EXERCISE

BALANCE SHEETS AS AT 31.12.20X0				
	Alpha Ltd		Beta Ltd	
	£000	£000	£000	£000
Fixed assets		640		410
Investment in Beta Ltd		500		–
Stock in trade	540		340	
Debtors	480		285	
Cash and bank	35		25	
Creditors	(425)	630	(435)	215
		1,770		625
		£000		£000
Share Capital		1,000		400
Share premium		200		100
Profit for the year		570		125
		1,770		625

When shares are issued by a subsidiary company at a premium, the procedure on consolidation is to cancel the investment against the balances in the Share Capital and Share Premium accounts of the subsidiary company.

To illustrate, let us assume that:

- the Balance Sheets of Alpha Ltd and Beta Ltd appear as stated on the left;
- all of Beta's Share Capital was issued to Alpha at a premium;
- Alpha's Balance Sheet reports as an investment the amount it paid for the shares in Beta.

To consolidate both Balance Sheets, every asset and liability in both are aggregated, cancelling the investments reported by Alpha as an asset at £500,000 against the balances in Beta's books of £400,000 in the Share Capital account and £100,000 in the Share Premium account. The Consolidated Balance Sheet would therefore appear as stated below.

It is important to appreciate that the consolidated values of assets and liabilities are not recorded in either Alpha's or Beta's books. Consolidation is merely a memorandum exercise done at a point of time – i.e. on each Balance Sheet date. To facilitate the cancellation involved in the consolidation process, a memorandum account called the

CONSOLIDATED BALANCE SHEET AS AT 31 DECEMBER 20X0		
	£000	£000
Fixed assets (640 + 410)		1,050
Stock in trade (540 + 340)	880	
Debtors (480 + 285)	765	
Cash/bank (35 + 25)	60	
Creditors (425 + 435)	(860)	845
		1,895
		£000
Ordinary shares of £1 (Alpha)		1,000
Share Premium a/c (Alpha)		200
Profit and Loss a/c (570 + 125)		695
		1,895

Cost of Control account is opened. This account compares the amount (£500,000) that it cost Alpha to acquire control of Beta Ltd with the amounts on Beta's Balance Sheet against which it is cancelled. The Cost of Control account in respect of the illustration we considered would appear as shown below.

COST OF CONTROL ACCOUNT			
	£000		£000
Investments	500	Share Capital	400
		Share Premium	100

Consolidation of Balance Sheets

Interaction 45.1

On 1 January 20X0 Humpty Ltd incorporated a subsidiary named Dumpty Ltd, investing £900,000 in 600,000 ordinary shares of £1 each in Dumpty, issued at a premium of 50p each.

The Balance Sheets of both at the year end appear as shown on the right.

Required: Prepare the Consolidated Balance Sheet of Humpty group as at 31 December 20X0.

BALANCE SHEETS AS AT 31 DECEMBER 20X0				
	Humpty Ltd		Dumpty Ltd	
Fixed assets:	£000	£000	£000	£000
Fixed assets at cost		2,460		980
Accum. depreciation		(1,240)		(98)
		1,220		882
Investments in Dumpty Ltd		900		
Current assets:				
Stock in trade	946		528	
Debtors	522		396	
Cash and bank	72		46	
Creditors	(648)	892	(595)	375
		3,012		1,257
		£000		£000
Ordinary shares of £1 each		2,000		600
Share Premium account		400		300
Profit and Loss account		612		357
		3,012		1,257

45.3 GOODWILL ARISING FROM CONSOLIDATION

If, instead of incorporating a subsidiary, a parent acquires a subsidiary from a third party, the amount paid for acquiring the subsidiary may have to be more than the sum of the market values of the subsidiary's net assets. For example, let us assume that:

BETA LTD'S BALANCE SHEET AS AT 1.1.20X0	
	£000
Motor vehicle	150
Furniture	60
Stock	210
Cash	30
	450
	£000
Share Capital	300
Share Premium	150
	450

- on 1.1.20X0 Jack (a third party) incorporated Beta Ltd;
- Beta issued Jack with 300,000 ordinary shares of £1 each, at £1.50 per share;
- the Balance Sheet of Beta Ltd on the day of incorporation appears as shown on the right;
- although the net assets of Beta are reported at only £450,000, Alpha had to pay Jack £475,000 in order to acquire all the shares.

The premium of £25,000 that Alpha Ltd pays Jack to acquire control of Beta Ltd, making it a subsidiary, is referred to as goodwill on acquisition. Such goodwill arises only upon consolidation.

45.3.1 Accounting for goodwill

BALANCE SHEETS AS AT 31.12.20X0				
	Alpha Ltd		Beta Ltd	
	£000	£000	£000	£000
Fixed assets:				
Motor vehicles	890		290	
Accum. depreciation	(267)	623	(44)	246
Furniture	650		160	
Accum. depreciation	(130)	520	(11)	149
Investment in Beta Ltd		475		–
Current assets:				
Stock in trade	762		358	
Debtors	484		412	
Cash and bank	58		76	
Creditors	(567)		(414)	
Taxation	(112)	625	(94)	338
		2,243		733
		£000		£000
Ordinary shares of £1		1,500		300
Share Premium a/c		300		150
Profit and Loss a/c		443		283
		2,243		733

The accepted accounting practice is to account for goodwill as an asset on the Consolidated Balance Sheet and to amortize it (write it off) systematically over the estimated period that the goodwill is expected to be of value to the group.

Let us proceed to assume that:

- a year after acquisition the Balance Sheets of both companies have been prepared as stated on the left;
- the group policy is to amortize goodwill equally over five years.

The Cost of Control account (shown below) identifies the goodwill of £25,000 as follows:

COST OF CONTROL ACCOUNT				
	£000		£000	
Alpha Ltd's investment	475	Beta Ltd's Share Capital	300	
		Share Premium	150	
		Goodwill	25	*
	475		475	

* The balancing figure.

In accordance with group policy the goodwill is amortized equally over five years. This means that £5,000 of goodwill is written off against the Consolidated Profit and Loss account of the first year ending on 31 December 20X0. The Consolidated Balance Sheet of Alpha Ltd and its subsidiary Beta Ltd would appear as stated on the right. As stated already, the consolidation process is only a memorandum exercise. The consolidated amounts of assets (including the goodwill) and the liabilities are not recorded anywhere on a double entry basis. Hence, when the Balance Sheets of both Alpha and Beta are consolidated again one year later, on 31 December 20X1, the comparison of Alpha's investment (of £475,000) with Beta's Share Capital and Share Premium account balances on the date of acquisition (of £300,000 and £150,000 respectively) will again reveal that goodwill of £25,000 was paid at acquisition. By that time, two years will have elapsed since acquisition and hence two instalments (of £5,000 each) would be written off goodwill.

CONSOLIDATED BALANCE SHEET AS AT 31.12.20X0			
		£000	£000
Fixed assets:			
Goodwill on consolidation			20
Motor vehicles	(890 + 290)	1,180	
Acc. depreciation	(267 + 44)	(311)	869
Furniture and fittings	(650 + 160)	810	
Acc. depreciation	(130 + 11)	(141)	669
Current assets:			
Stock in trade	(762 + 358)	1,120	
Debtors	(484 + 412)	896	
Cash and bank	(58 + 76)	134	
Creditors	(567 + 414)	(981)	
Taxation	(112 + 94)	(206)	963
			2,521
			£000
Ordinary shares of £1 each			1,500
Share Premium account			300
Consolidated Profit and Loss (443 + 283 − 5)			721
			2,521

Focus on goodwill amortization

Interaction 45.2

Horner Ltd acquired all the ordinary shares in Corner Ltd for £540,000 immediately after the latter was incorporated on 1 January 20X0. Their Balance Sheets on 31 December 20X8 have been drafted as stated on the right.

The group policy is to amortize goodwill equally over five years.

Required: Prepare the group's Consolidated Balance Sheet as at 31 December 20X8.

BALANCE SHEETS AS AT 31 DECEMBER 20X8				
	Horner Ltd		**Corner Ltd**	
Fixed assets:	£000	£000	£000	£000
Fixed assets at cost		2,400		960
Accum. depreciation		(960)		(432)
		1,440		528
Investments		640		85
Current assets:				
Stock in trade	748		624	
Debtors	634		596	
Cash and bank	28		32	
Creditors	(597)		(688)	
Taxation	(112)	701	(72)	492
		2,781		1,105
		£000		£000
Ordinary shares of £1		1,200		400
Share Premium a/c		240		80
Profit and Loss reserve		1,341		625
		2,781		1,105

45.4 CANCELLATION OF INTER-COMPANY INDEBTEDNESS

CONSOLIDATED BALANCE SHEET AS AT 31 DECEMBER 20X0		
	£000	£000
Fixed assets (640 + 410)		1,050
Stock in trade (540 + 340)	880	
Debtors (480 + 285)	# 765	
Cash/bank (35 + 25)	60	
Creditors (425 + 435)	# (860)	845
		1,895
		£000
Ordinary shares of £1		1,000
Share premium account		200
Profit and Loss reserve (570 + 125)		695
		1,895

Let us refer back to the case of Alpha and Beta and assume this time that, reported within the debtors stated in Alpha Ltd's Balance Sheet, is an amount of £75,000 due from Beta Ltd. Unless there is any cash or goods in transit between the two companies, the creditors reported in Beta's Balance Sheet ought to include the same amount as owed to Alpha Ltd. In that case, the Consolidated Balance Sheet we prepared for both companies (as repeated on the left) would be wrong because it includes the amount owed by one company in the group to the other both as a debtor and as a creditor.

The double-counting of the inter-company indebtedness does not in any way impair the correctness of the *net assets* of the group, which have been correctly reported as £1,895,000. What it does do, however, is to exaggerate the amounts stated in the Consolidated Balance Sheet as amounts receivable from its customers and owed to its suppliers. To correct the position, the debtors in Alpha's Balance Sheet should be stated without including £75,000 due from Beta and, correspondingly, the creditors in Beta's Balance Sheet should be stated without including the amount it owes Alpha.

The Consolidated Balance Sheet after so cancelling inter-company indebtedness would appear as shown on the right.

CONSOLIDATED BALANCE SHEET AS AT 31 DECEMBER 20X0		
	£000	£000
Fixed assets (640 + 410)		1,050
Stock in trade (540 + 340)	880	
Debtors (480 + 285 – 75)	690	
Cash/bank (35 + 25)	60	
Creditors (425 + 435 – 75)	(785)	845
		1,895
		£000
Ordinary shares of £1		1,000
Share Premium account		200
Profit and Loss Reserve (570 + 125)		695
		1,895

Interaction 45.3

Cancellation of inter-company indebtedness

Refer back to IQ 45.1. In addition to the information provided in that question, you are informed that creditors reported in Humpty Ltd's Balance Sheet includes £122,000 owed to Dumpty Ltd.

Required: Prepare the Consolidated Balance Sheet of Humpty group as at 31.12.20X0.

45.4.1 Items in transit

The cancellation of inter-company indebtedness during a consolidation process is facilitated if both companies involved are in agreement as to the amount one owes the other. Disagreement, other than that arising from a dispute, could arise because of:

- cash remitted by one not having reached the other – referred to as *cash in transit*;
- goods dispatched by one not having reached the other – referred to as *goods in transit*.

For example, Alpha's books may report Beta as a debtor for £50,000, whereas Beta would insist that it owes Alpha no more than £40,000. The difference may have arisen because £10,000 remitted by Beta immediately prior to the date of reporting is yet to reach Alpha. It is necessary that items in transit should be sorted out before inter-company indebtedness is cancelled. Sorting out the items in transit would not constitute a problem if one remembers that:

- if the item is in transit between a parent company and a subsidiary, the adjustment should always be in the books of the parent; and
- if the item is in transit between two subsidiaries, the adjustment should be in the books of the transferor.

In the example we have used for illustration, the remittance of £10,000 in transit is accounted for in Alpha's books by debiting a Cash in Transit account and crediting the Debtors account. Thereupon Alpha and Beta would agree that they owe each other £40,000 and this amount is cancelled as part of the consolidation process.

Focus on items in transit

Interaction 45.4

Refer back to IQ 45.2. In addition to the information stated in that question, you are informed that included within the debtors reported in Horner's Balance Sheet is £84,000 due from Corner. Corner Ltd agrees with the amount subject to a remittance of £18,000 being in transit as at 31 December 20X8.

Required: Prepare the Consolidated Balance Sheet of the group as at 31.12.20X8.

Multiple-choice question on cancellation of debts

Interaction 45.5

Balance Sheets as at 31.12.20X0 for Georgie Ltd and its fully owned subsidiary Porgie Ltd stated the Personal Ledger balances as stated on the right.

	Georgie	Porgie
Debtors	£654,000	£462,000
Creditors	£485,000	£418,000

Required: Identify the amounts at which debtors' and creditor's balances should be stated on the Consolidated Balance Sheet as at 31.12.20X0 in each of the following independent circumstances:

(i) Georgie's debtors include £126,000 due from Porgie. As at 31.12.20X0, a remittance of £25,000 from Porgie remains in transit.

	Debtors	Creditors
a	£990,000	£928,000
b	£1,116,000	£802,000
c	£1,015,000	£903,000

(ii) Georgie's creditors include £182,000 owed to Porgie. As at 31.12.20X0 a remittance of £42,000 remains in transit.

	Debtors	Creditors
a	£892,000	£656,000
b	£957,000	£903,000
c	£1,116,000	£721,000

(iii) Georgie's creditors include £214,000 owed to Porgie. As at 31.12.20X0 goods invoiced at £72,000 and a remittance of £45,000 have yet to reach their destination.

	Debtors	Creditors
a	£925,000	£666,000
b	£1,116,000	£549,000
c	£808,000	£903,000

45.5 ACCOUNTING FOR DIVIDENDS

A proposed dividend, stated as a liability in any company's Balance Sheet, is not really payable unless the shareholders approve the payment when financial statements are presented to them. For this reason, a company earning dividend by investing in another company should not account for the earning until the dividend is received – i.e. dividend income is accounted for on cash basis. Where, however, the dividend income is earned from a subsidiary, the parent company is free to account for the dividend earnings prior to receiving it. This is because the parent, being in control of the subsidiary, could be certain of receiving it.

If a subsidiary, fully owned by the parent, reports as a liability a proposed dividend of £60,000, the parent would account for it as shown below. The balance in the income account is credited to the parent company's Profit and Loss account. The balance in the asset account represents an amount due from the subsidiary – being the counterpart of the dividend liability reported in the books of the subsidiary.

DIVIDEND RECEIVABLE (INCOME) ACCOUNT		DIVIDEND RECEIVABLE (ASSET) ACCOUNT	
	£		£
Div. receivable	60,000	Div. receivable	60,000

Being another inter-company indebtedness, the asset in the parent's book, as well as the liability in the subsidiary's books, is cancelled.

Interaction 45.6

Focus on inter-company dividend

Bopeep Ltd acquired all 500,000 ordinary shares of Sheep Ltd on 1.7.20X0 for £860,000, immediately after Sheep's incorporation. The Balance Sheets of both have been prepared as shown here. You are further informed as follows:

(a) Included in creditors reported by Bopeep is £94,000 owed to Sheep Ltd. Sheep agrees with the amount subject to the following:
  – goods in transit invoiced by Sheep at £12,000; and
  – a remittance of £5,000 to Sheep yet to be received.
(b) The group policy is to amortize goodwill equally over ten years.

Required: Prepare the Consolidated Balance Sheet of Bopeep Ltd group as at 30 June 20X4.

BALANCE SHEETS AS AT 30 JUNE 20X4				
	Bopeep Ltd		Sheep Ltd	
Fixed assets:	£000	£000	£000	£000
Machinery	400		–	
Acc. depreciation	(120)	280	–	–
Furniture	240		320	
Acc. depreciation	(86)	154	(112)	208
Motor vehicles	180		240	
Acc. depreciation	(96)	84	(86)	154
Investments		995		85
Current assets:				
Stock in trade	644		582	
Debtors	592		496	
Cash and bank	36		48	
Creditors	(496)		(612)	
Taxation	(112)		(98)	
Dividend proposed	(60)	604	(45)	371
		2,117		818
		£000		£000
Ordinary shares of £1 each		1,200		450
Share Premium account		240		90
Profit and Loss reserve		677		278
		2,117		818

45.6 ELIMINATION OF WITHIN-GROUP UNREALIZED PROFIT

Each company, even if fully owned by another, is legally a separate entity. If Alpha sells goods costing £300,000 for £450,000 to Beta, even though Beta is fully owned by Alpha, the profit of £150,000 is earned by Alpha and may well be distributed as dividend to its shareholders. But when the veil of separate legal personality is lifted and both Balance Sheets are consolidated, so that both companies are treated as a single economic entity, these goods cannot be reported at £450,000 because that is not what they cost the group. It becomes necessary, therefore, as part of the consolidation process, to remove the profit that *for group purposes* is yet to be earned, so that stock may be reported on the Consolidated Balance Sheet at what it cost the group (i.e. £300,000).

Profit made by a company by selling goods to another *within* the group is regarded as 'yet to be earned', to the extent that the goods involved remain unsold with that other company. For example, of the goods sold by Alpha for £450,000 to Beta, if one-third remains with Beta by the year end, £50,000 (a profit margin of one-third on unsold goods of £150,000) is regarded as unearned for consolidation purposes. Such profits not yet earned are referred to as 'unrealized profit' (see Chapter 29).

Unrealized profit is accounted for by debiting the Profit and Loss account of the company that made that profit and crediting (removing the profit from) the stock in which that profit is included. In our example, the Profit and Loss account of Alpha is debited and the stock held by Beta credited with £50,000. As a result the unsold stock with Beta is reported on the Consolidated Balance Sheet at £100,000 instead of £150,000.

Focus on unrealized profit

Interaction 45.7

Twinkle plc acquired 600,000 ordinary shares of Star plc for £720,000 immediately after Star was incorporated on 1 May 20X0. Balance Sheets of both companies have been prepared as stated on the right. You are further informed as follows:

(a) Stock stated in Star's Balance Sheet includes, at £144,000, goods sold to it by Twinkle at cost plus 20 per cent.

(b) Included in debtors reported by Twinkle is an amount of £214,000 receivable from Star, whereas Star reports the amount owed to Twinkle as £196,000. Cash in transit accounts for the difference.

(c) The group policy is to amortize goodwill equally over ten years.

Required: Prepare a Consolidated Balance Sheet as at 30 April 20X6.

BALANCE SHEETS AS AT 30 APRIL 20X6				
	Twinkle plc		Star plc	
Fixed assets:	£000	£000	£000	£000
Machinery	800		–	
Acc. depreciation	(240)	560	–	–
Furniture	240		280	
Acc. depreciation	(86)	154	(124)	156
Motor vehicles	180		320	
Acc. depreciation	(96)	84	(128)	192
Investments		845		75
Current assets:				
Stock in trade	592		594	
Debtors	688		412	
Cash and bank	84		78	
Creditors	(596)		(592)	
Taxation	(108)		(74)	
Dividend proposed	(75)	585	(60)	358
		2,228		781
		£000		£000
Ordinary shares of £1 each		1,500		600
Share Premium account		150		30
Profit and Loss reserve		578		151
		2,228		781

45.7 FREEZING PROFIT PRIOR TO ACQUISITION

Let us assume that Alpha Ltd paid £650,000 to acquire all the shares in Beta Ltd, not immediately upon Beta's incorporation but after Beta had already earned a profit of £80,000 and that on the date of acquisition Beta's net asset position was as reported on the right. Since £650,000 had been paid for acquiring net assets of £560,000, it should be obvious that the difference of £90,000 had been paid for goodwill. This position should emerge whenever the two companies' accounts are consolidated. To establish that, let us assume that the Balance Sheets of both companies, a year later on 31

BALANCE SHEET AS AT 31.12.20X0	
	£000
Ordinary shares	400
Share Premium	80
Profit and Loss	80
	560

December 20X1, have been prepared as shown on the left. Since acquisition by Alpha, Beta's net assets have improved by £100,000. This is known as the ***post-acquisition profit***. In the process of consolidation, when both Balance Sheets are aggregated line by line, only the post-acquisition portion of Beta's Profit and Loss account balance can be added to that in Alpha's to state the Consolidated Profit and Loss account balance as £660,000. The profit that Beta already had at the point of acquisition (£80,000) is referred to as '*pre-acquisition profit*' and it should be matched, along with the balances in Beta's Share Capital and Share Premium accounts, with the amount Alpha paid for the control, to report the goodwill at the same amount of £90,000 – see the Cost of Control account shown below.

BALANCE SHEETS AS AT 31.12.20X1				
	Alpha Ltd		**Beta Ltd**	
	£000	£000	£000	£000
Fixed assets		720		360
Investment in Beta Ltd		650		
Stocks	560		265	
Debtors	480		185	
Cash and bank	45		40	
Creditors	(395)	690	(190)	300
		2,060		660
		£000		£000
Ordinary shares of £1		1,200		400
Share Premium a/c		300		80
Profit and Loss a/c		560		180
		2,060		660

COST OF CONTROL ACCOUNT

	£000		£000
Investment	650	Share capital	400
		Share Premium	80
		Profit and Loss a/c	80
		Goodwill a/c	90

This process of transferring the pre-acquisition portion of the subsidiary's Profit and Loss account balance to the Cost of Control account (rather than to the Consolidated Profit and Loss account) is known as 'freezing'. The principle is that only whatever is earned by the subsidiary *from the date of acquisition* should be regarded as the earnings of the group. Any amount earned by the subsidiary prior to the acquisition is not a group earning because it has been paid for by the parent (Alpha Ltd).

Interaction 45.8

Freezing a subsidiary's pre-acquisition profit

Refer back to IQ 45.7 but assume this time that, when Twinkle plc paid £720,000 to acquire all shares in Star plc on 1 May 20X0, Star had been in existence for several years and had by that date a balance of £40,000 in its Profit and Loss account.

Required: Prepare the Consolidated Balance Sheet of the group as at 30.4.20X6.

45.8 FAIR VALUATION AT THE POINT OF ACQUISITION

When Alpha paid £650,000 to acquire all the shares in Beta and Beta's net assets were as stated on the right, we concluded that Alpha had paid (the difference of) £90,000 for goodwill. This would be correct if the market value (referred to as 'fair value') of Beta's net assets on the date of acquisition was exactly as stated on Beta's Balance Sheet. If, on the other hand, an asset reported by Beta is valued in the market at £50,000 more, the value of Beta's net assets would be £560,000 + £50,000 = £610,000. Hence by paying £650,000 for these net

BALANCE SHEET AS AT 31.12.20X0	
	£000
Ordinary shares	400
Share Premium a/c	80
Profit and Loss Reserve	80
	560

assets, Alpha would have acquired Beta's goodwill for £650,000 − £610,000 = £40,000. What this means is that for correctly ascertaining the amount at which goodwill is acquired, two steps should be taken as follows:

- Step one: One (or more) of the subsidiary's assets that, on the date of acquisition, has a fair value different from the book value should be written up (or down) to the fair value, crediting (or debiting) the difference to a Fair Valuation account.
- Step two: The balance in the Fair Valuation account would represent an additional gain (or loss) as at the date of acquisition, which should also be taken into account as part of the subsidiary's net assets for comparison with the amount paid for its control.

Fair valuation of subsidiary's assets at acquisition

Interaction 45.9

Farmer Giles plc paid £640,000 to acquire 400,000 ordinary shares of £1 each in Bingo plc on 1.1.20X3, when Bingo had a Profit and Loss account balance of £60,000 and its investments were quoted on the London Stock Exchange at £220,000. The fair value of Bingo's other assets and liabilities were approximately equal to their book values. The group policy is to amortize goodwill equally over five years.

Required: Prepare the Consolidated Balance Sheet of Farmer Giles plc group as at 31.12.20X6.

BALANCE SHEETS AS AT 31.12.20X6				
	Farmer Giles plc		Bingo plc	
Fixed assets:	**£000**	**£000**	**£000**	**£000**
Motor vehicles	840		240	
Accum. deprn	(360)	480	(80)	160
Investment		640		140
Current assets:				
Stocks	376		320	
Debtors	598		428	
Cash and bank	24		72	
Creditors	(465)		(396)	
Taxation	(98)		(64)	
Dividend	(80)	355	(40)	320
		1,475		620
		£000		**£000**
Ordinary shares £1		800		400
Share Premium a/c		120		40
Profit and Loss a/c		555		180
		1,475		620

45.9 PARTLY OWNED SUBSIDIARIES

To be identified as a subsidiary, a company need not be fully owned. If Beta is controlled by Alpha, the former is recognized as a subsidiary and the latter as a parent.[2] To control Beta, Alpha should normally hold a majority of votes in Beta. Where, as is usual, each share in Beta carries one vote, Alpha would be Beta's parent if Alpha holds more than 50 per cent of Beta's ordinary shares. Let us consider a scenario where Alpha holds a majority (rather than the whole) of Beta's shares. The directors of Alpha would then have control over the net assets of Alpha and (by virtue of majority votes) of *the whole of* the net assets of Beta.

To report this position in the Consolidated Balance sheet, the whole of Beta's assets and liabilities are aggregated with those of Alpha. Then the amount of Beta's net assets belonging to outside shareholders is acknowledged as a long-term liability, which is named a *minority interest*, by transferring the appropriate portion of Beta's Share Capital and Reserves to a Minority Interest account.

To illustrate, let us assume that stated on the right are the Balance Sheets of Alpha plc and its subsidiary Beta plc and that:

- When Alpha plc paid £540,000 to acquire 300,000 ordinary shares in Beta plc on 1.1.20X3, Beta had a Profit and Loss balance of £32,000.
- Fair value of Beta's assets and liabilities on the date of acquisition was equal to the book values.
- The group policy is to amortize goodwill equally over six years.

Alpha owns 75 per cent of Beta (i.e. 300,000/400,000). Net assets of Beta on the date of acquisition were worth £472,000 (see calculation on the right). To acquire 75 per cent of £472,000, Alpha paid £540,000. Thus Beta's goodwill has been acquired for £540,000 − (75% of 472,000) = £186,000. Since outsiders hold 25 per cent of Beta's shares, 25 per cent of Beta's net assets on 31.12.20X5 should be reported as belonging to the minority interest (in money terms 25 per cent of £560,000 = £140,000).

Apart from aggregating the *whole* of every class of Beta's assets and liabilities with those of Alpha, the consolidation process will proceed as follows to produce the results we identified above:

BALANCE SHEETS AS AT 31.12.20X5		
	Alpha	Beta
	£000	£000
Fixed assets	860	320
Investment in Beta	540	–
Stocks	348	245
Debtors	416	326
Cash and bank	42	52
Creditors	(394)	(315)
Taxation	(72)	(48)
Dividend	(100)	(20)
	1,640	560
	£000	£000
Ord. shares of £1	1,000	400
Share Premium a/c	200	40
Profit and Loss a/c	440	120
	1,640	560

Beta:	£000
Share Capital	400
Share Premium	40
Profit and Loss	32
	472

(a) 25% of the balances in Beta's Share Capital, Share Premium and Profit and Loss accounts are transferred to a Minority Interest account (see below) to confirm that £140,000 of the net assets in Beta belong to shareholders outside the group.

(b) Seventy-five per cent of Beta's Share Capital, Share Premium and pre-acquisition portion (only) of the Profit and Loss account balance are transferred to the Cost of Control account.

(c) The balancing amount in the Cost of Control account is the cost of goodwill, which is amortized equally over six years at £31,000 per year.

BETA'S SHARE CAPITAL ACCOUNT

		£000		£000
a	Minority int.	100	Balance b/f	400
b	Cost of cont.	300		

BETA'S SHARE PREMIUM ACCOUNT

		£000		£000
a	Minority int.	10	Balance b/f	40
b	Cost of cont.	30		

BETA'S PROFIT AND LOSS ACCOUNT

		£000		£000
a	Minority int.	30	Balance b/f	120
b	Cost of cont.	24		
d	Consol. P&L	66		

MINORITY INTEREST ACCOUNT

	£000		£000	
		Beta:		
		Share Capital	100	a
		Share Premium	10	a
		Profit and Loss a/c	30	a
			140	

COST OF CONTROL ACCOUNT

	£000		£000	
Investments	540	Beta:		
		Share Capital	300	b
		Share Premium	30	b
		P&L – pre-acqui.	24	b
		Goodwill	186	c

CONSOLIDATED PROFIT AND LOSS ACCOUNT

		£000		£000	
c	Goodwill	93	Alpha plc's P&L	440	
			Beta's dividend	15	e
	Balance c/d	428	Beta post-acquisition	66	d
			Balance b/d	428	

(d) Beta's post-acquisition profit is (£120,000 – £32,000) = £88,000. The group share of it (75% of £88,000) is transferred to the Consolidated Profit and Loss account.

(e) Since Alpha holds only 75 per cent of shares in Beta, it could account for only 75 per cent of the dividend proposed by Beta. This is accounted for by debiting the Dividend Receivable (asset) account and crediting a Dividend Receivable (income) account with £15,000. The income is credited to the Consolidated Profit and Loss account. When, for cancellation of inter-company indebtedness, the asset is offset against the corresponding liability (dividend proposed) reported by Beta, an amount of £5,000 will be left in the liability account. This is the dividend that Beta plc proposes to pay minority shareholders. This should be stated in the Consolidated Balance Sheet with a suitable description among the current liabilities.

The Consolidated Balance Sheet as at 31 December 20X5 of Alpha and its partly owned subsidiary Beta would therefore appear as stated on the right.

CONSOLIDATED BALANCE SHEET AS AT 31.12.20X5

		£000
Fixed assets:		
Intangible – goodwill		93
Tangible		1,180
Current assets:		
Stocks	593	
Debtors	742	
Cash and bank	94	
Creditors due within one year		
Creditors	(709)	
Taxation	(120)	
Dividend payable to minority	(5)	
Dividend proposed	(100)	
Net current assets		495
		1,768
		£000
Capital and reserves:		
Called-up capital	1,000	
Share Premium account	200	
Consolidated Profit and Loss	428	1,628
Minority interest		140
		1,768

When consolidating partly owned subsidiaries, there would also arise a necessity to undertake the usual consolidation adjustments such as:

● cancellation of inter-company indebtedness;
● elimination of unrealized profit and;
● freezing the pre-acquisition profit of the subsidiary.

Whereas only the group share (in our example, 75 per cent) of the subsidiary's pre-acquisition profit is frozen (by transfer to the Cost of Control account) the whole of the inter-company indebtedness and unrealized profit[3] (rather than the group portion only) needs to be cancelled.

Interaction 45.10

Consolidated Balance Sheet with a partly owned subsidiary

Georgie Ltd paid £450,000 to acquire 300,000 ordinary shares of £1 each in Porgie Ltd on 1.1.20X2 when Porgie Ltd had a Profit and Loss account balance of £64,000 and its investments were quoted in the share market at £376,000. You are informed as follows:

(a) Stock held by Porgie as at 31.12.20X4 includes goods sold to it by Georgie for £84,000 at cost plus 20 per cent.
(b) Debtors stated in Georgie's Balance Sheet includes £48,000 due from Porgie. Porgie agrees with the amount subject to a remittance of £15,000 that it believes is in transit on this date.
(c) Group policy is to amortize goodwill equally over five years.

Required: Prepare the Consolidated Balance Sheet as at 31.12.20X4.

BALANCE SHEETS AS AT 31.12.20X4	Georgie	Porgie
	£000	£000
Tangible assets	720	440
Acc. depreciation	(284)	(176)
	436	264
Investments	625	340
Stock	598	296
Debtors	462	312
Cash and bank	34	28
Creditors	(396)	(398)
Taxation	(122)	(54)
Dividend	(75)	(40)
	1,562	748
	£000	£000
Ordinary shares of £1	1,000	400
Share Premium a/c	100	40
Profit and Loss a/c	462	308
	1,562	748

Interaction 45.11

Multiple-choice question on elimination unrealized profit

Wool Ltd is a subsidiary of Sheep plc. Identify the unrealized profit to be eliminated as at the Balance Sheet date, for purposes of consolidation, in each of the following alternative situations:

(i) Sheep plc holds £243,000 of goods invoiced to it by Wool Ltd, its fully owned subsidiary, at cost plus 50 per cent.

a	£121,500	
b	£60,450	
c	£81,000	

(ii) In addition to the information stated in (i) above, £63,000 worth of goods invoiced by Wool Ltd on the same terms remain in transit.

a	£81,000	
b	£102,000	
c	£153,000	

(iii) Wool Ltd holds £360,000 worth of goods invoiced to it by its parent Sheep plc. Sheep owns 80 per cent of Wool's equity and fixes its sale price to produce a gross profit ratio of 25 per cent.

a	£120,000	
b	£90,000	
c	£72,000	

References

1. Companies Act 1985, s. 229.
2. Companies Act 1985, s. 229.
3. FRS 10: *Goodwill and Intangible Assets*.

SOLUTIONS TO INTERACTIVE QUESTIONS

IQ 45.1 Consolidation of Balance Sheets

Note that when companies in a group are consolidated, to report their combined position as if they together constitute a single entity, amounts owing to each other within the group (intra-group indebtedness) are cancelled.

CONSOLIDATED BALANCE SHEET AS AT 31.12.20X0		£000	£000
Fixed assets:			
Fixed assets	(2,460 + 980)		3,440
Acc. depreciation	(1,240 + 98)		(1,338)
			2,102
Current assets:			
Stock in trade	(946 + 528)	1,474	
Debtors	(522 + 396)	918	
Cash and bank	(72 + 46)	118	
Creditors	(648 + 595)	(1,243)	1,267
			3,369
			£000
Ordinary shares of £1 each			2,000
Share Premium account			400
Profit and Loss a/c (612 + 357)			969
			3,369

IQ 45.2 Focus on goodwill amortization

For the consolidation, although nine years since the acquisition, the Cost of Control a/c identifies the same amount of goodwill as it would have in each of the previous eight years as follows:

COST OF CONTROL ACCOUNT

	£000		£000
Horner's Investments	540	*Corner's* Share Capital	400
		Share Premium	80
		Goodwill a/c	60

Every year, from the first one ending on 31 December 20X0, one-fifth of goodwill (£12,000) would have been written off. Hence, by the year ending 31 December 20X4, the whole of goodwill would have been amortized. Consolidated profit is reduced by goodwill. Note that both companies have investments in companies outside the group.

CONSOLIDATED BALANCE SHEET AS AT 31.12.20X8		£000	£000
Fixed assets	(2,400 + 960)		3,360
Acc. depreciation	(960 + 432)		(1,392)
			1,968
Investments	(100 + 85)		185
Current assets:			
Stock in trade	(748 + 624)	1,372	
Debtors	(634 + 596)	1,230	
Cash and bank	(28 + 32)	60	
Creditors	(597 + 688)	(1,285)	
Taxation	(112 + 72)	(184)	1,193
			3,346
			£000
Ordinary shares of £1			1,200
Share Premium account			240
Profit and Loss reserve (1,341 + 625 − 60)			1,906
			3,346

IQ 45.3 Cancellation of inter-company indebtedness

Note, again, that when companies in a group are consolidated in order to report their combined position as if they together constituted single entity, amounts owing to each other within the group (intra-group indebtedness) are cancelled.

The cancellation of the amount owed by Humpty to Dumpty (£122,000) does not affect the group's combined net assets, which remain £3,369,000.

CONSOLIDATED BALANCE SHEET AS AT 31.12.20X0

		£000	£000
Fixed assets:			
Fixed assets	(2,460 + 980)		3,440
Acc. depreciation	(1,240 + 98)		(1,338)
			2,102
Current assets:			
Stock in trade	(946 + 528)	1,474	
Debtors	(522 + 396 − 122)	796	
Cash and bank	(72 + 46)	118	
Creditors	(648 + 595 − 122)	(1,121)	1,267
			3,369

	£000
Ordinary shares of £1	2,000
Share Premium account	400
Profit and Loss a/c (612 + 357)	969
	3,369

IQ 45.4 Focus on items in transit

The cancellation of inter-company indebtedness is done as follows:

In Horner's books	£000	In Corner's books	£000
Debtors	634	Creditors	688
Cash in transit	(18)		
Cancellation	(66)	Cancellation	(66)
	550		622

Once Horner Ltd records the cash in transit, it would concede that only £66,000 is due from Corner Ltd. Having agreed on the amount of inter-company indebtedness, it is eliminated as part of the consolidation process. However, care should be taken to include the amount of cash in transit within the group's cash and bank balance.

The revised Consolidated Balance Sheet would appear as shown on the right.

CONSOLIDATED BALANCE SHEET AS AT 31.12.20X8

		£000	£000
Fixed assets	(2,400 + 960)		3,360
Acc. depreciation	(960 + 432)		(1,392)
			1,968
Investments	(100 + 85)		185
Current assets:			
Stock in trade	(748 + 624)	1,372	
Debtors	(550 + 596)	1,146	
Cash and bank	(28 + 32 + 18)	78	
Creditors	(597 + 622)	(1,219)	
Taxation	(112 + 72)	(184)	1,193
			3,346

	£000
Ordinary shares of £1	1,200
Share Premium account	240
Profit and Loss reserve (1,341 + 625 − 60)	1,906
	3,346

IQ 45.5 Multiple-choice question on cancellation of debts

(i) a, b;　　(ii) a, c;　　(iii) c, a.

IQ 45.6 Focus on inter-company dividend

1. Goodwill, ascertained as £320,000, is written off in ten equal instalments of £32,000. By 30.6.20X4 four instalments (£128,000) would be written off, leaving £192,000 to be reported as an asset.

2. Bopeep thought that the amount owed to Sheep was £94,000. Since a remittance of £5,000 is yet to reach Sheep, the amount is credited back to the Creditors account and debited to the Cash in Transit account. As a result, the amount owed to Sheep increases by that amount.

   When advised of goods in transit, a Goods in Transit account is debited and Creditors account credited with the invoice value of £12,000. When this too is taken into account, Bopeep owes Sheep (£94,000 + £5,000 + £12,000), namely £111,000, which then is the amount of inter-company indebtedness requiring to be cancelled.

3. Bopeep Ltd accounts for the dividend receivable from Sheep Ltd as follows:

COST OF CONTROL ACCOUNT

	£000		£000
Investments	860	Share Capital	450
		Share Premium	90
		Goodwill a/c	320

Bopeep's books	£000	Sheep's books	£000
Creditors	496	Debtors	496
Goods in transit	12		
Cash in transit	5		
Cancellation	(111)	Cancellation	(111)
	402		385

DIVIDEND RECEIVABLE (INCOME) ACCOUNT

	£000		£000
		Div. receivable	45

DIVIDEND RECEIVABLE (ASSET) ACCOUNT

	£000		£000
Div. receivable	45		

The income is credited to its Profit and Loss account and the asset, being another inter-company indebtedness, is cancelled against the liability in Sheep's books.

CONSOLIDATED BALANCE SHEET AS AT 30 JUNE 20X4

Fixed assets:		£000	£000
Intangible asset – Goodwill			192
Machinery	(400 + 0)	400	
Accum. depreciation	(120 + 0)	(120)	280
Furniture	(240 + 320)	560	
Accum. depreciation	(86 + 112)	(198)	362
Motor vehicles	(180 + 240)	420	
Accum. depreciation	(96 + 86)	(182)	238
Investments	(135 + 85)		220
Current assets:			
Stock in trade	(644 + 582 + 12)	1,238	
Debtors	(592 + 385)	977	
Cash and bank	(36 + 48 + 5)	89	
Creditors	(402 + 612)	(1,014)	
Taxation	(112 + 98)	(210)	
Dividend proposed	(60)	(60)	1,020
			2,312
			£000
Ordinary shares of £1 each			1,200
Share Premium account			240
Profit and Loss a/c (677 + 278 + 45 – 128)			872
			2,312

IQ 45.7 Focus on unrealized profit

1. Unrealized profit of £24,000 (one-sixth of £144,000) is eliminated from Twinkle's Profit and Loss account and the stock with Star.
2. Cancellation of inter-company indebtedness is shown on the right.

	Twinkle Debtors	Star Creditors
As reported in question	688	592
Cash in transit	(18)	–
Cancellation of inter-company debt	(196)	(196)
	474	396

3. Twinkle accounts for £60,000 dividend receivable from Star, debiting an asset account (which is cancelled against the liability in Star's books) and crediting an income account (which is reported in its Profit and Loss account).
4. Goodwill on acquisition is ascertained as shown in the Cost of Control account below. Since goodwill is amortized at £9,000 per year, £54,000 would have been written off by 30.4.20X6.
5. The consolidation adjustments made in Twinkle's Profit and Loss account are shown below (right).

COST OF CONTROL ACCOUNT

Twinkle's	£000	Star's	£000
Investment	720	Share Capital	600
		Share Premium	30
		Goodwill	90

PROFIT AND LOSS ACCOUNT

	£000		£000
Unrealized profit	24	Balance b/f	578
Goodwill w/off	54	Dividend – Star's	60
Balance c/d	711	Star plc	151
		Balance b/d	711

CONSOLIDATED BALANCE SHEET AS AT 30.4.20X6

		£000	£000
Fixed assets:			
Intangible assets: goodwill			36
Plant and machinery	(800 + 0)	800	
Acc. depreciation	(240 + 0)	(240)	560
Furniture and fittings	(240 + 280)	520	
Acc. depreciation	(86 + 124)	(210)	310
Motor vehicles	(180 + 320)	500	
Acc. depreciation	(96 + 128)	(224)	276
Investments	(845 − 720) + 75		200
Current assets:			
Stock in trade	592 + (594 − 24)	1,162	
Debtors	(474 + 412)	886	
Cash and bank	(84 + 18 + 78)	180	
Creditors	(596 + 396)	(992)	
Taxation	(108 + 74)	(182)	
Dividend proposed	(75)	(75)	979
			2,361

	£000
Ordinary shares of £1	1,500
Share Premium	150
Consolidated Profit and Loss account	711
	2,361

IQ 45.8 Freezing a subsidiary's pre-acquisition profit

CONSOLIDATED BALANCE SHEET AS AT 30.4.20X6

		£000	£000
Fixed assets:			
Intangible assets: goodwill			20
Plant and machinery	(800 + 0)	800	
Acc. depreciation	(240 + 0)	(240)	560
Furniture and fittings	(240 + 280)	520	
Acc. depreciation	(86 + 124)	(210)	310
Motor vehicles	(180 + 320)	500	
Acc. depreciation	(96 + 128)	(224)	276
Investments	(845 − 720) + 75		200
Current assets:			
Stock in trade	592 + (594 − 24)	1,162	
Debtors	(474 + 412)	886	
Cash and bank	(84 + 18 + 78)	180	
Creditors	(596 + 396)	(992)	
Taxation	(108 + 74)	(182)	
Dividend proposed	(75)	(75)	979
			2,345

	£000
Ordinary shares of £1	1,500
Share Premium	150
Consolidated Profit and Loss account	695
	2,345

Workings:

COST OF CONTROL ACCOUNT

	£000		£000
Investment	720	Star's:	
		Share Capital	600
		Share Premium a/c	30
		P&L – pre-acqui.	40
		Goodwill	50

STAR'S PROFIT AND LOSS ACCOUNT

	£000		£000
Cost of control	40	Balance	151
Consol. P&L	111		

CONSOLIDATED PROFIT AND LOSS ACCOUNT

	£000		£000
Unrealized profit	24	Twinkle's P&L	578
Goodwill w/off	30	Dividend receivable	60
Balance c/d	695	Star's P&L – post-acquisition	111
		Balance b/d	695

When Twinkle paid £720,000 Star's net assets were £670,000 (not £630,000 as stated in IQ45.7) because it had, by then, earned £40,000.

IQ 45.9 Fair valuation of subsidiary's assets at acquisition

To state Bingo's investments at fair value on the date of acquisition, £80,000 is debited to the Investments account and credited to the Fair Valuation account. Hence the net assets of Bingo plc as at 1.1.20X3 would have been £580,000 (see box below), for which Farmer Giles plc paid £640,000. The amount paid for goodwill, therefore, is £640,000 – £580,000 = £60,000.

Note that in the Consolidated Balance Sheet the investment held by Bingo plc is described as 'at cost'. This is because to the group these investments have cost £220,000.

The consolidated Profit and Loss account balance is made up as shown on the left.

Bingo plc assets	£000
Share Capital	400
Share Premium	40
Fair Valuation a/c	80
Profit and Loss	60
Net assets	580

Consolidated P&L a/c	£000
Farmer Giles P&L	555
Dividend – Bingo	40
Bingo P&L – post-acq.	120
Goodwill w/off	(48)
	667

CONSOLIDATED BALANCE SHEET AS AT 31.12.20X6		£000	£000
Fixed assets:			
Goodwill			12
Motor vehicles	(840 + 240)	1,080	
Acc. depreciation	(360 + 80)	(440)	640
Investment at cost			220
Current assets:			
Stocks	(376 + 320)	696	
Debtors	(598 + 428)	1,026	
Cash and bank	(24 + 72)	96	
Creditors	(465 + 396)	(861)	
Taxation	(98 + 64)	(162)	
Dividend	(80)	(80)	715
			1,587

	£000
Ordinary shares of £1	800
Share Premium account	120
Consolidated Profit and Loss a/c	667
	1,587

IQ 45.10 Consolidated Balance Sheet with a partly owned subsidiary

CONSOLIDATED BALANCE SHEET AS AT 31 DECEMBER 20X4		£000	£000	
Fixed assets:				
Intangible – goodwill			18	d
Tangible assets	(720 + 440)	1,160		
Acc. depreciation	(284 + 176)	(460)	700	
Investments	(175 + 376)		551	a
Current assets:				
Stocks	(598 + 296 – 14)	880		e
Debtors	(414 + 312)	726		f
Cash and bank	(34 + 28 + 15)	77		f
Creditors	(396 + 365)	(761)		f
Taxation	(122 + 54)	(176)		
Dividend payable to minority		(10)		g
Dividend proposed		(75)	661	
			1,930	
			£000	
Capital and Reserves:				
Ordinary shares of £1 each		1,000		
Share Premium account		100		
Consolidated Profit and Loss a/c		634	1,734	h
Minority interest			196	b
			1,930	

Notes:

(a) Porgie's investments, on the date of acquisition, are written up to their fair value, the gain being stated in a Fair Valuation account:

PORGIE'S INVESTMENTS ACCOUNT

	£000		£000
Balance b/f	340		
Fair Valuation a/c	36		

(b) Twenty-five per cent of the balances in Porgies' Share Capital, Share Premium, Fair Valuation and Profit and Loss accounts are transferred to a Minority Interest account:

MINORITY INTEREST ACCOUNT

	£000		£000
		Share Capital	100
		Share Premium	10
		Fair valuation	9
		Profit and Loss	77
			196

(c) Seventy-five per cent of balances in Porgie's Share Capital, Share Premium and Fair valuation accounts and 75 per cent of Porgie's pre-acquisition profit are matched, in a Cost of Control account, with the amount Georgie paid for the control, to determine the amount paid for goodwill as £45,000.

(d) In accordance with group policy, goodwill is amortized equally over five years at £9,000 per year. Since three years have passed since acquisition, £27,000 is written off to the Consolidated Profit and Loss account and the balance is stated in the Consolidated Balance Sheet as an intangible asset.

(e) Unrealized profit, calculated as one-sixth of £84,000, is debited to the Consolidated Profit and Loss account and credited to (removed from) Porgie's stock.

(f) £15,000 in transit from Porgie is accounted for in Georgie's books, crediting debtors and debiting cash in transit. Thereafter both parties would agree that the amount owed to each other is £33,000 and this amount is the inter-company indebtedness to be cancelled.

(g) Georgie would account for only 75 per cent of the dividend that Porgie proposes to pay. £30,000, which would then be stated as Dividend Receivable (an asset) in Georgie's books, is offset against the Dividend Proposed (liability) stated in Porgie's books, to leave a balance liability of £10,000 payable to minority.

(h) Out of the balance of £308,000 in Porgie's P&L, £64,000 was earned prior to acquisition. Hence 75 per cent of the post-acquisition profit of (£308,000 − £64,000) is recognized as the amount earned by the group.

COST OF CONTROL ACCOUNT

	£000		£000
Investments	450	Share Capital	300
		Share Premium	30
		Fair valuation	27
		Profit and Loss	48
		Goodwill	45

Georgie's debtors	£000	Porgies's creditors	£000
Balance b/f	462	Balance b/f	398
Cash in transit	(15)		
Inter-co. debt	(33)	Inter-co. debt	(33)
	414		365

CONSOLIDATED PROFIT AND LOSS ACCOUNT

		£000		£000	
e	Unrealized profit	14	Georgie's P&L	462	
d	Goodwill w/off	27	Dividend receivable	30	g
	Balance c/d	634	Porgie's post-acqui.	183	h

IQ 45.11 Multiple-choice question on elimination of unrealized profit

(i) c;   (ii) b;   (iii) b.

PROGRESSIVE QUESTIONS

PQ 45.1 Consolidation of Balance Sheets (with no pre-acquisition profit)

Muffet plc paid £720,000 to acquire all the shares in Tuffet plc soon after the latter was incorporated on 1 April 20X0. Their Balance Sheets have been drafted as shown here.

You are further informed as follows:

(a) Stock held by Muffet plc on 31 March 20X5 includes goods sold to it by Tuffet for £176,000 at cost plus one-third.

(b) Creditors stated in Muffet plc's Balance Sheet includes £246,000 owed to Tuffet. Tuffet's Balance Sheet includes Muffet as a debtor for £285,000. The difference has arisen from the following:
  – further goods invoiced by Tuffet at £24,000 (at cost plus one-third), which are yet to be received by Muffet plc;
  – a remittance in transit.

(c) The group policy is to amortize goodwill equally over ten years.

Required: Prepare the Consolidated Balance Sheet of Muffet plc group as at 31 March 20X5.

BALANCE SHEETS AS AT 31 MARCH 20X5

	Muffet plc		Tuffet plc	
Fixed assets:	£000	£000	£000	£000
Plant and machinery	720		540	
Acc. depreciation	(312)	408	(146)	394
Furniture and fittings	240		240	
Acc. depreciation	(108)	132	(96)	144
Investments		845		35
Current assets:				
Stock in trade	412		524	
Debtors	622		412	
Cash and bank	44		26	
Creditors	(594)		(468)	
Taxation	(112)		(64)	
Dividend proposed	(90)	282	(60)	370
		1,667		943
		£000		£000
Ordinary shares of 50p		900		500
Share Premium account		135		100
Profit and Loss account		632		343
		1,667		943

PQ 45.2 Group accounts involving pre-acquisition profits with a subsidiary

Willie plc paid £840,000 to acquire 600,000 ordinary shares of £1 each in Winkie plc on 1 January 20X0, when investments held by Winkie had a market value £60,000 in excess of book value and Winkie's Profit and Loss account balance was £96,000. The Balance Sheets of both companies have been set out on the right. Amounts stated on the Balance Sheets include the following:

(a) within Willie's stock, there are goods sold to it at £200,000 by Winkie;
(b) within Willie's creditors, £146,000 is owed to Winkie;
(c) within Winkie's debtors, £214,000 is receivable from Willie.

You are further informed as follows:

● Goods invoiced at £40,000 by Winkie to Willie remain in transit.
● Cash in transit explains any difference in trade debts.
● Winkie invoices goods to Willie at cost plus 25 per cent.
● The group policy is to amortize goodwill equally over six years.

Required: Prepare the Consolidated Balance Sheet for Willie plc group as at 31 December 20X6.

BALANCE SHEETS AS AT 31.12.20X6

	Willie	Winkie
	£000	£000
Fixed assets at cost	960	640
Acc. depreciation	(240)	(180)
	720	460
Investments	840	150
Stock in trade	754	620
Debtors	592	732
Cash and bank	74	16
Creditors	(654)	(548)
Taxation	(112)	(94)
Dividend proposed	(150)	(80)
	2,064	1,256
	£000	£000
Ordinary shares – £1	1,500	800
Share Premium a/c	300	80
Profit and Loss a/c	264	376
	2,064	1,256

INFLATION ACCOUNTING

In this chapter

We will learn of:

- inadequacy of accounts prepared on a historical cost basis
- current purchasing power (CPP) accounting
- current cost accounting (CCA)

46.1 INTRODUCTION

Until now, we have seen that business organizations have recorded their transactions at the cost *at the time* that they entered into the transactions. This is referred to as historical cost accounting (HCA). Before explaining alternatives to historical cost accounting, we will discuss its limitations by considering the four questions set out next.

46.1.1 Are the turnover and profit in the Profit and Loss account and the capital employed in the Balance Sheet comparable over time?

When making a prediction about the future, investors consider trends such as the rate of growth of turnover and rate of change in the return on capital employed over a period of say 3–5 years. However, HCA can be misleading because it does not take into account the impact of inflation. There may be apparent increases in turnover, profit or capital employed simply arising from the effect of the falling value of money, although there may have been no growth in real terms.

It is customary in the United Kingdom to measure inflation using the retail price index (RPI). The RPI measures changes in the average price of a collection of consumer goods as they affect the average household. It is published monthly. The UK government has currently set an annual inflation target of 2.5 per cent, and it is expected that the Bank of England will manage interest rates to achieve this target.

The RPI can be used as a means of restating historical figures in order to be able to compare years. For example, let us assume that Smooth Sailing Ltd reported turnover of £1,000,000 for each of the five years ended 31 March 1999. From the HCA accounts, the implication would be of a stable volume of sales. However, the RPI at 31 March in each relevant year was as follows:

Year ended 31 March	1995	1996	1997	1998	1999
RPI	147.5	151.5	155.4	160.8	164.1

If we restate the turnover in 1999 prices for each year using the RPI, the trend is as follows:

1995	£1,000,000 × 164.1/147.5 = £1,112,542
1996	£1,000,000 × 164.1/151.5 = £1,083,168
1997	£1,000,000 × 164.1/155.4 = £1,055,984
1998	£1,000,000 × 164.1/160.8 = £1,020,522
1999	£1,000,000 × 164.1/164.1 = £1,000,000

In real terms there has been a fall of 10 per cent in turnover since 1995.

46.1.2 Is the profit after tax a fair indication of the amount that an organization can afford to pay its owners and still maintain the level of net assets to support its current level of operations?

If the HCA profit after tax were fully distributed to the owners, then an organization would not be able to maintain its net assets at their current physical levels during times of inflation. The reasons include (a) charging insufficient depreciation, so that over the life of a fixed asset the accumulated depreciation provisions will be insufficient to provide for replacement at a higher replacement cost, and (b) charging insufficient in the Trading account for the cost of goods sold, so that the organization is unable to meet the increased cost of replacement.

For example, let us assume that a car dealer purchased a car for £10,000, held it in stock for three months, after which it was sold for £15,000. HCA accounts would record a profit of £5,000. However, if the cost of the next car rose to £13,500 then the dealer must retain £3,500 to finance the replacement of stock and the true profit is only £1,500.

46.1.3 Are the asset values in the Balance Sheet realistic?

Although current assets and current liabilities may approximate to their current value, the fixed assets may be carried at their depreciated historical cost, which might well bear little relation to their true current value.

Companies might revalue properties and maintain these at approximate current values by regular revaluation. Other fixed assets will, however, be reported at depreciated historical cost. It is not therefore possible for an investor to ascertain from HCA accounts the value of the business assets employed, nor to compare the entity's return on capital employed with those of other organizations.

46.1.4 Are the liability values in the Balance Sheet realistic?

Liabilities such as loans are recorded at the amount that is repayable. However, a borrower gains purchasing power during a period of inflation, while a lender loses to a similar extent. For example, a business that kept £10,000,000 on current account from 31 March 1995 to 31 March 1999 would have sustained an erosion of purchasing power of £11,125,423 [(£10,000,000/164.1 × 147.5) − £10,000,000]. Although this may be compensated for partly or wholly by interest received, HCA accounts do not measure this erosion of purchasing power.

46.2 WHAT IS INFLATION?

We can see from the above that we are considering two types of inflation.

One is the fall in the value of money, which affects *monetary assets* or liabilities such as cash, debtors, creditors and loan capital because the amount of these is fixed by contract regardless of changes in the general level of prices. We can measure the impact of the changing value of money by using a general price index, i.e. the RPI. The method of accounting for inflation using the RPI to restate the HCA accounts is generally known as current purchasing power (CPP) accounting.

The other is the change in the replacement cost of *non-monetary assets* such as fixed assets and stock. We can measure the impact of the changing value of the assets with which the business operates by using specific indices appropriate to the particular asset being considered, e.g. a computer hardware index, a commercial vehicle index etc. The method of accounting for inflation using specific indices to restate the HCA accounts is generally known as current cost accounting (CCA).

Each of these methods – CPP and CCA – is considered further below.

Measurement of profit in times of inflation

Interaction
46.1

Hymie Gold bought a house outside London in 1995 for £100,000. The house was valued in 1999 at £150,000. If he sells and moves closer to London he will need to pay £185,000 for a similar property.

Required: Discuss the following statements:

(a) Hymie has made a profit of £50,000.
(b) Hymie has made a profit of £38,745 after adjusting for an increase in the RPI:
 $\{£150,000 - [(100,000/147.5) \times 164.1]\}$.
(c) Hymie has made no profit because the replacement cost of his house is £150,000.

46.3 CURRENT PURCHASING POWER (CPP) ACCOUNTING

When we restate the historical cost of the items in the Profit and Loss account and Balance Sheet using the RPI, we are substituting a unit of purchasing power in place of the pound sterling. The effect of this is not to revalue the assets to a current value but simply to revalue the purchasing power of the money originally invested in those assets or being derived from those liabilities. This means that the CPP units attributed to non-monetary assets in the Balance Sheet will frequently bear no relation to their current market value.

Income and expenditure, assets and liabilities are all reported in pounds sterling in the financial accounts under the money-measurement concept at the cost incurred at the date of the transaction. Because the transactions will have occurred at different times, under CPP accounting we convert the monetary units to a common unit of purchasing power, i.e. by restating from the RPI at date of transaction to RPI at the date of the current Balance Sheet. This applies to the current year's accounts and also to the comparative figures from the previous year.

46.3.1 Non-monetary assets

These are restated applying the end of year RPI.

Interaction 46.2	**Non-monetary asset expressed in CPP unit**

Onslow Ltd is preparing its accounts for the year ended 30 June 20X1. On 1 July 20X0 the company had purchased machinery for £50,000. The RPI was 163.4 on 1 July 20X0 and 165.6 on 30 June 20X1. In the HCA accounts, the cost of the machinery will be shown as £50,000 on 30 June 20X1. In the CPP accounts, the £50,000 will be converted to the equivalent purchasing-power units at the end of the year. This would give £C50,673 [(50,000/163.4) × 165.6]. The director asked the accountant whether this meant that the machinery was now valued at £50,673.

Required: Explain to the director what the CPP figure represents.

46.3.2 Monetary assets

The end-of-year assets (cash, bank and debtors) and liabilities (creditors and loans) are not restated but the opening figures are restated in order to calculate the gain from owing money or the loss from being owed money.

Interaction 46.3	**Monetary assets/liabilities expressed in CPP unit**

Onslow Ltd has owed Mean Ltd £50,000 for the whole year. In the HCA accounts, the Balance Sheets at 30 June 20X0 and 30 June 20X1 will both show a figure of £50,000. However, Onslow Ltd will have gained purchasing power because the RPI general price level has risen. This means that the real value of £50,000 has declined over the year and it will therefore cost the company less to repay Mean Ltd.

In the 20X1 CPP accounts, the liability will be stated at £50,000 because it is a monetary liability with a value fixed at £50,000. The 20X0 comparative figure will be restated to the current end-year purchasing-power value i.e. £CPP50,673. The effect of this is to report that a liability of £CPP50,673 at 1 July 20X0 is only £C50,000 at 30 June 20X1, i.e. that there is a gain of £CPP673 through holding a monetary liability. The director of Onslow Ltd has asked you whether this £CPP673 could be distributed.

Required: Advise the director.

46.3.3 Shareholders' equity

Capital maintenance is an important aspect of CPP accounting. It is a *shareholder-based* approach that looks at the impact of inflation from the point of view of the shareholders. Only if the capital invested by the shareholders has maintained its purchasing power can the company be considered to have made a profit. This is achieved by excluding the amount required to bring the shareholders' equity back to its original purchasing power from the disclosed CPP profit. If the company were to pay a dividend in excess of the CPP profit – for instance, paying the whole of the historical cost profit as a dividend – the shareholders would, in purchasing power terms, be receiving a return of their capital investment.

46.3.4 Restating HCA accounts

There is a three step approach to restating HCA accounts, namely:

- **Step 1**: Restate the opening Balance Sheet using the RPI at the beginning of the accounting period and the RPI at the end in order to provide comparatives for the end of year (this means multiplying by RPI at the end and dividing by RPI at the date of the transaction).
- **Step 2**: Restate the Profit and Loss account for the year. Each item should be restated from RPI at the date of transaction to RPI at the end of year. In practice, however, it is usually assumed that items such as sales, purchases and most expenses accrue evenly over the year, and they may be converted using an average index.
- **Step 3**: Restate the Balance Sheet at the end of the accounting period into £CPP at end of year.

We will illustrate the step approach to restate the HCA accounts of Skye Ltd for the year ended 31 March 20X4.

Step 1: Restating the Balance Sheet as at 31 March 20X4 by:

	£	RPI for transaction	RPI at 31.3.20X4	£CPP
Premises purchased 1 April 20X0	20,000	147.5	164.1	22,251
Debtors	9,600	160.8	164.1	9,797
Bank	2,400	160.8	164.1	2,449
Creditors	(3,600)	160.8	164.1	(3,674)
	28,400			30,823
Shareholders' equity	28,400			30,823

Step 2: Restate the Profit and Loss account

The HCA profit for the year ended 31 March 20X4 was £12,400. This HCA profit will be reduced by the loss arising from the monetary assets held during the year as follows:

MONETARY ASSETS AT 1 APRIL 20X3			
		£	£
HCA (9,600 + 2,400 − 3,600)	=	8,400	
CPP (9,797 + 2,449 − 3,674)	=	8,572	172
Increase in net monetary assets during year arising from profit:			
HCA profit	=	12,400	
CPP restated (12,400 × 164.1/162.45)	=	12,526	126
Loss from holding monetary assets			298

Note: The index number 162.45 is the average for the year: $(164.1 + 160.8)/2$

Step 3: Restate the Balance Sheet at the end of the accounting period into £CPP at end of year

	£	RPI for transaction	RPI at 31.3.20X4	£CPP
Premises purchased 1 April 20X0	20,000	147.5	164.1	22,251
Debtors	12,000			12,000
Bank	14,800			14,800
Creditors	(6,000)			(6,000)
	40,800			43,051
Shareholders' equity	28,400			30,823
Profit for 20X4	12,400		Balancing figure*	12,228
	40,800			43,051

The CPP profit of £12,228 is £12,526 less a loss of £298 arising from holding monetary assets.

46.3.5 An appraisal of CPP accounting

The main advantage of CPP accounting is that the turnover, profit and capital employed in a business are comparable over time inasmuch as they are expressed in a common currency, namely the current purchasing power unit. This means that it is possible to compare the turnover between one year and another. However, if the HCA figures are not reliable, then restatement using the RPI does not rectify the position.

However, there are a number of criticisms of the method. First, we saw that if HCA profit were fully distributed then an organization would not be able to maintain its net assets at their current physical levels because the charges to the Profit and Loss account would be too low. Restatement using RPI has resulted in a lower profit but even this lower figure, if fully distributed, would result in too little being ploughed back to maintain the net assets.

Furthermore, the CPP value of an asset in the Balance Sheet will very rarely represent its true value. This is because non-monetary assets are converted from their historical cost to the equivalent pounds of purchasing power, using an index of general price changes. It would be quite possible for the replacement cost of a specific asset (e.g. a computer) to fall in cost while under CPP accounting it will be increased by applying the RPI change. In fact, CPP and replacement cost will only be equal if the increase in prices generally is exactly equal to the increase in the specific value of the asset.

Third, many users of accounts found it difficult to appreciate the concept of a 'current purchasing power pound' (£CPP) as a unit of measurement. They were familiar with £ sterling but not with a measurement unit that did not represent the amount that would be available if converted into cash.

Fourth, we have illustrated the loss arising from monetary assets under CPP and seen that it is deducted from CPP profit. Conversely, gains arising from monetary liabilities are added to the CPP profit, which means that highly geared companies disclose very high levels of CPP profit after taking credit for these gains on monetary liabilities. This is misleading inasmuch as the reported CPP profit is not available for distribution, being merely gains arising from the CPP indexation exercise.

Finally, CPP figures do not give a reasonable approximation to replacement costs; CPP accounts do not show the impact of inflation on the assets and liabilities of *individual* companies; and CPP is concerned with maintaining the purchasing power of the funds invested by the shareholders and is *proprietor-based* rather than *entity-based*.

46.4 CURRENT COST ACCOUNTING (CCA)

Current cost accounting is a system of value accounting whereby the operating assets of the business are revalued to their current value to the business at the end of each financial period. The basic concept of CCA is the maintenance of the operating capability of a business. This means maintaining the physical assets so that the business can continue to deliver the same amount of goods and services that it supplies from its existing resources. Because its focus is on the business entity rather than the shareholders' purchasing power, its approach to indexation is to apply an index that is specific to the asset being considered. The objective is to report each individual asset at what it is likely to cost to replace it. In practice this may be a difficult task because there may be no identical asset available to provide a current price, e.g. the asset might be obsolete with newer models and newer technologies.

46.4.1 The 'step' approach to preparing CCA accounts

We will illustrate the 'step' approach to preparing current cost accounts by applying specific price movement indices to the HCA accounts of Newera Ltd. This company commenced trading on 1 January 20X0 and prepared the following HCA accounts for the year ended 31 December 20X1. Depreciation is calculated at 10 per cent per annum using the straight-line method.

PROFIT AND LOSS ACCOUNT YEAR TO 31.12.20X1

		£000
Sales		300
Cost of sales		30
Gross profit		270
Depreciation	50	
Interest	20	
Expenses	80	150
Profit before tax		120
Tax		15
Profit after tax		105
Dividend		45
Retained profit		60

BALANCE SHEETS AS AT 31 DECEMBER

	20X1		20X0	
	£000	£000	£000	£000
Fixed assets:				
Cost		500		500
Depreciation		100		50
		400		450
Current assets:				
Stock	300		240	
Trade debtors	330		290	
Cash	20		10	
	650		540	
Current liabilities:				
Trade creditors	250		230	
Bank overdraft	90		110	
Tax	15		20	
Dividend	45		40	
	400		400	
Net current assets		250		140
		650		590
Less loans		100		100
		550		490
		£000		£000
Capital and reserves:				
Ordinary shares		450		450
Profit and Loss account		100		40
		550		490

The specific indices needed to translate the fixed assets and stocks in the Balance Sheet and to restate the Profit and Loss account to prepare the current cost accounts are as shown on the following page.

Fixed assets	Index	Index is needed to translate
At 1.1.20X0	120	Both Balance Sheets
At 31.12.20X0	150	Opening Balance Sheet
At 31.12.20X1	170	Closing Balance Sheet

Stock	Index	Index is needed to translate
At purchase*	152.4	Opening Balance Sheet
At 31.12.20X0	160.9	Opening Balance Sheet
At date 20X1 stock was bought	200.3	For translating the closing Balance Sheet
At 31 December 20X1	210.8	For translating the closing Balance Sheet
Average for 20X1	185.9	For translating the Profit and Loss account assuming sales and purchases occurred evenly during the year

* Index on the date when 20X0 stock was bought.

Step 1: Calculate the holding gain on fixed assets as at 31 December 20X0

Because the price index has increased from 120.0 at 1 January 20X0 to 150.0 at 31 December 20X0, the company has made a holding gain from holding the fixed assets during 20X0. This is a non-monetary gain that will be credited to a Current Cost Reserve in the Balance Sheet. It is calculated as follows:

	HCA	Index	CCA	Increase	Explanation
	£000		£000	£000	
Cost	500	150/120	625.0	125.0	Historical cost restated to current cost
Depreciation	50	150/120	62.5	12.5	Extra depreciation
	450		562.5	**112.5**	Net holding gain for 20X0 transferred to Current Cost Reserve in CC Balance Sheet

Step 2: Calculate the holding gain on stock as at 31 December 20X0

Because the price index has increased from 152.4 as at the date the stock was acquired to 160.9 as at 31 December 20X0, the company has made a holding gain from holding the stock on hand at the end of 20X0. This is a non-monetary gain that will be credited to a Current Cost Reserve in the Balance Sheet. It is calculated as follows:

	HCA	Index	CCA	Increase	Explanation
	£000		£000	£000	
Cost	240	160.9/152.4	253.386	13.386	Historical cost restated and credited to Current Cost Reserve in the balance sheet

Step 3: Prepare the current cost Balance Sheet

For the purpose of this illustration we are only restating the fixed assets and stock. In practice the Profit and Loss account would also be restated. A sample Balance Sheet is shown here. Note that the £125,886 credited to the Current Cost Reserve represents non-monetary holding gains of £112,500 on fixed assets and £13,386 on stock. Neither of these gains has been realized and therefore neither is available for distribution to shareholders. They are not gains in the commercial sense but merely a reflection of changes made to the carrying value of non-monetary items due to inflation as measured by the current cost method.

BALANCE SHEET AS AT 31.12.20X0		
Fixed assets:	£	£
Current cost		625,000
Depreciation		(62,500)
		562,500
Current assets:		
Stock	253,386	
Trade debtors	290,000	
Cash	10,000	
	553,386	
Current liabilities:		
Trade creditors	230,000	
Bank overdraft	110,000	
Tax	20,000	
Dividend	40,000	
	400,000	
Net current assets		153,386
		715,886
Less loans		(100,000)
		615,886
		£000
Capital and reserves:		
Ordinary shares		450,000
Current Cost Reserve		125,886
Profit and Loss account		40,000
		615,886

Step 4: Calculate the holding gain on fixed assets as at 31 December 20X1

Because the price index has increased from 150.0 at 1.1.20X1 to 170.0 at 31.12.20X1, the company has made a holding gain from holding the fixed assets during the year 20X1. This is a non-monetary gain that is credited to a Current Cost Reserve in the Balance Sheet. The calculation is as follows:

	HCA	Index	CCA	Explanation
	£000		£000	
Cost	500	170/120	708.333	Restated at CC
CC on 31.12.X0			625.000	CC from Step 1
			83.333	Holding gain

The net holding gain is transferred to Current Cost Reserve in CC Balance Sheet.

Step 5: Calculate the extra depreciation to be charged against the 20X1 profit

The depreciation charge in the 20X1 Profit and Loss account needs to be calculated as 10 per cent of the restated current cost of £708,333, i.e. £70,833, not 10 per cent of the historical cost of £500,000. This means that an *extra depreciation charge* is required of £20,833. This is called a 'depreciation adjustment'.

Step 6: Calculate the extra depreciation to be included in the accumulated depreciation in the Balance Sheet as at 31 December 20X1

The position that should be reported in the current cost Balance Sheet as at 31 December 20X1 is thus:

	£	£
Current cost of fixed assets as restated at 31 December 20X1		708,333
Less 10% Depreciation charge for 20X1	70,833	
Less 10% Depreciation charge for 20X0	70,834	
Accumulated depreciation		141,667
Net book value		566,666

However, the depreciation charge actually made in 20X0 was £62,500. This means that an additional £8,334 (£70,834 − £62,500) needs to be added to the accumulated depreciation. The accounting entries to achieve this are to credit the accumulated depreciation with £8,334 and to debit the Current Cost Reserve by the same amount.

Step 7: Calculate the holding gain on stock as at 31 December 20X1

Because the price index has increased from 200.3 as at the date the stock was acquired to 210.8 as at 31 December 20X1, the company has made a holding gain from holding the stock on hand at the end of 20X1. This is a non-monetary gain that will be credited to a Current Cost Reserve in the Balance Sheet. It is calculated as follows:

	HCA	Index	CCA	Increase
	£000		£000	£000
As at 31 December 20X1	300	210.8/200.3	315.726	15.726
As at 31 December 20X0 per Step 2			253.386	13.386
Credit change during 20X1 to Current Cost Reserve				2.340

Step 8: Calculate the effect of stock inflation on the Profit and Loss account

We have assumed that the purchases and sales have occurred evenly throughout 20X1, which means that it is appropriate to use the average index to calculate the amount that we need to increase the cost of sales by to reflect the inflation. The calculation is as follows:

	HCA	Index	CCA	Increase
	£000		**£000**	**£000**
Opening stock	240	185.9/152.4	292.756	52.756
Closing stock	(300)	185.9/200.3	(278.432)	21.568
Impact on cost of sales	(60)		14.324	74.324

The £74,324 is called a 'cost of sales adjustment' (COSA). It is deducted from the historical cost profit and credited to the Current Cost Reserve.

Step 9: Monetary working capital adjustment (MWCA)

We now need to transfer funds from the Profit and Loss account to the Current Cost Reserve to avoid it being distributed, in order to maintain the monetary working capital (i.e. debtors and creditors) at the current level of operating. This means we need to identify the change in debtors and creditors between the opening and closing Balance Sheet dates that arises from changes in the volume of business activity from the change that arises from inflation. It is the change that arises from inflation that we need to transfer from the Profit and Loss account to the Current Cost Reserve. It is calculated in two stages, as follows:

	20X1	20X0		
	£000	**£000**		**£000**
Stage 1 – Calculate the overall change:				
Trade debtors	330.000	290.000		
Trade creditors	250.000	230.000		
Monetary working capital (MWC)	80.000	60.000	Overall change	20.000
Stage 2 – Restate MWC at average	70.550	69.323	Volume change	1.227
			Price change	18.773

For Stage 2 £70,550 is calculated as £80,000 × 185.9/210.8 and £69,323 as £60,000 × 185.9/160.9.

Step 10: Construct the Current Cost Profit and Loss account for the year ended 31 December 20X1 after making the three adjustments

	£	£
Operating profit before interest and tax		140,000
Current cost adjustments:		
Depreciation adjustment	20,833	
Cost of Sales adjustment	74,324	
Monetary working capital adjustment	18,773	
		113,930
Current cost operating profit		26,070

This tells us that the company needs to retain £113,930 in order to maintain the operating capability of the business at the same level as in 20X0. If the company were to distribute more than £26,070, then it would need to obtain additional capital to maintain the current level of activity.

Step 11: Calculate the effect on the current cost adjustments of the company using funds other than those belonging to the shareholders

The objective of current cost accounting is to maintain the physical operating capacity of the company, i.e. its assets. This is achieved via extra depreciation, cost of sales adjustments and monetary working capital adjustments. However, if the company is partly financed by loans, then it gains purchasing power because inflation reduces the impact of a loan on a company, and its shareholders benefit from this. It is difficult to measure just how much shareholders benefit from loans and one approach has been to reduce the total current cost adjustments by a fraction known as a gearing adjustment.

The gearing adjustment formula is:

(Average loans/average shareholders' funds) × 100%

Average loans are calculated as follows:

	20X1	20X0	Average loans
	£000	£000	£000
Loans	100	100	
Overdraft	90	110	
Tax	15	20	
Cash	(20)	(10)	
	185	220	202.5

Average shareholders' funds are calculated as follows:

	20X1	20X0
	£000	£000
20X0 Shareholders' funds from Step 3		615.886
20X1 Shareholders' funds:		
As at 31 December 20X0	615.886	
Current cost adjustments in 20X1	113.930	
Less 20X0 depreciation restated	(8.334)	
	721.482	
Average shareholders' funds		668.684 (£615,886 + £721,482)/2

The gearing ratio for our example is calculated as:

$$[£202,500/(£202,500 + £668,684)] × 100\% = 23.2\%$$

The gearing adjustment is then calculated as 23.2% of £113,930 = £26,431.

Step 12: Restate the Current Cost Profit and Loss account for the year ended 31 December 20X1 taking into account the gearing ratio

	£	£
Operating profit before interest and tax		140,000
Current cost adjustments:		
Depreciation adjustment	20,833	
Cost of Sales adjustment	74,324	
Monetary working capital adjustment	18,773	113,930
Current cost operating profit		26,070
Gearing adjustment	26,431	
Interest payable	(20,000)	6,431
Current cost profit before tax		32,501
Taxation		(15,000)
Current cost profit after tax		17,501
Dividends		(45,000)
Current cost profit retained for year		(27,499)
Retained profit brought forward		40,000
CC retained profit		12,501

Step 13: Calculate the Current Cost Reserve as at 31 December 20X1

		£
Fixed assets holding gain at 31 December 20X0	(Step 1)	112,500
Stock holding gain at 31 December 20X0	(Step 2)	13,386
Fixed assets holding gain at 31 December 20X1	(Step 4)	83,333
Stock holding gain at 31 December 20X1	(Step 7)	2,340
Less Depreciation for 20X0 based on 20X1 current cost	(Step 6)	(8,334)
Cost of sales adjustment (COSA) for 20X1	(Step 8)	74,324
Monetary working capital adjustment (MWCA) for 20X1	(Step 9)	18,773
Gearing adjustment	(Step 11)	(26,431)
		269,891

Step 14: Prepare the Current Cost Balance Sheet as at 31 December 20X1

CURRENT COST BALANCE SHEET AS AT 31.12.20X0		
	£000	£000
Fixed assets:		
Current cost		708,333
Depreciation		141.667
		566,666
Current assets:		
Stock	315,726	
Trade debtors	330.000	
Cash	20.000	
	665.726	
Current liabilities:		
Trade creditors	250.000	
Bank overdraft	90.000	
Tax	15.000	
Proposed dividend	45.000	
	400.000	
Net current assets		265.726
		832,392
Less loans		(100.000)
		732.392
Capital and reserves:		
Ordinary shares		450.000
Current Cost Reserve		269,891
Profit and Loss account		12.501
		732.392

Interaction 46.4

How inflation erodes profit

Required: Explain why profits seem to fall when the effect of rising prices is taken into account.

SOLUTIONS TO INTERACTIVE QUESTIONS

IQ 46.1 Measurement of profit in times of inflation

Comments on Hymie's 'profit' are as follows:

(a) This view ignores the impact of changing prices. The inflation over the five years must be taken into account in measuring any profit.
(b) This view takes into account the fall in the value of money over the five-year period. The RPI increase in general price levels means that there has only been a gain of £38,745 in real terms.
(c) There has been a gain of £50,000 from holding the property but there is no profit available for spending on consumer products or holidays because the replacement cost is £150,000. Hymie might even consider that he has suffered a loss of £35,000 because the replacement cost nearer London is £185,000.

IQ 46.2 Non-monetary asset expressed in CPP unit

The CPP figure does not mean that machinery is valued at £CPP50,673 at 30 June 20X1. It is reporting that the expenditure of £50,000 at 1 July 20X0 would be equivalent to an expenditure of £CPP50,673 at the 30 June 20X1. The CPP accounting restatement has restated the value of the money invested and not the actual value of the asset itself.

IQ 46.3 Monetary assets/liabilities expressed in CPP unit

The £CPP673 is not available for distribution as cash. It merely reports that the company has benefited from owing money during a period of inflation.

IQ 46.4 How inflation erodes profit

Profits determined under the historical cost convention overstate profits when prices are rising because holding gains are treated as operating profit. We have seen that the depreciation charge needs to be increased using replacement cost as a base, the cost of sales is increased to reflect the rise in the cost of purchases, and there is a charge for the effect of inflation on the monetary working capital.

PROGRESSIVE QUESTIONS

PQ 46.1 Current purchasing power (CPP) accounting

Inflated Ltd acquired a market stall with opening stock on 1 July 20X0, and it carried on business as a market trader with all transactions on a cash basis. Purchases were made evenly through the year. The Profit and Loss account of the company for the year ended 30 June 20X1 and the opening and closing Balance Sheets are as follows:

PROFIT AND LOSS ACCOUNT YEAR TO 30 JUNE 20X1		
	£	£
Sales		4,500
Stock at 1 July 20X0	900	
Purchases	2,025	
	2,925	
Stock at 30 June 20X1	675	
Cost of sales		2,250
Gross profit		2,250
Expenses	1,125	
Depreciation	270	
		1,395
Net profit		855

BALANCE SHEETS		
	1 July 20X0	30 June 20X1
	£	£
Fixed assets:		
Machinery	1,350	1,350
Depreciation	–	(270)
Net book value	1,350	1,080
Current assets:		
Stock	900	675
Bank	–	1,350
	2,250	3,105
	£	£
Share Capital	450	450
Profit and Loss account		855
Debentures	1,800	1,800
	2,250	3,105

The retail price indices were:

1 July 20X0	160
31 December 20X0	220
30 June 20X1	280
Average	200

Required: Prepare a CPP Profit and Loss account for the year ended 30 June 20X1, and explain briefly the circumstances in which the £CPP figure is relevant for decision making.

PQ 46.2 Profit on the current cost basis

Refer back to the information in PQ 46.1. You are informed that the replacement cost of the stock sold at the date of sale was £2,750.

Required: Calculate the operating profit on the current cost basis, and explain briefly why this current cost operating profit is useful.

PQ 46.3 Analysis of a diagram (1) which shows the purchase on 1 January 20X0 and sale on 31 March 20X0 of a caravan by The Sussex Caravan Co. Ltd.

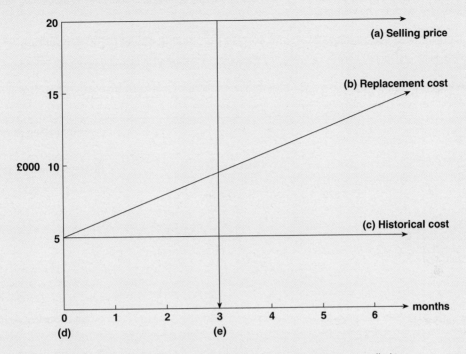

Required: Explain the limitations of historical cost accounting and the accounting terms applied to:

- (a) to (b), and (b) to (c), on the vertical axis;
- point (e), and (d) to (e), on the horizontal axis.

PQ 46.4 Analysis of a diagram (2)

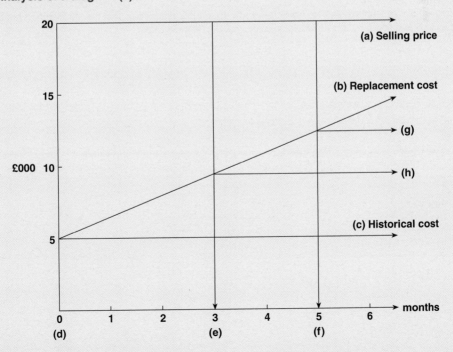

You are informed that the caravan was sold on credit and that the debtor was paid at point (f) on the horizontal axis.

Required: Explain the fundamental principle on which current cost accounting is based, and the accounting terms applied to (g) to (h), and (h) to (c), on the vertical scale.

PQ 46.5 Current cost accounting (CCA) and current purchasing power (CPP) accounting

(a) Explain the major differences between current cost accounting and current purchasing power accounting.

(b) Analysis of a diagram (3)

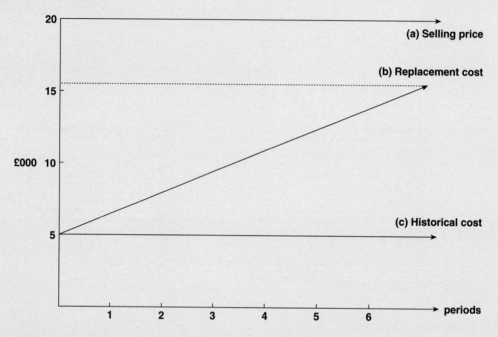

Required: Explain the accounting term for (a) to (b), (b) to (c), on the assumption that the caravan had not been sold at the end of period 6 and how the caravan would appear in a CCA Balance Sheet.

ANSWERS TO
PROGRESSIVE QUESTIONS

Notes:

- The rent demand will be marked by the cashier as PV1 and it will be filed in number sequence.
- The cash sales memo for the shop fittings will be marked as PV2 and filed.
- Similarly for each of the payments there will be a numbered voucher to support the payment.

It is customary for the owner/manager to initial each of the vouchers as authorization for the cashier to make a payment. This is a safeguard against the cashier paying for goods and services without the manager's approval, i.e. it avoids cash being misappropriated. It is also good business sense that invoices are not paid until the end of any period of credit that has been allowed by suppliers. In many businesses control over the timing of each payment is particularly important, e.g. cash might be scarce and payment for the purchase of goods delayed until after the sale of the goods.

CHAPTER 3

PQ 3.1 Multiple-choice question

1. (a) z (b) y (c) x (d) z (e) y
2. (a) y (b) x (c) z (d) y (e) z
3. (a) y (b) y (c) z (d) y (e) y (f) x
4. (a) x (b) y (c) y (d) x (e) x (f) x (g) y (h) x (i) x
5. (a) y (b) y (c) w (d) y (e) y (f) x (g) x (h) w

PQ 3.2 Preparation of a Category Quadrant

ASSETS	£
Premises	100,000
Fixtures	50,000
Vehicles	30,000
Cash	8,800

LIABILITIES	£
Capital	105,000

EXPENDITURE	£
Purchases	53,000
Rent	1,000
Lighting	500
Salaries	3,500
Insurance	200
Motor expenses	1,500
Office expenses	1,500

INCOME	£
Sales	145,000

Total uses	250,000	Total sources	250,000

CHAPTER 2

PQ 2.1 Sorting out the side

(a) y (b) x (c) y (d) x (e) y (f) z

PQ 2.2 Multiple-choice question

(a) y (b) z (c) z (d) y (e) z (f) y

PQ 2.3 Writing up the Cash account – Arnold

CASH ACCOUNT

Date	V	Particulars	F	Amount	Date	V	Particulars	F	Amount
20X0				£	20X0				£
1.1	a	Capital		15,000	2.1	b	Purchases		300
2.1	e	Sales		1,500	2.1	c	Rent		1,500
7.1	k	Sales		150	2.1	d	Stationery		90
					3.1	f	Purchases		150
					4.1	g	Stationery		60
					5.1	h	Motor Expenses		225
					6.1	i	Vehicle		1,500
					6.1	j	Drawings		450
							Balance c/d		4,275
				16,650					12,375
7.1		Balance b/d		12,375					16,650

PQ 2.4 Writing up the Cash account – Bennett

CASH ACCOUNT

Date	V	Particulars	F	Amount	Date	V	Particulars	F	Amount
20X0				£	20X0				£
1.4	R1	Capital		12,000	1.4	PV1	Rent		1,000
3.6	CS01	Sales		7,400	1.4	PV2	Shop fittings		1,200
					5.4	PV3	Purchases		2,400
					7.5	PV4	Wages		1,200
					9.5	PV5	Electricity		500
					1.6	PV6	Telephone		220
					8.6	PV7	Drawings		3,200
							Total payments		9,720
				19,400			Balance c/d		9,680
9.6		Balance b/d		9,680					19,400

PQ 3.3 Accounting for business transactions

	Transaction	Book of accounts	Name of the account	Class of account	Debit/ Credit	Balance + or – *
1	(a) Received £4,000 in cash as capital from Bert	Cash book	Cash account	Asset	Debit	Plus
	(b)	Real Ledger	Capital a/c	Liability	Credit	Plus
2	(a) Paid £100 as business rent	Cash book	Cash account	Asset	Credit	Minus
	(b)	Nominal Ledger	Rent account	Expenditure	Debit	Plus
3	(a) Paid £500 for business stationery	Cash book	Cash account	Asset	Credit	Minus
	(b)	Nominal Ledger	Stationery a/c	Expenditure	Debit	Plus
4	(a) Paid £150 as postage	Cash book	Cash account	Asset	Credit	Minus
	(b)	Nominal Ledger	Postage a/c	Expenditure	Debit	Plus
5	(a) Paid £10,000 for a van	Cash book	Cash account	Asset	Credit	Minus
	(b)	Real Ledger	Motor Vehicle a/c	Asset	Debit	Plus
6	(a) Paid £700 for business insurance	Cash book	Cash a/c	Asset	Credit	Minus
	(b)	Nominal Ledger	Insurance a/c	Expenditure	Debit	Plus
7	(a) Received £6,000 from selling medicine	Cash book	Cash account	Asset	Debit	Plus
	(b)	Nominal Ledger	Sales account	Income	Credit	Plus
8	(a) Paid £600 for steel cabinets	Cash book	Cash account	Asset	Credit	Minus
	(b)	Real Ledger	Furniture a/c	Asset	Debit	Plus
9	(a) Received £4,500 as a loan from Liza	Cash book	Cash account	Asset	Debit	Plus
	(b)	Real Ledger	Liza's Loan a/c	Liability	Credit	Plus
10	(a) Repaid £2,500 of Liza's loan	Cash book	Cash account	Asset	Credit	Minus
	(b)	Real Ledger	Liza's Loan a/c	Liability	Debit	Minus
11	(a) Paid £5,250 to buy medicine for sale	Cash book	Cash account	Asset	Credit	Minus
	(b)	Nominal Ledger	Purchases a/c	Expenditure	Debit	Plus
12	(a) Paid back £1,000 to Bert the owner	Cash book	Cash account	Asset	Credit	Minus
	(b)	Real Ledger	Capital account	Liability	Debit	Minus

* Whether the balance increases or decreases

(b) Payment vouchers, though received from various third parties, are filed in the sequence in which payments were made, and new voucher numbers are written on them to maintain cross-reference with the record in the Cash account.

(c) Posting to the ledger:

CASH ACCOUNT

Date	V	Particulars	F	Amount £	Date	V	Particulars	F	Amount £
20X0					20X0				
1.6	R01	Capital a/c	RL1	30,000	1.6	PV1	Motor Vehicle	RL31	18,000
1.6	CS01	Sales a/c	NL11	450	1.6	PV2	Purchases	NL1	1,540
1.6	CS02	Sales a/c	NL11	376	1.6	PV3	Stationery	NL21	24
2.6	CS03	Sales a/c	NL11	428	1.6	PV4	Staff Welfare	NL26	46
2.6	CS04	Sales a/c	NL11	540	1.6	PV5	Advertising	NL24	124
2.6	R02	Loan – S. Lawrie	RL21	2,500	1.6	PV6	Rent	NL28	1,000
2.6	CS05	Sales a/c	NL11	622	2.6	PV7	Postage	NL30	12
3.6	CS06	Sales a/c	NL11	568	2.6	PV8	Purchases	NL1	624
3.6	CS07	Sales a/c	NL11	245	2.6	PV9	Staff Welfare	NL26	14
3.6	CS08	Sales a/c	NL11	164	2.6	PV10	Advertising	NL24	33
3.6	CS09	Sales a/c	NL11	322	2.6	PV11	Staff Salary	NL34	200
3.6	CS10	Sales a/c	NL11	569	2.6	PV12	Purchases	NL1	165
4.6	CS11	Sales a/c	NL11	345	3.6	PV13	Staff salary	NL34	240
4.6	CS12	Sales a/c	NL11	140	3.6	PV14	Purchases	NL1	1,262
4.6	R03	Loan – S. Lawrie	RL21	1,500	3.6	PV15	Sagar's Drawing	RL1	465
4.6	CS13	Sales a/c	NL11	250	3.6	PV16	Staff Welfare	NL26	16
4.6	CS14	Sales a/c	NL11	372	3.6	PV17	Advertising	NL24	35
5.6	CS15	Sales a/c	NL11	459	4.6	PV18	Stationery	NL21	16
5.6	CS16	Sales a/c	NL11	165	4.6	PV19	Purchases	NL1	755
5.6	CS17	Sales a/c	NL11	544	4.6	PV20	Sagar's Drawing	RL1	245
5.6	CS18	Sales a/c	NL11	386	4.6	PV21	Staff Welfare	NL26	22
5.6	CS19	Sales a/c	NL11	240	4.6	PV22	Staff Salary	NL34	240
					4.6	PV23	Purchases	NL1	248
					4.6	PV24	Telephone	NL32	45
					5.6	PV25	Postage	NL30	15
					5.6	PV26	Staff Welfare	NL26	24
					5.6	PV27	Stationery	NL21	32
					5.6	PV28	Advertising	NL24	65
					5.6	-	Balance c/d	-	15,678
				41,185					41,185
6.6		Balance b/d		15,678					

CHAPTER 4

PQ 4.1 Multiple-choice question

1. (b)   2. (c)   3. (a)   4. (b)   5. (b)

PQ 4.2 Posting from the Cash account to the ledger

(a) Receipt vouchers with 'CS' prefix are cash sales memos issue in support of cash sales. Those with prefix 'R' are receipts, issued in acknowledgement of other amounts received.

NOMINAL LEDGER

NL1 PURCHASES ACCOUNT

			£000		£000
1.6	Cash a/c	CB1	1,540		
2.6	Cash a/c	CB1	624		
2.6	Cash a/c	CB1	165		
3.6	Cash a/c	CB1	1,262		
4.6	Cash a/c	CB1	755		
4.6	Cash a/c	CB1	248		
			4,594		

NL21 STATIONERY ACCOUNT

			£000		£000
1.6	Cash a/c	CB1	24		
2.6	Cash a/c	CB1	14		
5	Cash a/c	CB1	16		
5.6	Cash a/c	CB1	32		
			72		

NL24 ADVERTISING ACCOUNT

			£000		£000
1.6	Cash a/c	CB1	124		
2.6	Cash a/c	CB1	33		
4	Cash a/c	CB1	35		
6	Cash a/c	CB1	65		
			257		

NL26 STAFF WELFARE ACCOUNT

			£000		£000
1.6	Cash a/c	CB1	46		
2.6	Cash a/c	CB1	14		
3.6	Cash a/c	CB1	16		
4.6	Cash a/c	CB1	22		
5.6	Cash a/c	CB1	24		
			122		

NL34 STAFF SALARY ACCOUNT

			£000		£000
1.6	Cash a/c	CB1	200		
3.6	Cash a/c	CB1	240		
4.6	Cash a/c	CB1	240		
			680		

NL11 SALES ACCOUNT

	£000				£000
		1.6	Cash a/c	CB1	450
		1.6	Cash a/c	CB1	376
		2.6	Cash a/c	CB1	428
		2.6	Cash a/c	CB1	540
		2.6	Cash a/c	CB1	622
		3.6	Cash a/c	CB1	568
		3.6	Cash a/c	CB1	245
		3.6	Cash a/c	CB1	164
		3.6	Cash a/c	CB1	322
		4.6	Cash a/c	CB1	569
		4.6	Cash a/c	CB1	345
		4.6	Cash a/c	CB1	140
		4.6	Cash a/c	CB1	250
		4.6	Cash a/c	CB1	372
		5.6	Cash a/c	CB1	459
		5.6	Cash a/c	CB1	165
		5.6	Cash a/c	CB1	544
		5.6	Cash a/c	CB1	386
		5.6	Cash a/c	CB1	240
					7,185

NL28 RENT ACCOUNT

			£000		£000
1.6	Cash a/c	CB1	1,000		

NL30 POSTAGE ACCOUNT

			£000		£000
2.6	Cash a/c	CB1	12		
5.6	Cash a/c	CB1	15		
			27		

NL32 TELEPHONE ACCOUNT

			£000		£000
4.6	Cash a/c	CB1	45		

REAL LEDGER

RL1 CAPITAL ACCOUNT

			£				£
3.6	Cash a/c	CB1	465	1.6	Cash a/c	CB1	30,000
4.6	Cash a/c	CB1	245				
	Balance		29,290				
			30,000				30,000
				6.6	Balance		29,290

RL21 S. LAWRIE LOAN ACCOUNT

	£				£
		2.6	Cash a/c	CB1	2,500
		4.6	Cash a/c	CB1	1,500
					4,000

RL31 MOTOR VEHICLE ACCOUNT

			£		£
1.6	Cash a/c	CB1	18,000		

LIST OF BALANCES AS AT 5.6.20X0

Name of account	F	Dr	Cr
		£	£
Cash account	CB1	15,678	–
Purchases a/c	NL1	4,594	–
Sales a/c	NL11	–	7,185
Stationery a/c	NL21	72	–
Advertising a/c	NL24	257	–
Staff Welfare a/c	NL26	122	–
Rent a/c	NL28	1,000	–
Postage a/c	NL30	27	–
Telephone a/c	NL32	45	–
Staff Salaries a/c	NL34	680	–
Capital a/c	RL1	–	29,290
S. Lawrie Loan a/c	RL21	–	4,000
Motor Vehicles a/c	RL31	18,000	–
		40,475	40,475

CHAPTER 5

PQ 5.1 Multiple-choice question

(a) y   (b) y   (c) z   (d) x   (e) z   (f) z   (g) y

PQ 5.2 Preparation of a Trial Balance and identification of account balances

(a)

TRIAL BALANCE AS AT 31.3.20X0

	Debit	Credit
Sales account	–	86,000
Purchases account	62,500	–
Cash account	8,495	–
Salaries account	14,250	–
Rent account	3,000	–
Stationery account	240	–
Motor Vehicles account	12,000	–
Vehicle Maintenance account	220	–
Postage account	105	–
Staff Welfare account	325	–
Advertising account	1,200	–
Office Expenses account	165	–
Furniture account	8,000	–
Capital account	–	25,000
Audit Fees account	500	–
	111,000	111,000

(b)

	CLASS OF ACCOUNT
	Income
	Expenditure
	Asset
	Expenditure
	Expenditure
	Expenditure
	Asset
	Expenditure
	Expenditure
	Expenditure
	Expenditure
	Expenditure
	Asset
	Liability
	Expenditure

PQ 5.3 Withholding the balance in the Capital account

TRIAL BALANCE AS AT 31.12.20X0

	Debit	Credit
Stationery account	320	–
Salaries account	12,800	–
Electricity account	660	–
Sales account	–	94,500
Heating account	2,650	–
Postage account	125	–
Cash account	7,675	–
Furniture account	12,000	–
Loan from Peter account	–	3,000
Purchases account	68,400	–
Office Expenses account	1,465	–
Motor Vehicle account	18,000	–
Delivery Expenses account	1,250	–
Office Equipment account	6,600	–
Sales Commission account	2,555	–
Capital account	–	37,000
	134,500	134,500

PQ 5.4 Accounting control procedures to prevent errors

The errors/fraud may have been prevented by the following accounting control procedures:

(a) Pre-listing the amounts of the vouchers and checking against the amount paid through the Cash account would detect the error.

(b) Sequential number and checking the sequence entered in the Cash account would detect the error.

(c) Authorization by the manager for payment and checking that vouchers that have been paid were properly authorized would detect this type of fraud.

## CHAPTER 6

PQ 6.1 Balance Sheet equation

Three ways in which the cash balance can be improved are:

1. introduce more capital into business;
2. borrow more loan;
3. dispose of one or more vehicles.

The impact of each transaction on John's capital, liability and assets:	Capital	Liabilities	Vehicle	Cash
	£150,000	£50,000	£180,000	£20,000
(a) Introduced £10,000 more as capital	10,000			10,000
(b) Received £5,000 as transport charges	5,000			5,000
(c) Paid £1,000 as rent	(1,000)			(1,000)
(d) Paid £800 as salary to staff	(800)			(800)
(e) Borrowed £5,000 more from Mark		5,000		5,000
(f) Took £3,000 for John's household expenses	(3,000)			(3,000)
(g) Paid back £10,000 to Mark		(10,000)		(10,000)
(h) Paid £500 to mark as interest on loan	(500)			(500)
(i) Acquired another vehicle for £15,000			15,000	(15,000)
Balances as at completion	159,700	45,000	195,000	9,700

The Balance Sheet on completion of the stated transactions →

BALANCE SHEET AS AT XXXXXX	
	£
Motor vehicles	195,000
Cash	9,700
	204,700
	£
Capital – John Amber	159,700
Loan – Mark Batty	45,000
	204,700

PQ 6.2 Impact of each transaction on Balance Sheet items

(a) Movements during the year in Balance Sheet items were as follows:

Transactions	Cash account £	Shop premises £	Furniture £	Delivery van £	Stock £	Loan £	Capital £
Balance – 1.7.20X0	6,000	82,500	12,750	6,000	18,000	(50,250)	(75,000)
1. Cash sale	3,000	–	–	–	(2,400)	–	(600)
2. Van acquired	(5,000)	–	–	5,000	–	–	–
3. Purchases	(3,750)	–	–	–	3,750	–	–
4. Cash sale	2,250	–	–	–	(1,500)	–	(750)
5. Cash sale	4,200	–	–	–	(3,000)	–	(1,200)
6. Purchases	(4,500)	–	–	–	4,500	–	–
7. Wages	(600)	–	–	–	–	–	600
8. Rent	(375)	–	–	–	–	–	375
9. More capital	7,500	–	–	–	–	–	(7,500)
10. Drawings	–	–	–	–	(300)	–	300
11. Loan repaid	(1,500)	–	–	–	–	1,500	–
Balance 30.6.2001	7,225	82,500	12,750	11,000	19,050	(48,750)	(83,775)

Stated in parenthesis (brackets) are liabilities, increase of liability and reduction of asset.

Phillipa Gray's Balance Sheet as at 7 July 20X0 would appear as stated on the right.

It should be noted, however, that her fixed assets have not been depreciated. Depreciation would reduce the fixed assets and Phillipa's capital.

BALANCE SHEET AS AT 7.7.20X0		£
Fixed assets:		
Shop premises		82,500
Furniture		12,750
Delivery van		11,000
		106,250
Current assets:		
Stock	19,050	
Cash	7,225	
		26,275
		132,525
		£
Capital		83,775
Loan		48,750
		132,525

PQ 6.3 Adjusting for closing stock and depreciation

Capitalization of expenditure

PURCHASES ACCOUNT

	£		£
Balance b/f	62,500	Stock in trade a/c	6,500
		Balance c/d	56,000
Balance b/d	56,000		

STOCK IN TRADE ACCOUNT

	£		£
Purchases a/c	6,500		

The cost of goods remaining unsold at year end represents an asset because future economic benefits are expected to arise in the next accounting period when they are sold. Accordingly £6,500 is transferred from the expenditure (Purchases) account to an asset account named Stock in Trade. Transfer from an expenditure to an asset is known as 'capitalization'.

Writing off fixed assets

MOTOR VEHICLES ACCOUNT

	£		£
Balance b/f	12,000	Depreciation a/c	2,400
		Balance c/d	9,600
Balance b/d	9,600		

DEPRECIATION OF VEHICLES ACCOUNT

	£		£
M. Vehicles a/c	2,400		

FURNITURE ACCOUNT

	£		£
Balance b/f	8,000	Depreciation a/c	800
		Balance c/d	7,200
Balance b/d	7,200		

DEPRECIATION OF FURNITURE ACCOUNT

	£		£
Furniture a/c	800		

The transfer from an asset account to an expenditure account is known in the UK as writing off and in the USA as *expensing*.

TRADING AND PROFIT AND LOSS ACCOUNT FOR THE YEAR ENDED 31.3.20X0

Purchases a/c	56,000	Sales a/c	86,000
Gross profit c/d	30,000		
Salaries a/c	14,250	Gross profit b/d	30,000
Rent a/c	3,000		
Stationery a/c	240		
Postage a/c	105		
Depreciation – furniture	800		
Audit Fees a/c	500		
Office Expenses a/c	165		
Advertising account	1,200		
Staff Welfare a/c	325		
Vehicle Maintenance	220		
Depreciation – vehicles	2,400		
	23,205		
Profit c/d	6,795		
	6,795		
Capital a/c	6,795	Profit b/d	6,795

BALANCE SHEET AS AT 31.3.20X0

	£
Furniture account	7,200
Motor Vehicles account	9,600
Stock in Trade account	6,500
Cash account	8,495
	31,795
	£
Capital account	25,000
Profit for the year	6,795
	31,795

PQ 6.4 Adjusting for closing stock, an expense stock and depreciation

CLUE: Gross profit £41,400; net profit £14,490; Balance Sheet totals £54,490.

CHAPTER 7

PQ 7.1 Relations between payments and expenditure

ACCOUNT	DURING THE CURRENT YEAR		AS AT THE END OF THE YEAR	
	Payments	Expense	Prepayment	Accrual
(a) Vehicle maintenance	£135	£160	–	£25
(b) Insurance	£500	£625	–	£125
(c) Salaries	£2,545	£2,600	–	£55
(d) Rates	£355	£260	£95	–
(e) Telephone	£290	£370	–	£80

PQ 7.2 Relations among payments, expense, assets and liability

	BALANCE SHEET AS AT 31.12.20X0		DURING THE YEAR ENDED 31.12.2001		BALANCE SHEET AS AT 31.12.2001	
	Asset	Liability	Payment	Expense	Asset	Liability
(a) Rent	£400	–	£1,600	£1,600	£400	–
(b) Fuel	–	–	£855	£700	£155	–
(c) Office equipment	£8,000	–	–	£1,600	£6,400	–
(d) Motor vehicles	£5,500	–	£2,500	£2,000	£6,000	–
(e) Salaries	£300	–	£6,200	£6,900	–	£400
(f) Insurance	–	£300	£1,200	£1,200	–	£300
(g) Telephone	£160	–	£360	£420	£100	–

PQ 7.3 Accounting for income on an accruals basis

	BALANCE SHEET AS AT 31.12.20X0		DURING THE YEAR ENDED 31.12.2001		BALANCE SHEET AS AT 31.12.2001	
	Asset	Liability	Receipts	Income	Asset	Liability
(a) Commission earnings	£50	–	£565	£550	£35	–
(b) Interest receivable	£100	–	£900	£1,000	£200	00
(c) Rent receivable	–	£150	£1,300	£1,550	£100	–
(d) Commission earnings	£120	–	£1,600	£1,230	£300	£250
(e) Interest receivable	£100	–	£1,300	£1,500	–	–
(f) Rent receivable	£500	–	£7,000	£6,000	–	£500

PQ 7.4 Accounting for rent receivable

RENT RECEIVABLE ACCOUNT

20X0	£	20X0	£
31.12 Profit and Loss	8,000	31.12 Cash a/c	6,000
		31.12 Balance c/d	2,000
	8,000		8,000
2001		**2001**	
Balance b/d	2,000		
31.12 Profit and Loss	8,000	31.12 Cash a/c	12,000
31.12 Balance c/d	2,000		
		2002	
		Balance c/d	2,000

PROFIT AND LOSS ACCOUNT

Year ended 31.12	20X0	2001
Rent receivable	£8,000	£8,000

BALANCE SHEET

As at 31.12	20X0	2001
Current assets: Rent receivable	£2,000	
Current liability: Rent receivable*		£2,000

* Rent receivable reported as a current liability is a deferred income.

PQ 7.5 Accounting for expenses on an accruals basis

RENT ACCOUNT

		£			£
11.7.X9	Cash a/c	600	1.6.X9	Balance b/f	400
14.11X9	Cash a/c	800	31.5.X0	Profit and Loss	2,400
16.3.X0	Cash a/c	800			
31.5.X0	Balance c/d	600			
			1.6.X0	Balance b/d	600

INSURANCE ACCOUNT

		£			£
1.6.X9	Balance b/f	360	31.5.X0	Profit and Loss	1,160
24.9.X9	Cash a/c	1,200	31.5.X0	Balance c/d	400
1.6.X0	Balance b/d	400			

RATES ACCOUNT

		£			£
1.6.X9	Balance b/f	350	31.5.X0	Profit and Loss	1,450
3.10.X9	Cash a/c	700	31.5.X0	Balance c/d	400
8.4.X0	Cash a/c	800			
1.6.X0	Balance b/d	400			

PROFIT AND LOSS ACCOUNT FOR THE YEAR ENDED 31 MAY 20X0

	£
Rent	2,400
Insurance	1,160
Rates	1,450

BALANCE SHEET AS AT 31 MAY 20X0

	£
Current assets:	
Insurance prepaid	400
Rates prepaid	400
Current liabilities:	
Rent payable	(600)

PQ 7.6 Trial Balances extracted at different stages of accounting

TRIAL BALANCE AS AT 31.12.20X0

	£	£
Cash account	65,160	–
Capital account	–	100,000
Furniture account	12,000	–
Motor Vehicles account	20,000	–
Sales account	–	492,500
Purchases account	436,800	–
Postage and Telephone acc.	1,260	–
Sales Commission acc.	4,650	–
Staff Welfare account	3,750	–
Salaries and Wages account	28,200	–
Lighting and Heating account	2,280	–
Rent account	9,000	–
Advertising account	9,400	–
	592,500	592,500

Calculation of stock at end:	£	
Purchases	436,800	
Sales	492,500	
Less: gross profit: 20%	(98,500)	(394,000)
		42,800

TRIAL BALANCE AS AT 31.12.20X0

	£	£
Cash account	65,160	–
Capital account	–	100,000
Furniture account	10,800	–
Motor Vehicles account	16,000	–
Sales account	–	492,500
Purchases account	394,000	–
Postage and Telephone acc.	1,260	–
Sales commission acc.	4,650	–
Staff Welfare account	3,750	–
Salaries and Wages acc.	30,000	–
Lighting and Heating acc.	3,080	–
Rent account	6,000	–
Advertising account	9,400	–
Depreciation of Furniture	1,200	–
Depreciation of Vehicles	4,000	–
Salaries Accrued account	–	1,800
Heating Accrued account	–	800
Prepaid Rent account	3,000	–
Stock in Trade account	42,800	–
	595,100	595,100

TRADING AND PROFIT AND LOSS ACCOUNT FOR THE YEAR ENDED 31 DECEMBER 20X0

	£	£
Sales		492,500
Cost of goods sold		(394,000)
Gross profit		98,500
Administrative expenses:		
Postage/telephone	(1,260)	
Staff welfare	(3,750)	
Salaries and wages	(30,000)	
Light and heat	(3,080)	
Rent	(6,000)	
Depreciation – furniture	(1,200)	(45,290)
Distribution cost:		
Sales commission	(4,650)	
Advertising	(9,400)	
Depreciation – vehicles	(4,000)	(18,050)
Profit for the year		**35,160**

BALANCE SHEET AS AT 31.12.00

	£	£	£
FIXED ASSETS:			
Furniture at w.d.v.			10,800
Motor vehicles at w.d.v.			16,000
CURRENT ASSETS:			
Stock in trade		42,800	
Prepaid rent		3,000	
Cash in hand		65,160	
CURRENT LIABILITIES:			
Salaries accrued	(1,800)		
Heating accrued	(800)		108,360
			135,160
CAPITAL as at 1.1.20X0			100,000
Profit for the year			35,160
			135,160

CHAPTER 8

PQ 8.1 Accounting terminology

(a) The word 'credit' in relation to permitting a customer to delay paying for goods sold, means *belief* or *trust*.

(b) The conditions subject to which credit is allowed to anyone are called *credit terms*.

(c) The maximum period a trader agrees to await for cash in respect of a sale made is the *credit period*.

(d) The maximum amount up to which a trader agrees to sell on credit to a customer is the *credit limit*.

(e) The document that a customer is required to sign acknowledging the amount owed with regard to a credit sale is known alternatively as *an invoice, a credit sales memo* or *a debit note*.

(f) A reduction in price permitted usually to a fellow trader is known as *a trade discount*.

PQ 8.2 Appropriate book of prime entry for every transaction

(a) CB	(b) PDB	(c) CB	(d) CB	(e) CB	(f) CB
(g) PRDB	(h) CB	(i) SDB	(j) SRDB	(k) None	

PQ 8.3 The ledgers

(a) NL	(b) RL	(c) DL	(d) NL	(e) NL
(f) CL	(g) CB	(h) RL	(i) NL	(j) NL

PQ 8.4 Prime entry for sales and returns inwards

BOOKS OF PRIME ENTRY

SALES DAY BOOK

Date	V	Customer	F	Amount
20X0				**£**
2.1	484	S. Ally	21	14,500
4.1	485	Peter Gill	22	6,800
7.1	486	Jane Butt	23	11,200
11.1	487	S. Ally	21	6,200
12.1	488	Bob Smith	24	3,600
16.1	489	Sally John	25	5,400
22.1	490	Jane Butt	23	3,200
25.1	491	S. Ally	21	2,600
29.1	492	Peter Gill	22	2,900
		Sales a/c	11	56,400

SALES RETURNS DAY BOOK

Date	V	Customer	F	Amount
20X0				**£**
9.1	14	Peter Gill	22	1,400
14.1	15	S. Ally	21	2,200
19.1	16	Bob Smith	24	400
		Sales a/c	11	4,000

DEBTORS LEDGER

S. ALLY'S ACCOUNT L21

20X0		F	£	20X0		F	£
2.1	Sales D.Bk	1	14,500	14.1	Sales Ret.DB	1	2,200
11.1	Sales D.Bk	1	6,200	31.1	Balance c/d		21,100
25.1	Sales D.Bk	1	2,600				
			23,300				23,300
1.2	Balance b/d		21,100				

PETER GILL'S ACCOUNT L22

20X0		F	£	20X0		F	£
4.1	Sales D.Bk	1	6,800	9.1	Sales Ret.DB	1	1,400
29.1	Sales D.Bk	1	2,900	31.1	Balance c/d		8,300
			9,700				9,700
1.2	Balance b/d		8,300				

JANE BUTT'S ACCOUNT L23

20X0		F	£	20X0
7.1	Sales D.Bk	1	11,200	
22.1	Sales D.Bk	1	3,200	
			14,400	

BOB SMITH'S ACCOUNT L24

20X0		F	£	20X0		F	£
12.1	Sales D.Bk	1	3,600	19.1	Sales Ret.DB	1	400
				31.1	Balance c/d		3,200
			3,600				3,600
1.2	Balance b/d		3,200				

SALLY JOHN'S ACCOUNT L25

20X0		F	£	20X0
16.1	Sales D.Bk	1	5,400	

NOMINAL LEDGER

SALES ACCOUNT L11

20X0		F	£	20X0		F	£
31.1	Sales Ret. DB	1	4,000	31.1	Sales D.Bk	1	56,400

Notes:

1. The folio in which each account is located is stated within a box on the left hand top corner of each account.
2. There is a Voucher column in each of the day books. Every prime entry should be supported by a voucher.
3. Anyone writing up the day books fills in all columns other than the Folio column. The bookkeeper fills in the Folio column after he or she completes each posting. For example, after the total of the Sales Day Book is posted to the credit of the Sales account, the bookkeeper states Sales account's folio number L11 in the Sales Day Book.

PQ 8.5 Impact of errors on the Trial Balance

(a) y   (b) y   (c) x   (d) x   (e) y   (f) x   (g) z   (h) z

PQ 8.6 Source documents

		Source Document
(a)	1.1 Purchased goods from City Stores for £8,200	Invoice
(b)	1.1 Purchased more goods for sale for £3,800	Invoice
(c)	2.1 Sold goods for £1,200	Copy of cash sales memo
(d)	2.1 Sold goods to Sally Jones for £4,200	Copy of invoice
(e)	2.1 Acquired a motor vehicle for £6,000	Receipt
(f)	4.1 Paid £300 for office stationery	Receipt
(g)	4.1 Returned to City Stores goods for £1,200.	Credit note
(h)	5.1 Sold goods to Jim Mitchie for £7,200.	Copy of invoice
(i)	6.1 Received £5,000 as a long-term, interest-free loan from Zoë Budd	Copy of receipt
(j)	7.1 Paid £250 for advertising.	Receipt
(k)	7.1 Jim Mitchie returned goods sold to him for £1,500.	Copy of credit note

PQ 8.7 From commencement to first finalization – Grace Bert

THE BOOKS OF PRIME ENTRY

CASH ACCOUNT

Date	V	Particulars	F	Amount £	Date	V	Particulars	F	Amount £
20X0					20X0				
1.1	R01	Capital a/c	1	10,000	1.1	PV01	Purchases a/c	32	3,800
2.1	CS01	Sales a/c	31	1,200	2.1	PV02	Motor Vehicles a/c	3	6,000
6.1	R02	Zoe Loan a/c	2	5,000	4.1	PV03	Stationery a/c	33	300
9.1	CS02	Sales a/c	31	1,500	7.1	PV04	Advertising a/c	34	250
11.1	R03	Jim Michie a/c	21	3,000	10.1	PV05	Purchases a/c	32	2,400
14.1	CS03	Sales a/c	31	1,400	14.1	PV06	Stationery a/c	33	150
27.1	CS04	Sales a/c	31	1,800	17.1	PV07	Capital a/c	1	500
					19.1	PV08	Advertising a/c	34	150
					22.1	PV09	M. Vehicle Maint. a/c	36	90
					24.1	PV10	Salaries a/c	37	1,800
					27.1	PV11	Rent a/c	35	1,000
				23,900					16,440
1.2		Balance b/d		7,460	31.1		Balance c/d		7,460
									23,900

PURCHASES DAY BOOK

Date	V	Supplier	F	Amt. £
20X0				
1.1	1	City Stores	11	8,200
11.1	2	V.C. Ltd	12	4,600
19.1	3	City Stores	11	3,800
24.1	4	Latiff Bros	13	5,400
27.1	5	City Stores	11	2,600
		Purchases	32	24,600

SALES DAY BOOK

Date	V	Customer	F	Amt. £
20X0				
2.1	1	Sally Jones	22	4,200
5.1	2	Jim Mitchie	21	7,200
9.1	3	S.M. Patel	23	3,600
14.1	4	B. Cameron	24	1,600
19.1	5	S.M. Patel	23	2,200
22.1	6	Jim Mitchie	21	3,400
27.1	7	R. Rajan	25	
		Sales a/c	31	26,400

PURCHASE RETURNS DAY BOOK

Date	V	Supplier	F	Amount £
20X0				
4.1	1	City Stores	11	1,200
		Purchases	32	1,200

SALES RETURNS DAY BOOK

Date	V	Customer	F	Amount £
20X0				
7.1	1	Jim Mitchie	21	1,500
29.1	2	R. Rajan	25	900
		Sales a/c	31	2,400

REAL LEDGER

L1 — CAPITAL ACCOUNT

20X0			£	20X0			£
17.1	Cash bk	1	500	1.1	Cash bk	1	10,000
31.1	Balance c/d		9,500				
				1.2	Balance b/d		9,500

L2 — LOAN FROM ZOE BUD ACCOUNT

20X0			£	20X0			£
				6.1		1	5,000

L3 — MOTOR VEHICLES ACCOUNT

20X0			£	20X0			£
2.1	Cash bk	1	6,000				

Notes:

1. Until we encounter the supporting accounts in Chapter 9, the drawings by Grace (the owner) are debited to the Capital account and returns inwards and returns outwards are offset against purchases and sales respectively, without opening separate accounts to report them.
2. Motor vehicles are depreciated at 20 per cent of cost, but only for a month.

CREDITORS LEDGER

L11 — CITY STORE'S ACCOUNT

20X0			£	20X0			£
4.1	Purchases Retn Day Bk	PRDB1	1,200	1.1	Purchases Day Bk	PDB1	8,200
31.1	Balance c/d		13,400	19.1	Purchases Day Bk	PDB1	3,800
				27.1	Purchases Day Bk		2,600
			13,400				13,400
				1.2	Balance b/d		13,400

L12 — V.C. LTD'S ACCOUNT

20X0			£	20X0			£
				11.1	Purchases Day Bk	1	4,600

L13 — LATIFF BROS' ACCOUNT

20X0			£	20X0			£
				24.1	Purchases Day Bk	1	5,400

DEBTORS LEDGER

L21 JIM MITCHIE'S ACCOUNT

20X0			£	20X0			£
5.1	Sales Day Book	SDB1	7,200	7.1	Sales Retn Day Bk	SRDB1	1,500
22.1	Sales Day Book	SDB1	4,200	11.1	Cash book	CB1	3,300
				31.1	Balance c/d		6,900
1.2	Balance b/d		6,900				

L22 SALLY JONES'S ACCOUNT

20X0			£			£
2.1	Sales Day Book	SDB1	4,200			

L23 S.M. PATEL'S ACCOUNT

20X0			£			£
9.1	Sales Day Book	SDB1	3,600			
19.1	Sales Day Book	SDB1	2,200			
			5,800			

L24 BOB CAMERON'S ACCOUNT

20X0			£			£
14.1	Sales Day Book	SDB1	1,600			

L25 R. RAJAN'S ACCOUNT

20X0			£	20X0			£
27.1	Sales Day Book	SDB1	3,400	29.1	Sales Retn Day Bk	SRDB1	900
				31.1	Balance c/d		2,500
1.2	Balance b/d		2,500				

NOMINAL LEDGER

L31 SALES ACCOUNT

20X0			£	20X0			£
31.1	Sales Retn Day Bk	SRDB1	2,400	2.1	Cash book	CB1	1,200
31.1	Balance c/d		29,900	9.1	Cash book	CB1	1,500
				14.1	Cash book	CB1	1,400
				27.1	Cash book	CB1	1,800
				31.1	Sales Day Book	SDB1	26,400
			29,900				29,900
				1.2	Balance b/d		29,900

L32 PURCHASES ACCOUNT

20X0			£	20X0			£
1.1	Cash Book	CB1	3,800	31.1	Purchases Retn Day Bk	PRDB1	1,200
10.1	Cash Book	CB1	2,400	31.1	Balance c/d		29,600
31.1	Purchases Day Book	PDB1	24,600				
			29,600				29,600
1.2	Balance b/d		29,600				

L33 STATIONERY ACCOUNT

20X0			£	20X0		£
4.1	Cash bk	CB1	300			
14.1	Cash bk	CB1	150			
			450			

L34 ADVERTISING ACCOUNT

20X0			£	20X0		£
7.1	Cash bk	CB1	250			
14.1	Cash bk	CB1	150			
			400			

L35 RENT ACCOUNT

20X0			£	20X0		£
27.1	Cash bk	CB1	1,000			

L36 MOTOR VEHICLE MAINTENANCE ACCOUNT

20X0			£	20X0		£
22.1	Cash bk	CB1	90			

L37 SALARIES ACCOUNT

20X0			£	20X0		£
24.1	Cash bk	CB1	1,800			

TRIAL BALANCE AS AT 31.1.20X0

	Dr	Cr
Cash account	7,460	–
Capital account	–	9,500
Zoe Budd Loan	–	5,000
Motor Vehicle a/c	6,000	–
City Stores a/c	–	13,400
V.C. Ltd a/c	–	4,600
Latiff Bros a/c	–	5,400
Jim Mitchie	6,900	–
Sally Jone a/c	4,200	–
S.M. Patel a/c	5,800	–
Bob Cameron a/c	1,600	–
R. Rajan's a/c	2,500	–
Sales account	–	29,900
Purchases a/c	29,600	–
Stationery	450	–
Advertising a/c	400	–
Rent acount	1,000	–
M. Vehicle Maint.	90	–
Salaries account	1,800	–
	67,800	67,800

For the following month-end adjustments that the bookkeeper made as part of finalization, we have yet to find a prime entry book:

(a) accounting for stock remaining unsold by the accounting date;
(b) depreciating the motor vehicle for the month.

TRADING AND PROFIT AND LOSS ACCOUNT FOR THE MONTH ENDED 31.1.20X0

	£	£
Sales		29,900
Purchases	29,600	
Stock 31.20X0	(6,800)	(22,800)
Gross profit		7,100
ADMINISTRAT. EXPENSES		
Salaries	(1,800)	
Rent	(1,000)	
Stationery	(450)	(3,250)
DISTRIBUTION COST:		
Depre. of vehicles	(100)	
Advertising	(400)	
M. vehicle maintenance	(90)	(590)
PROFIT FOR THE MONTH		3,260

BALANCE SHEET AS AT 31.1.20X0

			£
FIXED ASSETS:			
Motor vehicles			5,900
CURRENT ASSETS:			
Stock in trade		6,800	
Trade debtors:			
Jim Mitchie	6,900		
Sally Jones	4,200		
S.M. Patel	5,800		
Bob Cameron	1,600		
R. Rajan	2,500	21,000	
Cash in hand		7,460	35,260
Trade creditors:			
City Stores	(13,400)		
V.C. Ltd	(4,600)		
Latiff Bros	(5,400)	(23,400)	11,860
			17,760

	£	£
Capital at commencement		10,000
Add: Profit for the month		3,260
Less: Drawings		(500)
		12,760
Zoe Budd's Loan		5,000
		17,760

PQ 8.8 From commencement to finalization – Jacob

CLUE: cash balance £2,900; day book totals: PDB £24,250, SDB £33,500, PRDB £500, SRDB £1,250; gross profit £10,750; net profit £7,300; debtors total £22,150; creditors total £9,000.

CHAPTER 9

PQ 9.1 Accounting for a fixed asset depreciated using the straight-line method

PLANT AND MACHINERY ACCOUNT

20X1		£	20X1		£
1.1	Cash a/c	24,000	31.12	Balance c/d	24,000
20X2			20X2		
1.1	Balance b/d	24,000	31.12	Balance c/d	54,000
1.4	Cash a/c	30,000			
20X3			20X3		
1.1	Balance b/d	54,000	1.7	Disposal a/c	24,000
1.7	Cash a/c	36,000	31.12	Balance c/d	66,000
20X4					
1.1	Balance b/d	66,000			

PROVISION FOR DEPRECIATION ACCOUNT

20X1		£	20X1		£
31.12	Balance c/d	2,400	31.12	Depreciat. a/c	2,400
20X2			20X2		
			1.1	Balance b/d	2,400
31.12	Balance c/d	7,050	31.12	Depreciat. a/c	4,650
20X3			20X3		
1.7	Disposal a/c	6,000	1.1	Balance b/d	7,050
			1.7	Depreciat. a/c	1,200
31.12	Balance c/d	7,050	31.12	Depreciat. a/c	4,800
			20X4		
			1.1	Balance b/d	7,050

DEPRECIATION OF MACHINERY ACCOUNT

20X1		£	20X1		£
31.12	Prov. for dep	2,400	31.12	Profit and Loss	2,400
20X2			20X2		
31.12	Prov. for dep	4,650	31.12	Profit and Loss	4,650
20X3			20X3		
1.7	Prov. for dep	1,200			
31.12	Prov. for dep	4,800	31.12	Profit and Loss	6,000

DISPOSAL OF MACHINERY ACCOUNT

20X3		£	20X3		£
1.7	Machinery	24,000	1.7	Prov. for dep	6,000
			1.7	Cash a/c	12,500
			31.12	P&L – Loss	5,500

BALANCE SHEET AS AT 31.12.20X3

	£
Fixed assets:	
Plant and machinery	66,000
Accumulated depreciation	(7,050)
	58,950

STATEMENT OF MOVEMENT OF PLANT AND MACHINERY

	£
Balance b/f	54,000
Acquisitions	36,000
Disposals	(24,000)
Balance c/f	66,000
Accumulated depreciation:	
Balance b/f	7,050
Depreciation in 20X3	6,000
Disposals	(6,000)
Balance c/f	7,050
Written down value	58,950

The statement of movement is merely presentation in the vertical format of the information in the asset account and the Provision for Depreciation account.

Notes:

1. Depreciation at 10% of £24,000 for a full year is £2,400.
2. Depreciation calculated as:
   - 10% of £24,000 for full year = £2,400
   - 10% of £30,000 for nine months = £2,250
3. Depreciation at 10% of £24,000 for six months = £1,200.
4. On disposal, transfer to the Disposal account the cost of the asset from the asset account and from the Provision for Depreciation account the accumulated depreciation as follows:
   - In 20X1 = £2,400
   - In 20X2 = £2,400
   - In 20X3 = £1,200
5. Depreciation on remaining machinery, to be written off on 31.12.20X3 is as follows:
   - 10% of £30,000 for full year = £3,000
   - 10% of £36,000 for six months = £1,800

PQ 9.2 Accounting for a fixed asset depreciated using the reducing balance method

PLANT AND MACHINERY ACCOUNT

20X1		£	20X1		£
1.1	Cash a/c	24,000	31.12	Balance c/d	24,000
20X2			**20X2**		
1.1	Balance b/d	24,000	31.12	Balance c/d	54,000
1.4	Cash a/c	30,000			
20X3			**20X3**		
1.1	Balance b/d	54,000	1.7	Disposal a/c	24,000
1.7	Cash a/c	36,000	31.12	Balance c/d	66,000
20X4					
1.1	Balance b/d	66,000			

PROVISION FOR DEPRECIATION ACCOUNT

20X1		£	20X1		£	
31.12	Balance c/d	4,800	31.12	Depreciat. a/c	4,800	1
20X2			**20X2**			
			1.1	Balance b/d	4,800	
31.12	Balance c/d	13,140	31.12	Depreciat. a/c	8,340	3
20X3			**20X3**			
1.7	Disposal a/c	10,176	1.1	Balance b/d	13,140	
			1.7	Depreciat. a/c	1,536	1
31.12	Balance c/d	13,200	31.12	Depreciat. a/c	8,700	4
			20X4			
			1.1	Balance b/d	13,200	

DEPRECIATION OF OF MACHINERY ACCOUNT

		£			£
20X1			**20X1**		
1 31.12	Prov. for dep	4,800	31.12	Profit and Loss	4,800
20X2			**20X2**		
3 31.12	Prov. for dep	8,340	31.12	Profit and Loss	8,340
20X3			**20X3**		
1.7	Prov. for dep	1,536	31.12	Profit and Loss	10,236
31.12	Prov. for dep	8,700			

DISPOSAL OF MACHINERY ACCOUNT

		£			£	
20X3			**20X3**			
1.7	Machinery	24,000	1.7	Provn. for depn	10,176	1
			1.7	Cash a/c	12,500	
			31.12	P&L – Loss	1,324	

BALANCE SHEET AS AT 31.12.20X3

	£
FIXED ASSETS	
Plant and machinery	66,000
Accumulated depreciation	(13,200)
	52,800

Notes:

1. Depreciation on lathe

		Ac. dep
Cost	24,000	
20X1 depre	(4,800)	4,800
WDV 1.1.01	19,200	
20X2 depre	(3,840)	3,840
WDV 1.1.02	15,360	
20X3 depre	(1,536)	1,536
		10,176

2. Depreciation of drill

Cost	30,000
20X2 depreciation	(4,500)
WDV on 1.1.20X2	25,500
20X3 depreciation	(5,100)

3. Depreciation in 20X2

Lathe	3,840
Drill	4,500

4. Depreciation in 20X3 on other machinery

Drill (see N.2)	5,100
New lathe	3,600

PQ 9.3 Assets involving conversion costs and enhancement costs

1. Costs incurred subsequent to acquiring an asset may be capitalized if it enhances the performance of the asset substantially more than previously assessed levels (see Chapter 14). Accordingly, the cost of the new motor (£21,500) as well as expenses of fitting it (£5,500) are capitalized because they improve fuel efficiency by 300 per cent. The amount so capitalized should be depreciated, using the straight-line method, over the remaining nine years of useful life of machine M39.

2. Of the amount paid for the luxury coach, £70,000 only is capitalized because this was incurred to acquire the asset and place it in the location and condition for use. Road tax is a period expense, and payment for the extended warranty is incurred in lieu of the repair bill, which would otherwise have to be met. These expenses are therefore written off.

3. Machine M42 should be capitalized at its cost price (£320,000) less trade discount (£64,000) plus carriage inwards of £4,000. £222,000 paid includes £2,000 paid for carriage outwards of M34. Hence that payment must be posted from the Cash account to the Disposal account to determine the gain or loss on the disposal. The remainder (£220,000) should be posted from the Cash account to the Machinery account. Since £40,000, the sale proceeds of machine M34, is withheld by the supplier as part-payment for M42, that amount is credited to the Disposal account and debited to the Machinery account. Thus M42 is recorded at its full cost of £260,000.

PLANT AND MACHINERY ACCOUNT

		£			£
1.4.20X4	Balance b/f	640,000	1.1.20X5	Disposal a/c	180,000
1.4.20X4	Cash a/c	27,000			
1.1.20X5	Cash a/c	220,000			
1.1.20X5	Disposal a/c	40,000	31.3.20X5	Balance c/d	747,000
		747,000			747,000
1.4.20X5	Balance b/d	747,000			

PROVISION FOR DEPRECIATION OF MACHINERY ACCOUNT

			£				£	
2	1.1.20X5	Disposal a/c	67,500		1.4.20X4	Balance b/f	126,000	
					1.1.20X5	Depreciation a/c	13,500	1
	31.3.20X5	Balance c/d	127,500		31.3.20X5	Depreciation a/c	55,500	2
			127,500				127,500	
					1.4.20X5	Balance b/d	127,500	

DEPRECIAITON OF PLANT AND MACHINERY ACCOUNT

			£			£
1	1.1.20X5	Provn for deprn.	13,500	31.3.20X5	Profit and Loss a/c	69,000
2	31.3.20X5	Provn for deprn.	55,500		(cost of sale)	

DISPOSAL OF MACHINERY ACCOUNT

		£			£	
1.1.20X5	Plant and machinery	180,000	1.1.20X5	Provn for deprn	67,500	2
1.1.20X5	Cash – carriage out	2,000	1.1.20X5	Plant and machinery	40,000	
			31.3.20X5	Profit and Loss a/c		
				– Loss on disposal	74,500	

MOTOR VEHICLES ACCOUNT

		£			£
1.4.20X4	Balance b/f	280,000	1.10.20X4	Disposal a/c	16,000
1.7.20X4	Cash a/c	70,000	31.3.20X5	Balance c/d	334,000
		334,000			334,000
1.4.20X5	Balance b/d	334,000			

PROVISION FOR DEPRECIATION OF MOTOR VEHICLES ACCOUNT

			£				£	
5	1.10.20X4	Disposal account	8,166		1.4.20X4	Balance b/f	80,000	
					1.10.20X4	Depreciation a/c	870	4
	31.3.20X5	Balance c/d	121,463		31.3.20X5	Depreciation a/c	48,759	6
			121,463				121,463	
					1.4.20X5	Balance b/d	121,463	

DEPRECIATION OF MOTOR VEHICLES ACCOUNT

			£			£
4	1.10.20X4	Provn for deprn	870	31.3.20X5	Profit and Loss a/c	49,629
6	31.3.20X5	Provn for deprn	48,759			
			49,629			49,629

DISPOSAL OF MOTOR VEHICLE ACCOUNT

		£			£	
1.10.20X4	Motor vehicles	16,000	1.10.20X4	Provn for deprn	8,166	5
31.3.20X5	P&L – gain	1,166	1.10.20X4	Cash account	9,000	

Notes:

1. Depreciation of machine M34 at 10% of £180,000 for nine months of use = £13,500.
2. Accumulated depreciation of machine M34 at 10% of £180,000 for three years and nine months = £67,500.
3. Depreciation of other machinery in the year to 31 March 20X1 is as follows:

M38:	10% of £260,000		£26,000
M39:	10% of £200,000	£20,000	
	One-ninth of enhancement cost of £270,000	£3,000	£23,000
M42:	10% of £260,000 for three months only		£6,500
			£55,500

4. Depreciation of the vehicle sold in the year is calculated as follows:

			Cumulative
Cost on 1.7.20X1	£16,000		
Depreciation at 20% of £16,000 for nine months	(2,400)		2,400
Written down value on 1.4.20X2	13,600		
Depreciation at 20% of £13,600	(2,720)	~	2,720
Written down value on 1.4.20X3	10,880		
Depreciation at 20% of £10,880	(2,176)	~	2,176
Written down value on 1.4.20X4	8,704		7,296
Depreciation at 20% of £8,704 for six months	(870)	~	870
	7,834	#	8,166 ##

The ~ symbol is used to show that the amount is extended.

5. Accumulated depreciation on the vehicle sold right upto 1.10.20X4 is £8,166, as marked with ## in working note 4 above.
6. Depreciation on other vehicles for the year to 31.3.20X5 is as follows:

Cost of all vehicles on 1.4.20X0	£280,000
Less: Cost of the vehicle sold	(£16,000)
Cost of other vehicles	£264,000
Accumulated provision for depreciation on all vehicle	£80,000
Less: Accumulated depre. on the one sold (marked # in note 4)	(£7,296)
Accumulated depreciation on other vehicles	(£72,704)
Written down value of other vehicles on 1.4.20X0	£191,296
Depreciation at 20% of £191,296	£38,259
Depreciation of luxury coach: 20% of £70,000 for nine months	£10,500

BALANCE SHEET AS AT 31 MARCH 20X5

	Cost £000	Accumulated depreciation £000	Written down value £000
Plant and machinery	747,000	(145,500)	601,500
Motor vehicles	334,000	(121,463)	212,537

PQ 9.4 Bad and doubtful debts

DEBTORS ACCOUNT

N		£		£	N
1	Balance b/f	426,400	Cash account	1,006,340	2
	Sales account	1,240,000	Discount allowed	65,060	3
			Return inwards	36,200	4
			Bad debts	28,600	5
			Balance c/d	530,200	6
		1,666,400		1,666,400	
	Balance b/d	530,200			

PROVISION FOR DOUBTFUL DEBTS ACCOUNT

N		£		£	N
5	Bad debts	28,600	Balance b/f	21,320	7
8	Balance c/d	26,510	Profit and Loss a/c	33,790	9
		55,110		55,110	
			Balance b/d	26,510	

Notes:
1. £405,080 × 100/95.
2. £585,540 + £420,800.
3. £585,540 × 10/90.
4. Another name for sales returns.
5. Bad debts are posted not to the expenditure account but to the supporting account.

6. Balancing figure.
7. 5% of £426,400.
8. 5% of £530,200.
9. Balancing figure written off to Profit and Loss account.

On the Balance Sheet as at 30 June 20X1 the debtors will be reported as shown here.

Debtors	£530,200
Less: Provision	(£26,510)
	£503,690

PQ 9.5 A Trial Balance featuring supporting accounts

TRADING AND PROFIT AND LOSS ACCOUNT FOR THE YEAR ENDED 30 JUNE 20X1

		£000	
Sales		965	
Less: Sales returns		(15)	1
		950	
Stock on 30.6.20X0		142	
Purchases	748		
Less: Returns	(21)	727	1
Stock on 30.6.20X1		(172)	
		697	1
Gross profit		253	
Administrative expenses:			
Salaries	85		2
Rent	18		3
Stationery	14		
Telephone and postage	14		2
Audit fees	4	(135)	2
Distribution cost:			
Advertising	35		
Sales commission	17		2
Depreciation – vehicles	36		4
Bad debts	31	(119)	5
Interest		(12)	2
Loss for the year		(13)	2

BALANCE SHEET AS AT 30 JUNE 20X1

	£000		
FIXED ASSETS:			
Motor vehicles – Cost	180		4
Acc depn	(100)	80	
CURRENT ASSETS:			
Stock in trade		172	
Debtors	230		
Prov. for doubtful debt	(23)	207	5
Prepaid rent		3	3
Cash and bank balance		31	
CURRENT LIABILITY:			
Accrued expenses	(19)		2
Interest payable	(12)	(31)	2
		382	2
		462	

	£000	
Capital	400	1
Loss for the year	(13)	
Drawings	(25)	362
12% Loan from Joe Rover		100
		462

Notes:

1. The balances in Sales Returns account, Purchases Returns account and Drawings account (supporting accounts) are shown as offset from the corresponding main accounts.
2. All amounts accrued (including interest) are accounted by debiting the respective expenditure accounts and crediting liability which is reported as a single figure on the Balance Sheet.
3. Prepaid rent is capitalized.
4. Depreciation on vehicles, at 20 per cent of £180,000, is debited to the expenditure account and credited to the supporting account, which would then have a balance of £100,000, which in turn is shown on the Balance Sheet as a deduction from the asset account.

5. The provision for doubtful debts, brought forward at £10,000, should be increased to £23,000 to cover 10 per cent of debtors remaining after writing off the amount due from Bill Lad.

BAD DEBTS ACCOUNT

	£000		£000
Debtors a/c	18	Profit and Loss	31
Prov. for d.debt	13		
	31		31

DEBTORS ACCOUNT

	£000		£000
Balance b/f	248	Bad debts	18
		Balance c/d	230
	248		248
Balance b/d	230		

PROVISION FOR DOUBTFUL DEBTS ACCOUNT

	£000		£000
		Balance b/f	10
Balance c/d	23	Bad debts a/c	13
	23		23
		Balance b/d	23

PQ 9.6 Recognizing the point at which a Trial Balance was extracted

(a) Identifying stock in trade

A Trial Balance extracted from the books of account on the last day of an accounting period, prior to making period-end adjustments, usually reports the opening stock. But the Trial Balance given in the question has been extracted after determining the cost of sales for the year. For determining the cost of sales, the opening stock is added to purchases and from the total the closing stock is deducted. The stock appearing in a Trial Balance extracted after these steps have been taken would, therefore, be the closing stock.

(b) Ascertaining whether assets were depreciated prior to extraction of the Trial Balance

Depreciation is an expenditure, which is reported in the account with a debit balance. The Trial Balance reports two depreciation accounts recording the expenditure arising from depreciation of furniture and vehicles. These have to be current year's expenditure because those of previous years would have been written off to the Profit and Loss accounts. Therefore, the Trial Balance has been extracted after furniture and vehicles have been depreciated for the current year.

(c) Financial statements for the current year:

DEBTORS ACCOUNT

		£000			£000
	Balance b/f	2,460		Sales a/c	240 ①
				Bad debts	20 ②
				Balance c/d	2,200
	Balance b/d	2,200			

SALES ACCOUNT

		£000		£000
①	Debtors a/c	240	Balance b/f	14,480
	Trading a/c	14,240		
		14,480		

BAD DEBTS ACCOUNT

		£000		£000
①	Balance b/f	32	Prov. for	
②	Debtors a/c	20	Doubtful	
③	P&L a/c	11	Debts a/c	63 ③
		63		

PROVISION FOR DOUBTFUL DEBTS ACCOUNT

		£000		£000
③	Bad debts	63	Balance b/f	195
	Balance c/d	132		
		195		
			Balance b/d	132

STOCK IN TRADE ACCOUNT

	£000		£000
Balance b/f	1,428		
Cost of sale	210 ①		
	1,638		

COST OF SALES ACCOUNT

	£000		£000
Balance b/f	11,840	Stock a/c	210 ①
		Trading a/c	11,630 ①

Notes:

1. Goods on 'sale or return' basis, accounted as sales, should be reversed and added to stock in hand.
2. The debt of £20 is written off.
3. Provision for doubtful debts is adjusted to 6 per cent of debtors outstanding at £2,200,000. This leaves an excess provision of £63,000, which, when transferred to the Bad Debts account, leaves a credit balance of £11,000 in that account. This is taken to the Profit and Loss account.

TRADING AND PROFIT AND LOSS ACCOUNT FOR THE YEAR ENDED 30 MARCH 20X1

	£000
Sales	14,240
Cost of sales	(11,630)
Gross profit	2,610
Administrative expenses:	
Salaries	628
Depreciation – furniture	45
Other admin. expenses	564
	(1,237)
Distribution cost:	
Advertising	218
Depreciation – vehicles	176
Bad debts	(11)
	(383)
Profit for the year	990

BALANCE SHEET AS AT 31.3.20X1

	Cost	Ac. depr	£000
FIXED ASSETS:			
Furniture	540	(189)	351
Motor vehicles	960	(528)	432
			783
CURRENT ASSETS:			
Stock in trade			1,638
Debtors	2,200		
Prov. for doubtful debt	(132)		
			2,068
Cash and bank balance			169
Creditors			(1,580)
			2,295
			3,078
Capital			2,200
Profit for the year			990
Drawings			(112)
			3,078

CHAPTER 10

PQ 10.1 Opening the books of a new retail outlet

PRIME ENTRY:

Cash introduced by Sheila is recorded in the cash book, which is also a book of prime entry. The prime entry for the the introduction by Sheila of the rest of the assets and liabilities is made in the Journal.

JOURNAL

	Dr	Dr	Cr
Sundries			
To Sundries			
Furniture account		36,000	–
Motor Vehicles account		24,000	–
Stock in Trade account		42,000	–
Trade Creditors account		–	39,000
Martin West Loan account		–	30,000
Capital account		–	33,000
Being assets and liabilities introduced as capital			

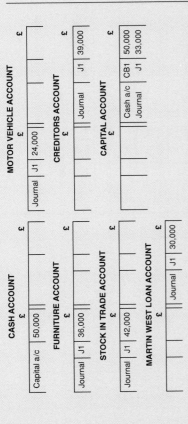

CASH ACCOUNT

	£
Capital a/c	50,000

FURNITURE ACCOUNT

		£
Journal	J1	36,000

STOCK IN TRADE ACCOUNT

		£
Journal	J1	42,000

MARTIN WEST LOAN ACCOUNT

		£
Journal	J1	30,000

MOTOR VEHICLE ACCOUNT

		£		£
Journal	J1	24,000		

CREDITORS ACCOUNT

	£			£
		Journal	J1	39,000

CAPITAL ACCOUNT

	£			£
		Cash a/c	CB1	50,000
		Journal	J1	33,000

After completing the posting, the bookkeeper records in the Folio column of each ledger account the folio number of the prime entry book in which the transaction was originally recorded.

PQ 10.2 Journal entries to account for transactions

(a) In discharge of the amount due from a customer, the vehicle is taken over and the remainder waived.

	Dr	
Sundries		
To Bob Salmon account	–	18,000
Motor Vehicles account	15,000	
Bad Debts account	3,000	

Being acceptance of a vehicle and waiver of balance in settlement of amount due from customer.

(b) £12,000 paid for machinery repairs and £24,000 paid as salary (after withholding ten instalments of £600 each from the pay sheet) would have been entered in the cash book and posted from there to respective expenditure accounts. A journal entry is needed only to transfer half of the cost of repair to the Salaries account.

	Dr	
Salaries account	6,000	–
To Machinery Repair a/c	–	6,000

Being recovery of cost of machine repair from the pay sheet.

(c) Because of uncertainty on whether goods gifted to charity were from those purchased in the current year or those left over from the previous year, the transaction is accounted for only after the balances in both the Opening Stock account and Purchases account are transferred to the Trading account.

	Dr	
Charity account	26,000	–
To Trading account	–	26,000

Being gifting of merchandise to charity.

(d) The difference in value (£38,000) paid in cash is entered in the cash book and posted from there to Plant and Machinery account. The transfer of the balances in respect of the used machinery from both asset account and its supporting account to a Disposal account is accounted for by one journal entry and the trading-in of the old for the new by a second entry.

	Dr	
Sundries		
To Plant and Machinery a/c	–	40,000
Provision for depreciation	28,000	–
Disposal of Machinery a/c	12,000	–

Being transfer of asset and its provision.

	Dr	
Plant and machinery a/c	12,000	–
To Disposal of machinery	–	12,000

Being trading in of old machinery for new.

PQ 10.3 Journal entries for the correction of errors

(a)
	Dr	
Sue Robert	1,800	–
To Sales account	–	1,800

Being correction of error

The difference between £14,200 and £12,400 is accounted for by debiting the customer's personal account and crediting Sales a/c.

(b)
	Dr	
Purchases account	16,450	–
To Calico plc account	–	16,450

Being correction of error

Purchases, left out of the Purchases Journal, are now accounted for.

(c)
	Dr	
Stationery account	400	–
To Purchases a/c	–	400

Being correction of error

The invoice, recorded in the Purchases Journal, would have been posted to the Purchases account.

(d)
	Dr	
Sales account	11,500	–
To Bad debt recoveries	–	11,500

Being correction of error

The wrong credit to the Sales account needs to be transferred to a Bad Debt Recoveries account.

(e)
	Dr	
Office Equipment a/c	16,000	–
To Stationery account	–	16,000

Being correction of error

	Dr	
Depreciation of equip.	1,200	–
To Prov. for Depre. a/c	–	1,200

Being accounting for depreciation of equipment

The cost of the asset needs to be transferred from the expenditure account and depreciated for nine months, in accordance with the policy of the entity.

(f)
	Dr	
Drawings account	2,000	–
To Rent and Rates a/c	–	2,000

Being correction of error

A payment for personal benefit of the owner, wrongly treated as expenditure, is recovered from the owner.

(g)
	Dr	
Stock loss a/c	3,500	–
To Stock in Trade a/c	–	3,500

Being accounting for depreciation of equipment

Stock reported as an asset should be written down to its realizable value.

PQ 10.4 Impact of error corrections on reported profit

	Gross profit	Operating profit
	£	£
As reported in the draft account:	976,800	172,400
(a) A sale not accounted for	1,800	1,800
(b) A purchase not accounted for	(16,450)	(16,450)
(c) Stationery wrongly expensed as Purchases	400	–
(d) Bad debt recovery stated as Sales	(11,500)	–
(e) An asset (office equipment) wrongly expensed (as stationery)	–	14,800
(f) Payment for owner's personal benefit treated as expenditure	–	2,000
(g) Stock (the Balance Sheet item) written down to realizable value	–	(3,500)
Revised figures for year ended 30.4.20X1	951,050	171,050

PQ 10.5 Establishment of a Suspense account

(a) c; (b) b; (c) a; (d) b; (e) c; (f) c; (g) b.

PQ 10.6 Correction of errors that may affect the Trial Balance

(a) Overcasting the Purchases Day Book inflates the debit balance in the Purchases a/c. To counteract that, a credit balance of £1,200 would have been placed in a Suspense account. Transferring that to the Purchases account would restore the correct balance in the latter account.

	Dr	
Suspense account	1,200	–
To Purchases a/c	–	1,200
Being rectification of error		

(b) Failure to post the payment would have created a debit shortfall on the Trial Balance, necessitating £800 to be debited to the Suspense account. Transferring that debit to the Creditors account remedies the error.

	Dr	
Lal Jason's a/c	800	–
To Suspense a/c	–	800
Being rectification of error		

(c) Similarly, failure to debit £1,200 to the Return Inwards account would have created a debit shortfall of the same amount in the Trial Balance, resulting in the amount being placed in suspense. By transferring the debit to the Returns Inwards account, the error is corrected.

	Dr	
Returns Inwards a/c	1,200	–
To Suspense a/c	–	1,200
Being rectification of error		

(d) The error, though one of principle, would not have disturbed the Trial Balance and therefore does not involve the Suspense account.

	Dr	
Stationery a/c	120	–
To Office equipment a/c	–	120
Being rectification of error		

(e) Omission of a zero would have caused a debit shortfall of £3,600 in the Trial Balance, resulting in a debit of that amount in the Suspense account. The error is rectified by transferring the debit to the Rent account.

	Dr	
Rent account	3,600	–
To Suspense a/c	–	3,600
Being rectification of error		

(f) The transposition error in posting would have caused an excess debit of £270 in the Trial Balance. To counterbalance the shortfall, that amount would have been credited to suspense. By transferring the credit to the Advertising account, the overstatement of that expense is corrected.

	Dr	
Suspense a/c	270	–
To Advertising a/c	–	270
Being rectification of error		

(g) Failure to credit the customer with the amount received causes a credit shortfall; and posting it instead to the debit side of the customer's account creates another credit shortfall. To make good both, £3,000 × 2 would have been credited to the Suspense account. Transfer of that credit to the customer's account will rectify the error.

	Dr	
Suspense a/c	6,000	–
To Mike Shane's a/c	–	6,000
Being rectification of error		

(h) Failure to credit the Return Outwards account would cause a credit shortfall in the Trial Balance. Debiting the Return Inwards account (a wrong account as well) causes a further credit shortfall. Hence the Suspense account would have been credited with £4,200 × 2 to make good both shortfalls. That credit has to be transferred partly to the Return Inwards account and partly to the Return Outwards account to rectify the errors.

	Dr	
Suspense account	8,400	–
To Return Outwards a/c	–	4,200
Return Inwards a/c	–	4,200
Being rectification of error		

(i) The error is a compound one. The easiest way of correcting the position would be to wipe off the erroneous accounting by one journal entry and account for it anew by another. The composite entry stated here summarizes both into a single journal entry. This would save time.

	Dr	
Joe Rogers account	6,250	–
To Jill Rogers account	–	265
Sales account	–	3,600
Suspense account	–	2,385
Being rectification of error		

(j) Failure to bring the prepaid rent as a debit balance causes a debit shortfall, while a further debit shortfall is caused when the balance is stated, instead, as a credit. The amount placed on the debit of the Suspense account would, therefore, be £6,000 × 2. This debit balance should be transferred to the Rent account to rectify the error.

	Dr	
Rent account	12,000	–
To Suspense a/c	–	12,000
Being rectification of error		

(k) There is no error in the books of account. An impression of an error was conveyed when a credit balance in the Accrued Rent account was listed on the Trial Balance as a debit balance. On the basis of the false impression, a credit balance of £3000 × 2 would have been placed in suspense. To remedy the position, the credit balance placed in the Suspense account is removed by a 'one-legged' journal entry.

	Dr	
Suspense a/c	6,000	–
Being rectification of error		

(l) Once again, there is no error in the books of account. Failure to include a credit in the Trial Balance would have conveyed a credit shortfall, to remedy which a credit would have been placed in the Suspense account. Again all that is necessary to rectify the position is to remove the credit placed in the Suspense account.

	Dr	
Suspense account	3,000	–
Being rectification of error		

SUSPENSE ACCOUNT

		£			£	
a	Journal	1,200	Balance b/f	4,885	~
f	Journal	270	b Journal	800	b
g	Journal	6,000	c Journal	1,200	c
h	Journal	8,400	e Journal	3,600	e
k	Journal	6,000	i Journal	2,385	i
l	Journal	3,000	j Journal	12,000	j
		24,870		24,870	

~ This is the amount of the imbalance in the Trial Balance which was placed in the Suspense account.

PQ 10.7 Elimination of the Suspense account to finalize the accounts

CLUES: No journal entry is needed for adjustment (a). Adjustments for information stated in (b), (d) and (e) would affect the Suspense account. Cost of sales £1,668; gross profit £1,258; salaries £512; stock at end £440; drawings £131.

PQ 10.8 Post-Balance Sheet elimination of the Suspense account balance

CLUES: Journal entries relating to information (b), (c) and (d) would eliminate the Suspense account balance. After corrections, gross profit = £686,000; net profit = £201,000; fixed assets = £580,000 less £235,000.

CHAPTER 11

PQ 11.1 An account and the side of its balance

Notes:

1. Accounts of a class and their balances fall into a regular pattern as follows:

Class of account	Account balance
Asset account	Debit
Liability account	Credit
Expenditure account	Debit
Income account	Credit
Supporting account	Usually opposite the balance in the main

TRIAL BALANCE AS AT 31.12.20X1

	£	£
Purchases	210,400	–
Stock on 31.12.20X0	29,600	–
Trade debtors	46,400	–
Sales	–	306,800
Rent	15,500	–
Discount allowed	2,400	–
Sales returns	5,200	–
Salaries	16,400	–
Advertising	6,850	–
Stationery	2,650	–
Capital	–	30,000
Discount received	–	2,100
Postage/telephone	950	–
Motor vehicles	24,000	–
Acc. depre. on vehicles	–	8,000
Drawings	2,500	–
Cash and bank	800	–
Staff welfare exp.	6,100	–
Trade creditors	–	26,200
Light and heat	3,350	–
	373,100	373,100

2. The discount allowed is an incentive given to customers to induce them to pay their dues ahead of the credit period permitted to them. An entity experiencing cash-flow problems may choose to allow a discount to its customers as a way of obtaining its cash requirements, rather than paying interest on borrowing the amount. The entity may itself earn such discounts by settling its own dues to its suppliers. Such discounts, known also as 'settlement discounts', are explained in Chapter 13.

TRADING AND PROFIT AND LOSS ACCOUNT FOR THE YEAR ENDED 31 DECEMBER 20X1

	£	£
Sales	306,800	
Less: Sales returns	(5,200)	301,600
Stock on 31.12.20X0	29,600	
Purchases	210,400	
Stock on 31.12.20X1	(38,400)	(201,600)
Gross profit		100,000
Discount received		2,100
ADMINISTRATIVE EXPENSES:		
Salaries	(19,600)	
Rent	(12,000)	
Stationery	(2,650)	
Postage/telephone	(1,850)	
Light/heat	(3,350)	
Staff welfare expense	(6,100)	
Bonus to staff	(13,000)	(58,550)
DISTRIBUTION COSTS		
Advertising	(7,650)	
Bad debts	(2,700)	
Depreciation – vehicles	(4,800)	(15,150)
INTEREST:		
Discount allowed		(2,400)
PROFIT FOR 20X1		26,000

BALANCE SHEET AS AT 31.12.20X1

	Cost £	Ac. dep £	W.D.V £
FIXED ASSETS:			
Motor vehicles	24,000	(12,800)	11,200
CURRENT ASSETS:			
Stock in trade			38,400
Trade debtors	46,000		
Prov. for doubtful debt	(2,300)		43,700
Prepaid rent			3,500
Cash and bank balance			800
CURRENT LIABILITIES:			
Trade creditors	(26,200)		
Accrued expense	(4,900)		
Provision for Bonus	(13,000)		(44,100)
WORKING CAPITAL			42,300
			53,500
Capital – Jim Hill			30,000
Profit for the year			26,000
Drawings			(2,500)
			53,500

3. Profit for the year, without taking staff bonus into account, is £39,000. Hence the bonus is one-third of the profit.

4. To avoid cluttering the Balance Sheet with excessive detail, amounts payable in respect of salary, advertising and telephone are reported in aggregate as accrued expenses.

PQ 11.2 Personal accounts and their balances

Party involved	Relationship	Side of balance	Category	N
Jeremy Holden	Customer for goods	Debit	Trade debtor	
Sony Rickman	Supplier of goods	Credit	Trade creditor	
Mike Johnson	Landlord	Credit	Expense creditor	1
London Electricity	Supplier of services	Credit	Expense creditor	1
Nancy Shaw	Customer for loan	Debit	Loan debtor	
Tim Morely	Sub-tenant	Debit	Rent debtor	2
City Bank	Lender	Credit	Loan creditor	3
London Truckers	Provider of service	Debit	Prepayments	

Notes:

1. Expense creditors are also known as accrued expenses.
2. Tim does not fall within any of the stated categories.
3. City Bank is a loan creditor for the amount of the loan and expense creditor for the interest.

PQ 11.3 A Trial Balance after all period-end adjustments

CLUES: Cost of sale £1,400; gross profit £700; rental income £12; admin. expenses £242; bad debts £6; bad debt recoveries (offset from distribution cost) £14; profit £391; fixed assets at written down value £912; drawings £21.

PQ 11.4 Accounting for deductions from pay and an insurance claim

1.

Stock on 30 April 20X1:		£000
Stock on 6 May 20X1:		126
Sales	42	
Return inwards	(2)	
	40	
Profit margin: 25%	(10)	
		30
Purchases	17	
Return outwards	(3)	
		(14)
		142

2. Carriage inwards and duty paid are part of the cost of placing the goods sold in the location.

3.

Cost of goods lost by fire:		£000
Opening stock		234
Purchases + carriage + duty		1,744
Sales less return inwards	2,400	
Profit margin at 25%	(600)	
		(1,800)
Stock on 30.4.20X1 – Note 1		(142)
Cost of stock lost by fire		36

4. The cost of goods lost by fire (£36,000) net of the insurance claim amount (£27,000) is written off.

5. Settlement discount allowed to customers for early settlement of their dues is an expense incurred by the entity for raising cash. The expense is, therefore, interest in disguise.

6. Income tax (PAYE) account and National Insurance account report liabilities owed to the respective departments in respect of amount withheld from the employee's pay and, in the case of the latter, in respect also of the National Insurance contribution that the employer is legally obliged to pay.

7. Gain on disposal of vehicle, being immaterial in amount, is regarded as a correction of an error in estimating depreciation and is included where the corresponding depreciation would be. If the amount had been material the gain has to be identified as an exceptional income (a topic dealt with in Chapter 42).

SALARIES ACCOUNT

	£000		£000
Balance b/f	166	Profit and Loss	330
National Insurance	24		
Income tax – PAYE	72		
Staff Loan	38		
National Insurance	30		

STAFF LOAN ACCOUNT

	£000		£000
Balance b/f	126	Salaries a/c	38
		Balance c/d	88
Balance b/d	88		

SALES ACCOUNT

	£000		£000
Vehicle disposal	56	Balance b/f	2,468
Return inwards	12		
Trading account	2,400		

DEBTORS ACCOUNT

	£000		£000
Balance b/f	665	Prov. for doubtful	5
		Balance c/d	660
Balance b/d	660		

MOTOR VEHICLES ACCOUNT

	£000		£000
Balance b/f	460	Vehicle disposal	60
		Balance c/d	400
Balance b/d	400		

PROVISION FOR DEPRECIATION – VEHICLES ACCOUNT

	£000		£000
Vehicle disposal	9	Balance b/f	117
Balance c/d	193	Depreciation a/c	5
		Depreciation a/c	80
		Balance b/d	193

LOSS BY FIRE ACCOUNT

	£000		£000
Trading account	36	Insurance claim	27
		Profit and Loss a/c	9

NATIONAL INSURANCE ACCOUNT

	£000		£000
Balance b/f	49	Salaries a/c	24
Balance c/d	5	Salaries a/c	30
		Balance b/d	5

INCOME TAX – PAYE ACCOUNT

	£000		£000
Balance b/f	60	Salaries a/c	72
Balance c/d	12	Balance b/d	12

RENT ACCOUNT

	£000		£000
Balance b/f	30	Drawings a/c	12
Balance c/d	6	Profit and Loss	24

ELECTRICITY ACCOUNT

	£000		£000
Balance b/f	15	Drawings a/c	3
		Profit and Loss	12

PROVISION FOR DOUBTFUL DEBTS ACCOUNT

	£000		£000
Debtors a/c	5	Balance b/f	16
Balance c/d	33	Profit and Loss	22
		Balance b/d	33

DEPRECIATION ON VEHICLES ACCOUNT

	£000		£000
Prov. for dep	5	Profit and Loss	85
Prov. for dep	80		

DISPOSAL OF MOTOR VEHICLE ACCOUNT

	£000		£000
Motor vehicle	60	Prov. for depr.	9
P&L – gain	5	Sales a/c	56

PROVISION FOR DEPRE. – FURNITURE

	£000		£000
Balance c/d	64	Balance b/f	42
		Depreciation a/c	22

TRADING AND PROFIT AND LOSS ACCOUNT FOR THE YEAR ENDED 30 APRIL 20X1

	£000	£000
Sales		2,400
Stock 1.5.20X0	234	
Purchases	1,648	
Carriage inwards	64	
Duty on imports	32	
Stock 30.4.20X1	(142)	
Stock lost	(36)	(1,800)
Gross profit		600
Administrative expenses:		
Salaries	330	
Rent	24	
Electricity	12	
Depreciation – furniture	22	
Loss by fire	9	(397)
Distribution cost:		
Carriage outwards	26	
Bad debts	22	
Depreciation – vehicles	85	
Gain – vehicle disposal	(5)	(128)
Interest:		
Discount allowed		(10)
Profit for the year		65

BALANCE SHEET AS AT 30 APRIL 20X1

	Cost	Ac. dep	£000
FIXED ASSETS:			
Furniture and fittings	220	(64)	156
Motor vehicles	400	(193)	207
			363
CURRENT ASSETS:			
Stock in trade			142
Debtors	660		
Prov. for doubtful debt	(33)	627	
Staff loan		88	
Cash and bank balance		48	905
CURRENT LIABILITY:			
Trade creditors	312		
Income tax – PAYE	12		
National Insurance	5		
Rent payable	6	(335)	
WORKING CAPITAL			570
			933
Capital			883
Profit			65
Drawings – Rent			(12)
Electricity			(3)
			933

MOTOR VEHICLES ACCOUNT

		£000			£000
	Balance b/f	370		Balance c/d	420
	Cash – trade in	32			
	Cash – servicing	18			
		420			420
x	Balance b/d	420	6	Disposal a/c	60
7	Disposal a/c	18		Vehicle maint.	18
				Balance c/d	360
		438			438
	Balance b/d	360			

PROVISION FOR DEPR. – VEHICLES ACCOUNT

		£000			£000
6	Disposal a/c	42		Balance b/f	64
	Balance c/d	95	5	Depreciation	6
				Depreciation	67
		137			137
				Balance b/d	95

MOTOR VEHICLE DISPOSAL ACCOUNT

		£000			£000
6	Motor vehicle	60		Prov. for depr	42
			7	Motor vehicle	18
		60			60

x: Balances as stated in the Trial Balance. The figures prior to these balances were the result of accounting entries prior to the extraction of the Trial Balance.

Notes:

1. The cost of the machine scrapped is removed both from the asset account and its supporting (Provision) account.
2. The cost of the new motor, regarded as an enhancement cost, is capitalized – i.e. transferred from the Machine Maintenance account to the Plant and Machinery account. The machinery to which the motor is fitted has only five more years left of its economic life. Therefore the enhancement cost should be written off over the five years using the straight-line method. This year's depreciation will only be for half a year.
3. Depreciation of machinery for the year is calculated as follows:

Cost of machinery as at 1.1.20X1	£560,000
Cost of machinery scrapped	(£88,000)
Cost of machinery fully depreciated	(£80,000)
Cost yet to be depreciated	£392,000

	£000
Depreciation for the year	
12.5% of £392,000	£49
On enhancement cost (see Note 2)	4
	53

4. Since furniture costing £60,000 has been fully depreciated, depreciation for the year on other furniture is 10% of £190,000 plus 10% of new furniture costing £30,000 for eight months of use.
5. The vehicle traded in is depreciated at 20 per cent of cost for six months of use until 1 July.
6. The cost of the vehicle traded in (£60,000) and the accumulated depreciation thereon for three years and six months of use (£42,000) are transferred to the Disposal account from the asset account and the supporting account respectively.
7. In the absence of any information on the value at which the used vehicle was traded in, it should be assumed that the trade-in value is the amount to which that vehicle had been written down by 1 July. This means that the cost of the new vehicle is the trade-in value of the used one (£18,000) plus the difference in value settled in cash (£32,000).

PQ 11.5 Asset disposal, trade-in and remaining in use after write-off

PLANT AND MACHINERY ACCOUNT

		£000			£000
x	Balance b/f	560	1	Machine scrap	88
2	Mach. mainten.	40		Balance c/d	512
		600			600
	Balance b/d	512			

PROVISION FOR DEPR. – MACHINERY ACCOUNT

		£000			£000
1	Machine scrap	88		Balance b/f	312
	Balance c/d	277	3	Depreciation	53
		365			365
				Balance b/d	277

FURNITURE AND FITTINGS ACCOUNT

		£000			£000
x	Balance b/d	250		Balance c/d	280
	Cash a/c	30			
		280			280
	Balance b/d	280			

PROVISION FOR DEPR. – FURNITURE ACCOUNT

		£000			£000
	Balance c/d	84		Balance b/f	63
			4	Depreciation	21
		84			84
				Balance b/d	84

8. Depreciation on other vehicles for the year is 20 per cent of £370,000 less the cost of the one traded in, plus 20 per cent of the cost of the new vehicle (£50,000) for six months of its use.

9. The amount paid for servicing vehicles, capitalized in error, is transferred to the Motor Vehicle Maintenance account.

TRADING AND PROFIT AND LOSS ACCOUNT FOR THE YEAR ENDED 31.12.20X1

	£000	£000
Sales		968
Stock 31.12.20X0	144	
Purchases	524	
Depreciation – machinery	53	
Machinery maintenance	14	
Stock – 31.12.20X1	(264)	(471)
Gross profit		497
Administrative expenses:		
Salaries	126	
Rent	36	
Postage and telephone	12	
Staff welfare	17	
Depreciation – furniture	21	
Other admin. expenses	10	(222)
Distribution cost:		
Sales commission	14	
Advertising	16	
Depreciation – vehicles	73	
Vehicle maintenance	29	
Bad debts	6	(138)
Operating profit		137
Dividend received		12
Discount received		29
Profit for the year		178

BALANCE SHEET AS AT 31.12.20X1

	Cost	Ac.dep	£000
FIXED ASSETS:			
Plant and machinery	512	(277)	235
Furniture and fitting	280	(84)	196
Motor vehicles	360	(95)	265
Trade investments			115
			811
CURRENT ASSETS:			
Stock in trade		264	
Debtors		116	
Cash and bank		49	
Creditors		(162)	267
			1,078

			£000
Capital			900
Profit for the year			178
			1,078

CHAPTER 13

PQ 13.1 Multiple-choice question

Only statements (a), (b) and (h) are true.

PQ 13.2 Two-column cash book

CASH BOOK

Date	V	Particulars	F	Cash £	Bank £	Date	V	Chq	Particulars	F	Cash £	Bank £
20X0						20X0						
1.1	R01	Capital a/c	C	10,000	–	1.1	PV01	–	Bank a/c	C	9,000	–
1.1	PV01	Cash a/c		–	9,000	1.1	PV02	–	Stationery		24	–
1.1	CS01	Sales a/c		300	–	1.1	PV03	0001	Purchases		–	2,400
2.1	R02	Peter Dudd		1,250	–	1.1	PV04	–	Advertising		65	–
2.1	CS02	Sales a/c		800	–	2.1	PV05	0002	Rent		–	1,500
2.1	R03	P. Richards		1,600	–	2.1	PV06	0003	Rocco Ltd		–	3,000
2.1	PV07	Cash a/c	C	–	3,861	2.1	PV07	–	Bank a/c	C	3,861	–
3.1	R04	Bank Loan a/c		–	15,000	3.1	PV08	0004	Motor Vehic.		–	16,500
3.1	CS03	Sales a/c		600	–	3.1	PV09	0005	Advertising		–	240
3.1	R05	S. Brown		1,500	–	3.1	PV10	–	Staff welfare		40	–
3.1	PV11	Cash a/c	C	–	2,700	3.1	PV11	–	Bank a/c	C	2,700	–
4.1	CS04	Sales a/c		850	–	3.1	PV12	0006	City Stores		–	3,850
4.1	R06	T. Dexter		2,800	–	4.1	PV13	0007	Advertising		–	450
5.1	–	Bank a/c	C	500	–	4.1	PV14	0008	Dawn Black		–	1,650
5.1	R07	S. Mohamed		1,450	–	4.1	PV15	–	Veh. maint.		420	–
5.1	PV18	Cash a/c	C	–	4,250	5.1	–	0009	Cash a/c	C	–	500
5.1	R08	Richard Day		–	3,200	5.1	PV16	–	S. Brown		–	1,500
5.1	R09	Laso plc		3,260	–	5.1	PV17	–	Wages a/c	C	650	–
						5.1	PV18	–	Bank a/c	C	4,250	–
						5.1	PV19	–	Rates a/c		275	–
						5.1	PV20	–	Bank charge		–	30
						5.1	–	–	Balance c/d		3,900	6,116
				24,910	38,011						24,910	38,011
6.1	–	Balance b/d		3,900	6,116							

PQ 13.3 Tracing items for a bank reconciliation statement

The disagreement is caused by the following:

	£	£
1. Deposits not cleared:		
Deposit on 5.1.20X0		4,250
2. Cheques not presented		
Cheque number 0005	240	
Cheque number 0007	450	690

BANK RECONCILIATION STATEMENT AS AT 5 JANUARY 20X0

	£
Balance as per bank statement	2,556
Add: Deposits awaiting clearance	4,250
	6,806
Less: cheques not presented	(690)
Balance at bank as in Cash Book	6,116

PQ 13.4 Ascertaining the actual balance at bank

(a) BANK RECONCILIATION STATEMENT AS AT 30 JUNE 20X0

	£
Balance as per bank statement	26,800
Deposits awaiting clearance	6,500
Cheques yet to be presented	(18,600)
Balance as per cash book	14,700

(b) BANK RECONCILIATION STATEMENT AS AT 30 JUNE 20X0

	£
Balance as per bank statement	42,750
Erroneous bank credit	(4,500)
Balance as it should have been	38,250
Effects awaiting clearance	14,650
Cheques yet to be presented	(74,200)
Overdraft as per cash book	(21,300)

(c) BANK RECONCILIATION STATEMENT AS AT 30 JUNE 20X0

	£
Overdraft as per bank statement	(72,400)
Cheques yet to be presented	(28,200)
Deposits yet to be cleared	116,200
Balance as per cash book	15,600

Note: Bear in mind that the actual balance at the bank should be reported in the Bank column of the cash book.

PQ 13.5 Bank reconciliation statements prepared as at two dates

As at	21.1.X0	26.1.X0
Deposits not cleared	£3,250	£1,840
Cheques not presented:		
Chq no: 24	£220	
Chq no: 25	£1,620	£1,840
Chq no: 27	£1,360	
Chq no: 30	£760	
Chq no: 32	£1,500	
Chq no: 33	£750	
Chq no: 34	£650	
Chq no: 36	£5,460	
Chq no: 37	£1,280	
Chq no: 38	£560	
		£12,320

BANK RECONCILIATION STATEMENT AS AT 21 JANUARY 20X0

	£
Overdraft as per bank statement	(150)
Cheques drawn but not presented	(1,840)
Deposits awaiting clearance	3,250
Balance as per cash book	1,260

BANK RECONCILIATION STATEMENT AS AT 26 JANUARY 20X0

	£
Overdraft as per cash book	(2,210)
Bank charges not accounted for	(55)
Rates not accounted for	(400)
Dividend income not accounted for	1,500
Actual overdraft (to be stated in cash book)	(1,165)
Deposits awaiting clearance	(1,840)
Cheques yet not presented for payment	12,320
Balance as stated in the bank statement	9,315

PQ 13.6 Adjusting the cash book prior to bank reconciliation

(a)

BANK ACCOUNT

	£		£	
Balance b/f	46,400	Suspense a/c		
b Bank Charges a/c	36	– Error in c/f	9,000	c
e John Curry's a/c	11,400	– Error in casting	120	d
		Insurance a/c	3,400	f
		Balance c/f	45,316	
Balance b/d	45,316			

(c)

BANK RECONCILIATION STATEMENT AS AT 31 MAY 20X0

	£
Balance as per cash book	45,316
Cheques not presented	36,840
Deposits yet to be cleared	(22,700)
Balance as in bank statement	59,456

Note: It is suggested that the aim of reconciliation is to arrive at the truth. Since the true balance at the bank is the one stated in the cash book, a bank reconciliation statement should preferably commence with the balance as stated in the bank statement and arrive at the one in the cash book. The peculiarity of this question, however, did not permit that approach.

(b) Journal entry to eliminate the balance in the Suspense account

Only errors stated as (c) and (d) would have disturbed the Trial Balance, by causing the debit balance in the Bank account to be inflated by £9,000 and £120 respectively. To correct the imbalance, £9,120 would have been placed to the credit of the Suspense account. The credit balance in the Suspense account will be eliminated when the credits made in the Bank account are posted to it. Since the cash book, in which the Bank account is placed, is itself a book of prime entry, no journal entry is needed to eliminate the balance in the Suspense account.

PQ 13.7 Bank balance – actual, and as stated in the bank statement

CASH BOOK – BANK ACCOUNT

	£		£
Balance b/f	14,680	C/F error	3,600
		Bank charges	136
		Drawings	900
		Balance c/d	10,044
Balance b/d	10,044*		

* Bank balance to appear in Balance Sheet.

BANK RECONCILIATION STATEMENT AS AT 14.9.20X1

	£
Balance as per cash book	10,044
Add: cheques not yet presented to the bank	18,260
Less: deposits awaiting clearance	(32,200)
Overdraft as it should be in bank statement	(3,896)
Deposit wrongly credited by the bank	10,000
Balance as stated in the bank statement	6,104

PQ 13.8 Role of bank reconciliation when finalizing accounts

(a) Journal entry for making correction of errors

The prime entry for correcting the errors stated in paragraphs (a) and (d) of the question is made in the cash book. Hence the only journal entry required for correcting the error in paragraph (b) is as follows:

£1,160 should have been debited to the Sales account and £10,440 to Suspense account. Since balances in both accounts have been transferred to the Trading and Profit and Loss account, that account is debited with the total amount of £11,600.

(b) The corrected profit and bank balance

Profit and Loss a/c	Dr	11,600	
To Mercy Alles (debtor)	DL?		11,600
Being correction of error			

	Profit for year to 31.12.20X0	Bank balance	N
	£	£	
As reported already	348,600	79,800	
Dividend income	3,600	3,600	1
Business rates	(2,800)	(2,800)	1
Bank charges	(16)	(16)	1
Error in posting receipt	(11,600)	–	2
Payment recorded twice	2,600	2,600	3
Corrected amounts	340,384	83,184	

Notes:

1. Profit as well as the bank balance improve by the dividend collected on a mandate and reduce by both bank charges and rates paid by direct debit.
2. Transferring the amount received from Mercy from the Profit and Loss account to her personal account reduces profit but has no impact on the bank balance.
3. When the double recording of a single payment is corrected, there will be an equivalent improvement in the profit and the bank balance.

(c)

BANK RECONCILIATION STATEMENT AS AT 31 DECEMBER 20X0	
	£
Balance at bank as per cash book	83,184
Add: Cheques yet to be presented	72,400
Less: Deposits yet not cleared	(22,600)
Balance as per bank statement	132,984

PQ 13.9 A three-column cash book

(a)

CASH BOOK

Date	V	Particulars	F	Disc.	Cash	Bank	Date	V	Chq	Particulars	F	Disc.	Cash	Bank
20X0				£	£	£	20X0					£	£	£
1.1	?	Balance b/f	?	–	650	12,740	1.1	?	476	Advertising a/c	?	–	–	450
1.1	?	Guy Thomas	?	400	7,600	–	1.1	?	477	Peter Tell a/c	?	1,200	–	13,800
1.1	?	Sales account	?	–	2,350	–	1.1	?	–	Staff Welfare	?	–	120	–
1.1	?	J. Wren a/c	?	325	6,175	–	1.1	?	478	Peter Paul a/c	?	650	–	5,850
1.1	?	M. Saunter a/c	?	360	6,840	–	1.1	?	–	Bank account	C	–	22,495	–
1.1	?	Cash account	C	–	–	22,495	1.1	–	–	Balance c/d		–	1,000	15,135
				1,085	23,615	35,235						1,850	23,615	35,235
2.1		Balance b/d	?		1,000	15,135							?	?

Notes:

1. The payment to Peter Tell is 92% of £15,000 owed to him = £13,800. The discount is £1,200.
2. The amount of £7,600 received from Guy Thomas is 95% of what he owes, which would be £8,000.
3. £6,175 received from Jerry Wren is again 95% of what he owes, which is £6,500.
4. £5,850 paid to Peter Paul is 90% of what is owed to him, which would therefore be £6,500.
5. Mike Saunter, who owes only £7,200 (net of returns), sends in a cheque for 95% of that amount.

(b) Posting of the transactions by the bookkeeper

1. The receipts are posted from the Cash account to the credit of respective personal accounts.
2. Receipts from sales are posted to the income account.
3. Payments to both Peters are posted to the debit of their respective personal accounts.
4. Payments for advertising and staff welfare are posted to the debit of the expenditure accounts.
5. Each item in the discount column on the debit side of the cash book is individually credited to the respective debtor's account, and the total of £1,085 is debited to Discount Allowed account.
6. Each item in the discount column on the credit side of the cash book is individually debited to the respective creditor's account and the total of £1,850 is credited to the Discount Received account.

PQ 13.10 Focus on discounts allowed and received

CLUE: While prime entry for the transactions would be in the cash book and the four day books, a journal entry would be needed for reversing the discount allowed to Mark. On completion of posting, the balances in various accounts would be as stated here.

Alpha's a/c	37,500	Sales a/c	143,600
Beta's a/c	19,900	Sales Return	1,200
Paul's a/c	108,300	Purchases	111,500
James' a/c	40,000	Purchases Return	9,800
John's a/c	4,500	Disc. allowed	2,980
Mark's a/c	21,400	Disc. received	5,570

PQ 13.11 Correction of errors and use of a Suspense account

(a) In the ledger, the Rent Accrued account appears correctly with a credit balance. By listing it as a debit balance, when preparing the Trial Balance, a credit shortfall of double that amount was created and placed in the Suspense account. The only correction needed is to remove that credit from the Suspense account by a one-legged journal entry.

Suspense a/c	Dr	4,800	–
Being elimination of amount wrongly placed in suspense.			

(b) Because of undercasting, the total of the day book debited to the Sales Returns account will be £2,100 short and, to meet the shortfall, that amount would have been debited to a Suspense account. To correct the error, the debit balance in the Suspense account should be transferred to the Sales Returns account.

Sales Returns a/c	Dr	2,100	–
To Suspense a/c		–	2,100
Being correction of error			

(c) The Trial Balance would have reported a debit shortfall of £8,500, because of (1) the failure to debit the Discount Allowed account with £4,250 and (2) crediting the Discount Received account with £4,250 without a matching debit for it. To mend that imbalance in the Trial Balance, the Suspense account would need to be debited with the difference of £8,500. To correct the errors, the debit balance in the Suspense account should be transferred partly to the Discount Received account (to remove the credit) and partly to the Discount Allowed account (to record the expenditure incurred by way of settlement discounts permitted to customers).

Sundries	Dr	
To Suspense a/c	–	8,500
Discount Received a/c	4,250	–
Discount Allowed a/c	4,250	–
Being correction of error.		

(d) The journal entry is exactly as was done in Mark's case in the last question. The cheque received from Tim Hall would have been for 95 per cent of the amount owed by him. When the cheque bounces, the discount he was allowed has to be reversed so that he may be reported as a debtor again for the full amount of £8,400 that he owed.

Tim Hill's a/c	Dr	420	–
To Discount allowed		–	420
Being reversal of discount allowed.			

SUSPENSE ACCOUNT

Balance* b/f	5,800	Journal (b)	2,100
Journal (a)	4,800	Journal (c)	8,500

* If the journal entries eliminate the whole of the balance placed in suspense, that balance must have been £5,800.

CHAPTER 14

PQ 14.1 Writing up Personal Ledger Control accounts

SALES LEDGER CONTROL ACCOUNT

	£		£ N
Balance b/f	348,250	Balance b/f (credit balances)	16,200
Sales a/c (credit sales)	412,200	Cash (amounts received)	368,500
Bank a/c (dishonoured cheques)	6,650	Discount allowed	15,950
Discount allowed – reversal	350	Sales returns	26,450
Debt collection expenses	150	Bad debts (written off)	3,800
Interest (charged on customer)	225	Purchase Ledg. Control (contra)	15,500
Balance c/d (credit balances)	17,200	Balance c/d	338,625
	785,025		785,025
Balance b/d	338,625	Balance b/d	17,200

PURCHASES LEDGER CONTROL ACCOUNT

	£		£
Balance b/f (debit bal.)	9,400	Balance b/f	225,700
Bank a/c (payments)	198,500	Purchases	264,600
Purchases returns	11,500	Balance c/d	11,500
Discount received	9,450		
Sales Ledger Control	15,500		
Balance c/d	257,450		
	501,800		501,800
Balance b/d	11,500	Balance b/d	257,450

Note: Debts written off in a prior year will not be included within the debtors. Hence the bad debt recoveries are irrelevant to the Control account and so are cash purchases/sales and carriage (both inwards and outwards).

PQ 14.2 Sales Ledger control from source information

(a) Posting from a Receipts Cash Book with analysis columns.

Conspicuous by its absence is the Folio column immediately before the Discount column. This is because each transaction is no longer posted individually. Instead, the total of the analysis columns are posted – £13,100 being credited (as one figure) to the Sales account and £415,296 being credited (again as a single figure) to the Debtors Ledger Control account (which would be in the Real Ledger because the Debtors Ledger is cut off on a self-balancing basis). The transactions, which cannot be analysed under these two columns, are stated in a Miscellaneous column, and every item in that column is posted individually to the Payments Cash Book and, in one case, to a Bank Loan account. The total of the Discount column in the Receipts Cash Book is, as usual, posted to the debit of the Discount Allowed account and credit of the Debtors Ledger Control account.

(b) SALES LEDGER CONTROL ACCOUNT

	£		£
Balance b/f	201,100	Balance b/f	17,650
Sales	484,070	Cash (received)	415,296
		Discount allowed	17,304
		Return inwards	15,300
		Bad debts	26,460
Balance c/d	3,940	Balance c/d	197,100
	689,110		689,110
Balance b/d	197,100	Balance b/d	3,940

(c) LIST OF DEBTORS AS AT 31.5.20X0

W.B. Rajaguru	£53,900
Parker and sons	£31,280
Rik Hunt and Co	£46,540
Jerry Haines plc	£29,260
Adam Young	£17,480
M. Ramanathan	£18,640
	£197,100
Lisa Jenkins Ltd (credit)	(£3,940)

PQ 14.3 Reconciliation of Debtors Control account balance with sum of individual balances

(a)

SALES LEDGER

W.B. RAJAGURU

Date	Particulars	£	Date	Particulars	£
1.5	Balance	62,450	11.5	Balance	3,750
3.5	Sales	26,200	11.5	Cash a/c	81,504
9.5	Sales	36,250	11.5	Discount	3,396
22.5	Sales	17,650	31.5	Balance	53,900
1.6	Balance	53,900			

RIK HUNT AND CO

Date	Particulars	£	Date	Particulars	£
1.5	Balance	34,550	9.5	Returns	1,250
7.5	Sales	20,200	24.5	Cash a/c	51,360
27.5	Sales	46,540	24.5	Discount	2,140
			31.5	Balance	46,540
1.6	Balance	46,540			

LISA JENKINS LTD

Date	Particulars	£	Date	Particulars	£
1.5	Balance	26,780	1.5	Return	1,840
3.5	Sales	17,460	3.5	Cash a/c	40,704
11.5	Sales	39,200	3.5	Discount	1,696
30.5	Sales	22,500	30.5	Cash a/c	59,232
31.5	Balance	3,940	30.5	Discount	2,468
			31.5	Returns	3,940
			1.6	Balance	3,940

JERRY HAINES PLC

Date	Particulars	£	Date	Particulars	£
1.5	Sales	36,450	1.5	Balance	6,400
11.5	Sales	18,560	1.5	Cash a/c	28,848
20.5	Sales	29,260	1.5	Discount	1,202
			11.5	Returns	1,660
			25.5	Cash a/c	16,224
			25.5	Discount	676
1.6	Balance	29,260	1.6	Balance	29,260

PARKER AND SONS

Date	Particulars	£	Date	Particulars	£
1.5	Balance	14,265	19.5	Cash a/c	41,184
1.5	Sales	28,635	19.5	Discount	1,716
19.5	Sales	34,140	21.5	Returns	2,860
			31.5	Balance	31,280
1.6	Balance	31,280			

ADAM YOUNG

Date	Particulars	£	Date	Particulars	£
1.5	Balance	36,595	18.4	Cash a/c	45,936
7.5	Sales	11,255	18.4	Discount	1,914
27.5	Sales	17,480	31.5	Balance	17,480
1.6	Balance	17,480			

M. RAMANATHAN

Date	Particulars	£	Date	Particulars	£
1.5	Balance	36,420	1.5	Balance	11,250
27.5	Sales	27,230	29.5	Cash a/c	50,304
31.5	Sales	18,640	29.5	Discount	2,096
			31.5	Balance	18,640
1.6	Balance	18,640			

ROB MURDOCH

Date	Particulars	£	Date	Particulars	£
1.5	Balance	26,460	27.5	Journal	26,460

Reconciliation of the Sales Ledger Control account balance on 31.3.20X0 with the sum of the individual debtors balances, in the Sales Ledger, on the same date.

	Control account balance	Sum of individual balances	N
Balance on 31.3. 20X0	330,600	322,800	1
(a) Error in posting to the customer's a/c (in the Sales Ledger)	–	(9,000)	2
(b) Casting error in Sales Day Book (affects Control a/c only)	(1,600)	–	3
(c) Dishonoured cheque – credit instead of debit in the customer's a/c	–	13,600	4
(d) Error in listing the customer's a/c – a debit balance instead of credit	–	(5,600)	3
(e) Casting error in Discount column (affects Control a/c only)	(600)	–	5
(g) Delivery charges recovered from customer in error	(160)	(160)	3
(h) Failure to write off bad debt (in the Control a/c only)	(2,600)	–	2
(i) Error in casting a customer's a/c (in the Sales Ledger)	–	3,000	5
(j) Unpaid debt recovery expenses still to be charged on customer	650	650	6
(k) Bad debt recovery credited in error to the Control a/c	7,200	–	3
(l) Contra offset not accounted in the Control accounts	(8,200)	–	
(l) Settlement discount not accounted at all (anywhere)	(225)	(225)	5
	325,065	325,065	

(b) Reasons for the adjustments made

1. The credit balance of £16,200 in the Sales Ledger Control account is netted against its debit balance for purposes of the reconciliation. The opening balance of £322,800, stated as the sum of all individual debtors' accounts, is the balancing figure arrived at on the basis of the reconciliation.

2. Errors identified in the posting to, casting of or listing out of individual customer's accounts require adjustment only in the Sales Ledger (second column).

3. A casting error in a book of prime entry affects only the Control account; and so would any error identified specifically as affecting the Control account.

4. Posting an item to the wrong side, as well as listing a balance on the wrong side, gives rise to a difference of double the amount involved.

5. The erroneous recovery of delivery charges from the customer, and the failure to account for the settlement discount and the unpaid debt recovery charges, affect the Control account as well as the individual personal accounts in the Sales Ledger.

6. Recovery of a debt written off in a previous year is an income and has no connection with the Sales Ledger Control account, which reports debts still receivable.

PQ 14.4 Reconciliation of Creditors Control account balance with sum of individual balances

Reconciliation of the balance in Purchase Ledger Control account with the sum of individual balances in Purchases Ledger	Control account balance	Purchases Ledger balances	N
Balances reported on 31.12.20X0 (net)	321,700	330,800	
(a) Creditor's balance listed on wrong side	–	(3,400)	1
(b) Credit note not posted to creditor's account	(3,600)	(3,600)	2
(c) Contra posted to wrong side of Control a/c	(16,400)	–	1
(d) Overcasting of Returns Outward Day Book	3,000	–	3
(e) Payment not posted to creditor's a/c	–	(19,100)	4
	304,700	304,700	

Notes:

1. Listing or posting to the wrong side causes a difference of twice the value involved.
2. It is assumed that the credit note is yet to be entered in the Returns Outwards Journal.
3. Overcasting of a book of prime entry affects only the Control account.
4. This is the balancing amount.

CHAPTER 15

PQ 15.1 Distinction of an asset from an expense

(a) Why the accounting treatment was incorrect:

(i) £14,200 paid for servicing machinery is an expenditure to be reported as part of the Machinery Maintenance account because the economic benefit arising from the servicing will not last substantially beyond the end of the current accounting period.

(ii) £7,500 paid for replacing the dynamo should also be written off as part of the Machinery Maintenance account because the cost maintains (rather than enhances) the performance of the machinery at existing levels.

(iii) £12,500 + £10,000 paid as stamp fees and for conveyancing should be capitalized as part of the cost of the property because the cost of an asset includes, beside its purchase price, *all directly attributable expenses to bring it to its intended use.* Without legally securing the title to the property, the entity will not be in a position to use the property.

(iv) £120,000 for a set of computer terminals should be capitalized because the payment gives the entity access to the terminals from which economic benefits may be expected to flow for several years.

(b) The impact of errors of principle on performance and position

	Profit	Net assets
As reported in the question	£1,246,000	£4,985,000
(a) Servicing cost capitalized in error	(£14,200)	(£14,200)
(b) Replacement of dynamo capitalized in error	(£7,500)	(£7,500)
(c) Conveyancing cost & stamp fees written off in error	£22,500	£22,500
(d) Computer terminals written off in error	£120,000	£120,000
Revised profit/position	£1,366,800	£5,105,800

PQ 15.2 The case of an intercontinental transport company

FREEHOLD LAND AND BUILDING ACCOUNT		N
Cash bk – price of property	585,500	1
Cash bk – compensation	25,000	2
Cash bk – stamp fees	2,500	3
Cash bk – registration fees	300	3
Cash bk – conveyancing	2,500	3
Cash bk – boundary wall	14,500	3
Cash bk – structural change	145,500	4
Cash bk – shatterproof glass	17,800	4
Cash bk – challenge to title	37,400	5
Cash bk – parking compound	126,200	4
	957,200	

PLANT AND MACHINERY ACCOUNT		N
Cash bk – cost of machine	214,500	1
Cash bk – freight/insurance	12,400	6
Cash bk – duty	46,500	6
Cash bk – reinforcing floor	12,600	4
Cash bk – iron pedestal	8,800	4
Cash bk – test runs	1,100	4
	295,900	

1. The cost of acquiring the asset (both premises and machinery) is capitalized because it gives the entity access to economic benefits, which will last for many future years.

2. The compensation paid to previous owner is capitalized because, unless he is relocated, the asset would not be available for its intended use.

3. Costs incurred in securing the title to the property and building a security fence to deny others access to the property are capitalized because these are steps essential for placing the asset within the entity's control.

4. The costs of structural alterations, installation of the shatterproof glass, and building the container compound are all capitalized because these are necessary for placing the premises in a condition for its intended use. Similarly, the cost of reinforcing the floor and building the iron pedestal are capitalized because these were incurred for placing machinery in a condition for its intended use. The cost of test runs are also capitalized because these are the start-up expenses without incurring which the asset would have been incapable of operating at normal levels.

5. The cost of defending the title, as part of the buying process, may be capitalized. The property may well have been acquired at a lower price because of a defective title. Remedying the defect in the title is therefore regarded as part of the cost of establishing access to, and control of, the economic benefits from the property.

6. Freight, insurance and duty are some of the costs incurred in bringing the machinery to the location of its intended use.

7. The costs of painting/colour-washing the premises and lubricating the machine are not capitalized on the premise that the amounts are not material and the benefits therefrom do not extend to a period significantly longer than an accounting period. One could, however, argue a case for capitalizing the first colour-washing and the first lubrication as necessary for the assets to be in a suitable condition for use.

8. Expenses on moving-in celebrations and relocating the machinery cannot be capitalized because capitalization should stop when the asset is ready for commercial use.

PQ 15.3 Costs incurred subsequent to the commencement of asset usage

(a) Cost of computerizing the designing of machine tools (£246,500) should be capitalized because the cost has clearly been incurred in anticipation of future economic benefits in the form of significant improvements to cash flows arising from the speed and precision designing of machine tools.

(b) Whether the cost of modifications to the machinery, to meet changes in customer needs, may be capitalized depends on whether the modifications are calculated to maintain the future economic benefits at already anticipated levels, or to extend it. If, for example, the economic life of the asset is significantly extended, the modification cost may be capitalized.

(c) The cost of repairing damage from vandalism should be written off because it would merely restore the performance of the asset to previously assessed levels.

(d) The refurbishment cost may be capitalized because it is a major overhaul that restores the economic benefits from the conveyor belts, which have been consumed and written off in the Profit and Loss account over its useful economic life.

CHAPTER 16

PQ 16.1 The concept of depreciation

(a) False: Depreciation on its own is not a source of funds for an entity. Funds are generated by the profit calculated, without including depreciation as an expense. This is because while all other expenses are matched by an equivalent outflow of the entity's funds (because they involve immediate or eventual cash payment), that is not the case with depreciation.

(b) True: The objective of depreciation is not valuation of the asset but allocation of its cost.

(c) i, ii, and iii: True, because each of them is a factor taken into account for determining depreciation.
iv: False, because market value is irrelevant so long as the asset remains in use in an ongoing entity.
v: False, because the expense on maintaining an asset in its current state of performance is an expenditure but it will not affect the amount of depreciation.

PQ 16.2 An assessment of the straight-line method of depreciation

The disadvantage of the straight-line method is that every year depreciation remains the same, whereas in early years repairs should be *low*. In later years there will be an *increasing* charge to the Profit and Loss account, in that there will be a *high* repair charge with the same depreciation.

Another disadvantage of the straight-line method is that if the asset is reduced to nil, care must be taken to see that the asset is not stolen or depreciated to a negative figure.

The assessment of depreciation involves the consideration of three factors: the *cost of the asset*, which is known; the probable *value realizable on ultimate disposal*, which can generally be estimated only within fairly wide limits; and the *length of time* during which the asset will be commercially useful to the organization. In most cases the last factor cannot be calculated precisely. Depreciation is therefore in most cases a matter of estimation based upon available experience and knowledge, rather than of accurate determination. The figures require adjustment from time to time in the light of changes in experience and expenditure, including prolongation of useful working life due to exceptional maintenance expenditure, curtailment due to excessive use, or obsolescence not allowed for in the original estimates of the commercially useful life of the asset.

PQ 16.3 The common depreciation methods

(a) SLM: because in this method, the depreciation once computed, the annual charge remains the same. The only adjustments required are when an asset is used only for a part of the period and when enhancement cost (which should be capitalized and therefore depreciated) has been incurred on the asset.

(b) RBM: because it writes off as depreciation a fixed percentage of a diminishing balance.

(c) SLM: because the loss of resale value (for example, in assets such as vehicles) is never at a consistent rate through the life of an asset.

(d) SLM: because the depreciation charge for a year is arrived at by allocating the depreciable cost equally over the UEL. On the other hand, there are others who would maintain that calculation of depreciation on RBM is simpler. Although the determination of the rate involves mathematical calculation (including an application of a formula), the calculation of depreciation to be written off in a year on RBM is simpler because all that it involves is the application of that rate to the closing balance in the corresponding asset account.

(e) RBM: because in this method the annual depreciation charge decreases with age.

(f) RBM: because in this method, unless the asset disposed of is deliberately removed from the account, the amount written off as depreciation will continue to be a stated percentage of whatever balance remains in the account.

(g) RBM: because in this method the decreasing depreciation charge is usually counterbalanced, with age, by the increasing repair bill.

(h) SLM: because in this method, although the depreciation charge remains constant, repair bills would tend to increase as the asset gets older.

PQ 16.4 Impact of depreciation on cash flow and asset replacement

(a) The bank balance at 31 December 20X0, 20X1 and 20X2 will be equal to the aggregate depreciation, i.e. £600, £1,200 and £1,800 respectively. The depreciation expense will have reduced the profits by £600 in each year and Smith always restricted his drawings to the amount of profit.

(b) The annual depreciation charge is not intended to provide funds for the replacement of the asset being depreciated. It is intended to allocate the cost less residual value over the expected economic life of the asset in as fair a way as possible. If there is the likelihood of inflation, Smith has two choices. The first is to restrict his drawings annually to leave £1,000 within the business, which, with the residual amount of £600 would be sufficient to replace at current prices; the second is to introduce additional capital into the business of £1,200 at the end of the three years.

PQ 16.5 Comparison of four depreciation methods

The correct answer is (c).

- Straight-line: $(50,000 - 10,000)/4 = 10,000$
- Reducing balance: $50,000 \times (1 - \sqrt[4]{10,000/50,000}) = 16,565$
- Machine hours: $(50,000 - 10,000)/40,000 \text{ hrs} \times 10,000 \text{ hours} = 10,000$
- Sum of digits: $(50,000 - 10,000) \times 4/10 = 16,000$

PQ 16.6 Further comparison of depreciation methods

(i) Straight-line method:
10% of £280,000 = £28,000

(ii) Reducing balance method:
20% of £114,688 = £22,938

(iii) Sum of the year's digits method:
6/55 of £280,000 = £30,545

(iv) Machine-hour rate method:
£280,000 × 108,000/864,000 = £35,000

(v) Production-unit method
£280,000 × 260,357/1,620,000 = £45,000

Reducing balance method:	£
Cost	280,000
31.12.X0: 20% of cost	(56,000)
WDV on 31.12.X0	224,000
31.12.X1: 20% of WDV	(44,800)
WDV on 31.12.X1	179,200
31.12.X2: 20% of WDV	(35,840)
WDV on 31.12.X2	143,360
31.12.X3: 20% of WDV	(28,672)
WDV on 31.12.X3	114,688

PQ 16.7 Comparison of straight-line method with sum of the year's digits method

The correct answer is the second.

Under the sum of the year's digits method, business Z will have written off:

Year 1 5/15
Year 2 4/15

Total 9/15 = 60%

Under the straight-line method, business Y will have written off:

Year 1 1/5
Year 2 1/5

Total 2/5 = 40%

This means that the net book value of Y is higher by 20 per cent and any loss will therefore be higher by this difference.

PQ 16.8 Change of estimate of useful economic life

● On a change of useful economic life, the book value (cost less amount written off) on that date should be written off over the revised economic life.

● The machine acquired for £320,000 on 1.7.20X0 would have been depreciated at £16,000 p.a. for three-and-a-half years until 1.1.20X4, leaving a book value on that date of £264,000.

● The book value on 1.1.20X4 (£264,000) should be written off over the revised three years of economic life at £88,000 per year.

CHAPTER 17

PQ 17.1 Where physical stock is lower than expected

(a) Reasons for Jerry's unhappiness with the results of the stocktaking

(i) According to the calculations shown here, the stock as at 31.12.20X0 should have been £581,000 rather than £546,000.

(ii) The stock levels may be too high. When the stock (£546,000) is compared with the cost of sales over the whole year (£4,287,000), it is revealed that (546/4,287 × 52 weeks = 6.62 weeks) almost seven weeks' supplies are carried as stock. Jerry should be conscious of the disadvantages of overstocking. These include the following:

● too much of the business's resources may be tied down in stock – by running down the stock the resources may be freed to be used more profitably elsewhere;

● excessive stock would involve increased storage costs and insurance expenses and higher risk of obsolescence and deterioration.

	£000	£000
Stock 1.1.X0		324
Purchases	4,620	
Purch. returns	(76)	4,544
		4,868
Sales	5,840	
Sales returns	(124)	
	5,716	
Profit margin	(1,429)	
Cost of goods sold		(4,287)
Stock should be		581

(b) Why stocktaking results are not what they ought to have been

● **Failure properly to attune purchases less returns and sales less returns with opening stock and closing stock.** For example, items purchased or returned by customers may, for some reason, have not been brought within the count; or items delivered to customers may not yet have been invoiced to them.

● **Errors in stocktaking.** For example, some items may have been counted wrong; some items (such as those in a bonded warehouse or in transit) may not have been counted at all; the costs may have been erroneously stated on stock sheets; or there could well have been either casting errors or carry-forward errors in the stock sheet.

● There may have been a deliberate departure, during the year, from the policy of fixing the sale price at cost plus one-third. For example, trade discounts may have been allowed to customers; or a decision taken not to pass on to customers any increase in the cost of placing the goods in the condition in which, and the location from which, they are sold.

● Goods disposed of otherwise than by sale (e.g. issued free for charity or as advertisements, or removed by the proprietor for personal use) may not have been accounted for.

● There may have been fraud – either misappropriation of takings by staff or shoplifting of goods by customers.

PQ 17.2 Impact on profit of errors in accounting for stock

(a) Revised performance results in each of the four years:

1. Bear in mind that one year's closing stock is the opening stock for next year. The casting error in the stock sheets as at 31.12.20X0 understated the stock on that date by £18,400. As a result, the cost of sale of that year would have been exaggerated and by that extent the profit of that year understated. Because of the same error, the opening stock in 20X1 would have been understated and therefore the profit reported would have been overstated.

2. Failure to account for the drawings would have inflated the cost of sale in that year by £16,000, and therefore the profit for that year would be understated by the same amount.

3. Because of the failure to include within the stock count goods still to be received on 31.12.20X1, the closing stock for that year is understated and hence the cost of sale overstated. Correspondingly, the opening stock for next year is also understated, and that would have inflated that year's profit by the same amount.

4. Loss arising from floods, recognized and written off in 20X3, occurred in 20X2 and should have been taken into account when reporting that year's performance.

5. Goods damaged by negligent handling are expected to be disposed of at £10,000 after they are reconditioned at a cost of £2,000. Hence, the realizable value of these goods is only £8,000 and therefore the loss by negligent handling, to be recognized in 20X3, is (£36,800 less £8,000) namely £28,800.

Accounting periods:	20X0	20X1	20X2	20X3	N
Performance as reported already	£76,500	(£58,000)	£124,600	£96,800	
(a) Casting error in stock sheets	18,400	(£18,400)	–	–	1
(b) Drawings not accounted for	–	£16,000	–	–	2
(c) Stock left out of inventory	–	£34,200	(£34,200)	–	3
(d) Damage caused by flooding	–	–	(£48,000)	£48,000	4
(e) Damaged caused by negligence	–	–	–	(£28,800)	5
Revised figures of annual performance	£94,900	(£26,200)	£42,400	£116,000	

(b) The impact on gross profit of the loss of stock by negligent handling

The cost of any goods lost or disposed of in any way other than sale should be removed for the purpose of ascertaining the cost of goods sold and of determining the gross profit. Without realizing that the goods in question had been damaged, the cost of these goods had been removed when ascertaining the cost of goods sold in year 20X2. Therefore, the recognition of the damage does not in any way affect the gross profit reported for 20X2. What is affected is the net profit for the year.

PQ 17.3 A trader takes stock after the year end

Note: The interval between the year end (31.12.20X0) and the date the stock was counted is referred to, in this answer, as the 'interregnum'.

Results of the stock count on 3–4 January 20X1:	£	£
		117,567
(b) Remove the sales in 20X0 that did not leave even until the count	80	
Profit margin (in 20X0 sales): 25% gross profit ratio	(20)	(60)
(c) Add back sales in the interregnum	19,590	
Less: Sales which did not leave until the count	(2,700)	
(d) Less: Goods returned prior to the count (hence included in it)	(96)	
	16,794	
Less: Profit margin in 20X1: 20/120 of £16,794	(2,799)	13,995
(e) Deduct: Purchases made in the interregnum		
(f) Add Purchases in 20X0 yet to be received even by date of count		(14,685)
		150
Cost of stock in trade as at 31.12.20X0		116,967

PQ 17.4 A manufacturer ascertains stock on the basis of a delayed inventory

	£	£
Results of stock inventory taken on 5 July 20X1		865,200
(a) Error in stock valuation:		
1,200 sets valued at £20 each	24,000	
100 dozens to be valued at £20 each dozen	(2,000)	(22,000)
(b) Sales in the interregnum (between 30.6.X1 and 5.7.20X1)	144,000	
Goods not delivered and included in the inventory	(48,000)	
Goods delivered within the interregnum	96,000	
Profit margin: 1/4 of £96,000	(24,000)	72,000
(c) Purchases in the interregnum	200,000	
Goods yet to arrive	(150,000)	(50,000)
(d) Purchases in the accounting period yet to be received on 5.7.20X1		75,000
Cost of goods remaining unsold – for Trading account purposes		940,200
(f) Office shelves at cost: 400 @ £300	120,000	
At realizable value: 400 @ £225	(90,000)	(30,000)
(g) Dining-room suite at cost	4,800	
Dining-room suite at realizable value (£6,000 less £1,500)	(4,500)	(300)
Stock at cost or lower realizable value for Balance Sheet purposes		909,900

(e) The lower realizable value is ignored in the case of the cabinet hinges because they are not for sale. It is assumed that when included in the cost of the cabinets, their cost is fully recoverable.

CHAPTER 18

PQ 18.1 Accounting for claims on a publisher

(i) Compensation for defamation of character:
The obligating event is the publication of the article on 15 May. It is therefore a present obligation, although it will be the verdict of the court that will confirm the

extent of damages. Solicitor's opinion confirms that a transfer of future economic benefit is probable. The amount, though reliably estimated at £150,000, remains uncertain until the court determines it. Hence a provision is required for the amount. A further damage the court may award is a possible obligation, which is yet to be confirmed by an uncertain event. Transfer of economic benefit in this regard is possible, although it is not possible to make a reliable estimate. Hence a Note should acknowledge the contingent liability, indicating its general nature, without necessarily disclosing any amounts (because that could prejudice Teenstar's interests).

(ii) Infringement of copyright: The obligating event was the infringement of the copyright that took place on 14 June 20X0. Hence the present obligation to transfer economic benefit existed on the previous Balance Sheet date as well, though it was not provided for on that date because the company was not aware of the claim. The transfer of economic benefit is probable. The amount, however, is uncertain. Hence, on the basis of the best estimate, a provision should be made at £25,000.

(iii) Wrongful dismissal: Because there was valid ground for the dismissal and therefore the chances of the claim succeeding remote, the possible obligation is ignored in accordance with FRS 12. However, company law requires disclosure of all contingent liabilities; and because Teenstar Ltd is a company, it has to disclose this liability in a Note.

REVISED FINANCIAL STATEMENTS:

INCOME STATEMENT FOR THE YEAR TO 30.6.20X1

	£000
Sale of newspaper	640
Cost of production	(210)
Gross profit	430
Distribution cost	(185)
Administrative exp.	(145)
Legal damages	(175)
Loss for the year	(75)

BALANCE SHEET AS AT 30.6.20X1

			£000
Fixed assets	480	(160)	320
Current assets:			
Stock		210	
Prepayment		35	
Cash/bank		45	
Creditors		(180)	
Prov. for damages		(175)	(65)
			255

	£000
Capital – 1.7.20X0	330
Loss for the year	(75)
	255

Notes:

Contingent liabilities. Litigation is in progress against the company, claiming damages both for personal defamation and an infringement of copyright laws. The information that FRS 12 requires to be disclosed is not fully disclosed on the ground that disclosure may seriously prejudice the outcome of the litigation. However, provision has been made in the accounts for reliable estimates of amounts the company may become liable for.

The claim for damages on grounds of wrongful dismissal of an employee has not been accounted for or stated in a Note because the chance of it succeeding is remote. However this may amount to a breach of company law requirement.

PQ 18.2 Accounting for claims on an oil explorer

(a) **Compensation for environmental contamination.** This is a possible liability to be confirmed by an uncertain event, i.e. whether or not the law will be passed. If passing of the law is virtually certain, then the transfer of future economic benefit (£12 million) is probable and a reliable estimate of the amount is available. Therefore, a provision should be made for the amount. At the same time, the assumption of this obligation would give Transoil access to future economic benefits that are likely to be substantially more than £12 million. Therefore £12 million is capitalized (not written off) and amortized over the periods in which economic benefits are expected to arise from explorations in Bolonia.

(b) **Capital construction necessary for future oil extraction.** There is no present liability arising from a past transaction as at 31.12.20X0. Having completed explorations by this date, the obligation to pay £26,000,000 for the capital construction would arise only if Transoil decides to extract oil, and that is yet to happen. Hence, in the financial statements as at 31.12.20X0, the liability for £26,000,000 is not recognized.

(c) **Removal of oil rig and restoration of seabed.** The obligating event is the continuation of oil extraction in Barona. Since legislation has been passed, the transfer of economic benefit is certain. Transoil would have experience of such decommissioning in other countries and therefore would be in a position to estimate with reasonable certainty the expenses that decommissioning would involve. Hence it will have to account for the decommissioning expenses of £38,000 as an accrued liability as at 31.12.20X0. The cost of decommissioning gives Transoil access to future economic benefits arising from sale of oil extracted in Barona. Thus, the amount may be capitalized and amortized over the years during which the future benefits are expected to arise.

(d) **Compensation for exploration related ailments.** The obligating event is not the extraction of oil, but a possible court verdict that upholds that lung cancer results from oil exploration efforts. Hence the claim for £54 million plus is a possible obligation the results of which will only be confirmed by events yet to happen. The transfer of economic benefits is by no means probable and the amount involved cannot be reliably estimated. In the circumstances, Transoil has only to disclose the contingent liability as a Note.

(e) **The promise of a hospital complex.** This represents a present obligation arising from a past event. The obligation is a constructive one (assumed by the chief executive's announcement) which creates a valid expectation in other parties – namely the residents of the Republic of Godavi. Transfer of future economic benefit is virtually certain. However, lacking experience in building hospital complexes, the amount estimated at £40 million cannot be certain. Therefore a provision is made for that amount when finalizing accounts for the year ended 31.12.20X0.

CHAPTER 19

PQ 19.1 A case study

Since Angela is still to approve the financial statements, all events stated as facts qualify to be considered as post-Balance Sheet events.

1. **Post-Balance Sheet confirmation of an asset's existence.** The invoice received in the post-Balance Sheet period confirms the shipping of the machinery 'FOB' (free on

PROFIT AND LOSS ACCOUNT FOR THE YEAR ENDED 31.12.20X0	
	£000
Sales	1,050
Cost of goods sold	(430)
Gross profit	620
Distribution cost	(235)
Administrative expenses	(255)
Interest	(12)
Profit for Year 20X0	118

BALANCE SHEET AS AT 31.12.20X0			
FIXED ASSETS:	Cost	Ac. dep.	£000
Machinery	580	(212)	368
Furniture	160	(46)	114
CURRENT ASSETS:			
Stock in trade		224	
Debtors		219	
Investments		255	
Cash/bank balance		23	
Creditors/accruals		(185)	
Compensation payable		(75)	
Payable for machine		(200)	261
			743
			£000
Capital – Angela Noall			525
Profit for 20X0			118
			643
Loan at 12% interest			100
			743

Notes:

1. **Exceptional items.** Expenses charged in the year include the following exceptional items:
   (a) £75,000 paid as compensation to staff involved in an industrial accident;
   (b) a bad debt of abnormal size, amounting to £45,000 arising from liquidation of a major customer.

2. **Non-adjusting post-Balance Sheet events:**
   (a) Reported at cost at £110,000 are investments held in a listed company that went into compulsory liquidation after the Balance Sheet date. No dividend is expected.
   (b) A line of activity accounting for one-third of the turnover in the year may not be sustained in future because the member of staff responsible for the production of that line left the services of the company after the Balance Sheet date.

	ASSETS				LIABILITIES			EXPENSES		
	Mach.	Stock	Debtor	Invest.	Supplier	Compens.	Distrib.	Admin.	Invest.
As stated in quest.	380,000	242,000	240,000	145,000	–	–	214,000	162,000	110,000
1. Machine acquired	200,000	–	–	–	(200,000)	–	–	–	–
2. Stock lost	–	(18,000)	–	–	–	–	–	18,000	–
3. Listed investment	–	–	–	110,000	–	–	–	–	(110,000)
4. Bad debts	–	–	(45,000)	–	–	–	45,000	–	–
5. Debt recovery	–	–	24,000	–	–	–	(24,000)	–	–
6. Compensation	–	–	–	–	–	(75,000)	–	75,000	–
7. Non adjusting	–	–	–	–	–	–	–	–	–
In the answer	580,000	224,000	219,000	255,000	(200,000)	(75,000)	235,000	255,000	–

board', a commercial expression which means that the Korean supplier is responsible for all expenses until delivering the goods to the ship, while all costs thereafter would be Angela's responsibility). At the point of delivery to the ship, the title to the goods passes to Angela. The machinery should therefore be reported as an asset at £200,000 on the Balance Sheet, while at the same time acknowledging that the same amount is owed to the Korean supplier.

2. **Loss of stock detected in the post-Balance Sheet period.** Unless there is convincing evidence that the rain seepage occurred after 31.12.20X0, the loss, although detected later, is assumed to have occurred in the current year. Stock that did not exist on 31.12.20X0 cannot be reported as an asset at that date.

3. **The case of investments held in companies listed in the Stock Exchange.** Investments held in companies listed in London Stock Exchange are readily realizable at the prices listed on that day. Thus, on 31.12.20X0 the shares in Joel plc had a realizable value of £113,600, which was higher than their cost of £110,000. Investments should, therefore, be stated on the Balance Sheet at cost. The loss in respect of these shares will have to be disclosed, however, as a note to the financial statements because those who make decisions on the basis of information on the financial statements ought to know of the material loss and the consequent liquidity problems likely to arise in the next accounting period.

4. **Irrecoverability of a trade debt established by a post-Balance Sheet event.** Unlike the investments in listed companies, a trade debt can only be recovered when the debtor decides to pay. If events in the post-Balance Sheet period establish that a debt is irrecoverable, the debt could not have been an asset as at the Balance Sheet date. The loss should therefore be recognized in the current year.

5. **Recovery in the post-Balance Sheet period of a debt written off prior to it.** The recovery of a debt in the post-Balance Sheet period establishes that the debt was an asset as at the Balance Sheet date. This is irrespective of how irrecoverable the debt may have appeared until then. The debt should, therefore, be restored as an asset on the Balance Sheet, reversing the write off.

6. **Confirmation by a post-Balance Sheet event of the existence and extent of a liability.** As we saw in Chapter 18, a liability exists if:
   • there is a present obligation (whether legal or constructive);
   • arising from a past event;
   • with no realistic way of avoiding the transfer of future economic benefit;
   • the extent of the transfer can be reliably estimated.
   There is undoubtedly a present obligation (constructive if not legal) to pay compensation and the obligation arose from a past event, which was the accident on 7 November. There is no realistic way of avoiding this obligation. The amount of the compensation payable is crystallized by the court decision within the post-Balance Sheet period. Therefore the Balance Sheet as at 31.12.20X0 should account for the compensation of £75,000 as a liability.

7. **A non-adjusting event which would have a material impact on the entity's future performance.** The performance reported in the Profit and Loss account is relied on as the basis of predicting future performance. Therefore the loss of Sue's services and the extent to which she contributed to the performance in the current period should be communicated as notes. Whether Clara could fill in the void is as yet a conjecture.

PQ 19.2 A second case study

1. **Loss of an important line of credit.** The loss of the revolving credit line, although occurring after the Balance Sheet date and therefore irrelevant to the position as at that date, is crucial for decisions to be made on the basis of the information because it may affect the liquidity as well as the future performance of the business. It is, therefore, a non-adjusting event to be disclosed in a Note. In the event that the denial of the line of credit imperils the ability of the business to survive, it will invalidate the assumption of going concern, making it necessary to redraft the financial statements on a gone-concern basis, i.e. the fixed assets would be valued at realizable values rather than at cost less accumulated depreciation and the current assets at net realizable values.

2. **Determination of the realizable value of unsold stock.** Stock should be reported at cost or lower realizable value. The disposal of stock specifically identified as dormant (at £214,500 + (20 per cent of £214,500) = £257,400, less 25 per cent) establishes the realizable value at £193,050, which is lower than cost. The stock should be reported at £193,050.

3. **The post-Balance Sheet loss of an asset.** Loss of machinery by fire does not affect the position as at the Balance Sheet date. It is therefore not an adjusting event. The machine in question will be reported on the Balance Sheet as at 30.6.20X0 at its written down value of £240,000. Whether the subsequent loss of the machine and the inability to recover the loss from insurance should be reported as a Note depends on the impact the loss would have on the capacity of the business, its performance in the future, and on its liquidity position (because of having to find resources to replace the machine).

4. **Post-Balance Sheet loss of a market.** The loss of a significant portion of the entity's market, in the post-Balance Sheet period, should be disclosed in a Note because of the serious impact it would have on the future performance and profitability of the business.

5. **Unreceived dividend income.** Although under the accruals concept the dividend from Hardput should be accounted for in the year ending 30.6.20X0 because it relates to the year, dividend earnings are never recognized as income until they are received. This is because, although proposed by its directors, the payment of the dividend by Hardput Ltd. depends on the approval by its shareholders. The dividend income is not, therefore, accounted for in the year. The amount being immaterial, it will not even be disclosed as a Note.

CHAPTER 20

PQ 20.1 Accounting for transactions of a VAT-registered trader

BOOKS OF PRIME ENTRY

PURCHASES DAY BOOK

20X0		F	£	Purch	VAT
1.1	Coolit Ltd	?	34,545	29,400	5,145
6.1	Coolit Ltd	?	17,625	15,000	2,625
			44,400		7,770
		NL?			RL?

SALES DAY BOOK

20X0		F	£	Sales	VAT
5.1	Comfy plc	?	14,100	12,000	2,100
6.1	Deckchair	?	18,800	16,000	2,800
14.1	Easy plc	?	14,100	12,000	2,100
24.1	Deckchair	?	14,100	12,000	2,100
				52,000	9,100
		NL?			RL?

NL = Nominal Ledger
RL = Real Ledger

CASH ACCOUNT

20X0		£	20X0		£
1.1	Capital a/c	100,000	1.1	Furniture a/c	24,000
9.1	Sales a/c	8,000	1.1	VAT a/c	4,200
9.1	VAT a/c	1,400	1.1	Advertising	1,400
20.1	Sales a/c	4,000	1.1	VAT a/c	77
20.1	VAT a/c	700	20.1	Motor Vehicle	38,775
22.1	Deckchair	18,800	3.1	Rent a/c	1,000
			17.1	Stationery a/c	200
			17.1	VAT a/c	35
			21.1	Advertising	600
			21.1	VAT a/c	105
			27.1	Salaries a/c	3,600
			30.1	Electricity a/c	240
			30.1	Gas a/c	360
			30.1	Telephone	160
			30.1	VAT a/c	133
			31.1	Balance c/d	58,975
		132,900			132,900
1.2	Balance	58,975			

JOURNAL

20X0			£	£
31.1	Drawings a/c	Dr	2,938	–
	To Trading a/c		–	2,500
	VAT a/c		–	438
	Being goods removed by proprietor for personal use.			

TRIAL BALANCE AS AT 31.1.2000

	£	£
Cash a/c	58,975	–
VAT account	1,120	–
Capital a/c	–	100,000
Purchases a/c	44,400	–
Sales a/c	–	64,000
Advertising a/c	1,040	–
Rent a/c	1,000	–
Stationery a/c	200	–
Salaries a/c	3,600	–
Electricity a/c	240	–
Gas a/c	360	–
Telephone a/c	160	–
Furniture a/c	24,000	–
Motor vehicles	38,775	–
Coolit Ltd a/c	–	52,170
Comfy plc a/c	14,100	–
Deckchair Ltd	14,100	–
Easy plc	14,100	–
	216,170	216,170

WORKING

VAT ACCOUNT

20X0		£	20X0		£
1.1	Cash – furniture	4,200	9.1	Cash – sales	1,400
1.1	Cash – advert.	77	20.1	Cash – sales	700
17.1	Cash – stationery	35	31.1	Sales Day Book	9,100
21.1	Cash – advert.	105			
30.1	Cash –	133			
31.1	Purch. Day Book	7,770	31.1	Balance c/d	1,120
		12,320			12,320
1.2	Balance b/d	1,120		Journal	438

TRADING AND PROFIT AND LOSS FOR THE MONTH ENDED 31.1.20X0

	£	£
Sales		64,000
Purchases	44,400	
Stock in trade	(2,500)	
Drawings	(2,500)	(39,400)
Gross profit		24,600
Distribution cost:		
Advertising	1,040	
Depre. of vehicle	646	(1,686)
Administrative expenses:		
Salaries	3,600	
Rent	1,000	
Depre. of furniture	200	
Stationery	200	
Electricity	240	
Gas	360	
Telephone	160	(5,760)
Profit for the month		17,154

BALANCE SHEET AS AT 31.1.20X0

	Cost	Ac. dep.	£
Fixed assets:			
Furniture	24,000	(200)	23,800
Motor vehicles	38,775	(646)	38,129
			61,929
Current assets:			
Stock in trade		2,500	
Trade debtors:			
Comfy plc	14,100		
Deckchair Ltd	14,100		
Easy plc	14,100	42,300	
VAT account		682	
Cash		58,975	
Creditors:			
Coolit plc		(52,170)	52,287
			114,216
Capital		100,000	
Profit for the month		17,154	
Drawings		(2,938)	
			114,216

1. Input VAT recoverable from the Department of Customs and Excise is reduced by the amount of VAT relating to the AC system taken by Bob for personal use.
2. Input VAT on motor vehicles is not recoverable.
3. Depreciation is calculated at the agreed percentage for one month.

PQ 20.2 Prime entry books with analysis columns to account for VAT

CLUES: Sales £50,000; purchases £53,200; wages £900, stationery £200; telephone £600; electricity £720; advertising £3,000; profit £3,000; expenses £214; furniture £2,566; vehicles £13,000; stock £28,200; due from VAT dept £3,654.

PQ 20.3 Finalization of accounts of a VAT-registered trader

TRADING AND PROFIT AND LOSS ACCOUNT FOR THE YEAR ENDED 30.6.20X1

	£	£000
Sales		3,000
Stock on 1.7.20X0	480	
Purchases	1,800	
Stock on 30.6.20X1	(360)	(1,920)
Gross profit		1,080
Administrative expenses:		
Salaries	216	
Rent	24	
Telephone	40	
Depre. – furniture	16.2	
Entertainment	94	
Stationery	120	(510.2)
Distribution cost:		
Depre. motor vehicle	83.7	
Bad debts	44	(127.7)
Profit for the year		442.1

BALANCE SHEET AS AT 30 JUNE 20X1

	Cost	Ac. dep.	£000
Fixed assets:			
Furniture	182	(88.2)	93.8
Motor vehicles	442	(279.7)	162.3
Current assets:			
Stock in trade			360
Debtors	640		
Provi. for doubtful debts	(32)	608	
Cash and bank		169	
Creditors	324		
VAT payable	107	(431)	706
			962.1

	£000
Capital	520
Profit for the year	442.1
	962.1

CUSTOMS AND EXCISE DEPT ACCOUNT

	£		£
Balance b/f	54	Sales a/c	525
Furniture a/c	14		
Purchases a/c	315		
Bad Debts a/c	7		
Telephone a/c	7		
Stationery a/c	21		
Balance c/d	107		
	525		525
		Balance b/d	107

Notes:

1. Input VAT on motor vehicles and entertainment cannot be reclaimed. Input VAT on all else has been debited to the Customs and Excise Dept, which has been credited with the output VAT collected with sales.
2. VAT relief is not available with regard to the adjustments to the general provision for bad debts.

CHAPTER 21

PQ 21.1 A basic interpretation of financial statements

Profitability:

(a) Return on capital employed

$$\frac{25+9}{200} \times 100 = 17\%$$

(b) Return on equity

$$\frac{25}{125} \times 100 = 20\%$$

Liquidity:

(a) Current ratio:

$$\frac{100}{50} = 2 \text{ times}$$

(b) Liquidity ratio:

$$\frac{37.500}{50,000} = 0.75 \text{ times}$$

Operational efficiency:

(a) Total asset turnover:

$$\frac{625}{200} = 3.125 \text{ times}$$

(b) Stock turnover:

$$\frac{425}{54.5 + 62.5/2} = 7.3 \text{ times}$$

Without more information on market rates of returns, industrial averages and performance in prior years, it is not possible to say whether 17 per cent ROCE and 20 per cent return on equity are satisfactory. However, 17 per cent ROCE makes affordable the payment of 12 per cent p.a. on loan capital.

Liquidity appears satisfactory because a current ratio of 2 is what is generally expected. That the liquidity ratio is less than unity may be of some concern. The degree of concern depends, however, on such matters as the ready realizability of stock, whether bank accommodation is readily available, and so on.

Operational efficiency of the business again cannot be assessed purely on the basis of total asset turnover of 3 and stock turnover in excess of 7, unless additional information is available on industrial averages and past performance.

Despite the reduction in sale price, the ratio of return on capital to sales, as well as the ratio of net profit to sales, have both improved, by 41 per cent and 23 per cent respectively. This has been achieved by pruning the administrative expenses and distribution cost by 57 per cent and 16 per cent respectively. This raises the suspicion, however, as to whether depreciation rates have been tampered with or necessary maintenance of fixed assets overlooked.

During the year all assets have been made to work harder. Total asset turnover and fixed asset turnover have improved by 12 per cent and 14 per cent respectively, while the turnover of working capital has improved by 181 per cent. Buying efficiency has improved as reflected by an improvement of 31 per cent in the stock turnover ratio. Credit control over customers has improved by 72 per cent as reflected by the debtors turnover ratio. In the meantime, greater attention is being paid to settling the suppliers in time, as reflected by 55 per cent improvement in the creditors turnover ratio.

Despite reducing sale prices by 24 per cent, because of more than commensurate expansion of sales (by 98 per cent) and pruning of costs, the business has become substantially more profitable. The return on capital employed ratio, at 27.84 per cent, is 59 per cent better than what it was in the previous year. The business is, therefore, amply justified in borrowing at 7% per annum.

The owner of the business is getting a return of 32.7 per cent which is an improvement of 87 per cent over that of the previous year.

The working capital ratio and liquidity ratio, which in 20X0 were both substantially lower than the rates normally regarded as desirable, have become even worse this year, the former by 17 per cent and the latter by 43 per cent. However, that does not appear to signify any liquidity problem because of the following reasons:

Sales in the year are almost double (+97.8 per cent) that of the previous year. One of the reasons for this appears to be a 24 per cent reduction in the sale price. An alternative explanation for the fall in the gross profit ratio may be that the business is unable to pass on to its customers an increased cost of goods.

PQ 21.2 Progress of an entity from one year to the next

Operational performance:

	In year to 31.12.20X1	In year to 31.12.20X0	+ or −
1. Gross profit ratio	$\frac{£115,900}{£764,200} \times 100 = 15.2\%$	$\frac{£77,280}{£386,400} \times 100 = 20\%$	−24%
2. Admin. expen. to sales ratio	$\frac{£37,650}{£764,200} \times 100 = 4.9\%$	$\frac{£43,400}{£386,400} \times 100 = 11.3\%$	−57%
3. Distrib. cost to sales ratio	$\frac{£24,650}{£764,200} \times 100 = 3.2\%$	$\frac{£14,680}{£386,400} \times 100 = 3.8\%$	−16%
4. Net profit to sales ratio	$\frac{£46,600}{£764,200} \times 100 = 6.1\%$	$\frac{£19,200}{£386,400} \times 100 = 4.97\%$	+23%
5. Return on capital to sales	$\frac{£53,600}{£764,200} \times 100 = 7.01\%$	$\frac{£19,200}{£386,400} \times 100 = 4.97\%$	+41%
6. Total asset turnover ratio	$\frac{£764,200}{119,200 + 265,800/2} = 4$ times	$\frac{£386,400}{100,000 + 119,200/2} = 3.5$ times	+12%
7. Fixed asset turnover ratio	$\frac{£764,200}{105,000 + 260,000/2} = 4.2$ times	$\frac{£386,400}{£105,000} = 3.7$ times	+14%
8. Working capital turnover ratio	$\frac{£764,200}{14,200 + 5,800/2} = 76$ times	$\frac{£386,400}{£14,200} = 27$ times	181%
9. Stock turnover ratio	$\frac{£648,300}{31,200 + 65,300/2} = 13.4$ times	$\frac{£309,120}{29,600 + 31,200/2} = 10$ times	+31%
10. Debtors turnover ratio	$\frac{£764,200}{19,700 + 25,700/2} = 33.7$ times	$\frac{£386,400}{£19,700} = 20$ times	+72%
11. Creditors turnover ratio	$\frac{£682,400}{52,300 + 96,700/2} = 9.2$ times	$\frac{£310,720}{£52,300} = 5.9$ times	+55%

Profitability:

	In year to 31.12.20X1	In year to 31.12.20X0	+ or −
1. Return on capital employed	$\frac{£46,600 + £7,000}{119,200 + 265,800/2} \times 100 = 27.84\%$	$\frac{£19,200}{100,000 + 119,200/2} \times 100 = 17.52\%$	+59%
2. Return to equity ratio	$\frac{£46,600}{119,200 + 165,800/2} \times 100 = 32.70\%$	$\frac{£19,200}{100,000 + 119,200/2} \times 100 = 17.52\%$	+87%

Liquidity:

	In year to 31.12.20X1	In year to 31.12.20X0	+ or −
1. Working capital ratio	$\frac{£102,500}{£96,700} = 1.06$ times	$\frac{£66,500}{£52,300} = 1.27$ times	−17%
2. Liquidity ratio	$\frac{£37,200}{£96,700} = 0.38$ times	$\frac{£35,300}{£52,300} = 0.67$ times	−43%
3. Stock days	$\frac{£65,300}{£648,300} \times 365 = 37$ days	$\frac{£31,200}{£309,120} \times 365 = 37$ days	0%
4. Debtors days	$\frac{£25,700}{£764,200} \times 365 = 12.3$ days	$\frac{£19,700}{£386,400} \times 365 = 18.6$ days	−34%
5. Creditors days	$\frac{£96,700}{£682,400} \times 365 = 51.7$ days	$\frac{£52,300}{£310,720} \times 365 = 61.4$ days	−16%

- the business does not have any bank loan or overdraft;
- the business is making such high levels of profit that it would not be difficult to find loan capital;
- the business continues to keep a good control over stock turnover and appears to be either making most of its sales on cash terms or extending very limited credit and enforcing tight credit control;
- the business is able to pay its creditors earlier than it did in the previous year.

The business continues to keep a tight grip on stock levels, carrying just about what is sufficient to cover a single month's sale.

If the sales are usually made on credit terms, the credit period appears to be only two weeks and this period is being strictly enforced. However, if the suppliers' credit period is one month, the business is still unable to comply with that period even though it has improved from the previous year's position.

Capital structure

	In year to 31.12.20X1	In year to 31.12.20X0	+ or –
1. Financing of fixed assets	$\dfrac{119{,}200 + 46{,}600 + 100{,}000}{260{,}000} \times 100 = 102\%$	$\dfrac{100{,}000 + 19{,}200}{£105{,}000} \times 100 = 113\%$	–10%
2. Gearing	$\dfrac{£100{,}000}{£119{,}200 + £46{,}600} \times 100 = 60\%$	$\dfrac{00}{£119{,}200} \times 100 = 00\%$	+60%
3. Interest cover	$\dfrac{£46{,}600 + £7{,}000}{£7{,}000} = 7.7$ times	No interest payable	

Though the whole of fixed assets is financed by long-term capital, the proportion of resources available as working capital is even lower than what it was in the previous year. Unless this position is one deliberately achieved, there may possibly be a situation of undercapitalization.

Having borrowed capital in the year, the business has just become geared; and at the given level of gearing, being 60 per cent, the business is now regarded as highly geared.

At current levels of earning, the interest cover available to loan creditors, at almost 8, is substantially high.

PQ 21.3 Return on capital employed

	Sales for the year	Net profit for the year	Interest on loan capital	Capital employed	Return on capital to sales ratio	Total asset turnover	Return on capital employed
(a)	£10,000	£800	£200	£5,000	10%	2	20%
(b)	£15,000	£1,600	£200	£8000	12%	1.875	22.5%
(c)	£10,000	£300	£200	£2,500	5%	4	20%
(d)	£20,000	£800	£200	£5,000	5%	4	20%
(e)	£40,000	£3,800	£200	£10,000	10%	4	40%
(f)	£20,000	£300	£200	£5,000	2.5%	4	10%

PQ 21.4 Interpretation from an investor's focus

General comment:
The business is still at an early stage. It is not unusual for a business at this stage to be unprofitable.

Operating efficiency:

- Sales in the second year have improved by 40 per cent in comparison with the first and, therefore, a projected increase is plausible but should be substantiated by detailed forecasts.
- Gross profit ratio in the second year has fallen by 10 per cent. It may be because of deliberate reduction in sale prices as a technique of boosting sales. Whether further reductions are contemplated to improve sales should be inquired into.

Year to 31.3	20X1	20X2
Gross profit ratio	40%	35.7%

- Fixed overheads: Whether the increase of £2,800 in fixed overheads arose wholly from the rent for enlarged premises should be established.
- Variable overheads: In proportion to the increase in sales, the variable overheads in the second year should have been £19,600, whereas they were £24,500. This could be because the rate of sales commission and the extent of advertising may have been increased for stimulating sales. Whether the expenses will remain at current levels or require increase should also be investigated.
- The net profit to sales ratio in the first year was 8 per cent. If the higher rental payment in the second year is ignored, the ratio in the second would have been 2 per cent.
- During the second year, as compared with the first:
  - total asset turnover improved by 35%;
  - fixed asset turnover improved by 36%;
  - working capital turnover improved by 51%;
  - stock turnover improved by 45%;
  - debtors turnover improved by 3%;
  - creditors turnover reduced (favourable) by 36%.

Year to 31.3	20X1	20X2
Total asset turnover	1.1	1.5
Fixed asset turnover	1.4	1.9
Working capital turnover	5.3	8
Stock turnover	7.6	11
Debtors turnover	7.2	7.4
Creditors turnover	15	9.6

The apparent improvements in these ratios, however, arose because of inadequate liquidity. For example, creditors on 31.3.20X2 and stock levels on that date are likely to have been substantially bigger if the business has had the resources or was able to obtain extended credit facility from suppliers.

Profitability:

- Return on capital employed in the first year was 9 per cent, and in the second year, if additional rent is not taken into account, was 3 per cent. To bring creditors within suppliers' credit period and to pay off the bank overdraft, William requires at least £6,000 as a loan from his mother on

PROJECTION – YEAR TO 31.3.20X3		
		£
Sales	as anticipated	150,000
Cost of sale		(96,450)
Gross profit	35.7% as in year 2	53,550
Fixed O/H	as in year 2	(11,200)
Variable O/H	25% year 2 levels	(37,500)
Interest	8% p.a. on £6,000	(480)
Profit anticipated (hopefully)		4,370

1.4.20X2. At best, the ROCE in the year to 31.3.20X3 (see workings on right) will be £(4,370 + 480)/£71,900 × 100% = 6.75%.

• Return on equity will be (4,370/64,400) × 100% = 6.8%.

Liquidity:

• William admits that liquidity of the business is strained. Ratios need not be calculated.

Conclusion:

• Though current levels of earning are substantially lower than what could be earned from employment, William may prefer the freedom and challenge of developing his own business.

• He must, however, work out his prospects by preparing three to five years of forecasts.

• He could ask for assistance from the Small Business section of his bank and from the Department of Trade and Industry.

• His mother should take comfort from her son's ability to pay her interest at rates she can earn elsewhere and that the interest cover is expected to be [(£4,370 + £480)/£480], which is more than 10 times.

PQ 21.5 Creating accounts from ratios

(a) Depreciation @ 10% of cost = £1,500
Fixed assets £1,500 × 100/10 = £15,000
Fixed assets at wdv by year end: £15,000 − £1,500 = £13,500

(b) Current asset ratio 1.5
Working capital is £11,500
Current assets = £11,500 × 3 = £34,500
Current Liabilities = £11,500 × 2 = £23,000 (creditors)

(c) Total assets: fixed asset (a) £13,500 + working capital £11,500 = £25,000

(d) Total asset turnover = 2
Total assets (c.) = £25,000
Sales = £25,000 × 2 = £50,000

(e) Debtors turnover = 8 times
Debtors: £50,000/8 = £6,250

(f) Acid test ratio 1.25 times
Current liability (b) £23,000
Liquid assets: £23,000 × 1.25 times = £28,750
Cash: liquid assets (£28,750) less debtors (e) £6,250 = £22,500

(g) Current assets (b) £34,500
Liquid assets (f) £28,750
Stock: current assets (£34,500) less liquid assets (£28,750) = £5,750

(h) Stock turnover ratio 5 times
Cost of sales: £5,750 × 5 = £28,750

(i) General expenses = 25% of sales: £50,000/4 = £12,500

(j) Capital employed (£25,000) + drawings (£3,000) − profit for the year (£7,250) = capital at commencement of the year.

TRADING AND PROFIT AND LOSS YEAR TO 31.5.20X0		N
	£	
Sales	50,000	d
Cost of sales	(28,750)	h
Gross profit	21,250	
Expenses	(12,500)	i
Depreciation	(1,500)	a
Profit	7,250	

BALANCE SHEET AS AT 31.5.20X0			
	£	£	
Fixed assets:		15,000	a
Less Depreciation		(1,500)	a
		13,500	
Current assets:			
Stock in trade	5,750		g
Debtors	6,250		e
Cash/bank	22,500		f
Creditors	(23,000)	11,500	b
		25,000	c
		£	
Capital		20,750	j
Profit for the year		7,250	
Drawings		(3,000)	
		25,000	

CHAPTER 23

PQ 23.1 The governing accounting concept

(a) The Prudence convention and the Matching working rule.
(b) The Matching working rule and the Prudence convention.
(c) The Prudence convention and the Non-aggregation working rule.
(d) The Separate Entity assumption.
(e) The Materiality convention.
(f) The Matching working rule and the Materiality convention.
(g) The Consistency convention.
(h) The Realization working rule and the Prudence convention.

PQ 23.2 Conflict among accounting concepts

(a) Instances of conflict:

• *Where the Matching working rule conflicts with the Materiality convention.* An office stapler costing £4 is written off as part of stationery in the year it was bought, based on 'Materiality convention', although because it would remain useful over several years, an appropriate portion of its cost should have been deferred to these years, in accordance with the Matching rule.

• *Where the Materiality convention conflicts with the Objectivity convention.* Threshold of materiality is a subjective decision. When ICI decides to round off each item in its financial statements to the nearest million pounds, it makes a subjective decision that amounts less than a million are not material to it – whereas such an amount is material to most other companies! In the same way, an item of office equipment costing, say, £1,000 may be material to and therefore capitalized by one entity and written off by another.

• *Where the Matching working rule conflicts with the Prudence convention.* The Matching working rule requires that the cost of developing a product that is expected to be marketed in a future year should be capitalized – reported as an asset in the year the cost is incurred and written off as expenditure in the years when the product

PROVISION FOR DEPRECIATION – MACHINERY

	£000		£000
Balance c/d	240	Balance b/f	180
		Loss on termination	60
	240		240
		Balance b/d	240

PROVISION FOR DOUBTFUL DEBTS ACCOUNT

	£000		£000
Balance c/d	97	Balance b/f	25
		Loss on termination	72
	97		97
		Balance b/d	97

generates sales income. The Prudence convention, however, requires the cost to be immediately written off because the product's ability to generate income would be a reality only when it happens and should not be counted on until then.

• Where the *Separate Entity* assumption conflicts with *Substance over Form convention*. If a house belonging to entity A is leased to entity B, the Separate Entity assumption requires that the house should appear as an asset on A's Balance Sheet. In contrast, the convention of Substance over form requires that the house should appear as an asset in B's Balance Sheet as well.

(b) Resolving the conflict of concepts

When an accountant finds that two or more concepts are at conflict, the choice of the concept to uphold is based not on whether that concept is one labelled as 'fundamental' but on what would assist in showing a true and fair view. For example, in the conflict cited as the first case above, the Materiality convention is upheld in preference to the Matching working rule, although the latter is the fundamental concept.

PQ 23.3 The assumption of going concern in jeopardy

Financial statements prepared without assuming that the entity will remain a going concern

CHAPTER 25

PQ 25.1 A case study

(a) **Subscriptions received in advance for a periodical.** On the critical-event approach to income recognition, the income on subscriptions received for a periodical can be recognized at the point where the production is completed. At that stage of the income-earning cycle, the transaction may be regarded as substantially completed because the major uncertainty that remained till then – namely whether the journal will still be in production – is resolved. Hence, at the end of the first year, if the issues relating to that year have been published, one-third of the amount received may be recognized as income and, similarly, one-third may be recognized in each of the next two years.

(b) **Sale of an item yet to be bought.** £90,000 received for supplying sugar should be reported as a liability and not recognized as an income. The revenue-earning cycle is initiated by this receipt, and uncertainties such as whether a buyer can be found and the price at which the sale can be effected are resolved already. But the earning cycle would not reach the critical stage to trigger income recognition unless significant uncertainties, which remain, are resolved. These uncertainties are whether that quantity of sugar can be bought, and at what cost. These uncertainties will be resolved when the quantity of sugar is bought, and that will be the stage for income recognition. By that stage, any remaining uncertainties – such as the cost of delivery – would be capable of reliable estimation.

(c) **Earnings on granting franchise right.** Such earnings are similar to – and could therefore be accounted for on the same basis as – rent, royalty and interest. Income of this kind, arising from permitting others to use one's resources, may be accounted for on the accretion approach. So long as, under the contract terms, there is a parallel increase in the claim on the person to whom the franchise is granted, the earning may be accounted on a time basis. £150,000 received in respect of five years may therefore be allocated on a time basis, recognizing one-fifth as income for the first year, and similar portions as income in each of the five years in which the other party thrives on the franchise. This is, however, a simplistic answer. In real life situations the franchise agreements are not standardized; the rights, duties and obligations assigned to each party to the agreement vary widely and will have to be taken into account for a proper allocation of the income to each of the accounting periods involved.

(d) **Mail-order goods remaining within the returnable period.** Mail-order companies usually deliver goods on approval, with an undertaking to accept them back within a specified period. This is generally done to compensate for the fact that the customer is induced to order goods without being provided with an opportunity to inspect them. Such situations, in which the title to the goods does not pass to the

TRADING AND PROFIT AND LOSS ACCOUNT FOR THE YEAR ENDED 30.6.20X1

	£000	£000
Sales		2,690
Stock - 30.6.20X0	826	
Purchases	2,086	
Depreciation – machinery	34	
Machinery maintenance	46	
Stock - 30.6.20X1	(840)	
		(2,152)
Gross profit		538
Administrative expenses:		
Salaries	300	
Rent	48	
Lighting and heating	29	
Other admin. expenses	198	
		(575)
Distribution cost:		
Depreciation – vehicles	42	
Vehicle maintenance	28	
Advertising	182	
		(252)
Interest		(24)
Operating loss		(313)
Loss on termination:		
Disposal of machinery	60	
Stock loss	315	
Bad debts	72	
Employee compensation	116	
		(563)
Loss carried forward		(876)

BALANCE SHEET AS AT 30 JUNE 20X1

	Cost	Acc. depn	£000
FIXED ASSETS:			
Motor vehicles	340	(240)	100
	420	(240)	180
CURRENT ASSETS:			
Stock in trade			525
Debtors	485		
Provn for doubtful debt	(97)		388
Cash and bank			16
CURRENT LIABILITY:			
Creditors	698		
Compensation	116		
Accrued expenses	62		
Interest accrued	24		
Bank loan	150		
Bank overdraft	60		(1,110)
			(181)
			99
			£000
Capital			975
Loss brought forward			(876)
			99

WORKINGS:	£000
Stock at cost	840
Profit margin	210
Usual sale price	1,050
50% discount	525
	525

CHAPTER 26

PQ 26.1 Multiple-choice question

1. (a); 2. (b); 3. (c); 4. (c); 5. (b)*; 6. (a); 7. (d); 8. (c)**; 9. (c)***;

Notes:

* When net assets at the end of the year are lower in value than at the beginning, reporting a loss, drawings should be offset against the loss and capital introduction added to the loss.

** Cash discount allowed is calculated as ($269,498/94) × 6 = £17,202.

*** Increase in the provision for doubtful debts would not appear in the Debtors Control account.

PQ 26.2 A mini question on incomplete records

Workings:

(a)   CASH ACCOUNT (SUMMARY)

	£		£
Balance b/f	2,160	Drawings	40,000
Debtors a/c	2,160,000	Creditors	1,731,600
		Salaries	180,000
		Expenses	154,800
		Fixed assets	16,400
		Balance c/d	39,360

STATEMENT OF AFFAIRS – 1.1.20X1

	£	£
Fixed assets (96,400 − 24,600)		71,800
Stock in trade	234,500	
Debtors	43,200	
Cash and bank balance	2,160	
Creditors	(97,200)	182,660
Capital as at 1.1.20X1		254,460

FIXED ASSETS ACCOUNT

	£		£
Balance b/f	96,400		
Cash book	16,400	Balance c/d	112,800

PROVISION FOR DEPRECIATION ACCOUNT

	£		£
		Balance b/f	24,600
Balance c/d	32,400	Depreciation	7,800

(b) PROFIT AND LOSS ACCOUNT FOR YEAR TO 31.12.20X1

	£
Sales	2,163,600
Cost of sale	(1,725,900)
Gross profit	437,700
Salaries	(180,000)
Depreciation	(7,800)
Expenses	(154,800)
Profit	95,100

customer until the approval period is over, are identified in the Sale of Goods Act 1979 (s. 2) as an 'agreement to sell' as distinct from a 'sale'. Therefore, until the approval period is over, the sale does not take place and accordingly the income cannot be recognized, because the earning cycle cannot be regarded as having reached the critical stage to trigger income recognition so long as a major uncertainty remains of a possible repudiation of the sale by the customer.

(e) **Sales subject to reservation of title.** The situation described is remarkably similar to the Romalpa case.[2] In this case, when the buyer faced bankruptcy proceedings, the unpaid seller was able to convince the courts that he remained the legal owner of the goods until the buyer paid for them. The unpaid seller based his claim on the premise that, by the small print on the invoice he had issued, he had reserved to himself the title to the goods sold until he received payments for them. If the decision of this case is accepted as the basis for income recognition, any sale made with similar reservations cannot be recognized as income until the proceeds are collected. But it is accepted that such reservations of title are of little significance in day-to-day commercial activity and are only made as a fallback position in the unlikely event of the buyer becoming bankrupt. The recommendations of the Institute of Chartered Accountants of England and Wales[3] is that in circumstances such as these the emphasis should be more on the commercial substance of the transaction rather than on its legal form. It is therefore submitted that unless the solvency of the customer and hence the collectibility of the debt are in doubt, the client should ignore the reservation of title in this manner and proceed to recognize the income from the sale of the machinery.

(f) **Revenue recognition on certain agricultural and mining produce.** The sale of tea is a trading transaction. It would, therefore, appear that revenue should be recognized on reaching the critical stage when a sale is made. In this case the income in respect of the stock held at the end of a year may be recognized as income only upon its sale in the following year. But by an established custom of the tea trade (adopted also for some other agricultural and mined products, such as precious metals) revenue recognition is permitted on the accretion approach provided the following conditions are satisfied:

● the item is one readily realizable in an active market, at readily determinable prices, without any significant effort;

● the market is able to absorb the quantity held in stock by the entity without significantly affecting the prices.

This custom of trade is recognized in the United States.[4] Therefore, the client may recognize the income in the year by valuing the unsold stock of tea at prices realized subsequent to the Balance Sheet date, net of the expenses of realization.

References

2. *Aluminium Industrie Vaassen BV v Romalpa Aluminium Ltd* [1976] 1 WLR 676 (Court of Appeal, January 1976).

3. Statement V24 in the ICAEW *Handbook*.

4. The *Statement of Financial Accounting Concepts No. 5*, issued by the Financial Accounting Standards Board.

PROVISION FOR DEPRECIATION ACCOUNT

	£		£	N
Disposal a/c	5,500	Balance b/f	120,000	6
Balance c/d	165,500	Depreciation	51,000	
	#			

FIXED ASSETS ACCOUNT

	£		£	N
Balance b/f	480,000	Disposal a/c	20,000	5
Cash a/c	60,000	Balance c/d	520,000	

PROVISION FOR DOUBTFUL DEBTS ACCOUNT

	£		£	N
		Balance b/f	8,100	2
Balance c/d	9,200	Bad Debts a/c	1,100	7
	#			

DISPOSAL OF FIXED ASSETS ACCOUNT

	£		£	N
F. Asset a/c	20,000	Prov. for dep	5,500	5
		Cash a/c	4,000	
		P&L – Loss	10,500	
			#	

BAD DEBTS ACCOUNT

	£		£
Total debtors	6,000	P&L a/c	7,100
Prov. for d.d	1,100		
	7,100		

TOTAL DEBTORS ACCOUNT

	£		£
Balance b/f	162,000	Cash a/c	954,600
Sales a/c	982,600	Bad debts	6,000
		Balance c/d	184,000
	#		

TOTAL CREDITORS ACCOUNT

	£		£
Cash a/c	628,200	Balance b/f	112,400
Balance c/d	198,600	Purchases	714,400
			#

SALARIES AND WAGES ACCOUNT

	£		£
Cash a/c	136,400	Balance b/f	24,500
Balance c/d	36,800	P&L a/c	148,700
	#		

BUSINESS RATES ACCOUNT

	£		£	N
Balance b/f	15,000	P&L a/c	6,000	4 / 9

	£
Balance c/d	21,000

RENT ACCOUNT

	£		£	N
Balance b/f	12,000	P&L a/c	24,000	3
Cash a/c	8,000			
Balance c/d	4,000			

CASH ACCOUNT

	£		£
Balance b/f	12,600	Fixed asset	60,000
Disposal	4,000	Creditors	628,200
Debtors	954,600	Salaries	136,400
		Advertising	26,600
		Rent	8,000
		Other exp.	75,200
		Drawings	35,400
		Balance c/d	1,400
			#

= balancing figures in each account

Notes:

1. Fixed assets, acquired on 1.7.20X0, have been depreciated using the straight-line method for two years and six months to 31.12.20X2.
2. Provision has been made for doubtful debts at 5 per cent of £162,000.
3. £72,000 prepaid as rent for 36 months would have expired except for £12,000 remaining.
4. Business rates remained unpaid on this date for two and a half years.
5. The Ford Escort van, already depreciated at £2,000 p.a. for two years and six months up to 31 December 20X2, has to be depreciated for further three months to 1 April 20X3.
6. The current year's charge for depreciation is made up of £500 on the Escort van, £4,500 on the Volkswagen and £46,000 on other assets.
7. Provision for doubtful debts is increased by £1,100 to cover 5 per cent of debtors at the year end.
8. Rent for the year = £2,000 × 12 months.
9. Expenditure on business rates for 20X1 is £6,000 irrespective of the amounts in arrears.

BALANCE SHEET AS AT 31.12.20X1

	£	£
Fixed assets	112,800	
Accumulated depreciation	(32,400)	80,400
Stock in trade	252,800	
Debtors	46,800	
Cash/bank	39,360	
Creditors	(109,800)	229,160
		309,560
Capital on 1.1.20X1		254,460
Profit for the year		95,100
Drawings		(40,000)
		309,560

DEBTORS CONTROL ACCOUNT

	£		£
Balance b/f	43,200	Cash book	2,160,000
Sales a/c	2,163,600	Balance c/d	46,800

COST OF SALE ACCOUNT

	£		£
Stock 1.1	234,500	Trading a/c	1,725,900
Purchases	1,744,200		
Stock 31.12	(252,800)		
	1,725,900		1,725,900

CREDITORS CONTROL ACCOUNT

	£		£
Cash book	1,731,600	Balance b/f	97,200
Balance c/d	109,800	Purchases	1,744,200
			1,744,200

PQ 26.3 Involving acquisition and disposal of fixed assets

CLUE: Capital at 1.4.20X0 £217,800; cost of goods sold £634,650; profit £126,050; drawings £35,050.

PQ 26.4 Information on assets and liabilities may be scattered

STATEMENT OF AFFAIRS AS AT 1.1.20X3

	£	£	£	N
Fixed assets			480,000	
Accumulated depreciation			(120,000)	1
			360,000	
Stock at cost			246,800	
Debtors	162,000			
Provision	(8,100)	153,900		2
Prepaid rent		12,000		3
Cash and bank		12,600		
Creditors	(112,400)			
Accruals	(24,500)			
Business rates	(15,000)	(151,900)	273,400	4
Capital – 1.1.20X3			633,400	

The two-column cash book written up on the basis of this information (see below) reveals the amount collected from all customers as £989,200. The cash and cheque payments to suppliers (£12,400 and £771,300), adjusted for amounts owed to them at the beginning and at the end of the year, reveal that purchases during the year are £735,000, and adjusted for opening and closing stock the cost of goods sold is ascertained as £693,000. Since goods are sold at cost plus 25 per cent, the goods costing £693,000 should have generated sales of £866,250. When the sales are accounted for, a difference of £20,950 crops up in the Debtors Control account and this amount is written off.

CASH BOOK

	Cash	Bank		Cash	Bank
	£	£		£	£
Balance b/f		51,600	Creditors	12,400	771,300
Cash a/c c	300	955,400	Rent	–	36,000
Debtors a/c	989,200	–	Salaries/wg	–	88,400
			Furniture	–	80,000
			Drawings a/c	11,800	15,000
			Bank a/c c	955,400	–
			Other exp.	9,600	27,400
			Balance c/d	300	–
Balance c/d	–	11,100			
Balance b/d	300	–	Balance b/d		11,100

DEBTORS CONTROL ACCOUNT

	£		£
Balance b/f	312,400	Cash a/c	989,200 ~
Sales a/c	866,250	Bad debts	20,950
		Balance c/d	168,500

CREDITORS CONTROL ACCOUNT

	£		£
Bank a/c	771,300	Balance b/f	245,400 #
Cash a/c	12,400	Purchases	735,000
Balance c/d	196,700		

SALARIES AND WAGES ACCOUNT

	£		£
Bank a/c	88,400	Balance b/f	12,600
Balance c/d	8,500	P&L a/c	84,300 #

FURNITURE ACCOUNT

	£		£
Balance b/f	60,000		
Bank a/c	80,000		

PROVISION FOR DEPRECIATION – FURNITURE ACCOUNT

	£		£
		Balance b/f	24,000
		Depreciation	12,000

OFFICE EQUIPMENT ACCOUNT

	£		£
Balance b/f	45,000		

PROVISION FOR DEPRECIATION – EQUIPMENT ACCOUNT

	£		£
		Balance b/f	10,400
		Depreciation	4,500

OTHER EXPENSES ACCOUNT

	£		£
Bank a/c	27,400	Balance b/f	20,200
Cash a/c	9,600	P&L a/c	30,700 #
Balance c/d	13,900		

: balancing figure in that account
~ : a figure derived from another account

TRADING AND PROFIT AND LOSS ACCOUNT FOR THE YEAR ENDED 31 DECEMBER 20X3

	£	£
Sales		982,600
Stock 1.1.20X3	246,800	
Purchases	714,400	
Stock – 31.12.20X3	(362,500)	(598,700)
Gross profit		383,900
Salaries and wages		(148,700)
Rent		(24,000)
Other expenses		(75,200)
Depreciation		(51,000)
Loss on disposal – asset		(10,500)
Business rates		(6,000)
Advertising		(26,600)
Bad debts		(7,100)
Profit for the year		34,800

BALANCE SHEET AS AT 31.12.20X3

	Cost	Acc.depn	W.D.V
	£	£	£
Fixed assets	520,000	(165,500)	354,500
Stock in trade			362,500
Debtors	184,000		
Prov. for d. debts	(9,200)		174,800
Cash/bank			1,400
Creditors	(198,600)		
Rent accrued	(4,000)		
Salaries accrued	(36,800)		
Business rates	(21,000)	(260,400)	278,300
			632,800
			£
Capital 1.1.20X3			633,400
Profit for 20X3			34,800
Drawings			(35,400)
			632,800

CHAPTER 27

PQ 27.1 Incomplete records involving bank reconciliations

The information obtained from the summary of bank statements requires adjustments for cheques yet to be presented and deposits awaiting clearance, to ascertain the real position, which should be stated in the cash book. For example, the bank balance stated in the bank statement as £27,200 at commencement of the year is increased by the deposits awaiting clearance on that date (of £24,400) to report the correct balance at the bank on that date of £51,600 in the cash book. Correspondingly, mindful of the fact that these deposits were made in the previous year, £24,400 should be removed from the amounts stated in the bank statements as current year's deposit. On the basis of similar adjustments, the correct position to be stated in the cash book is ascertained as follows:

BANK RECONCILIATION

	As stated in Question	Deposits not yet credited on 30.9.20X0	Deposits not yet credited on 30.9.20X1	Cheques not presented by 30.9.20X1	The correct position for Cash Book
Balance – 1.10.20X0	27,200	24,400	–	–	51,600
Bank lodgements	962,300	(24,400)	17,500	–	955,400
Purchases	(724,500)	–	–	(46,800)	(771,300)
Rent	(36,000)	–	–	–	(36,000)
Salaries and wages	(88,400)	–	–	–	(88,400)
Furniture	(80,000)	–	–	–	(80,000)
Drawings	(15,000)	–	–	–	(15,000)
Other expenses	(27,400)	–	–	–	(27,400)
Balance – 30.9.20X1	18,200	–	17,500	(46,800)	(11,100)

EQUIPMENT ACCOUNT

	£		£
Balance b/f	86,000		
3 Cash book	25,000		

PROVISION FOR DEPRECIATION – EQUIPMENTS

	£		£
		Balance b/f	25,800
		Depre. a/c	11,100

DEBTORS CONTROL ACCOUNT

	£		£
2 Balance b/f	161,000	Bad debts	43,475
# Sales a/c	882,400	Cash book	878,345
# VAT a/c	154,420	Balance c/d	276,000

PROVISION FOR DOUBTFUL DEBTS ACCOUNT

	£		£	
T. debtors	43,475	Balance b/f	8,050	2
Balance c/d	13,800	VAT a/c	6,475	4
		P&L a/c	42,750	#

CREDITORS CONTROL ACCOUNT

	£		£	
Cash book	501,495	Balance b/f	188,945	
Balance	216,200	Purchases	450,000	#
		VAT a/c	78,750	#

DISPOSAL OF MOTOR VEHICLES ACCOUNT

	£		£
M. vehicle	30,000	Prov. for dep.	24,000
P&L – gain	1,660	Cash book	7,660

SALARIES ACCOUNT

	£		£	
Cash book	200,260	Balance b/f	18,400	
Balance c/d	21,200	P&L a/c	203,060	#

VAT ACCOUNT

		£		£	
3	Equipment	4,375	Balance b/f	10,845	
~	Creditors	78,750	Debtors	154,420	
~	Expenses	12,250	Drawings	5,985	5
4	Bad debts	6,475			
	Cash book	32,500			
#	Balance	36,900			

EXPENSES ACCOUNT

	£		£	
Cash book	66,035	Balance b/f	10,810	
Balance c/d	27,025	P&L a/c	70,000	#
		VAT a/c	12,250	#

BALANCE SHEET AS AT 30.6.20X4

FIXED ASSETS:	Cost	Acc. depn	£
Motor vehicles	125,250	(49,050)	76,200
Equipment	111,000	(36,900)	74,100
			275,190
CURRENT ASSETS:			
Stock at cost		169,200	
Debtors	276,000		
Prov. for d.debts	(13,800)	262,200	
Cash and bank balance		815	
Creditors	(216,200)		
Salary accrued	(21,200)		
Rent accrued	(1,200)		
Other accruals	(27,025)		
VAT accrued	(36,900)	(307,325)	124,890
			275,190
			£
Capital 1.7.20X3			285,000
Profit for the year			56,875
Drawings			(66,685)
			275,190

TRADING AND PROFIT AND LOSS ACCOUNT FOR THE YEAR ENDED 30.6.20X4

	£	£
Sales		882,400
Stock 1.7.20X3	194,600	
Purchases	450,000	
Stock 30.6.20X4	(169,200)	
Drawings	(34,200)	(441,200)
Gross profit		441,200
Gain on disposal of veh.		1,660
Salaries		(203,060)
Rent		(30,000)
Entertainment		(4,025)
Other expenses		(70,000)
Depre. – vehicles		(25,050)
Depre. – equipment		(11,100)
Bad debts		(42,750)
Profit for the year		56,875

TRADING AND PROFIT AND LOSS ACCOUNT FOR THE YEAR ENDED 30.9.20X1

	£	£
Sales		866,250
Stock – 1.10.20X0	242,600	
Purchases	735,000	
Stock – 30.9.20X1	(284,600)	(693,000)
Gross profit		173,250
Salaries and wages		(84,300)
Rent		(36,000)
Accountancy fees		(5,000)
Depreciation – furniture		(12,000)
Depreciation – office equipment		(4,500)
Bad debts		(20,950)
Other expenses		(30,700)
Loss for the year		20,200

BALANCE SHEET AS AT 30 SEPTEMBER 20X1

	Cost	Acc.depre	W.D.V
	£	£	£
Furniture	140,000	(36,000)	104,000
Equipment	45,000	(14,900)	30,100
Stock in trade		284,600	
Trade debtors		168,500	
Cash in hand		300	
Trade creditors		(196,700)	
Salary accrued		(8,500)	
Other accruals		(13,900)	
Ac. fees owed		(5,000)	
Bank overdraft		(11,100)	(235,200)
			218,200
			352,300
			£
Capital – 1.10.20X0			399,300
Loss for the year			(20,200)
Drawings			(26,800)
			352,300

PQ 27.2 Another incomplete record involving bank reconciliations

CLUE: Balance at bank £500 at commencement and £29,500 at end; bank lodgements £445,000, apart from £4,700 for re-presentation of dishonoured cheques; cheque payments to creditors and electricity £85,600 and £6,600 respectively; drawings (by cheque) £38,000; sales £438,800; profit £74,000; capital at commencement and end of the year £30,000 and £66,000 respectively.

PQ 27.3 Incomplete records of a VAT-registered trader

CASH BOOK

	£		£
Balance b/f	34,250	Creditors	501,495
Disposal	7,660	Salaries	200,260
# Debtors	878,345	Rent	24,000
		Entertain.	4,025
		Equipment	25,000
		VAT – equip.	4,375
		Vehicles	35,250
		Expenses	66,035
		Drawings	26,500
		VAT a/c	32,500
		Balance c/d	815

RENT ACCOUNT

	£		£	
Cash book	24,000	P&L a/c	30,000	#
Balance c/d	6,000			

DRAWINGS ACCOUNT

	£		£
Cash book	26,500		
5 Trading a/c	34,200		
6 VAT a/c	5,985		

MOTOR VEHICLES ACCOUNT

	£		£
Balance b/f	120,000	Balance	30,000
Cash book	35,250	Disposal	125,250

PROVISION FOR DEPRECIATION – VEHICLES

	£		£
Disposal a/c	24,000	Balance b/f	48,000
Balance c/d	49,050	Depre. a/c	25,050

Notes:

1. The balancing figure in each of the following accounts is identified as # and the use of that figure in another account is indicated as ~. The balancing figures in the Total Debtors account, Total Creditors account and Expenses account are inclusive of VAT at 17.5 per cent and the VAT element thereof is accounted for appropriately. For example, the balancing figure of £1,036,820 in the Debtors Control account reports the sales in the year, inclusive of VAT, and is accounted for by crediting the Sales account and the VAT account in the ratio 100:17.5 respectively.

2. The debtors stated on the Balance Sheet on 30 June 20X3 are net of provisions for doubtful debts. The provision is calculated as 5/95 of £152,950. The provision at year end is 5 per cent of £276,000.

3. The VAT on the equipment is recoverable.

4. The bad debt relief applies.

5. Since gross profit is 50 per cent of sales, the other 50 per cent would be the cost of goods sold. The purchases for the year, adjusted for opening and closing stock, net of the cost of goods sold, would be the cost of goods removed by Carl's sons.

6. Since at the point of purchasing, input VAT would have been recovered, the VAT is payable to HM Customs and Excise when goods are removed for the personal use of the proprietor.

CHAPTER 28

PQ 28.1 Accounts of a social club

STATEMENT OF AFFAIRS AS AT 1.1.20X1

	£
Clubhouse	140,000
Furniture and fitting	16,800
Bar stock	6,440
Subs. receivable	1,850
Cash and bank	1,456
Creditors for bar	(4,760)
Accumulated Fund	161,786

SUBSCRIPTIONS RECEIVABLE (ASSET) ACCOUNT

	£		£
Balance b/d	1,850	Receipts and payments	60,228
Income and expenditure	60,198	Balance c/d	1,820
Balance b/d	1,820		

CREDITORS FOR BAR SUPPLIES ACCOUNT

	£		£
Receipts and payments	59,920	Balance b/f	4,760
Balance c/d	4,564	Bar purchases	59,724
		Balance b/d	4,564

INCOME AND EXPENDITURE ACCOUNT FOR THE YEAR ENDED 31.12.20X1

	£	£	£
Subscriptions receivable			60,198
Bar sales		98,560	
Less: Stock	6,440		
Purchases	59,724		
	(5,880)	(60,284)	38,276
Stock			
Salaries			(85,400)
Ground maintenance			(2,128)
Office supplies			(812)
Clubhouse expenses			(5,600)
Depreciation – furniture			(2,680)
Surplus of income over expense			1,854

BALANCE SHEET AS AT 31.12.20X1

	£	£
Clubhouse		140,000
Furniture and fittings		21,120
Subscriptions receivable	1,820	
Bar stock	5,880	
Cash and bank balance	504	
Creditors for bar supplies	(4,564)	
Accrued clubhouse exp.	(1,120)	2,520
		163,640
		£
Accumulated Fund on 1.1.20X1		161,786
Surplus of income over expenses		1,854
		163,640

PQ 28.2 Accounting for subscriptions receivable

SUBSCRIPTIONS INCOME

	on accruals basis	on receipts basis
A	£135,620	£122,640
B	£55,200	£55,080
C	£397,900	£374,100

A

SUBSCRIPTION RECEIVABLE (CONTROL) ACCOUNT

	£		£
Balance b/f	21,600	Rec. & paym.	9,460
Subscription	135,620	Rec. & paym.	124,580
Balance c/d	11,400	Balance c/d	34,580

SUBSCRIPTION RECEIVABLE (CONTROL) ACCOUNT

	£		£
Subscription	122,640	Balance b/f	9,460
Balance c/d	11,400	Rec. & paym.	124,580

B

SUBSCRIPTION RECEIVABLE (CONTROL) ACCOUNT

	£		£
Balance b/f	540	Rec. & paym.	300
Subscription	55,200	Rec. & paym.	55,020
Balance c/d	240	Balance c/d	660

SUBSCRIPTION RECEIVABLE (CONTROL) ACCOUNT

	£		£
Subscription	55,080	Balance b/f	300
Balance c/d	240	Rec. & paym.	55,020

C

SUBSCRIPTION RECEIVABLE (CONTROL) ACCOUNT

	£		£
Balance b/f	82,600	Rec. & paym.	27,600
Subscription	397,900	Rec. & paym.	368,500
Balance c/d	22,000	Balance c/d	106,400

SUBSCRIPTION RECEIVABLE (CONTROL) ACCOUNT

	£		£
Subscription	374,100	Balance b/f	27,600
Balance c/d	22,000	Rec. & paym.	368,500

PQ 28.3 The accounts of an association

CLUE: Membership subscription £50,400; crèche income (gross) £84,000 net of expenses £4,025; surplus of income over expenditure (£16,815) transferred to the Accumulated Fund.

PQ 28.4 Enrolment fees and special-purpose collections

STATEMENT OF AFFAIRS AS AT 1.1.20X3

	£	£
Clubhouse at cost		240,000
Furniture at w.d.v		72,500
Debtors for subscript.:		
Sporting members	28,400	
Social members	19,450	
Bar stock at cost	24,650	
Debtors – bar sales	6,450	
Sporting consumables	11,250	
Balance at bank	4,250	
Subsc. in advance:		
Sporting members	(1,450)	
Social members	(2,550)	
Bar creditors	(5,650)	
Refreshment creditors	(1,560)	
Owed to charity	(4,250)	78,990
		391,490
Mortgage loan		(125,000)
ACCUMULATED FUND		266,490

FURNITURE AND FITTINGS ACCOUNT

	£		£
Balance b/f	72,500	Depreciation	20,500
R & payments	30,000	Balance c/d	82,000
#			#

CREDITORS FOR BAR SUPPLIES ACCOUNT

	£		£
R & payments	66,600	Balance b/f	5,650
Balance c/d	4,400	Bar purchases	65,350
#			#

DEBTORS FOR BAR SALES ACCOUNT

	£		£
Balance b/f	6,450	R & payments	65,480
Bar sales	75,580	Balance c/d	16,550

SPORTS CONSUMABLES ACCOUNT

	£		£
Balance b/f	11,250	Income & exp.	19,300
R & payments	22,600	Balance c/d	14,550
#			#

CREDITORS FOR REFRESHMENT SUPPLIES ACCOUNT

	£		£
R & payments	16,850	Balance b/f	1,560
Balance c/d	3,450	Income & exp.	18,740
#			#

OWED TO MENTALLY HANDICAPPED ACCOUNT

	£		£
R & payments	6,200	Balance b/f	4,250
Balance c/d	5,700	R & payments	7,650
#			

SUBSCRIPTIONS RECEIVABLE ACCOUNT

	Sports	Social		Sports	Social
Balance b/f	28,400	19,450	Balance b/f	1,450	2,550
Subs. receivable	156,000	87,300	R & payments	131,920	75,450
Balance c/d	1,920	3,960	Bad debts	12,440	4,250
			Balance c/d	40,510	28,460
#					

Notes:

1. A Statement of Affairs is prepared at the commencement of the year to determine the Accumulated Fund on that date.
2. The symbol # indicates the balancing figure in each account.
3. For convenience, the Subscription Receivable account shows sports and social membership dues in two adjacent columns.

THE FINANCIAL STATEMENTS OF THE CLUB:

INCOME AND EXPENDITURE ACCOUNT FOR THE YEAR ENDED 31.12.20X3

	£	£	£
Subscriptions – sporting members			156,000
Subscriptions – social members			87,300
Enrolment fees			21,500
Bar sales		75,580	
Bar stock 1.1	24,650		
Bar purchases	65,350		
Bar stock 31.12	(21,500)	(68,500)	7,080
Staff salaries			(74,480)
Administrative expenses			(26,680)
Clubhouse maintenance			(22,450)
Depreciation of furniture			(20,500)
Sports goods consumed			(19,300)
Membership welfare			(14,260)
Sale of refreshments		21,345	
Cost of refreshments		(18,740)	2,605
Travel expenses on away matches			(14,260)
Bad debts written off			(16,690)
Interest paid			(6,875)
Surplus of income over expenditure			58,990

BALANCE SHEET AS AT 31.12.20X3

	£	£	£
Clubhouse			240,000
Furniture at written down value			82,000
Subsc. receivable – sports		40,510	
– social		28,460	
Stock of bar supplies		21,500	
Debtors for bar sales		16,550	
Sports consumables		14,550	
Balance at bank		1,340	
Subs. in advance – sports		(1,920)	
– social		(3,960)	
Creditors for bar supplies		(4,400)	
Creditors for refreshment		(3,450)	
Owed to charity		(5,700)	103,480
			425,480
Accumulated Fund – 1.1.20X3			266,490
Surplus for the year to 31.12.20X3			58,990
			325,480
Mortgage loan			100,000
			425,480

PQ 28.5 Receipts and Expenditure account

CLUE: Subscription income: sports £131,450, social £74,040; bar sales £82,200; misappropriation of bar takings £6,620; surplus of income over expenditure £44,490; Accumulated Fund at commencement £218,640 and at end £263,130.

PQ 28.6 Life membership fees and special funds

CLUE: Subscriptions receivable £566,000, received £527,500; misappropriation written off £41,295; Rutlish Fund and corresponding assets £96,545; surplus of income over expenditure £430,305; transfer to Rutlish Fund £39,180; Accumulated Fund £391,125; Life Membership Fund £70,200; bank balance £55,525.

CHAPTER 29

PQ 29.1 Accounting for a manufacturer

MANUFACTURING ACCOUNT
FOR THE YEAR ENDED 30.6.20X1

	£000	£000
Raw material consumed:		
Stock on 1.7.20X0	264	
Purchases	926	
Freight	75	
Duty	22	
Stock on 30.6.20X1	(164)	1,123
Productive wages		122
Prime cost		1,245
Factory overheads:		
Power	37	
Depreciation – machinery	32	
Depreciation – buildings	2	
Consumable stores	23	
Wages	65	
Electricity	4	
Rent	30	
Insurance	18	211
Work-in-progress: 30.6.20X0		93
Work-in-progress: 30.6.20X1		(109)
Factory cost of vanity cases		1,440
Manufacturing profit c/d		144
Transferred to Trading a/c		1,584

TRADING AND PROFIT AND LOSS ACCOUNT
FOR THE YEAR ENDED 30.6.20X1

	£000	£000
Sales		2,702
Stock on 1.7.20X0	187	
Transfer from Manufacturing a/c	1,584	
Stock on 30.6.20X1	(154)	(1,617)
Gross profit b/d		1,085
Manufacturing profit b/d	144	
Provision for unrealized profit	3	147
		1,232
Administrative expenses:		
Salaries and wages	135	
Telephone and postage	13	
Audit fees	15	
Depreciation of buildings	4	
Depreciation of furniture	26	
Stationery	10	
Electricity	12	
Rent	18	
Insurance	9	(242)
Distribution cost:		
Advertising	106	
Depreciation of buildings	2	
Depreciation of motor vehicles	64	
Salaries and wages	24	
Drivers and vehicle cleaners	18	
Electricity	4	
Rent	12	
Insurance	3	
Bad debts	21	
Sales commission	67	(321)
Profit for the year		669

BALANCE SHEET AS AT 30.6.20X1

Fixed assets:	Cost	Ac. dep.	£000
Freehold premises	620	(56)	564
Plant and machinery	640	(312)	328
Furniture and fittings	260	(143)	117
Motor vehicles	320	(216)	104
			1,113

Net current assets:			
Stock in trade:			
Raw materials		164	
Work in progress		109	
Finished goods	154		
Prov. for unrealized profit	(14)	140	
Stock of stationery		413	
Stock of consumable store		2	
Trade debtors		4	
Cash and bank balance		428	
Creditors		11	
		(217)	641
			1,754

		£000
Capital – Liz McDermot		1,200
Profit for the year		669
Drawings		(115)
		1,754

PROVISION FOR UNREALIZED PROFIT ACCOUNT

	£			£
Profit and Loss	3	Balance b/f		17
Balance c/d	14			
		Balance b/d		14

Notes:

1. Unrealized profit as at 30 June 20X0 = £187,000 × 10/110 = £17,000.
2. Unrealized profit as at 30 June 20X1 = £154,000 × 10/110 = £14,000.
3. The excess provision for unrealized profit is credited to the Profit and Loss account for the year.

PQ 29.2 Accounting for royalties

CLUE:	20X0	20X1	20X2	20X3	20X4
Copies published in each year	10,000	7,500	14,000	18,000	10,500
Royalty expensed (at £1.20 per copy)	£12,000	£9,000	£16,800	£21,600	£12,600
Royalty paid (in two instalments) in each year	£6,000	£15,000	£15,000	£15,000	£15,000
Shortworkings written off in the year	–	–	£1,200	–	–

PQ 29.3 To buy or to produce?

CLUE: Year to 31.3.20X3: units produced 2,540; royalty payable £63,500; shortworking written off £8,900; raw materials consumed £136,500; prime cost £342,700; factory overheads £152,600; factory profit £266,700; gross profit £245,500; provision for unrealized profit written off £19,375; profit for the year £86,925.

CHAPTER 30

PQ 30.1 Inadequacy of internal check at the tills

(a) The till operator records the transaction (sale) and has 'custody of the asset' – the cash received.

(b) One way that the till operator could perpetrate a fraud is, upon receiving the full amount from a customer, to record a lower sum on the till (or none at all). Another way is to record the full sales value but cancel the operation (or some items of the sale) after the total has been rung on the till. In collusion with customers, the possibilities for fraud proliferate.

(c) There are a number of ways of preventing the fraud:

(i) Encourage customers to insist on till rolls for the full amount tendered by them.

(ii) Use a video camera to record the till operator's work. This will have a 'policing effect' in that the existence of the video camera and the possibility of the till operator being detected may be deterrents.

(iii) Inspect the till roll and check cancelled items and the rate of cancelled items. If the percentage of cancelled items is high, it would suggest a fraud.

(iv) Check whether the gross profit remains similar to the gross profit margin fixed on the sale of the company's products. The gross profit margin can be checked with previous years, but this would not detect situations where the fraud has been carried out for a number of years.

(v) Carry out surprise counts of the cash in the till. This will detect cases where the full sum is received from the customer but a smaller sum is recorded on the till. The till operator misappropriates (steals) the excess of the cash in the till over the recorded sales, usually when he leaves at the end of the day. By performing surprise cash counts, fraud of this type can be found, as the cash counted will be significantly greater than the cash recorded on the till roll.

(vi) Bar code all products. This reduces the risk of fraud. Firstly, the amount rung up on the till depends on the price of the product recorded in the computer, and there will be special procedures when lower prices are used. With special prices input by the till operator, the till operator still scans the product and then enters the price manually. The computer records are checked to see whether the product with a lower price is one where prices were reduced, and the price input by the operator is checked to ascertain whether the price used was the officially reduced price. Also, the frequency of reduced prices is checked with the number of items reduced, and the till operator is asked to remove a label on the item and keep it in the till when there is a reduced price – the number of labels is checked to the number of reduced prices recorded on the till.

(vii) Use bar coding to deduct sales from the stock quantities. Any significant differences between the computer stock quantities and those counted in the store are investigated (for they may relate to items not recorded on the till). Special measures are used to check stock lines where there is an apparently large stock loss (i.e. the stock quantity on the computer is significantly more than the stock counted in the store).

PQ 30.2 Internal controls in the sales system

(a) The matters that should be checked when an order is received from a customer are as follows.

(i) The company should have a list of 'approved customers', and the customer should be on that list. If a customer is new, the creditworthiness of the customer should be checked. This can be performed by checking with a credit-rating company. For most new customers, either the customer will be asked to pay before the goods are delivered or a low credit limit will be allowed. When it is clear that the customer pays on time, the credit limit is increased.

(ii) A credit controller should authorize that goods can be sent to the customer. The credit controller determines the amount of credit that can be given to customers, checks the credit rating of customers, sets the credit limit and contacts customers when overdue amounts have not been received.

(iii) The price suggested on the order should be checked to the company's price list.

(iv) The goods ordered are checked for availability at the time specified for delivery on the purchase order.

(v) Some businesses send an order confirmation to the customer to confirm details on the purchase order (and specify any differences).

Assuming that everything is in order, the Sales Department will authorize the dispatch of goods to the customer. The Dispatch Department will dispatch the goods. In many computerized systems, the Sales Department will raise the dispatch note and at the same time the sales invoice will be produced and posted to the Sales Ledger. The Dispatch Department will dispatch the goods and the sales invoice will be sent to the customer. If there is a significant delay between checking the order and dispatching the goods, there will be an additional credit check of the customer just before the goods are sent to the customer. If the customer's balance is over the limit, or there are old outstanding items, then the credit controller may ask for a cheque from the customer before the goods are dispatched. Not dispatching goods to a customer is a good way of getting a prompt payment by a supplier.

(b) If the goods are sent to the customer through a carrier, the carrier should sign the dispatch note to acknowledge receipt of the goods. In this way, if the carrier does not deliver the goods to the customer, the business can claim compensation for the value of the goods lost. If the customer collects the goods, he/she should sign the dispatch note (in a similar way to the carrier). If the goods are delivered by the business to the customer, the customer should sign the dispatch note and this should be filed by the business. In this way, the business has evidence that the customer has received the goods, and it can insist that the customer pays for the goods.

PQ 30.3 Weaknesses in a purchases system

There are the following weaknesses in the purchasing system of Sherwood Wholesalers Ltd:

(a) The user department should issue a purchase requisition, which should be sequentially numbered, and it should list details of the items the department required. The head of the user department should authorize the purchase requisition. In the system stated in the question, there is no written purchase requisition.

(b) On receiving a purchase requisition, the Purchasing Department should consider whether the goods ordered are required by the user department, and check authorization by the department manager. The Purchasing Department should keep evidence of finding a suitable supplier. The supplier should be able to provide the goods at the lowest price consistent with quality and the delivery time. Some companies restrict suppliers to 'authorized suppliers', in which case the Purchasing Department should only order goods from an authorized supplier. The purchasing manager should authorize the purchase order before it is sent to the supplier.

(c) The Goods Received Department should check the goods received to the purchase order. If there is no purchase order, they should return the goods to the supplier. The Goods Received Department should issue a goods received note (GRN) that lists the goods received. The GRN should be signed by the goods received manager. The Goods Received Department should send a copy of the GRN to the Purchases Accounts Department, the Purchasing Department and the user department. With the current system, there is no check that the goods have been ordered, and so it will be possible for a supplier to send goods for which there is no purchase order (i.e. goods the company does not require).

(d) The Purchase Accounts Department should check the purchase invoice to the purchase order. The prices on the purchase invoice should be checked either to the purchase order or to the supplier's price list. The manager of the Purchase Accounts Department should initial the purchase invoice before it is posted to the purchase Ledger, confirming that the purchase invoice has been checked to the purchase order, the goods received note, the prices have been checked, and the calculations on the purchase invoice have been checked.

(e) Before signing the cheque, the chief accountant should check that the amount of the cheque and the payee agree to the details on the Purchase Ledger. If the supplier's credit is one month, the cheque paid at the end of May is for purchase invoices outstanding to the end of April. As the Purchase Accounts Department maintains the Purchase Ledger, it may be better for them (rather than the cashier) to make out the cheque.

(f) A person independent of all staff involved in purchasing transactions (including the Purchasing Department) should check suppliers' statements to the balances on the Purchase Ledger. That person should investigate differences, particularly old items on the supplier's statement that are not on the Purchase Ledger.

PQ 30.4 Internal controls in purchases system

(a) **Independent initiation of a purchase requisition**. It is important that different staff should authorize the purchase requisition from those who raise the purchase order, because this creates a division of duties and thus an effective system of internal control. The staff who raise the purchase requisition are authorizing (or initiating) the transaction and the Purchasing Department are executing the transaction. If the Purchasing Department both initiates and executes the transaction, it is possible for staff there to perpetrate a fraud as there is an inadequate division of duties. For instance, they could order a video camera for their personal use. As this purchase would have been made with an official purchase order, the company would not refuse delivery when the video camera arrived.

(b) **To minimize fraud related to ordering goods**. Even with a separate Purchasing Department (from the requisitioning department) there is still a risk of fraud, because the Purchasing Department has control over whom the goods are ordered from. Staff in the Purchasing Department could order goods from a supplier who gives a 'commission' to the member of staff ordering the goods. This type of fraud is controlled by having approved suppliers of goods and services, and an independent member of staff to check that prices charged by suppliers are not higher than those of alternative suppliers. Such a system of 'internal check' may not wholly prevent fraud but generally has a deterrent (i.e. the 'policing') effect.

(c) **Why the invoice should be received at the Accounts Department**. If the invoice was sent with the goods, the Goods Received Department would have both the goods (the 'asset') and the purchase invoice (which is 'recording the transaction'), and this would represent an inadequate division of duties. Sending the purchase invoice to the Accounts Department separates the duties of receiving the goods ('custody of the asset') and receiving and processing the purchase invoice ('recording the transaction'). This provides an effective division of duties.

(d) **Why goods received should be checked against copy purchase order**. The Goods Received Department should only accept goods that have been ordered by the company. If there is no purchase order, then the purchase of the goods will not have gone through the normal purchasing procedure. It is probable that the company has not ordered the goods, and hence does not want them. If they accept goods without an order, the company will probably have to pay for them, as acceptance of the goods is acknowledgement that the company requires the goods.

(e) **Processing of a purchase invoice**. The following checks should be performed when processing the purchase invoice:

- Details of the goods on the purchase invoice should be checked to the goods received, per the GRN and the supplier's delivery note. These checks will be for the quantity, description and part number of the goods received.
- Details on the purchase invoice should be checked to the purchase order (this would probably be performed by the Purchasing Department). These details should be recorded on the purchase order so as to prevent the same goods being received twice. The checks will be of the supplier's name and address, the quantity, part number and description of goods received (the goods received should not exceed those ordered). If the purchase order includes the price of the goods, this should be the same as that on the purchase invoice. Otherwise, the price on the invoice should be checked to a price list of the manufacturer (it is better to include the price on the purchase order).
- The calculations on the purchase invoice should be checked (i.e. price × quantity to the cost of goods received, the calculation of VAT and the total invoice value).
- The analysis of the invoice expense should be checked (i.e. that it is appropriate for the goods received).
- The invoice should be authorized by an independent responsible official. This independent check is important because if only the Accounts Department checks the items above, there would be a weakness in the division of duties and thus a risk of fraud and error.
- Then, the invoice can be posted to the Purchase Ledger (and the invoice expense and VAT would be recorded at the same time in the Purchases Day Book).

(f) **Why an independent person should check suppliers' statements**. It is important that the person who checks suppliers' statements to the balances on the Purchase Ledger should be independent of the processing of purchasing transactions, as this will ensure there is an effective system of 'internal check'. If the person checking suppliers' statements is not independent of processing of purchases transactions, there will be an inadequate division of duties.

(g) **What does checking of suppliers' statements involve?** Firstly, it should be pointed out that with a good purchases system, most of the balances on suppliers' statements should agree with the balances on the Purchase Ledger. Where differences are found, most of them will be 'timing errors'. Normally, the balance on the supplier's statement will be more than that on the Purchase Ledger. The two timing differences will be as follows:

1. Invoices are on the supplier's statement but not on the Purchase Ledger. If these invoices are dated close to the time of the check, then they are probably purchase invoices for goods received which have not completed the checks by staff and thus have not been posted to the Purchase Ledger. These types of difference can be accepted. However, if the invoice is dated some time back before the check, it should be investigated to determine why the invoice has not yet been posted to the Purchase Ledger. This could be due to slow processing of the invoice or some dispute (e.g. over the quality or quantity of the goods received or the price per unit charged).

2. Cash paid on the Purchase Ledger has not been recorded on the supplier's statement. This could be due to the cheques not being sent to the suppliers when they are written out (or printed by the computer). There may be a number of reasons for not sending cheques promptly, as the delay will reduce the company's bank overdraft and thus reduce the interest charge on the overdraft. Also, by delaying sending the cheques, the company may prevent the bank balance from exceeding the overdraft limit set by the bank. Another reason for the slow processing of cash paid could be the slow banking of cheques received by the supplier. Occasionally, this may highlight a 'teeming and lading fraud' in the supplier's business. Such a fraud would be more likely when the date the cheque is debited by the company's bank is significantly earlier than the date the cheque appears on the supplier's statement.

Differences can arise because of a variety of other reasons. For example, cash discount may have been accounted as earned whereas the supplier has disallowed the discount. Frequently, a 2.5 per cent discount is allowed for early settlement (i.e. paying for outstanding invoices). The date the cheque is cleared by the bank is a good indication of when the supplier received the cheque. If this date is after the date allowed for a discount, then the discount will be disallowed, so the discount on the Purchase Ledger will have to be cancelled. The date of the cheque is less reliable evidence of the date of payment, as sometimes companies hold cheques before sending them to the supplier. Checking the reconciliation of the Purchase Ledger Control account to the total of the balances on the Purchase Ledger and checking the bank reconciliation are other ways of highlighting errors in posting transactions to the Purchase Ledger. Any errors found from checking suppliers' statements to the balances on the Purchase Ledger should be corrected no later than the following month.

PQ 30.5 Control weakness in wages systems

(a) **Control weakness when the Wages Department deals with wage disputes.** The reason why there is weakness in control when the Wages Department deals with disputes about wages is that the Wages Department is recording the transaction and has put the money in the wage packets (custody of the asset). In dealing with disputes about wages, the Wages Department is dealing with alleged errors in recording wages transactions and the amount of cash they have put in the wage packet. Thus,

there is a serious weakness in the system of internal control. A separate department (or individual) should deal with disputes about wages, as this person will be in a position to detect errors (or fraud) by the Wages Department.

(b) **Control weakness when the Wages Department makes up the pay packets.** There are two weaknesses that should be mentioned. First, in making up the wage packets and paying employees, the Wages Department is both recording the transaction and has custody of the asset (cash in the wage packets). So, there is an inadequate division of duties and a weakness in the system of internal control. If the wages are paid out by a separate individual (e.g. the head of the department whose wages are being paid), this will be both a division of duties and he/she will be able to check whether the Wages Department has processed the transactions correctly.

A second way in which the Wages Department can commit a fraud is by creating 'fictitious' employees. These may well be totally fictitious employees; on the other hand the Wages Department can create a wage either before an employee has started work or after he/she has left – and the employee in the Wages Department will misappropriate the wage packet that represents these payments. This fraud can be detected by a senior employee checking the existence of employees on the payroll, or the department manager paying the wages to employees will find that employees are apparently being paid before they started work or after they have left (or are fictitious employees charged to the department). Separation from the Wages Department of dealing with unclaimed wages will either prevent or detect such a fraud.

(c) **Control weakness when the Wages Department calculates and pays its own wages.** Employees in the Wages Department will be responsible for recording their wage payments. This creates a weakness because it allows employees in the Wages Department to inflate their wage and thus perpetrate a fraud. This can be prevented by an independent person checking whether the wages of the staff in the Wages Department are reasonable, in terms of gross pay, deductions and net pay. Also, the person checking the payroll should investigate cases where the gross or net pay is unexpectedly high, and also investigate the existence of employees on the payroll of which he/she is not aware.

PQ 30.6 Checks in the petty cash system

The checks an independent person can perform on the petty cash system include:

(a) Counting the cash. The amount of cash should equal that recorded in the Petty Cash Book. When counting the petty cash, if there are some payments yet to be recorded in the Petty Cash Book, the cash counted plus the value of the items not recorded should equal the balance in the Petty Cash Book. The items not recorded in the Petty Cash Book should not include 'IOUs' (an amount owed by an employee to petty cash), unbanked employees' cheques and any other items that appear to suggest short-term loans made to employees from petty cash.

(b) Checking petty cash payments against vouchers, noting whether the amounts agree (be alert to whether £5.63 had been altered to £15.63), the amounts are reasonable, the 'vouchers' have been authorized (ideally by a responsible official) and, where possible, are supported by an externally produced evidence.

(c) Checking additions of receipts and payments in the Petty Cash Book and the posting of the analysed transactions to the appropriate accounts in the Nominal Ledger.

(d) Checking that all payments out of the cash book for petty cash are recorded in the Petty Cash Book.

(e) Checking that, when the petty cash float is reimbursed, the total petty cash is equal to the agreed petty cash float.

PQ 30.7 Verification of fixed assets

(a) **Verification of existence and value.** This comprises two separate activities. The first is to verify whether the fixed assets belonging to the entity are all recorded in the Fixed Asset Register. The second is to identify and inspect the assets recorded in the Fixed Asset Register. The Fixed Asset Register should give the location of the fixed asset. A person independent of the fixed asset system should begin by checking whether the totals of the cost and accumulated depreciation of the fixed assets in the Fixed Asset Register are the same as in the financial accounting records. When inspecting the asset, the following should be checked: the serial number on the fixed asset is the same as that recorded in the Fixed Asset Register; the description of the fixed asset is consistent with that in the Fixed Asset Register; and whether the fixed asset is in use and is in reasonable condition. It should be noted whether the fixed asset is not being used (is it better to sell it?) or is in poor condition (does it need repairs/refurbishment, and does its poor condition affect its performance; has there been neglect of the fixed asset, which could be rectified?).

(b) **Additional check for motor vehicles.** For motor vehicles, one normally checks the registration number of the vehicle, and this can be checked to both the Fixed Asset Register and the vehicle registration document. It is unusual to use the serial number of the motor vehicle (rather than the registration number) as they can be more difficult to find (although new motor cars in the UK usually have the serial number on the front windscreen). Checking the condition of the motor vehicle is important, and action should be taken if the vehicle looks neglected.

PQ 30.8 Disposing of fixed assets

The unauthorized disposal of fixed assets is a way of perpetrating a fraud. The employee may sell the fixed asset and misappropriate the proceeds. To overcome this weakness, there should be an approved system of disposing of fixed assets. The unauthorized disposal of fixed assets can be detected by periodically checking fixed assets from the Fixed Asset Register to the fixed asset (as described above). A further risk in disposing fixed assets is 'split consideration' where, for instance in the sale of a car, the purchaser pays £3,000 in cash, the employee misappropriates £1,000 and gives the balance of £2,000 to the cashier. A way of guarding against this possibility is to get the purchaser to sign a copy of the invoice that gives the actual sale proceeds, and a senior member of the business's staff should check that the sale proceeds of fixed assets are reasonable.

PQ 30.9 Nominal Ledger – checking the accountant's entries

The weakness in allowing the accountant to make entries in the Nominal Ledger is that there is likely to be little or no check over the entries he or she makes, which creates a risk of error (and, less commonly, fraud). So an independent person should check the entries by the accountant. That person should have some accounting knowledge and be senior to the accountant. The finance director would be a suitable person, but there may be problems when (in small companies) the finance director and the accountant

are the same person. If there is no senior person with accounting skills, this task could be undertaken by the internal auditor (who should report discrepancies to the managing director) or the external auditor, who reports on the company's annual financial statements. The accountant's entries should be checked for authorization and to supporting documentation. For example, an entry transferring an amount from the Staff Loan account to (say) the Staff Training account will require authorization at the appropriate level.

PQ 30.10 Controls to minimize abuse of company facilities

(a) With regard to concerns (i) to (iv) of the managing director:
(i) There are many ways of minimizing personal use of the telephone by employees. Some controls, although very effective, may prevent the smooth operation of the company; therefore the controls established may allow some private use of the telephone, while preventing or detecting significant personal use by employees. The controls include the following:

- Most telephones would be set up to allow only internal telephone calls. The only telephones set up for external calls would be those for members of staff who need to make external telephone calls in the course of their duty.
- The telephone bill for each telephone should be scrutinized by the department manager, who would investigate telephone calls that appear to be for excessive private use.
- Telephones could be restricted to calling only local numbers (i.e. they would not be allowed to call a number which starts with a '0').
- The use of the telephone outside normal working hours could be prevented, or only allowed by senior employees.

(ii) The main control over using a photocopier is the use of a personal card (like a credit card) for each employee. In this way, the photocopier can keep a record of the number of copies made by each employee. Then a senior member of staff can check that each employee's use of the photocopier is reasonable. This is not a wholly effective way of preventing employees from using the photocopier for personal use, as it would not detect when employees were obtaining a few copies. However, it should prevent employees obtaining a large number of copies for personal use. In addition, there should be a system where employees can pay for their private copies. The charge per copy should be reasonable: not too low as to encourage employees to obtain personal photocopies, but not too high to prevent them from 'owning up' in private use of the photocopier. The use of a book to record the use of a photocopier is less effective than a personal card, as some employees may not record their use of the photocopier in the book. There can be periodic checking by management of who is using the photocopier – this would be more as a deterrent, but it has a 'policing effect'.

(iii) The company can prevent the use of computer games on its computers by preventing such programs being loaded. However, this is more difficult with PCs on the employee's desk. There could be periodic checks of the local hard drives of PCs to check they do not contain computer games. There should be a rule that prohibits employees from using computer games, and action should be taken against employees using computer games in working hours.

Controlling access to the Internet is more difficult, as the company may allow employees access in order to perform their work effectively. Access to the

Internet could be limited to specified employees who require it for their work. Action could be taken against employees using the Internet who are not given this permission. This could be detected through monitoring the cost of telephone calls for Internet access, which could be allocated to each employee's terminal.

(iv) Postage of personal letters could be controlled by requiring all employees to send business letters through the department secretary. The secretary can put the stamp on each letter and post them, or send them to the central Postal Department for posting. The central Postal Department will only be permitted to post letters that are received from authorized sources (e.g. the department secretary). The authorized people will include staff in the Purchases and Sales Accounting Department, who send payments to suppliers and sales invoices and statements to customers.

(b) There are two reasons why a company might *not* introduce very strict controls over costs (a) (i) to (iv) above: the cost of implementing the controls, and the effect on employees of implementing the controls. The cost of implementing the controls should not be more than the savings; otherwise there will be a net cost (and reduction in profit) resulting in implementing the controls. On the second point, very tight controls may result in an adverse reaction by employees. So, it is probably worthwhile to allow employees to have a limited private use of these facilities. However, real abuse of these facilities by employees should be prevented (e.g. allowing an employee to run his/her business using the company's telephone), because that too can have an adverse effect on other employees if one employee is seen to be abusing the use of the facilities, and it could also encourage the other employees to make more private use of the company's facilities. Also, the company should realize that the cost of, for instance, using the company's telephone in working hours includes both the cost of the telephone calls and the amount of wages the company is paying the employee while he/she is using the telephone for private purposes. Some controls may be relatively easy to implement, such as a specified employee putting stamps on letters; this control will probably have no additional cost. But the risk of an employee being found using the company's mail for his personal use will be a deterrent to employees. The other controls in the list will probably be more expensive to implement, and probably less effective. However, the existence of a control will probably deter employees from the private use of the company's facilities. So it is important that there are some controls rather than none at all.

CHAPTER 31

PQ 31.1 Comparative appraisal of two investments

(a) **Payback method**

	Outlay	Year 1	Year 2	Year 3	Year 4	Year 5	Payback period
President	£40,000	£12,000	£16,000	£16,000	£16,000	£16,000	2 years and 9 mths
Royal	£60,000	£20,000	£20,000	£30,000	£40,000	£20,000	2 years and 8 mths

Net present value:

NPV	'President'		PV	'Royal'		PV
0	(40,000)	1.000	(40,000)	(60,000)	1.000	(60,000)
1	12,000	0.800	9,600	20,000	0.800	16,000
2	16,000	0.640	10,240	20,000	0.640	12,800
3	16,000	0.512	8,192	30,000	0.512	15,360
4	16,000	0.410	6,560	40,000	0.410	16,400
5	16,000	0.328	5,248	20,000	0.328	6,560
		NPV	(160)		NPV	7,120

(b) The 'Royal' should be chosen since it gives a positive net present value. With regard to payback, there is little to choose between the two models, with the 'President' being better by only one month, and given that all of the data is estimated, this difference is insignificant whereas the difference in the two net present values is very substantial.

PQ 31.2 Appraising the viability of a project

(a) **Calculate the payback period.**

Statement of net cash flow

Years	Sales	Variable cost	Net cash flow
1	£60,000	£13,000	£47,000
2	£75,000	£16,250	£58,750
3	£84,000	£18,200	£65,800
4	£96,000	£20,800	£75,200

First year: whole	£47,000	one year
Second year: whole	£58,750	one year
Third year: £59,250	£59,250	11 months
	£165,000	2 years 11 mths

(b) **The net present value (NPV) of the project**

Year	Net cash flow £	Discount factor £	Present value £
0	(165,000)	1.000	(165,000)
1	47,000	0.870	40,890
2	58,750	0.756	44,415
3	65,800	0.658	43,296.4
4	75,200	0.572	43,014.4
	£65,800		6,615.8

The NPV is positive or the project yields more than 15 per cent, and therefore it is acceptable.

(c) Report to the Directors explaining:

Report layout

   From

   To

Subject content

Date

(i) **Advantages of the payback method**
- Simple to understand by all staff.
- It gives fairly easily the period the business must wait until the cash invested is recouped.

PQ 31.4 Acquisition on HP terms including a trade-in

CLUE: Cranes are capitalized at their cash prices and depreciation, on reducing balance method, is time-apportioned. Interest on HP contract is calculated at 10 per cent and time-apportioned.

P&L account	20X0	20X1	20X2	20X3
Depreciation	(6,277)	(7,113)	(9,100)	(11,259)
Interest	(2,238)	(2,308)	(3,172)	(4,242)
Disposal gain	–	–	575	–

Balance Sheet	20X0	20X1	20X2	20X3
Crane at cost	41,844	41,844	62,550	62,550
Ac. depreciation	(6,277)	(13,390)	(6,255)	(17,514)
HP Vendor's a/c	(32,082)	(22,390)	(49,928)	(39,170)

PQ 31.5 Finance lease

CLUE: Present value of minimum lease payment (£20,000 × 3.170) = £63,400 = 99% of the fair value.

P&L account	20X1	20X2	20X3	20X4
Interest on FL	(4,755)	(5,443)	(3,959)	(2,326)
Depreciation	(9,510)	(12,680)	(12,680)	(12,680)

Balance Sheet	20X0	20X1	20X2	20X3
Machine	63,400	63,400	63,400	63,400
Ac. depreciation	(9,510)	(22,190)	(34,870)	(47,550)
Obligation – F.L	(68,155)	(53,598)	(37,557)	(19,883)

CHAPTER 32

PQ 32.1 Monthly cash budget

(a)

Sales calculated as follows:

	Qty	Price	Income	Cash receipts
October	1,080	20	21,600	5,400 in October 16,200 in November
November	1,760	20	35,200	8,800 in November 26,400 in December
December	2,040	20	40,800	10,200 in December 30,600 in January 20X2

Purchases calculated as follows:

	Qty	Price	Income	Cash payments
October	1,900	17	32,300	16,150 in October 16,150 in November
November	1,900	17	32,300	16,150 in November 16,150 in December
December	2,200	17	37,400	18,700 in December 18,700 in January 20X2

● As this method is generally used for short-term projects, there is less danger of false results occurring due to obsolescence.

● Payback identifies fast growth projects, thus minimizing risks.

(ii) **Points to be contained in the report concerning cash flow**

● Accounting profits are calculated using the accrual and matching concepts. Cash flow has little bearing.

● Profits cannot be spent unless they are in a cash form and cash flows are tangible and more objective.

● The timing of cash flows is more readily determined.

● It is more important to consider the expected life of the project and it could be misleading to use accounting profits that are related to distinctive periods.

● The cash-flow approach can disregard such accounting conventions as depreciation, stock value and revenue/expenditure classification as these can often be subjective.

PQ 31.3 Acquisition on hire purchase terms payable quarterly in advance

WBM Ltd. Profit and Loss for year ended and Balance sheet as at 31 December

PROFIT AND LOSS ACCOUNTS

	Interest	Depreciation
20X0	£364	£906
20X1	£965	£3,625
20X2	£171	£3,625
20X3	–	£3,625
20X4	–	£2,719

BALANCE SHEETS

Fixed asset	Cost	Ac. depre.	WDV
	£14,500	(£906)	£13,594
	£14,500	(£4,531)	£9,969
	£14,500	£(8,156)	£6,344
	£14,500	£(11,781)	£2,719
	£14,500	£(14,500)	–

Obligations under hire purchase:

Within one year	After one year
£7,035	£5,829
£5,829	–
–	–
–	–
–	–

Workings:

Quarter ended	Opening balance £	Deposit/ repayment £	Interest 11.65% £	Balance £	Closing balance £
1 October 20X0	14,500	2,000	364	12,500	12,864
1 January 20X1	12,864	2,000	316	10,864	11,180
1 April 20X1	11,180	2,000	267	9,180	9,447
1 July 20X1	9,447	2,000	217	7,447	7,664
1 October 20X1	7,664	2,000	165	5,664	5,829
1 January 20X2	5,829	2,000	112	3,829	3,941
1 April 20X2	3,941	2,000	59*	1,941	2,000
1 July 20X2	2,000	2,000	–	–	–

* £57 was rounded up to £59 to take account of all other rounding errors.

Cash budget for 3 months ended 31 December 20X1

	October	November	December
Cash receipts:			
Opening balance	–	308,000	249,590
Capital	680,000		
Sales: Cash	5,400	8,800	10,200
Debtors		16,200	26,400
	685,400	333,000	286,190
Cash payments:			
Property	238,000		
Equipment	102,000		
Fixtures		20,000	20,000
Vehicles		32,300	30,600
Purchases	16,150		34,850
Wages	13,600	13,600	13,600
Income tax			11,050
Expenses	4,930	14,790	14,790
Salaries	2,720	2,720	2,720
	377,400	83,410	127,610
Closing balance	308,000	249,590	158,580

(b) Comments

- Although there is a credit balance at the bank, it is declining.
- The monthly cash receipts from sales are not enough to cover the present level of cash expenses.
- The balance will be gradually depleted if there is no increase in sales or a cost reduction.
- The cash budget needs to be extended to cover a period of at least a year.

PQ 32.2 Purchases budget and cash budget

(a) Monthly purchases budget

	July		Aug		Sept		Oct		Nov		Dec		Jan	
Sales	100,000		150,000		200,000		250,000		300,000		350,000		350,000	
	S	DS	S	DS	S	DS	S	DS	S	DS	S	DS	S	DS
Inshore Deepsea	75,000	25,000	112,500	37,500	150,000	50,000	187,500	62,500	225,000	75,000	262,500	87,500	262,500	87,500
Profit	7,500	5,000	11,250	7,500	15,000	10,000	18,750	12,500	22,500	15,000	26,250	17,500	26,250	17,500
Cost	67,500	20,000	101,250	30,000	135,000	40,000	168,750	50,000	202,500	60,000	236,250	70,000	236,250	70,000

Purchases	July	Aug	Sept	Oct	Nov	Dec
	67,500	135,000	168,750	202,500	236,250	236,250
	20,000	40,000	50,000	60,000	70,000	70,000
	101,250					
	30,000					
	£218,750	£175,000	£218,750	£262,500	£306,250	£306,250

(b) Cash budget

	July	Aug	Sept	Oct	Nov	Dec
O/bal		162,500	37,500	12,500	(6,250)	(18,750)
Cash sales	125,000	75,000	100,000	125,000	150,000	175,000
Credit sales: Inshore	50,000	37,500	56,250	75,000	93,750	112,500
Deepsea			12,500	18,750	25,000	31,250
	175,000	275,000	206,250	231,250	262,500	300,000
Purchases		218,750	175,000	218,750	262,500	306,250
Wages	12,500	12,500	12,500	12,500	12,500	12,500
Other		6,250	6,250	6,250	6,250	6,250
	12,500	237,500	193,750	237,500	281,250	325,000
Monthly change	162,500	37,500	12,500	(6,250)	(18,750)	(25,000)

(c) Adverse implications

From the last line of the above workings, it can be seen that the business will run into an overdraft of £25,000 in December. This exceeds its agreed overdraft limit of £20,000. There are a number of ways of dealing with this, which include:

- Approaching the bank to extend the overdraft limit to £40,000. However, the bank will require a budget for the following year to see if the liquidity position is likely to worsen or improve.
- Increase sales or selling price to achieve a higher gross profit margin.
- Obtain longer credit terms from suppliers.
- Re-assess the viability of the business venture if the sales or gross profit margins cannot be improved.

PQ 32.3 Reconciliation of budgeted profit with actual

(a)

	Budget		Flexed budget		Actual	
Sales	2,000 × 40.0 =	80,000	1,600 × 40.0 =	64,000	1,600 × 40 =	64,000
Materials	2,000 × 12.0 =	24,000	1,600 × 12.0 =	19,200	1,600 × 13.2 =	21,120
Labour	2,000 × 8.0 =	16,000	1,600 × 8.0 =	12,800	1,600 × 8.4 =	13,440
Variable O/Hs	2,000 × 3.0 =	6,000	1,600 × 3.0 =	4,800	1,600 × 3.18 =	5,088
Fixed O/Hs	2,000 × 11.35 =	22,700	1,600 × 14.19 =	22,700	1,600 × 14.19 =	22,700
Profit/(Loss)	2,000 × 5.65 =	11,300	1,600 × 2.81 =	4,500	1,600 × 1.03 =	1,652

(b) Reconciliation

Budgeted profit		11,300
Volume variance		6,800
Profit		4,500
Cost variances:		
Material	(1,920)	
Labour	(640)	
Variable O/Hs	(288)	
		(2,848)
Actual profit		1,652

CHAPTER 33

PQ 33.1 The purpose of and case for standard costing

Standard costing is a system of cost accounting using *predetermined costs* for each element of cost for each item of production or service. *Actual costs* are compared with the standards and the differences, or variances, are identified and investigated to ascertain their causes in order that *corrective action* can be taken by the persons responsible.

Advantages include:

1. Standards are yardsticks for identifying levels of efficiency.
2. Deviations are quickly identified and action taken.
3. Management by exception can be practised.
4. As a result of (3), costs can be kept down.
5. Reports are relatively easily interpreted.
6. Cost control can be exercised.
7. A positive attitude is generated towards improving efficiency.
8. The method can be used when making policy decisions regarding production and pricing.
9. Incentive schemes can be based on the achievement of standards.
10. The method facilitates co-operation between members of staff.

Illustration

Total material	Standard 2,000 kg at £2	£4,000	
	Actual 1,950 kg at £2.20	£4,290	
cost variance		(£290)	Adv.

Material price variance	20p × 1,950 kg	£390	Adv.
Material usage variance	50 kg at £2	£100	Fav.
		(£290)	Adv.

Total labour	Standard 600 hrs at £5	£3,000	
	Actual 590 hrs at £5.50	£3,245	
cost variance		(£245)	Adv.

Labour rate variance	590 hrs at 50p	£295	Adv.
Labour efficiency variance	10 hrs at £5	£50	Fav.
		(£245)	Adv.

Reasons for variances

1. Unanticipated price increase; better-quality materials used.
2. Better quality materials, therefore less waste; higher-skilled labour, therefore less waste.
3. Unanticipated wage increase; higher-skilled staff.
4. Higher-skilled staff; better-quality materials that are easier to work with; better working practices.
5. Unrealistic standards set.

PQ 33.2 Variance analysis with flexed budget

The standard costs, based on a production of 360,000 packets, have to be flexed to the actual output of 300,000 packets, producing results as stated here.

Raw materials: 240,000 × 300/360 = 200,000 kg
Direct labour: 42,000 × 300/360 = 35,000 hours

Total material	Standard: 200,000 kg at 40p	£80,000	
	Actual: 210,000 kg at 38p	£79,800	
cost variance		£200	Fav.

Material price variance	2p × 210,000 kg	£4,200	Fav.
Material usage variance	10,000 kg × 40p	£4,000	Adv.
		£200	Fav.

Total labour	Standard: 35,000 hrs at £5.40	£189,000	
	Actual: 34,000 hrs at £5.50	£187,000	
cost variance		£2,000	Fav.

Labour rate variance	10p × 34,000 hrs	£3,400	Adv.
Labour efficiency variance	1,000 hrs × £5.40	£5,400	Fav.
		£2,000	Fav.

Budgeted amounts have been flexed for the actual output (300,000/360,000 units) to arrive at the standards.

(c) Profit statement for the year ended 31 May 20X0:

Output budgeted	Budgeted 360,000 units	Flexed budget 300,000 units	Actual
	£	£	£
Sales	450,000	375,000	375,000
	£	£	£
Raw materials	96,000	80,000	79,800
Direct labour	226,800	189,000	187,000
Fixed overheads	75,000	75,000	75,000
	(397,800)	(344,000)	(341,800)
Profit	52,200	31,000	33,200

PQ 33.3 Variance analysis and its use

Total material	Standard 38,400 kg at £6	£230,400	
	Actual 40,500 kg at £5.90	£238,950	
cost variance		(£8,550)	Adv.

Material price variance	10p at 40,500 kg	£4,050	Fav.
Material usage variance	2,100 kg at £6	£12,600	Adv.
		(£8,550)	Adv.

Total labour	Standard 115,200 hrs at £3.25	£374,400	
	Actual 118,000 hrs at £3.40	£401,200	
cost variance		(£26,800)	Adv.

Labour rate variance	118,000 hrs at 15p	£17,700	Adv.
Labour efficiency variance	2,800 hrs at £3.25	£9,100	Adv.
		(£26,800)	Adv.

Budgeted amounts have been flexed for the actual output (30,000/31,250 units) to arrive at the standards.

(b) Revenue statements for the month ending 31 March 20X0:

	Budgeted	Actual
Sales	1,500,000	1,612,000
Direct materials	240,000	238,950
Direct labour	390,000	401,200
Variable manufacturing overheads	75,000	78,750
Variable sales overheads	80,000	81,600
Administration costs	180,000	174,600
Selling and distribution costs	60,000	66,000
	1,025,000	1,041,100
Net profit	£475,000	£570,900

(c) Use of the variance analysis:

Generally – cut out unfavourable variances and continue processes that create favourable variances.

Materials – investigate causes of wastage; find solution to problem and if possible eradicate; set standard and test.

Price – investigate cause of saving; continue to use cheaper material/source.

Labour – investigate why fewer hours used; continue with the improved practice.

Wage – investigate why higher wage paid; if it is cost-effective, continue to adjust the standard; if not cost-effective, take remedial action.

(d) Possible action to avoid any adverse variances

Materials usage: If poor materials, change supplier, introduce better quality control, train staff and purchase better machinery

Labour rate: renegotiate wage contracts, install a system of piecework

CHAPTER 34

PQ 34.1 Absorption costing v. marginal costing

PROFIT STATEMENT YEAR ENDED 31.12.X1

	Absorption costing £	Absorption costing £	Marginal costing £	Marginal costing £
Sales		75,000		75,000
Costs:				
Direct material	22,500		22,500	
Direct labour	45,000		45,000	
Variable expenses	9,000		9,000	
	76,500		76,500	
Fixed overheads	18,000			
	94,500			
Less: Closing stock	(31,500)		(25,500)	
Cost of sales		(63,000)		(51,000)
Contribution				24,000
Fixed overheads				(18,000)
Profit		12,000		6,000

(b) The difference in net profit is due to the fixed expenses retained in closing stock value under the full cost method, i.e. fixed expenses/unit = (£18,000/22,500) = £0.80 per unit and for the stock increase this would be 7,500 units × £0.80, i.e. £6,000.

PQ 34.2 Profit using marginal costing

(a) Sale price per unit		£3.50
(b) Marginal cost per unit	(£396,000 + £72,000 + £36,000)/360,000 units	£1.40
(c) Contribution per unit	a – b	£2.10
(d) Total contribution	345,000 units × £2.10	£724,500
(e) Fixed overheads	£216,000 + £144,000	(£360,000)
(f) Profit	d – e	£364,500

PQ 34.3 Contribution and break-even point

Workings:

	Product A	Product B	Product C	Total
(a) Selling price per unit	£6.00	£4.90	£8.00	
(b) Variable cost per unit	£2.40	£3.34	£5.20	
(c) Contribution per unit	£3.60	£1.56	£2.80	
(d) Annual sales (in units)	500,000	1,200,000	480,000	2,180,000
(e) Annual contribution (c × d)	£1,800,000	£1,872,000	£1,344,000	£5,016,000
(f) Annual sales revenue (a × d)	£3,000,000	£5,880,000	£3,840,000	£12,720,000

(a) Weighted average contribution per £ of sales: £5,016,000/£12,720,000 × 100p = 39.43p.

(b) Break-even sales revenue: fixed overheads/weighted average contribution = £3,000,000/0.3943p = sales of £7,608,420.

(c) Margin of safety: total sales less break-even sales: £12,720,000 less £7,608,420 = £5,111,580 (or 40%).

The margin of safety is the fall in activity that must occur from the present activity level before break-even point is reached. The margin of safety may be affected by changes in price, mix or volume of sales. It will also be affected by changes in the rate of variable cost per unit or the total level of fixed cost.

PQ 34.4 Contemplated changes to product price and quality

(a) Whether to reduce price and incur costs

		Proposal (a)	Proposal (b)
(a) Sale prices proposed		£5.50	£5.10
(b) Variable costs		(£2.40)	(£2.40)
(c) Contribution	a – b	£3.10	£2.70
(d) Sales in units		700,000	800,000
(e) Annual contribution	c × d	£2,170,000	£2,160,000
(f) Contribution before the change		£1,800,000	£1,800,000
(g) Additional contribution	e – f	£370,000	£360,000
(h) Extra fixed cost contemplated		£365,000	£365,000
Additional profit (loss)		£5,000	(£5,000)

Aroma may proceed with the additional fixed costs but reduce the price to no lower than £5.50.

(b) Required sales of Product A

(Original contribution + extra fixed cost)/amended contribution per unit = (1,800,000 + 365,000)/3.1 = 698,387 units.

CHAPTER 35

PQ 35.1 Benefits of using computer systems

The benefits of using computer systems comprise:

- accuracy of processing;
- speed of processing;
- flexibility for analyses/reports.

On accuracy of processing, computer systems do not make calculation errors (provided there are no bugs in the programs). So, Trial Balances always balance, and if the data is entered correctly, the calculations will be performed accurately and the results will be accurate. Thus, there are no computational errors, unlike manual systems (where they are relatively common). However, computer systems do not wholly prevent errors in inputting data. If the operator inputs the wrong account number in a sales system, the sales invoice will be posted to the wrong account (provided this is a valid account). Using control totals, by checking the manually calculated total of items input to the computer equals the value of transactions accepted by the computer, the accuracy of processing by the computer can be improved further. The rules in a wages program concerning the calculation of tax and National Insurance deductions ensure the calculations are performed accurately and are consistent with the current tax and National Insurance legislation.

Using computers increases the speed that data is processed. For instance, in a wages system, the calculation of tax and National Insurance is a complex task to perform manually, using tax and National Insurance tables, which makes it both time-consuming and prone to error. With a wages computer program this task is performed more quickly and accurately. In one small company, the time taken to produce the payroll manually was 5 hours, whereas the time taken to produce it using a computer was only 45 minutes. In a Purchase Ledger system, when invoices are posted to the Purchase Ledger, the time saving is less than the payroll system described above but the accuracy of processing using a computer is much better than using a manual system. Also, the computer system allows greater analysis of the data to be performed much more quickly (e.g. calculating the age of debtors in a sales system).

Computer systems allow analyses and reports to be produced much more quickly and flexibly than a manual system. In a computer system an aged debtors report will only take the time required to print it, but in a manual system it could take too long for the accountant to prepare (particularly with Sales Ledger systems in Chapter 35, it can be seen that accounts). From the description of the EPOS system in Chapter 35, it can be seen that analysis of the data can be valuable for:

(a) ordering stock, in relation to both the time required and the quantity to be ordered (and this will include the decision to purchase no more stock);

(b) allocating the appropriate number of staff to the cash checkouts;

(c) highlighting loss of stock, by comparing physical stocktakes with the computer stock quantities – and action can be taken to reduce this loss of stock;

(d) reducing the selling price of slow-moving stock and seasonal stock (e.g. Christmas stock still held in January).

With spreadsheets, factors can be changed and the computer can recalculate the spreadsheet immediately, giving new results (e.g. a change in sales yielding a new profit and the effect on cash flow). In this way, the accountant can determine which factors have a significant effect on cash flow and profit, and thus take appropriate action.

Generally, computer systems produce a better 'audit trail' than manual systems. There should be a record of each entry made into an accounting system, whereas this is probably not true for manual systems. For instance, in the Sales Ledger system described in Chapter 35, an adjustment is posted to the Sales Ledger Suspense account. The accountant can print out that account, check each entry that comprises the total balance, and transfer the entries to the appropriate accounts (e.g. to the Bad Debts account). With a manual system, the record of such entries will probably be less clear, and so errors may occur in transferring balances from the Suspense account to the appropriate account in the Nominal Ledger. In a manual system, the reason for the Trial Balance not balancing will be due to one entry not being made in a (double entry) transaction, a figure being written down incorrectly or a total being added up incorrectly. As there will have been a large number of transactions, finding all these errors will probably be impossible. However, with a computer system this type of error cannot occur.

As a computer system can process data much quicker than a manual system, the accountant will produce reports and calculations using a computer system, which would be impossible to produce (in a reasonable time) using a manual system. With the additional information provided by the computer system, the accountant (or other employee) can have a better understanding of the operation of the business, and thus he or she will be able to manage it more effectively and profitably.

It is apparent that with many very large computer systems, it would be impossible to perform the task with a manual system. For instance, with a manual system it would not be possible to know the current stock quantities of each line of product in a supermarket, but this is quite easy with an EPOS system. The number of transactions in a banking system could not be performed using a manual system, and the use of 'hole in the wall' cash dispensers allows customers to obtain cash at any time and reduces the all-round costs of doing so, as it saves time for both bank employees and customers. The processing of credit card transactions could not be performed manually. With a computer, it can check whether the customer's credit limit is going to be exceeded with the current transaction (in which case it would refuse the transaction), and it can process the transaction immediately it takes place, thus ensuring the customer's balance is always correct.

PQ 35.2 Edit checks

The types of edit checks include the following:

(a) **Format check.** This will check that where an alphabetic character is required, the user has input only an alphabetic character (i.e. not a numeric character). Where a number is expected, the edit check will ensure that only a numeric character has been entered (i.e. 0–9). Most systems will not allow input of negative numbers, and so the format check will be to ensure there is no '–' input (e.g. negative sales invoices cannot be input, as they should be entered as a credit note). Where the amount is in £s and pence, the system will allow '.' as a decimal point, but only two numbers are allowed after the decimal point.

(b) **Check with standing data file.** For instance, when the operator inputs an account number 'B001', the computer will check there is an account with the number 'B001'. It will reject the account number if there is no account with the number 'B001' on the standing data file.

(c) **Reasonableness check.** The computer will check the quantity of items purchased/sold or the value of the entry is reasonable. It may be acceptable to have an order for 1,000 screws, but an order of 1,000 televisions would be unusual for a single retail store. Normally, a warning will be given when the size of the order is very large. If the system limits the value of an invoice to £999,999.99, then either a warning will be given or the data will be rejected if the value of the invoice is over this figure. Negative quantities will not be accepted for most entries (you cannot sell –1 televisions). The system can check the VAT value is reasonable (i.e. the goods value × the applicable VAT rate).

(d) **Check with transaction file.** In this situation, when a sales invoice is input to the system that suggests the customer's debt exceeds the credit limit, a warning will be given.

(e) **Checking that totals agree.** In inputting journal entries in a Nominal Ledger system, it will only accept the data if the value of debit entries equals the value of credit entries. In inputting the sales analysis of sales invoices (for posting to the Nominal Ledger), it will check the value of the analysed sales equals the total value.

CHAPTER 36

PQ 36.1 Ascertaining each partner's share of profit

(A) P&L APPROPRIATION ACCOUNT – YEAR ENDED 30.6.20X1

Salary:			Net profit b/d	*	284,484
Heron	12,000		Interest on drawings:		
Pelican	18,000		Heron	600	
Stork	6,000	36,000	Pelican	360	
Interest on capital:			Stork	186	1,146
Heron	36,000				
Pelican	24,000				
Stork	18,000	78,000			
Profit share:					
Heron	85,815				
Pelican	57,210				
Stork	28,605	171,630			
		285,630			285,630

* £284,484, the net profit for the year, is ascertained as the balancing figure. Drawings are taken to partners' Current accounts. Rent and interest on the loan, though paid to the partners, are charges against profit and are therefore debited to the Profit and Loss account rather than its appropriation section.

From the manner of sharing the residual profit it is evident that Heron, Pelican and Stork share profits in the ratio 3:2:1 respectively. Stork's share of the profit of £284,484 is as follows:

As salary	£6,000
As interest on capital	£18,000
As residual profit	£28,605
As interest on drawings	(£186)
	£52,419

Heron Current a/c	Dr 7,581	–
To Stork Current a/c		7,581
Being giving effect to Heron's guarantee to Stork.		

Heron Current a/c	Dr 4,968	–
To Pelican's Current a/c		4,968
Being giving effect to Heron's guarantee to Pelican.		

Guarantee (1): £60,000 less £52,419 = £7,581.
Guarantee (2): £52,419 less £40,000 = £12,419.
If Stork's share had been sealed at £40,000, Heron and Pelican would have shared £12,419 in the ratio 3:2 respectively. Under the guarantee, Heron has to take over Pelican's loss of two-fifths of £12,419.

PQ 36.2 An introductory question on partnership appropriation

1. A partner is entitled to get goods from his business at cost. Therefore, Senkoro's Current account is debited with the cost of goods removed for personal use by him, and the Trading account is credited, to remove the cost from the cost of goods sold in the year.

2. For the same reason, the cost of goods gifted to Msusa is credited to the Trading account and debited to the other two partners in the profit-sharing ratio, unless they agree to bear the cost in any other proportion.

3. Rent accrued as at the end of the year is credited to Msusa's Current account rather than opening too many accounts for the same person. Since rent is received for playing a role other than as a partner, the rent is treated as a charge rather than an appropriation.

4. On the other hand, Senkoro received a salary for doing what he should as a partner. Partner's salary is therefore an appropriation of profit.

5. Interest on Kibona's loan (calculated at 5 per cent per annum as per section 24 of the Partnership Act 1890) is also a charge on profit because it relates to an extra role.

6. Every partner, as a partner, has to contribute capital. Thus, interest on capital is also an appropriation of profit.

7. Residual profit is shared equally among the partners, as agreed among them.

PQ 36.4 Partnership appropriations including a guarantee

TRADING AND PROFIT AND LOSS ACCOUNT FOR THE YEAR ENDED 31 DECEMBER 20X1

	£	£	
Sales		994,800	
Stock – 1.1.20X1	116,500		
Purchases	668,900		
Donations	(30,000)		1
Stock – 31.12.20X1	(134,100)	(621,300)	
Gross profit c/d		373,500	2

	9 mths to 30.9.20X1	3 mths to 31.12.20X1	
Gross profit b/d	280,125	93,375	2
Salaries	(90,000)	(30,000)	3
Manager's salary	(13,500)	–	3
Rent	(27,000)	(9,000)	4
Administ. expenses	(46,800)	(15,600)	
Depre. on vehicles	(9,900)	(3,300)	2
Depre. on furniture	(1,500)	(500)	2
Donations	(22,500)	(7,500)	1
Advertising	(4,500)	(1,500)	2
Interest on loan	(4,500)	–	5
PROFIT	**59,925**	**25,975**	6
Interest on drawings:			
Tom	360	30	
Dick	315	15	
Salary – Tom	(18,000)	(6,000)	3
Interest on capital:			
Tom	(7,200)	(2,400)	
Dick	(4,800)	(1,600)	
Harry	–	(1,000)	
Profit share:			
Tom	(22,950)	(9,012)	8
Dick	(7,650)	(3,004)	
Harry	–	(3,004)	

Notes:

1. The cost of goods donated to charity is removed from the Trading account so that only the cost of goods sold may be compared with sales. On the assumption that the donations were made consistently throughout the year, the cost has been apportioned between the two periods on a time basis.

2. Because it is stated that all income and expenses have accrued consistently throughout the year, all expenses (both administrative and distribution) are apportioned between the two periods on a time basis.

3. The manager's salary relates to the first period. Tom's salary is time-apportioned and is treated as an appropriation. The remainder of staff salary is allocated on a time basis.

4. Rent, adjusted for accruals, is a charge on profit and is time-apportioned.

5. Interest on Harry's loan, until the date it was converted into capital, is a charge on profit and relates to the first period.

6. Interest on the amount drawn regularly by each partner is calculated at 6 per cent p.a. for the average period for which they were outstanding. Tom's drawing on 1.1.20X1 would have been outstanding for 12 months and that on 1.12.20X1 for 1 month.

Average of $(12 + 1)/2 = 6.5$ months. Interest on £12,000 @ 6 per cent for 6.5 months amounts to £390. To allocate this between the two periods, the average periods for which the drawings were outstanding in each of the two periods have to be worked out. As regards the first period, the drawing on 1.1.20X1 would have been outstanding for 12 months and that on 1.9.20X1 outstanding for 4 months, giving an average period of $(12 + 4)/2 = 8$ months. Similarly, as regards the second period, the drawing on 1.10.20X1 would have been outstanding for 3 months and that on 1.12.20X1 for 1 month, making an average of $(3 + 1)/2 = 2$ months. Interest amounting to £390 is hence allocated as shown here.

	£
£9,000 @ 6% for 8 months	360
£3,000 @ 6% for 2 months	30
	390

BALANCE SHEET AS AT 31.12.20X1

	Cost	Ac. dep.	£
Furniture	196,600	(111,100)	85,500
Motor vehicle	348,500	(140,500)	208,000
Stock		25,570	
Debtors		100,250	
Cash/bank balance		19,180	
Creditors		(91,550)	53,450
			346,950

		£
CAPITAL – Senkoro	100,000	
Kibona	100,000	
Msusa	40,000	240,000
CURRENT – Senkoro	25,700	
Kibona	23,000	
Msusa	8,250	56,950
		296,950
Kibona's Loan a/c		50,000
		346,950

TRADING AND PROFIT AND LOSS ACCOUNT FOR THE YEAR ENDED 31.12.20X1

	£	£
Sales		744,600
Stock – 31.12.20X0	78,450	
Purchases	416,500	
Drawing – Senkoro	(6,250)	
Wedding gift	(2,400)	
Stock – 31.12.20X1	(25,570)	(460,730)
Gross profit		283,870
Administrative expenses:		
Salaries	(96,500)	
Rent	(9,600)	
Stationery	(640)	
Telephone/postage	(1,860)	
Light and heat	(1,250)	
Depreciation – furniture	(9,500)	
Sundry expenses	(11,270)	(130,620)
Distribution cost:		
Advertising	(4,850)	
Vehicle maintenance	(24,600)	
Depreciation – vehicles	(52,000)	(81,450)
Interest on loan		(2,500)
Profit for the year		69,300
Salary – Senkoro		(12,000)
Interest on capital:		
– Senkoro	(12,000)	
– Kibona	(12,000)	
– Msusa	(4,800)	(28,800)
Profit share:		
– Senkoro	(9,500)	
– Kibona	(9,500)	
– Msusa	(9,500)	(28,500)

PARTNERS' CURRENT ACCOUNTS

	Senkoro	Kibona	Msusa		Senkoro	Kibona	Msusa
Balance b/f	–	–	3,650	Balance b/f	14,650	8,200	–
Drawings	4,000	8,000	6,000	Rent a/c	–	–	3,600
Goods removed	6,250	–	–	Salary	1,000	–	–
Wedding gift	1,200	1,200	–	Interest on loan	–	2,500	–
Balance c/d	25,700	23,000	8,250	Interest on capital	12,000	12,000	4,800
				Profit share	9,500	9,500	9,500

PQ 36.3 Deciding whether a charge on profit or an appropriation

CLUES: Royalty, rent and interest on loan, though paid to the partners, are rewards for roles not expected of partners. The partnership profit for the year, available for playing the roles expected of a partner, is £269,000.

A similar calculation is made for Dick. His drawing on 31.1.20X1 would have been outstanding for 11 months whereas the drawing on 30.9.20X1 would have been outstanding for 3 months, making an average for the first period of (11 + 3)/2 = 7 months. The drawing on 31.10.20X1 would have been outstanding for 2 months and that on 31.12.20X1 for zero months, making an average for the second period of (2 + 0)/2 = 1 month. Therefore, the interest of £330 is allocated as show here.

	£
£9,000 @ 6% for 7 months	315
£3,000 @ 6% for 1 month	15
	330

PARTNERS' CURRENT ACCOUNTS

N		Tom	Dick	Harry			Tom	Dick	Harry	N
6	Drawings	12,000	12,000	–		Rent a/c	–	–		4
	Interest on drawing					Interest on loan	–	1,500		5
	1.1.00 to 30.9.01	360	315	–		Interest on capital	–	1,000		7
	1.10.00 to 31.12.01	30	15	–		Profit – up to 30.9.01	9,600	6,400	–	8
9	Guarantee	1,996	–	–		Profit from 1.10.01	22,950	7,650	3,004	8
	Balance c/d	27,176	10,724	7,500		Guarantee	9,012	3,004	1,996	9
		27,176	10,724	7,500						

7. Interest at 8 per cent per annum on the fixed capital account balances of Tom and Dick is credited with interest on the two periods. Harry is credited with interest on his capital only for the period after he became a partner on 1.10.20X1.

8. The residual profit of the first period, enhanced by interest charged on partners' drawings and after appropriating Tom's salary as well as interest on both partners' capital balances, is apportioned between Tom and Dick in the ratio 3:1 respectively.

9. The guarantee is ignored until all appropriations are completed. At that stage, the amount Harry received as a partner (i.e. ignoring the interest received by him on the loan) is compared with the amount Tom guaranteed for him during the three months in which he was a partner.

Harry's guaranteed income	
Interest on capital	1,000
Share of profit	3,004
Total income as a partner	4,004
Amount guaranteed for three months	(6,000)
Difference to be made good	1,996

BALANCE SHEET AS AT 31.12.20X1

	Cost	Ac. dep	£
Furniture	44,000	(26,000)	18,000
Motor vehicles	96,000	(43,200)	52,800
Stock in trade		134,100	
Debtors		246,800	
Cash/bank		7,700	
Creditors		(164,000)	224,600
			295,400
CAPITAL: Tom		120,000	
Dick		80,000	
Harry		50,000	
			250,000
CURRENT: Tom		27,176	
Dick		10,724	
Harry		7,500	
			45,400
			295,400

PQ 36.5 Partnership appropriation with a negative guarantee

CLUES: Since sales did not accrue consistently from month to month, the gross profit (determined for the whole year as £373,500) and the distribution costs should be apportioned between the two periods on a turnover basis (2:1), while the administrative expenses should be apportioned on a time basis (3:1). Net profit up to 30 September is £30,400 and thereafter £55,500. As a partner during the last three months of the year, Harry would receive interest of £1,000 and profit of £8,909 and this exceeds the amount that Dick would like him to receive (£9,000) by £909. Had there been a ceiling of £9,000 on Harry's share of partnership profit, the excess of £909 would have been shared by Tom and Dick as £683 and £227 respectively. Dick would expect Tom to compensate him for the loss of £227.

PQ 36.6 Reappropriation of profits among partners

CLUE: The net impact of the error corrections on the performance reported in respect of years 20X0, 20X1 and 20X2 is an increase of £6,000, a decrease of £42,200 and a decrease of £30,000 respectively.

CHAPTER 37

PQ 37.1 Profit-sharing ratio after new partner's admission

	Old ratio	Working	New ratio
(a) Sane	3/5	less (3/5 of 1/4)	9/20
Wise	2/5	less (2/5 of 1/4)	6/20
Clever	–	1/4 which is the same as	5/20
(b) Sane	3/5	less (1/2 of 1/4)	19/40
Wise	2/5	less (1/2 of 1/4)	11/40
Clever	–	1/4 which is same as	10/40
(c) Sane	3/5	less 1/4	7/20
Wise	2/5	2/5 which is same as	8/20
Clever	–	1/4 which is same as	5/20

PQ 37.2 Adjustment for unrecorded goodwill

(a)

Clever Capital a/c	Dr 90	–	
To Sane Capital a/c		–	54
Wise Capital a/c		–	36
Being adjustment for unrecorded goodwill			

Working:

Sane	Wise	Clever
Cr 216	Cr 144	Dr 90
Dr 162	Dr 108	–
Cr 54	Cr 36	Dr 90

Explanation: Clever acquires unrecorded goodwill from Sane and Wise in the ratio 3:2 respectively.

(b)

Clever Capital a/c	Dr 90	–	
To Sane Capital a/c		–	45
Wise Capital a/c		–	45
Being adjustment for unrecorded goodwill			

Working:

Sane	Wise	Clever
Cr 216	Cr 144	Dr 90
Dr 171	Dr 99	–
Cr 54	Cr 45	Dr 90

Explanation: Clever acquires unrecorded goodwill equally from Sane and Wise.

(b)

CAPITAL ACCOUNTS

	Polly	Kelly	Molly		Polly	Kelly	Molly
Goodwill-new ratio	100,000	50,000	30,000	Balance b/f	200,000	150,000	–
Balance c/d	220,000	160,000	120,000	Cash introduced	–	–	150,000
				Goodwill-old ratio	120,000	60,000	–
	220,000	160,000	120,000		220,000	160,000	120,000
				Balance b/d	220,000	160,000	120,000

CURRENT ACCOUNTS

	Polly	Kelly	Molly		Polly	Kelly	Molly
Balance b/f	–	11,000	–	Balance b/f	18,000	–	–
Drawings	30,000	15,000	6,000	Interest to 1.3	8,000	6,000	–
				Interest after 1.3	4,400	3,200	2,400
				Profit to 1.3	60,000	30,000	–
Balance c/d	83,733	24,867	3,400	Profit after 1.3	23,333	11,667	7,000
	83,733	24,867	3,400	Balance b/d	83,733	24,867	3,400

PQ 37.4 Admission of a partner during an accounting period

(a) Why a continuing partner does not benefit from the adjustment for goodwill

Kumaran gets no compensation for any unrecorded asset because, even after Akilan's admission to partnership, he continues to get a one-third share of profit.

(b) The adjustment for goodwill may be performed in one of two methods

METHOD ONE

The easiest method of adjusting for unrecorded goodwill is to identify (as done above) the partner who deserves to be compensated, so that his Capital account is credited with the appropriate amount of the new partner's capital.

Unrecorded goodwill	Rajan	Kumaran	Akilan
SHARED in old ratio = 2:1	160,000	80,000	–
SHARED in new ratio = 3:2:1	120,000	80,000	40,000
Gain/loss	(40,000)	–	40,000

PARTNERS' CAPITAL ACCOUNTS

	Rajan	Kumaran	Akilan		Rajan	Kumaran	Akilan
				Balance b/f	300,000	100,000	–
				Cash book	40,000	–	100,000

METHOD TWO

The alternative method of achieving the same effect is to first account for goodwill, by crediting the continuing partners, and then eliminate the goodwill, debiting all the partners (including the new arrival) in their new profit-sharing ratio. Having in this way adjusted for unrecorded goodwill, the whole of the capital introduced by the new partner is posted from the cash book to his own Capital account.

(c)

Clever Capital a/c	Dr 90	–
To Sane Capital a/c	–	90
Being adjustment for unrecorded goodwill		

Cr 216	Cr 144	Dr 90
Dr 126	Dr 144	Dr 90
Cr 90	–	Dr 90

Clever acquires unrecorded goodwill wholly from Sane.

PQ 37.3 An elementary question on the admission of a new partner

(A) TRADING AND PROFIT AND LOSS ACCOUNT FOR THE YEAR ENDED 30 JUNE 20X1

	£000	£000
Sales		3,848
Stock on 1.7.20X0	214	
Purchases	2,174	
Stock on 30.6.20X1	(235)	(2,153)
		1,695
Distribution cost	484	
Administrative exp.	1,029	
Depreciation	26	(1,539)
Profit for the year		156

BALANCE SHEET AS AT 30 JUNE 20X1

	£000	£000	£000
Fixed assets	480	(246)	234
Stock in trade		235	
Debtors		469	
Cash and bank		92	
Creditors		(418)	378
			612

	Polly	Kelly	Molly	£000
Capital accounts	220,000	160,000	120,000	500
Current accounts	83,733	24,867	3,400	112
				612

APPROPRIATION OF PROFIT YEAR ENDED 30.6.20X1

8 MONTHS TO 1.3.20X1			
Profit apportioned 2:1		104,000	a
Interest on Capital:	Polly	(8,000)	b
	Kelly	(6,000)	b
	Molly	–	
Profit share	Polly	(60,000)	c
	Kelly	(30,000)	c
	Molly	–	

4 MONTHS TO 30.6.20X1			
Profit apportioned		52,000	a
Interest on Capital:	Polly	(4,400)	d
	Kelly	(3,200)	d
	Molly	(2,400)	d
Profit share	Polly	(23,333)	e
	Kelly	(11,667)	e
	Molly	(7,000)	e

	Old ratio	Less: given to Molly	New ratio
Polly	2/3	2/3 × 1/6	10/18
Kelly	1/3	1/3 × 1/6	5/18
Molly	–	1/6 is same as	3/18

Notes:

(a) Profit for the year is time-apportioned because income and expenses accrue evenly throughout the year.

(b) Interest at 6 per cent p.a. for eight months on the capital held prior to goodwill adjustment.

(c) Residual profit shared by Polly and Kelly in the old ratio of 2:1 respectively.

(d) Interest at 6 per cent p.a. for four months on capital after goodwill adjustment.

(e) Residual profit (£52,000 less £10,000) after Molly's admission to partnership is shared among Polly, Kelly and Molly in the ratio 10:5:3 respectively arrived at as shown here.

PARTNERS' CAPITAL ACCOUNTS

	Rajan	Kumaran	Akilan		Rajan	Kumaran	Akilan
Goodwill	120,000	80,000	40,000	Balance b/f	300,000	100,000	–
Balance	340,000	100,000	100,000	Goodwill	160,000	80,000	–
				Cash book	–	–	140,000

TRADING AND PROFIT AND LOSS ACCOUNT FOR THE YEAR ENDED 31.12.20X2

	£	3 mths to 31.3.20X2	9 mths to 31.12.20X2	Apportioned on basis of
Sales			984,250	
Stock – 31.12.20X1	186,400			
Purchases	692,650			
Stock 31.12.20X2	(214,500)		(664,550)	
Gross profit			319,700	
Gross profit		63,940	255,760	Turnover
Administrative expenses:				
Salaries		(22,500)	(67,500)	Time
Rent		(8,000)	(24,000)	Time
Depre. – furniture		(4,380)	(13,140)	Time
Admin. expense		(8,100)	(24,300)	Time
Distribution costs:				
Advertising		(3,561)	(14,244)	Turnover
Sales commission		(4,360)	(17,440)	Turnover
Bad debts		(1,440)	(5,760)	Turnover
Depre. – vehicles		(5,784)	(23,136)	Turnover
Depre. – gift vehicle		(640)	–	Allocated
Profit for the year		5,175	66,240	
Salary – Rajan		(6,000)	–	
Interest on capital:				
Rajan		(4,500)	(15,300)	
Kumaran		(1,500)	(4,500)	
Akilan		–	(4,500)	
Loss/Profit:				
Rajan		4,550	(15,300)	
Kumaran		2,275	(4,500)	

4. The 11 months' salary drawn by Rajan is debited to his Current account. At the point of appropriation, the salary he is entitled to in respect of the three months to 31 March 20X2 is credited to him.

5. The interest on capital credited to Rajan improves after the admission of the new partner because his capital base is improved on the date of the admission by the goodwill adjustment.

PARTNERS' CURRENT ACCOUNTS

	Rajan	Kumaran	Akilan		Rajan	Kumaran	Akilan
Salaries a/c	22,000	–	–	Salary – to 31.3.20X1	6,000	1,500	–
Loss to 31.3.X1	4,550	2,275	–	Interest to 31.3.20X1	4,500	4,500	4,500
Gift of car	6,080	6,080	–	Interest after 1.4.X1	15,300	4,500	4,500
Balance c/d	14,140	11,625	11,490	Profit after 1.4.20X1	20,970	13,980	6,990

(c) The financial statements of the partnership:

1. The car gifted to Akilan on 1.4.20X2 is depreciated up to that date (see calculations below) and its written down value on that date recovered equally from Rajan and Kumaran. Depreciation on vehicles (other than the one gifted), calculated using the reducing balance method (as shown here), is apportioned on a time basis because it is a distribution cost.

The car gifted:	£
Cost	20,000
Depre. to 31.12.20X1	(7,200)
WDV on 31.12.20X1	12,800
Depre. to 31.3.20X2	(640)
WDV on 1.4.20X2	12,160

MOTOR VEHICLES ACCOUNT

	£		£
Balance b/f	200,000	Gift a/c	20,000
		Balance c/d	180,000
Balance b/d	180,000		

PROVISION FOR DEPRECIATION ACCOUNT

	£		£
Gift a/c	7,840	Balance b/f	42,600
Balance c/d	64,320	Depre. – gift	640
		Depre. other	28,920
		Balance b/d	64,320

GIFT OF A VEHICLE TO A PARTNER ACCOUNT

	£		£
M.Vehicle	20,000	Prov. – depr.	7,840
		Current a/c	
		Rajan	6,080
		Kumaran	6,080

Depreciation on other vehicles	£
Cost of all vehicles	200,000
Cost of one gifted	(20,000)
Cost of others	180,000
Accum. depre. on all	42,600
Accum. depre. on gift	(7,200)
	35,400
Written down value – 31.12.20X2	144,600
Depreciation @ 20% for 20X2	28,920

2. Sales were not consistent from month to month. It becomes necessary, therefore, to arrive at a ratio of sales between the periods before and after Akilan's admission. Though Akilan was admitted to partnership on 1 April 20X2, the sales did not improve until 1 July. If the sales in each month to June are equated to 100 on a generalized scale, the sales in each month thereafter would be 150. Therefore, as shown in the box here, the turnover ratio between the periods before and after Akilan's admission is 1:4.

Turnover ratio:		Ratio
1.1 to 31.3.20X2	100 × 3 mths	300
1.4 to 31.3.20X2	100 × 3 mths	300
1.7 to 31.12.20X2	150 × 6 mths	900
		1,200

3. The gross profit and distribution cost are apportioned between the two periods on the turnover basis, while administrative expenses are apportioned on a time basis.

be shared among the partners in the ratio that they share operating profit, while the remainder of the gain (£156,000) is shared in the ratio of the partners' capital balances.

	Essai	Gulam
Capital	492	291
Current	27	(14)

Amount due to Karim on the date of retirement (Capital Amount due to Karim on the date of retirement (Capital account £843,000 + Current account £17,000 less cash paid £360,000) is transferred to a loan account, while the balances held by the remaining partners on 31 March 20X0 would be as stated here.

PQ 37.8 Death of a partner

CLUES: The credit balance of £11,900 reported in Brittle's account is the amount paid in by him as a rent agent for Hard. When the rent collected (£21,000) is debited to this account (crediting Hard's Current account) and rates, repairs and commission paid by him are credited (debiting Hard's Current account), this account balances off. Rent on premises occupied by Brittle (£3,600) recovered from his salary is accounted for by debiting the Salaries account and crediting Hard's Current account. The gain on surrender of the life policy (£36,000), together with the balance in the Life Policy Fund (£84,000), would be appropriated to the Capital accounts of Hard and Soft, as would be their share of goodwill. Operating results would be a loss of £2,505 until Soft's death and a profit of £4,415 thereafter (after charging an interest at 5 per cent p.a. on an amount of £36,000 owed to Soft's estate, as required by The Partnership Act 1890). Partners' balances as at 31.12.20X1 are as stated here.

	Hard	Brittle
Capital	230,000	75,000
Current	5,473	9,572

CHAPTER 38

PQ 38.1 Piecemeal disposal of a partnership business

(a) The preference to dispose of a business as a going concern

It is then possible to realize an amount for the goodwill built up over the years, and it is satisfying to see the business continue in operational existence.

(b) Closure of the partnership books:

REALIZATION ACCOUNT

		£				£
a	Machinery	348.5			Tarimo capital	16,000 d
a	Prov. for depn	(128.6)	219,900		Cash book:	
a	Motor vehicles	124.5			Machinery	114,500
a	Prov. for depn	(32.6)	91,900		Motor vehicle	76,500
	Stock		84,600		Stock	97,290 288,290
	Prepaid rent		2,500		Creditors	3,650 e
b	Maintenance		3,000		Capital: Tarimo	46,824
c	Bad debts		18,500		Kito	46,824
	Expenses		4,600		Mbwilo	23,412
			425,000			425,000

PQ 37.5 Goodwill valued by capitalizing super profits

CLUES: Average annual profit for three years until 1.10.20X3 is £81,000. Super profit (net of 6 per cent return on capital and fair remuneration to partners of £24,000) is £15,000, which when capitalized at 10 per cent, values goodwill at £150,000.

The new profit-sharing ratio among Anil, Ranil and Sunil would be 7:3:2 respectively. Partners' balances after adjusting for unrecorded assets and appropriating the profit to 31.12.20X3 would be as stated here. If it had not been agreed that Sunil would receive his share equally from his brothers, the profit-sharing ratio among Anil, Ranil and Sunil would have been 10:5:3 respectively.

	Anil	Ranil	Sunil
Capital a/c	394,500	304,500	71,000
Current a/c	137,222	27,055	(2,277)

PQ 37.6 A partnership with incomplete records

CLUES: The difference between the net assets at the beginning of each year (i.e. the sum of the partners' balances) and that at the end, adjusted for capital introductions and drawings, would be the profit/loss for the three years (£69,000) less 8 per cent return on capital employed on the date of valuation (£54,000) reveals a super profit of £15,000, which is capitalized at 20 per cent to value goodwill at £75,000. Since Gold waives his claim, goodwill is adjusted for by Nickel transferring £2,500 of his capital to each the other two partners. By 31.12.20X4, Gold, Silver, Copper and Nickel have capital balances of £253,000, £173,500 and £145,000 respectively.

PQ 37.7 Retirement of a partner

CLUES: £300,000 realized on surrendering the life policy includes £270,000 of premiums written off against operating profit. Hence £270,000 of the realization gain should

---

BALANCE SHEET AS AT 31 DECEMBER 20X2

	Cost	Ac. depr.	£
Furniture	210,000	(52,320)	157,680
Motor vehicles	180,000	(64,320)	115,680
Stock in trade		214,500	
Debtors		246,800	
Cash and bank balance		3,795	
Creditors		(161,200)	303,895
			577,255
			£
Capital – Rajan			340,000
Kumaran			100,000
Akilan			100,000
			540,000
Current a/c – Rajan		14,140	
Kumaran		11,625	
Akilan		11,490	37,255
			577,255

however, would have given the bank a claim against that asset in priority to other claimants against Tarimo's personal assets.

PQ 38.2   A basic question on going concern disposal of a partnership

(a) Closing the books of the partnership

REALIZATION ACCOUNT

N		£	£	N		£
a	Machinery	285,000		a	Creditors	96,600
	Provision	(112,600)	172,400	b	Cheerful Ltd	600,000
a	Vehicles	120,000				
	Provision	(45,000)	75,000			
a	Stock		248,600			
a	Debtors	164,000				
	Provision	(12,500)	151,500			
a	Cash/Bank		22,800			
	Gain:					
	Happy Capital a/c	15,780				
	Lucky Capital a/c	10,520				

CHEERFUL LIMITED ACCOUNT

		£			£	
b	Realization a/c	600,000		Investments a/c	600,000	d

INVESTMENTS ACCOUNT

		£			£	
d	Cheerful Ltd	600,000		Happy Capital	410,380	e
				Lucky Capital	189,620	e

CAPITAL ACCOUNTS

		Happy £	Lucky £		Happy £	Lucky £	
	Current a/c	–	20,900	Balance b/f	300,000	200,000	
e	Investments	410,380	189,620	Current a/c	94,600	–	
				Realization	15,780	10,520	e

Notes:

(a) When a business is disposed of as a going concern, unless agreed otherwise, all assets (including cash and bank) and all liabilities are taken over.

(b) The agreed purchase consideration is debited to Cheerful Ltd.

(c) The gain on disposal is appropriated between the partners in their profit-sharing ratio.

(d) Cheerful Ltd discharges the purchase consideration by an allotment of 400,000 ordinary shares, valuing each at £1.50 (i.e. at a premium of 50p each). In the partnership books these shares are accounted for as an asset in an Investment account at £600,000 because that is the amount they cost.

CASH BOOK

N		£			£	N
	Balance b/f	–		Realization – exp.	4,600	f
	Realization	288,290		Bank overdraft	14,225	f
c	Debtors	24,500		Creditors	32,850	f
				Accrued expen.	11,250	f
				Tarimo Loan	40,000	f
				Capital – Tarimo	108,376	f
		125		Kito	51,026	f
				Mbwilo	50,588	f

PARTNERS' CAPITAL ACCOUNTS

N		Tarimo	Kito	Mbwilo		Tarimo	Kito	Mbwilo	N
	Current a/c	–	2,150	6,000	Balance b/f	150,000	100,000	80,000	f
d	Realization a/c	16,000	–	–	Current a/c	3,200	–	–	
f	Realization-loss	46,824	46,824	23,412	Prov. for guarantee	18,000	–	–	b
f	Cash book	108,376	51,026	50,588					

Notes:

(a) For closing every account, the balances in each (other than cash and bank balance) should be transferred to the Realization account. This applies to every fixed asset account and its supporting account.

(b) The maintenance guarantee, accounted for in the partnership books at only £15,000, is taken over by Tarimo at £18,000. The loss of £3,000 is recorded in the Realization account.

(c) Upon recovering £24,500 from debtors, bad debt of £22,500 is offset against the provision for doubtful debts and the shortfall of £18,500 is accounted for as another loss on realization.

(d) The book value of the vehicle taken over by Tarimo is charged to his Capital account.

(e) On settling the suppliers with a payment of £32,850, the cash discount received is accounted for as a gain on realization.

(f) Cash realized on dissolution of the partnership should first be paid to meet expenses, then to meet the claims of third parties, then to pay any partner's loan, before the remainder is shared among the partners (not in any predetermined ratio) to meet exactly what their respective Capital accounts report as due to each of them at that stage.

(c) The effect of a personal guarantee/pledge given by a partner

The effect of the personal guarantee given by Tarimo and the pledge of his personal life policy is that if the assets of the partnership had proved insufficient to meet the amount owed by it to the bank, the bank would then have had recourse to the amounts realized by surrendering the life policy and ranked against Tarimo's personal assets for any shortfall. In the circumstances stated in the question, the bank did not have to exercise these rights because the amounts realized from the partnership's assets were adequate to meet its claim in full. In a partnership scenario, where individual partners are unlimitedly liable for the claims against the partnership, with or without the personal guarantee the bank could have ranked against Tarimo's personal assets. The pledge of his life policy,

(e) The investments are shared between the partners (in the absence of an agreement to the contrary) in such a manner as to satisfy the amounts due to them at the completion of the dissolution. If the shares had been shared, say, in the profit-sharing ratio, there would have arisen a need for a cash adjustment between the partners.

(b) To continue with the same profit-sharing arrangement
A limited company distributes profits as *dividends* to shareholders as a percentage of the par value of the shares held by each. If Happy and Lucky wish to share the company's profit in the same way as they did in the partnership, the shares in the company should be allotted to them in the ratio 3:2. On doing this, Lucky's account would report a deficiency of £50,380, which he has to make good by introducing that amount in cash.

CAPITAL ACCOUNTS

	Happy	Lucky		Happy	Lucky
Current a/c	–	20,900	Balance b/f	300,000	200,000
Investments	360,000	240,000	Current a/c	94,600	–
Cash book			Realization	15,780	10,520
			Cash book	–	50,380
	360,000	50,380			50,380

(c) Open the books of the new company:

VENDOR'S ACCOUNT

	£			£	
Creditors a/c	96,600	b	Machinery a/c	172,400	a
Provision for doubtful debt	12,500	b	Vehicles a/c	75,000	a
			Stock a/c	248,600	a
			Debtors a/c	164,000	a
Balance c/d	573,700	c	Cash book	22,800	a
Ordinary share capital a/c	600,000	d	Balance b/d	573,700	c
			Goodwill a/c	26,300	c

BALANCE SHEET AS AT 1 APRIL 20X1

		£
Goodwill at cost		26,300
Machinery at cost		172,400
Vehicles at cost		75,000
Stock in trade		248,600
Debtors	164,000	
Provision	(12,500)	151,500
Cash/bank		22,800
Creditors	(96,600)	326,300
		600,000

	£
Share Capital account:	
Ordinary shares of £1 each	400,000
Share Premium account	200,000
	600,000

Notes:

(a) Each asset acquired is recorded in an appropriate asset account at the value for which it was acquired, crediting a Vendor's account. The debtors amount, however, is recorded not at the acquisition value but at the gross amount receivable.

(b) Similarly, each liability taken over is credited in an appropriately named liability account, debiting the Vendor's account.

(c) The net asset taken over by the company amounts to £573,700. Yet the purchase consideration, discharged by an allotment of shares, is £600,000. The difference

of £26,300 is the amount Cheerful Ltd pays for the goodwill acquired from the partnership.

(d) The issue of shares, in discharge of the purchase consideration, is accounted for by debiting the Vendor's account with £600,000, crediting the Share Capital account with the par value of shares issued (£400,000) and crediting the Share Premium account with the difference (£200,000).

(e) Note that the amount of £26,300 reported by the partnership as gain on dissolution is reported by the company as the amount paid by them for goodwill.

PQ 38.3 Purchase consideration calculated on the basis of asset valuation

(a) Closing the books of the partnership
The first step in closing the books is the calculation of the purchase consideration by aggregating the values at which each of the assets (including cash and bank balance) is taken over and deducting therefrom the value of liabilities taken over.

PURCHASE CONSIDERATION

		£	
Assets at sale price			
Goodwill		120,000	a
Premises		300,000	a
Machinery		106,500	a
Furniture		56,000	b
Stock in trade		168,500	b
Debtors	246,400		
Provision	(24,640)	221,760	a
Cash		1,420	b
Liabilities taken over:			
Creditors		(196,500)	c
Accrued expenses		(26,600)	c
Purchase consideration		751,080	

Notes:

(a) Assets taken over at the values stated.

(b) Assets taken over at book values (in absence of any other information).

(c) Liabilities taken over.

(d) The Realization account is known also as Dissolution account.

(e) Every asset (along with corresponding supporting account) balance, including cash and bank balance, is transferred to the Dissolution account.

(f) Debtors, along with provision at *existing* levels in partnership books, are transferred to the Realization account.

(g) Expenses of dissolution are posted from the cash book to the Realization account.

(h) Creditors and accrued expenses taken over are credited to the Realization account.

(i) Investments appearing at £32,500 are taken over by Mandy, valued at £45,000 The gain of £12,500 is reported in the Realization account.

(j) Life policy, which did not appear in the books (because the premiums, when paid, had been written off), is surrendered, realizing £64,000.

(k) Cosmetics Ltd discharges the purchase consideration as follows:

Purchase consideration:	£751,080
600,000 shares @ £1.25	(£750,000)
Balance in cash	1,080

(l) Investments are allotted to the partners in their profit sharing ratio.

DISSOLUTION ACCOUNT

		£			£
e	Premises	320,000		Creditors	196,500	h
e	Provision	(64,000)	256,000	Accruals	26,600	h
e	Machinery	164,000		Gain on invest	12,500	i
e	Provision	(41,000)	123,000	Life policy	64,000	j
e	Furniture	80,000		Cosmetics Ltd		
e	Provision	(24,000)	56,000	Purchase	751,080	
e	Stock in trade		168,500	Consideration		
f	Debtors	246,400				
f	Provision	(12,320)	234,080			
e	Cash in hand		1,420			
g	Cash a/c – expenses		3,250			
h	Capital a/c – gain					
	Mandy	83,372				
	Daphne	62,529				
	Olive	62,529	208,430			

COSMETICS LTD

	£		£
Dissolution	751,080	Investments	750,000
		Cash book	1,080

INVESTMENTS ACCOUNT

	£		£
Cosmetics	750,000	Capital:	
		Mandy	300,000	–
		Daphne	225,000	–
		Olive	225,000	–

PARTNERS' CAPITAL ACCOUNTS

	Mandy	Daphne	Olive		Mandy	Daphne	Olive
Current a/c	15,200	–	–	Balance b/f	250,000	200,000	150,000
Investments	45,000	–	–	Current a/c	–	28,500	16,300
Investments				Dissolution	83,372	62,529	62,529
in cosmetics	300,000	225,000	225,000	Cash book	26,828		
Cash book	–	66,029	3,829				

CASH BOOK

	£		£
Balance b/f	1,420	Dissolution	1,420
Life policy	64,000	Expenses	3,250
Cosmetics	1,080	Bank overdraft	18,800
Mandy Capital	26,828	Daphne Capital	66,029
		Olive Capital	3,829

(b) Journal entries to open the books of a new company

	Dr	£	£
Sundries			
To Sundries			
Goodwill	120,000		
Business premises	300,000		
Machinery	106,500		
Furniture	56,000		
Stock in trade	168,500		
Debtors	246,400		
Cash book	1,420		
Prov. for doubtful debts			24,640
Creditors			196,500
Accrued expenses			26,600
Vendor's account			751,080

Being acquisition of assets and liabilities as per vending agreement dated ....

		£	£
Vendor's Account		751,080	–
To Ordinary share capital			600,000
Share Premium a/c		–	150,000
Cash book		–	1,080

Being discharge of the purchase consideration by the allotment of 600,000 Ordinary shares of £1 each at a premium of 25p each and payment of the balance in cash.

Notes:

(a) Vendors are given credit for each asset acquired from them at the value at which the asset is taken over. The exception, however, is debtors because the amount accounted for in the ledger should tally with the aggregate of various amounts receivable from each customer as listed by the vendor. The credit placed in the Provision for Doubtful Debts account ensures that the vendor does not get credit for any amount in excess of the value at which the debtors are taken over.

(b) Liabilities taken over are accounted for by crediting the appropriate liability account and debiting the Vendor's account.

(c) The issue of shares is accounted for by crediting the Share Capital account with the par value, crediting the Share Premium account with the premium, and debiting Vendor's account with the total of both.

(d) The amount paid in cash to discharge the purchase consideration is posted from the cash book to the debit of the Vendor's account.

(e) Cash transactions need not be journalized; but they have been because the question required it.

PQ 38.4 Calculation of the purchase consideration by reference to how it is discharged

(a) Closing the books of the partnership:

		£
Purchase consideration		600,000
1,200,000 SHARES @ 50p		600,000
Premium: 10% of par value		60,000
Fair value of shares		660,000
8% Debentures		90,000
Cash payment		16,300
Purchase consideration		766,300

Notes:

(a) In the absence of information on the value at which the goodwill is sold, purchase consideration cannot be calculated on the basis of valuing the net assets taken over. In the circumstances the purchase consideration is calculated by valuing what was received from Recovery Ltd in discharge of the purchase consideration – as shown in the box here.

(b) A debt is time-barred when the assistance of the law is no longer available for recovering it. The bad debt is written off against the provision, and the shortfall in the provision treated as a loss on dissolution.

(c) The compensation owed to Joe is accounted for in the partnership books by debiting an expenditure account and crediting a liability account, as shown here. The expenditure is transferred to a Realization account to take that loss into account when determining the gain or loss on dissolution; while the liability is also transferred to the Realization account just as all liabilities taken over are.

TOTAL DEBTORS ACCOUNT

	£		£
Balance b/f	182,500	Bad debts	12,500
		Realization	170,000

PROVISION FOR DOUBTFUL DEBTS ACCOUNT

	£		£
Bad debts	12,500	Balance b/f	9,400
		Realization	3,100

COMPENSATION PAYABLE (EXPENSE) ACCOUNT

	£		£
Compensation payable	24,000		

COMPENSATION PAYABLE (LIABILITY) ACCOUNT

	£		£
		Compensation payable	24,000

(d) All assets (including debtors net of those time-barred) and liabilities, including compensation payable to Joe, are transferred to the Realization account.

REALIZATION ACCOUNT

			£			£	
d	Goodwill		75,000	Creditors		164,800	d
d	Furniture	240,000		Accrued exp.		11,200	d
d	Provision	(48,000)	192,000	Compens. payable		24,000	d
d	Vehicles	180,000		Recovery Ltd.:			
d	Provision	(54,000)	126,000	Purchase			
d	Stock in trade		284,600	Consideration		766,300	a
d	Debtors		170,000				
d	Prepayments		3,500				
d	Cash/bank		32,200				
b	Bad debts		3,100				
c	Compens payable		24,000				
e	Gain on dissolution						
	Silent	33,540					
	Patient	22,360	55,900				

RECOVERY LIMITED ACCOUNT

	£		£
Realization a/c	766,300	Investments a/c	750,000
		Cash book	16,300

INVESTMENTS ACCOUNT

	£		£
Recovery Ltd	750,000	Silent Loan	90,000
		Silent Capital	440,000
		Patient Capital	220,000

PARTNERS' CAPITAL ACCOUNTS

	Silent £	Patient £		Silent £	Patient £
Current	–	15,200	Balance b/f	400,000	200,000
Investments	440,000	220,000	Current	35,600	–
Cash book	29,140	–	Realization	33,540	22,360
			Cash book	–	12,840

CASH BOOK

	£		£
Balance b/f	32,200	Realizat.	32,200
Recovery	16,300	Silent	29,140
Patient	12,840		

(c) Opening the books of the new company:

	Dr £	£
Sundries		
To Sundries		
Goodwill	266,600	
Furniture	192,000	
Motor vehicles	90,000	
Stock in trade	224,000	
Trade debtors	170,000	
Prov. for doubtful debts		8,500
Creditors		164,800
Accrued expenses		11,200
Compensation to Joe		24,000
Vendor's account		734,100

Being acquisition of assets and liabilities as per vending agreement dated ......

Vendor's account	750,000	–
To Ordinary share capital	–	600,000
Share Premium a/c	–	60,000
8% Debentures	–	90,000

Being discharge of the purchase consideration by the allotment of 600,000 ordinary shares of £1 each at a premium of 25p each, issue of 8% debentures and payment of the balance in cash.

CASH BOOK

	£		£
Vendor's a/c	32,200	Vendor's a/c	16,300
		Balance c/d	15,900
Balance b/d	15,900		

VENDOR'S ACCOUNT

	£		£
Journal	750,000	Journal	734,100
Cash book	16,300	Cash book	32,200

(e) The gain on dissolution is appropriated between the partners in their profit-sharing ratio.

(f) In discharge of the purchase consideration, the partners receive shares in Recovery Ltd valued at £660,000, debentures at £90,000, and £16,300 in cash.

(g) The debentures are allotted to Silent in discharge of the loan, while the shares are allotted to both partners in the ratio of their capital balances in the partnership.

(h) To close the books, Patient has to bring in £12,840 in cash and Silent to withdraw £29,140.

PQ 38.5 Converting the partnership books into those of a company

Notes:

(a) The balance in the provision for depreciation of premises is transferred to the asset account to determine the book value at the date of acquisition – which, when compared with the value at which premises are taken over (£300,000), reveals that the amount owed to the vendor would be £44,000 more than the balances in the partners' accounts.

(b) On the other hand, since machinery is taken over at a value of £16,500 lower than the book value, the amount owed to the vendor would be lower by that amount.

(c) Since Recovery Ltd wishes to increase the provision for doubtful debts by £12,320, it would be willing to pay the vendor that much less.

(d) When the Capital and Current account balances are transferred to the Vendor's account, it would appear that Recovery owes the vendor £629,600. This is:

- increased by the liability not taken over (bank overdraft of £18,800), the amount payable for goodwill (120,000) and the enhanced value (44,000) of the premises;
- reduced by the value of the asset not taken over (investments £32,500), the lower value of machinery (£16,500), and by the additional provision for doubtful debts (£12,320).

Thus the amount owed to the vendors = £629,600 + £120,000 + £18,800 + £44,000 – £32,500 – £12,320 = £751,080.

(e) The amount owed to the vendors is discharged by an allotment of 600,000 ordinary shares of 25p each and a payment of £1,080.

BUSINESS PREMISES ACCOUNT

	£		£
Balance b/f	320,000	Prov. for depre.	64,000
Purch. of Bus.	44,000	Balance c/d	300,000

PLANT AND MACHINERY ACCOUNT

	£		£
Balance b/f	164,000	Prov. for depre.	41,000
		Purch. of bus.	16,500
		Balance c/d	106,500

PROVISION FOR DOUBTFUL DEBTS ACCOUNT

	£		£
		Balance b/f	12,320
		Purch. of bus.	12,320

PURCHASE OF BUSINESS ACCOUNT

		£		£	
d	Mandy Current	15,200	Mandy Capital	250,000	
	Investments	32,500	Daphne Capital	200,000	
b	Machinery a/c	16,500	Olive Capital	150,000	
c	Prov. for d. debt	12,320	Daphne Current	28,500	
			Olive Current	16,300	d
e	Ord. share cap.	600,000	Bank overdraft	18,800	d
e	Share premium	150,000	Premises	44,000	a
e	Cash book	1,080	Goodwill a/c	120,000	

CHAPTER 40

PQ 40.1 Multiple-choice questions

	Share capital	Share premium
1.	c	a
2.	a	a
3.	c	c
4.	b	b

PQ 40.2 Accounting for share issue and forfeiture

(a) Abstract from the cash book:

CASH BOOK

		£			£
31.3	Application and allot. (on applic.)	360,000	31.3	Application and allot. (refund)	60,000
?	Application and allot. (on allotm.)	634,400			
?	First Call account	336,000			
15.8	Forfeited Shares a/c	10,800			
?	First Call account	4,200			
?	Final Call account	196,800			

(b) Ledger accounts:

APPLICATION AND ALLOTMENT ACCOUNT

			£				£	
1	31.3	Cash book	60,000	31.3	Cash book	360,000	1
2	31.3	Share capital	450,000	30.6	First Call a/c	634,400	~
2	31.3	Share premium	500,000	31.8	Final Call a/c	15,600	4
	31.7	Balance b/d	15,600	31.8	Forfeited shares	15,600	5

ORDINARY SHARES ACCOUNT

			£				£	
				31.3	Applic. & allot.	450,000	2
				31.8	First Call a/c	350,000	3
				31.8	Final Call a/c	198,800	8
	31.7	Forfeited shares	15,600	31.8	Forfeited shares	1,200	8
						1,000,000	

SHARE PREMIUM ACCOUNT

			£				£	
6	31.7	Forfeited shares	12,000	31.3	Applic. & allot.	500,000	2
~	31.12	Balance c/d	489,800	15.8	Forfeited shares	1,800	9
				1.1	Balance b/d	489,800	

FIRST CALL ACCOUNT

			£				£	
3	30.6	Share Capital	350,000	?	Cash book		336,000	4
				31.7	Balance c/d		14,000	5
4	31.7	Balance b/d	14,000	31.7	Forfeited shares		8,400	5
				?	Cash book		4,200	?
				31.12	Balance c/d		1,400	9
	1.1	Balance b/d	1,400					

FORFEITED SHARES ACCOUNT

			£				£	
5	31.7	Applic. & allot.	15,600	31.7	Share premium		12,000	6
5	31.7	First Call a/c	8,400	15.8	Cash book		10,800	7
9	15.8	Share premium	1,800	15.8	Balance c/d		3,000	?
	15.8	Balance b/d	3,000					
8	31.8	Share Capital	1,200					
			4,200					

FINAL CALL ACCOUNT

			£				£	
8	31.8	Share Capital	198,800	?	Cash book		196,800	?
				31.12	Balance c/d		2,000	x
	1.1	Balance b/d	2,000					

	£
Par value	1.00
First call	(0.35)
Final call	(0.20)
So far called up	0.45

Total payable	1.50
Par value each	(1.00)
Premium	0.50

Notes:

1. Receipt of application money on 1.2 million shares and refund of the same on 200,000.
2. So far called-up value is thus: one million shares at 45p each = £450,000.
3. First call of 35p each on one million shares.
4. 24,000 shares in arrears for allotment money and 40,000 shares in arrears for the first call.
5. Forfeiture of 24,000 shares which are in arrears for both allotment money and first call.
6. Reversal of unreceived share premium on the forfeited shares.
7. Issue of 18,000 forfeited shares at 60p each.
8. Final call made at 20p on 6,000 forfeited shares and on 994,000 in issue.
9. Gain on reissue of the forfeited shares transferred to Share Premium account.
x. Calls outstanding as at 31 December 20X0.
~ Balancing figures.

(c) **Extract from the balance sheet as at 31.12.20X0:**

	£	
Among the assets:		
Investments in own shares	4,200	6,000 forfeited shares yet to be reissued.
Called-up capital not paid	3,400	Arrears of first call (£1,400) plus final call (£2,000).
Share capital and reserves:		
Ordinary shares of £1 each	1,000,000	One million shares of £1 fully called-up.
Share Premium account	489,800	

PQ 40.3 Journal entries to account for share issue and forfeiture

31.3	Application and allotment a/c	Dr	950,000	–
	To Share Capital account		–	450,000
	To Share Premium account		–	500,000
	Being allotment of one million Ordinary shares of £1 each, 45p so far called up, at a premium of 50p each,			
30.6	First Call account	Dr	350,000	–
	To Share Capital account		–	350,000
	Being first call of 35p per share made on one million shares			
1.7	Forfeited Shares account	Dr	24,000	–
	To Application and Allotment a/c		–	15,600
	First Call account		–	8,400
	Being transfer of amounts in default, consequent to the forfeiture of 24,000 ordinary shares of £1 each, 80p called up.			
1.7	Share Premium account	Dr	12,000	–
	To Forfeited Shares account		–	12,000
	Being reversal of unreceived share premium in respect of the 24,000 forfeited shares.			
15.8	Forfeited Shares account	Dr	1,800	–
	To Share Premium account		–	1,800
	Being transfer of gain on re-issue of forfeited shares.			
31.8	Sundries	Dr	–	–
	To Share Capital account		–	200,000
	Forfeited Shares account			1,200
	Final Call account			198,800
	Being final call of 20p per share made on one million shares of £1 each, 6,000 of which are held in forfeiture.			

PQ 40.4 *Pro rata* allotment of shares

APPLICATION AND ALLOTMENT ACCOUNT

	£		£
Cash book	85,800	Cash book	445,800
Share capital	550,000	Cash book	372,450
Share premium	200,000	Balance c/d	17,550
Balance b/d	17,550		

ORDINARY SHARE CAPITAL ACCOUNT

	£
Balance b/f	3,150,000
Applic. & allot.	550,000
First call a/c	150,000
	3,850,000

FIRST CALL ACCOUNT

	£		£
Share capital	150,000	Cash book	139,500
		Balance c/d	10,500
Balance b/d	10,500		

SHARE PREMIUM ACCOUNT

	£
Applic. & allot.	200,000

CALL RECEIVED IN ADVANCE ACCOUNT

	£		£
		Cash book	4,500

	£
Allotment money on 4,500 @ £4.50	20,250
Excess paid on application (900 @ £3)	(2,700)
Amount in default on 31.12.20X2	17,550

Authorized capital	£6,000,000	600,000 shares of £10 each as stated in the Memorandum
Issued capital	£5,500,000	550,000 shares of £10 each allotted to shareholders
Called-up capital	£3,850,000	£7 so far called up: appears in the ledger account
Paid-up capital	£3,826,450	£3,850,000 + £4,500 (advance) – £17,550 and £10,500 (arrears)

PQ 40.5 Forfeiture and reissue of shares

APPLICATION AND ALLOTMENT ACCOUNT

	£		£
Cash book	85,800	Cash book	445,800
Share capital	550,000	Cash book	372,450
Share premium	200,000	Balance c/d	17,550
Balance b/d	17,550	Forfeited sh.	17,550

ORDINARY SHARE CAPITAL ACCOUNT

	£
Balance b/f	3,150,000
Applic. & allot.	550,000
First Call a/c	150,000
	3,850,000

FIRST CALL ACCOUNT

	£		£
Share capital	150,000	Cash book	139,500
		Balance c/d	10,500
Balance b/d	10,500	Forfeited sh.	10,500

SHARE PREMIUM ACCOUNT

	£		£
Forfeited sh.	9,000	Applic. & allot.	200,000
Balance c/d	199,950	Forfeited sh.	8,950
		Balance b/d	199,950

FORFEITED SHARES ACCOUNT

	£		£
Applic. & allot.	17,550	Share prem.	9,000
First Call a/c	10,500	Cash book	25,000
Share premium	8,950	Balance c/d	3,000
Balance b/d	3,000		

Notes:

1. Shares in default for either allotment or first call are forfeited. Hence 7,000 shares are involved.
2. The last part of the allotment money is assumed to be the share premium. Hence, it is assumed that 4,500 shares in arrears for allotment money have not paid any part of the premium.
3. Forfeited shares consist of two separate tranches as identified here. It would be prudent to assume that 2,000 forfeited shares remaining with the company are out of the second tranche.

Number of shares	Make up of book value			Book value	Value per share
	Allotment	Premium	First call		
4,500	£17,550	(£9,000)	£6,750	£15,300	£3.40
2,500	–	–	£3,750	£3,750	£1.50

Abstract from the Balance Sheet as at 31.12.20X3

Among assets: Investments in own shares	£3,000

Share capital and reserves:

Ordinary shares of £10 each £7 called up	£3,850,000
Share Premium account	£199,950

PQ 40.6 Redemption of debentures

(a) FRS 4 requires that at the point of issue, the debentures should be reported at the net proceeds of issue – i.e. net of the discount and the expenses of issue, which are stated in the Trial Balance within administrative expenses. Interest to be written off in the year is calculated at the effective rate (of 15 per cent) on £382,111 (the net proceeds on issue of debentures). The liability at the year end is reported at the net proceeds of issue, plus interest charge for the year (at the effective rate of 15 per cent), less interest actually paid in the year (at 5 per cent).

5% DEBENTURES ACCOUNT

	£		£
Discount on issue	100,000	Balance b/f	500,000
Issue expenses	17,889		
Balance c/d	382,111		
Interest paid	25,000	Balance b/d	382,111
Balance c/d	414,428	P&L: Interest	57,317
		Balance b/d	414,428

(b)

TRADING AND PROFIT AND LOSS ACCOUNT FOR THE YEAR ENDED 31.12.20X5

	£	£
Sales		1,618,000
Cost of sales		(982,000)
Gross profit		636,000
Distribution cost		(112,000)
Administrative expenses		(278,111)
Operating profit		245,889
Interest cost		(57,317)
Profit for the year		188,572

BALANCE SHEET AS AT 31.12.20X5

	£	£
Fixed assets	1,240,000	
Accumulated depreciation	(372,000)	868,000
Current assets:		
Stock in trade	365,000	
Debtors	512,000	
Cash and bank	54,000	
Creditors	(392,000)	539,000
		1,407,000
		£
Ordinary shares		600,000
Share Premium a/c		60,000
Profit and Loss b/f		144,000
Retained profit in the year		188,572
		992,572
5% Debentures		414,428
		1,407,000

(c) Appraisal of company financing:

Gearing ratio = 414,428/1,407,000 × 100% = 29.5%

The company is low geared

Interest cover: 245,889/57,317 = 4.3 times.

CHAPTER 41

PQ 41.1 Appropriations of a company profit

PROFIT AND LOSS (APPROPRIATION) ACCOUNT YEAR ENDED 31 DECEMBER

	20X1	20X2	20X3	20X4
	£000	£000	£000	£000
Profit before taxation	12,840	11,650	18,720	21,560
Taxation	(4,203)	(6,577)	(5,938)	(6,779)
Profit after taxation	8,637	5,073	12,782	14,781
Interim dividend paid	(2,400)	(2,400)	(3,600)	(3,600)
Final dividend proposed	(6,000)	(6,000)	(7,200)	(7,200)
Dividend Equalization Reserve	–	1,500	(1,000)	(2,000)
Fixed Asset Replacement Reserve	(500)	(500)	(500)	(500)
Profit and Loss Reserve b/f	2,600	2,337	10	492
Profit and Loss Reserve c/f	2,337	10	492	1,973

Tax charge:		£000
20X1:	Corporation Tax	3,965
	Underprovision	238
		4,203
20X2:	Corporation Tax	5,848
	Underprovision	729
		6,577
20X3:	Corporation Tax	5,924
	Underprovision	14
		5,938
20X4:	Corporation Tax	7,255
	Overprovision	(476)
		6,779

PQ 41.2 Final accounts of a manufacturing company

Points to note are as follows:

1. Value Added Tax on the furniture is (£47,000 × 17.5/117.5) = £7,000, included as part of the cost of furniture, and is recoverable from the Customs and Excise Department.
2. The opening stock of raw materials and work in progress have been absorbed into the amounts of manufacturing cost, stated in the Trial Balance.
3. The positioning, in this suggested answer, in the Profit and Loss account of the loss on disposal of machinery and the amount written off as a permanent fall in value of the investments is to satisfy the requirements of FRS 3 and company law respectively.

TRADING AND PROFIT AND LOSS ACCOUNT FOR THE YEAR ENDED 30 JUNE 20X5

	£000	£000	
Sales		8,748	
Stock – finished goods	462		
Manufacturing cost	6,428		
Depreciation – machinery	65		1
Stock – finished goods	(528)	(6,427)	
Gross profit		2,321	
Distribution cost:			
Advertising	294		
Sales commission	184		
Depreciation – vehicles	132		3
Rent	29		4
Electricity	12		4
Bad debts	28	(679)	4
Administrative expenses:			
Salaries	618		
Directors' fees	112		
Depreciation – furniture	53		2
Rent	87		4
Electricity	36		4
Telephone and postage	65	(971)	
Operating profit		671	
Disposal of machinery		(120)	
Dividend received		24	
Permanent fall in investments		(28)	
Interest and similar		(36)	5
Profit before taxation		511	
Taxation		(308)	
Profit after taxation		203	
Interim dividend paid		(120)	
Preference dividend proposed		(24)	
Final dividend proposed		(144)	6
Retained Loss		(85)	
Profit and Loss Reserve b/f		346	
Profit and Loss Reserve c/f		261	

BALANCE SHEET AS AT 30 JUNE 20X5

	Cost	Ac.dep.	£000	
Fixed assets:				
Machinery	940	(584)	356	1
Furniture and fittings	540	(242)	298	2
Vehicles	720	(366)	354	3
Investments			408	
Current assets:				
Stock – raw materials	238			
Work in progress	42			
Finished goods	528	808		
Debtors	760			
Provision for doubtful debt	(38)	722		7
Cash and bank		84		5
Current liability:				
Creditors	572			
Value Added Tax payable	105			
Interest accrued	18			
Taxation	286			
Preference dividend	24			
Final dividend proposed	144	(1,149)	465	6
			1,881	
			£000	
Share capital and reserves:				
Ordinary shares of 50p each			800	
8% Preference shares of £1			300	
Share Premium account			120	
Profit and Loss Reserve			261	
			1,481	5
Non-current liability:				
9% Debentures			400	
			1,881	

PQ 41.3 Corrections to financial statements prepared already

TRADING AND PROFIT AND LOSS ACCOUNT FOR THE YEAR ENDED 31.12.20X0

	£000	£000	
Sales		9,618	3
Stock – 1.1.20X0	614		
Purchases	7,286		
Stock – 31.12.20X0	(640)	(7,260)	7
Gross profit		2,358	
Distribution cost:			
Depreciation	296		
Advertising	104		
Bad debts	10	(410)	6
Administrative expenses:			
Salaries	849		
Directors' fees	72		
Depreciation	84		
Bank charges	7		
Audit fees	25		
Staff welfare	7		
Other expenses	282		8
Rates	15	(1,341)	2
Operating profit		607	
Dividend received		48	
Interest		6	
Interest and similar charge		(32)	2
Profit before taxation		629	
Taxation		(212)	
Profit after taxation		417	
Interim dividend paid		(60)	
Final dividend proposed		(96)	
		261	
Retained profit			
Balance b/f		415	
Balance c/f		676	

BALANCE SHEET AS AT 31.12.20X0

	Cost	Ac. dep.	£000	
Fixed assets:				
Furniture	960	(316)	644	
Motor vehicle	1,840	(980)	860	7
				4
Investments			485	6
Current assets:				
Stock		640		
Debtors	800			
Provision	(40)	760		
Loan to Tiny Ltd		60		
Current liability:				1
Creditors	738			
Taxation	198			
Bank overdraft	21			
Dividend	96	(1,053)	407	
			2,396	8
			£000	
Share capital and reserves:				
Ordinary shares of 50p each			1,200	
Share Premium account			120	
Profit and Loss account			676	
			1,996	
Non-current liability:				
8% Debentures			400	
			2,396	

Notes:

1.
Depreciation of machinery:	£000
5% of £480,000 for nine months	18
5% of £940,000 for full year	47
	65

2.
Depreciation of furniture	£000
10% of £40,000 for nine months	3
10% of £500,000 for full year	50
	53

3.
Depreciation of vehicles	£000
20% of £80,000 for 3 months	4
20% of £640,000 for full year	128
	132

4. Rent and electricity are apportioned between distribution and administration in the ratio 1:4 respectively.
5. A half-year's debenture interest, remaining unpaid, is accrued.
6. Final dividend is 9p per share on 1.6 million ordinary shares of 50p each in issue.
7. Value Added Tax payable is net of the amount recovered in respect of VAT on furniture.

MACHINERY ACCOUNT

Balance	1,420	Disposal	480
		Balance	940
	1,420		1,420
Balance	940		

PROV. FOR DEPN. – MACHINERY

Disposal	120	Balance	639
Balance	584	Depre.	65
	704		704
		Balance	584

FURNITURE ACCOUNT

Balance	500	Balance	547
Cash bk	47		
	547		547
Balance	547	VAT	7
		Balance	540
	547		547
Balance	540		

PROV. FOR DEPN. – FURNITURE

Balance	189	Balance	189
		Depreciat	53
	242		242
		Balance	242

DISPOSAL OF MACHINERY ACCOUNT

Machinery	480	Balance	240
		Prov. for dep	120
		P&L – loss	120
	480		480

VEHICLES ACCOUNT

Balance	640	Balance	720
Cash bk	80		
	720		720
Balance	720		

PROV. FOR DEPN. – VEHICLES

		Balance	234
		Depreci.	132
	366		366
		Balance	366

INVESTMENTS ACCOUNT

Balance	436	P&L – loss	28
		Balance	408
	436		436
Balance	408		

BAD DEBTS ACCOUNT

Balance	12	P&L a/c	28
Bad debts	16		
	28		28

TAXATION ACCOUNT (EXP)

Corp. Tax	286	P&L	308
Underpr.	22		
	308		308

PROVIS. FOR DOUBTFUL DEBTS

Balance	22	Balance	22
		Bad debts	16
	38		38
		Balance	38

SALES ACCOUNT

Debtors control	6	Balance b/f	9,618	3
Trading account	9,618			

DEBTORS CONTROL ACCOUNT

Balance b/f	9,624	Sales a/c	6
		Suspense a/c	8
		Balance c/d	800

BANK ACCOUNT

Interest a/c	6	Balance b/f	11	6
Balance c/d	21	Bank charge	1	2
		Rates	15	2

PROV. FOR DOUBTFUL DEBTS ACCOUNT

Bad debt a/c	1	Balance b/f	41	
Balance c/d	40			
	41		41	
		Balance b/f	41	

Notes:

1.

Bank reconciliation as at 31.12.20X0	£000
Balance as per bank statement	17,000
Lodgments yet to be credited	8,000
Cheques yet to be presented to bank	(46,000)
Actual overdraft as at 31.12.20X0	(21,000)

The bank reconciliation establishes that, as at 31.12.20X0, there was an overdraft of £21,000.

2. Bank charges and rates, as well as the interest received, are accounted for.

3. Overcasting of the Sales Day Book would have inflated the sales as well as the debtors by £6,000.

4. Correct amount receivable from debtors on 31.12 is found by adjusting the sum of individual debtors' balances, in the subsidiary ledger, for the error. See calculation in the box.

Sum of debtors accounts	£808,000
Cheque debited in error	(£8,000)
Correct amount of debtors	£800,000

5. The difference in the Control account, divided by two, is the total of the Discount column on the debit side of the cash book posted, in error, to the debit of the Debtors Control account. The amount would be £4,000, but when posted to the wrong side would have caused the Trial Balance to disagree by double that amount. To balance the Trial Balance, the difference of £8,000 would have been credited to the Suspense account. Posting £8,000 from the Debtors Control account to the Suspense account corrects the error and eliminates the Suspense account.

6. Provision for doubtful debts, when adjusted to cover 5 per cent of debtors (£800,000) would release £1,000 to offset from the bad debts expenditure.

7. The VAT element should be removed to report stock at cost as £752,000 × 100/117.5.

8. Preliminary expenses could be written off the balance in the Share Premium account (s. 130 of the Companies Act 1985).

PQ 41.4 An incomplete list of account balances

(a) Trading, Profit and Loss, and Balance Sheet for internal use:

TRADING AND PROFIT AND LOSS ACCOUNT FOR YEAR ENDED 30 JUNE 20X1

	£000	£000
Sales		9,478
Stock – 1.7.20X0	696	
Purchases	6,442	
Carriage inwards	142	
Stock – 30.6.20X1	(712)	(6,568)
Gross profit		2,910
Distribution costs:		
Advertising	186	
Bad debts	2	
Motor vehicle main	184	(372)
Administrative expenses:		
Salaries	963	
Rent and rates	246	
Stationery, postage and	72	
Audit fees	30	
Directors' emoluments	114	
Depreciation	590	(2,015)
Operating profit		523
Dividend received		42
Interest and similar charges		(27)
Profit before taxation		538
Taxation		(192)
Profit after taxation		346
Dividend proposed		(80)
Retained profit		266
Profit and Loss Reserve b/f		412
Profit and Loss Reserve c/f		678

BALANCE SHEET AS AT 30 JUNE 20X1

	Cost	Ac. dep.	£000
Fixed assets:			
Fixed assets:	5,900	(4,430)	1,470
Investments			286
Current assets:			
Stock in trade		712	
Debtors	560		
Provision	(28)	532	
Called-up share capital not paid		18	
Cash and bank balance		16	
Current liability:			
Creditors	662		
Audit fees accrued	30		
Bank overdraft	72		
Accrued expenses	168		
Interest accrued	27		
Taxation	214		
Dividend proposed	80	(1,253)	25
			1,781

		£000
Share capital and reserves:		
Ordinary shares of £1, 70p called up		700
Share Premium account		100
Calls received in advance		3
Profit and Loss Reserve		678
		1,481
Non-current liability:		
9% Debentures		300
		1,781

If the shares in arrears for the first call were forfeited, the Balance Sheet as at 30 June 20X1 will remain unchanged, except that the current asset entitled 'called-up share capital not paid' will instead be entitled 'investments in own shares'.

CHAPTER 42

PQ 42.1 No movements in fixed assets

PROFIT AND LOSS ACCOUNT FOR THE YEAR ENDED 31.12.20X1

	£000	
Turnover	4,510	a
Cost of sale	(3,106)	b
Gross profit	1,404	
Distribution cost	(363)	c
Administrative expenses	(877)	d
Operating profit	164	
Investment income	36	
Interest receivable and similar inc.	34	e
Interest payable and similar charg.	(64)	f
Profit before taxation	170	
Taxation	(20)	
Profit after taxation	150	
General reserve	(25)	
Interim dividend paid	(60)	
Final dividend proposed	(72)	g
Retained loss	(7)	

BALANCE SHEET AS AT 31.12.20X1

	Cost	Depn	£000	
Fixed assets:				
Land and building	1,200	(232)	968	h
Furniture	240	(84)	156	j
Investments			435	
Current assets:				
Stocks			427	
Debtors			456	
Cash and bank			476	
Creditors falling due within one year			(646)	
Net current assets			713	
Total assets less current liability			2,272	
Creditors due after more than one year				
12% Debentures			300	
Provision for liabilities and charges:				
Deferred taxation			42	
Capital and reserves:			£000	
Ordinary shares of 50p			1,200	
Share Premium account			300	
General reserve			25	
Profit and Loss Reserve			405	k
			1,930	
			2,272	

Notes and Schedules:

1. Expenses written off includes:

Directors' remuneration	£72,000
Directors' fees	£66,000
Depreciation	£28,000
Audit fees and expenses	£16,000
Salaries and wages	£374,000

2. Average number employed:

Directors	3
Senior executives	9
Other staff	42

3. Tax charge in the year:

Corporation Tax	£28,000
Over-provision for 20X0	(£8,000)
	£20,000

Workings (all in £000):

(a) Sales: £4,628 – £118 = £4,510.

(b) Cost of sales: £364 + £3,169 – £427 = £3,106.

(c) Distribution cost: £28 (bad debt) + £221 + £114 = £363.

(d) Admin. expenses: £(368 + 6) + £(16 + 12) + £12 + £72 + £21 + £180 + £66 + £42 + £82 = £877.

(e) Interest receivable: £22 + £12 discount received = £34.

(f) Interest payable: £(18 + 18 on debentures) + discount £28 = £64.

(g) Final dividend: 3p on 2,400,000 shares = £72.

(h) Land and building: £1,200 – £(216 + 16) = £968.

(j) Furniture: £240 – £(72 + 12) = £156.

(k) Profit and Loss Reserve: £412 – £7 retained loss = £405.

(l) Bad debt: £14 + £36 + £24 (c/f) – £46 (b/f) = £28.

PQ 42.2 Statement of fixed asset movements

PROFIT AND LOSS ACCOUNT FOR THE YEAR ENDED 31.12.20X4

	£000	
Turnover	6,342	a
Cost of sale	(3,204)	b
Gross profit	3,138	
Distribution cost	(425)	c
Administrative expenses	(808)	d
Operating profit	1,905	
Exceptional item:		
Loss on asset disposal	(120)	e
Investment income	48	
Interest and similar charges	(48)	f
Profit before taxation	1,785	
Taxation	(462)	
Profit after taxation	1,323	
Interim dividend paid	(120)	
Final dividend proposed	(180)	g
Retained profit	1,023	

BALANCE SHEET AS AT 31.12.20X4

	£000	
Fixed assets:		
Tangible assets	2,078	
Investments	425	
Current assets:		
Stocks	804	
Debtors	665	
Cash and bank	112	
Creditors falling due within one year	(1,361)	
Net current assets	220	
Total assets less current liability	2,723	
Creditors due after more than one year:		
12% Debentures	400	
Provision for liabilities and charges:		
Deferred taxation	74	
Capital and reserves:	£000	
Ordinary shares – 20p	600	
Share Premium account	120	
Profit and Loss Reserve	1,529	
	2,249	k
	2,723	

Tangible assets – statement of movements

Asset at cost	Land and Building	Machinery	Furniture	Total
	£000			£000
Balance b/f	2,100	760	120	2,980
Acquisition	–	80	40	120
Disposal	–	(240)	–	(240)
Balance c/d	2,100	600	160	2,860
Accumulated depreciation:				
Balance b/f	392	294	64	750
Depreciation	28	38	14	80
Disposal	–	(48)	–	(48)
Balance c/f	420	284	78	782
Written down value:				
as at 31.12.20X4	1,680	316	82	2,078

Expenses written off in the year include:	£000
Directors' remuneration	128
Directors' fees	66
Audit fees	15
Depreciation	80
Salaries and wages	762

Average number of employees	£000
Production workers	12
Factory supervisors	4
Administrative staff	3
Accounting staff	2
Salesmen	8
Directors	4

Stocks:	£000
Raw materials	322
Work in progress	54
Finished goods	428
	804

Creditors – falling due within one year	£000
Trade creditors	696
Accrued expense	57
Taxation	428
Dividend proposed	180
	1,361

Taxation charged in the year comprises of	£000
Corporation Tax – 20X4	428
Under-provision – 20X3	16
Deferred taxation	18
	462

Workings (all in £000):

(a) Turnover £6,458 – returns £116 = £6,342.

(b) Cost of sale: (Stocks £284 + £32 + £14) + (Depre £38 + £14) + (Elect & gas £36) + Overheads £112 + Freight & duty £284 + Purchases £2,418 + Power £54 Less (stocks £322 + £54 + £428) = £3,204.

(c) Distribution cost: Salary £144 + Depre £14 + Elect & gas £6 + Advt £96 + Sales commission £168 – bad debt £3 = £425.

(d) Administrative exp: (Salary £96 + £54 + £128) + Depre £14 + Audit £15 + Elect & gas £18 + stationery £21 + Rent £180 + Directors' fees £66 + Telephone & postage £34 + Sundries £182 = £808.

(e) Loss of disposal: Cost £240 – Accum. depre £48 = wdv £192 – proceeds £72 = loss on disposal £120.

(f) Debenture interest: Paid £24 + accrued £24 = £48.

(g) Final dividend proposed: 3,000,000 shares @ 6p = £180.

(h) Debtors: £724 – written off £24 – provision £35 = £665.

(i) Deferred taxation: Balance b/f £56 + amount set aside in the year £18 = £74.

(j) Profit and Loss Reserve: Balance b/f £506 + Retained profit £1,023 = £1,529.

(k) Accruals: Audit £15 + electricity & gas £18 + interest £24 = £57.

(l) Bad debts: Balance £6 + written off £24 + Provision c/f £35 less Provision b/f £68 = £3 credit balance.

PQ 42.3 An investor's decision

Investor ratios		Grill plc		Broil plc	
1	Earnings per share	776/16,000 × 100	4.85p	764/12,000 × 100	6.37p
2	Price earnings ratio	64/4.85	13.2	98/6.37	15.4
3	Earnings yield	4.85/64 × 100	7.6%	6.37/98 × 100	6.5%
4	Dividend yield	5/64 × 100	7.8%	4.5/98 × 100	4.6%
5	Dividend cover	776/800	97	764/540	141
6	Gearing	9,000/19,060 × 100	47.2%	Not geared	

Although both earnings yield and dividend yield are lower, the shares in Broil plc appear more promising because of the following reasons:

1. Earnings per share is better (6.37 – 4.85 = 1.52p per share better).

2. The PE ratio shows that investors have more confidence in the management and prospects of Broil plc. The chances are, therefore, that this confidence will translate into more improvement in the price of these shares.

3. Broil plc is pursuing a more prudent and sustainable dividend policy. While earning 6.4p per share, it is paying a dividend of only 4.5p per share. As the dividend cover ratio shows, it will be able to maintain this level of dividend despite a fall of up to 42 per cent in earnings. Grill plc, on the other hand, is earning 4.85p per share and paying a dividend of 5p per share. Its dividend policy is not sustainable even at current levels of earning.

4. Broil plc is not geared at all. Grill plc is significantly geared (though not highly geared). Any downturn in performance will, therefore, have a more than proportionate impact on the amounts available to ordinary shares.

CHAPTER 43

PQ 43.1 Multiple-choice question

(a) y;   (b) z;   (c) x;   (d) x;   (e) z;   (f) z;   (g) x.

PQ 43.2 Cash Flow Statement using the direct method and the indirect method

(a) On indirect method:

CASH FLOW STATEMENT YEAR ENDED 31.12.20X1

	£000	N
Operating activity	114	a
Capital expenditure:		
Asset acquisition	(80)	b
Equity: drawings	(26)	c
Cash inflow in 20X1	8	d

RECONCILIATION OF OPERATING PROFIT WITH CASH FLOW FROM OPERATING ACTIVITY

	£000
Operating profit	139
Depreciation	30
Stock increase	(68)
Debtors increase	(34)
Creditors increase	36
Accruals increase	11
Cash Flow	114

Notes:

(a) See reconciliation.

(b) £540,000 less £460,000.

(c) Given in the question.

(d) £32,000 less £24,000.

(b) On direct method

CASH FLOW STATEMENT FOR THE YEAR ENDED 31.12.20X1

	£000
Operating activity:	
From sales	932
On purchases	(676)
On expenses	(142)
	114
Capital expenditure:	
Asset acquisition	(80)
Equity: Drawings	(26)
Cash inflow in 20X1	8

(e)

		£000
Capital on 31.12.20X1		725
Add: Drawings		26
Less: Capital on 1.1.20X0		(612)
Profit in 20X1		139

TOTAL DEBTORS ACCOUNT

	£000		£000
Balance b/f	362	Cash*	932
Sales	966	Balance c/d	396

TOTAL CREDITORS ACCOUNT

	£000		£000
Cash*	676	Balance b/f	312
Balance c/d	348	Purchases	712

EXPENSES ACCOUNT

	£000		£000
Depreciat.	30	Balance	28
Cash*	142	P&L a/c	183
Balance	39		

COST OF SALE

		£000
Sales		966
Profit margin		(322)
Cost of sale		644

PURCHASES

		£000
Cost of sale		644
Closing stock		354
Opening stock		(286)
Purchases		712

EXPENSES

		£000
Gross profit		322
Profit for 20X1		(139)
Expenses		183

* Cash flows marked are all balancing figures.

PQ 43.3 Cash Flow Statement using the indirect method

CASH FLOW STATEMENT FOR THE YEAR ENDED 31.12.20X2

	£000	£000
Operating activity		420
Return on investment and servicing of finance		
Dividend received	18	
Interest paid	(64)	(46)
Capital expenditure and financial investments		
Insurance claim	5	
Furniture	(60)	
Motor vehicles	(126)	
Investments	(32)	(213)
Equity dividend		
Drawings		(26)
Management of liquid resources		
Fixed deposits		5
Finance		
Loan repayment		(150)
Cash outflow in the year		(10)

RECONCILIATION OF OPERATING PROFIT WITH CASH FLOW FROM OPERATION

	£000
Operating profit	343
Depreciation (30 + 43)	73
Stock decrease	40
Debtors increase	(61)
Creditors increase	18
Accruals increase (5–12)[b]	7
Cash inflow	420

Operating profit calculation:

	£000
Operating profit (balancing figure)	343
Dividend received	18
Loss on vehicle accident	(16)
Interest expense	(40)
Profit for the year (from Capital a/c)	305

Workings:

Cash flow in the year:

		£000
Cash and bank on 31.12.20X1	24	
Fixed deposit	(15)	9
Cash and bank on 31.12.20X2	9	
Fixed deposit	(10)	(1)
Outflow in the year		(10)

FURNITURE ACCOUNT

	£000		£000
Balance b/f	280	Balance c/d	340
Cash a/c[a]	60		

PROVISION FOR DEPRECIATION – FURNITURE

	£000		£000
Balance c/d	128	Balance b/f	98
		Depreciation	30

MOTOR VEHICLE ACCOUNT

	£000		£000
Balance b/f	360	Disposal a/c	36
Capital a/c	30	Balance c/d	480
Cash a/c[a]	126		

PROVISION FOR DEPRECIATION – VEHICLE

	£000		£000
Disposal a/c	15	Balance b/f	144
Balance c/d	172	Depreciation	43

VEHICLE DISPOSAL ACCOUNT

	£000		£000
M. Vehicle a/c	36	Prov. for depr	15
		Insurance	5
		P&L – loss	16

INVESTMENTS ACCOUNT

	£000		£000
Balance b/f	264	Balance c/f	296
Cash a/c[a]	32		

CAPITAL ACCOUNT

	£000		£000
Drawings	26	Balance b/f	673
Balance c/d	982	Motor vehicle	30
		Profit – balancing	305

a. Cash flows marked are all balancing figures.
b. Accruals reported are after removing interest accruals of £64,000 on 31.12.20X1 and £40,000 on 31.12.20X2.

PQ 43.4 Cash Flow Statement using the direct method

CASH FLOW STATEMENT FOR THE YEAR ENDED 30.6.20X1

	£000	£000
Operating activity:		
From sales	3,283	
For purchases	(2,430)	
Admin expense	(318)	
Distrib. cost	(125)	410
Return on investments and servicing of finance		
Interest paid		(51)
Capital expenditure and financial investment		
Plant and machinery	(200)	
Disposal of machinery	41	
Motor vehicles	(100)	
Disposal of vehicles	40	
Furniture	(30)	
Investments	(43)	(292)
Equity dividend		
Drawings		(56)
Management of liquid resources		
Investments		18
Financing		
Capital	30	
Loan repayment	(100)	(70)
Cash outflow		(41)

RECONCILIATION OF OPERATING PROFIT WITH CASH FLOW FROM OPERATION

	£000
Operating profit	283
Depreciation	162
Stock increase	(132)
Debtors increase	(42)
Creditors increase	96
Accruals increase	43
Cash Flow from op. activity	410

Workings:

Cash flow during the year:

		£000
Cash and bank balance on 30.6.20X0		36
Cash and bank balance on 30.6.20X1	11	
Overdraft as at 30.6.20X1	(16)	5
Outflow during the year		(41)

PLANT AND MACHINERY ACCOUNT

	£000		£000
Balance b/f	360	Disposal a/c	140
Cash a/c*	200	Balance c/d	420

PROVISION FOR DEPRECIATION – MACHINERY

	£000		£000
Disposal a/c	78	Balance b/f	124
Balance c/d	136	Depreciation	90

DISPOSAL OF MACHINERY ACCOUNT

	£000		£000
P. &Mach. a/c	140	Prov. for dep.	78
		P&L – Loss	21
		Cash a/c*	41

FURNITURE ACCOUNT

	£000		£000
Balance b/f	160	Balance c/d	190
Cash a/c*	30		

PROVISION FOR DEPRECIATION – FURNITURE

	£000		£000
Balance c/d	72	Balance b/f	54
		Depreciation	18

MOTOR VEHICLES ACCOUNT

	£000		£000
Balance b/f	280	Disposal a/c	60
Cash a/c*	100	Balance c/d	320

PROVISION FOR DEPRE. – VEHICLES

	£000		£000
Disposal a/c	34	Balance b/f	64
Balance c/d	84	Depreciation	54

PQ 43.5 Cash Flow Statement for a limited company

DEVELOPMENT COST

	£000		£000	
Balance b/f	120	Amortization	84	x
Cash book	122	Balance c/d	158	a

FURNITURE ACCOUNT

	£000		£000	
Balance b/f	964	Balance c/d	1,122	x
Cash book	158			b

PROVISION FOR DEPRECIATION-FURNITURE ACCOUNT

	£000		£000	
Balance c/d	324	Balance b/f	268	x
		Depreciation	56	

MOTOR VEHICLE ACCOUNT

	£000		£000	
Balance b/f	1,620	Disposal	80	x
Cash book	305	Balance c/d	1,845	c

PROVISION FOR DEPRECIATION-VEHICLE – ACCOUNT

	£000		£000	
Disposal a/c	36	Balance b/f	1,124	x
Balance c/d	1,346	Depreciation	258	p

MOTOR VEHICLE DISPOSAL ACCOUNT

	£000		£000	
Motor vehicle	80	Prov. for deprec.	36	d
		P&L – loss	18	x
		Cash book	26	e

FIXED ASSET – INVESTMENTS ACCOUNT

	£000		£000	
Balance b/f	333	P&L – write off	32	x
Cash book	173	Balance c/d	474	f

LIQUID RESOURCES ACCOUNT

	£000		£000	
Bal. – shares	31	Bal. – shares	54	x
Bal. – deposit	44	Bal. – deposit	25	x
Cash book	g			

INTEREST ACCOUNT

	£000		£000	
Cash book	72	Balance b/f	18	x
Balance c/d	12	P&L – expense	66	x

CASH FLOW STATEMENT FOR THE YEAR ENDED 30 JUNE 20X2

	£000	£000	
Operating activity:			
From sales	15,667		J
For purchases	(12,532)		L
For distrib. cost	(132)		M
For admin. exp.	(858)		N
		2,145	
Return on investment and servicing of finance			
Dividend received	54		h
Interest paid	(72)	(18)	o
Taxation		(710)	
Capital expenditure and financial investments			
Development cost	(122)		a
Furniture	(158)		b
Motor vehicles	(305)		c
Investments	(173)		f
Disposal of vehicle	26	(732)	e
Equity dividend paid			
Interim dividend	(240)		x
Final dividend	(540)	(780)	p
Management of liquid resources		(44)	g
Financing			
Redemption of deb.	(192)		q
Share capital	300		r
Share premium	122	230	s
Cash inflow in the year		91	

DISPOSAL OF VEHICLES ACCOUNT

	£000		£000
Motor vehicle	60	Prov. for depre.	34
P&L – gain	14	Cash a/c*	40

12% LOAN ACCOUNT

	£000		£000
Cash book*	100	Balance b/f	450
Balance c/f	350		

COST OF SALES ACCOUNT

	£000		£000
Stock b/f	654		
Purchases	2,526		
Depre. machine	90		
Stok at end	(786)		
	2,484		

ADMINISTRATIVE EXPENSES ACCOUNT

	£000		£000
Depre. Furniture	18	Balance b/f	82
Cash book*	318	Profit and Loss	366
Balance c/f	112		

DISTRIBUTION COST ACCOUNT

	£000		£000
Bad debts	14	Balance b/f	21
Depre. Vehicles	54	Profit and Loss	206
Cash book*	125		
Balance c/d	34		

FIXED ASSET INVESTMENTS ACCOUNT

	£000		£000
Balance b/f	169	Balance c/d	212
Cash a/c*	43		

LIQUID RESOURCES ACCOUNT

	£000		£000
Balance b/f	26	Cash book*	18
		Balance c/f	8

TOTAL DEBTORS ACCOUNT

	£000		£000
Balance b/f	552	Bad debts	14
Sales a/c	3,339	Cash book*	3,283
		Balance c/d	594

TOTAL CREDITORS ACCOUNT

	£000		£000
Cash book*	2,430	Balance b/f	628
Balance c/d	724	Purchases	2,526

CAPITAL ACCOUNT

	£000		£000
Drawing*	56	Balance b/f	814
Balance c/d	1,013	Cash book	30
		Profit	225

INTEREST ACCOUNT

	£000		£000
Cash bk*	51	P&L a/c	51

	20X0	20X1
Net debt as at 31.12		
12% Loan	(450)	(350)
Cash and bank balance	36	11
Bank overdraft	00	(16)
Liquid resources	26	8
Net debt as at 31.12	(388)	(347)

(B) RECONCILIATION OF CASH FLOW WITH NET DEBT

	£000
Repayment of loan	100
Cash outflow in the year	(41)
Reduction of liquid resources	(18)
Improvement in liquidity	41
Net debt on 1.1.20X1	(388)
Net debt on 31.12.20X1	(347)

* Cash flows marked are all balancing figures.

Brief comment on company's liquidity. Though the Cash Flow Statement shows a cash inflow of only £91,000, the improvement in liquidity is focused on in the statement of reconciliation with net debt. This shows that liquidity has in fact improved during the year by £295,000. As a result, from a net debt position of £165,000 the company has improved to a net fund position of £130,000.

PQ 43.6 Profit is not always matched by cash inflow

(a) Projection of performance in year 20X2

Sales: Since Debtor as at 31.12.20X1 ties up one month's sale

Sales in year 20X1 must have been £240,000 × 12 = £2,880,000

Therefore sales in year 20X2: £2,880,000 × 3 less 10% discount

£7,776,000

Gross profit: If cost price is £100 the new sale price will be

£100 + 50% profit less 10% discount = £135

Therefore gross profit in year 20X2: £7,776,000 × 35/135   2,016,000

Cost of sales in year 20X2: £7,776,000 – £2,016,000   5,760,000

Other expenses: £1,280,000 × 125%   1,600,000

The projected profit, ignoring depreciation, arising from the new thrust is £416,000 whereas it would have been a loss of £320,000 in 20X1.

PROFIT AND LOSS ACCOUNT YEAR TO 31 DECEMBER

	20X2		20X1
	£000	£000	£000
Sales		7,776	2,880
Stock (opening)	120		
Purchases	7,080		
Stock (closing)	(1,440)		
		(5,760)	(1,920)
Gross profit		2,016	960
Expenses		(1,600)	(1,280)
Profit (ignoring depreciation)		416	(320)

(b) Projection of cash flow in the year:

Debtors as at 31.12.20X2: Three months' sale: £7,776,000 × 3/12 = £1,944,000

Creditors as at 31.12/20X2: One month's purchases: £7,080,000/12 = £590,000

PROJECTED CASH FLOW

	£000
Balance b/f	35
Receipts from debtors	6,072
Payments to creditors	(6,610)
Expenses	(1,600)
Cash deficiency	(2,103)

TOTAL DEBTORS ACCOUNT

	£000		£000
Balance b/f	240	Cash a/c*	6,072
Sales	7,776	Balance c/f	1,944

TOTAL CREDITORS ACCOUNT

	£000		£000
Cash a/c*	6,610	Balance b/f	120
Balance c/d	590	Purchases	7,080

DEBTORS CONTROL ACCOUNT

	£000		£000	
Balance b/f	2,168	Bad debts a/c	22	x
Sales	15,977	Cash a/c	15,667	j
		Balance c/d	2,456	x

CREDITORS CONTROL ACCOUNT

	£000		£000	
Cash book	12,532	Balance b/f	1,942	x
Balance c/d	2,464	Purchases	13,054	k

COST OF SALES ACCOUNT

	£000		£000	
Stock 1.7.20X1	1,485	Trading account	12,495	
Purchases	13,054			
Amortization	84			
Stock 30.6.20X2	(2,128)			
	12,495		12,495	

ADMINISTRATIVE EXPENSES ACCOUNT

	£000		£000	
Balance b/f	42	Balance b/f	120	x
Depreciation	56	Profit and Loss a/c	948	x
Cash book	858			
Balance c/d	180	Balance c/d	68	x

DEBENTURE REDEMPTION ACCOUNT

	£000		£000	
Cash book	192	Debentures	160	x
		Sh. premium	32	x

ORDINARY SHARE CAPITAL ACCOUNT

	£000		£000	
Balance c/d	1,500	Balance b/f	1,200	x
		Cash book	300	r

SHARE PREMIUM ACCOUNT

	£000		£000	
Deb. redem.	32	Balance b/f	150	x
Balance c/d	240	Cash book	122	s

RECONCILIATION OF OPERATING PROFIT WITH CASH FLOW FROM OP. ACTIVITY

	£000
Operating profit	2,122
Depreciation (56 + 258)	314
Amortization	84
Stock decrease	(643)
Debtors increase	(288)
Prepayments increase	(26)
Creditors increase	522
Accruals increase	60
Cash flow in the year	2,145

RECONCILIATION OF CASH FLOW WITH NET DEBT

	£000
Debenture redemption	160
Cash inflow	91
Liquid resources increase	44
	295
Net debt on 1.7.20X2	(165)
Net funds on 30.6.20X2	130

DISTRIBUTION COST ACCOUNT

	£000		£000	
Depreciation	258	Profit and Loss	412	x
Bad debts	22			
Cash book	132			

TAXATION (LIABILITY) ACCOUNT

	£000		£000	
Cash book	685	Balance b/f	710	x
Balance c/d	870	Tax (exp) a/c	845	x

DIVIDEND PROPOSED (LIABILITY) ACCOUNT

	£000		£000	
Cash book	540	Balance b/f	540	x
Balance c/d	720	Dividend – exp	720	x

PROFIT AND LOSS ACCOUNT

	£000		£000	
Balance c/d	750	Balance b/f	520	x
		Retained prof.	230	x

Net (debt) funds as at

	30.6.20X1	30.6.20X2	
15% Debenture	(480)	(320)	x
Liquid resources	31	54	x
Fixed deposit	4	25	
Cash and bank balance	280	371	
	(165)	130	

PROJECTED CASH FLOW

	£000
Balance b/f	35
Receipts from debtors	6,072
Payment to creditors	(5,430)
Expenses	(1,600)
Cash deficiency	(923)

* balancing amount.

TOTAL CREDITORS ACCOUNT

	£000		£000
Cash a/c*	5,430	Balance b/f	120
Balance c/f	1,770	Purchases	7,080

Thus, despite the remarkable improvement in performance, an acute cash flow crisis is forecast. If three months' credit is negotiated from suppliers, there will still be a cash deficiency, but this time only of £923,000.

PQ 43.7 Focus on liquidity position

The correct answer in each case is option 'c'.

CHAPTER 44

PQ 44.1 Focus on the vehicles proposed to communicate information

The most appropriate vehicle would, in each case, be as follows:

(a) Statement of Corporate Objectives
(b) Cash Flow Statement
(c) Employment Report
(d) Statement of Corporate Objectives
(e) Statement of money exchange with the government/Statement of transactions in foreign currency
(f) Statement of Corporate Objectives (Environmental Reports are of recent origin)

Every effort is being made by the profession to enhance the predictive value of the information in the traditional financial statements, such as the Profit and Loss account. This is enhanced by:

● segmental reports;
● Operating and Financial Review.

PQ 44.2 Preparation of Value Added Statement

VALUE ADDED STATEMENT FOR THE YEAR ENDED 30 JUNE 20X1

	£000	
Turnover	8,684	
Less: Bought in materials and services	(6,122)	a
Loss on asset disposal	(124)	
Value added within entity	2,438	
Investment income	48	
Value added in the year	2,486	
Applied as follows:		
To employees	(1,428)	W
To providers of capital:		
As interest	60	
As dividend	180	(240)
To Government		
As Corporation Tax	148	
As import duty	214	(362)
Retained for maintenance and expansion		
As depreciation	291	b
As retained profit	165	(456)

Workings:

(a) Expenses:

	£000	£000
Cost of sale	5,268	
Distribution cost	962	
Administ. expenses	1,825	
		8,055
Duty paid		(214)
Depreciation:		
Building	29	
Machinery	106	
Furniture	68	
Motor vehicles	88	(291)
Salaries and wages		(1,428)
		6,122

(b) Depreciation as calculated above: £291,000.

CHAPTER 45

PQ 45.1 Consolidation of Balance Sheets (with no pre-acquisition profit)

CONSOLIDATED BALANCE SHEET AS AT 31 MARCH 20X5

		£000	£000
Fixed assets:			
Intangible asset – goodwill			60
Plant and machinery	720 + 540	1,260	
Accum. depreciation	312 + 146	(458)	802
Furniture and fittings	240 + 240	480	
Accum. depreciation	108 + 96	(204)	276
Investments	125 + 35		160
Current assets:			
Stock in trade	(412 + 24 – 50) + 524	910	
Debtors	622 + 127	749	
Cash and bank	(44 + 15) + 26	85	
Creditors	348 + 468	(816)	
Taxation	112 + 64	(176)	
Dividend proposed	90	(90)	662
			1,960

	£000
Ordinary shares of 50p each	900
Share premium account	135
Consolidated Profit and Loss a/c 692 + 293 – 60	925
	1,960

PQ 45.2 Group accounts involving pre-acquisition profits with the subsidiary

CONSOLIDATED BALANCE SHEET AS AT 31.12.20X6

		£000
Fixed assets	960 + 640	1,600
Acc. depn	(240 + 180)	(420)
		1,180
Investments	150 + 60(a)	210
Stock	754 + 620 + 40(b) – 48(c)	1,366
Debtors	592 + 518(d)	1,110
Cash/bank	74 + 16 + 28(e)	118
Creditors	508(d) + 548	(1,056)
Taxation	112 + 94	(206)
Minority div.	20(f)	(20)
Dividend proposed		(150)
		2,552

	£000
Ordinary shares of £1	1,500
Share Premium a/c	300
Consolidated Profit and Loss (h)	435
Minority Interest (i)	2,235
	317
	2,552

a) Gain on revaluation of Winkie's investments.

b) Stock in transit

c) Unrealized profit: 20% of £200,000 + £40,000

d) Cancellation of inter-company indebtedness:

As stated in the question:

	Willie's creditors	Winkie's debtors
Goods in transit (b)	654	732
Cash in transit (e)	40	
Inter-company indebtedness	28	
	(214)	(214)
	508	518

e) Cash in transit is ascertained as stated in the answer to PQ 45.1

f) Winkie's dividend, net of 75% credited to Consolidated Profit and Loss account.

h) P&L a/c

	Winkie	Willie	
As in question	376	264	As in question
Unrealised (c)	(48)	174	Winkie's P&L
	328	60	Winkie's dividend
Minority –25%	(82)	(63)	Goodwill w/off (i)
Cost of control	(72)	435	
Consol. P&L	(174)		

Notes:

1. When goods invoiced by Tuffet at £24,000 are taken into account, Muffet owes Tuffet £(246,000 + 24,000) = £270,000. Since Tuffet claims that it is owed £285,000, the difference of £15,000 would be the amount of Muffet's remittance still to reach Tuffet.

	Muffet creditors £000	Tuffet debtors £000
As in the Balance Sheet	594	412
Goods in transit	24	–
Cash in transit	15	–
Inter-company debt	(285)	(285)
	348	127

2. Profit made by Tuffet would be unrealized to the extent that its goods remain unsold with Muffet (£176,000) and are in transit (£24,000). Therefore unrealized profit to be eliminated from Tuffet's profit is one-quarter of £176,000 + £24,000 = £50,000.

3. Goodwill on acquisition is ascertained as set out below. At £12,000 per year, £60,000 of goodwill will have been written off over five years.

COST OF CONTROL ACCOUNT

	£000		£000
Muffet's		**Tuffet's**	
Investment	720	Share capital	500
		Share premium	100
		Goodwill	120

4. Profit and Loss accounts of the companies are adjusted as set out below. £60,000 of goodwill is written off from the total of both companies' profits.

	Muffet	Tuffet
Balances as reported	£632,000	£343,000
Dividend receivable	£60,000	–
Unrealized profit w/off	–	£50,000
	£692,000	£293,000

i)

COST OF CONTROL ACCOUNT		
Investments		840
Share capital	75%	(600)
Share premium account	75%	(60)
Revaluation gain (a)	75%	(45)
Pre-acquisition profit	75%	(72)
Winkie's profit net of unrealized portion		
Goodwill		63

MINORITY INTEREST		
	25%	200
	25%	20
	25%	15
	25%	82
		317

CHAPTER 46

PQ 46.1 Current purchasing power (CPP) accounting

(a) CPP Profit and Loss account

	£	RPI factor	CPP£		CPP£
Sales	4,500	280/200		1,575	6,300
Stock at 1 July 20X0	900	280/160		2,835	
Purchases	2,025	280/200		4,410	
	2,925				
Less: Stock at 30 June 20X1	675	280/200		945	
Cost of sales	2,250				3,465
Gross profit	2,250				2,835
Expenses	1,125	280/200		1,575	
Depreciation	270	280/160		473	
	1,395				2,048
Net profit	855				787
Add monetary gains:					
Loan	1,800	280/160	3,150 – 1,800	1,350	
Less monetary losses:					
Bank	1,350	280/200	1,890 – 1,350	(540)	
CPP £ Profit					1,597

The CPP Profit of CPP£1,597 represents the owners' spending power expressed in purchasing power units. It is not relevant if the business is to maintain its operating capacity.

PQ 46.2 Profit on the current cost basis

The gross profit of £2,250 calculated on the historical cost basis is reduced by £500 to £1,750 and the net profit is reduced from £855 to £355. The current cost profit of £355 is the maximum that the owners could withdraw from the business if they wished to maintain the scale of the operation. The £500 represents the holding gain and this is the amount that must be retained within the business in order to be able to maintain the existing level of stock holding and continue to trade at the same level.

PQ 46.3 Analysis of a diagram (1)

Limitations of historical cost accounting:

- The effect of inflation on purchasing power is often underestimated. For example, a compound rate of inflation as low as 3% means that the general price level will double in 20 years. If turnover were to have doubled during that period, the business would have only been standing still.
- The underlying assumption that there is a stable monetary unit is a delusion and distorts the reality of a business's turnover.
- The assumption also causes an overstatement of the profit because the cost of sales is understated, and if the whole of the historical profit were to be distributed the business would have reduced its operating capacity.
- It also overstates the profit and reports unrealistic fixed asset values. This means that the profits are overstated, with depreciation being understated, and the financial position is unrealistic, with fixed asset values being understated.
- HCA fails to recognize monetary gains from holding monetary liabilities and monetary losses arising from debtors.
- The return on capital employed is incorrect, with asset values being understated and profits being overstated.

Explaining accounting terms

- Point (a) to (b) on the vertical axis represents the operating profit.
- Point (b) to (c) on the axis represents the cost of sales adjustment (COSA).
- Point (e) is the date of sale.
- Point (d) to (e) on the horizontal axis represents the period of stockholding.

PQ 46.4 Analysis of a diagram (2)

The fundamental principle on which CCA is based

The principle is that of capital maintenance, with the capital being defined as the net operating assets. The current cost operating profit is the amount that remains after taking into account the impact of price changes on the funds needed to maintain the operating capability of the business. This means the figure after deducting the cost of sales adjustment, depreciation adjustment and monetary working capital adjustment.

The Current Cost Balance Sheet restates assets at their value to the business at current price levels. This means that fixed assets are restated at their net current replacement value, i.e. after deducting current cost depreciation and stock at current replacement value. This gives a more realistic picture of the resources employed within the business and allows a realistic return on capital employed to be calculated.

Explaining accounting terms

- Point (g) to (h) on the vertical scale represents the monetary working capital adjustment (MWCA)
- Point (h) to (c) represents the cost of sales adjustment (COSA) or realized holding gain.

PQ 46.5 Current cost accounting (CCA) and current purchasing power (CPP) accounting

(a) The major differences are that:

- CCA uses specific indices reflecting the change in price of specific fixed assets and stock items, whereas CPP accounting uses a general inflation index based on the Retail Price Index (RPI).
- CCA financial statements are expressed in £ sterling, whereas CPP financial statements are expressed in purchasing power units.
- CCA focuses on the operating capability of a business, i.e. its fixed assets and working capital, whereas CPP accounting focuses on the real return to shareholders on their capital inverted.

(b) (a) to (b) represents unrealized profit

(b) to (c) represents holding gain

The caravan would be reported as stock at £15,000 replacement cost. The holding gain of £10,000 would be reported in the current cost reserve.

SELECTION OF QUESTIONS FROM PAST EXAMINATIONS

Chapter 7 Period-end adjustments

AB, a sole trader, commenced trading on 1 January 1990. He has provided you with the following details of his telephone costs:

Quarterly rental payable in advance on 1 January, 1 April, 1 July and 1 October £15.

Particulars of Telephone calls payable in arrears are stated in the box on right.

He is to prepare his first accounts to 31.10.1990 and estimates that the cost of his calls for October 1990 will be £74.

He also pays rent quarterly in advance for his premises and has made payments as stated on right.

January to March 1990 paid 1.4.1990	£159
April to June 1990 paid 1.7.1990	£211
July to September 1990 paid 1.10.1990	£183

1 January 1990	£600
1 April 1990	£750
1 July 1990	£750
1 October 1990	£750

Required: (a) Prepare AB's ledger accounts for telephone and rent for the period 1 January to 31 October 1990, showing clearly the amounts to be transferred to the Profit and Loss account for the period together with balances carried down on 31 October 1990; (b) Explain the accruals concept. (CIMA)

Chapter 9 Supporting accounts

George Dunnon, a retailer, maintains a Provision for doubtful debts account, the balance in which is calculated by reference to the age of the debts outstanding at the end of the financial year. Information on debtors is stated on the right. Included in the debts over six months old were debts of £100 at 31 March 1996 and £320 at 31.3.1997, both of which were considered bad and were written off. The balance on the Provision for doubtful debts account at 1 April 1995 was £220.

Age of debts outstanding	Year ended 31.3.1996	Year ended 31.3.1997	Provision for doubtful debt
	£	£	%
0–1 month	4,000	3,000	1
1–3 months	12,000	8,000	2
3–6 months	4,100	4,500	3
over 6 months	1,800	2,400	4

Required: (a) Prepare the Provision for doubtful debts account for each of the two years ended 31.3.96 and 31.3.97; (b) Prepare an extract from George Dunnon's balance sheet as at 31.3.1997 showing how the information relating to the debtors would appear; (c) Explain the difference between a bad debt written off and a provision for doubtful debts; and (d) describe three actions George Dunnon could take to reduce the likelihood of bad debts occurring in the future. (AEB)

Chapter 10 The Journal

When Debbie Brown extracted her trial balance at 31 March 19X2 she found it did not agree. She opened a Suspense account, prepared her trading and profit and loss account and drew up her balance sheet as stated on the right. Subsequent checking of her records revealed the following errors which when corrected eliminated the Suspense account.

(i)   A cheque for £260 for acquiring a new display stand on 31 March 19x2 has been entered correctly in the Cash Book but posted to Shop fittings account as £200.

(ii) A credit note from XY Suppliers Ltd for £60 had been entered in Returns Outwards Day Book but has been posted to XY's account as £66.

(iii) Bank charges £21 appeared in the Cash Book but had not been posted.

(iv) An invoice for £139 for goods sold to Thompson had been correctly entered in the Sales Day Book but had been posted to Thompson's account as £193.

(v) The debit balance of £223 on Smith's account at 31 March 19X2 had been carried down as £253 and included in the Trial balance at that figure.

Required: (a) Set out the journal entries necessary to correct the errors; (b) Write up the Suspense account; (c) Prepare a statement showing the revised profit for the year; and (d) Prepare a corrected balance sheet. (AAT)

BALANCE SHEET AS AT 31 MARCH 19X2	£	£
Fixed assets:		
Shop fittings	1,500	
Accum. depreciation	(300)	1,200
Delivery van	3,200	
Accum. depreciation	(800)	2,400
Current assets:		
Stock	2,917	
Debtors	2,154	
Cash and bank	1,223	
Creditors	(1,888)	4,406
		8,006
		£
Capital 1 April 19X1	7,500	
Profit for the year	5,497	
Drawings	(5,000)	7,997
Suspense account		9
		8,006

Chapter 10 The Journal

After calculating net profit for the year ended 31 March 1998, WL has the following trial balance: A Suspense account was opened for the difference in the trial balance. Immediately after the production of the trial balance, the following errors were detected:

(i) A creditors account had been debited with £300 sales invoice (which had been correctly recorded in the Sales account).

(ii) The Heat & Light account had been credited with gas paid £150.

(iii) G. Gordon had been credited with a cheque for £800 received from another customer G. Goldman.

(iv) The Insurance account contained a credit entry for insurance Prepaid of £500, but the balance had not been carried down and hence had been omitted from the above trial balance.

(v) Purchase Returns had been over-cast by £700.

	Dr £	Cr £
Land and building at cost	10,000	
Building – depreciation at 31.3.1998		2,000
Plant at cost	12,000	
Plant – depreciation at 31.3.1998		3,000
Stocks	2,500	
Debtors	1,500	
Bank	8,250	
Creditors		1,700
Rent prepaid	400	
Wages accrued		300
Capital account		19,400
Profit for the year ended 31 March 1998		9,750
	34,650	36,150

Required: (a) Prepare journal entries to correct each of the above errors (narratives are not required); (b) Open the Suspense account at 31 March 1998 and enter the relevant corrections; (c) Name the type of error which had occurred in each of items (i), (ii) and (iii); (d) recalculate the net profit for the year to 31 March 1998; (e) Prepare a revised balance sheet as at 31 March 1998. (CIMA)

Chapter 13 The Bank accounts and bank reconciliation

Leo Conley's Cash Book and corresponding bank statement are shown below

CASH BOOK (BANK COLUMN ONLY)

Dr		£	Cr		£
1.4	McCreary Ltd	4,130	1.4	Balance b/d	4,690
2.4	Simpson & Hill	800	6.4	Morrison Ltd	46
3.4	Jake Computers	3,420	8.4	T Henry & Co	92
12.4	Harkin's Printing	221	16.4	Herbal Finance	110
20.4	L Hamilton	540	21.4	Treetop builders	249
24.4	J McCusker	120	26.4	Alvin's Advertising	75
26.4	H Morrison	399	28.4	Causeway Ltd	4,190
			30.4	Balance c/d	178
		9,630			9,630

Bank statement	Dr £	Cr £	Balance £
April			
1 Balance			4,690 Dr
2 McCreary Ltd		4,130	560 Dr
3 Simpson & Hill Ltd		800	240 Cr
5 Handy Insurance – DD	65		175 Cr
8 Jake's Computers		3,420	3,595 Cr
9 Morrison Ltd	46		3,549 Cr
12 T Henry & Co	92		3,457 Cr
14 Harkins Printing		221	3,678 Cr
25 Treetops Builders	249		3,429 Cr
26 J McCusker		120	3,549 Cr
27 Benson & Sons – CT		450	3,999 Cr
27 Bank Charges	66		3,933 Cr
29 Causeway Ltd	4,190		257 Dr
30 McCusker R/D	120		377 Dr

Required: (a) Update the cash book; (b) Prepare a bank reconciliation statement as at 30 April 1998; (c) Give reasons why a firm should prepare a bank reconciliation statement. (CCEA)

Chapter 14 Control accounts

A trial balance has an excess of debits over credits of £14,000 and a suspense account has been opened to make it balance. It is later discovered that: (a) the discounts allowed balance of £3,000 and the discount received balance of £7,000 have been entered on the wrong side of the trial balance; (b) The creditors control account balance of £233,786 has been included in the trial balance as £237,386; (c) An item of £500 had been omitted from the Sales Day Book; and (d) The balance on the current account with the senior partner's wife had been omitted from the trial balance.

Required: (a) set out how you would make the necessary corrections; and (b) show the suspense account, assuming that the corrections eliminated the balance placed in it. (ACCA)

Chapter 14 Control accounts

The Sales ledger control account of C Ltd is shown on the right. A list of individual customer balances at month end shows debit balances as £54,468.59 and credit balances as £52,080. The following facts have now been discovered:

1. No entries have been made in the Sales Ledger for the debt collection fees and bad debts written off.
2. The Sales Day Book has been over-added by £500.
3. The Sales Returns Day Book has been under-added by £10.
4. A credit balance of £673.46 has been taken as a debit balance in listing the customers' balances.
5. The account of a customer who settled by contra was debited with 378.82.
6. A debit balance on a customer's account of £347.58 has been stated in the list as £374.85.
7. The dishonoured cheque had been entered in the sales ledger as credit £601.75.

SALES LEDGER CONTROL

	£		£
Balance b/d	70,814.16	Balance b/d	1,198.73
Sales	54,738.36	Sales returns	2,344.39
Dishonour of cheque	607.15	Cash book	68,708.27
Debt collection fees	108.81	Contra	378.82
		Bad debts	474.16
Balance c/d	1,194.26	Balance c/d	54,358.37

Required: (a) Correct the Sales ledger control account; (b) reconcile the corrected control balances with the sum of the individual balances. (ACCA)

Chapter 15 Accounting for assets

Do you regard each of the following as an asset of a business for accounting purposes? Explain your answer:

(i) a screwdriver bought in 1987; (ii) a machine hired by the business; (iii) good reputation of the business with its customers. (ACCA)

Chapter 15 Accounting for assets

Sema plc, a company in heavy engineering industry, carried out an expansion programme in the 1986 financial year, in order to meet a permanent increase in contracts. The company selected a suitable site and commissioned a survey and valuation report, for which the fees were £1,500. On the basis of the report the site was acquired for £90,000. Solicitors' fees for drawing up the contract and conveyancing were £3,000. Fees of £8,700 were paid to the architects for preparing the building plans and overseeing the building work. This was carried out partly by the company's own work force (at a wages cost of £11,600), using company building materials (cost £76,800) and partly by sub-contractors who charged £69,400, of which £4,700 related to demolition of an existing building on the same site.

The completed building housed two hydraulic presses. The cost of press A was £97,000 (ex works) payable in a single lump sum two months after installation. Sema was given a trade discount of 10% and a cash discount for prompt payment of 2%. Hire of a transporter to collect the press and convey it to the new building was £2,900. Installation costs were £2,310 including hire of lifting gear, £1,400. Press B would have cost £105,800 (delivered) if it had been paid for in one lump sum. However Sema opted to pay three equal annual instalments of of £40,000 starting on the date of acquisition. Installation costs were £2,550 including hire of lifting gear £1,750.

Required: (a) Using such of the above information as is relevant write up the Premises account and Plant account; (b) State with reasons which of the above information were excluded from the accounts you wrote up. (ACCA)

Chapter 16 Depreciation of tangible fixed assets

The machinery register of Etheired Engineering plc on 1 January 1991 contained the items stated on the right. Depreciation policies are as follows:

Machines A & B on straight-line basis assuming zero scrap value after 10 years use.

Machine C on reducing balance basis at 20% p.a. assuming scrap value of £1,000.

Machine D & E on straight-line basis assuming a scrap value equal to 10% of cost after five years use. Relevant transactions during the year to 31 December 1991 were as follows:

(i) Machine B was taken in part exchange by the supplier of Machine F. The invoice for Machine F reads as stated on the right.

(ii) The motor in Machine E is discovered to be inadequate. By agreement it is replaced by a more powerful motor. The new motor costs £6,000 as compared with £4,000 for the original motor. The old inadequate motor is taken back by the supplier and full credit for the original £4,000 is given against the £6,000 cost of the new motor. This change is not expected to increase the life of the machine and it is agreed to treat this as a correction of the original cost. The depreciation policy for the new machine F is the same as for machines D and E.

Machine	Cost £	Year of purchase
A	10,000	1980
B	12,000	1984
C	15,000	1986
D	16,000	1989
E	20,000	1990

		£	£
New machine – list price		25,000	
trade discount		1,000	24,000
Allowance on your old machine			(2,000)
			22,000
Delivery of new machine		1,500	
Collection of old machine		1,000	2,500
			24,500

Required: Prepare a table showing for each machine: cost, depreciation to date, and net balance sheet figure and the Profit and Loss account entries for the year 1991. (ACCA)

Chapter 17 Stock in trade

Nick and Sally have approached their bank with a view to obtaining finance for a new project, trading in printed tee-shirts. The bank manager has requested a four year business plan and they have provided you with estimates as stated on the right. In the year to 30 June 1999 expenses are expected to be £1,000 and will increase by 10% per annum in each of the next three years. A printing machine will be purchased for £4,000 and come into operation on 1 July 1998. This machine will have an estimated life of four years and will have a scrap value of £500 at the end of this time.

Year to 30 June	Purchases	Sales
1999	1,000 @ £8	800 @ £12
2000	1,000 @ £10	800 @ £14
2001	1,000 @ £12	1,100 @ £16
2002	1,000 @ £14	1,300 @ £17

Required: (a) A statement showing the gross and net profits of each of the four years assuming use of the First In First Out method of pricing stores issues and straight line depreciation; (b) A statement showing gross and net profits for each of the four years assuming the use of Last In First Out method of pricing stores issue and reducing balance depreciation at a rate of 40% per annum; (c) Discuss the relative merits of the straight line and reducing balance methods of depreciation identifying the circumstances when each is appropriate. State which method is most appropriate for Nick and Sally situation; (d) Discuss the relative merits of the Last In first Out and First In first Out methods of pricing stores issues. State which approach is more appropriate for Nick and Sally's situation. (NEAB)

Chapter 20 Accounting for Value Added tax

Shown on the right is the Sales and Returns Inwards Day Book of XY, a sole trader, who employs a bookkeeper to maintain her personal account records but maintains the nominal ledger herself.

Required: (a) Explain the possible meaning of the entry on 17 February; (b) Explain how the realization concept would have been applied in determining the above entries; (c) Post the above transactions to the appropriate accounts in the nominal ledger and in the customer's personal accounts; and (d) Explain why a Provision for doubtful debts is usually calculated in respect of debtors; support your answers by reference to basic concepts. (CIMA)

Date	Customer	Goods	Vat	Total
1992		£	£	£
Feb-07	ANG Ltd	4,600	805	5,405
Feb-10	John's Stores	2,800	490	3,290
Feb-14	ML Limited	1,000	175	1,175
Feb-17	ML Limited	−600	−105	−705
Feb-25	ANG Ltd	1,200	210	1,410
		9,000	1,575	10,575

Chapter 21 Interpretation of financial statements

The directors of T plc are keen to reduce the company's bank overdraft by at least £600,000. They believe that this could be accomplished by better management of the company's trade debtors. In January 1997 one of the company's junior managers submitted a suggestion to the board that the company should offer trade debtors a 2% discount if they pay for purchases made during March 1997 before the end of the month. He estimated that 40% of the company's customers would take advantage of such an offer, thereby reducing the bank overdraft by the balance sheet date and reducing the debtors' turnover in days. The board rejected this suggestion, partly because of the cost of the discount but mainly because it would make the financial accounting misleading. Information stated on the right has been extracted from the financial statements for the year ended 31 March 1997. All sales occur evenly throughout the year.

Cash sales	£12.0 million
Credit sales	£14.0 million
Trade debtors	£2.2 million
Bank overdraft	£800,000

Required: (a) Calculate the debtor's turnover (in days) from the above figures; (b) Calculate a target debtor's turnover (in days) necessary to reduce T plc's trade debtors by £600,000; (c) Calculate the estimated debtors' balance and overdraft which would have been outstanding if the board had accepted the manager's suggestion; (d) Explain why the manager's proposal would have rendered the financial statements misleading and explain how the effects of the discount would have had to be accounted for. (CIMA)

Chapter 25 Revenue recognition

A firm produces a standard product. The stages of production and sale of the product are as follows:

Stage	A	B	C	D	E	F	G	H
Activity	Raw material	WIP – 1	WIP – 2	Finished goods	For sale	Sale agreed	Delivered	Paid for
Costs to date	£100	£120	£150	£170	£170	£170	£180	£180
Net realizable value	£80	£130	£190	£300	£300	£300	£300	£300

(a) What general rules do accountants apply when deciding when to recognize revenue on any transaction?
(b) Apply this rule to the above situation. State and explain the stage at which you think revenue will be recognized by accountants.
(c) How much would the gross profit on a unit of this product be? Why?
(d) Suggest arguments in favour of delaying the recognition of revenue until stage H.
(e) Suggest arguments in favour of recognizing revenue at appropriate successive amounts at stages B, C and D. (ACCA)

Chapter 26 Single entry and incomplete records (1)

Donald Barton is a sole trader. All his business payments are made by cheque and all receipts including cash sales are paid into the bank account. Stated on the right is a summary of the Bank account for the year ended 30 April 1999. Further information obtained from Donald's books: Discounts allowed to customers during the year amounted to £420. Donald received discounts of £389 from trade creditors. He also took goods from the business for his own use at a cost price of £350. Stock valued at cost £780 on 30 April 1999 has been damaged during the year and has a market value of £200.

Required: The trading and Profit and Loss account for the year ended 30 April 1999 and balance sheet as at 30 April 1999. (OCR)

Bank summary:	£		£
Balance at 1.5.1998	1,200	Creditors	49,600
Trade debtors	63,120	General expenses	12,620
Cash sales	20,000	Rent	4,000
		Drawings	15,000
		Fixtures	750

	30-Apr-98	30-Apr-99
Trade debtors	£3,800	£5,860
Trade creditors	£3,320	£4,250
General expenses owing	£620	£930
Stock at cost	£4,350	£6,200
Fixtures (net)	£1,200	£1,500
Rent prepaid	£300	£500

Chapter 27 Single entry and incomplete records (2)

Tom Noland commenced trading as a retailer of model railways on 1 August 1997. He did not keep a proper double entry bookkeeping system, nor did he keep adequate stock records. At 1 August 1997 the business assets were as stated on the right. On 30 April 1998 the shop was broken into and the cash float of £50 plus various items of stock were stolen. Tom Noland now has to complete an insurance claim to cover the loss. He is able to supply the following information:

Fixed assets	£26,400
Cash float	£50
Balance at bank	£2,850

(i) All sales are on cash basis. The net amount is banked daily after the payment of cash expenses and personal drawings.
(ii) All goods are sold at a mark-up of 100%.
(iii) Cash drawings are £500 per month.
(iv) A telephone bill of £45 for the quarter ended 31 May 1998 is unpaid.
(v) All creditors for goods purchased are paid by cheque.
(vi) Stock is generally maintained at a level of two months' average purchases.
(vii) Depreciation is to be charged on fixed assets at the rate of 20% per annum.
(viii) At the close of business on 30 April 1998 creditors for goods purchased were £1,550 and the remaining stock (after the burglary) was valued at £1320.
(ix) Cash and bank transactions for the period up to 30 April 1998 were as stated on the right.

	Cash £	Bank £
Business operating expenses	4,150	3,160
Payments to creditors for purchases	–	11,050
Cash banked	–	10,950
Cost of shelving (acquired on 1.8.1997)	–	1,600

Required: (a) Write up the Cash and Bank accounts for the nine months ended 30 April 1998; (b) Calculate the total loss for the purpose of the insurance claim; (c) Prepare a trading and profit and loss account for the nine months ended 30 April 1998 and a balance sheet as at that date; (d) Write a memorandum to Tom Noland explaining three benefits which may be derived from keeping adequate control of stock. (AEB)

Chapter 28 Accounting for non-trading concerns

The treasurer of the Players Sports and Social Club prepared the Receipts and Payments account for the year ended 31 December 1998 as stated on the right. It was felt by many members that this information was inadequate to give a full picture of the club's financial situation, and the Treasurer subsequently produced the following additional information:

	£	
Bank balance on 1 January 1998		1,470
Subscriptions re 1997		620
Subscriptions re 1998		14,080
Competition fees		2,590
Sale of van – 1 January 1998		1,000
Sale of dance ticket		1,778
Less:		21,538
Wages	8,450	
Printing and advertising	2,070	
Repairs to sports equipment	800	
Competition prizes	2,200	
Dance expenses	2,060	
New motor van (1 January 1998)	6,300	
Motor expenses	1,200	
Sundry expenses	1,180	(24,260)
Bank overdraft at 31 December 1998		(2,722)

(i) Assets and liabilities included as at

	1 January	31 December
Sports equipment	£6,200	£5,400
Members subscription due	£1,440	£1,620
Subscription in advance	–	£720
Stock of competition prizes	£850	£450
Office computer (Cost £2,000)	£1,600	£1,400

(ii) The van sold during the year had originally cost £4,000 and had been depreciated at 25% on the reducing balance method for exactly two years up to the date of sale. The new van is to be depreciated on the same basis as the previous one.

Required: An Income and Expenditure account for the year ended 31 December 1998 and a Balance sheet as at that date. (London Examinations)

Chapter 28 Accounting for non-trading concerns

BALANCE SHEET AS AT 31 DECEMBER 19X7	
	£
Half share in motorized roller	600
New sports equipment unsold	1,000
Used sports equip. at valuation	700
Rent (two months)	200
Subscriptions 19X7	60
Café stocks	800
Cash and bank	1,210
	4,570
	£
Insurance (3 months)	150
Subscriptions 19X8	120
Life subscriptions	1,400
Accumulated fund	2,900
	4,570

RECEIPTS AND PAYMENTS IN THE YEAR TO 31 DECEMBER 19X8			
	£		£
Subscriptions 19X7	40	Rent (12 months)	1,200
Subscriptions 19X8	1,100	Insurance (18 months)	900
Subscriptions 19X9	80	Suppliers of sports equip.	1,000
Life subscriptions	200	Café suppliers	1,900
Sale – new sports equipment	900	Wages – café manager	2,000
Sale – used sports equipment	14	Motorized roller repairs	450
Café takings	4,660		

1. Ownership and all expenses of the motorized roller are agreed to be shared equally with the Carefree Conveyancers Sports & Social club which occupies a nearby site. The roller cost £2,000 on 1.1.19X4 and has an estimated life of ten years.
2. Life subscriptions are brought into income equally over ten years, in a scheme begun in 19X3. Prior to 31.12.19X7, ten life subscriptions had been received.
3. Four more annual subscriptions of £20 had been promised relating to 19X8 but not yet received. Annual subscriptions promised but not received are carried forward for a maximum of 12 months.
4. New sports equipment is sold to members at cost plus 50%. Used sports equipment is sold off to members at book valuation. Half the sports equipment bought in the year has been used within the club and half made available for sale, new, to members. The used equipment at valuation figure is to remain at £700 in the balance sheet as at 31.12.19X8.
5. Closing café stocks are £850 and £80 is owed to suppliers at 31 December 19X8.

Required: (a) Profit on café operations and profit on sale of sports equipment; (b) the statement of subscription income for 19X8; (c) The income and expenditure statement for the year to 31 December 19X8 and a balance sheet as at that date; (d) why do life subscriptions appear as a liability? (ACCA)

Chapter 29 Accounts in manufacturing

Following balances have been extracted from the books of the Staghill Manufacturing Co. Ltd as at 30 April 1999.

Stock at 1 May 1998:	£
Raw material	26,740
Work in progress	23,170
Finished goods	37,440
Factory wages: direct	372,560
indirect	74,280
Royalty	6,500
Heating and lighting	26,650
General factory expense	47,080
Insurances	15,010
General office expenses	36,740
Purchase of raw material	278,630
Sales	1,163,750
Plant and machinery at cost	210,000
Prov. for depn – machinery	126,000
Provision for unrealized profit	6,240

(i) As at 30 April 1999 stocks were as stated on the right.

	£
Raw materials	24,390
Work in progress	24,640
Finished goods	36,720

(ii) Heating & lighting expenses are to be apportioned 2/3 to The factory and 1/3 to the company office.
(iii) At 30 April 1999 an electricity bill of £800 remained unpaid and insurance policies paid for the year ended 30 April 2000 amounted to £760.
(iv) The company depreciates plant & machinery at 10% per annum on cost.
(v) Finished goods are transferred from the factory to warehouse at cost plus 20%.

Required: (a) Prepare the Manufacturing, Trading & Profit and Loss account for the year ended 30 April 1999; (b) Identify and discuss two limitations of preparing a Manufacturing account; (c) Why do some businesses transfer finished goods to the Trading account at more than the cost? (AEB)

Chapter 30 Accounting systems and controls

The managing director of H plc read a news paper report of a fraud which had recently come to the attention of the police. The perpetrators had sent invoices to several thousand companies. These requested payment for an entry in a trade directory.

The directory did not, however, exist. The news paper report claimed that approximately 700 companies had paid £2,000 each for an entry in this alleged directory. H plc's managing director asked whether the company had received one of these invoices. It was discovered that H plc was one of the companies which had paid the £2,000 charge. The reason for this payment was investigated.

H plc's accounting system was recently computerized. All invoices are keyed straight into a standard accounting package. The company's accounting department is short-staffed and so the default settings on the package have been set to minimize the amount of clerical effort required to process transactions. If, for example, an invoice is received from a new supplier, the program will automatically allocate an account number and open an account in the Purchases Ledger. At the end of every month, the program calculates the amount which is due to each creditor; a cheque for each creditor is automatically printed out for the total of all the invoices from that creditor input during the month. When the system was first installed, the accountant used to review creditors' accounts prior to the cheque run as a check that the system was not being abused. This review was, however, discontinued because of pressure of work and because there were too many invoices to review properly.

The managing director was most disturbed by this description of the purchase system and decided that it was in urgent need of improvement. The company's accountant was ordered to redesign the system. The accountant was authorized to employ additional staff if the extra expense could be justified.

Required: (a) describe three weaknesses in H plc's existing purchases system; (b) explain how the purchases and creditors system should be reorganized. (CIMA)

Chapter 31 Fixed assets: appraisal and financing

A company is planning a capital investment for which the cash flows have been projected as stated on right. The company's cost of capital is 15%.

Required: (a) Calculate the Net Present Value of the investment; (b) Calculate the Internal Rate of Return (approximate); (c) Comment on whether the investment should be initialized and the factors to consider. (CIMA)

Time	Net Cash Flow	Time	Net Cash Flow
Now	−£10,000	At the end of year 4	+£4,000
At the end of year 1	+£500	At the end of year 5	+£5,000
At the end of year 2	+£2,000	At the end of year 6	+£2,500
At the end of year 3	+£3,000	At the end of year 7	+£2,000
		At the end of year 8	+£2,500

Chapter 32 Planning and control: budgeting

Lamb Ltd operates a system of budgetary control and it is now drawing up budgets for the first quarter of its next financial year beginning on 1 July 1998. It has been decided that production levels should be kept even during the four month period commencing July 1998, and that a closing stock of 10,000 units is required in September 1998. Market research details show that sales for July are expected to be 20,000 units and to increase by 6% in August, and by a further 6% in September (on August levels). There will be an opening stock of 8,344 units on 1 July 1998. Production in June was 41,600 units.

The variable cost of production per unit is £25 throughout the period, of which materials account for 50%. These materials are always bought the month before they are used in production. Until recently, suppliers gave two months' credit before requiring payment. However, a new arrangement is being phased in. From August, any purchases will be paid for in the next month. May was the last month for buying materials carrying two months credit. Of the purchases made in June, 50% will have to be paid in July, and the remainder in August. Of the purchases in July, 80% will have to be paid for in August and the remainder in September. Lamb Ltd sells 80% of its goods on credit terms. Credit customers pay in the month after receiving their goods. The selling price per unit of the product is £30. June sales were 20,000 units.

Required: (a) Outline the stages that Lamb Ltd would need to go through in order to draw up its overall budget, and the advantages it would gain from using a system of budgetary control; (b) Draw up monthly budgets for July, August and September 1998 for Lamb Ltd for: (i) stocks of finished goods in units; (ii) creditors in £s; (iii) debtors in £s. (Oxford)

Chapter 33 Standard costing and variance analysis: an introduction

A business is preparing to introduce standard costing. The Production Manager has recommended that standards are set based upon an attainable level of activity, but the Accountant believes that the standards should be based upon the ideal (optimum) level

	Ideal Level	Attainable Level	Current Level
Direct Costs Per Unit			
Material – Kilos	8	9	10
Price (per kilo)	£0.80	£1.00	£1.10
Labour – Rate (per hour)	£6.00	£6.40	£7.50
Production time	1 hour	1.25 hours	1.50 hours

Required: (a) a calculation of the cost for one unit of production at each of the three levels of output; (b) a discussion of the advantages of the standards for the next period being based on attainable levels. (London Examinations)

Chapter 34 Short-term decision making

J. Affia Ltd manufactures three products R,S and T, all of which are made from one basic raw material. Owing to a serious fire at the supplier's factory there will be a shortage of the basic raw material next year. The maximum amount of raw material available is £900,000. The budgeted cost and selling prices for the next year are as stated on the right. The total annual fixed costs are £650,000.

Required: (a) Calculate the maximum profit the company can make next year; (b) If there was no shortage of raw material,

Product	R	S	T
Sales (units)	16,000	21,000	18,000
Selling price (per unit)	£94	£92	£110
Variable cost per unit:			
Direct labour	£32	£38	£42
Direct material	£24	£20	£21
Variable overheads	£16	£15	£17

should the company accept a 'special order' for 4,000 units of product R at a special price of £82 per unit? Additional fixed costs of £10,000 would be incurred if the order is accepted. Calculate also the profit/loss for the special order outlining any other factors the company should take into account. (OCR)

Chapter 36 Partnership accounts (1): appropriations

For a number of years you have been employed in a senior position by a firm of certified accountants. The two partners, Checke and Tikk, have now offered to take you into the firm as a junior partner with effect from 1 April 1985. Hitherto Checke and Tikk have contributed £50,000 and £30,000 respectively as their capital. They receive interest on capital at 5% per annum and share profits in the ratio 3:2 respectively. After admission to the partnership you will be expected to continue managing the practice for which you will receive exactly half your present annual salary of £14,000 as partnership salary. You will also be expected to contribute £20,000 as capital for which you will receive interest at 5% per annum. The profit sharing ratio will then be altered to give you one sixth share of profits and losses, without disturbing the relative shares of the other two partners. For the year ended 31 March 1985 the total amount appropriated by the two partners was £34,000.

Required: Prepare a statement showing the details of the amounts appropriated to Checke and Tikk during the year ended 31 March 1985 together with details of amounts which would have been appropriated if you had been taken into partnership on 1 April 1984. (ACCA)

Chapter 37 Partnership accounts (2): unrecorded assets

Alpha and Beta are in partnership. They share profits equally after Alpha has been allowed a salary of £4,000 p.a. No interest is charged on drawings or allowed on current or capital accounts. The trial balance of the partnership on 31 December 1989, before adjusting for any of the items stated below, appears as stated on the right.

(i)   Closing stock in hand is £24,000.
(ii) On 31 December Alpha and Beta agreed to take Gamma into partnership, Gamma's loan being regarded from that date as his capital. Alpha, Beta and Gamma will share profits equally. Alpha will receive a salary of £4,000 p.a. as before and Gamma will be allowed a salary of £5,000 p.a. (half of what he received until then as manager). The three partners agree that the goodwill of the business on that date should be valued at £12,000 but is not to be recorded in the books. It is also agreed that land and buildings are to be revalued at a figure of £84,000 and that this revalued figure is to be recorded in the books.
(iii) Interest on the loans have not been paid.
(iv) Included in the sales are two items sold on sale or return for £3,000 each. Each item had cost £1,000. One of these items was in fact returned by 4 January 1990 and the other accepted by the customer on 6 January 1990.

	£000	£000
Capital – Alpha		30
– Beta		25
Current – Alpha		3
Beta		4
Drawings – Alpha	4	
– Beta	5	
Sales		200
Stock 1.1.1989	30	
Purchases	103	
Operating expenses	64	
Loan Beta (10%)		10
Loan Gamma (10%)		20
Land and building	60	
Machinery	70	
Depn – machinery 31.12.89		40
Debtors and creditors	40	33
Bank		11
	376	376

Required: (a) Submit with appropriately labeled headings (i) partners Capital accounts (ii) partners' Current accounts (iii) Trading Profit and Loss accounts for 1989 and balance sheet as at 31.12.1989; (b) Write a brief note to Gamma who cannot understand why his capital account balance seems so much less than those of others. (ACCA)

Chapter 38 Partnership accounts (3): dissolution and conversion

Alpha, Beta and Gamma were in partnership for many years sharing profits and losses in the ratio 5:3:2 respectively and making up their accounts to 31 December each year. Alpha died on 31 December 1997 and the partnership was dissolved as from that date. The partnership balance sheet on that date was as stated on the right.

In the period to March 1998 the following transactions took place and were dealt with in the partnership records:

(i)   Fixed assets – Land and buildings were sold for £380,000 and machinery for £88,000. Beta and Gamma took over the cars they were using valued at £9,000 and £14,000 respectively; the remaining cars were sold for £38,000.
(ii) Current assets: Stock was taken over by Gamma at an agreed value of £120,000. £68,400 was realized from debtors and the remainder taken over by Gamma at an agreed value of £20,000.
(iii) Current liabilities: Creditors were all settled for a total of £115,000.
(iv) Long term liability: Delta's loan was repaid on 31 March 1998 with interest accrued since 31 December 1997.
(v)   Expenses of dissolution £2,400 were paid.
(vi) Capital accounts: the final amounts due to or from the estate of Alpha, Beta and Gamma were paid/received on 31 March 1998.

BALANCE SHEET AS AT 31 DECEMBER 1997			
Fixed assets:	Cost	Depn.	£
Land and building	350,000	(50,000)	300,000
Plant and machinery	220,000	(104,100)	115,900
Motor vehicles	98,500	(39,900)	58,600
Current assets:			
Stock		110,600	
Debtors		89,400	
Cash and bank		12,600	
Creditors		(118,400)	94,200
			568,700
Loan – Delta at 10% per annum interest			(40,000)
			528,700
			£
Capital: Alpha			233,600
Beta			188,900
Gamma			106,200
			528,700

Prepare the following accounts showing the dissolution of the partnership (a) Realisation account; (b) Capital accounts; (c) Cash book. (ACCA)

Chapter 40 Companies (2): shares and debentures

Lawton plc has an authorized share capital of £2,000,000. At 31 January 1998 it had already issued 1,200,000 £1 ordinary shares at par. On 1 February 1998 it offered 400,000 ordinary shares to the public at a price of £1.50 each. The terms of the issue were 50 pence payable on application, *55* pence payable on allotment (including the premium), and the remainder to be called later. Applications were received by 27 February 1998 for 500,000 ordinary shares. On 12 March 1998 allotments were made as follows.

(i)   Applications for 75,000 shares were refused, and the money was returned to the applicants.
(ii) The remainder of the shares were issued on a pro-rata basis, any money over paid being retained towards the amount due on allotment.

All money due on allotment was received by 24 March 1998. The following calls were then made.

(i)   A first call of 25 pence per share on 10 April 1998, all of which was received by 20 April 1998.
(ii) A second and final call for the remaining money on the 8 May 1998. By 19 May 1998, all the money had been received except from an applicant who had been allocated 10,000 shares.

Required: Prepare the following ledger accounts to record the above transactions in the books of Lawton plc. (i) Application and Allotment Account; (ii) Bank Account; (iii) Ordinary Share Capital Account; (iv) Share Premium Account; (v) First Call Account; (vi) Second and Final Call Account. (Oxford)

Chapter 41 Companies (3): annual accounts for internal use

ABC Limited's trial balance at 31 March 1992 appears as stated below on the right:

	£	£
Freehold land at cost	60,000	–
Building at cost	50,000	–
Plant and equipment at cost	120,000	–
Motor vehicles at cost	32,000	–
Provision for depreciation:		
Buildings	–	20,000
Plant and equipment	–	74,000
Motor vehicles	–	16,800
Stock at 1 April 1991	74,000	–
Debtors and creditors	122,500	99,800
Cash at bank	3,500	–
Sales (all on credit)	–	249,760
Purchases (all on credit)	134,630	–
Returns	12,900	4,875
Discount allowed/received	3,200	1,850
Administrative expenses	22,150	–
Selling/distribution exp.	6,900	–
Ordinary shares of £1 each	–	100,000
Profit and Loss reserve	–	69,695
Suspense account	–	5,000

(i)   The balance in the suspense account represents the proceeds from the disposal of a motor van which had originally cost £14,000 and had a net book value of £6,000 on the date of disposal. The proceeds have been correctly entered in the bank account but no other entries have been made.
(ii) The closing stock of finished goods was valued at £124,875.
(iii) A review of the year end ledger accounts shows that the following accruals/prepayments are required.

	Accruals	Prepayments
Administrative expenses	£4,500	£12,000
Selling & distribution expenses	£5,300	£8,000

(iv) Depreciation is to be provided in full on all assets at year end using the following rates:
Buildings   4% p.a. on cost
Plant and equipment   20% p.a. on cost
Motor vehicles   25% p.a. on reducing balance method
(v)   The directors propose a final dividend of 5 pence per share.
(vi) The company's liability for corporation tax on the profits for the year has been estimated to be £15,000.

Prepare in vertical form (a) the company's Trading and Profit and Loss account for the year ended 31 March 1992; and (b) the company's balance sheet as at 31 March 1992. (CIMA)

Chapter 42 Company accounts (4): published financial statements

You are the accounting assistant in Cheapstake plc and your chief accountant has presented you with the trial balance as shown on the right, prepared by your predecessor. You are informed:

1. The credit Controller has stated that a bad debt of £25,000 needs to be written off and that the balance in the bad debts provision should be increased by 50%. He has also advised that a debt previously written off of £15,000 will be recovered and should be accrued.
2. Goodwill should be written off over ten years commencing from 1.1.1996.
3. Directors propose to pay preference dividend and a final ordinary dividend of 6p per share.
4. Stock on 31 December 1996 was £1,950,000.
5. There is an outstanding legal dispute with a customer who is claiming damages for faulty goods. This is not covered by insurance. Outcome is uncertain and the amount of damages not quantifiable.
6. Corporation tax on the year's profit is estimated at £105,000.
7. The building are to be depreciated at 10% p.a. on cost and the plant and machinery at 20% p.a. on cost. The land and building are subject to external revaluation every three years and the review in December 1996 reduces the value of land and buildings by £300,000. The balance in the Revaluation Reserve is gains on revaluing land and building. Assume that a third of the value relates to land.

TRIAL BALANCE AS AT 31 DECEMBER 1996		
	£000	£000
Administrative expenses	850	
Debenture interest (to 30.6.96)	25	
Distribution expenses	346	
Directors emoluments	150	
Purchases	4,329	
Sales		9,000
Rates and insurance	350	
Interim dividend	16	
Ordinary shares of £1 each		400
10% Preference shares of £1		600
Revaluation reserve		650
Profit and loss account reserve		550
Debentures 5%		1,000
Goodwill	300	
Land and buildings	4,800	
Acc. depreciation – 1.1.1996		1,750
Plant and machinery	1,500	
Acc. depreciation – 1.1.1996		600
Stock	2,154	
Trade debtors and creditors	1,500	1,750
Bank balance	200	
Provision for bad and doubtful debts		100
Deferred taxation		120
	16,520	16,520

8. Allocate expenditure as follows

	Distribution %	Administration %
Rates and insurance	50	50
Land and building depreciation	40	60
Plant and machinery depreciation	75	25
Goodwill amortization	–	100

Required: (a) Draft a Profit and Loss account and balance sheet for the year ended 31 December 1996 in compliance with Companies Act 1985. Notes to the accounts are not needed; (b) State what action you recommend in respect of the outstanding legal dispute. (ACCA)

Chapter 43 Cash Flow Statements

The accountant of Cambank plc has produced the Cash flow statement for the year ended 31 March 1998 for the company as shown on the right.

Cash Flow Statement – year ended 31 March 1998		£000
Net cash flow from operating activities		1,060
Returns on investments and servicing of finance		
Interest paid	(60)	
dividends paid	(290)	(350)
Tax paid		(180)
Investing activities		
purchase of tangible fixed assets	(1250)	
sale of fixed assets	275	(975)
Net cash outflow before financing		(445)
Financing		
issue of preference shares		400
Decrease in cash and cash equivalents		(45)

(I) RECONCILIATION OF OPERATING PROFIT TO NET CASH INFLOW FROM OPERATING ACTIVITY	
	£000
Operating profit	238
Depreciation	950
Increase in creditors	192
Increase in stocks	(130)
Increase in debtors	(190)
	1,060

An extract from the Balance Sheet as at 31 March 1998:	**£000**
Stocks	950
Debtors	450
Cash at bank	87
Creditors due within one year	
Creditors	(510)
Taxation	(200)
Dividend proposed	(190)

Analysis of Cash and cash equivalents during the year:

Balance at 1 April 1997	£132,000
Net Cash outflow	(£45,000)
Balance at 31 March 1998	£87,000

Required: (a) Explain clearly why in a Cash Flow Statement (i) depreciation is added to operating profit (ii) increase of stock is deducted from Cash flow (iii) increase of creditors is added to cash flow; (b) Prepare an extract of the company's balance Sheet as at 31 March 1997 showing in detail its working capital position; (c) Comment on the change in company's liquidity during the year ended 31 March 1998; (d) Explain how the preparation of a cash flow statement can be of use to a company's shareholders. (AEB)

Chapter 43 Cash Flow Statements

The following information relates to Z plc

PROFIT AND LOSS ACCOUNT FOR YEAR ENDED 30 SEPTEMBER 1998	
	£000
Turnover	8,000
Cost of sales	(4,500)
Gross profit	3,500
Other expenses	(1,000)
Interest	(14)
Profit before taxation	2,486
Taxation	(800)
Dividends	(700)
Retained profit	986
Profit and Loss balance b/f	4,400
Profit and Loss balance c/f	5,386

BALANCE SHEETS AT 30 SEPTEMBER

	1998		1997	
	£000	£000	£000	£000
Fixed assets		8,100		6,800
Current assets:				
Stocks	800		600	
Debtors	670		620	
Bank	80		300	
Current liabilities:				
Creditors	(420)		(340)	
Dividend proposed	(400)		(360)	
Taxation	(635)	95	(595)	225
		8,195		7,025
Long term loans		(1,200)		(1,400)
		6,995		5,625
		£000		£000
Share capital		1,100		1,000
Share premium		509		225
Profit and Loss		5,386		4,400
		6,995		5,625

During the year the company purchased fixed assets costing £1,900,000. Fixed assets which had a net book value of £310,000 were sold for £80,000.

Required: Prepare a cash flow statement for year ended 30.9.1998. (CIMA)

Chapter 45 Group accounts

You have been told that your employer Port plc acquired 45,000 ordinary shares of Starboard Ltd on 31 December 1994 when the balance on Starboard's Profit and Loss account was £300,000. In addition Port plc is able to appoint four of the five directors of Starboard Ltd thus exercising control over their activities.

You are given the following information:

● share capital of Port plc is 500,000 shares of £1 each and the Share capital of Starboard Ltd is 100,000 ordinary shares of £1.
● It is the accounting policy of Port plc to write off goodwill on acquisition equally over five years.
● Port plc has not accounted for its share of Starboard's proposed dividend.

Required: (a) Prepare a consolidated balance sheet of Port plc group as at 31 December 1996; (b) Explain why you have consolidated Starboard Ltd when Port plc owns less than 50% of the Ordinary shares in Starboard Ltd and in what circumstances consolidation would not have been appropriate. (ACCA – amended)

BALANCE SHEET AS AT 31 DECEMBER 1996				
	Port plc		Starboard Ltd	
		£000		£000
Fixed assets:				
Freehold property		400		300
Plant and machinery		200		150
Investments – Starboard		450		–
Current assets:				
Stock	150		100	
Debtors	170		80	
Bank	40		20	
Creditors due within on year				
Trade creditors	(120)		(100)	
Dividend	(50)	190	(20)	80
		1,240		530
		£000		£000
Capital and Reserves				
Ordinary shares		500		100
Profit and Loss account		740		430
		1,240		530

Chapter 46 Inflation accounting

Bruce finished his A-level course in June and decided to try to earn some money over the summer vacation. He knew that many students purchased text books during their course, for which they had no further use. He offered to buy these unwanted books for £2 each with the aim of selling them to the new intake of students in September for £3 each. He was fairly successful, buying a total of 250 books for £2 each and selling 235 for £3 each. The remaining books were rather specialized and as he did not expect to sell them before he went to university he donated them to the library.

On reflection he realized that he had met with some resistance when offering £2 for the books and decided that if he were to continue trading he would need to pay £2.50. During the three months he stored the books the general rate of inflation was 3%.

(a) Calculate the profit he earned under: (i) historic cost accounting; (ii) current cost (replacement cost) accounting; (iii) current purchasing power accounting; (b) Explain the usefulness to Bruce of each of the profit figures you have calculated. (NEAB)

INDEX

Index entries in **bold** refer to meanings and definitions.